GREAT BOOKS OF THE WESTERN WORLD

28. GILBERT
    GALILEO
    HARVEY
29. CERVANTES
30. FRANCIS BACON
31. DESCARTES
    SPINOZA
32. MILTON
33. PASCAL
34. NEWTON
    HUYGENS
35. LOCKE
    BERKELEY
    HUME
36. SWIFT
    STERNE
37. FIELDING
38. MONTESQUIEU
    ROUSSEAU
39. ADAM SMITH
40. GIBBON I
41. GIBBON II
42. KANT
43. AMERICAN STATE PAPERS
    THE FEDERALIST
    J. S. MILL
44. BOSWELL
45. LAVOISIER
    FOURIER
    FARADAY
46. HEGEL
47. GOETHE
48. MELVILLE
49. DARWIN
50. MARX
    ENGELS
51. TOLSTOY
52. DOSTOEVSKY
53. WILLIAM JAMES
54. FREUD

The Plays and Sonnets of William Shakespeare

Volume Two

Edited by William George Clarke *and* William Aldis Wright

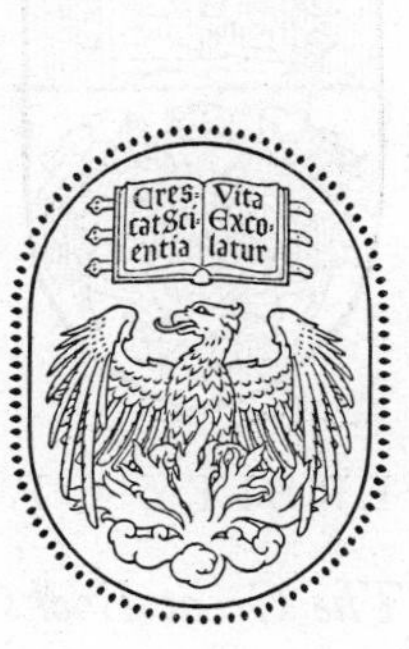

William Benton, *Publisher*

ENCYCLOPÆDIA BRITANNICA, INC.

CHICAGO · LONDON · TORONTO · GENEVA

THE UNIVERSITY OF CHICAGO

The Great Books
is published with the editorial advice of the faculties
of The University of Chicago

Contents, Volume Two

TWELFTH NIGHT
Or, What You Will

DRAMATIS PERSONÆ

ORSINO, DUKE OF ILLYRIA
SEBASTIAN, *brother to Viola*
ANTONIO, *a sea captain, friend to Sebastian*
A SEA CAPTAIN, *friend to Viola*
VALENTINE | *gentlemen attending on the Duke*
CURIO |
SIR TOBY BELCH, *uncle to Olivia*
SIR ANDREW AGUECHEEK
MALVOLIO, *steward to Olivia*
FABIAN | *servants to Olivia*
FESTE, A CLOWN |

TWO OFFICERS
A PRIEST
A SERVANT *to Olivia*

OLIVIA
VIOLA
MARIA, *Olivia's woman*

NON-SPEAKING: *Lords, Sailors, Officers, Musicians, and other Attendants*

SCENE: *A city in Illyria, and the sea-coast near it*

ACT I

SCENE I. *The Duke's palace*

Enter DUKE, CURIO, *and other Lords; Musicians attending.*

Duke. If music be the food of love, play on;
Give me excess of it, that, surfeiting,
The appetite may sicken, and so die.
That strain again! it had a dying fall:
O, it came o'er my ear like the sweet sound,
That breathes upon a bank of violets,
Stealing and giving odour! Enough; no more:
'Tis not so sweet now as it was before.
O spirit of love! how quick and fresh art thou,
That, notwithstanding thy capacity
Receiveth as the sea, nought enters there,
Of what validity and pitch soe'er,
But falls into abatement and low price,
Even in a minute: so full of shapes is fancy
That it alone is high fantastical.
Cur. Will you go hunt, my lord?
Duke. What, Curio?
Cur. The hart.
Duke. Why, so I do, the noblest that I have:
O, when mine eyes did see Olivia first,
Methought she purged the air of pestilence!
That instant was I turn'd into a hart;
And my desires, like fell and cruel hounds,
E'er since pursue me.

Enter VALENTINE.

How now! what news from her?
Val. So please my lord, I might not be admitted;
But from her handmaid do return this answer:
The element itself, till seven years' heat,
Shall not behold her face at ample view;
But, like a cloistress, she will veiled walk
And water once a day her chamber round
With eye-offending brine: all this to season
A brother's dead love, which she would keep fresh
And lasting in her sad remembrance.
Duke. O, she that hath a heart of that fine frame
To pay this debt of love but to a brother,
How will she love, when the rich golden shaft
Hath kill'd the flock of all affections else
That live in her; when liver, brain, and heart,
These sovereign thrones, are all supplied, and fill'd
Her sweet perfections with one self king!
Away before me to sweet beds of flowers:
Love-thoughts lie rich when canopied with bowers. [*Exeunt*.

SCENE II. *The sea-coast*

Enter VIOLA, *a* CAPTAIN, *and Sailors*.

Vio. What country, friends, is this?
Cap. This is Illyria, lady.
Vio. And what should I do in Illyria?
My brother he is in Elysium.
Perchance he is not drown'd: what think you, sailors?
Cap. It is perchance that you yourself were saved.
Vio. O my poor brother! and so perchance may he be.
Cap. True, madam: and, to comfort you with chance,

Assure yourself, after our ship did split,
When you and those poor numbers saved with you
Hung on our driving boat, I saw your brother,
Most provident in peril, bind himself,
Courage and hope both teaching him the practice,
To a strong mast that lived upon the sea;
Where, like Arion on the dolphin's back,
I saw him hold acquaintance with the waves
So long as I could see.

Vio. For saying so, there's gold:
Mine own escape unfoldeth to my hope,
Whereto thy speech serves for authority,
The like of him. Know'st thou this country?

Cap. Ay, madam, well; for I was bred and born
Not three hours' travel from this very place.

Vio. Who governs here?

Cap. A noble duke, in nature as in name.

Vio. What is his name?

Cap. Orsino.

Vio. Orsino! I have heard my father name him:
He was a bachelor then.

Cap. And so is now, or was so very late;
For but a month ago I went from hence,
And then 'twas fresh in murmur—as, you know,
What great ones do the less will prattle of—
That he did seek the love of fair Olivia.

Vio. What's she?

Cap. A virtuous maid, the daughter of a count
That died some twelvemonth since, then leaving her
In the protection of his son, her brother,
Who shortly also died: for whose dear love,
They say, she hath abjured the company
And sight of men.

Vio. O that I served that lady
And might not be delivered to the world,
Till I had made mine own occasion mellow,
What my estate is!

Cap. That were hard to compass;
Because she will admit no kind of suit,
No, not the Duke's.

Vio. There is a fair behaviour in thee, captain;
And though that nature with a beauteous wall
Doth oft close in pollution, yet of thee
I will believe thou hast a mind that suits
With this thy fair and outward character.
I prithee, and I'll pay thee bounteously,
Conceal me what I am, and be my aid
For such disguise as haply shall become
The form of my intent. I'll serve this duke:
Thou shalt present me as an eunuch to him:
It may be worth thy pains; for I can sing
And speak to him in many sorts of music
That will allow me very worth his service.
What else may hap to time I will commit;
Only shape thou thy silence to my wit.

Cap. Be you his eunuch, and your mute I'll be:
When my tongue blabs, then let mine eyes not see.

Vio. I thank thee: lead me on. [*Exeunt*.

SCENE III. *Olivia's house*

Enter SIR TOBY BELCH *and* MARIA.

Sir To. What a plague means my niece, to take the death of her brother thus? I am sure care's an enemy to life.

Mar. By my troth, Sir Toby, you must come in earlier o' nights: your cousin, my lady, takes great exceptions to your ill hours.

Sir To. Why, let her except, before excepted.

Mar. Ay, but you must confine yourself within the modest limits of order.

Sir To. Confine! I'll confine myself no finer than I am: these clothes are good enough to drink in; and so be these boots too: an they be not, let them hang themselves in their own straps.

Mar. That quaffing and drinking will undo you: I heard my lady talk of it yesterday: and of a foolish knight that you brought in one night here to be her wooer.

Sir To. Who, Sir Andrew Aguecheek?

Mar. Ay, he.

Sir To. He's as tall a man as any's in Illyria.

Mar. What's that to the purpose?

Sir To. Why, he has three thousand ducats a year.

Mar. Ay, he'll have but a year in all these ducats: he's a very fool and a prodigal.

Sir To. Fie, that you'll say so! he plays o' the viol-de-gamboys, and speaks three or four languages word for word without book, and hath all the good gifts of nature.

Mar. He hath indeed, almost natural: for besides that he's a fool, he's a great quarreller; and but that he hath the gift of a coward to allay the gust he hath in quarrelling, 'tis thought among the prudent he would quickly have the gift of a grave.

Sir To. By this hand, they are scoundrels and substractors that say so of him. Who are they?

Mar. They that add, moreover, he's drunk nightly in your company.

Sir. To. With drinking healths to my niece: I'll drink to her as long as there is a passage in my throat and drink in Illyria: he's a coward and a coystrill that will not drink to my niece till his brains turn o' the toe like a parish-top. What, wench! *Castiliano vulgo!* for here comes Sir Andrew Agueface.

Enter SIR ANDREW AGUECHEEK.

Sir And. Sir Toby Belch! how now, Sir Toby Belch!

Sir To. Sweet Sir Andrew!

Sir And. Bless you, fair shrew.

Mar. And you too, sir.

Sir To. Accost, Sir Andrew, accost.

Sir And. What's that?

Sir To. My niece's chambermaid.

Sir And. Good Mistress Accost, I desire better acquaintance.

Mar. My name is Mary, sir.

Sir And. Good Mistress Mary Accost—

Sir To. You mistake, knight: "accost" is front her, board her, woo her, assail her.

Sir And. By my troth, I would not undertake her in this company. Is that the meaning of "accost"?

Mar. Fare you well, gentlemen.

Sir To. An thou let part so, Sir Andrew, would thou mightst never draw sword again.

Sir And. An you part so, mistress, I would I might never draw sword again. Fair lady, do you think you have fools in hand?

Mar. Sir, I have not you by the hand.

Sir And. Marry, but you shall have; and here's my hand.

Mar. Now, sir, "thought is free." I pray you, bring your hand to the buttery-bar and let it drink.

Sir And. Wherefore, sweetheart? what's your metaphor?

Mar. It's dry, sir.

Sir And. Why, I think so: I am not such an ass but I can keep my hand dry. But what's your jest?

Mar. A dry jest, sir.

Sir And. Are you full of them?

Mar. Ay, sir, I have them at my fingers' ends: marry, now I let go your hand, I am barren. [*Exit.*

Sir To. O knight, thou lackest a cup of canary: when did I see thee so put down?

Sir And. Never in your life, I think; unless you see canary put me down. Methinks sometimes I have no more wit than a Christian or an ordinary man has: but I am a great eater of beef and I believe that does harm to my wit.

Sir To. No question.

Sir And. An I thought that, I'ld forswear it. I'll ride home to-morrow, Sir Toby.

Sir To. *Pourquoi*, my dear knight?

Sir And. What is *pourquoi*? do or not do? I would I had bestowed that time in the tongues that I have in fencing, dancing, and bear-baiting: O, had I but followed the arts!

Sir To. Then hadst thou had an excellent head of hair.

Sir And. Why, would that have mended my hair?

Sir To. Past question; for thou seest it will not curl by nature.

Sir And. But it becomes me well enough, does't not?

Sir To. Excellent; it hangs like flax on a distaff; and I hope to see a housewife take thee between her legs and spin it off.

Sir And. Faith, I'll home to-morrow, Sir Toby: your niece will not be seen; or if she be, it's four to one she'll none of me: the Count himself here hard by woos her.

Sir To. She'll none o' the Count: she'll not match above her degree, neither in estate, years, nor wit; I have heard her swear't. Tut, there's life in't, man.

Sir And. I'll stay a month longer. I am a fellow o' the strangest mind i' the world; I delight in masques and revels sometimes altogether.

Sir To. Art thou good at these kickshawses, knight?

Sir And. As any man in Illyria, whatsoever he be, under the degree of my betters; and yet I will not compare with an old man.

Sir To. What is thy excellence in a galliard, knight?

Sir And. Faith, I can cut a caper.

Sir To. And I can cut the mutton to't.

Sir And. And I think I have the back-trick simply as strong as any man in Illyria.

Sir To. Wherefore are these things hid? wherefore have these gifts a curtain before 'em? are they like to take dust, like Mistress Mall's picture? why dost thou not go to church in a galliard and come home in a coranto? My very walk should be a jig; I would not so much as make water but in a sink-a-pace. What dost thou mean? Is it a world to hide virtues in? I did think, by the excellent constitution of thy leg, it was formed under the star of a galliard.

Sir And. Ay, 'tis strong, and it does indifferent well in a flame-coloured stock. Shall we set about some revels?

Sir To. What shall we do else? were we not born under Taurus?

Sir And. Taurus! That's sides and heart.

Sir To. No, sir; it is legs and thighs. Let me see thee caper: ha! higher: ha, ha! excellent!

[*Exeunt.*

SCENE IV. *The Duke's palace*

Enter VALENTINE, *and* VIOLA *in man's attire.*

Val. If the Duke continue these favours towards you, Cesario, you are like to be much advanced: he hath known you but three days, and already you are no stranger.

Vio. You either fear his humour or my negligence, that you call in question the continuance of his love: is he inconstant, sir, in his favours?

Val. No, believe me.

Vio. I thank you. Here comes the count.

Enter DUKE, CURIO, *and Attendants.*

Duke. Who saw Cesario, ho?

Vio. On your attendance, my lord; here.

Duke. Stand you a while aloof. Cesario,
Thou know'st no less but all; I have unclasp'd
To thee the book even of my secret soul:
Therefore, good youth, address thy gait unto her;
Be not denied access, stand at her doors,
And tell them, there thy fixed foot shall grow
Till thou have audience.

Vio. Sure, my noble lord,
If she be so abandon'd to her sorrow
As it is spoke, she never will admit me.

Duke. Be clamorous and leap all civil bounds
Rather than make unprofited return.

Vio. Say I do speak with her, my lord, what then?

Duke. O, then unfold the passion of my love,
Surprise her with discourse of my dear faith:
It shall become thee well to act my woes;
She will attend it better in thy youth
Than in a nuncio's of more grave aspect.

Vio. I think not so, my lord.

Duke. Dear lad, believe it;
For they shall yet belie thy happy years,
That say thou art a man: Diana's lip
Is not more smooth and rubious; thy small pipe
Is as the maiden's organ, shrill and sound,
And all is semblative a woman's part.
I know thy constellation is right apt
For this affair. Some four or five attend him;
All, if you will; for I myself am best
When least in company. Prosper well in this,
And thou shalt live as freely as thy lord,
To call his fortunes thine.

Vio. I'll do my best
To woo your lady: [*Aside*] yet, a barful strife!
Whoe'er I woo, myself would be his wife.
[*Exeunt.*

SCENE V. *Olivia's house*

Enter MARIA *and* CLOWN.

Mar. Nay, either tell me where thou hast been, or I will not open my lips so wide as a bristle may enter in way of thy excuse: my lady will hang thee for thy absence.

Clo. Let her hang me: he that is well hanged in this world needs to fear no colours.

Mar. Make that good.

Clo. He shall see none to fear.

Mar. A good lenten answer: I can tell thee where that saying was born, of "I fear no colours."

Clo. Where, good Mistress Mary?

Mar. In the wars; and that may you be bold to say in your foolery.

Clo. Well, God give them wisdom that have it; and those that are fools, let them use their talents.

Mar. Yet you will be hanged for being so long absent; or to be turned away, is not that as good as a hanging to you?

Clo. Many a good hanging prevents a bad marriage; and, for turning away, let summer bear it out.

Mar. You are resolute, then?

Clo. Not so, neither; but I am resolved on two points.

Mar. That if one break, the other will hold; or, if both break, your gaskins fall.

Clo. Apt, in good faith; very apt. Well, go thy way; if Sir Toby would leave drinking, thou wert as witty a piece of Eve's flesh as any in Illyria.

Mar. Peace, you rogue, no more o' that. Here comes my lady: make your excuse wisely, you were best. [*Exit.*

Clo. Wit, an't be thy will, put me into good fooling! Those wits, that think they have thee, do very oft prove fools; and I, that am sure I lack thee, may pass for a wise man: for what says Quinapalus? "Better a witty fool than a foolish wit."

Enter LADY OLIVIA *with* MALVOLIO.

God bless thee, lady!

Oli. Take the fool away.

Clo. Do you not hear, fellows? Take away the lady.

Oli. Go to, you're a dry fool; I'll no more of you: besides, you grow dishonest.

Clo. Two faults, madonna, that drink and good counsel will amend: for give the dry fool drink, then is the fool not dry: bid the dishonest man mend himself; if he mend, he is no longer dishonest; if he cannot let the botcher mend him. Any thing that's mended is but patched: virtue that transgresses is but patched with sin; and sin that amends is but patched with virtue. If that this simple syllogism will serve, so; if it will not, what remedy? As there is no true cuckold but calamity, so beauty's a flower. The lady bade take away the fool; therefore, I say again, take her away.

Oli. Sir, I bade them take away you.

Clo. Misprision in the highest degree! Lady, *cucullus non facit monachum;* that's as much to say as I wear not motley in my brain. Good madonna, give me leave to prove you a fool.

Oli. Can you do it?

Clo. Dexteriously, good madonna.

Oli. Make your proof.

Clo. I must catechize you for it, madonna: good my mouse of virtue, answer me.

Oli. Well, sir, for want of other idleness, I'll bide your proof.

Clo. Good madonna, why mournest thou?

Oli. Good fool, for my brother's death.

Clo. I think his soul is in hell, madonna.

Oli. I know his soul is in heaven, fool.

Clo. The more fool, madonna, to mourn for your brother's soul being in heaven. Take away the fool, gentlemen.

Oli. What think you of this fool, Malvolio? doth he not mend?

Mal. Yes, and shall do till the pangs of death shake him: infirmity, that decays the wise, doth ever make the better fool.

Clo. God send you, sir, a speedy infirmity, for the better increasing your folly! Sir Toby will be sworn that I am no fox; but he will not pass his word for two pence that you are no fool.

Oli. How say you to that, Malvolio?

Mal. I marvel your ladyship takes delight in such a barren rascal: I saw him put down the other day with an ordinary fool that has no more brain than a stone. Look you now, he's out of his guard already; unless you laugh and minister occasion to him, he is gagged. I protest, I take these wise men, that crow so at these set kind of fools, no better than the fools' zanies.

Oli. O, you are sick of self-love, Malvolio, and taste with a distempered appetite. To be generous, guiltless, and of free disposition, is to take those things for bird-bolts that you deem cannon-bullets: there is no slander in an allowed fool, though he do nothing but rail; nor no railing in a known discreet man, though he do nothing but reprove.

Clo. Now Mercury endue thee with leasing, for thou speakest well of fools!

Re-enter MARIA.

Mar. Madam, there is at the gate a young gentleman much desires to speak with you.

Oli. From the Count Orsino, is it?

Mar. I know not, madam: 'tis a fair young man, and well attended.

Oli. Who of my people hold him in delay?

Mar. Sir Toby, madam, your kinsman.

Oli. Fetch him off, I pray you; he speaks nothing but madman: fie on him! [*Exit* MARIA.] Go you, Malvolio: if it be a suit from the Count, I am sick, or not at home; what you will, to dismiss it. [*Exit* MALVOLIO.] Now you see, sir, how your fooling grows old, and people dislike it.

Clo. Thou hast spoke for us, madonna, as if thy eldest son should be a fool; whose skull Jove cram with brains! for—here he comes—one of thy kin has a most weak *pia mater.*

Enter SIR TOBY.

Oli. By mine honour, half drunk. What is he at the gate, cousin?

Sir To. A gentleman.

Oli. A gentleman! what gentleman?

Sir To. 'Tis a gentleman here—a plague o' these pickle-herring! How now, sot!

Clo. Good Sir Toby!

Oli. Cousin, cousin, how have you come so early by this lethargy?

Sir To. Lechery! I defy lechery. There's one at the gate.

Oli. Ay, marry, what is he?

Sir To. Let him be the devil, an he will, I care not: give me faith, say I. Well, it's all one. [*Exit.*

Oli. What's a drunken man like, fool?

Clo. Like a drowned man, a fool, and a mad man: one draught above heat makes him a fool; the second mads him; and a third drowns him.

Oli. Go thou and seek the crowner, and let him sit o' my coz; for he's in the third degree of drink, he's drowned: go, look after him.

Clo. He is but mad yet, madonna; and the fool shall look to the madman. [*Exit.*

Re-enter MALVOLIO.

Mal. Madam, yond young fellow swears he will speak with you. I told him you were sick; he takes on him to understand so much, and therefore comes to speak with you. I told him you were asleep; he seems to have a foreknowledge of that too, and therefore comes to speak with you. What is to be said to him, lady? he's fortified against any denial.

Oli. Tell him he shall not speak with me.

Mal. Has been told so; and he says he'll stand at your door like a sheriff's post and be the supporter to a bench, but he'll speak with you.

Oli. What kind o' man is he?

Mal. Why, of mankind.

Oli. What manner of man?

Mal. Of very ill manner; he'll speak with you, will you or no.

Oli. Of what personage and years is he?

Mal. Not yet old enough for a man, nor young enough for a boy; as a squash is before 'tis a peascod, or a codling when 'tis almost an apple: 'tis with him in standing water, between boy and man. He is very well-favoured and he speaks very shrewishly; one would think his mother's milk were scarce out of him.

Oli. Let him approach: call in my gentlewoman.

Mal. Gentlewoman, my lady calls. [*Exit.*

Re-enter MARIA.

Oli. Give me my veil: come, throw it o'er my face.
We'll once more hear Orsino's embassy.

Enter VIOLA, *and Attendants.*

Vio. The honourable lady of the house, which is she?

Oli. Speak to me; I shall answer for her. Your will?

Vio. Most radiant, exquisite, and unmatchable beauty—I pray you, tell me if this be the lady of the house, for I never saw her: I would be loath to cast away my speech, for besides that it is excellently well penned, I have taken great pains to con it. Good beauties, let me sustain no scorn; I am very comptible, even to the least sinister usage.

Oli. Whence came you, sir?

Vio. I can say little more than I have studied, and that question's out of my part. Good gentle one, give me modest assurance if you be the lady of the house, that I may proceed in my speech.

Oli. Are you a comedian?

Vio. No, my profound heart: and yet, by the very fangs of malice I swear, I am not that I play. Are you the lady of the house?

Oli. If I do not usurp myself, I am.

Vio. Most certain, if you are she, you do usurp yourself; for what is yours to bestow is not yours to reserve. But this is from my commission: I will on with my speech in your praise, and then show you the heart of my message.

Oli. Come to what is important in't: I forgive you the praise.

Vio. Alas, I took great pains to study it, and 'tis poetical.

Oli. It is the more like to be feigned: I pray you, keep it in. I heard you were saucy at my gates, and allowed your approach rather to wonder at you than to hear you. If you be not mad, be gone; if you have reason, be brief: 'tis not that time of moon with me to make one in so skipping a dialogue.

Mar. Will you hoist sail, sir? here lies your way.

Vio. No, good swabber; I am to hull here a little longer. Some mollification for your giant, sweet lady. Tell me your mind: I am a messenger.

Oli. Sure, you have some hideous matter to deliver, when the courtesy of it is so fearful. Speak your office.

Vio. It alone concerns your ear. I bring no overture of war, no taxation of homage: I hold the olive in my hand; my words are as full of peace as matter.

Oli. Yet you began rudely. What are you? what would you?

Vio. The rudeness that hath appeared in me have I learned from my entertainment. What I am, and what I would, are as secret as maidenhead; to your ears, divinity, to any other's profanation.

Oli. Give us the place alone: we will hear this divinity. [*Exeunt* MARIA *and Attendants.*] Now, sir, what is your text?

Vio. Most sweet lady—

Oli. A comfortable doctrine, and much may be said of it. Where lies your text?

Vio. In Orsino's bosom.

Oli. In his bosom! In what chapter of his bosom?

Vio. To answer by the method, in the first of his heart.

Oli. O, I have read it: it is heresy. Have you no more to say?

Vio. Good madam, let me see your face.

Oli. Have you any commission from your lord to negotiate with my face? You are now out of your text: but we will draw the curtain and show you the picture. Look you, sir, such a one I was this present: is't not well done? [*Unveiling.*]

Vio. Excellently done, if God did all.

Oli. 'Tis in grain, sir; 'twill endure wind and weather.

Vio. 'Tis beauty truly blent, whose red and white
Nature's own sweet and cunning hand laid on:
Lady, you are the cruell'st she alive,
If you will lead these graces to the grave
And leave the world no copy.

Oli. O, sir, I will not be so hard-hearted; I will give out divers schedules of my beauty: it shall be inventoried, and every particle and utensil labelled to my will: as, item, two lips, indifferent red; item, two grey eyes, with lids to them; item, one neck, one chin, and so forth. Were you sent hither to praise me?

Vio. I see you what you are, you are too proud;
But, if you were the devil, you are fair.
My lord and master loves you. O such love

Could be but recompensed, though you were crown'd
The nonpareil of beauty!
Oli. How does he love me?
Vio. With adorations, fertile tears,
With groans that thunder love, with sighs of fire.
Oli. Your lord does know my mind; I cannot love him:
Yet I suppose him virtuous, know him noble,
Of great estate, of fresh and stainless youth;
In voices well divulged, free, learn'd, and valiant;
And in dimension and the shape of nature
A gracious person: but yet I cannot love him;
He might have took his answer long ago.
Vio. If I did love you in master's flame,
With such a suffering, such a deadly life,
In your denial I would find no sense;
I would not understand it.
Oli. Why, what would you?
Vio. Make me a willow cabin at your gate,
And call upon my soul within the house;
Write loyal cantons of contemned love
And sing them loud even in the dead of night;
Halloo your name to the reverberate hills
And make the babbling gossip of the air
Cry out "Olivia!" O, you should not rest
Between the elements of air and earth,
But you should pity me!
Oli. You might do much.
What is your parentage?
Vio. Above my fortunes, yet my state is well:
I am a gentleman.
Oli. Get you to your lord:
I cannot love him: let him send no more;
Unless, perchance, you come to me again,
To tell me how he takes it. Fare you well:
I thank you for your pains: spend this for me.
Vio. I am no fee'd post, lady; keep your purse:
My master, not myself, lacks recompense.
Love make his heart of flint that you shall love;
And let your fervour, like my master's, be
Placed in contempt! Farewell, fair cruelty. [*Exit.*
Oli. "What is your parentage?"
"Above my fortunes, yet my state is well:
I am a gentleman." I'll be sworn thou art;
Thy tongue, thy face, thy limbs, actions, and spirit,
Do give thee five-fold blazon: not too fast: soft, soft!
Unless the master were the man. How now!
Even so quickly may one catch the plague?
Methinks I feel this youth's perfections
With an invisible and subtle stealth
To creep in at mine eyes. Well, let it be.
What ho, Malvolio!

Re-enter MALVOLIO.

Mal. Here, madam, at your service.
Oli. Run after that same peevish messenger,
The County's man: he left this ring behind him,
Would I or not: tell him I'll none of it.
Desire him not to flatter with his lord,
Nor hold him up with hopes; I am not for him:
If that the youth will come this way to-morrow,
I'll give him reasons for't: hie thee, Malvolio.
Mal. Madam, I will. [*Exit.*
Oli. I do I know not what, and fear to find
Mine eye too great a flatterer for my mind.
Fate, show thy force: ourselves we do not owe;
What is decreed must be, and be this so. [*Exit.*

ACT II

SCENE I. *The sea-coast*

Enter ANTONIO *and* SEBASTIAN.

Ant. Will you stay no longer? nor will you not that I go with you?

Seb. By your patience, no. My stars shine darkly over me: the malignancy of my fate might perhaps distemper yours; therefore I shall crave of your leave that I may bear my evils alone: it were a bad recompense for your love, to lay any of them on you.

Ant. Let me yet know of you whither you are bound.

Seb. No, sooth, sir: my determinate voyage is mere extravagancy. But I perceive in you so excellent a touch of modesty that you will not extort from me what I am willing to keep in; therefore it charges me in manners the rather to express myself. You must know of me then, Antonio, my name is Sebastian, which I called Roderigo. My father was that Sebastian of Messaline, whom I know you have heard of. He left behind him myself and a sister, both born in an hour: if the heavens had been pleased, would we had so ended! but you, sir, altered that; for some hour before you took me from the breach of the sea was my sister drowned.

Ant. Alas the day!

Seb. A lady, sir, though it was said she much resembled me, was yet of many accounted beautiful: but, though I could not with such estimable wonder overfar believe that, yet thus far I will boldly publish her; she bore a mind that envy could not but call fair. She is drowned already, sir, with salt water, though I seem to drown her remembrance again with more.

Ant. Pardon me, sir, your bad entertainment.

Seb. O good Antonio, forgive me your trouble.

Ant. If you will not murder me for my love, let me be your servant.

Seb. If you will not undo what you have done, that is, kill him whom you have recovered, desire it not. Fare ye well at once: my bosom is full of kindness, and I am yet so near the manners of my mother, that upon the least occasion more mine eyes will tell tales of me. I am bound to the Count Orsino's court: farewell. [*Exit*.

Ant. The gentleness of all the gods go with thee!
I have many enemies in Orsino's court,
Else would I very shortly see thee there.
But, come what may, I do adore thee so,
That danger shall seem sport, and I will go.
[*Exit*.

SCENE II. *A street*

Enter VIOLA, MALVOLIO *following*.

Mal. Were not you even now with the Countess Olivia?

Vio. Even now, sir; on a moderate pace I have since arrived but hither.

Mal. She returns this ring to you, sir: you might have saved me my pains, to have taken it away yourself. She adds, moreover, that you should put your lord into a desperate assurance she will none of him: and one thing more, that you be never so hardy to come again in his affairs, unless it be to report your lord's taking of this. Receive it so.

Vio. She took the ring of me: I'll none of it.

Mal. Come, sir, you peevishly threw it to her; and her will is, it should be so returned: if it be worth stooping for, there it lies in your eye; if not, be it his that finds it. [*Exit*.

Vio. I left no ring with her: what means this lady?
Fortune forbid my outside have not charm'd her!
She made good view of me; indeed, so much,
That sure methought her eyes had lost her tongue,
For she did speak in starts distractedly.
She loves me, sure; the cunning of her passion
Invites me in this churlish messenger.
None of my lord's ring! why, he sent her none.
I am the man: if it be so, as 'tis,
Poor lady, she were better love a dream.
Disguise, I see, thou art a wickedness,
Wherein the pregnant enemy does much.
How easy is it for the proper-false
In women's waxen hearts to set their forms!
Alas, our frailty is the cause, not we!
For such as we are made of, such we be.
How will this fadge? my master loves her dearly;
And I, poor monster, fond as much on him;
And she, mistaken, seems to dote on me.
What will become of this? As I am man,
My state is desperate for my master's love;
As I am woman— now alas the day!—
What thriftless sighs shall poor Olivia breathe!
O time! thou must untangle this, not I;
It is too hard a knot for me to untie! [*Exit*.

SCENE III. *Olivia's house*

Enter SIR TOBY *and* SIR ANDREW.

Sir To. Approach, Sir Andrew: not to be abed after midnight is to be up betimes; and "*diluculo surgere*," thou know'st—

Sir And. Nay, by my troth, I know not: but I know, to be up late is to be up late.

Sir To. A false conclusion: I hate it as an unfilled can. To be up after midnight and to go to bed then, is early: so that to go to bed after midnight is to go bed betimes. Does not our life consist of the four elements?

Sir And. Faith, so they say; but I think it rather consists of eating and drinking.

Sir To. Thou'rt a scholar; let us therefore eat and drink. Marian, I say! a stoup of wine!

Enter CLOWN.

Sir And. Here comes the fool, i' faith.

Clo. How now, my hearts! did you never see the picture of "we three"?

Sir To. Welcome, ass. Now let's have a catch.

Sir And. By my troth, the fool has an excellent breast. I had rather than forty shillings I had such a leg, and so sweet a breath to sing, as the fool has. In sooth, thou wast in very gracious fooling last night, when thou spokest of Pigrogromitus, of the Vapians passing the equinoctial of Queubus: 'twas very good, i' faith. I sent thee sixpence for thy leman: hadst it?

Clo. I did impeticos thy gratillity; for Malvolio's nose is no whipstock: my lady has a white hand, and the Myrmidons are no bottle-ale houses.

Sir And. Excellent! why, this is the best fooling, when all is done. Now, a song.

Sir To. Come on; there is sixpence for you: let's have a song.

Sir And. There's a testril of me too: if one knight give a—

Clo. Would you have a love-song, or a song of good life?

Sir To. A love-song, a love-song.

Sir And. Ay, ay: I care not for good life.

Clo. [*Sings*]
"O mistress, where are you roaming?
O, stay and hear; your true love's coming,

That can sing both high and low:
Trip no further, pretty sweeting;
Journeys end in lovers meeting,
Every wise man's son doth know."

Sir And. Excellent good, i' faith.

Sir To. Good, good.

Clo. [*Sings*]
"What is love? 'tis not hereafter;
Present mirth hath present laughter;
What's to come is still unsure:
In delay there lies no plenty;
Then come kiss me, sweet and twenty,
Youth's a stuff will not endure."

Sir And. A mellifluous voice, as I am true knight.

Sir To. A contagious breath.

Sir And. Very sweet and contagious, i' faith.

Sir To. To hear by the nose, it is dulcet in contagion. But shall we make the welkin dance indeed? shall we rouse the night-owl in a catch that will draw three souls out of one weaver? shall we do that?

Sir And. An you love me, let's do't: I am dog at a catch.

Clo. By'r lady, sir, and some dogs will catch well.

Sir And. Most certain. Let our catch be, "Thou knave."

Clo. "Hold thy peace, thou knave," knight? I shall be constrained in't to call thee knave, knight.

Sir And. 'Tis not the first time I have constrained one to call me knave. Begin, fool: it begins "Hold thy peace."

Clo. I shall never begin if I hold my peace.

Sir And. Good, i' faith. Come, begin.

Catch sung.

Enter MARIA.

Mar. What a caterwauling do you keep here! If my lady have not called up her steward Malvolio and bid him turn you out of doors, never trust me.

Sir To. My lady's a Cataian, we are politicians, Malvolio's a Peg-a-Ramsey, and "Three merry men be we." Am not I consanguineous? am I not of her blood? Tilly-vally. Lady! [*Sings*]
"There dwelt a man in Babylon, lady, lady!"

Clo. Beshrew me, the knight's in admirable fooling.

Sir And. Ay, he does well enough if he be disposed, and so do I too: he does it with a better grace, but I do it more natural.

Sir To. [*Sings*] "O, the twelfth day of December"—

Mar. For the love o' God, peace!

Enter MALVOLIO.

Mal. My masters, are you mad? or what are you? Have you no wit, manners, nor honesty, but to gabble like tinkers at this time of night? Do ye make an alehouse of my lady's house, that ye squeak out your coziers' catches without any mitigation or remorse of voice? Is there no respect of place, persons, nor time in you?

Sir To. We did keep time, sir, in our catches. Sneck up!

Mal. Sir Toby, I must be round with you. My lady bade me tell you, that, though she harbours you as her kinsman, she's nothing allied to your disorders. If you can separate yourself and your misdemeanours, you are welcome to the house; if not, an it would please you to take leave of her, she is very willing to bid you farewell.

Sir To. "Farewell, dear heart, since I must needs be gone."

Mar. Nay, good Sir Toby.

Clo. "His eyes do show his days are almost done."

Mal. Is't even so?

Sir To. "But I will never die."

Clo. Sir Toby, there you lie.

Mal. This is much credit to you.

Sir To. "Shall I bid him go?"

Clo. "What an if you do?"

Sir To. "Shall I bid him go, and spare not?"

Clo. "O no, no, no, no, you dare not."

Sir To. Out o' tune, sir: ye lie. Art any more than a steward? Dost thou think, because thou art virtuous, there shall be no more cakes and ale?

Clo. Yes, by Saint Anne, and ginger shall be hot i' the mouth too.

Sir To. Thou'rt i' the right. Go, sir, rub your chain with crumbs. A stoup of wine, Maria!

Mal. Mistress Mary, if you prized my lady's favour at any thing more than contempt, you would not give means for this uncivil rule: she shall know of it, by this hand. [*Exit.*

Mar. Go shake your ears.

Sir And. 'Twere as good a deed as to drink when a man's a-hungry, to challenge him the field, and then to break promise with him and make a fool of him.

Sir To. Do't, knight: I'll write thee a challenge; or I'll deliver thy indignation to him by word of mouth.

Mar. Sweet Sir Toby, be patient for to-night: since the youth of the Count's was to-day with my lady, she is much out of quiet. For Monsieur Malvolio, let me alone with him: if I do not gull him into a nayword, and make him a common recreation, do not think I have wit enough to lie straight in my bed: I know I can do it.

Sir To. Possess us, possess us; tell us something of him.

Mar. Marry, sir, sometimes he is a kind of puritan.

Sir And. O, if I thought that, I'd beat him like a dog!

Sir To. What, for being a puritan? thy exquisite reason, dear knight?

Sir And. I have no exquisite reason for't, but I have reason good enough.

Mar. The devil a puritan that he is, or any thing constantly, but a time-pleaser; an affectioned ass, that cons state without book and utters it by great swarths: the best persuaded of himself, so crammed, as he thinks, with excellencies, that it is his grounds of faith that all that look on him love him; and on that vice in him will my revenge find notable cause to work.

Sir To. What wilt thou do?

Mar. I will drop in his way some obscure epistles of love; wherein, by the colour of his beard, the shape of his leg, the manner of his gait, the expressure of his eye, forehead, and complexion, he shall find himself most feelingly personated. I can write very like my lady your niece: on a forgotten matter we can hardly make distinction of our hands.

Sir To. Excellent! I smell a device.

Sir And. I have't in my nose too.

Sir To. He shall think, by the letters that thou wilt drop, that they come from my niece, and that she's in love with him.

Mar. My purpose is, indeed, a horse of that colour.

Sir And. And your horse now would make him an ass.

Mar. Ass, I doubt not.

Sir And. O, 'twill be admirable!

Mar. Sport royal, I warrant you: I know my physic will work with him. I will plant you two, and let the fool make a third, where he shall find the letter: observe his construction of it. For this night, to bed, and dream on the event. Farewell. [*Exit.*

Sir To. Good night, Penthesilea.

Sir And. Before me, she's a good wench.

Sir To. She's a beagle, true-bred, and one that adores me: what o' that?

Sir And. I was adored once too.

Sir To. Let's to bed, knight. Thou hadst need send for more money.

Sir And. If I cannot recover your niece, I am a foul way out.

Sir To. Send for money, knight: if thou hast her not i' the end, call me cut.

Sir And. If I do not, never trust me, take it how you will.

Sir To. Come, come, I'll go burn some sack; 'tis too late to go to bed now: come, knight; come, knight. [*Exeunt.*

SCENE IV. *The* DUKE'S *palace*

Enter DUKE, VIOLA, CURIO, *and others.*

Duke. Give me some music. Now, good morrow, friends.
Now, good Cesario, but that piece of song,
That old and antique song we heard last night:
Methought it did relieve my passion much,
More than light airs and recollected terms
Of these most brisk and giddy-paced times:
Come, but one verse.

Cur. He is not here, so please your lordship, that should sing it.

Duke. Who was it?

Cur. Feste, the jester, my lord; a fool that the lady Olivia's father took much delight in. He is about the house.

Duke. Seek him out, and play the tune the while. [*Exit* CURIO. *Music plays.*
Come hither, boy: if ever thou shalt love,
In the sweet pangs of it remember me;
For such as I am all true lovers are,
Unstaid and skittish in all motions else,
Save in the constant image of the creature
That is beloved. How dost thou like this tune?

Vio. It gives a very echo to the seat
Where Love is throned.

Duke. Thou dost speak masterly:
My life upon't, young though thou art, thine eye
Hath stay'd upon some favour that it loves:
Hath it not, boy?

Vio. A little, by your favour.

Duke. What kind of woman is't?

Vio. Of your complexion.

Duke. She is not worth thee, then. What years, i' faith?

Vio. About your years, my lord.

Duke. Too old, by heaven: let still the woman take
An elder than herself: so wears she to him,
So sways she level in her husband's heart:
For, boy, however we do praise ourselves,
Our fancies are more giddy and unfirm,
More longing, wavering, sooner lost and worn,
Than women's are.

Vio. I think it well, my lord.

Duke. Then let thy love be younger than thyself,
Or thy affection cannot hold the bent;

For women are as roses, whose fair flower
Being once display'd, doth fall that very hour.
Vio. And so they are: alas, that they are so;
To die, even when they to perfection grow!

Re-enter CURIO *and* CLOWN.

Duke. O, fellow, come, the song we had last night.
Mark it, Cesario, it is old and plain;
The spinsters and the knitters in the sun
And the free maids that weave their thread with bones
Do use to chant it: it is silly sooth,
And dallies with the innocence of love,
Like the old age.
Clo. Are you ready, sir?
Duke. Ay; prithee, sing.
Music.

SONG.

Clo. "Come away, come away, death,
And in sad cypress let me be laid;
Fly away, fly away, breath;
I am slain by a fair cruel maid.
My shroud of white, stuck all with yew,
O, prepare it!
My part of death, no one so true
Did share it.

Not a flower, not a flower sweet,
On my black coffin let there be strown;
Not a friend, not a friend greet
My poor corpse, where my bones shall be thrown:
A thousand thousand sighs to save,
Lay me, O, where
Sad true lover never find my grave,
To weep there!"

Duke. There's for thy pains.

Clo. No pains, sir; I take pleasure in singing, sir.

Duke. I'll pay thy pleasure then.

Clo. Truly, sir, and pleasure will be paid, one time or another.

Duke. Give me now leave to leave thee.

Clo. Now, the melancholy god protect thee; and the tailor make thy doublet of changeable taffeta, for thy mind is a very opal. I would have men of such constancy put to sea, that their business might be everything and their intent everywhere; for that's it that always makes a good voyage of nothing. Farewell. [*Exit*.

Duke. Let all the rest give place.
[CURIO *and Attendants retire*.
Once more, Cesario,
Get thee to yond same sovereign cruelty:
Tell her, my love, more noble than the world,
Prizes not quantity of dirty lands;
The parts that fortune hath bestow'd upon her,
Tell her, I hold as giddily as fortune;
But 'tis that miracle and queen of gems
That nature pranks her in attracts my soul.
Vio. But if she cannot love you, sir?
Duke. I cannot be so answer'd.
Vio. Sooth, but you must.
Say that some lady, as perhaps there is,
Hath for your love as great a pang of heart
As you have for Olivia: you cannot love her;
You tell her so; must she not then be answer'd?
Duke. There is no woman's sides
Can bide the beating of so strong a passion
As love doth give my heart; no woman's heart
So big, to hold so much; they lack retention.
Alas, their love may be call'd appetite,
No motion of the liver, but the palate,
That suffer surfeit, cloyment, and revolt;
But mine is all as hungry as the sea,
And can digest as much: make no compare
Between that love a woman can bear me
And that I owe Olivia.
Vio. Ay, but I know—
Duke. What dost thou know?
Vio. Too well what love women to men may owe:
In faith, they are as true of heart as we.
My father had a daughter loved a man,
As it might be, perhaps, were I a woman,
I should your lordship
Duke. And what's her history?
Vio. A blank, my lord. She never told her love,
But let concealment, like a worm i' the bud,
Feed on her damask cheek: she pined in thought,
And with a green and yellow melancholy
She sat like patience on a monument,
Smiling at grief. Was not this love indeed?
We men may say more, swear more: but indeed
Our shows are more than will; for still we prove
Much in our vows, but little in our love.
Duke. But died thy sister of her love, my boy?
Vio. I am all the daughters of my father's house,
And all the brothers too: and yet I know not.
Sir, shall I to this lady?
Duke. Ay, that's the theme.
To her in haste; give her this jewel; say
My love can give no place, bide no denay.
[*Exeunt*.

SCENE V. *Olivia's garden*

Enter SIR TOBY, SIR ANDREW, *and* FABIAN.

Sir To. Come thy ways, Signior Fabian.

Fab. Nay, I'll come: if I lose a scruple of this sport, let me be boiled to death with melancholy.

Sir To. Wouldst thou not be glad to have the niggardly rascally sheep-biter come by some notable shame?

Fab. I would exult, man: you know, he brought me out o' favour with my lady about a bear-baiting here.

Sir To. To anger him we'll have the bear again; and we will fool him black and blue: shall we not, Sir Andrew?

Sir And. An we do not, it is pity of our lives.

Sir To. Here comes the little villain.

Enter MARIA.

How now, my metal of India!

Mar. Get ye all three into the box-tree: Malvolio's coming down this walk: he has been yonder i' the sun practising behaviour to his own shadow this half hour: observe him, for the love of mockery; for I know this letter will make a contemplative idiot of him. Close, in the name of jesting! Lie thou there [*throws down a letter*]; for here comes the trout that must be caught with tickling. [*Exit.*

Enter MALVOLIO.

Mal. 'Tis but fortune; all is fortune. Maria once told me she did affect me: and I have heard herself come thus near, that, should she fancy, it should be one of my complexion. Besides, she uses me with a more exalted respect than any one else that follows her. What should I think on't?

Sir To. Here's an overweening rogue!

Fab. O, peace! Contemplation makes a rare turkey-cock of him: how he jets under his advanced plumes!

Sir And. 'Slight, I could so beat the rogue!

Sir To. Peace, I say.

Mal. To be Count Malvolio!

Sir To. Ah, rogue!

Sir And. Pistol him, pistol him.

Sir To. Peace, peace!

Mal. There is example for't; the lady of the Strachy married the yoeman of the wardrobe.

Sir And. Fie on him, Jezebel!

Fab. O, peace! now he's deeply in: look how imagination blows him.

Mal. Having been three months married to her, sitting in my state—

Sir To. O, for a stone-bow, to hit him in the eye!

Mal. Calling my officers about me, in my branched velvet gown; having come from a day-bed, where I have left Olivia sleeping—

Sir To. Fire and brimstone!

Fab. O, peace, peace!

Mal. And then to have the humour of state; and after a demure travel of regard, telling them I know my place as I would they should do theirs, to ask for my kinsman Toby—

Sir To. Bolts and shackles!

Fab. O peace, peace, peace! now, now.

Mal. Seven of my people, with an obedient start, make out for him: I frown the while; and perchance wind up my watch, or play with my—some rich jewel. Toby approaches; courtesies there to me—

Sir To. Shall this fellow live?

Fab. Though our silence be drawn from us with cars, yet peace.

Mal. I extend my hand to him thus, quenching my familiar smile with an austere regard of control—

Sir To. And does not Toby take you a blow o' the lips then?

Mal. Saying, "Cousin Toby, my fortunes having cast me on your niece give me this prerogative of speech"—

Sir To. What, what?

Mal. "You must amend your drunkenness."

Sir To. Out, scab!

Fab. Nay, patience, or we break the sinews of our plot.

Mal. "Besides, you waste the treasure of your time with a foolish knight"—

Sir And. That's me, I warrant you.

Mal. "One Sir Andrew"—

Sir And. I knew 'twas I; for many do call me fool.

Mal. What employment have we here?

Taking up the letter.

Fab. Now is the woodcock near the gin.

Sir To. O, peace! and the spirit of humours intimate reading aloud to him!

Mal. By my life, this is my lady's hand: these be her very *C*'s, her *U*'s and her *T*'s; and thus makes she her great *P*'s. It is, in contempt of question, her hand.

Sir And. Her *C*'s, her *U*'s and her *T*'s: why that?

Mal. [*Reads*] "To the unknown beloved, this, and my good wishes"—her very phrases! By your leave, wax. Soft! and the impressure her Lucrece, with which she uses to seal: 'tis my lady. To whom should this be?

Fab. This wins him, liver and all.

Mal. [*Reads*] "Jove knows I love:
But who?
Lips, do not move;
No man must know."

"No man must know." What follows? the numbers altered! "No man must know." If this should be thee, Malvolio?

Sir To. Marry, hang thee, brock!

Mal. [*Reads*]
"I may command where I adore;
But silence, like a Lucrece knife,
With bloodless stroke my heart doth
gore:
M, O, A, I, doth sway my life."

Fab. A fustian riddle!

Sir To. Excellent wench, say I.

Mal. "M, O, A, I, doth sway my life." Nay, but first, let me see, let me see, let me see.

Fab. What dish o'poison has she dressed him!

Sir To. And with what wing the staniel checks at it!

Mal. "I may command where I adore." Why, she may command me: I serve her; she is my lady. Why, this is evident to any formal capacity; there is no obstruction in this: and the end—what should that alphabetical position portend? If I could make that resemble something in me—Softly! *M, O, A, I*—

Sir To. O, ay, make up that: he is now at a cold scent.

Fab. Sowter will cry upon't for all this, though it be as rank as a fox.

Mal. *M*—Malvolio; *M*—why, that begins my name.

Fab. Did not I say he would work it out? the cur is excellent at faults.

Mal. *M*—but then there is no consonancy in the sequel; that suffers under probation: *A* should follow, but *O* does.

Fab. And *O* shall end, I hope.

Sir To. Ay, or I'll cudgel him, and make him cry *O!*

Mal. And then *I* comes behind.

Fab. Ay, an you had any eye behind you, you might see more detraction at your heels than fortunes before you.

Mal. *M, O, A, I;* this simulation is not as the former: and yet, to crush this a little, it would bow to me, for every one of these letters are in my name. Soft! here follows prose.

[*Reads*] "If this fall into thy hand, revolve. In my stars I am above thee; but be not afraid of greatness: some are born great, some achieve greatness, and some have greatness thrust upon 'em. Thy Fates open their hands; let thy blood and spirit embrace them; and, to inure thyself to what thou art like to be, cast thy humble slough and appear fresh. Be opposite with a kinsman, surly with servants; let thy tongue tang arguments of state; put thyself into the trick of singularity: she thus advises thee that sighs for thee. Remember who commended thy yellow stockings, and wished to see thee ever cross-gartered: I say, remember. Go to, thou art made, if thou desirest to be so; if not, let me see thee a steward still, the fellow of servants, and not worthy to touch Fortune's fingers. Farewell. She that would alter services with thee,
The Fortunate-Unhappy"

Daylight and champaign discovers not more: this is open. I will be proud, I will read politic authors, I will baffle Sir Toby, I will wash off gross acquaintance, I will be point-devise the very man. I do not now fool myself, to let imagination jade me; for every reason excites to this, that my lady loves me. She did commend my yellow stockings of late, she did praise my leg being cross-gartered; and in this she manifests herself to my love, and with a kind of injunction drives me to these habits of her liking. I thank my stars I am happy. I will be strange, stout, in yellow stockings, and cross-gartered, even with the swiftness of putting on. Jove and my stars be praised! Here is yet a postscript.

[*Reads*] "Thou canst not choose but know who I am. If thou entertainest my love, let it appear in thy smiling; thy smiles become thee well; therefore in my presence still smile, dear my sweet, I prithee."

Jove, I thank thee: I will smile; I will do everything that thou wilt have me. [*Exit*.

Fab. I will not give my part of this sport for a pension of thousands to be paid from the Sophy.

Sir To. I could marry this wench for this device.

Sir And. So could I too.

Sir To. And ask no other dowry with her but such another jest.

Sir And. Nor I neither.

Fab. Here comes my noble gull-catcher.

Re-enter MARIA.

Sir To. Wilt thou set thy foot o' my neck?

Sir And. Or o' mine either?

Sir To. Shall I play my freedom at tray-trip, and become thy bond-slave?

Sir And. I' faith, or I either?

Sir To. Why, thou hast put him in such a dream, that when the image of it leaves him he must run mad.

Mar. Nay, but say true; does it work upon him?

Sir To. Like aqua-vitæ with a midwife.

Mar. If you will then see the fruits of the sport, mark his first approach before my lady: he will come to her in yellow stockings, and 'tis a colour she abhors, and cross-gartered, a fashion she detests; and he will smile upon her, which will now be so unsuitable to her disposition, being addicted to a melancholy as she is, that it cannot but turn him into a notable contempt. If you will see it, follow me.

Sir To. To the gates of Tartar, thou most excellent devil of wit!

Sir And. I'll make one too. [*Exeunt.*

ACT III

SCENE I. *Olivia's garden*

Enter VIOLA, *and* CLOWN *with a tabor.*

Vio. Save thee, friend, and thy music: dost thou live by thy tabor?

Clo. No, sir, I live by the church.

Vio. Art thou a churchman?

Clo. No such matter, sir: I do live by the church; for I do live at my house, and my house doth stand by the church.

Vio. So thou mayst say, the king lies by a beggar, if a beggar dwell near him; or, the church stands by thy tabor, if thy tabor stand by the church.

Clo. You have said, sir. To see this age! A sentence is but a cheveril glove to a good wit: how quickly the wrong side may be turned outward!

Vio. Nay, that's certain; they that dally nicely with words may quickly make them wanton.

Clo. I would, therefore, my sister had had no name, sir.

Vio. Why, man?

Clo. Why, sir, her name's a word; and to dally with that word might make my sister wanton. But indeed words are very rascals since bonds disgraced them.

Vio. Thy reason, man?

Clo. Troth, sir, I can yield you none without words; and words are grown so false, I am loath to prove reason with them.

Vio. I warrant thou art a merry fellow and carest for nothing.

Clo. Not so, sir, I do care for something; but in my conscience, sir, I do not care for you: if that be to care for nothing, sir, I would it would make you invisible.

Vio. Art not thou the Lady Olivia's fool?

Clo. No, indeed, sir; the Lady Olivia has no folly: she will keep no fool, sir, till she be married; and fools are as like husbands as pilchards are to herrings; the husband's the bigger. I am indeed not her fool, but her corrupter of words.

Vio. I saw thee late at the Count Orsino's.

Clo. Foolery, sir, does walk about the orb like the sun, it shines everywhere. I would be sorry, sir, but the fool should be as oft with your master as with my mistress: I think I saw your wisdom there.

Vio. Nay, an thou pass upon me, I'll no more with thee. Hold, there's expenses for thee.

Clo. Now Jove, in his next commodity of hair, send thee a beard!

Vio. By my troth, I'll tell thee, I am almost sick for one; [*Aside*] though I would not have it grow on my chin. Is thy lady within?

Clo. Would not a pair of these have bred, sir?

Vio. Yes, being kept together and put to use.

Clo. I would play Lord Pandarus of Phrygia, sir, to bring a Cressida to this Troilus.

Vio. I understand you, sir; 'tis well begged.

Clo. The matter, I hope, is not great, sir, begging but a beggar: Cressida was a beggar. My lady is within, sir. I will construe to them whence you come; who you are and what you would are out of my welkin, I might say "element," but the word is over-worn. [*Exit.*

Vio. This fellow is wise enough to play the
fool;
And to do that well craves a kind of wit.
He must observe their mood on whom he jests,
The quality of persons, and the time,
And, like the haggard, check at every feather
That comes before his eye. This is a practice
As full of labour as a wise man's art:
For folly that he wisely shows is fit;
But wise men, folly-fall'n, quite taint their wit.

Enter SIR TOBY, *and* SIR ANDREW.

Sir To. Save you, gentleman.

Vio. And you, sir.

Sir And. *Dieu vous garde, monsieur.*

Vio. *Et vous aussi; votre serviteur.*

Sir And. I hope, sir, you are; and I am yours.

Sir To. Will you encounter the house? my niece is desirous you should enter, if your trade be to her.

Vio. I am bound to your niece, sir; I mean, she is the list of my voyage.

Sir To. Taste your legs, sir; put them to motion.

Vio. My legs do better understand me, sir, than I understand what you mean by bidding me taste my legs.

Sir To. I mean, to go, sir, to enter.

Vio. I will answer you with gait and entrance.
But we are prevented.

Enter OLIVIA *and* MARIA.

Most excellent accomplished lady, the heavens rain odours on you!

Sir And. That youth's a rare courtier: "Rain odours"; well.

Vio. My matter hath no voice, lady, but to your own most pregnant and vouchsafed ear.

Sir And. "Odours," "pregnant," and "vouchsafed"; I'll get 'em all three all ready.

Oli. Let the garden door be shut, and leave me to my hearing. [*Exeunt* SIR TOBY, SIR ANDREW, *and* MARIA.] Give me your hand, sir.

Vio. My duty, madam, and most humble service.

Oli. What is your name?

Vio. Cesario is your servant's name, fair princess.

Oli. My servant, sir! 'Twas never merry world
Since lowly feigning was call'd compliment:
You're servant to the Count Orsino, youth.

Vio. And he is yours, and his must needs be yours:
Your servant's servant is your servant, madam.

Oli. For him, I think not on him: for his thoughts,
Would they were blanks, rather than fill'd with me!

Vio. Madam, I come to whet your gentle thoughts
On his behalf.

Oli. O, by your leave, I pray you,
I bade you never speak again of him:
But, would you undertake another suit,
I had rather hear you to solicit that
Than music from the spheres.

Vio. Dear lady—

Oli. Give me leave, beseech you. I did send,
After the last enchantment you did here,
A ring in chase of you: so did I abuse
Myself, my servant, and, I fear me, you:
Under your hard construction must I sit,
To force that on you, in a shameful cunning,
Which you knew none of yours: what might you think?
Have you not set mine honour at the stake
And baited it with all the unmuzzled thoughts
That tyrannous heart can think? To one of your receiving
Enough is shown: a cypress, not a bosom,
Hideth my heart. So, let me hear you speak.

Vio. I pity you.

Oli. That's a degree to love.

Vio. No, not a grize; for 'tis a vulgar proof,
That very oft we pity enemies.

Oli. Why, then, methinks 'tis time to smile again.
O world, how apt the poor are to be proud!
If one should be a prey, how much the better
To fall before the lion than the wolf!

Clock strikes.

The clock upbraids me with the waste of time.
Be not afraid, good youth, I will not have you:
And yet, when wit and youth is come to harvest,
Your wife is like to reap a proper man:
There lies your way, due west.

Vio. Then westward-ho! Grace and good disposition
Attend your ladyship!
You'll nothing, madam, to my lord by me?

Oli. Stay:
I prithee, tell me what thou think'st of me.

Vio. That you do think you are not what you are.

Oli. If I think so, I think the same of you.

Vio. Then think you right: I am not what I am.

Oli. I would you were as I would have you be!

Vio. Would it be better, madam, than I am?
I wish it might, for now I am your fool.

Oli. O, what a deal of scorn looks beautiful
In the contempt and anger of his lip!
A murderous guilt shows not itself more soon
Than love that would seem hid: love's night is noon.
Cesario, by the roses of the spring,
By maidhood, honour, truth, and everything,
I love thee so, that, maugre all thy pride,
Nor wit nor reason can my passion hide.
Do not extort thy reasons from this clause,
For that I woo, thou therefore hast no cause;
But rather reason thus with reason fetter,
Love sought is good, but given unsought is better.

Vio. By innocence I swear, and by my youth,
I have one heart, one bosom, and one truth,
And that no woman has; nor never none
Shall mistress be of it, save I alone.
And so adieu, good madam: never more
Will I my master's tears to you deplore.

Oli. Yet come again; for thou perhaps mayst move
That heart, which now abhors, to like his love.
[*Exeunt*.

SCENE II. *Olivia's house*

Enter SIR TOBY, SIR ANDREW, *and* FABIAN.

Sir And. No, faith, I'll not stay a jot longer.

Sir To. Thy reason, dear venom, give thy reason.

Fab. You must needs yield your reason, Sir Andrew.

Sir And. Marry, I saw your niece do more favours to the Count's serving-man than ever she bestowed upon me; I saw 't i' the orchard.

Sir To. Did she see thee the while, old boy? Tell me that.

Sir And. As plain as I see you now.

Fab. This was a great argument of love in her toward you.

Sir And. 'Slight, will you make an ass o' me?

Fab. I will prove it legitimate, sir, upon the oaths of judgement and reason.

Sir To. And they have been grand-jurymen since before Noah was a sailor.

Fab. She did show favour to the youth in your sight only to exasperate you, to awake your dormouse valour, to put fire in your heart and brimstone in your liver. You should then have accosted her; and with some excellent jests, fire-new from the mint, you should have banged the youth into dumbness. This was looked for at your hand, and this was balked: the double gilt of this opportunity you let time wash off, and you are now sailed into the north of my lady's opinion; where you will hang like an icicle on a Dutchman's beard, unless you do redeem it by some laudable attempt either of valour or policy.

Sir And. An't be any way, it must be with valour; for policy I hate. I had as lief be a Brownist as a politician.

Sir To. Why, then, build me thy fortunes upon the basis of valour. Challenge me the Count's youth to fight with him; hurt him in eleven places; my niece shall take note of it; and assure thyself, there is no love-broker in the world can more prevail in man's commendation with woman than report of valour.

Fab. There is no way but this, Sir Andrew.

Sir. And. Will either of you bear me a challenge to him?

Sir To. Go, write it in a martial hand; be curst and brief; it is no matter how witty, so it be eloquent and full of invention: taunt him with the license of ink: if thou thou'st him some thrice, it shall not be amiss; and as many lies as will lie in thy sheet of paper, although the sheet were big enough for the bed of Ware in England, set 'em down: go, about it. Let there be gall enough in thy ink, though thou write with a goose-pen, no matter. About it.

Sir And. Where shall I find you?

Sir To. We'll call thee at the cubiculo: go.

[*Exit* SIR ANDREW.

Fab. This is a dear manikin to you, Sir Toby.

Sir To. I have been dear to him, lad, some two thousand strong, or so.

Fab. We shall have a rare letter from him: but you'll not deliver't?

Sir To. Never trust me, then; and by all means stir on the youth to an answer. I think oxen and wainropes cannot hale them together. For Andrew, if he were opened, and you find so much blood in his liver as will clog the foot of a flea, I'll eat the rest of the anatomy.

Fab. And his opposite, the youth, bears in his visage no great presage of cruelty.

Enter MARIA.

Sir To. Look, where the youngest wren of nine comes.

Mar. If you desire the spleen, and will laugh yoursleves into stitches, follow me. Yond gull Malvolio is turned heathen, a very renegado; for there is no Christian, that means to be saved by believing rightly, can ever believe such impossible passages of grossness. He's in yellow stockings.

Sir To. And cross-gartered?

Mar. Most villainously; like a pedant that keeps a school i' the church. I have dogged him, like his murderer. He does obey every point of the letter that I dropped to betray him. He does smile his face into more lines than is in the new map with the augmentation of the Indies: You have not seen such a thing as 'tis. I can hardly forbear hurling things at him. I know my lady will strike him: if she do, he'll smile and take't for a great favour.

Sir To. Come, bring us, bring us where he is.

[*Exeunt.*

SCENE III. *A street*

Enter SEBASTIAN *and* ANTONIO.

Seb. I would not by my will have troubled you;
But, since you make your pleasure of your pains,
I will no further chide you.

Ant. I could not stay behind you: my desire,
More sharp than filed steel, did spur me forth;
And not all love to see you, though so much
As might have drawn one to a longer voyage,
But jealousy what might befall your travel,
Being skilless in these parts; which to a stranger,
Unguided and unfriended, often prove
Rough and unhospitable: my willing love,
The rather by these arguments of fear,
Set forth in your pursuit.

Seb. My kind Antonio,
I can no other answer make but thanks,
And thanks; and ever thanks; and oft good turns
Are shuffled off with such uncurrent pay:
But, were my worth as is my conscience firm,
You should find better dealing. What's to do?

Shall we go see the reliques of this town?
Ant. To-morrow, sir: best first go see your lodging.
Seb. I am not weary, and 'tis long to night:
I pray you, let us satisfy our eyes
With the memorials and the things of fame
That do renown this city.
Ant. Would you'ld pardon me;
I do not without danger walk these streets:
Once, in a sea-fight, 'gainst the Count his galleys
I did some service; of such note indeed,
That were I ta'en here it would scarce be answer'd.
Seb. Belike you slew great number of his people.
Ant. The offence is not of such a bloody nature;
Albeit the quality of the time and quarrel
Might well have given us bloody argument.
It might have since been answer'd in repaying
What we took from them; which, for traffic's sake,
Most of our city did: only myself stood out;
For which, if I be lapsed in this place,
I shall pay dear.
Seb. Do not then walk too open.
Ant. It doth not fit me. Hold, sir, here's my purse.
In the south suburbs, at the Elephant,
Is best to lodge: I will bespeak our diet,
Whiles you beguile the time and feed your knowledge
With viewing of the town: there shall you have me.
Seb. Why I your purse?
Ant. Haply your eye shall light upon some toy
You have desire to purchase; and your store,
I think, is not for idle markets, sir.
Seb. I'll be your purse-bearer and leave you
For an hour.
Ant. To the Elephant.
Seb. I do remember. [*Exeunt.*

SCENE IV. *Olivia's garden*

Enter OLIVIA *and* MARIA.

Oli. I have sent after him: he says he'll come;
How shall I feast him? what bestow of him?
For youth is bought more oft than begg'd or borrow'd.
I speak too loud.
Where is Malvolio? he is sad and civil,
And suits well for a servant with my fortunes:
Where is Malvolio?

Mar. He's coming, madam; but in very strange manner. He is, sure, possessed, madam.

Oli. Why, what's the matter? does he rave?

Mar. No, madam, he does nothing but smile: your ladyship were best to have some guard about you, if he come; for, sure, the man is tainted in's wits.

Oli. Go call him hither. [*Exit* MARIA.] I am as mad as he,
If sad and merry madness equal be.

Re-enter MARIA, *with* MALVOLIO.

How now, Malvolio!

Mal. Sweet lady, ho, ho.

Oli. Smilest thou?
I sent for thee upon a sad occasion.

Mal. Sad, lady! I could be sad: this does make some obstruction in the blood, this cross-gartering; but what of that? if it please the eye of one, it is with me as the very true sonnet is, "Please one, and please all."

Oli. Why, how dost thou, man? what is the matter with thee?

Mal. Not black in my mind, though yellow in my legs. It did come to his hands, and commands shall be executed: I think we do know the sweet Roman hand.

Oli. Wilt thou go to bed, Malvolio?

Mal. To bed! ay, sweetheart, and I'll come to thee.

Oli. God comfort thee! Why dost thou smile so and kiss thy hand so oft?

Mar. How do you, Malvolio?

Mal. At your request! yes; nightingales answer daws.

Mar. Why appear you with this ridiculous boldness before my lady?

Mal. "Be not afraid of greatness": 'twas well writ.

Oli. What meanest thou by that, Malvolio?

Mal. "Some are born great"—

Oli. Ha!

Mal. "Some achieve greatness"—

Oli. What sayest thou?

Mal. "And some have greatness thrust upon them."

Oli. Heaven restore thee!

Mal. "Remember who commended thy yellow stockings"—

Oli. Thy yellow stockings!

Mal. "And wished to see thee cross-gartered."

Oli. Cross-gartered!

Mal. "Go to, thou art made, if thou desirest to be so"—

Oli. Am I made?

Mal. "If not, let me see thee a servant still."

Oli. Why, this is very midsummer madness.

Enter SERVANT.

Ser. Madam, the young gentleman of the Count Orsino's is returned: I could hardly entreat him back: he attends your ladyship's pleasure.

Oli. I'll come to him. [*Exit* SERVANT.] Good Maria, let this fellow be looked to. Where's my cousin Toby? Let some of my people have a special care of him: I would not have him miscarry for the half of my dowry.

[*Exeunt* OLIVIA *and* MARIA.

Mal. O, ho! do you come near me now? no worse man than Sir Toby to look to me! This concurs directly with the letter: she sends him on purpose, that I may appear stubborn to him; for she incites me to that in the letter. "Cast thy humble slough," says she; "be opposite with a kinsman, surly with servants; let thy tongue tang with arguments of state; put thyself into the trick of singularity"; and consequently sets down the manner how; as, a sad face, a reverend carriage, a slow tongue, in the habit of some sir of note, and so forth. I have limed her; but it is Jove's doing, and Jove make me thankful! And when she went away now, "Let this fellow be looked to": "fellow!" not Malvolio, nor after my degree, but "fellow." Why, every thing adheres together, that no dram of a scruple, no scruple of a scruple, no obstacle, no incredulous or unsafe circumstance—What can be said? Nothing that can be can come between me and the full prospect of my hopes. Well, Jove, not I, is the doer of this, and he is to be thanked.

Re-enter MARIA, *with* SIR TOBY *and* FABIAN.

Sir To. Which way is he, in the name of sanctity? If all the devils of hell be drawn in little, and Legion himself possessed him, yet I'll speak to him.

Fab. Here he is, here he is. How is't with you, sir? how is't with you, man?

Mal. Go off; I discard you: let me enjoy my private: go off.

Mar. Lo, how hollow the fiend speaks within him! did not I tell you? Sir Toby, my lady prays you to have a care of him.

Mal. Ah, ha! does she so?

Sir To. Go to, go to; peace, peace; we must deal gently with him: let me alone. How do you, Malvolio? how is't with you? What, man! defy the devil: consider, he's an enemy to mankind.

Mal. Do you know what you say?

Mar. La you, an you speak ill of the devil, how he takes it at heart! Pray God, he be not bewitched!

Fab. Carry his water to the wise woman.

Mar. Marry, and it shall be done to-morrow morning, if I live. My lady would not lose him for more than I'll say.

Mal. How now, mistress!

Mar. O Lord!

Sir To. Prithee, hold thy peace; this is not the way: do you not see you move him? let me alone with him.

Fab. No way but gentleness; gently, gently: the fiend is rough, and will not be roughly used.

Sir To. Why, how now, my bawcock! how dost thou, chuck?

Mal. Sir!

Sir To. Ay, Biddy, come with me. What, man! 'tis not for gravity to play at cherry-pit with Satan: hang him, foul collier!

Mar. Get him to say his prayers, good Sir Toby, get him to pray.

Mal. My prayers, minx!

Mar. No, I warrant you, he will not hear of godliness.

Mal. Go, hang yourselves all! you are idle shallow things: I am not of your element: you shall know more hereafter. [*Exit.*

Sir To. Is't possible?

Fab. If this were played upon a stage now, I could condemn it as an improbable fiction.

Sir To. His very genius hath taken the infection of the device, man.

Mar. Nay, pursue him now, lest the device take air and taint.

Fab. Why, we shall make him mad indeed.

Mar. The house will be the quieter.

Sir To. Come, we'll have him in a dark room and bound. My niece is already in the belief that he's mad: we may carry it thus, for our pleasure and his penance, till our very pastime, tired out of breath, prompt us to have mercy on him: at which time we will bring the device to the bar and crown thee for a finder of madmen. But see, but see.

Enter SIR ANDREW.

Fab. More matter for a May morning.

Sir And. Here's the challenge, read it. I warrant there's vinegar and pepper in't.

Fab. Is't so saucy?

Sir And. Ay, is't, I warrant him: do but read.

Sir To. Give me. [*Reads*] "Youth, whatsoever thou art, thou art but a scurvy fellow."

Fab. Good, and valiant.

Sir To. [*Reads*] "Wonder not, nor admire not in thy mind, why I do call thee so, for I will show thee no reason for't."

Fab. A good note; that keeps you from the blow of the law.

Sir To. [*Reads*] "Thou comest to the lady Olivia, and in my sight she uses thee kindly: but thou liest in thy throat; that is not the matter I challenge thee for."

Fab. Very brief, and to exceeding good sense —less.

Sir To. [*Reads*] "I will waylay thee going home; where if it be thy chance to kill me"—

Fab. Good.

Sir To. [*Reads*] "Thou killest me like a rogue and a villain."

Fab. Still you keep o' the windy side of the law: good.

Sir To. [*Reads*] "Fare thee well; and God have mercy upon one of our souls! He may have mercy upon mine; but my hope is better, and so look to thyself. Thy friend, as thou usest him, and thy sworn enemy. ANDREW AGUECHEEK." If this letter move him not, his legs cannot: I'll give't him.

Mar. You may have very fit occasion for't. He is now in some commerce with my lady, and will by and by depart.

Sir To. Go, Sir Andrew; scout me for him at the corner of the orchard like a bum-baily: so soon as ever thou seest him, draw; and, as thou drawest, swear horrible; for it comes to pass oft that a terrible oath, with a swaggering accent sharply twanged off, gives manhood more approbation than ever proof itself would have earned him. Away!

Sir And. Nay, let me alone for swearing. [*Exit*.

Sir. To. Now will not I deliver his letter: for the behaviour of the young gentleman gives him out to be of good capacity and breeding; his employment between his lord and my niece confirms no less: therefore this letter, being so excellently ignorant, will breed no terror in the youth: he will find it comes from a clodpole. But, sir, I will deliver his challenge by word of mouth; set upon Auguecheek a notable report of valour; and drive the gentleman, as I know his youth will aptly receive it, into a most hideous opinion of his rage, skill, fury, and impetuosity. This will so fright them both that they will kill one another by the look, like cockatrices.

Re-enter OLIVIA, *with* VIOLA.

Fab. Here he comes with your niece: give them way till he take leave, and presently after him.

Sir To. I will meditate the while upon some horrid message for a challenge

[*Exeunt* SIR TOBY, FABIAN, *and* MARIA.

Oli. I have said too much unto a heart of stone
And laid mine honour too unchary out:
There's something in me that reproves my fault;
But such a headstrong potent fault it is
That it but mocks reproof.

Vio. With the same 'haviour that your passion bears
Goes on my master's grief.

Oli. Here, wear this jewel for me, 'tis my picture;
Refuse it not; it hath no tongue to vex you;
And I beseech you come again to-morrow.
What shall you ask of me that I'll deny,
That honour saved may upon asking give?

Vio. Nothing but this; your true love for my master.

Oli. How with mine honour may I give him that
Which I have given to you?

Vio. I will acquit you.

Oli. Well, come again to-morrow. Fare thee well:
A fiend like thee might bear my soul to hell.

[*Exit*.

Re-enter SIR TOBY *and* FABIAN.

Sir To. Gentleman, God save thee.

Vio. And you, sir.

Sir To. That defence thou hast, betake thee to't: of what nature the wrongs are thou hast done him, I know not; but thy intercepter, full of despite, bloody as the hunter, attends thee at the orchard-end: dismount thy tuck, be yare in thy preparation, for thy assailant is quick, skilful and deadly.

Vio. You mistake, sir; I am sure no man hath any quarrel to me: my remembrance is very free and clear from any image of offence done to any man.

Sir To. You'll find it otherwise, I assure you: therefore, if you hold your life at any price, betake you to your guard; for your opposite hath in him what youth, strength, skill, and wrath can furnish man withal.

Vio. I pray you, sir, what is he?

Sir To. He is knight, dubbed with unhatched rapier and on carpet consideration; but he is a devil in private brawl; souls and bodies hath he divorced three; and his incensement at this moment is so implacable that satisfaction can be none but by pangs of death and sepulchre. Hob, nob, is his word; give't or take't.

Vio. I will return again into the house and desire some conduct of the lady. I am no fighter. I have heard of some kind of men that put quarrels purposely on others, to taste their valour: belike this is a man of that quirk.

Sir To. Sir, no; his indignation derives itself out of a very competent injury: therefore, get you on and give him his desire. Back you shall not to the house, unless you undertake that with me which with as much safety you might answer him: therefore, on, or strip your sword stark naked; for meddle you must, that's certain, or forswear to wear iron about you.

Vio. This is as uncivil as strange. I beseech you, do me this courteous office, as to know of the knight what my offence to him is: it is something of my negligence, nothing of my purpose.

Sir To. I will do so. Signior Fabian, stay you by this gentleman till my return. [*Exit.*

Vio. Pray you, sir, do you know of this matter?

Fab. I know the knight is incensed against you, even to a mortal arbitrement; but nothing of the circumstance more.

Vio. I beseech you, what manner of man is he?

Fab. Nothing of that wonderful promise, to read him by his form, as you are like to find him in the proof of his valour. He is, indeed, sir, the most skilful, bloody, and fatal opposite that you could possibly have found in any part of Illyria. Will you walk towards him? I will make your peace with him if I can.

Vio. I shall be much bound to you for't. I am one that had rather go with sir priest than sir knight. I care not who knows so much of my mettle. [*Exeunt.*

Re-enter SIR TOBY, *with* SIR ANDREW.

Sir To. Why, man, he's a very devil; I have not seen such a firago. I had a pass with him, rapier, scabbard, and all, and he gives me the stuck in with such a mortal motion that it is inevitable; and on the answer, he pays you as surely as your feet hit the ground they step on. They say he has been fencer to the Sophy.

Sir And. Pox on't, I'll not meddle with him.

Sir To. Ay, but he will not now be pacified: Fabian can scarce hold him yonder.

Sir And. Plague on't, an I thought he had been valiant and so cunning in fence, I'd have seen him damned ere I'd have challenged him. Let him let the matter slip and I'll give him my horse, grey Capilet.

Sir To. I'll make the motion: stand here, make a good show on't: this shall end without the perdition of souls. [*Aside*] Marry, I'll ride your horse as well as I ride you.

Re-enter FABIAN *and* VIOLA.

[*To Fabian*] I have his horse to take up the quarrel: I have persuaded him the youth's a devil.

Fab. He is as horribly conceited of him; and pants and looks pale, as if a bear were at his heels.

Sir To. [*To* VIOLA] There's no remedy, sir; he will fight with you for's oath sake: marry, he hath better bethought him of his quarrel, and he finds that now scarce to be worth talking of: therefore draw, for the supportance of his vow; he protests he will not hurt you.

Vio. [*Aside*] Pray God defend me! A little thing would make me tell them how much I lack of a man.

Fab. Give ground, if you see him furious.

Sir To. Come, Sir Andrew, there's no remedy; the gentleman will, for his honour's sake, have one bout with you; he cannot by the duello avoid it: but he has promised me, as he is a gentleman and a soldier, he will not hurt you. Come on; to't.

Sir And. Pray God, he keep his oath!

Vio. I do assure you, 'tis against my will.

They draw.

Enter ANTONIO.

Ant. Put up your sword. If this young gentleman
Have done offence, I take the fault on me;
If you offend him, I for him defy you.

Sir To. You, sir! why, what are you?

Ant. One, sir, that for his love dares yet do more
Than you have heard him brag to you he will.

Sir To. Nay, if you be an undertaker, I am for you.

They draw.

Enter OFFICERS.

Fab. O good Sir Toby, hold! Here come the officers.

Sir To. I'll be with you anon.

Vio. Pray, sir, put your sword up, if you please.

Sir And. Marry, will I, sir; and, for that I promised you, I'll be as good as my word: he will bear you easily and reins well.

1st Off. This is the man; do thy office.

2nd Off. Antonio, I arrest thee at the suit of Count Orsino.

Ant. You do mistake me, sir.

1st Off. No, sir, no jot; I know your favour well,
Though now you have no sea-cap on your head.
Take him away: he knows I know him well.

Ant. I must obey. [*To* VIOLA] This comes with seeking you.
But there's no remedy; I shall answer it.
What will you do, now my necessity

Makes me to ask you for my purse? It grieves me
Much more for what I cannot do for you
Than what befalls myself. You stand amazed;
But be of comfort.

2nd Off. Come, sir, away.

Ant. I must entreat of you some of that money.

Vio. What money, sir?
For the fair kindness you have show'd me here,
And, part, being prompted by your present trouble,
Out of my lean and low ability
I'll lend you something: my having is not much;
I'll make division of my present with you:
Hold, there's half my coffer.

Ant. Will you deny me now?
Is't possible that my deserts to you
Can lack persuasion? Do not tempt my misery,
Lest that it make me so unsound a man
As to upbraid you with those kindnesses
That I have done for you.

Vio. I know of none;
Nor know I you by voice or any feature.
I hate ingratitude more in a man
Than lying, vainness, babbling, drunkenness,
Or any taint of vice whose strong corruption
Inhabits our frail blood.

Ant. O heavens themselves!

2nd Off. Come, sir, I pray you, go.

Ant. Let me speak a little. This youth that you see here
I snatch'd one half out of the jaws of death,
Relieved him with such sanctity of love,
And to his image, which methought did promise
Most venerable worth, did I devotion.

1st Off. What's that to us? The time goes by: away!

Ant. But O how vile an idol proves this god!
Thou hast, Sebastian, done good feature shame.
In nature there's no blemish but the mind;
None can be call'd deform'd but the unkind:
Virtue is beauty, but the beauteous evil
Are empty trunks o'erflourish'd by the devil.

1st Off. The man grows mad: away with him!
Come, come, sir.

Ant. Lead me on. [*Exit with* OFFICERS.

Vio. Methinks his words do from such passion fly,
That he believes himself: so do not I.
Prove true, imagination, O, prove true,
That I, dear brother, be now ta'en for you!

Sir To. Come hither, knight; come hither, Fabian: we'll whisper o'er a couplet or two of most sage saws.

Vio. He named Sebastian: I my brother know
Yet living in my glass; even such and so
In favour was my brother, and he went
Still in this fashion, colour, ornament,
For him I imitate. O, if it prove,
Tempests are kind and salt waves fresh in love. [*Exit*.

Sir To. A very dishonest paltry boy, and more a coward than a hare: his dishonesty appears in leaving his friend here in necessity and denying him; and for his cowardship, ask Fabian.

Fab. A coward, a most devout coward, religious in it.

Sir And. 'Slid, I'll after him again and beat him.

Sir To. Do; cuff him soundly, but never draw thy sword.

Sir And. An I do not— [*Exit*.

Fab. Come, let's see the event.

Sir To. I dare lay any money 'twill be nothing yet. [*Exeunt*.

ACT IV

SCENE I. *Before Olivia's house*

Enter SEBASTIAN *and* CLOWN.

Clo. Will you make me believe that I am not sent for you?

Seb. Go to, go to, thou art a foolish fellow:
Let me be clear of thee.

Clo. Well held out, i' faith! No, I do not know you; nor I am not sent to you by my lady, to bid you come speak with her; nor your name is not Master Cesario; nor this is not my nose neither. Nothing that is so is so.

Seb. I prithee, vent thy folly somewhere else:
Thou know'st not me.

Clo. Vent my folly! He has heard that word of some great man and now applies it to a fool. Vent my folly! I am afraid this great lubber, the world, will prove a cockney. I prithee now, ungird thy strangeness and tell me what I shall vent to my lady: shall I vent to her that thou art coming?

Seb. I prithee, foolish Greek, depart from me:
There's money for thee: if you tarry longer,
I shall give worse payment.

Clo. By my troth, thou hast an open hand. These wise men that give fools money get themselves a good report—after fourteen years' purchase.

Enter SIR ANDREW, SIR TOBY, *and* FABIAN.

Sir And. Now, sir, have I met you again? there's for you.

Seb. Why, there's for thee, and there, and there.
Are all the people mad?

Sir To. Hold, sir, or I'll throw your dagger o'er the house.

Clo. This will I tell my lady straight: I would not be in some of your coats for two pence. [*Exit*.

Sir To. Come on, sir; hold.

Sir And. Nay, let him alone: I'll go another way to work with him; I'll have an action of battery against him, if there be any law in Illyria: though I struck him first, yet it's no matter for that.

Seb. Let go thy hand.

Sir To. Come, sir, I will not let you go. Come, my young soldier, put up your iron: you are well fleshed; come on.

Seb. I will be free from thee. What wouldst thou now?
If thou darest tempt me further, draw thy sword.

Sir To. What, what? Nay, then I must have an ounce or two of this malapert blood from you.

Enter OLIVIA.

Oli. Hold, Toby; on thy life I charge thee, hold!
Sir To. Madam!
Oli. Will it be ever thus? Ungracious wretch,
Fit for the mountains and the barbarous caves,
Where manners ne'er were preach'd! out of my sight!
Be not offended, dear Cesario.
Rudesby, be gone!
[*Exeunt* SIR TOBY, SIR ANDREW, *and* FABIAN.
I prithee, gentle friend,
Let thy fair wisdom, not thy passion, sway
In this uncivil and unjust extent
Against thy peace. Go with me to my house,
And hear thou there how many fruitless pranks
This ruffian hath botch'd up, that thou thereby
Mayst smile at this: thou shalt not choose but go:
Do not deny. Beshrew his soul for me,
He started one poor heart of mine in thee.
Seb. What relish is in this? how runs the stream?
Or I am mad, or else this is a dream:
Let fancy still my sense in Lethe steep;
If it be thus to dream, still let me sleep!
Oli. Nay, come, I prithee; would thou'ldst be ruled by me!
Seb. Madam, I will.
Oli. O, say so, and so be! [*Exeunt*.

SCENE II. *Olivia's house*

Enter MARIA *and* CLOWN.

Mar. Nay, I prithee, put on this gown and this beard; make him believe thou art Sir Topas the curate: do it quickly; I'll call Sir Toby the whilst. [*Exit*.

Clo. Well, I'll put it on, and I will dissemble myself in 't; and I would I were the first that ever dissembled in such a gown. I am not tall enough to become the function well, nor lean enough to be thought a good student; but to be said an honest man and a good housekeeper goes as fairly as to say a careful man and a great scholar. The competitors enter.

Enter SIR TOBY *and* MARIA.

Sir To. Jove bless thee, master Parson.

Clo. *Bonos dies*, Sir Toby: for, as the old hermit of Prague, that never saw pen and ink, very wittily said to a niece of King Gorboduc, "That that is is"; so I, being master Parson, am master Parson; for, what is "that" but "that," and "is" but "is"?

Sir To. To him, Sir Topas.

Clo. What, ho, I say! peace in this prison!

Sir To. The knave counterfeits well; a good knave.

Mal. [*Within*] Who calls there?

Clo. Sir Topas the curate, who comes to visit Malvolio the lunatic.

Mal. Sir Topas, Sir Topas, good Sir Topas, go to my lady.

Clo. Out, hyperbolical fiend! how vexest thou this man! talkest thou nothing but of ladies?

Sir To. Well said, master Parson.

Mal. Sir Topas, never was man thus wronged: good Sir Topas, do not think I am mad: they have laid me here in hideous darkness.

Clo. Fie, thou dishonest Satan! I call thee by the most modest terms; for I am one of those gentle ones that will use the devil himself with courtesy: sayest thou that house is dark?

Mal. As hell, Sir Topas.

Clo. Why, it hath bay windows transparent as barricadoes, and the clearstores toward the south north are as lustrous as ebony; and yet complainest thou of obstruction?

Mal. I am not mad, Sir Topas: I say to you, this house is dark.

Clo. Madman, thou errest: I say, there is no darkness but ignorance; in which thou art more puzzled than the Egyptians in their fog.

Mal. I say, this house is as dark as ignorance, though ignorance were as dark as hell; and I say, there was never man thus abused. I am no more mad than you are: make the trial of it in any constant question.

Clo. What is the opinion of Pythagoras concerning wild fowl?

Mal. That the soul of our grandam might haply inhabit a bird.

Clo. What thinkest thou of his opinion?

Mal. I think nobly of the soul, and no way approve his opinion.

Clo. Fare thee well. Remain thou still in darkness: thou shalt hold the opinion of Pythagoras ere I will allow of thy wits, and fear to kill a woodcock, lest thou dispossess the soul of thy grandam. Fare thee well.

Mal. Sir Topas, Sir Topas!

Sir To. My most exquisite Sir Topas!

Clo. Nay, I am for all waters.

Mar. Thou mightst have done this without thy beard and gown: he sees thee not.

Sir To. To him in thine own voice, and bring me word how thou findest him: I would we were well rid of this knavery. If he may be conveniently delivered, I would he were, for I am now so far in offence with my niece that I cannot pursue with any safety this sport to the upshot. Come by and by to my chamber.

[*Exeunt* SIR TOBY *and* MARIA.

Clo. [*Singing*] "Hey, Robin, jolly Robin,
Tell me how thy lady does."

Mal. Fool!

Clo. "My lady is unkind, perdy."

Mal. Fool!

Clo. "Alas, why is she so?"

Mal. Fool, I say!

Clo. "She loves another"—Who calls, ha?

Mal. Good fool, as ever thou wilt deserve well at my hand, help me to a candle, and pen, ink and paper: as I am a gentleman, I will live to be thankful to thee for't.

Clo. Master Malvolio?

Mal. Ay, good fool.

Clo. Alas, sir, how fell you besides your five wits?

Mal. Fool, there was never man so notoriously abused: I am as well in my wits, fool, as thou art.

Clo. But as well? then you are mad indeed, if you be no better in your wits than a fool.

Mal. They have here propertied me; keep me in darkness, send ministers to me, asses, and do all they can to face me out of my wits.

Clo. Advise you what you say; the minister is here. Malvolio, Malvolio, thy wits the heavens restore! endeavour thyself to sleep, and leave thy vain bibble babble.

Mal. Sir Topas!

Clo. Maintain no words with him, good fellow. Who, I, sir? not I, sir. God be wi' you, good Sir Topas. Marry, amen. I will, sir, I will.

Mal. Fool, fool, fool, I say!

Clo. Alas, sir, be patient. What say you, sir? I am shent for speaking to you.

Mal. Good fool, help me to some light and some paper: I tell thee, I am as well in my wits as any man in Illyria.

Clo. Well-a-day that you were, sir!

Mal. By this hand, I am. Good fool, some ink, paper, and light; and convey what I will set down to my lady: it shall advantage thee more than ever the bearing of letter did.

Clo. I will help you to't. But tell me true, are you not mad indeed? or do you but counterfeit?

Mal. Believe me, I am not; I tell thee true.

Clo. Nay, I'll ne'er believe a madman till I see his brains. I will fetch you light and paper and ink.

Mal. Fool, I'll requite it in the highest degree: I prithee, be gone.

Clo. [*Singing*] "I am gone, sir,
And anon, sir,
I'll be with you again,
In a trice,
Like to the old Vice,
Your need to sustain;

Who, with dagger of lath,
In his rage and his wrath,
Cries, ah, ha! to the devil:
Like a mad lad,
Pare thy nails, dad;
Adieu, good man devil."

[*Exit.*

SCENE III. *Olivia's garden*

Enter SEBASTIAN.

Seb. This is the air; that is the glorious sun;
This pearl she gave me, I do feel't and see't;
And though 'tis wonder that enwraps me thus,
Yet 'tis not madness. Where's Antonio, then?
I could not find him at the Elephant:
Yet there he was; and there I found this credit,
That he did range the town to seek me out.
His counsel now might do me golden service;
For though my soul disputes well with my sense
That this may be some error, but no madness,
Yet doth this accident and flood of fortune
So far exceed all instance, all discourse,
That I am ready to distrust mine eyes
And wrangle with my reason that persuades me
To any other trust but that I am mad
Or else the lady's mad; yet, if 'twere so,
She could not sway her house, command her followers,
Take and give back affairs and their dispatch
With such a smooth, discreet, and stable bearing
As I perceive she does: there's something in't
That is deceivable. But here the lady comes.

Enter OLIVIA *and* PRIEST.

Oli. Blame not this haste of mine. If you mean well,
Now go with me and with this holy man
Into the chantry by: there, before him,
And underneath that consecrated roof,
Plight me the full assurance of your faith;
That my most jealous and too doubtful soul
May live at peace. He shall conceal it
Whiles you are willing it shall come to note,

What time we will our celebration keep
According to my birth. What do you say?

Seb. I'll follow this good man, and go with you;
And, having sworn truth, ever will be true.

Oliv. Then lead the way, good father; and heavens so shine,
That they may fairly note this act of mine!
[*Exeunt*.

ACT V

Scene i. *Before Olivia's house*

Enter Clown *and* Fabian.

Fab. Now, as thou lovest me, let me see his letter.

Clo. Good Master Fabian, grant me another request.

Fab. Anything.

Clo. Do not desire to see this letter.

Fab. This is, to give a dog, and in recompense desire my dog again.

Enter Duke, Viola, Curio, *and Lords*.

Duke. Belong you to the Lady Olivia, friends?

Clo. Ay, sir; we are some of her trappings.

Duke. I know thee well: how dost thou, my good fellow?

Clo. Truly, sir, the better for my foes and the worse for my friends.

Duke. Just the contrary; the better for thy friends.

Clo. No, sir, the worse.

Duke. How can that be?

Clo. Marry, sir, they praise me and make an ass of me; now my foes tell me plainly I am an ass: so that by my foes, sir, I profit in the knowledge of myself, and by my friends I am abused: so that, conclusions to be as kisses, if your four negatives make your two affirmatives, why then, the worse for my friends and the better for my foes.

Duke. Why, this is excellent.

Clo. By my troth, sir, no; though it please you to be one of my friends.

Duke. Thou shalt not be the worse for me: there's gold.

Clo. But that it would be double-dealing, sir, I would you could make it another.

Duke. O, you give me ill counsel.

Clo. Put your grace in your pocket, sir, for this once, and let your flesh and blood obey it.

Duke. Well, I will be so much a sinner, to be a double-dealer: there's another.

Clo. Primo, secundo, tertio, is a good play; and the old saying is, the third pays for all: the triplex, sir, is a good tripping measure; or the bells of Saint Bennet, sir, may put you in mind; one, two, three.

Duke. You can fool no more money out of me at this throw: if you will let your lady know I am here to speak with her, and bring her along with you, it may awake my bounty further.

Clo. Marry, sir, lullaby to your bounty till I come again. I go, sir; but I would not have you to think that my desire of having is the sin of covetousness: but, as you say, sir, let your bounty take a nap, I will awake it anon. [*Exit*.

Vio. Here comes the man, sir, that did rescue me.

Enter Antonio *and* Officers.

Duke. That face of his I do remember well;
Yet, when I saw it last, it was besmear'd
As black as Vulcan in the smoke of war:
A bawbling vessel was he captain of,
For shallow draught and bulk unprizable,
With which such scathful grapple did he make
With the most noble bottom of our fleet,
That very envy and the tongue of loss
Cried fame and honour on him. What's the matter?

1st Off. Orsino, this is that Antonio
That took the *Phœnix* and her fraught from Candy;
And this is he that did the *Tiger* board,
When your young nephew Titus lost his leg:
Here in the streets, desperate of shame and state,
In private brabble did we apprehend him.

Vio. He did me kindness, sir, drew on my side;
But in conclusion put strange speech upon me:
I know not what 'twas but distraction.

Duke. Notable pirate! thou salt-water thief!
What foolish boldness brought thee to their mercies,
Whom thou, in terms so bloody and so dear,
Hast made thine enemies?

Ant. Orsino, noble sir,
Be pleased that I shake off these names you give me:
Antonio never yet was thief or pirate,
Though I confess, on base and ground enough,
Orsino's enemy. A witchcraft drew me hither:
That most ingrateful boy there by your side,
From the rude sea's enraged and foamy mouth
Did I redeem; a wreck past hope he was.
His life I gave him and did thereto add
My love, without retention or restraint,
All his in dedication; for his sake
Did I expose myself, pure for his love,
Into the danger of this adverse town;
Drew to defend him when he was beset:
Where being apprehended, his false cunning,

Not meaning to partake with me in danger,
Taught him to face me out of his acquaintance,
And grew a twenty years removed thing
While one would wink; denied me mine own purse,
Which I had recommended to his use
Not half an hour before.

Vio. How can this be?

Duke. When came he to this town?

Ant. To-day, my lord; and for three months before,
No interim, not a minute's vacancy,
Both day and night did we keep company.

Enter OLIVIA *and Attendants.*

Duke. Here comes the Countess: now heaven walks on earth.
But for thee, fellow; fellow, thy words are madness:
Three months this youth hath tended upon me;
But more of that anon. Take him aside.

Oli. What would my lord, but that he may not have,
Wherein Olivia may seem serviceable?
Cesario, you do not keep promise with me.

Vio. Madam!

Duke. Gracious Olivia—

Oli. What do you say, Cesario? Good my lord—

Vio. My lord would speak; my duty hushes me.

Oli. If it be aught to the old tune, my lord,
It is as fat and fulsome to mine ear
As howling after music.

Duke. Still so cruel?

Oli. Still so constant, lord.

Duke. What, to perverseness? you uncivil lady,
To whose ingrate and unauspicious altars
My soul the faithfull'st offerings hath breathed out
That e'er devotion tender'd! What shall I do?

Oli. Even what it please my lord, that shall become him.

Duke. Why should I not, had I the heart to do it,
Like to the Egyptian thief at point of death,
Kill what I love?—a savage jealousy
That sometime savours nobly. But hear me this:
Since you to non-regardance cast my faith,
And that I partly know the instrument
That screws me from my true place in your favour,
Live you the marble-breasted tyrant still;
But this your minion, whom I know you love,
And whom, by heaven I swear, I tender dearly,
Him will I tear out of that cruel eye,
Where he sits crowned in his master's spite.
Come, boy, with me; my thoughts are ripe in mischief:
I'll sacrifice the lamb that I do love,
To spite a raven's heart within a dove.

Vio. And I, most jocund, apt, and willingly,
To do you rest, a thousand deaths would die.

Oli. Where goes Cesario?

Vio. After him I love
More than I love these eyes, more than my life,
More, by all mores, than e'er I shall love wife.
If I do feign, you witnesses above
Punish my life for tainting of my love!

Oli. Ay me, detested! how am I beguiled!

Vio. Who does beguile you? who does do you wrong?

Oli. Hast thou forgot thyself? is it so long?
Call forth the holy father.

Duke. Come, away!

Oli. Whither, my lord? Cesario, husband, stay.

Duke. Husband!

Oli. Ay, husband: can he that deny?

Duke. Her husband, sirrah!

Vio. No, my lord, not I.

Oli. Alas, it is the baseness of thy fear
That makes thee strangle thy propriety:
Fear not, Cesario; take thy fortunes up;
Be that thou know'st thou art, and then thou art
As great as that thou fear'st.

Enter PRIEST.

O, welcome, father!
Father, I charge thee, by thy reverence,
Here to unfold, though lately we intended
To keep in darkness what occasion now
Reveals before 'tis ripe, what thou dost know
Hath newly pass'd between this youth and me.

Priest. A contract of eternal bond of love,
Confirm'd by mutual joinder of your hands,
Attested by the holy close of lips,
Strengthen'd by interchangement of your rings;
And all the ceremony of this compact
Seal'd in my function, by my testimony:
Since when, my watch hath told me, toward my grave
I have travell'd but two hours.

Duke. O thou dissembling cub! what wilt thou be
When time hath sow'd a grizzle on thy case?
Or will not else thy craft so quickly grow,
That thine own trip shall be thine overthrow?
Farewell, and take her; but direct thy feet
Where thou and I henceforth may never meet.

Vio. My lord, I do protest—

Oli. O, do not swear!
Hold little faith, though thou hast too much fear.

Enter SIR ANDREW.

Sir And. For the love of God, a surgeon! Send one presently to Sir Toby.

Oli. What's the matter?

Sir And. He has broke my head across and has given Sir Toby a bloody coxcomb too: for the love of God, your help! I had rather than forty pound I were at home.

Oli. Who has done this, Sir Andrew?

Sir And. The Count's gentleman, one Cesario: we took him for a coward, but he's the very devil incardinate.

Duke. My gentleman, Cesario?

Sir And. 'Od's lifelings, here he is! You broke my head for nothing; and that that I did, I was set on to do't by Sir Toby.

Vio. Why do you speak to me? I never hurt you:
You drew your sword upon me without cause;
But I bespake you fair, and hurt you not.

Sir And. If a bloody coxcomb be a hurt, you have hurt me: I think you set nothing by a bloody coxcomb.

Enter SIR TOBY *and* CLOWN.

Here comes Sir Toby halting; you shall hear more: but if he had not been in drink, he would have tickled you othergates than he did.

Duke. How now, gentleman! how is't with you?

Sir To. That's all one: has hurt me, and there's the end on't. Sot, didst see Dick surgeon, sot?

Clo. O, he's drunk, Sir Toby, an hour agone; his eyes were set at eight i' the morning.

Sir To. Then he's a rogue, and a passy measures panyn: I hate a drunken rogue.

Oli. Away with him! Who hath made this havoc with them?

Sir And. I'll help you, Sir Toby, because we'll be dressed together.

Sir To. Will you help? an ass-head and a coxcomb and a knave, a thin-faced knave, a gull!

Oli. Get him to bed, and let his hurt be look'd to. [*Exeunt* CLOWN, FABIAN, SIR TOBY, *and* SIR ANDREW.

Enter SEBASTIAN.

Seb. I am sorry, madam, I have hurt your kinsman;
But, had it been the brother of my blood,
I must have done no less with wit and safety.
You throw a strange regard upon me, and by that
I do perceive it hath offended you:
Pardon me, sweet one, even for the vows
We made each other but so late ago.

Duke. One face, one voice, one habit, and two persons,
A natural perspective, that is and is not!

Seb. Antonio, O my dear Antonio!
How have the hours rack'd and tortured me,
Since I have lost thee!

Ant. Sebastian are you?

Seb. Fear'st thou that, Antonio?

Ant. How have you made division of yourself?
An apple, cleft in two, is not more twin
Than these two creatures. Which is Sebastian?

Oli. Most wonderful!

Seb. Do I stand there? I never had a brother;
Nor can there be that deity in my nature,
Of here and everywhere. I had a sister,
Whom the blind waves and surges have devour'd.
Of charity, what kin are you to me?
What countryman? what name? what parentage?

Vio. Of Messaline: Sebastian was my father;
Such a Sebastian was my brother too,
So went he suited to his watery tomb.
If spirits can assume both form and suit
You come to fright us.

Seb. A spirit I am indeed;
But am in that dimension grossly clad
Which from the womb I did participate.
Were you a woman, as the rest goes even,
I should my tears let fall upon your cheek,
And say "Thrice-welcome, drowned Viola!"

Vio. My father had a mole upon his brow.

Seb. And so had mine.

Vio. And died that day when Viola from her birth
Had number'd thirteen years.

Seb. O, that record is lively in my soul!
He finished indeed his mortal act
That day that made my sister thirteen years.

Vio. If nothing lets to make us happy both
But this my masculine usurp'd attire,
Do not embrace me till each circumstance
Of place, time, fortune, do cohere and jump
That I am Viola: which to confirm,
I'll bring you to a captain in this town,
Where lie my maiden weeds; by whose gentle help
I was preserved to serve this noble count.
All the occurrence of my fortune since
Hath been between this lady and this lord.

Seb. [*To* OLIVIA] So comes it, lady, you have been mistook:
But nature to her bias drew in that.
You would have been contracted to a maid;
Nor are you therein, by my life, deceived,
You are betroth'd both to a maid and man.

Duke. Be not amazed; right noble is his blood.

If this be so, as yet the glass seems true,
I shall have share in this most happy wreck.
[*To* VIOLA] Boy, thou hast said to me a thousand times
Thou never shouldst love woman like to me.
Vio. And all those sayings will I over-swear;
And all those swearings keep as true in soul
As doth that orbed continent the fire
That severs day from night.
Duke. Give me thy hand;
And let me see thee in thy woman's weeds.
Vio. The captain that did bring me first on shore
Hath my maid's garments: he upon some action
Is now in durance, at Malvolio's suit,
A gentleman, and follower of my lady's.
Oli. He shall enlarge him: fetch Malvolio hither:
And yet, alas, now I remember me,
They say, poor gentleman, he's much distract.

Re-enter CLOWN *with a letter, and* FABIAN.

A most extracting frenzy of mine own
From my remembrance clearly banish'd his.
How does he, sirrah?

Clo. Truly, madam, he holds Belzebub at the stave's end as well as a man in his case may do: has here writ a letter to you; I should have given 't you to-day morning, but as a madman's epistles are no gospels, so it skills not much when they are delivered.

Oli. Open 't, and read it.

Clo. Look then to be well edified when the fool delivers the madman. [*Reads*] "By the Lord, madam"—

Oli. How now! art thou mad?

Clo. No, madam, I do but read madness: an your ladyship will have it as it ought to be, you must allow Vox.

Oli. Prithee, read i' thy right wits.

Clo. So I do, madonna; but to read his right wits is to read thus: therefore perpend, my princess, and give ear.

Oli. Read it you, sirrah. [*To* FABIAN.]

Fab. [*Reads*] "By the Lord, madam, you wrong me, and the world shall know it: though you have put me into darkness and given your drunken cousin rule over me, yet have I the benefit of my senses as well as your ladyship. I have your own letter that induced me to the semblance I put on; with the which I doubt not but to do myself much right, or you much shame. Think of me as you please. I leave my duty a little unthought of and speak out of my injury.

The madly-used Malvolio."

Oli. Did he write this?

Clo. Ay, madam.

Duke. This savours not much of distraction.

Oli. See him deliver'd, Fabian; bring him hither.
[*Exit* FABIAN.
My lord, so please you, these things further thought on,
To think me as well a sister as a wife,
One day shall crown the alliance on't, so please you,
Here at my house and at my proper cost.
Duke. Madam, I am most apt to embrace your offer.
[*To* VIOLA] Your master quits you; and for your service done him,
So much against the mettle of your sex,
So far beneath your soft and tender breeding,
And since you call'd me master for so long,
Here is my hand: you shall from this time be
Your master's mistress.
Oli. A sister! you are she.

Re-enter FABIAN, *with* MALVOLIO.

Duke. Is this the madman?
Oli. Ay, my lord, this same.
How now, Malvolio!
Mal. Madam, you have done me wrong,
Notorious wrong.
Oli. Have I, Malvolio? no.
Mal. Lady, you have. Pray you, peruse that letter.
You must not now deny it is your hand:
Write from it, if you can, in hand or phrase;
Or say 'tis not your seal, not your invention:
You can say none of this: well, grant it then
And tell me, in the modesty of honour,
Why you have given me such clear lights of favour,
Bade me come smiling and cross-garter'd to you,
To put on yellow stockings and to frown
Upon Sir Toby and the lighter people;
And, acting this in an obedient hope,
Why have you suffer'd me to be imprison'd,
Kept in a dark house, visited by the priest,
And made the most notorious geck and gull
That e'er invention play'd on? tell me why.
Oli. Alas, Malvolio, this is not my writing,
Though, I confess, much like the character:
But out of question 'tis Maria's hand.
And now I do bethink me, it was she
First told me thou wast mad; then camest in smiling,
And in such forms which here were presupposed
Upon thee in the letter. Prithee, be content:

This practice hath most shrewdly pass'd upon
thee;
But when we know the grounds and authors of it,
Thou shalt be both the plaintiff and the judge
Of thine own cause.
Fab. Good madam, hear me speak,
And let no quarrel nor no brawl to come
Taint the condition of this present hour,
Which I have wonder'd at. In hope it shall not,
Most freely I confess, myself and Toby
Set this device against Malvolio here,
Upon some stubborn and uncourteous parts
We had conceived against him: Maria writ
The letter at Sir Toby's great importance;
In recompense whereof he hath married her.
How with a sportful malice it was follow'd,
May rather pluck on laughter than revenge;
If that the injuries be justly weigh'd
That have on both sides pass'd.

Oli. Alas, poor fool, how have they baffled thee!

Clo. Why, "some are born great, some achieve greatness, and some have greatness thrown upon them." I was one, sir, in this interlude; one Sir Topas, sir; but that's all one. "By the Lord, fool, I am not mad." But do you remember? "Madam, why laugh you at such a barren rascal? an you smile not, he's gagged"; and thus the whirligig of time brings in his revenges.

Mal. I'll be revenged on the whole pack of you. [*Exit.*

Oli. He hath been most notoriously abused.

Duke. Pursue him, and entreat him to a peace:
He hath not told us of the captain yet:
When that is known and golden time convents,
A solemn combination shall be made
Of our dear souls. Meantime, sweet sister,
We will not part from hence. Cesario, come;
For so you shall be, while you are a man;
But when in other habits you are seen,
Orsino's mistress and his fancy's queen.
[*Exeunt all, except* CLOWN.

Clo. [*Sings*]
"When that I was and a little tiny boy,
With hey, ho, the wind and the rain,
A foolish thing was but a toy,
For the rain it raineth every day.

But when I came to man's estate,
With hey, ho, &c.
'Gainst knaves and thieves men shut their
gate,
For the rain, &c.

But when I came, alas! to wive,
With hey, ho, &c.
By swaggering could I never thrive,
For the rain, &c.

But when I came unto my beds,
With hey, ho, &c.
With toss-pots still had drunken heads,
For the rain, &c.

A great while ago the world begun,
With hey, ho, &c.
But that's all one, our play is done,
And we'll strive to please you every day."
[*Exit.*

HAMLET, Prince of Denmark

DRAMATIS PERSONÆ

CLAUDIUS, *King of Denmark*
HAMLET, *son to the late, and nephew to the present, King*
POLONIUS, *Lord Chamberlain*
HORATIO, *friend to Hamlet*
LAERTES, *son to Polonius*
VOLTIMAND, CORNELIUS, ROSENCRANTZ, GUILDENSTERN, OSRIC, A GENTLEMAN — *Courtiers*
A PRIEST
MARCELLUS, BERNARDO — *Officers*
FRANCISCO, *a soldier*
REYNALDO, *servant to Polonius*
FIVE PLAYERS
TWO CLOWNS, *gravediggers*
FORTINBRAS, *Prince of Norway*
A CAPTAIN
ENGLISH AMBASSADORS
A LORD
A SOLDIER
TWO MESSENGERS
A SERVANT *to Horatio*
DANES
GHOST *of Hamlet's father*

GERTRUDE, *Queen of Denmark, and mother to Hamlet*
OPHELIA, *daughter to Polonius*

NON-SPEAKING: *Lords, Ladies, Officers, Soldiers, Sailors, and other Attendants*

SCENE: *Denmark*

ACT I

SCENE I. *Elsinore: a platform before the castle*

FRANCISCO *at his post. Enter to him* BERNARDO.

Ber. Who's there?
Fran. Nay, answer me: stand, and unfold yourself.
Ber. Long live the king!
Fran. Bernardo?
Ber. He.
Fran. You come most carefully upon your hour.
Ber. 'Tis now struck twelve; get thee to bed, Francisco.
Fran. For this relief much thanks: 'tis bitter cold,
And I am sick at heart.
Ber. Have you had quiet guard?
Fran. Not a mouse stirring.
Ber. Well, good night.
If you do meet Horatio and Marcellus,
The rivals of my watch, bid them make haste.
Fran. I think I hear them. Stand, ho! Who's there?

Enter HORATIO *and* MARCELLUS.

Hor. Friends to this ground.
Mar. And liegemen to the Dane.
Fran. Give you good night.
Mar. O, farewell, honest soldier:
Who hath relieved you?
Fran. Bernardo has my place.
Give you good night. [*Exit.*
Mar. Holla! Bernardo!
Ber. Say,
What, is Horatio there?
Hor. A piece of him.
Ber. Welcome, Horatio: welcome, good Marcellus.
Mar. What, has this thing appear'd again tonight?
Ber. I have seen nothing.
Mar. Horatio says 'tis but our fantasy,
And will not let belief take hold of him
Touching this dreaded sight, twice seen of us:
Therefore I have entreated him along
With us to watch the minutes of this night,
That if again this apparition come,
He may approve our eyes and speak to it.
Hor. Tush, tush, 'twill not appear.
Ber. Sit down awhile;
And let us once again assail your ears,
That are so fortified against our story,
What we have two nights seen.
Hor. Well, sit we down,
And let us hear Bernardo speak of this.
Ber. Last night of all,
When yond same star that's westward from the pole

Had made his course to illume that part of heaven
Where now it burns, Marcellus and myself,
The bell then beating one—

Enter GHOST.

Mar. Peace, break thee off; look, where it comes again!
Ber. In the same figure, like the King that's dead.
Mar. Thou art a scholar; speak to it, Horatio.
Ber. Looks it not like the King? mark it, Horatio.
Hor. Most like: it harrows me with fear and wonder.
Ber. It would be spoke to.
Mar. Question it, Horatio.
Hor. What art thou that usurp'st this time of night,
Together with that fair and warlike form
In which the majesty of buried Denmark
Did sometimes march? by heaven I charge thee, speak!
Mar. It is offended.
Ber. See, it stalks away!
Hor. Stay! speak, speak! I charge thee, speak!
[*Exit* GHOST.
Mar. 'Tis gone, and will not answer.
Ber. How now, Horatio! you tremble and look pale:
Is not this something more than fantasy?
What think you on't?
Hor. Before my God, I might not this believe
Without the sensible and true avouch
Of mine own eyes.
Mar. Is it not like the King?
Hor. As thou art to thyself:
Such was the very armour he had on
When he the ambitious Norway combated;
So frown'd he once, when, in an angry parle,
He smote the sledded Polacks on the ice.
'Tis strange.
Mar. Thus twice before, and jump at this dead hour,
With martial stalk hath he gone by our watch.
Hor. In what particular thought to work I know not;
But in the gross and scope of my opinion,
This bodes some strange eruption to our state.
Mar. Good now, sit down, and tell me, he that knows,
Why this same strict and most observant watch
So nightly toils the subject of the land,
And why such daily cast of brazen cannon,
And foreign mart for implements of war;
Why such impress of shipwrights, whose sore task
Does not divide the Sunday from the week;
What might be toward, that this sweaty haste
Doth make the night joint-labourer with the day:
Who is't that can inform me?
Hor. That can I;
At least, the whisper goes so. Our last king,
Whose image even but now appear'd to us,
Was, as you know, by Fortinbras of Norway,
Thereto prick'd on by a most emulate pride,
Dared to the combat; in which our valiant Hamlet—
For so this side of our known world esteem'd him—
Did slay this Fortinbras; who, by a seal'd compact,
Well ratified by law and heraldry,
Did forfeit, with his life, all those his lands
Which he stood seized of, to the conqueror:
Against the which, a moiety competent
Was gaged by our king; which had return'd
To the inheritance of Fortinbras,
Had he been vanquisher; as, by the same covenant,
And carriage of the article design'd,
His fell to Hamlet. Now, sir, young Fortinbras,
Of unimproved mettle hot and full,
Hath in the skirts of Norway here and there
Shark'd up a list of lawless resolutes,
For food and diet, to some enterprise
That hath a stomach in't; which is no other—
As it doth well appear unto our state—
But to recover of us, by strong hand
And terms compulsatory, those foresaid lands
So by his father lost: and this, I take it,
Is the main motive of our preparations,
The source of this our watch and the chief head
Of this post-haste and romage in the land.
Ber. I think it be no other but e'en so:
Well may it sort that this portentous figure
Comes armed through our watch; so like the King
That was and is the question of these wars.
Hor. A mote it is to trouble the mind's eye.
In the most high and palmy state of Rome,
A little ere the mightiest Julius fell,
The graves stood tenantless and the sheeted dead
Did squeak and gibber in the Roman streets.
As stars with trains of fire and dews of blood,
Disasters in the sun; and the moist star
Upon whose influence Neptune's empire stands
Was sick almost to doomsday with eclipse.
And even the like precurse of fierce events,
As harbingers preceding still the fates
And prologue to the omen coming on,

Have heaven and earth together demonstrated
Unto our climatures and countrymen.
But soft, behold! lo, where it comes again!

Re-enter GHOST.

I'll cross it, though it blast me. Stay, illusion!
If thou hast any sound, or use of voice,
Speak to me:
If there be any good thing to be done,
That may to thee do ease and grace to me,
Speak to me:
If thou art privy to thy country's fate,
Which, happily, foreknowing may avoid,
O, speak!
Or if thou hast uphoarded in thy life
Extorted treasure in the womb of earth,
For which, they say, you spirits oft walk in death,
Speak of it: [*Cock crows.*] stay, and speak!
Stop it, Marcellus.

Mar. Shall I strike at it with my partisan?

Hor. Do, if it will not stand.

Ber. 'Tis here!

Hor. 'Tis here!

Mar. 'Tis gone! [*Exit* GHOST.
We do it wrong, being so majestical,
To offer it the show of violence;
For it is, as the air, invulnerable,
And our vain blows malicious mockery.

Ber. It was about to speak, when the cock crew.

Hor. And then it started like a guilty thing
Upon a fearful summons. I have heard,
The cock, that is the trumpet to the morn,
Doth with his lofty and shrill-sounding throat
Awake the god of day; and, at his warning,
Whether in sea or fire, in earth or air,
The extravagant and erring spirit hies
To his confine: and of the truth herein
This present object made probation.

Mar. It faded on the crowing of the cock.
Some say that ever 'gainst that season comes
Wherein our Saviour's birth is celebrated,
The bird of dawning singeth all night long:
And then, they say, no spirit dare stir abroad;
The nights are wholesome; then no planets strike,
No fairy takes, nor witch hath power to charm,
So hallow'd and so gracious is the time.

Hor. So have I heard and do in part believe it.
But, look, the morn, in russet mantle clad,
Walks o'er the dew of yon high eastward hill:
Break we our watch up; and by my advice,
Let us impart what we have seen to-night
Unto young Hamlet; for, upon my life,
This spirit, dumb to us, will speak to him.
Do you consent we shall acquaint him with it,
As needful in our loves, fitting our duty?

Mar. Let's do't, I pray; and I this morning know
Where we shall find him most conveniently.
[*Exeunt*.

SCENE II. *A room of state in the castle*

Enter the KING, QUEEN, HAMLET, POLONIUS, LAERTES, VOLTIMAND, CORNELIUS, *Lords, and Attendants*.

King. Though yet of Hamlet our dear brother's death
The memory be green, and that it us befitted
To bear our hearts in grief and our whole kingdom
To be contracted in one brow of woe,
Yet so far hath discretion fought with nature
That we with wisest sorrow think on him,
Together with remembrance of ourselves.
Therefore our sometime sister, now our queen,
The imperial jointress to this warlike state,
Have we, as 'twere with a defeated joy—
With an auspicious and a dropping eye,
With mirth in funeral and with dirge in marriage,
In equal scale weighing delight and dole—
Taken to wife: nor have we herein barr'd
Your better wisdoms, which have freely gone
With this affair along. For all, our thanks.
Now follows, that you know, young Fortinbras,
Holding a weak supposal of our worth,
Or thinking by our late dear brother's death
Our state to be disjoint and out of frame,
Colleagued with the dream of his advantage,
He hath not fail'd to pester us with message,
Importing the surrender of those lands
Lost by his father, with all bonds of law,
To our most valiant brother. So much for him.
Now for ourself and for this time of meeting:
Thus much the business is: we have here writ
To Norway, uncle of young Fortinbras—
Who, impotent and bed-rid, scarcely hears
Of this his nephew's purpose—to suppress
His further gait herein; in that the levies,
The lists, and full proportions are all made
Out of his subject: and we here dispatch
You, good Cornelius, and you, Voltimand,
For bearers of this greeting to old Norway;
Giving to you no further personal power
To business with the king, more than the scope
Of these delated articles allow.
Farewell, and let your haste commend your duty.

Cor., *Vol.* In that and all things will we show our duty.

King. We doubt it nothing: heartily farewell.
[*Exeunt* VOLTIMAND *and* CORNELIUS.
And now, Laertes, what's the news with you?
You told us of some suit; what is't, Laertes?

You cannot speak of reason to the Dane,
And lose your voice: what wouldst thou beg, Laertes,
That shall not be my offer, not thy asking?
The head is not more native to the heart,
The hand more instrumental to the mouth,
Than is the throne of Denmark to thy father.
What wouldst thou have, Laertes?

Laer. My dread lord,
Your leave and favour to return to France;
From whence though willingly I came to Denmark,
To show my duty in your coronation,
Yet now, I must confess, that duty done,
My thoughts and wishes bend again toward France
And bow them to your gracious leave and pardon.

King. Have you your father's leave? What says Polonius?

Pol. He hath, my lord, wrung from me my slow leave
By laboursome petition, and at last
Upon his will I seal'd my hard consent:
I do beseech you, give him leave to go.

King. Take thy fair hour, Laertes; time be thine,
And thy best graces spend it at thy will!
But now, my cousin Hamlet, and my son—

Ham. [*Aside*] A little more than kin, and less than kind.

King. How is it that the clouds still hang on you?

Ham. Not so, my lord; I am too much i' the sun.

Queen. Good Hamlet, cast thy nighted colour off,
And let thine eye look like a friend on Denmark.
Do not for ever with thy vailed lids
Seek for thy noble father in the dust.
Thou know'st 'tis common; all that lives must die,
Passing through nature to eternity.

Ham. Ay, madam, it is common.

Queen. If it be,
Why seems it so particular with thee?

Ham. Seems, madam! nay, it is; I know not "seems."
'Tis not alone my inky cloak, good mother,
Nor customary suits of solemn black,
Nor windy suspiration of forced breath,
No, nor the fruitful river in the eye,
Nor the dejected 'haviour of the visage,
Together with all forms, moods, shapes of grief,
That can denote me truly: these indeed seem,
For they are actions that a man might play:
But I have that within which passeth show;
These but the trappings and the suits of woe.

King. 'Tis sweet and commendable in your nature, Hamlet,
To give these mourning duties to your father:
But, you must know, your father lost a father;
That father lost, lost his, and the survivor bound
In filial obligation for some term
To do obsequious sorrow: but to persever
In obstinate condolement is a course
Of impious stubbornness; 'tis unmanly grief;
It shows a will most incorrect to heaven,
A heart unfortified, a mind impatient,
An understanding simple and unschool'd:
For what we know must be and is as common
As any the most vulgar thing to sense,
Why should we in our peevish opposition
Take it to heart? Fie! 'tis a fault to heaven,
A fault against the dead, a fault to nature,
To reason most absurd; whose common theme
Is death of fathers, and who still hath cried,
From the first corse till he that died to-day,
"This must be so." We pray you, throw to earth
This unprevailing woe, and think of us
As of a father: for let the world take note,
You are the most immediate to our throne;
And with no less nobility of love
Than that which dearest father bears his son,
Do I impart toward you. For your intent
In going back to school in Wittenberg,
It is most retrograde to our desire:
And we beseech you, bend you to remain
Here, in the cheer and comfort of our eye,
Our chiefest courtier, cousin, and our son.

Queen. Let not thy mother lose her prayers, Hamlet:
I pray thee, stay with us; go not to Wittenberg.

Ham. I shall in all my best obey you, madam.

King. Why, 'tis a loving and a fair reply:
Be as ourself in Denmark. Madam, come;
This gentle and unforced accord of Hamlet
Sits smiling to my heart: in grace whereof,
No jocund health that Denmark drinks to-day,
But the great cannon to the clouds shall tell,
And the King's rouse the heavens shall bruit again,
Re-speaking earthly thunder. Come away.

[*Exeunt all but* HAMLET.

Ham. O, that this too too solid flesh would melt,
Thaw, and resolve itself into a dew!
Or that the Everlasting had not fix'd
His canon 'gainst self-slaughter! O God! God!
How weary, stale, flat, and unprofitable,
Seem to me all the uses of this world!
Fie on't! ah fie! 'tis an unweeded garden,

That grows to seed; things rank and gross in nature
Possess it merely. That it should come to this!
But two months dead: nay, not so much, not two:
So excellent a king; that was, to this,
Hyperion to a satyr; so loving to my mother
That he might not beteem the winds of heaven
Visit her face too roughly. Heaven and earth!
Must I remember? why, she would hang on him,
As if increase of appetite had grown
By what it fed on: and yet, within a month—
Let me not think on't—Frailty, thy name is woman!—
A little month, or ere those shoes were old
With which she follow'd my poor father's body,
Like Niobe, all tears: why she, even she—
O God! a beast, that wants discourse of reason,
Would have mourn'd longer—married with my uncle,
My father's brother, but no more like my father
Than I to Hercules: within a month:
Ere yet the salt of most unrighteous tears
Had left the flushing in her galled eyes,
She married. O, most wicked speed, to post
With such dexterity to incestuous sheets!
It is not nor it cannot come to good:
But break, my heart; for I must hold my tongue.

Enter HORATIO, MARCELLUS, *and* BERNARDO.

Hor. Hail to your lordship!
Ham. I am glad to see you well:
Horatio—or I do forget myself.
Hor. The same, my lord, and your poor servant ever.
Ham. Sir, my good friend; I'll change that name with you:
And what make you from Wittenberg, Horatio?
Marcellus?
Mar. My good lord—
Ham. I am very glad to see you. Good even, sir.
But what, in faith, make you from Wittenberg?
Hor. A truant disposition, good my lord.
Ham. I would not hear your enemy say so,
Nor shall you do mine ear that violence,
To make it truster of your own report
Against yourself: I know you are no truant.
But what is your affair in Elsinore?
We'll teach you to drink deep ere you depart.
Hor. My lord, I came to see your father's funeral.
Ham. I pray thee, do not mock me, fellow-student;
I think it was to see my mother's wedding.
Hor. Indeed, my lord, it follow'd hard upon.
Ham. Thrift, thrift, Horatio! the funeral baked meats
Did coldly furnish forth the marriage tables.
Would I had met my dearest foe in heaven
Or ever I had seen that day, Horatio!
My father!—methinks I see my father.
Hor. Where, my lord?
Ham. In my mind's eye, Horatio.
Hor. I saw him once; he was a goodly king.
Ham. He was a man, take him for all in all,
I shall not look upon his like again.
Hor. My lord, I think I saw him yesternight.
Ham. Saw? who?
Hor. My lord, the King your father.
Ham. The King my father!
Hor. Season your admiration for a while
With an attent ear, till I may deliver,
Upon the witness of these gentlemen,
This marvel to you.
Ham. For God's love, let me hear.
Hor. Two nights together had these gentlemen,
Marcellus and Bernardo, on their watch,
In the dead vast and middle of the night,
Been thus encounter'd. A figure like your father,
Armed at point exactly, cap-a-pie,
Appears before them, and with solemn march
Goes slow and stately by them: thrice he walk'd
By their oppress'd and fear-surprised eyes,
Within his truncheon's length; whilst they, distill'd
Almost to jelly with the act of fear,
Stand dumb and speak not to him. This to me
In dreadful secrecy impart they did;
And I with them the third night kept the watch:
Where, as they had deliver'd, both in time,
Form of the thing, each word made true and good,
The apparition comes: I knew your father;
These hands are not more like.
Ham. But where was this?
Mar. My lord, upon the platform where we watch'd.
Ham. Did you not speak to it?
Hor. My lord, I did;
But answer made it none: yet once methought
It lifted up it head and did address
Itself to motion, like as it would speak;
But even then the morning cock crew loud,
And at the sound it shrunk in haste away,
And vanish'd from our sight.
Ham. 'Tis very strange.
Hor. As I do live, my honour'd lord, 'tis true;
And we did think it writ down in our duty
To let you know of it.
Ham. Indeed, indeed, sirs, but this troubles me.
Hold you the watch to-night?
Mar., *Ber.* We do, my lord.
Ham. Arm'd, say you?

Mar.
Ber. } Arm'd, my lord.
Ham. From top to toe?
Mar.
Ber. } My lord, from head to foot.
Ham. Then saw you not his face?
Hor. O, yes, my lord; he wore his beaver up.
Ham. What, look'd he frowningly?
Hor. A countenance more in sorrow than in anger.
Ham. Pale or red?
Hor. Nay, very pale.
Ham. And fix'd his eyes upon you?
Hor. Most constantly.
Ham. I would I had been there.
Hor. It would have much amazed you.
Ham. Very like, very like. Stay'd it long?
Hor. While one with moderate haste might tell a hundred.
Mar.
Ber. } Longer, longer.
Hor. Not when I saw't.
Ham. His beard was grizzled, no?
Hor. It was, as I have seen it in his life,
A sable silver'd.
Ham. I will watch to-night;
Perchance 'twill walk again.
Hor. I warrant it will.
Ham. If it assume my noble father's person,
I'll speak to it, though hell itself should gape
And bide me hold my peace. I pray you all,
If you have hitherto conceal'd this sight,
Let it be tenable in your silence still;
And whatsoever else shall hap to-night,
Give it an understanding, but no tongue:
I will requite your loves. So, fare you well:
Upon the platform, 'twixt eleven and twelve,
I'll visit you.
All. Our duty to your honour.
Ham. Your loves, as mine to you: farewell.
[*Exeunt all but* HAMLET.
My father's spirit in arms! all is not well;
I doubt some foul play. Would the night were come!
Till then sit still, my soul. Foul deeds will rise,
Though all the earth o'erwhelm them, to men's eyes. [*Exit.*

SCENE III. *A room in Polonius' house*

Enter LAERTES *and* OPHELIA.

Laer. My necessaries are embark'd: farewell:
And, sister, as the winds give benefit
And convoy is assistant, do not sleep,
But let me hear from you.
Oph. Do you doubt that?
Laer. For Hamlet and the trifling of his favour,
Hold it a fashion and a toy in blood,
A violet in the youth of primy nature,
Forward, not permanent, sweet, not lasting,
The perfume and suppliance of a minute;
No more.
Oph. No more but so?
Laer. Think it no more:
For nature, crescent, does not grow alone
In thews and bulk, but, as this temple waxes,
The inward service of the mind and soul
Grows wide withal. Perhaps he loves you now,
And now no soil nor cautel doth besmirch
The virtue of his will: but you must fear,
His greatness weigh'd, his will is not his own;
For he himself is subject to his birth.
He may not, as unvalued persons do,
Carve for himself; for on his choice depends
The safety and health of this whole state;
And therefore must his choice be circumscribed
Unto the voice and yielding of that body
Whereof he is the head. Then if he says he loves you,
It fits your wisdom so far to believe it
As he in his particular act and place
May give his saying deed; which is no further
Than the main voice of Denmark goes withal.
Then weigh what loss your honour may sustain,
If with too credent ear you list his songs,
Or lose your heart, or your chaste treasure open
To his unmaster'd importunity.
Fear it, Ophelia, fear it, my dear sister,
And keep you in the rear of your affection,
Out of the shot and danger of desire.
The chariest maid is prodigal enough,
If she unmask her beauty to the moon:
Virtue itself 'scapes not calumnious strokes:
The canker galls the infants of the spring,
Too oft before their buttons be disclosed,
And in the morn and liquid dew of youth
Contagious blastments are most imminent.
Be wary then; best safety lies in fear:
Youth to itself rebels, though none else near.
Oph. I shall the effect of this good lesson keep,
As watchman to my heart. But, good my brother,
Do not, as some ungracious pastors do,
Show me the steep and thorny way to heaven;
Whiles, like a puff'd and reckless libertine,
Himself the primrose path of dalliance treads,
And recks not his own rede.
Laer. O, fear me not.
I stay too long: but here my father comes.

Enter POLONIUS.

A double blessing is a double grace;
Occasion smiles upon a second leave.

Pol. Yet here, Laertes! aboard, aboard, for shame!
The wind sits in the shoulder of your sail,
And you are stay'd for. There; my blessing with thee!
And these few precepts in thy memory
See thou character. Give thy thoughts no tongue,
Nor any unproportion'd thought his act.
Be thou familiar, but by no means vulgar.
Those friends thou hast, and their adoption tried,
Grapple them to thy soul with hoops of steel;
But do not dull thy palm with entertainment
Of each new-hatch'd, unfledged comrade. Beware
Of entrance to a quarrel, but being in,
Bear't that the opposed may beware of thee.
Give every man thy ear, but few thy voice;
Take each man's censure, but reserve thy judgement.
Costly thy habit as thy purse can buy,
But not express'd in fancy; rich, not gaudy;
For the apparel oft proclaims the man,
And they in France of the best rank and station
Are of a most select and generous chief in that.
Neither a borrower nor a lender be;
For loan oft loses both itself and friend,
And borrowing dulls the edge of husbandry.
This above all: to thine own self be true,
And it must follow, as the night the day,
Thou canst not then be false to any man.
Farewell: my blessing season this in thee!

Laer. Most humbly do I take my leave, my lord.

Pol. The time invites you; go; your servants tend.

Laer. Farewell, Ophelia; and remember well
What I have said to you.

Oph. 'Tis in my memory lock'd,
And you yourself shall keep the key of it.

Laer. Farewell. [*Exit.*

Pol. What is't, Ophelia, he hath said to you?

Oph. So please you, something touching the Lord Hamlet.

Pol. Marry, well bethought:
'Tis told me, he hath very oft of late
Given private time to you; and you yourself
Have of your audience been most free and bounteous:
If it be so, as so 'tis put on me,
And that in way of caution, I must tell you,
You do not understand yourself so clearly
As it behoves my daughter and your honour.
What is between you? give me up the truth.

Oph. He hath, my lord, of late made many tenders
Of his affection to me.

Pol. Affection! pooh! you speak like a green girl,
Unsifted in such perilous circumstance.
Do you believe his tenders, as you call them?

Oph. I do not know, my lord, what I should think.

Pol. Marry, I'll teach you: think yourself a baby;
That you have ta'en these tenders for true pay,
Which are not sterling. Tender yourself more dearly;
Or—not to crack the wind of the poor phrase,
Running it thus—you'll tender me a fool.

Oph. My lord, he hath importuned me with love
In honourable fashion.

Pol. Ay, fashion you may call it; go to, go to.

Oph. And hath given countenance to his speech, my lord,
With almost all the holy vows of heaven.

Pol. Ay, springes to catch woodcocks. I do know,
When the blood burns, how prodigal the soul
Lends the tongue vows: these blazes, daughter,
Giving more light than heat, extinct in both,
Even in their promise, as it is a-making,
You must not take for fire. From this time
Be somewhat scanter of your maiden presence;
Set your entreatments at a higher rate
Than a command to parley. For Lord Hamlet,
Believe so much in him, that he is young,
And with a larger tether may he walk
Than may be given you: in few, Ophelia,
Do not believe his vows; for they are brokers,
Not of that dye which their investments show,
But mere implorators of unholy suits,
Breathing like sanctified and pious bawds,
The better to beguile. This is for all:
I would not, in plain terms, from this time forth,
Have you so slander any moment leisure,
As to give words or talk with the Lord Hamlet.
Look to't, I charge you: come your ways.

Oph. I shall obey, my lord. [*Exeunt.*

SCENE IV. *The platform*

Enter HAMLET, HORATIO, *and* MARCELLUS.

Ham. The air bites shrewdly; it is very cold.

Hor. It is a nipping and an eager air.

Ham. What hour now?

Hor. I think it lacks of twelve.

Mar. No, it is struck.

Hor. Indeed? I heard it not: then it draws near the season
Wherein the spirit held his wont to walk.

A flourish of trumpets, and ordnance shot off, within.

What does this mean, my lord?

Ham. The King doth wake to-night and takes his rouse,
Keeps wassail, and the swaggering up-spring reels;
And, as he drains his draughts of Rhenish down,
The kettle-drum and trumpet thus bray out
The triumph of his pledge.
Hor. Is it a custom?
Ham. Ay, marry, is't:
But to my mind, though I am native here
And to the manner born, it is a custom
More honour'd in the breach than the observance.
This heavy-headed revel east and west
Makes us traduced and tax'd of other nations:
They clepe us drunkards, and with swinish phrase
Soil our addition; and indeed it takes
From our achievements, though perform'd at height,
The pith and marrow of our attribute.
So, oft it chances in particular men,
That for some vicious mole of nature in them,
As, in their birth—wherein they are not guilty,
Since nature cannot choose his origin—
By the o'ergrowth of some complexion,
Oft breaking down the pales and forts of reason,
Or by some habit that too much o'er-leavens
The form of plausive manners, that these men,
Carrying, I say, the stamp of one defect,
Being nature's livery, or fortune's star—
Their virtues else—be they as pure as grace,
As infinite as man may undergo—
Shall in the general censure take corruption
From that particular fault: the dram of eale
Doth all the noble substance of a doubt
To his own scandal.
Hor. Look, my lords, it comes!

Enter GHOST.

Ham. Angels and ministers of grace defend us!
Be thou a spirit of health or goblin damn'd,
Bring with thee airs from heaven or blasts from hell,
Be thy intents wicked or charitable,
Thou comest in such a questionable shape
That I will speak to thee. I'll call thee Hamlet,
King, father, royal Dane: O, answer me!
Let me not burst in ignorance; but tell
Why thy canonized bones, hearsed in death,
Have burst their cerements; why the sepulchre,
Wherein we saw thee quietly inurn'd,
Hath oped his ponderous and marble jaws,
To cast thee up again. What may this mean,
That thou, dead corse, again in complete steel
Revisit'st thus the glimpses of the moon,
Making night hideous; and we fools of nature
So horridly to shake our disposition
With thoughts beyond the reaches of our souls?
Say, why is this? wherefore? what should we do?

GHOST *beckons* HAMLET.

Hor. It beckons you to go away with it,
As if it some impartment did desire
To you alone.
Mar. Look, with what courteous action
It waves you to a more removed ground:
But do not go with it.
Hor. No, by no means.
Ham. It will not speak; then I will follow it.
Hor. Do not, my lord.
Ham. Why what should be the fear?
I do not set my life at a pin's fee;
And for my soul, what can it do to that,
Being a thing immortal as itself?
It waves me forth again: I'll follow it.
Hor. What if it tempt you toward the flood, my lord,
Or to the dreadful summit of the cliff
That beetles o'er his base into the sea,
And there assume some other horrible form,
Which might deprive your sovereignty of reason
And draw you into madness? think of it.
The very place puts toys of desperation,
Without more motive, into every brain
That looks so many fathoms to the sea
And hears it roar beneath.
Ham. It waves me still.
Go on; I'll follow thee.
Mar. You shall not go, my lord.
Ham. Hold off your hands.
Hor. Be ruled; you shall not go.
Ham. My fate cries out,
And makes each petty artery in this body
As hardy as the Nemean lion's nerve.
Still am I call'd. Unhand me, gentlemen.
By heaven, I'll make a ghost of him that lets me!
I say, away! Go on; I'll follow thee.
[*Exeunt* GHOST *and* HAMLET.
Hor. He waxes desperate with imagination.
Mar. Let's follow; 'tis not fit thus to obey him.
Hor. Have after. To what issue will this come?
Mar. Something is rotten in the state of Denmark.
Hor. Heaven will direct it.
Mar. Nay, let's follow him. [*Exeunt.*

SCENE V. *Another part of the platform*

Enter GHOST *and* HAMLET.

Ham. Where wilt thou lead me? speak; I'll go no further.
Ghost. Mark me.
Ham. I will.
Ghost. My hour is almost come,

When I to sulphurous and tormenting flames
Must render up myself.
Ham. Alas, poor ghost!
Ghost. Pity me not, but lend thy serious hearing
To what I shall unfold.
Ham. Speak; I am bound to hear.
Ghost. So art thou to revenge, when thou shalt hear.
Ham. What?
Ghost. I am thy father's spirit,
Doom'd for a certain term to walk the night,
And for the day confined to fast in fires,
Till the foul crimes done in my days of nature
Are burnt and purged away. But that I am forbid
To tell the secrets of my prison-house,
I could a tale unfold whose lightest word
Would harrow up thy soul, freeze thy young blood,
Make thy two eyes, like stars, start from their spheres,
Thy knotted and combined locks to part
And each particular hair to stand an end,
Like quills upon the fretful porpentine.
But this eternal blazon must not be
To ears of flesh and blood. List, list, O, list!
If thou didst ever thy dear father love—
Ham. O God!
Ghost. Revenge his foul and most unnatural murder.
Ham. Murder!
Ghost. Murder most foul, as in the best it is;
But this most foul, strange, and unnatural.
Ham. Haste me to know't, that I, with wings as swift
As meditation or the thoughts of love,
May sweep to my revenge.
Ghost. I find thee apt;
And duller shouldst thou be than the fat weed
That roots itself in ease on Lethe wharf,
Wouldst thou not stir in this. Now, Hamlet, hear:
'Tis given out that, sleeping in my orchard,
A serpent stung me; so the whole ear of Denmark
Is by a forged process of my death
Rankly abused: but know, thou noble youth,
The serpent that did sting thy father's life
Now wears his crown.
Ham. O my prophetic soul!
My uncle!
Ghost. Ay, that incestuous, that adulterate beast,
With witchcraft of his wit, with traitorous gifts—
O wicked wit and gifts, that have the power
So to seduce!—won to his shameful lust
The will of my most seeming-virtuous queen:
O Hamlet, what a falling-off was there!
From me, whose love was of that dignity
That it went hand in hand even with the vow
I made to her in marriage, and to decline
Upon a wretch whose natural gifts were poor
To those of mine!
But virtue, as it never will be moved,
Though lewdness court it in a shape of heaven,
So lust, though to a radiant angel link'd,
Will sate itself in a celestial bed,
And prey on garbage.
But, soft! methinks I scent the morning air;
Brief let me be. Sleeping within my orchard,
My custom always of the afternoon,
Upon my secure hour thy uncle stole,
With juice of cursed hebenon in a vial,
And in the porches of my ears did pour
The leperous distilment; whose effect
Holds such an enmity with blood of man
That swift as quicksilver it courses through
The natural gates and alleys of the body,
And with a sudden vigour it doth posset
And curd, like eager droppings into milk,
The thin and wholesome blood. So did it mine;
And a most instant tetter bark'd about,
Most lazar-like, with vile and loathsome crust,
All my smooth body.
Thus was I, sleeping, by a brother's hand
Of life, of crown, of queen, at once dispatch'd:
Cut off even in the blossoms of my sin,
Unhousel'd, disappointed, unaneled,
No reckoning made, but sent to my account
With all my imperfections on my head.
O, horrible! O, horrible! most horrible!
If thou hast nature in thee, bear it not;
Let not the royal bed of Denmark be
A couch for luxury and damned incest.
But, howsoever thou pursuest this act,
Taint not thy mind, nor let thy soul contrive
Against thy mother aught: leave her to heaven
And to those thorns that in her bosom lodge,
To prick and sting her. Fare thee well at once!
The glow-worm shows the matin to be near,
And 'gins to pale his uneffectual fire:
Adieu, adieu! Hamlet, remember me. [*Exit.*
Ham. O all you host of heaven! O earth! what else?
And shall I couple hell? O, fie! Hold, hold, my heart;
And you, my sinews, grow not instant old,
But bear me stiffly up. Remember thee!
Ay, thou poor ghost, while memory holds a seat
In this distracted globe. Remember thee!
Yea, from the table of my memory
I'll wipe away all trivial fond records,
All saws of books, all forms, all pressures past,
That youth and observation copied there;

And thy commandment all alone shall live
Within the book and volume of my brain,
Unmix'd with baser matter. Yes, by heaven!
O most pernicious woman!
O villain, villain, smiling, damned villain!
My tables—meet it is I set it down,
That one may smile, and smile, and be a villain;
At least I'm sure it may be so in Denmark:
Writing.
So, uncle, there you are. Now to my word;
It is "Adieu, adieu! remember me."
I have sworn't.
Mar., *Hor.* [*Within*] My lord, my lord—
Mar. [*Within*] Lord Hamlet—
Hor. [*Within*] Heaven secure him!
Ham. So be it!
Hor. [*Within*] Hillo, ho, ho, my lord!
Ham. Hillo, ho, ho, boy! come, bird, come.

Enter HORATIO *and* MARCELLUS.

Mar. How is't, my noble lord?
Hor. What news, my lord?
Ham. O, wonderful!
Hor. Good my lord, tell it.
Ham. No; you'll reveal it.
Hor. Not I, my lord, by heaven.
Mar. Nor I, my lord.
Ham. How say you, then; would heart of man once think it?
But you'll be secret?
Hor., *Mar.* Ay, by heaven, my lord.
Ham. There's ne'er a villain dwelling in all Denmark
But he's an arrant knave.
Hor. There needs no ghost, my lord, come from the grave
To tell us this.
Ham. Why, right; you are i' the right;
And so, without more circumstance at all,
I hold it fit that we shake hands and part:
You, as your business and desire shall point you;
For every man has business and desire,
Such as it is; and for mine own poor part,
Look you, I'll go pray.
Hor. These are but wild and whirling words, my lord.
Ham. I'm sorry they offend you, heartily;
Yes, 'faith, heartily.
Hor. There's no offence, my lord.
Ham. Yes, by Saint Patrick, but there is, Horatio,
And much offence too. Touching this vision here,
It is an honest ghost, that let me tell you,
For your desire to know what is between us,
O'ermaster 't as you may. And now, good friends,
As you are friends, scholars, and soldiers,
Give me one poor request.
Hor. What is't, my lord? we will.
Ham. Never make known what you have seen to-night.
Hor., *Mar.* My Lord, we will not.
Ham. Nay, but swear't.
Hor. In faith,
My lord, not I.
Mar. Nor I, my lord, in faith.
Ham. Upon my sword.
Mar. We have sworn, my lord, already.
Ham. Indeed, upon my sword, indeed.
Ghost. [*Beneath*] Swear.
Ham. Ah, ha, boy! say'st thou so? art thou there, truepenny?
Come on—you hear this fellow in the cellarage—
Consent to swear.
Hor. Propose the oath, my lord.
Ham. Never to speak of this that you have seen,
Swear by my sword.
Ghost. [*Beneath*] Swear.
Ham. *Hic et ubique?* then we'll shift our ground.
Come higher, gentlemen,
And lay your hands again upon my sword:
Never to speak of this that you have heard,
Swear by my sword.
Ghost. [*Beneath*] Swear.
Ham. Well said, old mole! canst work i' the earth so fast?
A worthy pioner! Once more remove, good friends.
Hor. O day and night, but this is wondrous strange!
Ham. And therefore as a stranger give it welcome.
There are more things in heaven and earth, Horatio,
Than are dreamt of in your philosophy.
But come;
Here, as before, never, so help you mercy,
How strange or odd soe'er I bear myself,
As I perchance hereafter shall think meet
To put an antic disposition on,
That you, at such times seeing me, never shall,
With arms encumber'd thus, or this head-shake,
Or by pronouncing of some doubtful phrase,
As "Well, well, we know," or "We could, an if we would,"
Or "If we list to speak," or "There be, an if they might,"
Or such ambiguous giving out, to note
That you know aught of me: this not to do,

So grace and mercy at your most need help you,
Swear.

Ghost. [*Beneath*] Swear.

Ham. Rest, rest, perturbed spirit! [*They swear*.] So, gentlemen,
With all my love I do commend me to you:
And what so poor a man as Hamlet is
May do, to express his love and friending to you,
God willing, shall not lack. Let us go in together;
And still your fingers on your lips, I pray.
The time is out of joint: O cursed spite,
That ever I was born to set it right!
Nay, come, let's go together. [*Exeunt*.

ACT II

SCENE I. *A room in Polonius' house*

Enter POLONIUS *and* REYNALDO.

Pol. Give him this money and these notes, Reynaldo.

Rey. I will, my lord.

Pol. You shall do marvellous wisely, good Reynaldo,
Before you visit him, to make inquire
Of his behaviour.

Rey. My lord, I did intend it.

Pol. Marry, well said; very well said. Look you, sir,
Inquire me first what Danskers are in Paris;
And how, and who, what means, and where they keep,
What company, at what expense; and finding
By this encompassment and drift of question
That they do know my son, come you more nearer
Than your particular demands will touch it.
Take you, as 'twere, some distant knowledge of him;
As thus, "I know his father and his friends,
And in part him": do you mark this, Reynaldo?

Rey. Ay, very well, my lord.

Pol. "And in part him; but" you may say "not well:
But, if't be he I mean, he's very wild;
Addicted so and so": and there put on him
What forgeries you please; marry, none so rank
As may dishonour him; take heed of that;
But, sir, such wanton, wild, and usual slips
As are companions noted and most known
To youth and liberty.

Rey. As gaming, my lord.

Pol. Ay, or drinking, fencing, swearing, quarrelling,
Drabbing: you may go so far.

Rey. My lord, that would dishonour him.

Pol. 'Faith, no; as you may season it in the charge.
You must not put another scandal on him,
That he is open to incontinency;
That's not my meaning. But breathe his faults so quaintly
That they may seem the taints of liberty,
The flash and outbreak of a fiery mind,
A savageness in unreclaimed blood,
Of general assault.

Rey. But, my good lord—

Pol. Wherefore should you do this?

Rey. Ay, my lord,
I would know that.

Pol. Marry, sir, here's my drift;
And, I believe, it is a fetch of wit.
You laying these slight sullies on my son,
As 'twere a thing a little soil'd i' the working,
Mark you,
Your party in converse, him you would sound,
Having ever seen in the prenominate crimes
The youth you breathe of guilty, be assured
He closes with you in this consequence;
"Good sir," or so, or "friend," or "gentleman,"
According to the phrase or the addition
Of man and country.

Rey. Very good, my lord.

Pol. And then, sir, does he this—he does—
what was I about to say? By the mass, I was
about to say something. Where did I leave?

Rey. At "closes in the consequence," at "friend or so," and "gentleman."

Pol. At "closes in the consequence," ay, marry;
He closes thus: "I know the gentleman;
I saw him yesterday, or t'other day,
Or then, or then; with such, or such; and, as you say,
There was a' gaming; there o'ertook in's rouse;
There falling out at tennis": or perchance,
"I saw him enter such a house of sale,"
Videlicet, a brothel, or so forth.
See you now;
Your bait of falsehood takes this carp of truth:
And thus do we of wisdom and of reach,
With windlasses and with assays of bias,
By indirections find directions out.
So by my former lecture and advice,
Shall you my son. You have me, have you not?

Rey. My lord, I have.

Pol. God be wi' you; fare you well.

Rey. Good my lord!

Pol. Observe his inclination in yourself.

Rey. I shall, my lord.

Pol. And let him ply his music.

Rey. Well, my lord.

Pol. Farewell! [*Exit* REYNALDO.

Enter OPHELIA.

How now, Ophelia! what's the matter?
Oph. O, my lord, my lord, I have been so affrighted!
Pol. With what, i' the name of God?
Oph. My lord, as I was sewing in my closet,
Lord Hamlet, with his doublet all unbraced;
No hat upon his head; his stockings foul'd,
Ungarter'd, and down-gyved to his ancle;
Pale as his shirt; his knees knocking each other;
And with a look so piteous in purport
As if he had been loosed out of hell
To speak of horrors—he comes before me.
Pol. Mad for thy love?
Oph. My lord, I do not know;
But truly, I do fear it.
Pol. What said he?
Oph. He took me by the wrist and held me hard;
Then goes he to the length of all his arm;
And, with his other hand thus o'er his brow,
He falls to such perusal of my face
As he would draw it. Long stay'd he so;
At last, a little shaking of mine arm
And thrice his head thus waving up and down,
He raised a sigh so piteous and profound
As it did seem to shatter all his bulk
And end his being. That done, he lets me go;
And, with his head over his shoulder turn'd,
He seem'd to find his way without his eyes;
For out o'doors he went without their helps,
And, to the last, bended their light on me.
Pol. Come, go with me: I will go seek the King.
This is the very ecstasy of love,
Whose violent property fordoes itself
And leads the will to desperate undertakings
As oft as any passion under heaven
That does afflict our natures. I am sorry.
What, have you given him any hard words of late?
Oph. No, my good lord, but, as you did command,
I did repel his letters and denied
His access to me.
Pol. That hath made him mad.
I am sorry that with better heed and judgement
I had not quoted him. I fear'd he did but trifle,
And meant to wreck thee; but, beshrew my jealousy!
By heaven, it is as proper to our age
To cast beyond ourselves in our opinions
As it is common for the younger sort
To lack discretion. Come, go we to the King:
This must be known; which, being kept close, might move
More grief to hide than hate to utter love.
[*Exeunt.*

SCENE II. *A room in the castle*

Enter KING, QUEEN, ROSENCRANTZ, GUILDENSTERN, *and Attendants.*

King. Welcome, dear Rosencrantz and Guildenstern!
Moreover that we much did long to see you,
The need we have to use you did provoke
Our hasty sending. Something have you heard
Of Hamlet's transformation; so call it,
Sith nor the exterior nor the inward man
Resembles that it was. What it should be,
More than his father's death, that thus hath put him
So much from the understanding of himself,
I cannot dream of. I entreat you both
That, being of so young days brought up with him,
And sith so neighbour'd to his youth and humour,
That you vouchsafe your rest here in our court
Some little time; so by your companies
To draw him on to pleasures, and to gather,
So much as from occasion you may glean,
Whether aught, to us unknown, afflicts him thus,
That, open'd, lies within our remedy.
Queen. Good gentlemen, he hath much talk'd of you;
And sure I am two men there are not living
To whom he more adheres. If it will please you
To show us so much gentry and good will
As to expend your time with us awhile,
For the supply and profit of our hope,
Your visitation shall receive such thanks
As fits a king's remembrance.
Ros. Both your Majesties
Might, by the sovereign power you have of us,
Put your dread pleasures more into command
Than to entreaty.
Guil. But we both obey,
And here give up ourselves, in the full bent
To lay our service freely at your feet,
To be commanded.
King. Thanks, Rosencrantz and gentle Guildenstern.
Queen. Thanks, Guildenstern and gentle Rosencrantz:
And I beseech you instantly to visit
My too much changed son. Go, some of you,
And bring these gentlemen where Hamlet is.
Guil. Heavens make our presence and our practices
Pleasant and helpful to him!
Queen. Ay, amen!

[*Exeunt* ROSENCRANTZ, GUILDENSTERN, *and some Attendants.*

Enter POLONIUS.

Pol. The ambassadors from Norway, my good lord,
Are joyfully return'd.
King. Thou still hast been the father of good news.
Pol. Have I, my lord? I assure my good liege,
I hold my duty, as I hold my soul,
Both to my God and to my gracious king:
And I do think, or else this brain of mine
Hunts not the trail of policy so sure
As it hath used to do, that I have found
The very cause of Hamlet's lunacy.
King. O, speak of that; that do I long to hear.
Pol. Give first admittance to the ambassadors;
My news shall be the fruit to that great feast.
King. Thyself do grace to them, and bring them in. [*Exit* POLONIUS.
He tells me, my dear Gertrude, he hath found
The head and source of all your son's distemper.
Queen. I doubt it is no other but the main;
His father's death, and our o'erhasty marriage.
King. Well, we shall sift him.

Re-enter POLONIUS, *with* VOLTIMAND *and* CORNELIUS.

Welcome, my good friends!
Say, Voltimand, what from our brother Norway?
Volt. Most fair return of greetings and desires.
Upon our first, he sent out to suppress
His nephew's levies; which to him appear'd
To be a preparation 'gainst the Polack;
But, better look'd into, he truly found
It was against your Highness: whereat grieved,
That so to his sickness, age and impotence
Was falsely borne in hand, sends out arrests
On Fortinbras; which he, in brief, obeys;
Receives rebuke from Norway, and in fine
Makes vow before his uncle never more
To give the assay of arms against your Majesty.
Whereon old Norway, overcome with joy,
Gives him three thousand crowns in annual fee,
And his commission to employ those soldiers,
So levied as before, against the Polack:
With an entreaty, herein further shown,
Giving a paper.
That it might please you to give quiet pass
Through your dominions for this enterprise,
On such regards of safety and allowance
As therein are set down.
King. It likes us well;
And at our more consider'd time we'll read,
Answer, and think upon this business.
Meantime we thank you for your well-took labour.
Go to your rest; at night we'll feast together.
Most welcome home!
[*Exeunt* VOLTIMAND *and* CORNELIUS.
Pol. This business is well ended.
My liege, and madam, to expostulate
What majesty should be, what duty is,
Why day is day, night night, and time is time,
Were nothing but to waste night, day, and time.
Therefore, since brevity is the soul of wit,
And tediousness the limbs and outward flourishes,
I will be brief: your noble son is mad.
Mad call I it; for, to define true madness,
What is't but to be nothing else but mad?
But let that go.
Queen. More matter, with less art.
Pol. Madam, I swear I use no art at all.
That he is mad, 'tis true: 'tis true 'tis pity;
And pity 'tis 'tis true. A foolish figure;
But farewell it, for I will use no art.
Mad let us grant him, then; and now remains
That we find out the cause of this effect,
Or rather say, the cause of this defect,
For this effect defective comes by cause.
Thus it remains and the remainder thus.
Perpend.
I have a daughter—have while she is mine—
Who, in her duty and obedience, mark,
Hath given me this. Now gather, and surmise.
Reads.
"To the celestial and my soul's idol, the most beautified Ophelia"—
That's an ill phrase, a vile phrase; "beautified" is a vile phrase: but you shall hear. Thus: [*Reads.*]
"In her excellent white bosom, these, &c."
Queen. Came this from Hamlet to her?
Pol. Good madam, stay awhile; I will be faithful. [*Reads.*]
"Doubt thou the stars are fire;
Doubt that the sun doth move;
Doubt truth to be a liar;
But never doubt I love.
"O dear Ophelia, I am ill at these numbers; I have not art to reckon my groans: but that I love thee best, O most best, believe it. Adieu.
"Thine evermore, most dear lady, whilst this machine is to him, Hamlet"
This, in obedience, hath my daughter shown me,
And more above, hath his solicitings,
As they fell out by time, by means, and place,
All given to mine ear.
King. But how hath she
Received his love?
Pol. What do you think of me?
King. As of a man faithful and honourable.

Pol. I would fain prove so. But what might you think,
When I had seen this hot love on the wing—
As I perceived it, I must tell you that,
Before my daughter told me—what might you,
Or my dear Majesty your queen here, think,
If I had play'd the desk or table-book,
Or given my heart a winking, mute and dumb,
Or look'd upon this love with idle sight;
What might you think? No, I went round to work,
And my young mistress thus I did bespeak:
"Lord Hamlet is a prince, out of thy star;
This must not be": and then I prescripts gave her,
That she should lock herself from his resort,
Admit no messengers, receive no tokens.
Which done, she took the fruits of my advice;
And he, repulsed—a short tale to make—
Fell into a sadness, then into a fast,
Thence to a watch, thence into a weakness,
Thence to a lightness, and, by this declension,
Into the madness wherein now he raves,
And all we mourn for.

King. Do you think 'tis this?

Queen. It may be, very likely.

Pol. Hath there been such a time—I'd fain know that—
That I have positively said "'Tis so,"
When it proved otherwise?

King. Not that I know.

Pol. [*Pointing to his head and shoulder*] Take this from this, if this be otherwise:
If circumstances lead me, I will find
Where truth is hid, though it were hid indeed
Within the centre.

King. How may we try it further?

Pol. You know, sometimes he walks four hours together
Here in the lobby.

Queen. So he does indeed.

Pol. At such a time I'll loose my daughter to him:
Be you and I behind an arras then;
Mark the encounter. If he love her not
And be not from his reason fall'n thereon,
Let me be no assistant for a state,
But keep a farm and carters.

King. We will try it.

Queen. But, look, where sadly the poor wretch comes reading.

Pol. Away, I do beseech you, both away:
I'll board him presently.

[*Exeunt* KING, QUEEN, *and Attendants.*

Enter HAMLET, *reading.*

O, give me leave,
How does my good Lord Hamlet?

Ham. Well, God-a-mercy.

Pol. Do you know me, my lord?

Ham. Excellent well; you are a fishmonger.

Pol. Not I, my lord.

Ham. Then I would you were so honest a man.

Pol. Honest, my lord!

Ham. Ay, sir; to be honest, as this world goes, is to be one man picked out of ten thousand.

Pol. That's very true, my lord.

Ham. For if the sun breed maggots in a dead dog, being a god kissing carrion—Have you a daughter?

Pol. I have, my lord.

Ham. Let her not walk i' the sun. Conception is a blessing, but not as your daughter may conceive. Friend, look to 't.

Pol. [*Aside*] How say you by that? Still harping on my daughter: yet he knew me not at first; he said I was a fishmonger: he is far gone, far gone, and truly in my youth I suffered much extremity for love; very near this. I'll speak to him again. What do you read, my lord?

Ham. Words, words, words.

Pol. What is the matter, my lord?

Ham. Between who?

Pol. I mean, the matter that you read, my lord.

Ham. Slanders, sir: for the satirical rogue says here that old men have grey beards, that their faces are wrinkled, their eyes purging thick amber and plum-tree gum and that they have a plentiful lack of wit, together with most weak hams; all which, sir, though I most powerfully and potently believe, yet I hold it not honesty to have it thus set down, for yourself, sir, should be old as I am, if like a crab you could go backward.

Pol. [*Aside*] Though this be madness, yet there is method in't. Will you walk out of the air, my lord?

Ham. Into my grave.

Pol. Indeed, that is out o' the air. [*Aside*] How pregnant sometimes his replies are! a happiness that often madness hits on, which reason and sanity could not so prosperously be delivered of. I will leave him, and suddenly contrive the means of meeting between him and my daughter.—My honourable lord, I will most humbly take my leave of you.

Ham. You cannot, sir, take from me any thing that I will more willingly part withal: except my life, except my life, except my life.

Pol. Fare you well, my lord.

Ham. These tedious old fools!

Enter ROSENCRANTZ *and* GUILDENSTERN

Pol. You go to seek the Lord Hamlet; there he is.

Ros. [*To* POLONIUS] God save you, sir!

[*Exit* POLONIUS.

Guil. My honoured lord!

Ros. My most dear lord!

Ham. My excellent good friends! How dost thou, Guildenstern? Ah, Rosencrantz! Good lads, how do ye both?

Ros. As the indifferent children of the earth.

Guil. Happy, in that we are not over-happy;
On fortune's cap we are not the very button.

Ham. Nor the soles of her shoe?

Ros. Neither, my lord.

Ham. Then you live about her waist, or in the middle of her favours?

Guil. 'Faith, her privates we.

Ham. In the secret parts of fortune? O, most true; she is a strumpet. What's the news?

Ros. None, my lord, but that the world's grown honest.

Ham. Then is doomsday near. But your news is not true. Let me question more in particular. What have you, my good friends, deserved at the hands of fortune, that she sends you to prison hither?

Guil. Prison, my lord!

Ham. Denmark's a prison.

Ros. Then is the world one.

Ham. A goodly one; in which there are many confines, wards, and dungeons, Denmark being one o' the worst.

Ros. We think not so, my lord.

Ham. Why, then, 'tis none to you; for there is nothing either good or bad, but thinking makes it so. To me it is a prison.

Ros. Why then, your ambition makes it one; 'tis too narrow for your mind.

Ham. O God, I could be bounded in a nutshell and count myself a king of infinite space, were it not that I have bad dreams.

Guil. Which dreams indeed are ambition, for the very substance of the ambitious is merely the shadow of a dream.

Ham. A dream itself is but a shadow.

Ros. Truly, and I hold ambition of so airy and light a quality that it is but a shadow's shadow.

Ham. Then are our beggars bodies, and our monarchs and outstretched heroes the beggars' shadows. Shall we to the court? for, by my fay, I cannot reason.

Ros. } *Guil.* } We'll wait upon you.

Ham. No such matter. I will not sort you with the rest of my servants, for, to speak to you like an honest man, I am most dreadfully attended. But, in the beaten way of friendship, what make you at Elsinore?

Ros. To visit you, my lord; no other occasion.

Ham. Beggar that I am, I am even poor in thanks; but I thank you: and sure, dear friends, my thanks are too dear a halfpenny. Were you not sent for? Is it your own inclining? Is it a free visitation? Come, deal justly with me. Come, come; nay, speak.

Guil. What should we say, my lord?

Ham. Why, any thing, but to the purpose. You were sent for; and there is a kind of confession in your looks which your modesties have not craft enough to colour. I know the good king and queen have sent for you.

Ros. To what end, my lord?

Ham. That you must teach me. But let me conjure you, by the rights of our fellowship, by the consonancy of our youth, by the obligation of our ever-preserved love, and by what more dear a better proposer could charge you withal, be even and direct with me, whether you were sent for, or no?

Ros. [*Aside to* GUILDENSTERN] What say you?

Ham. [*Aside*] Nay, then, I have an eye of you.—If you love me, hold not off.

Guil. My lord, we were sent for.

Ham. I will tell you why; so shall my anticipation prevent your discovery, and your secrecy to the king and queen moult no feather. I have of late—but wherefore I know not—lost all my mirth, forgone all custom of exercises; and indeed it goes so heavily with my disposition that this goodly frame, the earth, seems to me a sterile promontory, this most excellent canopy, the air, look you, this brave o'erhanging firmament, this majestical roof fretted with golden fire, why, it appears no other thing to me than a foul and pestilent congregation of vapours. What a piece of work is a man! how noble in reason! how infinite in faculty! in form and moving how express and admirable! in action how like an angel! in apprehension how like a god! the beauty of the world! the paragon of animals! And yet, to me, what is this quintessence of dust? man delights not me: no, nor woman neither, though by your smiling you seem to say so.

Ros. My lord, there was no such stuff in my thoughts.

Ham. Why did you laugh then, when I said "man delights not me"?

Ros. To think, my lord, if you delight not in man, what lenten entertainment the players shall receive from you. We coted them on the way; and hither are they coming, to offer you service.

Ham. He that plays the king shall be welcome; his majesty shall have tribute of me; the adventurous knight shall use his foil and target; the lover shall not sigh *gratis;* the humorous man shall end his part in peace; the clown shall make those laugh whose lungs are tickle o' the sere; and the lady shall say her mind freely, or the blank verse shall halt for't. What players are they?

Ros. Even those you were wont to take delight in, the tragedians of the city.

Ham. How chances it they travel? their residence, both in reputation and profit, was better both ways.

Ros. I think their inhibition comes by the means of the late innovation.

Ham. Do they hold the same estimation they did when I was in the city? are they so followed?

Ros. No, indeed, are they not.

Ham. How comes it? do they grow rusty?

Ros. Nay, their endeavour keeps in the wonted pace; but there is, sir, an aery of children, little eyases, that cry out on the top of question, and are most tyrannically clapped for't. These are now the fashion, and so berattle the common stages—so they call them—that many wearing rapiers are afraid of goose-quills and dare scarce come thither.

Ham. What, are they children? who maintains 'em? how are they escoted? Will they pursue the quality no longer than they can sing? will they not say afterwards, if they should grow themselves to common players—as it is most like, if their means are no better—their writers do them wrong, to make them exclaim against their own succession?

Ros. 'Faith, there has been much to do on both sides; and the nation holds it no sin to tarre them to controversy. There was, for a while, no money bid for argument, unless the poet and the player went to cuffs in the question.

Ham. Is't possible?

Guil. O, there has been much throwing about of brains.

Ham. Do the boys carry it away?

Ros. Ay, that they do, my lord; Hercules and his load too.

Ham. It is not very strange; for mine uncle is King of Denmark, and those that would make mows at him while my father lived, give twenty, forty, fifty, an hundred ducats a-piece for his picture in little. 'Sblood, there is something in this more than natural, if philosophy could find it out.

Flourish of trumpets within.

Guil. There are the players.

Ham. Gentlemen, you are welcome to Elsinore. Your hands, come then. The appurtenance of welcome is fashion and ceremony. Let me comply with you in this garb, lest my extent to the players, which, I tell you, must show fairly outward, should more appear like entertainment than yours. You are welcome; but my uncle-father and aunt-mother are deceived.

Guil. In what, my dear lord?

Ham. I am but mad north-north-west. When the wind is southerly I know a hawk from a handsaw.

Re-enter POLONIUS.

Pol. Well be with you, gentlemen!

Ham. Hark you, Guildenstern; and you too: at each ear a hearer: that great baby you see there is not yet out of his swaddling-clouts.

Ros. Happily he's the second time come to them; for they say an old man is twice a child.

Ham. I will prophesy he comes to tell me of the players; mark it. [*Aloud.*] You say right, sir: o'Monday morning; 'twas so indeed.

Pol. My lord, I have news to tell you.

Ham. My lord, I have news to tell you. When Roscius was an actor in Rome—

Pol. The actors are come hither, my lord.

Ham. Buz, buz!

Pol. Upon mine honour—

Ham. Then came each actor on his ass—

Pol. The best actors in the world, either for tragedy, comedy, history, pastoral, pastoral-comical, historical-pastoral, tragical-historical, tragical-comical-historical-pastoral, scene individable, or poem unlimited; Seneca cannot be too heavy, nor Plautus too light. For the law of writ and the liberty, these are the only men.

Ham. O Jephthah, judge of Israel, what a treasure hadst thou!

Pol. What a treasure had he, my lord?

Ham. Why,

"One fair daughter, and no more,
The which he loved passing well."

Pol. [*Aside*] Still on my daughter.

Ham. Am I not i' the right, old Jephthah?

Pol. If you call me Jephthah, my lord, I have a daughter that I love passing well.

Ham. Nay, that follows not.

Pol. What follows, then, my lord?

Ham. Why,

"As by lot, God wot,"

and then, you know,

"It came to pass, as most like it was"—

the first row of the pious chanson will show you more; for look, where my abridgement comes.

Enter four or five PLAYERS.

You are welcome, masters; welcome, all. I am glad to see thee well. Welcome, good friends.

O, my old friend! thy face is valanced since I saw thee last; comest thou to beard me in Denmark? What, my young lady and mistress! By'r lady, your ladyship is nearer to heaven than when I saw you last, by the altitude of a chopine. Pray God, your voice, like a piece of uncurrent gold, be not cracked within the ring. Masters, you are all welcome. We'll e'en to't like French falconers, fly at anything we see: we'll have a speech straight. Come, give us a taste of your quality; come, a passionate speech.

1st Play. What speech, my lord?

Ham. I heard thee speak me a speech once, but it was never acted; or, if it was, not above once; for the play, I remember, pleased not the million; 'twas caviare to the general; but it was—as I received it, and others, whose judgements in such matters cried in the top of mine—an excellent play, well digested in the scenes, set down with as much modesty as cunning. I remember, one said there were no sallets in the lines to make the matter savoury, nor no matter in the phrase that might indict the author of affectation; but called it an honest method, as wholesome as sweet, and by very much more handsome than fine. One speech in it I chiefly loved: 'twas Æneas' tale to Dido; and thereabout of it especially, where he speaks of Priam's slaughter. If it live in your memory, begin at this line: let me see, let me see—
"The rugged Pyrrhus, like the Hyrcanian beast"
—it is not so. It begins with Pyrrhus:
"The rugged Pyrrhus, he whose sable arms,
Black as his purpose, did the night resemble
When he lay couched in the ominous horse,
Hath now this dread and black complexion smear'd
With heraldry more dismal; head to foot
Now is he total gules; horridly trick'd
With blood of fathers, mothers, daughters, sons,
Baked and impasted with the parching streets,
That lend a tyrannous and damned light
To their lord's murder: roasted in wrath and fire,
And thus o'er-sized with coagulate gore,
With eyes like carbuncles, the hellish Pyrrhus
Old grandsire Priam seeks."
So, proceed you.

Pol. 'Fore God, my lord, well spoken, with good accent and good discretion.

1st Play. "Anon he finds him
Striking too short at Greeks; his antique sword,
Rebellious to his arm, lies where it falls,
Repugnant to command. Unequal match'd,
Pyrrhus at Priam drives; in rage strikes wide;
But with the whiff and wind of his fell sword
The unnerved father falls. Then senseless Ilium,
Seeming to feel this blow, with flaming top
Stoops to his base, and with a hideous crash
Takes prisoner Pyrrhus' ear; for, lo! his sword,
Which was declining on the milky head
Of reverend Priam, seem'd i' the air to stick.
So, as a painted tyrant, Pyrrhus stood,
And like a neutral to his will and matter,
Did nothing.
But, as we often see, against some storm,
A silence in the heavens, the rack stand still,
The bold winds speechless, and the orb below
As hush as death, anon the dreadful thunder
Doth rend the region, so, after Pyrrhus' pause,
Aroused vengeance sets him new a-work;
And never did the Cyclops' hammers fall
On Mars's armour forged for proof eterne
With less remorse than Pyrrhus' bleeding sword
Now falls on Priam.
Out, out, thou strumpet, Fortune! All you gods,
In general synod, take away her power;
Break all the spokes and fellies from her wheel,
And bowl the round nave down the hill of heaven,
As low as to the fiends!"

Pol. This is too long.

Ham. It shall to the barber's, with your beard. Prithee, say on; he's for a jig or a tale of bawdry, or he sleeps. Say on; come to Hecuba.

1st Play. "But who, O, who had seen the mobled queen—"

Ham. "The mobled queen"?

Pol. That's good; "mobled queen" is good.

1st Play. "Run barefoot up and down, threatening the flames
With bisson rheum; a clout upon that head
Where late the diadem stood, and for a robe,
About her lank and all o'er-teemed loins,
A blanket, in the alarm of fear caught up;
Who this had seen, with tongue in venom steep'd,
'Gainst Fortune's state would treason have pronounced:
But if the gods themselves did see her then
When she saw Pyrrhus make malicious sport
In mincing with his sword her husband's limbs,
The instant burst of clamour that she made,
Unless things mortal move them not at all,
Would have made milch the burning eyes of heaven,

And passion in the gods."

Pol. Look, whether he has not turned his colour and has tears in's eyes. Pray you, no more.

Ham. 'Tis well; I'll have thee speak out the rest soon. Good my lord, will you see the players well bestowed? Do you hear, let them be well used; for they are the abstract and brief chronicles of the time; after your death you were better have a bad epitaph than their ill report while you live.

Pol. My lord, I will use them according to their desert.

Ham. God's bodykins, man, much better. Use every man after his desert, and who should 'scape whipping? Use them after your own honour and dignity; the less they deserve, the more merit is in your bounty. Take them in.

Pol. Come, sirs.

Ham. Follow him, friends: we'll hear a play to-morrow. [*Exit* POLONIUS *with all the* PLAYERS *but the* FIRST.] Dost thou hear me, old friend; can you play "The Murder of Gonzago"?

1st Play. Ay, my lord.

Ham. We'll ha't to-morrow night. You could, for a need, study a speech of some dozen or sixteen lines, which I would set down and insert in't, could you not?

1st Play. Ay, my lord.

Ham. Very well. Follow that lord; and look you mock him not. [*Exit* FIRST PLAYER.] My good friends, I'll leave you till night: you are welcome to Elsinore.

Ros. Good my lord!

Ham. Ay, so, God be wi' ye; [*Exeunt* ROSENCRANTZ *and* GUILDENSTERN.] Now I am alone.
O, what a rogue and peasant slave am I!
Is it not monstrous that this player here,
But in a fiction, in a dream of passion,
Could force his soul so to his own conceit
That from her working all his visage wann'd,
Tears in his eyes, distraction in's aspect,
A broken voice, and his whole function suiting
With forms to his conceit? and all for nothing!
For Hecuba!
What's Hecuba to him, or he to Hecuba,
That he should weep for her? What would he do,
Had he the motive and the cue for passion
That I have? He would drown the stage with tears
And cleave the general ear with horrid speech,
Make mad the guilty and appal the free,
Confound the ignorant, and amaze indeed
The very faculties of eyes and ears.
Yet I,
A dull and muddy-mettled rascal, peak,
Like John-a-dreams, unpregnant of my cause,
And can say nothing; no, not for a king,
Upon whose property and most dear life
A damn'd defeat was made. Am I a coward?
Who calls me villain? breaks my pate across?
Plucks off my beard, and blows it in my face?
Tweaks me by the nose? gives me the lie i' the throat,
As deep as to the lungs? who does me this?
Ha!
'Swounds, I should take it: for it cannot be
But I am pigeon-liver'd and lack gall
To make oppression bitter, or ere this
I should have fatted all the region kites
With this slave's offal. Bloody, bawdy villain!
Remorseless, treacherous, lecherous, kindless villain!
O, vengeance!
Why, what an ass am I! This is most brave,
That I, the son of a dear father murder'd,
Prompted to my revenge by heaven and hell,
Must, like a whore, unpack my heart with words,
And fall a-cursing, like a very drab,
A scullion!
Fie upon't! foh! About, my brain! I have heard
That guilty creatures sitting at a play
Have by the very cunning of the scene
Been struck so to the soul that presently
They have proclaim'd their malefactions;
For murder, though it have no tongue, will speak
With most miraculous organ. I'll have these players
Play something like the murder of my father
Before mine uncle. I'll observe his looks;
I'll tent him to the quick. If he but blench,
I know my course. The spirit that I have seen
May be the devil; and the devil hath power
To assume a pleasing shape; yea, and perhaps
Out of my weakness and my melancholy,
As he is very potent with such spirits,
Abuses me to damn me. I'll have grounds
More relative than this. The play's the thing
Wherein I'll catch the conscience of the King.
[*Exit*.

ACT III

SCENE I. *A room in the castle*

Enter KING, QUEEN, POLONIUS, OPHELIA, ROSENCRANTZ, *and* GUILDENSTERN.

King. And can you, by no drift of circumstance,
Get from him why he puts on this confusion,
Grating so harshly all his days of quiet
With turbulent and dangerous lunacy?

Ros. He does confess he feels himself distracted;
But from what cause he will by no means speak.

Guil. Nor do we find him forward to be sounded,

But, with a crafty madness, keeps aloof,
When we would bring him on to some confession
Of his true state.

Queen. Did he receive you well?

Ros. Most like a gentleman.

Guil. But with much forcing of his disposition.

Ros. Niggard of question; but, of our demands,
Most free in his reply.

Queen. Did you assay him
To any pastime?

Ros. Madam, it so fell out, that certain players
We o'er-raught on the way; of these we told
him,
And there did seem in him a kind of joy
To hear of it. They are about the court,
And, as I think, they have already order
This night to play before him.

Pol. 'Tis most true.
And he beseech'd me to entreat your Majesties
To hear and see the matter.

King. With all my heart; and it doth much content me
To hear him so inclined.
Good gentlemen, give him a further edge,
And drive his purpose on to these delights.

Ros. We shall, my lord.

[*Exeunt* ROSENCRANTZ *and* GUILDENSTERN.

King. Sweet Gertrude, leave us too;
For we have closely sent for Hamlet hither,
That he, as 'twere by accident, may here
Affront Ophelia.
Her father and myself, lawful espials,
Will so bestow ourselves that, seeing, unseen,
We may of their encounter frankly judge,
And gather by him, as he is behaved,
If't be the affliction of his love or no
That thus he suffers for.

Queen. I shall obey you.
And for your part, Ophelia, I do wish
That your good beauties be the happy cause
Of Hamlet's wildness: so shall I hope your virtues
Will bring him to his wonted way again,
To both your honours.

Oph. Madam, I wish it may. [*Exit* QUEEN.

Pol. Ophelia, walk you here. Gracious, so
please you,
We will bestow ourselves. [*To* OPHELIA] Read
on this book;
That show of such an exercise may colour
Your loneliness. We are oft to blame in this—
'Tis too much proved—that with devotion's visage
And pious action we do sugar o'er
The devil himself.

King. [*Aside*] O, 'tis too true!
How smart a lash that speech doth give my conscience!
The harlot's cheek, beautied with plastering art,
Is not more ugly to the thing that helps it
Than is my deed to my most painted word:
O heavy burthen!

Pol. I hear him coming: let's withdraw, my lord.

[*Exeunt* KING *and* POLONIUS.

Enter HAMLET.

Ham. To be, or not to be: that is the question.
Whether 'tis nobler in the mind to suffer
The slings and arrows of outrageous fortune,
Or to take arms against a sea of troubles,
And by opposing end them? To die; to sleep;
No more; and by a sleep to say we end
The heart-ache and the thousand natural shocks
That flesh is heir to, 'tis a consummation
Devoutly to be wish'd. To die, to sleep;
To sleep? perchance to dream. Ay, there's the
rub;
For in that sleep of death what dreams may come
When we have shuffled off this mortal coil,
Must give us pause. There's the respect
That makes calamity of so long life;
For who would bear the whips and scorns of
time,
The oppressor's wrong, the proud man's contumely,
The pangs of despised love, the law's delay,
The insolence of office and the spurns
That patient merit of the unworthy takes,
When he himself might his quietus make
With a bare bodkin? who would fardels bear,
To grunt and sweat under a weary life,
But that the dread of something after death,
The undiscover'd country from whose bourn
No traveller returns, puzzles the will
And makes us rather bear those ills we have
Than fly to others that we know not of?
Thus conscience does make cowards of us all;
And thus the native hue of resolution
Is sicklied o'er with the pale cast of thought,
And enterprises of great pitch and moment
With this regard their currents turn awry,
And lose the name of action.—Soft you now!
The fair Ophelia! Nymph, in thy orisons
Be all my sins remember'd.

Oph. Good my lord,
How does your honour for this many a day?

Ham. I humbly thank you; well, well, well.

Oph. My lord, I have remembrances of yours,
That I have longed long to re-deliver;
I pray you, now receive them.

Ham. No, not I;
I never gave you aught.

Oph. My honour'd lord, you know right well you did;
And, with them, words of so sweet breath composed
As made the things more rich. Their perfume lost,
Take these again; for to the noble mind
Rich gifts wax poor when givers prove unkind.
There, my lord.

Ham. Ha, ha! are you honest?

Oph. My lord?

Ham. Are you fair?

Oph. What means your lordship?

Ham. That if you be honest and fair, your honesty should admit no discourse to your beauty.

Oph. Could beauty, my lord, have better commerce than with honesty?

Ham. Ay, truly; for the power of beauty will sooner transform honesty from what it is to a bawd than the force of honesty can translate beauty into his likeness. This was sometime a paradox, but now the time gives it proof. I did love you once.

Oph. Indeed, my lord, you made me believe so.

Ham. You should not have believed me; for virtue cannot so inoculate our old stock but we shall relish of it. I loved you not.

Oph. I was the more deceived.

Ham. Get thee to a nunnery; why wouldst thou be a breeder of sinners? I am myself indifferent honest; but yet I could accuse me of such things that it were better my mother had not borne me. I am very proud, revengeful, ambitious, with more offences at my beck than I have thoughts to put them in, imagination to give them shape, or time to act them in. What should such fellows as I do crawling between earth and heaven? We are arrant knaves, all; believe none of us. Go thy ways to a nunnery. Where's your father?

Oph. At home, my lord.

Ham. Let the doors be shut upon him, that he may play the fool nowhere but in's own house. Farewell.

Oph. O, help him, you sweet heavens!

Ham. If thou dost marry, I'll give thee this plague for thy dowry: be thou as chaste as ice, as pure as snow, thou shalt not escape calumny. Get thee to a nunnery, go. Farewell. Or, if thou wilt needs marry, marry a fool; for wise men know well enough what monsters you make of them. To a nunnery, go, and quickly too. Farewell.

Oph. O heavenly powers, restore him!

Ham. I have heard of your paintings too, well enough; God has given you one face, and you make yourselves another. You jig, you amble, and you lisp, and nick-name God's creatures, and make your wantonness your ignorance. Go to, I'll no more on't; it hath made me mad. I say, we will have no more marriages. Those that are married already, all but one, shall live; the rest shall keep as they are. To a nunnery, go. [*Exit.*

Oph. O, what a noble mind is here o'erthrown!
The courtier's, soldier's, scholar's, eye, tongue, sword,
The expectancy and rose of the fair state,
The glass of fashion and the mould of form,
The observed of all observers, quite, quite down!
And I, of ladies most deject and wretched,
That suck'd the honey of his music vows,
Now see that noble and most sovereign reason,
Like sweet bells jangled, out of tune and harsh;
That unmatch'd form and feature of blown youth
Blasted with ecstasy: O, woe is me,
To have seen what I have seen, see what I see!

Re-enter KING *and* POLONIUS.

King. Love! his affections do not that way tend;
Nor what he spake, though it lack'd form a little,
Was not like madness. There's something in his soul,
O'er which his melancholy sits on brood;
And I do doubt the hatch and the disclose
Will be some danger; which for to prevent,
I have in quick determination
Thus set it down: he shall with speed to England,
For the demand of our neglected tribute.
Haply the seas and countries different
With variable objects shall expel
This something-settled matter in his heart,
Whereon his brains still beating puts him thus
From fashion of himself. What think you on't?

Pol. It shall do well: but yet do I believe
The origin and commencement of his grief
Sprung from neglected love. How now, Ophelia!
You need not tell us what Lord Hamlet said;
We heard it all. My lord, do as you please;
But, if you hold it fit, after the play
Let his queen mother all alone entreat him
To show his grief: let her be round with him;
And I'll be placed, so please you, in the ear
Of all their conference. If she find him not,
To England send him, or confine him where
Your wisdom best shall think.

King. It shall be so.
Madness in great ones must not unwatch'd go.
[*Exeunt.*

SCENE II. *A hall in the castle*

Enter HAMLET *and* PLAYERS.

Ham. Speak the speech, I pray you, as I pronounced it to you, trippingly on the tongue: but if you mouth it, as many of your players do, I had as lief the town-crier spoke my lines. Nor do not saw the air too much with your hand, thus, but use all gently; for in the very torrent, tempest, and, as I may say, the whirlwind of passion, you must acquire and beget a temperance that may give it smoothness. O, it offends me to the soul to hear a robustious periwig-pated fellow tear a passion to tatters, to very rags, to split the ears of the groundlings, who for the most part are capable of nothing but inexplicable dumb-shows and noise. I would have such a fellow whipped for o'erdoing Termagant. It out-herods Herod. Pray you, avoid it.

1st Play. I warrant your honour.

Ham. Be not too tame neither, but let your own discretion be your tutor. Suit the action to the word, the word to the action; with this special observance, that you o'erstep not the modesty of nature; for anything so overdone is from the purpose of playing, whose end, both at the first and now, was and is, to hold, as 'twere, the mirror up to nature; to show virtue her own feature, scorn her own image, and the very age and body of the time his form and pressure. Now this overdone, or come tardy off, though it make the unskilful laugh, cannot but make the judicious grieve; the censure of the which one must in your allowance o'erweigh a whole theatre of others. O, there be players that I have seen play, and heard others praise, and that highly, not to speak it profanely, that, neither having the accent of Christians nor the gait of Christian, pagan, nor man, have so strutted and bellowed that I have thought some of nature's journeymen had made men and not made them well, they imitated humanity so abominably.

1st Play. I hope we have reformed that indifferently with us, sir.

Ham. O, reform it altogether. And let those that play your clowns speak no more than is set down for them; for there be of them that will themselves laugh, to set on some quantity of barren spectators to laugh too; though, in the mean time, some necessary question of the play be then to be considered: that's villainous, and shows a most pitiful ambition in the fool that uses it. Go, make you ready. [*Exeunt* PLAYERS.

Enter POLONIUS, ROSENCRANTZ, *and* GUILDENSTERN.

How now, my lord! will the King hear this piece of work?

Pol. And the Queen too, and that presently.

Ham. Bid the players make haste. [*Exit* POLONIUS.] Will you two help to hasten them?

Ros. } *Guil.* } We will, my lord.

[*Exeunt* ROSENCRANTZ *and* GUILDENSTERN.

Ham. What ho! Horatio!

Enter HORATIO.

Hor. Here, sweet lord, at your service.

Ham. Horatio, thou art e'en as just a man
As e'er my conversation coped withal.

Hor. O, my dear lord—

Ham. Nay, do not think I flatter;
For what advancement may I hope from thee
That no revenue hast but thy good spirits,
To feed and clothe thee? Why should the poor be flatter'd?
No, let the candied tongue lick absurd pomp,
And crook the pregnant hinges of the knee
Where thrift may follow fawning. Dost thou hear?
Since my dear soul was mistress of her choice
And could of men distinguish, her election
Hath seal'd thee for herself; for thou hast been
As one, in suffering all, that suffers nothing,
A man that fortune's buffets and rewards
Hast ta'en with equal thanks; and blest are those
Whose blood and judgement are so well commingled,
That they are not a pipe for fortune's finger
To sound what stop she please. Give me that man
That is not passion's slave, and I will wear him
In my heart's core, ay, in my heart of heart,
As I do thee.—Something too much of this.—
There is a play to-night before the King.
One scene of it comes near the circumstance
Which I have told thee of my father's death:
I prithee, when thou seest that act afoot,
Even with the very comment of thy soul
Observe mine uncle. If his occulted guilt
Do not itself unkennel in one speech,
It is a damned ghost that we have seen,
And my imaginations are as foul
As Vulcan's stithy. Give him heedful note;
For I mine eyes will rivet to his face,
And after we will both our judgements join
In censure of his seeming.

Hor. Well, my lord.
If he steal aught the whilst this play is playing,
And 'scape detecting, I will pay the theft.

Ham. They are coming to the play; I must be idle.
Get you a place.

Danish march. A flourish. Enter KING, QUEEN, POLONIUS, OPHELIA, ROSENCRANTZ, GUILDENSTERN, *and others.*

King. How fares our cousin Hamlet?

Ham. Excellent, i' faith; of the chameleon's dish. I eat the air, promise-crammed. You cannot feed capons so.

King. I have nothing with this answer, Hamlet; these words are not mine.

Ham. No, nor mine now. [*To* POLONIUS] My lord, you played once i' the university, you say?

Pol. That did I, my lord; and was accounted a good actor.

Ham. What did you enact?

Pol. I did enact Julius Cæsar. I was killed i' the Capitol; Brutus killed me.

Ham. It was a brute part of him to kill so capital a calf there. Be the players ready?

Ros. Ay, my lord; they stay upon your patience.

Queen. Come hither, my dear Hamlet, sit by me.

Ham. No, good mother, here's metal more attractive.

Pol. [*To the* KING] O, ho! do you mark that?

Ham. Lady, shall I lie in your lap?

[*Lying down at* OPHELIA'*s feet.*

Oph. No, my lord.

Ham. I mean, my head upon your lap?

Oph. Ay, my lord.

Ham. Do you think I meant country matters?

Oph. I think nothing, my lord.

Ham. That's a fair thought to lie between maids' legs.

Oph. What is, my lord?

Ham. Nothing.

Oph. You are merry, my lord.

Ham. Who, I?

Oph. Ay, my lord.

Ham. O God, your only jig-maker. What should a man do but be merry? for, look you, how cheerfully my mother looks, and my father died within these two hours.

Oph. Nay, 'tis twice two months, my lord.

Ham. So long? Nay then, let the devil wear black, for I'll have a suit of sables. O heavens! die two months ago, and not forgotten yet? Then there's hope a great man's memory may outlive his life half a year; but, by'r lady, he must build churches, then; or else shall he suffer not thinking on, with the hobby-horse, whose epitaph is "For, O, for, O, the hobby-horse is forgot."

Hautboys play. The dumb-show enters.

Enter a King and a Queen very lovingly; the Queen embracing him, and he her. She kneels and makes show of protestation unto him. He takes her up, and declines his head upon her neck; lays him down upon a bank of flowers. She, seeing him asleep, leaves him. Anon comes in a fellow, takes off his crown, kisses it, and pours poison in the King's ears, and exit. The Queen returns; finds the King dead, and makes passionate action. The Poisoner, with some two or three Mutes, comes in again, seeming to lament with her. The dead body is carried away. The Poisoner wooes the Queen with gifts; she seems loath and unwilling awhile, but in the end accepts his love. [*Exeunt.*

Oph. What means this, my lord?

Ham. Marry, this is miching mallecho; it means mischief.

Oph. Belike this show imports the argument of the play.

Enter PROLOGUE.

Ham. We shall know by this fellow. The players cannot keep counsel; they'll tell all.

Oph. Will he tell us what this show meant?

Ham. Ay, or any show that you'll show him. Be not you ashamed to show, he'll not shame to tell you what it means.

Oph. You are naught, you are naught: I'll mark the play.

Pro. For us, and for our tragedy,
Here stooping to your clemency,
We beg your hearing patiently. [*Exit.*

Ham. Is this a prologue, or the posy of a ring?

Oph. 'Tis brief, my lord.

Ham. As woman's love.

Enter two Players as KING *and* QUEEN.

P. King. Full thirty times hath Phœbus' cart gone round
Neptune's salt wash and Tellus' orbed ground,
And thirty dozen moons with borrow'd sheen
About the world have times twelve thirties been,
Since love our hearts and Hymen did our hands
Unite commutual in most sacred bands.

P. Queen. So many journeys may the sun and moon
Make us again count o'er ere love be done!
But, woe is me, you are so sick of late,
So far from cheer and from your former state,
That I distrust you. Yet, though I distrust,
Discomfort you, my lord, it nothing must;
For women's fear and love holds quantity,
In neither aught, or in extremity.
Now, what my love is, proof hath made you know;
And as my love is sized, my fear is so.
Where love is great, the littlest doubts are fear;
Where little fears grow great, great love grows there.

P. King. 'Faith, I must leave thee, love, and shortly too;
My operant powers their functions leave to do;
And thou shalt live in this fair world behind,
Honour'd, beloved; and haply one as kind
For husband shalt thou—

P. Queen. O, confound the rest!
Such love must needs be treason in my breast.
In second husband let me be accurst!
None wed the second but who kill'd the first.

Ham. [*Aside*] Wormwood, wormwood.

P. Queen. The instances that second marriage move
Are base respects of thrift, but none of love:
A second time I kill my husband dead,
When second husband kisses me in bed.

P. King. I do believe you think what now you speak;
But what we do determine oft we break.
Purpose is but the slave to memory,
Of violent birth, but poor validity:
Which now, like fruit unripe, sticks on the tree;
But fall, unshaken, when they mellow be.
Most necessary 'tis that we forget
To pay ourselves what to ourselves is debt:
What to ourselves in passion we propose,
The passion ending, doth the purpose lose.
The violence of either grief or joy
Their own enactures with themselves destroy.
Where joy most revels, grief doth most lament;
Grief joys, joy grieves, on slender accident.
This world is not for aye, nor 'tis not strange
That even our loves should with our fortunes change;
For 'tis a question left us yet to prove,
Whether love lead fortune, or else fortune love.
The great man down, you mark his favourite flies;
The poor advanced makes friends of enemies.
And hitherto doth love on fortune tend;
For who not needs shall never lack a friend,
And who in want a hollow friend doth try,
Directly seasons him his enemy.
But, orderly to end where I begun,
Our wills and fates do so contrary run
That our devices still are overthrown;
Our thoughts are ours, their ends none of our own.
So think thou wilt no second husband wed;
But die thy thoughts when thy first lord is dead.

P. Queen. Nor earth to me give food, nor heaven light!
Sport and repose lock from me day and night!
To desperation turn my trust and hope!
An anchor's cheer in prison be my scope!
Each opposite that blanks the face of joy
Meet what I would have well and it destroy!
Both here and hence pursue me lasting strife,
If, once a widow, ever I be wife!

Ham. If she should break it now!

P. King. 'Tis deeply sworn. Sweet, leave me here awhile;
My spirits grow dull, and fain I would beguile
The tedious day with sleep. [*Sleeps*.]

P. Queen. Sleep rock thy brain;
And never come mischance between us twain!
[*Exit*.

Ham. Madam, how like you this play?

Queen. The lady doth protest too much, methinks.

Ham. O, but she'll keep her word.

King. Have you heard the argument? Is there no offence in 't?

Ham. No, no, they do but jest, poison in jest; no offence i' the world.

King. What do you call the play?

Ham. "The Mouse-trap." Marry, how? Tropically. This play is the image of a murder done in Vienna. Gonzago is the duke's name; his wife, Baptista. You shall see anon; 'tis a knavish piece of work, but what o' that? your Majesty and we that have free souls, it touches us not. Let the galled jade wince, our withers are unwrung.

Enter LUCIANUS.

This is one Lucianus, nephew to the king.

Oph. You are as good as a chorus, my lord.

Ham. I could interpret between you and your love, if I could see the puppets dallying.

Oph. You are keen, my lord, you are keen.

Ham. It would cost you a groaning to take off my edge.

Oph. Still better, and worse.

Ham. So you must take your husbands. Begin, murderer; pox, leave thy damnable faces, and begin. Come, "the croaking raven doth bellow for revenge."

Luc. Thoughts black, hands apt, drugs fit, and time agreeing;
Confederate season, else no creature seeing;
Thou mixture rank, of midnight weeds collected,
With Hecate's ban thrice blasted, thrice infected,
Thy natural magic and dire property,
On wholesome life usurp immediately.

Pours the poison into the sleeper's ears.

Ham. He poisons him i' the garden for's estate. His name's Gonzago; the story is extant, and writ in choice Italian. You shall see anon how the murderer gets the love of Gonzago's wife.

Oph. The King rises.

Ham. What, frighted with false fire!

Queen. How fares my lord?

Pol. Give o'er the play.

King. Give me some light. Away!

All. Lights, lights, lights!

[*Exeunt all but* HAMLET *and* HORATIO.

Ham. Why, let the stricken deer go weep,
The hart ungalled play;
For some must watch, while some must sleep;
So runs the world away.

Would not this, sir, and a forest of feathers—if the rest of my fortunes turn Turk with me—with two Provincial roses on my razed shoes, get me a fellowship in a cry of players, sir?

Hor. Half a share.

Ham. A whole one, I.
For thou dost know, O Damon dear,
This realm dismantled was
Of Jove himself; and now reigns here
A very, very—pajock.

Hor. You might have rhymed.

Ham. O good Horatio, I'll take the ghost's word for a thousand pound. Didst perceive?

Hor. Very well, my lord.

Ham. Upon the talk of the poisoning?

Hor. I did very well note him.

Ham. Ah, ha! Come, some music! come, the recorders!
For if the king like not the comedy,
Why then, belike, he likes it not, perdy.
Come, some music!

Re-enter ROSENCRANTZ *and* GUILDENSTERN.

Guil. Good my lord, vouchsafe me a word with you.

Ham. Sir, a whole history.

Guil. The King, sir—

Ham. Ay, sir, what of him?

Guil. Is in his retirement marvellous distempered.

Ham. With drink, sir?

Guil. No, my lord, rather with choler.

Ham. Your wisdom should show itself more richer to signify this to his doctor; for, for me to put him to his purgation would perhaps plunge him into far more choler.

Guil. Good my lord, put your discourse into some frame and start not so wildly from my affair.

Ham. I am tame, sir; pronounce.

Guil. The Queen, your mother, in most great affliction of spirit, hath sent me to you.

Ham. You are welcome.

Guil. Nay, good my lord, this courtesy is not of the right breed. If it shall please you to make me a wholesome answer, I will do your mother's commandment; if not, your pardon and my return shall be the end of my business.

Ham. Sir, I cannot.

Guil. What, my lord?

Ham. Make you a wholesome answer; my wit's diseased. But, sir, such answer as I can make, you shall command; or, rather, as you say, my mother. Therefore no more, but to the matter. My mother, you say,—

Ros. Then thus she says; your behaviour hath struck her into amazement and admiration.

Ham. O wonderful son, that can so astonish a mother! But is there no sequel at the heels of this mother's admiration? Impart.

Ros. She desires to speak with you in her closet, ere you go to bed.

Ham. We shall obey, were she ten times our mother. Have you any further trade with us?

Ros. My lord, you once did love me.

Ham. So I do still, by these pickers and stealers.

Ros. Good my lord, what is your cause of distemper? you do, surely, bar the door upon your own liberty, if you deny your griefs to your friend.

Ham. Sir, I lack advancement.

Ros. How can that be, when you have the voice of the King himself for your succession in Denmark?

Ham. Ay, sir, but, "While the grass grows"—the proverb is something musty.

Re-enter PLAYERS *with recorders.*

O, the recorders! let me see one. To withdraw with you:—why do you go about to recover the wind of me, as if you would drive me into a toil?

Guil. O, my lord, if my duty be too bold, my love is too unmannerly.

Ham. I do not well understand that. Will you play upon this pipe?

Guil. My lord, I cannot.

Ham. I pray you.

Guil. Believe me, I cannot.

Ham. I do beseech you.

Guil. I know no touch of it, my lord.

Ham. 'Tis as easy as lying. Govern these ventages with your fingers and thumb, give it breath with your mouth, and it will discourse most eloquent music. Look you, these are the stops.

Guil. But these cannot I command to any utterance of harmony; I have not the skill.

Ham. Why, look you now, how unworthy a thing you make of me! You would play upon me; you would seem to know my stops; you would pluck out the heart of my mystery; you would sound me from my lowest note to the top of my compass; and there is much music, excellent voice, in this little organ, yet cannot you make it speak. 'Sblood, do you think I am easier to be played on than a pipe? Call me what instrument you will, though you can fret me, yet you cannot play upon me.

Enter POLONIUS.

God bless you, sir!

Pol. My lord, the Queen would speak with you, and presently.

Ham. Do you see yonder cloud that's almost in shape of a camel?

Pol. By the mass, and 'tis like a camel, indeed.

Ham. Methinks it is like a weasel.

Pol. It is backed like a weasel.

Ham. Or like a whale?

Pol. Very like a whale.

Ham. Then I will come to my mother by and by. They fool me to the top of my bent. I will come by and by.

Pol. I will say so.

Ham. By and by is easily said. [*Exit* POLONIUS.]
Leave me, friends.

[*Exeunt all but* HAMLET.

'Tis now the very witching time of night,
When churchyards yawn and hell itself breathes out
Contagion to this world. Now could I drink hot blood,
And do such bitter business as the day
Would quake to look on. Soft! now to my mother.
O heart, lose not thy nature; let not ever
The soul of Nero enter this firm bosom.
Let me be cruel, not unnatural.
I will speak daggers to her, but use none;
My tongue and soul in this be hypocrites;
How in my words soever she be shent,
To give them seals never, my soul, consent!

[*Exit.*

SCENE III. *A room in the castle*

Enter KING, ROSENCRANTZ, *and* GUILDENSTERN.

King. I like him not, nor stands it safe with us
To let his madness range. Therefore prepare you;
I your commission will forthwith dispatch,
And he to England shall along with you:
The terms of our estate may not endure
Hazard so near us as doth hourly grow
Out of his lunacies.

Guil. We will ourselves provide.
Most holy and religious fear it is
To keep those many many bodies safe
That live and feed upon your Majesty.

Ros. The single and peculiar life is bound,
With all the strength and armour of the mind,
To keep itself from noyance; but much more
That spirit upon whose weal depend and rest
The lives of many. The cease of majesty
Dies not alone; but, like a gulf, doth draw
What's near it with it. It is a massy wheel,
Fix'd on the summit of the highest mount,
To whose huge spokes ten thousand lesser things
Are mortised and adjoin'd; which, when it falls,
Each small annexment, petty consequence,
Attends the boisterous ruin. Never alone
Did the King sigh, but with a general groan.

King. Arm you, I pray you, to this speedy voyage;
For we will fetters put upon this fear,
Which now goes too free-footed.

Ros.
Guil. } We will haste us.

[*Exeunt* ROSENCRANTZ *and* GUILDENSTERN.

Enter POLONIUS.

Pol. My lord, he's going to his mother's closet:
Behind the arras I'll convey myself,
To hear the process; I'll warrant she'll tax him home:
And, as you said, and wisely was it said,
'Tis meet that some more audience than a mother,
Since nature makes them partial, should o'erhear
The speech, of vantage. Fare you well, my liege.
I'll call upon you ere you go to bed,
And tell you what I know.

King. Thanks, dear my lord.

[*Exit* POLONIUS.

O, my offence is rank, it smells to heaven;
It hath the primal eldest curse upon't,
A brother's murder. Pray can I not,
Though inclination be as sharp as will.
My stronger guilt defeats my strong intent;
And, like a man to double business bound,
I stand in pause where I shall first begin,
And both neglect. What if this cursed hand
Were thicker than itself with brother's blood,
Is there not rain enough in the sweet heavens
To wash it white as snow? Whereto serves mercy
But to confront the visage of offence?
And what's in prayer but this two-fold force,
To be forestalled ere we come to fall,
Or pardon'd being down? Then I'll look up;
My fault is past. But, O, what form of prayer
Can serve my turn? "Forgive me my foul murder"?

That cannot be; since I am still possess'd
Of those effects for which I did the murder,
My crown, mine own ambition, and my queen.
May one be pardon'd and retain the offence?
In the corrupted currents of this world
Offence's gilded hand may shove by justice,
And oft 'tis seen the wicked prize itself
Buys out the law: but 'tis not so above;
There is no shuffling, there the action lies
In his true nature; and we ourselves compell'd,
Even to the teeth and forehead of our faults,
To give in evidence. What then? what rests?
Try what repentance can. What can it not?
Yet what can it when one can not repent?
O wretched state! O bosom black as death!
O limed soul, that, struggling to be free,
Art more engaged! Help, angels! Make assay!
Bow, stubborn knees; and, heart with strings of steel,
Be soft as sinews of the new-born babe!
All may be well. [*Retires and kneels*.

Enter HAMLET.

Ham. Now might I do it pat, now he is praying;
And now I'll do't. And so he goes to heaven;
And so am I revenged. That would be scann'd.
A villain kills my father; and for that,
I, his sole son, do this same villain send
To heaven.
O, this is hire and salary, not revenge.
He took my father grossly, full of bread;
With all his crimes broad blown, as flush as May;
And how his audit stands who knows save heaven?
But in our circumstance and course of thought,
'Tis heavy with him. And am I then revenged,
To take him in the purging of his soul,
When he is fit and season'd for his passage?
No!
Up, sword; and know thou a more horrid hent.
When he is drunk asleep, or in his rage,
Or in the incestuous pleasure of his bed;
At gaming, swearing, or about some act
That has no relish of salvation in't;
Then trip him, that his heels may kick at heaven,
And that his soul may be as damn'd and black
As hell, whereto it goes. My mother stays.
This physic but prolongs thy sickly days. [*Exit*.

King. [*Rising*] My words fly up, my thoughts remain below.
Words without thoughts never to heaven go.
[*Exit*.

SCENE IV. *The Queen's closet*

Enter QUEEN *and* POLONIUS.

Pol. He will come straight. Look you lay home to him.
Tell him his pranks have been too broad to bear with,
And that your Grace hath screen'd and stood between
Much heat and him. I'll sconce me even here.
Pray you, be round with him.

Ham. [*Within*] Mother, mother, mother!

Queen. I'll warrant you,
Fear me not. Withdraw, I hear him coming.
[POLONIUS *hides behind the arras*.

Enter HAMLET.

Ham. Now, mother, what's the matter?

Queen. Hamlet, thou hast thy father much offended.

Ham. Mother, you have my father much offended.

Queen. Come, come, you answer with an idle tongue.

Ham. Go, go, you question with a wicked tongue.

Queen. Why, how now, Hamlet!

Ham. What's the matter now?

Queen. Have you forgot me?

Ham No, by the rood, not so:
You are the Queen, your husband's brother's wife;
And—would it were not so!—you are my mother.

Queen. Nay, then, I'll set those to you that can speak.

Ham. Come, come, and sit you down; you shall not budge;
You go not till I set you up a glass
Where you may see the inmost part of you.

Queen. What wilt thou do? thou wilt not murder me?
Help, help, ho!

Pol. [*Behind*] What, ho! help, help, help!

Ham. [*Drawing*] How now! a rat? Dead, for a ducat, dead!
Makes a pass through the arras.

Pol. [*Behind*] O, I am slain! [*Falls and dies*.

Queen. O me, what hast thou done?

Ham. Nay, I know not:
Is it the King?

Queen. O, what a rash and bloody deed is this!

Ham. A bloody deed! almost as bad, good mother,
As kill a king, and marry with his brother.

Queen. As kill a king!

Ham. Ay, lady, 'twas my word.
Lifts up the arras and discovers Polonius.
Thou wretched, rash, intruding fool, farewell!
I took thee for thy better. Take thy fortune;
Thou find'st to be too busy is some danger.

Leave wringing of your hands. Peace! sit you down,
And let me wring your heart; for so I shall,
If it be made of penetrable stuff,
If damned custom have not brass'd it so
That it be proof and bulwark against sense.

Queen. What have I done, that thou darest wag thy tongue
In noise so rude against me?

Ham. Such an act
That blurs the grace and blush of modesty,
Calls virtue hypocrite, takes off the rose
From the fair forehead of an innocent love
And sets a blister there, makes marriage-vows
As false as dicers' oaths; O, such a deed
As from the body of contraction plucks
The very soul, and sweet religion makes
A rhapsody of words. Heaven's face doth glow;
Yea, this solidity and compound mass,
With tristful visage, as against the doom,
Is thought-sick at the act.

Queen. Ay me, what act,
That roars so loud, and thunders in the index?

Ham. Look here, upon this picture, and on this,
The counterfeit presentment of two brothers.
See, what a grace was seated on this brow;
Hyperion's curls; the front of Jove himself;
An eye like Mars, to threaten and command;
A station like the herald Mercury
New-lighted on a heaven-kissing hill;
A combination and a form indeed,
Where every god did seem to set his seal,
To give the world assurance of a man.
This was your husband. Look you now, what follows:
Here is your husband; like a mildew'd ear,
Blasting his wholesome brother. Have you eyes?
Could you on this fair mountain leave to feed,
And batten on this moor? Ha! have you eyes?
You cannot call it love; for at your age
The hey-day in the blood is tame, it's humble,
And waits upon the judgement; and what judgement
Would step from this to this? Sense, sure, you have,
Else could you not have motion; but sure, that sense
Is apoplex'd; for madness would not err,
Nor sense to ecstasy was ne'er so thrall'd
But it reserved some quantity of choice,
To serve in such a difference. What devil was't
That thus hath cozen'd you at hoodman-blind?
Eyes without feeling, feeling without sight,
Ears without hands or eyes, smelling sans all,
Or but a sickly part of one true sense
Could not so mope.
O shame! where is thy blush? Rebellious hell,
If thou canst mutine in a matron's bones,
To flaming youth let virtue be as wax,
And melt in her own fire. Proclaim no shame
When the compulsive ardour gives the charge,
Since frost itself as actively doth burn
And reason panders will.

Queen. O Hamlet, speak no more.
Thou turn'st mine eyes into my very soul;
And there I see such black and grained spots
As will not leave their tinct.

Ham. Nay, but to live
In the rank sweat of an enseamed bed,
Stew'd in corruption, honeying and making love
Over the nasty sty—

Queen. O, speak to me no more;
These words, like daggers, enter in mine ears;
No more, sweet Hamlet!

Ham. A murderer and a villain;
A slave that is not twentieth part the tithe
Of your precedent lord; a vice of kings;
A cutpurse of the empire and the rule,
That from a shelf the precious diadem stole,
And put it in his pocket!

Queen. No more!

Ham. A king of shreds and patches—

Enter GHOST.

Save me, and hover o'er me with your wings,
You heavenly guards! What would your gracious figure?

Queen. Alas, he's mad!

Ham. Do you not come your tardy son to chide,
That, lapsed in time and passion, lets go by
The important acting of your dread command?
O, say!

Ghost. Do not forget! This visitation
Is but to whet thy almost blunted purpose.
But, look, amazement on thy mother sits.
O, step between her and her fighting soul.
Conceit in weakest bodies strongest works.
Speak to her, Hamlet.

Ham. How is it with you, lady?

Queen. Alas, how is't with you,
That you do bend your eye on vacancy
And with the incorporal air do hold discourse?
Forth at your eyes your spirits wildly peep;
And, as the sleeping soldiers in the alarm,
Your bedded hair, like life in excrements,
Start up, and stand an end. O gentle son,
Upon the heat and flame of thy distemper
Sprinkle cool patience. Whereon do you look?

Ham. On him, on him! Look you, how pale he glares!
His form and cause conjoin'd, preaching to stones,
Would make them capable. Do not look upon me;
Lest with this piteous action you convert
My stern effects; then what I have to do
Will want true colour, tears perchance for blood.
Queen. To whom do you speak this?
Ham. Do you see nothing there?
Queen. Nothing at all; yet all that is I see.
Ham. Nor did you nothing hear?
Queen. No, nothing but ourselves.
Ham. Why, look you there! look, how it steals away!
My father, in his habit as he lived!
Look, where he goes, even now, out at the portal!
[*Exit* GHOST.
Queen. This is the very coinage of your brain.
This bodiless creation ecstasy
Is very cunning in.
Ham. Ecstasy!
My pulse, as yours, doth temperately keep time,
And makes as healthful music. It is not madness
That I have utter'd. Bring me to the test,
And I the matter will re-word; which madness
Would gambol from. Mother, for love of grace,
Lay not that flattering unction to your soul,
That not your trespass, but my madness speaks.
It will but skin and film the ulcerous place,
Whiles rank corruption, mining all within,
Infects unseen. Confess yourself to heaven;
Repent what's past; avoid what is to come;
And do not spread the compost on the weeds,
To make them ranker. Forgive me this my virtue;
For in the fatness of these pursy times
Virtue itself of vice must pardon beg,
Yea, curb and woo for leave to do him good.
Queen. O Hamlet, thou hast cleft my heart in twain.
Ham. O, throw away the worser part of it,
And live the purer with the other half.
Good night; but go not to mine uncle's bed.
Assume a virtue, if you have it not.
That monster, custom, who all sense doth eat,
Of habits devil, is angel yet in this,
That to the use of actions fair and good
He likewise gives a frock or livery,
That aptly is put on. Refrain to-night,
And that shall lend a kind of easiness
To the next abstinence; the next more easy;
For use almost can change the stamp of nature,
And either master the devil, or throw him out
With wondrous potency. Once more, good night;
And when you are desirous to be bless'd,
I'll blessing beg of you. For this same lord,
[*Pointing to Polonius.*
I do repent; but heaven hath pleased it so,
To punish me with this and this with me,
That I must be their scourge and minister.
I will bestow him, and will answer well
The death I gave him. So, again, good night.
I must be cruel, only to be kind.
Thus bad begins and worse remains behind.
One word more, good lady.
Queen. What shall I do?
Ham. Not this, by no means, that I bid you do:
Let the bloat king tempt you again to bed;
Pinch wanton on your cheek; call you his mouse;
And let him, for a pair of reechy kisses,
Or paddling in you neck with his damn'd fingers,
Make you to ravel all this matter out,
That I essentially am not in madness,
But mad in craft. 'Twere good you let him know;
For who, that's but a queen, fair, sober, wise,
Would from a paddock, from a bat, a gib,
Such dear concernings hide? who would do so?
No, in despite of sense and secrecy,
Unpeg the basket on the house's top,
Let the birds fly, and, like the famous ape,
To try conclusions, in the basket creep,
And break your own neck down.
Queen. Be thou assured, if words be made of breath,
And breath of life, I have no life to breathe
What thou hast said to me.
Ham. I must to England; you know that?
Queen. Alack,
I had forgot. 'Tis so concluded on.
Ham. There's letters seal'd, and my two school-fellows,
Whom I will trust as I will adders fang'd,
They bear the mandate; they must sweep my way,
And marshal me to knavery. Let it work;
For 'tis the sport to have the enginer
Hoist with his own petar; and 't shall go hard
But I will delve one yard below their mines,
And blow them at the moon. O, 'tis most sweet,
When in one line two crafts directly meet.
This man shall set me packing.
I'll lug the guts into the neighbour room.
Mother, good night. Indeed this counsellor
Is now most still, most secret, and most grave,
Who was in life a foolish prating knave.
Come, sir, to draw toward an end with you.
Good night, mother.
[*Exeunt severally;* HAMLET *dragging in Polonius.*

ACT IV

Scene i. *A room in the castle*

Enter KING, QUEEN, ROSENCRANTZ, *and* GUILDENSTERN.

King. There's matter in these sighs; these profound heaves
You must translate; 'tis fit we understand them.
Where is your son?
Queen. Bestow this place on us a little while.
[*Exeunt* ROSENCRANTZ *and* GUILDENSTERN.
Ah, mine own lord, what have I seen to-night!
King. What, Gertrude? How does Hamlet?
Queen. Mad as the sea and wind, when both contend
Which is the mightier. In his lawless fit,
Behind the arras hearing something stir,
Whips our his rapier, cries, "A rat, a rat!"
And, in this brainish apprehension, kills
The unseen good old man.
King. O heavy deed!
It had been so with us, had we been there.
His liberty is full of threats to all;
To you yourself, to us, to every one.
Alas, how shall this bloody deed be answer'd?
It will be laid to us, whose providence
Should have kept short, restrain'd, and out of haunt,
This mad young man. But so much was our love,
We would not understand what was most fit;
But, like the owner of a foul disease,
To keep it from divulging, let it feed
Even on the pith of life. Where is he gone?
Queen. To draw apart the body he hath kill'd,
O'er whom his very madness, like some ore
Among a mineral of metals base,
Shows itself pure; he weeps for what is done.
King. O Gertrude, come away!
The sun no sooner shall the mountains touch,
But we will ship him hence, and this vile deed
We must, with all our majesty and skill,
Both countenance and excuse. Ho, Guildenstern!

Re-enter ROSENCRANTZ *and* GUILDENSTERN.

Friends both, go join you with some further aid.
Hamlet in madness hath Polonius slain,
And from his mother's closet hath he dragg'd him.
Go seek him out; speak fair, and bring the body
Into the chapel. I pray you, haste in this.
[*Exeunt* ROSENCRANTZ *and* GUILDENSTERN.
Come, Gertrude, we'll call up our wisest friends;
And let them know, both what we mean to do,
And what's untimely done; so, haply, slander,
Whose whisper o'er the world's diameter,
As level as the cannon to his blank,
Transports his poison'd shot, may miss our name,
And hit the woundless air. O, come away!
My soul is full of discord and dismay. [*Exeunt.*

Scene ii. *Another room in the castle*

Enter HAMLET.

Ham. Safely stowed.
Ros. / *Guil.* [*Within*] Hamlet! Lord Hamlet!
Ham. But soft, what noise? who calls on Hamlet? O, here they come.

Enter ROSENCRANTZ *and* GUILDENSTERN.

Ros. What have you done, my lord, with the dead body?
Ham. Compounded it with dust, whereto 'tis kin.
Ros. Tell us where 'tis, that we may take it thence
And bear it to the chapel.
Ham. Do not believe it.
Ros. Believe what?
Ham. That I can keep your counsel and not mine own. Besides, to be demanded of a sponge, what replication should be made by the son of a king?
Ros. Take you me for a sponge, my lord?
Ham. Ay, sir, that soaks up the King's countenance, his rewards, his authorities. But such officers do the King best service in the end. He keeps them, like an ape, in the corner of his jaw; first mouthed, to be last swallowed. When he needs what you have gleaned, it is but squeezing you, and, sponge, you shall be dry again.
Ros. I understand you not, my lord.
Ham. I am glad of it. A knavish speech sleeps in a foolish ear.
Ros. My lord, you must tell us where the body is, and go with us to the King.
Ham. The body is with the King, but the King is not with the body. The King is a thing—
Guil. A thing, my lord!
Ham. Of nothing. Bring me to him. Hide fox, and all after. [*Exeunt.*

Scene iii. *Another room in the castle*

Enter KING *attended.*

King. I have sent to seek him, and to find the body.
How dangerous is it that this man goes loose!
Yet must not we put the strong law on him.
He's loved of the distracted multitude,
Who like not in their judgement, but their eyes:

And where 'tis so, the offender's scourge is weigh'd,
But never the offence. To bear all smooth and even,
This sudden sending him away must seem
Deliberate pause. Diseases desperate grown
By desperate appliance are relieved,
Or not at all.

Enter ROSENCRANTZ.

How now! what hath befall'n?

Ros. Where the dead body is bestow'd, my lord,
We cannot get from him.

King. But where is he?

Ros. Without, my lord; guarded, to know your pleasure.

King. Bring him before us.

Ros. Ho, Guildenstern! bring in my lord.

Enter HAMLET *and* GUILDENSTERN.

King. Now, Hamlet, where's Polonius?

Ham. At supper.

King. At supper! where?

Ham. Not where he eats, but where he is eaten. A certain convocation of politic worms are e'en at him. Your worm is your only emperor for diet. We fat all creatures else to fat us, and we fat ourselves for maggots. Your fat king and your lean beggar is but variable service, two dishes, but to one table; that's the end.

King. Alas, alas!

Ham. A man may fish with the worm that hath eat of a king, and eat of the fish that hath fed of that worm.

King. What dost thou mean by this?

Ham. Nothing but to show you how a king may go a progress through the guts of a beggar.

King. Where is Polonius?

Ham. In heaven; send thither to see. If your messenger find him not there, seek him i' the other place yourself. But indeed, if you find him not within this month, you shall nose him as you go up the stairs into the lobby.

King. Go seek him there. [*To some Attendants*.

Ham. He will stay till you come.

[*Exeunt Attendants*.

King. Hamlet, this deed, for thine especial safety—
Which we do tender, as we dearly grieve
For that which thou hast done—must send thee hence
With fiery quickness. Therefore prepare thyself;
The bark is ready, and the wind at help,
The associates tend, and everything is bent
For England.

Ham. For England!

King. Ay, Hamlet.

Ham. Good.

King. So is it, if thou knew'st our purposes.

Ham. I see a cherub that sees them. But, come; for England! Farewell, dear mother.

King. Thy loving father, Hamlet.

Ham. My mother. Father and mother is man and wife; man and wife is one flesh; and so, my mother. Come, for England! [*Exit*.

King. Follow him at foot; tempt him with speed aboard;
Delay it not; I'll have him hence to-night.
Away! for every thing is seal'd and done
That else leans on the affair. Pray you, make haste.

[*Exeunt* ROSENCRANTZ *and* GUILDENSTERN.

And, England, if my love thou hold'st at aught—
As my great power thereof may give thee sense,
Since yet thy cicatrice looks raw and red
After the Danish sword, and thy free awe
Pays homage to us—thou mayst not coldly set
Our sovereign process; which imports at full,
By letters congruing to that effect,
The present death of Hamlet. Do it, England;
For like the hectic in my blood he rages,
And thou must cure me. Till I know 'tis done,
Howe'er my haps, my joys were ne'er begun.

[*Exit*.

SCENE IV. *A plain in Denmark*

Enter FORTINBRAS, *a* CAPTAIN, *and Soldiers, marching*.

For. Go, captain, from me greet the Danish king:
Tell him that, by his license, Fortinbras
Craves the conveyance of a promised march
Over his kingdom. You know the rendezvous.
If that his Majesty would aught with us,
We shall express our duty in his eye;
And let him know so.

Cap. I will do't, my lord.

For. Go softly on.

[*Exeunt* FORTINBRAS *and Soldiers*.

Enter HAMLET, ROSENCRANTZ, GUILDENSTERN, *and others*.

Ham. Good sir, whose powers are these?

Cap. They are of Norway, sir.

Ham. How purposed, sir, I pray you?

Cap. Against some part of Poland.

Ham. Who commands them, sir?

Cap. The nephew to old Norway, Fortinbras.

Ham. Goes it against the main of Poland, sir,
Or for some frontier?
Cap. Truly to speak, and with no addition,
We go to gain a little patch of ground
That hath in it no profit but the name.
To pay five ducats, five, I would not farm it;
Nor will it yield to Norway or the Pole
A ranker rate, should it be sold in fee.
Ham. Why, then the Polack never will defend it.
Cap. Yes, it is already garrison'd.
Ham. Two thousand souls and twenty thousand ducats
Will not debate the question of this straw.
This is the imposthume of much wealth and peace,
That inward breaks, and shows no cause without
Why the man dies. I humbly thank you, sir.
Cap. God be wi' you, sir. [*Exit*.
Ros. Will't please you go, my lord?
Ham. I'll be with you straight. Go a little before. [*Exeunt all except* HAMLET.
How all occasions do inform against me,
And spur my dull revenge! What is a man,
If his chief good and market of his time
Be but to sleep and feed? a beast, no more.
Sure, he that made us with such large discourse,
Looking before and after, gave us not
That capability and god-like reason
To fust in us unused. Now, whether it be
Bestial oblivion, or some craven scruple
Of thinking too precisely on the event,
A thought which, quarter'd, hath but one part wisdom
And ever three parts coward, I do not know
Why yet I live to say "This thing's to do";
Sith I have cause and will and strength and means
To do't. Examples gross as earth exhort me;
Witness this army of such mass and charge
Led by a delicate and tender prince,
Whose spirit with divine ambition puff'd
Makes mouths at the invisible event,
Exposing what is mortal and unsure
To all that fortune, death, and danger dare,
Even for an egg-shell. Rightly to be great
Is not to stir without great argument,
But greatly to find quarrel in a straw
When honour's at the stake. How stand I then,
That have a father kill'd, a mother stain'd,
Excitements of my reason and my blood,
And let me sleep? while, to my shame, I see
The imminent death of twenty thousand men,
That, for a fantasy and trick of fame,
Go to their graves like beds, fight for a plot
Whereon the numbers cannot try the cause,
Which is not tomb enough and continent
To hide the slain? O, from this time forth,
My thoughts be bloody, or be nothing worth!
[*Exit*.

SCENE V. *Elsinore: a room in the castle*

Enter QUEEN, HORATIO, *and a* GENTLEMAN.

Queen. I will not speak with her.
Gent. She is importunate, indeed distract.
Her mood will needs be pitied.
Queen. What would she have?
Gent. She speaks much of her father; says she hears
There's tricks i' the world; and hems, and beats her heart;
Spurns enviously at straws; speaks things in doubt,
That carry but half sense. Her speech is nothing,
Yet the unshaped use of it doth move
The hearers to collection; they aim at it,
And botch the words up fit to their own thoughts;
Which, as her winks, and nods, and gestures yield them,
Indeed would make one think there might be thought,
Though nothing sure, yet much unhappily.
Hor. 'Twere good she were spoken with; for she may strew
Dangerous conjectures in ill-breeding minds.
Queen. Let her come in. [*Exit* HORATIO.
To my sick soul, as sin's true nature is,
Each toy seems prologue to some great amiss;
So full of artless jealousy is guilt,
It spills itself in fearing to be spilt.

Re-enter HORATIO, *with* OPHELIA.

Oph. Where is the beauteous majesty of Denmark?
Queen. How now, Ophelia!
Oph. [*Sings*] "How should I your true love know
From another one?
By his cockle hat and staff,
And his sandal shoon."
Queen. Alas, sweet lady, what imports this song?
Oph. Say you? nay, pray you, mark.
[*Sings*] "He is dead and gone, lady,
He is dead and gone;
At his head a grass-green turf,
At his heels a stone."
Queen. Nay, but, Ophelia—
Oph. Pray you, mark.
[*Sings*] "White his shroud as the mountain snow"—

Enter KING.

Queen. Alas, look here, my lord.

Oph. [*Sings*] "Larded with sweet flowers;
Which bewept to the grave did go
With true-love showers."

King. How do you, pretty lady?

Oph. Well, God 'ild you! They say the owl was a baker's daughter. Lord, we know what we are, but know not what we may be. God be at your table!

King. Conceit upon her father.

Oph. Pray you, let's have no words of this; but when they ask you what it means, say you this:
[*Sings*] "To-morrow is Saint Valentine's day,
All in the morning betime,
And I a maid at your window,
To be your Valentine.
Then up he rose, and donn'd his clothes,
And dupp'd the chamber-door;
Let in the maid, that out a maid
Never departed more."

King. Pretty Ophelia!

Oph. Indeed, la, without an oath, I'll make an end on't:
[*Sings*] "By Gis and by Saint Charity,
Alack, and fie for shame!
Young men will do't, if they come to't;
By cock, they are to blame.
Quoth she, before you tumbled me,
You promised me to wed.
So would I ha' done, by yonder sun,
An thou hadst not come to my bed."

King. How long hath she been thus?

Oph. I hope all will be well. We must be patient; but I cannot choose but weep, to think they should lay him i' the cold ground. My brother shall know of it; and so I thank you for your good counsel. Come, my coach! Good night, ladies; good night, sweet ladies; good night, good night. [*Exit*.

King. Follow her close; give her good watch, I pray you. [*Exit* HORATIO.
O, this is the poison of deep grief; it springs
All from her father's death. O Gertrude, Gertrude,
When sorrows come, they come not single spies,
But in battalions. First, her father slain;
Next, your son gone; and he most violent author
Of his own just remove; the people muddied,
Thick and unwholesome in their thoughts and whispers,
For good Polonius' death; and we have done but greenly,
In hugger-mugger to inter him; poor Ophelia
Divided from herself and her fair judgement,
Without the which we are pictures, or mere beasts;
Last, and as much containing as all these,
Her brother is in secret come from France;
Feeds on his wonder, keeps himself in clouds,
And wants not buzzers to infect his ear
With pestilent speeches of his father's death;
Wherein necessity, of matter beggar'd,
Will nothing stick our person to arraign
In ear and ear. O my dear Gertrude, this,
Like to a murdering-piece, in many places
Gives me superfluous death.

A noise within.

Queen. Alack, what noise is this?

Enter another GENTLEMAN.

King. Where are my Switzers? Let them guard the door.
What is the matter?

Gent. Save yourself, my lord:
The ocean, overpeering of his list,
Eats not the flats with more impetuous haste
Than young Laertes, in a riotous head,
O'erbears your officers. The rabble call him lord;
And, as the world were now but to begin,
Antiquity forgot, custom not known,
The ratifiers and props of every word,
They cry, "Choose we: Laertes shall be king:"
Caps, hands, and tongues, applaud it to the clouds:
"Laertes shall be king, Laertes king!"

Queen. How cheerfully on the false trail they cry!
O, this is counter, you false Danish dogs!

King. The doors are broke.

Noise within.

Enter LAERTES, *armed;* DANES *following*.

Laer. Where is this king? Sirs, stand you all without.

Danes. No, let's come in.

Laer. I pray you, give me leave.

Danes. We will, we will.

[*They retire without the door*.

Laer. I thank you; keep the door. O thou vile king,
Give me my father!

Queen. Calmly, good Laertes.

Laer. That drop of blood that's calm proclaims me bastard,
Cries cuckold to my father, brands the harlot
Even here, between the chaste unsmirched brow
Of my true mother.

King. What is the cause, Laertes,
That thy rebellion looks so giant-like?
Let him go, Gertrude; do not fear our person:
There's such divinity doth hedge a king,
That treason can but peep to what it would,

Acts little of his will. Tell me, Laertes,
Why thou art thus incensed. Let him go, Gertrude.
Speak, man.
Laer. Where is my father?
King. Dead.
Queen. But not by him.
King. Let him demand his fill.
Laer. How came he dead? I'll not be juggled with.
To hell, allegiance! vows, to the blackest devil!
Conscience and grace, to the profoundest pit!
I dare damnation. To this point I stand,
That both the worlds I give to negligence,
Let come what comes; only I'll be revenged
Most throughly for my father.
King. Who shall stay you?
Laer. My will, not all the world:
And for my means, I'll husband them so well,
They shall go far with little.
King. Good Laertes,
If you desire to know the certainty
Of your dear father's death, is't writ in your revenge,
That, swoopstake, you will draw both friend and foe,
Winner and loser?
Laer. None but his enemies.
King. Will you know them then?
Laer. To his good friends thus wide I'll ope my arms;
And like the kind life-rendering pelican,
Repast them with my blood.
King. Why, now you speak
Like a good child and a true gentleman.
That I am guiltless of your father's death,
And am most sensibly in grief for it,
It shall as level to your judgement pierce
As day does to your eye
Danes. [*Within*] Let her come in.
Laer. How now! what noise is that?

Re-enter OPHELIA.

O heat, dry up my brains! tears seven times salt,
Burn out the sense and virtue of mine eye!
By heaven, thy madness shall be paid with weight,
Till our scale turn the beam. O rose of May!
Dear maid, kind sister, sweet Ophelia!
O heavens! is't possible, a young maid's wits
Should be as mortal as an old man's life?
Nature is fine in love, and where 'tis fine,
It sends some precious instance of itself
After the thing it loves.
Oph. [*Sings*]
"They bore him barefaced on the bier;
Hey non nonny, nonny, hey nonny;
And in his grave rain'd many a tear"—
Fare you well, my dove!
Laer. Hadst thou thy wits, and didst persuade revenge,
It could not move thus.
Oph. [*Sings*] "You must sing a-down a-down,
An you call him a-down-a."
O, how the wheel becomes it! It is the false steward, that stole his master's daughter.
Laer. This nothing's more than matter.
Oph. There's rosemary, that's for remembrance; pray, love, remember; and there is pansies, that's for thoughts.
Laer. A document in madness, thoughts and remembrance fitted.
Oph. There's fennel for you, and columbines; there's rue for you, and here's some for me; we may call it herb-grace o'Sundays. O, you must wear your rue with a difference. There's a daisy. I would give you some violets, but they withered all when my father died. They say he made a good end—
[*Sings*] "For bonny sweet Robin is all my joy."
Laer. Thought and affliction, passion, hell itself,
She turns to favour and to prettiness.
Oph. [*Sings*] "And will he not come again?
And will he not come again?
No, no, he is dead;
Go to thy death-bed;
He never will come again.

His beard was as white as snow,
All flaxen was his poll.
He is gone, he is gone,
And we cast away moan.
God ha' mercy on his soul!"
And of all Christian souls, I pray God. God be wi' ye. [*Exit*.
Laer. Do you see this, O God?
King. Laertes, I must commune with your grief,
Or you deny me right. Go but apart,
Make choice of whom your wisest friends you will,
And they shall hear and judge 'twixt you and me.
If by direct or by collateral hand
They find us touch'd, we will our kingdom give,
Our crown, our life, and all that we call ours,
To you in satisfaction; but if not,
Be you content to lend your patience to us,
And we shall jointly labour with your soul
To give it due content.
Laer. Let this be so;
His means of death, his obscure funeral—

No trophy, sword, nor hatchment o'er his bones,
No noble rite nor formal ostentation—
Cry to be heard, as 'twere from heaven to earth,
That I must call't in question.

King. So you shall;
And where the offence is let the great axe fall.
I pray you, go with me. [*Exeunt*.

SCENE VI. *Another room in the castle*

Enter HORATIO *and a* SERVANT.

Hor. What are they that would speak with me?

Serv. Sailors, sir. They say they have letters for you.

Hor. Let them come in. [*Exit* SERVANT.
I do not know from what part of the world
I should be greeted, if not from lord Hamlet.

Enter SAILORS.

1st Sail. God bless you, sir.

Hor. Let him bless thee too.

1st Sail. He shall, sir, an't please Him. There's a letter for you, sir. It comes from the ambassador that was bound for England; if your name be Horatio, as I am let to know it is.

Hor. [*Reads*] "Horatio, when thou shalt have overlooked this, give these fellows some means to the King; they have letters for him. Ere we were two days old at sea, a pirate of very warlike appointment gave us chase. Finding ourselves too slow of sail, we put on a compelled valour, and in the grapple I boarded them. On the instant they got clear of our ship; so I alone became their prisoner. They have dealt with me like thieves of mercy, but they knew what they did; I am to do a good turn for them. Let the King have the letters I have sent; and repair thou to me with as much speed as thou wouldst fly death. I have words to speak in thine ear will make thee dumb; yet are they much too light for the bore of the matter. These good fellows will bring thee where I am. Rosencrantz and Guildenstern hold their course for England; of them I have much to tell thee. Farewell.

"He that thou knowest thine, Hamlet"

Come, I will make you way for these your letters;
And do't the speedier, that you may direct me
To him from whom you brought them. [*Exeunt*.

SCENE VII. *Another room in the castle*

Enter KING *and Laertes*.

King. Now must your conscience my acquittance seal,
And you must put me in your heart for friend,
Sith you have heard, and with a knowing ear,
That he which hath your noble father slain
Pursued my life.

Laer. It well appears: but tell me
Why you proceeded not against these feats,
So crimeful and so capital in nature,
As by your safety, wisdom, all things else,
You mainly were stirr'd up.

King. O, for two special reasons;
Which may to you, perhaps, seem much unsinew'd,
But yet to me they are strong. The Queen his mother
Lives almost by his looks; and for myself—
My virtue or my plague, be it either which—
She's so conjunctive to my life and soul,
That, as the star moves not but in his sphere,
I could not but by her. The other motive,
Why to a public count I might not go,
Is the great love the general gender bear him;
Who, dipping all his faults in their affection,
Would, like the spring that turneth wood to stone,
Convert his gyves to graces; so that my arrows,
Too slightly timber'd for so loud a wind,
Would have reverted to my bow again,
And not where I had aim'd them.

Laer. And so have I a noble father lost;
A sister driven into desperate terms,
Whose worth, if praises may go back again,
Stood challenger on mount of all the age
For her perfections. But my revenge will come.

King. Break not your sleeps for that. You must not think
That we are made of stuff so flat and dull
That we can let our beard be shook with danger
And think it pastime. You shortly shall hear more.
I loved your father, and we love ourself;
And that, I hope, will teach you to imagine—

Enter a MESSENGER.

How now! what news?

Mess. Letters, my lord, from Hamlet.
This to your Majesty; this to the Queen.

King. From Hamlet! who brought them?

Mess. Sailors, my lord, they say; I saw them not:
They were given me by Claudio; he received them
Of him that brought them.

King. Laertes, you shall hear them.
Leave us. [*Exit* MESSENGER.
[*Reads*] "High and mighty, You shall know I am set naked on your kingdom. To-morrow shall I beg leave to see your kingly eyes, when I shall, first asking your pardon thereunto, recount the

occasion of my sudden and more strange return.
"Hamlet"
What should this mean? Are all the rest come
back?
Or is it some abuse, and no such thing?
Laer. Know you the hand?
King. 'Tis Hamlet's character. "Naked!"
And in a postscript here, he says "alone."
Can you advise me?
Laer. I'm lost in it, my lord. But let him come;
It warms the very sickness in my heart,
That I shall live and tell him to his teeth,
"Thus didest thou."
King. If it be so, Laertes—
As how should it be so? how otherwise?—
Will you be ruled by me?
Laer. Ay, my lord;
So you will not o'errule me to a peace.
King. To thine own peace. If he be now re-
turn'd,
As checking at his voyage, and that he means
No more to undertake it, I will work him
To an exploit, now ripe in my device,
Under the which he shall not choose but fall;
And for his death no wind of blame shall breathe,
But even his mother shall uncharge the practice
And call it accident.
Laer. My lord, I will be ruled;
The rather, if you could devise it so
That I might be the organ.
King. It falls right.
You have been talk'd of since your travel much,
And that in Hamlet's hearing, for a quality
Wherein, they say, you shine: your sum of
parts
Did not together pluck such envy from him
As did that one, and that, in my regard,
Of the unworthiest siege.
Laer. What part is that, my lord?
King. A very riband in the cap of youth,
Yet needful too; for youth no less becomes
The light and careless livery that it wears
Than settled age his sables and his weeds,
Importing health and graveness. Two months
since,
Here was a gentleman of Normandy;
I've seen myself, and served against, the French,
And they can well on horseback: but this gallant
Had witchcraft in't; he grew unto his seat;
And to such wondrous doing brought his horse,
As had he been incorpsed and demi-natured
With the brave beast. So far he topp'd my
thought,
That I, in forgery of shapes and tricks,
Come short of what he did.
Laer. A Norman was't?
King. A Norman.
Laer. Upon my life, Lamond.
King. The very same.
Laer. I know him well. He is the brooch indeed
And gem of all the nation.
King. He made confession of you,
And gave you such a masterly report
For art and exercise in your defence
And for your rapier most especial,
That he cried out, 'twould be a sight indeed,
If one could match you. The scrimers of their
nation,
He swore, had neither motion, guard, nor eye,
If you opposed them. Sir, this report of his
Did Hamlet so envenom with his envy
That he could nothing do but wish and beg
Your sudden coming o'er, to play with him.
Now, out of this—
Laer. What out of this, my lord?
King. Laertes, was your father dear to you?
Or are you like the painting of a sorrow,
A face without a heart?
Laer. Why ask you this?
King. Not that I think you did not love your
father;
But that I know love is begun by time;
And that I see, in passages of proof,
Time qualifies the spark and fire of it.
There lives within the very flame of love
A kind of wick or snuff that will abate it;
And nothing is at a like goodness still;
For goodness, growing to a plurisy,
Dies in his own too much. That we would do,
We should do when we would; for this "would"
changes
And hath abatements and delays as many
As there are tongues, are hands, are accidents;
And then this "should" is like a spendthrift sigh,
That hurts by easing. But, to the quick o' the
ulcer—
Hamlet comes back. What would you undertake,
To show yourself your father's son in deed
More than in words?
Laer. To cut his throat i' the church.
King. No place, indeed, should murder sanc-
tuarize;
Revenge should have no bounds. But, good
Laertes,
Will you do this, keep close within your cham-
ber.
Hamlet return'd shall know you are come home.
We'll put on those shall praise your excellence
And set a double varnish on the fame
The Frenchman gave you, bring you in fine to-
gether
And wager on your heads. He, being remiss,

Most generous and free from all contriving,
Will not peruse the foils; so that, with ease,
Or with a little shuffling, you may choose
A sword unbated, and in a pass of practice
Requite him for your father.
Laer. I will do 't;
And, for that purpose, I'll anoint my sword.
I bought an unction of a mountebank,
So mortal that, but dip a knife in it,
Where it draws blood no cataplasm so rare,
Collected from all simples that have virtue
Under the moon, can save the thing from death
That is but scratch'd withal. I'll touch my point
With this contagion, that, if I gall him slightly,
It may be death.
King. Let's further think of this;
Weigh what convenience both of time and means
May fit us to our shape: if this should fail,
And that our drift look through our bad performance,
'Twere better not assay'd: therefore this project
Should have a back or second, that might hold,
If this should blast in proof. Soft! let me see:
We'll make a solemn wager on your cunnings.
I ha't:
When in your motion you are hot and dry—
As make your bouts more violent to that end—
And that he calls for drink, I'll have prepared him
A chalice for the nonce, whereon but sipping,
If he by chance escape your venom'd stuck,
Our purpose may hold there.

Enter QUEEN.

How now, sweet queen!
Queen. One woe doth tread upon another's heel,
So fast they follow. Your sister's drown'd, Laertes.
Laer. Drown'd! O, where?
Queen. There is a willow grows aslant a brook,
That shows his hoar leaves in the glassy stream;
There with fantastic garlands did she come
Of crow-flowers, nettles, daisies, and long purples
That liberal shepherds give a grosser name,
But our cold maids do dead men's fingers call them;
There, on the pendent boughs her coronet weeds
Clambering to hang, an envious sliver broke;
When down her weedy trophies and herself
Fell in the weeping brook. Her clothes spread wide;
And, mermaid-like, awhile they bore her up;
Which time she chanted snatches of old tunes;
As one incapable of her own distress,
Or like a creature native and indued
Unto that element. But long it could not be
Till that her garments, heavy with their drink,
Pull'd the poor wretch from her melodious lay
To muddy death.
Laer. Alas, then, she is drown'd?
Queen. Drown'd, drown'd.
Laer. Too much of water hast thou, poor Ophelia,
And therefore I forbid my tears. But yet
It is our trick; Nature her custom holds,
Let shame say what it will; when these are gone,
The woman will be out. Adieu, my lord:
I have a speech of fire, that fain would blaze,
But that this folly douts it. [*Exit.*
King. Let's follow, Gertrude.
How much I had to do to calm his rage!
Now fear I this will give it start again;
Therefore let's follow. [*Exeunt.*

ACT V

SCENE I. *A churchyard*

Enter TWO CLOWNS, *with spades, &c.*

1st Clo. Is she to be buried in Christian burial that wilfully seeks her own salvation?

2nd Clo. I tell thee she is; and therefore make her grave straight. The crowner hath sat on her, and finds it Christian burial.

1st Clo. How can that be, unless she drowned herself in her own defence?

2nd Clo. Why, 'tis found so.

1st Clo. It must be *se offendendo;* it cannot be else. For here lies the point: if I drown myself wittingly, it argues an act, and an act hath three branches; it is, to act, to do, and to perform: argal, she drowned herself wittingly.

2nd Clo. Nay, but hear you, goodman delver—

1st Clo. Give me leave. Here lies the water; good. Here stands the man; good. If the man go to this water, and drown himself, it is, will he, nill he, he goes—mark you that. But if the water come to him and drown him, he drowns not himself; argal, he that is not guilty of his own death shortens not his own life.

2nd Clo. But is this law?

1st Clo. Ay, marry, is't; crowner's quest law.

2nd Clo. Will you ha' the truth on't? If this had not been a gentlewoman, she should have been buried out o' Christian burial.

1st Clo. Why, there thou say'st; and the more pity that great folk should have countenance in this world to drown or hang themselves, more than their even Christian. Come, my spade. There is no ancient gentlemen but gardeners, ditchers, and grave-makers; they hold up Adam's profession.

2nd Clo. Was he a gentleman?

1st Clo. A' was the first that ever bore arms.

2nd Clo. Why, he had none.

1st Clo. What, art a heathen? How dost thou understand the Scripture? The Scripture says "Adam digged"; could he dig without arms? I'll put another question to thee. If thou answerest me not to the purpose, confess thyself—

2nd Clo. Go to.

1st Clo. What is he that builds stronger than either the mason, the shipwright, or the carpenter?

2nd Clo. The gallows-maker; for that frame outlives a thousand tenants.

1st Clo. I like thy wit well, in good faith. The gallows does well; but how does it well? it does well to those that do ill. Now thou dost ill to say the gallows is built stronger than the church; argal, the gallows may do well to thee. To't again, come.

2nd Clo. "Who builds stronger than a mason, a shipwright, or a carpenter?"

1st Clo. Ay, tell me that, and unyoke.

2nd Clo. Marry, now I can tell.

1st Clo. To't.

2nd Clo. Mass, I cannot tell.

Enter HAMLET *and* HORATIO, *at a distance.*

1st Clo. Cudgel thy brains no more about it, for your dull ass will not mend his pace with beating; and, when you are asked this question next, say "a grave-maker": the houses that he makes last till doomsday. Go, get thee to Yaughan: fetch me a stoup of liquor.

[*Exit* SECOND CLOWN.

He digs, and sings.

"In youth, when I did love, did love,
Methought it was very sweet,
To contract, O, the time, for, ah, my behove,
O, methought, there was nothing meet."

Ham. Has this fellow no feeling of his business, that he sings at grave-making?

Hor. Custom hath made it in him a property of easiness.

Ham. 'Tis e'en so. The hand of little employment hath the daintier sense.

1st Clo. [*Sings*]

"But age, with his stealing steps,
Hath claw'd me in his clutch,
And hath shipped me intil the land,
As if I had never been such."

Throws up a skull.

Ham. That skull had a tongue in it, and could sing once. How the knave jowls it to the ground, as if it were Cain's jaw-bone, that did the first murder! It might be the pate of a politician, which this ass now o'er-reaches; one that would circumvent God, might it not?

Hor. It might, my lord.

Ham. Or of a courtier; which could say "Good morrow, sweet lord! How dost thou, good lord?" This might be my Lord Such-a-one, that praised my Lord Such-a-one's horse, when he meant to beg it; might it not?

Hor. Ay, my lord.

Ham. Why, e'en so; and now my Lady Worm's; chapless, and knocked about the mazzard with a sexton's spade. Here's fine revolution, an we had the trick to see't. Did these bones cost no more the breeding, but to play at loggats with 'em? mine ache to think on't.

1st Clo. [*Sings*]

"A pick-axe, and a spade, a spade,
For and a shrouding sheet;
O, a pit of clay for to be made
For such a guest is meet."

Throws up another skull.

Ham. There's another. Why may not that be the skull of a lawyer? Where be his quiddities now, his quillets, his cases, his tenures, and his tricks? Why does he suffer this rude knave now to knock him about the sconce with a dirty shovel, and will not tell him of his action of battery? Hum! This fellow might be in's time a great buyer of land, with his statutes, his recognizances, his fines, his double vouchers, his recoveries. Is this the fine of his fines, and the recovery of his recoveries, to have his fine pate full of fine dirt? Will his vouchers vouch him no more of his purchases, and double ones too, than the length and breadth of a pair of indentures? The very conveyances of his lands will hardly lie in this box; and must the inheritor himself have no more, ha?

Hor. Not a jot more, my lord.

Ham. Is not parchment made of sheep-skins?

Hor. Ay, my lord, and of calf-skins too.

Ham. They are sheep and calves which seek out assurance in that. I will speak to this fellow. Whose grave's this, sirrah?

1st Clo. Mine, sir.

[*Sings*] "O, a pit of clay for to be made
For such a guest is meet."

Ham. I think it be thine, indeed; for thou liest in't.

1st Clo. You lie out on't, sir, and therefore it is not yours. For my part, I do not lie in't, and yet it is mine.

Ham. Thou dost lie in't, to be in't and say it is thine. 'Tis for the dead, not for the quick; therefore thou liest.

1st Clo. 'Tis a quick lie, sir; 'twill away again, from me to you.

Ham. What man dost thou dig it for?

1st Clo. For no man, sir.

Ham. What woman, then?

1st Clo. For none, neither.

Ham. Who is to be buried in't?

1st Clo. One that was a woman, sir; but, rest her soul, she's dead.

Ham. How absolute the knave is! we must speak by the card, or equivocation will undo us. By the Lord, Horatio, these three years I have taken note of it; the age is grown so picked that the toe of the peasant comes so near the heel of the courtier, he galls his kibe. How long hast thou been a grave-maker?

1st Clo. Of all the days i' the year, I came to 't that day that our last king Hamlet overcame Fortinbras.

Ham. How long is that since?

1st Clo. Cannot you tell that? every fool can tell that. It was the very day that young Hamlet was born; he that is mad, and sent into England.

Ham. Ay, marry, why was he sent into England?

1st Clo. Why, because he was mad. He shall recover his wits there; or, if he do not, it's no great matter there.

Ham. Why?

1st Clo. 'Twill not be seen in him there; there the men are as mad as he.

Ham. How came he mad?

1st Clo. Very strangely, they say.

Ham. How strangely?

1st Clo. Faith, e'en with losing his wits.

Ham. Upon what ground?

1st Clo. Why, here in Denmark. I have been sexton here, man and boy, thirty years.

Ham. How long will a man lie i' the earth ere he rot?

1st Clo. I' faith, if he be not rotten before he die —as we have many pocky corses now-a-days, that will scarce hold the laying in—he will last you some eight year or nine year. A tanner will last you nine year.

Ham. Why he more than another?

1st Clo. Why, sir, his hide is so tanned with his trade, that he will keep out water a great while; and your water is a sore decayer of your whoreson dead body. Here's a skull now; this skull has lain in the earth three and twenty years.

Ham. Whose was it?

1st Clo. A whoreson mad fellow's it was. Whose do you think it was?

Ham. Nay, I know not.

1st Clo. A pestilence on him for a mad rogue! a' poured a flagon of Rhenish on my head once. This same skull, sir, was Yorick's skull, the King's jester.

Ham. This?

1st Clo. E'en that.

Ham. Let me see. [*Takes the skull.*] Alas, poor Yorick! I knew him, Horatio; a fellow of infinite jest, of most excellent fancy. He hath borne me on his back a thousand times; and now, how abhorred in my imagination it is! my gorge rises at it. Here hung those lips that I have kissed I know not how oft. Where be your gibes now? your gambols? your songs? your flashes of merriment, that were wont to set the table on a roar? Not one now, to mock your own grinning? quite chap-fallen? Now get you to my lady's chamber, and tell her, let her paint an inch thick, to this favour she must come; make her laugh at that. Prithee, Horatio, tell me one thing.

Hor. What's that, my lord?

Ham. Dost thou think Alexander looked o' this fashion i' the earth?

Hor. E'en so.

Ham. And smelt so? pah!

Puts down the skull.

Hor. E'en so, my lord.

Ham. To what base uses we may return, Horatio! Why may not imagination trace the noble dust of Alexander, till he find it stopping a bung-hole?

Hor. 'Twere to consider too curiously, to consider so.

Ham. No, faith, not a jot; but to follow him thither with modesty enough, and likelihood to lead it; as thus: Alexander died, Alexander was buried, Alexander returneth into dust; the dust is earth; of earth we make loam; and why of that loam, whereto he was converted, might they not stop a beer-barrel?

Imperious Cæsar, dead and turn'd to clay,
Might stop a hole to keep the wind away.
O, that that earth, which kept the world in awe,
Should patch a wall to expel the winter's flaw!

But soft, but soft! aside: here comes the King,

Enter PRIESTS, *&c. in procession; the corpse of* OPHELIA, LAERTES *and Mourners following;* KING, QUEEN, *their trains, &c.*

The Queen, the courtiers. Who is this they follow?
And with such maimed rites? This doth betoken
The corse they follow did with desperate hand
Fordo it own life. 'Twas of some estate.
Couch we awhile, and mark.

[*Retiring with* HORATIO.

Laer. What ceremony else?
Ham. That is Laertes,
A very noble youth; mark.
Laer. What ceremony else?
1st Priest. Her obsequies have been as far enlarged
As we have warranty. Her death was doubtful;
And, but that great command o'ersways the order,
She should in ground unsanctified have lodged
Till the last trumpet; for charitable prayers,
Shards, flints, and pebbles should be thrown on her:
Yet here she is allow'd her virgin crants,
Her maiden strewments, and the bringing home
Of bell and burial.
Laer. Must there no more be done?
First Priest. No more be done.
We should profane the service of the dead
To sing a requiem and such rest to her
As to peace-parted souls.
Laer. Lay her i' the earth,
And from her fair and unpolluted flesh
May violets spring! I tell thee, churlish priest,
A ministering angel shall my sister be,
When thou liest howling.
Ham. What, the fair Ophelia!
Queen. Sweets to the sweet; farewell!
Scattering flowers.
I hoped thou shouldst have been my Hamlet's wife;
I thought thy bride-bed to have deck'd, sweet maid,
And not have strew'd thy grave.
Laer. O, treble woe
Fall ten times treble on that cursed head,
Whose wicked deed thy most ingenious sense
Deprived thee of! Hold off the earth awhile,
Till I have caught her once more in mine arms.
Leaps into the grave.
Now pile your dust upon the quick and dead,
Till of this flat a mountain you have made,
To o'ertop old Pelion, or the skyish head
Of blue Olympus.
Ham. [*Advancing*] What is he whose grief
Bears such an emphasis? whose phrase of sorrow
Conjures the wandering stars, and makes them stand
Like wonder-wounded hearers? This is I,
Hamlet the Dane. [*Leaps into the grave*.]
Laer. The devil take thy soul!
Grappling with him.
Ham. Thou pray'st not well.
I prithee, take thy fingers from my throat;
For, though I am not splenitive and rash,
Yet have I something in me dangerous,
Which let thy wiseness fear: hold off thy hand.
King. Pluck them asunder.
Queen. Hamlet, Hamlet!
All. Gentlemen—
Hor. Good my lord, be quiet.
The Attendants part them, and they come out of the grave.
Ham. Why, I will fight with him upon this theme
Until my eyelids will no longer wag.
Queen. O my son, what theme?
Ham. I loved Ophelia. Forty thousand brothers
Could not, with all their quantity of love,
Make up my sum. What wilt thou do for her?
King. O, he is mad, Laertes.
Queen. For love of God, forbear him.
Ham. 'Swounds, show me what thou'lt do.
Woo't weep? woo't fight? woo't fast? woo't tear thyself?
Woo't drink up eisel? eat a crocodile?
I'll do't. Dost thou come here to whine?
To outface me with leaping in her grave?
Be buried quick with her, and so will I;
And, if thou prate of mountains, let them throw
Millions of acres on us, till our ground,
Singeing his pate against the burning zone,
Make Ossa like a wart! Nay, an thou'lt mouth,
I'll rant as well as thou.
Queen. This is mere madness,
And thus awhile the fit will work on him;
Anon, as patient as the female dove,
When that her golden couplets are disclosed,
His silence will sit drooping.
Ham. Hear you, sir;
What is the reason that you use me thus?
I loved you ever. But it is no matter;
Let Hercules himself do what he may,
The cat will mew and dog will have his day.
[*Exit*.
King. I pray you, good Horatio, wait upon him.
[*Exit* HORATIO.
[*To* LAERTES] Strengthen your patience in our last night's speech;
We'll put the matter to the present push.
Good Gertrude, set some watch over your son.
This grave shall have a living monument.
An hour of quiet shortly shall we see;
Till then, in patience our proceeding be. [*Exeunt*.

SCENE II. *A hall in the castle*

Enter HAMLET *and* HORATIO.

Ham. So much for this, sir; now shall you see the other;
You do remember all the circumstance?
Hor. Remember it, my lord!

Ham. Sir, in my heart there was a kind of fighting,
That would not let me sleep. Methought I lay
Worse than the mutines in the bilboes. Rashly,
And praised be rashness for it, let us know,
Our indiscretion sometimes serves us well,
When our deep plots do pall; and that should teach us
There's a divinity that shapes our ends,
Rough-hew them how we will—
Hor. That is most certain.
Ham. Up from my cabin,
My sea-gown scarf'd about me, in the dark
Groped I to find out them; had my desire,
Finger'd their packet, and in fine withdrew
To mine own room again; making so bold,
My fears forgetting manners, to unseal
Their grand commission; where I found, Horatio—
O royal knavery!—an exact command,
Larded with many several sorts of reasons
Importing Denmark's health and England's too,
With, ho! such bugs and goblins in my life,
That, on the supervise, no leisure bated,
No, not to stay the grinding of the axe,
My head should be struck off.
Hor. Is't possible?
Ham. Here's the commission; read it at more leisure.
But wilt thou hear me how I did proceed?
Hor. I beseech you.
Ham. Being thus be-netted round with villainies—
Ere I could make a prologue to my brains,
They had begun the play—I sat me down,
Devised a new commission, wrote it fair.
I once did hold it, as our statists do,
A baseness to write fair and labour'd much
How to forget that learning, but, sir, now
It did me yeoman's service. Wilt thou know
The effect of what I wrote?
Hor. Ay, good my lord.
Ham. An earnest conjuration from the King,
As England was his faithful tributary,
As love between them like the palm might flourish,
As peace should still her wheaten garland wear
And stand a comma 'tween their amities,
And many such-like as's of great charge,
That, on the view and knowing of these contents,
Without debatement further, more or less,
He should the bearers put to sudden death,
Not shriving-time allow'd.
Hor. How was this seal'd?
Ham. Why, even in that was heaven ordinant.
I had my father's signet in my purse,
Which was the model of that Danish seal;
Folded the writ up in form of the other,
Subscribed it, gave't the impression, placed it safely,
The changeling never known. Now, the next day
Was our sea-fight; and what to this was sequent
Thou know'st already.
Hor. So Guildenstern and Rosencrantz go to't.
Ham. Why, man, they did make love to this employment;
They are not near my conscience; their defeat
Does by their own insinuation grow.
'Tis dangerous when the baser nature comes
Between the pass and fell incensed points
Of mighty opposites.
Hor. Why, what a king is this!
Ham. Does it not, thinks't thee, stand me now upon—
He that hath kill'd my king and whored my mother,
Popp'd in between the election and my hopes,
Thrown out his angle for my proper life,
And with such cozenage—is't not perfect conscience,
To quit him with this arm? and is't not to be damn'd,
To let this canker of our nature come
In further evil?
Hor. It must be shortly known to him from England
What is the issue of the business there.
Ham. It will be short; the interim is mine,
And a man's life's no more than to say "One."
But I am very sorry, good Horatio,
That to Laertes I forgot myself;
For, by the image of my cause, I see
The portraiture of his. I'll court his favours.
But, sure, the bravery of his grief did put me
Into a towering passion.
Hor. Peace! who comes here?

Enter OSRIC.

Osr. Your lordship is right welcome back to Denmark.

Ham. I humbly thank you, sir. Dost know this water-fly?

Hor. No, my good lord.

Ham. Thy state is the more gracious; for 'tis a vice to know him. He hath much land, and fertile; let a beast be lord of beasts, and his crib shall stand at the King's mess. 'Tis a chough; but, as I say, spacious in the possession of dirt.

Osr. Sweet lord, if your lordship were at leisure, I should impart a thing to you from his majesty.

Ham. I will receive it, sir, with all diligence of

spirit. Put your bonnet to his right use; 'tis for the head.

Osr. I thank your lordship, it is very hot.

Ham. No, believe me, 'tis very cold; the wind is northerly.

Osr. It is indifferent cold, my lord, indeed.

Ham. But yet methinks it is very sultry and hot for my complexion.

Osr. Exceedingly, my lord; it is very sultry—as 'twere—I cannot tell how. But, my lord, his Majesty bade me signify to you that he has laid a great wager on your head. Sir, this is the matter,—

Ham. I beseech you, remember—

HAMLET *moves him to put on his hat.*

Osr. Nay, good my lord; for mine ease, in good faith. Sir, here is newly come to court Laertes; believe me, an absolute gentleman, full of most excellent differences, of very soft society and great showing; indeed, to speak feelingly of him, he is the card or calendar of gentry, for you shall find in him the continent of what part a gentleman would see.

Ham. Sir, his definement suffers no perdition in you; though, I know, to divide him inventorially would dizzy the arithmetic of memory, and yet but yaw neither, in respect of his quick sail. But, in the verity of extolment, I take him to be a soul of great article; and his infusion of such dearth and rareness, as, to make true diction of him, his semblable is his mirror; and who else would trace him, his umbrage, nothing more.

Osr. Your lordship speaks most infallibly of him.

Ham. The concernancy, sir? why do we wrap the gentleman in our more rawer breath?

Osr. Sir?

Hor. Is't not possible to understand in another tongue? You will do't, sir, really.

Ham. What imports the nomination of this gentleman?

Osr. Of Laertes?

Hor. His purse is empty already; all's golden words are spent.

Ham. Of him, sir.

Osr. I know you are not ignorant—

Ham. I would you did, sir; yet, in faith, if you did, it would not much approve me. Well, sir?

Osr. You are not ignorant of what excellence Laertes is—

Ham. I dare not confess that, lest I should compare with him in excellence; but, to know a man well, were to know himself.

Osr. I mean, sir, for his weapon; but in the imputation laid on him by them, in his meed he's unfellowed.

Ham. What's his weapon?

Osr. Rapier and dagger.

Ham. That's two of his weapons; but, well.

Osr. The King, sir, hath wagered with him six Barbary horses, against the which he has imponed, as I take it, six French rapiers and poniards, with their assigns, as girdle, hangers, and so. Three of the carriages, in faith, are very dear to fancy, very responsive to the hilts, most delicate carriages, and of very liberal conceit.

Ham. What call you the carriages?

Hor. I knew you must be edified by the margent ere you had done.

Osr. The carriages, sir, are the hangers.

Ham. The phrase would be more german to the matter, if we could carry cannon by our sides; I would it might be hangers till then. But, on: six Barbary horses against six French swords, their assigns, and three liberal-conceited carriages; that's the French bet against the Danish. Why is this "imponed," as you call it?

Osr. The King, sir, hath laid, that in a dozen passes between yourself and him, he shall not exceed you three hits. He hath laid on twelve for nine; and it would come to immediate trial, if your lordship would vouchsafe the answer.

Ham. How if I answer "no"?

Osr. I mean, my lord, the opposition of your person in trial.

Ham. Sir, I will walk here in the hall; if it please his Majesty, 'tis the breathing time of day with me; let the foils be brought, the gentleman willing, and the King hold his purpose, I will win for him an I can; if not, I will gain nothing but my shame and the odd hits.

Osr. Shall I re-deliver you e'en so?

Ham. To this effect, sir; after what flourish your nature will.

Osr. I commend my duty to your lordship.

Ham. Yours, yours. [*Exit* OSRIC.] He does well to commend it himself; there are no tongues else for's turn.

Hor. This lapwing runs away with the shell on his head.

Ham. He did comply with his dug, before he sucked it. Thus has he—and many more of the same breed that I know the drossy age dotes on—only got the tune of the time and outward habit of encounter; a kind of yesty collection, which carries them through and through the most fond and winnowed opinions; and do but blow them to their trial, the bubbles are out.

Enter A LORD.

Lord. My Lord, his Majesty commended him to you by young Osric, who brings back to him, that you attend him in the hall. He sends to know if your pleasure hold to play with Laertes, or that you will take longer time.

Ham. I am constant to my purposes; they follow the King's pleasure. If his fitness speaks, mine is ready; now or whensoever, provided I be so able as now.

Lord. The King and Queen and all are coming down.

Ham. In happy time.

Lord. The Queen desires you to use some gentle entertainment to Laertes before you fall to play.

Ham. She well instructs me. [*Exit* LORD.

Hor. You will lose this wager, my lord.

Ham. I do not think so; since he went into France, I have been in continual practice; I shall win at the odds. But thou wouldst not think how ill all's here about my heart. But it is no matter.

Hor. Nay, good my lord—

Ham. It is but foolery; but it is such a kind of gain-giving, as would perhaps trouble a woman.

Hor. If your mind dislike anything, obey it. I will forestall their repair hither, and say you are not fit.

Ham. Not a whit, we defy augury. There's a special providence in the fall of a sparrow. If it be now, 'tis not to come; if it be not to come, it will be now; if it be not now, yet it will come; the readiness is all. Since no man has aught of what he leaves, what is't to leave betimes? Let be.

Enter KING, QUEEN, LAERTES, OSRIC, *Lords, and Attendants with foils and gauntlets; a table and flagons of wine on it.*

King. Come, Hamlet, come, and take this hand
from me.

The KING *puts* LAERTES' *hand into* HAMLET'S.

Ham. Give me your pardon, sir. I've done you
wrong;
But pardon't, as you are a gentleman.
This presence knows,
And you must needs have heard, how I am pun-
ish'd
With sore distraction. What I have done,
That might your nature, honour, and exception
Roughly awake, I here proclaim was madness.
Was't Hamlet wrong'd Laertes? Never Hamlet:
If Hamlet from himself be ta'en away,
And when he's not himself does wrong Laertes,
Then Hamlet does it not, Hamlet denies it.
Who does it, then? His madness. If't be so,
Hamlet is of the faction that is wrong'd;
His madness is poor Hamlet's enemy.
Sir, in this audience,
Let my disclaiming from a purposed evil
Free me so far in your most generous thoughts,
That I have shot mine arrow o'er the house,
And hurt my brother.

Laer. I am satisfied in nature,
Whose motive, in this case, should stir me most
To my revenge; but in my terms of honour
I stand aloof, and will no reconcilement,
Till by some elder masters, of known honour,
I have a voice and precedent of peace,
To keep my name ungored. But till that time,
I do receive your offer'd love like love,
And will not wrong it.

Ham. I embrace it freely;
And will this brother's wager frankly play.
Give us the foils. Come on.

Laer. Come, one for me.

Ham. I'll be your foil, Laertes; in mine ignor-
ance
Your skill shall, like a star i' the darkest night,
Stick fiery off indeed.

Laer. You mock me, sir.

Ham. No, by this hand.

King. Give them the foils, young Osric. Cousin
Hamlet,
You know the wager?

Ham. Very well, my lord;
Your Grace hath laid the odds o' the weaker side.

King. I do not fear it; I have seen you both;
But since he is better'd, we have therefore odds.

Laer. This is too heavy, let me see another.

Ham. This likes me well. These foils have all a
length?

They prepare to play.

Osr. Ay, my good lord.

King. Set me the stoups of wine upon that table.
If Hamlet give the first or second hit,
Or quit in answer of the third exchange,
Let all the battlements their ordnance fire;
The King shall drink to Hamlet's better breath;
And in the cup an union shall he throw,
Richer than that which four successive kings
In Denmark's crown have worn. Give me the
cups;
And let the kettle to the trumpet speak,
The trumpet to the cannoneer without,
The cannons to the heavens, the heavens to earth,
"Now the King drinks to Hamlet." Come,
begin;
And you, the judges, bear a wary eye.

Ham. Come on, sir.

Laer. Come, my lord.

They play.

Ham. One.

Laer. No.

Ham. Judgement.

Osr. A hit, a very palpable hit.

Laer. Well; again.

King. Stay; give me drink. Hamlet, this pearl is thine;
Here's to thy health.
Trumpets sound, and cannon shot off within.
Give him the cup.
Ham. I'll play this bout first; set it by awhile.
Come. [*They play*.] Another hit; what say you?
Laer. A touch, a touch, I do confess.
King. Our son shall win.
Queen. He's fat, and scant of breath.
Here, Hamlet, take my napkin, rub thy brows.
The Queen carouses to thy fortune, Hamlet.
Ham. Good madam!
King. Gertrude, do not drink.
Queen. I will, my lord; I pray you, pardon me.
King. [*Aside*] It is the poison'd cup; it is too late.
Ham. I dare not drink yet, madam; by and by.
Queen. Come, let me wipe thy face.
Laer. My lord, I'll hit him now.
King. I do not think't.
Laer. [*Aside*] And yet 'tis almost 'gainst my conscience.
Ham. Come, for the third, Laertes; you but dally.
I pray you, pass with your best violence;
I am afeard you make a wanton of me.
Laer. Say you so? come on.
They play.
Osr. Nothing, neither way.
Laer. Have at you now!
LAERTES *wounds* HAMLET; *then, in scuffling, they change rapiers, and* HAMLET *wounds* LAERTES.
King. Part them; they are incensed.
Ham. Nay, come, again.
The QUEEN *falls*.
Osr. Look to the Queen there, ho!
Hor. They bleed on both sides. How is it, my lord?
Osr. How is't, Laertes?
Laer. Why, as a woodcock to mine own springe, Osric;
I am justly kill'd with mine own treachery.
Ham. How does the Queen?
King. She swounds to see them bleed.
Queen. No, no, the drink, the drink—O my dear Hamlet—
The drink, the drink! I am poison'd. [*Dies*.
Ham. O villainy! Ho! let the door be lock'd;
Treachery! Seek it out.
Laer. It is here, Hamlet. Hamlet, thou art slain.
No medicine in the world can do thee good;
In thee there is not half an hour of life;
The treacherous instrument is in thy hand,
Unbated and envenom'd. The foul practice
Hath turn'd itself on me; lo, here I lie,
Never to rise again. Thy mother's poison'd.
I can no more. The King, the King's to blame.
Ham. The point envenom'd too!
Then, venom, to thy work.
Stabs the KING.
All. Treason! treason!
King. O, yet defend me, friends; I am but hurt.
Ham. Here, thou incestuous, murderous, damned Dane,
Drink off this potion. Is thy union here?
Follow my mother. [KING *dies*.
Laer. He is justly served;
It is a poison temper'd by himself.
Exchange forgiveness with me, noble Hamlet.
Mine and my father's death come not upon thee,
Nor thine on me! [*Dies*.
Ham. Heaven make thee free of it! I follow thee.
I am dead, Horatio. Wretched Queen, adieu!
You that look pale and tremble at this chance,
That are but mutes or audiences to this act,
Had I but time—as this fell sergeant, Death,
Is strict in his arrest—O, I could tell you—
But let it be. Horatio, I am dead;
Thou livest; report me and my cause aright
To the unsatisfied.
Hor. Never believe it.
I am more an antique Roman than a Dane;
Here's yet some liquor left.
Ham. As thou'rt a man,
Give me the cup. Let go! By heaven, I'll have't.
O good Horatio, what a wounded name,
Things standing thus unknown, shall live behind me!
If thou didst ever hold me in thy heart,
Absent thee from felicity awhile,
And in this harsh world draw thy breath in pain,
To tell my story.
March afar off, and shot within.
What warlike noise is this?
Osr. Young Fortinbras, with conquest come from Poland,
To the ambassadors of England gives
This warlike volley.
Ham. O, I die, Horatio;
The potent poison quite o'er-crows my spirit.
I cannot live to hear the news from England,
But I do prophesy the election lights
On Fortinbras; he has my dying voice.
So tell him, with the occurrents, more and less,
Which have solicited. The rest is silence. [*Dies*.
Hor. Now cracks a noble heart. Good night, sweet prince;
And flights of angels sing thee to thy rest!
Why does the drum come hither?
March within.

Enter FORTINBRAS, *the* ENGLISH AMBASSADORS, *and others*.

Fort. Where is this sight?
Hor. What is it ye would see?
If aught of woe or wonder, cease your search.
Fort. This quarry cries on havoc. O proud Death,
What feast is toward in thine eternal cell,
That thou so many princes at a shot
So bloodily hast struck?
1st Amb. The sight is dismal;
And our affairs from England come too late.
The ears are senseless that should give us hearing,
To tell him his commandment is fulfill'd, 381
That Rosencrantz and Guildenstern are dead.
Where should we have our thanks?
Hor. Not from his mouth,
Had it the ability of life to thank you.
He never gave commandment for their death.
But since, so jump upon this bloody question,
You from the Polack wars, and you from England,
Are here arrived, give order that these bodies
High on a stage be placed to the view; 389
And let me speak to the yet unknowing world
How these things came about. So shall you hear
Of carnal, bloody, and unnatural acts,
Of accidental judgements, casual slaughters,
Of deaths put on by cunning and forced cause,
And, in this upshot, purposes mistook
Fall'n on the inventors' heads: all this can I
Truly deliver.
Fort. Let us haste to hear it,
And call the noblest to the audience.
For me, with sorrow I embrace my fortune.
I have some rights of memory in this kingdom,
Which now to claim my vantage doth invite me.
Hor. Of that I shall have also cause to speak,
And from his mouth whose voice will draw on more.
But let this same be presently perform'd,
Even while men's minds are wild; lest more mischance,
On plots and errors, happen.
Fort. Let four captains
Bear Hamlet, like a soldier, to the stage;
For he was likely, had he been put on,
To have proved most royally; and, for his passage,
The soldiers' music and the rites of war 410
Speak loudly for him.
Take up the bodies. Such a sight as this
Becomes the field, but here shows much amiss.
Go, bid the soldiers shoot.

[*A dead march. Exeunt, bearing off the dead bodies; after which a peal of ordnance is shot off*.

THE MERRY WIVES OF WINDSOR

DRAMATIS PERSONÆ

Sir John Falstaff
Fenton, *a gentleman*
Shallow, *a country justice*
Slender, *cousin to Shallow*
Ford, Page — *two gentlemen dwelling at Windsor*
William Page, *a boy, son to Page*
Sir Hugh Evans, *a Welsh parson*
Doctor Caius, *a French physician*
Host *of the Garter Inn*
Bardolph, Pistol, Nym — *sharpers attending on Falstaff*

Robin, *page to Falstaff*
Simple, *servant to Slender*
John Rugby, *servant to Doctor Caius*
Two Servants *to Ford*

Mistress Ford
Mistress Page
Anne Page, *her daughter*
Mistress Quickly, *servant to Doctor Caius*
Some Children, *as fairies*

Non-Speaking: *Servants to Page and Ford*

Scene: *Windsor, and the neighborhood*

ACT I

Scene i. *Windsor: before Page's house*

Enter JUSTICE SHALLOW, SLENDER, *and* SIR HUGH EVANS.

Shal. Sir Hugh, persuade me not; I will make a Star chamber matter of it. If he were twenty Sir John Falstaffs, he shall not abuse Robert Shallow, esquire.

Slen. In the county of Gloucester, justice of peace and "Coram."

Shal. Ay, cousin Slender, and "Custalorum."

Slen. Ay, and "Rato-lorum" too; and a gentleman born, master parson; who writes himself "Armigero," in any bill, warrant, quittance, or obligation, "Armigero."

Shal. Ay, that I do; and have done any time these three hundred years.

Slen. All his successors gone before him hath done't; and all his ancestors that come after him may. They may give the dozen white luces in their coat.

Shal. It is an old coat.

Evans. The dozen white louses do become an old coat well; it agrees well, passant; it is a famiiar beast to man, and signifies love.

Shal. The luce is the fresh fish; the salt fish is an old coat.

Slen. I may quarter, coz.

Shal. You may, by marrying.

Evans. It is marring indeed, if he quarter it.

Shal. Not a whit.

Evans. Yes, py'r lady; if he has a quarter of your coat, there is but three skirts for yourself, in my simple conjectures. But that is all one. If Sir John Falstaff have committed disparagements unto you, I am of the church, and will be glad to do my benevolence to make atonements and compremises between you.

Shal. The council shall hear it; it is a riot.

Evans. It is not meet the council hear a riot; there is no fear of Got in a riot. The council, look you, shall desire to hear the fear of Got, and not to hear a riot; take your vizaments in that.

Shal. Ha! o' my life, if I were young again, the sword should end it.

Evans. It is petter that friends is the sword, and end it; and there is also another device in my prain, which peradventure prings goot discretions with it: there is Anne Page, which is daughter to Master Thomas Page, which is pretty virginity.

Slen. Mistress Anne Page? She has brown hair, and speaks small like a woman.

Evans. It is that fery person for all the orld, as just as you will desire; and seven hundred pounds of moneys, and gold and silver, is her grandsire upon his death's-bed—Got deliver to a joyful resurrections!—give, when she is able to overtake seventeen years old. It were a goot motion if we leave our pribbles and prabbles, and desire a marriage between Master Abraham and Mistress Anne Page.

Slen. Did her grandsire leave her seven hundred pound?

Evans. Ay, and her father is make her a petter penny.

Slen. I know the young gentlewoman; she has good gifts.

Evans. Seven hundred pounds and possibilities is goot gifts.

Shal. Well, let us see honest Master Page. Is Falstaff there?

Evans. Shall I tell you a lie? I do despise a liar as I do despise one that is false, or as I despise one that is not true. The knight, Sir John, is there; and, I beseech you, be ruled by your well-willers. I will peat the door for Master Page. [*Knocks*] What, hoa! Got pless your house here!

Page. [*Within*] Who's there?

Enter PAGE.

Evans. Here is Got's plessing, and your friend, and Justice Shallow; and here young Master Slender, that peradventures shall tell you another tale, if matters grow to your likings.

Page. I am glad to see your worships well. I thank you for my venison, Master Shallow.

Shal. Master Page, I am glad to see you. Much good do it your good heart! I wished your venison better; it was ill killed. How doth good Mistress Page?—and I thank you always with my heart, la! with my heart.

Page. Sir, I thank you.

Shal. Sir, I thank you; by yea and no, I do.

Page. I am glad to see you, good Master Slender.

Slen. How does your fallow greyhound, sir? I heard say he was outrun on Cotsall.

Page. I could not be judged, sir.

Slen. You'll not confess, you'll not confess.

Shal. That he will not. 'Tis your fault, 'tis your fault; 'tis a good dog.

Page. A cur, sir.

Shal. Sir, he's a good dog, and a fair dog; can there be more said? he is good and fair. Is Sir John Falstaff here?

Page. Sir, he is within; and I would I could do a good office between you.

Evans. It is spoke as a Christians ought to speak.

Shal. He hath wronged me, Master Page.

Page. Sir, he doth in some sort confess it.

Shal. If it be confessed, it is not redressed. Is not that so, Master Page? He hath wronged me; indeed he hath; at a word, he hath, believe me: Robert Shallow, esquire, saith, he is wronged.

Page. Here comes Sir John.

Enter SIR JOHN FALSTAFF, BARDOLPH, NYM, *and* PISTOL.

Fal. Now, Master Shallow, you'll complain of me to the King?

Shal. Knight, you have beaten my men, killed my deer, and broke open my lodge.

Fal. But not kissed your keeper's daughter?

Shal. Tut, a pin! this shall be answered.

Fal. I will answer it straight; I have done all this.
That is now answered.

Shal. The council shall know this.

Fal. 'Twere better for you if it were known in counsel: you'll be laughed at.

Evans. *Pauca verba*, Sir John; goot worts.

Fal. Good worts! good cabbage. Slender, I broke your head; what matter have you against me?

Slen. Marry, sir, I have matter in my head against you; and against your cony-catching rascals, Bardolph, Nym, and Pistol.

Bard. You Banbury cheese!

Slen. Ay, it is no matter.

Pist. How now, Mephostophilus!

Slen. Ay, it is no matter.

Nym. Slice, I say! *pauca, pauca*. Slice! that's my humour.

Slen. Where's Simple, my man? Can you tell, cousin?

Evans. Peace, I pray you. Now let us understand. There is three umpires in this matter, as I understand; that is, Master Page, *fidelicet* Master Page; and there is myself, *fidelicet* myself; and the three party is, lastly and finally, mine host of the Garter.

Page. We three, to hear it and end it between them.

Evans. Fery goot. I will make a prief of it in my note-book; and we will afterwards ork upon the cause with as great discreetly as we can.

Fal. Pistol!

Pist. He hears with ears.

Evans. The tevil and his tam! what phrase is this, "He hears with ear"? why, it is affectations.

Fal. Pistol, did you pick Master Slender's purse?

Slen. Ay, by these gloves, did he, or I would I might never come in mine own great chamber again else, of seven groats in mill-sixpences, and two Edward shovel-boards, that cost me two shilling and two pence a-piece of Yead Miller, by these gloves.

Fal. Is this true, Pistol?

Evans. No; it is false, if it is a pick-purse.

Pist. Ha, thou mountain-foreigner! Sir John and master mine,
I combat challenge of this latten bilbo.
Word of denial in thy *labras* here!
Word of denial! Froth and scum, thou liest!

Slen. By these gloves, then, 'twas he.

Nym. Be avised, sir, and pass good humours. I will say "marry trap" with you, if you run the nuthook's humour on me; that is the very note of it.

Slen. By this hat, then, he in the red face had it; for though I cannot remember what I did when you made me drunk, yet I am not altogether an ass.

Fal. What say you, Scarlet and John?

Bard. Why, sir, for my part, I say the gentleman had drunk himself out of his five sentences.

Evans. It is his five senses. Fie, what the ignorance is!

Bard. And being fap, sir, was, as they say, cashiered; and so conclusions passed the careires.

Slen. Ay, you spake in Latin then too; but 'tis no matter; I'll ne'er be drunk whilst I live again, but in honest, civil, godly company, for this trick. If I be drunk, I'll be drunk with those that have the fear of God, and not with drunken knaves.

Evans. So Got udge me, that is a virtuous mind.

Fal. You hear all these matters denied, gentlemen; you hear it.

Enter ANNE PAGE, *with wine;* MISTRESS FORD *and* MISTRESS PAGE, *following*.

Page. Nay, daughter, carry the wine in; we'll drink within. [*Exit* ANNE PAGE.

Slen. O heaven! this is Mistress Anne Page.

Page. How now, Mistress Ford!

Fal. Mistress Ford, by my troth, you are very well met. By your leave, good mistress.
Kisses her.

Page. Wife, bid these gentlemen welcome. Come, we have a hot venison pasty to dinner. Come, gentlemen, I hope we shall drink down all unkindness.
[*Exeunt all except* SHALLOW, SLENDER, *and* EVANS.

Slen. I had rather than forty shillings I had my Book of Songs and Sonnets here.

Enter SIMPLE.

How now, Simple! where have you been? I must wait on myself, must I? You have not the Book of Riddles about you, have you?

Sim. Book of Riddles! why, did you not lend it to Alice Shortcake upon All-hallowmas last, a fortnight afore Michaelmas?

Shal. Come, coz; come, coz; we stay for you. A word with you, coz; marry, this, coz: there is, as 'twere, a tender, a kind of tender, made afar off by Sir Hugh here. Do you understand me?

Slen. Ay, sir, you shall find me reasonable; if it be so, I shall do that that is reason.

Shal. Nay, but understand me.

Slen. So I do, sir.

Evans. Give ear to his motions, Master Slender. I will description the matter to you, if you be capacity of it.

Slen. Nay, I will do as my cousin Shallow says. I pray you, pardon me; he's a justice of peace in his country, simple though I stand here.

Evans. But that is not the question. The question is concerning your marriage.

Shal. Ay, there's the point, sir.

Evans. Marry, is it; the very point of it; to Mistress Anne Page.

Slen. Why, if it be so, I will marry her upon any reasonable demands.

Evans. But can you affection the 'oman? Let us command to know that of your mouth or of your lips; for divers philosophers hold that the lips is parcel of the mouth. Therefore, precisely, can you carry your good will to the maid?

Shal. Cousin Abraham Slender, can you love her?

Slen. I hope, sir, I will do as it shall become one that would do reason.

Evans. Nay, Got's lords and his ladies! you must speak possitable, if you can carry her your desires towards her.

Shal. That you must. Will you, upon good dowry, marry her?

Slen. I will do a greater thing than that, upon your request, cousin, in any reason.

Shal. Nay, conceive me, conceive me, sweet coz; what I do is to pleasure you, coz. Can you love the maid?

Slen. I will marry her, sir, at your request; but if there be no great love in the beginning, yet heaven may decrease it upon better acquaintance, when we are married and have more occasion to know one another. I hope, upon familiarity will grow more contempt. But if you say, "Marry her," I will marry her; that I am freely dissolved, and dissolutely.

Evans. It is a fery discretion answer; save the fall is in the ort "dissolutely": the ort is, according to our meaning, "resolutely." His meaning is good.

Shal. Ay, I think my cousin meant well.

Slen. Ay, or else I would I might be hanged, la!

Shal. Here comes fair Mistress Anne.

Re-enter ANNE PAGE.

Would I were young for your sake, Mistress Anne!

Anne. The dinner is on the table; my father desires your worships' company.

Shal. I will wait on him, fair Mistress Anne.

Evans. Od's plessed will! I will not be absence at the grace. [*Exeunt* SHALLOW *and* EVANS.

Anne. Will't please your worship to come in, sir?

Slen. No, I thank you, forsooth, heartily; I am very well.

Anne. The dinner attends you, sir.

Slen. I am not a-hungry, I thank you, forsooth. Go, sirrah, for all you are my man, go wait upon my cousin Shallow. [*Exit* SIMPLE.] A justice of peace sometime may be beholding to his friend for a man. I keep but three men and a boy yet, till my mother be dead. But what though? Yet I live like a poor gentleman born.

Anne. I may not go in without your worship. They will not sit till you come.

Slen. I' faith, I'll eat nothing; I thank you as much as though I did.

Anne. I pray you, sir, walk in.

Slen. I had rather walk here, I thank you. I bruised my shin th' other day with playing at sword and dagger with a master of fence; three veneys for a dish of stewed prunes; and, by my troth, I cannot abide the smell of hot meat since. Why do your dogs bark so? be there bears i' the town?

Anne. I think there are, sir; I heard them talked of.

Slen. I love the sport well; but I shall as soon quarrel at it as any man in England. You are afraid, if you see the bear loose, are you not?

Anne. Ay, indeed, sir.

Slen. That's meat and drink to me, now. I have seen Sackerson loose twenty times, and have taken him by the chain; but, I warrant you, the women have so cried and shrieked at it, that it passed. But women, indeed, cannot abide 'em; they are very ill-favoured rough things.

Re-enter PAGE.

Page. Come, gentle Master Slender, come; we stay for you.

Slen. I'll eat nothing, I thank you, sir.

Page. By cock and pie, you shall not choose, sir! come, come.

Slen. Nay, pray you, lead the way.

Page. Come on, sir.

Slen. Mistress Anne, yourself shall go first.

Anne. Not I, sir; pray you, keep on.

Slen. Truly, I will not go first; truly, la! I will not do you that wrong.

Anne. I pray you, sir.

Slen. I'll rather be unmannerly than troublesome. You do yourself wrong, indeed, la! [*Exeunt*.

SCENE II. *The same*

Enter SIR HUGH EVANS *and* SIMPLE.

Evans. Go your ways, and ask of Doctor Caius' house which is the way; and there dwells one Mistress Quickly, which is in the manner of his nurse, or his dry nurse, or his cook, or his laundry, his washer, and his wringer.

Sim. Well, sir.

Evans. Nay, it is petter yet. Give her this letter; for it is a 'oman that altogether's acquaintance with Mistress Anne Page; and the letter is, to desire and require her to solicit your master's desires to Mistress Anne Page. I pray you, be gone. I will make an end of my dinner; there's pippins and cheese to come. [*Exeunt*.

SCENE III. *A room in the Garter Inn*

Enter FALSTAFF, HOST, BARDOLPH, NYM, PISTOL, *and* ROBIN.

Fal. Mine host of the Garter!

Host. What says my bully-rook? speak scholarly and wisely.

Fal. Truly, mine host, I must turn away some of my followers.

Host. Discard, bully Hercules; cashier. Let them wag; trot, trot.

Fal. I sit at ten pounds a week.

Host. Thou'rt an emperor, Cæsar, Keisar, and Pheezar. I will entertain Bardolph; he shall draw, he shall tap. Said I well, bully Hector?

Fal. Do so, good mine host.

Host. I have spoke; let him follow. [*To* BARDOLPH.] Let me see thee froth and lime. I am at a word; follow. [*Exit*.

Fal. Bardolph, follow him. A tapster is a good trade; an old cloak makes a new jerkin; a withered serving-man a fresh tapster. Go; adieu.

Bard. It is a life that I have desired. I will thrive.

Pist. O base Hungarian wight! wilt thou the spigot wield? [*Exit* BARDOLPH.

Nym. He was gotten in drink. Is not the humour conceited?

Fal. I am glad I am so acquit of this tinderbox; his thefts were too open; his filching was like an unskilful singer; he kept not time.

Nym. The good humour is to steal at a minute's rest.

Pist. "Convey," the wise it call. "Steal!" foh! a fico for the phrase!

Fal. Well, sirs, I am almost out at heels.

Pist. Why, then, let kibes ensue.

Fal. There is no remedy; I must cony-catch; I must shift.

Pist. Young ravens must have food.

Fal. Which of you know Ford of this town?

Pist. I ken the wight. He is of substance good.

Fal. My honest lads, I will tell you what I am about.

Pist. Two yards, and more.

Fal. No quips now, Pistol! Indeed, I am in the waist two yards about; but I am now about no waste; I am about thrift. Briefly, I do mean to make love to Ford's wife. I spy entertainment in her; she discourses, she carves, she gives the leer of invitation. I can construe the action of her familiar style; and the hardest voice of her behaviour, to be Englished rightly, is, "I am Sir John Falstaff's."

Pist. He hath studied her will, and translated her will, out of honesty into English.

Nym. The anchor is deep: will that humour pass?

Fal. Now, the report goes she has all the rule of her husband's purse. He hath a legion of angels.

Pist. As many devils entertain; and "To her, boy," say I.

Nym. The humour rises; it is good. Humour me the angels.

Fal. I have writ me here a letter to her; and here another to Page's wife, who even now gave me good eyes too, examined my parts with most judicious œillades; sometimes the beam of her view gilded my foot, sometimes my portly belly.

Pist. Then did the sun on dunghill shine.

Nym. I thank thee for that humour.

Fal. O, she did so course o'er my exteriors with such a greedy intention, that the appetite of her eye did seem to scorch me up like a burning-glass! Here's another letter to her. She bears the purse too; she is a region in Guiana, all gold and bounty. I will be cheater to them both, and they shall be exchequers to me; they shall be my East and West Indies, and I will trade to them both. Go bear thou this letter to Mistress Page; and thou this to Mistress Ford. We will thrive, lads, we will thrive.

Pist. Shall I Sir Pandarus of Troy become,
And by my side wear steel? then, Lucifer take all!

Nym. I will run no base humour. Here, take the humour-letter; I will keep the haviour of reputation.

Fal. [*To* ROBIN] Hold, sirrah, bear you these letters tightly;
Sail like my pinnace to these golden shores.
Rogues, hence, avaunt! vanish like hailstones go;
Trudge, plod away o' the hoof; seek shelter, pack!
Falstaff will learn the humour of the age,
French thrift, you rogues; myself and skirted page. [*Exeunt* FALSTAFF *and* ROBIN.

Pist. Let vultures gripe thy guts! for gourd and fullam holds,
And high and low beguiles the rich and poor.
Tester I'll have in pouch when thou shalt lack,
Base Phrygian Turk!

Nym. I have operations which be humours of revenge.

Pist. Wilt thou revenge?

Nym. By welkin and her star!

Pist. With wit or steel?

Nym. With both the humours, I.
I will discuss the humour of this love to Page.

Pist. And I to Ford shall eke unfold
How Falstaff, varlet vile,
His dove will prove, his gold will hold,
And his soft couch defile.

Nym. My humour shall not cool. I will incense Page to deal with poison; I will possess him with yellowness, for the revolt of mine is dangerous. That is my true humour.

Pist. Thou art the Mars of malecontents. I second thee; troop on. [*Exeunt*.

SCENE IV. *A room in Doctor Caius's house.*

Enter MISTRESS QUICKLY, SIMPLE, *and* RUGBY.

Quick. What, John Rugby! I pray thee, go to the casement, and see if you can see my master, Master Doctor Caius, coming. If he do, i' faith, and find any body in the house, here will be an old abusing of God's patience and the King's English.

Rug. I'll go watch.

Quick. Go; and we'll have a posset for't soon at night, in faith, at the latter end of a sea-coal fire. [*Exit* RUGBY.] An honest, willing, kind fellow, as ever servant shall come in house withal, and, I warrant you, no tell-tale nor no breed-bate: his worst fault is, that he is given to prayer; he is something peevish that way; but nobody but has his fault; but let that pass. Peter Simple, you say your name is?

Sim. Ay, for fault of a better.

Quick. And Master Slender's your master?

Sim. Ay, forsooth.

Quick. Does he not wear a great round beard, like a glover's paring-knife?

Sim. No, forsooth; he hath but a little wee face, with a little yellow beard, a Cain-coloured beard.

Quick. A softly-sprighted man, is he not?

Sim. Ay, forsooth; but he is as tall a man of his

hands as any is between this and his head; he hath fought with a warrener.

Quick. How say you? O, I should remember him. Does he not hold up his head, as it were, and strut in his gait?

Sim. Yes, indeed, does he.

Quick. Well, heaven send Anne Page no worse fortune! Tell Master Parson Evans I will do what I can for your master. Anne is a good girl, and I wish—

Re-enter RUGBY.

Rug. Out, alas! here comes my master.

Quick. We shall all be shent. Run in here, good young man; go into this closet. He will not stay long. [*Shuts* SIMPLE *in the closet*.] What, John Rugby! John! what, John, I say! Go, John, go inquire for my master; I doubt he be not well, that he comes not home.

[*Singing*] And down, down, adown-a, &c.

Enter DOCTOR CAIUS.

Caius. Vat is you sing? I do not like des toys. Pray you, go and vetch me in my closet *un boitier vert*, a box, a green-a box: do intend vat I speak? a green-a box.

Quick. Ay, forsooth; I'll fetch it you. [*Aside*] I am glad he went not in himself: if he had found the young man, he would have been horn-mad.

Caius. *Fe, fe, fe, fe! ma foi, il fait fort chaud. Je m'en vais à la cour—la grande affaire.*

Quick. Is it this, sir?

Caius. *Oui; mette le au mon pocket: dépêche*, quickly. Vere is dat knave Rugby?

Quick. What, John Rugby! John!

Rug. Here, sir!

Caius. You are John Rugby, and you are Jack Rugby. Come, take-a your rapier, and come after my heel to the court.

Rug. 'Tis ready, sir, here in the porch.

Caius. By my trot, I tarry too long. Od's me! *Qu' ai-j'oublie!* dere is some simples in my closet, dat I vill not for the varld I shall leave behind.

Quick. Ay me, he'll find the young man there, and be mad!

Caius. *O diable, diable!* vat is in my closet? Villain! larron! [*Pulling* SIMPLE *out*.] Rugby, my rapier!

Quick. Good master, be content.

Caius. Wherefore shall I be content-a?

Quick. The young man is an honest man.

Caius. What shall de honest man do in my closet? dere is no honest man dat shall come in my closet.

Quick. I beseech you, be not so phlegmatic. Hear the truth of it: he came of an errand to me from Parson Hugh.

Caius. Vell.

Sim. Ay, forsooth; to desire her to—

Quick. Peace, I pray you.

Caius. Peace-a your tongue. Speak-a your tale.

Sim. To desire this honest gentlewoman, your maid, to speak a good word to Mistress Anne Page for my master in the way of marriage.

Quick. This is all, indeed, la! but I'll ne'er put my finger in the fire, and need not.

Caius. Sir Hugh send-a you? Rugby, *baillez* me some paper. Tarry you a little-a while.

Writes.

Quick. [*Aside to* SIMPLE] I am glad he is so quiet. If he had been throughly moved, you should have heard him so loud and so melancholy. But notwithstanding, man, I'll do you your master what good I can; and the very yea and the no is, the French doctor, my master—I may call him my master, look you, for I keep his house; and I wash, wring, brew, bake, scour, dress meat and drink, make the beds, and do all myself—

Sim. [*Aside to* QUICKLY] 'Tis a great charge to come under one body's hand.

Quick. [*Aside to* SIMPLE] Are you avised o' that? you shall find it a great charge; and to be up early and down late; but notwithstanding—to tell you in your ear; I would have no words of it—my master himself is in love with Mistress Anne Page; but notwithstanding that, I know Anne's mind—that's neither here nor there.

Caius. You jack'nape, give-a this letter to Sir Hugh; by gar, it is a shallenge: I will cut his troat in de park; and I will teach a scurvy jack-a-nape priest to meddle or make. You may be gone; it is not good you tarry here. By gar, I will cut all his two stones; by gar, he shall not have a stone to throw at his dog. [*Exit* SIMPLE.

Quick. Alas, he speaks but for his friend.

Caius. It is no matter-a ver dat. Do not you tell-a me dat I shall have Anne Page for myself? By gar, I vill kill de Jack priest; and I have appointed mine host of de Jarteer to measure our weapon. By gar, I will myself have Anne Page.

Quick. Sir, the maid loves you, and all shall be well. We must give folks leave to prate; what, the good-jer!

Caius. Rugby, come to the court with me. By gar, if I have not Anne Page, I shall turn your head out of my door. Follow my heels Rugby.

[*Exeunt* CAIUS *and* RUGBY.

Quick. You shall have An fool's-head of your own. No, I know Anne's mind for that. Never a woman in Windsor knows more of Anne's mind than I do; nor can do more than I do with her, I thank heaven.

Fent. [*Within*] Who's within there? ho!

Quick. Who's there, I trow! Come near the house, I pray you.

Enter FENTON.

Fent. How now, good woman! how dost thou?

Quick. The better that it pleases your good worship to ask.

Fent. What news? how does pretty Mistress Anne?

Quick. In truth, sir, and she is pretty, and honest, and gentle; and one that is your friend, I can tell you that by the way; I praise heaven for it.

Fent. Shall I do any good, thinkest thou? shall I not lose my suit?

Quick. Troth, sir, all is in His hands above. But notwithstanding, Master Fenton. I'll be sworn on a book, she loves you. Have not your worship a wart above your eye?

Fent. Yes, marry, have I; what of that?

Quick. Well, thereby hangs a tale. Good faith, it is such another Nan; but, I detest, an honest maid as ever broke bread. We had an hour's talk of that wart. I shall never laugh but in that maid's company! But indeed she is given too much to allicholy and musing; but for you—well, go to.

Fent. Well, I shall see her to-day. Hold, there's money for thee; let me have thy voice in my behalf. If thou seest her before me, commend me.

Quick. Will I? i' faith, that we will; and I will tell your worship more of the wart the next time we have confidence; and of other wooers.

Fent. Well, farewell; I am in great haste now.

Quick. Farewell to your worship. [*Exit* FENTON.] Truly, an honest gentleman; but Anne loves him not; for I know Anne's mind as well as another does. Out upon't! what have I forgot? [*Exit.*

ACT II

SCENE I. *Before Page's house*

Enter MISTRESS PAGE, *with a letter.*

Mrs. Page. What, have I 'scaped love-letters in the holiday-time of my beauty, and am I now a subject for them? Let me see. [*Reads.*] "Ask me no reason why I love you; for though Love use Reason for his physician, he admits him not for his counsellor. You are not young, no more am I; go to then, there's sympathy. You are merry, so am I; ha, ha! then there's more sympathy. You love sack, and so do I; would you desire better sympathy? Let it suffice thee, Mistress Page—at the least, if the love of soldier can suffice—that I love thee. I will not say, pity me; 'tis not a soldier-like phrase: but I say, love me. By me,

Thine own true knight,
By day or night,
Or any kind of light,
With all his might
For thee to fight, John Falstaff"

What a Herod of Jewry is this! O wicked, wicked world! One that is well-nigh worn to pieces with age to show himself a young gallant! What an unweighed behaviour hath this Flemish drunkard picked—with the devil's name!—out of my conversation, that he dares in this manner assay me? Why, he hath not been thrice in my company! What should I say to him? I was then frugal of my mirth. Heaven forgive me! Why, I'll exhibit a bill in the parliament for the putting down of men. How shall I be revenged on him? for revenged I will be, as sure as his guts are made of puddings.

Enter MISTRESS FORD.

Mrs. Ford. Mistress Page! trust me, I was going to your house.

Mrs. Page. And, trust me, I was coming to you. You look very ill.

Mrs. Ford. Nay, I'll ne'er believe that; I have to show to the contrary.

Mrs. Page. Faith, but you do, in my mind.

Mrs. Ford. Well, I do then; yet I say I could show you to the contrary. O Mistress Page, give me some counsel!

Mrs. Page. What's the matter, woman?

Mrs. Ford. O woman, if it were not for one trifling respect, I could come to such honour!

Mrs. Page. Hang the trifle, woman! take the honour. What is it? dispense with trifles; what is it?

Mrs. Ford. If I would but go to hell for an eternal moment or so, I could be knighted.

Mrs. Page. What? thou liest! Sir Alice Ford! These knights will hack; and so thou shouldst not alter the article of thy gentry.

Mrs. Ford. We burn daylight. Here, read, read; perceive how I might be knighted. I shall think the worse of fat men, as long as I have an eye to make difference of men's liking; and yet he would not swear; praised women's modesty; and gave such orderly and well-behaved reproof to all uncomeliness, that I would have sworn his disposition would have gone to the truth of his words; but they do no more adhere and keep place together than the Hundredth Psalm to the tune of "Green Sleeves." What tempest, I trow, threw this whale, with so many tuns of oil in his belly, ashore at Windsor? How shall I be revenged on him? I think the best way were to entertain him with hope, till the wicked fire of lust have melted him in his own grease. Did you ever hear the like?

Mrs. Page. Letter for letter, but that the name of Page and Ford differs! To thy great comfort in this mystery of ill opinions, here's the twin-brother of thy letter: but let thine inherit first; for, I protest, mine never shall. I warrant he hath a thousand of these letters, writ with blank space for different names—sure, more—and these are of the second edition. He will print them, out of doubt; for he cares not what he puts into the press, when he would put us two. I had rather be a giantess, and lie under Mount Pelion. Well, I will find you twenty lascivious turtles ere one chaste man.

Mrs. Ford. Why, this is the very same; the very hand, the very words. What doth he think of us?

Mrs. Page. Nay, I know not. It makes me almost ready to wrangle with mine own honesty. I'll entertain myself like one that I am not acquainted withal; for, sure, unless he know some strain in me that I know not myself, he would never have boarded me in this fury.

Mrs. Ford. "Boarding," call you it? I'll be sure to keep him above deck.

Mrs. Page. So will I. If he come under my hatches, I'll never to sea again. Let's be revenged on him. Let's appoint him a meeting, give him a show of comfort in his suit and lead him on with a fine-baited delay, till he hath pawned his horse to mine host of the Garter.

Mrs. Ford. Nay, I will consent to act any villainy against him, that may not sully the chariness of our honesty. O, that my husband saw this letter! it would give eternal food to his jealousy.

Mrs. Page. Why, look where he comes; and my good man too. He's as far from jealousy as I am from giving him cause; and that I hope is an unmeasurable distance.

Mrs. Ford. You are the happier woman.

Mrs. Page. Let's consult together against this greasy knight. Come hither. [*They retire.*

Enter FORD *with* PISTOL, *and* PAGE *with* NYM.

Ford. Well, I hope it be not so.

Pist. Hope is a curtal dog in some affairs.
Sir John affects thy wife.

Ford. Why, sir, my wife is not young.

Pist. He wooes both high and low, both rich and poor,
Both young and old, one with another, Ford;
He loves the gallimaufry. Ford, perpend.

Ford. Love my wife!

Pist. With liver burning hot. Prevent, or go thou,
Like Sir Actæon he, with Ringwood at thy heels,
O, odious is the name!

Ford. What name, sir?

Pist. The horn, I say. Farewell.
Take heed, have open eye, for thieves do foot by night.
Take heed, ere summer comes or cuckoo-birds do sing.
Away, Sir Corporal Nym!
Believe it, Page; he speaks sense. [*Exit.*

Ford. [*Aside*] I will be patient; I will find out this.

Nym. [*To* PAGE] And this is true; I like not the humour of lying. He hath wronged me in some humours. I should have borne the humoured letter to her; but I have a sword and it shall bite upon my necessity. He loves your wife; there's the short and the long. My name is Corporal Nym; I speak and I avouch; 'tis true; my name is Nym and Falstaff loves your wife. Adieu. I love not the humour of bread and cheese, and there's the humour of it. Adieu. [*Exit.*

Page. "The humour of it," quoth a'! Here's a fellow frights English out of his wits.

Ford. I will seek out Falstaff.

Page. I never heard such a drawling, affecting rogue.

Ford. If I do find it! Well.

Page. I will not believe such a Cataian, though the priest o' the town commended him for a true man.

Ford. 'Twas a good sensible fellow. Well.

Page. How how, Meg!

MISTRESS PAGE *and* MISTRESS FORD *come forward.*

Mrs. Page. Whither go you, George? Hark you.

Mrs. Ford. How now, sweet Frank! why art thou melancholy?

Ford. I melancholy! I am not melancholy. Get you home, go.

Mrs. Ford. Faith, thou hast some crotchets in thy head. Now, will you go, Mistress Page?

Mrs. Page. Have with you. You'll come to dinner, George. [*Aside to* MISTRESS FORD] Look who comes yonder. She shall be our messenger to this paltry knight.

Mrs. Ford. [*Aside* to MISTRESS PAGE] Trust me, I thought on her: she'll fit it.

Enter MISTRESS QUICKLY.

Mrs. Page. You are come to see my daughter Anne?

Quick. Ay, forsooth; and, I pray, how does good Mistress Anne?

Mrs. Page. Go in with us and see. We have an hour's talk with you.

[*Exeunt* MISTRESS PAGE, MISTRESS FORD, *and* MISTRESS QUICKLY.

Page. How now, Master Ford!

Ford. You heard what this knave told me, did you not?

Page. Yes; and you heard what the other told me?

Ford. Do you think there is truth in them?

Page. Hang 'em, slaves! I do not think the knight would offer it; but these that accuse him in his intent towards our wives are a yoke of his discarded men; very rogues, now they be out of service.

Ford. Were they his men?

Page. Marry, were they.

Ford. I like it never the better for that. Does he lie at the Garter?

Page. Ay, marry, does he. If he should intend this voyage towards my wife, I would turn her loose to him; and what he gets more of her than sharp words, let it lie on my head.

Ford. I do not misdoubt my wife; but I would be loath to turn them together. A man may be too confident. I would have nothing lie on my head. I cannot be thus satisfied.

Page. Look where my ranting host of the Garter comes. There is either liquor in his pate or money in his purse when he looks so merrily.

Enter HOST.

How now, mine host!

Host. How now, bully-rook! thou'rt a gentleman. Cavaleiro-justice, I say!

Enter Shallow.

Shal. I follow, mine host, I follow. Good even and twenty, good Master Page! Master Page, will you go with us? we have sport in hand.

Host. Tell him, cavaleiro-justice; tell him, bully-rook.

Shal. Sir, there is a fray to be fought between Sir Hugh the Welsh priest and Caius the French doctor.

Ford. Good mine host o' the Garter, a word with you. [*Drawing him aside.*]

Host. What sayest thou, my bully-rook?

Shal. [*To* PAGE] Will you go with us to behold it? My merry host hath had the measuring of their weapons; and, I think, hath appointed them contrary places; for, believe me, I hear the parson is no jester. Hark, I will tell you what our sport shall be. [*They converse apart.*]

Host. Hast thou no suit against my knight, my guest-cavaleire?

Ford. None, I protest; but I'll give you a pottle of burnt sack to give me recourse to him and tell him my name is Brook; only for a jest.

Host. My hand, bully; thou shalt have egress and regress—said I well?—and thy name shall be Brook. It is a merry knight. Will you go, An-heires?

Shal. Have with you, mine host.

Page. I have heard the Frenchman hath good skill in his rapier.

Shal. Tut, sir, I could have told you more. In these times you stand on distance, your passes, stoccadoes, and I know not what. 'Tis the heart, Master Page; 'tis here, 'tis here. I have seen the time, with my long sword I would have made you four tall fellows skip like rats.

Host. Here, boys, here, here! shall we wag?

Page. Have with you. I had rather hear them scold than fight.

[*Exeunt* HOST, SHALLOW, *and* PAGE.

Ford. Though Page be a secure fool, and stands so firmly on his wife's frailty, yet I cannot put off my opinion so easily. She was in his company at Page's house; and what they made there, I know not. Well, I will look further into 't; and I have a disguise to sound Falstaff. If I find her honest, I lose not my labour; if she be otherwise, 'tis labour well bestowed. [*Exit.*

SCENE II. *A room in the Garter Inn*

Enter FALSTAFF *and* PISTOL.

Fal. I will not lend thee a penny.

Pist. Why, then the world's mine oyster,
Which I with sword will open.

Fal. Not a penny. I have been content, sir, you should lay my countenance to pawn. I have grated upon my good friends for three reprieves for you and your coach-fellow Nym; or else you had looked through the grate, like a geminy of baboons. I am damned in hell for swearing to gentlemen my friends, you were good soldiers and tall fellows; and when Mistress Bridget lost the handle of her fan, I took't upon mine honour thou hadst it not.

Pist. Didst not thou share? hadst thou not fifteen pence?

Fal. Reason, you rogue, reason: thinkest thou I'll endanger my soul gratis? At a word, hang no more about me, I am no gibbet for you. Go. A short knife and a throng! To your manor of Pickt-hatch! Go. You'll not bear a letter for me, you rogue! you stand upon your honour. Why thou unconfinable baseness, it is as much as I can do to keep the terms of my honour precise. I, I, I myself sometimes, leaving the fear of God on the left hand and hiding mine honour in my necessity, am fain to shuffle, to hedge and to lurch; and yet you, rogue, will ensconce your rags, your cat-a-mountain looks, your red-lattice phrases, and your bold-beating oaths, under the shelter of your honour! You will not do it, you!

Pist. I do relent. What would thou more of man?

Enter ROBIN.

Rob. Sir, here's a woman would speak with you.

Fal. Let her approach.

Enter MISTRESS QUICKLY.

Quick. Give your worship good morrow.

Fal. Good morrow, good wife.

Quick. Not so, an't please your worship.

Fal. Good maid, then.

Quick. I'll be sworn,
As my mother was, the first hour I was born.

Fal. I do believe the swearer. What with me?

Quick. Shall I vouchsafe your worship a word or two?

Fal. Two thousand, fair woman; and I'll vouchsafe thee the hearing.

Quick. There is one Mistress Ford, sir—I pray, come a little nearer this ways—I myself dwell with Master Doctor Caius—

Fal. Well, on. Mistress Ford, you say—

Quick. Your worship says very true. I pray your worship, come a little nearer this ways.

Fal. I warrant thee, nobody hears; mine own people, mine own people.

Quick. Are they so? God bless them and make them His servants!

Fal. Well, Mistress Ford; what of her?

Quick. Why, sir, she's a good creature. Lord, Lord! your worship's a wanton! Well, heaven forgive you and all of us, I pray!

Fal. Mistress Ford; come, Mistress Ford—

Quick. Marry, this is the short and the long of it; you have brought her into such a canaries as 'tis wonderful. The best courtier of them all, when the court lay at Windsor, could never have brought her to such a canary. Yet there has been knights, and lords, and gentlemen, with their coaches, I warrant you, coach after coach, letter after letter, gift after gift; smelling so sweetly, all musk, and so rushling, I warrant you, in silk and gold; and in such alligant terms; and in such wine and sugar of the best and the fairest, that would have won any woman's heart; and, I warrant you, they could never get an eye-wink of her. I had myself twenty angels given me this morning; but I defy all angels, in any such sort, as they say, but in the way of honesty; and, I warrant you, they could never get her so much as sip on a cup with the proudest of them all; and yet there has been earls, nay, which is more, pensioners; but, I warrant you, all is one with her.

Fal. But what says she to me? be brief, my good she-Mercury.

Quick. Marry, she hath received your letter, for the which she thanks you a thousand times; and she gives you to notify that her husband will be absence from his house between ten and eleven.

Fal. Ten and eleven?

Quick. Ay, forsooth; and then you may come and see the picture, she says, that you wot of. Master Ford, her husband, will be from home. Alas! the sweet woman leads an ill life with him. He's a very jealousy man. She leads a very frampold life with him, good heart.

Fal. Ten and eleven. Woman, commend me to her; I will not fail her.

Quick. Why, you say well. But I have another messenger to your worship. Mistress Page hath her hearty commendations to you too; and let me tell you in your ear, she's as fartuous a civil modest wife, and one, I tell you, that will not miss you morning nor evening prayer, as any is in Windsor, whoe'er be the other; and she bade me tell your worship that her husband is seldom from home; but she hopes there will come a time. I never knew a woman so dote upon a man. Surely I think you have charms, la; yes, in truth.

Fal. Not I, I assure thee. Setting the attraction of my good parts aside I have no other charms.

Quick. Blessing on your heart for't!

Fal. But, I pray thee, tell me this: has Ford's wife and Page's wife acquainted each other how they love me?

Quick. That were a jest indeed! they have not so little grace, I hope. That were a trick indeed! But Mistress Page would desire you to send her your little page, of all loves. Her husband has a marvellous infection to the little page; and truly Master Page is an honest man. Never a wife in Windsor leads a better life than she does: do what she will, say what she will, take all, pay all, go to bed when she list, rise when she list, all is as she will; and truly she deserves it; for if there be a kind woman in Windsor, she is one. You must send her your page; no remedy.

Fal. Why, I will.

Quick. Nay, but do so, then; and, look you, he may come and go between you both; and in any case have a nay-word, that you may know one another's mind, and the boy never need to understand any thing; for 'tis not good that children should know any wickedness. Old folks, you know, have discretion, as they say, and know the world.

Fal. Fare thee well. Commend me to them both. There's my purse; I am yet thy debtor. Boy, go along with this woman. [*Exeunt* MISTRESS QUICKLY *and* ROBIN.] This news distracts me!

Pist. This punk is one of Cupid's carriers.
Clap on more sails; pursue; up with your fights;
Give fire; she is my prize, or ocean whelm them all! [*Exit.*

Fal. Sayest thou so, old Jack? go thy ways; I'll make more of thy old body than I have done. Will they yet look after thee? Wilt thou, after the expense of so much money, be now a gainer? Good body, I thank thee. Let them say 'tis grossly done; so it be fairly done, no matter.

Enter BARDOLPH.

Bard. Sir John, there's one Master Brook below would fain speak with you, and be acquainted with you; and hath sent your worship a morning's draught of sack.

Fal. Brook is his name?

Bard. Ay, sir.

Fal. Call him in. [*Exit* BARDOLPH.] Such Brooks are welcome to me, that o'erflow such liquor. Ah, ha! Mistress Ford and Mistress Page, have I encompassed you? go to; via!

Re-enter BARDOLPH, *with* FORD *disguised.*

Ford. Bless you, sir!

Fal. And you, sir! Would you speak with me?

Ford. I make bold to press with so little preparation upon you.

Fal. You're welcome. What's your will? Give us leave, drawer. [*Exit* BARDOLPH.

Ford. Sir, I am a gentleman that have spent much; my name is Brook.

Fal. Good Master Brook, I desire more acquaintance of you.

Ford. Good Sir John, I sue for yours, not to charge you; for I must let you understand I think myself in better plight for a lender than you are, the which hath something emboldened me to this unseasoned intrusion; for they say, if money go before, all ways do lie open.

Fal. Money is a good soldier, sir, and will on.

Ford. Troth, and I have a bag of money here troubles me. If you will help to bear it, Sir John, take all, or half, for easing me of the carriage.

Fal. Sir, I know not how I may deserve to be your porter.

Ford. I will tell you, sir, if you will give me the hearing.

Fal. Speak, good Master Brook. I shall be glad to be your servant.

Ford. Sir, I hear you are a scholar—I will be brief with you—and you have been a man long known to me, though I had never so good means, as desire, to make myself acquainted with you. I shall discover a thing to you, wherein I must very much lay open mine own imperfection; but, good Sir John, as you have one eye upon my follies, as you hear them unfolded, turn another into the register of your own; that I may pass with a reproof the easier, sith you yourself know how easy it is to be such an offender.

Fal. Very well, sir; proceed.

Ford. There is a gentlewoman in this town; her husband's name is Ford.

Fal. Well, sir.

Ford. I have long loved her, and, I protest to you, bestowed much on her; followed her with a doting observance; engrossed opportunities to meet her; fee'd every slight occasion that could but niggardly give me sight of her; not only bought many presents to give her, but have given largely to many to know what she would have given; briefly, I have pursued her as love hath pursued me; which hath been on the wing of all occasions. But whatsoever I have merited, either in my mind or in my means, meed, I am sure, I have received none; unless experience be a jewel that I have purchased at an infinite rate, and that hath taught me to say this:
"Love like a shadow flies when substance love pursues;
Pursuing that that flies, and flying what pursues."

Fal. Have you received no promise of satisfaction at her hands?

Ford. Never.

Fal. Have you importuned her to such a purpose?

Ford. Never.

Fal. Of what quality was your love, then?

Ford. Like a fair house built on another man's ground; so that I have lost my edifice by mistaking the place where I erected it.

Fal. To what purpose have you unfolded this to me?

Ford. When I have told you that, I have told you all. Some say, that though she appear honest to me, yet in other places she enlargeth her mirth so far that there is shrewd construction made of her. Now, Sir John, here is the heart of my purpose: you are a gentleman of excellent breeding, admirable discourse, of great admittance, authentic in your place and person, generally allowed for your many war-like, court-like, and learned preparations.

Fal. O, sir!

Ford. Believe it, for you know it. There is money; spend it, spend it; spend more; spend all I have; only give me so much of your time in exchange of it, as to lay an amiable siege to the honesty of this Ford's wife. Use your art of wooing; win her to consent to you; if any man may, you may as soon as any.

Fal. Would it apply well to the vehemency of your affection, that I should win what you would enjoy? Methinks you prescribe to yourself very preposterously.

Ford. O, understand my drift. She dwells so securely on the excellency of her honour, that the folly of my soul dares not present itself. She is too bright to be looked against. Now, could I come to her with any detection in my hand, my desires had instance and argument to commend themselves. I could drive her then from the ward of her purity, her reputation, her marriage-vow, and a thousand other her defences, which now are too too strongly embattled against me. What say you to't, Sir John?

Fal. Master Brook, I will first make bold with your money; next, give me your hand; and last, as I am a gentleman, you shall, if you will, enjoy Ford's wife.

Ford. O good sir!

Fal. I say you shall.

Ford. Want no money, Sir John; you shall want none.

Fal. Want no Mistress Ford, Master Brook; you shall want none. I shall be with her, I may tell you, by her own appointment; even as you came in to me, her assistant or go-between parted from me. I say I shall be with her between ten and eleven; for at that time the jealous rascally knave her husband will be forth. Come you to me at night; you shall know how I speed.

Ford. I am blest in your acquaintance. Do you know Ford, sir?

Fal. Hang him, poor cuckoldly knave! I know him not. Yet I wrong him to call him poor; they say the jealous wittolly knave hath masses of money; for the which his wife seems to me well-favoured. I will use her as the key of the cuckoldly rogue's coffer; and there's my harvest-home.

Ford. I would you knew Ford, sir, that you might avoid him if you saw him.

Fal. Hang him, mechanical salt-butter rogue! I will stare him out of his wits; I will awe him with my cudgel; it shall hang like a meteor o'er the cuckold's horns. Master Brook, thou shalt know I will predominate over the peasant, and thou shalt lie with his wife. Come to me soon at night. Ford's a knave, and I will aggravate his style; thou, Master Brook, shalt know him for knave and cuckold. Come to me soon at night. [*Exit*.

Ford. What a damned Epicurean rascal is this! My heart is ready to crack with impatience. Who says this is improvident jealousy? my wife hath sent to him; the hour is fixed; the match is made. Would any man have thought this? See the hell of having a false woman! My bed shall be abused, my coffers ransacked, my reputation gnawn at; and I shall not only receive this villainous wrong, but stand under the adoption of abominable terms, and by him that does me this wrong. Terms! names! Amaimon sounds well; Lucifer, well; Barbason, well; yet they are devils' additions, the names of fiends; but Cuckold! Wittol!—Cuckold! the devil himself hath not such a name. Page is an ass, a secure ass. He will trust his wife; he will not be jealous. I will rather trust a Fleming with my butter, Parson Hugh the Welshman with my cheese, an Irishman with my aqua-vitæ bottle, or a thief to walk my ambling gelding, than my wife with herself. Then she plots, then she ruminates, then she devises; and what they think in their hearts they may effect, they will break their hearts but they will effect. God be praised for my jealousy! Eleven o'clock the hour. I will prevent this, detect my wife, be revenged on Falstaff, and laugh at Page. I will about it; better three hours too soon than a minute too late. Fie, fie, fie! cuckold! cuckold! cuckold! [*Exit*.

SCENE III. *A field near Windsor*

Enter CAIUS *and* RUGBY.

Caius. Jack Rugby!

Rug. Sir?

Caius. Vat is de clock, Jack?

Rug. 'Tis past the hour, sir, that Sir Hugh promised to meet.

Caius. By gar, he has save his soul, dat he is no come; he has pray his Pible well, dat he is no come. By gar, Jack Rugby, he is dead already, if he be come.

Rug. He is wise, sir; he knew your worship would kill him, if he came.

Caius. By gar, de herring is no dead so as I vill kill him. Take your rapier, Jack; I vill tell you how I vill kill him.

Rug. Alas, sir, I cannot fence.

Caius. Villainy, take your rapier.

Rug. Forbear; here's company.

Enter HOST, SHALLOW, SLENDER, *and* PAGE.

Host. Bless thee, bully doctor!

Shal. Save you, Master Doctor Caius!

Page. Now, good master doctor!

Slen. Give you good morrow, sir.

Caius. Vat be all you, one, two, tree, four, come for?

Host. To see thee fight, to see thee foin, to see thee traverse; to see thee here, to see thee there; to see thee pass thy punto, thy stock, thy reverse, thy distance, thy montant. Is he dead, my Ethiopian? is he dead, my Francisco? ha, bully! What says my Æsculapius? my Galen? my heart of elder? ha! is he dead, bully stale? is he dead?

Caius. By gar, he is de coward Jack priest of de vorld; he is not show his face.

Host. Thou art a Castalion-King-Urinal. Hector of Greece, my boy!

Caius. I pray you, bear vitness that me have stay six or seven, two, tree hours for him, and he is no come.

Shal. He is the wiser man, master doctor. He is a curer of souls, and you a curer of bodies; if you should fight, you go against the hair of your professions. Is it not true, Master Page?

Page. Master Shallow, you have yourself been a great fighter, though now a man of peace.

Shal. Bodykins, Master Page, though I now be old and of the peace, if I see a sword out, my finger itches to make one. Though we are justices and doctors and churchmen, Master Page, we have some salt of our youth in us; we are the sons of women, Master Page.

Page. 'Tis true, Master Shallow.

Shal. It will be found so, Master Page. Master Doctor Caius, I am come to fetch you home. I am sworn of the peace. You have showed yourself a wise physician, and Sir Hugh hath shown himself a wise and patient churchman. You must go with me, master doctor.

Host. Pardon, guest-justice. A word, Mounseur Mockwater.

Caius. Mock-vater! vat is dat?

Host. Mock-water, in our English tongue, is valour, bully.

Caius. By gar, den, I have as mush mock-vater as de Englishman. Scurvy jack-dog priest! by gar, me vill cut his ears.

Host. He will clapper-claw thee tightly, bully.

Caius. Clapper-de-claw! vat is dat?

Host. That is, he will make thee amends.

Caius. By gar, me do look he shall clapper-de-claw me; for, by gar, me vill have it.

Host. And I will provoke him to't, or let him wag.

Caius. Me tank you for dat.

Host. And, moreover, bully—but first, master guest, and Master Page, and eke Cavaleiro Slender, go you through the town to Frogmore. [*Aside to them*.]

Page. Sir Hugh is there, is he?

Host. He is there. See what humour he is in; and I will bring the doctor about by the fields. Will it do well?

Shal. We will do it.

Page, Shal., and Slen. Adieu, good master doctor.

[*Exeunt* PAGE, SHALLOW, *and* SLENDER.

Caius. By gar, me vill kill de priest; for he speak for a jack-an-ape to Anne Page.

Host. Let him die; sheathe thy impatience, throw cold water on thy choler; go about the fields with me through Frogmore. I will bring thee where Mistress Anne Page is, at a farmhouse a-feasting; and thou shalt woo her. Cried I aim? said I well?

Caius. By gar, me dank you vor dat. By gar, I love you; and I shall procure-a you de good guest, de earl, de knight, de lords, de gentlemen, my patients.

Host. For the which I will be thy adversary toward Anne Page. Said I well?

Caius. By gar, 'tis good; vell said.

Host. Let us wag, then.

Caius. Come at my heels, Jack Rugby. [*Exeunt*.

ACT III

SCENE I. *A field near Frogmore*

Enter SIR HUGH EVANS *and* SIMPLE.

Evans. I pray you now, good Master Slender's serving-man, and friend Simple by your name, which way have you looked for Master Caius, that calls himself doctor of physic?

Sim. Marry, sir, the pittie-ward, the parkward, every way; old Windsor way, and every way but the town way.

Evans. I most fehemently desire you you will also look that way.

Sim. I will, sir. [*Exit*.

Evans. 'Pless my soul, how full of chollors I am, and trempling of mind! I shall be glad if he have deceived me. How melancholies I am! I will knog his urinals about his knave's costard when I have good opportunities for the ork. 'Pless my soul! [*Sings*.]

"To shallow rivers, to whose falls
Melodious birds sings madrigals;
There will we make our peds of roses,
And a thousand fragrant posies.
To shallow"—

Mercy on me! I have a great dispositions to cry. [*Sings*.]

"Melodious birds sing madrigals—

When as I sat in Pabylon—
And a thousand vagram posies.
To shallow" &c.

Re-enter SIMPLE.

Sim. Yonder he is coming, this way, Sir Hugh.

Evans. He's welcome. [*Sings*.]
"To shallow rivers, to whose falls"—
Heaven prosper the right! What weapons is he?

Sim. No weapons, sir. There comes my master, Master Shallow, and another gentleman, from Frogmore, over the stile, this way.

Evans. Pray you, give me my gown; or else keep it in your arms.

Enter PAGE, SHALLOW, *and* SLENDER.

Shal. How now, master Parson! Good morrow, good Sir Hugh. Keep a gamester from the dice, and a good student from his book, and it is wonderful.

Slen. [*Aside*] Ah, sweet Anne Page!

Page. 'Save you, good Sir Hugh!

Evans. 'Pless you from his mercy sake, all of you!

Shal. What, the sword and the word! do you study them both, master parson?

Page. And youthful still! in your doublet and hose this raw rheumatic day!

Evans. There is reasons and causes for it.

Page. We are come to you to do a good office, master parson.

Evans. Fery well; what is it?

Page. Yonder is a most reverend gentleman, who, belike having received wrong by some person, is at most odds with his own gravity and patience that ever you saw.

Shal. I have lived fourscore years and upward; I never heard a man of his place, gravity and learning, so wide of his own respect.

Evans. What is he?

Page. I think you know him; Master Doctor Caius, the renowned French physician.

Evans. Got's will, and his passion of my heart! I had as lief you would tell me of a mess of porridge.

Page. Why?

Evans. He has no more knowledge in Hibocrates and Galen—and he is a knave besides; a cowardly knave as you would desires to be acquainted withal.

Page. I warrant you, he's the man should fight with him.

Slen. [*Aside*] O sweet Anne Page!

Shal. It appears so by his weapons. Keep them asunder; here comes Doctor Caius.

Enter HOST, CAIUS, *and* RUGBY.

Page. Nay, good master parson, keep in your weapon.

Shal. So do you, good master doctor.

Host. Disarm them, and let them question. Let them keep their limbs whole and hack our English.

Caius. I pray you, let-a me speak a word with your ear. Vherefore vill you not meet-a me?

Evans. [*Aside to* CAIUS] Pray you, use your patience. In good time.

Caius. By gar, you are de coward, de Jack dog, John ape.

Evans. [*Aside to* CAIUS] Pray you, let us not be laughing-stocks to other men's humours; I desire you in friendship, and I will one way or other make you amends. [*Aloud*] I will knog your urinals about your knave's cogscomb for missing your meetings and appointments.

Caius. *Diable!* Jack Rugby—mine host de Jarteer—have I not stay for him to kill him? have I not, at de place I did appoint?

Evans. As I am a Christians soul now, look you, this is the place appointed. I'll be judgement by mine host of the Garter.

Host. Peace, I say, Gallia and Gaul, French and Welsh, soul-curer and body-curer!

Caius. Ay, dat is very good; excellent.

Host. Peace, I say! hear mine host of the Garter. Am I politic? am I subtle? am I a Machiavel? Shall I lose my doctor? no; he gives me the potions and the motions. Shall I lose my parson, my priest, my Sir Hugh? no; he gives me the proverbs and the no-verbs. Give me thy hand terrestrial; so. Give me thy hand, celestial; so. Boys of art, I have deceived you both; I have directed you to wrong places. Your hearts are mighty, your skins are whole, and let burnt sack be the issue. Come, lay their swords to pawn. Follow me, lads of peace; follow, follow, follow.

Shal. Trust me, a mad host. Follow, gentlemen, follow.

Slen. [*Aside*] O sweet Anne Page!

[*Exeunt* SHALLOW, SLENDER, PAGE, *and* HOST.

Caius. Ha, do I perceive dat? have you make-a de sot of us, ha, ha?

Evans. This is well; he has made us his vlouting-stog. I desire you that we may be friends; and let us knog our prains together to be revenge on this same scall, scurvy, cogging companion, the host of the Garter

Caius. By gar, with all my heart. He promise to bring me where is Anne Page; by gar, he deceive me too.

Evans. Well, I will smite his noddles. Pray you, follow. [*Exeunt*.

SCENE II. *A street*

Enter MISTRESS PAGE *and* ROBIN.

Mrs. Page. Nay, keep your way, little gallant; you were wont to be a follower, but now you are a leader. Whether had you rather lead mine eyes, or eye your master's heels?

Rob. I had rather, forsooth, go before you like a man than follow him like a dwarf.

Mrs. Page. O, you are a flattering boy. Now I see you'll be a courtier.

Enter FORD.

Ford. Well met, Mistress Page. Whither go you?

Mrs. Page. Truly, sir, to see your wife. Is she at home?

Ford. Ay; and as idle as she may hang together, for want of company. I think, if your husbands were dead, you two would marry.

Mrs. Page. Be sure of that—two other husbands.

Ford. Where had you this pretty weathercock?

Mrs. Page. I cannot tell what the dickens his name is my husband had him of. What do you call your knight's name, sirrah?

Rob. Sir John Falstaff.

Ford. Sir John Falstaff!

Mrs. Page. He, he; I can never hit on's name. There is such a league between my good man and he! Is your wife at home indeed?

Ford. Indeed she is.

Mrs. Page. By your leave, sir. I am sick till I see her. [*Exeunt* MISTRESS PAGE *and* ROBIN.

Ford. Has Page any brains? hath he any eyes? hath he any thinking? Sure, they sleep; he hath no use of them. Why, this boy will carry a letter twenty mile, as easy as a cannon will shoot point-blank twelve score. He pieces out his wife's inclination; he gives her folly motion and advantage; and now she's going to my wife, and Falstaff's boy with her. A man may hear this shower sing in the wind. And Falstaff's boy with her! Good plots, they are laid; and our revolted wives share damnation together. Well; I will take him, then torture my wife, pluck the borrowed veil of modesty from the so seeming Mistress Page, divulge Page himself for a secure and wilful Actæon; and to these violent proceedings all my neighbours shall cry aim. [*Clock heard*.] The clock gives me my cue, and my assurance bids me search. There I shall find Falstaff. I shall be rather praised for this than mocked; for it is as positive as the earth is firm that Falstaff is there. I will go.

Enter PAGE, SHALLOW, SLENDER, HOST, SIR HUGH EVANS, CAIUS, *and* RUGBY.

Shal., *Page*, *&c*. Well met, Master Ford.

Ford. Trust me, a good knot. I have good cheer at home; and I pray you all go with me.

Shal. I must excuse myself, Master Ford.

Slen. And so must I, sir. We have appointed to dine with Mistress Anne, and I would not break with her for more money than I'll speak of.

Shal. We have lingered about a match between Anne Page and my cousin Slender, and this day we shall have our answer.

Slen. I hope I have your good will, father Page.

Page. You have, Master Slender; I stand wholly for you; but my wife, master doctor, is for you altogether.

Caius. Ay, be-gar; and de maid is love-a me. My nursh-a Quickly tell me so mush.

Host. What say you to young Master Fenton? he capers, he dances, he has eyes of youth, he writes verses, he speaks holiday, he smells April and May. He will carry't, he will carry't; 'tis in his buttons; he will carry't.

Page. Not by my consent, I promise you. The gentleman is of no having. He kept company with the wild prince and Poins; he is of too high a region; he knows too much. No, he shall not knit a knot in his fortunes with the finger of my substance. If he take her, let him take her simply; the wealth I have waits on my consent, and my consent goes not that way.

Ford. I beseech you heartily, some of you go home with me to dinner. Besides your cheer, you shall have sport; I will show you a monster. Master doctor, you shall go; so shall you, Master Page; and you, Sir Hugh.

Shal. Well, fare you well. We shall have the freer wooing at Master Page's.

[*Exeunt* SHALLOW *and* SLENDER.

Caius. Go home, John Rugby; I come anon.

[*Exit* RUGBY.

Host. Farewell, my hearts. I will to my honest knight Falstaff, and drink canary with him.

[*Exit*.

Ford. [*Aside*] I think I shall drink in pipewine first with him; I'll make him dance. Will you go, gentles?

All. Have with you to see this monster.

[*Exeunt*.

SCENE III. *A room in Ford's house*

Enter MISTRESS FORD *and* MISTRESS PAGE.

Mrs. Ford. What, John! What, Robert!

Mrs. Page. Quickly, quickly! Is the buck-basket—

Mrs. Ford. I warrant. What, Robin, I say!

Enter Servants with a basket.

Mr. Page. Come, come, come.

Mrs. Ford. Here, set it down.

Mrs. Page. Give your men the charge; we must be brief.

Mrs. Ford. Marry, as I told you before, John and Robert, be ready here hard by in the brew-house; and when I suddenly call you, come forth, and without any pause or staggering take this basket on your shoulders. That done, trudge with it in all haste, and carry it among the whitsters in Datchet-mead, and there empty it in the muddy ditch close by the Thames side.

Mrs. Page. You will do it?

Mrs. Ford. I ha' told them over and over; they lack no direction. Be gone, and come when you are called [*Exeunt Servants.*

Mrs. Page. Here comes little Robin.

Enter ROBIN.

Mrs. Ford. How now, my eyas-musket! what news with you?

Rob. My master, Sir John, is come in at your back-door, Mistress Ford, and requests your company.

Mrs. Page. You little Jack-a-Lent, have you been true to us?

Rob. Ay, I'll be sworn. My master knows not of your being here and hath threatened to put me into everlasting liberty if I tell you of it; for he swears he'll turn me away.

Mrs. Page. Thou'rt a good boy. This secrecy of thine shall be a tailor to thee and shall make thee a new doublet and hose. I'll go hide me.

Mrs. Ford. Do so. Go tell thy master I am alone. [*Exit* ROBIN.] Mistress Page, remember you your cue.

Mrs. Page. I warrant thee; if I do not act it, hiss me. [*Exit.*

Mrs. Ford. Go to, then. We'll use this unwholesome humidity, this gross watery pumpion; we'll teach him to know turtles from jays.

Enter FALSTAFF.

Fal. "Have I caught thee, my heavenly jewel?" Why, now let me die, for I have lived long enough. This is the period of my ambition. O this blessed hour!

Mrs. Ford. O sweet Sir John!

Fal. Mistress Ford, I cannot cog, I cannot prate, Mistress Ford. Now shall I sin in my wish: I would thy husband were dead. I'll speak it before the best lord; I would make thee my lady.

Mrs. Ford. I your lady, Sir John! alas, I should be a pitiful lady!

Fal. Let the court of France show me such another. I see how thine eye would emulate the diamond. Thou hast the right arched beauty of the brow that becomes the ship-tire, the tire-valiant, or any tire of Venetian admittance.

Mrs. Ford. A plain kerchief, Sir John. My brows become nothing else; nor that well neither.

Fal. By the Lord, thou art a traitor to say so. Thou wouldst make an absolute courtier; and the firm fixture of thy foot would give an excellent motion to thy gait in a semi-circled farthingale. I see what thou wert, if Fortune thy foe were not, Nature thy friend. Come, thou canst not hide it.

Mrs. Ford. Believe me, there's no such thing in me.

Fal. What made me love thee? let that persuade thee there's something extraordinary in thee. Come, I cannot cog and say thou art this and that, like a many of these lisping hawthorn-buds, that come like women in men's apparel, and smell like Bucklersbury in simple time; I cannot. But I love thee; none but thee; and thou deservest it.

Mrs. Ford. Do not betray me, sir. I fear you love Mistress Page.

Fal. Thou mightst as well say I love to walk by the Counter-gate, which is as hateful to me as the reek of a lime-kiln.

Mrs. Ford. Well, heaven knows how I love you; and you shall one day find it.

Fal. Keep in that mind; I'll deserve it.

Mrs. Ford. Nay, I must tell you, so you do; or else I could not be in that mind.

Rob. [*Within*] Mistress Ford, Mistress Ford! here's Mistress Page at the door, sweating and blowing and looking wildly, and would needs speak with you presently.

Fal. She shall not see me. I will ensconce me behind the arras.

Mrs. Ford. Pray you, do so. She's a very tattling woman. [FALSTAFF *hides himself.*

Re-enter MISTRESS PAGE *and* ROBIN.

What's the matter? how now!

Mrs. Page. O Mistress Ford, what have you done? You're shamed, you're overthrown, you're undone for ever!

Mrs. Ford. What's the matter, good Mistress Page?

Mrs. Page. O well-a-day, Mistress Ford! having an honest man to your husband, to give him such cause of suspicion!

Mrs. Ford. What cause of suspicion?

Mrs. Page. What cause of suspicion! Out upon you! how am I mistook in you!

Mrs. Page. Why, alas, what's the matter?

Mrs. Page. Your husband's coming hither, woman, with all the officers in Windsor, to search for a gentleman that he says is here now in the house by your consent, to take an ill advantage of his absence. You are undone.

Mrs. Ford. 'Tis not so, I hope.

Mrs. Page. Pray heaven it be not so, that you have such a man here! but 'tis most certain your husband's coming, with half Windsor at his heels, to search for such a one. I come before to tell you. If you know yourself clear, why, I am glad of it; but if you have a friend here, convey, convey him out. Be not amazed; call all your senses to you; defend your reputation, or bid farewell to your good life for ever.

Mrs. Ford. What shall I do? There is a gentleman my dear friend; and I fear not mine own shame so much as his peril. I had rather than a thousand pound he were out of the house.

Mrs. Page. For shame! never stand "you had rather" and "you had rather." Your husband's here at hand; bethink you of some conveyance. In the house you cannot hide him. O, how have you deceived me! Look, here is a basket. If he be of any reasonable stature, he may creep in here; and throw foul linen upon him, as if it were going to bucking, or—it is whiting-time—send him by your two men to Datchet-mead.

Mrs. Ford. He's too big to go in there. What shall I do?

Fal. [*Coming forward*] Let me see't, let me see't, O, let me see't! I'll in, I'll in. Follow your friend's counsel. I'll in.

Mrs. Page. What, Sir John Falstaff! Are these your letters, knight?

Fal. I love thee. Help me away. Let me creep in here. I'll never—

Gets into the basket; they cover him with foul linen.

Mrs. Page. Help to cover your master, boy. Call your men, Mistress Ford. You dissembling knight!

Mrs. Ford. What, John! Robert! John!

[*Exit* ROBIN.

Re-enter Servants.

Go take up these clothes here quickly. Where's the cowl-staff? look, how you drumble! Carry them to the laundress in Datchet-mead; quickly, come.

Enter FORD, PAGE, CAIUS, *and* SIR HUGH EVANS.

Ford. Pray you, come near. If I suspect without cause, why then make sport at me; then let me be your jest; I deserve it. How now! whither bear you this?

Serv. To the laundress, forsooth.

Mrs. Ford. Why, what have you to do whither they bear it? You were best meddle with buck-washing.

Ford. Buck! I would I could wash myself of the buck! Buck, buck, buck! Ay, buck; I warrant you, buck; and of the season too, it shall appear. [*Exeunt Servants with the basket.*] Gentlemen, I have dreamed to-night; I'll tell you my dream. Here, here, here be my keys. Ascend my chambers; search, seek, find out. I'll warrant we'll unkennel the fox. Let me stop this way first. [*Locking the door.*] So, now uncape.

Page. Good Master Ford, be contented. You wrong yourself too much.

Ford. True, Master Page. Up, gentlemen; you shall see sport anon: follow me, gentlemen.

[*Exit.*

Evans. This is fery fantastical humours and jealousies.

Caius. By gar, 'tis no the fashion of France; it is not jealous in France.

Page. Nay, follow him, gentlemen; see the issue of his search.

[*Exeunt* PAGE, CAIUS, *and* EVANS.

Mrs. Page. Is there not a double excellency in this?

Mrs. Ford. I know not which pleases me better, that my husband is deceived, or Sir John.

Mrs. Page. What a taking was he in when your husband asked who was in the basket!

Mrs. Ford. I am half afraid he will have need of washing; so throwing him into the water will do him a benefit.

Mrs. Page. Hang him, dishonest rascal! I would all of the same strain were in the same distress.

Mrs. Ford. I think my husband hath some special suspicion of Falstaff's being here; for I never saw him so gross in his jealousy till now.

Mrs. Page. I will lay a plot to try that; and we will yet have more tricks with Falstaff. His dissolute disease will scarce obey this medicine.

Mrs. Ford. Shall we send that foolish carrion, Mistress Quickly, to him, and excuse his throwing into the water; and give him another hope, to betray him to another punishment?

Mrs. Page. We will do it. Let him be sent for tomorrow, eight o'clock, to have amends.

Re-enter FORD, PAGE, CAIUS, *and* SIR HUGH EVANS.

Ford. I cannot find him. May be the knave bragged of that he could not compass.

Mrs. Page. [*Aside to* MISTRESS FORD] Heard you that?

Mrs. Ford. You use me well, Master Ford, do you?

Ford. Ay, I do so.

Mrs. Ford. Heaven make you better than your thoughts!

Ford. Amen!

Mrs. Page. You do yourself mighty wrong, Master Ford.

Ford. Ay, ay; I must bear it.

Evans. If there be any pody in the house, and in the chambers, and in the coffers, and in the presses, heaven forgive my sins at the day of judgment!

Caius. By gar, nor I too. There is no bodies.

Page. Fie, fie, Master Ford! are you not ashamed? What spirit, what devil suggests this imagination? I would not ha' your distemper in this kind for the wealth of Windsor Castle.

Ford. 'Tis my fault, Master Page. I suffer for it.

Evans. You suffer for a pad conscience. Your wife is as honest a'omans as I will desires among five thousand, and five hundred too.

Caius. By gar, I see 'tis an honest woman.

Ford. Well, I promised you a dinner. Come, come, walk in the Park. I pray you, pardon me; I will hereafter make known to you why I have done this. Come, wife; come, Mistress Page. I pray you, pardon me; pray heartily, pardon me.

Page. Let's go in, gentlemen; but, trust me, we'll mock him. I do invite you to-morrow morning to my house to breakfast. After, we'll a-birding together; I have a fine hawk for the bush. Shall it be so?

Ford. Anything.

Evans. If there is one, I shall make two in the company.

Caius. If dere be one or two, I shall make-a the turd.

Ford. Pray you, go, Master Page.

Evans. I pray you now, remembrance to-morrow on the lousy knave, mine host.

Caius. Dat is good; by gar, with all my heart!

Evans. A lousy knave, to have his gibes and his mockeries! *Exeunt*.

SCENE IV. *A room in Page's house*

Enter FENTON *and* ANNE PAGE.

Fent. I see I cannot get thy father's love;
Therefore no more turn me to him, sweet Nan.

Anne. Alas, how then?

Fent. Why, thou must be thyself.
He doth object I am too great of birth;
And that, my state being gall'd with my expense,
I seek to heal it only by his wealth.
Besides these, other bars he lays before me,
My riots past, my wild societies;
And tells me 'tis a thing impossible
I should love thee but as a property.

Anne. May be he tells you true.

Fent. No, heaven so speed me in my time to come!
Albeit I will confess thy father's wealth
Was the first motive that I woo'd thee, Anne;
Yet, wooing thee, I found thee of more value
Than stamps in gold or sums in sealed bags;
And 'tis the very riches of thyself
That now I aim at.

Anne. Gentle Master Fenton,
Yet seek my father's love; still seek it, sir.
If opportunity and humblest suit
Cannot attain it, why, then—hark you hither!
[*They converse apart*.

Enter SHALLOW, SLENDER, *and* MISTRESS QUICKLY.

Shal. Break their talk, Mistress Quickly. My kinsman shall speak for himself.

Slen. I'll make a shaft or a bolt on't. 'Slid, 'tis but venturing.

Shal. Be not dismayed.

Slen. No, she shall not dismay me. I care not for that, but that I am afeard.

Quick. Hark ye; Master Slender would speak a word with you.

Anne. I come to him. [*Aside*] This is my father's choice.
O, what a world of vile ill-favour'd faults
Looks handsome in three hundred pounds a-year!

Quick. And how does good Master Fenton?
Pray you, a word with you.

Shal. She's coming; to her, coz. O boy, thou hadst a father!

Slen. I had a father, Mistress Anne; my uncle can tell you good jests of him. Pray you, uncle, tell Mistress Anne the jest, how my father stole two geese out of a pen, good uncle.

Shal. Mistress Anne, my cousin loves you.

Slen. Ay, that I do; as well as I love any woman in Gloucestershire.

Shal. He will maintain you like a gentlewoman.

Slen. Ay, that I will, come cut and long-tail, under the degree of a squire.

Shal. He will make you a hundred and fifty pounds jointure.

Anne. Good Master Shallow, let him woo for himself.

Shal. Marry, I thank you for it; I thank you for that good comfort. She calls you, coz. I'll leave you.

Anne. Now, Master Slender—

Slen. Now, good Mistress Anne—

Anne. What is your will?

Slen. My will! 'od's heartlings, that's a pretty

jest indeed! I ne'er made my will yet, I thank heaven; I am not such a sickly creature, I give heaven praise.

Anne. I mean, Master Slender, what would you with me?

Slen. Truly, for mine own part, I would little or nothing with you. Your father and my uncle hath made motions. If it be my luck, so; if not, happy man be his dole! They can tell you how things go better than I can. You may ask your father; here he comes.

Enter PAGE *and* MISTRESS PAGE.

Page. Now, Master Slender. Love him, daughter Anne.
Why, how now! what does Master Fenton here?
You wrong me, sir, thus still to haunt my house.
I told you, sir, my daughter is disposed of.

Fent. Nay, Master Page, be not impatient.

Mrs. Page. Good Master Fenton, come not to my child.

Page. She is no match for you.

Fent. Sir, will you hear me?

Page. No, good Master Fenton.
Come, Master Shallow; come, son Slender, in.
Knowing my mind, you wrong me, Master Fenton.

[*Exeunt* PAGE, SHALLOW *and* SLENDER.

Quick. Speak to Mistress Page.

Fent. Good Mistress Page, for that I love your daughter
In such a righteous fashion as I do,
Perforce, against all checks, rebukes and manners,
I must advance the colours of my love
And not retire. Let me have your good will.

Anne. Good mother, do not marry me to yond fool.

Mrs. Page. I mean it not; I seek you a better husband.

Quick. That's my master, master doctor.

Anne. Alas, I had rather be set quick i' the earth
And bowl'd to death with turnips!

Mrs. Page. Come, trouble not yourself. Good Master Fenton,
I will not be your friend nor enemy.
My daughter will I question how she loves you,
And as I find her, so am I affected.
Till then farewell, sir; she must needs go in;
Her father will be angry.

Fent. Farewell, gentle mistress: farewell, Nan.

[*Exeunt* MISTRESS PAGE *and Anne*.

Quick. This is my doing, now: "Nay," said I, "will you cast away your child on a fool, and a physician? Look on Master Fenton." This is my doing.

Fent. I thank thee; and I pray thee, once to-night
Give my sweet Nan this ring. There's for thy pains.

Quick. Now heaven send thee good fortune! [*Exit* FENTON.] A kind heart he hath. A woman would run through fire and water for such a kind heart. But yet I would my master had Mistress Anne; or I would Master Slender had her; or, in sooth, I would Master Fenton had her. I will do what I can for them all three; for so I have promised, and I'll be as good as my word; but speciously for Master Fenton. Well, I must of another errand to Sir John Falstaff from my two mistresses. What a beast am I to slack it! [*Exit*.

SCENE V. *A room in the Garter Inn*

Enter FALSTAFF *and* BARDOLPH.

Fal. Bardolph, I say—

Bard. Here, sir.

Fal. Go fetch me a quart of sack; put a toast in't. [*Exit* BARDOLPH.] Have I lived to be carried in a basket, like a barrow of butcher's offal, and to be thrown in the Thames? Well, if I be served such another trick, I'll have my brains ta'en out and buttered, and give them to a dog for a new year's gift. The rogues slighted me into the river with as little remorse as they would have drowned a blind bitch's puppies, fifteen i' the litter; and you may know by my size that I have a kind of alacrity in sinking; if the bottom were as deep as hell, I should down. I had been drowned, but that the shore was shelvy and shallow—a death that I abhor; for the water swells a man; and what a thing should I have been when I had been swelled! I should have been a mountain of mummy.

Re-enter BARDOLPH *with sack*.

Bard. Here's Mistress Quickly, sir, to speak with you.

Fal. Come, let me pour in some sack to the Thames water; for my belly's as cold as if I had swallowed snowballs for pills to cool the reins. Call her in.

Bard. Come in, woman!

Enter MISTRESS QUICKLY.

Quick. By your leave; I cry you mercy. Give your worship good morrow.

Fal. Take away these chalices. Go brew me a pottle of sack finely.

Bard. With eggs, sir?

Fal. Simple of itself; I'll no pullet-sperm in my brewage. [*Exit* BARDOLPH.] How now!

Quick. Marry, sir, I come to your worship from Mistress Ford.

Fal. Mistress Ford! I have had ford enough; I was thrown into the ford; I have my belly full of ford.

Quick. Alas the day! good heart, that was not her fault. She does so take on with her men; they mistook their erection.

Fal. So did I mine, to build upon a foolish woman's promise.

Quick. Well, she laments, sir, for it, that it would yearn your heart to see it. Her husband goes this morning a-birding; she desires you once more to come to her between eight and nine. I must carry her word quickly. She'll make you amends, I warrant you.

Fal. Well, I will visit her. Tell her so; and bid her think what a man is. Let her consider his frailty, and then judge of my merit.

Quick. I will tell her.

Fal. Do so. Between nine and ten, sayest thou?

Quick. Eight and nine, sir.

Fal. Well, be gone. I will not miss her.

Quick. Peace be with you, sir. [*Exit.*

Fal. I marvel I hear not of Master Brook; he sent me word to stay within. I like his money well. O, here he comes.

Enter FORD.

Ford. Bless you, sir!

Fal. Now, master Brook, you come to know what hath passed between me and Ford's wife?

Ford. That, indeed, Sir John, is my business.

Fal. Master Brook, I will not lie to you. I was at her house the hour she appointed me.

Ford. And sped you, sir?

Fal. Very ill-favouredly, Master Brook.

Ford. How so, sir? Did she change her determination?

Fal. No, Master Brook; but the peaking Cornuto her husband, Master Brook, dwelling in a continual 'larum of jealousy, comes me in the instant of our encounter, after we had embraced, kissed, protested, and, as it were, spoke the prologue of our comedy; and at his heels a rabble of his companions, thither provoked and instigated by his distemper, and, forsooth, to search his house for his wife's love.

Ford. What, while you were there?

Fal. While I was there.

Fal. And did he search for you, and could not find you?

Fal. You shall hear. As good luck would have it, comes in one Mistress Page; gives intelligence of Ford's approach; and, in her invention and Ford's wife's distraction, they conveyed me into a buck-basket.

Ford. A buck-basket!

Fal. By the Lord, a buck-basket! rammed me in with foul shirts and smocks, socks, foul stockings, greasy napkins; that, Master Brook, there was the rankest compound of villainous smell that ever offended nostril.

Ford. And how long lay you there?

Fal. Nay, you shall hear, Master Brook, what I have suffered to bring this woman to evil for your good. Being thus crammed in the basket, a couple of Ford's knaves, his hinds, were called forth by their mistress to carry me in the name of foul clothes to Datchet-lane. They took me on their shoulders; met the jealous knave their master in the door, who asked them once or twice what they had in their basket; I quaked for fear, lest the lunatic knave would have searched it; but fate, ordaining he should be a cuckold, held his hand. Well, on went he for a search, and away went I for foul clothes. But mark the sequel, Master Brook. I suffered the pangs of three several deaths; first, an intolerable fright, to be detected with a jealous rotten bell-wether; next, to be compassed, like a good bilbo, in the circumference of a peck, hilt to point, heel to head; and then, to be stopped in, like a strong distillation, with stinking clothes that fretted in their own grease. Think of that—a man of my kidney—think of that—that am as subject to heat as butter; a man of continual dissolution and thaw—it was a miracle to 'scape suffocation. And in the height of this bath, when I was more than half stewed in grease, like a Dutch dish, to be thrown into the Thames, and cooled, glowing hot, in that surge, like a horse-shoe; think of that—hissing hot—think of that, Master Brook.

Ford. In good sadness, sir, I am sorry that for my sake you have suffered all this. My suit then is desperate; you'll undertake her no more?

Fal. Master Brook, I will be thrown into Etna, as I have been into Thames, ere I will leave her thus. Her husband is this morning gone a-birding. I have received from her another embassy of meeting; 'twixt eight and nine is the hour, Master Brook.

Ford. 'Tis past eight already, sir.

Fal. Is it? I will then address me to my appointment. Come to me at your convenient leisure, and you shall know how I speed; and the conclusion shall be crowned with your enjoying her. Adieu. You shall have her, Master Brook; Master Brook, you shall cuckold Ford. [*Exit.*

Ford. Hum! ha! is this a vision? is this a dream?

do I sleep? Master Ford, awake! awake, Master Ford! there's a hole made in your best coat, Master Ford. This 'tis to be married! this 'tis to have linen and buck-baskets! Well, I will proclaim myself what I am. I will now take the lecher; he is at my house; he cannot 'scape me; 'tis impossible he should. He cannot creep into a halfpenny purse, nor into a pepper-box; but, lest the devil that guides him should aid him, I will search impossible places. Though what I am I cannot avoid, yet to be what I would not shall not make me tame. If I have horns to make one mad, let the proverb go with me: I'll be horn-mad. [*Exit.*

ACT IV

SCENE I. *A street*

Enter MISTRESS PAGE, MISTRESS QUICKLY, *and* WILLIAM.

Mrs. Page. Is he at Master Ford's already, think'st thou?

Quick. Sure he is by this, or will be presently. But, truly, he is very courageous mad about his throwing into the water. Mistress Ford desires you to come suddenly.

Mrs. Page. I'll be with her by and by; I'll but bring my young man here to school. Look, where his master comes; 'tis a playing-day, I see.

Enter SIR HUGH EVANS.

How now, Sir Hugh! no school to-day?

Evans. No; Master Slender is let the boys leave to play.

Quick. Blessing of his heart!

Mrs. Page. Sir Hugh, my husband says my son profits nothing in the world at his book. I pray you, ask him some questions in his accidence.

Evans. Come hither, William; hold up your head; come.

Mrs. Page. Come on, sirrah; hold up your head; answer your master, be not afraid.

Evans. William, how many numbers is in nouns?

Will. Two.

Quick. Truly, I thought there had been one number more, because they say, "Od's nouns."

Evans. Peace your tattlings! What is "fair," William?

Will. Pulcher.

Quick. Polecats! there are fairer things than polecats, sure.

Evans. You are a very simplicity 'oman. I pray you, peace. What is *lapis*, William?

Will. A stone.

Evans. And what is "a stone," William?

Will. A pebble.

Evans. No, it is *lapis*. I pray you, remember in your prain.

Will. Lapis.

Evans. That is a good William. What is he, William, that does lend articles?

Will. Articles are borrowed of the pronoun, and be thus declined: *Singulariter*, *nominativo*, *hic*, *hæc*, *hoc*.

Evans. Nominativo, *hig*, *hag*, *hog*; pray you, mark: *genitivo*, *hujus*. Well, what is your accusative case?

Will. Accusativo, *hinc*.

Evans. I pray you, have your remembrance, child; *accusativo*, *hung*, *hang*, *hog*.

Quick. "Hang-hog" is Latin for bacon, I warrant you.

Evans. Leave your prabbles, 'oman, What is the focative case, William?

Will. O—*vocativo*, *O*.

Evans. Remember, William; focative is *caret*.

Quick. And that's a good root.

Evans. 'Oman, forbear.

Mrs. Page. Peace!

Evans. What is your genitive case plural, William?

Will. Genitive case!

Evans. Ay.

Will. Genitive—*horum*, *harum*, *horum*.

Quick. Vengeance of Jenny's case! fie on her! never name her, child, if she be a whore.

Evans. For shame, 'oman.

Quick. You do ill to teach the child such words. He teaches him to hick and to hack, which they'll do fast enough of themselves, and to call "horum." Fie upon you!

Evans. 'Oman, art thou lunatics? hast thou no understandings for thy cases and the numbers of the genders? Thou art as foolish Christian creatures as I would desires.

Mrs. Page. Prithee, hold thy peace.

Evans. Show me now, William, some declensions of your pronouns.

Will. Forsooth, I have forgot.

Evans. It is *qui*, *quæ*, *quod*. If you forget your *quies*, your *quæs*, and your *quods*, you must be preeches. Go your ways, and play; go.

Mrs. Page. He is a better scholar than I thought he was.

Evans. He is a good sprag memory. Farewell, Mistress Page.

Mrs. Page. Adieu, good Sir Hugh.

[*Exit* SIR HUGH.]

Get you home, boy. Come, we stay too long.

[*Exeunt.*

SCENE II. *A room in Ford's house*

Enter FALSTAFF *and* MISTRESS FORD.

Fal. Mistress Ford, your sorrow hath eaten up my sufferance. I see you are obsequious in your love, and I profess requital to a hair's breadth; not only, Mistress Ford, in the simple office of love, but in all the accoutrement, complement and ceremony of it. But are you sure of your husband now?

Mrs. Ford. He's a-birding, sweet Sir John.

Mrs. Page. [*Within*] What, ho, gossip Ford! what, ho!

Mrs. Ford. Step into the chamber, Sir John.

[*Exit* FALSTAFF.

Enter MISTRESS PAGE.

Mrs. Page. How now, sweetheart! who's at home besides yourself?

Mrs. Ford. Why, none but mine own people.

Mrs. Page. Indeed!

Mrs. Ford. No, certainly. [*Aside to her*] Speak louder.

Mrs. Page. Truly, I am so glad you have nobody here.

Mrs. Ford. Why?

Mrs. Page. Why, woman, your husband is in his old lines again. He so takes on yonder with my husband; so rails against all married mankind; so curses all Eve's daughters, of what complexion soever; and so buffets himself on the forehead, crying, "Peer out, peer out!" that any madness I ever yet beheld seemed but tameness, civility, and patience, to this his distemper he is in now. I am glad the fat knight is not here.

Mrs. Ford. Why, does he talk of him?

Mrs. Page. Of none but him; and swears he was carried out, the last time he searched for him, in a basket; protests to my husband he is now here, and hath drawn him and the rest of their company from their sport, to make another experiment of his suspicion. But I am glad the knight is not here; now he shall see his own foolery.

Mrs. Ford. How near is he, Mistress Page?

Mrs. Page. Hard by; at street end; he will be here anon.

Mrs. Ford. I am undone! The knight is here.

Mrs. Page. Why then you are utterly shamed, and he's but a dead man. What a woman are you!—Away with him, away with him! better shame than murder.

Mrs. Ford. Which way should he go? how should I bestow him? Shall I put him into the basket again?

Re-enter FALSTAFF.

Fal. No, I'll come no more i' the basket. May I not go out ere he come?

Mrs. Page. Alas, three of Master Ford's brothers watch the door with pistols, that none shall issue out; otherwise you might slip away ere he came. But what make you here?

Fal. What shall I do? I'll creep up into the chimney.

Mrs. Ford. There they always use to discharge their birding-pieces. Creep into the kiln-hole.

Fal. Where is it?

Mrs. Ford. He will seek there, on my word. Neither press, coffer, chest, trunk, well, vault, but he hath an abstract for the remembrance of such places, and goes to them by his note. There is no hiding you in the house.

Fal. I'll go out then.

Mrs. Page. If you go out in your own semblance, you die, Sir John. Unless you go out disguised—

Mrs. Ford. How might we disguise him?

Mrs. Page. Alas the day, I know not! There is no woman's gown big enough for him; otherwise he might put on a hat, a muffler and a kerchief, and so escape.

Fal. Good hearts, devise something. Any extremity rather than a mischief.

Mrs. Ford. My maid's aunt, the fat woman of Brentford, has a gown above.

Mrs. Page. On my word, it will serve him; she's as big as he is; and there's her thrummed hat and her muffler too. Run up, Sir John.

Mrs. Ford. Go, go, sweet Sir John. Mistress Page and I will look some linen for your head.

Mrs. Page. Quick, quick! we'll come dress you straight. Put on the gown the while.

[*Exit* FALSTAFF.

Mrs. Ford. I would my husband would meet him in this shape. He cannot abide the old woman of Brentford; he swears she's a witch; forbade her my house and hath threatened to beat her.

Mrs. Page. Heaven guide him to thy husband's cudgel, and the devil guide his cudgel afterwards!

Mrs. Ford. But is my husband coming?

Mrs. Page. Ay, in good sadness, is he; and talks of the basket too, howsoever he hath had intelligence.

Mrs. Ford. We'll try that; for I'll appoint my men to carry the basket again, to meet him at the door with it, as they did last time.

Mrs. Page. Nay, but he'll be here presently. Let's go dress him like the witch of Brentford.

Mrs. Ford. I'll first direct my men what they

shall do with the basket. Go up; I'll bring linen for him straight. [*Exit.*

Mrs. Page. Hang him, dishonest varlet! we cannot misuse him enough.
We'll leave a proof, by that which we will do,
Wives may be merry, and yet honest too.
We do not act that often jest and laugh;
'Tis old, but true, Still swine eats all the draff. [*Exit.*

Re-enter MISTRESS FORD *with* TWO SERVANTS.

Mrs. Ford. Go, sirs, take the basket again on your shoulders. Your master is hard at door; if he bid you set it down, obey him. Quickly, dispatch. [*Exit.*

1st Serv. Come, come, take it up.

2nd Serv. Pray heaven it be not full of knight again.

1st Serv. I hope not; I had as lief bear so much lead.

Enter FORD, PAGE, SHALLOW, CAIUS, *and* SIR HUGH EVANS.

Ford. Ay, but if it prove true, Master Page, have you any way then to unfool me again? Set down the basket, villain! Somebody call my wife. Youth in a basket! O you pandarly rascals! there's a knot, a ging, a pack, a conspiracy against me. Now shall the devil be shamed. What, wife, I say! Come, come forth! Behold what honest clothes you send forth to bleaching!

Page. Why, this passes, Master Ford; you are not to go loose any longer; you must be pinioned.

Evans. Why, this is lunatics! this is mad as a mad dog!

Shal. Indeed, Master Ford, this is not well, indeed.

Ford. So say I too, sir.

Re-enter MISTRESS FORD.

Come hither, Mistress Ford; Mistress Ford, the honest woman, the modest wife, the virtuous creature, that hath the jealous fool to her husband! I suspect without cause, mistress, do I?

Mrs. Ford. Heaven be my witness you do, if you suspect me in any dishonesty.

Ford. Well said, brazen-face! hold it out. Come forth, sirrah!

Pulling clothes out of the basket.

Page. This passes!

Mrs. Ford. Are you not ashamed? let the clothes alone.

Ford. I shall find you anon.

Evans. 'Tis unreasonable! Will you take up your wife's clothes? Come away.

Ford. Empty the basket, I say!

Mrs. Ford. Why, man, why?

Ford. Master Page, as I am a man, there was one conveyed out of my house yesterday in this basket. Why may not he be there again? In my house I am sure he is. My intelligence is true; my jealousy is reasonable. Pluck me out all the linen.

Mrs. Ford. If you find a man there, he shall die a flea's death.

Page. Here's no man.

Shal. By my fidelity, this is not well, Master Ford; this wrongs you.

Evans. Master Ford, you must pray, and not follow the imaginations of your own heart. This is jealousies.

Ford. Well, he's not here I seek for.

Page. No, nor nowhere else but in your brain.

Ford. Help to search my house this one time. If I find not what I seek, show no colour for my extremity; let me for ever be your table-sport; let them say of me, "As jealous as Ford, that searched a hollow walnut for his wife's leman." Satisfy me once more; once more search with me.

Mrs. Ford. What, ho, Mistress Page! come you and the old woman down; my husband will come into the chamber.

Ford. Old woman! what old woman's that?

Mrs Ford. Why, it is my maid's aunt of Brentford.

Ford. A witch, a quean, an old cozening quean! Have I not forbid her my house? She comes of errands, does she? We are simple men; we do not know what's brought to pass under the profession of fortune-telling. She works by charms, by spells, by the figure, and such daubery as this is, beyond our element. We know nothing. Come down, you witch, you hag, you; come down, I say!

Mrs. Ford. Nay, good, sweet husband! Good gentlemen, let him not strike the old woman.

Re-enter FALSTAFF *in woman's clothes, and* MISTRESS PAGE.

Mrs. Page. Come, Mother Prat; come, give me your hand.

Ford. I'll prat her. [*Beating him*] Out of my door, you witch, you hag, you baggage, you polecat, you ronyon! out, out! I'll conjure you, I'll fortune-tell you. [*Exit* FALSTAFF.

Mrs. Page. Are you not ashamed? I think you have killed the poor woman.

Mrs. Ford. Nay, he will do it. 'Tis a goodly credit for you.

Ford. Hang her, witch!

Evans. By yea and no, I think the 'oman is a

witch indeed. I like not when a 'oman has a great peard; I spy a great peard under his muffler.

Ford. Will you follow, gentlemen? I beseech you, follow; see but the issue of my jealousy. If I cry out thus upon no trail, never trust me when I open again.

Page. Let's obey his humour a little further. Come, gentlemen.

[*Exeunt* FORD, PAGE, SHALLOW, CAIUS, *and* EVANS.

Mrs. Page. Trust me, he beat him most pitifully.

Mrs. Ford. Nay, by the mass, that he did not; he beat him most unpitifully, methought.

Mrs. Page. I'll have the cudgel hallowed and hung o'er the altar; it hath done meritorious service.

Mrs. Ford. What think you? may we, with the warrant of womanhood and the witness of a good conscience, pursue him with any further revenge?

Mrs. Page. The spirit of wantonness is, sure, scared out of him. If the devil have him not in fee-simple, with fine and recovery, he will never, I think, in the way of waste, attempt us again.

Mrs. Ford. Shall we tell our husbands how we have served him?

Mrs. Page. Yes, by all means; if it be but to scrape the figures out of your husband's brains. If they can find in their hearts the poor unvirtuous fat knight shall be any further afflicted, we two will still be the ministers.

Mrs. Ford. I'll warrant they'll have him publicly shamed; and methinks there would be no period to the jest, should he not be publicly shamed.

Mrs. Page. Come, to the forge with it then; shape it. I would not have things cool. [*Exeunt*.

SCENE III. *A room in the Garter Inn*

Enter HOST *and* BARDOLPH.

Bard. Sir, the Germans desire to have three of your horses. The Duke himself will be tomorrow at court, and they are going to meet him.

Host. What duke should that be comes so secretly? I hear not of him in the court. Let me speak with the gentlemen. They speak English?

Bard. Ay, sir; I'll call them to you.

Host. They shall have my horses; but I'll make them pay; I'll sauce them. They have had my house a week at command; I have turned away my other guests. They must come off; I'll sauce them. Come. [*Exeunt*.

SCENE IV. *A room in Ford's house*

Enter PAGE, FORD, MISTRESS PAGE, MISTRESS FORD, *and* SIR HUGH EVANS.

Evans. 'Tis one of the best discretions of a 'oman as ever I did look upon.

Page. And did he send you both these letters at an instant?

Mrs. Page. Within a quarter of an hour.

Ford. Pardon me, wife. Henceforth do what thou wilt.
I rather will suspect the sun with cold
Than thee with wantonness. Now doth thy honour stand,
In him that was of late an heretic,
As firm as faith.

Page. 'Tis well, 'tis well; no more.
Be not as extreme in submission
As in offence.
But let our plot go forward. Let our wives
Yet once again, to make us public sport,
Appoint a meeting with this old fat fellow,
Where we may take him and disgrace him for it.

Ford. There is no better way than that they spoke of.

Page. How? to send him word they'll meet him in the park at midnight? Fie, fie! he'll never come.

Evans. You say he has been thrown in the rivers and has been grievously peaten as an old 'oman. Methinks there should be terrors in him that he should not come; methinks his flesh is punished, he shall have no desires.

Page. So think I too.

Mrs. Ford. Devise but how you'll use him when he comes,
And let us two devise to bring him thither.

Mrs. Page. There is an old tale goes that Herne the hunter,
Sometime a keeper here in Windsor forest,
Doth all the winter-time, at still midnight,
Walk round about an oak, with great ragg'd horns;
And there he blasts the tree and takes the cattle
And makes milch-kine yield blood and shakes a chain
In a most hideous and dreadful manner.
You have heard of such a spirit, and well you know
The superstitious idle-headed eld
Received and did deliver to our age
This tale of Herne the hunter for a truth.

Page. Why, yet there want not many that do fear
In deep of night to walk by this Herne's oak.
But what of this?

Mrs. Ford. Marry, this is our device;
That Falstaff at that oak shall meet with us.

Page. Well, let it not be doubted but he'll come;
And in this shape when you have brought him thither,
What shall be done with him? what is your plot?

Mrs. Page. That likewise have we thought upon, and thus:
Nan Page, my daughter, and my little son
And three or four more of their growth we'll dress
Like urchins, ouphes, and fairies, green and white,
With rounds of waxen tapers on their heads,
And rattles in their hands. Upon a sudden,
As Falstaff, she, and I are newly met,
Let them from forth a sawpit rush at once
With some diffused song. Upon their sight,
We two in great amazedness will fly.
Then let them all encircle him about
And, fairy-like, to pinch the unclean knight,
And ask him why, that hour of fairy revel,
In their so sacred paths he dares to tread
In shape profane.

Mrs. Ford. And till he tell the truth,
Let the supposed fairies pinch him sound
And burn him with their tapers.

Mrs. Page. The truth being known,
We'll all present ourselves, dis-horn the spirit,
And mock him home to Windsor.

Ford. The children must
Be practised well to this, or they'll ne'er do't.

Evans. I will teach the children their behaviors; and I will be like a jack-an-apes also, to burn the knight with my taber.

Ford. That will be excellent. I'll go buy them vizards.

Mrs. Page. My Nan shall be the queen of all the fairies,
Finely attired in a robe of white.

Page. That silk will I go buy. [*Aside*] And in that time
Shall Master Slender steal my Nan away
And marry her at Eton. Go send to Falstaff straight.

Ford. Nay, I'll to him again in name of Brook.
He'll tell me all his purpose. Sure, he'll come.

Mrs. Page. Fear not you that. Go get us properties
And tricking for our fairies.

Evans. Let us about it. It is admirable pleasures and fery honest knaveries.

[*Exeunt* PAGE, FORD, *and* EVANS.

Mrs. Page. Go, mistress Ford,
Send quickly to Sir John, to know his mind.

[*Exit* MISTRESS FORD.

I'll to the doctor. He hath my good will,
And none but he, to marry with Nan Page.
That Slender, though well landed, is an idiot;
And he my husband best of all affects.
The doctor is well money'd, and his friends
Potent at court. He, none but he, shall have her,
Though twenty thousand worthier come to crave her.

[*Exit*.

SCENE V. *A room in the Garter Inn*

Enter HOST *and* SIMPLE.

Host. What wouldst thou have, boor? what, thick-skin? speak, breathe, discuss; brief, short, quick, snap.

Sim. Marry, sir, I come to speak with Sir John Falstaff from Master Slender.

Host. There's his chamber, his house, his castle, his standing-bed and truckle-bed; 'tis painted about with the story of the Prodigal, fresh and new. Go knock and call; he'll speak like an Anthropophaginian unto thee. Knock, I say.

Sim. There's an old woman, a fat woman, gone up into his chamber. I'll be so bold as stay, sir, till she come down; I come to speak with her, indeed.

Host. Ha! a fat woman! the knight may be robbed. I'll call. Bully knight! bully Sir John! speak from thy lungs military. Art thou there? it is thine host, thine Ephesian, calls.

Fal. [*Above*] How now, mine host!

Host. Here's a Bohemian-Tartar tarries the coming down of thy fat woman. Let her descend, bully, let her descend; my chambers are honourable. Fie! privacy? fie!

Enter FALSTAFF.

Fal. There was, mine host, an old fat woman even now with me; but she's gone.

Sim. Pray you, sir, was't not the wise woman of Brentford?

Fal. Ay, marry, was it, mussel-shell. What would you with her?

Sim. My master, sir, Master Slender, sent to her, seeing her go through the streets, to know, sir, whether one Nym, sir, that beguiled him of a chain, had the chain or no.

Fal. I spake with the old woman about it.

Sim. And what says she, I pray, sir?

Fal. Marry, she says that the very same man that beguiled Master Slender of his chain cozened him of it.

Sim. I would I could have spoken with the woman herself; I had other things to have spoken with her too from him.

Fal. What are they? let us know.

Host. Ay, come; quick.

Sim. I may not conceal them, sir.

Host. Conceal them, or thou diest.

Sim. Why, sir, they were nothing but about Mistress Anne Page; to know if it were my master's fortune to have her or no.

Fal. 'Tis, 'tis his fortune.

Sim. What, sir?

Fal. To have her, or no. Go; say the woman told me so.

Sim. May I be bold to say so, sir?

Fal. Ay, sir; like who more bold.

Sim. I thank your worship. I shall make my master glad with these tidings. [*Exit.*

Host. Thou art clerkly, thou art clerkly, Sir John. Was there a wise woman with thee?

Fal. Ay, that there was, mine host; one that hath taught me more wit than ever I learned before in my life; and I paid nothing for it neither, but was paid for my learning.

Enter BARDOLPH.

Bard. Out, alas, sir! cozenage, mere cozenage!

Host. Where be my horses? speak well of them, varletto.

Bard. Run away with the cozeners; for so soon as I came beyond Eton, they threw me off from behind one of them, in a slough of mire; and set spurs and away, like three German devils, three Doctor Faustuses.

Host. They are gone but to meet the Duke, villain. Do not say they be fled; Germans are honest men.

Enter SIR HUGH EVANS.

Evans. Where is mine host?

Host. What is the matter, sir?

Evans. Have a care of your entertainments. There is a friend of mine come to town, tells me there is three cozen-germans that has cozened all the hosts of Readins, of Maidenhead, of Colebrook, of horses and money. I tell you for good will, look you. You are wise and full of gibes and vlouting-stocks, and 'tis not convenient you should be cozened. Fare you well. [*Exit.*

Enter DOCTOR CAIUS.

Caius. Vere is mine host de Jarteer?

Host. Here, master doctor, in perplexity and doubtful dilemma.

Caius. I cannot tell vat is dat; but it is tell-a me dat you make grand preparation for a duke de Jamany. By my trot, dere is no duke dat the court is know to come. I tell you for good vill: adieu. [*Exit.*

Host. Hue and cry, villain, go! Assist me, knight. I am undone! Fly, run, hue and cry, villain! I am undone! [*Exeunt* HOST *and* BARDOLPH.

Fal. I would all the world might be cozened; for I have been cozened and beaten too. If it should come to the ear of the court, how I have been transformed and how my transformation hath been washed and cudgelled, they would melt me out of my fat drop by drop and liquor fishermen's boots with me. I warrant they would whip me with their fine wits till I were as crestfallen as a dried pear. I never prospered since I forswore myself at primero. Well, if my wind were but long enough to say my prayers, I would repent.

Enter MISTRESS QUICKLY.

Now, whence come you?

Quick. From the two parties, forsooth.

Fal. The devil take one party and his dam the other! and so they shall be both bestowed. I have suffered more for their sakes, more than the villainous inconstancy of man's disposition is able to bear.

Quick. And have not they suffered? Yes, I warrant; speciously one of them; Mistress Ford, good heart, is beaten black and blue, that you cannot see a white spot about her.

Fal. What tellest thou me of black and blue? I was beaten myself into all the colours of the rainbow; and I was like to be apprehended for the witch of Brentford. But that my admirable dexterity of wit, my counterfeiting the action of an old woman, delivered me, the knave constable had set me i' the stocks, i' the common stocks, for a witch.

Quick. Sir, let me speak with you in your chamber. You shall hear how things go; and, I warrant, to your content. Here is a letter will say somewhat. Good hearts, what ado here is to bring you together! Sure, one of you does not serve heaven well, that you are so crossed.

Fal. Come up into my chamber. [*Exeunt.*

SCENE VI. *Another room in the Garter Inn*

Enter FENTON *and* HOST.

Host. Master Fenton, talk not to me; my mind is heavy. I will give over all.

Fent. Yet hear me speak. Assist me in my purpose,
And, as I am a gentleman, I'll give thee
A hundred pound in gold more than your loss.

Host. I will hear you, Master Fenton; and I will at the least keep your counsel.

Fent. From time to time I have acquainted you
With the dear love I bear to fair Anne Page;
Who mutually hath answer'd my affection,
So far forth as herself might be her chooser,
Even to my wish. I have a letter from her
Of such contents as you will wonder at;
The mirth whereof so larded with my matter,
That neither singly can be manifested,
Without the show of both. Fat Falstaff
Hath a great scene. The image of the jest

I'll show you here at large. Hark, good mine
host.
To-night at Herne's oak, just 'twixt twelve and
one,
Must my sweet Nan present the Fairy Queen;
The purpose why, is here; in which disguise,
While other jests are something rank on foot,
Her father hath commanded her to slip
Away with Slender and with him at Eton
Immediately to marry. She hath consented.
Now, sir,
Her mother, ever strong against that match
And firm for Doctor Caius, hath appointed
That he shall likewise shuffle her away,
While other sports are tasking of their minds,
And at the deanery, where a priest attends,
Straight marry her. To this her mother's plot
She seemingly obedient likewise hath
Made promise to the doctor. Now, thus it rests:
Her father means she shall be all in white,
And in that habit, when Slender sees his time
To take her by the hand and bid her go,
She shall go with him. Her mother hath intended,
The better to denote her to the doctor,
For they must all be mask'd and vizarded,
That quaint in green she shall be loose enrobed,
With ribands pendent, flaring 'bout her head;
And when the doctor spies his vantage ripe,
To pinch her by the hand, and, on that token,
The maid hath given consent to go with him.

Host. Which means she to deceive, father or
mother?

Fent. Both, my good host, to go along with me.
And here it rests, that you'll procure the vicar
To stay for me at church 'twixt twelve and one,
And, in the lawful name of marrying,
To give our hearts united ceremony.

Host. Well, husband your device; I'll to the
vicar.
Bring you the maid, you shall not lack a priest.

Fent. So shall I evermore be bound to thee;
Besides, I'll make a present recompense. [*Exeunt*.

ACT V

SCENE I. *A room in the Garter Inn*

Enter FALSTAFF *and* MISTRESS QUICKLY.

Fal. Prithee, no more prattling; go. I'll hold. This is the third time; I hope good luck lies in odd numbers. Away! go. They say there is divinity in odd numbers, either in nativity, chance, or death. Away!

Quick. I'll provide you a chain; and I'll do what I can to get you a pair of horns.

Fal. Away, I say; time wears. Hold up your head, and mince. [*Exit* MISTRESS QUICKLY.

Enter FORD.

How now, Master Brook! Master Brook, the matter will be known to-night, or never. Be you in the Park about midnight, at Herne's oak, and you shall see wonders.

Ford. Went you not to her yesterday, sir, as you told me you had appointed?

Fal. I went to her, Master Brook, as you see, like a poor old man; but I came from her, Master Brook, like a poor old woman. That same knave Ford, her husband, hath the finest mad devil of jealousy in him, Master Brook, that ever governed frenzy. I will tell you. He beat me grievously, in the shape of a woman; for in the shape of man, Master Brook, I fear not Goliath with a weaver's beam; because I know also life is a shuttle. I am in haste; go along with me. I'll tell you all, Master Brook. Since I plucked geese, played truant, and whipped top, I knew not what 'twas to be beaten till lately. Follow me. I'll tell you strange things of this knave Ford, on whom to-night I will be revenged, and I will deliver his wife into your hand. Follow. Strange things in hand, Master Brook! Follow. [*Exeunt*.

SCENE II. *Windsor Park*

Enter PAGE, SHALLOW, *and* SLENDER.

Page. Come, come; we'll couch i' the castle-ditch till we see the light of our fairies. Remember, son Slender, my daughter.

Slen. Ay, forsooth; I have spoke with her and we have a nay-word how to know one another. I come to her in white, and cry "mum"; she cries "budget"; and by that we know one another.

Shal. That's good too; but what needs either your "mum" or her "budget"? the white will decipher her well enough. It hath struck ten o'clock.

Page. The night is dark; light and spirits will become it well. Heaven prosper our sport! No man means evil but the devil, and we shall know him by his horns. Let's away; follow me. [*Exeunt*.

SCENE III. *A street leading to the Park*

Enter MISTRESS PAGE, MISTRESS FORD, *and* DOCTOR CAIUS.

Mrs. Page. Master doctor, my daughter is in green. When you see your time, take her by the hand, away with her to the deanery, and dispatch it quickly. Go before into the Park. We two must go together.

Caius. I know vat I have to do. Adieu.

Mrs. Page. Fare you well, sir. [*Exit* CAIUS.] My husband will not rejoice so much at the abuse of

Falstaff as he will chafe at the doctor's marrying my daughter. But 'tis no matter; better a little chiding than a great deal of heart-break.

Mrs. Ford. Where is Nan now and her troop of fairies, and the Welsh devil Hugh?

Mrs. Page. They are all couched in a pit hard by Herne's oak, with obscured lights; which, at the very instant of Falstaff's and our meeting, they will at once display to the night.

Mrs. Ford. That cannot choose but amaze him.

Mrs. Page. If he be not amazed, he will be mocked; if he be amazed, he will every way be mocked.

Mrs. Ford. We'll betray him finely.

Mrs. Page. Against such lewdsters and their lechery
Those that betray them do no treachery.

Mrs. Ford. The hour draws on. To the oak, to the oak! [*Exeunt.*

Scene iv. *Windsor Park*

Enter Sir Hugh Evans *disguised, with others as Fairies.*

Evans. Trib, trib, fairies; come; and remember your parts. Be pold, I pray you; follow me into the pit; and when I give the watch-'ords, do as I pid you. Come, come; trib, trib. [*Exeunt.*

Scene v. *Another part of the Park*

Enter Falstaff *disguised as Herne with a buck's head upon him.*

Fal. The Windsor bell hath struck twelve; the minute draws on. Now, the hot-blooded gods assist me! Remember, Jove, thou wast a bull for thy Europa; love set on thy horns. O powerful love! that, in some respects, makes a beast a man, in some other, a man a beast. You were also, Jupiter, a swan for the love of Leda. O omnipotent Love! how near the god drew to the complexion of a goose! A fault done first in the form of a beast. O Jove, a beastly fault! And then another fault in the semblance of a fowl; think on't, Jove; a foul fault! When gods have hot backs, what shall poor men do? For me, I am here a Windsor stag; and the fattest, I think, i' the forest. Send me a cool rut-time, Jove, or who can blame me to piss my tallow? Who comes here? my doe?

Enter Mistress Ford *and* Mistress Page.

Mrs. Ford. Sir John! art thou there, my deer? my male deer?

Fal. My doe with the black scut! Let the sky rain potatoes; let it thunder to the tune of "Green Sleeves," hail kissing-comfits and snow eringoes; let there come a tempest of provocation, I will shelter me here.

Mrs. Ford. Mistress Page is come with me, sweetheart.

Fal. Divide me like a bribe buck, each a haunch. I will keep my sides to myself, my shoulders for the fellow of this walk, and my horns I bequeath your husbands. Am I a woodman, ha? Speak I like Herne the hunter? Why, now is Cupid a child of conscience; he makes restitution. As I am a true spirit, welcome!

Noise within.

Mrs. Page. Alas, what noise?

Mrs. Ford. Heaven forgive our sins!

Fal. What should this be?

Mrs. Ford.
Mrs. Page. } Away, away! [*They run off.*

Fal. I think the devil will not have me damned, lest the oil that's in me should set hell on fire; he would never else cross me thus.

Enter Sir Hugh Evans, *disguised as a Satyr;* Pistol, *as Hobgoblin;* Mistress Quickly, Anne Page, *and others, as Fairies, with tapers.*

Quick. Fairies, black, grey, green, and white,
You moonshine revellers, and shades of night,
You orphan heirs of fixed destiny,
Attend your office and your quality.
Crier Hobgoblin, make the fairy oyes.

Pist. Elves, list your names; silence, you airy toys.
Cricket, to Windsor chimneys shalt thou leap:
Where fires thou find'st unraked and hearths unswept,
There pinch the maids as blue as bilberry;
Our radiant queen hates sluts and sluttery.

Fal. They are fairies; he that speaks to them shall die.
I'll wink and couch; no man their works must eye.

Lies down upon his face.

Evans. Where's Bede? Go you, and where you find a maid
That, ere she sleep, has thrice her prayers said,
Raise up the organs of her fantasy;
Sleep she as sound as careless infancy.
But those as sleep and think not on their sins,
Pinch them, arms, legs, backs, shoulders, sides, and shins.

Quick. About, about;
Search Windsor Castle, elves, within and out.
Strew good luck, ouphes, on every sacred room;
That it may stand till the perpetual doom
In state as wholesome as in state 'tis fit,
Worthy the owner, and the owner it.
The several chairs of order look you scour

With juice of balm and every precious flower;
Each fair instalment, coat, and several crest,
With loyal blazon, evermore be blest!
And nightly, meadow-fairies, look you sing,
Like to the Garter's compass, in a ring.
The expressure that it bears, green let it be,
More fertile-fresh than all the field to see;
And "*Honi soit qui mal y pense*" write
In emerald tufts, flowers purple, blue, and white;
Like sapphire, pearl, and rich embroidery,
Buckled below fair knighthood's bending knee.
Fairies use flowers for their charactery.
Away; disperse. But till 'tis one o'clock,
Our dance of custom round about the oak
Of Herne the hunter, let us not forget.

Evans. Pray you, lock hand in hand; yourselves in order set;
And twenty glow-worms shall our lanterns be,
To guide our measure round about the tree.
But, stay; I smell a man of middle-earth.

Fal. Heavens defend me from that Welsh fairy, lest he transform me to a piece of cheese!

Pist. Vile worm, thou wast o'erlook'd even in thy birth.

Quick. With trial-fire touch me his finger-end.
If he be chaste, the flame will back descend
And turn him to no pain; but if he start,
It is the flesh of a corrupted heart.

Pist. A trial, come.

Evans. Come, will this wood take fire?

They burn him with their tapers.

Fal. Oh, Oh, Oh!

Quick. Corrupt, corrupt, and tainted in desire!
About him, fairies; sing a scornful rhyme;
And, as you trip, still pinch him to your time.

SONG

Fie on sinful fantasy!
Fie on lust and luxury!
Lust is but a bloody fire,
Kindled with unchaste desire,
Fed in heart, whose flames aspire
As thoughts do blow them, higher and higher.
Pinch him, fairies, mutually;
Pinch him for his villainy;
Pinch him, and burn him, and turn him about,
Till candles and starlight and moonshine be out.

During this song they pinch FALSTAFF. DOCTOR CAIUS *comes one way, and steals away a boy in green;* SLENDER *another way, and takes off a boy in white; and* FENTON *comes, and steals away* ANNE PAGE. *A noise of hunting is heard within. All the Fairies run away.* FALSTAFF *pulls off his buck's head, and rises.*

Enter PAGE, FORD, MISTRESS PAGE *and* MISTRESS FORD.

Page. Nay, do not fly; I think we have watch'd you now.
Will none but Herne the hunter serve your turn?

Mrs. Page. I pray you, come, hold up the jest no higher.
Now, good Sir John, how like you Windsor wives?
See you these, husband? do not these fair yokes
Become the forest better than the town?

Ford. Now, sir, who's a cuckold now? Master Brook, Falstaff's a knave, a cuckoldly knave; here are his horns, Master Brook; and, Master Brook, he hath enjoyed nothing of Ford's but his buck-basket, his cudgel, and twenty pounds of money, which must be paid to Master Brook; his horses are arrested for it, Master Brook.

Mrs. Ford. Sir John, we have had ill luck; we could never meet. I will never take you for my love again; but I will always count you my deer.

Fal. I do begin to perceive that I am made an ass.

Ford. Ay, and an ox too; both the proofs are extant.

Fal. And these are not fairies? I was three or four times in the thought they were not fairies; and yet the guiltiness of my mind, the sudden surprise of my powers, drove the grossness of the foppery into a received belief, in despite of the teeth of all rhyme and reason, that they were fairies. See now how wit may be made a Jack-a-Lent, when 'tis upon ill employment!

Evans. Sir John Falstaff, serve Got, and leave your desires, and fairies will not pinse you.

Ford. Well said, fairy Hugh.

Evans. And leave your jealousies too, I pray you.

Ford. I will never mistrust my wife again, till thou art able to woo her in good English.

Fal. Have I laid my brain in the sun and dried it, that it wants matter to prevent so gross o'er-reaching as this? Am I ridden with a Welsh goat too? shall I have a coxcomb of frize? 'Tis time I were choked with a piece of toasted cheese.

Evans. Seese is not good to give putter; your belly is all putter.

Fal. "Seese" and "putter"! have I lived to stand at the taunt of one that makes fritters of English? This is enough to be the decay of lust and late-walking through the realm.

Mrs. Page. Why, Sir John, do you think, though we would have thrust virtue out of our hearts by the head and shoulders and have given ourselves without scruple to hell, that ever the devil could have made you our delight?

Ford. What, a hodge-pudding? a bag of flax?

Mrs. Page. A puffed man?

Page. Old, cold, withered, and of intolerable entrails?

Ford. And one that is as slanderous as Satan?

Page. And as poor as Job?

Ford. And as wicked as his wife?

Evans. And given to fornications, and to taverns and sack and wine and metheglins, and to drinkings and swearings and starings, pribbles and prabbles?

Fal. Well, I am your theme; you have the start of me. I am dejected; I am not able to answer the Welsh flannel; ignorance itself is a plummet o'er me. Use me as you will.

Ford. Marry, sir, we'll bring you to Windsor, to one Master Brook, that you have cozened of money, to whom you should have been a pandar. Over and above that you have suffered, I think to repay that money will be a biting affliction.

Page. Yet be cheerful, knight. Thou shalt eat a posset to-night at my house; where I will desire thee to laugh at my wife, that now laughs at thee. Tell her Master Slender hath married her daughter.

Mrs. Page. [*Aside*] Doctors doubt that. If Anne Page be my daughter, she is, by this, Doctor Caius' wife.

Enter SLENDER.

Slen. Whoa, ho! ho, father Page!

Page. Son, how now! how now, son! have you dispatched?

Slen. Dispatched! I'll make the best in Gloucestershire know on't; would I were hanged, la, else!

Page. Of what, son?

Slen. I came yonder at Eton to marry Mistress Anne Page, and she's a great lubberly boy. If it had not been i' the church, I would have swinged him, or he should have swinged me. If I did not think it had been Anne Page, would I might never stir!—and 'tis a postmaster's boy.

Page. Upon my life, then, you took the wrong.

Slen. What need you tell me that? I think so, when I took a boy for a girl. If I had been married to him, for all he was in woman's apparel, I would not have had him.

Page. Why, this is your own folly. Did not I tell you how you should know my daughter by her garments?

Slen. I went to her in white, and cried "mum," and she cried "budget," as Anne and I had appointed; and yet it was not Anne, but a postmaster's boy.

Mrs. Page. Good George, be not angry: I knew of your purpose; turned my daughter into green; and, indeed, she is now with the doctor at the deanery, and there married.

Enter CAIUS.

Caius. Vere is Mistress Page? By gar, I am cozened. I ha' married *un garcon*, a boy; *un paysan*, by gar, a boy; it is not Anne Page. By gar, I am cozened.

Mrs. Page. Why, did you take her in green?

Caius. Ay, by gar, and 'tis a boy. By gar, I'll raise all Windsor. [*Exit.*

Ford. This is strange. Who hath got the right Anne?

Page. My heart misgives me. Here comes Master Fenton.

Enter FENTON *and* ANNE PAGE.

How now, Master Fenton!

Anne. Pardon, good father! good my mother,
pardon!

Page. Now, mistress, how chance you went not with Master Slender?

Mrs. Page. Why went you not with master doctor, maid?

Fent. You do amaze her. Hear the truth of it.
You would have married her most shamefully,
Where there was no proportion held in love.
The truth is, she and I, long since contracted,
Are now so sure that nothing can dissolve us.
The offence is holy that she hath committed;
And this deceit loses the name of craft,
Of disobedience, or unduteous title,
Since therein she doth evitate and shun
A thousand irreligious cursed hours,
Which forced marriage would have brought
upon her.

Ford. Stand not amazed; here is no remedy.
In love the heavens themselves do guide the
state;
Money buys lands, and wives are sold by fate.

Fal. I am glad, though you have ta'en a special stand to strike at me, that your arrow hath glanced.

Page. Well, what remedy? Fenton, heaven give
thee joy!
What cannot be eschew'd must be embraced.

Fal. When night-dogs run, all sorts of deer are
chased.

Mrs. Page. Well, I will must no further. Master
Fenton,
Heaven give you many, many merry days!
Good husband, let us every one go home,
And laugh this sport o'er by a country fire;
Sir John and all.

Ford. Let it be so. Sir John,
To Master Brook you yet shall hold your word;
For he to-night shall lie with Mistress Ford.
[*Exeunt.*

TROILUS AND CRESSIDA

DRAMATIS PERSONÆ

PRIAM, *King of Troy*
HECTOR, TROILUS, PARIS, DEIPHOBUS, HELENUS — *his sons*
MARGARELON, *a bastard son of Priam*
ÆNEAS, ANTENOR — *Trojan commanders*
CALCHAS, *a Trojan priest, taking part with the Greeks*
PANDARUS, *uncle to Cressida*
AGAMEMNON, *the Grecian general*
MENELAUS, *his brother*
ACHILLES, AJAX, ULYSSES, NESTOR, DIOMEDES, PATROCLUS — *Grecian commanders*

THERSITES, *a deformed and scurrilous Grecian*
ALEXANDER, *servant to Cressida*
A BOY, *servant to Troilus*
A SERVANT *to Paris*
A SERVANT *to Diomedes*
A MYRMIDON

HELEN, *wife to Menelaus*
ANDROMACHE, *wife to Hector*
CASSANDRA, *daughter to Priam, a prophetess*
CRESSIDA, *daughter to Calchas*

NON-SPEAKING: *Trojan and Greek soldiers, Myrmidons, and Attendants*

SCENE: *Troy, and the Grecian camp before it*

PROLOGUE

In Troy, there lies the scene. From isles of Greece
The princes orgulous, their high blood chafed,
Have to the port of Athens sent their ships,
Fraught with the ministers and instruments
Of cruel war. Sixty and nine, that wore
Their crownets regal, from the Athenian bay
Put forth toward Phrygia; and their vow is made
To ransack Troy, within whose strong immures
The ravish'd Helen, Menelaus' queen,
With wanton Paris sleeps; and that's the quarrel.
To Tenedos they come;
And the deep-drawing barks do there disgorge
Their warlike fraughtage. Now on Dardan plains
The fresh and yet unbruised Greeks do pitch
Their brave pavilions. Priam's six-gated city,
Dardan, and Tymbria, Helias, Chetas, Troien,
And Antenorides, with massy staples
And corresponsive and fulfilling bolts,
Sperr up the sons of Troy.
Now expectation, tickling skittish spirits,
On one and other side, Trojan and Greek,
Sets all on hazard: and hither am I come
A prologue arm'd, but not in confidence
Of author's pen or actor's voice, but suited
In like conditions as our argument,
To tell you, fair beholders, that our play
Leaps o'er the vaunt and firstlings of those broils,
Beginning in the middle, starting thence away
To what may be digested in a play.
Like or find fault; do as your pleasures are;
Now good or bad, 'tis but the chance of war.

ACT I

SCENE I. *Troy: before Priam's palace*

Enter TROILUS *armed, and* PANDARUS.

Tro. Call here my varlet; I'll unarm again.
Why should I war without the walls of Troy,
That find such cruel battle here within?
Each Trojan that is master of his heart,
Let him to field; Troilus, alas! hath none.

Pan. Will this gear ne'er be mended?

Tro. The Greeks are strong and skilful to their strength,
Fierce to their skill and to their fierceness valiant;
But I am weaker than a woman's tear,
Tamer than sleep, fonder than ignorance,
Less valiant than the virgin in the night,
And skilless as unpractised infancy.

Pan. Well, I have told you enough of this. For my part, I'll not meddle nor make no further. He that will have a cake out of the wheat must needs tarry the grinding.

Tro. Have I not tarried?

Pan. Ay, the grinding; but you must tarry the bolting.

Tro. Have I not tarried?

Pan. Ay, the bolting, but you must tarry the leavening.

Tro. Still have I tarried.

Pan. Ay, to the leavening; but here's yet in the word "hereafter" the kneading, the making of the cake, the heating of the oven, and the baking; nay, you must stay the cooling too, or you may chance to burn your lips.

Tro. Patience herself, what goddess e'er she be,
Doth lesser blench at sufferance than I do.
At Priam's royal table do I sit;
And when fair Cressid comes into my thoughts—
So, traitor! "When she comes!" When is she thence?

Pan. Well, she looked yesternight fairer than ever I saw her look, or any woman else.

Tro. I was about to tell thee:—when my heart,
As wedged with a sigh, would rive in twain,
Lest Hector or my father should perceive me,
I have, as when the sun doth light a storm,
Buried this sigh in wrinkle of a smile.
But sorrow, that is couch'd in seeming gladness,
Is like that mirth fate turns to sudden sadness.

Pan. An her hair were not somewhat darker than Helen's—well, go to—there were no more comparison between the women. But, for my part, she is my kinswoman; I would not, as they term it, praise her, but I would somebody had heard her talk yesterday, as I did. I will not dispraise your sister Cassandra's wit, but—

Tro. O Pandarus! I tell thee, Pandarus—
When I do tell thee, there my hopes lie drown'd,
Reply not in how many fathoms deep
They lie indrench'd. I tell thee I am mad
In Cressid's love. Thou answer'st, "She is fair";
Pour'st in the open ulcer of my heart
Her eyes, her hair, her cheek, her gait, her voice,
Handlest in thy discourse, O, that her hand,
In whose comparison all whites are ink,
Writing their own reproach, to whose soft seizure
The cygnet's down is harsh and spirit of sense
Hard as the palm of ploughman. This thou tell'st me,
As true thou tell'st me, when I say I love her;
But, saying thus, instead of oil and balm,
Thou lay'st in every gash that love hath given me
The knife that made it.

Pan. I speak no more than truth.

Tro. Thou dost not speak so much.

Pan. Faith, I'll not meddle in't. Let her be as she is. If she be fair, 'tis the better for her; and she be not, she has the mends in her own hands.

Tro. Good Pandarus, how now, Pandarus!

Pan. I have had my labour for my travail; ill-thought on of her and ill-thought on of you; gone between and between, but small thanks for my labour.

Tro. What, art thou angry, Pandarus? what, with me?

Pan. Because she's kin to me, therefore she's not so fair as Helen. An she were not kin to me, she would be as fair on Friday as Helen is on Sunday. But what care I? I care not an she were a black-a-moor; 'tis all one to me.

Tro. Say I she is not fair?

Pan. I do not care whether you do or no. She's a fool to stay behind her father; let her to the Greeks; and so I'll tell her the next time I see her. For my part, I'll meddle nor make no more i' the matter.

Tro. Pandarus—

Pan. Not I.

Tro. Sweet Pandarus—

Pan. Pray you, speak no more to me. I will leave all as I found it, and there an end.

[*Exit* PANDARUS. *An alarum.*

Tro. Peace, you ungracious clamours! peace, rude sounds!
Fools on both sides! Helen must needs be fair,
When with your blood you daily paint her thus.
I cannot fight upon this argument;
It is too starved a subject for my sword.
But Pandarus—O gods, how do you plague me!
I cannot come to Cressid but by Pandar;
And he's as tetchy to be woo'd to woo
As she is stubborn-chaste against all suit.
Tell me, Apollo, for thy Daphne's love,
What Cressid is, what Pandar, and what we?
Her bed is India; there she lies, a pearl;
Between our Ilium and where she resides,
Let it be call'd the wild and wandering flood,
Ourself the merchant, and this sailing Pandar
Our doubtful hope, our convoy, and our bark.

Alarum. Enter ÆNEAS.

Æne. How now, Prince Troilus! wherefore not afield?

Tro. Because not there. This woman's answer sorts,
For womanish it is to be from thence.
What news, Æneas, from the field to-day?

Æne. That Paris is returned home and hurt.

Tro. By whom, Æneas?

Æne. Troilus, by Menelaus.

Tro. Let Paris bleed; 'tis but a scar to scorn;
Paris is gored with Menelaus' horn.

Alarum.

Æne. Hark, what good sport is out of town to-day!

Tro. Better at home, if "would I might" were "may."

But to the sport abroad. Are you bound thither?
Æne. In all swift haste.
Tro. Come, go we then together.
[*Exeunt*.

SCENE II. *The same: a street*

Enter CRESSIDA *and her man* ALEXANDER.

Cres. Who were those went by?
Alex. Queen Hecuba and Helen.
Cres. And whither go they?
Alex. Up to the eastern tower,
Whose height commands as subject all the vale,
To see the battle. Hector, whose patience
Is, as a virtue, fix'd, to-day was moved.
He chid Andromache and struck his armorer,
And, like as there were husbandry in war,
Before the sun rose he was harness'd light,
And to the field goes he; where every flower
Did, as a prophet, weep what it foresaw
In Hector's wrath.
Cres. What was his cause of anger?
Alex. The noise goes, this: there is among the Greeks
A lord of Trojan blood, nephew to Hector;
They call him Ajax.
Cres. Good; and what of him?
Alex. They say he is a very man *per se*,
And stands alone.

Cres. So do all men, unless they are drunk, sick, or have no legs.

Alex. This man, lady, hath robbed many beasts of their particular additions; he is as valiant as the lion, churlish as the bear, slow as the elephant; a man into whom nature hath so crowded humours that his valour is crushed into folly, his folly sauced with discretion. There is no man hath a virtue that he hath not a glimpse of, nor any man an attaint but he carries some stain of it. He is melancholy without cause, and merry against the hair; he hath the joints of everything, but everything so out of joint that he is a gouty Briareus, many hands and no use, or purblind Argus, all eyes and no sight.

Cres. But how should this man, that makes me smile, make Hector angry?

Alex. They say he yesterday coped Hector in the battle and struck him down, the disdain and shame whereof hath ever since kept Hector fasting and waking.

Cres. Who comes here?

Alex. Madam, your uncle Pandarus.

Enter PANDARUS.

Cres. Hector's a gallant man.

Alex. As may be in the world, lady.

Pan. What's that? what's that?

Cres. Good morrow, uncle Pandarus.

Pan. Good morrow, cousin Cressid. What do you talk of? Good morrow, Alexander. How do you, cousin? When were you at Ilium?

Cres. This morning, uncle.

Pan. What were you talking of when I came? Was Hector armed and gone ere ye came to Ilium? Helen was not up, was she?

Cres. Hector was gone, but Helen was not up.

Pan. E'en so. Hector was stirring early.

Cres. That were we talking of, and of his anger.

Pan. Was he angry?

Cres. So he says here.

Pan. True, he was so. I know the cause too. He'll lay about him to-day, I can tell them that; and there's Troilus will not come far behind him; let them take heed of Troilus, I can tell them that too.

Cres. What, is he angry too?

Pan. Who, Troilus? Troilus is the better man of the two.

Cres. O Jupiter! there's no comparison.

Pan. What, not between Troilus and Hector? Do you know a man if you see him?

Cres. Ay, if I ever saw him before and knew him.

Pan. Well, I say Troilus is Troilus.

Cres. Then you say as I say; for, I am sure, he is not Hector.

Pan. No, nor Hector is not Troilus in some degrees.

Cres. 'Tis just to each of them; he is himself.

Pan. Himself! Alas, poor Troilus! I would he were.

Cres. So he is.

Pan. Condition, I had gone barefoot to India.

Cres. He is not Hector.

Pan. Himself! no, he's not himself; would a' were himself! Well, the gods are above; time must friend or end. Well, Troilus, well; I would my heart were in her body. No, Hector is not a better man than Troilus.

Cres. Excuse me.

Pan. He is elder.

Cres. Pardon me, pardon me.

Pan. Th' other's not come to't; you shall tell me another tale, when th' other's come to't. Hector shall not have his wit this year.

Cres. He shall not need it, if he have his own.

Pan. Nor his qualities.

Cres. No matter.

Pan. Nor his beauty.

Cres. 'Twould not become him; his own's better.

Pan. You have no judgement, niece. Helen herself swore th' other day that Troilus, for a brown favour—for so 'tis, I must confess—not brown neither—

Cres. No, but brown.

Pan. 'Faith, to say truth, brown and not brown.

Cres. To say the truth, true and not true.

Pan. She praised his complexion above Paris.

Cres. Why, Paris hath colour enough.

Pan. So he has.

Cres. Then Troilus should have too much. If she praised him above, his complexion is higher than his; he having colour enough, and the other higher, is too flaming a praise for a good complexion. I had as lief Helen's golden tongue had commended Troilus for a copper nose.

Pan. I swear to you, I think Helen loves him better than Paris.

Cres. Then she's a merry Greek indeed.

Pan. Nay, I am sure she does. She came to him th' other day into the compassed window—and, you know, he has not past three or four hairs on his chin—

Cres. Indeed, a tapster's arithmetic may soon bring his particulars therein to a total.

Pan. Why, he is very young; and yet will he, within three pound, lift as much as his brother Hector.

Cres. Is he so young a man and so old a lifter?

Pan. But to prove to you that Helen loves him: she came and puts me her white hand to his cloven chin—

Cres. Juno have mercy! how came it cloven?

Pan. Why, you know, 'tis dimpled. I think his smiling becomes him better than any man in all Phrygia.

Cres. O, he smiles valiantly.

Pan. Does he not?

Cres. O yes, an 'twere a cloud in autumn.

Pan. Why, go to, then. But to prove to you that Helen loves Troilus—

Cres. Troilus will stand to the proof, if you'll prove it so.

Pan. Troilus! why, he esteems her no more than I esteem an addle egg.

Cres. If you love an addle egg as well as you love an idle head, you would eat chickens i' the shell.

Pan. I cannot choose but laugh, to think how she tickled his chin; indeed, she has a marvellous white hand, I must needs confess—

Cres. Without the rack.

Pan. And she takes upon her to spy a white hair on his chin.

Cres. Alas, poor chin! many a wart is richer.

Pan. But there was such laughing! Queen Hecuba laughed that her eyes ran o'er.

Cres. With mill-stones.

Pan. And Cassandra laughed.

Cres. But there was more temperate fire under the pot of her eyes. Did her eyes run o'er too?

Pan. And Hector laughed.

Cres. At what was all this laughing?

Pan. Marry, at the white hair that Helen spied on Troilus' chin.

Cres. An't had been a green hair, I should have laughed too.

Pan. They laughed not so much at the hair as at his pretty answer.

Cres. What was his answer?

Pan. Quoth she, "Here's but two and fifty hairs on your chin, and one of them is white."

Cres. This is her question.

Pan. That's true; make no question of that. "Two and fifty hairs," quoth he, "and one white. That white hair is my father, and all the rest are his sons." "Jupiter!" quoth she, "which of these hairs is Paris my husband?" "The forked one," quoth he, "pluck't out, and give it him." But there was such laughing! and Helen so blushed, and Paris so chafed, and all the rest so laughed, that it passed.

Cres. So let it now; for it has been a great while going by.

Pan. Well, cousin, I told you a thing yesterday; think on't.

Cres. So I do.

Pan. I'll be sworn 'tis true; he will weep you, an 'twere a man born in April.

Cres. And I'll spring up in his tears, an 'twere a nettle against May.

A retreat sounded.

Pan. Hark! they are coming from the field: shall we stand up here, and see them as they pass toward Ilium? good niece, do, sweet niece Cressida.

Cres. At your pleasure.

Pan. Here, here, here's an excellent place; here we may see most bravely. I'll tell you them all by their names as they pass by; but mark Troilus above the rest.

Cres. Speak not so loud.

ÆNEAS *passes.*

Pan. That's Æneas; is not that a brave man? he's one of the flowers of Troy, I can tell you. But mark Troilus; you shall see anon.

ANTENOR *passes.*

Cres. Who's that?

Pan. That's Antenor; he has a shrewd wit, I can tell you; and he's a man good enough; he's one o' the soundest judgements in Troy, whosoever, and a proper man of person. When comes Troilus? I'll show you Troilus anon. If he see me, you shall see him nod at me.

Cres. Will he give you the nod?

Pan. You shall see.

Cres. If he do, the rich shall have more.

HECTOR *passes.*

Pan. That's Hector, that, that, look you, that; there's a fellow! Go thy way, Hector! There's a brave man, niece. O brave Hector! Look how he looks! there's a countenance! is't not a brave man?

Cres. O, a brave man!

Pan. Is a' not? it does a man's heart good. Look you what hacks are on his helmet! Look you yonder, do you see? Look you there; there's no jesting; there's laying on, take't off who will, as they say. There be hacks!

Cres. Be those with swords?

Pan. Swords! anything, he cares not; an the devil come to him, it's all one. By God's lid, it does one's heart good. Yonder comes Paris, yonder comes Paris.

PARIS *passes.*

Look ye yonder, niece; is't not a gallant man too, is't not? Why, this is brave now. Who said he came hurt home to-day? he's not hurt. Why, this will do Helen's heart good now, ha! Would I could see Troilus now! You shall see Troilus anon.

HELENUS *passes.*

Cres. Who's that?

Pan. That's Helenus. I marvel where Troilus is. That's Helenus. I think he went not forth to-day. That's Helenus.

Cres. Can Helenus fight, uncle?

Pan. Helenus? no. Yes, he'll fight indifferent well. I marvel where Troilus is. Hark! do you not hear the people cry "Troilus"? Helenus is a priest.

Cres. What sneaking fellow comes yonder?

TROILUS *passes.*

Pan. Where? yonder? that's Deiphobus. 'Tis Troilus! there's a man, niece! Hem! Brave Troilus! the prince of chivalry!

Cres. Peace, for shame, peace!

Pan. Mark him; note him. O brave Troilus! Look well upon him, niece. Look you how his sword is bloodied, and his helm more hacked than Hector's, and how he looks, and how he goes! O admirable youth! he ne'er saw three and twenty. Go thy way, Troilus, go thy way! Had I a sister were a grace, or a daughter a goddess, he should take his choice. O admirable man! Paris? Paris is dirt to him; and, I warrant, Helen, to change, would give an eye to boot.

Cres. Here come more.

Forces pass.

Pan. Asses, fools, dolts! chaff and bran, chaff and bran! porridge after meat! I could live and die i' the eyes of Troilus. Ne'er look, ne'er look; the eagles are gone; crows and daws, crows and daws! I had rather be such a man as Troilus than Agamemnon and all Greece.

Cres. There is among the Greeks Achilles, a better man than Troilus.

Pan. Achilles! a drayman, a porter, a very camel.

Cres. Well, well.

Pan. "Well, well!" Why, have you any discretion? have you any eyes? do you know what a man is? Is not birth, beauty, good shape, discourse, manhood, learning, gentleness, virtue, youth, liberality, and such like, the spice and salt that season a man?

Cres. Ay, a minced man; and then to be baked with no date in the pie, for then the man's date's out.

Pan. You are such a woman! one knows not at what ward you lie.

Cres. Upon my back, to defend my belly; upon my wit, to defend my wiles; upon my secrecy, to defend mine honesty; my mask, to defend my beauty; and you, to defend all these; and at all these wards I lie, at a thousand watches.

Pan. Say one of your watches.

Cres. Nay, I'll watch you for that; and that's one of the chiefest of them too. If I cannot ward what I would not have hit, I can watch you for telling how I took the blow; unless it swell past hiding, and then it's past watching.

Pan. You are such another!

Enter TROILUS'S BOY.

Boy. Sir, my lord would instantly speak with you.

Pan. Where?

Boy. At your own house; there he unarms him.

Pan. Good boy, tell him I come. [*Exit* BOY.]
I doubt he be hurt. Fare ye well, good niece.

Cres. Adieu, uncle.

Pan. I'll be with you, niece, by and by.

Cres. To bring, uncle?

Pan. Ay, a token from Troilus.

Cres. By the same token, you are a bawd.

[*Exit* PANDARUS.

Words, vows, gifts, tears, and love's full sacrifice,

He offers in another's enterprise.
But more in Troilus thousand fold I see
Than in the glass of Pandar's praise may be;
Yet hold I off. Women are angels, wooing.
Things won are done; joy's soul lies in the doing.
That she beloved knows nought that knows not this:
Men prize the thing ungain'd more than it is.
That she was never yet that ever knew
Love got so sweet as when desire did sue.
Therefore this maxim out of love I teach:
Achievement is command; ungain'd, beseech.
Then though my heart's content firm love doth bear,
Nothing of that shall from mine eyes appear.
[*Exeunt.*

SCENE III. *The Grecian camp: before Agamemnon's tent*

Sennet. Enter AGAMEMNON, NESTOR, ULYSSES, MENELAUS, *and others.*

Agam. Princes,
What grief hath set the jaundice on your cheeks?
The ample proposition that hope makes
In all designs begun on earth below
Fails in the promised largeness. Checks and disasters
Grow in the veins of actions highest rear'd,
As knots, by the conflux of meeting sap,
Infect the sound pine and divert his grain
Tortive and errant from his course of growth.
Nor, princes, is it matter new to us
That we come short of our suppose so far
That after seven years' siege yet Troy walls stand;
Sith every action that hath gone before,
Whereof we have record, trial did draw
Bias and thwart, not answering the aim,
And that unbodied figure of the thought
That gave't surmised shape. Why then, you princes,
Do you with cheeks abash'd behold our works,
And call them shames? which are indeed nought else
But the protractive trials of great Jove
To find persistive constancy in men;
The fineness of which metal is not found
In fortune's love; for then the bold and coward,
The wise and fool, the artist and unread,
The hard and soft, seem all affined and kin.
But, in the wind and tempest of her frown,
Distinction, with a broad and powerful fan,
Puffing at all, winnows the light away;
And what hath mass or matter, by itself
Lies rich in virtue and unmingled.
Nest. With due observance of thy godlike seat,
Great Agamemnon, Nestor shall apply
Thy latest words. In the reproof of chance
Lies the true proof of men. The sea being smooth,
How many shallow bauble boats dare sail
Upon her patient breast, making their way
With those of nobler bulk!
But let the ruffian Boreas once enrage
The gentle Thetis, and anon behold
The strong-ribb'd bark through liquid mountains cut,
Bounding between the two moist elements,
Like Perseus' horse; where's then the saucy boat
Whose weak untimber'd sides but even now
Co-rivall'd greatness? Either to harbour fled,
Or made a toast for Neptune. Even so
Doth valour's show and valour's worth divide
In storms of fortune; for in her ray and brightness
The herd hath more annoyance by the breese
Than by the tiger; but when the splitting wind
Makes flexible the knees of knotted oaks,
And flies fled under shade, why, then the thing of courage
As roused with rage, with rage doth sympathize,
And with an accent tuned in selfsame key
Retorts to chiding fortune.
Ulyss. Agamemnon,
Thou great commander, nerve and bone of Greece,
Heart of our numbers, soul and only spirit,
In whom the tempers and the minds of all
Should be shut up, hear what Ulysses speaks.
Besides the applause and approbation
The which, [*To* AGAMEMNON] most mighty for thy place and sway,
[*To* NESTOR] And thou most reverend for thy stretch'd-out life,
I give to both your speeches, which were such
As Agamemnon and the hand of Greece
Should hold up high in brass, and such again
As venerable Nestor, hatch'd in silver,
Should with a bond of air, strong as the axle-tree
On which heaven rides, knit all the Greekish ears
To his experienced tongue, yet let it please both,
Thou great, and wise, to hear Ulysses speak.
Agam. Speak, Prince of Ithaca; and be't of less expect
That matter needless, of importless burden,
Divide thy lips, than we are confident,
When rank Thersites opes his mastic jaws,
We shall hear music, wit, and oracle.
Ulyss. Troy, yet upon his basis, had been down,
And the great Hector's sword had lack'd a master,
But for these instances.

The specialty of rule hath been neglected;
And, look, how many Grecian tents do stand
Hollow upon this plain, so many hollow factions.
When that the general is not like the hive
To whom the foragers shall all repair,
What honey is expected? Degree being vizarded,
The unworthiest shows as fairly in the mask.
The heavens themselves, the planets, and this centre
Observe degree, priority, and place,
Insisture, course, proportion, season, form,
Office, and custom, in all line of order;
And therefore is the glorious planet Sol
In noble eminence enthroned and sphered
Amidst the other; whose medicinable eye
Corrects the ill aspects of planets evil,
And posts, like the commandment of a king,
Sans check, to good and bad. But when the planets
In evil mixture to disorder wander,
What plagues and what portents! what mutiny!
What raging of the sea! shaking of earth!
Commotion in the winds! frights, changes, horrors,
Divert and crack, rend and deracinate
The unity and married calm of states
Quite from their fixure! O, when degree is shaked,
Which is the ladder to all high designs,
The enterprise is sick! How could communities,
Degrees in schools and brotherhoods in cities,
Peaceful commerce from dividable shores,
The primogenitive and due of birth,
Prerogative of age, crowns, sceptres, laurels,
But by degree, stand in authentic place?
Take but degree away, untune that string,
And, hark, what discord follows! Each thing meets
In mere oppugnancy. The bounded waters
Should lift their bosoms higher than the shores
And make a sop of all this solid globe.
Strength should be lord of imbecility,
And the rude son should strike his father dead.
Force should be right; or rather, right and wrong,
Between whose endless jar justice resides,
Should lose their names, and so should justice too.
Then everything includes itself in power,
Power into will, will into appetite;
And appetite, an universal wolf,
So doubly seconded with will and power,
Must make perforce an universal prey,
And last eat up himself. Great Agamemnon,
This chaos, when degree is suffocate,
Follows the choking.
And this neglection of degree it is
That by a pace goes backward, with a purpose
It hath to climb. The general's disdain'd
By him one step below, he by the next,
That next by him beneath; so every step,
Exampled by the first pace that is sick
Of his superior, grows to an envious fever
Of pale and bloodless emulation.
And 'tis this fever that keeps Troy on foot,
Not her own sinews. To end a tale of length,
Troy in our weakness stands, not in her strength.
Nest. Most wisely hath Ulysses here discover'd
The fever whereof all our power is sick.
Agam. The nature of the sickness found, Ulysses,
What is the remedy?
Ulyss. The great Achilles, whom opinion crowns
The sinew and the forehand of our host,
Having his ear full of his airy fame,
Grows dainty of his worth and in his tent
Lies mocking our designs. With him Patroclus
Upon a lazy bed the livelong day
Breaks scurril jests,
And with ridiculous and awkward action,
Which, slanderer, he imitation calls,
He pageants us. Sometime, great Agamemnon,
Thy topless deputation he puts on,
And, like a strutting player, whose conceit
Lies in his hamstring, and doth think it rich
To hear the wooden dialogue and sound
'Twixt his stretch'd footing and the scaffoldage—
Such to-be-pitied and o'er-wrested seeming
He acts thy greatness in; and when he speaks,
'Tis like a chime a-mending; with terms unsquared,
Which, from the tongue of roaring Typhon dropp'd,
Would seem hyperboles. At this fusty stuff
The large Achilles, on his press'd bed lolling,
From his deep chest laughs out a loud applause;
Cries "Excellent! 'tis Agamemnon just.
Now play me Nestor; hem, and stroke thy beard,
As he being drest to some oration."
That's done, as near as the extremest ends
Of parallels, as like as Vulcan and his wife.
Yet god Achilles still cries "Excellent!
'Tis Nestor right. Now play him me, Patroclus,
Arming to answer in a night alarm."
And then, forsooth, the faint defects of age
Must be the scene of mirth; to cough and spit,
And, with a palsy-fumbling on his gorget,
Shake in and out the rivet. And at this sport
Sir Valour dies; cries "O, enough, Patroclus;
Or give me ribs of steel! I shall split all
In pleasure of my spleen." And in this fashion,

All our abilities, gifts, natures, shapes,
Severals and generals of grace exact,
Achievements, plots, orders, preventions,
Excitements to the field, or speech for truce,
Success or loss, what is or is not, serves
As stuff for these two to make paradoxes.
Nest. And in the imitation of these twain—
Who, as Ulysses says, opinion crowns
With an imperial voice—many are infect.
Ajax is grown self-will'd, and bears his head
In such a rein, in full as proud a place
As broad Achilles; keeps his tent like him;
Makes factious feasts; rails on our state of war,
Bold as an oracle, and sets Thersites,
A slave whose gall coins slanders like a mint,
To match us in comparisons with dirt,
To weaken and discredit our exposure,
How rank soever rounded in with danger.
Ulyss. They tax our policy, and call it cowardice,
Count wisdom as no member of the war,
Forestall prescience, and esteem no act
But that of hand. The still and mental parts,
That do contrive how many hands shall strike,
When fitness calls them on, and know by measure
Of their observant toil the enemies' weight—
Why, this hath not a finger's dignity.
They call this bed-work, mappery, closet-war;
So that the ram that batters down the wall,
For the great swing and rudeness of his poise,
They place before his hand that made the engine,
Or those that with the fineness of their souls
By reason guide his execution.
Nest. Let this be granted, and Achilles' horse
Makes many Thetis' sons.
A tucket.
Agam. What trumpet? look, Menelaus.
Men. From Troy.

Enter ÆNEAS.

Agam. What would you 'fore our tent?
Æne. Is this great Agamemnon's tent, I pray you?
Agam. Even this.
Æne. May one that is a herald and a prince
Do a fair message to his kingly ears?
Agam. With surety stronger than Achilles' arm
'Fore all the Greekish heads, which with one voice
Call Agamemnon head and general.
Æne. Fair leave and large security. How may
A stranger to those most imperial looks
Know them from eyes of other mortals?
Agam. How!
Æne. Ay;
I ask, that I might waken reverence,
And bid the cheek be ready with a blush
Modest as morning when she coldly eyes
The youthful Phœbus.
Which is that god in office, guiding men?
Which is the high and mighty Agamemnon?
Agam. This Trojan scorns us; or the men of Troy
Are ceremonious courtiers.
Æne. Courtiers as free, as debonair, unarm'd,
As bending angels; that's their fame in peace.
But when they would seem soldiers, they have galls,
Good arms, strong joints, true swords; and, Jove's accord,
Nothing so full of heart. But peace, Æneas,
Peace, Trojan; lay thy finger on thy lips!
The worthiness of praise distains his worth,
If that the praised himself bring the praise forth.
But what the repining enemy commends,
That breath fame blows; that praise, sole pure, transcends.
Agam. Sir, you of Troy, call you yourself Æneas?
Æne. Ay, Greek, that is my name.
Agam. What's your affair, I pray you?
Æne. Sir, pardon; 'tis for Agamemnon's ears.
Agam. He hears nought privately that comes from Troy.
Æne. Nor I from Troy come not to whisper him.
I bring a trumpet to awake his ear,
To set his sense on the attentive bent,
And then to speak.
Agam. Speak frankly as the wind;
It is not Agamemnon's sleeping hour.
That thou shalt know, Trojan, he is awake,
He tells thee so himself.
Æne. Trumpet, blow loud,
Send thy brass voice through all these lazy tents;
And every Greek of mettle, let him know,
What Troy means fairly shall be spoke aloud.
Trumpet sounds.
We have, great Agamemnon, here in Troy
A prince call'd Hector—Priam is his father—
Who in this dull and long-continued truce
Is rusty grown. He bade me take a trumpet,
And to this purpose speak. Kings, princes, lords!
If there be one among the fair'st of Greece
That holds his honour higher than his ease,
That seeks his praise more than he fears his peril,
That knows his valour, and knows not his fear,
That loves his mistress more than in confession,
With truant vows to her own lips he loves,

And dare avow her beauty and her worth
In other arms than hers—to him this challenge.
Hector, in view of Trojans and of Greeks,
Shall make it good, or do his best to do it,
He hath a lady, wiser, fairer, truer,
Than ever Greek did compass in his arms,
And will to-morrow with his trumpet call
Midway between your tents and walls of Troy,
To rouse a Grecian that is true in love.
If any come, Hector shall honour him;
If none, he'll say in Troy when he retires,
The Grecian dames are sunburnt and not worth
The splinter of a lance. Even so much.

Agam. This shall be told our lovers, Lord Æneas;
If none of them have soul in such a kind,
We left them all at home. But we are soldiers;
And may that soldier a mere recreant prove,
That means not, hath not, or is not in love!
If then one is, or hath, or means to be,
That one meets Hector; if none else, I am he.

Nest. Tell him of Nestor, one that was a man
When Hector's grandsire suck'd. He is old now;
But if there be not in our Grecian host
One noble man that hath one spark of fire
To answer for his love, tell him from me
I'll hide my silver beard in a gold beaver
And in my vantbrace put this wither'd brawn,
And meeting him will tell him that my lady
Was fairer than his grandam and as chaste
As may be in the world. His youth in flood,
I'll prove this truth with my three drops of blood.

Æne. Now heavens forbid such scarcity of youth!

Ulyss. Amen.

Agam. Fair Lord Æneas, let me touch your hand;
To our pavilion shall I lead you, sir.
Achilles shall have word of this intent;
So shall each lord of Greece, from tent to tent.
Yourself shall feast with us before you go
And find the welcome of a noble foe.

[*Exeunt all but* ULYSSES *and* NESTOR.

Ulyss. Nestor!

Nest. What says Ulysses?

Ulyss. I have a young conception in my brain;
Be you my time to bring it to some shape.

Nest. What is't?

Ulyss. This 'tis:
Blunt wedges rive hard knots. The seeded pride
That hath to this maturity blown up
In rank Achilles must or now be cropp'd,
Or, shedding, breed a nursery of like evil,
To overbulk us all.

Nest. Well, and how?

Ulyss. This challenge that the gallant Hector sends,
However it is spread in general name,
Relates in purpose only to Achilles.

Nest. The purpose is perspicuous even as substance,
Whose grossness little characters sum up.
And, in the publication, make no strain,
But that Achilles, were his brain as barren
As banks of Libya—though, Apollo knows,
'Tis dry enough—will with great speed of judgement,
Ay, with celerity, find Hector's purpose
Pointing on him.

Ulyss. And wake him to the answer, think you?

Nest. Yes, 'tis most meet. Whom may you else oppose,
That can from Hector bring his honour off,
If not Achilles? Though't be a sportful combat,
Yet in the trial much opinion dwells;
For here the Trojans taste our dear'st repute
With their finest palate; and trust to me, Ulysses,
Our imputation shall be oddly poised
In this wild action; for the success,
Although particular, shall give a scantling
Of good or bad unto the general;
And in such indexes, although small pricks
To their subsequent volumes, there is seen
The baby figure of the giant mass
Of things to come at large. It is supposed
He that meets Hector issues from our choice;
And choice, being mutual act of all our souls,
Makes merit her election, and doth boil,
As 'twere from forth us all, a man distill'd
Out of our virtues; who miscarrying,
What heart receives from hence the conquering part,
To steel a strong opinion to themselves?
Which entertain'd, limbs are his instruments,
In no less working than are swords and bows
Directive by the limbs.

Ulyss. Give pardon to my speech.
Therefore 'tis meet Achilles meet not Hector.
Let us, like merchants, show our foulest wares,
And think, perchance, they'll sell; if not,
The lustre of the better yet to show,
Shall show the better. Do not consent
That ever Hector and Achilles meet;
For both our honour and our shame in this
Are dogg'd with two strange followers.

Nest. I see them not with my old eyes. What are they?

Ulyss. What glory our Achilles shares from Hector,

Were he not proud, we all should share with
him.
But he already is too insolent;
And we were better parch in Afric sun
Than in the pride and salt scorn of his eyes,
Should he 'scape Hector fair. If he were foil'd,
Why then, we did our main opinion crush
In taint of our best man. No, make a lottery;
And, by device, let blockish Ajax draw
The sort to fight with Hector. Among ourselves
Give him allowance for the better man;
For that will physic the great Myrmidon
Who broils in loud applause, and make him fall
His crest that prouder than blue Iris bends.
If the dull brainless Ajax come safe off,
We'll dress him up in voices. If he fail,
Yet go we under our opinion still
That we have better men. But, hit or miss,
Our project's life this shape of sense assumes:
Ajax employ'd plucks down Achilles' plumes.

Nest. Ulysses,
Now I begin to relish thy advice;
And I will give a taste of it forthwith
To Agamemnon. Go we to him straight.
Two curs shall tame each other; pride alone
Must tarre the mastiffs on, as 'twere their bone.
[*Exeunt.*

ACT II

Scene I. *A part of the Grecian camp*

Enter AJAX *and* THERSITES.

Ajax. Thersites!

Ther. Agamemnon, how if he had boils? full, all over, generally?

Ajax. Thersites!

Ther. And those boils did run? Say so: did not the general run then? Were not that a botchy core?

Ajax. Dog!

Ther. Then would come some matter from him; I see none now.

Ajax. Thou bitch-wolf's son, canst thou not hear? [*Beating him*] Feel, then.

Ther. The plague of Greece upon thee, thou mongrel beef-witted lord!

Ajax. Speak then, thou vinewedst leaven, speak. I will beat thee into handsomeness.

Ther. I shall sooner rail thee into wit and holiness; but, I think, thy horse will sooner con an oration than thou learn a prayer without book. Thou canst strike, canst thou? A red murrain o' thy jade's tricks!

Ajax. Toadstool, learn me the proclamation.

Ther. Dost thou think I have no sense, thou strikest me thus?

Ajax. The proclamation!

Ther. Thou art proclaimed a fool, I think.

Ajax. Do not, porpentine, do not; my fingers itch.

Ther. I would thou didst itch from head to foot and I had the scratching of thee; I would make thee the loathsomest scab in Greece. When thou art forth in the incursions, thou strikest as slow as another.

Ajax. I say, the proclamation!

Ther. Thou grumblest and railest every hour on Achilles, and thou art as full of envy at his greatness as Cerberus is at Proserpina's beauty, ay, that thou barkest at him.

Ajax. Mistress Thersites!

Ther. Thou shouldst strike him.

Ajax. Cobloaf!

Ther. He would pun thee into shivers with his fist, as a sailor breaks a biscuit.

Ajax. [*Beating him*] You whoreson cur!

Ther. Do, do.

Ajax. Thou stool for a witch!

Ther. Ay, do, do; thou sodden-witted lord! Thou hast no more brain than I have in mine elbows; an assinego may tutor thee. Thou scurvy-valiant ass! thou art here but to thrash Trojans; and thou art bought and sold among those of any wit, like a barbarian slave. If thou use to beat me, I will begin at thy heel, and tell what thou art by inches, thou thing of no bowels, thou!

Ajax. You dog!

Ther. You scurvy lord!

Ajax. [*Beating him*] You cur!

Ther. Mars his idiot! do, rudeness; do, camel; do, do.

Enter ACHILLES *and* PATROCLUS.

Achil. Why, how now, Ajax! wherefore do you thus? How now, Thersites! what's the matter, man?

Ther. You see him there, do you?

Achil. Ay; what's the matter?

Ther. Nay, look upon him.

Achil. So I do. What's the matter?

Ther. Nay, but regard him well.

Achil. "Well!" why, I do so.

Ther. But yet you look not well upon him; for, whosoever you take him to be, he is Ajax.

Achil. I know that, fool.

Ther. Ay, but that fool knows not himself.

Ajax. Therefore I beat thee.

Ther. Lo, lo, lo, lo, what modicums of wit he utters! his evasions have ears thus long. I have bobbed his brain more than he has beat my bones. I will buy nine sparrows for a penny, and his *pia mater* is not worth the ninth part of a sparrow. This lord, Achilles, Ajax, who wears his wit in his belly and his guts in his head, I'll tell you what I say of him.

Achil. What?

Ther. I say, this Ajax—

AJAX *offers to beat him.*

Achil. Nay, good Ajax.

Ther. Has not so much wit—

Achil. Nay, I must hold you.

Ther. As will stop the eye of Helen's needle, for whom he comes to fight.

Achil. Peace, fool!

Ther. I would have peace and quietness, but the fool will not. He there, that he. Look you there.

Ajax. O thou damned cur! I shall—

Achil. Will you set your wit to a fool's?

Ther. No, I warrant you; for a fool's will shame it.

Patr. Good words, Thersites.

Achil. What's the quarrel?

Ajax. I bade the vile owl go learn me the tenour of the proclamation, and he rails upon me.

Ther. I serve thee not.

Ajax. Well, go to, go to.

Ther. I serve here voluntary.

Achil. Your last service was sufferance, 'twas not voluntary. No man is beaten voluntary; Ajax was here the voluntary, and you as under an impress.

Ther. E'en so; a great deal of your wit, too, lies in your sinews, or else there be liars. Hector shall have a great catch, if he knock out either of your brains. A' were as good crack a fusty nut with no kernel.

Achil. What, with me too, Thersites?

Ther. There's Ulysses and old Nestor, whose wit was mouldy ere your grandsires had nails on their toes, yoke you like draught-oxen and make you plough up the wars.

Achil. What, what?

Ther. Yes, good sooth. To, Achilles! to, Ajax! to!

Ajax. I shall cut out your tongue.

Ther. 'Tis no matter; I shall speak as much as thou afterwards.

Patr. No more words, Thersites; peace!

Ther. I will hold my peace when Achilles' brach bids me, shall I?

Achil. There's for you Patroclus.

Ther. I will see you hanged, like clotpoles, ere I come any more to your tents. I will keep where there is wit stirring and leave the faction of fools. [*Exit.*

Patr. A good riddance.

Achil. Marry, this, sir, is proclaim'd through all our host:
That Hector, by the fifth hour of the sun,
Will with a trumpet 'twixt our tents and Troy
To-morrow morning call some knight to arms
That hath a stomach; and such a one that dare
Maintain—I know not what; 'tis trash. Farewell.

Ajax. Farewell. Who shall answer him?

Achil. I know not. 'Tis put to lottery; otherwise
He knew his man.

Ajax. O, meaning you. I will go learn more of it. [*Exeunt.*

SCENE II. *Troy: a room in Priam's palace*

Enter PRIAM, HECTOR, TROILUS, PARIS, *and* HELENUS.

Pri. After so many hours, lives, speeches spent,
Thus once again says Nestor from the Greeks:
"Deliver Helen, and all damage else—
As honour, loss of time, travail, expense,
Wounds, friends, and what else dear that is consumed
In hot digestion of this cormorant war—
Shall be struck off." Hector, what say you to't?

Hect. Though no man lesser fears the Greeks than I
As far as toucheth my particular,
Yet, dread Priam,
There is no lady of more softer bowels,
More spongy to suck in the sense of fear,
More ready to cry out, "Who knows what follows?"
Than Hector is. The wound of peace is surety,
Surety secure; but modest doubt is call'd
The beacon of the wise, the tent that searches
To the bottom of the worst. Let Helen go.
Since the first sword was drawn about this question,
Every tithe soul, 'mongst many thousand dismes,
Hath been as dear as Helen; I mean, of ours.
If we have lost so many tenths of ours,
To guard a thing not ours nor worth to us,
Had it our name, the value of one ten,
What merit's in that reason which denies
The yielding of her up?

Tro. Fie, fie, my brother!
Weigh you the worth and honour of a king
So great as our dread father in a scale
Of common ounces? will you with counters sum
The past proportion of his infinite?
And buckle in a waist most fathomless
With spans and inches so diminutive
As fears and reasons? fie, for godly shame!

Hel. No marvel, though you bite so sharp at reasons,

You are so empty of them. Should not our father
Bear the great sway of his affairs with reasons,
Because your speech hath none that tells him so?
Tro. You are for dreams and slumbers, brother priest;
You fur your gloves with reason. Here are your reasons:
You know an enemy intends you harm;
You know a sword employ'd is perilous,
And reason flies the object of all harm.
Who marvels then, when Helenus beholds
A Grecian and his sword, if he do set
The very wings of reason to his heels
And fly like chidden Mercury from Jove,
Or like a star disorb'd? Nay, if we talk of reason,
Let's shut our gates and sleep. Manhood and honour
Should have hare-hearts, would they but fat their thoughts
With this cramm'd reason. Reason and respect
Make livers pale and lustihood deject.
Hect. Brother, she is not worth what she doth cost
The holding.
Tro. What is aught, but as 'tis valued?
Hect. But value dwells not in particular will;
It holds his estimate and dignity
As well wherein 'tis precious of itself
As in the prizer. 'Tis mad idolatry
To make the service greater than the god;
And the will dotes that is attributive
To what infectiously itself affects,
Without some image of the affected merit.
Tro. I take to-day a wife, and my election
Is led on in the conduct of my will;
My will enkindled by mine eyes and ears,
Two traded pilots 'twixt the dangerous shores
Of will and judgement: how may I avoid,
Although my will distaste what it elected,
The wife I chose? there can be no evasion
To blench from this and to stand firm by honour.
We turn not back the silks upon the merchant,
When we have soil'd them, nor the remainder viands
We do not throw in unrespective sieve,
Because we now are full. It was thought meet
Paris should do some vengeance on the Greeks.
Your breath of full consent bellied his sails;
The seas and winds, old wranglers, took a truce
And did him service; he touch'd the ports desired,
And for an old aunt whom the Greeks held captive,
He brought a Grecian queen, whose youth and freshness
Wrinkles Apollo's, and makes stale the morning.
Why keep we her? the Grecians keep our aunt.
Is she worth keeping? why, she is a pearl,
Whose price hath launch'd above a thousand ships,
And turn'd crown'd kings to merchants.
If you'll avouch 'twas wisdom Paris went—
As you must needs, for you all cried "Go, go"—
If you'll confess he brought home noble prize—
As you must needs, for you all clapp'd your hands,
And cried "Inestimable!"—why do you now
The issue of your proper wisdoms rate,
And do a deed that fortune never did,
Beggar the estimation which you prized
Richer than sea and land? O, theft most base,
That we have stol'n what we do fear to keep!
But, thieves, unworthy of a thing so stol'n,
That in their country did them that disgrace,
We fear to warrant in our native place!
Cas. [*Within*] Cry, Trojans, cry!
Pri. What noise? what shriek is this?
Tro. 'Tis our mad sister, I do know her voice.
Cas. [*Within*] Cry, Trojans!
Hect. It is Cassandra.

Enter CASSANDRA, *raving*.

Cas. Cry, Trojans, cry! lend me ten thousand eyes,
And I will fill them with prophetic tears.
Hect. Peace, sister, peace!
Cas. Virgins and boys, mid-age and wrinkled eld,
Soft infancy, that nothing canst but cry,
Add to my clamours! let us pay betimes
A moiety of that mass of moan to come.
Cry, Trojans, cry! practise your eyes with tears!
Troy must not be, nor goodly Ilion stand;
Our firebrand brother, Paris, burns us all.
Cry, Trojans, cry! a Helen and a woe:
Cry, cry! Troy burns, or else let Helen go. [*Exit.*
Hect. Now, youthful Troilus, do not these high strains
Of divination in our sister work
Some touches of remorse? or is your blood
So madly hot that no discourse of reason,
No fear of bad success in a bad cause,
Can qualify the same?
Tro. Why, brother Hector,
We may not think the justness of each act
Such and no other than event doth form it,
Nor once deject the courage of our minds,
Because Cassandra's mad. Her brain-sick raptures
Cannot distaste the goodness of a quarrel
Which hath our several honours all engaged
To make it gracious. For my private part,
I am no more touch'd than all Priam's sons;

And Jove forbid there should be done amongst us
Such things as might offend the weakest spleen
To fight for and maintain!

Par. Else might the world convince of levity
As well my undertakings as your counsels;
But I attest the gods, your full consent
Gave wings to my propension and cut off
All fears attending on so dire a project.
For what, alas, can these my single arms?
What propugnation is in one man's valour,
To stand the push and enmity of those
This quarrel would excite? Yet, I protest,
Were I alone to pass the difficulties
And had as ample power as I have will,
Paris should ne'er retract what he hath done,
Nor faint in the pursuit.

Pri. Paris, you speak
Like one besotted on your sweet delights.
You have the honey still, but these the gall;
So to be valiant is no praise at all.

Par. Sir, I propose not merely to myself
The pleasures such a beauty brings with it;
But I would have the soil of her fair rape
Wiped off, in honourable keeping her.
What treason were it to the ransack'd queen,
Disgrace to your great worths and shame to me,
Now to deliver her possession up
On terms of base compulsion! Can it be
That so degenerate a strain as this
Should once set footing in your generous bosoms?
There's not the meanest spirit on our party
Without a heart to dare or sword to draw
When Helen is defended, nor none so noble
Whose life were ill bestow'd or death unfamed
Where Helen is the subject; then, I say,
Well may we fight for her whom, we know well,
The world's large spaces cannot parallel.

Hect. Paris and Troilus, you have both said well,
And on the cause and question now in hand
Have glozed, but superficially; not much
Unlike young men, whom Aristotle thought
Unfit to hear moral philosophy.
The reasons you allege do more conduce
To the hot passion of distemper'd blood
Than to make up a free determination
'Twixt right and wrong, for pleasure and revenge
Have ears more deaf than adders to the voice
Of any true decision. Nature craves
All dues be render'd to their owners. Now,
What nearer debt in all humanity
Than wife is to the husband? If this law
Of nature be corrupted through affection,
And that great minds, of partial indulgence
To their benumbed wills, resist the same,
There is a law in each well-order'd nation
To curb those raging appetites that are
Most disobedient and refractory.
If Helen then be wife to Sparta's king,
As it is known she is, these moral laws
Of nature and of nations speak aloud
To have her back return'd. Thus to persist
In doing wrong extenuates not wrong,
But makes it much more heavy. Hector's opinion
Is this in way of truth; yet ne'ertheless,
My spritely brethren, I propend to you
In resolution to keep Helen still,
For 'tis a cause that hath no mean dependance
Upon our joint and several dignities.

Tro. Why, there you touch'd the life of our design.
Were it not glory that we more affected
Than the performance of our heaving spleens,
I would not wish a drop of Trojan blood
Spent more in her defence. But, worthy Hector,
She is a theme of honour and renown,
A spur to valiant and magnanimous deeds,
Whose present courage may beat down our foes,
And fame in time to come canonize us;
For, I presume, brave Hector would not lose
So rich advantage of a promised glory
As smiles upon the forehead of this action
For the wide world's revenue.

Hect. I am yours,
You valiant offspring of great Priamus.
I have a roisting challenge sent amongst
The dull and factious nobles of the Greeks
Will strike amazement to their drowsy spirits.
I was advertised their great general slept,
Whilst emulation in the army crept.
This, I presume, will wake him. [*Exeunt*.

SCENE III. *The Grecian camp: before Achilles' tent*

Enter THERSITES, *solus*.

Ther. How now, Thersites! what, lost in the labyrinth of thy fury! Shall the elephant Ajax carry it thus? he beats me, and I rail at him. O, worthy satisfaction! would it were otherwise; that I could beat him, whilst he railed at me. 'Sfoot, I'll learn to conjure and raise devils, but I'll see some issue of my spiteful execrations. Then there's Achilles, a rare enginer! If Troy be not taken till these two undermine it, the walls will stand till they fall of themselves. O thou great thunder-darter of Olympus, forget that thou art Jove, the king of gods, and, Mercury, lose all the serpentine craft of thy caduceus, if ye take not that little little less than little wit from them that they have! which short-armed ignorance itself knows is so abundant scarce, it will not in circumvention deliver a fly from a spider, without drawing their massy irons and cutting the web. After this, the vengeance on the whole camp! or rather, the bone-ache! for that, methinks, is the curse dependent on those that war for a placket. I have said my prayers and devil Envy say Amen. What ho! my Lord Achilles!

Enter PATROCLUS.

Patr. Who's there? Thersites! Good Thersites, come in and rail.

Ther. If I could have remembered a gilt counterfeit, thou wouldst not have slipped out of my contemplation. But it is no matter; thyself upon thyself! The common curse of mankind, folly and ignorance, be thine in great revenue! Heaven bless thee from a tutor, and discipline come not near thee! Let thy blood be thy direction till thy death! then if she that lays thee out says thou art a fair corse, I'll be sworn and sworn upon't she never shrouded any but lazars. Amen. Where's Achilles?

Patr. What, art thou devout? wast thou in prayer?

Ther. Ay. The heavens hear me!

Enter ACHILLES.

Achil. Who's there?

Patr. Thersites, my lord.

Achil. Where, where? Art thou come? why, my cheese, my digestion, why hast thou not served thyself in to my table so many meals? Come, what's Agamemnon?

Ther. Thy commander, Achilles. Then tell me, Patroclus, what's Achilles?

Patr. Thy lord, Thersites. Then tell me, I pray thee, what's thyself?

Ther. Thy knower, Patroclus. Then tell me, Patroclus, what art thou?

Patr. Thou mayst tell that knowest.

Achil. O, tell, tell.

Ther. I'll decline the whole question. Agamemnon commands Achilles; Achilles is my lord; I am Patroclus' knower, and Patroclus is a fool.

Patr. You rascal!

Ther. Peace, fool! I have not done.

Achil. He is a privileged man. Proceed, Thersites.

Ther. Agamemnon is a fool; Achilles is a fool; Thersites is a fool, and, as aforesaid, Patroclus is a fool.

Achil. Derive this; come.

Ther. Agamemnon is a fool to offer to command Achilles; Achilles is a fool to be commanded of Agamemnon; Thersites is a fool to serve such a fool, and Patroclus is a fool positive.

Patr. Why am I a fool?

Ther. Make that demand of the prover. It suffices me thou art. Look you, who comes here?

Achil. Patroclus, I'll speak with nobody. Come in with me, Thersites. [*Exit*.

Ther. Here is such patchery, such juggling and such knavery! All the argument is a cuckold and a whore; a good quarrel to draw emulous factions and bleed to death upon. Now, the dry serpigo on the subject! and war and lechery confound all! [*Exit*.

Enter AGAMEMNON, ULYSSES, NESTOR, DIOMEDES, *and* AJAX.

Agam. Where is Achilles?

Patr. Within his tent; but ill disposed, my lord.

Agam. Let it be known to him that we are here.
He shent our messengers; and we lay by
Our appertainments, visiting of him.
Let him be told so, lest perchance he think
We dare not move the question of our place,
Or know not what we are.

Patr. I shall say so to him. [*Exit*.

Ulyss. We saw him at the opening of his tent. He is not sick.

Ajax. Yes, lion-sick, sick of proud heart. You may call it melancholy, if you will favour the may; but, by my head, 'tis pride. But why, why? let him show us the cause. A word, my lord. [*Takes* AGAMEMNON *aside*.

Nest. What moves Ajax thus to bay at him?

Ulyss. Achilles hath inveigled his fool from him.

Nest. Who, Thersites?

Ulyss. He.

Nest. Then will Ajax lack matter, if he have lost his argument.

Ulyss. No, you see, he is his argument that has his argument, Achilles.

Nest. All the better; their fraction is more our wish than their faction. But it was a strong composure a fool could disunite.

Ulyss. The amity that wisdom knits not, folly may easily untie. Here comes Patroclus.

Re-enter PATROCLUS.

Nest. No Achilles with him.

Ulyss. The elephant hath joints, but none for courtesy. His legs are legs for necessity, not for flexure.

Patr. Achilles bids me say, he is much sorry,
If any thing more than your sport and pleasure
Did move your greatness and this noble state
To call upon him; he hopes it is no other

But for your health and your digestion sake,
An after-dinner's breath.
Agam. Hear you, Patroclus.
We are too well acquainted with these answers;
But his evasion, wing'd thus swift with scorn,
Cannot outfly our apprehensions.
Much attribute he hath, and much the reason
Why we ascribe it to him; yet all his virtues,
Not virtuously on his own part beheld,
Do in our eyes begin to lose their gloss,
Yea, like fair fruit in an unwholesome dish,
Are like to rot untasted. Go and tell him
We come to speak with him; and you shall not sin,
If you do say we think him over-proud
And under-honest, in self-assumption greater
Than in the note of judgement; and worthier than himself
Here tend the savage strangeness he puts on,
Disguise the holy strength of their command,
And underwrite in an observing kind
His humorous predominance; yea, watch
His pettish lunes, his ebbs, his flows, as if
The passage and whole carriage of this action
Rode on his tide. Go tell him this, and add,
That if he overhold his price so much,
We'll none of him; but let him, like an engine
Not portable, lie under this report:
"Bring action hither, this cannot go to war."
A stirring dwarf we do allowance give
Before a sleeping giant. Tell him so.
Patr. I shall; and bring his answer presently. [*Exit.*
Agam. In second voice we'll not be satisfied;
We come to speak with him. Ulysses, enter you. [*Exit* ULYSSES.
Ajax. What is he more than another?
Agam. No more than what he thinks he is.
Ajax. Is he so much? Do you not think he thinks himself a better man than I am?
Agam. No question.
Ajax. Will you subscribe his thought, and say he is?
Agam. No, noble Ajax; you are as strong, as valiant, as wise, no less noble, much more gentle, and altogether more tractable.
Ajax. Why should a man be proud? How doth pride grow? I know not what pride is.
Agam. Your mind is the clearer, Ajax, and your virtues the fairer. He that is proud eats up himself; pride is his own glass, his own trumpet, his own chronicle; and whatever praises itself but in the deed, devours the deed in the praise.
Ajax. I do hate a proud man, as I hate the engendering of toads.
Nest. [*Aside.*] Yet he loves himself. Is't not strange?

Re-enter ULYSSES.

Ulysses. Achilles will not to the field tomorrow.
Agam. What's his excuse?
Ulyss. He doth rely on none,
But carries on the stream of his dispose
Without observance or respect of any,
In will peculiar and in self-admission.
Agam. Why will he not upon our fair request
Untent his person and share the air with us?
Ulyss. Things small as nothing, for request's sake only,
He makes important. Possess'd he is with greatness,
And speaks not to himself but with a pride
That quarrels at self-breath. Imagined worth
Holds in his blood such swoln and hot discourse
That 'twixt his mental and his active parts
Kingdom'd Achilles in commotion rages
And batters down himself. What should I say?
He is so plaguy proud that the death-tokens of it
Cry "No recovery."
Agam. Let Ajax go to him.
Dear lord, go you and greet him in his tent.
'Tis said he holds you well, and will be led
At your request a little from himself.
Ulyss. O Agamemnon, let it not be so!
We'll consecrate the steps that Ajax makes
When they go from Achilles. Shall the proud lord
That bastes his arrogance with his own seam
And never suffers matter of the world
Enter his thoughts, save such as do revolve
And ruminate himself, shall he be worshipp'd
Of that we hold an idol more than he?
No, this thrice worthy and right valiant lord
Must not so stale his palm, nobly acquired;
Nor, by my will, assubjugate his merit,
As amply titled as Achilles is,
By going to Achilles.
That were to enlard his fat already pride
And add more coals to Cancer when he burns
With entertaining great Hyperion.
This lord go to him! Jupiter forbid,
And say in thunder "Achilles go to him."
Nest. [*Aside to* DIOMEDES.] O, this is well; he rubs the vein of him.
Dio. [*Aside to* NESTOR.] And how his silence drinks up this applause!
Ajax. If I go to him, with my armed fist
I'll pash him o'er the face.
Agam. O, no, you shall not go.

Ajax. An a' be proud with me, I'll pheeze his pride.
Let me go to him.
Ulyss. Not for the worth that hangs upon our quarrel.
Ajax. A paltry, insolent fellow!
Nest. [*Aside*.] How he describes himself!
Ajax. Can he not be sociable?
Ulyss. [*Aside*.] The raven chides blackness.
Ajax. I'll let his humours blood.

Agam. [*Aside*.] He will be the physician that should be the patient.

Ajax. An all men were o' my mind—
Ulyss. [*Aside*.] Wit would be out of fashion.

Ajax. A' should not bear it so, a' should eat swords first. Shall pride carry it?

Nest [*Aside*.] An 'twould, you'ld carry half.
Ulyss. [*Aside*.] A' would have ten shares.
Ajax. I will knead him; I'll make him supple.

Nest. [*Aside*] He's not yet through warm. Force him with praises. Pour in, pour in; his ambition is dry.

Ulyss. [*To* AGAMEMNON.] My lord, you feed too much on this dislike.

Nest. Our noble general, do not do so.
Dio. You must prepare to fight without Achilles.
Ulyss. Why, 'tis this naming of him does him harm.
Here is a man—but 'tis before his face;
I will be silent.
Nest. Wherefore should you so?
He is not emulous, as Achilles is.
Ulyss. Know the whole world, he is as valiant.
Ajax. A whoreson dog, that shall palter thus with us!
Would he were a Trojan!
Nest. What a vice were it in Ajax now—
Ulyss. If he were proud—
Dio. Or covetous of praise—
Ulyss. Ay, or surly borne—
Dio. Or strange, or self-affected!
Ulyss. Thank the heavens, lord, thou art of sweet composure;
Praise him that got thee, she that gave thee suck.
Famed be thy tutor, and thy parts of nature
Thrice famed, beyond all erudition.
But he that disciplined thy arms to fight,
Let Mars divide eternity in twain,
And give him half; and, for thy vigour,
Bull-bearing Milo his addition yield
To sinewy Ajax. I will not praise thy wisdom,
Which, like a bourn, a pale, a shore, confines
Thy spacious and dilated parts. Here's Nestor;
Instructed by the antiquary times,
He must, he is, he cannot but be wise.
But pardon, father Nestor, were your days
As green as Ajax' and your brain so temper'd,
You should not have the eminence of him,
But be as Ajax.
Ajax. Shall I call you father?
Nest. Ay, my good son.
Dio. Be ruled by him, Lord Ajax.
Ulyss. There is no tarrying here; the hart Achilles
Keeps thicket. Please it our great general
To call together all his state of war;
Fresh kings are come to Troy; to-morrow
We must with all our main of power stand fast;
And here's a lord—come knights from east to west,
And cull their flower, Ajax shall cope the best.
Agam. Go we to council. Let Achilles sleep:
Light boats sail swift, though greater hulks draw deep. [*Exeunt*.

ACT III

SCENE I. *Troy: Priam's palace*

Enter a SERVANT *and* PANDARUS.

Pan. Friend, you! pray you, a word. Do not you follow the young Lord Paris?

Serv. Ay, sir, when he goes before me.

Pan. You depend upon him, I mean?

Serv. Sir, I do depend upon the lord.

Pan. You depend upon a noble gentleman; I must needs praise him.

Serv. The lord be praised!

Pan. You know me, do you not?

Serv. Faith, sir, superficially.

Pan. Friend, know me better; I am the Lord Pandarus.

Serv. I hope I shall know your honour better.

Pan. I do desire it.

Serv. You are in the state of grace.

Pan. Grace! not so, friend; honour and lordship are my titles. [*Music within*.] What music is this?

Serv. I do but partly know, sir. It is music in parts.

Pan. Know you the musicians?

Serv. Wholly, sir.

Pan. Who play they to?

Serv. To the hearers, sir.

Pan. At whose pleasure, friend?

Serv. At mine, sir, and theirs that love music.

Pan. Command, I mean, friend.

Serv. Who shall I command, sir?

Pan. Friend, we understand not one another; I am too courtly and thou art too cunning. At whose request do these men play?

Serv. That's to't indeed, sir. Marry, sir, at the

request of Paris my lord, who's there in person; with him, the mortal Venus, the heart-blood of beauty, love's invisible soul—

Pan. Who, my cousin Cressida?

Serv. No, sir, Helen. Could you not find out that by her attributes?

Pan. It should seem, fellow, that thou hast not seen the Lady Cressida. I come to speak with Paris from the Prince Troilus. I will make a complimental assault upon him, for my business seethes.

Serv. Sodden business! there's a stewed phrase indeed!

Enter PARIS *and* HELEN, *attended.*

Pan. Fair be to you, my lord, and to all this fair company! fair desires, in all fair measure fairly guide them! especially to you, fair queen fair thoughts be your fair pillow!

Helen. Dear lord, you are full of fair words.

Pan. You speak your fair pleasure, sweet queen. Fair prince here is good broken music.

Par. You have broke it, cousin, and, by my life, you shall make it whole again; you shall piece it out with a piece of your performance. Nell, he is full of harmony.

Pan. Truly, lady, no.

Helen. O, sir—

Pan. Rude, in sooth; in good sooth, very rude.

Par. Well said, my lord! well, you say so in fits.

Pan. I have business to my lord, dear queen. My lord, will you vouchsafe me a word?

Helen. Nay, this shall not hedge us out. We'll hear you sing, certainly.

Pan. Well, sweet queen, you are pleasant with me. But, marry, thus, my lord: my dear lord and most esteemed friend, your brother Troilus—

Helen. My Lord Pandarus; honey-sweet lord—

Pan. Go to, sweet queen, go to!—commends himself most affectionately to you—

Helen. You shall not bob us out of our melody. If you do, our melancholy upon your head!

Pan. Sweet queen, sweet queen! that's a sweet queen, i' faith.

Helen. And to make a sweet lady sad is a sour offence.

Pan. Nay, that shall not serve your turn; that shall it not, in truth, la. Nay, I care not for such words; no, no. And, my lord, he desires you, that if the King call for him at supper, you will make his excuse.

Helen. My Lord Pandarus—

Pan. What says my sweet queen, my very very sweet queen?

Par. What exploit's in hand? where sups he to-night?

Helen. Nay, but, my lord—

Pan. What says my sweet queen? My cousin will fall out with you. You must not know where he sups.

Par. I'll lay my life, with my disposer Cressida.

Pan. No, no, no such matter; you are wide. Come, your disposer is sick.

Par. Well, I'll make excuse.

Pan. Ay, good my lord. Why should you say Cressida? no, your poor disposer's sick.

Par. I spy.

Pan. You spy! what do you spy? Come, give me an instrument. Now, sweet queen.

Helen. Why, this is kindly done.

Pan. My niece is horribly in love with a thing you have, sweet queen.

Helen. She shall have it, my lord, if it be not my lord Paris.

Pan. He! no, she'll none of him; they two are twain.

Helen. Falling in, after falling out, may make them three.

Pan. Come, come, I'll hear no more of this; I'll sing you a song now.

Helen. Ay, ay, prithee now. By my troth, sweet lord, thou hast a fine forehead.

Pan. Ay, you may, you may.

Helen. Let thy song be love. This love will undo us all. O Cupid, Cupid, Cupid!

Pan. Love! ay, that it shall, i' faith.

Par. Ay, good now, love, love, nothing but love.

Pan. In good troth, it begins so.

[*Sings.*] "Love, love, nothing but love, still more!
For, O, love's bow
Shoots buck and doe.
The shaft confounds,
Not that it wounds,
But tickles still the sore.
These lovers cry Oh! oh! they die!
Yet that which seems the wound to kill,
Doth turn oh! oh! to ha! ha! he!
So dying love lives still.
Oh! oh! a while, but ha! ha! ha!
Oh! oh! groans out for ha! ha! ha!
Heigh-ho!

Helen. In love, i' faith, to the very tip of the nose.

Par. He eats nothing but doves, love, and that breeds hot blood, and hot blood begets hot thoughts, and hot thoughts beget hot deeds, and hot deeds is love.

Pan. Is this the generation of love? hot blood, hot thoughts, and hot deeds? Why, they are vipers. Is love a generation of vipers? Sweet lord, who's a-field to-day?

Par. Hector, Deiphobus, Helenus, Antenor, and all the gallantry of Troy. I would fain have armed to-day, but my Nell would not have it so. How chance my brother Troilus went not?

Helen. He hangs the lip at something. You know all, Lord Pandarus.

Pan. Not I, honey-sweet queen. I long to hear how they sped to-day. You'll remember your brother's excuse?

Par. To a hair.

Pan. Farewell, sweet queen.

Helen. Commend me to your niece.

Pan. I will, sweet queen. [*Exit.*

A retreat sounded.

Par. They're come from field. Let us to Priam's hall,
To greet the warriors. Sweet Helen, I must woo you
To help unarm our Hector. His stubborn buckles,
With these your white enchanting fingers touch'd,
Shall more obey than to the edge of steel
Or force of Greekish sinews; you shall do more
Than all the island kings—disarm great Hector.

Helen. 'Twill make us proud to be his servant, Paris;
Yea, what he shall receive of us in duty
Gives us more palm in beauty than we have,
Yea, overshines ourself.

Par. Sweet, above thought I love thee. [*Exeunt.*

SCENE II. *The same: Pandarus' orchard*

Enter PANDARUS *and* TROILUS' BOY, *meeting.*

Pan. How now! where's thy master? at my cousin Cressida's?

Boy. No, sir; he stays for you to conduct him thither.

Pan. O, here he comes.

Enter TROILUS.

How now, how now!

Tro. Sirrah, walk off. [*Exit* BOY.

Pan. Have you seen my cousin?

Tro. No, Pandarus. I stalk about her door,
Like a strange soul upon the Stygian banks
Staying for waftage. O, be thou my Charon,
And give me swift transportance to those fields
Where I may wallow in the lily-beds
Proposed for the deserver! O gentle Pandarus,
From Cupid's shoulder pluck his painted wings,
And fly with me to Cressid!

Pan. Walk here i' the orchard, I'll bring her straight. [*Exit.*

Tro. I am giddy; expectation whirls me round.
The imaginary relish is so sweet
That it enchants my sense. What will it be,
When that the watery palate tastes indeed
Love's thrice repured nectar? death, I fear me,
Swooning destruction, or some joy too fine,
Too subtle-potent, tuned too sharp in sweetness,
For the capacity of my ruder powers.
I fear it much; and I do fear besides,
That I shall lose distinction in my joys;
As doth a battle, when they charge on heaps
The enemy flying.

Re-enter PANDARUS.

Pan. She's making her ready, she'll come straight. You must be witty now. She does so blush, and fetches her wind so short, as if she were frayed with a sprite. I'll fetch her. It is the prettiest villain; she fetches her breath as short as a new-ta'en sparrow. [*Exit.*

Tro. Even such a passion doth embrace my bosom.
My heart beats thicker than a feverous pulse;
And all my powers do their bestowing lose,
Like vassalage at unawares encountering
The eye of majesty.

Re-enter PANDARUS *with* CRESSIDA.

Pan. Come, come, what need you blush? shame's a baby. Here she is now; swear the oaths now to her that you have sworn to me. What, are you gone again? you must be watched ere you be made tame, must you? Come your ways, come your ways; an you draw backward, we'll put you i' the fills. Why do you not speak to her? Come, draw this curtain, and let's see your picture. Alas the day, how loath you are to offend daylight! an 'twere dark, you'ld close sooner. So, so; rub on, and kiss the mistress. How now! a kiss in fee-farm! build there, carpenter; the air is sweet. Nay, you shall fight your hearts out ere I part you. The falcon as the tercel, for all the ducks i' the river. Go to, go to.

Tro. You have bereft me of all words, lady.

Pan. Words pay no debts, give her deeds; but she'll bereave you o' the deeds too, if she call your activity in question. What, billing again? Here's "In witness whereof the parties interchangeably"— Come in, come in. I'll go get a fire. [*Exit.*

Cres. Will you walk in, my lord?

Tro. O Cressida, how often have I wished me thus!

Cres. Wished, my lord! The gods grant—
O my lord!

Tro. What should they grant? what makes this pretty abruption? What too curious dreg espies my sweet lady in the fountain of our love?

Cres. More dregs than water, if my fears have eyes.

Tro. Fears make devils of cherubins; they never see truly.

Cres. Blind fear, that seeing reason leads, finds safer footing than blind reason stumbling without fear. To fear the worst oft cures the worse.

Tro. O, let my lady apprehend no fear; in all Cupid's pageant there is presented no monster.

Cres. Nor nothing monstrous neither?

Tro. Nothing, but our undertakings; when we vow to weep seas, live in fire, eat rocks, tame tigers; thinking it harder for our mistress to devise imposition enough than for us to undergo any difficulty imposed. This is the monstruosity in love, lady, that the will is infinite and the execution confined, that the desire is boundless and the act a slave to limit.

Cres. They say all lovers swear more performance than they are able and yet reserve an ability that they never perform, vowing more than the perfection of ten and discharging less than the tenth part of one. They that have the voice of lions and the act of hares, are they not monsters?

Tro. Are there such? such are not we. Praise us as we are tasted, allow us as we prove; our head shall go bare till merit crown it. No perfection in reversion shall have a praise in present; we will not name desert before his birth, and, being born, his addition shall be humble. Few words to fair faith. Troilus shall be such to Cressid as what envy can say worst shall be a mock for his truth, and what truth can speak truest not truer than Troilus.

Cres. Will you walk in, my lord?

Re-enter PANDARUS.

Pan. What, blushing still? have you not done talking yet.

Cres. Well, uncle, what folly I commit, I dedicate to you.

Pan. I thank you for that; if my lord get a boy of you, you'll give him me. Be true to my lord; if he flinch, chide me for it.

Tro. You know now your hostages; your uncle's word and my firm faith.

Pan. Nay, I'll give my word for her too Our kindred, though they be long ere they are wooed, they are constant being won. They are burs, I can tell you; they'll stick where they are thrown.

Cres. Boldness comes to me now, and brings me heart.
Prince Troilus, I have loved you night and day
For many weary months.

Tro. Why was my Cressid then so hard to win?

Cres. Hard to seem won; but I was won, my lord,
With the first glance that ever—pardon me—
If I confess much, you will play the tyrant.
I love you now; but not, till now, so much
But I might master it. In faith, I lie;
My thoughts were like unbridled children, grown
Too headstrong for their mother. See, we fools!
Why have I blabb'd? who shall be true to us,
When we are so unsecret to ourselves?
But, though I loved you well, I woo'd you not;
And yet, good faith, I wish'd myself a man,
Or that we women had men's privilege
Of speaking first. Sweet, bid me hold my tongue,
For in this rapture I shall surely speak
The thing I shall repent. See, see, your silence,
Cunning in dumbness, from my weakness draws
My very soul of counsel! stop my mouth.

Tro. And shall, albeit sweet music issues thence.

Pan. Pretty, i' faith.

Cres. My lord, I do beseech you, pardon me;
'Twas not my purpose, thus to beg a kiss.
I am ashamed. O heavens! what have I done?
For this time will I take my leave, my lord.

Tro. Your leave, sweet Cressid!

Pan. Leave! an you take leave till to-morrow morning—

Cres. Pray you, content you.

Tro. What offends you, lady?

Cres. Sir, mine own company.

Tro. You cannot shun
Yourself.

Cres. Let me go and try.
I have a kind of self resides with you;
But an unkind self, that itself will leave,
To be another's fool. I would be gone.
Where is my wit? I know not what I speak.

Tro. Well know they what they speak that speak so wisely.

Cres. Perchance, my lord, I show more craft than love;
And fell so roundly to a large confession,
To angle for your thoughts. But you are wise,
Or else you love not, for to be wise and love
Exceeds man's might; that dwells with gods above.

Tro. O that I thought it could be in a woman—
As, if it can, I will presume in you—
To feed for aye her lamp and flames of love;
To keep her constancy in plight and youth,

Outliving beauty's outward, with a mind
That doth renew swifter then blood decays!
Or that persuasion could but thus convince me,
That my integrity and truth to you
Might be affronted with the match and weight
Of such a winnow'd purity in love;
How were I then uplifted! but, alas!
I am as true as truth's simplicity
And simpler than the infancy of truth.

Cres. In that I'll war with you.

Tro. O virtuous fight,
When right with right wars who shall be most right!
True swains in love shall in the world to come
Approve their truths by Troilus. When their rhymes,
Full of protest, of oath and big compare,
Want similes, truth tired with iteration,
As true as steel, as plantage to the moon,
As sun to day, as turtle to her mate,
As iron to adamant, as earth to the centre,
Yet, after all comparisons of truth,
As truth's authentic author to be cited,
"As true as Troilus" shall crown up the verse,
And sanctify the numbers.

Cres. Prophet may you be!
If I be false, or swerve a hair from truth,
When time is old and hath forgot itself,
When waterdrops have worn the stones of Troy,
And blind oblivion swallow'd cities up,
And mighty states characterless are grated
To dusty nothing, yet let memory,
From false to false, among false maids in love,
Upbraid my falsehood! when they've said "as false
As air, as water, wind, or sandy earth,
As fox to lamb, as wolf to heifer's calf,
Pard to the hind, or stepdame to her son,"
"Yea," let them say, to stick the heart of falsehood,
"As false as Cressid."

Pan. Go to, a bargain made. Seal it, seal it; I'll be the witness. Here I hold your hand, here my cousin's. If ever you prove false one to another, since I have taken such pains to bring you together, let all pitiful goers-between be called to the world's end after my name; call them all Pandars; let all constant men be Troiluses, all false women Cressids, and all brokers-between Pandars! say, amen.

Tro. Amen.

Cres. Amen.

Pan. Amen. Whereupon I will show you a chamber with a bed; which bed, because it shall not speak of your pretty encounters, press it to death. Away!
And Cupid grant all tongue-tied maidens here
Bed, chamber, Pandar to provide this gear!
[*Exeunt*.

SCENE III. *The Grecian camp: before Achilles' tent*

Enter AGAMEMNON, ULYSSES, DIOMEDES, NESTOR, AJAX, MENELAUS, *and* CALCHAS.

Cal. Now, princes, for the service I have done you,
The advantage of the time prompts me aloud
To call for recompense. Appear it to your mind
That, through the sight I bear in things to love,
I have abandon'd Troy, left my possession,
Incurr'd a traitor's name; exposed myself,
From certain and possess'd conveniences,
To doubtful fortunes; sequestering from me all
That time, acquaintance, custom, and condition
Made tame and most familiar to my nature,
And here, to do you service, am become
As new into the world, strange, unacquainted.
I do beseech you, as in way of taste,
To give me now a little benefit,
Out of those many register'd in promise,
Which, you say, live to come in my behalf.

Agam. What wouldst thou of us, Trojan? make demand.

Cal. You have a Trojan prisoner, call'd Antenor,
Yesterday took. Troy holds him very dear.
Oft have you—often have you thanks therefore—
Desired my Cressid in right great exchange,
Whom Troy hath still denied. But this Antenor,
I know, is such a wrest in their affairs
That their negotiations all must slack,
Wanting his manage; and they will almost
Give us a prince of blood, a son of Priam,
In change of him. Let him be sent, great princes,
And he shall buy my daughter; and her presence
Shall quite strike off all service I have done,
In most accepted pain.

Agam. Let Diomedes bear him,
And bring us Cressid hither. Calchas shall have
What he requests of us. Good Diomed,
Furnish you fairly for this interchange.
Withal bring word if Hector will to-morrow
Be answer'd in his challenge. Ajax is ready.

Dio. This shall I undertake; and 'tis a burden
Which I am proud to bear.
[*Exeunt* DIOMEDES *and* CALCHAS.

Enter ACHILLES *and* PATROCLUS, *before their tent*.

Ulyss. Achilles stands i' the entrance of his tent.
Please it our general to pass strangely by him,
As if he were forgot; and, princes all,
Lay negligent and loose regard upon him.

I will come last. 'Tis like he'll question me
Why such unplausive eyes are bent on him.
If so, I have derision medicinable,
To use between your strangeness and his pride,
Which his own will shall have desire to drink.
It may do good; pride hath no other glass
To show itself but pride, for supple knees
Feed arrogance and are the proud man's fees.
Agam. We'll execute your purpose, and put on
A form of strangeness as we pass along;
So do each lord, and either greet him not,
Or else disdainfully, which shall shake him more
Than if not look'd on. I will lead the way.
Achil. What, comes the general to speak with me?
You know my mind, I'll fight no more 'gainst Troy.
Agam. What says Achilles? would he aught with us?
Nest. Would you, my lord, aught with the general?
Achil. No.
Nest. Nothing, my lord.
Agam. The better.
[*Exeunt* AGAMEMNON *and* NESTOR.
Achil. Good day, good day.
Men. How do you? how do you? [*Exit*.
Achil. What, does the cuckold scorn me?
Ajax. How now, Patroclus!
Achil. Good morrow, Ajax.
Ajax. Ha?
Achil. Good morrow.
Ajax. Ay, and good next day too. [*Exit*.
Achil. What mean these fellows? Know they not Achiles?
Patr. They pass by strangely. They were used to bend,
To send their smiles before them to Achilles;
To come as humbly as they used to creep
To holy altars.
Achil. What, am I poor of late?
'Tis certain, greatness, once fall'n out with fortune,
Must fall out with men too. What the declined is
He shall as soon read in the eyes of others
As feel in his own fall; for men, like butterflies,
Show not their mealy wings but to the summer,
And not a man, for being simply man,
Hath any honour, but honour for those honours
That are without him, as place, riches, favour,
Prizes of accident as oft as merit;
Which when they fall, as being slippery standers,
The love that lean'd on them as slippery too,
Do one pluck down another and together
Die in the fall. But 'tis not so with me:
Fortune and I are friends: I do enjoy
At ample point all that I did possess,
Save these men's looks; who do, methinks, find out
Something not worth in me such rich beholding
As they have often given. Here is Ulysses;
I'll interrupt his reading.
How now, Ulysses!
Ulyss. Now, great Thetis' son!
Achil. What are you reading?
Ulyss. A strange fellow here
Writes me: "That man, how dearly ever parted,
How much in having, or without or in,
Cannot make boast to have that which he hath,
Nor feels not what he owes, but by reflection;
As when his virtues shining upon others
Heat them and they retort that heat again
To the first giver."
Achil. This is not strange, Ulysses.
The beauty that is borne here in the face
The bearer knows not, but commends itself
To other's eyes; nor doth the eye itself,
That most pure spirit of sense, behold itself,
Not going from itself; but eye to eye opposed
Salutes each other with each other's form;
For speculation turns not to itself,
Till it hath travell'd and is mirror'd there
Where it may see itself. This is not strange at all.
Ulyss. I do not strain at the position—
It is familiar—but at the author's drift;
Who, in his circumstance, expressly proves
That no man is the lord of anything,
Though in and of him there be much consisting,
Till he communicate his parts to others;
Nor doth he of himself know them for aught
Till he behold them form'd in the applause
Where they're extended; who, like an arch, reverberates
The voice again, or, like a gate of steel
Fronting the sun, receives and renders back
His figure and his heat. I was much wrapt in this;
And apprehended here immediately
The unknown Ajax.
Heavens, what a man is there! a very horse,
That has he knows not what. Nature, what things there are
Most abject in regard and dear in use!
What things again most dear in the esteem
And poor in worth! Now shall we see to-morrow—
An act that very chance doth throw upon him—
Ajax renown'd. O heavens, what some men do,
While some men leave to do!
How some men creep in skittish fortune's hall,
Whiles others play the idiots in her eyes!
How one man eats into another's pride,
While pride is fasting in his wantonness!

To see these Grecian lords!—why, even already
They clap the lubber Ajax on the shoulder,
As if his foot were on brave Hector's breast
And great Troy shrieking.
Achil. I do believe it; for they pass'd by me
As misers do by beggars, neither gave to me
Good word nor look. What, are my deeds forgot?
Ulyss. Time hath, my lord, a wallet at his back,
Wherein he puts alms for Oblivion,
A great-sized monster of ingratitudes.
Those scraps are good deeds past; which are devour'd
As fast as they are made, forgot as soon
As done. Perseverance, dear my lord,
Keeps honour bright; to have done is to hang
Quite out of fashion, like a rusty mail
In monumental mockery. Take the instant way;
For honour travels in a strait so narrow,
Where one but goes abreast. Keep then the path;
For Emulation hath a thousand sons
That one by one pursue. If you give way,
Or hedge aside from the direct forthright,
Like to an enter'd tide, they all rush by
And leave you hindmost;
Or, like a gallant horse fall'n in first rank,
Lie there for pavement to the abject rear,
O'er-run and trampled on. Then what they do in present,
Though less than yours in past, must o'ertop yours;
For time is like a fashionable host
That slightly shakes his parting guest by the hand,
And with his arms outstretch'd, as he would fly,
Grasps in the comer. Welcome ever smiles,
And farewell goes out sighing. O, let not virtue seek
Remuneration for the thing it was;
For beauty, wit,
High birth, vigour of bone, desert in service,
Love, friendship, charity, are subjects all
To envious and calumniating Time.
One touch of nature makes the whole world kin,
That all with one consent praise new-born gawds,
Though they are made and moulded of things past,
And give to dust that is a little gilt
More laud than gilt o'er-dusted.
The present eye praises the present object.
Then marvel not, thou great and complete man,
That all the Greeks begin to worship Ajax;
Since things in motion sooner catch the eye
Than what not stirs. The cry went once on thee,
And still it might, and yet it may again,
If thou wouldst not entomb thyself alive
And case thy reputation in thy tent;
Whose glorious deeds, but in these fields of late,
Made emulous missions 'mongst the gods themselves
And drave great Mars to faction.
Achil. Of this my privacy
I have strong reasons.
Ulyss. But 'gainst your privacy
The reasons are more potent and heroical.
'Tis known, Achilles, that you are in love
With one of Priam's daughters.
Achil. Ha! known!
Ulyss. Is that a wonder?
The providence that's in a watchful state
Knows almost every grain of Plutus' gold,
Finds bottom in the uncomprehensive deeps,
Keeps place with thought and almost, like the gods,
Does thoughts unveil in their dumb cradles.
There is a mystery—with whom relation
Durst never meddle—in the soul of state;
Which hath an operation more divine
Than breath or pen can give expressure to:
All the commerce that you have had with Troy
As perfectly is ours as yours, my lord;
And better would it fit Achilles much
To throw down Hector than Polyxena.
But it must grieve young Pyrrhus now at home,
When fame shall in our islands sound her trump,
And all the Greekish girls shall tripping sing,
"Great Hector's sister did Achilles win,
But our great Ajax bravely beat down him."
Farewell, my lord. I as your lover speak;
The fool slides o'er the ice that you should break.
[*Exit.*
Patr. To this effect, Achilles, have I moved you.
A woman impudent and mannish grown
Is not more loathed than an effeminate man
In time of action. I stand condemn'd for this;
They think my little stomach to the war
And your great love to me restrains you thus.
Sweet, rouse yourself; and the weak wanton Cupid
Shall from your neck unloose his amorous fold,
And, like a dew-drop from the lion's mane,
Be shook to air.
Achil. Shall Ajax fight with Hector?
Patr. Ay, and perhaps receive much honour by him.
Achil. I see my reputation is at stake;
My fame is shrewdly gored.
Patr. O, then, beware;
Those wounds heal ill that men do give themselves.
Omission to do what is necessary

Seals a commission to a blank of danger;
And danger, like an ague, subtly taints
Even then when we sit idly in the sun.

Achil. Go call Thersites hither, sweet Patroclus.
I'll send the fool to Ajax and desire him
To invite the Trojan lords after the combat
To see us here unarm'd. I have a woman's longing,
An appetite that I am sick withal,
To see great Hector in his weeds of peace,
To talk with him and to behold his visage,
Even to my full of view.

Enter THERSITES.

A labour saved!

Ther. A wonder!

Achil. What?

Ther. Ajax goes up and down the field, asking for himself.

Achil. How so?

Ther. He must fight singly to-morrow with Hector, and is so prophetically proud of an heroical cudgelling that he raves in saying nothing.

Achil. How can that be?

Ther. Why, he stalks up and down like a peacock—a stride and a stand; ruminates like an hostess that hath no arithmetic but her brain to set down her reckoning; bites his lip with a politic regard, as who should say, "There were wit in this head, an 'twould out"; and so there is, but it lies as coldly in him as fire in a flint, which will not show without knocking. The man's undone for ever; for if Hector break not his neck i' the combat, he'll break 't himself in vain-glory. He knows not me. I said, "Good morrow, Ajax"; and he replies, "Thanks, Agamemnon." What think you of this man that takes me for the general? He's grown a very land-fish, languageless, a monster. A plague of opinion! a man may wear it on both sides, like a leather jerkin.

Achil. Thou must be my ambassador to him, Thersites.

Ther. Who, I? why, he'll answer nobody; he professes not answering. Speaking is for beggars; he wears his tongue in's arms. I will put on his presence; let Patroclus make demands to me, you shall see the pageant of Ajax.

Achil. To him, Patroclus. Tell him I humbly desire the valiant Ajax to invite the most valorous Hector to come unarmed to my tent, and to procure safe-conduct for his person of the magnanimous and most illustrious six-or-seven-times-honoured captain-general of the Grecian army, Agamemnon, et cetera. Do this.

Patr. Jove bless great Ajax!

Ther. Hum!

Patr. I come from the worthy Achilles—

Ther. Ha!

Patr. Who most humbly desires you to invite Hector to his tent—

Ther. Hum!

Patr. And to procure safe-conduct from Agamemnon.

Ther. Agamemnon!

Patr. Ay, my lord.

Ther. Ha!

Patr. What say you to't?

Ther. God b' wi' you, with all my heart.

Patr. Your answer, sir.

Ther. If to-morrow be a fair day, by eleven o'clock it will go one way or other. Howsoever, he shall pay for me ere he has me.

Patr. Your answer, sir.

Ther. Fare you well, with all my heart.

Achil. Why, but he is not in this tune, is he?

Ther. No, but he's out o' tune thus. What music will be in him when Hector has knocked out his brains, I know not; but, I am sure, none, unless the fiddler Apollo get his sinews to make catlings on.

Achil. Come, thou shalt bear a letter to him straight.

Ther. Let me bear another to his horse; for that's the more capable creature.

Achil. My mind is troubled, like a fountain stirr'd;
And I myself see not the bottom of it.

[*Exeunt* ACHILLES *and* PATROCLUS.

Ther. Would the fountain of your mind were clear again, that I might water an ass at it! I had rather be a tick in a sheep than such a valiant ignorance. [*Exit*.

ACT IV

SCENE I. *Troy: a street*

Enter, from one side, ÆNEAS, *and Servant with a torch; from the other,* PARIS, DEIPHOBUS, ANTENOR, DIOMEDES, *and others, with torches.*

Par. See, ho! who is that there?

Dei. It is the Lord Æneas.

Æne. Is the prince there in person?
Had I so good occasion to lie long
As you, Prince Paris, nothing but heavenly business
Should rob my bed-mate of my company.

Dio. That's my mind too. Good morrow, Lord Æneas.

Par. A valiant Greek, Æneas—take his hand—
Witness the process of your speech, wherein
You told how Diomed, a whole week by days,

Did haunt you in the field.
Æne. Health to you, valiant sir,
During all question of the gentle truce;
But when I meet you arm'd, as black defiance
As heart can think or courage execute.
Dio. The one and other Diomed embraces.
Our bloods are now in calm; and, so long, health!
But when contention and occasion meet,
By Jove, I'll play the hunter for thy life
With all my force, pursuit and policy.
Æne. And thou shalt hunt a lion that will fly
With his face backward. In humane gentleness,
Welcome to Troy! now, by Anchises' life,
Welcome, indeed! By Venus' hand I swear,
No man alive can love in such a sort
The thing he means to kill more excellently.
Dio. We sympathise. Jove, let Æneas live,
If to my sword his fate be not the glory,
A thousand complete courses of the sun!
But, in mine emulous honour, let him die,
With every joint a wound, and that to-morrow!
Æne. We know each other well.
Dio. We do; and long to know each other worse.
Par. This is the most despiteful gentle greeting,
The noblest hateful love, that e'er I heard of.
What business, lord, so early?
Æne. I was sent for to the King; but why, I know not.
Par. His purpose meets you. 'Twas to bring this Greek
To Calchas' house, and there to render him,
For the enfreed Antenor, the fair Cressid.
Let's have your company, or, if you please,
Haste there before us. I constantly do think—
Or rather, call my thought a certain knowledge—
My brother Troilus lodges there to-night.
Rouse him and give him note of our approach,
With the whole quality wherefore. I fear
We shall be much unwelcome.
Æne. That I assure you.
Troilus had rather Troy were borne to Greece
Than Cressid borne from Troy.
Par. There is no help;
The bitter disposition of the time
Will have it so. On, lord; we'll follow you.
Æne. Good morrow, all. [*Exit with Servant.*
Par. And tell me, noble Diomed, faith, tell me true,
Even in the soul of sound good-fellowship,
Who, in your thoughts, merits fair Helen best,
Myself or Menelaus?
Dio. Both alike:
He merits well to have her, that doth seek her,
Not making any scruple of her soilure,
With such a hell of pain and world of charge,
And you as well to keep her, that defend her,
Not palating the taste of her dishonour,
With such a costly loss of wealth and friends:
He, like a puling cuckold, would drink up
The lees and dregs of a flat tamed piece;
You, like a lecher, out of whorish loins
Are pleased to breed out your inheritors.
Both merits poised, each weighs nor less nor more;
But he as he, the heavier for a whore.
Par. You are too bitter to your countrywoman.
Dio. She's bitter to her country. Hear me, Paris:
For every false drop in her bawdy veins
A Grecian's life hath sunk; for every scruple
Of her contaminated carrion weight,
A Trojan hath been slain. Since she could speak,
She hath not given so many good words breath
As for her Greeks and Trojans suffer'd death.
Par. Fair Diomed, you do as chapmen do,
Dispraise the thing that you desire to buy.
But we in silence hold this virtue well,
We'll but commend what we intend to sell.
Here lies our way. [*Exeunt.*

SCENE II. *The same: court of Pandarus' house*

Enter TROILUS *and* CRESSIDA.

Tro. Dear, trouble not yourself. The morn is cold.
Cres. Then, sweet my lord, I'll call mine uncle down;
He shall unbolt the gates.
Tro. Trouble him not;
To bed, to bed. Sleep kill those pretty eyes,
And give as soft attachment to thy senses
As infants' empty of all thought!
Cres. Good morrow, then.
Tro. I prithee now, to bed.
Cres. Are you a-weary of me?
Tro. O Cressida! but that the busy day,
Waked by the lark, hath roused the ribald crows,
And dreaming night will hide our joys no longer,
I would not from thee.
Cres. Night hath been too brief.
Tro. Beshrew the witch! with venomous wights she stays
As tediously as hell, but flies the grasps of love
With wings more momentary-swift than thought.
You will catch cold and curse me.
Cres. Prithee, tarry.
You men will never tarry.
O foolish Cressid! I might have still held off,
And then you would have tarried. Hark! there's one up.
Pan. [*Within*] What, 's all the doors open here?
Tro. It is your uncle.

Cres. A pestilence on him! now will he be mocking.
I shall have such a life!

Enter PANDARUS.

Pan. How now, how now! how go maidenheads? Here, you maid! where's my cousin Cressid?

Cres. Go hang yourself, you naughty mocking uncle!
You bring me to do, and then you flout me too.

Pan. To do what? to do what? let her say what. What have I brought you to do?

Cres. Come, come, beshrew your heart! you'll ne'er be good,
Nor suffer others.

Pan. Ha, ha! Alas, poor wretch! ah, poor *capocchia!* hast not slept to-night? would he not, a naughty man, let it sleep? a bugbear take him!

Cres. Did not I tell you? Would he were knock'd i' the head!

Knocking within.

Who's that at door? good uncle, go and see.
My lord, come you again into my chamber.
You smile and mock me, as if I meant naughtily.

Tro. Ha, ha!

Cres. Come, you are deceived, I think of no such thing.

Knocking within.

How earnestly they knock! Pray you, come in.
I would not for half Troy have you seen here.

[*Exeunt* TROILUS *and* CRESSIDA.

Pan. Who's there? what's the matter? will you beat down the door? How now! what's the matter?

Enter ÆNEAS.

Æne. Good morrow, lord, good morrow.

Pan. Who's there? my Lord Æneas! By my troth,
I knew you not. What news with you so early?

Æne. Is not Prince Troilus here?

Pan. Here! what should he do here?

Æne. Come, he is here, my lord; do not deny him.
It doth import him much to speak with me.

Pan. Is he here, say you? 'tis more than I know, I'll be sworn. For my own part, I came in late. What should he do here?

Æne. Who!—nay, then. Come, come, you'll do him wrong ere you're ware. You'll be so true to him, to be false to him. Do not you know of him, but yet go fetch him hither; go.

Re-enter TROILUS.

Tro. How now! what's the matter?

Æne. My lord, I scarce have leisure to salute you,
My matter is so rash. There is at hand
Paris your brother, and Deiphobus,
The Grecian Diomed, and our Antenor
Deliver'd to us; and for him forthwith,
Ere the first sacrifice, within this hour,
We must give up to Diomedes' hand
The Lady Cressida.

Tro. Is it so concluded?

Æne. By Priam and the general state of Troy.
They are at hand and ready to effect it.

Tro. How my achievements mock me!
I will go meet them. And, my Lord Æneas,
We met by chance; you did not find me here.

Æne. Good, good, my lord; the secrets of nature
Have not more gift in taciturnity.

[*Exeunt* TROILUS *and* ÆNEAS.

Pan. Is't possible? no sooner got but lost? The devil take Antenor! the young prince will go mad. A plague upon Antenor! I would they had broke 's neck!

Re-enter CRESSIDA.

Cres. How now! what's the matter? who was here?

Pan. Ah, ah!

Cres. Why sigh you so profoundly? where's my lord? gone! Tell me, sweet uncle, what's the matter?

Pan. Would I were as deep under the earth as I am above!

Cres. O the gods! what's the matter?

Pan. Prithee, get thee in. Would thou hadst ne'er been born! I knew thou wouldst be his death. O, poor gentleman! A plague upon Antenor!

Cres. Good uncle, I beseech you, on my knees I beseech you, what's the matter?

Pan. Thou must be gone, wench, thou must be gone; thou art changed for Antenor; thou must to thy father, and be gone from Troilus. 'Twill be his death; 'twill be his bane; he cannot bear it.

Cres. O you immortal gods! I will not go.

Pan. Thou must.

Cres. I will not, uncle. I have forgot my father;
I know no touch of consanguinity;
No kin, no love, no blood, no soul so near me
As the sweet Troilus. O you gods divine!
Make Cressid's name the very crown of falsehood,
If ever she leave Troilus! Time, force, and death,
Do to this body what extremes you can;
But the strong base and building of my love

Is as the very centre of the earth,
Drawing all things to it. I'll go in and weep—

Pan. Do, do.

Cres. Tear my bright hair and scratch my praised cheeks,
Crack my clear voice with sobs and break my heart
With sounding Troilus. I will not go from Troy. [*Exeunt.*

SCENE III. *The same: street before Pandarus' house*

Enter PARIS, TROILUS, ÆNEAS, DEIPHOBUS, ANTENOR, *and* DIOMEDES

Par. It is great morning, and the hour prefix'd
Of her delivery to this valiant Greek
Comes fast upon. Good my brother Troilus,
Tell you the lady what she is to do,
And haste her to the purpose.

Tro. Walk into her house;
I'll bring her to the Grecian presently;
And to his hand when I deliver her,
Think it an altar, and thy brother Troilus
A priest there offering to it his own heart. [*Exit.*

Par. I know what 'tis to love;
And would, as I shall pity, I could help!
Please you walk in, my lords. [*Exeunt.*

SCENE IV. *The same: Pandarus' house*

Enter PANDARUS *and* CRESSIDA.

Pan. Be moderate, be moderate.

Cres. Why tell you me of moderation?
The grief is fine, full, perfect, that I taste,
And violenteth in a sense as strong
As that which causeth it. How can I moderate it?
If I could temporize with my affection,
Or brew it to a weak and colder palate,
The like allayment could I give my grief.
My love admits no qualifying dross;
No more my grief, in such a precious loss.

Pan. Here, here, here he comes.

Enter TROILUS.

Ah, sweet ducks!

Cres. O Troilus! Troilus! [*Embracing him.*]

Pan. What a pair of spectacles is here! Let me embrace too. "O heart," as the goodly saying is,

"—O heart, heavy heart,
Why sigh'st thou without breaking?"

where he answers again,

"Because thou canst not ease thy smart
By friendship nor by speaking."

There was never a truer rhyme. Let us cast away nothing, for we may live to have need of such a verse. We see it, we see it. How now, lambs?

Tro. Cressid, I love thee in so strain'd a purity,
That the bless'd gods, as angry with my fancy,
More bright in zeal than the devotion which
Cold lips blow to their deities, take thee from me.

Cres. Have the gods envy?

Pan. Ay, ay, ay, ay; 'tis too plain a case.

Cres. And is it true that I must go from Troy?

Tro. A hateful truth.

Cres. What, and from Troilus too?

Tro. From Troy and Troilus.

Cres. Is it possible?

Tro. And suddenly; where injury of chance
Puts back leave-taking, justles roughly by
All time of pause, rudely beguiles our lips
Of all rejoindure, forcibly prevents
Our lock'd embrasures, strangles our dear vows
Even in the birth of our own labouring breath.
We two, that with so many thousand sighs
Did buy each other, must poorly sell ourselves
With the rude brevity and discharge of one.
Injurious time now with a robber's haste
Crams his rich thievery up, he knows not how.
As many farewells as be stars in heaven,
With distinct breath and consign'd kisses to them,
He fumbles up into a loose adieu,
And scants us with a single famish'd kiss,
Distasted with the salt of broken tears.

Æne. [*Within*] My lord, is the lady ready?

Tro. Hark! you are call'd. Some say the Genius so
Cries "come" to him that instantly must die.
Bid them have patience; she shall come anon.

Pan. Where are my tears? rain, to lay this wind, or my heart will be blown up by the root. [*Exit.*

Cres. I must then to the Grecians?

Tro. No remedy.

Cres. A woful Cressid 'mongst the merry Greeks!
When shall we see again?

Tro. Hear me, my love. Be thou but true of heart—

Cres. I true! how now! what wicked deem is this?

Tro. Nay, we must use expostulation kindly,
For it is parting from us.
I speak not "be thou true," as fearing thee,
For I will throw my glove to Death himself,
That there's no maculation in thy heart;
But "be thou true," say I, to fashion in
My sequent protestation; be thou true,
And I will see thee.

Cres. O, you shall be exposed, my lord, to dangers
As infinite as imminent! but I'll be true.
Tro. And I'll grow friend with danger. Wear this sleeve.
Cres. And you this glove. When shall I see you?
Tro. I will corrupt the Grecian sentinels,
To give thee nightly visitation.
But yet be true.
Cres. O heavens! "be true" again!
Tro. Hear why I speak it, love.
The Grecian youths are full of quality;
They're loving, well composed with gifts of nature,
Flowing and swelling o'er with arts and exercise:
How novelty may move, and parts with person,
Alas, a kind of godly jealousy—
Which, I beseech you, call a virtuous sin—
Makes me afeard.
Cres. O heavens! you love me not.
Tro. Die I a villain, then!
In this I do not call your faith in question
So mainly as my merit. I cannot sing,
Nor heel the high lavolt, nor sweeten talk,
Nor play at subtle games; fair virtues all,
To which the Grecians are most prompt and pregnant.
But I can tell that in each grace of these
There lurks a still and dumb-discoursive devil
That tempts most cunningly. But be not tempted.
Cres. Do you think I will?
Tro. No.
But something may be done that we will not:
And sometimes we are devils to ourselves,
When we will tempt the frailty of our powers,
Presuming on their changeful potency.
Æne. [*Within*] Nay, good my lord—
Tro. Come, kiss; and let us part.
Par. [*Within*] Brother Troilus!
Tro. Good brother, come you hither;
And bring Æneas and the Grecian with you.
Cres. My lord, will you be true?
Tro. Who, I? alas, it is my vice, my fault.
Whiles others fish with craft for great opinion,
I with great truth catch mere simplicity;
Whilst some with cunning gild their copper crowns,
With truth and plainness I do wear mine bare.
Fear not my truth; the moral of my wit
Is "plain and true"; there's all the reach of it.

Enter ÆNEAS, PARIS, ANTENOR, DEIPHOBUS, *and* DIOMEDES.

Welcome, Sir Diomed! here is the lady
Which for Antenor we deliver you.
At the port, lord, I'll give her to thy hand;
And by the way possess thee what she is.
Entreat her fair; and, by my soul, fair Greek,
If e'er thou stand at mercy of my sword,
Name Cressid, and thy life shall be as safe
As Priam is in Ilion.
Dio. Fair Lady Cressid,
So please you, save the thanks this prince expects.
The lustre in your eye, heaven in your cheek,
Pleads your fair usage; and to Diomed
You shall be mistress and command him wholly.
Tro. Grecian, thou dost not use me courteously,
To shame the zeal of my petition to thee
In praising her. I tell thee, lord of Greece,
She is as far high-soaring o'er thy praises
As thou unworthy to be call'd her servant.
I charge thee use her well, even for my charge;
For, by the dreadful Pluto, if thou dost not,
Though the great bulk Achilles be thy guard,
I'll cut thy throat.
Dio. O, be not moved, Prince Troilus.
Let me be privileged by my place and message,
To be a speaker free. When I am hence,
I'll answer to my lust; and know you, lord,
I'll nothing do on charge. To her own worth
She shall be prized; but that you say "be't so,"
I'll speak it in my spirit and honour, "no."
Tro. Come, to the port. I'll tell thee, Diomed,
This brave shall oft make thee to hide thy head.
Lady, give me your hand, and, as we walk,
To our own selves bend we our needful talk.
[*Exeunt* TROILUS, CRESSIDA, *and* DIOMEDES.
Trumpet within.
Par. Hark! Hector's trumpet.
Æne. How have we spent this morning!
The prince must think me tardy and remiss,
That swore to ride before him to the field.
Par. 'Tis Troilus' fault. Come, come, to field with him.
Dei. Let us make ready straight.
Æne. Yea, with a bridegroom's fresh alacrity,
Let us address to tend on Hector's heels.
The glory of our Troy doth this day lie
On his fair worth and single chivalry. [*Exeunt*.

SCENE V. *The Grecian camp: lists set out*

Enter AJAX, *armed;* AGAMEMNON, ACHILLES, PATROCLUS, MENELAUS, ULYSSES, NESTOR, *and others*.

Agam. Here art thou in appointment fresh and fair,
Anticipating time with starting courage.
Give with thy trumpet a loud note to Troy,
Thou dreadful Ajax; that the appalled air

May pierce the head of the great combatant
And hale him hither.
Ajax. Thou, trumpet, there's my purse.
Now crack thy lungs, and split thy brazen pipe.
Blow, villain, till thy sphered bias cheek
Outswell the colic of puff'd Aquilon.
Come, stretch thy chest, and let thy eyes spout blood;
Thou blow'st for Hector

Trumpet sounds.

Ulyss. No trumpet answers.
Achil. 'Tis but early days.
Agam. Is not yond Diomed, with Calchas' daughter?
Ulyss. 'Tis he, I ken the manner of his gait;
He rises on the toe. That spirit of his
In aspiration lifts him from the earth.

Enter DIOMEDES, *with* CRESSIDA.

Agam. Is this the Lady Cressid?
Dio. Even she.
Agam. Most dearly welcome to the Greeks, sweet lady.
Nest. Our general doth salute you with a kiss.
Ulyss. Yet is the kindness but particular;
'Twere better she were kiss'd in general.
Nest. And very courtly counsel. I'll begin.
So much for Nestor.
Achil. I'll take that winter from your lips, fair lady.
Achilles bids you welcome.
Men. I had good argument for kissing once.
Patr. But that's no argument for kissing now;
For thus popp'd Paris in his hardiment,
And parted thus you and your argument.
Ulyss. O deadly gall, and theme of all our scorns!
For which we lose our heads to gild his horns.
Patr. The first was Menelaus' kiss; this, mine.
Patroclus kisses you.
Men. O, this is trim!
Patr. Paris and I kiss evermore for him.
Men. I'll have my kiss, sir. Lady, by your leave.
Cres. In kissing, do you render or receive?
Patr. Both take and give.
Cres. I'll make my match to live,
The kiss you take is better than you give;
Therefore no kiss.
Men. I'll give you boot, I'll give you three for one.
Cres. You're an odd man; give even, or give none.
Men. An odd man, lady! every man is odd.
Cres. No, Paris is not; for you know 'tis true,
That you are odd, and he is even with you.
Men. You fillip me o' the head.
Cres. No, I'll be sworn.
Ulyss. It were no match, your nail against his horn.
May I, sweet lady, beg a kiss of you?
Cres. You may.
Ulyss. I do desire it.
Cres. Why, beg, then.
Ulyss. Why then for Venus' sake, give me a kiss,
When Helen is a maid again, and his.
Cres. I am your debtor, claim it when 'tis due.
Ulyss. Never's my day, and then a kiss of you.
Dio. Lady, a word: I'll bring you to your father. [*Exit with* CRESSIDA.
Nest. A woman of quick sense.
Ulyss. Fie, fie upon her!
There's language in her eye, her cheek, her lip,
Nay, her foot speaks; her wanton spirits look out
At every joint and motive of her body.
O, these encounterers, so glib of tongue,
That give accosting welcome ere it comes,
And wide unclasp the tables of their thoughts
To every ticklish reader! set them down
For sluttish spoils of opportunity
And daughters of the game.

Trumpet within.

All. The Trojans' trumpet.
Agam. Yonder comes the troop.

Enter HECTOR, *armed*; ÆNEAS, TROILUS, *and other* TROJANS, *with Attendants*.

Æne. Hail, all you state of Greece! what shall be done
To him that victory commands? or do you purpose
A victor shall be known? will you the knights
Shall to the edge of all extremity
Pursue each other, or shall be divided
By any voice or order of the field?
Hector bade ask.
Agam. Which way would Hector have it?
Æne. He cares not; he'll obey conditions.
Achil. 'Tis done like Hector; but securely done,
A little proudly, and great deal misprizing
The knight opposed.
Æne. If not Achilles, sir,
What is your name?
Achil. If not Achilles, nothing.
Æne. Therefore Achilles. But, whate'er, know this:
In the extremity of great and little,
Valour and pride excel themselves in Hector;
The one almost as infinite as all,

The other blank as nothing. Weigh him well,
And that which looks like pride is courtesy.
This Ajax is half made of Hector's blood;
In love whereof, half Hector stays at home;
Half heart, half hand, half Hector comes to seek
This blended knight, half Trojan and half Greek.

Achil. A maiden battle, then? O, I perceive you.

Re-enter DIOMEDES.

Agam. Here is Sir Diomed. Go, gentle kinght,
Stand by our Ajax. As you and Lord Æneas
Consent upon the order of their fight,
So be it; either to the uttermost,
Or else a breath. The combatants being kin
Half stints their strife before their strokes begin.

AJAX *and* HECTOR *enter the lists.*

Ulyss. They are opposed already.

Agam. What Trojan is that same that looks so heavy?

Ulyss. The youngest son of Priam, a true knight,
Not yet mature, yet matchless, firm of word,
Speaking in deeds and deedless in his tongue;
Not soon provoked nor being provoked soon calm'd;
His heart and hand both open and both free;
For what he has he gives, what thinks he shows;
Yet gives he not till judgement guide his bounty,
Nor dignifies an impair thought with breath;
Manly as Hector, but more dangerous;
For Hector in his blaze of wrath subscribes
To tender objects, but he in heat of action
Is more vindicative than jealous love.
They call him Troilus, and on him erect
A second hope, as fairly built as Hector.
Thus says Æneas; one that knows the youth
Even to his inches, and with private soul
Did in great Ilion thus translate him to me.

Alarum. HECTOR *and* AJAX *fight.*

Agam. They are in action.

Nest. Now, Ajax, hold thine own!

Tro. Hector, thou sleep'st;
Awake thee!

Agam. His blows are well disposed. There, Ajax!

Dio. You must no more.

Trumpets cease.

Æne. Princes, enough, so please you.

Ajax. I am not warm yet; let us fight again.

Dio. As Hector pleases.

Hec. Why, then will I no more.
Thou art, great lord, my father's sister's son,
A cousin-german to great Priam's seed;
The obligation of our blood forbids
A gory emulation 'twixt us twain.
Were thy commixtion Greek and Trojan so
That thou couldst say, "This hand is Grecian all,
And this is Trojan; the sinews of this leg
All Greek, and this all Troy; my mother's blood
Runs on the dexter cheek, and this sinister
Bounds in my father's"; by Jove multipotent,
Thou shouldst not bear from me a Greekish member
Wherein my sword had not impressure made
Of our rank feud; but the just gods gainsay
Thay any drop thou borrow'dst from thy mother,
My sacred aunt, should by my mortal sword
Be drain'd! Let me embrace thee, Ajax.
By him that thunders, thou hast lusty arms;
Hector would have them fall upon him thus.
Cousin, all honour to thee!

Ajax. I thank thee, Hector.
Thou art too gentle and too free a man.
I came to kill thee, cousin, and bear hence
A great addition earned in thy death.

Hect. Not Neoptolemus so mirable,
On whose bright crest Fame with her loud'st Oyes
Cries "This is he," could promise to himself
A thought of added honour torn from Hector.

Æne. There is expectance here from both the sides,
What further you will do.

Hect. We'll answer it;
The issue is embracement. Ajax, farewell.

Ajax. If I might in entreaties find success—
As seld I have the chance—I would desire
My famous cousin to our Grecian tents.

Dio. 'Tis Agamemnon's wish, and great Achilles
Doth long to see unarm'd the valiant Hector.

Hect. Æneas, call my brother Troilus to me,
And signify this loving interview
To the expecters of our Trojan part;
Desire them home. Give me thy hand, my cousin;
I will go eat with thee and see your knights.

Ajax. Great Agamemnon comes to meet us here.

Hect. The worthiest of them tell me name by name;
But for Achilles, mine own searching eyes
Shall find him by his large and portly size.

Agam. Worthy of arms! as welcome as to one
That would be rid of such an enemy;
But that's no welcome. Understand more clear,
What's past and what's to come is strew'd with husks
And formless ruin of oblivion;
But in this extant moment, faith and troth,
Strain'd purely from all hollow bias-drawing,
Bids thee, with most divine integrity,

From heart of very heart, great Hector, welcome.
Hect. I thank thee, most imperious Agamemnon.
Agam. [*To* TROILUS] My well-famed lord of Troy, no less to you.
Men. Let me confirm my princely brother's greeting.
You brace of warlike brothers, welcome hither.
Hect. Who must we answer?
Æne. The noble Menelaus.
Hect. O, you, my lord? by Mars his gauntlet, thanks!
Mock not, that I affect the untraded oath;
Your quondam wife swears still by Venus' glove.
She's well, but bade me not commend her to you.
Men. Name her not now, sir; she's a deadly theme.
Hect. O, pardon; I offend.
Nest. I have, thou gallant Trojan, seen thee oft
Labouring for destiny make cruel way
Through ranks of Greekish youth, and I have seen thee,
As hot as Perseus, spur thy Phrygian steed,
Despising many forfeits and subduements,
When thou hast hung thy advanced sword i' the air,
Not letting it decline on the declined,
That I have said to some my standers by
"Lo, Jupiter is yonder, dealing life!"
And I have seen thee pause and take thy breath,
When that a ring of Greeks have hemm'd thee in,
Like an Olympian wrestling. This have I seen;
But this thy countenance, still lock'd in steel,
I never saw till now. I knew thy grandsire,
And once fought with him. He was a soldier good;
But, by great Mars, the captain of us all,
Never like thee. Let an old man embrace thee;
And, worthy warrior, welcome to our tents.
Æne. 'Tis the old Nestor.
Hect. Let me embrace thee, good old chronicle,
That hast so long walk'd hand in hand with time.
Most reverend Nestor, I am glad to clasp thee.
Nest. I would my arms could match thee in contention,
As they contend with thee in courtesy.
Hect. I would they could.
Nest. Ha!
By this white beard, I'd fight with thee tomorrow.
Well, welcome, welcome!—I have seen the time.
Ulyss. I wonder now how yonder city stands
When we have here her base and pillar by us.
Hect. I know your favour, Lord Ulysses, well.
Ah, sir, there's many a Greek and Trojan dead,
Since first I saw yourself and Diomed
In Ilion, on your Greekish embassy.
Ulyss. Sir, I foretold you then what would ensue.
My prophecy is but half his journey yet;
For yonder walls, that pertly front your town,
Yond towers, whose wanton tops do buss the clouds,
Must kiss their own feet.
Hect. I must not believe you.
There they stand yet, and modestly I think,
The fall of every Phrygian stone will cost
A drop of Grecian blood. The end crowns all,
And that old common arbitrator, Time,
Will one day end it.
Ulyss. So to him we leave it.
Most gentle and most valiant Hector, welcome.
After the general, I beseech you next
To feast with me and see me at my tent.
Achil. I shall forestall thee, Lord Ulysses, thou!
Now, Hector, I have fed mine eyes on thee;
I have with exact view perused thee, Hector,
And quoted joint by joint.
Hect. Is this Achilles?
Achil. I am Achilles.
Hect. Stand fair, I pray thee. Let me look on thee.
Achil. Behold thy fill.
Hect. Nay, I have done already.
Achil. Thou art too brief. I will the second time,
As I would buy thee, view thee limb by limb.
Hect. O, like a book of sport thou'lt read me o'er;
But there's more in me than thou understand'st.
Why dost thou so oppress me with thine eye?
Achil. Tell me, you heavens, in which part of his body
Shall I destroy him? whether there, or there, or there?
That I may give the local wound a name
And make distinct the very breach whereout
Hector's great spirit flew. Answer me, heavens!
Hect. It would discredit the blest gods, proud man,
To answer such a question. Stand again.
Think'st thou to catch my life so pleasantly
As to prenominate in nice conjecture
Where thou wilt hit me dead?
Achil. I tell thee, yea.
Hect. Wert thou an oracle to tell me so,
I'd not believe thee. Henceforth guard thee well;
For I'll not kill thee there, nor there, nor there;
But, by the forge that stithied Mars his helm,
I'll kill thee everywhere, yea, o'er and o'er.
You wisest Grecians, pardon me this brag;
His insolence draws folly from my lips;

But I'll endeavour deeds to match these words,
Or may I never—
Ajax. Do not chafe thee, cousin:
And you, Achilles, let these threats alone,
Till accident or purpose bring you to't.
You may have every day enough of Hector,
If you have stomach; the general state, I fear,
Can scarce entreat you to be odd with him.
Hect. I pray you, let us see you in the field.
We have had pelting wars, since you refused
The Grecian's cause.
Achil. Dost thou entreat me, Hector?
To-morrow do I meet thee, fell as death;
To-night all friends.
Hect. Thy hand upon that match.
Agam. First, all you peers of Greece, go to my tent;
There in the full convive we. Afterwards,
As Hector's leisure and your bounties shall
Concur together, severally entreat him.
Beat loud the tabourines, let the trumpets blow,
That this great soldier may his welcome know.
[*Exeunt all except* TROILUS *and* ULYSSES.
Tro. My Lord Ulysses, tell me, I beseech you,
In what place of the field doth Calchas keep?
Ulyss. At Menelaus' tent, most princely Troilus.
There Diomed doth feast with him to-night;
Who neither looks upon the heaven nor earth,
But gives all gaze and bent of amorous view
On the fair Cressid.
Tro. Shall I, sweet lord, be bound to you so much,
After we part from Agamemnon's tent,
To bring me thither?
Ulyss. You shall command me, sir.
As gentle tell me, of what honour was
This Cressida in Troy? Had she no lover there
That wails her absence?
Tro. O, sir, to such as boasting show their scars
A mock is due. Will you walk on, my lord?
She was beloved, she loved; she is, and doth;
But still sweet love is food for fortune's tooth.
[*Exeunt.*

ACT V

SCENE I. *The Grecian camp: before Achilles' tent*

Enter ACHILLES *and* PATROCLUS.

Achil. I'll heat his blood with Greekish wine to-night,
Which with my scimitar I'll cool to-morrow.
Patroclus, let us feast him to the height.
Patr. Here comes Thersites.

Enter THERSITES.

Achil. How now, thou core of envy!
Thou crusty batch of nature, what's the news?
Ther. Why, thou picture of what thou seemest, and idol of idiot-worshippers, here's a letter for thee.

Achil. From whence, fragment?

Ther. Why, thou full dish of fool, from Troy.

Patr. Who keeps the tent now?

Ther. The surgeon's box, or the patient's wound.

Patr. Well said, adversity! and what need these tricks?

Ther. Prithee, be silent, boy; I profit not by thy talk. Thou art thought to be Achilles' male varlet.

Patr. Male varlet, you rogue! what's that?

Ther. Why, his masculine whore. Now, the rotten diseases of the south, the guts-griping, ruptures, catarrhs, loads o' gravel i' the back, lethargies, cold palsies, raw eyes, dirt-rotten livers, wheezing lungs, bladders full of imposthume, sciaticas, limekilns i' the palm, incurable bone-ache, and the rivelled fee-simple of the tetter, take and take again such preposterous discoveries!

Patr. Why, thou damnable box of envy, thou, what meanest thou to curse thus?

Ther. Do I curse thee?

Patr. Why, no, you ruinous butt, you whoreson indistinguishable cur, no.

Ther. No! why art thou then exasperate, thou idle immaterial skein of sleave-silk, thou green sarcenet flap for a sore eye, thou tassel of a prodigal's purse, thou? Ah, how the poor world is pestered with such waterflies, diminutives of nature!

Patr. Out, gall!

Ther. Finch-egg!

Achil. My sweet Patroclus, I am thwarted quite
From my great purpose in to-morrow's battle.
Here is a letter from Queen Hecuba,
A token from her daughter, my fair love,
Both taxing me and gaging me to keep
An oath that I have sworn. I will not break it.
Fall Greeks; fail fame; honour or go or stay;
My major vow lies here, this I'll obey.
Come, come, Thersites, help to trim my tent.
This night in banqueting must all be spent.
Away, Patroclus!
[*Exeunt* ACHILLES *and* PATROCLUS.

Ther. With too much blood and too little brain, these two may run mad; but, if with too much brain and too little blood they do, I'll be a curer of madmen. Here's Agamemnon, an honest fellow enough, and one that loves quails; but he has not so much brain as ear-wax: and the goodly transformation of Jupiter there, his brother, the bull—the primitive statue, and oblique memorial of cuckolds; a thrifty shoeing-horn in a chain, hanging at his brother's leg—to what form but that he is, should wit larded with malice and malice forced with wit turn him to? To an ass, were nothing; he is both ass and ox; to an ox, were nothing; he is both ox and ass. To be a dog, a mule, a cat, a fitchew, a toad, a lizard, an owl, a puttock, or a herring without a roe, I would not care; but to be Menelaus! I would conspire against destiny. Ask me not what I would be, if I were not Thersites; for I care not to be the louse of a lazar, so I were not Menelaus. Hoy-day! spirits and fires!

Enter HECTOR, TROILUS, AJAX, AGAMEMNON, ULYSSES, NESTOR, MENELAUS, *and* DIOMEDES, *with lights.*

Agam. We go wrong, we go wrong.
Ajax. No, yonder 'tis;
There, where we see the lights.
Hect. I trouble you.
Ajax. No, not a whit.
Ulyss. Here comes himself to guide you.

Re-enter ACHILLES.

Achil. Welcome, brave Hector; welcome, princes all.
Agam. So now, fair Prince of Troy, I bid good night.
Ajax commands the guard to tend on you.
Hect. Thanks and good night to the Greeks' general.
Men. Good night, my lord.
Hect. Good night, sweet Lord Menelaus.

Ther. Sweet draught! "Sweet" quoth 'a! Sweet sink, sweet sewer.

Achil. Good night and welcome, both at once, to those
That go or tarry.
Agam. Good night.
[*Exeunt* AGAMEMNON *and* MENELAUS.
Achil. Old Nestor tarries; and you too, Diomed,
Keep Hector company an hour or two.
Dio. I cannot, lord; I have important business,
The tide whereof is now. Good night, great Hector.
Hect. Give me your hand.
Ulyss. [*Aside to* TROILUS] Follow his torch; he goes to Calchas' tent.
I'll keep you company.
Tro. Sweet sir, you honour me.
Hect. And so, good night.
[*Exit* DIOMEDES; ULYSSES *and* TROILUS *following.*
Achil. Come, come, enter my tent.
[*Exeunt* ACHILLES, HECTOR, AJAX, *and* NESTOR.

Ther. That same Diomed's a false-hearted rogue, a most unjust knave; I will no more trust him when he leers than I will a serpent when he hisses. He will spend his mouth, and promise, like Brabbler the hound; but when he performs, astronomers foretell it; it is prodigious, there will come some change; the sun borrows of the moon, when Diomed keeps his word. I will rather leave to see Hector, than not to dog him. They say he keeps a Trojan drab, and uses the traitor Calchas' tent. I'll after. Nothing but lechery! all incontinent varlets! [*Exit.*

SCENE II. *The same: before Calchas' tent*

Enter DIOMEDES.

Dio. What, are you up here, ho? speak.
Cal. [*Within*] Who calls?
Dio. Diomed. Calchas, I think. Where's your daughter?
Cal. [*Within*] She comes to you.

Enter TROILUS *and* ULYSSES, *at a distance; after them* THERSITES.

Ulyss. Stand where the torch may not discover us.

Enter CRESSIDA.

Tro. Cressid comes forth to him.
Dio. How now, my charge!
Cres. Now, my sweet guardian! Hark, a word with you. [*Whispers.*]
Tro. Yea, so familiar!
Ulyss. She will sing any man at first sight.

Ther. And any man may sing her, if he can take her cliff; she's noted.

Dio. Will you remember?
Cres. Remember! yes.
Dio. Nay, but do, then;
And let your mind be coupled with your words.
Tro. What should she remember?
Ulyss. List.
Cres. Sweet honey Greek, tempt me no more to folly.
Ther. Roguery!
Dio. Nay, then—
Cres. I'll tell you what—
Dio. Foh, foh! come, tell a pin. You are forsworn.
Cres. In faith, I cannot. What would you have me do?
Ther. A juggling trick—to be secretly open.

Dio What did you swear you would bestow on me?
Cres. I prithee, do not hold me to mine oath;
Bid me do anything but that, sweet Greek.
Dio. Good night.
Tro. Hold, patience!
Ulyss. How now, Trojan!
Cres. Diomed—
Dio. No, no, good night. I'll be your fool no more.
Tro. Thy better must.
Cres. Hark, one word in your ear.
Tro. O plague and madness!
Ulyss. You are moved, prince; let us depart, I pray you,
Lest your displeasure should enlarge itself
To wrathful terms. This place is dangerous;
The time right deadly; I beseech you, go.
Tro. Behold, I pray you!
Ulyss. Nay, good my lord, go off.
You flow to great distraction; come, my lord.
Tro. I pray thee, stay.
Ulyss. You have not patience; come.
Tro. I pray, stay; by hell and all hell's torments,
I will not speak a word!
Dio. And so, good night.
Cres. Nay, but you part in anger.
Tro. Doth that grieve thee?
O wither'd truth!
Ulyss. Why, how now, lord!
Tro. By Jove,
I will be patient.
Cres. Guardian!—why, Greek!
Dio. Foh, foh! adieu; you palter.
Cres. In faith, I do not. Come hither once again.
Ulyss. You shake, my lord, at something. Will you go?
You will break out.
Tro. She strokes his cheek!
Ulyss. Come, Come.
Tro. Nay, stay; by Jove, I will not speak a word.
There is between my will and all offences
A guard of patience. Stay a little while.
Ther. How the devil Luxury, with his fat rump and potato-finger, tickles these together!
Fry, lechery, fry!
Dio. But will you, then?
Cres. In faith, I will, la; never trust me else.
Dio. Give me some token for the surety of it.
Cres. I'll fetch you one. [*Exit*.
Ulyss. You have sworn patience.
Tro. Fear me not, sweet lord;
I will not be myself, nor have cognition
Of what I feel. I am all patience.

Re-enter CRESSIDA.

Ther. Now the pledge; now, now, now!
Cres. Here, Diomed, keep this sleeve.
Tro. O beauty! where is thy faith?
Ulyss. My lord—
Tro. I will be patient; outwardly I will.
Cres. You look upon that sleeve; behold it well.
He loved me—O false wench!—Give't me again.
Dio. Whose was't?
Cres. It is no matter, now I have't again.
I will not meet with you to-morrow night.
I prithee, Diomed, visit me no more.
Ther. Now she sharpens. Well said, whetstone!
Dio. I shall have it.
Cres. What, this?
Dio. Ay, that.
Cres. O, all you gods! O pretty, pretty pledge!
Thy master now lies thinking in his bed
Of thee and me, and sighs, and takes my glove,
And gives memorial dainty kisses to it,
As I kiss thee. Nay, do not snatch it from me;
He that takes that doth take my heart withal.
Dio. I had your heart before, this follows it.
Tro. I did swear patience.
Cres. You shall not have it, Diomed; faith, you shall not;
I'll give you something else.
Dio. I will have this. Whose was it?
Cres. It is no matter.
Dio. Come, tell me whose it was.
Cres. 'Twas one's that loved me better than you will.
But, now you have it, take it.
Dio. Whose was it?
Cres. By all Diana's waiting-women yond,
And by herself, I will not tell you whose.
Dio. To-morrow will I wear it on my helm,
And grieve his spirit that dares not challenge it.
Tro. Wert thou the devil, and worest it on thy horn,
It should be challenged.
Cres. Well, well, 'tis done, 'tis past. And yet it is not;
I will not keep my word.
Dio. Why, then, farewell;
Thou never shalt mock Diomed again.
Cres. You shall not go. One cannot speak a word,
But it straight starts you.
Dio. I do not like this fooling.
Ther. Nor I, by Pluto. But that that likes not you pleases me best.
Dio. What, shall I come? the hour?

Cres. Ay, come—O Jove!—do come—I shall be plagued.
Dio. Farewell till then.
Cres. Good night. I prithee, come.
[*Exit* DIOMEDES.
Troilus, farewell! one eye yet looks on thee;
But with my heart the other eye doth see.
Ah, poor our sex! this fault in us I find,
The error of our eye directs our mind.
What error leads must err; O, then conclude
Minds sway'd by eyes are full of turpitude. [*Exit*.
Ther. A proof of strength she could not publish more.
Unless she said, "My mind is now turn'd whore."
Ulyss. All's done, my lord.
Tro. It is.
Ulyss. Why stay we, then?
Tro. To make a recordation to my soul
Of every syllable that here was spoke.
But if I tell how these two did co-act,
Shall I not lie in publishing a truth?
Sith yet there is a credence in my heart,
An esperance so obstinately strong,
That doth invert the attest of eyes and ears,
As if those organs had deceptious functions,
Created only to calumniate.
Was Cressid here?
Ulyss. I cannot conjure, Trojan.
Tro. She was not, sure.
Ulyss. Most sure she was.
Tro. Why, my negation hath no taste of madness.
Ulyss. Nor mine, my lord. Cressid was here but now.
Tro. Let it not be believed for womanhood!
Think, we had mothers; do not give advantage
To stubborn critics, apt, without a theme,
For depravation, to square the general sex
By Cressid's rule: rather think this not Cressid.
Ulyss. What hath she done, Prince, that can soil our mothers?
Tro. Nothing at all, unless that this were she.
Ther. Will he swagger himself out on's own eyes?
Tro. This she? no, this is Diomed's Cressida.
If beauty have a soul, this is not she;
If souls guide vows, if vows be sanctimonies,
If sanctimony be the gods' delight,
If there be rule in unity itself,
This is not she. O madness of discourse,
That cause sets up with and against itself!
Bi-fold authority! where reason can revolt
Without perdition, and loss assume all reason
Without revolt: this is, and is not, Cressid.
Within my soul there doth conduce a fight
Of this strange nature that a thing inseparate
Divides more wider than the sky and earth,
And yet the spacious breadth of this division
Admits no orifex for a point as subtle
As Ariachne's broken woof to enter.
Instance, O instance! strong as Pluto's gates;
Cressid is mine, tied with the bonds of heaven.
Instance, O instance! strong as heaven itself;
The bonds of heaven are slipp'd, dissolved, and loosed;
And with another knot, five-finger-tied,
The fractions of her faith, orts of her love,
The fragments, scraps, the bits and greasy relics
Of her o'er-eaten faith, are bound to Diomed.
Ulyss. May worthy Troilus be half attach'd
With that which here his passion doth express?
Tro. Ay, Greek; and that shall be divulged well
In characters as red as Mars his heart
Inflamed with Venus. Never did young man fancy
With so eternal and so fix'd a soul.
Hark, Greek: as much as I do Cressid love,
So much by weight hate I her Diomed.
That sleeve is mine that he'll bear on his helm;
Were it a casque composed by Vulcan's skill,
My sword should bite it; not the dreadful spout
Which shipmen do the hurricano call,
Constringed in mass by the almighty sun,
Shall dizzy with more clamour Neptune's ear
In his descent than shall my prompted sword
Falling on Diomed.
Ther. He'll tickle it for his concupy.
Tro. O Cressid! O false Cressid! false, false, false!
Let all untruths stand by thy stained name
And they'll seem glorious.
Ulyss. O, contain yourself;
Your passion draws ears hither.

Enter ÆNEAS.

Æne. I have been seeking you this hour, my lord.
Hector, by this, is arming him in Troy;
Ajax, your guard, stays to conduct you home.
Tro. Have with you, Prince. My courteous lord, adieu.
Farewell, revolted fair! and, Diomed,
Stand fast, and wear a castle on thy head!
Ulyss. I'll bring you to the gates.
Tro. Accept distracted thanks.
[*Exeunt* TROILUS, ÆNEAS, *and* ULYSSES.
Ther. Would I could meet that rogue Diomed! I would croak like a raven; I would bode, I would bode. Patroclus will give me anything for the intelligence of this whore. The parrot will not do more for an almond than he for a commo-

dious drab. Lechery, lechery; still, wars and lechery; nothing else holds fashion. A burning devil take them! [*Exit.*

SCENE III. *Troy: before Priam's palace*

Enter HECTOR *and* ANDROMACHE.

And. When was my lord so much ungently temper'd,
To stop his ears against admonishment?
Unarm, unarm, and do not fight to-day.
Hect. You train me to offend you; get you in.
By all the everlasting gods, I'll go!
And. My dreams will, sure, prove ominous to the day.
Hect. No more, I say.

Enter CASSANDRA.

Cas. Where is my brother Hector?
And. Here, sister; arm'd, and bloody in intent.
Consort with me in loud and dear petition,
Pursue we him on knees; for I have dream'd
Of bloody turbulence, and this whole night
Hath nothing been but shapes and forms of slaughter.
Cas. O, 'tis true.
Hect. Ho! bid my trumpet sound.
Cas. No notes of sally, for the heavens, sweet brother.
Hect. Be gone, I say. The gods have heard me swear.
Cas. The gods are deaf to hot and peevish vows.
They are polluted offerings, more abhorr'd
Than spotted livers in the sacrifice.
And. O, be persuaded! do not count it holy
To hurt by being just. It is as lawful,
For we would give much, to use violent thefts,
And rob in the behalf of charity.
Cas. It is the purpose that makes strong the vow;
But vows to every purpose must not hold.
Unarm, sweet Hector.
Hect. Hold you still, I say;
Mine honour keeps the weather of my fate.
Life every man holds dear; but the brave man
Holds honour far more precious-dear than life.

Enter TROILUS.

How now, young man! mean'st thou to fight to-day?
And. Cassandra, call my father to persuade.
[*Exit* CASSANDRA.
Hect. No, faith, young Troilus; doff thy harness, youth;
I am to-day i' the vein of chivalry.
Let grow thy sinews till their knots be strong,
And tempt not yet the brushes of the war.
Unarm thee, go, and doubt thou not, brave boy,
I'll stand to-day for thee and me and Troy.
Tro. Brother, you have a vice of mercy in you,
Which better fits a lion than a man.
Hect. What vice is that, good Troilus? chide me for it.
Tro. When many times the captive Grecian falls,
Even in the fan and wind of your fair sword,
You bid them rise, and live.
Hect. O, 'tis fair play.
Tro. Fool's play, by heaven, Hector.
Hect. How now! how now!
Tro. For the love of all the gods,
Let's leave the hermit pity with our mothers,
And when we have our armours buckled on,
The venom'd vengeance ride upon our swords,
Spur them to ruthful work, rein them from ruth.
Hect. Fie, savage, fie!
Tro. Hector, then 'tis wars.
Hect. Troilus, I would not have you fight to-day.
Tro. Who should withold me?
Not fate, obedience, nor the hand of Mars
Beckoning with fiery truncheon my retire;
Not Priamus and Hecuba on knees,
Their eyes o'ergalled with recourse of tears;
Nor you, my brother, with your true sword drawn,
Opposed to hinder me, should stop my way,
But by my ruin.

Re-enter CASSANDRA, *with* PRIAM.

Cas. Lay hold upon him, Priam, hold him fast.
He is thy crutch; now if thou lose thy stay,
Thou on him leaning, and all Troy on thee,
Fall all together.
Pri. Come, Hector, come, go back.
Thy wife hath dream'd; thy mother hath had visions;
Cassandra doth foresee; and I myself
Am like a prophet suddenly enrapt
To tell thee that this day is ominous.
Therefore, come back.
Hect. Æneas is a-field;
And I do stand engaged to many Greeks,
Even in the faith of valour, to appear
This morning to them.
Pri. Ay, but thou shalt not go.
Hect. I must not break my faith.
You know me dutiful; therefore, dear sir,
Let me not shame respect; but give me leave
To take that course by your consent and voice,
Which you do here forbid me, royal Priam.
Cas. O Priam, yield not to him!
And. Do not, dear father.

Hect. Andromache, I am offended with you.
Upon the love you bear me, get you in.
[*Exit* ANDROMACHE.

Tro. This foolish, dreaming, superstitious girl
Makes all these bodements.

Cas. O, farewell, dear Hector!
Look, how thou diest! look, how thy eye turns pale!
Look, how thy wounds do bleed at many vents!
Hark, how Troy roars! how Hecuba cries out!
How poor Andromache shrills her dolours forth!
Behold, distraction, frenzy, and amazement,
Like witless antics, one another meet,
And all cry, Hector! Hector's dead! O Hector!

Tro. Away! away!

Cas. Farewell; yet, soft! Hector, I take my leave.
Thou dost thyself and all our Troy deceive. [*Exit.*

Hect. You are amazed, my liege, at her exclaim.
Go in and cheer the town. We'll forth and fight,
Do deeds worth praise, and tell you them at night.

Pri. Farewell! the gods with safety stand about thee!
[*Exeunt severally* PRIAM *and* HECTOR. *Alarums.*

Tro. They are at it, hark! Proud Diomed, believe,
I come to lose my arm, or win my sleeve.

Enter PANDARUS.

Pan. Do you hear, my lord? do you hear?

Tro. What now?

Pan. Here's a letter come from yond poor girl.

Tro. Let me read.

Pan. A whoreson tisick, a whoreson rascally tisick so troubles me, and the foolish fortune of this girl; and what one thing, what another, that I shall leave you one o' these days. And I have a rheum in mine eyes too, and such an ache in my bones that, unless a man were cursed, I cannot tell what to think on't. What says she there?

Tro. Words, words, mere words, no matter from the heart;
The effect doth operate another way.
Tearing the letter.
Go, wind, to wind, there turn and change together.
My love with words and errors still she feeds;
But edifies another with her deeds.
[*Exeunt severally.*

SCENE IV. *Plains between Troy and the Grecian camp*

Alarums: excursions. Enter THERSITES.

Ther. Now they are clapper-clawing one another; I'll go look on. That dissembling abominable varlet, Diomed, has got that same scurvy doting foolish young knave's sleeve of Troy there in his helm. I would fain see them meet; that that same young Trojan ass, that loves the whore there, might send that Greekish whoremasterly villain, with the sleeve, back to the dissembling luxurious drab, of a sleeveless errand. O' the t'other side, the policy of those crafty swearing rascals, that stale old mouse-eaten dry cheese, Nestor, and that same dog-fox, Ulysses, is not proved worth a blackberry. They set me up, in policy, that mongrel cur, Ajax, against that dog of as bad a kind, Achilles. And now is the cur Ajax prouder than the cur Achilles, and will not arm to-day; whereupon the Grecians begin to proclaim barbarism, and policy grows into an ill opinion. Soft! here comes sleeve, and t'other.

Enter DIOMEDES, TROILUS *following.*

Tro. Fly not; for shouldst thou take the river Styx,
I would swim after.

Dio. Thou dost miscall retire.
I do not fly, but advantageous care
Withdrew me from the odds of multitude.
Have at thee!

Ther. Hold thy whore, Grecian!—now for thy whore, Trojan!—now the sleeve, now the sleeve!
[*Exeunt* TROILUS *and* DIOMEDES, *fighting.*

Enter HECTOR.

Hect. What art thou, Greek? art thou for Hector's match?
Art thou of blood and honour?

Ther. No, no, I am a rascal; a scurvy railing knave; a very filthy rogue.

Hect. I do believe thee. Live. [*Exit.*

Ther. God-a-mercy, that thou wilt believe me; but a plague break thy neck for frighting me! What's become of the wenching rogues? I think they have swallowed one another. I would laugh at that miracle. Yet, in a sort, lechery eats itself. I'll seek them. [*Exit.*

SCENE V. *Another part of the plains*

Enter DIOMEDES *and a Servant.*

Dio. Go, go, my servant, take thou Troilus' horse;
Present the fair steed to my lady Cressid.
Fellow, commend my service to her beauty;
Tell her I have chastised the amorous Trojan,
And am her knight by proof.

Serv. I go, my lord. [*Exit.*

Enter AGAMEMNON.

Agam. Renew, renew! The fierce Polydamas
Hath beat down Menon; bastard Margarelon
Hath Doreus prisoner,
And stands colossus-wise, waving his beam,
Upon the pashed corses of the kings
Epistrophus and Cedius; Polyxenes is slain,
Amphimachus and Thoas deadly hurt,
Patroclus ta'en or slain, and Palamedes
Sore hurt and bruised. The dreadful Sagittary
Appals our numbers. Haste we, Diomed,
To reinforcement, or we perish all.

Enter NESTOR.

Nest. Go, bear Patroclus' body to Achilles;
And bid the snail-paced Ajax arm for shame.
There is a thousand Hectors in the field.
Now here he fights on Galathe his horse,
And there lacks work; anon he's there afoot,
And there they fly or die, like scaled sculls
Before the belching whale; then is he yonder,
And there the strawy Greeks, ripe for his edge,
Fall down before him, like the mower's swath.
Here, there, and everywhere, he leaves and takes,
Dexterity so obeying appetite
That what he will he does, and does so much
That proof is call'd impossibility.

Enter ULYSSES.

Ulyss. O, courage, courage, Princes! great Achilles
Is arming, weeping, cursing, vowing vengeance.
Patroclus' wounds have roused his drowsy blood,
Together with his mangled Myrmidons,
That noseless, handless, hack'd, and chipp'd, come to him,
Crying on Hector. Ajax hath lost a friend
And foams at mouth, and he is arm'd and at it,
Roaring for Troilus, who hath done to-day
Mad and fantastic execution,
Engaging and redeeming of himself
With such a careless force and forceless care
As if that luck, in very spite of cunning,
Bade him win all.

Enter AJAX.

Ajax. Troilus! thou coward Troilus! [*Exit.*
Dio. Ay, there, there.
Nest. So, so, we draw together.

Enter ACHILLES.

Achil. Where is this Hector?
Come, come, thou boy-queller, show thy face;
Know what it is to meet Achilles angry.
Hector! where's Hector? I will none but Hector.
[*Exeunt.*

SCENE VI. *Another part of the plains*

Enter AJAX.

Ajax. Troilus, thou coward Troilus, show thy head!

Enter DIOMEDES.

Dio. Troilus, I say! where's Troilus?
Ajax. What wouldst thou?
Dio. I would correct him.
Ajax. Were I the general, thou shouldst have my office
Ere that correction. Troilus, I say! what, Troilus!

Enter TROILUS.

Tro. O traitor Diomed! turn thy false face, thou traitor,
And pay thy life thou owest me for my horse!
Dio. Ha, art thou there?
Ajax. I'll fight with him alone. Stand, Diomed.
Dio. He is my prize; I will not look upon.
Tro. Come, both you cogging Greeks; have at you both! [*Exeunt, fighting.*

Enter HECTOR.

Hect. Yea, Troilus? O, well fought, my youngest brother!

Enter ACHILLES.

Achil. Now do I see thee, ha! have at thee, Hector!
Hect. Pause, if thou wilt.
Achil. I do disdain thy courtesy, proud Trojan.
Be happy that my arms are out of use;
My rest and negligence befriends thee now,
But thou anon shalt hear of me again;
Till when, go seek thy fortune. [*Exit.*
Hect. Fare thee well.
I would have been much more a fresher man,
Had I expected thee. How now, my brother!

Re-enter TROILUS.

Tro. Ajax hath ta'en Æneas. Shall it be?
No, by the flame of yonder glorious heaven,
He shall not carry him; I'll be ta'en too,
Or bring him off. Fate, hear me what I say!
I reck not though I end my life to-day. [*Exit.*

Enter one in sumptuous armour.

Hect. Stand, stand, thou Greek; thou art a goodly mark.
No, wilt thou not? I like thy armour well;
I'll frush it and unlock the rivets all,
But I'll be master of it. Wilt thou not, beast, abide?

Why, then fly on, I'll hunt thee for thy hide.
[*Exeunt.*

SCENE VII. *Another part of the plains*

Enter ACHILLES, *with* MYRMIDONS.

Achil. Come here about me, you my Myrmidons;
Mark what I say. Attend me where I wheel:
Strike not a stroke, but keep yourselves in breath;
And when I have the bloody Hector found,
Empale him with your weapons round about;
In fellest manner execute your aims.
Follow me, sirs, and my proceedings eye.
It is decreed Hector the great must die. [*Exeunt.*

Enter MENELAUS *and* PARIS, *fighting; then* THERSITES.

Ther. The cuckold and the cuckold-maker are at it. Now bull! now, dog! 'Loo, Paris, 'loo! now my double-henned sparrow! 'loo, Paris, 'loo! The bull has the game; ware horns, ho!

[*Exeunt* PARIS *and* MENELAUS.

Enter MARGARELON.

Mar. Turn, slave, and fight.

Ther. What are thou?

Mar. A bastard son of Priam's.

Ther. I am a bastard too; I love bastards. I am a bastard begot, bastard instructed, bastard in mind, bastard in valour, in everything illegitimate. One bear will not bite another, and wherefore should one bastard? Take heed, the quarrel's most ominous to us. If the son of a whore fight for a whore, he tempts judgement. Farewell, bastard. [*Exit.*

Mar. The devil take thee, coward! [*Exit.*

SCENE VIII. *Another part of the plains*

Enter HECTOR.

Hect. Most putrefied core, so fair without,
Thy goodly armour thus hath cost thy life.
Now is my day's work done; I'll take good breath.
Rest, sword; thou hast thy fill of blood and death.
Puts off his helmet and hangs his shield behind him.

Enter ACHILLES *and* MYRMIDONS.

Achil. Look, Hector, how the sun begins to set;
How ugly night comes breathing at his heels.
Even with the vail and darkening of the sun,
To close the day up, Hector's life is done.

Hect. I am unarm'd; forego this vantage, Greek.

Achil. Strike, fellows, strike; this is the man I seek. [HECTOR *falls.*
So, Ilion, fall thou next! now, Troy, sink down!
Here lies thy heart, thy sinews, and thy bone.
On, Myrmidons, and cry you all amain,
"Achilles hath the mighty Hector slain."
A retreat sounded.
Hark! a retire upon our Grecian part.

Myr. The Trojan trumpets sound the like, my lord.

Achil. The dragon wing of night o'erspreads the earth,
And, stickler-like, the armies separates.
My half-supp'd sword, that frankly would have fed,
Pleased with this dainty bait, thus goes to bed.
Sheathes his sword.
Come, tie his body to my horse's tail;
Along the field I will the Trojan trail. [*Exeunt.*

SCENE IX. *Another part of the plains*

Enter AGAMEMNON, AJAX, MENELAUS, NESTOR, DIOMEDES, *and others, marching. Shouts within.*

Agam. Hark! hark! what shout is that?

Nest. Peace, drums!

[*Within*] Achilles! Achilles! Hector's slain! Achilles!

Dio. The bruit is, Hector's slain, and by Achilles.

Ajax. If it be so, yet bragless let it be;
Great Hector was a man as good as he.

Agam. March patiently along. Let one be sent
To pray Achilles see us at our tent.
If in his death the gods have us befriended,
Great Troy is ours, and our sharp wars are ended. [*Exeunt, marching.*

SCENE X. *Another part of the plains*

Enter ÆNEAS *and Trojans.*

Æne. Stand, ho! yet are we masters of the field.
Never go home; here starve we out the night.

Enter TROILUS.

Tro. Hector is slain.

All. Hector! the gods forbid!

Tro. He's dead; and at the murderer's horse's tail,
In beastly sort, dragg'd through the shameful field.
Frown on, you heavens, effect your rage with speed!
Sit, gods, upon your thrones, and smile at Troy!
I say, at once let your brief plagues be mercy,
And linger not our sure destructions on!

Æne. My lord, you do discomfort all the host.

Tro. You understand me not that tell me so.
I do not speak of flight, of fear, of death,
But dare all imminence that gods and men

Address their dangers in. Hector is gone.
Who shall tell Priam so, or Hecuba?
Let him that will a screech-owl aye be call'd,
Go in to Troy, and say there, "Hector's dead!"
There is a word will Priam turn to stone;
Make wells and Niobes of the maids and wives,
Cold statues of the youth, and, in a word,
Scare Troy out of itself. But, march away.
Hector is dead; there is no more to say.
Stay yet. You vile abominable tents,
Thus proudly pight upon our Phrygian plains,
Let Titan rise as early as he dare.
I'll through and through you! and, thou great-sized coward,
No space of earth shall sunder our two hates.
I'll haunt thee like a wicked conscience still,
That mouldeth goblins swift as frenzy's thoughts.
Strike a free march to Troy! with comfort go;
Hope of revenge shall hide our inward woe.

[*Exeunt* ÆNEAS *and Trojans.*

As TROILUS *is going out, enter, from the other side,* PANDARUS.

Pan. But hear you, hear you!

Tro. Hence, broker-lackey! ignomy and shame
Pursue thy life, and live aye with thy name!

[*Exit.*

Pan. A goodly medicine for my aching bones! O world! world! world! thus is the poor agent despised! O traitors and bawds, how earnestly are you set a-work, and how ill requited! why should our endeavour be so loved and the performance so loathed? what verse for it? what instance for it? Let me see:

"Full merrily the humble-bee doth sing,
Till he hath lost his honey and his sting;
And being once subdued in armed tail,
Sweet honey and sweet notes together fail."

Good traders in the flesh, set this in your painted cloths.
As many as be here of Pandar's hall,
Your eyes, half out, weep out at Pandar's fall;
Or if you cannot weep, yet give some groans,
Though not for me, yet for your aching bones.
Brethren and sisters of the hold-door trade,
Some two months hence my will shall here be made.
It should be now, but that my fear is this,
Some galled goose of Winchester would hiss.
Till then I'll sweat and seek about for eases,
And at that time bequeathe you my diseases.

[*Exit.*

ALL'S WELL THAT ENDS WELL

DRAMATIS PERSONÆ

KING OF FRANCE
DUKE OF FLORENCE
BERTRAM, *Count of Rousillon*
LAFEU, *an old lord*
PAROLLES, *a follower of Bertram*
TWO FRENCH LORDS *in the Florentine service*
RINALDO, *steward to the Countess*
A CLOWN, *servant to the Countess*
THREE FRENCH LORDS, *attending on the King*
A GENTLEMAN, *a stranger*
TWO SOLDIERS
A MESSENGER

COUNTESS OF ROUSILLON, *mother to Bertram*
HELENA, *a gentlewoman protected by the Countess*
A WIDOW *of Florence*
DIANA, *daughter to the Widow*
MARIANA, *neighbour and friend to the Widow*

NON-SPEAKING: *Lords, Officers; Soldiers, French and Florentine; Violenta, neighbour and friend to the Widow; Attendants*

SCENE: *Rousillon, Paris, Florence, Marseilles*

ACT I

SCENE I. *Rousillon: the Count's palace*

Enter BERTRAM, *the* COUNTESS OF ROUSILLON, HELENA, *and* LAFEU, *all in black.*

Count. In delivering my son from me, I bury a second husband.

Ber. And I in going, madam, weep o'er my father's death anew; but I must attend his Majesty's command, to whom I am now in ward, evermore in subjection.

Laf. You shall find of the King a husband, madam; you, sir, a father. He that so generally is at all times good must of necessity hold his virtue to you, whose worthiness would stir it up where it wanted rather than lack it where there is such abundance.

Count. What hope is there of his Majesty's amendment?

Laf. He hath abandoned his physicians, madam; under whose practices he hath persecuted time with hope, and finds no other advantage in the process but only the losing of hope by time.

Count. This young gentlewoman had a father—O, that "had"! how sad a passage 'tis!—whose skill was almost as great as his honesty; had it stretched so far, would have made nature immortal, and death should have play for lack of work. Would, for the King's sake, he were living! I think it would be the death of the King's disease.

Laf. How called you the man you speak of, madam?

Count. He was famous, sir, in his profession, and it was his great right to be so: Gerard de Narbon.

Laf. He was excellent indeed, madam. The King very lately spoke of him admiringly and mourningly. He was skilful enough to have lived still, if knowledge could be set up against mortality.

Ber. What is it, my good lord, the King languishes of?

Laf. A fistula, my lord.

Ber. I heard not of it before.

Laf. I would it were not notorious. Was this gentlewoman the daughter of Gerard de Narbon?

Count. His sole child, my lord, and bequeathed to my overlooking. I have those hopes of her good that her education promises; her dispositions she inherits, which makes fair gifts fairer; for where an unclean mind carries virtuous qualities, there commendations go with pity; they are virtues and traitors too. In her they are the better for their simpleness; she derives her honesty and achieves her goodness.

Laf. Your commendations, madam, get from her tears.

Count. 'Tis the best brine a maiden can season her praise in. The remembrance of her father never approaches her heart but the tyranny of her sorrows takes all livelihood from her cheek. No more of this, Helena; go to, no more; lest it be rather thought you affect a sorrow than have it.

Hel. I do affect a sorrow indeed, but I have it too.

Laf. Moderate lamentation is the right of the dead, excessive grief the enemy to the living.

Count. If the living be enemy to the grief, the excess makes it soon mortal.

Ber. Madam, I desire your holy wishes.

Laf. How understand we that?

Count. Be thou blest, Bertram, and succeed thy father
In manners, as in shape! thy blood and virtue
Contend for empire in thee, and thy goodness
Share with thy birthright! Love all, trust a few,
Do wrong to none. Be able for thine enemy
Rather in power than use, and keep thy friend
Under thy own life's key. Be check'd for silence,
But never tax'd for speech. What heaven more will,
That thee may furnish and my prayers pluck down,
Fall on thy head! Farewell, my lord;
'Tis an unseason'd courtier; good my lord,
Advise him.

Laf. He cannot want the best
That shall attend his love.

Count Heaven bless him! Farewell, Bertram.
[*Exit.*

Ber. [*To* HELENA] The best wishes that can be forged in your thoughts be servants to you! Be comfortable to my mother, your mistress, and make much of her.

Laf. Farewell, pretty lady. You must hold the credit of your father.
[*Exeunt* BERTRAM *and* LAFEU.

Hel. O, were that all! I think not on my father;
And these great tears grace his remembrance more
Than those I shed for him. What was he like?
I have forgot him. My imagination
Carries no favour in't but Bertram's.
I am undone; there is no living, none,
If Bertram be away. 'Twere all one
That I should love a bright particular star
And think to wed it, he is so above me.
In his bright radiance and collateral light
Must I be comforted, not in his sphere.
The ambition in my love thus plagues itself.
The hind that would be mated by the lion
Must die for love. 'Twas pretty, though a plague,
To see him every hour; to sit and draw
His arched brows, his hawking eye, his curls,
In our heart's table; heart too capable
Of every line and trick of his sweet favour.
But now he's gone, and my idolatrous fancy
Must sanctify his reliques. Who comes here?

Enter PAROLLES.

[*Aside*] One that goes with him. I love him for his sake;
And yet I know him a notorious liar,
Think him a great way fool, solely a coward;
Yet these fix'd evils sit so fit in him,
That they take place, when virtue's steely bones
Look bleak i' the cold wind. Withal, full oft we see
Cold wisdom waiting on superfluous folly.

Par. Save you, fair queen!

Hel. And you, monarch!

Par. No.

Hel. And no.

Par. Are you meditating on virginity?

Hel. Ay. You have some stain of soldier in you; let me ask you a question. Man is enemy to virginity; how may we barricado it against him?

Par. Keep him out.

Hel. But he assails; and our virginity, though valiant, in the defence yet is weak. Unfold to us some warlike resistance.

Par. There is none. Man, sitting down before you, will undermine you and blow you up.

Hel. Bless our poor virginity from underminers and blowers up! Is there no military policy, how virgins might blow up men?

Par. Virginity being blown down, man will quicklier be blown up. Marry, in blowing him down again, with the breach yourselves made, you lose your city. It is not politic in the commonwealth of nature to preserve virginity. Loss of virginity is rational increase and there was never virgin got till virginity was first lost. That you were made of is metal to make virgins. Virginity by being once lost may be ten times found; by being ever kept, it is ever lost. 'Tis too cold a companion; away with 't!

Hel. I will stand for 't a little, though therefore I die a virgin.

Par. There's little can be said in 't; 'tis against the rule of nature. To speak on the part of virginity, is to accuse your mothers, which is most infallible disobedience. He that hangs himself is a virgin. Virginity murders itself; and should be buried in highways out of all sanctified limit, as a desperate offendress against nature. Virginity breeds mites, much like a cheese; consumes itself to the very paring, and so dies with feeding his own stomach. Besides, virginity is peevish, proud, idle, made of self-love, which is the most inhibited sin in the canon. Keep it not; you cannot choose but lose by 't. Out with 't! within ten year it will make itself ten, which is a goodly increase; and the principal itself not much the worse. Away with 't!

Hel. How might one do, sir, to lose it to her own liking?

Par. Let me see. Marry, ill, to like him that ne'er it likes. 'Tis a commodity will lose the gloss with lying; the longer kept, the less worth. Of with 't while 'tis vendible; answer the time of request. Virginity, like an old courtier, wears her cap out of fashion; richly suited, but unsuitable; just like the brooch and the tooth-pick, which wear not now. Your date is better in your pie and your porridge than in your cheek. And your virginity, your old virginity, is like one of our French withered pears, it looks ill, it eats drily; marry, 'tis a withered pear; it was formerly better; marry, yet 'tis a withered pear. Will you anything with it?

Hel. Not my virginity yet . . . . . .
There shall your master have a thousand loves,
A mother and a mistress and a friend,
A phœnix, captain, and an enemy,
A guide, a goddess, and a sovereign,
A counsellor, a traitress, and a dear;
His humble ambition, proud humility,
His jarring concord, and his discord dulcet,
His faith, his sweet disaster; with a world
Of pretty, fond, adoptious christendoms,
That blinking Cupid gossips. Now shall he—
I know not what he shall. God send him well!
The court's a learning place, and he is one—

Par. What one, i' faith?

Hel. That I wish well. 'Tis pity—

Par. What's pity?

Hel. That wishing well had not a body in't,
Which might be felt; that we, the poorer born,
Whose baser stars do shut us up in wishes,
Might with effects of them follow our friends,
And show what we alone must think, which never
Returns us thanks.

Enter PAGE.

Page. Monsieur Parolles, my lord calls for you. [*Exit.*

Par. Little Helen, farewell. If I can remember thee, I will think of thee at court.

Hel. Monsieur Parolles, you were born under a charitable star.

Par. Under Mars, I.

Hel. I especially think, under Mars.

Par. Why under Mars?

Hel. The wars have so kept you under that you must needs be born under Mars.

Par. When he was predominant.

Hel. When he was retrograde, I think, rather.

Par. Why think you so?

Hel. You go so much backward when you fight.

Par. That's for advantage.

Hel. So is running away, when fear proposes the safety. But the composition that your valour and fear makes in you is a virtue of a good wing, and I like the wear well.

Par. I am so full of business, I cannot answer thee acutely. I will return perfect courtier; in the which, my instruction shall serve to naturalize thee, so thou wilt be capable of a courtier's counsel and understand what advice shall thrust upon thee; else thou diest in thine unthankfulness, and thine ignorance makes thee away. Farewell. When thou hast leisure, say thy prayers; when thou hast none, remember thy friends. Get thee a good husband, and use him as he uses thee. So farewell. [*Exit.*

Hel. Our remedies oft in ourselves do lie,
Which we ascribe to heaven. The fated sky
Gives us free scope, only doth backward pull
Our slow designs when we ourselves are dull.
What power is it which mounts my love so high,
That makes me see, and cannot feed mine eye?
The mightiest space in fortune nature brings
To join like likes and kiss like native things.
Impossible be strange attempts to those
That weigh their pains in sense and do suppose
What hath been cannot be. Who ever strove
To show her merit that did miss her love?
The King's disease—my project may deceive me,
But my intents are fix'd and will not leave me. [*Exit.*

SCENE II. *Paris: the King's palace*

Flourish of cornets. Enter the KING OF FRANCE, *with letters,* LORDS, *and divers Attendants.*

King. The Florentines and Senoys are by the ears,
Have fought with equal fortune, and continue
A braving war.

1st Lord. So 'tis reported, sir.

King. Nay, 'tis most credible; we here receive it
A certainty, vouch'd from our cousin Austria,
With caution that the Florentine will move us
For speedy aid; wherein our dearest friend
Prejudicates the business and would seem
To have us make denial.

1st Lord. His love and wisdom,
Approved so to your Majesty, may plead
For amplest credence.

King. He hath arm'd our answer,
And Florence is denied before he comes.
Yet, for our gentlemen that mean to see
The Tuscan service, freely have they leave
To stand on either part.

2nd Lord. It well may serve
A nursery to our gentry who are sick

For breathing and exploit.
King. What's he comes here?

Enter BERTRAM, LAFEU, *and* PAROLLES.

1st Lord. It is the Count Rousillon, my good lord,
Young Bertram.
King. Youth, thou bear'st thy father's face;
Frank nature, rather curious than in haste,
Hath well composed thee. Thy father's moral parts
Mayst thou inherit too! Welcome to Paris.
Ber. My thanks and duty are your Majesty's.
King. I would I had that corporal soundness now,
As when thy father and myself in friendship
First tried our soldiership! He did look far
Into the service of the time and was
Discipled of the bravest. He lasted long;
But on us both did haggish age steal on
And wore us out of act. It much repairs me
To talk of your good father. In his youth
He had the wit which I can well observe
To-day in our young lords; but they may jest
Till their own scorn return to them unnoted
Ere they can hide their levity in honour
So like a courtier. Contempt nor bitterness
Were in his pride or sharpness; if they were,
His equal had awaked them, and his honour,
Clock to itself, knew the true minute when
Exception bid him speak, and at this time
His tongue obey'd his hand. Who were below him
He used as creatures of another place
And bow'd his eminent top to their low ranks,
Making them proud of his humility,
In their poor praise he humbled. Such a man
Might be a copy to these younger times;
Which, follow'd well, would demonstrate them now
But goers backward.
Ber. His good remembrance, sir,
Lies richer in your thoughts than on his tomb;
So in approof lives not his epitaph
As in your royal speech.
King. Would I were with him! He would always say—
Methinks I hear him now; his plausive words
He scatter'd not in ears, but grafted them,
To grow there and to bear—"Let me not live"—
This is good melancholy oft began,
On the catastrophe and heel of pastime,
When it was out—"Let me not live," qouth he,
"After my flame lacks oil, to be the snuff
Of younger spirits, whose apprehensive senses
All but new things disdain; whose judgments are
Mere fathers of their garments; whose constancies
Expire before their fashions." This he wish'd.
I after him do after him wish too,
Since I nor wax nor honey can bring home,
I quickly were dissolved from my hive,
To give some labourers room.
2nd Lord. You are loved, sir;
They that least lend it you shall lack you first.
King. I fill a place, I know't. How long is't, Count,
Since the physician at your father's died?
He was much famed.
Ber. Some six months since, my lord
King. If he were living, I would try him yet.
Lend me an arm; the rest have worn me out
With several applications. Nature and sickness
Debate it at their leisure. Welcome, Count;
My son's no dearer.
Ber. Thank your Majesty.
[*Exeunt. Flourish.*

SCENE III. *Rousillon: The Count's palace*

Enter COUNTESS, STEWARD, *and* CLOWN.

Count. I will now hear; what say you of this gentlewoman?

Stew. Madam, the care I have had to even your content, I wish might be found in the calendar of my past endeavours; for then we wound our modesty and make foul the clearness of our deservings, when of ourselves we publish them.

Count. What does this knave here? Get you gone, sirrah. The complaints I have heard of you I do not all believe. 'Tis my slowness that I do not; for I know you lack not folly to commit them, and have ability enough to make such knaveries yours.

Clo. 'Tis not unknown to you, madam, I am a poor fellow.

Count. Well, sir.

Clo. No, madam, 'tis not so well that I am poor, though many of the rich are damned; but, if I may have your ladyship's good will to go to the world, Isbel the woman and I will do as we may.

Count. Wilt thou needs be a beggar?

Clo. I do beg your good will in this case.

Count. In what case?

Clo. In Isbel's case and mine own. Service is no heritage; and I think I shall never have the blessing of God till I have issue o' my body; for they say barnes are blessings.

Count. Tell me thy reason why thou wilt marry.

Clo. My poor body, madam, requires it. I am driven on by the flesh; and he must needs go that the devil drives.

Count. Is this all your worship's reason?

Clo. Faith, madam, I have other holy reasons, such as they are.

Count. May the world know them?

Clo. I have been, madam, a wicked creature, as you and all flesh and blood are; and, indeed, I do marry that I may repent.

Count. Thy marriage, sooner than thy wickedness.

Clo. I am out o' friends, madam; and I hope to have friends for my wife's sake.

Count. Such friends are thine enemies, knave.

Clo. You're shallow, madam, in great friends; for the knaves come to do that for me which I am aweary of. He that ears my land spares my team and gives me leave to in the crop; if I be his cuckold, he's my drudge. He that comforts my wife is the cherisher of my flesh and blood; he that cherishes my flesh and blood loves my flesh and blood; he that loves my flesh and blood is my friend; ergo, he that kisses my wife is my friend. If men could be contented to be what they are, there were no fear in marriage; for young Charbon the puritan and old Poysam the papist, howsome'er their hearts are severed in religion, their heads are both one; they may joul horns together, like any deer i' the herd.

Count. Wilt thou ever be a foul-mouthed and calumnious knave?

Clo. A prophet I, madam; and I speak the truth the next way:

"For I the ballad will repeat,
Which men full true shall find;
Your marriage comes by destiny,
Your cuckoo sings by kind."

Count. Get you gone, sir; I'll talk with you more anon.

Stew. May it please you, madam, that he bid Helen come to you. Of her I am to speak.

Count. Sirrah, tell my gentlewoman I would speak with her; Helen, I mean.

Clo. [*Sings.*]

"Was this fair face the cause, quoth she,
Why the Grecians sacked Troy?
Fond done, done fond,
Was this King Priam's joy?
With that she sighed as she stood,
With that she sighed as she stood,
And gave this sentence then;
Among nine bad if one be good,
Among nine bad if one be good,
There's yet one good in ten."

Count. What, one good in ten? you corrupt the song, sirrah.

Clo. One good woman in ten, madam; which is a purifying o' the song. Would God would serve the world so all the year! we'd find no fault with the tithe-woman, if I were the parson. One in ten, quoth a'! An we might have a good woman born but one every blazing star, or at an earthquake, 'twould mend the lottery well; a man may draw his heart out, ere a' pluck one.

Count. You'll be gone, sir knave, and do as I command you.

Clo. That man should be at woman's command, and yet no hurt done! Though honesty be no puritan, yet it will do no hurt; it will wear the surplice of humility over the black gown of a big heart. I am going, forsooth. The business is for Helen to come hither. [*Exit.*

Count. Well, now.

Stew. I know, madam, you love your gentlewoman entirely.

Count. Faith, I do. Her father bequeathed her to me; and she herself, without other advantage, may lawfully make title to as much love as she finds. There is more owing her than is paid; and more shall be paid her than she'll demand.

Stew. Madam, I was very late more near her than I think she wished me. Alone she was, and did communicate to herself her own words to her own ears; she thought, I dare vow for her, they touched not any stranger sense. Her matter was, she loved your son. Fortune, she said, was no goddess, that had put such difference betwixt their two estates; Love no god, that would not extend his might, only where qualities were level; Dian no queen of virgins, that would suffer her poor knight surprised, without rescue in the first assault or ransom afterward. This she delivered in the most bitter touch of sorrow that e'er I heard virgin exclaim in, which I held my duty speedily to acquaint you withal; sithence, in the loss that may happen, it concerns you something to know it.

Count. You have discharged this honestly; keep it to yourself. Many likelihoods informed me of this before, which hung so tottering in the balance that I could neither believe nor misdoubt. Pray you, leave me. Stall this in your bosom; and I thank you for your honest care. I will speak with you further anon.

[*Exit* STEWARD.

Enter HELENA.

Even so it was with me when I was young.
If ever we are nature's, these are ours; this thorn
Doth to our rose of youth rightly belong;
Our blood to us, this to our blood is born;
It is the show and seal of nature's truth,
Where love's strong passion is impress'd in youth.
By our remembrances of days foregone,

Such were our faults, or then we thought them none.
Her eye is sick on't; I observe her now.
Hel. What is your pleasure, madam?
Count. You know, Helen,
I am a mother to you.
Hel. Mine honourable mistress.
Count. Nay, a mother.
Why not a mother? When I said "a mother,"
Methought you saw a serpent: what's in "mother,"
That you start at it? I say, I am your mother;
And put you in the catalogue of those
That were enwombed mine. 'Tis often seen
Adoption strives with nature and choice breeds
A native slip to us from foreign seeds.
You ne'er oppress'd me with a mother's groan
Yet I express to you a mother's care.
God's mercy, maiden! does it curd thy blood
To say I am thy mother? What's the matter,
That this distemper'd messenger of wet,
The many-colour'd Iris, rounds thine eye?
Why? that you are my daughter?
Hel. That I am not.
Count. I say, I am your mother.
Hel. Pardon, madam;
The Count Rousillon cannot be my brother.
I am from humble, he from honour'd name;
No note upon my parents, his all noble.
My master, my dear lord he is; and I
His servant live, and will his vassal die.
He must not be my brother.
Count. Nor I your mother?
Hel. You are my mother, madam; would you were—
So that my lord your son were not my brother—
Indeed my mother! or were you both our mothers,
I care no more for than I do for heaven,
So I were not his sister. Can't no other,
But, I your daughter, he must be my brother?
Count. Yes, Helen, you might be my daughter-in-law.
God shield you mean it not! daughter and mother
So strive upon your pulse. What, pale again?
My fear hath catch'd your fondness. Now I see
The mystery of your loneliness, and find
Your salt tears' head: Now to all sense 'tis gross
You love my son; invention is ashamed,
Against the proclamation of thy passion,
To say thou dost not; therefore tell me true;
But tell me then, 'tis so; for, look, thy cheeks
Confess it, th' one to th' other; and thine eyes
See it so grossly shown in thy behaviours
That in their kind they speak it. Only sin
And hellish obstinacy tie thy tongue,
That truth should be suspected. Speak, is't so?
If it be so, you have wound a goodly clew;
If it be not, forswear 't. Howe'er, I charge thee,
As heaven shall work in me for thine avail,
To tell me truly.
Hel. Good madam, pardon me!
Count. Do you love my son?
Hel. Your pardon, noble mistress!
Count. Love you my son?
Hel. Do not you love him, madam?
Count. Go not about; my love hath in't a bond,
Whereof the world takes note. Come, come, disclose
The state of your affection; for your passions
Have to the full appeach'd.
Hel. Then, I confess,
Here on my knee, before high heaven and you,
That before you, and next unto high heaven,
I love your son.
My friends were poor, but honest; so's my love.
Be not offended; for it hurts not him
That he is loved of me. I follow him not
By any token of presumptuous suit;
Nor would I have him till I do deserve him;
Yet never know how that desert should be.
I know I love in vain, strive against hope;
Yet in this captious and intenible sieve
I still pour in the waters of my love
And lack not to lose still. Thus, Indian-like,
Religious in mine error, I adore
The sun, that looks upon his worshipper,
But knows of him no more. My dearest madam,
Let not your hate encounter with my love
For loving where you do; but if yourself,
Whose aged honour cites a virtuous youth,
Did ever in so true a flame of liking
Wish chastely and love dearly, that your Dian
Was both herself and love; O, then, give pity
To her, whose state is such that cannot choose
But lend and give where she is sure to lose;
That seeks not to find that her search implies,
But riddle-like lives sweetly where she dies!
Count. Had you not lately an intent—speak truly—
To go to Paris?
Hel. Madam, I had.
Count. Wherefore? tell true.
Hel. I will tell truth; by grace itself I swear.
You know my father left me some prescriptions
Of rare and proved effects, such as his reading
And manifest experience had collected
For general sovereignty; and that he will'd me
In heedfull'st reservation to bestow them,
As notes whose faculties inclusive were
More than they were in note. Amongst the rest
There is a remedy, approved, set down,
To cure the desperate languishings whereof

The King is render'd lost.
Count. This was your motive
For Paris, was it? speak.
Hel. My lord your son made me to think of this;
Else Paris and the medicine and the King
Had from the conversation of my thoughts
Haply been absent then.
Count. But think you, Helen,
If you should tender your supposed aid,
He would receive it? he and his physicians
Are of a mind; he, that they cannot help him,
They, that they cannot help. How shall they credit
A poor unlearned virgin, when the schools,
Embowell'd of their doctrine, have left off
The danger to itself?
Hel. There's something in't,
More than my father's skill, which was the greatest
Of his profession, that his good receipt
Shall for my legacy be sanctified
By the luckiest stars in heaven; and, would your honour
But give me leave to try success, I'd venture
The well-lost life of mine on his Grace's cure
By such a day and hour.
Count. Dost thou believe 't?
Hel. Ay, madam, knowingly.
Count. Why, Helen, thou shalt have my leave and love,
Means and attendants and my loving greetings
To those of mine in court. I'll stay at home
And pray God's blessing into thy attempt.
Be gone to-morrow; and be sure of this,
What I can help thee to thou shalt not miss.
[*Exeunt.*

ACT II

SCENE I. *Paris: the King's palace*

Flourish of cornets. Enter the KING, *attended with divers young* LORDS *taking leave for the Florentine war,* BERTRAM, *and* PAROLLES.

King. Farewell, young lords; these warlike principles
Do not throw from you; and you, my lords, farewell!
Share the advice betwixt you; if both gain, all
The gift doth stretch itself as 'tis received,
And is enough for both.
1st Lord. 'Tis our hope, sir,
After well enter'd soldiers, to return
And find your Grace in health.
King. No, no, it cannot be; and yet my heart
Will not confess he owes the malady
That doth my life besiege, Farewell, young lords;
Whether I live or die, be you the sons
Of worthy Frenchmen; let higher Italy—
Those bated that inherit but the fall
Of the last monarchy—see that you come
Not to woo honour, but to wed it; when
The bravest questant shrinks, find what you seek,
That fame may cry you loud. I say, farewell.
2nd Lord. Health, at your bidding, serve your majesty!
King. Those girls of Italy, take heed of them.
They say, our French lack language to deny,
If they demand. Beware of being captives,
Before you serve.
Both. Our hearts receive your warnings.
King. Farewell. Come hither to me.
[*Exit, attended.*
1st Lord. O my sweet lord, that you will stay behind us!
Par. 'Tis not his fault, the spark.
2nd Lord. O, 'tis brave wars!
Par. Most admirable. I have seen those wars!
Ber. I am commanded here, and kept a coil with
"Too young" and "the next year" and "'tis too early."
Par. An thy mind stand to't, boy, steal away bravely.
Ber. I shall stay here the forehorse to a smock,
Creaking my shoes on the plain masonry,
Till honour be bought up and no sword worn
But one to dance with! By heaven, I'll steal away.
1st Lord. There's honour in the theft.
Par. Commit it, Count.
2nd Lord. I am your accessary; and so, farewell.
Ber. I grow to you, and our parting is a tortured body.
1st Lord. Farewell, captain.
2nd Lord. Sweet Monsieur Parolles!

Par. Noble heroes, my sword and yours are kin. Good sparks and lustrous, a word, good metals: you shall find in the regiment of the Spinii one Captain Spurio, with his cicatrice, an emblem of war, here on his sinister cheek; it was this very sword entrenched it. Say to him, I live; and observe his reports for me.

1st Lord. We shall, noble captain.
[*Exeunt* LORDS.

Par. Mars dote on you for his novices! what will ye do?

Ber. Stay. The King!

Re-enter KING. BERTRAM *and* PAROLLES *retire.*

Par. [*To* BERTRAM.] Use a more spacious ceremony to the noble lords; you have restrained yourself within the list of too cold an adieu. Be more expressive to them; for they wear themselves in the cap of the time, there do muster true gait, eat, speak, and move under the influence of the most received star; and though the devil lead the measure, such are to be followed. After them, and take a more dilated farewell.

Ber. And I will do so.

Par. Worthy fellows; and like to prove most sinewy sword-men.

[*Exeunt* BERTRAM *and* PAROLLES.

Enter LAFEU.

Laf. [*Kneeling*] Pardon, my lord, for me and for my tidings.

King. I'll fee thee to stand up.

Laf. Then here's a man stands, that has brought his pardon.
I would you had kneel'd, my lord, to ask me mercy,
And that at my bidding you could so stand up.

King. I would I had; so I had broke thy pate,
And ask'd thee mercy for't.

Laf. Good faith, across. But, my good lord, 'tis thus;
Will you be cured of your infirmity?

King. No.

Laf. O, will you eat no grapes, my royal fox?
Yes, but you will my noble grapes, an if
My royal fox could reach them. I have seen a medicine
That's able to breathe life into a stone,
Quicken a rock, and make you dance canary
With spritely fire and motion; whose simple touch
Is powerful to araise King Pepin, nay,
To give great Charlemain a pen in's hand
And write to her a love-line.

King. What "her" is this?

Laf. Why, Doctor She. My lord, there's one arrived,
If you will see her. Now, by my faith and honour,
If seriously I may convey my thoughts
In this my light deliverance, I have spoke
With one that, in her sex, her years, profession,
Wisdom, and constancy, hath amazed me more
Than I dare blame my weakness. Will you see her,
For that is her demand, and know her business?
That done, laugh well at me.

King. Now, good Lafeu,
Bring in the admiration; that we with thee
May spend our wonder too, or take off thine
By wondering how thou took'st it.

Laf. Nay, I'll fit you,
And not be all day neither [*Exit.*

King. Thus he his special nothing ever prologues.

Re-enter LAFEU, *with* HELENA.

Laf. Nay, come your ways.

King. This haste hath wings indeed.

Laf. Nay, come your ways;
This is his majesty; say your mind to him.
A traitor you do look like; but such traitors
His Majesty seldom fears. I am Cressid's uncle,
That dare leave two together; fare you well.
[*Exit.*

King. Now, fair one, does your business follow us?

Hel. Ay, my good lord.
Gerard de Narbon was my father;
In what he did profess, well found.

King. I knew him.

Hel. The rather will I spare my praises towards him;
Knowing him is enough. On's bed of death
Many receipts he gave me; chiefly one,
Which, as the dearest issue of his practice,
And of his old experience the only darling,
He bade me store up, as a triple eye,
Safer than mine own two, more dear; I have so;
And, hearing your high Majesty is touch'd
With that malignant cause wherein the honour
Of my dear father's gift stands chief in power,
I come to tender it and my appliance
With all bound humbleness.

King. We thank you, maiden;
But may not be so credulous of cure,
When our most learned doctors leave us and
The congregated college have concluded
That labouring art can never ransom nature
From her inaidible estate; I say we must not
So stain our judgement, or corrupt our hope,
To prostitute our past-cure malady
To empirics, or to dissever so
Our great self and our credit, to esteem
A senseless help when help past sense we deem.

Hel. My duty then shall pay me for my pains.
I will no more enforce mine office on you;
Humbly entreating from your royal thoughts
A modest one, to bear me back again.

King. I cannot give thee less, to be call'd grateful.
Thou thought'st to help me; and such thanks I give
As one near death to those that wish him live.
But what at full I know, thou know'st no part,
I knowing all my peril, thou no art.

Hel. What I can do can do no hurt to try,

Since you set up your rest 'gainst remedy
He that of greatest works is finisher
Oft does them by the weakest minister.
So holy writ in babes hath judgement shown,
When judges have been babes; great floods have flown
From simple sources, and great seas have dried
When miracles have by the greatest been denied.
Oft expectation fails and most oft there
Where most it promises, and oft it hits
Where hope is coldest and despair most fits

King. I must not hear thee; fare thee well, kind maid;
Thy pains not used must by thyself be paid.
Proffers not took reap thanks for their reward.

Hel. Inspired merit so by breath is barr'd.
It is not so with Him that all things knows
As 'tis with us that square our guess by shows;
But most it is presumption in us when
The help of heaven we count the act of men.
Dear sir, to my endeavours give consent;
Of heaven, not me, make an experiment.
I am not an impostor that proclaim
Myself against the level of mine aim;
But know I think and think I know most sure
My art is not past power nor you past cure.

King. Art thou so confident? within what space
Hopest thou my cure?

Hel. The great'st grace lending grace,
Ere twice the horses of the sun shall bring
Their fiery torcher his diurnal ring,
Ere twice in murk and occidental damp
Moist Hesperus hath quench'd his sleepy lamp,
Or four and twenty times the pilot's glass
Hath told the thievish minutes how they pass,
What is infirm from your sound parts shall fly,
Health shall live free and sickness freely die.

King. Upon thy certainty and confidence
What darest thou venture?

Hel. Tax of impudence,
A strumpet's boldness, a divulged shame
Traduced by odious ballads, my maiden's name
Sear'd otherwise; nay, worse—if worse—extended
With vilest torture let my life be ended.

King. Methinks in thee some blessed spirit doth speak
His powerful sound within an organ weak;
And what impossibility would slay
In common sense, sense saves another way.
Thy life is dear; for all that life can rate
Worth name of life in thee hath estimate,
Youth, beauty, wisdom, courage, all
That happiness and prime can happy call.
Thou this to hazard needs must intimate
Skill infinite or monstrous desperate.
Sweet practiser, thy physic I will try,
That ministers thine own death if I die.

Hel. If I break time, or flinch in property
Of what I spoke, unpitied let me die,
And well deserved. Not helping, death's my fee;
But, if I help, what do you promise me?

King. Make thy demand.

Hel. But will you make it even?

King. Ay, by my sceptre and my hopes of heaven.

Hel. Then shalt thou give me with thy kingly hand
What husband in thy power I will command,
Exempted be from me the arrogance
To choose from forth the royal blood of France,
My low and humble name to propagate
With any branch or image of thy state;
But such a one, thy vassal, whom I know
Is free for me to ask, thee to bestow.

King. Here is my hand; the premises observed,
Thy will by my performance shall be served.
So make the choice of thy own time, for I,
Thy resolved patient, on thee still rely.
More should I question thee, and more I must,
Though more to know could not be more to trust,
From whence thou camest, how tended on; but rest
Unquestion'd welcome and undoubted blest.
Give me some help here, ho! If thou proceed
As high as word, my deed shall match thy meed.
[*Flourish. Exeunt.*

SCENE II. *Rousillon: the Count's palace*

Enter COUNTESS *and* CLOWN.

Count. Come on, sir; I shall now put you to the height of your breeding.

Clo. I will show myself highly fed and lowly taught. I know my business is but to the court.

Count. To the court! why, what place make you special, when you put off that with such contempt? But to the court!

Clo. Truly, madam, if God have lent a man any manners, he may easily put it off at court. He that cannot make a leg, put off's cap, kiss his hand and say nothing, has neither leg, hands, lip, nor cap; and indeed such a fellow, to say precisely, were not for the court; but for me, I have an answer will serve all men.

Count. Marry, that's a bountiful answer that fits all questions.

Clo. It is like a barber's chair that fits all buttocks, the pin-buttock, the quatch-buttock, the brawn buttock, or any buttock.

Count. Will your answer serve fit to all questions?

Clo. As fit as ten groats is for the hand of an attorney, as your French crown for your taffeta punk, as Tib's rush for Tom's forefinger, as a pancake for Shrove Tuesday, a morris for May-day, as the nail to his hole, the cuckold to his horn, as a scolding quean to a wrangling knave, as the nun's lip to the friar's mouth, nay, as the pudding to his skin.

Count. Have you, I say, an answer of such fitness for all questions?

Clo. From below your duke to beneath your constable, it will fit any question.

Count. It must be an answer of most monstrous size that must fit all demands.

Clo. But a trifle neither, in good faith, if the learned should speak truth of it. Here it is, and all that belongs to't. Ask me if I am a courtier: it shall do you no harm to learn.

Count. To be young again, if we could, I will be a fool in question, hoping to be the wiser by your answer. I pray you, sir, are you a courtier?

Clo. O Lord, sir! There's a simple putting off. More, more, a hundred of them.

Count. Sir, I am a poor friend of yours, that loves you.

Clo. O Lord, sir! Thick, thick, spare not me.

Count. I think, sir, you can eat none of this homely meat.

Clo. O Lord, sir! Nay, put me to't, I warrant you.

Count. You were lately whipped, sir, as I think.

Clo. O Lord, sir! spare not me.

Count. Do you cry, "O Lord, sir!" at your whipping, and "spare not me"? Indeed your "O Lord, sir!" is very sequent to your whipping; you would answer very well to a whipping, if you were but bound to't.

Clo. I ne'er had worse luck in my life in my "O Lord, sir!" I see things may serve long, but not serve ever.

Count. I play the noble housewife with the time,
To entertain't so merrily with a fool.

Clo. O Lord, sir! why, there's serves well again.

Count. An end, sir; to your business. Give Helen this,
And urge her to a present answer back.
Commend me to my kinsmen and my son.
This is not much.

Clo. Not much commendation to them.

Count. Not much employment for you. You understand me?

Clo. Most fruitfully; I am there before my legs.

Count. Haste you again. [*Exeunt severally.*

SCENE III. *Paris: the King's palace*

Enter BERTRAM, LAFEU, *and* PAROLLES.

Laf. They say miracles are past; and we have our philosophical persons, to make modern and familiar, things supernatural and causeless. Hence is it that we make trifles of terrors, ensconcing ourselves into seeming knowledge, when we should submit ourselves to an unknown fear.

Par. Why, 'tis the rarest argument of wonder that hath shot out in our latter times.

Ber. And so 'tis.

Laf. To be relinquished of the artists—

Par. So I say.

Laf. Both of Galen and Paracelsus.

Par. So I say.

Laf. Of all the learned and authentic fellows—

Par. Right; so I say.

Laf. That gave him out incurable—

Par. Why, there 'tis; so say I too.

Laf. Not to be helped—

Par. Right; as 'twere, a man assured of a—

Laf. Uncertain life, and sure death.

Par. Just, you say well; so would I have said.

Laf. I may truly say, it is a novelty to the world.

Par. It is, indeed; if you will have it in showing, you shall read it in—what do ye call there?

Laf. A showing of a heavenly effect in an earthly actor.

Par. That's it; I would have said the very same.

Laf. Why, your dolphin is not lustier. 'Fore me, I speak in respect—

Par. Nay, 'tis strange, 'tis very strange, that is the brief and the tedious of it; and he's of a most facinerious spirit that will not acknowledge it to be the—

Laf. Very hand of heaven.

Par. Ay, so I say.

Laf. In a most weak—[*pausing*] and debile minister, great power, great transcendence; which should, indeed, give us a further use to be made than alone the recovery of the King, as to be—[*pausing*] generally thankful.

Par. I would have said it; you say well. Here comes the King.

Enter KING, HELENA, *and Attendants.*

LAFEU *and* PAROLLES *retire.*

Laf. *Lustig*, as the Dutchman says. I'll like a maid the better, whilst I have a tooth in my head. Why, he's able to lead her a coranto.

Par. *Mort du vinaigre!* is not this Helen?

Laf. 'Fore God, I think so.

King. Go, call before me all the lords in court.
Sit, my preserver, by thy patient's side;

And with this healthful hand, whose banish'd sense
Thou hast repeal'd, a second time receive
The confirmation of my promised gift,
Which but attends thy naming.

Enter three or four LORDS.

Fair maid, send forth thine eye. This youthful parcel
Of noble bachelors stand at my bestowing,
O'er whom both sovereign power and father's voice
I have to use: thy frank election make;
Thou hast power to choose, and they none to forsake.

Hel. To each of you one fair and virtuous mistress
Fall, when Love please! marry, to each, but one!

Laf. I'd give bay Curtal and his furniture,
My mouth no more were broken than these boys',
And writ as little beard.

King. Peruse them well.
Not one of those but had a noble father.

Hel. Gentlemen,
Heaven hath through me restored the King to health.

All. We understand it, and thank heaven for you.

Hel. I am a simple maid, and therein wealthiest,
That I protest I simply am a maid.
Please it your Majesty, I have done already.
The blushes in my cheeks thus whisper me,
"We blush that thou shouldst choose; but, be refused,
Let the white death sit on thy cheek for ever;
We'll ne'er come there again."

King. Make choice; and, see,
Who shuns thy love shuns all his love in me.

Hel. Now, Dian, from thy altar do I fly,
And to imperial Love, that god most high,
Do my sighs stream. Sir, will you hear my suit?

1st Lord. And grant it.

Hel. Thanks, sir; all the rest is mute.

Laf. I had rather be in this choice than throw ames-ace for my life.

Hel. The honour, sir, that flames in your fair eyes,
Before I speak, too threateningly replies.
Love make your fortunes twenty times above
Her that so wishes and her humble love!

2nd Lord. No better, if you please.

Hel. My wish receive,
Which great Love grant! and so, I take my leave.

Laf. Do all they deny her? An they were sons of mine, I'd have them whipped; or I would send them to the Turk, to make eunuchs of.

Hel. Be not afraid that I your hand should take;
I'll never do you wrong for your own sake.
Blessing upon your vows! and in your bed
Find fairer fortune, if you ever wed!

Laf. These boys are boys of ice, they'll none have her. Sure, they are bastards to the English; the French ne'er got 'em.

Hel. You are too young, too happy, and too good,
To make yourself a son out of my blood.

4th Lord. Fair one, I think not so.

Laf. There's one grape yet; I am sure thy father drunk wine. But if thou be'st not an ass, I am a youth of fourteen; I have known thee already.

Hel. [*To* BERTRAM] I dare not say I take you; but I give
Me and my service, ever whilst I live,
Into your guiding power. This is the man.

King. Why, then, young Bertram, take her; she's thy wife.

Ber. My wife, my liege! I shall beseech your Highness,
In such a business give me leave to use
The help of mine own eyes.

King. Know'st thou not, Bertram,
What she has done for me?

Ber. Yes, my good lord;
But never hope to know why I should marry her.

King. Thou know'st she has raised me from my sickly bed.

Ber. But follows it, my lord, to bring me down
Must answer for your raising? I know her well.
She had her breeding at my father's charge.
A poor physician's daughter my wife! Disdain
Rather corrupt me ever!

King. 'Tis only title thou disdain'st in her, the which
I can build up. Strange is it that our bloods,
Of colour, weight, and heat, pour'd all together,
Would quite confound distinction, yet stand off
In differences so mighty. If she be
All that is virtuous, save what thou dislikest,
A poor physician's daughter, thou dislikest
Of virtue for the name. But do not so.
From lowest place when virtuous things proceed,
The place is dignified by the doer's deed.
Where great additions swell's, and virtue none,
It is a dropsied honour. Good alone
Is good without a name. Vileness is so;
The property by what it is should go,
Not by the title. She is young, wise, fair;
In these to nature she's immediate heir,
And these breed honour. That is honour's scorn,
Which challenges itself as honour's born
And is not like the sire. Honours thrive,

When rather from our acts we them derive
Than our foregoers. The mere word's a slave
Debosh'd on every tomb, on every grave
A lying trophy, and as oft is dumb
Where dust and damn'd oblivion is the tomb
Of honour'd bones indeed. What should be said?
If thou canst like this creature as a maid,
I can create the rest. Virtue and she
Is her own dower; honour and wealth from me.

Ber. I cannot love her, nor will strive to do't.

King. Thou wrong'st thyself, if thou shouldst strive to choose.

Hel. That you are well restored, my lord, I'm glad.
Let the rest go.

King. My honour's at the stake; which to defeat,
I must produce my power. Here, take her hand,
Proud scornful boy, unworthy this good gift;
That dost in vile misprision shackle up
My love and her desert; that canst not dream,
We, poising us in her defective scale,
Shall weigh thee to the beam; that wilt not know,
It is in us to plant thine honour where
We please to have it grow. Check thy contempt.
Obey our will, which travails in thy good.
Believe not thy disdain, but presently
Do thine own fortunes that obedient right
Which both thy duty owes and our power claims;
Or I will throw thee from my care for ever
Into the staggers and the careless lapse
Of youth and ignorance; both my revenge and hate
Loosing upon thee, in the name of justice,
Without all terms of pity. Speak; thine answer.

Ber. Pardon, my gracious lord; for I submit
My fancy to your eyes. When I consider
What great creation and what dole of honour
Flies where you bid it, I find that she, which late
Was in my nobler thoughts most base, is now
The praised of the King; who, so ennobled,
Is as 'twere born so.

King. Take her by the hand,
And tell her she is thine; to whom I promise
A counterpoise, if not to thy estate
A balance more replete.

Ber. I take her hand.

King. Good fortune and the favour of the King
Smile upon this contract; whose ceremony
Shall seem expedient on the now-born brief,
And be perform'd to-night. The solemn feast
Shall more attend upon the coming space,
Expecting absent friends. As thou lovest her,
Thy love's to me religious; else, does err.

[*Exeunt all but* LAFEU *and* PAROLLES.

Laf. [*Advancing*] Do you hear, monsieur? a word with you.

Par. Your pleasure, sir?

Laf. Your lord and master did well to make his recantation.

Par. Recantation! My lord! my master!

Laf. Ay; is it not a language I speak?

Par. A most harsh one, and not to be understood without bloody succeeding. My master!

Laf. Are you companion to the Count Rousillon?

Par. To any count, to all counts, to what is man.

Laf. To what is count's man. Count's master is of another style.

Par. You are too old, sir; let it satisfy you, you are too old.

Laf. I must tell thee, sirrah, I write man; to which title age cannot bring thee.

Par. What I dare too well do, I dare not do.

Laf. I did think thee, for two ordinaries, to be a pretty wise fellow; thou didst make tolerable vent of thy travel; it might pass. Yet the scarfs and the bannerets about thee did manifoldly dissuade me from believing thee a vessel of too great a burthen. I have now found thee; when I lose thee again, I care not. Yet art thou good for nothing but taking up; and that thou'rt scarce worth.

Par. Hadst thou not the privilege of antiquity upon thee—

Laf. Do not plunge thyself too far in anger, lest thou hasten thy trial; which if—Lord have mercy on thee for a hen! So, my good window of lattice, fare thee well. Thy casement I need not open, for I look through thee. Give me thy hand.

Par. My lord, you give me most egregious indignity.

Laf. Ay, with all my heart; and thou art worthy of it.

Par. I have not, my lord, deserved it.

Laf. Yes, good faith, every dram of it; and I will not bate thee a scruple.

Par. Well, I shall be wiser.

Laf. Even as soon as thou canst, for thou hast to pull at a smack o' the contrary. If ever thou be'st bound in thy scarf and beaten, thou shalt find what it is to be proud of thy bondage. I have a desire to hold my acquaintance with thee, or rather my knowledge, that I may say in the default, "He is a man I know."

Par. My lord, you do me most insupportable vexation.

Laf. I would it were hell-pains for thy sake, and my poor doing eternal; for doing I am past, as I will by thee, in what motion age will give me leave. [*Exit*.

Par. Well, thou hast a son shall take this disgrace off me; scurvy, old, filthy, scurvy lord! Well, I must be patient; there is no fettering of authority. I'll beat him, by my life, if I can meet him with any convenience, an he were double and double a lord. I'll have no more pity of his age than I would have of—I'll beat him, an if I could but meet him again.

Re-enter LAFEU.

Laf. Sirrah, your lord and master's married; there's news for you. You have a new mistress.

Par. I most unfeignedly beseech your lordship to make some reservation of your wrongs. He is my good lord. Whom I serve above is my master.

Laf. Who? God?

Par. Ay, sir.

Laf. The devil it is that's thy master. Why dost thou garter up thy arms o' this fashion? dost make hose of thy sleeves? do other servants so? Thou wert best set thy lower part where thy nose stands. By mine honour, if I were but two hours younger, I'd beat thee. Methinks, thou art a general offence, and every man should beat thee. I think thou wast created for men to breathe themselves upon thee.

Par. This is hard and undeserved measure, my lord.

Laf. Go to, sir; you were beaten in Italy for picking a kernel out of a pomegranate; you are a vagabond and no true traveller; you are more saucy with lords and honourable personages than the commission of your birth and virtue gives you heraldry. You are not worth another word, else I'd call you knave. I leave you. [*Exit*.

Par. Good, very good; it is so then. Good, very good; let it be concealed awhile.

Re-enter BERTRAM.

Ber. Undone, and forfeited to cares forever!
Par. What's the matter, sweetheart?
Ber. Although before the solemn priest I have sworn,
I will not bed her.
Par. What, what, sweetheart?
Ber. O my Parolles, they have married me!
I'll to the Tuscan wars, and never bed her.
Par. France is a dog-hole, and it no more merits
The tread of a man's foot. To the wars!
Ber. There's letters from my mother. What the import is, I know not yet.
Par. Ay, that would be known. To the wars, my boy, to the wars!
He wears his honour in a box unseen,
That hugs his kicky-wicky here at home,
Spending his manly marrow in her arms,
Which should sustain the bound and high curvet
Of Mars's fiery steed. To other regions
France is a stable; we that dwell in't jades;
Therefore, to the war!
Ber. It shall be so. I'll send her to my house,
Acquaint my mother with my hate to her,
And wherefore I am fled; write to the King
That which I durst not speak: his present gift
Shall furnish me to those Italian fields,
Where noble fellows strike. War is no strife
To the dark house and the detested wife.
Par. Will this *capriccio* hold in thee? art sure?
Ber. Go with me to my chamber, and advise me.
I'll send her straight away. To-morrow
I'll to the wars, she to her single sorrow.
Par. Why, these balls bound; there's noise in it. 'Tis hard!
A young man married is a man that's marr'd;
Therefore away, and leave her bravely; go.
The King has done you wrong; but, hush, 'tis so.
[*Exeunt*.

SCENE IV. *Paris: the King's palace*

Enter HELENA *and* CLOWN.

Hel. My mother greets me kindly. Is she well?

Clo. She is not well; but yet she has her health. She's very merry; but yet she is not well; but thanks be given, she's very well and wants nothing i' the world; but yet she is not well.

Hel. If she be very well, what does she ail, that she's not very well?

Clo. Truly, she's very well indeed, but for two things.

Hel. What two things?

Clo. One, that she's not in heaven, whither God send her quickly! the other, that she's in earth, from whence God send her quickly!

Enter PAROLLES.

Par. Bless you, my fortunate lady!

Hel. I hope, sir, I have your good will to have mine own good fortunes.

Par. You had my prayers to lead them on; and to keep them on, have them still. O, my knave, how does my old lady?

Clo. So that you had her wrinkles and I her money, I would she did as you say.

Par. Why, I say nothing.

Clo. Marry, you are the wiser man; for many a man's tongue shakes out his master's undoing. To say nothing, to do nothing, to know nothing, and to have nothing, is to be a great part of your title; which is within a very little of nothing.

Par. Away! thou'rt a knave.

Clo. You should have said, sir, before a knave thou'rt a knave; that's, before me thou'rt a knave; this had been truth, sir.

Par. Go to, thou art a witty fool; I have found thee.

Clo. Did you find me in yourself, sir? or were you taught to find me? The search, sir, was profitable; and much fool may you find in you, even to the world's pleasure and the increase of laughter.

Par. A good knave, i' faith, and well fed.
Madam, my lord will go away to-night;
A very serious business calls on him.
The great prerogative and rite of love,
Which, as your due, time claims, he does acknowledge;
But puts it off to a compell'd restraint;
Whose want, and whose delay, is strew'd with sweets,
Which they distil now in the curbed time,
To make the coming hour o'erflow with joy
And pleasure drown the brim.

Hel. What's his will else?

Par. That you take your instant leave o' the King,
And make this haste as your own good proceeding,
Strengthen'd with what apology you think
May make it probable need.

Hel. What more commands he?

Par. That, having this obtain'd, you presently
Attend his further pleasure.

Hel. In everything I wait upon his will.

Par. I shall report it so.

Hel. I pray you. [*Exit* PAROLLES.]
Come, sirrah. [*Exeunt.*

SCENE V. *Paris: the King's palace*

Enter LAFEU *and* BERTRAM.

Laf. But I hope your lordship thinks not him a soldier.

Ber. Yes, my lord, and of very valiant approof.

Laf. You have it from his own deliverance.

Ber. And by other warranted testimony.

Laf. Then my dial goes not true. I took this lark for a bunting.

Ber. I do assure you, my lord, he is very great in knowledge and accordingly valiant.

Laf. I have then sinned against his experience and transgressed against his valour; and my state that way is dangerous, since I cannot yet find in my heart to repent. Here he comes; I pray you, make us friends; I will pursue the amity.

Enter PAROLLES.

Par. [*To* BERTRAM] These things shall be done, sir.

Laf. Pray you, sir, who's his tailor?

Par. Sir?

Laf. O, I know him well, I, sir; he, sir, 's a good workman, a very good tailor.

Ber. [*Aside to* PAROLLES] Is she gone to the King?

Par. She is.

Ber. Will she away to-night?

Par. As you'll have her.

Ber. I have writ my letters, casketed my treasure,
Given order for our horses; and to-night,
When I should take possession of the bride,
End ere I do begin.

Laf. A good traveller is something at the latter end of a dinner; but one that lies three thirds and uses a known truth to pass a thousand nothings with, should be once heard and thrice beaten. God save you, captain.

Ber. Is there any unkindness between my lord and you, monsieur?

Par. I know not how I have deserved to run into my lord's displeasure.

Laf. You have made shift to run into 't, boots and spurs and all, like him that leaped into the custard; and out of it you'll run again, rather than suffer question for your residence.

Ber. It may be you have mistaken him, my lord.

Laf. And shall do so ever, though I took him at 's prayers. Fare you well, my lord; and believe this of me, there can be no kernel in this light nut; the soul of this man is his clothes. Trust him not in matter of heavy consequence; I have kept of them tame, and know their natures. Farewell, monsieur. I have spoken better of you than you have or will to deserve at my hand; but we must do good against evil. [*Exit.*

Par. An idle lord, I swear.

Ber. I think so.

Par. Why, do you not know him?

Ber. Yes, I do know him well, and common speech
Gives him a worthy pass. Here comes my clog.

Enter HELENA.

Hel. I have, sir, as I was commanded from you,
Spoke with the King and have procured his leave
For present parting; only he desires
Some private speech with you.

Ber. I shall obey his will.
You must not marvel, Helen, at my course,
Which holds not colour with the time, nor does
The ministration and required office
On my particular. Prepared I was not
For such a business; therefore am I found
So much unsettled. This drives me to entreat you
That presently you take your way for home;
And rather muse than ask why I entreat you,

For my respects are better than they seem
And my appointments have in them a need
Greater than shows itself at the first view
To you that know them not. This to my mother:
Giving a letter.
'Twill be two days ere I shall see you, so
I leave you to your wisdom.
Hel. Sir, I can nothing say,
But that I am your most obedient servant.
Ber. Come, come, no more of that.
Hel. And ever shall
With true observance seek to eke out that
Wherein toward me my homely stars have fail'd
To equal my great fortune.
Ber. Let that go.
My haste is very great. Farewell; hie home.
Hel. Pray, sir, your pardon.
Ber. Well, what would you say?
Hel. I am not worthy of the wealth I owe,
Nor dare I say 'tis mine, and yet it is;
But, like a timorous thief, most fain would steal
What law does vouch mine own.
Ber. What would you have?
Hel. Something; and scarce so much; nothing, indeed.
I would not tell you what I would, my lord.
Faith, yes;
Strangers and foes do sunder, and not kiss.
Ber. I pray you, stay not, but in haste to horse.
Hel. I shall not break your bidding, good my lord.
Ber. Where are my other men, monsieur? Farewell. [*Exit* HELENA.
Go thou toward home; where I will never come
Whilst I can shake my sword or hear the drum.
Away, and for our flight.
Par. Bravely, *coragio!*
[*Exeunt.*

ACT III

SCENE I. *Florence: the Duke's palace*

Flourish. Enter the DUKE OF FLORENCE, *attended; the two French* LORDS, *with a troop of soldiers.*

Duke. So that from point to point now have you heard
The fundamental reasons of this war,
Whose great decision hath much blood let forth
And more thirsts after.
1st Lord. Holy seems the quarrel
Upon your Grace's part; black and fearful
On the opposer.
Duke. Therefore we marvel much our cousin France
Would in so just a business shut his bosom
Against our borrowing prayers.
2nd Lord. Good my lord,
The reasons of our state I cannot yield,
But like a common and an outward man,
That the great figure of a council frames
By self-unable motion; therefore dare not
Say what I think of it, since I have found
Myself in my incertain grounds to fail
As often as I guess'd.
Duke. Be it his pleasure.
1st Lord. But I am sure the younger of our nature,
That surfeit on their ease, will day by day
Come here for physic.
Duke. Welcome shall they be;
And all the honours that can fly from us
Shall on them settle. You know your places well;
When better fall, for your avails they fell.
To-morrow to the field. [*Flourish. Exeunt.*

SCENE II. *Rousillon: the Count's palace*

Enter COUNTESS *and* CLOWN.

Count. It hath happened all as I would have had it, save that he comes not along with her

Clo. By my troth, I take my young lord to be a very melancholy man.

Count. By what observance, I pray you?

Clo. Why, he will look upon his boot and sing; mend the ruff and sing; ask questions and sing; pick his teeth and sing. I know a man that had this trick of melancholy sold a goodly manor for a song.

Count. Let me see what he writes, and when he means to come. [*Opening a letter.*]

Clo. I have no mind to Isbel since I was at court. Our old ling and our Isbels o' the country are nothing like your old ling and your Isbels o' the court. The brains of my Cupid's knocked out, and I begin to love, as an old man loves money, with no stomach.

Count. What have we here?

Clo. E'en that you have there. [*Exit.*

Count. [*Reads*] "I have sent you a daughter-in-law. She hath recovered the King, and undone me. I have wedded her, not bedded her; and sworn to make the 'not' eternal. You shall hear I am run away. Know it before the report come. If there be breadth enough in the world, I will hold a long distance. My duty to you.

Your unfortunate son,
Bertram"

This is not well, rash and unbridled boy,
To fly the favours of so good a King;
To pluck his indignation on thy head
By the misprising of a maid too virtuous
For the contempt of empire.

Re-enter CLOWN.

Clo. O madam, yonder is heavy news within between two soldiers and my young lady!

Count. What is the matter?

Clo. Nay, there is some comfort in the news, some comfort; your son will not be killed so soon as I thought he would.

Count. Why should he be killed?

Clo. So say I, madam, if he run away, as I hear he does. The danger is in standing to't; that's the loss of men, though it be the getting of children. Here they come will tell you more; for my part, I only hear your son was run away. [*Exit.*

Enter HELENA *and* TWO FRENCH LORDS

1st Lord. Save you, good madam.
Hel. Madam, my lord is gone, for ever gone.
2nd Lord. Do not say so.
Count. Think upon patience. Pray you, gentlemen,
I have felt so many quirks of joy and grief
That the first face of neither, on the start,
Can woman me unto't. Where is my son, I pray you?
2nd Lord. Madam, he's gone to serve the duke of Florence.
We met him thitherward; for thence we came,
And, after some dispatch in hand at court,
Thither we bend again.
Hel. Look on his letter, madam; here's my passport.

[*Reads*] "When thou canst get the ring upon my finger which never shall come off, and show me a child begotten of thy body that I am father to, then call me husband; but in such a 'then' I write a 'never.' "

This is a dreadful sentence.
Count. Brought you this letter, gentlemen?
1st Lord. Ay, madam;
And for the contents' sake are sorry for our pains.
Count. I prithee, lady, have a better cheer;
If thou engrossest all the griefs are thine,
Thou robb'st me of a moiety. He was my son;
But I do wash his name out of my blood,
And thou art all my child. Towards Florence is he?
2nd Lord. Ay, madam.
Count. And to be a soldier?
2nd Lord. Such is his noble purpose; and, believe 't,
The Duke will lay upon him all the honour
That good convenience claims.
Count. Return you thither?
1st Lord. Ay, madam, with the swiftest wing of speed.
Hel. [*Reads*] "Till I have no wife, I have nothing in France."
'Tis bitter.
Count. Find you that there?
Hel. Ay, madam.
1st Lord. 'Tis but the boldness of his hand, haply, which his heart was not consenting to.
Count. Nothing in France, until he have no wife!
There's nothing here that is too good for him
But only she; and she deserves a lord
That twenty such rude boys might tend upon
And call her hourly mistress. Who was with him?
1st Lord. A servant only, and a gentleman
Which I have sometime known.
Count. Parolles, was it not?
1st Lord. Ay, my good lady, he.
Count. A very tainted fellow, and full of wickedness.
My son corrupts a well-derived nature
With his inducement.
1st Lord. Indeed, good lady,
The fellow has a deal of that too much,
Which holds him much to have.
Count. You're welcome, gentlemen.
I will entreat you, when you see my son,
To tell him that his sword can never win
The honour that he loses. More I'll entreat you
Written to bear along.
2nd Lord. We serve you, madam,
In that and all your worthiest affairs.
Count. Not so, but as we change our courtesies.
Will you draw near?
[*Exeunt* COUNTESS *and the* TWO LORDS.
Hel. "Till I have no wife, I have nothing in France."
Nothing in France, until he has no wife!
Thou shalt have none, Rousillon, none in France;
Then hast thou all again. Poor lord! is't I
That chase thee from thy country and expose
Those tender limbs of thine to the event
Of the none-sparing war? and is it I
That drive thee from the sportive court, where thou
Wast shot at with fair eyes, to be the mark
Of smoky muskets? O you leaden messengers,
That ride upon the violent speed of fire,
Fly with false aim; move the still-peering air,
That sings with piercing; do not touch my lord.
Whoever shoots at him, I set him there;
Whoever charges on his forward breast,
I am the caitiff that do hold him to 't;
And, though I kill him not, I am the cause

His death was so effected. Better 'twere
I met the ravin lion when he roar'd
With sharp constraint of hunger; better 'twere
That all the miseries which nature owes
Were mine at once. No, come thou home, Rousillon,
Whence honour but of danger wins a scar,
As oft it loses all. I will be gone;
My being here it is that holds thee hence.
Shall I stay here to do't? no, no, although
The air of paradise did fan the house
And angels officed all. I will be gone,
That pitiful rumour may report my flight,
To consolate thine ear. Come, night; end, day!
For with the dark, poor thief, I'll steal away.
[*Exit*.

SCENE III. *Florence: before the Duke's palace*

Flourish. Enter the DUKE OF FLORENCE, BERTRAM, PAROLLES, *Soldiers, Drum, and Trumpets.*

Duke. The general of our horse thou art; and we,
Great in our hope, lay our best love and credence
Upon thy promising fortune.
Ber. Sir, it is
A charge too heavy for my strength, but yet
We'll strive to bear it for your worthy sake
To the extreme edge of hazard.
Duke. Then go thou forth;
And fortune play upon thy prosperous helm,
As thy auspicious mistress!
Ber. This very day,
Great Mars, I put myself into thy file;
Make me but like my thoughts, and I shall prove
A lover of thy drum, hater of love. [*Exeunt*.

SCENE IV. *Rousillon: the Count's palace*

Enter COUNTESS *and* STEWARD.

Count. Alas! and would you take the letter of her?
Might you not know she would do as she has done,
By sending me a letter? Read it again.
Stew. [*Reads*]
"I am Saint Jaques' pilgrim, thither gone.
Ambitious love hath so in me offended,
That barefoot plod I the cold ground upon,
With sainted vow my faults to have amended.
Write, write, that from the bloody course of war
My dearest master, your dear son, may hie.
Bless him at home in peace, whilst I from far
His name with zealous fervour sanctify.
His taken labours bid him me forgive;
I, his despiteful Juno, sent him forth
From courtly friends, with camping foes to live,
Where death and danger dogs the heels of worth.
He is too good and fair for Death and me,
Whom I myself embrace, to set him free."
Count. Ah, what sharp stings are in her mildest words!
Rinaldo, you did never lack advice so much,
As letting her pass so. Had I spoke with her,
I could have well diverted her intents,
Which thus she hath prevented.
Stew. Pardon me, madam.
If I had given you this at over-night,
She might have been o'erta'en; and yet she writes,
Pursuit would be but vain.
Count. What angel shall
Bless this unworthy husband? he cannot thrive,
Unless her prayers, whom heaven delights to hear
And loves to grant, reprieve him from the wrath
Of greatest justice. Write, write, Rinaldo,
To this unworthy husband of his wife;
Let every word weigh heavy of her worth
That he does weigh too light. My greatest grief,
Though little he do feel it, set down sharply.
Dispatch the most convenient messenger.
When haply he shall hear that she is gone,
He will return; and hope I may that she,
Hearing so much, will speed her foot again,
Led hither by pure love. Which of them both
Is dearest to me, I have no skill in sense
To make distinction. Provide this messenger.
My heart is heavy and mine age is weak;
Grief would have tears, and sorrow bids me speak. [*Exeunt*.

SCENE V. *Florence: without the walls. A tucket afar off*

Enter an old WIDOW *of Florence*, DIANA, VIOLENTA, *and* MARIANA, *with other Citizens.*

Wid. Nay, come; for if they do approach the city, we shall lose all the sight.

Dia. They say the French Count has done most honourable service.

Wid. It is reported that he has taken their greatest commander; and that with his own hand he slew the Duke's brother. [*Tucket*.] We have lost our labour; they are gone a contrary way. Hark! you may know by their trumpets.

Mar. Come, let's return again, and suffice ourselves with the report of it. Well, Diana, take heed of this French earl. The honour of a maid is her name; and no legacy is so rich as honesty.

Wid. I have told my neighbour how you have been solicited by a gentleman his companion.

Mar. I know that knave; hang him! one Parolles; a filthy officer he is in those suggestions for the young earl. Beware of them, Diana; their promises, enticements, oaths, tokens, and all these engines of lust, are not the things they go under. Many a maid hath been seduced by them; and the misery is, example, that so terrible shows in the wreck of maidenhood, cannot for all that dissuade succession, but that they are limed with the twigs that threaten them. I hope I need not to advise you further; but I hope your own grace will keep you where you are, though there were no further danger known but the modesty which is so lost.

Dia. You shall not need to fear me.

Wid. I hope so.

Enter HELENA, *disguised like a Pilgrim.*

Look, here comes a pilgrim. I know she will lie at my house; thither they send one another. I'll question her. God save you, pilgrim! whither are you bound?

Hel. To Saint Jaques le Grand.
Where do the palmers lodge, I do beseech you?

Wid. At the Saint Francis here beside the port.

Hel. Is this the way?

Wid. Ay, marry, is't.

A march afar.

Hark you! they come this way.
If you will tarry, holy pilgrim,
But till the troops come by,
I will conduct you where you shall be lodged;
The rather, for I think I know your hostess
As ample as myself.

Hel. Is it yourself?

Wid. If you shall please so, pilgrim.

Hel. I thank you, and will stay upon your leisure.

Wid. You came, I think, from France?

Hel. I did so.

Wid. Here you shall see a countryman of yours
That has done worthy service. 51

Hel. His name, I pray you.

Dia. The Count Rousillon. Know you such a one?

Hel. But by the ear, that hears most nobly of him.
His face I know not.

Dia. Whatsome'er he is,
He's bravely taken here. He stole from France,
As 'tis reported, for the King had married him
Against his liking. Think you it is so?

Hel. Ay, surely, mere the truth. I know his lady.

Dia. There is a gentleman that serves the Count
Reports but coarsely of her.

Hel. What's his name?

Dia. Monsieur Parolles.

Hel. O, I believe with him,
In argument of praise, or to the worth
Of the great Count himself, she is too mean
To have her name repeated. All her deserving
Is a reserved honesty, and that
I have not heard examined.

Dia. Alas, poor lady!
'Tis a hard bondage to become the wife
Of a detesting lord.

Wid. I warrant, good creature, wheresoe'er she is,
Her heart weighs sadly. This young maid might do her
A shrewd turn, if she pleased.

Hel. How do you mean?
May be the amorous Count solicits her
In the unlawful purpose.

Wid. He does indeed;
And brokes with all that can in such a suit
Corrupt the tender honour of a maid.
But she is arm'd for him and keeps her guard
In honestest defence.

Mar. The gods forbid else!

Wid. So, now they come.

Drum and Colours.

Enter BERTRAM, PAROLLES, *and the whole army.*

That is Antonio, the Duke's eldest son;
That, Escalus.

Hel. Which is the Frenchman?

Dia. He;
That with the plume. 'Tis a most gallant fellow.
I would he loved his wife. If he were honester
He were much goodlier. Is't not a handsome gentleman?

Hel. I like him well.

Dia. 'Tis pity he is not honest. Yond's that same knave
That leads him to these places. Were I his lady,
I would poison that vile rascal.

Hel. Which is he?

Dia. That jack-an-apes with scarfs. Why is he melancholy?

Hel. Perchance he's hurt i' the battle.

Par. Lose our drum! well.

Mar. He's shrewdly vexed at something. Look, he has spied us.

Wid. Marry, hang you!

Mar. And your courtesy, for a ring-carrier!

[*Exeunt* BERTRAM, PAROLLES, *and army.*

Wid. The troop is past. Come, pilgrim, I will bring you
Where you shall host. Of enjoin'd penitents
There's four or five, to great Saint Jaques bound,
Already at my house.

Hel. I humbly thank you.
Please it this matron and this gentle maid
To eat with us to-night, the charge and thanking
Shall be for me; and, to requite you further,
I will bestow some precepts of this virgin
Worthy the note.

Both. We'll take your offer kindly.
[*Exeunt.*

SCENE VI. *Camp before Florence*

Enter BERTRAM *and the* TWO FRENCH LORDS.

2nd Lord. Nay, good my lord, put him to't; let him have his way.

1st Lord. If your lordship find him not a hilding, hold me no more in your respect.

2nd Lord. On my life, my lord, a bubble.

Ber. Do you think I am so far deceived in him?

2nd Lord. Believe it, my lord, in mine own direct knowledge, without any malice, but to speak of him as my kinsman, he's a most notable coward, an infinite and endless liar, an hourly promise-breaker, the owner of no one good quality worthy your lordship's entertainment.

1st Lord. It were fit you knew him; lest, reposing too far in his virtue, which he hath not, he might at some great and trusty business in a main danger fail you.

Ber. I would I knew in what particular action to try him.

1st Lord. None better than to let him fetch off his drum, which you hear him so confidently undertake to do.

2nd Lord. I, with a troop of Florentines, will suddenly surprise him; such I will have, whom I am sure he knows not from the enemy. We will bind and hoodwink him so that he shall suppose no other but that he is carried into the leaguer of the adversaries, when we bring him to our own tents. Be but your lordship present at his examination. If he do not, for the promise of his life and in the highest compulsion of base fear, offer to betray you and deliver all the intelligence in his power against you, and that with the divine forfeit of his soul upon oath, never trust my judgement in anything.

1st Lord. O, for the love of laughter, let him fetch his drum; he says he has a stratagem for't. When your lordship sees the bottom of his success in 't, and to what metal this counterfeit lump of ore will be melted, if you give him not John Drum's entertainment, your inclining cannot be removed. Here he comes.

Enter PAROLLES.

2nd Lord. [*Aside to* BERTRAM] O, for the love of laughter, hinder not the honour of his design. Let him fetch off his drum in any hand.

Ber. How now, monsieur! this drum sticks sorely in your disposition.

1st Lord. A pox on't, let it go; 'tis but a drum.

Par. "But a drum"! is't "but a drum"? A drum so lost! There was excellent command—to charge in with our horse upon our own wings, and to rend our own soldiers!

1st Lord. That was not to be blamed in the command of the service. It was a disaster of war that Cæsar himself could not have prevented, if he had been there to command.

Ber. Well, we cannot greatly condemn our success. Some dishonour we had in the loss of that drum; but it is not to be recovered.

Par. It might have been recovered.

Ber. It might; but it is not now.

Par. It is to be recovered; but that the merit of service is seldom attributed to the true and exact performer, I would have that drum or another, or "*hic jacet.*"

Ber. Why, if you have a stomach, to't, monsieur; if you think your mystery in stratagem can bring this instrument of honour again into his native quarter, be magnanimous in the enterprise and go on; I will grace the attempt for a worthy exploit. If you speed well in it, the Duke shall both speak of it, and extend to you what further becomes his greatness, even to the utmost syllable of your worthiness.

Par. By the hand of a soldier, I will undertake it.

Ber. But you must not now slumber in it.

Par. I'll about it this evening; and I will presently pen down my dilemmas, encourage myself in my certainty, put myself into my mortal preparation; and by midnight look to hear further from me.

Ber. May I be bold to acquaint his Grace you are gone about it?

Par. I know not what the success will be, my lord; but the attempt I vow.

Ber. I know thou'rt valiant; and, to the possibility of thy soldiership, will subscribe for thee. Farewell.

Par. I love not many words. [*Exit.*

2nd Lord. No more than a fish loves water. Is not this a strange fellow, my lord, that so confidently seems to undertake this business, which he knows is not to be done; damns himself to do and dares better be damned than to do 't?

1st Lord. You do not know him, my lord, as we do. Certain it is that he will steal himself into a man's favour and for a week escape a great deal of discoveries; but when you find him out, you have him ever after.

Ber. Why, do you think he will make no deed

at all of this that so seriously he does address himself unto?

2nd Lord. None in the world; but return with an invention and clap upon you two or three probable lies. But we have almost embossed him; you shall see his fall to-night; for indeed he is not for your lordship's respect.

1st Lord. We'll make you some sport with the fox ere we case him. He was first smoked by the old lord Lafeu. When his disguise and he is parted, tell me what a sprat you shall find him; which you shall see this very night.

2nd Lord. I must go look my twigs. He shall be caught.
Ber. Your brother he shall go along with me.
2nd Lord. As't please your lordship. I'll leave you. [*Exit*.
Ber. Now will I lead you to the house, and show you
The lass I spoke of.
1st Lord. But you say she's honest.
Ber. That's all the fault. I spoke with her but once
And found her wondrous cold; but I sent to her,
By this same coxcomb that we have i' the wind,
Tokens and letters which she did re-send;
And this is all I have done. She's a fair creature.
Will you go see her?
1st Lord. With all my heart, my lord.
[*Exeunt*.

SCENE VII. *Florence: the Widow's house*

Enter HELENA *and* WIDOW.

Hel. If you misdoubt me that I am not she,
I know not how I shall assure you further,
But I shall lose the grounds I work upon.
Wid. Though my estate be fallen, I was well born,
Nothing acquainted with these businesses;
And would not put my reputation now
In any staining act.
Hel. Nor would I wish you.
First, give me trust, the Count he is my husband,
And what to your sworn counsel I have spoken
Is so from word to word; and then you cannot,
By the good aid that I of you shall borrow,
Err in bestowing it.
Wid. I should believe you;
For you have show'd me that which well approves
You're great in fortune.
Hel. Take this purse of gold,
And let me buy your friendly help thus far,
Which I will over-pay and pay again
When I have found it. The Count he wooes your daughter,
Lays down his wanton siege before her beauty,
Resolved to carry her. Let her in fine consent,
As we'll direct her how 'tis best to bear it.
Now his important blood will nought deny
That she'll demand. A ring the County wears,
That downward hath succeeded in his house
From son to son, some four or five descents
Since the first father wore it. This ring he holds
In most rich choice; ye in his idle fire,
To buy his will, it would not seem too dear,
Howe'er repented after.
Wid. Now I see
The bottom of your purpose.
Hel. You see it lawful, then. It is no more,
But that your daughter, ere she seems as won,
Desires this ring; appoints him an encounter;
In fine, delivers me to fill the time,
Herself most chastely absent. After this,
To marry her, I'll add three thousand crowns
To what is past already.
Wid. I have yielded.
Instruct my daughter how she shall persever,
That time and place with this deceit so lawful
May prove coherent. Every night he comes
With musics of all sorts and songs composed
To her unworthiness. It nothing steads us
To chide him from our eaves; for he persists
As if his life lay on 't.
Hel. Why then to-night
Let us assay our plot; which, if it speed,
Is wicked meaning in a lawful deed
And lawful meaning in a lawful act,
Where both not sin, and yet a sinful fact.
But let's about it. [*Exeunt*.

ACT IV

SCENE I. *Without the Florentine camp*

Enter SECOND FRENCH LORD, *with five or six other* SOLDIERS *in ambush*.

2nd Lord. He can come no other way but by this hedge-corner. When you sally upon him, speak what terrible language you will. Though you understand it not yourselves, no matter; for we must not seem to understand him, unless some one among us whom we must produce for an interpreter.

1st Sold. Good captain, let me be the interpreter.

2nd Lord. Art not acquainted with him? knows he not thy voice?

1st Sold. No, sir, I warrant you.

2nd Lord. But what linsey-woolsey hast thou to speak to us again?

1st Sold. E'en such as you speak to me.

2nd Lord. He must think us some band of strangers i' the adversary's entertainment. Now he hath a smack of all neighbouring languages; therefore we must every one be a man of his own fancy, not to know what we speak one to another; so we seem to know, is to know straight our purpose: choughs' language, gabble enough, and good enough. As for you, interpreter, you must seem very politic. But couch, ho! here he comes, to beguile two hours in a sleep, and then to return and swear the lies he forges.

Enter PAROLLES.

Par. Ten o'clock; within these three hours 'twill be time enough to go home. What shall I say I have done? It must be a very plausive invention that carries it. They begin to smoke me; and disgraces have of late knocked too often at my door. I find my tongue is too foolhardy; but my heart hath the fear of Mars before it and of his creatures, not daring the reports of my tongue.

2nd Lord. [*Aside, in ambush*.] This is the first truth that e'er thine own tongue was guilty of.

Par. What the devil should move me to undertake the recovery of this drum, being not ignorant of the impossibility, and knowing I had no such purpose? I must give myself some hurts, and say I got them in exploit. Yet slight ones will not carry it; they will say, "Came you off with so little?" and great ones I dare not give. Wherefore, what's the instance? Tongue, I must put you into a butter-woman's mouth and buy myself another of Bajazet's mule, if you prattle me into these perils.

2nd Lord. Is it possible he should know what he is, and be that he is?

Par. I would the cutting of my garments would serve the turn, or the breaking of my Spanish sword.

2nd Lord. We cannot afford you so.

Par. Or the baring of my beard; and to say it was in stratagem.

2nd Lord. 'Twould not do.

Par. Or to drown my clothes, and say I was stripped.

2nd Lord. Hardly serve.

Par. Though I swore I leaped from the window of the citadel—

2nd Lord. How deep?

Par. Thirty fathom.

2nd Lord. Three great oaths would scarce make that be believed.

Par. I would I had any drum of the enemy's: I would swear I recovered it.

2nd Lord. You shall hear one anon.

Par. A drum now of the enemy's—

[*Alarum within*.

2nd Lord. *Throca movousus, cargo, cargo, cargo*.

All. *Cargo, cargo, cargo, villianda par corbo, cargo*.

Par. O, ransom, ransom! do not hide mine eyes.

They seize and blindfold him.

1st Sold. *Boskos thromuldo boskos*.

Par. I know you are the Muskos' regiment,
And I shall lose my life for want of language.
If there be here German, or Dane, low Dutch,
Italian, or French, let him speak to me; I'll
Discover that which shall undo the Florentine.

1st Sold. *Boskos vauvado:* I understand thee, and can speak thy tongue. *Kerelybonto*, sir, betake thee to thy faith, for seventeen poniards are at thy bosom.

Par. O!

1st Sold. O, pray, pray, pray! *Manka revania dulche*.

2nd Lord. *Oscorbidulchos volivorco*.

1st Sold. The general is content to spare thee yet;
And, hoodwink'd as thou art, will lead thee on
To gather from thee. Haply thou mayst inform
Something to save thy life.

Par. O, let me live!
And all the secrets of our camp I'll show,
Their force, their purposes; nay, I'll speak that
Which you will wonder at.

1st Sold. But wilt thou faithfully?

Par. If I do not, damn me.

1st Sold. *Acordo linta*.
Come on; thou art granted space.

[*Exit, with* PAROLLES *guarded. A short alarum within*.

2nd Lord. Go, tell the Count Rousillon, and my brother,
We have caught the woodcock, and will keep him muffled
Till we do hear from them.

2nd Sold. Captain, I will.

2nd Lord. A' will betray us all unto ourselves;
Inform on that.

2nd. Sold. So I will, sir.

2nd. Lord. Till then I'll keep him dark and safely lock'd. [*Exeunt*.

SCENE II. *Florence: the Widow's house*

Enter BERTRAM *and* DIANA.

Ber. They told me that your name was Fontibell.

Dia. No, my good lord, Diana.

Ber. Titled goddess;
And worth it, with addition! But, fair soul,

In your fine frame hath love no quality?
If the quick fire of youth light not your mind,
You are no maiden, but a monument.
When you are dead, you should be such a one
As you are now, for you are cold and stern;
And now you should be as your mother was
When your sweet self was got.
Dia. She then was honest.
Ber. So should you be.
Dia. No.
My mother did but duty; such, my lord,
As you owe to your wife.
Ber. No more o'that;
I prithee, do not strive against my vows.
I was compell'd to her; but I love thee
By love's own sweet constraint, and will for ever
Do thee all rights of service.
Dia. Ay, so you serve us
Till we serve you; but when you have our roses,
You barely leave our thorns to prick ourselves
And mock us with our bareness.
Ber. How have I sworn!
Dia. 'Tis not the many oaths that makes the truth,
But the plain single vow that is vow'd true.
What is not holy, that we swear not by,
But take the High'st to witness. Then, pray you, tell me,
If I should swear by God's great attributes,
I loved you dearly, would you believe my oaths,
When I did love you ill? This has no holding,
To swear by Him whom I protest to love,
That I will work against Him; therefore your oaths
Are words and poor conditions, but unseal'd,
At least in my opinion.
Ber. Change it, change it;
Be not so holy-cruel. Love is holy;
And my integrity ne'er knew the crafts
That you do charge men with. Stand no more off,
But give thyself unto my sick desires,
Who then recover. Say thou art mine, and ever
My love as it begins shall so persever.
Dia. I see that men make ropes in such a scarre
That we'll forsake ourselves. Give me that ring.
Ber. I'll lend it thee, my dear; but have no power
To give it from me.
Dia. Will you not, my lord?
Ber. It is an honour 'longing to our house,
Bequeathed down from many ancestors;
Which were the greatest obloquy i' the world
In me to lose.
Dia. Mine honour's such a ring,
My chastity's the jewel of our house,
Bequeathed down from many ancestors;
Which were the greatest obloquy i' the world
In me to lose. Thus your own proper wisdom
Brings in the champion Honour on my part,
Against your vain assault.
Ber. Here, take my ring.
My house, mine honour, yea, my life, be thine,
And I'll be bid by thee.
Dia. When midnight comes, knock at my chamber-window.
I'll order take my mother shall not hear.
Now will I charge you in the band of truth,
When you have conquer'd my yet maiden bed,
Remain there but an hour, nor speak to me.
My reasons are most strong; and you shall know them
When back again this ring shall be deliver'd;
And on your finger in the night I'll put
Another ring, that what in time proceeds
May token to the future our past deeds.
Adieu, till then; then, fail not. You have won
A wife of me, though there my hope be done.
Ber. A heaven on earth I have won by wooing thee. [*Exit.*
Dia. For which live long to thank both heaven and me!
You may so in the end.
My mother told me just how he would woo,
As if she sat in's heart; she says all men
Have the like oaths. He had sworn to marry me
When his wife's dead; therefore I'll lie with him
When I am buried. Since Frenchmen are so braid,
Marry that will, I live and die a maid.
Only in this disguise I think't no sin
To cozen him that would unjustly win. [*Exit.*

SCENE III. *The Florentine camp.*

Enter the TWO FRENCH LORDS *and some two or three* SOLDIERS.

1st Lord. You have not given him his mother's letter?

2nd Lord. I have delivered it an hour since. There is something in't that stings his nature; for on the reading it he changed almost into another man.

1st Lord. He has much worthy blame laid upon him for shaking off so good a wife and so sweet a lady.

2nd Lord. Especially he hath incurred the everlasting displeasure of the King, who had even tuned his bounty to sing happiness to him. I will tell you a thing, but you shall let it dwell darkly with you.

1st Lord. When you have spoken, 'tis dead, and I am the grave of it.

2nd Lord. He hath perverted a young gentlewoman here in Florence, of a most chaste renown; and this night he fleshes his will in the spoil of her honour. He hath given her his monumental ring, and thinks himself made in the unchaste composition.

1st Lord. Now, God delay our rebellion! as we are ourselves, what things are we!

2nd Lord. Merely our own traitors. And as in the common course of all treasons, we still see them reveal themselves, till they attain to their abhorred ends, so he that in this action contrives against his own nobility, in his proper stream o'erflows himself.

1st Lord. Is it not meant damnable in us to be trumpeters of our unlawful intents? We shall not then have his company to-night?

2nd Lord. Not till after midnight; for he is dieted to his hour.

1st Lord. That approaches apace; I would gladly have him see his company anatomized, that he might take a measure of his own judgements, wherein so curiously he had set this counterfeit.

2nd Lord. We will not meddle with him till he come; for his presence must be the whip of the other.

1st Lord. In the mean time, what hear you of these wars?

2nd Lord. I hear there is an overture of peace.

1st Lord. Nay, I assure you, a peace concluded.

2nd Lord. What will Count Rousillon do then? will he travel higher, or return again into France?

1st Lord. I perceive, by this demand, you are not altogether of his council.

2nd Lord. Let it be forbid, sir; so should I be a great deal of his act.

1st Lord. Sir, his wife some two months since fled from his house. Her pretence is a pilgrimage to Saint Jaques le Grand; which holy undertaking with most austere sanctimony she accomplished; and, there residing, the tenderness of her nature became as a prey to her grief; in fine, made a groan of her last breath, and now she sings in heaven.

2nd Lord. How is this justified?

1st Lord. The stronger part of it by her own letters, which makes her story true, even to the point of her death. Her death itself, which could not be her office to say is come, was faithfully confirmed by the rector of the place.

2nd Lord. Hath the Count all this intelligence?

1st Lord. Ay, and the particular confirmations, point from point, to the full arming of the verity.

2nd Lord. I am heartily sorry that he'll be glad of this.

1st Lord. How mightily sometimes we make us comforts of our losses!

2nd Lord. And how mightily some other times we drown our gain in tears! The great dignity that his valour hath here acquired for him shall at home be encountered with a shame as ample.

1st Lord. The web of our life is of a mingled yarn, good and ill together. Our virtues would be proud, if our faults whipped them not; and our crimes would despair, if they were not cherished by our virtues.

Enter a MESSENGER.

How now! where's your master?

Mess. He met the Duke in the street, sir, of whom he hath taken a solemn leave. His lordship will next morning for France. The Duke hath offered him letters of commendations to the King.

2nd Lord. They shall be no more than needful there, if they were more than they can commend.

1st Lord. They cannot be too sweet for the King's tartness. Here's his lordship now.

Enter BERTRAM.

How now, my lord! is 't not after midnight?

Ber. I have to-night dispatched sixteen businesses, a month's length a-piece, by an abstract of success. I have congied with the Duke, done my adieu with his nearest; buried a wife, mourned for her; writ to my lady mother I am returning; entertained my convoy; and between these main parcels of dispatch effected many nicer needs. The last was the greatest, but that I have not ended yet.

2nd Lord. If the business be of any difficulty, and this morning your departure hence, it requires haste of your lordship.

Ber. I mean, the business is not ended, as fearing to hear of it hereafter. But shall we have this dialogue beween the fool and the soldier? Come, bring forth this counterfeit module, has deceived me, like a double-meaning prophesier.

2nd Lord. Bring him forth. Has sat i' the stocks all night, poor gallant knave.

Ber. No matter; his heels have deserved it, in usurping his spurs so long. How does he carry himself?

2nd Lord. I have told your lordship already, the stocks carry him. But to answer you as you would be understood; he weeps like a wench that had shed her milk. He hath confessed himself to Morgan, whom he supposes to be a friar, from the time of his remembrance to this very instant disaster of his setting i' the stocks; and what think you he hath confessed?

Ber. Nothing of me, has a'?

2nd Lord. His confession is taken, and it shall be read to his face. If your lordship be in't, as I believe you are, you must have the patience to hear it.

Enter PAROLLES *guarded, and* FIRST SOLDIER.

Ber. A plague upon him! muffled! he can say nothing of me. Hush, hush!

1st Lord. Hoodman comes! *Portotartarosa*.

1st Sold. He calls for the tortures. What will you say without 'em?

Par. I will confess what I know without constraint. If ye pinch me like a pasty, I can say no more.

1st Sold. *Bosko chimurcho*.

1st Lord. *Boblibindo chicurmurco*.

1st Sold. You are a merciful general. Our general bids you answer to what I shall ask you out of a note.

Par. And truly, as I hope to live.

1st Sold. [*Reads*] "First demand of him how many horse the Duke is strong." What say you to that?

Par. Five or six thousand; but very weak and unserviceable. The troops are all scattered, and the commanders very poor rogues, upon my reputation and credit and as I hope to live.

1st Sold. Shall I set down your answer so?

Par. Do. I'll take the sacrament on't, how and which way you will.

Ber. All's one to him. What a past-saving slave is this!

1st Lord. You're deceived, my lord; this is Monsieur Parolles, the gallant militarist—that was his own phrase—that had the whole theoric of war in the knot of his scarf, and the practice in the chape of his dagger.

2nd Lord. I will never trust a man again for keeping his sword clean, nor believe he can have everything in him by wearing his apparel neatly.

1st Sold. Well, that's set down.

Par. Five or six thousand horse, I said—I will say true—or thereabouts, set down, for I'll speak truth.

1st Lord. He's very near the truth in this.

Ber. But I con him no thanks for't, in the nature he delivers it.

Par. Poor rogues, I pray you, say.

1st Sold. Well, that's set down.

Par. I humbly thank you, sir. A truth's a truth, the rogues are marvellous poor.

1st Sold. [*Reads*] "Demand of him, of what strength they are a-foot." What say you to that?

Par. By my troth, sir, if I were to live this present hour, I will tell true. Let me see: Spurio, a hundred and fifty; Sebastian, so many; Corambus, so many; Jaques, so many; Guiltian, Cosmo, Lodowick, and Gratii, two hundred and fifty each; mine own company, Chitopher, Vaumond, Bentii, two hundred and fifty each: so that the muster-file, rotten and sound, upon my life, amounts not to fifteen thousand poll; half of the which dare not shake the snow from off their cassocks, lest they shake themselves to pieces.

Ber. What shall be done to him?

1st Lord. Nothing, but let him have thanks. Demand of him my condition, and what credit I have with the Duke.

1st Sold. Well, that's set down. [*Reads*] "You shall demand of him, whether one Captain Dumain be i' the camp, a Frenchman; what his reputation is with the Duke; what his valour, honesty, and expertness in wars; or whether he thinks it were not possible, with well-weighing sums of gold, to corrupt him to a revolt." What say you to this? what do you know of it?

Par. I beseech you, let me answer to the particular of the inter'gatories. Demand them singly.

1st Sold. Do you know this Captain Dumain?

Par. I know him. A' was a botcher's 'prentice in Paris, from whence he was whipped for getting the shrieve's fool with child—a dumb innocent, that could not say him nay.

FIRST LORD *raises his hand as if to strike him*.

Ber. Nay, by your leave, hold your hands; though I know his brains are forfeit to the next tile that falls.

1st Sold. Well, is this captain in the Duke of Florence's camp?

Par. Upon my knowledge, he is, and lousy.

1st Lord. Nay, look not so upon me; we shall hear of your lordship anon.

1st Sold. What is his reputation with the Duke?

Par. The Duke knows him for no other but a poor officer of mine; and writ to me this other day to turn him out o' the band. I think I have his letter in my pocket.

1st Sold. Marry, we'll search.

Par. In good sadness, I do not know; either it is there, or it is upon a file with the Duke's other letters in my tent.

1st Sold. Here 'tis; here's a paper; shall I read it to you?

Par. I do not know if it be it or no.

Ber. Our interpreter does it well.

1st Lord. Excellently.

1st Sold. [*Reads*] "Dian, the Count's a fool, and full of gold"—

Par. That is not the Duke's letter, sir; that is an advertisement to a proper maid in Florence, one Diana, to take heed of the allurement of one Count Rousillon, a foolish idle boy, but for all that very ruttish. I pray you, sir, put it up again.

1st Sold. Nay, I'll read it first, by your favour.

Par. My meaning in't, I protest, was very honest in the behalf of the maid; for I knew the young Count to be a dangerous and lascivious boy, who is a whale to virginity and devours up all the fry it finds.

Ber. Damnable both-sides rogue!

1st Sold. [*Reads*] "When he swears oaths, bid him drop gold, and take it;
After he scores, he never pays the score.
Half won is match well made; match, and well make it;
He ne'er pays after-debts, take it before;
And say a soldier, Dian, told thee this,
Men are to mell with, boys are not to kiss.
For count of this, the Count's a fool, I know it,
Who pays before, but not when he does owe it.
Thine, as he vowed to thee in thine ear,
Parolles"

Ber. He shall be whipped through the army with this rhyme in in's forehead.

2nd Lord. This is your devoted friend, sir, the manifold linguist and the armipotent soldier.

Ber. I could endure anything before but a cat, and now he's a cat to me.

1st Sold. I perceive, sir, by the general's looks, we shall be fain to hang you.

Par. My life, sir, in any case. Not that I am afraid to die; but that, my offences being many, I would repent out the remainder of nature. Let me live, sir, in a dungeon, i' the stocks, or any where, so I may live.

1st Sold. We'll see what may be done, so you confess freely; therefore, once more to this Captain Dumain. You have answered to his reputation with the Duke and to his valour. What is his honesty?

Par. He will steal, sir, an egg out of a cloister; for rapes and ravishments he parallels Nessus; he professes not keeping of oaths; in breaking 'em he is stronger than Hercules; he will lie, sir, with such volubility, that you would think truth were a fool; drunkenness is his best virtue, for he will be swine-drunk; and in his sleep he does little harm, save to his bed-clothes about him; but they know his conditions and lay him in straw. I have but little more to say, sir, of his honesty. He has everything that an honest man should not have; what an honest man should have, he has nothing.

1st Lord. I begin to love him for this.

Ber. For this description of thine honesty?
A pox upon him for me, he's more and more a cat.

1st Sold. What say you to his expertness in war?

Par. Faith, sir, has led the drum before the English tragedians; to belie him, I will not, and more of his soldiership I know not; except, in that country he had the honour to be the officer at a place there called Mile-end, to instruct for the doubling of files. I would do the man what honour I can, but of this I am not certain.

1st Lord. He hath out-villained villainy so far that the rarity redeems him.

Ber. A pox on him, he's a cat still.

1st Sold. His qualities being at this poor price, I need not to ask you if gold will corrupt him to revolt.

Par. Sir, for a *quart d'écu* he will sell the fee-simple of his salvation, the inheritance of it; and cut the entail from all remainders, and a perpetual succession for it perpetually.

1st Sold. What's his brother, the other Captain Dumain?

2nd Lord. Why does he ask him of me?

1st Sold. What's he?

Par. E'en a crow o' the same nest; not altogether so great as the first in goodness, but greater a great deal in evil. He excels his brother for a coward, yet his brother is reputed one of the best that is; in a retreat he outruns any lackey; marry, in coming on he has the cramp.

1st Sold. If your life be saved, will you undertake to betray the Florentine?

Par. Ay, and the captain of his horse, Count Rousillon.

1st Sold. I'll whisper with the general, and know his pleasure.

Par. [*Aside*] I'll no more drumming; a plague of all drums! Only to seem to deserve well, and to beguile the supposition of that lascivious young boy the Count, have I run into this danger. Yet who would have suspected an ambush where I was taken?

1st Sold. There is no remedy, sir, but you must die. The general says, you that have so traitorously discovered the secrets of your army and made such pestiferous reports of men very nobly held, can serve the world for no honest use; therefore you must die. Come, headsman, off with his head.

Par. O Lord, sir, let me live, or let me see my death!

1st Sold. That shall you, and take your leave of all your friends. [*Unblinding him.*]
So, look about you. Know you any here?

Ber. Good morrow, noble captain.

2nd Lord. God bless you, Captain Parolles.

1st Lord. God save you, noble captain.

2nd Lord. Captain, what greeting will you to my Lord Lafeu? I am for France.

1st Lord. Good captain, will you give me a copy of the sonnet you writ to Diana in behalf of the Count Rousillon? an I were not a very coward, I'd compel it of you: but fare you well.

[*Exeunt* BERTRAM *and* LORDS.

1st Sold. You are undone, captain, all but your scarf; that has a knot on't yet.

Par. Who cannot be crushed with a plot?

1st Sold. If you could find out a country where but women were that had received so much shame, you might begin an impudent nation. Fare ye well, sir; I am for France too. We shall speak of you there.

[*Exit with* SOLDIERS.

Par. Yet am I thankful. If my heart were great,
'Twould burst at this. Captain I'll be no more;
But I will eat and drink, and sleep as soft
As captain shall. Simply the thing I am
Shall make me live. Who knows himself a braggart,
Let him fear this, for it will come to pass
That every braggart shall be found an ass.
Rust, sword! cool, blushes! and, Parolles, live
Safest in shame! being fool'd, by foolery thrive!
There's place and means for every man alive.
I'll after them. [*Exit.*

SCENE IV. *Florence: the Widow's house*

Enter HELENA, WIDOW, *and* DIANA.

Hel. That you may well perceive I have not wrong'd you,
One of the greatest in the Christian world
Shall be my surety; 'fore whose throne 'tis needful,
Ere I can perfect mine intents, to kneel.
Time was, I did him a desired office,
Dear almost as his life; which gratitude
Through flinty Tartar's bosom would peep forth,
And answer, thanks. I duly am inform'd
His Grace is at Marseilles; to which place
We have convenient convoy. You must know
I am supposed dead. The army breaking,
My husband hies him home; where, heaven aiding,
And by the leave of my good lord the King,
We'll be before our welcome.

Wid. Gentle madam,
You never had a servant to whose trust
Your business was more welcome.

Hel. Nor you, mistress,
Ever a friend whose thoughts more truly labour
To recompense your love. Doubt not but heaven
Hath brought me up to be your daughter's dower,
As it hath fated her to be my motive
And helper to a husband. But, O strange men!
That can such sweet use make of what they hate,
When saucy trusting of the cozen'd thoughts
Defiles the pitchy night. So lust doth play
With what it loathes for that which is away.
But more of this hereafter. You, Diana,
Under my poor instructions yet must suffer
Something in my behalf.

Dia. Let death and honesty
Go with your impositions, I am yours
Upon your will to suffer.

Hel. Yet, I pray you.
But with the word the time will bring on summer,
When briers shall have leaves as well as thorns,
And be as sweet as sharp. We must away;
Our waggon is prepared, and time revives us.
All's well that ends well. Still the fine's the crown;
Whate'er the course, the end is the renown.

[*Exeunt.*

SCENE V. *Rousillon: the Count's palace*

Enter COUNTESS, LAFEU, *and* CLOWN

Laf. No, no, no, your son was misled with a snipt-taffeta fellow there, whose villainous saffron would have made all the unbaked and doughy youth of a nation in his colour. Your daughter-in-law had been alive at this hour, and your son here at home, more advanced by the King than by that red-tailed humble-bee I speak of.

Count. I would I had not known him; it was the death of the most virtuous gentlewoman that ever nature had praise for creating. If she had partaken of my flesh, and cost me the dearest groans of a mother, I could not have owed her a more rooted love.

Laf. 'Twas a good lady, 'twas a good lady; we may pick a thousand salads ere we light on such another herb.

Clo. Indeed, sir, she was the sweet-marjoram of the salad, or rather, the herb of grace.

Laf. They are not herbs, you knave; they are nose-herbs.

Clo. I am no great Nebuchadnezzar, sir; I have not much skill in grass.

Laf. Whether dost thou profess thyself, a knave or a fool?

Clo. A fool, sir, at a woman's service, and a knave at a man's.

Laf. Your distinction?

Clo. I would cozen the man of his wife and do his service.

Laf. So you were a knave at his service, indeed.

Clo. And I would give his wife my bauble, sir, to do her service.

Laf. I will subscribe for thee, thou art both knave and fool.

Clo. At your service.

Laf. No, no, no.

Clo. Why, sir, if I cannot serve you, I can serve as great a prince as you are.

Laf. Who's that? a Frenchman?

Clo. Faith, sir, a' has an English name; but his fisnomy is more hotter in France than there.

Laf. What prince is that?

Clo. The Black Prince, sir; alias, the Prince of Darkness; alias, the devil,

Laf. Hold thee, there's my purse. I give thee not this to suggest thee from thy master thou talkest of; serve him still.

Clo. I am a woodland fellow, sir, that always loved a great fire; and the master I speak of ever keeps a good fire. But, sure, he is the prince of the world; let his nobility remain in's court. I am for the house with the narrow gate, which I take to be too little for pomp to enter. Some that humble themselves may; but the many will be too chill and tender, and they'll be for the flowery way that leads to the broad gate and the great fire.

Laf. Go thy ways, I begin to be aweary of thee; and I tell thee so before, because I would not fall out with thee. Go thy ways. Let my horses be well looked to, without any tricks.

Clo. If I put any tricks upon 'em, sir, they shall be jades' tricks; which are their own right by the law of nature. [*Exit*.

Laf. A shrewd knave and an unhappy.

Count. So he is. My lord that's gone made himself much sport out of him. By his authority he remains here, which he thinks is a patent for his sauciness; and, indeed, he has no pace, but runs where he will.

Laf. I like him well; 'tis not amiss. And I was about to tell you, since I heard of the good lady's death and that my lord your son was upon his return home, I moved the King my master to speak in the behalf of my daughter; which, in the minority of them both, his Majesty, out of a self-gracious remembrance, did first propose. His Highness hath promised me to do it; and, to stop up the displeasure he hath conceived against your son, there is no fitter matter. How does your ladyship like it?

Count. With very much content, my lord; and I wish it happily effected.

Laf. His Highness comes post from Marseilles, of as able body as when he numbered thirty. He will be here to-morrow, or I am deceived by him that in such intelligence hath seldom failed.

Count. It rejoices me, that I hope I shall see him ere I die. I have letters that my son will be here to-night. I shall beseech your lordship to remain with me till they meet together.

Laf. Madam, I was thinking with what manners I might safely be admitted.

Count. You need but plead your honourable privilege.

Laf. Lady, of that I have made a bold charter; but I thank my God it holds yet.

Re-enter CLOWN.

Clo. O madam, yonder's my lord your son with a patch of velvet on's face. Whether there be a scar under't or no, the velvet knows; but 'tis a goodly patch of velvet. His left cheek is a cheek of two pile and a half, but his right cheek is worn bare.

Laf. A scar nobly got, or a noble scar, is a good livery of honour; so belike is that.

Clo. But it is your carbonadoed face.

Laf. Let us go see your son, I pray you. I long to talk with the young noble soldier.

Clo. Faith, there's a dozen of 'em, with delicate fine hats and most courteous feathers which bow the head and nod at every man. [*Exeunt*.

ACT V

SCENE I. *Marseilles: a street*

Enter HELENA, WIDOW, *and* DIANA, *with two Attendants*.

Hel. But this exceeding posting day and night
Must wear your spirits low; we cannot help it.
But since you have made the days and nights as one,
To wear your gentle limbs in my affairs,
Be bold you do so grow in my requital
As nothing can unroot you. In happy time;

Enter a GENTLEMAN, A STRANGER.

This man may help me to his Majesty's ear,
If he would spend his power. God save you, sir.

Gent. And you.

Hel. Sir, I have seen you in the court of France.

Gent. I have been sometimes there.

Hel. I do presume, sir, that you are not fallen
From the report that goes upon your goodness;
And therefore, goaded with most sharp occasions,
Which lay nice manners by, I put you to
The use of your own virtues, for the which
I shall continue thankful.

Gent. What's your will?

Hel. That it will please you
To give this poor petition to the King,
And aid me with that store of power you have
To come into his presence.

Gent. The King's not here.

Hel. Not here, sir!
Gent. Not, indeed.
He hence removed last night and with more haste
Than is his use.
Wid. Lord, how we lose our pains!
Hel. All's well that ends well yet,
Though time seem so adverse and means unfit.
I do beseech you, whither is he gone?
Gent. Marry, as I take it, to Rousillon,
Whither I am going.
Hel. I do beseech you, sir,
Since you are like to see the King before me,
Commend the paper to his gracious hand,
Which I presume shall render you no blame
But rather make you thank your pains for it.
I will come after you with what good speed
Our means will make us means.
Gent. This I'll do for you.
Hel. And you shall find yourself to be well thank'd,
Whate'er falls more. We must to horse again.
Go, go, provide. [*Exeunt.*

SCENE II. *Rousillon: before the Count's palace*

Enter CLOWN, *and* PAROLLES, *following.*

Par. Good Monsieur Lavache, give my Lord Lafeu this letter. I have ere now, sir, been better known to you, when I have held familiarity with fresher clothes; but I am now, sir, muddied in fortune's mood, and smell somewhat strong of her strong displeasure.

Clo. Truly, fortune's displeasure is but sluttish, if it smell so strongly as thou speakest of. I will henceforth eat no fish of fortune's buttering. Prithee, allow the wind.

Par. Nay, you need not to stop your nose, sir; I spake but by a metaphor.

Clo. Indeed, sir, if your metaphor stink, I will stop my nose; or against any man's metaphor. Prithee, get thee further.

Par. Pray you, sir, deliver me this paper.

Clo. Foh! prithee, stand away. A paper from fortune's close-stool to give to a nobleman! Look, here he comes himself.

Enter LAFEU.

Here is a purr of fortune's, sir, or of fortune's cat—but not a musk-cat—that has fallen into the unclean fishpond of her displeasure, and, as he says, is muddied withal. Pray you, sir, use the carp as you may; for he looks like a poor, decayed, ingenious, foolish, rascally knave. I do pity his distress in my similes of comfort and leave him to your lordship. [*Exit.*

Par. My lord, I am a man whom fortune hath cruelly scratched.

Laf. And what would you have me to do? 'Tis too late to pare her nails now. Wherein have you played the knave with fortune, that she would scratch you, who of herself is a good lady and would not have knaves thrive long under her? There's a *quart d'écu* for you. Let the justices make you and fortune friends. I am for other business.

Par. I beseech your honour to hear me one single word.

Laf. You beg a single penny more. Come, you shall ha't; save your word.

Par. My name, my good Lord, is Parolles.

Laf. You beg more than "word," then. Cox my passion! give me your hand. How does your drum?

Par. O my good lord, you were the first that found me!

Laf. Was I, in sooth? and I was the first that lost thee.

Par. It lies in you, my lord, to bring me in some grace, for you did bring me out.

Laf. Out upon thee, knave! dost thou put upon me at once both the office of God and the devil? One brings thee in grace and the other brings thee out. [*Trumpets sound.*] The King's coming; I know by his trumpets. Sirrah, inquire further after me; I had talk of you last night. Though you are a fool and a knave, you shall eat; go to, follow.

Par. I praise God for you. [*Exeunt.*

SCENE III. *Rousillon: the Count's palace*

Flourish. Enter KING, COUNTESS, LAFEU, *the* TWO FRENCH LORDS, *with Attendants.*

King. We lost a jewel of her; and our esteem
Was made much poorer by it; but your son,
As mad in folly, lack'd the sense to know
Her estimation home.
Count. 'Tis past, my liege;
And I beseech your Majesty to make it
Natural rebellion, done i' the blaze of youth;
When oil and fire, too strong for reason's force,
O'erbears it and burns on.
King. My honour'd lady,
I have forgiven and forgotten all;
Though my revenges were high bent upon him,
And watch'd the time to shoot.
Laf. This I must say,
But first I beg my pardon, the young lord
Did to his Majesty, his mother, and his lady
Offence of mighty note; but to himself
The greatest wrong of all. He lost a wife
Whose beauty did astonish the survey
Of richest eyes, whose words all ears took captive,

Whose dear perfection hearts that scorn'd to serve
Humbly call'd mistress.

King. Praising what is lost
Makes the remembrance dear. Well, call him hither;
We are reconciled, and the first view shall kill
All repetition. Let him not ask our pardon;
The nature of his great offence is dead,
And deeper than oblivion we do bury
The incensing relics of it. Let him approach,
A stranger, no offender; and inform him
So 'tis our will he should.

1st Lord. I shall, my liege. [*Exit.*

King. What says he to your daughter? have you spoke?

Laf. All that he is hath reference to your highness.

King. Then shall we have a match. I have letters sent me
That set him high in fame.

Enter BERTRAM.

Laf. He looks well on't.

King. I am not a day of season,
For thou mayst see a sunshine and a hail
In me at once; but to the brightest beams
Distracted clouds give way; so stand thou forth;
The time is fair again.

Ber. My high-repented blames,
Dear sovereign, pardon to me.

King. All is whole;
Not one word more of the consumed time.
Let's take the instant by the forward top;
For we are old, and on our quick'st decrees
The inaudible and noiseless foot of Time
Steals ere we can effect them. You remember
The daughter of this lord?

Ber. Admiringly, my liege, at first
I stuck my choice upon her, ere my heart
Durst make too bold a herald of my tongue;
Where the impression of mine eye infixing,
Contempt his scornful perspective did lend me,
Which warp'd the line of every other favour;
Scorn'd a fair colour, or express'd it stolen;
Extended or contracted all proportions
To a most hideous object; thence it came
That she whom all men praised and whom myself,
Since I have lost, have loved, was in mine eye
The dust that did offend it.

King. Well excused.
That thou didst love her, strikes some scores away
From the great compt; but love that comes too late,
Like a remorseful pardon slowly carried,
To the great sender turns a sour offence,
Crying, "That's good that's gone." Our rash faults
Make trivial price of serious things we have,
Not knowing them until we know their grave.
Oft our displeasures, to ourselves unjust,
Destroy our friends and after weep their dust.
Our own love waking cries to see what's done,
While shame full late sleeps out the afternoon.
Be this sweet Helen's knell, and now forget her.
Send forth your amorous token for fair Maudlin.
The main consents are had; and here we'll stay
To see our widower's second marriage day.

Count. Which better than the first, O dear heaven, bless!
Or, ere they meet, in me, O nature, cease!

Laf. Come on, my son, in whom my house's name
Must be digested, give a favour from you
To sparkle in the spirits of my daughter,
That she may quickly come. [BERTRAM *gives a ring.*] By my old beard,
And every hair that's on't, Helen, that's dead,
Was a sweet creature. Such a ring as this,
The last that e'er I took her leave at court,
I saw upon her finger.

Ber. Hers it was not.

King. Now, pray you, let me see it; for mine eye,
While I was speaking, oft was fasten'd to't.
This ring was mine; and, when I gave it Helen,
I bade her, if her fortunes ever stood
Necessitied to help, that by this token
I would relieve her. Had you that craft, to reave her
Of what should stead her most?

Ber. My gracious sovereign,
Howe'er it pleases you to take it so,
The ring was never hers.

Count. Son, on my life,
I have seen her wear it; and she reckon'd it
At her life's rate.

Laf. I am sure I saw her wear it.

Ber. You are deceived, my lord; she never saw it.
In Florence was it from a casement thrown me,
Wrapp'd in a paper, which contain'd the name
Of her that threw it. Noble she was, and thought
I stood engaged; but when I had subscribed
To mine own fortune and inform'd her fully
I could not answer in that course of honour
As she had made the overture, she ceased
In heavy satisfaction and would never
Receive the ring again.

King. Plutus himself,

That knows the tinct and multiplying medicine,
Hath not in nature's mystery more science
Than I have in this ring. 'Twas mine, 'twas Helen's,
Whoever gave it you. Then, if you know
That you are well acquainted with yourself,
Confess 'twas hers, and by what rough enforcement
You got it from her. She call'd the saints to surety
That she would never put it from her finger,
Unless she gave it to yourself in bed,
Where you have never come, or sent it us
Upon her great disaster.

Ber. She never saw it.

King. Thou speak'st it falsely, as I love mine honour;
And makest conjectural fears to come into me,
Which I would fain shut out. If it should prove
That thou art so inhuman—'twill not prove so—
And yet I know not. Thou didst hate her deadly,
And she is dead; which nothing, but to close
Her eyes myself, could win me to believe,
More than to see this ring. Take him away.

Guards seize BERTRAM.

My fore-past proofs, howe'er the matter fall,
Shall tax my fears of little vanity,
Having vainly fear'd too little. Away with him!
We'll sift this matter further.

Ber. If you shall prove
This ring was ever hers, you shall as easy
Prove that I husbanded her bed in Florence,
Where yet she never was. [*Exit, guarded.*

King. I am wrapp'd in dismal thinkings.

Enter a GENTLEMAN.

Gent. Gracious sovereign,
Whether I have been to blame or no, I know not.
Here's a petition from a Florentine,
Who hath for four or five removes come short
To tender it herself. I undertook it,
Vanquish'd thereto by the fair grace and speech
Of the poor suppliant, who by this I know
Is here attending. Her business looks in her
With an importing visage; and she told me,
In a sweet verbal brief, it did concern
Your Highness with herself.

King. [*Reads*] "Upon his many protestations to marry me when his wife was dead, I blush to say it, he won me. Now is the Count Rousillon a widower. His vows are forfeited to me, and my honour's paid to him. He stole from Florence, taking no leave, and I follow him to his country for justice. Grant it me, O king! in you it best lies; otherwise a seducer flourishes, and a poor maid is undone. Diana Capilet"

Laf. I will buy me a son-in-law in a fair, and toll for this. I'll none of him.

King. The heavens have thought well on thee, Lafeu,
To bring forth this discovery. Seek these suitors.
Go speedily and bring again the Count.
I am afeard the life of Helen, lady,
Was foully snatch'd.

Count. Now, justice on the doers!

Re-enter BERTRAM, *guarded*.

King. I wonder, sir, sith wives are monsters to you,
And that you fly them as you swear them lordship,
Yet you desire to marry.

Enter WIDOW *and* DIANA.

What woman's that?

Dia. I am, my lord, a wretched Florentine,
Derived from the ancient Capilet.
My suit, as I do understand, you know,
And therefore know how far I may be pitied.

Wid. I am her mother, sir, whose age and honour
Both suffer under this complaint we bring,
And both shall cease, without your remedy.

King. Come hither, Count; do you know these women?

Ber. My lord, I neither can nor will deny
But that I know them. Do they charge me further?

Dia. Why do you look so strange upon your wife?

Ber. She's none of mine, my lord.

Dia. If you shall marry,
You give away this hand, and that is mine;
You give away heaven's vows, and those are mine;
You give away myself, which is known mine;
For I by vow am so embodied yours,
That she which marries you must marry me,
Either both or none.

Laf. Your reputation comes too short for my daughter; you are no husband for her.

Ber. My lord, this is a fond and desperate creature,
Whom sometime I have laugh'd with. Let your Highness
Lay a more noble thought upon mine honour
Than for to think that I would sink it here.

King. Sir, for my thoughts, you have them ill to friend
Till your deeds gain them; fairer prove your honour
Than in my thought it lies.

Dia. Good my lord,
Ask him upon his oath if he does think
He had not my virginity.
King. What say'st thou to her?
Ber. She's impudent, my lord.
And was a common gamester to the camp.
Dia. He does me wrong, my lord; if I were so,
He might have bought me at a common price.
Do not believe him. O, behold this ring,
Whose high respect and rich validity
Did lack a parallel; yet for all that
He gave it to a commoner o' the camp,
If I be one.
Count. He blushes, and 'tis it.
Of six preceding ancestors, that gem,
Conferr'd by testament to the sequent issue,
Hath it been owed and worn. This is his wife;
That ring's a thousand proofs.
King. Methought you said
You saw one here in court could witness it.
Dia. I did, my lord, but loath am to produce
So bad an instrument. His name's Parolles.
Laf. I saw the man to-day, if man he be.
King. Find him, and bring him hither.
[*Exit an Attendant*.
Ber. What of him?
He's quoted for a most perfidious slave,
With all the spots o' the world tax'd and debosh'd;
Whose nature sickens but to speak a truth.
Am I or that or this for what he'll utter,
That will speak anything?
King. She hath that ring of yours.
Ber. I think she has. Certain it is I liked her,
And boarded her i' the wanton way of youth.
She knew her distance and did angle for me,
Madding my eagerness with her restraint,
As all impediments in fancy's course
Are motives of more fancy; and, in fine,
Her infinite cunning, with her modern grace,
Subdued me to her rate. She got the ring;
And I had that which any inferior might
At market-price have bought.
Dia. I must be patient.
You, that have turn'd off a first so noble wife,
May justly diet me. I pray you yet;
Since you lack virtue, I will lose a husband;
Send for your ring, I will return it home,
And give me mine again.
Ber. I have it not.
King. What ring was yours, I pray you?
Dia. Sir, much like
The same upon your finger.
King. Know you this ring? this ring was his of late.
Dia. And this was it I gave him, being abed.
King. The story then goes false, you threw it him
Out of a casement.
Dia. I have spoke the truth.

Enter PAROLLES.

Ber. My lord, I do confess the ring was hers.
King. You boggle shrewdly, every feather starts you.
Is this the man you speak of?
Dia. Ay, my lord.
King. Tell me, sirrah, but tell me true, I charge you,
Not fearing the displeasure of your master,
Which on your just proceeding I'll keep off,
By him and by this woman here what know you?

Par. So please your Majesty, my master hath been an honourable gentleman. Tricks he hath had in him, which gentlemen have.

King. Come, come, to the purpose. Did he love this woman?

Par. Faith, sir, he did love her; but how?

King. How, I pray you?

Par. He did love her, sir, as a gentleman loves a woman.

King. How is that?

Par. He loved her, sir, and loved her not.

King. As thou art a knave, and no knave. What an equivocal companion is this!

Par. I am a poor man, and at your Majesty's command.

Laf. He's a good drum, my lord, but a naughty orator.

Dia. Do you know he promised me marriage?

Par. Faith, I know more than I'll speak.

King. But wilt thou not speak all thou knowest?

Par. Yes, so please your Majesty. I did go between them, as I said; but more than that, he loved her; for indeed he was mad for her, and talked of Satan and of Limbo and of Furies and I know not what; yet I was in that credit with them at that time that I knew of their going to bed, and of other motions, as promising her marriage, and things which would derive me ill will to speak of; therefore I will not speak what I know.

King. Thou hast spoken all already, unless thou canst say they are married; but thou art too fine in thy evidence; therefore stand aside.
This ring, you say, was yours?
Dia. Ay, my good lord.
King. Where did you buy it? or who gave it you?
Dia. It was not given me, nor I did not buy it.
King. Who lent it you?
Dia. It was not lent me neither.

King. Where did you find it, then?
Dia. I found it not.
King. If it were yours by none of all these ways,
How could you give it him?
Dia. I never gave it him.

Laf. This woman's an easy glove, my lord; she goes off and on at pleasure.

King. This ring was mine; I gave it his first wife.
Dia. It might be yours or hers, for aught I know.
King. Take her away; I do not like her now;
To prison with her; and away with him.
Unless thou tell'st me where thou hadst this ring,
Thou diest within this hour.
Dia. I'll never tell you.
King. Take her away.
Dia. I'll put in bail, my liege.
King. I think thee now some common customer.
Dia. By Jove, if ever I knew man, 'twas you.
King. Wherefore hast thou accused him all this while?
Dia. Because he's guilty, and he is not guilty;
He knows I am no maid, and he'll swear to't;
I'll swear I am a maid, and he knows not.
Great King, I am no strumpet, by my life;
I am either maid, or else this old man's wife.
King. She does abuse our ears. To prison with her.
Dia. Good mother, fetch my bail. Stay, royal sir. [*Exit* WIDOW.
The jeweller that owes the ring is sent for,
And he shall surety me. But for this lord,
Who hath abused me, as he knows himself,
Though yet he never harm'd me, here I quit him.
He knows himself my bed he hath defiled;
And at that time he got his wife with child.
Dead though she be, she feels her young one kick.
So there's my riddle: one that's dead is quick:
And now behold the meaning.

Re-enter WIDOW, *with* HELENA.

King. Is there no exorcist
Beguiles the truer office of mine eyes?
Is't real that I see?
Hel. No, my good lord;
'Tis but the shadow of a wife you see,
The name and not the thing.
Ber. Both, both. O, pardon!
Hel. O my good lord, when I was like this maid,
I found you wondrous kind. There is your ring;
And, look you, here's your letter; this it says:
"When from my finger you can get this ring
And are by me with child," &c. This is done.
Will you be mine, now you are doubly won?
Ber. If she, my liege, can make me know this clearly,
I'll love her dearly, ever, ever dearly.
Hel. If it appear not plain and prove untrue,
Deadly divorce step between me and you!
O my dear mother, do I see you living?
Laf. Mine eyes smell onions; I shall weep anon:
[*To* PAROLLES] Good Tom Drum, lend me a handkercher. So,
I thank thee; wait on me home, I'll make sport with thee.
Let thy courtesies alone, they are scurvy ones.
King. Let us from point to point this story know,
To make the even truth in pleasure flow.
[*To* DIANA] If thou be'st yet a fresh uncropped flower,
Choose thou thy husband, and I'll pay thy dower;
For I can guess that by thy honest aid
Thou kept'st a wife herself, thyself a maid.
Of that and all the progress, more and less,
Resolvedly more leisure shall express.
All yet seems well; and if it end so meet,
The bitter past, more welcome is the sweet.
[*Flourish*.

EPILOGUE

King. The king's a beggar, now the play is done.
All is well ended, if this suit be won,
That you express content; which we will pay,
With strife to please you, day exceeding day.
Ours be your patience then, and yours our parts;
Your gentle hands lend us, and take our hearts.
[*Exeunt*.

MEASURE FOR MEASURE

DRAMATIS PERSONÆ

VINCENTIO, *the Duke*
ANGELO, *the Deputy*
ESCALUS, *an ancient Lord*
CLAUDIO, *a young gentleman*
LUCIO, *a fantastic*
TWO GENTLEMEN
PROVOST
THOMAS | *two friars*
PETER | *two friars*
A JUSTICE
VARRIUS
ELBOW, *a simple constable*
FROTH, *a foolish gentleman*
POMPEY, *servant to Mistress Overdone*
ABHORSON, *an executioner*
BARNARDINE, *a dissolute prisoner*
A BOY
A MESSENGER
A SERVANT *to Angelo*

ISABELLA, *sister to Claudio*
MARIANA, *bethrothed to Angelo*
JULIET, *beloved of Claudio*
FRANCISCA, *a nun*
MISTRESS OVERDONE, *a bawd*

NON-SPEAKING: *Lords, Officers, Citizens, and Attendants*

SCENE: *Vienna*

ACT I

SCENE I. *An apartment in the Duke's palace*

Enter DUKE, ESCALUS, *Lords and Attendants.*

Duke. Escalus.
Escal. My lord.
Duke. Of government the properties to unfold,
Would seem in me to affect speech and discourse;
Since I am put to know that your own science
Exceeds, in that, the lists of all advice
My strength can give you. Then no more remains,
But that to your sufficiency . . . . .
. . . . as your worth is able,
And let them work. The nature of our people,
Our city's institutions, and the terms
For common justice, you're as pregnant in
As art and practice hath enriched any
That we remember. There is our commission,
From which we would not have you warp. Call hither,
I say, bid come before us Angelo.
[*Exit an Attendant.*
What figure of us think you he will bear?
For you must know, we have with special soul
Elected him our absence to supply,
Lent him our terror, dress'd him with our love,
And given his deputation all the organs
Of our own power. What think you of it?
Escal. If any in Vienna be of worth
To undergo such ample grace and honour,
It is Lord Angelo.
Duke. Look where he comes.

Enter ANGELO.

Ang. Always obedient to your Grace's will,
I come to know your pleasure.
Duke. Angelo,
There is a kind of character in thy life
That to the observer doth thy history
Fully unfold. Thyself and thy belongings
Are not thine own so proper as to waste
Thyself upon thy virtues, they on thee.
Heaven doth with us as we with torches do,
Not light them for themselves; for if our virtues
Did not go forth of us, 'twere all alike
As if we had them not. Spirits are not finely touch'd
But to fine issues, nor Nature never lends
The smallest scruple of her excellence
But, like a thrifty goddess, she determines
Herself the glory of a creditor,
Both thanks and use. But I do bend my speech
To one that can my part in him advertise;
Hold therefore, Angelo:
In our remove be thou at full ourself;
Mortality and mercy in Vienna
Live in thy tongue and heart. Old Escalus,
Though first in question, is thy secondary.
Take thy commission.
Ang. Now, good my lord,
Let there be some more test made of my metal,
Before so noble and so great a figure
Be stamp'd upon it.
Duke. No more evasion.
We have with a leaven'd and prepared choice
Proceeded to you; therefore take your honours.
Our haste from hence is of so quick condition

That it prefers itself and leaves unquestion'd
Matters of needful value. We shall write to you,
As time and our concernings shall importune,
How it goes with us, and do look to know
What doth befall you here. So, fare you well.
To the hopeful execution do I leave you
Of your commissions.

Ang. Yet give leave, my lord,
That we may bring you something on the way.

Duke. My haste may not admit it;
Nor need you, on mine honour, have to do
With any scruple; your scope is as mine own,
So to enforce or qualify the laws
As to your soul seems good. Give me your hand;
I'll privily away. I love the people,
But do not like to stage me to their eyes.
Though it do well, I do not relish well
Their loud applause and Aves vehement;
Nor do I think the man of safe discretion
That does affect it. Once more, fare you well.

Ang. The heavens give safety to your purposes!

Escal. Lead forth and bring you back in happiness!

Duke. I thank you. Fare you well. [*Exit.*

Escal. I shall desire you, sir, to give me leave
To have free speech with you; and it concerns me
To look into the bottom of my place.
A power I have, but of what strength and nature
I am not yet instructed.

Ang. 'Tis so with me. Let us withdraw together,
And we may soon our satisfaction have
Touching that point.

Escal. I'll wait upon your honour. [*Exeunt.*

SCENE II. *A street*

Enter LUCIO *and* TWO GENTLEMEN.

Lucio. If the Duke with the other dukes come not to composition with the King of Hungary, why then all the dukes fall upon the King.

1st Gent. Heaven grant us its peace, but not the King of Hungary's!

2nd Gent. Amen.

Lucio. Thou concludest like the sanctimonious pirate, that went to sea with the Ten Commandments, but scraped one out of the table.

2nd Gent. "Thou shalt not steal"?

Lucio. Ay, that he razed.

1st Gent. Why, 'twas a commandment to command the captain and all the rest from their functions; they put forth to steal. There's not a soldier of us all, that, in the thanksgiving before meat, do relish the petition well that prays for peace.

2nd Gent. I never heard any soldier dislike it.

Lucio. I believe thee; for I think thou never wast where grace was said.

2nd Gent. No? a dozen times at least.

1st Gent. What, in metre?

Lucio. In any proportion or in any language.

1st Gent. I think, or in any religion.

Lucio. Ay, why not? Grace is grace, despite of all controversy; as, for example, thou thyself art a wicked villain, despite of all grace.

1st Gent. Well, there went but a pair of shears between us.

Lucio. I grant; as there may between the lists and the velvet. Thou art the list.

1st Gent. And thou the velvet. Thou art good velvet; thou'rt a three-piled piece, I warrant thee. I had as lief be a list of an English kersey as be piled, as thou art piled, for a French velvet. Do I speak feelingly now?

Lucio. I think thou dost; and, indeed, with most painful feeling of thy speech. I will, out of thine own confession, learn to begin thy health; but, whilst I live, forget to drink after thee.

1st Gent. I think I have done myself wrong, have I not?

2nd Gent. Yes, that thou hast, whether thou art tainted or free.

Lucio. Behold, behold, where Madam Mitigation comes! I have purchased as many diseases under her roof as come to—

2nd Gent. To what, I pray?

Lucio. Judge.

2nd Gent. To three thousand dolours a year.

1st Gent. Ay, and more.

Lucio. A French crown more.

1st Gent. Thou art always figuring diseases in me; but thou art full of error; I am sound.

Lucio. Nay, not as one would say, healthy; but so sound as things that are hollow. Thy bones are hollow; impiety has made a feast of thee.

Enter MISTRESS OVERDONE.

1st Gent. How now! which of your hips has the most profound sciatica?

Mrs Ov. Well, well; there's one yonder arrested and carried to prison was worth five thousand of you all.

2nd Gent. Who's that, I pray thee?

Mrs Ov. Marry, sir, that's Claudio, Signior Claudio.

1st Gent. Claudio to prison? 'tis not so.

Mrs Ov. Nay, but I know 'tis so. I saw him arrested, saw him carried away; and, which is more, within these three days his head to be chopped off.

Lucio. But, after all this fooling, I would not have it so. Art thou sure of this?

Mrs Ov. I am too sure of it; and it is for getting Madam Julietta with child.

Lucio. Believe me, this may be. He promised to meet me two hours since, and he was ever precise in promise-keeping.

2nd Gent. Besides, you know, it draws something near to the speech we had to such a purpose.

1st Gent. But, most of all, agreeing with the proclamation.

Lucio. Away! let's go learn the truth of it.

[*Exeunt* LUCIO *and* GENTLEMEN.

Mrs Ov. Thus, what with the war, what with the sweat, what with the gallows, and what with poverty, I am custom-shrunk.

Enter POMPEY.

How now! what's the news with you?

Pom. Yonder man is carried to prison.

Mrs Ov. Well; what has he done?

Pom. A woman.

Mrs Ov. But what's his offence?

Pom. Groping for trouts in a peculiar river.

Mrs Ov. What, is there a maid with child by him?

Pom. No, but there's a woman with maid by him. You have not heard of the proclamation, have you?

Mrs Ov. What proclamation, man?

Pom. All houses in the suburbs of Vienna must be plucked down.

Mrs Ov. And what shall become of those in the city?

Pom. They shall stand for seed. They had gone down too, but that a wise burgher put in for them.

Mrs Ov. But shall all our houses of resort in the suburbs be pulled down?

Pom. To the ground, mistress.

Mrs Ov. Why, here's a change indeed in the commonwealth! What shall become of me?

Pom. Come; fear not you; good counsellors lack no clients. Though you change your place, you need not change your trade; I'll be your tapster still. Courage! there will be pity taken on you; you that have worn your eyes almost out in the service, you will be considered.

Mrs Ov. What's to do here, Thomas tapster? let's withdraw.

Pom. Here comes Signior Claudio, led by the provost to prison; and there's Madam Juliet.

[*Exeunt*.

Enter PROVOST, CLAUDIO, JULIET, *and Officers*.

Claud. Fellow, why dost thou show me thus to the world?
Bear me to prison, where I am committed.

Prov. I do it not in evil disposition,
But from Lord Angelo by special charge.

Claud. Thus can the demigod Authority
Make us pay down for our offence by weight
The words of heaven; on whom it will, it will;
On whom it will not, so; yet still 'tis just.

Re-enter LUCIO *and* TWO GENTLEMEN.

Lucio. Why, how now, Claudio! whence comes this restraint?

Claud. From too much liberty, my Lucio, liberty.
As surfeit is the father of much fast,
So every scope by the immoderate use
Turns to restraint. Our natures do pursue,
Like rats that ravin down their proper bane,
A thirsty evil; and when we drink we die.

Lucio. If I could speak so wisely under an arrest, I would send for certain of my creditors. And yet, to say the truth, I had as lief have the foppery of freedom as the morality of imprisonment. What's thy offence, Claudio?

Claud. What but to speak of would offend again.

Lucio. What, is't murder?

Claud. No.

Lucio. Lechery?

Claud. Call it so.

Prov. Away, sir! you must go.

Claud. One word, good friend. Lucio, a word with you.

Lucio. A hundred, if they'll do you any good.
Is lechery so look'd after?

Claud. Thus stands it with me. Upon a true contract
I got possession of Julietta's bed;
You know the lady; she is fast my wife,
Save that we do the denunciation lack
Of outward order. This we came not to,
Only for propagation of a dower
Remaining in the coffer of her friends,
From whom we thought it meet to hide our love
Till time had made them for us. But it chances
The stealth of our most mutual entertainment
With character too gross is writ on Juliet.

Lucio. With child, perhaps?

Claud. Unhappily, even so.
And the new deputy now for the Duke—
Whether it be the fault and glimpse of newness,
Or whether that the body public be
A horse whereon the governor doth ride,
Who, newly in the seat, that it may know
He can command, lets it straight feel the spur;
Whether the tyranny be in his place,
Or in his eminence that fills it up,

I stagger in: but this new governor
Awakes me all the enrolled penalties
Which have, like unscour'd armour, hung by the wall
So long that nineteen zodiacs have gone round
And none of them been worn; and, for a name,
Now puts the drowsy and neglected act
Freshly on me. 'Tis surely for a name.

Lucio. I warrant it is; and thy head stands so tickle on thy shoulders that a milkmaid, if she be in love, may sigh it off. Send after the Duke and appeal to him.

Claud. I have done so, but he's not to be found.
I prithee, Lucio, do me this kind service.
This day my sister should the cloister enter
And there receive her approbation.
Acquaint her with the danger of my state;
Implore her, in my voice, that she make friends
To the strict deputy; bid herself assay him;
I have great hope in that; for in her youth
There is a prone and speechless dialect,
Such as move men; beside, she hath prosperous art
When she will play with reason and discourse,
And well she can persuade.

Lucio. I pray she may; as well for the encouragement of the like, which else would stand under grievous imposition, as for the enjoying of thy life, who I would be sorry should be thus foolishly lost at a game of tick-tack. I'll to her.

Claud. I thank you, good friend Lucio.
Lucio. Within two hours.
Claud. Come, officer, away!
[*Exeunt.*

SCENE III. *A monastery*

Enter DUKE *and* FRIAR THOMAS.

Duke. No, holy father; throw away that thought.
Believe not that the dribbling dart of love
Can pierce a complete bosom. Why I desire thee
To give me secret harbour, hath a purpose
More grave and wrinkled than the aims and ends
Of burning youth.
Fri. T. May your Grace speak of it?
Duke. My holy sir, none better knows than you
How I have ever loved the life removed
And held in idle price to haunt assemblies
Where youth, and cost, and witless bravery keeps.
I have deliver'd to Lord Angelo,
A man of stricture and firm abstinence,
My absolute power and place here in Vienna,
And he supposes me travell'd to Poland;
For so I have strew'd it in the common ear,
And so it is received. Now, pious sir,
You will demand of me why I do this?
Fri. T. Gladly, my lord.
Duke. We have strict statutes and most biting laws,
The needful bits and curbs to headstrong weeds,
Which for this nineteen years we have let slip;
Even like an o'ergrown lion in a cave,
That goes not out to prey. Now, as fond fathers,
Having bound up the threatening twigs of birch,
Only to stick it in their children's sight
For terror, not to use, in time the rod
Becomes more mock'd than fear'd; so our decrees,
Dead to infliction, to themselves are dead,
And liberty plucks justice by the nose,
The baby beats the nurse, and quite athwart
Goes all decorum.
Fri. T. It rested in your Grace
To unloose this tied-up justice when you pleased;
And it in you more dreadful would have seem'd
Than in Lord Angelo.
Duke. I do fear, too dreadful.
Sith 'twas my fault to give the people scope,
'Twould be my tyranny to strike and gall them
For what I bid them do; for we bid this be done,
When evil deeds have their permissive pass
And not the punishment. Therefore indeed, my father,
I have on Angelo imposed the office;
Who may, in the ambush of my name, strike home,
And yet my nature never in the fight
To do in slander. And to behold his sway,
I will, as 'twere a brother of your order,
Visit both prince and people; therefore, I prithee,
Supply me with the habit and instruct me
How I may formally in person bear me
Like a true friar. Moe reasons for this action
At our more leisure shall I render you;
Only, this one: Lord Angelo is precise;
Stands at a guard with envy; scarce confesses
That his blood flows, or that his appetite
Is more to bread than stone; hence shall we see,
If power change purpose, what our seemers be.
[*Exeunt.*

SCENE IV. *A nunnery*

Enter ISABELLA *and* FRANCISCA.

Isab. And have you nuns no farther privileges?
Fran. Are not these large enough?
Isab. Yes, truly. I speak not as desiring more;
But rather wishing a more strict restraint
Upon the sisterhood, the votarists of Saint Clare.
Lucio. [*Within*] Ho! Peace be in this place!
Isab. Who's that which calls?

Fran. It is a man's voice. Gentle Isabella,
Turn you the key, and know his business of him;
You may, I may not; you are yet unsworn.
When you have vow'd, you must not speak with men
But in the presence of the prioress;
Then, if you speak, you must not show your face,
Or, if you show your face, you must not speak.
He calls again; I pray you, answer him. [*Exit*.
Isab. Peace and prosperity! Who is't that calls?

Enter LUCIO.

Lucio. Hail, virgin, if you be, as those cheek-roses
Proclaim you are no less! Can you so stead me
As bring me to the sight of Isabella,
A novice of this place and the fair sister
To her unhappy brother Claudio?
Isab. Why "her unhappy brother"? let me ask,
The rather for I now must make you know
I am that Isabella and his sister.
Lucio. Gentle and fair, your brother kindly greets you.
Not to be weary with you, he's in prison.
Isab. Woe me! for what?
Lucio. For that which, if myself might be his judge,
He should receive his punishment in thanks.
He hath got his friend with child.
Isab. Sir, make me not your story.
Lucio. It is true.
I would not—though 'tis my familiar sin
With maids to seem the lapwing and to jest,
Tongue far from heart—play with all virgins so.
I hold you as a thing ensky'd and sainted,
By your renouncement an immortal spirit,
And to be talk'd with in sincerity,
As with a saint.
Isab. You do blaspheme the good in mocking me.
Lucio. Do not believe it. Fewness and truth, 'tis thus:
Your brother and his lover have embraced;
As those that feed grow full, as blossoming time
That from the seedness the bare fallow brings
To teeming foison, even so her plenteous womb
Expresseth his full tilth and husbandry.
Isab. Some one with child by him? My cousin Juliet?
Lucio. Is she your cousin?
Isab. Adoptedly; as school-maids change their names
By vain though apt affection.
Lucio. She it is.
Isab. O, let him marry her.
Lucio. This is the point.
The Duke is very strangely gone from hence;
Bore many gentlemen, myself being one,
In hand and hope of action; but we do learn
By those that know the very nerves of state,
His givings-out were of an infinite distance
From his true-meant design. Upon his place,
And with full line of his authority,
Governs Lord Angelo; a man whose blood
Is very snow-broth; one who never feels
The wanton stings and motions of the sense,
But doth rebate and blunt his natural edge
With profits of the mind, study, and fast.
He—to give fear to use and liberty,
Which have for long run by the hideous law,
As mice by lions—hath pick'd out an act,
Under whose heavy sense your brother's life
Falls into forfeit; he arrests him on it;
And follows close the rigour of the statute,
To make him an example. All hope is gone,
Unless you have the grace by your fair prayer
To soften Angelo. And that's my pith of business
'Twixt you and your poor brother.
Isab. Doth he so seek his life?
Lucio. Has censured him
Already; and, as I hear, the Provost hath
A warrant for his execution.
Isab. Alas! what poor ability's in me
To do him good?
Lucio. Assay the power you have.
Isab. My power? Alas, I doubt—
Lucio. Our doubts are traitors
And make us lose the good we oft might win
By fearing to attempt. Go to Lord Angelo,
And let him learn to know, when maidens sue,
Men give like gods; but when they weep and kneel,
All their petitions are as freely theirs
As they themselves would owe them.
Isab. I'll see what I can do.
Lucio. But speedily.
Isab. I will about it straight;
No longer staying but to give the Mother
Notice of my affair. I humbly thank you.
Commend me to my brother. Soon at night
I'll send him certain word of my success.
Lucio. I take my leave of you.
Isab. Good sir, adieu.
[*Exeunt*.

ACT II

SCENE I. *A hall in Angelo's house*

Enter ANGELO, ESCALUS, *and a* JUSTICE, PROVOST, *Officers, and other Attendants, behind*.

Ang. We must not make a scarecrow of the law,

Setting it up to fear the birds of prey,
And let it keep one shape, till custom make it
Their perch and not their terror.

Escal. Ay, but yet
Let us be keen, and rather cut a little,
Than fall, and bruise to death. Alas, this gentleman,
Whom I would save, had a most noble father!
Let but your honour know,
Whom I believe to be most strait in virtue,
That, in the working of your own affections,
Had time cohered with place or place with wishing,
Or that the resolute acting of your blood
Could have attain'd the effect of your own purpose,
Whether you had not sometime in your life
Err'd in this point which now you censure him,
And pull'd the law upon you.

Ang. 'Tis one thing to be tempted, Escalus,
Another thing to fall. I not deny,
The jury, passing on the prisoner's life,
May in the sworn twelve have a thief or two
Guiltier than him they try. What's open made to justice,
That justice seizes. What know the laws
That thieves do pass on thieves? 'Tis very pregnant,
The jewel that we find, we stoop and take't
Because we see it; but what we do not see
We tread upon, and never think of it.
You may not so extenuate his offence
For I have had such faults; but rather tell me,
When I, that censure him, do so offend,
Let mine own judgement pattern out my death,
And nothing come in partial. Sir, he must die.

Escal. Be it as your wisdom will.

Ang. Where is the Provost?

Prov. Here, if it like your honour.

Ang. See that Claudio
Be executed by nine to-morrow morning.
Bring him his confessor, let him be prepared;
For that's the utmost of his pilgrimage.

[*Exit* PROVOST.

Escal. [*Aside*] Well, heaven forgive him! and forgive us all!
Some rise by sin, and some by virtue fall.
Some run from brakes of vice, and answer none;
And some condemned for a fault alone.

Enter ELBOW, *and Officers with* FROTH *and* POMPEY.

Elb. Come, bring them away. If these be good people in a commonweal that do nothing but use their abuses in common houses, I know no law. Bring them away.

Ang. How now, sir! What's your name? and what's the matter?

Elb. If it please your honour, I am the poor Duke's constable, and my name is Elbow. I do lean upon justice, sir, and do bring in here before your good honour two notorious benefactors.

Ang. Benefactors? Well; what benefactors are they? are they not malefactors?

Elb. If it please your honour, I know not well what they are; but precise villains they are, that I am sure of; and void of all profanation in the world that good Christians ought to have.

Escal. This comes off well; here's a wise officer.

Ang. Go to; what quality are they of? Elbow is your name? why dost thou not speak, Elbow?

Pom. He cannot, sir; he's out at elbow.

Ang. What are you, sir?

Elb. He, sir! a tapster, sir; parcel-bawd; one that serves a bad woman; whose house, sir, was, as they say, plucked down in the suburbs; and now she professes a hot-house, which, I think, is a very ill house too.

Escal. How know you that?

Elb. My wife, sir, whom I detest before heaven and your honour—

Escal. How? thy wife?

Elb. Ay, sir; whom, I thank heaven, is an honest woman—

Escal. Dost thou detest her therefore?

Elb. I say, sir, I will detest myself also, as well as she, that this house, if it be not a bawd's house, it is pity of her life, for it is a naughty house.

Escal. How dost thou know that, constable?

Elb. Marry, sir, by my wife; who, if she had been a woman cardinally given, might have been accused in fornication, adultery, and all uncleanliness there.

Escal. By the woman's means?

Elb. Ay, sir, by Mistress Overdone's means; but as she spit in his face, so she defied him.

Pom. Sir, if it please your honour, this is not so.

Elb. Prove it before these varlets here, thou honourable man; prove it.

Escal. Do you hear how he misplaces?

Pom. Sir, she came in great with child; and longing, saving your honour's reverence, for stewed prunes; sir, we had but two in the house, which at that very distant time stood, as it were, in a fruit-dish, a dish of some three-pence; your honours have seen such dishes; they are not China dishes, but very good dishes—

Escal. Go to, go to; no matter for the dish, sir.

Pom. No, indeed, sir, not of a pin; you are therein in the right; but to the point. As I say, this Mistress Elbow, being, as I say, with child, and being great-bellied, and longing, as I said, for prunes; and having but two in the dish, as I said, Master Froth here, this very man, having eaten the rest, as I said, and, as I say, paying for them very honestly; for, as you know, Master Froth, I could not give you three-pence again.

Froth. No, indeed.

Pom. Very well; you being then, if you be remembered, cracking the stones of the foresaid prunes—

Froth. Ay, so I did indeed.

Pom. Why, very well; I telling you then, if you be remembered, that such a one and such a one were past cure of the thing you wot of, unless they kept very good diet, as I told you—

Froth. All this is true.

Pom. Why, very well, then—

Escal. Come, you are a tedious fool; to the purpose. What was done to Elbow's wife, that he hath cause to complain of? Come me to what was done to her.

Pom. Sir, your honour cannot come to that yet.

Escal. No, sir, nor I mean it not.

Pom. Sir, but you shall come to it, by your honour's leave, And, I beseech you, look into Master Froth here, sir; a man of fourscore pound a year; whose father died at Hallowmas. Was't not at Hallowmas, Master Froth?

Froth. All-hallond eve.

Pom. Why, very well; I hope here be truths.
He, sir, sitting, as I say, in a lower chair, sir; 'twas in the Bunch of Grapes, where indeed you have a delight to sit, have you not?

Froth. I have so; because it is an open room
and good for winter.

Pom. Why, very well, then; I hope here be truths.

Ang. This will last out a night in Russia,
When nights are longest there. I'll take my leave,
And leave you to the hearing of the cause;
Hoping you'll find good cause to whip them all.

Escal. I think no less. Good morrow to your lordship. [*Exit* ANGELO.
Now, sir, come on. What was done to Elbow's wife, once more?

Pom. Once, sir? there was nothing done to her once.

Elb. I beseech you, sir, ask him what this man did to my wife.

Pom. I beseech your honour, ask me.

Escal. Well, sir; what did this gentleman to her?

Pom. I beseech you, sir, look in this gentleman's face. Good Master Froth, look upon his honour; 'tis for a good purpose. Doth your honour mark his face?

Escal. Ay, sir, very well.

Pom. Nay, I beseech you, mark it well.

Escal. Well, I do so.

Pom. Doth your honour see any harm in his face?

Escal. Why, no.

Pom. I'll be supposed upon a book, his face is the worst thing about him. Good, then; if his face be the worst thing about him, how could Master Froth do the constable's wife any harm? I would know that of your honour.

Escal. He's in the right. Constable, what say you to it?

Elb. First, an it like you, the house is a respected house; next, this is a respected fellow; and his mistress is a respected woman.

Pom. By this hand, sir, his wife is a more respected person than any of us all.

Elb. Varlet, thou liest; thou liest, wicked varlet! the time is yet to come that she was ever respected with man, woman, or child.

Pom. Sir, she was respected with him before he married with her.

Escal. Which is the wiser here? Justice or Iniquity? Is this true?

Elb. O thou caitiff! O thou varlet! O thou wicked Hannibal! I respected with her before I was married to her! If ever I was respected with her, or she with me, let not your worship think me the poor Duke's officer. Prove this, thou wicked Hannibal, or I'll have mine action of battery on thee.

Escal. If he took you a box o' the ear, you might have your action of slander too.

Elb. Marry, I thank your good worship for it. What is't your worship's pleasure I shall do with this wicked caitiff?

Escal. Truly, officer, because he hath some offences in him that thou wouldst discover if thou couldst, let him continue in his courses till thou knowest what they are.

Elb. Marry, I thank your worship for it.
Thou seest, thou wicked varlet, now, what's come upon thee. Thou art to continue now, thou varlet; thou art to continue.

Escal. Where were you born, friend?

Froth. Here in Vienna, sir.

Escal. Are you of fourscore pounds a year?

Froth. Yes, an't please you, sir.

Escal. So. What trade are you of, sir?

Pom. A tapster; a poor widow's tapster.

Escal. Your mistress' name?

Pom. Mistress Overdone.

Escal. Hath she had any more than one husband?

Pom. Nine, sir; Overdone by the last.

Escal. Nine! Come hither to me, Master Froth. Master Froth, I would not have you acquainted with tapsters; they will draw you, Master Froth, and you will hang them. Get you gone, and let me hear no more of you.

Froth. I thank your worship. For mine own part, I never come into any room in a taphouse, but I am drawn in.

Escal. Well, no more of it, Master Froth: farewell. [*Exit* FROTH.] Come you hither to me, Master tapster. What's your name, Master tapster?

Pom. Pompey.

Escal. What else?

Pom. Bum, sir.

Escal. Troth, and your bum is the greatest thing about you; so that in the beastliest sense you are Pompey the Great. Pompey, you are partly a bawd, Pompey, howsoever you colour it in being a tapster, are you not? Come, tell me true; it shall be the better for you.

Pom. Truly, sir, I am a poor fellow that would live.

Escal. How would you live, Pompey? by being a bawd? What do you think of the trade, Pompey? is it a lawful trade?

Pom. If the law would allow it, sir.

Escal. But the law will not allow it, Pompey; nor it shall not be allowed in Vienna.

Pom. Does your worship mean to geld and splay all the youth of the city?

Escal. No, Pompey.

Pom. Truly, sir, in my poor opinion, they will to't then. If your worship will take order for the drabs and the knaves, you need not to fear the bawds.

Escal. There are pretty orders beginning, I can tell you. It is but heading and hanging.

Pom. If you head and hang all that offend that way but for ten year together, you'll be glad to give out a commission for more heads. If this law hold in Vienna ten year, I'll rent the fairest house in it after three-pence a bay. If you live to see this come to pass, say Pompey told you so.

Escal. Thank you, good Pompey; and, in requital of your prophecy, hark you, I advise you, let me not find you before me again upon any complaint whatsoever; no, not for dwelling where you do. If I do, Pompey, I shall beat you to your tent, and prove a shrewd Cæsar to you; in plain dealing, Pompey, I shall have you whipt. So, for this time, Pompey, fare you well.

Pom. I thank your worship for your good counsel; [*aside*] but I shall follow it as the flesh and fortune shall better determine.
Whip me? No, no; let carman whip his jade;
The valiant heart's not whipt out of his trade.
[*Exit.*

Escal. Come hither to me, Master Elbow; come hither, Master constable. How long have you been in this place of constable?

Elb. Seven year and a half, sir.

Escal. I thought, by your readiness in the office, you had continued in it some time. You say, seven years together?

Elb. And a half, sir.

Escal. Alas, it hath been great pains to you. They do you wrong to put you so oft upon't. Are there not men in your ward sufficient to serve it?

Elb. Faith, sir, few of any wit in such matters. As they are chosen, they are glad to choose me for them; I do it for some piece of money, and go through with all.

Escal. Look you bring me in the names of some six or seven, the most sufficient of your parish.

Elb. To your worship's house, sir?

Escal. To my house. Fare you well.
[*Exit* ELBOW.
What's o'clock, think you?

Just. Eleven, sir.

Escal. I pray you home to dinner with me.

Just. I humbly thank you.

Escal. It grieves me for the death of Claudio;
But there's no remedy.

Just. Lord Angelo is severe.

Escal. It is but needful.
Mercy is not itself, that oft looks so;
Pardon is still the nurse of second woe.
But yet—poor Claudio! There is no remedy.
Come, sir.
[*Exeunt.*

SCENE II. *Another room in the same*

Enter PROVOST *and a* SERVANT

Serv. He's hearing of a cause; he will come straight.
I'll tell him of you.

Prov. Pray you, do. [*Exit* SERVANT.] I'll know
His pleasure; may be he will relent. Alas,
He hath but as offended in a dream!
All sects, all ages smack of this vice; and he
To die for't!

Enter ANGELO.

Ang. Now, what's the matter, provost?

Prov. Is it your will Claudio shall die tomorrow?

Ang. Did not I tell thee yea? hadst thou not order?

Why dost thou ask again?
Prov. Lest I might be too rash.
Under your good correction, I have seen,
When, after execution, judgement hath
Repented o'er his doom.
Ang. Go to; let that be mine.
Do you your office, or give up your place,
And you shall well be spared.
Prov. I crave your honour's pardon.
What shall be done, sir, with the groaning Juliet?
She's very near her hour.
Ang. Dispose of her
To some more fitter place, and that with speed.

Re-enter SERVANT.

Serv. Here is the sister of the man condemn'd
Desires access to you.
Ang. Hath he a sister?
Prov. Ay, my good lord; a very virtuous maid,
And to be shortly of a sisterhood,
If not already.
Ang. Well, let her be admitted.
[*Exit* SERVANT.
See you the fornicatress be removed.
Let her have needful, but not lavish, means;
There shall be order for't.

Enter ISABELLA *and* LUCIO.

Prov. God save your honour!
Ang. Stay a little while. [*To* ISABELLA.] You're welcome; what's your will?
Isab. I am a woeful suitor to your honour,
Please but your honour hear me.
Ang. Well; what's your suit?
Isab. There is a vice that most I do abhor,
And most desire should meet the blow of justice;
For which I would not plead, but that I must;
For which I must not plead, but that I am
At war 'twixt will and will not.
Ang. Well; the matter?
Isab. I have a brother is condemn'd to die.
I do beseech you, let it be his fault,
And not my brother.
Prov. [*Aside*] Heaven give thee moving graces!
Ang. Condemn the fault, and not the actor of it?
Why, every fault's condemn'd ere it be done.
Mine were the very cipher of a function,
To fine the faults whose fine stands in record,
And let go by the actor.
Isab. O just but severe law!
I had a brother, then. Heaven keep your honour!
Lucio. [*Aside to* ISABELLA.] Giv't not o'er so. To him again, entreat him;
Kneel down before him, hang upon his gown.
You are too cold; if you should need a pin,
You could not with more tame a tongue desire it.
To him, I say!
Isab. Must he needs die?
Ang. Maiden, no remedy.
Isab. Yes; I do think that you might pardon him,
And neither heaven nor man grieve at the mercy.
Ang. I will not do't.
Isab. But can you, if you would?
Ang. Look, what I will not, that I cannot do.
Isab. But might you do't, and do the world no wrong,
If so your heart were touch'd with that remorse
As mine is to him?
Ang He's sentenced; 'tis too late.
Lucio. [*Aside to* ISABELLA] You are too cold.
Isab. Too late? why, no; I, that do speak a word,
May call it back again. Well, believe this,
No ceremony that to great ones 'longs,
Not the king's crown, nor the deputed sword,
The marshal's truncheon, nor the judge's robe,
Become them with one half so good a grace
As mercy does.
If he had been as you and you as he,
You would have slipt like him; but he, like you,
Would not have been so stern.
Ang. Pray you, be gone.
Isab. I would to heaven I had your potency,
And you were Isabel! should it then be thus?
No; I would tell what 'twere to be a judge,
And what a prisoner.
Lucio. [*Aside to* ISABELLA] Ay, touch him; there's the vein.
Ang. Your brother is a forfeit of the law.
And you but waste your words.
Isab. Alas, alas!
Why, all the souls that were were forfeit once;
And He that might the vantage best have took
Found out the remedy. How would you be,
If He, which is the top of judgement, should
But judge you as you are? O, think on that;
And mercy then will breathe within your lips,
Like man new made.
Ang. Be you content, fair maid;
It is the law, not I, condemn your brother.
Were he my kinsman, brother, or my son,
It should be thus with him. He must die to-morrow.
Isab. To-morrow! O, that's sudden! Spare him, spare him!
He's not prepared for death. Even for our kitchens
We kill the fowl of season. Shall we serve Heaven
With less respect than we do minister

To our gross selves? Good, good my lord, bethink you;
Who is it that hath died for this offence?
There's many have committed it.

Lucio. [*Aside to* ISABELLA] Ay, well said.

Ang. The law hath not been dead, though it hath slept.
Those many had not dared to do that evil,
If the first that did the edict infringe
Had answer'd for his deed. Now 'tis awake,
Takes note of what is done; and, like a prophet,
Looks in a glass that shows what future evils,
Either new, or by remissness new-conceived,
And so in progress to be hatch'd and born,
Are now to have no successive degrees,
But, ere they live, to end.

Isab. Yet show some pity.

Ang. I show it most of all when I show justice;
For then I pity those I do not know,
Which a dismiss'd offence would after gall;
And do him right that, answering one foul wrong,
Lives not to act another. Be satisfied;
Your brother dies to-morrow; be content.

Isab. So you must be the first that gives this sentence,
And he, that suffers. O, it is excellent
To have a giant's strength; but it is tyrannous
To use it like a giant.

Lucio. [*Aside to* ISABELLA] That's well said.

Isab. Could great men thunder
As Jove himself does, Jove would ne'er be quiet,
For every pelting, petty officer
Would use his heaven for thunder;
Nothing but thunder! Merciful Heaven,
Thou rather with thy sharp and sulphurous bolt
Split'st the unwedgeable and gnarled oak
Than the soft myrtle; but man, proud man,
Drest in a little brief authority,
Most ignorant of what he's most assured,
His glassy essence, like an angry ape,
Plays such fantastic tricks before high heaven
As make the angels weep; who, with our spleens,
Would all themselves laugh mortal.

Lucio. [*Aside to* ISABELLA] O, to him, to him, wench! he will relent;
He's coming; I perceive't.

Prov. [*Aside*] Pray heaven she win him!

Isab. We cannot weigh our brother with ourself.
Great men may jest with saints; 'tis wit in them,
But in the less foul profanation.

Lucio [*Aside.*] Thou'rt i' the right girl; more o' that.

Isab. That in the captain's but a choleric word,
Which in the soldier is flat blasphemy.

Lucio. [*Aside to* ISABELLA.] Art avised o' that? more on't.

Ang. Why do you put these sayings upon me?

Isab. Because authority, though it err like others,
Hath yet a kind of medicine in itself
That skins the vice o' the top. Go to your bosom;
Knock there, and ask your heart what it doth know
That's like my brother's fault. If it confess
A natural guiltiness such as is his,
Let it not sound a thought upon your tongue
Against my brother's life.

Ang. [*Aside*] She speaks, and 'tis
Such sense that my sense breeds with it. Fare you well.

Isab. Gentle my lord, turn back.

Ang. I will bethink me. Come again to-morrow.

Isab. Hark how I'll bribe you. Good my lord, turn back.

Ang. How! bribe me?

Isab. Ay, with such gifts that heaven shall share with you.

Lucio. [*Aside to* ISABELLA] You had marr'd all else.

Isab. Not with fond shekels of the tested gold,
Or stones whose rates are either rich or poor
As fancy values them; but with true prayers
That shall be up at heaven and enter there
Ere sun-rise, prayers from preserved souls,
From fasting maids whose minds are dedicate
To nothing temporal.

Ang. Well; come to me to-morrow.

Lucio. [*Aside to* ISABELLA] Go to; 'tis well; away!

Isab. Heaven keep your honour safe!

Ang. [*Aside*] Amen.
For I am that way going to temptation,
Where prayers cross.

Isab. At what hour to-morrow
Shall I attend your lordship?

Ang. At any time 'fore noon.

Isab. 'Save your honour!

[*Exeunt* ISABELLA, LUCIO, *and* PROVOST.

Ang. From thee, even from thy virtue!
What's this, what's this? Is this her fault or mine?
The tempter or the tempted, who sins most?
Ha!
Not she; nor doth she tempt; but it is I
That, lying by the violet in the sun,
Do as the carrion does, not as the flower,
Corrupt with virtuous season. Can it be
That modesty may more betray our sense
Than woman's lightness? Having waste ground enough,
Shall we desire to raze the sanctuary
And pitch our evils there? O, fie, fie, fie!

What dost thou, or what art thou, Angelo?
Dost thou desire her foully for those things
That make her good? O, let her brother live!
Thieves for their robbery have authority
When judges steal themselves. What, do I love her,
That I desire to hear her speak again,
And feast upon her eyes? What is't I dream on?
O cunning enemy, that, to catch a saint,
With saints dost bait thy hook! Most dangerous
Is that temptation that doth goad us on
To sin in loving virtue. Never could the strumpet,
With all her double vigour, art and nature,
Once stir my temper; but this virtuous maid
Subdues me quite. Ever till now,
When men were fond, I smiled and wonder'd how. [*Exit.*

SCENE III. *A room in a prison*

Enter, severally, DUKE *disguised as a friar, and* PROVOST.

Duke. Hail to you, Provost! so I think you are.
Prov. I am the Provost. What's your will, good friar?
Duke. Bound by my charity and my blest order,
I come to visit the afflicted spirits
Here in the prison. Do me the common right
To let me see them and to make me know
The nature of their crimes, that I may minister
To them accordingly.
Prov. I would do more than that, If more were needful.

Enter JULIET.

Look, here comes one; a gentlewoman of mine,
Who, falling in the flaws of her own youth,
Hath blister'd her report. She is with child;
And he that got it, sentenced; a young man
More fit to do another such offence
Than die for this.
Duke. When must he die?
Prov. As I do think, to-morrow.
I have provided for you: stay awhile, [*To* JULIET.
And you shall be conducted.
Duke. Repent you, fair one, of the sin you carry?
Jul. I do; and bear the shame most patiently.
Duke. I'll teach you how you shall arraign your conscience,
And try your penitence, if it be sound,
Or hollowly put on.
Jul. I'll gladly learn.
Duke. Love you the man that wrong'd you
Jul. Yes, as I love the woman that wrong'd him.
Duke. So then it seems your most offenceful act
Was mutually committed?
Jul. Mutually.
Duke. Then was your sin of heavier kind than his.
Jul. I do confess it, and repent it, father.
Duke. 'Tis meet so, daughter; but lest you do repent,
As that the sin hath brought you to this shame,
Which sorrow is always toward ourselves, not heaven,
Showing we would not spare heaven as we love it,
But as we stand in fear—
Jul. I do repent me, as it is an evil,
And take the shame with joy.
Duke. There rest.
Your partner, as I hear, must die to-morrow,
And I am going with instruction to him.
Grace go with you, *Benedicite!* [*Exit.*
Jul. Must die to-morrow! O injurious love,
That respites me a life whose very comfort
Is still a dying horror!
Prov. 'Tis pity of him. [*Exeunt.*

SCENE IV. *A room in Angelo's house.*

Enter ANGELO.

Ang. When I would pray and think, I think and pray
To several subjects. Heaven hath my empty words;
Whilst my invention, hearing not my tongue,
Anchors on Isabel; Heaven in my mouth,
As if I did but only chew his name;
And in my heart the strong and swelling evil
Of my conception. The state, whereon I studied,
Is like a good thing, being often read,
Grown fear'd and tedious; yea, my gravity,
Wherein—let no man hear me—I take pride,
Could I with boot change for an idle plume,
Which the air beats for vain. O place, O form,
How often dost thou with thy case, thy habit,
Wrench awe from fools and tie the wiser souls
To thy false seeming! Blood, thou art blood.
Let's write good angel on the devil's horn;
'Tis not the devil's crest.

Enter a SERVANT.

How now! who's there?
Serv. One Isabel, a sister, desires access to you.
Ang. Teach her the way. [*Exit* SERVANT] O heavens!
Why does my blood thus muster to my heart,
Making both it unable for itself,
And dispossessing all my other parts
Of necessary fitness?
So play the foolish throngs with one that swoons;
Come all to help him, and so stop the air

By which he should revive; and even so
The general, subject to a well-wish'd king,
Quit their own part, and in obsequious fondness
Crowd to his presence, where their untaught love
Must needs appear offence.

Enter ISABELLA.

How now, fair maid?
Isab. I am come to know your pleasure.
Ang. That you might know it, would much better please me
Than to demand what 'tis. Your brother cannot live.
Isab. Even so. Heaven keep your honour!
Ang. Yet may he live awhile; and, it may be,
As long as you or I. Yet he must die.
Isab. Under your sentence?
Ang. Yea.
Isab. When, I beseech you? that in his reprieve,
Longer or shorter, he may be so fitted
That his soul sicken not.
Ang. Ha! fie, these filthy vices! It were as good
To pardon him that hath from nature stolen
A man already made, as to remit
Their saucy sweetness that do coin heaven's image
In stamps that are forbid. 'Tis all as easy
Falsely to take away a life true made
As to put metal in restrained means
To make a false one.
Isab. 'Tis set down so in heaven, but not in earth.
Ang. Say you so? then I shall pose you quickly.
Which had you rather, that the most just law
Now took your brother's life; or, to redeem him,
Give up your body to such sweet uncleanness
As she that he hath stain'd?
Isab. Sir, believe this,
I had rather give my body than my soul.
Ang. I talk not of your soul. Our compell'd sins
Stand more for number than for accompt.
Isab. How say you?
Ang. Nay, I'll not warrant that; for I can speak
Against the thing I say. Answer to this:
I, now the voice of the recorded law,
Pronounce a sentence on your brother's life.
Might there not be a charity in sin
To save this brother's life?
Isab. Please you to do't,
I'll take it as a peril to my soul,
It is no sin at all, but charity.
Ang. Pleased you to do't at peril of your soul,
Were equal poise of sin and charity.
Isab. That I do beg his life, if it be sin,
Heaven let me bear it! you granting of my suit,
If that be sin, I'll make it my morn prayer
To have it added to the faults of mine,
And nothing of your answer.
Ang. Nay, but hear me.
Your sense pursues not mine. Either you are ignorant,
Or seem so craftily; and that's not good.
Isab. Let me be ignorant, and in nothing good,
But graciously to know I am no better.
Ang. Thus wisdom wishes to appear most bright
When it doth tax itself; as these black masks
Proclaim an enshield beauty ten times louder
Than beauty could, display'd. But mark me;
To be received plain, I'll speak more gross.
Your brother is to die.
Isab. So.
Ang. And his offence is so, as it appears,
Accountant to the law upon that pain.
Isab. True.
Ang. Admit no other way to save his life—
As I subscribe not that, nor any other,
But in the loss of question—that you, his sister,
Finding yourself desired of such a person,
Whose credit with the judge, or own great place,
Could fetch your brother from the manacles
Of the all-building law; and that there were
No earthly mean to save him, but that either
You must lay down the treasures of your body
To this supposed, or else to let him suffer;
What would you do?
Isab. As much for my poor brother as myself:
That is, were I under the terms of death,
The impression of keen whips I'd wear as rubies,
And strip myself to death, as to a bed
That longing have been sick for, ere I'd yield
My body up to shame.
Ang. Then must your brother die.
Isab. And 'twere the cheaper way.
Better it were a brother died at once,
Than that a sister, by redeeming him,
Should die for ever.
Ang. Were not you then as cruel as the sentence
That you have slander'd so?
Isab. Ignomy in ransom and free pardon
Are of two houses. Lawful mercy
Is nothing kin to foul redemption.
Ang. You seem'd of late to make the law a tyrant;
And rather proved the sliding of your brother
A merriment than a vice.
Isab. O, pardon me, my lord; it oft falls out,
To have what we would have, we speak not what we mean.
I something do excuse the thing I hate,
For his advantage that I dearly love.
Ang. We are all frail.

Isab. Else let my brother die,
If not a fedary, but only he
Owe and succeed thy weakness.
Ang. Nay, women are frail too.
Isab. Ay, as the glasses where they view themselves;
Which are as easy broke as they make forms.
Women! Help Heaven! men their creation mar
In profiting by them. Nay, call us ten times frail
For we are soft as our complexions are,
And credulous to false prints.
Ang. I think it well;
And from this testimony of your own sex—
Since I suppose we are made to be no stronger
Than faults may shake our frames—let me be bold;
I do arrest your words. Be that you are,
That is, a woman; if you be more, you're none;
If you be one, as you are well express'd
By all external warrants, show it now,
By putting on the destined livery.
Isab. I have no tongue but one; gentle my lord,
Let me entreat you speak the former language.
Ang. Plainly conceive, I love you.
Isab. My brother did love Juliet,
And you tell me that he shall die for it.
Ang. He shall not, Isabel, if you give me love.
Isab. I know your virtue hath a license in't,
Which seems a little fouler than it is,
To pluck on others.
Ang. Believe me, on mine honour,
My words express my purpose.
Isab. Ha! little honour to be much believed,
And most pernicious purpose! Seeming, seeming!
I will proclaim thee, Angelo; look for't.
Sign me a present pardon for my brother,
Or with an outstretch'd throat I'll tell the world aloud
What man thou art.
Ang. Who will believe thee, Isabel?
My unsoil'd name, the austereness of my life,
My vouch against you, and my place i' the state,
Will so your accusation overweigh,
That you shall stifle in your own report
And smell of calumny. I have begun,
And now I give my sensual race the rein.
Fit thy consent to my sharp appetite;
Lay by all nicety and prolixious blushes,
That banish what they sue for; redeem thy brother
By yielding up thy body to my will;
Or else he must not only die the death,
But thy unkindness shall his death draw out
To lingering sufferance. Answer me to-morrow,
Or, by the affection that now guides me most,
I'll prove a tyrant to him. As for you,
Say what you can, my false o'erweighs your true. [*Exit.*
Isab. To whom should I complain? Did I tell this,
Who would believe me? O perilous mouths,
That bear in them one and the self-same tongue,
Either of condemnation or approof;
Bidding the law make court'sy to their will;
Hooking both right and wrong to the appetite,
To follow as it draws! I'll to my brother:
Though he hath fall'n by prompture of the blood,
Yet hath he in him such a mind of honour
That, had he twenty heads to tender down
On twenty bloody blocks, he'ld yield them up,
Before his sister should her body stoop
To such abhorr'd pollution.
Then, Isabel, live chaste, and, brother, die;
More than our brother is our chastity.
I'll tell him yet of Angelo's request,
And fit his mind to death, for his soul's rest.
[*Exit.*

ACT III

Scene i. *A room in the prison*

Enter DUKE *disguised as before,* CLAUDIO, *and* PROVOST.

Duke. So then you hope of pardon from Lord Angelo?
Claud. The miserable have no other medicine
But only hope.
I've hope to live, and am prepared to die.
Duke. Be absolute for death; either death or life
Shall thereby be the sweeter. Reason thus with life:
If I do lose thee, I do lose a thing
That none but fools would keep. A breath thou art,
Servile to all the skyey influences,
That dost this habitation, where thou keep'st,
Hourly afflict. Merely, thou art Death's fool;
For him thou labour'st by thy flight to shun
And yet runn'st toward him still. Thou art not noble;
For all the accommodations that thou bear'st
Are nursed by baseness. Thou'rt by no means valiant;
For thou dost fear the soft and tender fork
Of a poor worm. Thy best of rest is sleep,
And that thou oft provokest; yet grossly fear'st
Thy death, which is no more. Thou art not thyself;
For thou exist'st on many a thousand grains

That issue out of dust. Happy thou art not;
For what thou hast not, still thou strivest to get,
And what thou hast, forget'st. Thou are not certain;
For thy complexion shifts to strange effects,
After the moon. If thou art rich, thou'rt poor;
For, like an ass whose back with ingots bows,
Thou bear'st thy heavy riches but a journey,
And death unloads thee. Friend hast thou none;
For thine own bowels, which do call thee sire,
The mere effusion of thy proper loins,
Do curse the gout, serpigo, and the rheum,
For ending thee no sooner. Thou hast nor youth nor age,
But, as it were, an after-dinner's sleep,
Dreaming on both; for all thy blessed youth
Becomes as aged, and doth beg the alms
Of palsied eld; and when thou art old and rich,
Thou hast neither heat, affection, limb, nor beauty,
To make thy riches pleasant. What's yet in this
That bears the name of life? Yet in this life
Lie hid moe thousand deaths; yet death we fear,
That makes these odds all even.

Claud. I humbly thank you.
To sue to live, I find I seek to die;
And, seeking death, find life. Let it come on.

Isab. [*Within*] What, ho! Peace here, grace and good company!

Prov. Who's there? come in. The wish deserves a welcome.

Duke. Dear sir, ere long I'll visit you again.

Claud. Most holy sir, I thank you.

Enter ISABELLA.

Isab. My business is a word or two with Claudio.

Prov. And very welcome. Look, signior, here's your sister.

Duke. Provost, a word with you.

Prov. As many as you please.

Duke. Bring me to hear them speak, where I may be concealed. [*Exeunt* DUKE *and* PROVOST.

Claud. Now, sister, what s the comfort?

Isab. Why,
As all comforts are; most good, most good indeed.
Lord Angelo, having affairs to heaven,
Intends you for his swift ambassador,
Where you shall be an everlasting leiger;
Therefore your best appointment make with speed;
To-morrow you set on.

Claud. Is there no remedy?

Isab. None, but such remedy as, to save a head,
To cleave a heart in twain.

Claud. But is there any?

Isab. Yes, brother, you may live.
There is a devilish mercy in the judge,
If you'll implore it, that will free your life,
But fetter you till death.

Claud. Perpetual durance?

Isab. Ay, just; perpetual durance, a restraint,
Though all the world's vastidity you had,
To a determined scope.

Claud. But in what nature?

Isab. In such a one as, you consenting to't,
Would bark your honour from that trunk you bear,
And leave you naked.

Claud. Let me know the point.

Isab. O, I do fear thee, Claudio; and I quake,
Lest thou a feverous life shouldst entertain,
And six or seven winters more respect
Than a perpetual honour. Darest thou die?
The sense of death is most in apprehension;
And the poor beetle that we tread upon,
In corporal sufferance finds a pang as great
As when a giant dies

Claud. Why give you me this shame?
Think you I can a resolution fetch
From flowery tenderness? If I must die,
I will encounter darkness as a bride,
And hug it in mine arms.

Isab. There spake my brother; there my father's grave
Did utter forth a voice. Yes, thou must die.
Thou art too noble to conserve a life
In base appliances. This outward-sainted deputy,
Whose settled visage and deliberate word
Nips youth i' the head and follies doth emmew
As falcon doth the fowl, is yet a devil;
His filth within being cast, he would appear
A pond as deep as hell.

Claud. The prenzie Angelo!

Isab. O, 'tis the cunning livery of hell,
The damned'st body to invest and cover
In prenzie guards! Dost thou think, Claudio?
If I would yield him my virginity,
Thou mightst be freed.

Claud. O heavens! it cannot be.

Isab. Yes, he would give't thee, from this rank offence,
So to offend him still. This night's the time
That I should do what I abhor to name,
Or else thou diest to-morrow.

Claud. Thou shalt not do't.

Isab. O, were it but my life,
I' throw it down for your deliverance
As frankly as a pin.

Claud. Thanks, dear Isabel.

Isab. Be ready, Claudio, for your death to-morrow.

Claud. Yes. Has he affections in him,
That thus can make him bite the law by the nose,
When he would force it? Sure, it is no sin;
Or of the deadly seven it is the least.

Isab. Which is the least?

Claud. If it were damnable, he being so wise,
Why would he for the momentary trick
Be perdurably fined? O Isabel!

Isab. What says my brother?

Claud. Death is a fearful thing.

Isab. And shamed life a hateful.

Claud. Ay, but to die, and go we know not where;
To lie in cold obstruction and to rot;
This sensible warm motion to become
A kneaded clod; and the delighted spirit
To bathe in fiery floods, or to reside
In thrilling region of thick-ribbed ice;
To be imprison'd in the viewless winds,
And blown with restless violence round about
The pendent world; or to be worse than worst
Of those that lawless and incertain thought
Imagine howling; 'tis too horrible!
The weariest and most loathed worldly life
That age, ache, penury, and imprisonment
Can lay on nature is a paradise
To what we fear of death.

Isab. Alas, alas!

Claud. Sweet sister, let me live.
What sin you do to save a brother's life,
Nature dispenses with the deed so far
That it becomes a virtue.

Isab. O you beast!
O faithless coward! O dishonest wretch!
Wilt thou be made a man out of my vice?
Is't not a kind of incest, to take life
From thine own sister's shame? What should I think?
Heaven shield my mother play'd my father fair!
For such a warped slip of wilderness
Ne'er issued from his blood. Take my defiance!
Die, perish! Might but my bending down
Reprieve thee from thy fate, it should proceed.
I'll pray a thousand prayers for thy death,
No word to save thee.

Claud. Nay, hear me, Isabel.

Isab. O, fie, fie, fie!
Thy sin's not accidental, but a trade.
Mercy to thee would prove itself a bawd.
'Tis best that thou diest quickly.

Claud. O hear me, Isabella!

Re-enter DUKE.

Duke. Vouchsafe a word, young sister, but one word.

Isab. What is your will?

Duke. Might you dispense with your leisure,
I would by and by have some speech with you. The satisfaction I would require is likewise your own benefit.

Isab. I have no superfluous leisure; my stay must be stolen out of other affairs; but I will attend you awhile. [*Walks apart*.

Duke. Son, I have overheard what hath passed between you and your sister. Angelo had never the purpose to corrupt her; only he hath made an assay of her virtue to practise his judgement with the disposition of natures. She, having the truth of honour in her, hath made him that gracious denial which he is most glad to receive. I am confessor to Angelo, and I know this to be true; therefore prepare yourself to death. Do not satisfy your resolution with hopes that are fallible; to-morrow you must die; go to your knees and make ready.

Claud. Let me ask my sister pardon. I am so out of love with life that I will sue to be rid of it.

Duke. Hold you there! Farewell. [*Exit Claudio*.] Provost, a word with you!

Re-enter PROVOST.

Prov. What's your will, father?

Duke. That now you are come, you will be gone. Leave me awhile with the maid. My mind promises with my habit no loss shall touch her by my company.

Prov. In good time.

[*Exit* PROVOST. ISABELLA *comes forward*.

Duke. The hand that hath made you fair hath made you good; the goodness that is cheap in beauty makes beauty brief in goodness; but grace, being the soul of your complexion, shall keep the body of it ever fair. The assault that Angelo hath made to you, fortune hath conveyed to my understanding; and, but that frailty hath examples for his falling, I should wonder at Angelo. How will you do to content this substitute, and to save your brother?

Isab. I am now going to resolve him. I had rather my brother die by the law than my son should be unlawfully born. But, O, how much is the good Duke deceived in Angelo! If ever he return and I can speak to him, I will open my lips in vain, or discover his government.

Duke. That shall not be much amiss; yet, as the matter now stands, he will avoid your accusation; he made trial of you only. Therefore fasten your ear on my advisings. To the love I have in doing good a remedy presents itself. I do make myself believe that you may most uprighteously do a poor wronged lady a merited benefit; redeem your brother from the angry law; do no stain to your own gracious person; and much please the absent Duke, if peradventure he shall ever return to have hearing of this business.

Isab. Let me hear you speak farther. I have spirit to do anything that appears not foul in the truth of my spirit.

Duke. Virtue is bold, and goodness never fearful. Have you not heard speak of Mariana, the sister of Frederick the great soldier who miscarried at sea?

Isab. I have heard of the lady, and good words went with her name.

Duke. She should this Angelo have married; was affianced to her by oath, and the nuptial appointed; between which time of the contract and limit of the solemnity, her brother Frederick was wrecked at sea, having in that perished vessel the dowry of his sister. But mark how heavily this befell to the poor gentlewoman. There she lost a noble and renowned brother, in his love toward her ever most kind and natural; with him, the portion and sinew of her fortune, her marriage dowry; with both, her combinate husband, this well-seeming Angelo.

Isab. Can this be so? did Angelo so leave her?

Duke. Left her in her tears, and dried not one of them with his comfort; swallowed his vows whole, pretending in her discoveries of dishonour; in few, bestowed her on her own lamentation, which she yet wears for his sake; and he, a marble to her tears, is washed with them, but relents not.

Isab. What a merit were it in death to take this poor maid from the world! What corruption in this life, that it will let this man live! But how out of this can she avail?

Duke. It is a rupture that you may easily heal; and the cure of it not only saves your brother, but keeps you from dishonour in doing it.

Isab. Show me how, good father.

Duke. This forenamed maid hath yet in her the countinuance of her first affection; his unjust unkindness, that in all reason should have quenched her love, hath, like an impediment in the current, made it more violent and unruly. Go you to Angelo; answer his requiring with a plausible obedience; agree with his demands to the point; only refer yourself to this advantage, first, that your stay with him may not be long; that the time may have all shadow and silence in it; and the place answer to convenience. This being granted in course—and now follows all—we shall advise this wronged maid to stead up your appointment, go in your place; if the encounter acknowledge itself hereafter, it may compel him to her recompense: and here, by this, is your brother saved, your honour untainted, the poor Mariana advantaged, and the corrupt deputy scaled. The maid will I frame and make fit for his attempt. If you think well to carry this as you may, the doubleness of the benefit defends the deceit from reproof. What think you of it?

Isab. The image of it gives me content already; and I trust it will grow to a most prosperous perfection.

Duke. It lies much in your holding up. Haste you speedily to Angelo. If for this night he entreat you to his bed, give him promise of satisfaction. I will presently to Saint Luke's; there, at the moated grange, resides this dejected Mariana. At that place call upon me; and dispatch with Angelo, that it may be quickly.

Isab. I thank you for this comfort. Fare you well, good father. [*Exeunt severally.*

SCENE II. *The street before the prison.*

Enter, on one side, DUKE *disguised as before; on the other,* ELBOW, *and Officers with* POMPEY.

Elb. Nay, if there be no remedy for it, but that you will needs buy and sell men and women like beasts, we shall have all the world drink brown and white bastard.

Duke. O heavens! what stuff is here?

Pom. 'Twas never merry world since, of two usuries, the merriest was put down, and the worser allowed by order of law a furred gown to keep him warm; and furred with fox and lambskins too, to signify, that craft, being richer than innocency, stands for the facing.

Elb. Come your way, sir. 'Bless you, good father friar.

Duke. And you, good brother father. What offence hath this man made you, sir?

Elb. Marry, sir, he hath offended the law; and, sir, we take him to be a thief too, sir; for we have found upon him, sir, a strange picklock, which we have sent to the deputy.

Duke. Fie, sirrah! a bawd, a wicked bawd!
The evil that thou causest to be done,
That is thy means to live. Do thou but think
What 'tis to cram a maw or clothe a back
From such a filthy vice; say to thyself,
From their abominable and beastly touches
I drink, I eat, array myself, and live.
Canst thou believe thy living is a life,
So stinkingly depending? Go mend, go mend.

Pom. Indeed, it does stink in some sort, sir; but yet, sir, I would prove—

Duke. Nay, if the devil have given thee proofs for sin,
Thou wilt prove his. Take him to prison, officer.
Correction and instruction must both work
Ere this rude beast will profit.

Elb. He must before the deputy, sir; he has given him warning. The deputy cannot abide a whoremaster. If he be a whoremonger, and comes before him, he were as good go a mile on his errand.

Duke. That we were all, as some would seem to be,
From our faults, as faults from seeming, free!

Elb. His neck will come to your waist—a cord, sir.

Pom. I spy comfort; I cry bail. Here's a gentleman and a friend of mine.

Enter LUCIO.

Lucio. How now, noble Pompey! What, at the wheels of Cæsar? art thou led in triumph? What, is there none of Pygmalion's images, newly made woman, to be had now, for putting the hand in the pocket and extracting it clutched? What reply, ha? What sayest thou to this tune, matter and method? Is't not drowned i' the last rain, ha? What sayest thou, Trot? Is the world as it was, man? Which is the way? Is it sad, and few words? or how? The trick of it?

Duke. Still thus, and thus; still worse!

Lucio. How doth my dear morsel, thy mistress? Procures she still, ha?

Pom. Troth, sir, she hath eaten up all her beef, and she is herself in the tub.

Lucio. Why, 'tis good; it is the right of it; it must be so. Ever your fresh whore and your powdered bawd; an unshunned consequence; it must be so. Art going to prison, Pompey?

Pom. Yes, faith, sir.

Lucio. Why, 'tis not amiss, Pompey. Farewell. Go say I sent thee thither. For debt, Pompey? or how?

Elb. For being a bawd, for being a bawd.

Lucio. Well, then, imprison him. If imprisonment be the due of a bawd, why, 'tis his right. Bawd is he doubtless, and of antiquity too: bawd-born. Farewell, good Pompey. Commend me to the prison, Pompey. You will turn good husband now, Pompey; you will keep the house.

Pom. I hope, sir, your good worship will be my bail.

Lucio. No, indeed, will I not, Pompey; it is not the wear. I will pray, Pompey, to increase your bondage. If you take it not patiently, why, your mettle is the more. Adieu, trusty Pompey. 'Bless you, friar.

Duke. And you.

Lucio. Does Bridget paint still, Pompey, ha?

Elb. Come your ways, sir; come.

Pom. You will not bail me, then, sir?

Lucio. Then, Pompey, nor now. What news abroad, friar? what news?

Elb. Come your ways, sir; come.

Lucio. Go to kennel, Pompey; go. [*Exeunt* ELBOW, POMPEY *and Officers*.] What news, friar, of the Duke?

Duke. I know none. Can you tell me of any?

Lucio. Some say he is with the Emperor of Russia; other some, he is in Rome: but where is he, think you?

Duke. I know not where; but wheresoever, I wish him well.

Lucio. It was a mad fantastical trick of him to steal from the state, and usurp the beggary he was never born to. Lord Angelo dukes it well in his absence; he puts transgression to't.

Duke. He does well in't.

Lucio. A little more lenity to lechery would do no harm in him; something too crabbed that way, friar.

Duke. It is too general a vice, and severity must cure it.

Lucio. Yes, in good sooth, the vice is of a great kindred; it is well allied; but it is impossible to extirp it quite, friar, till eating and drinking be put down. They say this Angelo was not made by man and woman after this downright way of creation. Is it true, think you?

Duke. How should he be made, then?

Lucio. Some report a sea-maid spawned him; some, that he was begot between two stock-fishes. But it is certain that when he makes water his urine is congealed ice; that I know to be true: and he is a motion generative; that's infallible.

Duke. You are pleasant, sir, and speak apace.

Lucio. Why, what a ruthless thing is this in him, for the rebellion of a codpiece to take away the life of a man! Would the Duke that is absent have done this? Ere he would have hanged a man for the getting a hundred bastards, he would have paid for the nursing a thousand. He had some feeling of the sport; he knew the service, and that instructed him to mercy.

Duke. I never heard the absent Duke much detected for women; he was not inclined that way.

Lucio. O, sir, you are deceived.

Duke. 'Tis not possible.

Lucio. Who, not the Duke? yes, your beggar of fifty; and his use was to put a ducat in her clack-dish. The Duke had crotchets in him. He would be drunk too; that let me inform you.

Duke. You do him wrong, surely.

Lucio. Sir, I was an inward of his. A shy fellow was the Duke; and I believe I know the cause of his withdrawing.

Duke. What, I prithee, might be the cause?

Lucio. No, pardon; 'tis a secret must be locked within the teeth and the lips. But this I can let you understand, the greater file of the subject held the Duke to be wise.

Duke. Wise! why, no question but he was.

Lucio. A very superficial, ignorant, unweighing fellow.

Duke. Either this is envy in you, folly, or mistaking. The very stream of his life and the business he hath helmed must upon a warranted need give him a better proclamation. Let him be but testimonied in his own bringings-forth, and he shall appear to the envious a scholar, a statesman, and a soldier. Therefore you speak unskilfully; or if your knowledge be more it is much darkened in your malice.

Lucio. Sir, I know him, and I love him.

Duke. Love talks with better knowledge, and knowledge with dearer love.

Lucio. Come, sir, I know what I know.

Duke. I can hardly believe that, since you know not what you speak. But, if ever the Duke return, as our prayers are he may, let me desire you to make your answer before him. If it be honest you have spoke, you have courage to maintain it. I am bound to call upon you; and, I pray you, your name?

Lucio. Sir, my name is Lucio; well known to the Duke.

Duke. He shall know you better, sir, if I may live to report you.

Lucio. I fear you not.

Duke. O, you hope the Duke will return no more; or you imagine me too unhurtful an opposite. But indeed I can do you little harm; you'll forswear this again.

Lucio. I'll be hanged first. Thou art deceived in me, friar. But no more of this. Canst thou tell if Claudio die to-morrow or no?

Duke. Why should he die, sir?

Lucio. Why? For filling a bottle with a tundish. I would the Duke we talk of were returned again. This ungenitured agent will unpeople the province with continency; sparrows must not build in his house-eaves, because they are lecherous. The Duke yet would have dark deeds darkly answered; he would never bring them to light. Would he were returned! Marry, this Claudio is condemned for untrussing. Farewell, good friar; I prithee, pray for me. The Duke, I say to thee again, would eat mutton on Fridays. He's not past it yet, and I say to thee, he would mouth with a beggar, though she smelt brown bread and garlic. Say that I said so. Farewell. [*Exit*.

Duke. No might nor greatness in mortality
Can censure 'scape; back-wounding calumny
The whitest virtue strikes. What king so strong
Can tie the gall up in the slanderous tongue?
But who comes here?

Enter ESCALUS, PROVOST, *and Officers with* MISTRESS OVERDONE.

Escal. Go; away with her to prison!

Mrs Ov. Good my lord, be good to me; your honour is accounted a merciful man; good my lord.

Escal. Double and treble admonition, and still forfeit in the same kind! This would make mercy swear and play the tyrant.

Prov. A bawd of eleven years' continuance, may it please your honour.

Mrs Ov. My lord, this is one Lucio's information against me. Mistress Kate Keepdown was with child by him in the Duke's time; he promised her marriage. His child is a year and a quarter old, come Philip and Jacob. I have kept it myself; and see how he goes about to abuse me!

Escal. That fellow is a fellow of much license. Let him be called before us. Away with her to prison! Go to; no more words. [*Exeunt Officers with* MISTRESS OVERDONE] Provost, my brother Angelo will not be altered; Claudio must die to-morrow. Let him be furnished with divines, and have all charitable preparation. If my brother wrought by my pity, it should not be so with him.

Prov. So please you, this friar hath been with him, and advised him for the entertainment of death.

Escal. Good even, good father.

Duke. Bliss and goodness on you!

Escal. Of whence are you?

Duke. Not of this country, though my chance is now
To use it for my time. I am a brother
Of gracious order, late come from the See
In special business from his Holiness.

Escal. What news abroad i' the world?

Duke. None, but that there is so great a fever on goodness that the dissolution of it must cure it. Novelty is only in request; and it is as dangerous to be aged in any kind of course, as it is virtuous to be constant in any undertaking. There is scarce truth enough alive to make societies secure; but security enough to make fellowships accurst. Much upon this riddle runs the wisdom of the world. This news is old enough, yet it is every day's news. I pray you, sir, of what disposition was the Duke?

Escal. One that, above all other strifes, contended especially to know himself.

Duke. What pleasure was he given to?

Escal. Rather rejoicing to see another merry, than merry at anything which professed to make him rejoice; a gentleman of all temperance. But leave we him to his events, with a prayer they may prove prosperous; and let me desire to know how you find Claudio prepared. I am made to understand that you have lent him visitation.

Duke. He professes to have received no sinister measure from his judge, but most willingly humbles himself to the determination of justice; yet had he framed to himself, by the instruction of his frailty, many deceiving promises of life; which I by my good leisure have discredited to him, and now is he resolved to die.

Escal. You have paid the heavens your function, and the prisoner the very debt of your calling. I have laboured for the poor gentleman to the extremest shore of my modesty; but my brother justice have I found so severe that he hath forced me to tell him he is indeed Justice.

Duke. If his own life answer the straitness of his proceeding, it shall become him well; wherein if he chance to fail, he hath sentenced himself.

Escal. I am going to visit the prisoner. Fare you well.

Duke. Peace be with you!

[*Exeunt* ESCALUS *and* PROVOST.

He who the sword of heaven will bear
Should be as holy as severe;
Pattern in himself to know,
Grace to stand, and virtue go;
More nor less to others paying
Than by self-offences weighing.
Shame to him whose cruel striking
Kills for faults of his own liking!
Twice treble shame on Angelo,
To weed my vice and let his grow!
O, what may man within him hide,
Though angel on the outward side!
How may likeness made in crimes,
Making practice on the times,
To draw with idle spiders' strings
Most ponderous and substantial things!
Craft against vice I must apply.
With Angelo to-night shall lie
His old betrothed but despised;
So disguise shall, by the disguised,
Pay with falsehood false exacting,
And perform an old contracting. [*Exit*.

ACT IV

SCENE I. *The moated grange at St. Luke's*

Enter MARIANA *and a* BOY.

BOY [*sings*].

"Take, O, take those lips away,
That so sweetly were forsworn;
And those eyes, the break of day,
Lights that do mislead the morn;
But my kisses bring again, bring again;
Seals of love, but seal'd in vain, seal'd in vain."

Mari. Break off thy song, and haste thee quick away:
Here comes a man of comfort, whose advice
Hath often still'd my brawling discontent.

[*Exit* BOY.

Enter DUKE *disguised as before*.

I cry you mercy, sir; and well could wish
You had not found me here so musical.
Let me excuse me, and believe me so,
My mirth it much displeased, but pleased my woe.

Duke. 'Tis good; though music oft hath such a charm
To make bad good, and good provoke to harm.
I pray you, tell me, hath anybody inquired for me here to-day? much upon this time have I promised here to meet.

Mari. You have not been inquired after. I have sat here all day.

Enter ISABELLA.

Duke. I do constantly believe you. The time is come even now. I shall crave your forbearance a little. May be I will call upon you anon, for some advantage to yourself.

Mari. I am always bound to you. [*Exit*.

Duke. Very well met, and well come.
What is the news from this good deputy?

Isab. He hath a garden circummured with brick,
Whose western side is with a vineyard back'd;
And to that vineyard is a planched gate,
That makes his opening with this bigger key.
This other doth command a little door
Which from the vineyard to the garden leads;
There have I made my promise
Upon the heavy middle of the night
To call upon him.

Duke. But shall you on your knowledge find this way?

Isab. I have ta'en a due and wary note upon't.
With whispering and most guilty diligence,
In action all of precept, he did show me
The way twice o'er.

Duke. Are there no other tokens

Between you 'greed concerning her observance?
Isab. No, none, but only a repair i' the dark;
And that I have possess'd him my most stay
Can be but brief; for I have made him know
I have a servant comes with me along,
That stays upon me, whose persuasion is
I come about my brother.
Duke. 'Tis well borne up.
I have not yet made known to Mariana
A word of this. What, ho! within! come forth!

Re-enter MARIANA.

I pray you, be acquainted with this maid;
She comes to do you good.
Isab. I do desire the like.
Duke. Do you persuade yourself that I respect you?
Mari. Good friar, I know you do, and have found it.
Duke. Take, then, this your companion by the hand,
Who hath a story ready for your ear.
I shall attend your leisure; but make haste;
The vaporous night approaches.
Mari. Will't please you walk aside?
[*Exeunt* MARIANA *and* ISABELLA.
Duke. O place and greatness! millions of false eyes
Are stuck upon thee. Volumes of report
Run with these false and most contrarious quests
Upon thy doings; thousand escapes of wit
Make thee the father of their idle dreams
And rack thee in their fancies.

Re-enter MARIANA *and* ISABELLA.

Welcome, how agreed?
Isab. She'll take the enterprise upon her, father,
If you advise it.
Duke. It is not my consent,
But my entreaty too.
Isab. Little have you to say
When you depart from him, but, soft and low,
"Remember now my brother."
Mari. Fear me not.
Duke. Nor, gentle daughter, fear you not at all.
He is your husband on a pre-contract.
To bring you thus together, 'tis no sin,
Sith that the justice of your title to him
Doth flourish the deceit. Come, let us go.
Our corn's to reap, for yet our tithe's to sow.
[*Exeunt.*

SCENE II. *A room in the prison*

Enter PROVOST *and* POMPEY.

Prov. Come hither, sirrah. Can you cut off a man's head?

Pom. If the man be a bachelor, sir, I can; but if he be a married man, he's his wife's head, and I can never cut off a woman's head.

Prov. Come, sir, leave me your snatches, and yield me a direct answer. To-morrow morning are to die Claudio and Barnardine. Here is in our prison a common executioner, who in his office lacks a helper. If you will take it on you to assist him, it shall redeem you from your gyves; if not, you shall have your full time of imprisonment and your deliverance with an unpitied whipping, for you have been a notorious bawd.

Pom. Sir, I have been an unlawful bawd time out of mind; but yet I will be content to be a lawful hangman. I would be glad to receive some instruction from my fellow partner.

Prov. What, ho! Abhorson! Where's Abhorson, there?

Enter ABHORSON.

Abhor. Do you call, sir?

Prov. Sirrah, here's a fellow will help you to-morrow in your execution. If you think it meet, compound with him by the year, and let him abide here with you; if not, use him for the present and dismiss him. He cannot plead his estimation with you; he hath been a bawd.

Abhor. A bawd, sir? fie upon him! he will discredit our mystery.

Prov. Go to, sir; you weigh equally; a feather will turn the scale. [*Exit.*

Pom. Pray, sir, by your good favour—for surely, sir, a good favour you have, but that you have a hanging look—do you call, sir, your occupation a mystery?

Abhor. Ay, sir; a mystery.

Pom. Painting, sir, I have heard say, is a mystery; and your whores, sir, being members of my occupation, using painting, do prove my occupation a mystery; but what mystery there should be in hanging, if I should be hanged, I cannot imagine.

Abhor. Sir, it is a mystery.

Pom. Proof?

Abhor. Every true man's apparel fits your thief. If it be too little for your thief, your true man thinks it big enough; if it be too big for your thief, your thief thinks it little enough; so every true man's apparel fits your thief.

Re-enter PROVOST.

Prov. Are you agreed?

Pom. Sir, I will serve him; for I do find your hangman is a more penitent trade than your bawd; he doth oftener ask forgiveness.

Prov. You, sirrah, provide your block and your axe to-morrow four o'clock.

Abhor. Come on, bawd; I will instruct thee in my trade; follow.

Pom. I do desire to learn, sir; and I hope, if you have occasion to use me for your own turn, you shall find me yare; for truly, sir, for your kindness I owe you a good turn.

Prov. Call hither Barnardine and Claudio:
[*Exeunt* POMPEY *and* ABHORSON.
The one has my pity; not a jot the other,
Being a murderer, though he were my brother.

Enter CLAUDIO.

Look, here's the warrant, Claudio, for thy death.
'Tis now dead midnight, and by eight to-morrow
Thou must be made immortal. Where's Barnardine?

Claud. As fast lock'd up in sleep as guiltless labour
When it lies starkly in the traveller's bones.
He will not wake.

Prov. Who can do good on him?
Well, go, prepare yourself. [*Knocking within.*]
But, hark, what noise?
Heaven give your spirits comfort!
[*Exit* CLAUDIO.]
By and by.
I hope it is some pardon or reprieve
For the most gentle Claudio.

Enter DUKE *disguised as before.*

Welcome, father.

Duke. The best and wholesomest spirits of the night
Envelope you, good Provost! Who call'd here of late?

Prov. None, since the curfew rung.

Duke. Not Isabel?

Prov. No.

Duke. They will, then, ere't be long.

Prov. What comfort is for Claudio?

Duke. There's some in hope.

Prov. It is a bitter deputy.

Duke. Not so, not so; his life is parallel'd
Even with the stroke and line of his great justice.
He doth with holy abstinence subdue
That in himself which he spurs on his power
To qualify in others. Were he meal'd with that
Which he corrects, then were he tyrannous;
But this being so, he's just.
Knocking within.
Now are they come.
[*Exit* PROVOST.
This is a gentle Provost: seldom when
The steeled gaoler is the friend of men.
Knocking within.
How now! what noise? That spirit's possess'd with haste
That wounds the unsisting postern with these strokes.

Re-enter PROVOST.

Prov. There he must stay until the officer
Arise to let him in. He is call'd up.

Duke. Have you no countermand for Claudio yet,
But he must die to-morrow?

Prov. None, sir, none.

Duke. As near the dawning, Provost, as it is,
You shall hear more ere morning.

Prov. Happily
You something know; yet I believe there comes
No countermand; no such example have we.
Besides, upon the very siege of justice
Lord Angelo hath to the public ear
Profess'd the contrary.

Enter a MESSENGER.

This is his lordship's man.

Duke. And here comes Claudio's pardon.

Mes. [*Giving a paper.*] My lord hath sent you this note; and by me this further charge, that you swerve not from the smallest article of it, neither in time, matter, or other circumstance. Good morrow; for, as I take it, it is almost day.

Prov. I shall obey him. [*Exit* MESSENGER.

Duke. [*Aside*] This is his pardon, purchased by such sin
For which the pardoner himself is in.
Hence hath offence his quick celerity,
When it is borne in high authority.
When vice makes mercy, mercy's so extended,
That for the fault's love is the offender friended.
Now, sir, what news?

Prov. I told you. Lord Angelo, belike thinking me remiss in mine office, awakens me with this unwonted putting-on; methinks strangely, for he hath not used it before.

Duke. Pray you, let's hear.

Prov. [*Reads*]
"Whatsoever you may hear to the contrary, let Claudio be executed by four of the clock; and in the afternoon Barnardine. For my better satisfaction, let me have Claudio's head sent me by five. Let this be duly performed; with a thought that more depends on it than we must yet deliver. Thus fail not to do your office, as you will answer it at your peril."
What say you to this, sir?

Duke. What is that Barnardine who is to be executed in the afternoon?

Prov. A Bohemian born, but here nursed up and bred; one that is a prisoner nine years old.

Duke. How came it that the absent Duke had not either delivered him to his liberty or executed him? I have heard it was ever his manner to do so.

Prov. His friends still wrought reprieves for him; and, indeed, his fact, till now in the government of Lord Angelo, came not to an undoubtful proof.

Duke. It is now apparent?

Prov. Most manifest, and not denied by himself.

Duke. Hath he borne himself penitently in prison? how seems he to be touched?

Prov. A man that apprehends death no more dreadfully but as a drunken sleep; careless, reckless, and fearless of what's past, present, or to come; insensible of mortality, and desperately mortal.

Duke. He wants advice.

Prov. He will hear none. He hath evermore had the liberty of the prison; give him leave to escape hence, he would not; drunk many times a day, if not many days entirely drunk. We have very oft awaked him, as if to carry him to execution, and showed him a seeming warrant for it; it hath not moved him at all.

Duke. More of him anon. There is written in your brow, Provost, honesty and constancy. If I read it not truly, my ancient skill beguiles me; but, in the boldness of my cunning, I will lay my self in hazard. Claudio, whom here you have warrant to execute, is no greater forfeit to the law than Angelo who hath sentenced him. To make you understand this in a manifested effect, I crave but four days' respite; for the which you are to do me both a present and a dangerous courtesy.

Prov. Pray, sir, in what?

Duke. In the delaying death.

Prov. Alack, how may I do it, having the hour limited, and an express command, under penalty, to deliver his head in the view of Angelo? I may make my case as Claudio's, to cross this in the smallest.

Duke. By the vow of mine order I warrant you, if my instructions may be your guide. Let this Barnardine be this morning executed, and his head borne to Angelo.

Prov. Angelo hath seen them both, and will discover the favour.

Duke. O, death's a great disguiser; and you may add to it. Shave the head, and tie the beard; and say it was the desire of the penitent to be so bared before his death: you know the course is common. If anything fall to you upon this, more than thanks and good fortune, by the saint whom I profess, I will plead against it with my life.

Prov. Pardon me, good father; it is against my oath.

Duke. Were you sworn to the Duke, or to the deputy?

Prov. To him, and to his substitutes.

Duke. You will think you have made no offence, if the Duke avouch the justice of your dealing?

Prov. But what likelihood is in that?

Duke. Not a resemblance, but a certainty. Yet since I see you fearful, that neither my coat, integrity, nor persuasion can with ease attempt you, I will go further than I meant, to pluck all fears out of you. Look you, sir, here is the hand and seal of the Duke. You know the character, I doubt not; and the signet is not strange to you.

Prov. I know them both.

Duke. The contents of this is the return of the Duke. You shall anon over-read it at your pleasure; where you shall find, within these two days he will be here. This is a thing that Angelo knows not; for he this very day receives letters of strange tenour; perchance of the Duke's death; perchance entering into some monastery; but, by chance, nothing of what is writ. Look, the unfolding star calls up the shepherd. Put not yourself into amazement how these things should be. All difficulties are but easy when they are known. Call your executioner, and off with Barnardine's head. I will give him a present shrift and advise him for a better place. Yet you are amazed; but this shall absolutely resolve you. Come away; it is almost clear dawn. [*Exeunt.*

SCENE III. *Another room in the same*

Enter POMPEY.

Pom. I am as well acquainted here as I was in our house of profession. One would think it were Mistress Overdone's own house, for here be many of her old customers. First, here's young Master Rash; he's in for a commodity of brown paper and old ginger, nine-score and seventeen pounds; of which he made five marks, ready money. Marry, then ginger was not much in request, for the old women were all dead. Then is there here one Master Caper, at the suit of Master Three-pile the mercer, for some four suits of peach-coloured satin, which now peaches him a beggar. Then have we here young Dizy, and young Master Deep-vow, and Master Copper-spur, and Master Starve-lackey the rapier and dagger man, and young Drop-heir that killed lusty Pudding, and Master Forthlight the tilter, and brave Master Shooty the great traveller, and wild Half-can that stabbed Pots, and, I think, forty more; all great doers in our trade, and are now "for the Lord's sake."

Enter ABHORSON.

Abhor. Sirrah, bring Barnardine hither.

Pom. Master Barnardine! you must rise and be hanged, Master Barnardine!

Abhor. What, ho, Barnardine!

Bar. [*Within*] A pox o' your throats! Who makes that noise there? What are you?

Pom. Your friends, sir; the hangman. You must be so good, sir, to rise and be put to death.

Bar. [*Within*] Away, you rogue, away! I am sleepy.

Abhor. Tell him he must awake, and that quickly too.

Pom. Pray, Master Barnardine, awake till you are executed, and sleep afterwards.

Abhor. Go in to him, and fetch him out.

Pom. He is coming, sir, he is coming; I hear his straw rustle.

Abhor. Is the axe upon the block, sirrah?

Pom. Very ready, sir.

Enter BARNARDINE.

Bar. How now, Abhorson? what's the news with you?

Abhor. Truly, sir, I would desire you to clap into your prayers; for, look you, the warrant's come.

Bar. You rogue, I have been drinking all night; I am not fitted for 't.

Pom. O, the better, sir; for he that drinks all night, and is hanged betimes in the morning, may sleep the sounder all the next day.

Enter DUKE *disguised as before*.

Abhor. Look you, sir; here comes your ghostly father. Do we jest now, think you?

Duke. Sir, induced by my charity, and hearing how hastily you are to depart, I am come to advise you, comfort you, and pray with you.

Bar. Friar, not I. I have been drinking hard all night, and I will have more time to prepare me, or they shall beat out my brains with billets. I will not consent to die this day, that's certain.

Duke. O, sir, you must; and therefore I beseech you
Look forward on the journey you shall go.

Bar. I swear I will not die to-day for any man's persuasion.

Duke. But hear you.

Bar. Not a word. If you have anything to say to me, come to my ward; for thence will not I to-day. [*Exit*.

Duke. Unfit to live or die, O gravel heart!
After him, fellows; bring him to the block.
[*Exeunt* ABHORSON *and* POMPEY.

Enter PROVOST.

Prov. Now, sir, how do you find the prisoner?

Duke. A creature unprepared, unmeet for death;
And to transport him in the mind he is
Were damnable.

Prov. Here in the prison, father,
There died this morning of a cruel fever
One Ragozine, a most notorious pirate,
A man of Claudio's years; his beard and head
Just of his colour. What if we do omit
This reprobate till he were well inclined;
And satisfy the deputy with the visage
Of Ragozine, more like to Claudio?

Duke. O, 'tis an accident that heaven provides!
Dispatch it presently; the hour draws on
Prefix'd by Angelo. See this be done,
And sent according to command; whiles I
Persuade this rude wretch willingly to die.

Prov. This shall be done, good father, presently.
But Barnardine must die this afternoon;
And how shall we continue Claudio,
To save me from the danger that might come
If he were known alive?

Duke. Let this be done.
Put them in secret holds, both Barnardine and Claudio.
Ere twice the sun hath made his journal greeting
To the under generation, you shall find
Your safety manifested.

Prov. I am your free dependant.

Duke. Quick, dispatch, and send the head to Angelo. [*Exit* PROVOST.
Now will I write letters to Angelo—
The Provost, he shall bear them—whose contents
Shall witness to him I am near at home,
And that, by great injunctions, I am bound
To enter publicly. Him I'll desire
To meet me at the consecrated fount
A league below the city; and from thence,
By cold gradation and well-balanced form,
We shall proceed with Angelo.

Re-enter PROVOST.

Prov. Here is the head; I'll carry it myself.

Duke. Convenient is it. Make a swift return;
For I would commune with you of such things
That want no ear but yours.

Prov. I'll make all speed. [*Exit*.

Isab. [*Within*] Peace, ho, be here!

Duke. The tongue of Isabel. She's come to know
If yet her brother's pardon be come hither.

But I will keep her ignorant of her good,
To make her heavenly comforts of despair,
When it is least expected.

Enter ISABELLA.

Isab. Ho, by your leave!
Duke. Good morning to you, fair and gracious daughter.
Isab. The better, given me by so holy a man.
Hath yet the deputy sent my brother's pardon?
Duke. He hath released him, Isabel, from the world.
His head is off and sent to Angelo.
Isab. Nay, but it is not so.
Duke. It is no other. Show your wisdom, daughter,
In your patience.
Isab. O, I will to him and pluck out his eyes!
Duke. You shall not be admitted to his sight.
Isab. Unhappy Claudio! wretched Isabel!
Injurious world! most damned Angelo!
Duke. This nor hurts him nor profits you a jot;
Forbear it therefore; give your cause to heaven.
Mark what I say, which you shall find
By every syllable a faithful verity.
The Duke comes home to-morrow; nay, dry your eyes;
One of our convent, and his confessor,
Gives me this instance. Already he hath carried
Notice to Escalus and Angelo,
Who do prepare to meet him at the gates,
There to give up their power. If you can, pace your wisdom
In that good path that I would wish it go,
And you shall have your bosom on this wretch,
Grace of the Duke, revenges to your heart,
And general honour.
Isab. I am directed by you.
Duke. This letter, then, to Friar Peter give;
'Tis that he sent me of the Duke's return.
Say, by this token, I desire his company
At Mariana's house to-night. Her cause and yours
I'll perfect him withal, and he shall bring you
Before the Duke, and to the head of Angelo
Accuse him home and home. For my poor self,
I am combined by a sacred vow
And shall be absent. Wend you with this letter.
Command these fretting waters from your eyes
With a light heart; trust not my holy order,
If I pervert your course. Who's here?

Enter LUCIO.

Lucio. Good even. Friar, where's the Provost?
Duke. Not within, sir.

Lucio. O pretty Isabella, I am pale at mine heart to see thine eyes so red. Thou must be patient. I am fain to dine and sup with water and bran; I dare not for my head fill my belly; one fruitful meal would set me to't. But they say the Duke will be here to-morrow. By my troth, Isabel, I loved thy brother. If the old fantastical Duke of dark corners had been at home, he had lived. [*Exit* ISABELLA.

Duke. Sir, the Duke is marvellous little beholding to your reports; but the best is, he lives not in them.

Lucio. Friar, thou knowest not the Duke so well as I do. He's a better woodman than thou takest him for.

Duke. Well, you'll answer this one day. Fare ye well.

Lucio. Nay, tarry; I'll go along with thee. I can tell thee pretty tales of the Duke.

Duke. You have told me too many of him already, sir, if they be true; if not true, none were enough.

Lucio. I was once before him for getting a wench with child.

Duke. Did you such a thing?

Lucio. Yes, marry, did I; but I was fain to forswear it. They would else have married me to the rotten medlar.

Duke. Sir, your company is fairer than honest. Rest you well.

Lucio. By my troth, I'll go with thee to the lane's end. If bawdy talk offend you, we'll have very little of it. Nay, friar, I am a kind of burr; I shall stick. [*Exeunt.*

SCENE IV. *A room in Angelo's house*

Enter ANGELO *and* ESCALUS.

Escal. Every letter he hath writ hath disvouched other.

Ang. In most uneven and distracted manner. His actions show much like to madness; pray Heaven his wisdom be not tainted! And why meet him at the gates, and redeliver our authorities there?

Escal. I guess not.

Ang. And why should we proclaim it in an hour before his entering, that if any crave redress of injustice, they should exhibit their petitions in the street?

Escal. He shows his reason for that: to have a dispatch of complaints, and to deliver us from devices hereafter, which shall then have no power to stand against us.

Ang. Well, I beseech you, let it be proclaimed betimes i' the morn; I'll call you at your house. Give notice to such men of sort and suit as are to meet him.

Escal. I shall, sir. Fare you well.
Ang. Good night. [*Exit* ESCALUS.
This deed unshapes me quite, makes me unpregnant
And dull to all proceedings. A deflower'd maid!
And by an eminent body that enforced
The law against it! But that her tender shame
Will not proclaim against her maiden loss,
How might she tongue me! Yet reason dares her no;
For my authority bears of a credent bulk,
That no particular scandal once can touch
But it confounds the breather. He should have lived,
Save that his riotous youth, with dangerous sense,
Might in the times to come have ta'en revenge,
By so receiving a dishonour'd life
With ransom of such shame. Would yet he had lived!
Alack, when once our grace we have forgot,
Nothing goes right; we would, and we would not,
[*Exit*.

SCENE V. *Fields without the town*

Enter DUKE *in his own habit, and* FRIAR PETER.

Duke. These letters at fit time deliver me.
Giving letters.
The Provost knows our purpose and our plot.
The matter being afoot, keep your instruction,
And hold you ever to our special drift;
Though sometimes you do blench from this to that,
As cause doth minister. Go call at Flavius' house,
And tell him where I stay. Give the like notice
To Valentinus, Rowland, and to Crassus,
And bid them bring the trumpets to the gate;
But send me Flavius first.
Fri. P. It shall be speeded well. [*Exit*.

Enter VARRIUS.

Duke. I thank thee, Varrius; thou hast made good haste.
Come, we will walk. There's other of our friends
Will greet us here anon, my gentle Varrius.
[*Exeunt*.

SCENE VI. *Street near the city gate*

Enter ISABELLA *and* MARIANA.

Isab. To speak so indirectly I am loath.
I would say the truth; but to accuse him so,
That is your part. Yet I am advised to do it;
He says, to veil full purpose.
Mari. Be ruled by him.
Isab. Besides, he tells me that, if peradventure
He speak against me on the adverse side,
I should not think it strange; for 'tis a physic
That's bitter to sweet end.
Mari. I would Friar Peter—
Isab. O, peace! the friar is come.

Enter FRIAR PETER.

Fri. P. Come, I have found you out a stand most fit,
Where you may have such vantage on the Duke,
He shall not pass you. Twice have the trumpets sounded,
The generous and gravest citizens
Have hent the gates, and very near upon
The Duke is entering; therefore, hence, away!
[*Exeunt*.

ACT V

SCENE I. *The city gate*

MARIANA *veiled*, ISABELLA, *and* FRIAR PETER, *at their stand. Enter* DUKE, VARRIUS, *Lords*, ANGELO, ESCALUS, LUCIO, PROVOST, *Officers, and Citizens, at several doors*.

Duke. My very worthy cousin, fairly met!
Our old and faithful friend, we are glad to see you.
Ang. }
Escal. } Happy return be to your royal Grace!
Duke. Many and hearty thankings to you both.
We have made inquiry of you; and we hear
Such goodness of your justice, that our soul
Cannot but yield you forth to public thanks,
Forerunning more requital.
Ang. You make my bonds still greater.
Duke. O, your desert speaks loud; and I should wrong it
To lock it in the wards of covert bosom,
When it deserves, with characters of brass,
A forted residence 'gainst the tooth of time
And razure of oblivion. Give me your hand,
And let the subject see, to make them know
That outward courtesies would fain proclaim
Favours that keep within. Come, Escalus,
You must walk by us on our other hand;
And good supporters are you.

FRIAR PETER *and* ISABELLA *come forward*.

Fri. P. Now is your time. Speak loud and kneel before him.
Isab. Justice, O royal Duke! Vail your regard
Upon a wrong'd, I would fain have said, a maid!
O worthy Prince, dishonour not your eye
By throwing it on any other object
Till you have heard me in my true complaint
And given me justice, justice, justice, justice!
Duke. Relate your wrongs; in what? by whom? be brief.

Here is Lord Angelo shall give you justice:
Reveal yourself to him.
Isab. O worthy Duke,
You bid me seek redemption of the devil.
Hear me yourself; for that which I must speak
Must either punish me, not being believed,
Or wring redress from you. Hear me, O hear me, here!
Ang. My lord, her wits, I fear me, are not firm.
She hath been a suitor to me for her brother
Cut off by course of justice—
Isab. By course of justice!
Ang. And she will speak most bitterly and strange.
Isab. Most strange, but yet most truly, will I speak:
That Angelo's forsworn; is it not strange?
That Angelo's a murderer; is't not strange?
That Angelo is an adulterous thief,
An hypocrite, a virgin-violator;
Is it not strange and strange?
Duke. Nay, it is ten times strange.
Isab. It is not truer he is Angelo
Than this is all as true as it is strange.
Nay, it is ten times true; for truth is truth
To the end of reckoning.
Duke. Away with her! Poor soul,
She speaks this in the infirmity of sense.
Isab. O Prince, I conjure thee, as thou believest
There is another comfort than this world,
That thou neglect me not, with that opinion
That I am touch'd with madness! Make not impossible
That which but seems unlike. 'Tis not impossible
But one, the wicked'st caitiff on the ground,
May seem as shy, as grave, as just, as absolute
As Angelo; even so may Angelo,
In all his dressings, characts, titles, forms,
Be an arch-villain; believe it, royal prince.
If he be less, he's nothing; but he's more,
Had I more name for badness.
Duke. By mine honesty,
If she be mad—as I believe no other—
Her madness hath the oddest frame of sense,
Such a dependency of thing on thing,
As e'er I heard in madness.
Isab. O gracious Duke,
Harp not on that, nor do not banish reason
For inequality; but let your reason serve
To make the truth appear where it seems hid,
And hide the false seems true.
Duke. Many that are not mad
Have, sure, more lack of reason. What would you say?
Isab. I am the sister of one Claudio,
Condemn'd upon the act of fornication
To lose his head; condemn'd by Angelo.
I, in probation of a sisterhood,
Was sent to by my brother; one Lucio
As then the messenger—
Lucio. That's I, an't like your Grace.
I came to her from Claudio, and desired her
To try her gracious fortune with Lord Angelo
For her poor brother's pardon.
Isab. That's he indeed.
Duke. You were not bid to speak.
Lucio. No, my good lord;
Nor wish'd to hold my peace.
Duke. I wish you now, then;
Pray you, take note of it; and when you have
A business for yourself, pray Heaven you then
Be perfect.
Lucio. I warrant your honour.
Duke. The warrant's for yourself; take heed to 't.
Isab. This gentleman told somewhat of my tale—
Lucio. Right.
Duke. It may be right; but you are i' the wrong
To speak before your time. Proceed.
Isab. I went
To this pernicious caitiff deputy—
Duke. That's somewhat madly spoken.
Isab. Pardon it;
The phrase is to the matter.
Duke. Mended again. The matter; proceed.
Isab. In brief, to set the needless process by,
How I persuaded, how I pray'd, and kneel'd,
How he refell'd me, and how I replied—
For this was of much length—the vile conclusion
I now begin with grief and shame to utter.
He would not, but by gift of my chaste body
To his concupiscible intemperate lust,
Release my brother; and, after much debatement,
My sisterly remorse confutes mine honour,
And I did yield to him; but the next morn betimes,
His purpose surfeiting, he sends a warrant
For my poor brother's head.
Duke. This is most likely!
Isab. O, that it were as like as it is true!
Duke. By heaven, fond wretch, thou know'st not what thou speak'st,
Or else thou art suborn'd against his honour
In hateful practice. First, his integrity
Stands without blemish. Next, it imports no reason
That with such vehemency he should pursue
Faults proper to himself. If he had so offended,
He would have weigh'd thy brother by himself

And not have cut him off. Some one hath set you on.
Confess the truth, and say by whose advice
Thou camest here to complain.
Isab. And is this all?
Then, O you blessed ministers above,
Keep me in patience, and with ripen'd time
Unfold the evil which is here wrapt up
In countenance! Heaven shield your Grace from woe,
As I, thus wrong'd, hence unbelieved go!
Duke. I know you'd fain be gone. An officer!
To prison with her! Shall we thus permit
A blasting and a scandalous breath to fall
On him so near us? This needs must be a practice.
Who knew of your intent and coming hither?
Isab. One that I would were here, Friar Lodowick.
Duke. A ghostly father, belike. Who knows that Lodowick?
Lucio. My lord, I know him; 'tis a meddling friar;
I do not like the man. Had he been lay, my lord,
For certain words he spake against your Grace
In your retirement, I had swinged him soundly.
Duke. Words against me! this is a good friar, belike!
And to set on this wretched woman here
Against our substitute! Let this friar be found.
Lucio. But yesternight, my lord, she and that friar,
I saw them at the prison. A saucy friar,
A very scurvy fellow.
Fri. P. Blessed be your royal Grace!
I have stood by, my lord, and I have heard
Your royal ear abused. First, hath this woman
Most wrongfully accused your substitute,
Who is as free from touch or soil with her
As she from one ungot.
Duke. We did believe no less.
Know you that Friar Lodowick that she speaks of?
Fri. P. I know him for a man divine and holy;
Not scurvy, nor a temporary meddler,
As he's reported by this gentleman;
And, on my trust, a man that never yet
Did, as he vouches, misreport your Grace.
Lucio. My lord, most villainously; believe it.
Fri. P. Well, he in time may come to clear himself;
But at this instant he is sick, my lord,
Of a strange fever. Upon his mere request,
Being come to knowledge that there was complaint
Intended 'gainst Lord Angelo, came I hither,
To speak, as from his mouth, what he doth know
Is true and false; and what he with his oath
And all probation will make up full clear,
Whensoever he's convented. First, for this woman,
To justify this worthy nobleman,
So vulgarly and personally accused,
Her shall you hear disproved to her eyes,
Till she herself confess it.
Duke. Good friar, let's hear it.
[ISABELLA *is carried off guarded; and* MARIANA *comes forward.*
Do you not smile at this, Lord Angelo?
O heaven, the vanity of wretched fools!
Give us some seats. Come, cousin Angelo;
In this I'll be impartial; be you judge
Of your own cause. Is this the witness, friar?
First, let her show her face, and after speak.
Mari. Pardon, my lord; I will not show my face
Until my husband bid me.
Duke. What, are you married?
Mari. No, my lord.
Duke. Are you a maid?
Mari. No, my lord.
Duke. A widow, then?
Mari. Neither, my lord.
Duke. Why, you are nothing then: neither maid, widow, nor wife?
Lucio. My lord, she may be a punk; for many of them are neither maid, widow, nor wife.
Duke. Silence that fellow. I would he had some cause
To prattle for himself.
Lucio. Well, my lord.
Mari. My lord, I do confess I ne'er was married;
And I confess besides I am no maid;
I have known my husband; yet my husband
Knows not that ever he knew me.
Lucio. He was drunk then my lord. It can be no better.
Duke. For the benefit of silence, would thou wert so too!
Lucio. Well, my lord.
Duke. This is no witness for Lord Angelo.
Mari. Now I come to't, my lord.
She that accuses him of fornication,
In self-same manner doth accuse my husband,
And charges him, my lord, with such a time
When I'll depose I had him in mine arms
With all the effect of love.
Ang. Charges she more than me?
Mari. Not that I know.
Duke. No? you say your husband.
Mari. Why, just, my lord, and that is Angelo,
Who thinks he knows that he ne'er knew my body,

But knows he thinks that he knows Isabel's.

Ang. This is a strange abuse. Let's see thy face.

Mari. My husband bids me; now I will unmask. [*Unveiling*.]
This is that face, thou cruel Angelo,
Which once thou sworest was worth the looking on;
This is the hand which, with a vow'd contract,
Was fast belock'd in thine; this is the body
That took away the match from Isabel,
And did supply thee at thy garden-house
In her imagined person.

Duke. Know you this woman?

Lucio. Carnally, she says.

Duke. Sirrah, no more!

Lucio. Enough, my lord.

Ang. My lord, I must confess I know this woman;
And five years since there was some speech of marriage
Betwixt myself and her; which was broke off,
Partly for that her promised proportions
Came short of composition, but in chief
For that her reputation was disvalued
In levity; since which time of five years
I never spake with her, saw her, nor heard from her,
Upon my faith and honour.

Mari. Noble Prince,
As there comes light from heaven and words from breath,
As there is sense in truth and truth in virtue,
I am affianced this man's wife as strongly
As words could make up vows; and, my good lord,
But Tuesday night last gone in's garden-house
He knew me as a wife. As this is true,
Let me in safety raise me from my knees;
Or else for ever be confixed here,
A marble monument!

Ang. I did but smile till now.
Now, good my lord, give me the scope of justice;
My patience here is touch'd. I do perceive
These poor informal women are no more
But instruments of some more mightier member
That sets them on. Let me have way, my lord,
To find this practice out.

Duke. Ay, with my heart;
And punish them to your height of pleasure
Thou foolish friar, and thou pernicious woman,
Compact with her that's gone, think'st thou thy oaths,
Though they would swear down each particular saint,
Were testimonies against his worth and credit
That's seal'd in approbation? You, Lord Escalus,
Sit with my cousin; lend him your kind pains
To find out this abuse, whence 'tis derived.
There is another friar that set them on;
Let him be sent for.

Fri. P. Would he were here, my lord! for he indeed
Hath set the women on to this complaint.
Your Provost knows the place where he abides
And he may fetch him.

Duke. Go do it instantly. [*Exit* PROVOST.
And you, my noble and well-warranted cousin,
Whom it concerns to hear this matter forth,
Do with your injuries as seems you best,
In any chastisement. I for a while will leave you;
But stir not you till you have well determined
Upon these slanderers.

Escal. My lord, we'll do it throughly. [*Exit* DUKE.
Signior Lucio, did not you say you knew that Friar Lodowick to be a dishonest person?

Lucio. *Cucullus non facit monachum:* honest in nothing but in his clothes; and one that hath spoke most villainous speeches of the Duke.

Escal. We shall entreat you to abide here till he come and enforce them against him. We shall find this friar a notable fellow.

Lucio. As any in Vienna, on my word.

Escal. Call that same Isabel here once again; I would speak with her. [*Exit an Attendant*.] Pray you, my lord, give me leave to question; you shall see how I'll handle her.

Lucio. Not better than he, by her own report.

Escal. Say you?

Lucio. Marry, sir, I think, if you handled her privately, she would sooner confess; perchance, publicly, she'll be ashamed.

Escal. I will go darkly to work with her.

Lucio. That's the way; for women are light at midnight.

Re-enter Officers with ISABELLA; *and* PROVOST *with the* DUKE *in his friar's habit*.

Escal. Come on, mistress. Here's a gentlewoman denies all that you have said.

Lucio. My lord, here comes the rascal I spoke of; here with the Provost.

Escal. In very good time. Speak not you to him till we call upon you.

Lucio. Mum.

Escal. Come, sir; did you set these women on to slander Lord Angelo? they have confessed you did.

Duke. 'Tis false.

Escal. How! know you where you are?

Duke. Respect to your great place! and let the devil
Be sometime honour'd for his burning throne!
Where is the Duke? 'tis he should hear me speak.

Escal. The Duke's in us; and we will hear you speak.
Look you speak justly.

Duke. Boldly, at least. But, O, poor souls,
Come you to seek the lamb here of the fox?
Good night to your redress! Is the Duke gone?
Then is your cause gone too. The Duke's unjust,
Thus to retort your manifest appeal,
And put your trial in the villain's mouth
Which here you come to accuse.

Lucio. This is the rascal; this is he I spoke of.

Escal. Why, thou unreverend and unhallow'd friar,
Is't not enough thou hast suborn'd these women
To accuse this worthy man, but, in foul mouth
And in the witness of his proper ear,
To call him villain? and then to glance from him
To the Duke himself, to tax him with injustice?
Take him hence; to the rack with him! We'll touse you
Joint by joint, but we will know his purpose.
What, "unjust"!

Duke. Be not so hot; the Duke
Dare no more stretch this finger of mine than he
Dare rack his own. His subject am I not,
Nor here provincial. My business in this state
Made me a looker on here in Vienna,
Where I have seen corruption boil and bubble
Till it o'er-run the stew; laws for all faults,
But faults so countenanced, that the strong statutes
Stand like the forfeits in a barber's shop,
As much in mock as mark.

Escal. Slander to the state! Away with him to prison!

Ang. What can you vouch against him, Signior Lucio?
Is this the man that you did tell us of?

Lucio. 'Tis he, my lord. Come hither, goodman baldpate. Do you know me?

Duke. I remember you, sir, by the sound of your voice. I met you at the prison, in the absence of the Duke.

Lucio. O, did you so? And do you remember what you said of the Duke?

Duke. Most notedly, sir.

Lucio. Do you so, sir? And was the Duke a fleshmonger, a fool, and a coward, as you then reported him to be?

Duke. You must, sir, change persons with me, ere you make that my report. You, indeed, spoke so of him; and much more, much worse.

Lucio. O thou damnable fellow! Did not I pluck thee by the nose for thy speeches?

Duke. I protest I love the Duke as I love myself.

Ang. Hark, how the villain would close now, after his treasonable abuses!

Escal. Such a fellow is not to be talked withal. Away with him to prison. Where is the Provost? Away with him to prison! lay bolts enough upon him. Let him speak no more. Away with those giglots too, and with the other confederate companion!

Duke. [*To* PROVOST] Stay, sir; stay awhile.

Ang. What, resists he? Help him, Lucio.

Lucio. Come, sir; come, sir; come, sir; foh, sir! Why, you bald-pated, lying rascal, you must be hooded, must you? Show your knave's visage, with a pox to you! show your sheep-biting face, and be hanged an hour! Will't not off?

Pulls off the friar's hood, and discovers the Duke.

Duke. Thou art the first knave that e'er madest a Duke.
First, Provost, let me bail these gentle three.
[*To* LUCIO] Sneak not away, sir; for the friar and you
Must have a word anon. Lay hold on him.

Lucio. This may prove worse than hanging.

Duke. [*To* ESCALUS] What you have spoke I pardon. Sit you down.
We'll borrow place of him. [*To* ANGELO] Sir, by your leave.
Hast thou or word, or wit, or impudence,
That yet can do thee office? If thou hast,
Rely upon it till my tale be heard,
And hold no longer out.

Ang. O my dread lord,
I should be guiltier than my guiltiness,
To think I can be undiscernible,
When I perceive your Grace, like power divine,
Hath look'd upon my passes. Then, good Prince,
No longer session hold upon my shame,
But let my trial be mine own confession.
Immediate sentence then and sequent death
Is all the grace I beg.

Duke. Come hither, Mariana.
Say, wast thou e'er contracted to this woman?

Ang. I was, my lord.

Duke. Go take her hence, and marry her instantly.
Do you the office, friar; which consummate,
Return him here again. Go with him, Provost.

[*Exeunt* ANGELO, MARIANA, FRIAR PETER *and* PROVOST.

Escal. My lord, I am more amazed at his dishonour

Than at the strangeness of it.
Duke. Come hither, Isabel.
Your friar is now your Prince. As I was then
Advertising and holy to your business,
Not changing heart with habit, I am still
Attorney'd at your service.
Isab. O, give me pardon,
That I, your vassal, have employ'd and pain'd
Your unknown sovereignty!
Duke. You are pardon'd, Isabel.
And now, dear maid, be you as free to us.
Your brother's death, I know, sits at your heart;
And you may marvel why I obscured myself,
Labouring to save his life, and would not rather
Make rash remonstrance of my hidden power
Than let him so be lost. O most kind maid,
It was the swift celerity of his death,
Which I did think with slower foot came on,
That brain'd my purpose. But, peace be with him!
That life is better life, past fearing death,
Than that which lives to fear. Make it your comfort,
So happy is your brother.
Isab. I do, my lord.

Re-enter ANGELO, MARIANA, FRIAR PETER, *and* PROVOST.

Duke. For this new-married man approaching here,
Whose salt imagination yet hath wrong'd
Your well defended honour, you must pardon
For Mariana's sake. But as he adjudged your brother—
Being criminal, in double violation
Of sacred chastity and of promise-breach
Thereon dependent, for your brother's life—
The very mercy of the law cries out
Most audible, even from his proper tongue,
"An Angelo for Claudio, death for death!"
Haste still pays haste, and leisure answers leisure;
Like doth quit like, and MEASURE still FOR MEASURE.
Then, Angelo, thy fault's thus manifested;
Which, though thou wouldst deny, denies thee vantage.
We do condemn thee to the very block
Where Claudio stoop'd to death, and with like haste.
Away with him!
Mari. O my most gracious lord,
I hope you will not mock me with a husband.
Duke. It is your husband mock'd you with a husband.
Consenting to the safeguard of your honour,
I thought your marriage fit; else imputation,
For that he knew you, might reproach your life
And choke your good to come. For his possessions,
Although by confiscation they are ours,
We do instate and widow you withal,
To buy you a better husband.
Mari. O my dear lord,
I crave no other, nor no better man.
Duke. Never crave him; we are definitive.
Mari. Gentle my liege— [*Kneeling.*]
Duke. You do but lose your labour.
Away with him to death! [*To* LUCIO] Now, sir, to you.
Mari. O my good lord! Sweet Isabel, take my part;
Lend me your knees, and all my life to come
I'll lend you all my life to do you service.
Duke. Against all sense you do importune her.
Should she kneel down in mercy of this fact,
Her brother's ghost his paved bed would break,
And take her hence in horror.
Mari. Isabel,
Sweet Isabel, do yet but kneel by me;
Hold up your hands, say nothing; I'll speak all.
They say, best men are moulded out of faults;
And, for the most, become much more the better
For being a little bad; so may my husband.
O Isabel, will you not lend a knee?
Duke. He dies for Claudio's death.
Isab. Most bounteous sir, [*Kneeling.*]
Look, if it please you, on this man condemn'd,
As if my brother lived. I partly think
A due sincerity govern'd his deeds,
Till he did look on me. Since it is so,
Let him not die. My brother had but justice,
In that he did the thing for which he died.
For Angelo,
His act did not o'ertake his bad intent,
And must be buried but as an intent
That perish'd by the way. Thoughts are no subjects;
Intents but merely thoughts.
Mari. Merely, my lord.
Duke. Your suit's unprofitable; stand up, I say.
I have bethought me of another fault.
Provost, how came it Claudio was beheaded
At an unusual hour?
Prov. It was commanded so.
Duke. Had you a special warrant for the deed?
Prov. No, my good lord; it was by private message.
Duke. For which I do discharge you of your office.
Give up your keys.
Prov. Pardon me, noble lord.

I thought it was a fault, but knew it not;
Yet did repent me, after more advice;
For testimony whereof, one in the prison,
That should by private order else have died,
I have reserved alive.

Duke. What's he?

Prov. His name is Barnardine.

Duke. I would thou hadst done so by Claudio.
Go fetch him hither; let me look upon him.

[*Exit* PROVOST.

Escal. I am sorry, one so learned and so wise
As you, Lord Angelo, have still appear'd,
Should slip so grossly, both in the heat of blood,
And lack of temper'd judgement afterward.

Ang. I am sorry that such sorrow I procure;
And so deep sticks it in my penitent heart
That I crave death more willingly than mercy;
'Tis my deserving, and I do entreat it.

Re-enter PROVOST, *with* BARNARDINE, CLAUDIO *muffled, and* JULIET.

Duke. Which is that Barnardine?

Prov. This, my lord.

Duke. There was a friar told me of this man.
Sirrah, thou art said to have a stubborn soul,
That apprehends no further than this world,
And squarest thy life according. Thou'rt condemn'd;
But, for those earthly faults, I quit them all;
And pray thee take this mercy to provide
For better times to come. Friar, advise him;
I leave him to your hand. What muffled fellow's that?

Prov. This is another prisoner that I saved,
Who should have died when Claudio lost his head;
As like almost to Claudio as himself.

Unmuffles CLAUDIO.

Duke. [*To* ISABELLA] If he be like your brother, for his sake
Is he pardon'd; and, for your lovely sake,
Give me your hand and say you will be mine,
He is my brother too; but fitter time for that.
By this Lord Angelo perceives he's safe;
Methinks I see a quickening in his eye.
Well, Angelo, your evil quits you well.
Look that you love your wife; her worth worth yours.
I find an apt remission in myself;
And yet here's one in place I cannot pardon.
[*To* LUCIO] You, sirrah, that knew me for a fool, a coward,
One all of luxury, an ass, a madman;
Wherein have I so deserved of you,
That you extol me thus?

Lucio. 'Faith, my lord, I spoke it but according to the trick. If you will hang me for it, you may; but I had rather it would please you I might be whipt.

Duke. Whipt first, sir, and hanged after.
Proclaim it, Provost, round about the city,
Is any woman wrong'd by this lewd fellow,
As I have heard him swear himself there's one
Whom he begot with child, let her appear,
And he shall marry her; the nuptial finish'd,
Let him be whipt and hang'd.

Lucio. I beseech your Highness, do not marry me to a whore. Your Highness said even now, I made you a Duke. Good my lord, do not recompense me in making me a cuckold.

Duke. Upon mine honour, thou shalt marry her.
Thy slanders I forgive; and therewithal
Remit thy other forfeits. Take him to prison;
And see our pleasure herein executed.

Lucio. Marrying a punk, my lord, is pressing to death, whipping, and hanging.

Duke. Slandering a prince deserves it.

[*Exeunt Officers with* LUCIO.

She, Claudio, that you wrong'd, look you restore.
Joy to you, Mariana! Love her, Angelo;
I have confess'd her and I know her virtue.
Thanks, good friend Escalus, for thy much goodness;
There's more behind that is more gratulate.
Thanks, Provost, for thy care and secrecy;
We shall employ thee in a worthier place.
Forgive him, Angelo, that brought you home
The head of Ragozine for Claudio's;
The offence pardons itself. Dear Isabel,
I have a motion much imports your good;
Whereto if you'll a willing ear incline,
What's mine is yours and what is yours is mine.
So, bring us to our palace, where we'll show
What's yet behind, that's meet you all should know.

[*Exeunt.*

OTHELLO, the Moor of Venice

DRAMATIS PERSONÆ

DUKE OF VENICE
BRABANTIO, *a Senator*
TWO SENATORS
GRATIANO, *brother to Brabantio*
LODOVICO, *kinsman to Brabantio*
OTHELLO, *a noble Moor in the service of the Venetian state*
CASSIO, *his lieutenant*
IAGO, *his ancient*
RODERIGO, *a Venetian gentleman*
MONTANO, *Othello's predecessor in the government of Cyprus*
CLOWN, *servant to Othello*
TWO GENTLEMEN, *of Venice*
FOUR GENTLEMEN, *of Cyprus*

AN OFFICER
A HERALD
A MESSENGER
A SAILOR
A MUSICIAN

DESDEMONA, *daughter to Brabantio and wife to Othello*
EMILIA, *wife to Iago*
BIANCA, *mistress to Cassio*

NON-SPEAKING: *Officers, Gentlemen, Musicians, and Attendants*

SCENE: *Venice, and a Sea-port in Cyprus*

ACT I

SCENE I. *Venice: a street*

Enter RODERIGO *and* IAGO.

Rod. Tush! never tell me; I take it much unkindly
That thou, Iago, who hast had my purse
As if the strings were thine, shouldst know of this.

Iago. 'Sblood, but you will not hear me.
If ever I did dream of such a matter,
Abhor me.

Rod. Thou told'st me thou didst hold him in thy hate.

Iago. Despise me, if I do not. Three great ones of the city,
In personal suit to make me his lieutenant,
Off-capp'd to him; and, by the faith of man,
I know my price, I am worth no worse a place.
But he, as loving his own pride and purposes,
Evades them, with a bombast circumstance
Horribly stuff'd with epithets of war,
And, in conclusion,
Nonsuits my mediators; for, "Certes," says he,
"I have already chose my officer."
And what was he?
Forsooth, a great arithmetician,
One Michael Cassio, a Florentine,
A fellow almost damn'd in a fair wife;
That never set a squadron in the field,
Nor the division of a battle knows
More than a spinster; unless the bookish theoric,
Wherein the toged consuls can propose
As masterly as he. Mere prattle, without practice,
Is all his soldiership. But he, sir, had the election;
And I, of whom his eyes had seen the proof
At Rhodes, at Cyprus and on other grounds
Christian and heathen, must be be-lee'd and calm'd
By debitor and creditor; this counter-caster,
He, in good time, must his lieutenant be,
And I—God bless the mark!—his Moorship's ancient.

Rod. By heaven, I rather would have been his hangman.

Iago. Why, there's no remedy; 'tis the curse of service,
Preferment goes by letter and affection,
And not by old gradation, where each second
Stood heir to the first. Now, sir, be judge yourself
Whether I in any just term am affined
To love the Moor.

Rod. I would not follow him then.

Iago. O, sir, content you;
I follow him to serve my turn upon him.
We cannot all be masters, nor all masters
Cannot be truly follow'd. You shall mark
Many a duteous and knee-crooking knave
That, doting on his own obsequious bondage,
Wears out his time, much like his master's ass,
For nought but provender, and when he's old, cashier'd.
Whip me such honest knaves. Others there are
Who, trimm'd in forms and visages of duty,
Keep yet their hearts attending on themselves,
And, throwing but shows of service on their lords,

Do well thrive by them and when they have lined their coats
Do themselves homage. These fellows have some soul;
And such a one do I profess myself. For, sir,
It is as sure as you are Roderigo,
Were I the Moor, I would not be Iago.
In following him, I follow but myself;
Heaven is my judge, not I for love and duty,
But seeming so, for my peculiar end;
For when my outward action doth demonstrate
The native act and figure of my heart
In compliment extern, 'tis not long after
But I will wear my heart upon my sleeve
For daws to peck at. I am not what I am.

Rod. What a full fortune does the thick-lips owe,
If he can carry't thus!

Iago. Call up her father,
Rouse him. Make after him, poison his delight,
Proclaim him in the streets. Incense her kinsmen,
And, though he in a fertile climate dwell,
Plague him with flies. Though that his joy be joy,
Yet throw such changes of vexation on't,
As it may lose some colour.

Rod. Here is her father's house; I'll call aloud.

Iago. Do, with like timorous accent and dire yell
As when, by night and negligence, the fire
Is spied in populous cities.

Rod. What, ho, Brabantio! Signior Brabantio, ho!

Iago. Awake! what, ho, Brabantio! thieves! thieves! thieves!
Look to your house, your daughter, and your bags!
Thieves! thieves!

BRABANTIO *appears above, at a window.*

Bra. What is the reason of this terrible summons?
What is the matter there?

Rod. Signior, is all your family within?

Iago. Are your doors lock'd?

Bra. Why, wherefore ask you this?

Iago. 'Zounds, sir, you're robb'd; for shame, put on your gown;
Your heart is burst, you have lost half your soul;
Even now, now, very now, an old black ram
Is tupping your white ewe. Arise, arise;
Awake the snorting citizens with the bell,
Or else the devil will make a grandsire of you.
Arise, I say.

Bra. What, have you lost your wits?

Rod. Most reverend signior, do you know my voice?

Bra. Not I. What are you?

Rod. My name is Roderigo.

Bra. The worser welcome.
I have charged thee not to haunt about my doors.
In honest plainness thou hast heard me say
My daughter is not for thee; and now, in madness,
Being full of supper and distempering draughts,
Upon malicious bravery, dost thou come
To start my quiet.

Rod. Sir, sir, sir—

Bra. But thou must needs be sure
My spirit and my place have in them power
To make this bitter to thee.

Rod. Patience, good sir.

Bra. What tell'st thou me of robbing? this is Venice;
My house is not a grange.

Rod. Most grave Brabantio,
In simple and pure soul I come to you.

Iago. 'Zounds, sir, you are one of those that will not serve God, if the devil bid you. Because we come to do you service and you think we are ruffians, you'll have your daughter covered with a Barbary horse; you'll have your nephews neigh to you; you'll have coursers for cousins and gennets for germans.

Bra. What profane wretch art thou?

Iago. I am one, sir, that comes to tell you your daughter and the Moor are now making the beast with two backs.

Bra. Thou art a villain.

Iago. You are—a senator.

Bra. This thou shalt answer; I know thee, Roderigo.

Rod. Sir, I will answer anything. But, I beseech you,
If't be your pleasure and most wise consent,
As partly I find it is, that your fair daughter,
At this odd-even and dull watch o' the night,
Transported, with no worse nor better guard
But with a knave of common hire, a gondolier,
To the gross clasps of a lascivious Moor—
If this be known to you and your allowance,
We then have done you bold and saucy wrongs;
But if you know not this, my manners tell me
We have your wrong rebuke. Do not believe
That, from the sense of all civility,
I thus would play and trifle with your reverence.
Your daughter, if you have not given her leave,
I say again, hath made a gross revolt;
Tying her duty, beauty, wit, and fortunes
In an extravagant and wheeling stranger

Of here and everywhere. Straight satisfy yourself.
If she be in her chamber or your house,
Let loose on me the justice of the state
For thus deluding you.
Bra. Strike on the tinder, ho!
Give me a taper! call up all my people!
This accident is not unlike my dream;
Belief of it oppresses me already.
Light, I say! light! [*Exit above.*
Iago. Farewell; for I must leave you.
It seems not meet, nor wholesome to my place,
To be produced—as, if I stay, I shall—
Against the Moor; for, I do know, the state,
However this may gall him with some check,
Cannot with safety cast him, for he's embark'd
With such loud reason to the Cyprus wars,
Which even now stand in act, that, for their souls,
Another of his fathom they have none
To lead their business; in which regard,
Though I do hate him as I do hell-pains,
Yet, for necessity of present life,
I must show out a flag and sign of love,
Which is indeed but sign. That you shall surely find him,
Lead to the Sagittary the raised search;
And there will I be with him. So, farewell.
[*Exit.*

Enter, below, BRABANTIO, *and Servants with torches.*

Bra. It is too true an evil; gone she is;
And what's to come of my despised time
Is nought but bitterness. Now, Roderigo,
Where didst thou see her? O unhappy girl!
With the Moor, say'st thou? Who would be a father!
How didst thou know 'twas she? O, she deceives me
Past thought! What said she to you? Get more tapers.
Raise all my kindred. Are they married, think you?
Rod. Truly, I think they are.
Bra. O heaven! How got she out? O treason of the blood!
Fathers, from hence trust not your daughters' minds
By what you see them act. Is there not charms
By which the property of youth and maidhood
May be abused? Have you not read, Roderigo,
Of some such thing?
Rod. Yes, sir, I have indeed.
Bra. Call up my brother. O, would you had had her!
Some one way, some another. Do you know
Where we may apprehend her and the Moor?
Rod. I think I can discover him, if you please
To get good guard and go along with me.
Bra. Pray you, lead on. At every house I'll call;
I may command at most. Get weapons, ho!
And raise some special officers of night.
On, good Roderigo; I'll deserve your pains.
[*Exeunt.*

SCENE II. *Another street*

Enter OTHELLO, IAGO, *and Attendants with torches.*

Iago. Though in the trade of war I have slain men,
Yet do I hold it very stuff o' the conscience
To do no contrived murder. I lack iniquity
Sometimes to do me service. Nine or ten times
I had thought to have yerk'd him here under the ribs.
Oth. 'Tis better as it is.
Iago. Nay, but he prated,
And spoke such scurvy and provoking terms
Against your honour
That, with the little godliness I have,
I did full hard forbear him. But, I pray you, sir,
Are you fast married? Be assured of this,
That the magnifico is much beloved,
And hath in his effect a voice potential
As double as the Duke's. He will divorce you;
Or put upon you what restraint and grievance
The law, with all his might to enforce it on,
Will give him cable.
Oth. Let him do his spite;
My services which I have done the signiory
Shall out-tongue his complaints. 'Tis yet to know—
Which, when I know that boasting is an honour,
I shall promulgate—I fetch my life and being
From men of royal siege, and my demerits
May speak unbonneted to as proud a fortune
As this that I have reach'd; for know, Iago,
But that I love the gentle Desdemona,
I would not my unhoused free condition
Put into circumscription and confine
For the sea's worth. But, look! what lights come yond?
Iago. Those are the raised father and his friends.
You were best go in.
Oth. Not I; I must be found.
My parts, my title, and my perfect soul
Shall manifest me rightly. Is it they?
Iago. By Janus, I think no.
Enter CASSIO, *and certain* OFFICERS *with torches.*

Oth. The servants of the Duke, and my lieutenant.
The goodness of the night upon you, friends!
What is the news?
Cas. The Duke does greet you, general,
And he requires your haste-post-haste appearance,
Even on the instant.
Oth. What is the matter, think you?
Cas. Something from Cyprus, as I may divine;
It is a business of some heat. The galleys
Have sent a dozen sequent messengers
This very night at one another's heels,
And many of the consuls, raised and met,
Are at the Duke's already. You have been hotly call'd for;
When, being not at your lodging to be found,
The senate hath sent about three several quests
To search you out.
Oth. 'Tis well I am found by you.
I will but spend a word here in the house,
And go with you. [*Exit.*
Cas. Ancient, what makes he here?
Iago. 'Faith, he to-night hath boarded a land carack.
If it prove lawful prize, he's made for ever.
Cas. I do not understand.
Iago. He's married.
Cas. To who?

Re-enter OTHELLO.

Iago. Marry, to—Come, captain, will you go?
Oth. Have with you.
Cas. Here comes another troop to seek for you.
Iago. It is Brabantio. General, be advised;
He comes to bad intent.

Enter BRABANTIO, RODERIGO, *and Officers with torches and weapons.*

Oth. Holla! stand there!
Rod. Signior, it is the Moor.
Bra. Down with him, thief!
They draw on both sides.
Iago. You, Roderigo! come, sir, I am for you.
Oth. Keep up your bright swords, for the dew will rust them.
Good signior, you shall more command with years
Than with your weapons. 61
Bra. O thou foul thief, where hast thou stow'd my daughter?
Damn'd as thou art, thou hast enchanted her;
For I'll refer me to all things of sense,
If she in chains of magic were not bound,
Whether a maid so tender, fair, and happy,
So opposite to marriage that she shunn'd
The wealthy curled darlings of our nation,
Would ever have, to incur a general mock,
Run from her guardage to the sooty bosom
Of such a thing as thou—to fear, not to delight.
Judge me the world, if 'tis not gross in sense
That thou hast practised on her with foul charms,
Abused her delicate youth with drugs or minerals
That weaken motion. I'll have't disputed on;
'Tis probable and palpable to thinking.
I therefore apprehend and do attach thee
For an abuser of the world, a practiser
Of arts inhibited and out of warrant.
Lay hold upon him. If he do resist,
Subdue him at his peril.
Oth. Hold your hands,
Both you of my inclining, and the rest.
Were it my cue to fight, I should have known it
Without a prompter. Where will you that I go
To answer this your charge?
Bra. To prison, till fit time
Of law and course of direct session
Call thee to answer.
Oth. What if I do obey?
How may the Duke be therewith satisfied,
Whose messengers are here about my side,
Upon some present business of the state
To bring me to him?
1st Off. 'Tis true, most worthy signior;
The Duke's in council, and your noble self,
I am sure, is sent for.
Bra. How! the Duke in council!
In this time of the night! Bring him away.
Mine's not an idle cause. The Duke himself,
Or any of my brothers of the state,
Cannot but feel this wrong as 'twere their own;
For if such actions may have passage free,
Bond-slaves and pagans shall our statesmen be.
[*Exeunt.*

SCENE III. *A council-chamber*

The DUKE *and* SENATORS *sitting at a table;* OFFICERS *attending.*

Duke. There is no composition in these news
That gives them credit.
1st Sen. Indeed, they are disproportion'd;
My letters say a hundred and seven galleys.
Duke. And mine, a hundred and forty.
2nd Sen. And mine, two hundred.
But though they jump not on a just account—
As in these cases, where the aim reports,
'Tis oft with difference—yet do they all confirm
A Turkish fleet, and bearing up to Cyprus.
Duke. Nay, it is possible enough to judgement.
I do not so secure me in the error,
But the main article I do approve
In fearful sense.

Sailor. [*Within*] What, ho! what, ho! what, ho!
1st Off. A messenger from the galleys.

Enter a SAILOR.

Duke. Now, what's the business?
Sail. The Turkish preparation makes for Rhodes;
So was I bid report here to the state
By Signior Angelo.
Duke. How say you by this change?
1st Sen. This cannot be,
By no assay of reason; 'tis a pageant,
To keep us in false gaze. When we consider
The importancy of Cyprus to the Turk,
And let ourselves again but understand,
That as it more concerns the Turk than Rhodes,
So may he with more facile question bear it,
For that it stands not in such warlike brace,
But altogether lacks the abilities
That Rhodes is dress'd in. If we make thought of this,
We must not think the Turk is so unskilful
To leave that latest which concerns him first,
Neglecting an attempt of ease and gain
To wake and wage a danger profitless.
Duke. Nay, in all confidence, he's not for Rhodes.
1st Off. Here is more news.

Enter a MESSENGER.

Mess. The Ottomites, reverend and gracious,
Steering with due course towards the isle of Rhodes,
Have there injointed them with an after fleet.
1st Sen. Ay, so I thought. How many, as you guess?
Mess. Of thirty sail; and now they do re-stem
Their backward course, bearing with frank appearance
Their purposes toward Cyprus. Signior Montano,
Your trusty and most valiant servitor,
With his free duty recommends you thus,
And prays you to believe him.
Duke. 'Tis certain, then, for Cyprus.
Marcus Luccicos, is not he in town?
1st Sen. He's now in Florence.
Duke. Write from us to him; post-post-haste dispatch.
1st Sen. Here comes Brabantio and the valiant Moor.

Enter BRABANTIO, OTHELLO, IAGO, RODERIGO, *and Officers*.

Duke. Valiant Othello, we must straight employ you
Against the general enemy Ottoman.
[*To* BRABANTIO] I did not see you; welcome, gentle signior;
We lack'd your counsel and your help to-night.
Bra. So did I yours. Good your Grace, pardon me;
Neither my place nor aught I heard of business
Hath raised me from my bed, nor doth the general care
Take hold on me, for my particular grief
Is of so flood-gate and o'erbearing nature
That it engluts and swallows other sorrows
And it is still itself.
Duke. Why, what's the matter?
Bra. My daughter! O, my daughter!
All. Dead?
Bra. Ay, to me;
She is abused, stol'n from me, and corrupted
By spells and medicines bought of mountebanks;
For nature so preposterously to err,
Being not deficient, blind, or lame of sense,
Sans witchcraft could not.
Duke. Whoe'er he be that in this foul proceeding
Hath thus beguiled your daughter of herself
And you of her, the bloody book of law
You shall yourself read in the bitter letter
After your own sense, yea, though our proper son
Stood in your action.
Bra. Humbly I thank your Grace.
Here is the man, this Moor, whom now, it seems,
Your special mandate for the state affairs
Hath hither brought.
All. We are very sorry for't.
Duke. [*To* OTHELLO] What, in your own part, can you say to this?
Bra. Nothing, but this is so.
Oth. Most potent, grave, and reverend signiors,
My very noble and approved good masters,
That I have ta'en away this old man's daughter,
It is most true; true, I have married her:
The very head and front of my offending
Hath this extent, no more. Rude am I in my speech,
And little bless'd with the soft phrase of peace.
For since these arms of mine had seven years' pith,
Till now some nine moons wasted, they have used
Their dearest action in the tented field,
And little of this great world can I speak
More than pertains to feats of broil and battle,
And therefore little shall I grace my cause
In speaking for myself. Yet, by your gracious patience,
I will a round unvarnish'd tale deliver

Of my whole course of love; what drugs, what charms,
What conjuration, and what mighty magic,
For such proceeding I am charged withal,
I won his daughter.

Bra. A maiden never bold;
Of spirit so still and quiet that her motion
Blush'd at herself; and she, in spite of nature,
Of years, of country, credit, everything,
To fall in love with what she fear'd to look on!
It is a judgement maim'd and most imperfect
That will confess perfection so could err
Against all rules of nature, and must be driven
To find out practices of cunning hell,
Why this should be. I therefore vouch again
That with some mixtures powerful o'er the blood,
Or with some dram conjured to this effect,
He wrought upon her.

Duke. To vouch this is no proof,
Without more wider and more overt test
Than these thin habits and poor likelihoods
Of modern seeming do prefer against him.

1st Sen. But, Othello, speak.
Did you by indirect and forced courses
Subdue and poison this young maid's affections?
Or came it by request and such fair question
As soul to soul affordeth?

Oth. I do beseech you,
Send for the lady to the Sagittary,
And let her speak of me before her father.
If you do find me foul in her report,
The trust, the office I do hold of you,
Not only take away, but let your sentence
Even fall upon my life.

Duke. Fetch Desdemona hither.

Oth. Ancient, conduct them; you best know the place. [*Exeunt* IAGO *and Attendants.*
And, till she come, as truly as to heaven
I do confess the vices of my blood,
So justly to your grave ears I'll present
How I did thrive in this fair lady's love,
And she in mine.

Duke. Say it, Othello.

Oth. Her father loved me; oft invited me;
Still question'd me the story of my life,
From year to year, the battles, sieges, fortunes,
That I have pass'd.
I ran it through, even from my boyish days,
To the very moment that he bade me tell it;
Wherein I spake of most disastrous chances,
Of moving accidents by flood and field,
Of hair-breadth scapes i' the imminent deadly breach,
Of being taken by the insolent foe
And sold to slavery, of my redemption thence
And portance in my travels' history;
Wherein of antres vast and deserts idle,
Rough quarries, rocks, and hills whose heads touch heaven,
It was my hint to speak—such was the process—
And of the Cannibals that each other eat,
The Anthropophagi and men whose heads
Do grow beneath their shoulders. This to hear
Would Desdemona seriously incline;
But still the house-affairs would draw her thence,
Which ever as she could with haste dispatch,
She'd come again, and with a greedy ear
Devour up my discourse; which I observing,
Took once a pliant hour, and found good means
To draw from her a prayer of earnest heart
That I would all my pilgrimage dilate,
Whereof by parcels she had something heard,
But not intentively. I did consent,
And often did beguile her of her tears
When I did speak of some distressful stroke
That my youth suffer'd. My story being done,
She gave me for my pains a world of sighs.
She swore, in faith, 'twas strange, 'twas passing strange,
'Twas pitiful, 'twas wondrous pitiful.
She wish'd she had not heard it, yet she wish'd
That heaven had made her such a man. She thank'd me,
And bade me, if I had a friend that loved her,
I should but teach him how to tell my story,
And that would woo her. Upon this hint I spake:
She loved me for the dangers I had pass'd,
And I loved her that she did pity them.
This only is the witchcraft I have used.
Here comes the lady; let her witness it.

Enter DESDEMONA, IAGO, *and Attendants.*

Duke. I think this tale would win my daughter too.
Good Brabantio,
Take up this mangled matter at the best;
Men do their broken weapons rather use
Than their bare hands.

Bra. I pray you, hear her speak.
If she confess that she was half the wooer,
Destruction on my head, if my bad blame
Light on the man! Come hither, gentle mistress.
Do you perceive in all this noble company
Where most you owe obedience?

Des. My noble father,
I do perceive here a divided duty:
To you I am bound for life and education;
My life and education both do learn me
How to respect you; you are the lord of duty;

I am hitherto your daughter. But here's my husband,
And so much duty as my mother show'd
To you, preferring you before her father,
So much I challenge that I may profess
Due to the Moor my lord.

Bra. God be wi' you! I have done.
Please it your Grace, on to the state-affairs.
I had rather to adopt a child than get it.
Come hither, Moor.
I here do give thee that with all my heart
Which, but thou hast already, with all my heart
I would keep from thee. For your sake, jewel,
I am glad at soul I have no other child;
For thy escape would teach me tyranny,
To hang clogs on them. I have done, my lord.

Duke. Let me speak like yourself, and lay a sentence,
Which, as a grise or step, may help these lovers
Into your favour.
When remedies are past, the griefs are ended
By seeing the worst, which late on hopes depended.
To mourn a mischief that is past and gone
Is the next way to draw new mischief on.
What cannot be preserved when fortune takes,
Patience her injury a mockery makes.
The robb'd that smiles steals something from the thief;
He robs himself that spends a bootless grief.

Bra. So let the Turk of Cyprus us beguile;
We lose it not, so long as we can smile.
He bears the sentence well that nothing bears
But the free comfort which from thence he hears,
But he bears both the sentence and the sorrow
That, to pay grief, must of poor patience borrow.
These sentences, to sugar, or to gall,
Being strong on both sides, are equivocal.
But words are words; I never yet did hear
That the bruised heart was pierced through the ear.
I humbly beseech you, proceed to the affairs of state.

Duke. The Turk with a most mighty preparation makes for Cyprus. Othello, the fortitude of the place is best known to you; and though we have there a substitute of most allowed sufficiency, yet opinion, a sovereign mistress of effects, throws a more safer voice on you. You must therefore be content to slubber the gloss of your new fortunes with this more stubborn and boisterous expedition.

Oth. The tyrant custom, most grave senators,
Hath made the flinty and steel couch of war
My thrice-driven bed of down. I do agnize
A natural and prompt alacrity
I find in hardness, and do undertake
These present wars against the Ottomites.
Most humbly therefore bending to your state,
I crave fit disposition for my wife,
Due reference of place and exhibition,
With such accommodation and besort
As levels with her breeding.

Duke. If you please,
Be 't at her father's.

Bra. I'll not have it so.

Oth. Nor I.

Des. Nor I; I would not there reside,
To put my father in impatient thoughts
By being in his eye. Most gracious Duke,
To my unfolding lend your prosperous ear;
And let me find a charter in your voice,
To assist my simpleness.

Duke. What would you, Desdemona?

Des. That I did love the Moor to live with him,
My downright violence and storm of fortunes
May trumpet to the world. My heart's subdued
Even to the very quality of my lord.
I saw Othello's visage in his mind,
And to his honours and his valiant parts
Did I my soul and fortunes consecrate.
So that, dear lords, if I be left behind,
A moth of peace, and he go to the war,
The rites for which I love him are bereft me,
And I a heavy interim shall support
By his dear absence. Let me go with him.

Oth. Let her have your voices.
Vouch with me, Heaven, I therefore beg it not,
To please the palate of my appetite,
Nor to comply with heat—the young affects
In me defunct—and proper satisfaction,
But to be free and bounteous to her mind;
And Heaven defend your good souls, that you think
I will your serious and great business scant
For she is with me. No, when light-wing'd toys
Of feather'd Cupid seel with wanton dullness
My speculative and officed instruments,
That my disports corrupt and taint my business,
Let housewives make a skillet of my helm,
And all indign and base adversities
Make head against my estimation!

Duke. Be it as you shall privately determine,
Either for her stay or going. The affair cries haste,
And speed must answer it.

1st Sen. You must away to-night

Oth. With all my heart.

Duke. At nine i' the morning here we'll meet again.

Othello, leave some officer behind,
And he shall our commission bring to you,
With such things else of quality and respect
As doth import you.

Oth. So please your Grace, my ancient;
A man he is of honesty and trust.
To his conveyance I assign my wife,
With what else needful your good Grace shall think
To be sent after me.

Duke. Let it be so.
Good night to every one. [*To* BRABANTIO] And, noble signior,
If virtue no delighted beauty lack,
Your son-in-law is far more fair than black.

1st Sen. Adieu, brave Moor; use Desdemona well.

Bra. Look to her, Moor, if thou hast eyes to see;
She has deceived her father, and may thee.

[*Exeunt* DUKE, SENATORS, *Officers, &c.*

Oth. My life upon her faith! Honest Iago,
My Desdemona must I leave to thee.
I prithee, let thy wife attend on her;
And bring them after in the best advantage.
Come, Desdemona; I have but an hour
Of love, of worldly matters and direction,
To spend with thee. We must obey the time.

[*Exeunt* OTHELLO *and* DESDEMONA.

Rod. Iago—

Iago. What say'st thou, noble heart?

Rod. What will I do, thinkest thou?

Iago. Why, go to bed and sleep.

Rod. I will incontinently drown myself.

Iago. If thou dost, I shall never love thee after. Why, thou silly gentleman!

Rod. It is silliness to live when to live is torment; and then have we a prescription to die when Death is our physician.

Iago. O villainous! I have looked upon the world for four times seven years; and since I could distinguish betwixt a benefit and an injury, I never found a man that knew how to love himself. Ere I would say I would drown myself for the love of a guinea-hen, I would change my humanity with a baboon.

Rod. What should I do? I confess it is my shame to be so fond; but it is not in my virtue to amend it.

Iago. Virtue! a fig! 'tis in ourselves that we are thus or thus. Our bodies are our gardens, to the which our wills are gardeners; so that if we will plant nettles, or sow lettuce, set hyssop and weed up thyme, supply it with one gender of herbs, or distract it with many, either to have it sterile with idleness or manured with industry, why, the power and corrigible authority of this lies in our wills. If the balance of our lives had not one scale of reason to poise another of sensuality, the blood and baseness of our natures would conduct us to most preposterous conclusions; but we have reason to cool our raging motions, our carnal stings, our unbitted lusts, whereof I take this that you call love to be a sect or scion.

Rod. It cannot be.

Iago. It is merely a lust of the blood and a permission of the will. Come, be a man. Drown thyself! drown cats and blind puppies. I have professed me thy friend and I confess me knit to thy deserving with cables of perdurable toughness; I could never better stead thee than now. Put money in thy purse; follow thou the wars; defeat thy favour with an usurped beard; I say, put money in thy purse. It cannot be that Desdemona should long continue her love to the Moor—put money in thy purse—nor he his to her. It was a violent commencement, and thou shalt see an answerable sequestration—put but money in thy purse. These Moors are changeable in their wills—fill thy purse with money—the food that to him now is as luscious as locusts, shall be to him shortly as bitter as coloquintida. She must change for youth; when she is sated with his body, she will find the error of her choice; she must have change, she must; therefore put money in thy purse. If thou wilt needs damn thyself, do it a more delicate way than drowning. Make all the money thou canst. If sanctimony and a frail vow betwixt an erring barbarian and a supersubtle Venetian be not too hard for my wits and all the tribe of hell, thou shalt enjoy her; therefore make money. A pox of drowning thyself! it is clean out of the way. Seek thou rather to be hanged in compassing thy joy than to be drowned and go without her.

Rod. Wilt thou be fast to my hopes, if I depend on the issue?

Iago. Thou art sure of me. Go, make money. I have told thee often, and I re-tell thee again and again, I hate the Moor; my cause is hearted; thine hath no less reason. Let us be conjunctive in our revenge against him. If thou canst cuckold him, thou dost thyself a pleasure, me a sport. There are many events in the womb of time which will be delivered. Traverse! go, provide thy money. We will have more of this to-morrow. Adieu.

Rod. Where shall we meet i' the morning?

Iago. At my lodging.

Rod. I'll be with thee betimes.

Iago. Go to, farewell. Do you hear, Roderigo?
Rod. What say you?
Iago. No more of drowning, do you hear?
Rod. I am changed. I'll go sell all my land. [*Exit*.
Iago. Thus do I ever make my fool my purse;
For I mine own gain'd knowledge should profane,
If I would time expend with such a snipe,
But for my sport and profit. I hate the Moor;
And it is thought abroad that 'twixt my sheets
He has done my office. I know not if't be true;
But I, for mere suspicion in that kind,
Will do as if for surety. He holds me well;
The better shall my purpose work on him.
Cassio's a proper man; let me see now;
To get his place and to plume up my will
In double knavery—How, how?—Let's see—
After some time, to abuse Othello's ear
That he is too familiar with his wife.
He hath a person and a smooth dispose
To be suspected, framed to make women false.
The Moor is of a free and open nature
That thinks men honest that but seem to be so,
And will as tenderly be led by the nose
As asses are.
I have't. It is engender'd. Hell and night
Must bring this monstrous birth to the world's light. [*Exit*.

ACT II

SCENE I. *A Sea-port in Cyprus: an open place near the quay*

Enter MONTANO *and* TWO GENTLEMEN.

Mon. What from the cape can you discern at sea?
1st Gent. Nothing at all; it is a high-wrought flood.
I cannot, 'twixt the heaven and the main,
Descry a sail.
Mon. Methinks the wind hath spoke aloud at land;
A fuller blast ne'er shook our battlements.
If it hath ruffian'd so upon the sea,
What ribs of oak, when mountains melt on them,
Can hold the mortise? What shall we hear of this?
2nd Gent. A segregation of the Turkish fleet.
For do but stand upon the foaming shore,
The chidden billow seems to pelt the clouds;
The wind-shaked surge, with high and monstrous mane,
Seems to cast water on the burning bear,
And quench the guards of the ever-fixed pole.
I never did like molestation view
On the enchafed flood.
Mon. If that the Turkish fleet
Be not enshelter'd and embay'd, they are drown'd;
It is impossible they bear it out.

Enter a THIRD GENTLEMAN.

3rd Gent. News, lads! our wars are done.
The desperate tempest hath so bang'd the Turks
That their designment halts. A noble ship of Venice
Hath seen a grievous wreck and sufferance
On most part of their fleet.
Mon. How! is this true?
3rd Gent. The ship is here put in.
A Veronese, Michael Cassio,
Lieutenant to the warlike Moor Othello,
Is come on shore; the Moor himself at sea,
And is in full commission here for Cyprus.
Mon. I am glad on't; 'tis a worthy governor.
3rd Gent. But this same Cassio, though he speak of comfort
Touching the Turkish loss, yet he looks sadly,
And prays the Moor be safe, for they were parted
With foul and violent tempest.
Mon. Pray heavens he be;
For I have served him, and the man commands
Like a full soldier. Let's to the seaside, ho!
As well to see the vessel that's come in
As to throw out our eyes for brave Othello,
Even till we make the main and the aerial blue
An indistinct regard.
3rd Gent. Come, let's do so;
For every minute is expectancy
Of more arrivance.

Enter CASSIO.

Cas. Thanks, you the valiant of this warlike isle,
That so approve the Moor! O, let the heavens
Give him defence against the elements,
For I have lost him on a dangerous sea.
Mon. Is he well shipp'd?
Cas. His bark is stoutly timber'd, and his pilot
Of very expert and approved allowance;
Therefore my hopes, not surfeited to death,
Stand in bold cure.
A cry within, "A sail, a sail, a sail!"

Enter a FOURTH GENTLEMAN.

Cas. What noise?
4th Gent. The town is empty; on the brow o' the sea
Stand ranks of people, and they cry, "A sail!"
Cas. My hopes do shape him for the governor.
Guns heard.

2nd Gent. They do discharge their shot of courtesy.
Our friends at least.
Cas. I pray you, sir, go forth,
And give us truth who 'tis that is arrived.
2nd Gent. I shall. [*Exit*.
Mon. But, good lieutenant, is your general wived?
Cas. Most fortunately. He hath achieved a maid
That paragons description and wild fame;
One that excels the quirks of blazoning pens,
And in the essential vesture of creation
Does tire the ingener.

Re-enter SECOND GENTLEMAN.

How now! who has put in?
2nd. Gent. 'Tis one Iago, ancient to the general.
Cas. He has had most favourable and happy speed.
Tempests themselves, high seas and howling winds,
The gutter'd rocks and congregated sands—
Traitors ensteep'd to clog the guiltless keel—
As having sense of beauty, do omit
Their mortal natures, letting go safely by
The divine Desdemona.
Mon. What is she?
Cas. She that I spake of, our great captain's captain,
Left in the conduct of the bold Iago,
Whose footing here anticipates our thoughts
A se'nnight's speed. Great Jove, Othello guard,
And swell his sail with thine own powerful breath,
That he may bless this bay with his tall ship,
Make love's quick pants in Desdemona's arms,
Give renew'd fire to our extincted spirits,
And bring all Cyprus comfort!

Enter DESDEMONA, EMILIA, IAGO, RODERIGO, *and Attendants*.

O, behold,
The riches of the ship is come on shore!
Ye men of Cyprus, let her have your knees.
Hail to thee, lady! and the grace of heaven,
Before, behind thee, and on every hand,
Enwheel thee round!
Des. I thank you, valiant Cassio.
What tidings can you tell me of my lord?
Cas. He is not yet arrived; nor know I aught
But that he's well and will be shortly here.
Des. O, but I fear—how lost you company?
Cas. The great contention of the sea and skies
Parted our fellowship—But, hark! a sail.
Within, "A sail, a sail!" *Guns heard*.
2nd Gent. They give their greeting to the citadel.
This likewise is a friend.
Cas. See for the news. [*Exit* GENTLEMAN.
Good ancient, you are welcome. [*To* EMILIA]
Welcome, mistress.
Let it not gall your patience, good Iago,
That I extend my manners; 'tis my breeding
That gives me this bold show of courtesy.
Kissing her.
Iago. Sir, would she give you so much of her lips
As of her tongue she oft bestows on me,
You'd have enough.
Des. Alas, she has no speech.
Iago. In faith, too much;
I find it still, when I have list to sleep.
Marry, before your ladyship, I grant,
She puts her tongue a little in her heart,
And chides with thinking.
Emil. You have little cause to say so.
Iago. Come on, come on; you are pictures out of doors,
Bells in your parlours, wild-cats in your kitchens,
Saints in your injuries, devils being offended,
Players in your housewifery, and housewives in your beds.
Des. O, fie upon thee, slanderer!
Iago. Nay, it is true, or else I am a Turk;
You rise to play and go to bed to work.
Emil. You shall not write my praise.
Iago. No, let me not.
Des. What wouldst thou write of me, if thou shouldst praise me?
Iago. O gentle lady, do not put me to't;
For I am nothing, if not critical.
Des. Come on, assay. There's one gone to the harbour?
Iago. Ay, madam.
Des. I am not merry; but I do beguile
The thing I am by seeming otherwise.
Come, how wouldst thou praise me?
Iago. I am about it; but indeed my invention
Comes from my pate as birdlime does from frize;
It plucks out brains and all. But my Muse labours,
And thus she is deliver'd.
If she be fair and wise, fairness and wit,
The one's for use, the other useth it.
Des. Well praised! How if she be black and witty?
Iago. If she be black, and thereto have a wit,
She'll find a white that shall her blackness fit.
Des. Worse and worse.
Emil. How if fair and foolish?
Iago. She never yet was foolish that was fair;
For even her folly help'd her to an heir.

Des. These are old fond paradoxes to make fools laugh i' the alehouse. What miserable praise hast thou for her that's foul and foolish?

Iago. There's none so foul and foolish thereunto,
But does foul pranks which fair and wise ones do.

Des. O heavy ignorance! thou praisest the worst best. But what praise couldst thou bestow on a deserving woman indeed, one that, in the authority of her merit, did justly put on the vouch of very malice itself?

Iago. She that was ever fair and never proud,
Had tongue at will and yet was never loud,
Never lack'd gold and yet went never gay,
Fled from her wish and yet said, "Now I may";
She that being anger'd, her revenge being nigh,
Bade her wrong stay and her displeasure fly,
She that in wisdom never was so frail
To change the cod's head for the salmon's tail,
She that could think and ne'er disclose her mind,
See suitors following and not look behind,
She was a wight, if ever such wight were—

Des. To do what?

Iago. To suckle fools and chronicle small beer.

Des. O most lame and impotent conclusion! Do not learn of him, Emilia, though he be thy husband. How say you, Cassio? is he not a most profane and liberal counsellor?

Cas. He speaks home, madam. You may relish him more in the soldier than in the scholar.

Iago. [*Aside*] He takes her by the palm; ay, well said, whisper. With as little a web as this will I ensnare as great a fly as Cassio. Ay, smile upon her, do; I will gyve thee in thine own courtship. You say true; 'tis so, indeed. If such tricks as these strip you out of your lieutenantry, it had been better you had not kissed your three fingers so oft, which now again you are most apt to play the sir in. Very good; well kissed! an excellent courtesy! 'tis so, indeed. Yet again your fingers to your lips? would they were clyster-pipes for your sake! [*Trumpet within.*] The Moor! I know his trumpet.

Cas. 'Tis truly so.

Des. Let's meet him and receive him.

Cas. Lo, where he comes!

Enter OTHELLO *and Attendants.*

Oth. O my fair warrior!

Des. My dear Othello!

Oth. It gives me wonder great as my content
To see you here before me. O my soul's joy!
If after every tempest come such calms,
May the winds blow till they have waken'd death!
And let the labouring bark climb hills of seas
Olympus-high and duck again as low
As hell's from heaven! If it were now to die,
'Twere now to be most happy; for, I fear,
My soul hath her content so absolute
That not another comfort like to this
Succeeds in unknown fate.

Des. The heavens forbid
But that our loves and comforts should increase,
Even as our days do grow!

Oth. Amen to that, sweet powers!
I cannot speak enough of this content;
It stops me here; it is too much of joy.
And this, and this, the greatest discords be
Kissing her.
That e'er our hearts shall make!

Iago. [*Aside*] O, you are well tuned now!
But I'll set down the pegs that make this music,
As honest as I am.

Oth. Come, let us to the castle.
News, friends; our wars are done, the Turks are drown'd.
How does my old acquaintance of this isle?
Honey, you shall be well desired in Cyprus;
I have found great love amongst them. O my sweet,
I prattle out of fashion, and I dote
In mine own comforts. I prithee, good Iago,
Go to the bay and disembark my coffers.
Bring thou the master to the citadel;
He is a good one, and his worthiness
Does challenge much respect. Come, Desdemona,
Once more, well met at Cyprus.

[*Exeunt* OTHELLO, DESDEMONA, *and Attendants.*

Iago. Do thou meet me presently at the harbour. Come hither. If thou be'st valiant—as, they say, base men being in love have then a nobility in their natures more than is native to them—list me. The lieutenant to-night watches on the court of guard. First, I must tell thee this —Desdemona is directly in love with him.

Rod. With him! why, 'tis not possible.

Iago. Lay thy finger thus, and let thy soul be instructed. Mark me with what violence she first loved the Moor, but for bragging and telling her fantastical lies; and will she love him still for prating? let not thy discreet heart think it. Her eye must be fed; and what delight shall she have to look on the devil? When the blood is made dull with the act of sport, there should be, again to inflame it and to give satiety a fresh appetite, loveliness in favour, sympathy in years, manners, and beauties; all which the Moor is defective in. Now, for want of these required conveniences, her delicate tenderness will find itself abused, begin to heave the gorge, disrelish and abhor the Moor; very nature will instruct her in it and compel her to some second choice. Now, sir, this granted—as it is a most pregnant and unforced position—who stands so eminent in the degree of this fortune as Cassio does? a knave very voluble; no further conscionable than in putting on the mere form of civil and humane seeming, for the better compassing of his salt and most hidden loose affection? Why, none; why, none; a slipper and subtle knave, a finder of occasions, that has an eye can stamp and counterfeit advantages, though true advantage never present itself; a devilish knave. Besides, the knave is handsome, young, and hath all those requisites in him that folly and green minds look after; a pestilent complete knave; and the woman hath found him already.

Rod. I cannot believe that in her; she's full of most blessed condition.

Iago. Blessed fig's-end! the wine she drinks is made of grapes. If she had been blessed, she would never have loved the Moor. Blessed pudding! Didst thou not see her paddle with the palm of his hand? didst not mark that?

Rod. Yes, that I did; but that was but courtesy.

Iago. Lechery, by this hand; an index and obscure prologue to the history of lust and foul thoughts. They met so near with their lips that their breaths embraced together. Villainous thoughts, Roderigo! when these mutualities so marshal the way, hard at hand comes the master and main exercise, the incorporate conclusion. Pish! But, sir, be you ruled by me; I have brought you from Venice. Watch you to-night; for the command, I'll lay't upon you. Cassio knows you not. I'll not be far from you. Do you find some occasion to anger Cassio, either by speaking too loud, or tainting his discipline; or from what other course you please, which the time shall more favourably minister.

Rod. Well.

Iago. Sir, he is rash and very sudden in choler, and haply may strike at you. Provoke him, that he may; for even out of that will I cause these of Cyprus to mutiny; whose qualification shall come into no true taste again but by the displanting of Cassio. So shall you have a shorter journey to your desires by the means I shall then have to prefer them; and the impediment most profitably removed, without the which there were no expectation of our prosperity.

Rod. I will do this, if I can bring it to any opportunity.

Iago. I warrant thee. Meet me by and by at the citadel. I must fetch his necessaries ashore. Farewell.

Rod. Adieu. [*Exit*.

Iago. That Cassio loves her, I do well believe it;
That she loves him, 'tis apt and of great credit.
The Moor, howbeit that I endure him not,
Is of a constant, loving, noble nature,
And I dare think he'll prove to Desdemona
A most dear husband. Now, I do love her too;
Not out of absolute lust, though peradventure
I stand accountant for as great a sin,
But partly led to diet my revenge,
For that I do suspect the lusty Moor
Hath leap'd into my seat; the thought whereof
Doth, like a poisonous mineral, gnaw my inwards;
And nothing can or shall content my soul
Till I am even'd with him, wife for wife,
Or failing so, yet that I put the Moor
At least into a jealousy so strong
That judgement cannot cure. Which thing to do,
If this poor trash of Venice, whom I trash
For his quick hunting, stand the putting on,
I'll have our Michael Cassio on the hip,
Abuse him to the Moor in the rank garb—
For I fear Cassio with my night-cap too—
Make the Moor thank me, love me, and reward me,
For making him egregiously an ass
And practising upon his peace and quiet
Even to madness. 'Tis here, but yet confused;
Knavery's plain face is never seen till used. [*Exit*.

SCENE II. *A street*

Enter a HERALD *with a proclamation; People following*.

Her. It is Othello's pleasure, our noble and valiant general, that, upon certain tidings now arrived, importing the mere perdition of the Turkish fleet, every man put himself into triumph; some to dance, some to make bonfires, each man to what sport and revels his addiction leads him; for, besides these beneficial news, it is the celebration of his nuptial. So much was his pleasure should be proclaimed. All offices are open, and there is full liberty of feasting from this present hour of five till the bell have told eleven. Heaven bless the isle of Cyprus and our noble general Othello! [*Exeunt*.

SCENE III. *A hall in the castle*

Enter OTHELLO, DESDEMONA, CASSIO, *and Attendants*.

Oth. Good Michael, look you to the guard to-night.
Let's teach ourselves that honourable stop,
Not to outsport discretion.

Cas. Iago hath direction what to do;

But, notwithstanding, with my personal eye
Will I look to't.

Oth. Iago is most honest.
Michael, good night. To-morrow with your earliest
Let me have speech with you. [*To Desdemona*] Come, my dear love,
The purchase made, the fruits are to ensue;
That profit's yet to come 'tween me and you.
Good night.

[*Exeunt* OTHELLO, DESDEMONA, *and Attendants*.

Enter IAGO.

Cas. Welcome, Iago; we must to the watch.

Iago. Not this hour, lieutenant; 'tis not yet ten o'clock. Our general cast us thus early for the love of his Desdemona; who let us not therefore blame. He hath not yet made wanton the night with her; and she is sport for Jove.

Cas. She's a most exquisite lady.

Iago. And, I'll warrant her, full of game.

Cas. Indeed, she's a most fresh and delicate creature.

Iago. What an eye she has! methinks it sounds a parley of provocation.

Cas. An inviting eye; and yet methinks right modest.

Iago. And when she speaks, is it not an alarum to love?

Cas. She is indeed perfection.

Iago. Well, happiness to their sheets! Come, lieutenant, I have a stoup of wine; and here without are a brace of Cyprus gallants that would fain have a measure to the health of black Othello.

Cas. Not to-night, good Iago. I have very poor and unhappy brains for drinking. I could well wish courtesy would invent some other custom of entertainment.

Iago. O, they are our friends; but one cup; I'll drink for you.

Cas. I have drunk but one cup to-night, and that was craftily qualified too, and, behold, what innovation it makes here. I am unfortunate in the infirmity, and dare not task my weakness with any more.

Iago. What, man! 'tis a night of revels. The gallants desire it.

Cas. Where are they?

Iago. Here at the door; I pray you, call them in.

Cas. I'll do't; but it dislikes me. [*Exit.*

Iago. If I can fasten but one cup upon him,
With that which he hath drunk to-night already,
He'll be as full of quarrel and offence
As my young mistress' dog. Now, my sick fool Roderigo,
Whom love hath turn'd almost the wrong side out,
To Desdemona hath to-night caroused
Potations pottle-deep; and he's to watch.
Three lads of Cyprus, noble swelling spirits,
That hold their honours in a wary distance,
The very elements of this warlike isle,
Have I to-night fluster'd with flowing cups,
And they watch too. Now, 'mongst this flock of drunkards,
Am I to put our Cassio in some action
That may offend the isle. But here they come.
If consequence do but approve my dream,
My boat sails freely, both with wind and stream.

Re-enter CASSIO; *with him* MONTANO *and* GENTLEMEN; *Servants following with wine.*

Cas. 'Fore God, they have given me a rouse already.

Mon. Good faith, a little one; not past a pint, as I am a soldier.

Iago. Some wine, ho!
[*Sings*] "And let me the canakin clink, clink;
And let me the canakin clink.
A soldier's a man;
A life's but a span;
Why, then, let a soldier drink."
Some wine, boys!

Cas. 'Fore God, an excellent song.

Iago. I learned it in England, where, indeed, they are most potent in potting; your Dane, your German, and your swag-bellied Hollander—Drink, ho!—are nothing to your English.

Cas. Is your Englishman so expert in his drinking?

Iago. Why, he drinks you, with facility, your Dane dead drunk; he sweats not to overthrow your Almain; he gives your Hollander a vomit, ere the next pottle can be filled.

Cas. To the health of our general!

Mon. I am for it, lieutenant; and I'll do you justice.

Iago. O sweet England!
"King Stephen was a worthy peer,
His breeches cost him but a crown;
He held them sixpence all too dear,
With that he call'd the tailor lown.

"He was a wight of high renown,
And thou art but of low degree.
'Tis pride that pulls the country down;
Then take thine auld cloak about thee."
Some wine, ho!

Cas. Why, this is a more exquisite song than the other.

Iago. Will you hear 't again?

Cas. No; for I hold him to be unworthy of his place that does those things. Well, God's above all; and there be souls must be saved, and there be souls must not be saved.

Iago. It's true, good lieutenant.

Cas. For mine own part—no offence to the general, nor any man of quality—I hope to be saved.

Iago. And so do I too, lieutenant.

Cas. Ay, but, by your leave, not before me; the lieutenant is to be saved before the ancient. Let's have no more of this; let's to our affairs.—Forgive us our sins!—Gentlemen, let's look to our business. Do not think, gentlemen, I am drunk. This is my ancient; this is my right hand, and this is my left. I am not drunk now; I can stand well enough, and speak well enough.

All. Excellent well.

Cas. Why, very well then; you must not think then that I am drunk. [*Exit.*

Mon. To the platform, masters; come, let's set the watch.

Iago. You see this fellow that is gone before;
He is a soldier fit to stand by Cæsar
And give direction; and do but see his vice.
'Tis to his virtue a just equinox,
The one as long as the other; 'tis pity of him.
I fear the trust Othello puts him in,
On some odd time of his infirmity,
Will shake this island.

Mon. But is he often thus?

Iago. 'Tis evermore the prologue to his sleep.
He'll watch the horologe a double set,
If drink rock not his cradle.

Mon. It were well
The general were put in mind of it.
Perhaps he sees it not; or his good nature
Prizes the virtue that appears in Cassio,
And looks not on his evils. Is not this true?

Enter RODERIGO.

Iago. [*Aside to him*] How now, Roderigo!
I pray you, after the lieutenant; go.
[*Exit* RODERIGO.

Mon. And 'tis great pity that the noble Moor
Should hazard such a place as his own second
With one of an ingraft infirmity.
It were an honest action to say
So to the Moor.

Iago. Not I, for this fair island.
I do love Cassio well; and would do much
To cure him of this evil—But, hark! what noise?

Cry within: "Help! help!"

Re-enter CASSIO, *driving in* RODERIGO.

Cas. You rogue! you rascal!

Mon. What's the matter, lieutenant?

Cas. A knave teach me my duty!
I'll beat the knave into a twiggen bottle.

Rod. Beat me!

Cas. Dost thou prate, rogue?

Striking RODERIGO.

Mon. Nay, good lieutenant;

Staying him.

I pray you, sir, hold your hand.

Cas. Let me go, sir,
Or I'll knock you o'er the mazzard.

Mon. Come, come, you're drunk.

Cas. Drunk! [*They fight.*]

Iago. [*Aside to* RODERIGO] Away, I say; go out, and cry a mutiny. [*Exit* RODERIGO.
Nay, good lieutenant—alas, gentlemen—
Help, ho!—Lieutenant—sir—Montano—sir—
Help, masters!—Here's a goodly watch indeed!

Bell rings.

Who's that which rings the bell?—Diablo, ho!
The town will rise. God's will, lieutenant, hold!
You will be shamed for ever.

Re-enter OTHELLO *and Attendants.*

Oth. What is the matter here?

Mon. 'Zounds, I bleed still; I am hurt to the death. [*Faints.*]

Oth. Hold, for your lives!

Iago. Hold, ho! Lieutenant—sir—Montano—gentlemen—
Have you forgot all sense of place and duty?
Hold! the general speaks to you; hold, hold, for shame!

Oth. Why, how now, ho! from whence ariseth this?
Are we turn'd Turks, and to ourselves do that
Which Heaven hath forbid the Ottomites?
For Christian shame, put by this barbarous brawl.
He that stirs next to carve for his own rage
Holds his soul light; he dies upon his motion.
Silence that dreadful bell; it frights the isle
From her propriety. What is the matter, masters?
Honest Iago, that look'st dead with grieving,
Speak, who began this? on thy love, I charge thee.

Iago. I do not know. Friends all but now, even now,
In quarter, and in terms like bride and groom
Devesting them for bed; and then, but now—
As if some planet had unwitted men—
Swords out, and tilting one at other's breast,
In opposition bloody. I cannot speak
Any beginning to this peevish odds;
And would in action glorious I had lost

Those legs that brought me to a part of it!
Oth. How comes it, Michael, you are thus forgot?
Cas. I pray you, pardon me; I cannot speak.
Oth. Worthy Montano, you were wont be civil;
The gravity and stillness of your youth
The world hath noted, and your name is great
In mouths of wisest censure. What's the matter,
That you unlace your reputation thus
And spend your rich opinion for the name
Of a night-brawler? give me answer to it.
Mon. Worthy Othello, I am hurt to danger.
Your officer, Iago, can inform you—
While I spare speech, which something now offends me—
Of all that I do know; nor know I aught
By me that's said or done amiss this night;
Unless self-charity be sometimes a vice,
And to defend ourselves it be a sin
When violence assails us.
Oth. Now, by heaven,
My blood begins my safer guides to rule;
And passion, having my best judgement collied,
Assays to lead the way. If I once stir,
Or do but lift this arm, the best of you
Shall sink in my rebuke. Give me to know
How this foul rout began, who set it on;
And he that is approved in this offence,
Though he had twinn'd with me, both at a birth,
Shall lose me. What! in a town of war,
Yet wild, the people's hearts brimful of fear,
To manage private and domestic quarrel,
In night, and on the court and guard of safety!
'Tis monstrous. Iago, who began 't?
Mon. If partially affined, or leagued in office,
Thou dost deliver more or less than truth,
Thou art no soldier.
Iago. Touch me not so near.
I had rather have this tongue cut from my mouth
Than it should do offence to Michael Cassio;
Yet, I persuade myself, to speak the truth
Shall nothing wrong him. Thus it is, general.
Montano and myself being in speech,
There comes a fellow crying out for help;
And Cassio following him with determined sword,
To execute upon him. Sir, this gentleman
Steps in to Cassio, and entreats his pause.
Myself the crying fellow did pursue,
Lest by his clamour—as it so fell out—
The town might fall in fright. He, swift of foot,
Outran my purpose; and I return'd the rather
For that I heard the clink and fall of swords,
And Cassio high in oath; which till to-night
I ne'er might say before. When I came back—
For this was brief—I found them close together,
At blow and thrust; even as again they were
When you yourself did part them.
More of this matter cannot I report.
But men are men; the best sometimes forget.
Though Cassio did some little wrong to him,
As men in rage strike those that wish them best,
Yet surely Cassio, I believe, received
From him that fled some strange indignity
Which patience could not pass.
Oth. I know, Iago,
Thy honesty and love doth mince this matter,
Making it light to Cassio. Cassio, I love thee;
But never more be officer of mine.

Re-enter DESDEMONA, *attended.*

Look, if my gentle love be not raised up!
I'll make thee an example.
Des. What's the matter?
Oth. All's well now, sweeting; come away to bed.
Sir, for your hurts, myself will be your surgeon.
Lead him off. [*To* MONTANO, *who is led off.*
Iago, look with care about the town,
And silence those whom this vile brawl distracted.
Come, Desdemona; 'tis the soldiers' life
To have their balmy slumbers waked with strife.
[*Exeunt all but* IAGO *and* CASSIO.
Iago. What, are you hurt, lieutenant?
Cas. Ay, past all surgery.
Iago. Marry, heaven forbid!

Cas. Reputation, reputation, reputation! O, I have lost my reputation! I have lost the immortal part of myself, and what remains is bestial. My reputation, Iago, my reputation!

Iago. As I am an honest man, I thought you had received some bodily wound; there is more sense in that than in reputation. Reputation is an idle and most false imposition; oft got without merit, and lost without deserving. You have lost no reputation at all, unless you repute yourself such a loser. What, man! there are ways to recover the general again. You are but now cast in his mood, a punishment more in policy than in malice; even so as one would beat his offenceless dog to affright an imperious lion. Sue to him again, and he's yours.

Cas. I will rather sue to be despised than to deceive so good a commander with so slight, so drunken, and so indiscreet an officer. Drunk? and speak parrot? and squabble? swagger? swear? and discourse fustian with one's own shadow? O thou invisible spirit of wine, if thou hast no name to be known by, let us call thee devil!

Iago. What was he that you followed with your sword? What had he done to you?

Cas. I know not.

Iago. Is't possible?

Cas. I remember a mass of things, but nothing distinctly; a quarrel, but nothing wherefore. O God, that men should put an enemy in their mouths to steal away their brains! that we should, with joy, pleasance, revel, and applause, transform ourselves into beasts!

Iago. Why, but you are now well enough. How came you thus recovered?

Cas. It hath pleased the devil drunkenness to give place to the devil wrath. One unperfectness shows me another, to make me frankly despise myself.

Iago. Come, you are too severe a moraler. As the time, the place, and the condition of this country stands, I could heartily wish this had not befallen; but, since it is as it is, mend it for your own good.

Cas. I will ask him for my place again; he shall tell me I am a drunkard! Had I as many mouths as Hydra, such an answer would stop them all. To be now a sensible man, by and by a fool, and presently a beast! O strange! Every inordinate cup is unblessed and the ingredient is a devil.

Iago. Come, come, good wine is a good familiar creature, if it be well used; exclaim no more against it. And, good lieutenant, I think you think I love you.

Cas. I have well approved it, sir. I drunk!

Iago. You or any man living may be drunk at a time, man. I'll tell you what you shall do. Our general's wife is now the general. I may say so in this respect, for that he hath devoted and given up himself to the contemplation, mark, and denotement of her parts and graces. Confess yourself freely to her; importune her help to put you in your place again. She is of so free, so kind, so apt, so blessed a disposition, she holds it a vice in her goodness not to do more than she is requested. This broken joint between you and her husband entreat her to splinter; and, my fortunes against any lay worth naming, this crack of your love shall grow stronger than it was before.

Cas. You advise me well.

Iago. I protest, in the sincerity of love and honest kindness.

Cas. I think it freely; and betimes in the morning I will beseech the virtuous Desdemona to undertake for me. I am desperate of my fortunes if they check me here.

Iago. You are in the right. Good night, lieutenant; I must to the watch.

Cas. Good night, honest Iago. [*Exit*.

Iago. And what's he then that says I play the villain?
When this advice is free I give and honest,
Probal to thinking and indeed the course
To win the Moor again? For 'tis most easy
The inclining Desdemona to subdue
In any honest suit; she's framed as fruitful
As the free elements. And then for her
To win the Moor—were't to renounce his baptism,
All seals and symbols of redeemed sin,
His soul is so enfetter'd to her love,
That she may make, unmake, do what she list,
Even as her appetite shall play the god
With his weak function. How am I then a villain
To counsel Cassio to this parallel course,
Directly to his good? Divinity of hell!
When devils will the blackest sins put on,
They do suggest at first with heavenly shows,
As I do now; for whiles this honest fool
Plies Desdemona to repair his fortunes
And she for him pleads strongly to the Moor,
I'll pour this pestilence into his ear,
That she repeals him for her body's lust;
And by how much she strives to do him good,
She shall undo her credit with the Moor.
So will I turn her virtue into pitch,
And out of her own goodness make the net
That shall enmesh them all.

Re-enter RODERIGO.

How now, Roderigo!

Rod. I do follow here in the chase, not like a hound that hunts, but one that fills up the cry. My money is almost spent; I have been to-night exceedingly well cudgelled; and I think the issue will be, I shall have so much experience for my pains, and so, with no money at all and a little more wit, return again to Venice.

Iago. How poor are they that have not patience!
What wound did ever heal but by degrees?
Thou know'st we work by wit, and not by witchcraft;
And wit depends on dilatory time.
Does't not go well? Cassio hath beaten thee,
And thou, by that small hurt, hast cashier'd Cassio.
Though other things grow fair against the sun,
Yet fruits that blossom first will first be ripe.
Content thyself awhile. By the mass, 'tis morning;
Pleasure and action make the hours seem short.
Retire thee; go where thou art billeted.
Away, I say; thou shalt know more hereafter.

Nay, get thee gone. [*Exit* RODERIGO.] Two things are to be done:
My wife must move for Cassio to her mistress;
I'll set her on;
Myself the while to draw the Moor apart,
And bring him jump when he may Cassio find
Soliciting his wife. Ay, that's the way;
Dull not device by coldness and delay. [*Exit.*

ACT III

SCENE I. *Before the castle*

Enter CASSIO *and some* MUSICIANS.

Cas. Masters, play here; I will content your pains;
Something that's brief; and bid "Good morrow, general."
Music.

Enter CLOWN.

Clo. Why, masters, have your instruments been in Naples, that they speak i' the nose thus?

1st Mus. How, sir, how!

Clo. Are these, I pray you, wind-instruments?

1st Mus. Ay, marry, are they, sir.

Clo. O, thereby hangs a tail.

1st Mus. Whereby hangs a tale, sir?

Clo. Marry, sir, by many a wind-instrument that I know. But, masters, here's money for you; and the general so likes your music, that he desires you, for love's sake, to make no more noise with it.

1st Mus. Well, sir, we will not.

Clo. If you have any music that may not be heard, to't again; but, as they say, to hear music the general does not greatly care.

1st Mus. We have none such, sir.

Clo. Then put up your pipes in your bag, for I'll away. Go; vanish into air; away!

[*Exeunt* MUSICIANS.

Cas. Dost thou hear, my honest friend?

Clo. No, I hear not your honest friend; I hear you.

Cas. Prithee, keep up thy quillets. There's a poor piece of gold for thee. If the gentlewoman that attends the general's wife be stirring, tell her there's one Cassio entreats her a little favour of speech. Wilt thou do this?

Clo. She is stirring, sir. If she will stir hither,
I shall seem to notify unto her.

Cas. Do, good my friend. [*Exit* CLOWN.

Enter IAGO.

In happy time, Iago.

Iago. You have not been a-bed, then?

Cas. Why, no; the day had broke
Before we parted. I have made bold, Iago,
To send in to your wife. My suit to her
Is that she will to virtuous Desdemona
Procure me some access.

Iago. I'll send her to you presently;
And I'll devise a mean to draw the Moor
Out of the way, that your converse and business
May be more free.

Cas. I humbly thank you for't. [*Exit* IAGO.
I never knew
A Florentine more kind and honest.

Enter EMILIA.

Emil. Good morrow, good lieutenant. I am sorry
For your displeasure; but all will sure be well.
The general and his wife are talking of it;
And she speaks for you stoutly. The Moor replies
That he you hurt is of great fame in Cyprus
And great affinity and that in wholesome wisdom
He might not but refuse you, but he protests he loves you
And needs no other suitor but his likings
To take the safest occasion by the front
To bring you in again.

Cas. Yet, I beseech you,
If you think fit, or that it may be done,
Give me advantage of some brief discourse
With Desdemona alone.

Emil. Pray you, come in.
I will bestow you where you shall have time
To speak your bosom freely.

Cas. I am much bound to you. [*Exeunt.*

SCENE II. *A room in the castle*

Enter OTHELLO, IAGO, *and* GENTLEMEN.

Oth. These letters give, Iago, to the pilot;
And by him do my duties to the Senate.
That done, I will be walking on the works;
Repair there to me.

Iago. Well, my good lord, I'll do 't.

Oth. This fortification, gentlemen, shall we see 't?

Gent. We'll wait upon your lordship. [*Exeunt.*

SCENE III. *The garden of the castle*

Enter DESDEMONA, CASSIO, *and* EMILIA.

Des. Be thou assured, good Cassio, I will do
All my abilities in thy behalf.

Emil. Good madam, do. I warrant it grieves my husband,
As if the case were his.

Des. O, that's an honest fellow. Do not doubt, Cassio,
But I will have my lord and you again

As friendly as you were.
Cas. Bounteous madam,
Whatever shall become of Michael Cassio,
He's never anything but your true servant.
Des. I know't; I thank you. You do love my lord;
You have known him long; and be you well assured
He shall in strangeness stand no further off
Than in a politic distance.
Cas. Ay, but, lady,
That policy may either last so long,
Or feed upon such nice and waterish diet,
Or breed itself so out of circumstance,
That, I being absent and my place supplied,
My general will forget my love and service.
Des. Do not doubt that; before Emilia here
I give thee warrant of thy place. Assure thee,
If I do vow a friendship, I'll perform it
To the last article. My lord shall never rest;
I'll watch him tame and talk him out of patience;
His bed shall seem a school, his board a shrift;
I'll intermingle everything he does
With Cassio's suit. Therefore be merry, Cassio;
For thy solicitor shall rather die
Than give thy cause away.

Enter OTHELLO *and* IAGO.

Emil. Madam, here comes my lord.
Cas. Madam, I'll take my leave.
Des. Why, stay, and hear me speak.
Cas. Madam, not now; I am very ill at ease,
Unfit for mine own purposes.
Des. Well, do your discretion. [*Exit* CASSIO.
Iago. Ha! I like not that.
Oth. What dost thou say?
Iago. Nothing, my lord; or if—I know not what.
Oth. Was not that Cassio parted from my wife?
Iago. Cassio, my lord! No, sure, I cannot think it,
That he would steal away so guilty-like,
Seeing you coming.
Oth. I do believe 'twas he.
Des. How now, my lord!
I have been talking with a suitor here,
A man that languishes in your displeasure.
Oth. Who is't you mean?
Des. Why, your lieutenant, Cassio. Good my lord,
If I have any grace or power to move you,
His present reconciliation take;
For if he be not one that truly loves you,
That errs in ignorance and not in cunning,
I have no judgement in an honest face.
I prithee, call him back.
Oth. Went he hence now?
Des. Ay, sooth; so humbled
That he hath left part of his grief with me,
To suffer with him. Good love, call him back.
Oth. Not now, sweet Desdemona; some other time.
Des. But shall't be shortly?
Oth. The sooner, sweet, for you.
Des. Shall 't be to-night at supper?
Oth. No, not to-night.
Des. To-morrow dinner, then?
Oth. I shall not dine at home;
I meet the captains at the citadel.
Des. Why, then, to-morrow night; or Tuesday morn;
On Tuesday noon, or night; on Wednesday morn.
I prithee, name the time, but let it not
Exceed three days. In faith, he's penitent;
And yet his trespass, in our common reason—
Save that, they say, the wars must make examples
Out of their best—is not almost a fault
To incur a private check. When shall he come?
Tell me, Othello. I wonder in my soul
What you would ask me that I should deny,
Or stand so mammering on. What! Michael Cassio,
That came a-wooing with you, and so many a time,
When I have spoke of you dispraisingly,
Hath ta'en your part; to have so much to do
To bring him in! Trust me, I could do much—
Oth. Prithee, no more. Let him come when he will;
I will deny thee nothing.
Des. Why, this is not a boon;
'Tis as I should entreat you wear your gloves,
Or feed on nourishing dishes, or keep you warm,
Or sue to you to do a peculiar profit
To your own person. Nay, when I have a suit
Wherein I mean to touch your love indeed,
It shall be full of poise and difficult weight
And fearful to be granted.
Oth. I will deny thee nothing;
Whereon, I do beseech thee, grant me this,
To leave me but a little to myself.
Des. Shall I deny you? no. Farewell, my lord.
Oth. Farewell, my Desdemona. I'll come to thee straight.
Des. Emilia, come. Be as your fancies teach you;
Whate'er you be, I am obedient.
[*Exeunt* DESDEMONA *and* EMILIA.

Oth. Excellent wretch! Perdition catch my soul,
But I do love thee! and when I love thee not,
Chaos is come again.
Iago. My noble lord—
Oth. What dost thou say, Iago?
Iago. Did Michael Cassio, when you woo'd my lady,
Know of your love?
Oth. He did, from first to last. Why dost thou ask?
Iago. But for a satisfaction of my thought;
No further harm.
Oth. Why of thy thought, Iago?
Iago. I did not think he had been acquainted with her.
Oth. O, yes; and went between us very oft.
Iago. Indeed!
Oth. Indeed! ay, indeed. Discern'st thou aught in that?
Is he not honest?
Iago. Honest, my lord!
Oth. Honest! ay, honest.
Iago. My lord, for aught I know.
Oth. What dost thou think?
Iago. Think, my lord!
Oth. Think, my lord!
By heaven, he echoes me,
As if there were some monster in his thought
Too hideous to be shown. Thou dost mean something.
I heard thee say even now, thou likedst not that,
When Cassio left my wife. What didst not like?
And when I told thee he was of my counsel
In my whole course of wooing, thou criedst "Indeed!"
And didst contract and purse thy brow together,
As if thou then hadst shut up in thy brain
Some horrible conceit. If thou dost love me,
Show me thy thought.
Iago. My lord, you know I love you.
Oth. I think thou dost;
And, for I know thou'rt full of love and honesty,
And weigh'st thy words before thou givest them breath,
Therefore these stops of thine fright me the more;
For such things in a false disloyal knave
Are tricks of custom, but in a man that's just
They are close delations, working from the heart
That passion cannot rule.
Iago. For Michael Cassio,
I dare be sworn I think that he is honest.
Oth. I think so too.
Iago. Men should be what they seem;
Or those that be not, would they might seem none!
Oth. Certain, men should be what they seem.
Iago. Why, then, I think Cassio's an honest man.
Oth. Nay, yet there's more in this.
I prithee, speak to me as to thy thinkings,
As thou dost ruminate, and give thy worst of thoughts
The worst of words.
Iago. Good my lord, pardon me.
Though I am bound to every act of duty,
I am not bound to that all slaves are free to.
Utter my thoughts? Why, say they are vile and false;
As where's that palace whereinto foul things
Sometimes intrude not? who has a breast so pure,
But some uncleanly apprehensions
Keep leets and law-days and in session sit
With meditations lawful?
Oth. Thou dost conspire against thy friend, Iago,
If thou but think'st him wrong'd and makest his ear
A stranger to thy thoughts.
Iago. I do beseech you—
Though I perchance am vicious in my guess,
As, I confess, it is my nature's plague
To spy into abuses, and oft my jealousy
Shapes faults that are not—that your wisdom yet,
From one that so imperfectly conceits,
Would take no notice, nor build yourself a trouble
Out of his scattering and unsure observance.
It were not for your quiet nor your good,
Nor for my manhood, honesty, or wisdom,
To let you know my thoughts.
Oth. What dost thou mean?
Iago. Good name in man and woman, dear my lord,
Is the immediate jewel of their souls.
Who steals my purse steals trash; 'tis something, nothing;
'Twas mine, 'tis his, and has been slave to thousands;
But he that filches from me my good name
Robs me of that which not enriches him
And makes me poor indeed.
Oth. By heaven, I'll know thy thoughts.
Iago. You cannot, if my heart were in your hand;
Nor shall not, whilst 'tis in my custody.
Oth. Ha!
Iago. O, beware, my lord, of jealousy;
It is the green-eyed monster which doth mock
The meat it feeds on. That cuckold lives in bliss
Who, certain of his fate, loves not his wronger;

But, O, what damned minutes tells he o'er
Who dotes, yet doubts, suspects, yet strongly loves!
Oth. O misery!
Iago. Poor and content is rich and rich enough,
But riches fineless is as poor as winter
To him that ever fears he shall be poor.
Good heaven, the souls of all my tribe defend
From jealousy!
Oth. Why, why is this?
Think'st thou I'd make a life of jealousy,
To follow still the changes of the moon
With fresh suspicions? No; to be once in doubt
Is once to be resolved. Exchange me for a goat,
When I shall turn the business of my soul
To such exsufflicate and blown surmises,
Matching thy inference. 'Tis not to make me jealous
To say my wife is fair, feeds well, loves company,
Is free of speech, sings, plays, and dances well;
Where virtue is, these are more virtuous.
Nor from mine own weak merits will I draw
The smallest fear or doubt of her revolt;
For she had eyes, and chose me. No, Iago;
I'll see before I doubt; when I doubt, prove;
And on the proof, there is no more but this—
Away at once with love or jealousy!
Iago. I am glad of it; for now I shall have reason
To show the love and duty that I bear you
With franker spirit; therefore, as I am bound,
Receive it from me. I speak not yet of proof.
Look to your wife; observe her well with Cassio;
Wear your eye thus, not jealous nor secure.
I would not have your free and noble nature,
Out of self-bounty, be abused; look to't.
I know our country disposition well;
In Venice they do let heaven see the pranks
They dare not show their husbands; their best conscience
Is not to leave't undone, but keep't unknown.
Oth. Dost thou say so?
Iago. She did deceive her father, marrying you;
And when she seem'd to shake and fear your looks,
She loved them most.
Oth. And so she did.
Iago. Why, go to then;
She that, so young, could give out such a seeming,
To seel her father's eyes up close as oak—
He thought 'twas witchcraft—but I am much to blame;
I humbly do beseech you of your pardon
For too much loving you.
Oth. I am bound to thee for ever.
Iago. I see this hath a little dash'd your spirits.
Oth. Not a jot, not a jot.
Iago. I' faith, I fear it has.
I hope you will consider what is spoke
Comes from my love. But I do see you're moved.
I am to pray you not to strain my speech
To grosser issues nor to larger reach
Than to suspicion.
Oth. I will not.
Iago. Should you do so, my lord,
My speech should fall into such vile success
As my thoughts aim not at. Cassio's my worthy friend—
My lord, I see you're moved.
Oth. No, not much moved.
I do not think but Desdemona's honest.
Iago. Long live she so! and long live you to think so!
Oth. And yet, how nature erring from itself—
Iago. Ay, there's the point; as—to be bold with you—
Not to affect many proposed matches
Of her own clime, complexion, and degree,
Whereto we see in all things nature tends—
Foh! one may smell in such a will most rank,
Foul disproportion, thoughts unnatural.
But pardon me; I do not in position
Distinctly speak of her; though I may fear
Her will, recoiling to her better judgement,
May fall to match you with her country forms
And happily repent.
Oth. Farewell, farewell.
If more thou dost perceive, let me know more;
Set on thy wife to observe. Leave me, Iago.
Iago. [*Going*] My lord, I take my leave.
Oth. Why did I marry? This honest creature doubtless
Sees and knows more, much more, than he unfolds.
Iago. [*Returning*] My lord, I would I might entreat your honour
To scan this thing no further; leave it to time.
Though it be fit that Cassio have his place,
For, sure, he fills it up with great ability,
Yet, if you please to hold him off awhile,
You shall by that perceive him and his means.
Note, if your lady strain his entertainment
With any strong or vehement importunity;
Much will be seen in that. In the mean time,
Let me be thought too busy in my fears—
As worthy cause I have to fear I am—
And hold her free, I do beseech your honour.
Oth. Fear not my government.
Iago. I once more take my leave. [*Exit.*
Oth. This fellow's of exceeding honesty,

And knows all qualities, with a learned spirit,
Of human dealings. If I do prove her haggard,
Though that her jesses were my dear heart-strings,
I'd whistle her off and let her down the wind,
To prey at fortune. Haply, for I am black
And have not those soft parts of conversation
That chamberers have, or for I am declined
Into the vale of years—yet that's not much—
She's gone. I am abused; and my relief
Must be to loathe her. O curse of marriage,
That we can call these delicate creatures ours,
And not their appetites! I had rather be a toad,
And live upon the vapour of a dungeon,
Than keep a corner in the thing I love
For others' uses. Yet, 'tis the plague of great ones;
Prerogatived are they less than the base;
'Tis destiny unshunnable, like death.
Even then this forked plague is fated to us
When we do quicken. Desdemona comes;

Re-enter DESDEMONA *and* EMILIA.

If she be false, O, then heaven mocks itself!
I'll not believe 't.
Des. How now, my dear Othello!
Your dinner, and the generous islanders
By you invited, do attend your presence.
Oth. I am to blame.
Des. Why do you speak so faintly?
Are you not well?
Oth. I have a pain upon my forehead here.
Des. 'Faith, that's with watching; 'twill away again.
Let me but bind it hard, within this hour
It will be well.
Oth. Your napkin is too little.
He puts the handkerchief from him; and it drops.
Let it alone. Come, I'll go in with you.
Des. I am very sorry that you are not well.
[*Exeunt* OTHELLO *and* DESDEMONA.
Emil. I am glad I have found this napkin;
This was her first remembrance from the Moor.
My wayward husband hath a hundred times
Woo'd me to steal it; but she so loves the token,
For he conjured her she should ever keep it,
That she reserves it evermore about her
To kiss and talk to. I'll have the work ta'en out,
And give't Iago. What he will do with it
Heaven knows, not I;
I nothing but to please his fantasy.

Re-enter IAGO.

Iago. How now! what do you here alone?
Emil. Do not you chide; I have a thing for you.
Iago. A thing for me? it is a common thing—
Emil. Ha!
Iago. To have a foolish wife.
Emil. O, is that all? What will you give me now
For that same handkerchief?
Iago. What handkerchief?
Emil. What handkerchief!
Why, that the Moor first gave to Desdemona;
That which so often you did bid me steal.
Iago. Hast stol'n it from her?
Emil. No, 'faith; she let it drop by negligence,
And, to the advantage, I, being here, took 't up.
Look, here it is.
Iago. A good wench; give it me.
Emil. What will you do with't, that you have been so earnest
To have me filch it?
Iago. [*Snatching it*] Why, what's that to you?
Emil. If it be not for some purpose of import,
Give 't me again. Poor lady, she'll run mad
When she shall lack it.
Iago. Be not acknown on't; I have use for it.
Go, leave me. [*Exit* EMILIA.
I will in Cassio's lodging lose this napkin,
And let him find it. Trifles light as air
Are to the jealous confirmations strong
As proofs of holy writ; this may do something.
The Moor already changes with my poison.
Dangerous conceits are, in their natures, poisons,
Which at the first are scarce found to distaste,
But with a little act upon the blood,
Burn like the mines of sulphur. I did say so.
Look, where he comes!

Re-enter OTHELLO.

Not poppy, nor mandragora,
Nor all the drowsy syrups of the world,
Shall ever medicine thee to that sweet sleep
Which thou owedst yesterday.
Oth. Ha! ha! false to me?
Iago. Why, how now, general! no more of that.
Oth. Avaunt! be gone! thou hast set me on the rack.
I swear 'tis better to be much abused
Than but to know 't a little.
Iago. How now, my lord!
Oth. What sense had I of her stol'n hours of lust?
I saw 't not, thought it not, it harm'd not me.
I slept the next night well, was free and merry;
I found not Cassio's kisses on her lips.
He that is robb'd, not wanting what is stol'n,
Let him not know 't, and he's not robb'd at all.
Iago. I am sorry to hear this.
Oth. I had been happy, if the general camp,
Pioners and all, had tasted her sweet body,
So I had nothing known. O, now, for ever
Farewell the tranquil mind! farewell content!

Farewell the plumed troop, and the big wars,
That make ambition virtue! O, farewell!
Farewell the neighing steed, and the shrill trump,
The spirit-stirring drum, the ear-piercing fife,
The royal banner, and all quality,
Pride, pomp, and circumstance of glorious war!
And, O you mortal engines, whose rude throats
The immortal Jove's dread clamours counterfeit,
Farewell! Othello's occupation's gone!

Iago. Is't possible, my lord?

Oth. Villain, be sure thou prove my love a whore,
Be sure of it; give me the ocular proof;
Or, by the worth of man's eternal soul,
Thou hadst been better have been born a dog
Than answer my waked wrath!

Iago. Is't come to this?

Oth. Make me to see't; or, at the least, so prove it
That the probation bear no hinge nor loop
To hang a doubt on; or woe upon thy life!

Iago. My noble lord—

Oth. If thou dost slander her and torture me,
Never pray more; abandon all remorse;
On horror's head horrors accumulate;
Do deeds to make heaven weep, all earth amazed;
For nothing canst thou to damnation add
Greater than that.

Iago. O grace! O heaven forgive me!
Are you a man? have you a soul or sense?
God be wi' you; take mine office. O wretched fool,
That livest to make thine honesty a vice!
O monstrous world! Take note, take note, O world,
To be direct and honest is not safe.
I thank you for this profit; and from hence
I'll love no friend, sith love breeds such offence.

Oth. Nay, stay. Thou shouldst be honest.

Iago. I should be wise, for honesty's a fool
And loses that it works for.

Oth. By the world,
I think my wife be honest and think she is not;
I think that thou art just and think thou art not.
I'll have some proof. Her name, that was as fresh
As Dian's visage, is now begrimed and black
As mine own face. If there be cords, or knives,
Poison, or fire, or suffocating streams,
I'll not endure it. Would I were satisfied!

Iago. I see, sir, you are eaten up with passion.
I do repent me that I put it to you.
You would be satisfied?

Oth. Would! nay, I will.

Iago. And may; but, how? how satisfied, my lord?
Would you, the supervisor, grossly gape on—
Behold her topp'd?

Oth. Death and damnation! O!

Iago. It were a tedious difficulty, I think,
To bring them to that prospect. Damn them then,
If ever mortal eyes do see them bolster
More than their own! What then? how then?
What shall I say? Where's satisfaction?
It is impossible you should see this,
Were they as prime as goats, as hot as monkeys,
As salt as wolves in pride, and fools as gross
As ignorance made drunk. But yet, I say,
If imputation and strong circumstances,
Which lead directly to the door of truth,
Will give you satisfaction, you may have 't.

Oth. Give me a living reason she's disloyal.

Iago. I do not like the office;
But, sith I am enter'd in this cause so far,
Prick'd to 't by foolish honesty and love,
I will go on. I lay with Cassio lately;
And, being troubled with a raging tooth,
I could not sleep.
There are a kind of men so loose of soul,
That in their sleeps will mutter their affairs;
One of this kind is Cassio.
In sleep I heard him say, "Sweet Desdemona,
Let us be wary, let us hide our loves";
And then, sir, would he gripe and wring my hand,
Cry, "O sweet creature!" and then kiss me hard,
As if he pluck'd up kisses by the roots
That grew upon my lips; then laid his leg
Over my thigh, and sigh'd, and kiss'd; and then
Cried, "Cursed fate that gave thee to the Moor!"

Oth. O monstrous! monstrous!

Iago. Nay, this was but his dream.

Oth. But this denoted a foregone conclusion.
'Tis a shrewd doubt, though it be but a dream.

Iago. And this may help to thicken other proofs
That do demonstrate thinly.

Oth. I'll tear her all to pieces.

Iago. Nay, but be wise; yet we see nothing done;
She may be honest yet. Tell me but this,
Have you not sometimes seen a handkerchief
Spotted with strawberries in your wife's hand?

Oth. I gave her such a one; 'twas my first gift

Iago. I know not that; but such a handkerchief—
I am sure it was your wife's—did I to-day
See Cassio wipe his beard with.

Oth. If it be that—

Iago. If it be that, or any that was hers,
It speaks against her with the other proofs.

Oth. O, that the slave had forty thousand lives!
One is too poor, too weak for my revenge.

Now do I see 'tis true. Look here, Iago;
All my fond love thus do I blow to heaven.
'Tis gone.
Arise, black vengeance, from thy hollow cell!
Yield up, O love, thy crown and hearted throne
To tyrannous hate! Swell, bosom, with thy
fraught,
For 'tis of aspics' tongues!

Iago. Yet be content.

Oth. O, blood, blood, blood!

Iago. Patience, I say; your mind perhaps may
change.

Oth. Never, Iago. Like to the Pontic sea,
Whose icy current and compulsive course
Ne'er feels retiring ebb, but keeps due on
To the Propontic and the Hellespont,
Even so my bloody thoughts, with violent pace,
Shall ne'er look back, ne'er ebb to humble love,
Till that a capable and wide revenge
Swallow them up. Now, by yond marble
heaven,
[*Kneels*] In the due reverence of a sacred vow
I here engage my words.*

Iago. Do not rise yet.
[*Kneels*] Witness, you ever-burning lights above,
You elements that clip us round about,
Witness that here Iago doth give up
The execution of his wit, hands, heart,
To wrong'd Othello's service! Let him com-
mand,
And to obey shall be in me remorse,
What bloody business ever. [*They rise.*]

Oth. I greet thy love,
Not with vain thanks, but with acceptance
bounteous,
And will upon the instant put thee to 't.
Within these three days let me hear thee say
That Cassio's not alive.

Iago. My friend is dead; 'tis done at your request.
But let her live.

Oth. Damn her, lewd minx! O, damn her!
Come, go with me apart; I will withdraw,
To furnish me with some swift means of death
For the fair devil. Now art thou my lieutenant.

Iago. I am your own for ever. [*Exeunt.*

SCENE IV. *Before the castle*

Enter DESDEMONA, EMILIA, *and* CLOWN.

Des. Do you know, sirrah, where Lieutenant Cassio lies?

Clo. I dare not say he lies anywhere.

Des. Why, man?

Clo. He's a soldier, and for one to say a soldier lies, is stabbing.

Des. Go to. Where lodges he?

Clo. To tell you where he lodges, is to tell you where I lie.

Des. Can anything be made of this?

Clo. I know not where he lodges, and for me to devise a lodging and say he lies here or he lies there, were to lie in mine own throat.

Des. Can you inquire him out, and be edified by report?

Clo. I will catechize the world for him; that is, make questions, and by them answer.

Des. Seek him, bid him come hither. Tell him I have moved my lord on his behalf, and hope all will be well.

Clo. To do this is within the compass of man's wit; and therefore I will attempt the doing it. [*Exit.*

Des. Where should I lose that handkerchief,
Emilia?

Emil. I know not, madam.

Des. Believe me, I had rather have lost my purse
Full of crusadoes; and, but my noble Moor
Is true of mind and made of no such baseness
As jealous creatures are, it were enough
To put him to ill thinking.

Emil. Is he not jealous?

Des. Who, he? I think the sun where he was
born
Drew all such humours from him.

Emil. Look, where he comes.

Des. I will not leave him now till Cassio
Be call'd to him.

Enter OTHELLO.

How is't with you, my lord?

Oth. Well, my good lady. [*Aside*] O, hardness
to dissemble!—
How do you, Desdemona?

Des. Well, my good lord.

Oth. Give me your hand. This hand is moist, my
lady.

Des. It yet hath felt no age nor known no sorrow.

Oth. This argues fruitfulness and liberal heart;
Hot, hot, and moist. This hand of yours requires
A sequester from liberty, fasting, and prayer,
Much castigation, exercise devout;
For here's a young and sweating devil here,
That commonly rebels. 'Tis a good hand,
A frank one.

Des. You may, indeed, say so;
For 'twas that hand that gave away my heart.

Oth. A liberal hand. The hearts of old gave
hands;
But our new heraldry is hands, not hearts.

Des. I cannot speak of this. Come now, your
promise.

Oth. What promise, chuck?
Des. I have sent to bid Cassio come speak with you.
Oth. I have a salt and sorry rheum offends me;
Lend my thy handkerchief.
Des. Here, my lord.
Oth. That which I gave you.
Des. I have it not about me.
Oth. Not?
Des. No, indeed, my lord.
Oth. That is a fault.
That handkerchief
Did an Egyptian to my mother give;
She was a charmer, and could almost read
The thoughts of people. She told her, while she kept it,
'Twould make her amiable and subdue my father
Entirely to her love, but if she lost it
Or made a gift of it, my father's eye
Should hold her loathed and his spirits should hunt
After new fancies. She, dying, gave it me;
And bid me, when my fate would have me wive,
To give it her. I did so; and take heed on 't;
Make it a darling like your precious eye;
To lose 't or give 't away were such perdition
As nothing else could match.
Des. Is't possible?
Oth. 'Tis true; there's magic in the web of it.
A sibyl, that had number'd in the world
The sun to course two hundred compasses,
In her prophetic fury sew'd the work;
The worms were hallow'd that did breed the silk;
And it was dyed in mummy which the skilful
Conserved of maidens' hearts.
Des. Indeed! is't true?
Oth. Most veritable; therefore look to 't well.
Des. Then would to God that I had never seen 't!
Oth. Ha! wherefore?
Des. Why do you speak so startingly and rash?
Oth. Is't lost? is't gone? speak, is it out o' the way?
Des. Heaven bless us!
Oth. Say you?
Des. It is not lost; but what an if it were?
Oth. How!
Des. I say, it is not lost.
Oth. Fetch't, let me see't.
Des. Why, so I can, sir, but I will not now.
This is a trick to put me from my suit.
Pray you, let Cassio be received again.
Oth. Fetch me the handkerchief. My mind misgives.
Des. Come, come;
You'll never meet a more sufficient man.
Oth. The handkerchief!
Des. I pray, talk me of Cassio.
Oth. The handkerchief!
Des. A man that all his time
Hath founded his good fortunes on your love,
Shared dangers with you—
Oth. The handkerchief!
Des. In sooth, you are to blame.
Oth. Away! [*Exit.*
Emil. Is not this man jealous?
Des. I ne'er saw this before.
Sure, there's some wonder in this handkerchief.
I am most unhappy in the loss of it.
Emil. 'Tis not a year or two shows us a man.
They are all but stomachs, and we all but food;
They eat us hungerly, and when they are full,
They belch us. Look you, Cassio and my husband!

Enter CASSIO *and* IAGO.

Iago. There is no other way; 'tis she must do 't.
And, lo, the happiness! go, and importune her.
Des. How now, good Cassio! what's the news with you?
Cas. Madam, my former suit. I do beseech you
That by your virtuous means I may again
Exist, and be a member of his love
Whom I with all the office of my heart
Entirely honour. I would not be delay'd.
If my offence be of such mortal kind
That nor my service past, nor present sorrows,
Nor purposed merit in futurity,
Can ransom me into his love again,
But to know so must be my benefit;
So shall I clothe me in a forced content,
And shut myself up in some other course,
To fortune's alms.
Des. Alas, thrice-gentle Cassio!
My advocation is not now in tune;
My lord is not my lord; nor should I know him,
Were he in favour as in humour alter'd.
So help me every spirit sanctified,
As I have spoken for you all my best
And stood within the blank of his displeasure
For my free speech! you must awhile be patient.
What I can do I will; and more I will
Than for myself I dare. Let that suffice you.
Iago. Is my lord angry?
Emil. He went hence but now,
And certainly in strange unquietness.
Iago. Can he be angry? I have seen the cannon,
When it hath blown his ranks into the air,
And, like the devil, from his very arm
Puff'd his own brother—and can he be angry?
Something of moment then. I will go meet him.
There's matter in 't indeed, if he be angry.

Des. I prithee, do so. [*Exit* IAGO.
Something, sure, of state,
Either from Venice, or some unhatch'd practice
Made demonstrable here in Cyprus to him,
Hath puddled his clear spirit; and in such cases
Men's natures wrangle with inferior things,
Though great ones are their object. 'Tis even so;
For let our finger ache, and it indues
Our other healthful members even to that sense
Of pain. Nay, we must think men are not gods,
Nor of them look for such observances
As fit the bridal. Beshrew me much, Emilia,
I was, unhandsome warrior as I am,
Arraigning his unkindness with my soul;
But now I find I had suborn'd the witness,
And he's indicted falsely.
Emil. Pray heaven it be state-matters, as you think,
And no conception nor no jealous toy
Concerning you.
Des. Alas the day! I never gave him cause.
Emil. But jealous souls will not be answer'd so;
They are not ever jealous for the cause,
But jealous for they are jealous. 'Tis a monster
Begot upon itself, born on itself.
Des. Heaven keep that monster from Othello's mind!
Emil. Lady, amen.
Des. I will go seek him. Cassio, walk here about.
If I do find him fit, I'll move your suit
And seek to effect it to my uttermost.
Cas. I humbly thank your ladyship.
[*Exeunt* DESDEMONA *and* EMILIA.

Enter BIANCA.

Bian. Save you, friend Cassio!
Cas. What make you from home?
How is it with you, my most fair Bianca?
I' faith, sweet love, I was coming to your house.
Bian. And I was going to your lodging, Cassio.
What, keep a week away? seven days and nights?
Eight score eight hours? and lovers' absent hours,
More tedious than the dial eight score times?
O weary reckoning!
Cas. Pardon me, Bianca.
I have this while with leaden thoughts been press'd;
But I shall, in a more continuate time,
Strike off this score of absence. Sweet Bianca,
Giving her Desdemona's handkerchief.
Take me this work out.
Bian. O Cassio, whence came this?
This is some token from a newer friend.
To the felt absence now I feel a cause;
Is't come to this? Well, well.
Cas. Go to, woman!
Throw your vile guesses in the devil's teeth,
From whence you have them. You are jealous now
That this is from some mistress, some remembrance.
No, in good troth, Bianca.
Bian. Why, whose is it?
Cas. I know not, sweet. I found it in my chamber.
I like the work well. Ere it be demanded—
As like enough it will—I'd have it copied.
Take it, and do't; and leave me for this time.
Bian. Leave you! wherefore?
Cas. I do attend here on the general;
And think it no addition, nor my wish,
To have him see me woman'd.
Bian. Why, I pray you?
Cas. Not that I love you not.
Bian. But that you do not love me.
I pray you, bring me on the way a little,
And say if I shall see you soon at night.
Cas. 'Tis but a little way that I can bring you;
For I attend here; but I'll see you soon.
Bian. 'Tis very good; I must be circumstanced.
[*Exeunt*.

ACT IV

SCENE I. *Cyprus: before the castle*

Enter OTHELLO *and* IAGO.

Iago. Will you think so?
Oth. Think so, Iago!
Iago. What,
To kiss in private?
Oth. An unauthorized kiss.
Iago. Or to be naked with her friend in bed
An hour or more, not meaning any harm?
Oth. Naked in bed, Iago, and not mean harm!
It is hypocrisy against the devil.
They that mean virtuously, and yet do so,
The devil their virtue tempts, and they tempt heaven.
Iago. So they do nothing, 'tis a venial slip.
But if I give my wife a handkerchief—
Oth. What then?
Iago. Why, then, 'tis hers, my lord; and, being hers,
She may, I think, bestow't on any man.
Oth. She is protectress of her honour too.
May she give that?
Iago. Her honour is an essence that's not seen;
They have it very oft that have it not.
But, for the handkerchief—
Oth. By heaven, I would most gladly have forgot it.

Thou said'st—O, it comes o'er my memory,
As doth the raven o'er the infected house,
Boding to all—he had my handkerchief.
Iago. Ay, what of that?
Oth. That's not so good now.
Iago. What,
If I had said I had seen him do you wrong?
Or heard him say—as knaves be such abroad,
Who having, by their own importunate suit,
Or voluntary dotage of some mistress,
Convincèd or supplied them, cannot choose
But they must blab—
Oth. Hath he said anything?
Iago. He hath, my lord; but be you well assured,
No more than he'll unswear.
Oth. What hath he said?
Iago. 'Faith, that he did—I know not what he did.
Oth. What? what?
Iago. Lie—
Oth. With her?
Iago. With her, on her; what you will.
Oth. Lie with her! lie on her! We say lie on her, when they belie her. Lie with her! that's fulsome. —Handkerchief—confessions—handkerchief!— To confess, and be hanged for his labour—first, to be hanged, and then to confess.—I tremble at it. Nature would not invest herself in such shadowing passion without some instruction. It is not words that shake me thus. Pish! Noses, ears, and lips.—Is't possible?—Confess—handkerchief!—O devil! [*Falls in a trance*.]
Iago. Work on,
My medicine, work! Thus credulous fools are caught;
And many worthy and chaste dames even thus,
All guiltless, meet reproach. What, ho! my lord!
My lord, I say! Othello!

Enter CASSIO.

How now, Cassio!
Cas. What's the matter?
Iago. My lord is fall'n into an epilepsy.
This is his second fit; he had one yesterday.
Cas. Rub him about the temples.
Iago. No, forbear;
The lethargy must have his quiet course;
If not, he foams at mouth and by and by
Breaks out to savage madness. Look, he stirs.
Do you withdraw yourself a little while,
He will recover straight. When he is gone,
I would on great occasion speak with you.
[*Exit* CASSIO.
How is it, general? have you not hurt your head?
Oth. Dost thou mock me?
Iago. I mock you! no, by heaven.
Would you would bear your fortune like a man!
Oth. A hornèd man's a monster and a beast.
Iago. There's many a beast then in a populous city,
And many a civil monster.
Oth. Did he confess it?
Iago. Good sir, be a man;
Think every bearded fellow that's but yoked
May draw with you. There's millions now alive
That nightly lie in those unproper beds
Which they dare swear peculiar; your case is better.
O, 'tis the spite of hell, the fiend's arch-mock,
To lip a wanton in a secure couch,
And to suppose her chaste! No, let me know;
And knowing what I am, I know what she shall be.
Oth. O, thou art wise; 'tis certain.
Iago. Stand you awhile apart;
Confine yourself but in a patient list.
Whilst you were here o'erwhelmed with your grief—
A passion most unsuiting such a man—
Cassio came hither. I shifted him away,
And laid good 'scuse upon your ecstasy,
Bade him anon return and here speak with me;
The which he promised. Do but encave yourself,
And mark the fleers, the gibes, and notable scorns,
That dwell in every region of his face;
For I will make him tell the tale anew,
Where, how, how oft, how long ago, and when
He hath, and is again to cope your wife.
I say, but mark his gesture. Marry, patience;
Or I shall say you are all in all in spleen,
And nothing of a man.
Oth. Dost thou hear, Iago?
I will be found most cunning in my patience;
But—dost thou hear?—most bloody.
Iago. That's not amiss;
But yet keep time in all. Will you withdraw?
[OTHELLO *retires*.
Now will I question Cassio of Bianca,
A housewife that by selling her desires
Buys herself bread and clothes; it is a creature
That dotes on Cassio; as 'tis the strumpet's plague
To beguile many and be beguiled by one.
He, when he hears of her, cannot refrain
From the excess of laughter. Here he comes.

Re-enter CASSIO.

As he shall smile, Othello shall go mad;
And his unbookish jealousy must construe

Poor Cassio's smiles, gestures, and light behaviour,
Quite in the wrong. How do you now, lieutenant?

Cas. The worser that you give me the addition
Whose want even kills me.

Iago. Ply Desdemona well, and you are sure on't.
[*Speaking lower*] Now, if this suit lay in Bianca's power,
How quickly should you speed!

Cas. Alas, poor caitiff!

Oth. Look, how he laughs already!

Iago. I never knew woman love man so.

Cas. Alas, poor rogue! I think, i' faith, she loves me.

Oth. Now he denies it faintly, and laughs it out.

Iago. Do you hear, Cassio?

Oth. Now he importunes him
To tell it o'er. Go to; well said, well said.

Iago. She gives it out that you shall marry her.
Do you intend it?

Cas. Ha, ha, ha!

Oth. Do you triumph, Roman? do you triumph?

Cas. I marry her! what? a customer! Prithee, bear some charity to my wit; do not think it so unwholesome. Ha, ha, ha!

Oth. So, so, so, so; they laugh that win.

Iago. 'Faith, the cry goes that you shall marry her.

Cas. Prithee, say true.

Iago. I am a very villain else.

Oth. Have you scored me? Well.

Cas. This is the monkey's own giving out: she is persuaded I will marry her, out of her own love and flattery, not out of my promise.

Oth. Iago beckons me; now he begins the story.

Cas. She was here even now; she haunts me in every place. I was the other day talking on the sea-bank with certain Venetians; and thither comes the bauble, and, by this hand, she falls me thus about my neck—

Oth. Crying, "O dear Cassio!" as it were; his gesture imports it.

Cas. So hangs, and lolls, and weeps upon me; so hales, and pulls me. Ha, ha, ha!

Oth. Now he tells how she plucked him to my chamber. O, I see that nose of yours, but not that dog I shall throw it to.

Cas. Well, I must leave her company.

Iago. Before me! look, where she comes.

Cas. 'Tis such another fitchew! marry, a perfumed one.

Enter BIANCA.

What do you mean by this haunting of me?

Bian. Let the devil and his dam haunt you! What did you mean by that same handkerchief you gave me even now? I was a fine fool to take it. I must take out the work?—A likely piece of work, that you should find it in your chamber, and not know who left it there! This is some minx's token, and I must take out the work? There; give it your hobby-horse. Wheresoever you had it, I'll take out no work on't.

Cas. How now, my sweet Bianca! how now! how now!

Oth. By heaven, that should be my handkerchief!

Bian. An you'll come to supper to-night, you may; an you will not, come when you are next prepared for. [*Exit.*

Iago. After her, after her.

Cas. 'Faith, I must; she'll rail in the street else.

Iago. Will you sup there?

Cas. 'Faith, I intend so.

Iago. Well, I may chance to see you; for I would very fain speak with you.

Cas. Prithee, come; will you?

Iago. Go to; say no more. [*Exit* CASSIO.

Oth. [*Advancing*] How shall I murder him, Iago?

Iago. Did you perceive how he laughed at his vice?

Oth. O Iago!

Iago. And did you see the handkerchief?

Oth. Was that mine?

Iago. Yours, by this hand; and to see how he prizes the foolish woman your wife! she gave it him, and he hath given it his whore.

Oth. I would have him nine years a-killing. A fine woman! a fair woman! a sweet woman!

Iago. Nay, you must forget that.

Oth. Ay, let her rot, and perish, and be damned to-night; for she shall not live. No, my heart is turned to stone; I strike it, and it hurts my hand. O, the world hath not a sweeter creature! She might lie by an emperor's side and command him tasks.

Iago. Nay, that's not your way.

Oth. Hang her! I do but say what she is: so delicate with her needle; an admirable musician: O! she will sing the savageness out of a bear. Of so high and plenteous wit and invention—

Iago. She's the worse for all this.

Oth. O, a thousand thousand times. And then, of so gentle a condition!

Iago. Ay, too gentle.

Oth. Nay, that's certain; but yet the pity of it, Iago! O Iago, the pity of it, Iago!

Iago. If you are so fond over her iniquity, give her patent to offend; for, if it touch not you, it comes near nobody.

Oth. I will chop her into messes. Cuckold me!
Iago. O, 'tis foul in her.
Oth. With mine officer!
Iago. That's fouler.
Oth. Get me some poison, Iago; this night. I'll not expostulate with her, lest her body and beauty unprovide my mind again. This night, Iago.
Iago. Do it not with poison; strangle her in her bed, even the bed she hath contaminated.
Oth. Good, good; the justice of it pleases; very good.
Iago. And for Cassio, let me be his undertaker. You shall hear more by midnight.
Oth. Excellent good.
A trumpet within.
What trumpet is that same?
Iago. Something from Venice, sure. 'Tis Lodovico
Come from the Duke. And, see, your wife is with him.

Enter LODOVICO, DESDEMONA, *and Attendants.*

Lod. Save you, worthy general!
Oth. With all my heart, sir.
Lod. The Duke and Senators of Venice greet you. [*Gives him a letter.*]
Oth. I kiss the instrument of their pleasures.
Opens the letter, and reads.
Des. And what's the news, good cousin Lodovico?
Iago. I am very glad to see you, signior;
Welcome to Cyprus.
Lod. I thank you. How does Lieutenant Cassio?
Iago. Lives, sir.
Des. Cousin, there's fall'n between him and my lord
An unkind breach; but you shall make all well.
Oth. Are you sure of that?
Des. My lord?
Oth. [*Reads*] "This fail you not to do, as you will"—
Lod. He did not call; he's busy in the paper.
Is there division 'twixt my lord and Cassio?
Des. A most unhappy one. I would do much
To atone them, for the love I bear to Cassio.
Oth. Fire and brimstone!
Des. My lord?
Oth. Are you wise?
Des. What, is he angry?
Lod. May be the letter moved him;
For, as I think, they do command him home,
Deputing Cassio in his government.
Des. Trust me, I am glad on't.
Oth. Indeed!
Des. My lord?
Oth. I am glad to see you mad.
Des. Why, sweet Othello—
Oth. [*Striking her*] Devil!
Des. I have not deserved this.
Lod. My lord, this would not be believed in Venice,
Though I should swear I saw't. 'Tis very much.
Make her amends; she weeps.
Oth. O devil, devil!
If that the earth could teem with woman's tears,
Each drop she falls would prove a crocodile.
Out of my sight!
Des. I will not stay to offend you. [*Going*.
Lod. Truly, an obedient lady.
I do beseech your lordship, call her back.
Oth. Mistress!
Des. My lord?
Oth. What would you with her, sir?
Lod. Who, I, my lord?
Oth. Ay; you did wish that I would make her turn.
Sir, she can turn, and turn, and yet go on,
And turn again; and she can weep, sir, weep;
And she's obedient, as you say, obedient,
Very obedient. Proceed you in your tears.
Concerning this, sir—O well-painted passion!—
I am commanded home. Get you away;
I'll send for you anon. Sir, I obey the mandate,
And will return to Venice. Hence, avaunt!
[*Exit* DESDEMONA.
Cassio shall have my place. And, sir, to-night,
I do entreat that we may sup together.
You are welcome, sir, to Cyprus.—Goats and monkeys! [*Exit*.
Lod. Is this the noble Moor whom our full Senate
Call all in all sufficient? Is this the nature
Whom passion could not shake? whose solid virtue
The shot of accident, nor dart of chance,
Could neither graze nor pierce?
Iago. He is much changed.
Lod. Are his wits safe? Is he not light of brain?
Iago. He's that he is; I may not breathe my censure
What he might be. If what he might he is not,
I would to heaven he were!
Lod. What, strike his wife!
Iago. 'Faith, that was not so well; yet would I knew
That stroke would prove the worst!
Lod. Is it his use?
Or did the letters work upon his blood
And new-create this fault?
Iago. Alas, alas!
It is not honesty in me to speak

What I have seen and known. You shall observe him,
And his own courses will denote him so
That I may save my speech. Do but go after,
And mark how he continues.

Lod. I am sorry that I am deceived in him. [*Exeunt.*

SCENE II. *A room in the castle*

Enter OTHELLO *and* EMILIA.

Oth. You have seen nothing then?

Emil. Nor ever heard, nor ever did suspect.

Oth. Yes, you have seen Cassio and she together.

Emil. But then I saw no harm, and then I heard
Each syllable that breath made up between them.

Oth. What, did they never whisper?

Emil. Never, my lord.

Oth. Nor send you out o' the way?

Emil. Never.

Oth. To fetch her fan, her gloves, her mask, nor nothing?

Emil. Never, my lord.

Oth. That's strange.

Emil. I durst, my lord, to wager she is honest,
Lay down my soul at stake. If you think other,
Remove your thought; it doth abuse your bosom.
If any wretch have put this in your head,
Let heaven requite it with the serpent's curse!
For, if she be not honest, chaste, and true,
There's no man happy; the purest of their wives
Is foul as slander.

Oth. Bid her come hither; go. [*Exit* EMILIA.
She says enough; yet she's a simple bawd
That cannot say as much. This is a subtle whore,
A closet lock and key of villainous secrets;
And yet she'll kneel and pray; I have seen her do't.

Enter DESDEMONA *with* EMILIA.

Des. My lord, what is your will?

Oth. Pray, chuck, come hither.

Des. What is your pleasure?

Oth. Let me see your eyes;
Look in my face.

Des. What horrible fancy's this?

Oth. [*To* EMILIA] Some of your function, mistress;
Leave procreants alone and shut the door;
Cough, or cry "hem," if anybody come.
Your mystery, your mystery; nay, dispatch. [*Exit* EMILIA.

Des. Upon my knees, what doth your speech import?
I understand a fury in your words,
But not the words.

Oth. Why, what art thou?

Des. Your wife, my lord; your true
And loyal wife.

Oth. Come, swear it, damn thyself;
Lest, being like one of heaven, the devils themselves
Should fear to seize thee; therefore be double damn'd.
Swear thou art honest.

Des. Heaven doth truly know it.

Oth. Heaven truly knows that thou art false as hell.

Des. To whom, my lord? with whom? how am I false?

Oth. O Desdemona! away! away! away!

Des. Alas the heavy day! Why do you weep?
Am I the motive of these tears, my lord?
If haply you my father do suspect
An instrument of this your calling back,
Lay not your blame on me. If you have lost him,
Why, I have lost him too.

Oth. Had it pleased heaven
To try me with affliction; had they rain'd
All kinds of sores and shames on my bare head,
Steep'd me in poverty to the very lips,
Given to captivity me and my utmost hopes,
I should have found in some place of my soul
A drop of patience; but, alas, to make me
A fixed figure for the time of scorn
To point his slow unmoving finger at!
Yet could I bear that too; well, very well;
But there, where I have garner'd up my heart,
Where either I must live, or bear no life;
The fountain from the which my current runs,
Or else dries up; to be discarded thence!
Or keep it as a cistern for foul toads
To knot and gender in! Turn thy complexion there,
Patience, thou young and rose-lipp'd cherubin—
Ay, there, look grim as hell!

Des. I hope my noble lord esteems me honest.

Oth. O, ay; as summer flies are in the shambles,
That quicken even with blowing. O thou weed,
Who art so lovely fair and smell'st so sweet
That the sense aches at thee, would thou hadst ne'er been born!

Des. Alas, what ignorant sin have I committed?

Oth. Was this fair paper, this most goodly book,
Made to write "whore" upon? What committed!
Committed! O thou public commoner!
I should make very forges of my cheeks,
That would to cinders burn up modesty,
Did I but speak thy deeds. What committed!
Heaven stops the nose at it and the moon winks,

The bawdy wind that kisses all it meets
Is hush'd within the hollow mine of earth,
And will not hear it. What committed!
Impudent strumpet!

Des. By heaven, you do me wrong.

Oth. Are not you a strumpet?

Des. No, as I am a Christian.
If to preserve this vessel for my lord
From any other foul unlawful touch
Be not to be a strumpet, I am none.

Oth. What, not a whore?

Des. No, as I shall be saved.

Oth. Is't possible?

Des. O, heaven forgive us!

Oth. I cry you mercy, then.
I took you for that cunning whore of Venice
That married with Othello. [*Raising his voice*]
You, mistress,
That have the office opposite to Saint Peter,
And keep the gate of hell!

Re-enter EMILIA.

You, you, ay, you!
We have done our course; there's money for your pains.
I pray you, turn the key and keep our counsel. [*Exit.*

Emil. Alas, what does this gentleman conceive?
How do you, madam? how do you, my good lady?

Des. 'Faith, half asleep.

Emil. Good madam, what's the matter with my lord?

Des. With who?

Emil. Why, with my lord, madam.

Des. Who is thy lord?

Emil. He that is yours, sweet lady.

Des. I have none. Do not talk to me, Emilia;
I cannot weep; nor answer have I none,
But what should go by water. Prithee, to-night
Lay on my bed my wedding sheets, remember;
And call thy husband hither.

Emil. Here's a change indeed! [*Exit.*

Des. 'Tis meet I should be used so, very meet.
How have I been behaved, that he might stick
The small'st opinion on my least misuse?

Re-enter EMILIA *with* IAGO.

Iago. What is your pleasure, madam? How is't with you?

Des. I cannot tell. Those that do teach young babes
Do it with gentle means and easy tasks.
He might have chid me so; for, in good faith,
I am a child to chiding.

Iago. What's the matter, lady?

Emil. Alas, Iago, my lord hath so bewhored her,
Thrown such despite and heavy terms upon her,
As true hearts cannot bear.

Des. Am I that name, Iago?

Iago. What name, fair lady?

Des. Such as she says my lord did say I was.

Emil. He call'd her whore. A beggar in his drink
Could not have laid such terms upon his callet.

Iago. Why did he so?

Des. I do not know; I am sure I am none such.

Iago. Do not weep, do not weep. Alas the day!

Emil. Hath she forsook so many noble matches,
Her father and her country and her friends,
To be call'd whore? would it not make one weep?

Des. It is my wretched fortune.

Iago. Beshrew him for't!
How comes this trick upon him?

Des. Nay, Heaven doth know.

Emil. I will be hang'd, if some eternal villain,
Some busy and insinuating rogue,
Some cogging, cozening slave, to get some office,
Have not devised this slander; I'll be hang'd else.

Iago. Fie, there is no such man; it is impossible.

Des. If any such there be, Heaven pardon him!

Emil. A halter pardon him! and hell gnaw his bones!
Why should he call her whore? who keeps her company?
What place? what time? what form? what likelihood?
The Moor's abused by some most villainous knave,
Some base notorious knave, some scurvy fellow.
O heaven, that such companions thou'dst unfold,
And put in every honest hand a whip
To lash the rascals naked through the world
Even from the east to the west!

Iago. Speak within door.

Emil. O, fie upon them! Some such squire he was
That turn'd your wit the seamy side without,
And made you to suspect me with the Moor.

Iago. You are a fool; go to.

Des. O good Iago,
What shall I do to win my lord again?
Good friend, go to him; for, by this light of heaven,
I know not how I lost him. Here I kneel.
If e'er my will did trespass 'gainst his love,
Either in discourse of thought or actual deed,
Or that mine eyes, mine ears, or any sense,
Delighted them in any other form;
Or that I do not yet, and ever did,
And ever will—though he do shake me off

To beggarly divorcement—love him dearly,
Comfort forswear me! Unkindness may do much;
And his unkindness may defeat my life,
But never taint my love. I cannot say "whore."
It doth abhor me now I speak the word;
To do the act that might the addition earn
Not the world's mass of vanity could make me.

Iago. I pray you, be content; 'tis but his humour.
The business of the state does him offence,
And he does chide with you.

Des. If 'twere no other—

Iago. 'Tis but so, I warrant.

Trumpets within.

Hark, how these instruments summon to supper!
The messengers of Venice stay the meat.
Go in, and weep not; all things shall be well.

[*Exeunt* DESDEMONA *and* EMILIA.

Enter RODERIGO.

How now, Roderigo!

Rod. I do not find that thou dealest justly with me.

Iago. What in the contrary?

Rod. Every day thou daffest me with some device, Iago; and rather, as it seems to me now, keepest from me all conveniency than suppliest me with the least advantage of hope. I will indeed no longer endure it, nor am I yet persuaded to put up in peace what already I have foolishly suffered.

Iago. Will you hear me, Roderigo?

Rod. 'Faith, I have heard too much, for your words and performances are no kin together.

Iago. You charge me most unjustly.

Rod. With nought but truth. I have wasted myself out of my means. The jewels you have had from me to deliver to Desdemona would half have corrupted a votarist. You have told me she hath received them and returned me expectations and comforts of sudden respect and acquaintance, but I find none.

Iago. Well; go to; very well.

Rod. Very well! go to! I cannot go to, man; nor 'tis not very well. Nay, I think it is scurvy, and begin to find myself fopped in it.

Iago. Very well.

Rod. I tell you 'tis not very well. I will make myself known to Desdemona. If she will return me my jewels, I will give over my suit and repent my unlawful solicitation; if not, assure yourself I will seek satisfaction of you.

Iago. You have said now.

Rod. Ay, and said nothing but what I protest intendment of doing.

Iago. Why, now I see there's mettle in thee, and even from this instant do build on thee a better opinion than ever before. Give me thy hand, Roderigo. Thou hast taken against me a most just exception; but yet, I protest, I have dealt most directly in thy affair.

Rod. It hath not appeared.

Iago. I grant indeed it hath not appeared, and your suspicion is not without wit and judgement. But, Roderigo, if thou hast that in thee indeed, which I have greater reason to believe now than ever, I mean purpose, courage, and valour, this night show it. If thou the next night following enjoy not Desdemona, take me from this world with treachery and devise engines for my life.

Rod. Well, what is it? is it within reason and compass?

Iago. Sir, there is especial commission come from Venice to depute Cassio in Othello's place.

Rod. Is that true? why, then Othello and Desdemona return again to Venice.

Iago. O, no; he goes into Mauritania and takes away with him the fair Desdemona, unless his abode be lingered here by some accident; wherein none can be so determinate as the removing of Cassio.

Rod. How do you mean, removing of him?

Iago. Why, by making him uncapable of Othello's place; knocking out his brains.

Rod. And that you would have me to do?

Iago. Ay, if you dare do yourself a profit and a right. He sups to-night with a harlotry, and thither will I go to him; he knows not yet of his honourable fortune. If you will watch his going thence, which I will fashion to fall out between twelve and one, you may take him at your pleasure. I will be near to second your attempt, and he shall fall between us. Come, stand not amazed at it, but go along with me; I will show you such a necessity in his death that you shall think yourself bound to put it on him. It is now high supper-time, and the night grows to waste. About it.

Rod. I will hear further reason for this.

Iago. And you shall be satisfied. [*Exeunt*.

SCENE III. *Another room in the castle*

Enter OTHELLO, LODOVICO, DESDEMONA, EMILIA, *and Attendants*.

Lod. I do beseech you, sir, trouble yourself no further.

Oth. O, pardon me; 'twill do me good to walk.

Lod. Madam, good night; I humbly thank your ladyship.

Des. Your honour is most welcome.

Oth. Will you walk, sir?
O—Desdemona—

Des. My lord?

Oth. Get you to bed on the instant; I will be returned forthwith. Dismiss your attendant there. Look it be done.

Des. I will, my lord.

[*Exeunt* OTHELLO, LODOVICO, *and Attendants.*

Emil. How goes it now? he looks gentler than he did.

Des. He says he will return incontinent.
He hath commanded me to go to bed,
And bade me to dismiss you.

Emil. Dismiss me!

Des. It was his bidding; therefore, good Emilia,
Give me my nightly wearing, and adieu.
We must not now displease him.

Emil. I would you had never seen him!

Des. So would not I. My love doth so approve him,
That even his stubbornness, his checks, his frowns—
Prithee, unpin me—have grace and favour in them.

Emil. I have laid those sheets you bade me on the bed.

Des. All's one. Good faith, how foolish are our minds!
If I do die before thee, prithee, shroud me
In one of those same sheets.

Emil. Come, come, you talk.

Des. My mother had a maid call'd Barbara;
She was in love, and he she loved proved mad
And did forsake her. She had a song of "Willow",
An old thing 'twas, but it express'd her fortune,
And she died singing it. That song to-night
Will not go from my mind; I have much to do,
But to go hang my head all at one side,
And sing it like poor Barbara. Prithee, dispatch.

Emil. Shall I go fetch your night-gown?

Des. No, unpin me here.
This Lodovico is a proper man.

Emil. A very handsome man.

Des. He speaks well.

Emil. I know a lady in Venice would have walked barefoot to Palestine for a touch of his nether lip.

Des. [*Singing*] "The poor soul sat sighing by a sycamore tree,
Sing all a green willow;
Her hand on her bosom, her head on her knee,
Sing willow, willow, willow.
The fresh streams ran by her, and murmur'd her moans;
Sing willow, willow, willow;
Her salt tears fell from her, and soften'd the stones"—
Lay by these:—
[*Singing*] "Sing willow, willow, willow";
Prithee, hie thee; he'll come anon—
[*Singing*] "Sing all a green willow must be my garland.
Let nobody blame him; his scorn I approve"—
Nay, that's not next.—Hark! who is't that knocks?

Emil. It's the wind.

Des. [*Singing*] "I call'd my love false love; but what said he then?
Sing willow, willow, willow.
If I court moe women, you'll couch with moe men."
So, get thee gone; good night. Mine eyes do itch;
Doth that bode weeping?

Emil. 'Tis neither here nor there.

Des. I have heard it said so. O, these men, these men!
Dost thou in conscience think—tell me, Emilia—
That there be women do abuse their husbands
In such gross kind?

Emil. There be some such, no question.

Des. Wouldst thou do such a deed for all the world?

Emil. Why, would not you?

Des. No, by this heavenly light!

Emil. Nor I neither by this heavenly light;
I might do't as well i' the dark.

Des. Wouldst thou do such a deed for all the world?

Emil. The world's a huge thing; it is a great price.
For a small vice.

Des. In troth, I think thou wouldst not.

Emil. In troth, I think I should; and undo't when I had done. Marry, I would not do such a thing for a joint-ring, nor for measures of lawn, nor for gowns, petticoats, nor caps, nor any petty exhibition; but, for the whole world—why, who would not make her husband a cuckold to make him a monarch? I should venture purgatory for't.

Des. Beshrew me, if I would do such a wrong
For the whole world.

Emil. Why, the wrong is but a wrong i' the world; and having the world for your labour, 'tis a wrong in your own world, and you might quickly make it right.

Des. I do not think there is any such woman.

Emil. Yes, a dozen; and as many to the vantage as would store the world they played for.
But I do think it is their husbands' faults

If wives do fall. Say that they slack their duties,
And pour our treasures into foreign laps,
Or else break out in peevish jealousies,
Throwing restraint upon us; or say they strike us,
Or scant our former having in despite;
Why, we have galls, and though we have some grace,
Yet have we some revenge. Let husbands know
Their wives have sense like them; they see and smell
And have their palates both for sweet and sour,
As husbands have. What is it that they do
When they change us for others? Is it sport?
I think it is. And doth affection breed it?
I think it doth. Is't frailty that thus errs?
It is so too. And have not we affections,
Desires for sport, and frailty, as men have?
Then let them use us well; else let them know,
The ills we do, their ills instruct us so.

Des. Good night, good night. Heaven me such uses send,
Not to pick bad from bad, but by bad mend!
[*Exeunt.*

ACT V

SCENE I. *Cyprus: a street*

Enter IAGO *and* RODERIGO.

Iago. Here, stand behind this bulk; straight will he come.
Wear thy good rapier bare, and put it home.
Quick, quick; fear nothing; I'll be at thy elbow.
It makes us, or it mars us; think on that,
And fix most firm thy resolution.

Rod. Be near at hand; I may miscarry in't.

Iago. Here, at thy hand; be bold, and take thy stand. [*Retires.*

Rod. I have no great devotion to the deed;
And yet he hath given me satisfying reasons.
'Tis but a man gone. Forth, my sword; he dies.

Iago. I have rubb'd this young quat almost to the sense,
And he grows angry. Now, whether he kill Cassio,
Or Cassio him, or each do kill the other,
Every way makes my gain. Live Roderigo,
He calls me to a restitution large
Of gold and jewels that I bobb'd from him,
As gifts to Desdemona;
It must not be. If Cassio do remain,
He hath a daily beauty in his life
That makes me ugly; and, besides, the Moor
May unfold me to him; there stand I in much peril.
No, he must die. But so; I hear him coming.

Enter CASSIO.

Rod. I know his gait, 'tis he.—Villain, thou diest! [*Makes a pass at* CASSIO.]

Cas. That thrust had been mine enemy indeed,
But that my coat is better than thou know'st.
I will make proof of thine.

Draws, and wounds RODERIGO.

Rod. O, I am slain!

IAGO *from behind wounds* CASSIO *in the leg, and exit.*

Cas. I am maim'd for ever. Help, ho! murder! murder! [*Falls.*]

Enter OTHELLO.

Oth. The voice of Cassio. Iago keeps his word.

Rod. O, villain that I am!

Oth. It is even so.

Cas. O, help, ho! light! a surgeon!

Oth. 'Tis he. O brave Iago, honest and just,
That hast such noble sense of thy friend's wrong!
Thou teachest me. Minion, your dear lies dead,
And your unblest fate hies; strumpet, I come.
Forth of my heart those charms, thine eyes, are blotted;
Thy bed, lust-stain'd, shall with lust's blood be spotted. [*Exit.*

Enter LODOVICO *and* GRATIANO.

Cas. What, ho! no watch? no passage? murder! murder!

Gra. 'Tis some mischance; the cry is very direful.

Cas. O, help!

Lod. Hark!

Rod. O wretched villain!

Lod. Two or three groan. It is a heavy night,
These may be counterfeits; let's think't unsafe
To come in to the cry without more help.

Rod. Nobody come? then shall I bleed to death.

Lod. Hark!

Re-enter IAGO, *with a light.*

Gra. Here's one comes in his shirt, with light and weapons.

Iago. Who's there? whose noise is this that cries on murder?

Lod. We do not know.

Iago. Did not you hear a cry?

Cas. Here, here! for heaven's sake, help me!

Iago. What's the matter?

Gra. This is Othello's ancient, as I take it.

Lod. The same indeed; a very valiant fellow.

Iago. What are you here that cry so grievously?

Cas. Iago? O, I am spoil'd, undone by villains!
Give me some help.

Iago. O me, lieutenant! what villains have done this?
Cas. I think that one of them is hereabout,
And cannot make away.
Iago. O treacherous villains!
What are you there? come in, and give some help. [*To* LODOVICO *and* GRATIANO.]
Rod. O, help me here!
Cas. That's one of them.
Iago. O murderous slave! O villain!
Stabs RODERIGO.
Rod. O damn'd Iago! O inhuman dog!
Iago. Kill men i' the dark! Where be these bloody thieves?
How silent is this town! Ho! murder! murder!
What may you be? are you of good or evil?
Lod. As you shall prove us, praise us.
Iago. Signior Lodovico?
Lod. He, sir.
Iago. I cry you mercy. Here's Cassio hurt by villains.
Gra. Cassio!
Iago. How is't, brother!
Cas. My leg is cut in two.
Iago. Marry, heaven forbid!
Light, gentlemen. I'll bind it with my shirt.

Enter BIANCA.

Bian. What is the matter, ho? who is't that cried?
Iago. Who is't that cried!
Bian. O my dear Cassio! my sweet Cassio!
O Cassio, Cassio, Cassio!
Iago. O notable strumpet! Cassio, may you suspect
Who they should be that have thus mangled you?
Cas. No.
Gra. I am sorry to find you thus. I have been to seek you.
Iago. Lend me a garter. So. O, for a chair,
To bear him easily hence!
Bian. Alas, he faints! O Cassio, Cassio, Cassio!
Iago. Gentlemen all, I do suspect this trash
To be a party in this injury.
Patience awhile, good Cassio. Come, come;
Lend me a light. Know we this face or no?
Alas, my friend and my dear countryman
Roderigo! no. Yes, sure. O heaven! Roderigo.
Gra. What, of Venice?
Iago. Even he, sir. Did you know him?
Gra. Know him! ay.
Iago. Signior Gratiano? I cry you gentle pardon;
These bloody accidents must excuse my manners,
That so neglected you.
Gra. I am glad to see you.
Iago. How do you, Cassio? O, a chair, a chair!
Gra. Roderigo!
Iago. He, he, 'tis he. [*A chair brought in*.]
O, that's well said; the chair.
Some good man bear him carefully from hence;
I'll fetch the general's surgeon. [*To* BIANCA]
For you, mistress,
Save you your labour. He that lies slain here, Cassio,
Was my dear friend. What malice was between you?
Cas. None in the world; nor do I know the man.
Iago. [*To* BIANCA] What, look you pale? O, bear him out o' the air.
[CASSIO *and* RODERIGO *are borne off*.
Stay you, good gentlemen. Look you pale, mistress?
Do you perceive the gastness of her eye?
Nay, if you stare, we shall hear more anon.
Behold her well; I pray you, look upon her;
Do you see, gentlemen? nay, guiltiness will speak,
Though tongues were out of use.

Enter EMILIA.

Emil. 'Las, what's the matter? what's the matter, husband?
Iago. Cassio hath here been set on in the dark
By Roderigo and fellows that are scaped.
He's almost slain, and Roderigo dead.
Emil. Alas, good gentleman! alas, good Cassio!
Iago. This is the fruit of whoring. Prithee, Emilia,
Go know of Cassio where he supp'd to-night.
[*To* BIANCA] What, do you shake at that?
Bian. He supp'd at my house; but I therefore shake not.
Iago. O, did he so? I charge you, go with me.
Emil. Fie, fie upon thee, strumpet!
Bian. I am no strumpet; but of life as honest
As you that thus abuse me.
Emil. As I! foh! fie upon thee!
Iago. Kind gentlemen, let's go see poor Cassio dress'd.
Come, mistress, you must tell's another tale.
Emilia, run you to the citadel,
And tell my lord and lady what hath happ'd.
Will you go on? I pray. [*Aside*] This is the night
That either makes me or fordoes me quite.
[*Exeunt*.

SCENE II. *A bedchamber in the castle:* DESDEMONA *in bed asleep; a light burning*

Enter OTHELLO.

Oth. It is the cause, it is the cause, my soul—

Let me not name it to you, you chaste stars!—
It is the cause. Yet I'll not shed her blood;
Nor scar that whiter skin of hers than snow,
And smooth as monumental alabaster.
Yet she must die, else she'll betray more men.
Put out the light, and then put out the light.
If I quench thee, thou flaming minister,
I can again thy former light restore,
Should I repent me; but once put out thy light,
Thou cunning'st pattern of excelling nature,
I know not where is that Promethean heat
That can thy light relume. When I have pluck'd the rose,
I cannot give it vital growth again,
It must needs wither. I'll smell it on the tree.
Kissing her.
Ah, balmy breath, that dost almost persuade
Justice to break her sword! One more, one more.
Be thus when thou art dead, and I will kill thee,
And love thee after. One more, and this the last;
So sweet was ne'er so fatal. I must weep,
But they are cruel tears. This sorrow's heavenly;
It strikes where it doth love. She wakes.
Des. Who's there? Othello?
Oth. Ay, Desdemona.
Des. Will you come to bed, my lord?
Oth. Have you pray'd to-night, Desdemona?
Des. Ay, my lord.
Oth. If you bethink yourself of any crime
Unreconciled as yet to Heaven and grace,
Solicit for it straight.
Des. Alas, my lord, what do you mean by that?
Oth. Well, do it, and be brief; I will walk by.
I would not kill thy unprepared spirit;
No; heaven forfend! I would not kill thy soul.
Des. Talk you of killing?
Oth. Ay, I do.
Des. Then Heaven
Have mercy on me!
Oth. Amen, with all my heart!
Des. If you say so, I hope you will not kill me.
Oh. Hum!
Des. And yet I fear you; for you are fatal then
When your eyes roll so. Why I should fear I know not,
Since guiltiness I know not; but yet I feel I fear.
Oth. Think on thy sins.
Des. They are loves I bear to you.
Oth. Ay, and for that thou diest.
Des. That death's unnatural that kills for loving.
Alas, why gnaw you so your nether lip?
Some bloody passion shakes your very frame.
These are portents; but yet I hope, I hope,
They do not point on me.
Oth. Peace, and be still!
Des. I will so. What's the matter?
Oth. That handkerchief which I so loved and gave thee
Thou gavest to Cassio.
Des. No, by my life and soul!
Send for the man, and ask him.
Oth. Sweet soul, take heed,
Take heed of perjury; thou art on thy death-bed.
Des. Ay, but not yet to die.
Oth. Yes, presently;
Therefore confess thee freely of thy sin;
For to deny each article with oath
Cannot remove nor choke the strong conception
That I do groan withal. Thou art to die.
Des. Then Lord have mercy on me!
Oth. I say, amen.
Des. And have you mercy too! I never did
Offend you in my life; never loved Cassio
But with such general warranty of heaven
As I might love; I never gave him token.
Oth. By heaven, I saw my handkerchief in's hand.
O perjured woman! thou dost stone my heart,
And makest me call what I intend to do
A murder, which I thought a sacrifice.
I saw the handkerchief.
Des. He found it then;
I never gave it him. Send for him hither;
Let him confess a truth.
Oth. He hath confess'd.
Des. What, my lord?
Oth. That he hath used thee.
Des. How? unlawfully?
Oth. Ay.
Des. He will not say so.
Oth. No, his mouth is stopp'd;
Honest Iago hath ta'en order for't.
Des. O! my fear interprets. What, is he dead?
Oth. Had all his hairs been lives, my great revenge
Had stomach for them all.
Des. Alas! he is betray'd and I undone.
Oth. Out, strumpet! weep'st thou for him to my face?
Des. O, banish me, my lord, but kill me not!
Oth. Down, strumpet!
Des. Kill me to-morrow; let me live to-night!
Oth. Nay, if you strive—
Des. But half an hour!
Oth. Being done, there is no pause.
Des. But while I say one prayer!
Oth. It is too late
He stifles her.
Emil. [*Within*] My lord, my lord! what, ho! my lord, my lord!
Oth. What noise is this? Not dead? not yet quite dead?

I that am cruel am yet merciful;
I would not have thee linger in thy pain.
So, so.

Emil. [*Within*] What, ho! my lord, my lord!

Oth. Who's there?

Emil. [*Within*] O, good my lord, I would speak a word with you!

Oth. Yes, 'tis Emilia.—By and by.—She's dead.—
'Tis like she comes to speak of Cassio's death.
The noise was here. Ha! no more moving?
Still as the grave.—Shall she come in? were't good?—
I think she stirs again. No.—What's best to do?
If she come in, she'll sure speak to my wife.
My wife! my wife! what wife? I have no wife.
O, insupportable! O heavy hour!
Methinks it should be now a huge eclipse
Of sun and moon, and that the affrighted globe
Should yawn at alteration.

Emil. [*Within*] I do beseech you
That I may speak with you, O, good my lord!

Oth. I had forgot thee. O, come in, Emilia.
Soft; by and by. Let me the curtains draw.
Where art thou? [*Unlocks the door.*]

Enter EMILIA.

What's the matter with thee now?

Emil. O, my good lord, yonder's foul murders done!

Oth. What, now?

Emil. But now, my lord.

Oth. It is the very error of the moon;
She comes more nearer earth than she was wont,
And makes men mad.

Emil. Cassio, my lord, hath kill'd a young Venetian
Call'd Roderigo.

Oth. Roderigo kill'd!
And Cassio kill'd!

Emil. No, Cassio is not kill'd.

Oth. Not Cassio kill'd! then murder's out of tune,
And sweet revenge grows harsh.

Des. O, falsely, falsely murder'd!

Emil. Alas, what cry is that?

Oth. That! what?

Emil. Out, and alas! that was my lady's voice.
Help! help, ho! help! O lady, speak again!
Sweet Desdemona! O sweet mistress, speak!

Des. A guiltless death I die.

Emil. O, who hath done this deed?

Des. Nobody; I myself. Farewell.
Commend me to my kind lord. O, farewell! [*Dies.*

Oth. Why, how should she be murder'd?

Emil. Alas, who knows?

Oth. You heard her say herself, it was not I.

Emil. She said so. I must needs report the truth.

Oth. She's, like a liar, gone to burning hell.
'Twas I that kill'd her.

Emil. O, the more angel she,
And you the blacker devil!

Oth. She turn'd to folly, and she was a whore.

Emil. Thou dost belie her, and thou art a devil.

Oth. She was false as water.

Emil. Thou art rash as fire to say
That she was false. O, she was heavenly true!

Oth. Cassio did top her; ask thy husband else.
O, I were damn'd beneath all depth in hell,
But that I did proceed upon just grounds
To this extremity. Thy husband knew it all.

Emil. My husband!

Oth. Thy husband.

Emil. That she was false to wedlock?

Oth. Ay, with Cassio. Nay, had she been true,
If Heaven would make me such another world
Of one entire and perfect chrysolite,
I'd not have sold her for it.

Emil. My husband!

Oth. Ay, 'twas he that told me first.
An honest man he is, and hates the slime
That sticks on filthy deeds.

Emil. My husband!

Oth. What needs this iteration, woman? I say thy husband.

Emil. O mistress, villainy hath made mocks with love!
My husband say that she was false!

Oth. He, woman;
I say thy husband. Dost understand the word?
My friend, thy husband, honest, honest Iago.

Emil. If he say so, may his pernicious soul
Rot half a grain a day! he lies to the heart.
She was too fond of her most filthy bargain.

Oth. Ha!

Emil. Do thy worst.
This deed of thine is no more worthy heaven
Than thou wast worthy her.

Oth. Peace, you were best.

Emil. Thou hast not half that power to do me harm
As I have to be hurt. O gull! O dolt!
As ignorant as dirt! thou hast done a deed—
I care not for thy sword; I'll make thee known,
Though I lost twenty lives.—Help! help, ho! help!
The Moor hath kill'd my mistress! Murder! murder!

Enter MONTANO, GRATIANO, IAGO, *and others.*

Mon. What is the matter? How now, general!

Emil. O, are you come, Iago? you have done well,
That men must lay their murders on your neck.
Gra. What is the matter?
Emil. Disprove this villain, if thou be'st a man.
He says thou told'st him that his wife was false.
I know thou didst not, thou'rt not such a villain.
Speak, for my heart is full.
Iago. I told him what I thought, and told no more
Than what he found himself was apt and true.
Emil. But did you ever tell him she was false?
Iago. I did.
Emil. You told a lie; an odious, damned lie;
Upon my soul, a lie, a wicked lie.
She false with Cassio!—did you say with Cassio?
Iago. With Cassio, mistress. Go to, charm your tongue.
Emil. I will not charm my tongue; I am bound to speak.
My mistress here lies murder'd in her bed—
All. O heavens forfend!
Emil. And your reports have set the murder on.
Oth. Nay, stare not, masters. It is true, indeed.
Gra. 'Tis a strange truth.
Mon. O monstrous act!
Emil. Villainy, villainy, villainy!
I think upon 't, I think, I smell 't. O villainy!
I thought so then. I'll kill myself for grief.
O villainy, villainy!
Iago. What, are you mad? I charge you, get you home.
Emil. Good gentlemen, let me have leave to speak;
'Tis proper I obey him, but not now.
Perchance, Iago, I will ne'er go home.
Oth. O! O! O! [*He falls on the bed.*]
Emil. Nay, lay thee down and roar;
For thou hast kill'd the sweetest innocent
That e'er did lift up eye.
Oth. [*Rising*] O, she was foul!
I scarce did know you, uncle. There lies your niece,
Whose breath, indeed, these hands have newly stopp'd.
I know this act shows horrible and grim.
Gra. Poor Desdemona! I am glad thy father's dead.
Thy match was mortal to him, and pure grief
Shore his old thread in twain. Did he live now,
This sight would make him do a desperate turn,
Yea, curse his better angel from his side,
And fall to reprobation.
Oth. 'Tis pitiful; but yet Iago knows
That she with Cassio hath the act of shame
A thousand times committed; Cassio confess'd it.
And she did gratify his amorous works
With that recognizance and pledge of love
Which I first gave her; I saw it in his hand;
It was a handkerchief, an antique token
My father gave my mother.
Emil. O heaven! O heavenly powers!
Iago. Come, hold your peace.
Emil. 'Twill out, 'twill out! I peace!
No, I will speak as liberal as the north.
Let heaven and men and devils, let them all,
All, all, cry shame against me, yet I'll speak.
Iago. Be wise, and get you home.
Emil. I will not.

IAGO *offers to stab* EMILIA.

Gra. Fie!
Your sword upon a woman?
Emil. O thou dull Moor! that handkerchief thou speak'st of
I found by fortune and did give my husband;
For often, with a solemn earnestness,
More than indeed belong'd to such a trifle,
He begg'd of me to steal it.
Iago. Villainous whore!
Emil. She give it Cassio! No, alas! I found it,
And I did give't my husband.
Iago. Filth, thou liest!
Emil. By heaven, I do not, I do not, gentlemen.
O murderous coxcomb! what should such a fool
Do with so good a woman?
Oth. Are there no stones in heaven
But what serve for the thunder?—Precious villain!

He runs at IAGO. IAGO, *from behind, stabs Emilia, and exit.*

Gra. The woman falls; sure, he hath kill'd his wife.
Emil. Ay, ay. O, lay me by my mistress' side.
Gra. He's gone, but his wife's kill'd.
Mon. 'Tis a notorious villain. Take you this weapon,
Which I have here recover'd from the Moor.
Come, guard the door without; let him not pass,
But kill him rather. I'll after that same villain,
For 'tis a damned slave.

[*Exeunt* MONTANO *and* GRATIANO.

Oth. I am not valiant neither,
But every puny whipster gets my sword.
But why should honour outlive honesty?
Let it go all.
Emil. What did thy song bode, lady?
Hark, canst thou hear me? I will play the swan,
And die in music. [*Singing*] 'Willow, willow, willow."—
Moor, she was chaste; she loved thee, cruel Moor;
So come my soul to bliss, as I speak true;

So speaking as I think, I die, I die. [*Dies*.
Oth. I have another weapon in this chamber;
It is a sword of Spain, the ice-brook's temper.
O, here it is. Uncle, I must come forth.
Gra. [*Within*] If thou attempt it, it will cost thee dear.
Thou hast no weapon, and perforce must suffer.
Oth. Look in upon me then and speak with me,
Or, naked as I am, I will assault thee.

Re-enter GRATIANO.

Gra. What is the matter?
Oth. Behold, I have a weapon;
A better never did itself sustain
Upon a soldier's thigh. I have seen the day
That, with this little arm and this good sword,
I have made my way through more impediments
Than twenty times your stop. But, O vain boast!
Who can control his fate? 'tis not so now.
Be not afraid, though you do see me weapon'd;
Here is my journey's end, here is my butt,
And very sea-mark of my utmost sail.
Do you go back dismay'd? 'tis a lost fear;
Man but a rush against Othello's breast,
And he retires. Where should Othello go?
Now, how dost thou look now? O ill-starr'd wench!
Pale as thy smock! when we shall meet at compt,
This look of thine will hurl my soul from heaven,
And fiends will snatch at it. Cold, cold, my girl!
Even like thy chastity. O cursed slave!
Whip me, ye devils,
From the possession of this heavenly sight!
Blow me about in winds! roast me in sulphur!
Wash me in steep-down gulfs of liquid fire!
O Desdemona! Desdemona! dead!
Oh! Oh! Oh!

Enter LODOVICO, MONTANO, CASSIO *carried in a chair, and Officers with* IAGO, *prisoner*.

Lod. Where is this rash and most unfortunate man?
Oth. That's he that was Othello. Here I am.
Lod. Where is that viper? bring the villain forth.
Oth. I look down towards his feet; but that's a fable.
If that thou be'st a devil, I cannot kill thee.
Wounds IAGO.
Lod. Wrench his sword from him.
Iago. I bleed, sir; but not kill'd.
Oth. I am not sorry neither. I'd have thee live;
For, in my sense, 'tis happiness to die.
Lod. O thou Othello, that wert once so good,
Fall'n in the practice of a damned slave,
What shall be said to thee?
Oth. Why, anything;
An honourable murderer, if you will;
For nought I did in hate, but all in honour.
Lod. This wretch hath part confess'd his villainy.
Did you and he consent in Cassio's death?
Oth. Ay.
Cas. Dear general, I never gave you cause.
Oth. I do believe it, and I ask you pardon.
Will you, I pray, demand that demi-devil
Why he hath thus ensnared my soul and body?
Iago. Demand me nothing. What you know, you know.
From this time forth I never will speak word.
Lod. What, not to pray?
Gra. Torments will ope your lips.
Oth. Well, thou dost best.
Lod. Sir, you shall understand what hath befall'n,
Which, as I think, you know not. Here is a letter
Found in the pocket of the slain Roderigo;
And here another. The one of them imports
The death of Cassio to be undertook
By Roderigo.
Oth. O villain!
Cas. Most heathenish and most gross!
Lod. Now here's another discontented paper,
Found in his pocket too; and this, it seems,
Roderigo meant to have sent this damned villain;
But that belike Iago in the interim
Came in and satisfied him.
Oth. O the pernicious caitiff!
How came you, Cassio, by that handkerchief
That was my wife's?
Cas. I found it in my chamber;
And he himself confess'd but even now
That there he dropp'd it for a special purpose
Which wrought to his desire.
Oth. O fool! fool! fool!
Cas. There is besides in Roderigo's letter,
How he upbraids Iago, that he made him
Brave me upon the watch; whereon it came
That I was cast. And even but now he spake,
After long seeming dead, Iago hurt him,
Iago set him on.
Lod. You must forsake this room, and go with us;
Your power and your command is taken off,
And Cassio rules in Cyprus. For this slave,
If there be any cunning cruelty
That can torment him much and hold him long,
It shall be his. You shall close prisoner rest,
Till that the nature of your fault be known
To the Venetian state. Come, bring him away.
Oth. Soft you; a word or two before you go.
I have done the state some service, and they know't.

No more of that. I pray you, in your letters,
When you shall these unlucky deeds relate,
Speak of me as I am; nothing extenuate,
Nor set down aught in malice. Then must you speak
Of one that loved not wisely but too well;
Of one not easily jealous, but being wrought
Perplex'd in the extreme; of one whose hand,
Like the base Indian, threw a pearl away
Richer than all his tribe; of one whose subdued eyes,
Albeit unused to the melting mood,
Drop tears as fast as the Arabian trees
Their medicinal gum. Set you down this;
And say besides, that in Aleppo once,
Where a malignant and a turban'd Turk
Beat a Venetian and traduced the state,
I took by the throat the circumcised dog,
And smote him, thus. [*Stabs himself*.]

Lod. O bloody period!

Gra. All that's spoke is marr'd.

Oth. I kiss'd thee ere I kill'd thee. No way but this,
Killing myself, to die upon a kiss.
[*Falls on the bed and dies*.

Cas. This did I fear, but thought he had no weapon;
For he was great of heart.

Lod. [*To* IAGO] O Spartan dog,
More fell then anguish, hunger, or the sea!
Look on the tragic loading of this bed;
This is thy work. The object poisons sight;
Let it be hid. Gratiano, keep the house,
And seize upon the fortunes of the Moor,
For they succeed on you. To you, lord governor,
Remains the censure of this hellish villain;
The time, the place, the torture. O, enforce it!
Myself will straight aboard; and to the state
This heavy act with heavy heart relate. [*Exeunt*.

KING LEAR

DRAMATIS PERSONÆ

LEAR, *King of Britain*
KING OF FRANCE
DUKE OF BURGUNDY
DUKE OF CORNWALL
DUKE OF ALBANY
EARL OF KENT
EARL OF GLOUCESTER
EDGAR, *son to Gloucester*
EDMUND, *bastard son to Gloucester*
CURAN, *a courtier*
OLD MAN, *tenant to Gloucester*
A DOCTOR
FOOL
OSWALD, *steward to Goneril*
TWO CAPTAINS
A GENTLEMAN, *attendant on Cordelia*
A GENTLEMAN, *attendant on Lear*
A KNIGHT, *attendant on Lear*
A HERALD
THREE SERVANTS *to Cornwall*
TWO MESSENGERS
GONERIL, REGAN, CORDELIA — *daughters to Lear*

NON-SPEAKING: *Knights of Lear's train, Captains, Soldiers, and Attendants*

SCENE: *Britain*

ACT I

SCENE I. *King Lear's palace*

Enter KENT, GLOUCESTER, *and* EDMUND.

Kent. I thought the King had more affected the Duke of Albany than Cornwall.

Glou. It did always seem so to us; but now, in the division of the kingdom, it appears not which of the Dukes he values most; for equalities are so weighed, that curiosity in neither can make choice of either's moiety.

Kent. Is not this your son, my lord?

Glou. His breeding, sir, hath been at my charge. I have so often blushed to acknowledge him, that now I am brazed to it.

Kent. I cannot conceive you.

Glou. Sir, this young fellow's mother could; whereupon she grew round-wombed, and had, indeed, sir, a son for her cradle ere she had a husband for her bed. Do you smell a fault?

Kent. I cannot wish the fault undone, the issue of it being so proper.

Glou. But I have, sir, a son by order of law, some year elder than this, who yet is no dearer in my account. Though this knave came something saucily into the world before he was sent for, yet was his mother fair; there was good sport at his making, and the whoreson must be acknowledged. Do you know this noble gentleman, Edmund?

Edm. No, my lord.

Glou. My lord of Kent. Remember him hereafter as my honourable friend.

Edm. My services to your lordship.

Kent. I must love you, and sue to know you better.

Edm. Sir, I shall study deserving.

Glou. He hath been out nine years, and away he shall again. The King is coming.

Sennet. Enter KING LEAR, CORNWALL, ALBANY, GONERIL, REGAN, CORDELIA, *and Attendants*.

Lear. Attend the lords of France and Burgundy, Gloucester.

Glou. I shall, my liege.

[*Exeunt* GLOUCESTER *and* EDMUND.

Lear. Meantime we shall express our darker purpose.
Give me the map there. Know that we have divided
In three our kingdom; and 'tis our fast intent
To shake all cares and business from our age;
Conferring them on younger strengths, while we
Unburthen'd crawl toward death. Our son of Cornwall,
And you, our no less loving son of Albany,
We have this hour a constant will to publish
Our daughters' several dowers, that future strife
May be prevented now. The Princes, France and Burgundy,
Great rivals in our youngest daughter's love,
Long in our court have made their amorous sojourn,
And here are to be answer'd. Tell me, my daughters—
Since now we will divest us, both of rule,
Interest of territory, cares of state—
Which of you shall we say doth love us most?
That we our largest bounty may extend

Where nature doth with merit challenge. Goneril,
Our eldest-born, speak first.
Gon. Sir, I love you more than words can wield the matter;
Dearer than eye-sight, space, and liberty;
Beyond what can be valued, rich or rare;
No less than life, with grace, health, beauty, honour;
As much as child e'er loved, or father found;
A love that makes breath poor, and speech unable;
Beyond all manner of so much I love you.
Cor. [*Aside*] What shall Cordelia do? Love, and be silent.
Lear. Of all these bounds, even from this line to this,
With shadowy forests and with champains rich'd,
With plenteous rivers and wide-skirted meads,
We make thee lady; to thine and Albany's issue
Be this perpetual. What says our second daughter,
Our dearest Regan, wife to Cornwall? Speak.
Reg. Sir, I am made
Of the self-same metal that my sister is,
And prize me at her worth. In my true heart
I find she names my very deed of love;
Only she comes too short; that I profess
Myself an enemy to all other joys,
Which the most precious square of sense possesses;
And find I am alone felicitate
In your dear Highness' love.
Cor. [*Aside*] Then poor Cordelia!
And yet not so; since, I am sure, my love's
More richer than my tongue.
Lear. To thee and thine hereditary ever
Remain this ample third of our fair kingdom;
No less in space, validity, and pleasure,
Than that conferr'd on Goneril. Now, our joy,
Although the last, not least; to whose young love
The vines of France and milk of Burgundy
Strive to be interess'd; what can you say to draw
A third more opulent than your sisters? Speak.
Cor. Nothing, my lord.
Lear. Nothing!
Cor. Nothing.
Lear. Nothing will come of nothing. Speak again.
Cor. Unhappy that I am, I cannot heave
My heart into my mouth. I love your Majesty
According to my bond; nor more nor less.
Lear. How, how, Cordelia! mend your speech a little,
Lest it may mar your fortunes.
Cor. Good my lord,
You have begot me, bred me, loved me. I
Return those duties back as are right fit,
Obey you, love you, and most honour you.
Why have my sisters husbands, if they say
They love you all? Haply, when I shall wed,
That lord whose hand must take my plight shall carry
Half my love with him, half my care and duty.
Sure, I shall never marry like my sisters,
To love my father all.
Lear. But goes thy heart with this?
Cor. Ay, good my lord.
Lear. So young, and so untender?
Cor. So young, my lord, and true.
Lear. Let it be so; thy truth, then, be thy dower;
For, by the sacred radiance of the sun,
The mysteries of Hecate, and the night;
By all the operation of the orbs
From whom we do exist, and cease to be;
Here I disclaim all my paternal care,
Propinquity and property of blood,
And as a stranger to my heart and me
Hold thee, from this, for ever. The barbarous Scythian,
Or he that makes his generation messes
To gorge his appetite, shall to my bosom
Be as well neighbour'd, pitied, and relieved,
As thou my sometime daughter.
Kent. Good my liege—
Lear. Peace, Kent!
Come not between the dragon and his wrath.
I loved her most, and thought to set my rest
On her kind nursery. Hence, and avoid my sight!
So be my grave my peace, as here I give
Her father's heart from her! Call France; who stirs?
Call Burgundy. Cornwall and Albany,
With my two daughters' dowers digest this third.
Let pride, which she calls plainness, marry her.
I do invest you jointly with my power,
Pre-eminence, and all the large effects
That troop with majesty. Ourself, by monthly course,
With reservation of an hundred knights,
By you to be sustain'd, shall our abode
Make with you by due turns. Only we still retain
The name, and all the additions to a king;
The sway, revenue, execution of the rest,
Beloved sons, be yours; which to confirm,
This coronet part betwixt you. [*Giving the crown.*
Kent. Royal Lear,
Whom I have ever honour'd as my king,
Loved as my father, as my master follow'd,
As my great patron thought on in my prayers—
Lear. The bow is bent and drawn, make from the shaft.
Kent. Let it fall rather, though the fork invade
The region of my heart: be Kent unmannerly,

When Lear is mad. What wilt thou do, old man?
Think'st thou that duty shall have dread to speak,
When power to flattery bows? To plainness honour's bound
When majesty stoops to folly. Reverse thy doom;
And, in thy best consideration, check
This hideous rashness. Answer my life my judgement,
Thy youngest daughter does not love thee least;
Nor are those empty-hearted whose low sound
Reverbs no hollowness.

Lear. Kent, on thy life, no more.

Kent. My life I never held but as a pawn
To wage against thy enemies; nor fear to lose it,
Thy safety being the motive.

Lear. Out of my sight!

Kent. See better, Lear; and let me still remain
The true blank of thine eye.

Lear. Now, by Apollo—

Kent. Now, by Apollo, king,
Thou swear'st thy gods in vain.

Lear. O, vassal! miscreant!

Laying his hand on his sword.

Alb., *Corn.* Dear sir, forbear.

Kent. Do;
Kill thy physician, and the fee bestow
Upon thy foul disease. Revoke thy doom;
Or, whilst I can vent clamour from my throat,
I'll tell thee thou dost evil.

Lear. Hear me, recreant!
On thine allegiance, hear me!
Since thou hast sought to make us break our vow,
Which we durst never yet, and with strain'd pride
To come between our sentence and our power,
Which nor our nature nor our place can bear,
Our potency made good, take thy reward.
Five days we do allot thee, for provision
To shield thee from diseases of the world;
And on the sixth to turn thy hated back
Upon our kingdom. If, on the tenth day following,
Thy banish'd trunk be found in our dominions,
The moment is thy death. Away! by Jupiter,
This shall not be revoked.

Kent. Fare thee well, king! Sith thus thou wilt appear,
Freedom lives hence, and banishment is here.
[*To* CORDELIA] The gods to their dear shelter take thee, maid,
That justly think'st, and hast most rightly said!
[*To* REGAN *and* GONERIL] And your large speeches may your deeds approve,
That good effects may spring from words of love.
Thus Kent, O Princes, bids you all adieu;
He'll shape his old course in a country new. [*Exit.*

Flourish. Re-enter GLOUCESTER, *with* FRANCE, BURGUNDY, *and Attendants.*

Glou. Here's France and Burgundy, my noble lord.

Lear. My Lord of Burgundy,
We first address towards you, who with this king
Hath rivall'd for our daughter: what, in the least,
Will you require in present dower with her,
Or cease your quest of love?

Bur. Most royal Majesty,
I carve no more than what your Highness offer'd,
Nor will you tender less.

Lear. Right noble Burgundy,
When she was dear to us, we did hold her so;
But now her price is fall'n. Sir, there she stands:
If aught within that little seeming substance,
Or all of it, with our displeasure pieced,
And nothing more, may fitly like your Grace,
She's there, and she is yours.

Bur. I know no answer.

Lear. Will you, with those infirmities she owes,
Unfriended, new-adopted to our hate,
Dower'd with our curse, and stranger'd with our oath,
Take her, or leave her?

Bur. Pardon me, royal sir;
Election makes not up on such conditions.

Lear. Then leave her, sir; for, by the power that made me,
I tell you all her wealth. [*To* FRANCE] For you, great king,
I would not from your love make such a stray,
To match you where I hate; therefore beseech you
To avert your liking a more worthier way
Than on a wretch whom nature is ashamed
Almost to acknowledge hers.

France. This is most strange,
That she, that even but now was your best object,
The argument of your praise, balm of your age,
Most best, most dearest, should in this trice of time
Commit a thing so monstrous, to dismantle
So many folds of favour. Sure, her offence
Must be of such unnatural degree,
That monsters it, or your fore-vouch'd affection
Fall'n into taint; which to believe of her,
Must be a faith that reason without miracle
Could never plant in me.

Cor. I yet beseech your Majesty—
If for I want that glib and oily art

To speak and purpose not; since what I well intend,
I'll do't before I speak—that you make known
It is no vicious blot, murder, or foulness,
No unchaste action, or dishonour'd step,
That hath deprived me of your grace and favour;
But even for want of that for which I am richer,
A still-soliciting eye, and such a tongue
As I am glad I have not, though not to have it
Hath lost me in your liking.

Lear. Better thou
Hadst not been born than not to have pleased me better.

France. Is it but this—a tardiness in nature
Which often leaves the history unspoke
That it intends to do? My Lord of Burgundy,
What say you to the lady? Love's not love
When it is mingled with regards that stand
Aloof from the entire point. Will you have her?
She is herself a dowry.

Bur. Royal Lear,
Give but that portion which yourself proposed,
And here I take Cordelia by the hand,
Duchess of Burgundy.

Lear. Nothing. I have sworn; I am firm.

Bur. I am sorry, then, you have so lost a father
That you must lose a husband.

Cor. Peace be with Burgundy!
Since that respects of fortune are his love,
I shall not be his wife.

France. Fairest Cordelia, that art most rich, being poor;
Most choice, forsaken; and most loved, despised!
Thee and thy virtues here I seize upon,
Be it lawful I take up what's cast away.
Gods, gods! 'tis strange that from their cold'st neglect
My love should kindle to inflamed respect.
Thy dowerless daughter, king, thrown to my chance,
Is queen of us, of ours, and our fair France.
Not all the dukes of waterish Burgundy
Can buy this unprized precious maid of me.
Bid them farewell, Cordelia, though unkind;
Thou losest here, a better where to find.

Lear. Thou hast her, France. Let her be thine; for we
Have no such daughter, nor shall ever see
That face of hers again. Therefore be gone
Without our grace, our love, our benison.
Come, noble Burgundy.

[*Flourish. Exeunt all but* FRANCE, GONERIL, REGAN, *and* CORDELIA.

France. Bid farewell to your sisters.

Cor. The jewels of our father, with wash'd eyes
Cordelia leaves you. I know you what you are;
And like a sister am most loath to call
Your faults as they are named. Use well our father;
To your professed bosoms I commit him.
But yet, alas, stood I within his grace,
I would prefer him to a better place.
So, farewell to you both.

Reg. Prescribe not us our duties.

Gon. Let your study
Be to content your lord, who hath received you
At fortune's alms. You have obedience scanted,
And well are worth the want that you have wanted.

Cor. Time shall unfold what plaited cunning hides;
Who cover faults, at last shame them derides.
Well may you prosper!

France. Come, my fair Cordelia.

[*Exeunt* FRANCE *and* CORDELIA.

Gon. Sister, it is not a little I have to say of what most nearly appertains to us both. I think our father will hence to-night.

Reg. That's most certain, and with you; next month with us.

Gon. You see how full of changes his age is; the observation we have made of it hath not been little. He always loved our sister most; and with what poor judgement he hath now cast her off appears too grossly.

Reg. 'Tis the infirmity of his age. Yet he hath ever but slenderly known himself.

Gon. The best and soundest of his time hath been but rash; then must we look to receive from his age, not alone the imperfections of long-engraffed condition, but therewithal the unruly waywardness that infirm and choleric years bring with them.

Reg. Such unconstant starts are we like to have from him as this of Kent's banishment.

Gon. There is further compliment of leave-taking between France and him. Pray you, let's hit together. If our father carry authority with such dispositions as he bears, this last surrender of his will but offend us.

Reg. We shall further think on't.

Gon. We must do something, and i' the heat.

[*Exeunt*.

SCENE II. *The Earl of Gloucester's castle*

Enter EDMUND, *with a letter*.

Edm. Thou, nature, art my goddess; to thy law
My services are bound. Wherefore should I
Stand in the plague of custom, and permit
The curiosity of nations to deprive me,

For that I am some twelve or fourteen moonshines
Lag of a brother? Why bastard? wherefore base?
When my dimensions are as well compact,
My mind as generous, and my shape as true,
As honest madam's issue? Why brand they us
With base? with baseness? bastardy? base, base?
Who, in the lusty stealth of nature, take
More composition and fierce quality
Than doth, within a dull, stale, tired bed,
Go to the creating a whole tribe of fops,
Got 'tween asleep and wake? Well, then,
Legitimate Edgar, I must have your land.
Our father's love is to the bastard Edmund
As to the legitimate. Fine word, "legitimate!"
Well, my legitimate, if this letter speed,
And my invention thrive, Edmund the base
Shall top the legitimate. I grow; I prosper.
Now, gods, stand up for bastards!

Enter GLOUCESTER.

Glou. Kent banish'd thus! and France in choler parted!
And the King gone to-night! subscribed his power!
Confined to exhibition! All this done
Upon the gad! Edmund, how now! what news?

Edm. So please your lordship, none.

Putting up the letter.

Glou. Why so earnestly seek you to put up that letter?

Edm. I know no news, my lord.

Glou. What paper were you reading?

Edm. Nothing, my lord.

Glou. No? What needed, then, that terrible dispatch of it into your pocket? the quality of nothing hath not such need to hide itself. Let's see. Come, if it be nothing, I shall not need spectacles.

Edm. I beseech you, sir, pardon me. It is a letter from my brother that I have not all o'er-read; and for so much as I have perused, I find it not fit for your o'er-looking.

Glou. Give me the letter, sir.

Edm. I shall offend, either to detain or give it. The contents, as in part I understand them, are to blame.

Glou. Let's see, let's see.

Edm. I hope, for my brother's justification, he wrote this but as an essay or taste of my virtue.

Glou. [*Reads*] "This policy and reverence of age makes the world bitter to the best of our times; keeps our fortunes from us till our oldness cannot relish them. I begin to find an idle and fond bondage in the oppression of aged tyranny; who sways, not as it hath power, but as it is suffered. Come to me, that of this I may speak more. If our father would sleep till I waked him, you should enjoy half his revenue for ever, and live the beloved of your brother, Edgar" Hum, conspiracy! "Sleep till I waked him, you should enjoy half his revenue." My son Edgar! Had he a hand to write this? a heart and brain to breed it in? When came this to you? who brought it?

Edm. It was not brought me, my lord; there's the cunning of it; I found it thrown in at the casement of my closet.

Glou. You know the character to be your brother's?

Edm. If the matter were good, my lord, I durst swear it were his; but, in respect of that, I would fain think it were not.

Glou. It is his.

Edm. It is his hand, my lord; but I hope his heart is not in the contents.

Glou. Hath he never heretofore sounded you in this business?

Edm. Never, my lord; but I have heard him oft maintain it to be fit that, sons at perfect age, and fathers declining, the father should be as ward to the son, and the son manage his revenue.

Glou. O villain, villain! His very opinion in the letter! Abhorred villain! Unnatural, detested, brutish villain! worse than brutish! Go, sirrah, seek him; I'll apprehend him. Abominable villain! Where is he?

Edm. I do not well know, my lord. If it shall please you to suspend your indignation against my brother till you can derive from him better testimony of his intent, you shall run a certain course; where, if you violently proceed against him, mistaking his purpose, it would make a great gap in your own honour, and shake in pieces the heart of his obedience. I dare pawn down my life for him, that he hath writ this to feel my affection to your honour, and to no other pretence of danger.

Glou. Think you so?

Edm. If your honour judge it meet, I will place you where you shall hear us confer of this, and by an auricular assurance have your satisfaction; and that without any further delay than this very evening.

Glou. He cannot be such a monster—

Edm. Nor is not, sure.

Glou. To his father, that so tenderly and entirely loves him. Heaven and earth! Edmund, seek him out; wind me into him, I pray you. Frame the business after your own wisdom. I would unstate myself, to be in a due resolution.

Edm. I will seek him, sir, presently; convey

the business as I shall find means, and acquaint you withal.

Glou. These late eclipses in the sun and moon portend no good to us. Though the wisdom of nature can reason it thus and thus, yet nature finds itself scourged by the sequent effects. Love cools, friendship falls off, brothers divide; in cities, mutinies; in countries, discord; in palaces, treason; and the bond cracked 'twixt son and father. This villain of mine comes under the prediction; there's son against father. The King falls from bias of nature; there's father against child. We have seen the best of our time: machinations, hollowness, treachery, and all ruinous disorders, follow us disquietly to our graves. Find out this villain, Edmund; it shall lose thee nothing; do it carefully. And the noble and true-hearted Kent banished! his offence, honesty! 'Tis strange. [*Exit.*

Edm. This is the excellent foppery of the world, that, when we are sick in fortune—often the surfeit of our own behaviour—we make guilty of our disasters the sun, the moon, and the stars, as if we were villains by necessity, fools by heavenly compulsion, knaves, thieves, and treachers, by spherical predominance, drunkards, liars, and adulterers, by an enforced obedience of planetary influence, and all that we are evil in, by a divine thrusting on. An admirable evasion of whoremaster man, to lay his goatish disposition to the charge of a star! My father compounded with my mother under the dragon's tail; and my nativity was under *Ursa major;* so that it follows, I am rough and lecherous. Tut, I should have been that I am, had the maidenliest star in the firmament twinkled on my bastardizing. Edgar—

Enter EDGAR.

and pat he comes like the catastrophe of the old comedy. My cue is villainous melancholy, with a sigh like Tom o' Bedlam. O, these eclipses do portend these divisions! *fa, sol, la, mi.*

Edg. How now, brother Edmund! what serious contemplation are you in?

Edm. I am thinking, brother, of a prediction I read this other day, what should follow these eclipses.

Edg. Do you busy yourself about that?

Edm. I promise you, the effects he writes of succeed unhappily; as of unnaturalness between the child and the parent; death, dearth, dissolutions of ancient amities; divisions in state, menaces and maledictions against king and nobles; needless diffidences, banishment of friends, dissipation of cohorts, nuptial breaches, and I know not what.

Edg. How long have you been a sectary astronomical?

Edm. Come, come; when saw you my father last?

Edg. Why, the night gone by.

Edm. Spake you with him?

Edg. Ay, two hours together.

Edm. Parted you in good terms? Found you no displeasure in him by word or countenance?

Edg. None at all.

Edm. Bethink yourself wherein you may have offended him; and at my entreaty forbear his presence till some little time hath qualified the heat of his displeasure, which at this instant so rageth in him, that with the mischief of your person it would scarcely allay.

Edg. Some villain hath done me wrong.

Edm. That's my fear. I pray you, have a continent forbearance till the speed of his rage goes slower; and, as I say, retire with me to my lodging, from whence I will fitly bring you to hear my lord speak. Pray ye, go; there's my key. If you do stir abroad, go armed.

Edg. Armed, brother!

Edm. Brother, I advise you to the best; go armed. I am no honest man if there be any good meaning towards you. I have told you what I have seen and heard; but faintly, nothing like the image and horror of it. Pray you, away.

Edg. Shall I hear from you anon?

Edm. I do serve you in this business.

[*Exit* EDGAR.

A credulous father! and a brother noble,
Whose nature is so far from doing harms
That he suspects none; on whose foolish honesty
My practices ride easy! I see the business.
Let me, if not by birth, have lands by wit;
All with me's meet that I can fashion fit. [*Exit.*

SCENE III. *The Duke of Albany's palace*

Enter GONERIL, *and* OSWALD, *her steward.*

Gon. Did my father strike my gentleman for chiding of his fool?

Osw. Yes, madam.

Gon. By day and night he wrongs me; every hour
He flashes into one gross crime or other,
That sets us all at odds. I'll not endure it.
His knights grow riotous, and himself upbraids us
On every trifle. When he returns from hunting,
I will not speak with him; say I am sick.
If you come slack of former services,
You shall do well; the fault of it I'll answer.

Osw. He's coming, madam; I hear him.

Horns within.

Gon. Put on what weary negligence you please,

You and your fellows; I'd have it come to question.
If he dislike it, let him to our sister,
Whose mind and mine, I know, in that are one,
Not to be over-ruled. Idle old man,
That still would manage those authorities
That he hath given away! Now, by my life,
Old fools are babes again; and must be used
With checks as flatteries—when they are seen abused.
Remember what I tell you.

Osw. Well, madam.

Gon. And let his knights have colder looks among you;
What grows of it, no matter; advise your fellows so.
I would breed from hence occasions, and I shall,
That I may speak. I'll write straight to my sister,
To hold my very course. Prepare for dinner.
[*Exeunt.*

Scene iv. *A hall in the same*

Enter kent, *disguised.*

Kent. If but as well I other accents borrow,
That can my speech defuse, my good intent
May carry through itself to that full issue
For which I razed my likeness. Now, banish'd Kent,
If thou canst serve where thou dost stand condemn'd,
So may it come, thy master, whom thou lovest,
Shall find thee full of labours.

Horns within. Enter lear, knights, *and Attendants.*

Lear. Let me not stay a jot for dinner; go get it ready. [*Exit an Attendant.*] How now! what art thou?

Kent. A man, sir.

Lear. What dost thou profess? what wouldst thou with us?

Kent. I do profess to be no less than I seem; to serve him truly that will put me in trust; to love him that is honest; to converse with him that is wise, and says little; to fear judgement; to fight when I cannot choose; and to eat no fish.

Lear. What art thou?

Kent. A very honest-hearted fellow, and as poor as the King.

Lear. If thou be as poor for a subject as he is for a king, thou art poor enough. What wouldst thou?

Kent. Service.

Lear. Who wouldst thou serve?

Kent. You.

Lear. Dost thou know me, fellow?

Kent. No, sir; but you have that in your countenance which I would fain call master.

Lear. What's that?

Kent. Authority.

Lear. What services canst thou do?

Kent. I can keep honest counsel, ride, run, mar a curious tale in telling it, and deliver a plain message bluntly. That which ordinary men are fit for, I am qualified in; and the best of me is diligence.

Lear. How old art thou?

Kent. Not so young, sir, to love a woman for singing, nor so old to dote on her for anything. I have years on my back forty eight.

Lear. Follow me; thou shalt serve me. If I like thee no worse after dinner, I will not part from thee yet. Dinner, ho, dinner! Where's my knave? my Fool? Go you, and call my Fool hither. [*Exit an Attendant.*

Enter oswald.

You, you, sirrah, where's my daughter?

Osw. So please you— [*Exit.*

Lear. What says the fellow there? Call the clotpoll back. [*Exit a* knight.] Where's my Fool, ho? I think the world's asleep.

Re-enter knight.

How now! where's that mongrel?

Knight. He says, my lord, your daughter is not well.

Lear. Why came not the slave back to me when I called him.

Knight. Sir, he answered me in the roundest manner, he would not.

Lear. He would not!

Knight. My lord, I know not what the matter is; but, to my judgement, your Highness is not entertained with that ceremonious affection as you were wont; there's a great abatement of kindness appears as well in the general dependants as in the Duke himself also and your daughter.

Lear. Ha! sayest thou so?

Knight. I beseech you, pardon me, my lord, If I be mistaken; for my duty cannot be silent when I think your Highness wronged.

Lear. Thou but rememberest me of mine own conception. I have perceived a most faint neglect of late, which I have rather blamed as mine own jealous curiosity than as a very pretence and purpose of unkindness. I will look further into't. But where's my Fool? I have not seen him this two days.

Knight. Since my young lady's going into France, sir, the Fool hath much pined away.

Lear. No more of that; I have noted it well. Go you, and tell my daughter I would speak with her. [*Exit an Attendant*.] Go you, call hither my Fool. [*Exit an Attendant*.

Re-enter OSWALD.

O, you sir, you, come you hither, sir. Who am I, sir?

Osw. My lady's father.

Lear. "My lady's father"! my lord's knave! You whoreson dog! you slave! you cur!

Osw. I am none of these, my lord; I beseech your pardon.

Lear. Do you bandy looks with me, you rascal? [*Striking him*.]

Osw. I'll not be struck, my lord.

Kent. Nor tripped neither, you base foot-ball player. [*Tripping up his heels*.]

Lear. I thank thee, fellow; thou servest me, and I'll love thee.

Kent. Come, sir, arise, away! I'll teach you differences. Away, away! If you will measure your lubber's length again, tarry. But away! go to; have you wisdom? so. [*Pushes* OSWALD *out*.

Lear. Now, my friendly knave, I thank thee. There's earnest of thy service.

Giving KENT *money*.

Enter FOOL.

Fool. Let me hire him too. Here's my coxcomb. [*Offering* KENT *his cap*.]

Lear. How now, my pretty knave! how dost thou?

Fool. Sirrah, you were best take my coxcomb.

Kent. Why, Fool?

Fool. Why, for taking one's part that's out of favour. Nay, an thou canst not smile as the wind sits, thou'lt catch cold shortly. There, take my coxcomb. Why, this fellow has banished two on 's daughters, and did the third a blessing against his will; if thou follow him, thou must needs wear my coxcomb. How now, nuncle! Would I had two coxcombs and two daughters!

Lear. Why, my boy?

Fool. If I gave them all my living, I'd keep my coxcombs myself. There's mine; beg another of thy daughters.

Lear. Take heed, sirrah; the whip.

Fool. Truth's a dog must to kennel; he must be whipped out, when Lady the brach may stand by the fire and stink.

Lear. A pestilent gall to me!

Fool. Sirrah, I'll teach thee a speech.

Lear. Do.

Fool. Mark it, nuncle:

"Have more than thou showest,
Speak less than thou knowest,
Lend less than thou owest,
Ride more than thou goest,
Learn more than thou trowest,
Set less than thou throwest,
Leave thy drink and thy whore,
And keep in-a-door,
And thou shalt have more
Than two tens to a score."

Kent. This is nothing, fool.

Fool. Then 'tis like the breath of an unfee'd lawyer; you gave me nothing for't. Can you make no use of nothing, nuncle?

Lear. Why, no, boy; nothing can be made out of nothing.

Fool. [*To* KENT] Prithee, tell him, so much the rent of his land comes to. He will not believe a Fool.

Lear. A bitter fool!

Fool. Dost thou know the difference, my boy, between a bitter fool and a sweet fool?

Lear. No, lad; teach me.

Fool. "That lord that counsell'd thee
To give away thy land,
Come place him here by me,
Do thou for him stand.
The sweet and bitter fool
Will presently appear;
The one in motley here,
The other found out there."

Lear. Dost thou call me fool, boy?

Fool. All thy other titles thou hast given away; that thou wast born with.

Kent. This is not altogether fool, my lord.

Fool. No, faith, lords and great men will not let me; if I had a monopoly out, they would have part on't. And ladies too, they will not let me have all fool to myself; they'll be snatching. Give me an egg, nuncle, and I'll give thee two crowns.

Lear. What two crowns shall they be?

Fool. Why, after I have cut the egg i' the middle, and eat up the meat, the two crowns of the egg. When thou clovest thy crown i' the middle, and gavest away both parts, thou borest thy ass on thy back o'er the dirt. Thou hadst little wit in thy bald crown when thou gavest thy golden one away. If I speak like myself in this, let him be whipped that first finds it so.

[*Singing*] "Fools had ne'er less wit in a year;
For wise men are grown foppish,
They know not how their wits to wear,
Their manners are so apish."

Lear. When were you wont to be so full of songs, sirrah?

Fool. I have used it, nuncle, ever since thou

madest thy daughters thy mother; for when thou gavest them the rod, and put'st down thine own breeches,

[*Singing*] "Then they for sudden joy did weep,
And I for sorrow sung,
That such a king should play bo-peep,
And go the fools among."

Prithee, nuncle, keep a schoolmaster that can teach thy Fool to lie. I would fain learn to lie.

Lear. An you lie, sirrah, we'll have you whipped.

Fool. I marvel what kin thou and thy daughters are. They'll have me whipped for speaking true, thou'lt have me whipped for lying; and sometimes I am whipped for holding my peace. I had rather be any kind o' thing than a Fool; and yet I would not be thee, nuncle; thou hast pared thy wit o' both sides, and left nothing i' the middle. Here comes one o' the parings.

Enter GONERIL.

Lear. How now, daughter! what makes that frontlet on? Methinks you are too much of late i' the frown.

Fool. Thou wast a pretty fellow when thou hadst no need to care for her frowning; now thou art an O without a figure. I am better than thou art now; I am a fool, thou art nothing. [*To* GONERIL] Yes, forsooth, I will hold my tongue; so your face bids me, though you say nothing. Mum, mum,

"He that keeps nor crust nor crum,
Weary of all, shall want some."

[*Pointing to* LEAR] That's a shealed peascod.

Gon. Not only, sir, this your all-licensed Fool,
But other of your insolent retinue
Do hourly carp and quarrel, breaking forth
In rank and not-to-be-endured riots. Sir,
I had thought, by making this well known unto you,
To have found a safe redress; but now grow fearful
By what yourself too late have spoke and done,
That you protect this course, and put it on
By your allowance; which if you should, the fault
Would not 'scape censure, nor the redresses sleep,
Which, in the tender of a wholesome weal,
Might in their working do you that offence,
Which else were shame, that then necessity
Will call discreet proceeding.

Fool. For, you know, nuncle,
"The hedge-sparrow fed the cuckoo so long,
That it had it head bit off by it young."

So, out went the candle, and we were left darkling.

Lear. Are you our daughter?

Gon. Come, sir.
I would you would make use of that good wisdom,
Whereof I know you are fraught; and put away
These dispositions, that of late transform you
From what you rightly are.

Fool. May not an ass know when the cart draws the horse? "Whoop, Jug! I love thee."

Lear. Doth any here know me? This is not Lear.
Doth Lear walk thus? speak thus? Where are his eyes?
Either his notion weakens, his discernings
Are lethargied—Ha! waking? 'tis not so.
Who is it that can tell me who I am?

Fool. Lear's shadow.

Lear. I would learn that; for, by the marks of sovereignty, knowledge, and reason, I should be false persuaded I had daughters.

Fool. Which they will make an obedient father.

Lear. Your name, fair gentlewoman?

Gon. This admiration, sir, is much o' the savour
Of other your new pranks. I do beseech you
To understand my purposes aright.
As you are old and reverend, you should be wise.
Here do you keep a hundred knights and squires;
Men so disorder'd, so debosh'd and bold,
That this our court, infected with their manners,
Shows like a riotous inn. Epicurism and lust
Make it more like a tavern or a brothel
Than a graced palace. The shame itself doth speak
For instant remedy. Be then desired
By her, that else will take the thing she begs,
A little to disquantity your train;
And the remainder, that shall still depend
To be such men as may besort your age,
And know themselves and you.

Lear. Darkness and devils!
Saddle my horses; call my train together.
Degenerate bastard! I'll not trouble thee;
Yet have I left a daughter.

Gon. You strike my people; and your disorder'd rabble
Make servants of their betters.

Enter ALBANY.

Lear. Woe, that too late repents—[*To* ALBANY] O, sir, are you come?
Is it your will? Speak, sir. Prepare my horses.
Ingratitude, thou marble-hearted fiend,
More hideous when thou show'st thee in a child
Than the sea-monster!

Alb. Pray, sir, be patient.

Lear. [*To* GONERIL] Detested kite! thou liest.

My train are men of choice and rarest parts,
That all particulars of duty know,
And in the most exact regard support
The worships of their name. O most small fault,
How ugly didst thou in Cordelia show!
That, like an engine, wrench'd my frame of nature
From the fix'd place; drew from my heart all love,
And added to the gall. O Lear, Lear, Lear!
Beat at this gate, that let thy folly in,
Striking his head.
And thy dear judgement out! Go, go, my people.
Alb. My lord, I am guiltless, as I am ignorant
Of what hath moved you.
Lear. It may be so, my lord.
Hear, Nature, hear; dear goddess, hear!
Suspend thy purpose, if thou didst intend
To make this creature fruitful!
Into her womb convey sterility!
Dry up in her the organs of increase;
And from her derogate body never spring
A babe to honour her! If she must teem,
Create her child of spleen; that it may live,
And be a thwart disnatured torment to her!
Let it stamp wrinkles in her brow of youth;
With cadent tears fret channels in her cheeks;
Turn all her mother's pains and benefits
To laughter and contempt; that she may feel
How sharper than a serpent's tooth it is
To have a thankless child! Away, away! [*Exit.*
Alb. Now, gods that we adore, whereof comes this?
Gon. Never afflict yourself to know the cause;
But let his disposition have that scope
That dotage gives it.

Re-enter LEAR.

Lear. What, fifty of my followers at a clap!
Within a fortnight!
Alb. What's the matter, sir?
Lear. I'll tell thee. [*To* GONERIL] Life and death! I am ashamed
That thou hast power to shake my manhood thus;
That these hot tears, which break from me perforce,
Should make thee worth them. Blasts and fogs upon thee!
The untented woundings of a father's curse
Pierce every sense about thee! Old fond eyes,
Beweep this cause again, I'll pluck ye out,
And cast you, with the waters that you lose,
To temper clay. Yea, is it come to this?
Let it be so: yet have I left a daughter,
Who, I am sure, is kind and comfortable.
When she shall hear this of thee, with her nails
She'll flay thy wolvish visage. Thou shalt find
That I'll resume the shape which thou dost think
I have cast off for ever. Thou shalt, I warrant thee.
[*Exeunt* LEAR, KENT, *and Attendants.*
Gon. Do you mark that, my lord?
Alb. I cannot be so partial, Goneril,
To the great love I bear you—
Gon. Pray you, content. What, Oswald, ho!
[*To the* FOOL] You, sir, more knave than fool, after your master.
Fool. Nuncle Lear, nuncle Lear, tarry and take the Fool with thee.
"A fox, when one has caught her,
And such a daughter,
Should sure to the slaughter,
If my cap would buy a halter.
So the Fool follows after." [*Exit.*
Gon. This man hath had good counsel; a hundred knights!
'Tis politic and safe to let him keep
At point a hundred knights; yes, that, on every dream,
Each buzz, each fancy, each complaint, dislike,
He may enguard his dotage with their powers,
And hold our lives in mercy. Oswald, I say!
Alb. Well, you may fear too far.
Gon. Safer than trust too far.
Let me still take away the harms I fear,
Not fear still to be taken. I know his heart.
What he hath utter'd I have writ my sister.
If she sustain him and his hundred knights,
When I have show'd the unfitness—

Re-enter OSWALD.

How now, Oswald!
What, have you writ that letter to my sister?
Osw. Yes, madam.
Gon. Take you some company, and away to horse.
Inform her full of my particular fear;
And thereto add such reasons of your own
As may compact it more. Get you gone;
And hasten your return. [*Exit* OSWALD.] No, no, my lord,
This milky gentleness and course of yours
Though I condemn not, yet, under pardon,
You are much more attask'd for want of wisdom
Than praised for harmful mildness.
Alb. How far your eyes may pierce I cannot tell.
Striving to better, oft we mar what's well.
Gon. Nay, then—
Alb. Well, well; the event. [*Exeunt.*

Scene v. *Court before the same*

Enter Lear, Kent, *and* Fool.

Lear. Go you before to Gloucester with these letters. Acquaint my daughter no further with anything you know than comes from her demand out of the letter. If your diligence be not speedy, I shall be there afore you.

Kent. I will not sleep, my lord, till I have delivered your letter. [*Exit.*

Fool. If a man's brains were in's heels, were't not in danger of kibes?

Lear. Ay, boy.

Fool. Then, I prithee, be merry; thy wit shall ne'er go slip-shod.

Lear. Ha, ha, ha!

Fool. Shalt see thy other daughter will use thee kindly; for though she's as like this as a crab's like an apple, yet I can tell what I can tell.

Lear. Why, what canst thou tell, my boy?

Fool. She will taste as like this as a crab does to a crab. Thou canst tell why one's nose stands i' the middle on's face?

Lear. No.

Fool. Why, to keep one's eyes of either side 's nose; that what a man cannot smell out, he may spy into.

Lear. I did her wrong—

Fool. Canst tell how an oyster makes his shell?

Lear. No.

Fool. Nor I neither; but I can tell why a snail has a house.

Lear. Why?

Fool. Why, to put his head in; not to give it away to his daughters, and leave his horns without a case.

Lear. I will forget my nature. So kind a father! Be my horses ready?

Fool. Thy asses are gone about 'em. The reason why the seven stars are no more than seven is a pretty reason.

Lear. Because they are not eight?

Fool. Yes, indeed. Thou wouldst make a good fool.

Lear. To take 't again perforce! Monster ingratitude!

Fool. If thou wert my fool, nuncle, I'd have thee beaten for being old before thy time.

Lear. How's that?

Fool. Thou shouldst not have been old till thou hadst been wise.

Lear. O, let me not be mad, not mad, sweet
  heaven!
Keep me in temper. I would not be mad!

Enter Gentleman.

How now! are the horses ready?

Gent. Ready, my lord.

Lear. Come, boy.

Fool. She that's a maid now, and laughs at my
  departure,
Shall not be a maid long, unless things be cut
  shorter. [*Exeunt.*

ACT II

Scene i. *The Earl of Gloucester's castle*

Enter Edmund, *and* Curan *meets him.*

Edm. Save thee, Curan.

Cur. And you, sir. I have been with your father, and given him notice that the Duke of Cornwall and Regan his duchess will be here with him this night.

Edm. How comes that?

Cur. Nay, I know not. You have heard of the news abroad; I mean the whispered ones, for they are yet but ear-kissing arguments?

Edm. Not I. Pray you, what are they?

Cur. Have you heard of no likely wars toward, 'twixt the Dukes of Cornwall and Albany?

Edm. Not a word.

Cur. You may do, then, in time. Fare you well, sir. [*Exit.*

Edm. The Duke be here to-night? The better!
  best!
This weaves itself perforce into my business.
My father hath set guard to take my brother;
And I have one thing, of a queasy question,
Which I must act. Briefness and fortune, work!
Brother, a word; descend, Brother, I say!

Enter Edgar.

My father watches. O sir, fly this place;
Intelligence is given where you are hid;
You have now the good advantage of the night.
Have you not spoken 'gainst the Duke of Corn-
  wall?
He's coming hither; now, i' the night, i' the
  haste,
And Regan with him. Have you nothing said
Upon his party 'gainst the Duke of Albany?
Advise yourself.

Edg. I am sure on't, not a word.

Edm. I hear my father coming. Pardon me;
In cunning I must draw my sword upon you:
Draw; seem to defend yourself; now quit you
  well.
Yield. Come before my father. Light, ho, here!
Fly, brother. Torches, torches! So, farewell.
[*Exit* Edgar
Some blood drawn on me would beget opinion
Wounds his arm.

Of my more fierce endeavour. I have seen drunkards
Do more than this in sport. Father, father!
Stop, stop! No help?

Enter GLOUCESTER, *and Servants with torches.*

Glou. Now, Edmund, where's the villain?
Edm. Here stood he in the dark, his sharp sword out,
Mumbling of wicked charms, conjuring the moon
To stand auspicious mistress—
Glou. But where is he?
Edm. Look, sir, I bleed.
Glou. Where is the villain, Edmund?
Edm. Fled this way, sir. When by no means he could—
Glou. Pursue him, ho! Go after. [*Exeunt some Servants.*] By no means what?
Edm. Persuade me to the murder of your lordship;
But that I told him, the revenging gods
'Gainst parricides did all their thunders bend;
Spoke, with how manifold and strong a bond
The child was bound to the father; sir, in fine,
Seeing how loathly opposite I stood
To his unnatural purpose, in fell motion,
With his prepared sword, he charges home
My unprovided body, lanced mine arm.
But when he saw my best alarum'd spirits,
Bold in the quarrel's right, rousèd to the encounter,
Or whether gasted by the noise I made,
Full suddenly he fled.
Glou. Let him fly far.
Not in this land shall he remain uncaught;
And found—dispatch. The noble Duke my master,
My worthy arch and patron, comes to-night.
By his authority I will proclaim it,
That he which finds him shall deserve our thanks,
Bringing the murderous coward to the stake;
He that conceals him, death.
Edm. When I dissuaded him from his intent,
And found him pight to do it, with curst speech
I threaten'd to discover him; he replied,
"Thou unpossessing bastard! dost thou think,
If I would stand against thee, would the reposal
Of any trust, virtue, or worth in thee
Make thy words faith'd? No. What I should deny—
As this I would; ay, though thou didst produce
My very character—I'd turn it all
To thy suggestion, plot, and damned practice.
And thou must make a dullard of the world,
If they not thought the profits of my death
Were very pregnant and potential spurs
To make thee seek it."
Glou. Strong and fasten'd villain!
Would he deny his letter? I never got him.
Tucket within.
Hark, the Duke's trumpets! I know not why he comes.
All ports I'll bar; the villain shall not 'scape;
The Duke must grant me that. Besides, his picture
I will send far and near, that all the kingdom
May have due note of him; and of my land,
Loyal and natural boy, I'll work the means
To make thee capable.

Enter CORNWALL, REGAN, *and Attendants.*

Corn. How now, my noble friend! since I came hither,
Which I can call but now, I have heard strange news.
Reg. If it be true, all vengeance comes too short
Which can pursue the offender. How dost, my lord?
Glou. O, madam, my old heart is crack'd, is crack'd!
Reg. What, did my father's godson seek your life?
He whom my father named? your Edgar?
Glou. O, lady, lady, shame would have it hid!
Reg. Was he not companion with the riotous knights
That tend upon my father?
Glou. I know not, madam. 'Tis too bad, too bad.
Edm. Yes, madam, he was of that consort.
Reg. No marvel, then, though he were ill affected.
'Tis they have put him on the old man's death,
To have the expense and waste of his revenues.
I have this present evening from my sister
Been well inform'd of them; and with such cautions,
That if they come to sojourn at my house,
I'll not be there.
Corn. Nor I, assure thee, Regan.
Edmund, I hear that you have shown your father
A child-like office.
Edm. 'Twas my duty, sir.
Glou. He did bewray his practice; and received
This hurt you see, striving to apprehend him.
Corn. Is he pursued?
Glou. Ay, my good lord.
Corn. If he be taken, he shall never more
Be fear'd of doing harm. Make your own purpose,
How in my strength you please. For you, Edmund,

Whose virtue and obedience doth this instant
So much commend itself, you shall be ours.
Natures of such deep trust we shall much need;
You we first seize on.

Edm. I shall serve you, sir,
Truly, however else.

Glou. For him I thank your Grace.

Corn. You know not why we came to visit you—

Reg. Thus out of season, threading dark-eyed night.
Occasions, noble Gloucester, of some poise,
Wherein we must have use of your advice.
Our father he hath writ, so hath our sister,
Of differences, which I least thought it fit
To answer from our home; the several messengers
From hence attend dispatch. Our good old friend,
Lay comforts to your bosom; and bestow
Your needful counsel to our business,
Which craves the instant use.

Glou. I serve you, madam.
Your Graces are right welcome. [*Exeunt.*

SCENE II. *Before Gloucester's castle*

Enter KENT *and* OSWALD, *severally.*

Osw. Good dawning to thee, friend. Art of this house?

Kent. Ay.

Osw. Where may we set our horses?

Kent. I' the mire.

Osw. Prithee, if thou lovest me, tell me.

Kent. I love thee not.

Osw. Why, then, I care not for thee.

Kent. If I had thee in Lipsbury pinfold, I would make thee care for me.

Osw. Why dost thou use me thus? I know thee not.

Kent. Fellow, I know thee.

Osw. What dost thou know me for?

Kent. A knave; a rascal; an eater of broken meats; a base, proud, shallow, beggarly, three-suited, hundred-pound, filthy, worsted-stocking knave; a lily-livered, action-taking knave, a whoreson, glass-gazing, superserviceable, finical rogue; one-trunk-inheriting slave; one that wouldst be a bawd, in way of good service, and art nothing but the composition of a knave, beggar, coward, pandar, and the son and heir of a mongrel bitch; one whom I will beat into clamorous whining, if thou deniest the least syllable of thy addition.

Osw. Why, what a monstrous fellow art thou, thus to rail on one that is neither known of thee nor knows thee!

Kent. What a brazen-faced varlet art thou, to deny thou knowest me! Is it two days ago since I tripped up thy heels, and beat thee before the King? Draw, you rogue; for, though it be night, yet the moon shines; I'll make a sop o' the moonshine of you. Draw, you whoreson cullionly barber-monger, draw.

Drawing his sword.

Osw. Away! I have nothing to do with thee.

Kent. Draw, you rascal. You come with letters against the King; and take vanity the puppet's part against the royalty of her father. Draw, you rogue, or I'll so carbonado your shanks. Draw, you rascal; come your ways.

Osw. Help, ho! murder! help!

Kent. Strike, you slave; stand, rogue, stand; you neat slave, strike. [*Beating him.*]

Osw. Help, ho! murder! murder!

Enter EDMUND, *with his rapier drawn,* CORNWALL, REGAN, GLOUCESTER, *and Servants.*

Edm. How now! What's the matter?

Kent. With you, goodman boy, an you please. Come, I'll flesh ye; come on, young master.

Glou. Weapons! arms! What's the matter here?

Corn. Keep peace, upon your lives;
He dies that strikes again. What is the matter?

Reg. The messengers from our sister and the King.

Corn. What is your difference? speak.

Osw. I am scarce in breath, my lord.

Kent. No marvel, you have so bestirred your valour. You cowardly rascal, nature disclaims in thee. A tailor made thee.

Corn. Thou art a strange fellow. A tailor make a man?

Kent. Ay, a tailor, sir. A stone-cutter or a painter could not have made him so ill, though he had been but two hours at the trade.

Corn. Speak yet, how grew your quarrel?

Osw. This ancient ruffian, sir, whose life I have spared at suit of his gray beard—

Kent. Thou whoreson zed! thou unnecessary letter! My lord, if you will give me leave, I will tread this unbolted villain into mortar, and daub the walls of a jakes with him. Spare my gray beard, you wagtail?

Corn. Peace, sirrah!
You beastly knave, know you no reverence?

Kent. Yes, sir; but anger hath a privilege.

Corn. Why art thou angry?

Kent. That such a slave as this should wear a sword,
Who wears no honesty. Such smiling rogues as these,
Like rats, oft bite the holy cords a-twain

Which are too intrinse t' unloose; smooth every passion
That in the natures of their lords rebel;
Bring oil to fire, snow to their colder moods;
Renege, affirm, and turn their halcyon beaks
With every gale and vary of their masters,
Knowing nought, like dogs, but following.
A plague upon your epileptic visage!
Smile you my speeches, as I were a fool?
Goose, if I had you upon Sarum plain,
I'd drive ye cackling home to Camelot.

Corn. What, art thou mad, old fellow?

Glou. How fell you out? say that.

Kent. No contraries hold more antipathy
Than I and such a knave.

Corn. Why dost thou call him knave? What's his offence?

Kent. His countenance likes me not.

Corn. No more, perchance, does mine, nor his, nor hers.

Kent. Sir, 'tis my occupation to be plain.
I have seen better faces in my time
Than stands on any shoulder that I see
Before me at this instant.

Corn. This is some fellow,
Who, having been praised for bluntness, doth affect
A saucy roughness, and constrains the garb
Quite from his nature. He cannot flatter, he,
An honest mind and plain, he must speak truth!
An they will take it, so; if not, he's plain.
These kind of knaves I know, which in this plainness
Harbour more craft and more corrupter ends
Than twenty silly ducking observants
That stretch their duties nicely.

Kent. Sir, in good sooth, in sincere verity,
Under the allowance of your great aspect,
Whose influence, like the wreath of radiant fire
On flickering Phœbus' front—

Corn. What mean'st by this?

Kent. To go out of my dialect, which you discommend so much. I know, sir, I am no flatterer. He that beguiled you in a plain accent was a plain knave; which for my part I will not be, though I should win your displeasure to entreat me to't.

Corn. What was the offence you gave him?

Osw. I never gave him any.
It pleased the King his master very late
To strike at me, upon his misconstruction;
When he, conjunct, and flattering his displeasure,
Tripp'd me behind; being down, insulted, rail'd,
And put upon him such a deal of man,
That worthied him, got praises of the King
For him attempting who was self-subdued;
And, in the fleshment of this dread exploit,
Drew on me here again.

Kent. None of these rogues and cowards
But Ajax is their fool.

Corn. Fetch forth the stocks!
You stubborn ancient knave, you reverend braggart,
We'll teach you—

Kent. Sir, I am too old to learn.
Call not your stocks for me. I serve the King;
On whose employment I was sent to you:
You shall do small respect, show too bold malice
Against the grace and person of my master,
Stocking his messenger.

Corn. Fetch forth the stocks! As I have life and honour,
There shall he sit till noon.

Reg. Till noon! till night, my lord; and all night too.

Kent. Why, madam, if I were your father's dog,
You should not use me so.

Reg. Sir, being his knave, I will.

Corn. This is a fellow of the self-same colour
Our sister speaks of. Come, bring away the stocks!

Stocks brought out.

Glou. Let me beseech your Grace not to do so:
His fault is much, and the good King his master
Will check him for 't. Your purposed low correction
Is such as basest and contemned'st wretches
For pilferings and most common trespasses
Are punish'd with. The King must take it ill
That he's so slightly valued in his messenger,
Should have him thus restrain'd.

Corn. I'll answer that.

Reg. My sister may receive it much more worse,
To have her gentleman abused, assaulted,
For following her affairs. Put in his legs.

KENT *is put in the stocks.*

Come, my good lord, away.

[*Exeunt all but* GLOUCESTER *and* KENT.

Glou. I am sorry for thee, friend; 'tis the Duke's pleasure,
Whose disposition, all the world well knows,
Will not be rubb'd nor stopp'd. I'll entreat for thee.

Kent. Pray, do not, sir. I have watched and travell'd hard;
Some time I shall sleep out, the rest I'll whistle.
A good man's fortune may grow out at heels.
Give you good morrow!

Glou. The Duke's to blame in this; 'twill be ill taken. [*Exit.*

Kent. Good King, that must approve the common saw,
Thou out of heaven's benediction comest
To the warm sun!
Approach, thou beacon to this under globe,
That by thy comfortable beams I may
Peruse this letter! Nothing almost sees miracles
But misery. I know 'tis from Cordelia,
Who hath most fortunately been inform'd
Of my obscured course; and [*reads*] "shall find time
From this enormous state, seeking to give
Losses their remedies." All weary and o'er-watch'd,
Take vantage, heavy eyes, not to behold
This shameful lodging.
Fortune, good night. Smile once more; turn thy wheel! [*Sleeps.*

SCENE III. *A wood*

Enter EDGAR.

Edg. I heard myself proclaim'd;
And by the happy hollow of a tree
Escaped the hunt. No port is free; no place
That guard and most unusual vigilance
Does not attend my taking. Whiles I may 'scape,
I will preserve myself. And am bethought
To take the basest and most poorest shape
That ever penury, in contempt of man,
Brought near to beast. My face I'll grime with filth;
Blanket my loins; elf all my hair in knots;
And with presented nakedness out-face
The winds and persecutions of the sky.
The country gives me proof and precedent
Of Bedlam beggars, who, with roaring voices,
Strike in their numb'd and mortified bare arms
Pins, wooden pricks, nails, sprigs of rosemary;
And with this horrible object, from low farms,
Poor pelting villages, sheep-cotes, and mills,
Sometime with lunatic bans, sometime with prayers,
Enforce their charity. Poor Turlygod! poor Tom!
That's something yet. Edgar I nothing am. [*Exit.*

SCENE IV. *Before Gloucester's castle.* KENT *in the stocks*

Enter LEAR, FOOL, *and* GENTLEMAN.

Lear. 'Tis strange that they should so depart from home,
And not send back my messenger.
Gent. As I learn'd,
The night before there was no purpose in them
Of this remove.
Kent. Hail to thee, noble master!
Lear. Ha!
Makest thou this shame thy pastime?
Kent. No, my lord.
Fool. Ha, ha! he wears cruel garters. Horses are tied by the heads, dogs and bears by the neck, monkeys by the loins, and men by the legs. When a man's over-lusty at legs, then he wears wooden nether-stocks.
Lear. What's he that hath so much thy place mistook
To set thee here?
Kent. It is both he and she;
Your son and daughter.
Lear. No.
Kent. Yes.
Lear. No, I say.
Kent. I say, yea.
Lear. No, no, they would not.
Kent. Yes, they have.
Lear. By Jupiter, I swear, no.
Kent. By Juno, I swear, ay.
Lear. They durst not do't;
They could not, would not do't; 'tis worse than murder,
To do upon respect such violent outrage.
Resolve me, with all modest haste, which way
Thou mightst deserve, or they impose, this usage,
Coming from us.
Kent. My lord, when at their home
I did commend your Highness' letters to them,
Ere I was risen from the place that show'd
My duty kneeling, came there a reeking post,
Stew'd in his haste, half breathless, panting forth
From Goneril his mistress salutations;
Deliver'd letters, spite of intermission,
Which presently they read. On whose contents,
They summon'd up their meiny, straight took horse;
Commanded me to follow and attend
The leisure of their answer; gave me cold looks;
And meeting here the other messenger,
Whose welcome, I perceived, had poison'd mine—
Being the very fellow that of late
Display'd so saucily against your Highness—
Having more man than wit about me, drew.
He raised the house with loud and coward cries.
Your son and daughter found this trespass worth
The shame which here it suffers.
Fool. Winter's not gone yet, if the wild-geese fly that way.
"Fathers that wear rags
Do make their children blind;
But fathers that bear bags

Shall see their children kind.
Fortune, that arrant whore,
Ne'er turns the key to the poor."
But, for all this, thou shalt have as many dolours for thy daughters as thou canst tell in a year.

Lear. O, how this mother swells up toward my heart!
Hysterica passio, down, thou climbing sorrow,
Thy element's below! Where is this daughter?

Kent. With the Earl, sir, here within.

Lear. Follow me not;
Stay here. [*Exit*.

Gent. Made you no more offence but what you speak of?

Kent. None.
How chance the King comes with so small a train?

Fool. An thou hadst been set i' the stocks for that question, thou hadst well deserved it.

Kent. Why, fool?

Fool. We'll set thee to school to an ant, to teach thee there's no labouring i' the winter. All that follow their noses are led by their eyes but blind men; and there's not a nose among twenty but can smell him that's stinking. Let go thy hold when a great wheel runs down a hill, lest it break thy neck with following it; but the great one that goes up the hill, let him draw thee after. When a wise man gives thee better counsel, give me mine again. I would have none but knaves follow it, since a fool gives it.

"That sir which serves and seeks for gain,
And follows but for form,
Will pack when it begins to rain,
And leave thee in the storm.
But I will tarry; the Fool will stay,
And let the wise man fly.
The knave turns fool that runs away;
The Fool no knave, perdy."

Kent. Where learned you this, Fool?

Fool. Not i' the stocks, fool.

Re-enter LEAR, *with* GLOUCESTER.

Lear. Deny to speak with me? They are sick? they are weary?
They have travell'd all the night? Mere fetches;
The images of revolt and flying off.
Fetch me a better answer.

Glou. My dear lord,
You know the fiery quality of the Duke;
How unremovable and fix'd he is
In his own course.

Lear. Vengeance! plague! death! confusion!
Fiery? what quality? Why, Gloucester, Gloucester,
I'd speak with the Duke of Cornwall and his wife.

Glou. Well, my good lord, I have inform'd them so.

Lear. Inform'd them! Dost thou understand me, man?

Glou. Ay, my good lord.

Lear. The King would speak with Cornwall; the dear father
Would with his daughter speak, commands her service.
Are they "inform'd" of this? My breath and blood!
"Fiery"? the fiery Duke? Tell the hot Duke that—
No, but not yet; may be he is not well.
Infirmity doth still neglect all office
Whereto our health is bound; we are not ourselves
When nature, being oppress'd, commands the mind
To suffer with the body. I'll forbear;
And am fall'n out with my more headier will,
To take the indisposed and sickly fit
For the sound man. Death on my state! wherefore [*Looking on* KENT]
Should he sit here? This act persuades me
That this remotion of the Duke and her
Is practice only. Give me my servant forth.
Go tell the Duke and 's wife I'd speak with them,
Now, presently. Bid them come forth and hear me,
Or at their chamber-door I'll beat the drum
Till it cry sleep to death.

Glou. I would have all well betwixt you. [*Exit*.

Lear. O me, my heart, my rising heart! but, down!

Fool. Cry to it, nuncle, as the cockney did to the eels when she put 'em i' the paste alive; she knapped 'em o' the coxcombs with a stick, and cried, "Down, wantons, down!" 'Twas her brother that, in pure kindness to his horse, buttered his hay.

Enter CORNWALL, REGAN, GLOUCESTER, *and Servants*.

Lear. Good morrow to you both.

Corn. Hail to your Grace!

KENT *is set at liberty*.

Reg. I am glad to see your Highness.

Lear. Regan, I think you are; I know what reason
I have to think so. If thou shouldst not be glad,
I would divorce me from thy mother's tomb,
Sepulchring an adultress. [*To* KENT] O, are you free?

Some other time for that. Beloved Regan,
Thy sister's naught. O Regan, she hath tied
Sharp-tooth'd unkindness, like a vulture, here.
Points to his heart.
I can scarce speak to thee; thou'lt not believe
With how depraved a quality—O Regan!
Reg. I pray you, sir, take patience. I have hope
You less know how to value her desert
Than she to scant her duty.
Lear. Say, how is that?
Reg. I cannot think my sister in the least
Would fail her obligation. If, sir, perchance
She have restrain'd the riots of your followers,
'Tis on such ground, and to such wholesome end,
As clears her from all blame.
Lear. My curses on her!
Reg. O, sir, you are old;
Nature in you stands on the very verge
Of her confine. You should be ruled and led
By some discretion that discerns your state
Better than you yourself. Therefore, I pray you
That to our sister you do make return;
Say you have wrong'd her, sir.
Lear. Ask her forgiveness?
Do you but mark how this becomes the house:
"Dear daughter, I confess that I am old;
Kneeling.
Age is unnecessary. On my knees I beg
That you'll vouchsafe me raiment, bed, and food."
Reg. Good sir, no more; these are unsightly tricks.
Return you to my sister.
Lear. [*Rising*] Never, Regan.
She hath abated me of half my train;
Look'd black upon me; struck me with her tongue,
Most serpent-like, upon the very heart.
All the stored vengeances of heaven fall
On her ingrateful top! Strike her young bones,
You taking airs, with lameness!
Corn. Fie, sir, fie!
Lear. You nimble lightnings, dart your blinding flames
Into her scornful eyes! Infect her beauty,
You fen-suck'd fogs, drawn by the powerful sun,
To fall and blast her pride!
Reg. O the blest gods! so will you wish on me,
When the rash mood is on.
Lear. No, Regan, thou shalt never have my curse.
Thy tender-hefted nature shall not give
Thee o'er to harshness. Her eyes are fierce; but thine
Do comfort and not burn. 'Tis not in thee
To grudge my pleasures, to cut off my train,
To bandy hasty words, to scant my sizes,
And in conclusion to oppose the bolt
Against my coming in. Thou better know'st
The offices of nature, bond of childhood,
Effects of courtesy, dues of gratitude;
Thy half o' the kingdom hast thou not forgot,
Wherein I thee endow'd.
Reg. Good sir, to the purpose.
Lear. Who put my man i' the stocks?
Tucket within.
Corn. What trumpet's that?
Reg. I know't, my sister's. This approves her letter,
That she would soon be here.

Enter OSWALD.

Is your lady come?
Lear. This is a slave, whose easy-borrow'd pride
Dwells in the fickle grace of her he follows.
Out, varlet, from my sight!
Corn. What means your Grace?
Lear. Who stock'd my servant? Regan, I have good hope
Thou didst not know on't. Who comes here? O heavens,

Enter GONERIL.

If you do love old men, if your sweet sway
Allow obedience, if yourselves are old,
Make it your cause; send down, and take my part!
[*To* GONERIL] Art not ashamed to look upon this beard?
O Regan, wilt thou take her by the hand?
Gon. Why not by the hand, sir? How have I offended?
All's not offence that indiscretion finds
And dotage terms so.
Lear. O sides, you are too tough;
Will you yet hold? How came my man i' the stocks?
Corn. I set him there, sir; but his own disorders
Deserved much less advancement.
Lear. You! did you?
Reg. I pray you, father, being weak, seem so.
If, till the expiration of your month,
You will return and sojourn with my sister,
Dismissing half your train, come then to me.
I am now from home, and out of that provision
Which shall be needful for your entertainment.
Lear. Return to her, and fifty men dismiss'd?
No, rather I abjure all roofs, and choose
To wage against the enmity o' the air;
To be a comrade with the wolf and owl—
Necessity's sharp pinch! Return with her?

Why, the hot-blooded France, that dowerless took
Our youngest born, I could as well be brought
To knee his throne, and, squire-like, pension beg
To keep base life afoot. Return with her?
Persuade me rather to be slave and sumpter
To this detested groom. [*Pointing at* OSWALD.]
Gon. At your choice, sir.
Lear. I prithee, daughter, do not make me mad.
I will not trouble thee, my child; farewell.
We'll no more meet, no more see one another.
But yet thou art my flesh, my blood, my daughter;
Or rather a disease that's in my flesh,
Which I must needs call mine; thou art a boil,
A plague-sore, an embossed carbuncle,
In my corrupted blood. But I'll not chide thee;
Let shame come when it will, I do not call it.
I do not bid the thunder-bearer shoot,
Nor tell tales of thee to high-judging Jove.
Mend when thou canst; be better at thy leisure.
I can be patient; I can stay with Regan,
I and my hundred knights.
Reg. Not altogether so.
I look'd not for you yet, nor am provided
For your fit welcome. Give ear, sir, to my sister;
For those that mingle reason with your passion
Must be content to think you old, and so—
But she knows what she does.
Lear. Is this well spoken?
Reg. I dare avouch it, sir. What, fifty followers?
Is it not well? What should you need of more?
Yea, or so many, sith that both charge and danger
Speak 'gainst so great a number? How, in one house,
Should many people, under two commands,
Hold amity? 'Tis hard; almost impossible.
Gon. Why might not you, my lord, receive attendance
From those that she calls servants or from mine?
Reg. Why not, my lord? If then they chanced to slack you,
We could control them. If you will come to me—
For now I spy a danger—I entreat you
To bring but five and twenty. To no more
Will I give place or notice.
Lear. I gave you all—
Reg. And in good time you gave it.
Lear. Made you my guardians, my depositaries;
But kept a reservation to be follow'd
With such a number. What, must I come to you
With five and twenty, Regan? said you so?
Reg. And speak't again, my lord; no more with me.
Lear. Those wicked creatures yet do look well-favour'd,
When others are more wicked; not being the worst
Stands in some rank of praise. [*To* GONERIL] I'll go with thee.
Thy fifty yet doth double five and twenty,
And thou art twice her love.
Gon. Hear me, my lord.
What need you five and twenty, ten, or five,
To follow in a house where twice so many
Have a command to tend you?
Reg. What need one?
Lear. O, reason not the need. Our basest beggars
Are in the poorest thing superfluous.
Allow not nature more than nature needs,
Man's life's as cheap as beast's. Thou art a lady;
If only to go warm were gorgeous,
Why, nature needs not what thou gorgeous wear'st,
Which scarcely keeps thee warm. But, for true need—
You heavens, give me that patience, patience I need!
You see me here, you gods, a poor old man,
As full of grief as age; wretched in both!
If it be you that stirs these daughters' hearts
Against their father, fool me not so much
To bear it tamely; touch me with noble anger,
And let not women's weapons, water-drops,
Stain my man's cheeks! No, you unnatural hags,
I will have such revenges on you both,
That all the world shall—I will do such things—
What they are, yet I know not; but they shall be
The terrors of the earth. You think I'll weep;
No, I'll not weep.
I have full cause of weeping; but this heart
Shall break into a hundred thousand flaws,
Or ere I'll weep. O Fool, I shall go mad!
[*Exeunt* LEAR, GLOUCESTER, KENT, *and* FOOL.
Storm and tempest.
Corn. Let us withdraw; 'twill be a storm.
Reg. This house is little. The old man and his people
Cannot be well bestow'd.
Gon. 'Tis his own blame; hath put himself from rest,
And must needs taste his folly.
Reg. For his particular, I'll receive him gladly,
But not one follower.
Gon. So am I purposed.
Where is my lord of Gloucester?
Corn. Follow'd the old man forth. He is return'd.

Re-enter GLOUCESTER.

Glou. The King is in high rage.
Corn. Whither is he going?
Glou. He calls to horse; but will I know not whither.
Corn. 'Tis best to give him way; he leads himself.
Gon. My lord, entreat him by no means to stay.
Glou. Alack, the night comes on, and the bleak winds
Do sorely ruffle; for many miles about
There's scarce a bush.
Reg. O, sir, to wilful men,
The injuries that they themselves procure
Must be their schoolmasters. Shut up your doors.
He is attended with a desperate train;
And what they may incense him to, being apt
To have his ear abused, wisdom bids fear.
Corn. Shut up your doors, my lord; 'tis a wild night;
My Regan counsels well. Come out o' the storm.
[*Exeunt*.

ACT III

Scene i. *A heath*

Storm still. Enter KENT *and a* GENTLEMAN, *meeting*.

Kent. Who's there, besides foul weather?
Gent. One minded like the weather, most unquietly.
Kent. I know you. Where's the King?
Gent. Contending with the fretful element;
Bids the wind blow the earth into the sea,
Or swell the curled waters 'bove the main,
That things might change or cease; tears his white hair,
Which the impetuous blasts, with eyeless rage,
Catch in their fury, and make nothing of;
Strives in his little world of man to out-scorn
The to-and-fro-conflicting wind and rain.
This night, wherein the cub-drawn bear would couch,
The lion and the belly-pinched wolf
Keep their fur dry, unbonneted he runs,
And bids what will take all.
Kent. But who is with him?
Gent. None but the Fool; who labours to out-jest
His heart-struck injuries.
Kent. Sir, I do know you;
And dare, upon the warrant of my note,
Commend a dear thing to you. There is division,
Although as yet the face of it be cover'd
With mutual cunning, 'twixt Albany and Cornwall;
Who have—as who have not, that their great stars
Throned and set high?—servants, who seem no less,
Which are to France the spies and speculations
Intelligent of our state; what hath been seen,
Either in snuffs and packings of the Dukes,
Or the hard rein which both of them have borne
Against the old kind King; or something deeper,
Whereof perchance these are but furnishings;
But, true it is, from France there comes a power
Into this scatter'd kingdom; who already,
Wise in our negligence, have secret feet
In some of our best ports, and are at point
To show their open banner. Now to you.
If on my credit you dare build so far
To make your speed to Dover, you shall find
Some that will thank you, making just report
Of how unnatural and bemadding sorrow
The King hath cause to plain.
I am a gentleman of blood and breeding;
And, from some knowledge and assurance, offer
This office to you.
Gent. I will talk further with you.
Kent. No, do not.
For confirmation that I am much more
Than my out-wall, open this purse, and take
What it contains. If you shall see Cordelia—
As fear not but you shall—show her this ring;
And she will tell you who your fellow is
That yet you do not know. Fie on this storm!
I will go seek the King.
Gent. Give me your hand. Have you no more to say?
Kent. Few words, but, to effect, more than all yet;
That, when we have found the King—in which your pain
That way, I'll this—he that first lights on him
Holla the other. [*Exeunt severally*.

Scene ii. *Another part of the heath. Storm still*

Enter LEAR *and* FOOL.

Lear. Blow, winds, and crack your cheeks! rage! blow!
You cataracts and hurricanes, spout
Till you have drench'd our steeples, drown'd the cocks!
You sulphurous and thought-executing fires,
Vaunt-couriers to oak-cleaving thunderbolts,
Singe my white head! And thou, all-shaking thunder,
Smite flat the thick rotundity o' the world!
Crack nature's moulds, all germens spill at once,

That make ingrateful man!
Fool. O nuncle, court holy-water in a dry house is better than this rain-water out o' door. Good nuncle, in, and ask thy daughters' blessing. Here's a night pities neither wise man nor fool.
Lear. Rumble thy bellyful! Spit, fire! spout, rain!
Nor rain, wind, thunder, fire, are my daughters.
I tax not you, you elements, with unkindness;
I never gave you kingdom, call'd you children,
You owe me no subscription. Then let fall
Your horrible pleasure; here I stand, your slave,
A poor, infirm, weak, and despised old man:
But yet I call you servile ministers,
That have with two pernicious daughters join'd
Your high engender'd battles 'gainst a head
So old and white as this. O! O! 'tis foul!
Fool. He that has a house to put's head in has a good head-piece.
"The cod-piece that will house
Before the head has any,
The head and he shall louse;
So beggars marry many.
The man that makes his toe
What he his heart should make
Shall of a corn cry woe,
And turn his sleep to wake."
For there was never yet fair woman but she made mouths in a glass.
Lear. No, I will be the pattern of all patience;
I will say nothing.

Enter KENT.

Kent. Who's there?
Fool. Marry, here's grace and a cod-piece; that's a wise man and a fool.
Kent. Alas, sir, are you here? things that love night
Love not such nights as these; the wrathful skies
Gallow the very wanderers of the dark,
And make them keep their caves. Since I was man,
Such sheets of fire, such bursts of horrid thunder,
Such groans of roaring wind and rain, I never
Remember to have heard. Man's nature cannot carry
The affliction nor the fear.
Lear. Let the great gods,
That keep this dreadful pother o'er our heads,
Find out their enemies now. Tremble, thou wretch,
That hast within thee undivulged crimes,
Unwhipp'd of justice. Hide thee, thou bloody hand;
Thou perjured, and thou simular man of virtue
That art incestuous. Caitiff, to pieces shake,
That under covert and convenient seeming
Hast practised on man's life. Close pent-up guilts,
Rive your concealing continents, and cry
These dreadful summoners grace. I am a man
More sinn'd against than sinning.
Kent. Alack, bare-headed!
Gracious my lord, hard by here is a hovel;
Some friendship will it lend you 'gainst the tempest.
Repose you there; while I to this hard house—
More harder than the stones whereof 'tis raised;
Which even but now, demanding after you,
Denied me to come in—return, and force
Their scanted courtesy.
Lear. My wits begin to turn.
Come on, my boy. How dost, my boy? art cold?
I am cold myself. Where is this straw, my fellow?
The art of our necessities is strange,
That can make vile things precious. Come, your hovel.
Poor fool and knave, I have one part in my heart
That's sorry yet for thee.
Fool. [*Singing*] "He that has and a little tiny wit—
With hey, ho, the wind and the rain—
Must make content with his fortunes fit,
For the rain it raineth every day."
Lear. True, my good boy. Come, bring us to this hovel. [*Exeunt* LEAR *and* KENT.
Fool. This is a brave night to cool a courtezan.
I'll speak a prophecy ere I go:
When priests are more in word than matter;
When brewers mar their malt with water;
When nobles are their tailors' tutors;
No heretics burn'd, but wenches' suitors;
When every case in law is right;
No squire in debt, nor no poor knight;
When slanders do not live in tongues;
Nor cutpurses come not to throngs;
When usurers tell their gold i' the field;
And bawds and whores do churches build;
Then shall the realm of Albion
Come to great confusion.
Then comes the time, who lives to see't,
That going shall be used with feet.
This prophecy Merlin shall make; for I live before his time. [*Exit*.

SCENE III. *Gloucester's castle*

Enter GLOUCESTER *and* EDMUND.

Glou. Alack, alack, Edmund, I like not this unnatural dealing. When I desired their leave that I might pity him, they took from me the use of mine own house; charged me, on pain of their perpetual displeasure, neither to speak of him, entreat for him, nor any way sustain him.

Edm. Most savage and unnatural!

Glou. Go to; say you nothing. There's a division betwixt the Dukes; and a worse matter than that. I have received a letter this night; 'tis dangerous to be spoken; I have locked the letter in my closet. These injuries the King now bears will be revenged home; there's part of a power already footed. We must incline to the King. I will seek him, and privily relieve him. Go you and maintain talk with the Duke, that my charity be not of him perceived. If he ask for me, I am ill and gone to bed. Though I die for it, as no less is threatened me, the King my old master must be relieved. There is some strange thing toward, Edmund; pray you, be careful. [*Exit.*

Edm. This courtesy, forbid thee, shall the Duke
Instantly know; and of that letter too.
This seems a fair deserving, and must draw me
That which my father loses; no less than all.
The younger rises when the old doth fall. [*Exit.*

Scene iv. *The heath: before a hovel*

Enter LEAR, KENT, *and* FOOL.

Kent. Here is the place, my lord; good my lord, enter.
The tyranny of the open night's too rough
For nature to endure.

Storm still.

Lear. Let me alone.
Kent. Good my lord, enter here.
Lear. Wilt break my heart?
Kent. I had rather break mine own. Good my lord, enter.
Lear. Thou think'st 'tis much that this contentious storm
Invades us to the skin. So 'tis to thee;
But where the greater malady is fix'd,
The lesser is scarce felt. Thou'dst shun a bear;
But if thy flight lay toward the raging sea,
Thou'dst meet the bear i' the mouth. When the mind's free,
The body's delicate. The tempest in my mind
Doth from my senses take all feeling else
Save what beats there. Filial ingratitude!
Is it not as this mouth should tear this hand
For lifting food to't? But I will punish home.
No, I will weep no more. In such a night
To shut me out! Pour on; I will endure.
In such a night as this! O Regan, Goneril!
Your old kind father, whose frank heart gave all—
O, that way madness lies; let me shun that;
No more of that.
Kent. Good my lord, enter here.
Lear. Prithee, go in thyself; seek thine own ease.
This tempest will not give me leave to ponder
On things would hurt me more. But I'll go in.
[*To the* FOOL] In, boy; go first. You houseless poverty—
Nay, get thee in. I'll pray, and then I'll sleep.

FOOL *goes in.*

Poor naked wretches, wheresoe'er you are,
That bide the pelting of this pitiless storm,
How shall your houseless heads and unfed sides,
Your loop'd and window'd raggedness, defend you
From reasons such as these? O, I have ta'en
Too little care of this! Take physic, pomp;
Expose thyself to feel what wretches feel,
That thou mayst shake the superflux to them,
And show the heavens more just.

Edg. [*Within*] Fathom and half, fathom and half! Poor Tom!

The FOOL *runs out from the hovel.*

Fool. Come not in here, nuncle, here's a spirit.
Help me, help me!
Kent. Give me thy hand. Who's there?

Fool. A spirit, a spirit. He says his name's poor Tom.

Kent. What art thou that dost grumble there i' the straw? Come forth.

Enter EDGAR *disguised as a madman.*

Edg. Away! the foul fiend follows me!
Through the sharp hawthorn blows the cold wind.
Hum! go to thy cold bed and warm thee.
Lear. Hast thou given all to thy two daughters?
And art thou come to this?

Edg. Who gives anything to poor Tom? whom the foul fiend hath led through fire and through flame, through ford and whirlipool, o'er bog and quagmire; that hath laid knives under his pillow, and halters in his pew; set ratsbane by his porridge; made him proud of heart, to ride on a bay trotting-horse over four-inched bridges, to course his own shadow for a traitor. Bless thy five wits! Tom's a-cold—O, do de, do de, do de. Bless thee from whirlwinds, star-blasting and taking! Do poor Tom some charity, whom the foul fiend vexes. There could I have him now—and there—and there again, and there.

Storm still.

Lear. What, have his daughters brought him to this pass?
Couldst thou save nothing? Didst thou give them all?

Fool. Nay, he reserved a blanket, else we had been all shamed.

Lear. Now, all the plagues that in the pendulous air
Hang fated o'er men's faults light on thy daughters!

Kent. He hath no daughters, sir.

Lear. Death, traitor! nothing could have subdued nature
To such a lowness but his unkind daughters.
Is it the fashion, that discarded fathers
Should have thus little mercy on their flesh?
Judicious punishment! 'twas this flesh begot
Those pelican daughters.

Edg. "Pillicock sat on Pillicock-hill."
Halloo, halloo, loo, loo!

Fool. This cold night will turn us all to fools and madmen.

Edg. Take heed o' the foul fiend. Obey thy parents; keep thy word justly; swear not; commit not with man's sworn spouse; set not thy sweet heart on proud array. Tom's a-cold.

Lear. What hast thou been?

Edg. A serving-man, proud in heart and mind; that curled my hair; wore gloves in my cap; served the lust of my mistress' heart, and did the act of darkness with her; swore as many oaths as I spake words, and broke them in the sweet face of heaven: one that slept in the contriving of lust, and waked to do it. Wine loved I deeply, dice dearly; and in woman out-paramoured the Turk: false of heart, light of ear, bloody of hand; hog in sloth, fox in stealth, wolf in greediness, dog in madness, lion in prey. Let the creaking of shoes nor the rustling of silks betray thy poor heart to woman. Keep thy foot out of brothels, thy hand out of plackets, thy pen from lenders' books, and defy the foul fiend.
Still through the hawthorn blows the cold wind:
Says suum, mun, ha, no, nonny.
Dolphin my boy, my boy, sessa! let him trot by.

Storm still.

Lear. Why, thou wert better in thy grave than to answer with thy uncovered body this extremity of the skies. Is man no more than this? Consider him well. Thou owest the worm no silk, the beast no hide, the sheep no wool, the cat no perfume. Ha! here's three on 's are sophisticated! Thou art the thing itself. Unaccommodated man is no more but such a poor, bare, forked animal as thou art. Off, off, you lendings! come, unbutton here. [*Tearing off his clothes.*]

Fool. Prithee, nuncle, be contented; 'tis a naughty night to swim in. Now a little fire in a wild field were like an old lecher's heart; a small spark, all the rest on 's body cold. Look, here comes a walking fire.

Enter GLOUCESTER, *with a torch.*

Edg. This is the foul fiend Flibbertigibbet. He begins at curfew, and walks till the first cock; he gives the web and the pin, squints the eye, and makes the hare-lip; mildews the white wheat, and hurts the poor creature of earth.
"St. Withold footed thrice the old;
He met the night-mare, and her nine-fold;
Bid her alight,
And her troth plight,
And, aroint thee, witch, aroint thee!"

Kent. How fares your Grace?

Lear. What's he?

Kent. Who's there? What is't you seek?

Glou. What are you there? Your names?

Edg. Poor Tom; that eats the swimming frog, the toad, the tadpole, the wall-newt, and the water; that in the fury of his heart, when the foul fiend rages, eats cow-dung for sallets; swallows the old rat and the ditch-dog; drinks the green mantle of the standing pool; who is whipped from tithing to tithing, and stock-punished, and imprisoned; who hath had three suits to his back, six shirts to his body, horse to ride, and weapon to wear;
But mice and rats, and such small deer,
Have been Tom's food for seven long year.
Beware my follower. Peace, Smulkin; peace, thou fiend!

Glou. What, hath your Grace no better company?

Edg. The prince of darkness is a gentleman.
Modo he's call'd, and Mahu.

Glou. Our flesh and blood is grown so vile, my lord,
That it doth hate what gets it.

Edg. Poor Tom 's a-cold.

Glou. Go in with me; my duty cannot suffer
To obey in all your daughters' hard commands.
Though their injunction be to bar my doors,
And let this tyrannous night take hold upon you,
Yet have I ventured to come seek you out,
And bring you where both fire and food is ready.

Lear. First let me talk with this philosopher.
What is the cause of thunder?

Kent. Good my lord, take his offer; go into the house.

Lear. I'll talk a word with this same learned Theban.
What is your study?

Edg. How to prevent the fiend, and to kill vermin.

Lear. Let me ask you one word in private.

Kent. Importune him once more to go, my lord;
His wits begin to unsettle.
Glou. Canst thou blame him?
Storm still.
His daughters seek his death. Ah, that good Kent!
He said it would be thus, poor banish'd man!
Thou say'st the King grows mad; I'll tell thee, friend,
I am almost mad myself. I had a son,
Now outlaw'd from my blood; he sought my life,
But lately, very late. I loved him, friend;
No father his son dearer. Truth to tell thee,
The grief hath crazed my wits. What a night's this!
I do beseech your Grace—
Lear. O, cry you mercy, sir.
Noble philosopher, your company.
Edg. Tom 's a-cold.
Glou. In, fellow, there, into the hovel. Keep thee warm.
Lear. Come, let's in all.
Kent. This way, my lord.
Lear. With him;
I will keep still with my philosopher.
Kent. Good my lord, sooth him; let him take the fellow.
Glou. Take him you on.
Kent. Sirrah, come on; go along with us.
Lear. Come, good Athenian.
Glou. No words, no words; hush.
Edg. "Child Rowland to the dark tower came,
His word was still, 'Fie, foh, and fum,
I smell the blood of a British man.' "
[*Exeunt.*

SCENE V. *Gloucester's castle*

Enter CORNWALL *and* EDMUND.

Corn. I will have my revenge ere I depart his house.

Edm. How, my lord, I may be censured that nature thus gives way to loyalty, something fears me to think of.

Corn. I now perceive, it was not altogether your brother's evil disposition made him seek his death; but a provoking merit, set a-work by a reproveable badness in himself.

Edm. How malicious is my fortune that I must repent to be just! this is the letter he spoke of, which approves him an intelligent party to the advantages of France. O heavens! that this treason were not, or not I the detector!

Corn. Go with me to the Duchess.

Edm. If the matter of this paper be certain, you have mighty business in hand.

Corn. True or false, it hath made thee Earl of Gloucester. Seek out where thy father is, that he may be ready for our apprehension.

Edm. [*Aside*] If I find him comforting the King, it will stuff his suspicion more fully.—I will persevere in my course of loyalty, though the conflict be sore between that and my blood.

Corn. I will lay trust upon thee; and thou shalt find a dearer father in my love. [*Exeunt.*

SCENE VI. *A chamber in a farmhouse adjoining the castle*

Enter GLOUCESTER, LEAR, KENT, FOOL, *and* EDGAR.

Glou. Here is better than the open air; take it thankfully. I will piece out the comfort with what addition I can. I will not be long from you.

Kent. All the power of his wits have given way to his impatience. The gods reward your kindness! [*Exit* GLOUCESTER.

Edg. Frateretto calls me; and tells me Nero is an angler in the lake of darkness. Pray, innocent, and beware the foul fiend.

Fool. Prithee, nuncle, tell me whether a madman be a gentleman or a yeoman?

Lear. A king, a king!

Fool. No, he's a yeoman that has a gentleman to his son; for he's a mad yeoman that sees his son a gentleman before him.

Lear. To have a thousand with red burning spits
Come hissing in upon 'em—

Edg. The foul fiend bites my back.

Fool. He's mad that trusts in the tameness of a wolf, a horse's health, a boy's love, or a whore's oath.

Lear. It shall be done; I will arraign them straight.
[*To* EDGAR] Come, sit thou here, most learned justicer;
[*To the* FOOL] Thou, sapient sir, sit here. Now, you she foxes!

Edg. Look, where he stands and glares!
Wantest thou eyes at trial, madam?
"Come o'er the bourn, Bessy, to me"—

Fool. "Her boat hath a leak,
And she must not speak
Why she dares not come over to thee."

Edg. The foul fiend haunts poor Tom in the voice of a nightingale. Hopdance cries in Tom's belly for two white herring. Croak not, black angel; I have no food for thee.

Kent. How do you, sir? Stand you not so amazed.
Will you lie down and rest upon the cushions?

Lear. I'll see their trial first. Bring in the evidence.

[*To* EDGAR] Thou robed man of justice, take thy place;
[*To the* FOOL] And thou, his yoke-fellow of equity,
Bench by his side. [*To* KENT] You are o' the commission,
Sit you too.

Edg. Let us deal justly.
"Sleepest or wakest thou, jolly shepherd?
Thy sheep be in the corn;
And for one blast of thy minikin mouth,
Thy sheep shall take no harm."
Pur! the cat is gray.

Lear. Arraign her first; 'tis Goneril. I here take my oath before this honourable assembly, she kicked the poor King her father.

Fool. Come hither, mistress. Is your name Goneril?

Lear. She cannot deny it.

Fool. Cry you mercy, I took you for a joint-stool.

Lear. And here's another, whose warp'd looks proclaim
What store her heart is made on. Stop her there!
Arms, arms, sword, fire! Corruption in the place!
False justicer, why hast thou let her 'scape?

Edg. Bless thy five wits!

Kent. O pity! Sir, where is the patience now
That you so oft have boasted to retain?

Edg. [*Aside*] My tears begin to take his part so much,
They'll mar my counterfeiting.

Lear. The little dogs and all,
Tray, Blanch, and Sweetheart, see, they bark at me.

Edg. Tom will throw his head at them. Avaunt, you curs!
Be thy mouth or black or white,
Tooth that poisons if it bite;
Mastiff, greyhound, mongrel grim,
Hound or spaniel, brach or lym,
Or bobtail tike or trundle-tail,
Tom will make them weep and wail;
For, with throwing thus my head,
Dogs leap the hatch, and all are fled.
Do de, de, de. Sessa! come, march to wakes and fairs and market-towns. Poor Tom, thy horn is dry.

Lear. Then let them anatomize Regan; see what breeds about her heart. Is there any cause in nature that makes these hard hearts? [*To* EDGAR] You, sir, I entertain for one of my hundred; only I do not like the fashion of your garments. you will say they are Persian attire; but let them be changed.

Kent. Now, good my lord, lie here and rest awhile.

Lear. Make no noise, make no noise; draw the curtains; so, so, so. We'll go to supper i' the morning. So, so, so.

Fool. And I'll go to bed at noon.

Re-enter GLOUCESTER.

Glou. Come hither, friend; where is the King my master?

Kent. Here, sir; but trouble him not, his wits are gone.

Glou. Good friend, I prithee, take him in thy arms;
I have o'erheard a plot of death upon him.
There is a litter ready; lay him in't,
And drive towards Dover, friend, where thou shalt meet
Both welcome and protection. Take up thy master.
If thou shouldst dally half an hour, his life,
With thine and all that offer to defend him,
Stand in assured loss. Take up, take up;
And follow me, that will to some provision
Give thee quick conduct.

Kent. Oppressed nature sleeps.
This rest might yet have balm'd thy broken sinews,
Which, if convenience will not allow,
Stand in hard cure. [*To the* FOOL] Come, help to bear thy master:
Thou must not stay behind.

Glou. Come, come, away.

[*Exeunt all but* EDGAR.

Edg. When we our betters see bearing our woes,
We scarcely think our miseries our foes.
Who alone suffers, suffers most i' the mind,
Leaving free things and happy shows behind;
But then the mind much sufferance doth o'erskip,
When grief hath mates, and bearing fellowship.
How light and portable my pain seems now,
When that which makes me bend makes the King bow,
He childed as I father'd! Tom, away!
Mark the high noises; and thyself bewray,
When false opinion, whose wrong thought defiles thee,
In thy just proof, repeals and reconciles thee.
What will hap more to-night, safe 'scape the King!
Lurk, lurk. [*Exit*.

SCENE VII. *Gloucester's castle*

Enter CORNWALL, REGAN, GONERIL, EDMUND, *and Servants*.

Corn. Post speedily to my lord your husband; show him this letter. The army of France is landed. Seek out the villain Gloucester.

[*Exeunt some of the Servants.*

Reg. Hang him instantly.
Gon. Pluck out his eyes.
Corn. Leave him to my displeasure. Edmund, keep you our sister company. The revenges we are bound to take upon your traitorous father are not fit for your beholding. Advise the Duke, where you are going, to a most festinate preparation; we are bound to the like. Our posts shall be swift and intelligent betwixt us. Farewell, dear sister; farewell, my Lord of Gloucester.

Enter OSWALD.

How now! where's the King?
Osw. My lord of Gloucester hath convey'd him hence.
Some five or six and thirty of his knights,
Hot questrists after him, met him at gate;
Who, with some other of the lord's dependants,
Are gone with him towards Dover; where they boast
To have well-armed friends.
Corn. Get horses for your mistress.
Gon. Farewell, sweet lord, and sister.
Corn. Edmund, farewell.

[*Exeunt* GONERIL, EDMUND, *and* OSWALD.

Go seek the traitor Gloucester,
Pinion him like a thief, bring him before us.

[*Exeunt other Servants.*

Though well we may not pass upon his life
Without the form of justice, yet our power
Shall do a courtesy to our wrath, which men
May blame, but not control. Who's there? the traitor?

Enter GLOUCESTER, *brought in by two or three* SERVANTS.

Reg. Ingrateful fox! 'tis he.
Corn. Bind fast his corky arms.
Glou. What mean your Graces? Good my friends, consider
You are my guests. Do me no foul play, friends.
Corn. Bind him, I say.

SERVANTS *bind him.*

Reg. Hard, hard. O filthy traitor!
Glou. Unmerciful lady as you are, I'm none.
Corn. To this chair bind him. Villain, thou shalt find—

REGAN *plucks his beard.*

Glou. By the kind gods, 'tis most ignobly done
To pluck me by the beard.
Reg. So white, and such a traitor!
Glou. Naughty lady,
These hairs, which thou dost ravish from my chin,
Will quicken, and accuse thee. I am your host.
With robbers' hands my hospitable favours
You should not ruffle thus. What will you do?
Corn. Come, sir, what letters had you late from France?
Reg. Be simple answerer, for we know the truth.
Corn. And what confederacy have you with the traitors
Late footed in the kingdom?
Reg. To whose hands have you sent the lunatic King?
Speak.
Glou. I have a letter guessingly set down,
Which came from one that's of a neutral heart,
And not from one opposed.
Corn. Cunning.
Reg. And false.
Corn. Where hast thou sent the King?
Glou. To Dover.
Reg. Wherefore to Dover? Wast thou not charged at peril—
Corn. Wherefore to Dover? Let him first answer that.
Glou. I am tied to the stake, and I must stand the course.
Reg. Wherefore to Dover, sir?
Glou. Because I would not see thy cruel nails
Pluck out his poor old eyes; nor thy fierce sister
In his anointed flesh stick boarish fangs.
The sea, with such a storm as his bare head
In hell-black night endured, would have bouy'd up,
And quench'd the stelled fires;
Yet, poor old heart, he holp the heavens to rain.
If wolves had at thy gate howl'd that stern time,
Thou shouldst have said, "Good porter, turn the key,"
All cruels else subscribed; but I shall see
The winged vengeance overtake such children.
Corn. See't shalt thou never. Fellows, hold the chair.
Upon these eyes of thine I'll set my foot.
Glou. He that will think to live till he be old,
Give me some help! O cruel! O you gods!
Reg. One side will mock another; the other too.
Corn. If you see vengeance—
1st Serv. Hold your hand, my lord.
I have served you ever since I was a child;
But better service have I never done you
Than now to bid you hold.
Reg. How now, you dog!
1st Serv. If you did wear a beard upon your chin,

I'd shake it on this quarrel. What do you mean?
Corn. My villain!
They draw and fight.
1st Serv. Nay, then, come on, and take the chance of anger.
Reg. Give me thy sword. A peasant stand up thus!
Takes a sword, and runs at him behind.
1st Serv. O, I am slain! My lord, you have one eye left
To see some mischief on him. O! [*Dies.*
Corn. Lest it see more, prevent it. Out, vile jelly!
Where is thy lustre now?
Glou. All dark and comfortless. Where's my son Edmund?
Edmund, enkindle all the sparks of nature,
To quit this horrid act.
Reg. Out, treacherous villain!
Thou call'st on him that hates thee. It was he
That made the overture of thy treasons to us;
Who is too good to pity thee.
Glou. O my follies! then Edgar was abused.
Kind gods, forgive me that, and prosper him!
Reg. Go thrust him out at gates, and let him smell
His way to Dover. [*Exit one with* GLOUCESTER.]
How is't, my lord? how look you?
Corn. I have received a hurt. Follow me, lady.
Turn out that eyeless villain; throw this slave
Upon the dunghill. Regan, I bleed apace.
Untimely comes this hurt; give me your arm.
[*Exit* CORNWALL, *led by* REGAN.
2nd Serv. I'll never care what wickedness I do,
If this man come to good.
3rd Serv. If she live long,
And in the end meet the old course of death,
Women will all turn monsters.
2nd. Serv. Let's follow the old Earl, and get the Bedlam
To lead him where he would. His roguish madness
Allows itself to anything.
3rd Servant. Go thou. I'll fetch some flax and whites of eggs
To apply to his bleeding face. Now, Heaven help him! [*Exeunt severally.*

ACT IV

SCENE I. *The heath*

Enter EDGAR.

Edg. Yet better thus, and known to be contemn'd,
Than still contemn'd and flatter'd. To be worst,
The lowest and most dejected thing of fortune,
Stands still in esperance, lives not in fear.
The lamentable change is from the best;
The worst returns to laughter. Welcome, then,
Thou unsubstantial air that I embrace!
The wretch that thou hast blown unto the worst
Owes nothing to thy blasts. But who comes here?

Enter GLOUCESTER, *led by an* OLD MAN.

My father, poorly led? World, world, O world!
But that thy strange mutations make us hate thee,
Life would not yield to age.
Old Man. O, my good lord, I have been your tenant, and your father's tenant, these fourscore years.
Glou. Away, get thee away; good friend, be gone.
Thy comforts can do me no good at all;
Thee they may hurt.
Old Man. Alack, sir, you cannot see your way.
Glou. I have no way, and therefore want no eyes;
I stumbled when I saw. Full oft 'tis seen,
Our means secure us, and our mere defects
Prove our commodities. O dear son Edgar,
The food of thy abused father's wrath!
Might I but live to see thee in my touch,
I'd say I had eyes again!
Old Man. How now! Who's there?
Edg. [*Aside*] O gods! Who is't can say, "I am at the worst"?
I am worse than e'er I was.
Old Man. 'Tis poor mad Tom.
Edg. [*Aside*] And worse I may be yet; the worst is not
So long as we can say, "This is the worst."
Old Man. Fellow, where goest?
Glou. Is it a beggar-man?
Old Man. Madman and beggar too.
Glou. He has some reason, else he could not beg.
I' the last night's storm I such a fellow saw;
Which made me think a man a worm. My son
Came then into my mind; and yet my mind
Was then scarce friends with him. I have heard more since.
As flies to wanton boys, are we to the gods,
They kill us for their sport.
Edg. [*Aside*] How should this be?
Bad is the trade that must play fool to sorrow,
Angering itself and others.—Bless thee, master!
Glou. Is that the naked fellow?
Old Man. Ay, my lord.
Glou. Then, prithee, get thee gone. If, for my sake,
Thou wilt o'ertake us, hence a mile or twain,
I' the way toward Dover, do it for ancient love;
And bring some covering for this naked soul,

Who I'll entreat to lead me.
Old Man. Alack, sir, he is mad.
Glou. 'Tis the times' plague, when madmen lead the blind.
Do as I bid thee, or rather do thy pleasure;
Above the rest, be gone.
Old Man. I'll bring him the best 'parel that I have,
Come on't what will. [*Exit.*
Glou. Sirrah, naked fellow—
Edg. Poor Tom's a-cold. [*Aside*] I cannot daub it further.
Glou. Come hither, fellow.
Edg. [*Aside*] And yet I must.—Bless thy sweet eyes, they bleed.
Glou. Know'st thou the way to Dover?

Edg. Both stile and gate, horse-way and foot-path. Poor Tom hath been scared out of his good wits. Bless thee, good man's son, from the foul fiend! five fiends have been in poor Tom at once; of lust, as Obidicut; Hobbididance, prince of dumbness; Mahu, of stealing; Modo, of murder; Flibbertigibbet, of mopping and mowing, who since possesses chambermaids and waiting-women. So, bless thee, master!

Glou. Here, take this purse, thou whom the heavens' plagues
Have humbled to all strokes. That I am wretched
Makes thee the happier. Heavens, deal so still!
Let the superfluous and lust-dieted man,
That slaves your ordinance, that will not see
Because he doth not feel, feel your power quickly;
So distribution should undo excess,
And each man have enough. Dost thou know Dover?
Edg. Ay, master.
Glou. There is a cliff, whose high and bending head
Looks fearfully in the confined deep.
Bring me but to the very brim of it,
And I'll repair the misery thou dost bear
With something rich about me. From that place
I shall no leading need.
Edg. Give me thy arm:
Poor Tom shall lead thee. [*Exeunt.*

SCENE II. *Before the Duke of Albany's palace*

Enter GONERIL *and* EDMUND.

Gon. Welcome, my lord. I marvel our mild husband
Not met us on the way.

Enter OSWALD.

Now, where's your master?
Osw. Madam, within; but never man so changed.
I told him of the army that was landed;
He smiled at it. I told him you were coming;
His answer was, "The worse"; of Gloucester's treachery,
And of the loyal service of his son,
When I inform'd him, then he call'd me sot,
And told me I had turn'd the wrong side out.
What most he should dislike seems pleasant to him;
What like, offensive.
Gon. [*To* EDMUND] Then shall you go no further.
It is the cowish terror of his spirit,
That dares not undertake. He'll not feel wrongs
Which tie him to an answer. Our wishes on the way
May prove effects. Back, Edmund, to my brother;
Hasten his musters and conduct his powers.
I must change arms at home, and give the distaff
Into my husband's hands. This trusty servant
Shall pass between us. Ere long you are like to hear,
If you dare venture in your own behalf,
A mistress's command. Wear this; spare speech;
Giving a favour.
Decline your head. This kiss, if it durst speak,
Would stretch thy spirits up into the air.
Conceive, and fare thee well.
Edm. Yours in the ranks of death.
Gon. My most dear Gloucester!
[*Exit* EDMUND.
O, the difference of man and man!
To thee a woman's services are due;
My fool usurps my body.
Osw. Madam, here comes my lord.
[*Exit.*

Enter ALBANY.

Gon. I have been worth the whistle.
Alb. O Goneril!
You are not worth the dust which the rude wind
Blows in your face. I fear your disposition.
That nature, which contemns it origin,
Cannot be border'd certain in itself;
She that herself will sliver and disbranch
From her material sap, perforce must wither
And come to deadly use.
Gon. No more; the text is foolish.
Alb. Wisdom and goodness to the vile seem vile;
Filths savour but themselves. What have you done?
Tigers, not daughters, what have you perform'd?
A father, and a gracious aged man,

Whose reverence even the head-lugg'd bear would lick,
Most barbarous, most degenerate! have you madded.
Could my good brother suffer you to do it?
A man, a prince, by him so benefited!
If that the heavens do not their visible spirits
Send quickly down to tame these vile offences,
It will come,
Humanity must perforce prey on itself,
Like monsters of the deep.

Gon. Milk-liver'd man!
That bear'st a cheek for blows, a head for wrongs;
Who hast not in thy brows an eye discerning
Thine honour from thy suffering; that not know'st
Fools do those villains pity who are punish'd
Ere they have done their mischief. Where's thy drum?
France spreads his banners in our noiseless land,
With plumed helm thy state begins to threat;
Whiles thou, a moral fool, sit'st still, and criest,
"Alack, why does he so?"

Alb. See thyself, devil!
Proper deformity seems not in the fiend!
So horrid as in woman.

Gon. O vain fool!

Alb. Thou changed and self-cover'd thing, for shame,
Be-monster not thy feature. Were 't my fitness
To let these hands obey my blood,
They are apt enough to dislocate and tear
Thy flesh and bones. Howe'er thou art a fiend,
A woman's shape doth shield thee.

Gon. Marry, your manhood now—

Enter a MESSENGER.

Alb. What news?

Mess. O, my good lord, the Duke of Cornwall's dead;
Slain by his servant, going to put out
The other eye of Gloucester.

Alb. Gloucester's eyes!

Mess. A servant that he bred, thrill'd with remorse,
Opposed against the act, bending his sword
To his great master; who, thereat enraged,
Flew on him, and amongst them fell'd him dead;
But not without that harmful stroke, which since
Hath pluck'd him after.

Alb. This shows you are above,
You justicers, that these our nether crimes
So speedily can venge! But, O poor Gloucester!
Lost he his other eye?

Mess. Both, both, my lord.
This letter, madam, craves a speedy answer;
'Tis from your sister.

Gon. [*Aside*] One way I like this well;
But being widow, and my Gloucester with her,
May all the building in my fancy pluck
Upon my hateful life; another way,
The news is not so tart.—I'll read, and answer.
[*Exit.*

Alb. Where was his son when they did take his eyes?

Mess. Come with my lady hither.

Alb. He is not here.

Mess. No, my good lord; I met him back again.

Alb. Knows he the wickedness?

Mess. Ay, my good lord; 'twas he inform'd against him;
And quit the house on purpose, that their punishment
Might have the freer course.

Alb. Gloucester, I live
To thank thee for the love thou show'dst the King,
And to revenge thine eyes. Come hither, friend.
Tell me what more thou know'st. [*Exeunt.*

SCENE III. *The French camp near Dover*

Enter KENT *and a* GENTLEMAN.

Kent. Why the King of France is so suddenly gone back know you the reason?

Gent. Something he left imperfect in the state, which since his coming forth is thought of; which imports to the kingdom so much fear and danger, that his personal return was most required and necessary.

Kent. Who hath he left behind him general?

Gent. The Marshal of France, Monsieur La Far.

Kent. Did your letters pierce the Queen to any demonstration of grief?

Gent. Ay, sir; she took them, read them in my presence;
And now and then an ample tear trill'd down
Her delicate cheek. It seem'd she was a queen
Over her passion; who, most rebel-like,
Sought to be king o'er her.

Kent. O, then it moved her.

Gent. Not to a rage: patience and sorrow strove
Who should express her goodliest. You have seen
Sunshine and rain at once: her smiles and tears
Were like a better way; those happy smilets,
That play'd on her ripe lip, seem'd not to know
What guests were in her eyes; which parted thence,
As pearls from diamonds dropp'd. In brief,
Sorrow would be a rarity most beloved,

If all could so become it.
Kent. Made she no verbal question?
Gent. 'Faith, once or twice she heaved the name of "father"
Pantingly forth, as if it press'd her heart;
Cried "Sisters! sisters! Shame of ladies! sisters!
Kent! father! sisters! What, i' the storm? i' the night?
Let pity not be believed!" There she shook
The holy water from her heavenly eyes,
And clamour moisten'd; then away she started
To deal with grief alone.
Kent. It is the stars,
The stars above us, govern our conditions;
Else one self mate and mate could not beget
Such different issues. You spoke not with her since?
Gent. No.
Kent. Was this before the King returned?
Gent. No, since.
Kent. Well, sir, the poor distressed Lear's i' the town;
Who sometime, in his better tune, remembers
What we are come about, and by no means
Will yield to see his daughter.
Gent. Why, good sir?
Kent. A sovereign shame so elbows him. His own unkindness,
That stripp'd her from his benediction, turn'd her
To foreign casualties, gave her dear rights
To his dog-hearted daughters, these things sting
His mind so venomously, that burning shame
Detains him from Cordelia.
Gent. Alack, poor gentleman!
Kent. Of Albany's and Cornwall's powers you heard not?
Gent. 'Tis so, they are afoot.
Kent. Well, sir, I'll bring you to our master Lear,
And leave you to attend him. Some dear cause
Will in concealment wrap me up awhile;
When I am known aright, you shall not grieve
Lending me this acquaintance. I pray you, go
Along with me. [*Exeunt.*

SCENE IV. *The same: a tent*

Enter, with drum and colours, CORDELIA, DOCTOR, *and Soldiers.*

Cor. Alack, 'tis he. Why, he was met even now
As mad as the vex'd sea; singing aloud;
Crown'd with rank fumiter and furrow-weeds,
With bur-docks, hemlock, nettles, cuckoo-flowers,
Darnel, and all the idle weeds that grow
In our sustaining corn. A century send forth;
Search every acre in the high-grown field,
And bring him to our eye. [*Exit an Officer.*]
What can man's wisdom
In the restoring his bereaved sense?
He that helps him take all my outward worth.
Doct. There is means, madam.
Our foster-nurse of nature is repose,
The which he lacks; that to provoke in him,
Are many simples operative, whose power
Will close the eye of anguish.
Cor. All blest secrets,
All you unpublish'd virtues of the earth,
Spring with my tears! be aidant and remediate
In the good man's distress! Seek, seek for him;
Lest his ungovern'd rage dissolve the life
That wants the means to lead it.

Enter a MESSENGER.

Mess. News, madam;
The British powers are marching hitherward.
Cor. 'Tis known before; our preparation stands
In expectation of them. O dear father,
It is thy business that I go about;
Therefore great France
My mourning and important tears hath pitied.
No blown ambition doth our arms incite,
But love, dear love, and our aged father's right.
Soon may I hear and see him! [*Exeunt.*

SCENE V. *Gloucester's castle*

Enter REGAN *and* OSWALD.

Reg. But are my brother's powers set forth?
Osw. Ay, madam.
Reg. Himself in person there?
Osw. Madam, with much ado.
Your sister is the better soldier.
Reg. Lord Edmund spake not with your lord at home?
Osw. No, madam.
Reg. What might import my sister's letter to him?
Osw. I know not, lady.
Reg. 'Faith, he is posted hence on serious matter.
It was great ignorance, Gloucester's eyes being out,
To let him live; where he arrives he moves
All hearts against us. Edmund, I think, is gone,
In pity of his misery, to dispatch
His nighted life, moreover, to descry
The strength o' the enemy.
Osw. I must needs after him, madam, with my letter.
Reg. Our troops set forth to-morrow. Stay with us;
The ways are dangerous.

Osw. I may not, madam.
My lady charged my duty in this business.
Reg. Why should she write to Edmund? Might not you
Transport her purposes by word? Belike,
Something—I know not what. I'll love thee much,
Let me unseal the letter.
Osw. Madam, I had rather—
Reg. I know your lady does not love her husband;
I am sure of that. And at her late being here
She gave strange œillades and most speaking looks
To noble Edmund. I know you are of her bosom.
Osw. I, madam?
Reg. I speak in understanding; you are, I know't.
Therefore I do advise you, take this note.
My lord is dead; Edmund and I have talk'd;
And more convenient is he for my hand
Than for your lady's. You may gather more.
If you do find him, pray you, give him this;
And when your mistress hears thus much from you,
I pray, desire her call her wisdom to her.
So, fare you well.
If you do chance to hear of that blind traitor,
Preferment falls on him that cuts him off.
Osw. Would I could meet him, madam! I should show
What party I do follow.
Reg. Fare thee well. [*Exeunt.*

SCENE VI. *Fields near Dover*

Enter GLOUCESTER, *and* EDGAR *dressed like a peasant.*

Glou. When shall we come to the top of that same hill?
Edg. You do climb up it now. Look, how we labour.
Glou. Methinks the ground is even.
Edg. Horrible steep.
Hark, do you hear the sea?
Glou. No, truly.
Edg. Why, then, your other senses grow imperfect
By your eyes' anguish.
Glou. So may it be, indeed.
Methinks thy voice is alter'd; and thou speak'st
In better phrase and matter than thou didst.
Edg. You're much deceived. In nothing am I changed
But in my garments.
Glou. Methinks you're better spoken.
Edg. Come on, sir; here's the place. Stand still. How fearful
And dizzy 'tis, to cast one's eyes so low!
The crows and choughs that wing the midway air
Show scarce so gross as beetles. Half way down
Hangs one that gathers samphire, dreadful trade!
Methinks he seems no bigger than his head.
The fishermen, that walk upon the beach,
Appear like mice; and yond tall anchoring bark,
Diminish'd to her cock; her cock, a buoy
Almost too small for sight. The murmuring surge,
That on the unnumber'd idle pebbles chafes,
Cannot be heard so high. I'll look no more;
Lest my brain turn, and the deficient sight
Topple down headlong.
Glou. Set me where you stand.
Edg. Give me your hand. You are now within a foot
Of the extreme verge. For all beneath the moon
Would I not leap upright.
Glou. Let go my hand.
Here, friend, 's another purse; in it a jewel
Well worth a poor man's taking. Fairies and gods
Prosper it with thee! Go thou farther off;
Bid me farewell, and let me hear thee going.
Edg. Now fare you well, good sir.
Glou. With all my heart.
Edg. Why I do trifle thus with his despair
Is done to cure it.
Glou. [*Kneeling*] O you mighty gods!
This world I do renounce, and, in your sights,
Shake patiently my great affliction off.
If I could bear it longer, and not fall
To quarrel with your great opposeless wills,
My snuff and loathed part of nature should
Burn itself out. If Edgar live, O, bless him!
Now, fellow, fare thee well. [*He falls forward.*
Edg. Gone, sir; farewell.
And yet I know not how conceit may rob
The treasury of life, when life itself
Yields to the theft. Had he been where he thought,
By this, had thought been past. Alive or dead?
Ho, you sir! friend! Hear you, sir! speak!
Thus might he pass indeed. Yet he revives.
What are you, sir?
Glou. Away, and let me die.
Edg. Hadst thou been aught but gossamer, feathers, air,
So many fathom down precipitating,
Thou'dst shiver'd like an egg. But thou dost breathe;
Hast heavy substance; bleed'st not; speak'st; art sound.
Ten masts at each make not the altitude
Which thou hast perpendicularly fell.

Thy life's a miracle. Speak yet again.
Glou. But have I fall'n, or no?
Edg. From the dread summit of this chalky bourn.
Look up a-height; the shrill-gorged lark so far
Cannot be seen or heard. Do but look up.
Glou. Alack, I have no eyes.
Is wretchedness deprived that benefit,
To end itself by death? 'Twas yet some comfort,
When misery could beguile the tyrant's rage,
And frustrate his proud will.
Edg. Give me your arm.
Up: so. How is't? Feel you your legs? You stand.
Glou. Too well, too well.
Edg. This is above all strangeness.
Upon the crown o' the cliff, what thing was that
Which parted from you?
Glou. A poor unfortunate beggar.
Edg. As I stood here below, methought his eyes
Were two full moons; he had a thousand noses,
Horns whelk'd and waved like the enridged sea.
It was some fiend; therefore, thou happy father,
Think that the clearest gods, who make them honours
Of men's impossibilities, have preserved thee.
Glou. I do remember now. Henceforth I'll bear
Affliction till it do cry out itself
"Enough, enough," and die. That thing you speak of,
I took it for a man; often 'twould say
"The fiend, the fiend." He led me to that place.
Edg. Bear free and patient thoughts. But who comes here?

Enter LEAR, *fantastically dressed with wild flowers.*

The safer sense will ne'er accommodate
His master thus.
Lear. No, they cannot touch me for coining; I am the king himself.
Edg. O thou side-piercing sight!
Lear. Nature's above art in that respect. There's your press-money. That fellow handles his bow like a crow-keeper. Draw me a clothier's yard. Look, look, a mouse! Peace, peace; this piece of toasted cheese will do't. There's my gauntlet; I'll prove it on a giant. Bring up the brown bills. O, well flown, bird! i' the clout, i' the clout. Hewgh! Give the word.
Edg. Sweet marjoram.
Lear. Pass.
Glou. I know that voice.
Lear. Ha! Goneril, with a white beard! They flattered me like a dog; and told me I had white hairs in my beard ere the black ones were there. To say "ay" and "no" to everything that I said!—"Ay" and "no" too was no good divinity. When the rain came to wet me once, and the wind to make me chatter; when the thunder would not peace at my bidding; there I found 'em, there I smelt 'em out. Go to, they are not men o' their words. They told me I was every thing; 'tis a lie, I am not ague-proof.
Glou. The trick of that voice I do well remember.
Is't not the King?
Lear. Ay, every inch a king!
When I do stare, see how the subject quakes.
I pardon that man's life. What was thy cause?
Adultery?
Thou shalt not die. Die for adultery! No:
The wren goes to't, and the small gilded fly
Does lecher in my sight.
Let copulation thrive; for Gloucester's bastard son
Was kinder to his father than my daughters
Got 'tween the lawful sheets.
To't, luxury, pell-mell; for I lack soldiers.
Behold yond simpering dame,
Whose face between her forks presages snow;
That minces virtue, and does shake the head
To hear of pleasure's name;
The fitchew, nor the soiled horse, goes to't
With a more riotous appetite.
Down from the waist they are Centaurs,
Though women all above;
But to the girdle do the gods inherit,
Beneath is all the fiends';
There's hell, there's darkness, there's the sulphurous pit,
Burning, scalding, stench, consumption; fie, fie, fie! pah, pah! Give me an ounce of civet, good apothecary, to sweeten my imagination. There's money for thee.
Glou. O, let me kiss that hand!
Lear. Let me wipe it first; it smells of mortality.
Glou. O ruin'd piece of nature! This great world
Shall so wear out to nought. Dost thou know me?
Lear. I remember thine eyes well enough. Dost thou squiny at me? No, do thy worst, blind Cupid; I'll not love. Read thou this challenge; mark but the penning of it.
Glou. Were all the letters suns, I could not see one.
Edg. I would not take this from report; it is,
And my heart breaks at it.
Lear. Read.
Glou. What, with the case of eyes?
Lear. O, ho, are you there with me? No eyes in your head, nor no money in your purse? Your eyes are in a heavy case, your purse in a light. Yet you see how this world goes.
Glou. I see it feelingly.

Lear. What, art mad? A man may see how this world goes with no eyes. Look with thine ears: see how yond justice rails upon yond simple thief. Hark, in thine ear: change places; and, handy-dandy, which is the justice, which is the thief? Thou hast seen a farmer's dog bark at a beggar?

Glou. Ay, sir.

Lear. And the creature run from the cur?
There thou mightst behold the great image of authority: a dog's obeyed in office.
Thou rascal beadle, hold thy bloody hand!
Why dost thou lash that whore? Strip thine own back;
Thou hotly lust'st to use her in that kind
For which thou whipp'st her. The usurer hangs the cozener.
Through tatter'd clothes small vices do appear;
Robes and furr'd gowns hide all. Plate sin with gold,
And the strong lance of justice hurtless breaks;
Arm it in rags, a pigmy's straw does pierce it.
None does offend, none, I say, none; I'll able 'em.
Take that of me, my friend, who have the power
To seal the accuser's lips. Get thee glass eyes;
And, like a scurvy politician, seem
To see the things thou dost not. Now, now, now, now.
Pull off my boots: harder, harder; so.

Edg. O, matter and impertinency mix'd!
Reason in madness!

Lear. If thou wilt weep my fortunes, take my eyes.
I know thee well enough; thy name is Gloucester.
Thou must be patient; we came crying hither.
Thou know'st, the first time that we smell the air,
We wawl and cry. I will preach to thee; mark.

Glou. Alack, alack the day!

Lear. When we are born, we cry that we are come
To this great stage of fools. This' a good block;
It were a delicate stratagem, to shoe
A troop of horse with felt. I'll put't in proof;
And when I have stol'n upon these sons-in-law,
Then, kill, kill, kill, kill, kill, kill!

Enter a GENTLEMAN, *with Attendants*.

Gent. O, here he is. Lay hand upon him. Sir,
Your most dear daughter—

Lear. No rescue? What, a prisoner? I am even
The natural fool of fortune. Use me well;
You shall have ransom. Let me have surgeons;
I am cut to the brains.

Gent. You shall have anything.

Lear. No seconds? all myself?
Why, this would make a man a man of salt,
To use his eyes for garden water-pots,
Ay, and laying autumn's dust.

Gent. Good sir—

Lear. I will die bravely, like a bridegroom. What!
I will be jovial. Come, come; I am a king,
My masters, know you that.

Gent. You are a royal one, and we obey you.

Lear. Then there's life in't. Nay, if you get it, you shall get it with running. Sa, sa, sa, sa.

[*Exit running; Attendants follow*.

Gent. A sight most pitiful in the meanest wretch,
Past speaking of in a king! Thou hast one daughter,
Who redeems nature from the general curse
Which twain have brought her to.

Edg. Hail, gentle sir.

Gent. Sir, speed you. What's your will?

Edg. Do you hear aught, sir, of a battle toward?

Gent. Most sure and vulgar. Every one hears that,
Which can distinguish sound.

Edg. But, by your favour,
How near's the other army?

Gent. Near and on speedy foot; the main descry
Stands on the hourly thought.

Edg. I thank you, sir. That's all.

Gent. Though that the Queen on special cause is here,
Her army is moved on.

Edg. I thank you, sir.

[*Exit* GENTLEMAN.

Glou. You ever-gentle gods, take my breath from me;
Let not my worser spirit tempt me again
To die before you please!

Edg. Well pray you, father.

Glou. Now, good sir, what are you?

Edg. A most poor man, made tame to fortune's blows;
Who, by the art of known and feeling sorrows,
Am pregnant to good pity. Give me your hand,
I'll lead you to some biding.

Glou. Hearty thanks.
The bounty and the benison of Heaven
To boot, and boot!

Enter OSWALD.

Osw. A proclaim'd prize! Most happy!
That eyeless head of thine was first framed flesh
To raise my fortunes. Thou old unhappy traitor,
Briefly thyself remember; the sword is out
That must destroy thee.

Glou. Now let thy friendly hand

Put strength enough to't.

EDGAR *interposes.*

Osw. Wherefore, bold peasant,
Darest thou support a publish'd traitor? Hence;
Lest that the infection of his fortune take
Like hold on thee. Let go his arm.

Edg. Chill not let go, zir, without vurther 'casion.

Osw. Let go, slave, or thou diest!

Edg. Good gentleman, go your gait, and let poor volk pass. An chud ha' bin zwaggered out of my life, 'twould not ha' bin zo long as 'tis by a vortnight. Nay, come not near th' old man; keep out, che vor ye, or ise try whether your costard or my ballow be the harder. Chill be plain with you.

Osw. Out, dunghill!

Edg. Chill pick your teeth, zir. Come; no matter vor your foins.

They fight, and EDGAR *knocks him down.*

Osw. Slave, thou hast slain me. Villain, take my purse.
If ever thou wilt thrive, bury my body;
And give the letters which thou find'st about me
To Edmund Earl of Gloucester; seek him out
Upon the British party. O, untimely death!
[*Dies.*

Edg. I know thee well. A serviceable villain;
As duteous to the vices of thy mistress
As badness would desire.

Glou. What, is he dead?

Edg. Sit you down, father; rest you.
Let's see these pockets. The letters that he speaks of
May be my friends. He's dead; I am only sorry
He had no other death's-man. Let us see;
Leave, gentle wax; and, manners, blame us not.
To know our enemies' minds, we'd rip their hearts;
Their papers, is more lawful.

[*Reads*] "Let our reciprocal vows be remembered. You have many opportunities to cut him off. If your will want not, time and place will be fruitfully offered. There is nothing done, if he return the conqueror. Then am I the prisoner, and his bed my gaol; from the loathed warmth whereof deliver me, and supply the place for your labour.

"Your—wife, so I would say—
"Affectionate servant,
"Goneril"

O undistinguish'd space of woman's will!
A plot upon her virtuous husband's life;
And the exchange my brother! Here, in the sands,
Thee I'll rake up, the post unsanctified
Of murderous lechers. And in the mature time
With this ungracious paper strike the sight
Of the death-practised Duke; for him 'tis well
That of thy death and business I can tell.

Glou. The King is mad. How stiff is my vile sense,
That I stand up, and have ingenious feeling
Of my huge sorrows! Better I were distract.
So should my thoughts be sever'd from my griefs,
And woes by wrong imaginations lose
The knowledge of themselves.

Edg. Give me your hand:

Drum afar off.

Far off, methinks, I hear the beaten drum.
Come, father, I'll bestow you with a friend.
[*Exeunt.*

SCENE VII. *A tent in the French camp.* LEAR *on a bed asleep, soft music playing;* GENTLEMAN, *and others attending*

Enter CORDELIA, KENT, *and* DOCTOR.

Cor. O thou good Kent, how shall I live and work,
To match thy goodness? My life will be too short,
And every measure fail me.

Kent. To be acknowledged, madam, is o'erpaid.
All my reports go with the modest truth;
Nor more nor clipp'd, but so.

Cor. Be better suited;
These weeds are memories of those worser hours.
I prithee, put them off.

Kent. Pardon me, dear madam;
Yet to be known shortens my made intent.
My boon I make it, that you know me not
Till time and I think meet.

Cor. Then be't so, my good lord. [*To the* DOCTOR] How does the King?

Doct. Madam, sleeps still.

Cor. O you kind gods,
Cure this great breach in his abused nature!
The untuned and jarring senses, O, wind up
Of this child-changed father!

Doct. So please your Majesty
That we may wake the King? He hath slept long.

Cor. Be govern'd by your knowledge, and proceed
I' the sway of your own will. Is he array'd?

Gent. Ay, madam; in the heaviness of his sleep
We put fresh garments on him.

Doct. Be by, good madam, when we do awake him;
I doubt not of his temperance.

Cor. Very well.

Doct. Please you, draw near. Louder the music there!
Cor. O my dear father! Restoration hang
Thy medicine on my lips; and let this kiss
Repair those violent harms that my two sisters
Have in thy reverence made!
Kent. Kind and dear Princess!
Cor. Had you not been their father, these white flakes
Had challenged pity of them. Was this a face
To be opposed against the warring winds?
To stand against the deep dread-bolted thunder?
In the most terrible and nimble stroke
Of quick, cross lightning? to watch—poor perdu!—
With this thin helm? Mine enemy's dog,
Though he had bit me, should have stood that night
Against my fire; and wast thou fain, poor father,
To hovel thee with swine and rogues forlorn
In short and musty straw? Alack, alack!
'Tis wonder that thy life and wits at once
Had not concluded all. He wakes; speak to him.
Doct. Madam, do you; 'tis fittest.
Cor. How does my royal lord? How fares your Majesty?
Lear. You do me wrong to take me out o' the grave.
Thou art a soul in bliss; but I am bound
Upon a wheel of fire, that mine own tears
Do scald like molten lead.
Cor. Sir, do you know me?
Lear. You are a spirit, I know. When did you die?
Cor. Still, still, far wide!
Doct. He's scarce awake. Let him alone awhile.
Lear. Where have I been? Where am I? Fair daylight?
I am mightily abused. I should e'en die with pity,
To see another thus. I know not what to say.
I will not swear these are my hands. Let's see;
I feel this pin prick. Would I were assured
Of my condition!
Cor. O, look upon me, sir,
And hold your hands in benediction o'er me.
No, sir, you must not kneel.
Lear. Pray, do not mock me.
I am a very foolish fond old man,
Fourscore and upward, not an hour more nor less;
And, to deal plainly,
I fear I am not in my perfect mind.
Methinks I should know you, and know this man;
Yet I am doubtful; for I am mainly ignorant
What place this is; and all the skill I have
Remembers not these garments; nor I know not
Where I did lodge last night. Do not laugh at me;
For, as I am a man, I think this lady
To be my child Cordelia.
Cor. And so I am, I am.
Lear. Be your tears wet? yes, 'faith. I pray, weep not.
If you have poison for me, I will drink it.
I know you do not love me; for your sisters
Have, as I do remember, done me wrong.
You have some cause, they have not.
Cor. No cause, no cause.
Lear. Am I in France?
Kent. In your own kingdom, sir.
Lear. Do not abuse me.
Doct. Be comforted, good madam. The great rage,
You see, is kill'd in him; and yet it is danger
To make him even o'er the time he has lost.
Desire him to go in; trouble him no more
Till further settling.
Cor. Will't please your Highness walk?
Lear. You must bear with me.
Pray you now, forget and forgive. I am old and foolish.
[*Exeunt all but* KENT *and* GENTLEMAN.

Gent. Holds it true, sir, that the Duke of Cornwall was so slain?

Kent. Most certain, sir.

Gent. Who is conductor of his people?

Kent. As 'tis said, the bastard son of Gloucester.

Gent. They say Edgar, his banished son, is with the Earl of Kent in Germany.

Kent. Report is changeable. 'Tis time to look about; the powers of the kingdom approach apace.

Gent. The arbitrement is like to be bloody. Fare you well, sir. [*Exit.*

Kent. My point and period will be thoroughly wrought,
Or well or ill, as this day's battle's fought.
[*Exit.*

ACT V

SCENE I. *The British camp, near Dover*

Enter, with drum and colours, EDMUND, REGAN, *Gentlemen, and Soldiers.*

Edm. Know of the Duke if his last purpose hold,
Or whether since he is advised by aught
To change the course. He's full of alteration
And self-reproving; bring his constant pleasure.
[*To a Gentleman, who goes out.*
Reg. Our sister's man is certainly miscarried.
Edm. 'Tis to be doubted, madam.

Reg. Now, sweet lord,
You know the goodness I intend upon you.
Tell me—but truly—but then speak the truth,
Do you not love my sister?
Edm. In honour'd love.
Reg. But have you never found my brother's way
To the forfended place?
Edm. That thought abuses you.
Reg. I am doubtful that you have been conjunct
And bosom'd with her, as far as we call hers.
Edm. No, by mine honour, madam.
Reg. I never shall endure her. Dear my lord,
Be not familiar with her.
Edm. Fear me not.
She and the Duke her husband!

Enter, with drum and colours, ALBANY, GONERIL, *and Soldiers.*

Gon. [*Aside*] I had rather lose the battle than that sister
Should loosen him and me.
Alb. Our very loving sister, well be-met.
Sir, this I hear; the King is come to his daughter,
With others whom the rigour of our state
Forced to cry out. Where I could not be honest,
I never yet was valiant; for this business,
It toucheth us, as France invades our land,
Not bolds the King, with others, whom, I fear,
Most just and heavy causes make oppose.
Edm. Sir, you speak nobly.
Reg. Why is this reason'd?
Gon. Combine together 'gainst the enemy;
For these domestic and particular broils
Are not the question here.
Alb. Let's then determine
With the ancient of war on our proceedings.
Edm. I shall attend you presently at your tent.
Reg. Sister, you'll go with us?
Gon. No.
Reg. 'Tis most convenient; pray you, go with us.
Gon. [*Aside*] O, ho, I know the riddle.—I will go.

As they are going out, enter EDGAR *disguised.*

Edg. If e'er your Grace had speech with man so poor,
Hear me one word.
Alb. I'll overtake you. Speak.
[*Exeunt all but* ALBANY *and* EDGAR.
Edg. Before you fight the battle, ope this letter.
If you have victory, let the trumpet sound
For him that brought it. Wretched though I seem,
I can produce a champion that will prove
What is avouched there. If you miscarry,
Your business of the world hath so an end,
And machination ceases. Fortune love you!
Alb. Stay till I have read the letter.
Edg. I was forbid it.
When time shall serve, let but the herald cry,
And I'll appear again.
Alb. Why, fare thee well. I will o'erlook thy paper. [*Exit* EDGAR.

Re-enter EDMUND.

Edm. The enemy's in view; draw up your powers.
Here is the guess of their true strength and forces
By diligent discovery; but your haste
Is now urged on you.
Alb. We will greet the time. [*Exit.*
Edm. To both these sisters have I sworn my love;
Each jealous of the other, as the stung
Are of the adder. Which of them shall I take?
Both? one? or neither? Neither can be enjoy'd,
If both remain alive. To take the widow
Exasperates, makes mad her sister Goneril;
And hardly shall I carry out my side,
Her husband being alive. Now then we'll use
His countenance for the battle; which being done,
Let her who would be rid of him devise
His speedy taking off. As for the mercy
Which he intends to Lear and to Cordelia,
The battle done, and they within our power,
Shall never see his pardon; for my state
Stands on me to defend, not to debate. [*Exit.*

SCENE II. *A field between the two camps*

Alarum within. Enter, with drum and colours, LEAR, CORDELIA, *and Soldiers, over the stage; and exeunt.*

Enter EDGAR *and* GLOUCESTER.

Edg. Here, father, take the shadow of this tree
For your good host; pray that the right may thrive.
If ever I return to you again,
I'll bring you comfort.
Glou. Grace go with you, sir!
[*Exit* EDGAR.

Alarum and retreat within. Re-enter EDGAR.

Edg. Away, old man; give me thy hand; away!
King Lear hath lost, he and his daughter ta'en.
Give me thy hand; come on.
Glou. No farther, sir; a man may rot even here.
Edg. What, in ill thoughts again? Men must endure

Their going hence, even as their coming hither;
Ripeness is all. Come on.
Glou. And that's true too. [*Exeunt.*

SCENE III. *The British camp near Dover*

Enter, in conquest, with drum and colours, EDMUND; LEAR *and* CORDELIA, *prisoners; Captain, Soldiers, &c.*

Edm. Some officers take them away. Good guard,
Until their greater pleasures first be known
That are to censure them.
Cor. We are not the first
Who, with best meaning, have incurr'd the worst.
For thee, oppressed King, am I cast down;
Myself could else out-frown false Fortune's frown.
Shall we not see these daughters and these sisters?
Lear. No, no, no, no! Come, let's away to prison.
We two alone will sing like birds i' the cage;
When thou dost ask me blessing, I'll kneel down,
And ask of thee forgiveness; so we'll live,
And pray, and sing, and tell old tales, and laugh
At gilded butterflies, and hear poor rogues
Talk of court news; and we'll talk with them too,
Who loses and who wins; who's in, who's out;
And take upon's the mystery of things,
As if we were God's spies; and we'll wear out,
In a wall'd prison, packs and sects of great ones,
That ebb and flow by the moon.
Edm. Take them away.
Lear. Upon such sacrifices, my Cordelia,
The gods themselves throw incense. Have I caught thee?
He that parts us shall bring a brand from heaven,
And fire us hence like foxes. Wipe thine eyes;
The good-years shall devour them, flesh and fell,
Ere they shall make us weep. We'll see 'em starve first.
Come. [*Exeunt* LEAR *and* CORDELIA, *guarded.*
Edm. Come hither, captain; hark.
Take thou this note [*giving a paper*]; go follow them to prison.
One step I have advanced thee; if thou dost
As this instructs thee, thou dost make thy way
To noble fortunes. Know thou this, that men
Are as the time is; to be tender-minded
Does not become a sword. Thy great employment
Will not bear question; either say thou'lt do 't,
Or thrive by other means.
Capt. I'll do 't, my lord.
Edm. About it; and write happy when thou hast done.
Mark, I say, instantly; and carry it so
As I have set it down.
Capt. I cannot draw a cart, nor eat dried oats;
If it be man's work, I'll do 't. [*Exit.*

Flourish. Enter ALBANY, GONERIL, REGAN, *another* CAPTAIN, *and Soldiers.*

Alb. Sir, you have shown to-day your valiant strain,
And fortune led you well. You have the captives
That were the opposites of this day's strife;
We do require them of you, so to use them
As we shall find their merits and our safety
May equally determine.
Edm. Sir, I thought it fit
To send the old and miserable King
To some retention and appointed guard;
Whose age has charms in it, whose title more,
To pluck the common bosom on his side,
And turn our impress'd lances in our eyes
Which do command them. With him I sent the Queen;
My reason all the same; and they are ready
To-morrow, or at further space, to appear
Where you shall hold your session. At this time
We sweat and bleed; the friend hath lost his friend;
And the best quarrels, in the heat, are cursed
By those that feel their sharpness.
The question of Cordelia and her father
Requires a fitter place.
Alb. Sir, by your patience,
I hold you but a subject of this war,
Not as a brother.
Reg. That's as we list to grace him.
Methinks our pleasure might have been demanded,
Ere you had spoke so far. He led our powers;
Bore the commission of my place and person;
The which immediacy may well stand up,
And call itself your brother.
Gon. Not so hot:
In his own grace he doth exalt himself,
More than in your addition.
Reg. In my rights,
By me invested, he compeers the best.
Gon. That were the most, if he should husband you.
Reg. Jesters do oft prove prophets.
Gon. Holla, holla!
That eye that told you so look'd but a-squint.
Reg. Lady, I am not well; else I should answer
From a full-flowing stomach. General,
Take thou my soldiers, prisoners, patrimony;

Dispose of them, of me; the walls are thine.
Witness the world, that I create thee here
My lord and master.
Gon. Mean you to enjoy him?
Alb. The let-alone lies not in your good will.
Edm. Nor in thine, lord.
Alb. Half-blooded fellow, yes.
Reg. [*To* EDMUND] Let the drum strike, and prove my title thine.
Alb. Stay yet; hear reason. Edmund, I arrest thee
On capital treason; and, in thine attaint,
This gilded serpent [*pointing to* GONERIL]. For your claim, fair sister,
I bar it in the interest of my wife;
'Tis she is sub-contracted to this lord,
And I, her husband, contradict your bans.
If you will marry, make your loves to me,
My lady is bespoke.
Gon. An interlude!
Alb. Thou art arm'd, Gloucester. Let the trumpet sound.
If none appear to prove upon thy head
Thy heinous, manifest, and many treasons,
There is my pledge [*throwing down a glove*]; I'll prove it on thy heart,
Ere I taste bread, thou art in nothing less
Than I have here proclaim'd thee.
Reg. Sick, O, sick!
Gon. [*Aside*] If not, I'll ne'er trust medicine.
Edm. There's my exchange [*throwing down a glove*]. What in the world he is
That names me traitor, villain-like he lies.
Call by thy trumpet; he that dares approach,
On him, on you, who not? I will maintain
My truth and honour firmly.
Alb. A herald, ho!
Edm. A herald, ho, a herald!
Alb. Trust to thy single virtue; for thy soldiers,
All levied in my name, have in my name
Took their discharge.
Reg. My sickness grows upon me.
Alb. She is not well; convey her to my tent.
[*Exit* REGAN, *led.*

Enter a HERALD.

Come hither, herald. Let the trumpet sound,
And read out this.
Capt. Sound, trumpet! [*A trumpet sounds.*

Her. [*Reads*] "If any man of quality or degree within the lists of the army will maintain upon Edmund, supposed Earl of Gloucester, that he is a manifold traitor, let him appear by the third sound of the trumpet. He is bold in his defence."

Edm. Sound! [*First trumpet.*]
Her. Again! [*Second trumpet.*]
Her. Again! [*Third trumpet.*]
Trumpet answers within.

Enter EDGAR, *at the third sound, armed, with a trumpet before him.*

Alb. Ask him his purposes, why he appears
Upon this call o' the trumpet.
Her. What are you?
Your name, your quality? and why you answer
This present summons?
Edg. Know, my name is lost;
By treason's tooth bare-gnawn and canker-bit.
Yet am I noble as the adversary
I come to cope.
Alb. Which is that adversary?
Edg. What's he that speaks for Edmund Earl of Gloucester?
Edm. Himself. What say'st thou to him?
Edg. Draw thy sword,
That, if my speech offend a noble heart,
Thy arm may do thee justice; here is mine.
Behold, it is the privilege of mine honours,
My oath, and my profession. I protest,
Maugre thy strength, youth, place, and eminence,
Despite thy victor sword and fire-new fortune,
Thy valour and thy heart, thou art a traitor;
False to thy gods, thy brother, and thy father;
Conspirant 'gainst this high-illustrious prince;
And, from the extremest upward of thy head
To the descent and dust below thy foot,
A most toad-spotted traitor. Say thou "No,"
This sword, this arm, and my best spirits are bent
To prove upon thy heart, whereto I speak,
Thou liest.
Edm. In wisdom I should ask thy name;
But, since thy outside looks so fair and warlike,
And that thy tongue some say of breeding breathes,
What safe and nicely I might well delay
By rule of knighthood, I disdain and spurn.
Back do I toss these treasons to thy head;
With the hell-hated lie o'erwhelm thy heart;
Which, for they yet glance by and scarcely bruise,
This sword of mine shall give them instant way,
Where they shall rest for ever. Trumpets, speak!
Alarums. They fight. EDMUND *falls.*
Alb. Save him, save him!
Gon. This is practice, Gloucester.
By the law of arms thou wast not bound to answer
An unknown opposite; thou art not vanquish'd,
But cozen'd and beguiled.
Alb. Shut your mouth, dame,

Or with this paper shall I stop it. Hold, sir.
Thou worse than any name, read thine own evil.
No tearing, lady; I perceive you know it.
Gives the letter to EDMUND.
Gon. Say, if I do, the laws are mine, not thine.
Who can arraign me for't?
Alb. Most monstrous! oh!
Know'st thou this paper?
Gon. Ask me not what I know. [*Exit.*
Alb. Go after her. She's desperate; govern her.
Edm. What you have charged me with, that have I done;
And more, much more; the time will bring it out.
'Tis past, and so am I. But what art thou
That hast this fortune on me? If thou'rt noble,
I do forgive thee.
Edg. Let's exchange charity.
I am no less in blood than thou art, Edmund;
If more, the more thou hast wrong'd me.
My name is Edgar, and thy father's son.
The gods are just, and of our pleasant vices
Make instruments to plague us.
The dark and vicious place where thee he got
Cost him his eyes.
Edm. Thou hast spoken right, 'tis true;
The wheel is come full circle; I am here.
Alb. Methought thy very gait did prophesy
A royal nobleness. I must embrace thee.
Let sorrow split my heart, if ever I
Did hate thee or thy father!
Edg. Worthy Prince, I know't.
Alb. Where have you hid yourself?
How have you known the miseries of your father?
Edg. By nursing them, my lord. List a brief tale;
And when 'tis told, O, that my heart would burst!
The bloody proclamation to escape,
That follow'd me so near,—O, our lives' sweetness!
That we the pain of death would hourly die
Rather than die at once!—taught me to shift
Into a madman's rags; to assume a semblance
That very dogs disdain'd; and in this habit
Met I my father with his bleeding rings,
Their precious stones new lost; became his guide,
Led him, begg'd for him, saved him from despair;
Never—O fault!—reveal'd myself unto him,
Until some half-hour past, when I was arm'd.
Not sure, though hoping, of this good success,
I ask'd his blessing, and from first to last
Told him my pilgrimage. But his flaw'd heart,
Alack, too weak the conflict to support!
'Twixt two extremes of passion, joy and grief,
Burst smilingly.
Edm. This speech of yours hath moved me,
And shall perchance do good. But speak you on;
You look as you had something more to say.
Alb. If there be more, more woeful, hold it in;
For I am almost ready to dissolve,
Hearing of this.
Edg. This would have seem'd a period
To such as love not sorrow; but another,
To amplify too much, would make much more,
And top extremity.
Whilst I was big in clamour came there in a man,
Who, having seen me in my worst estate,
Shunn'd my abhorr'd society; but then, finding
Who 'twas that so endured, with his strong arms
He fasten'd on my neck, and bellow'd out
As he'd burst heaven; threw him on my father;
Told the most piteous tale of Lear and him
That ever ear received; which in recounting
His grief grew puissant, and the strings of life
Began to crack. Twice then the trumpets sounded,
And there I left him tranced.
Alb. But who was this?
Edg. Kent, sir, the banish'd Kent; who in disguise
Follow'd his enemy King, and did him service
Improper for a slave.

Enter a GENTLEMAN, *with a bloody knife.*

Gent. Help, help, O, help!
Edg. What kind of help?
Alb. Speak, man.
Edg. What means that bloody knife?
Gent. 'Tis hot, it smokes;
It came even from the heart of—O, she's dead!
Alb. Who dead? speak, man.
Gent. Your lady, sir, your lady. And her sister
By her is poisoned; she hath confess'd it.
Edm. I was contracted to them both. All three
Now marry in an instant.
Edg. Here comes Kent.
Alb. Produce their bodies, be they alive or dead.
This judgment of the heavens, that makes us tremble,
Touches us not with pity. [*Exit* GENTLEMAN.

Enter KENT.

O, is this he?
The time will not allow the compliment
Which very manners urges.
Kent. I am come
To bid my King and master aye good night.
Is he not here?

Alb. Great thing of us forgot!
Speak, Edmund, where's the King? and where's Cordelia?
See'st thou this object, Kent?

The bodies of GONERIL *and* REGAN *are brought in.*

Kent. Alack, why thus?
Edm. Yet Edmund was beloved.
The one the other poison'd for my sake,
And after slew herself.
Alb. Even so. Cover their faces.
Edm. I pant for life. Some good I mean to do,
Despite of mine own nature. Quickly send,
Be brief in it, to the castle; for my writ
Is on the life of Lear and on Cordelia.
Nay, send in time.
Alb. Run, run, O, run!
Edg. To who, my lord? Who hath the office? send
Thy token of reprieve.
Edm. Well thought on. Take my sword,
Give it the captain.
Alb. Haste thee, for thy life. [*Exit* EDGAR.
Edm. He hath commission from thy wife and me
To hang Cordelia in the prison, and
To lay the blame upon her own despair,
That she fordid herself.
Alb. The gods defend her! Bear him hence awhile. [EDMUND *is borne off.*

Re-enter LEAR, *with* CORDELIA *dead in his arms;* EDGAR, CAPTAIN, *and others following.*

Lear. Howl, howl, howl, howl! O, you are men of stones!
Had I your tongues and eyes, I'd use them so
That heaven's vault should crack. She's gone for ever!
I know when one is dead, and when one lives;
She's dead as earth. Lend me a looking-glass;
If that her breath will mist or stain the stone,
Why, then she lives.
Kent. Is this the promised end?
Edg. Or image of that horror?
Alb. Fall, and cease!
Lear. This feather stirs; she lives! if it be so,
It is a chance which does redeem all sorrows
That ever I have felt.
Kent. [*Kneeling*] O my good master!
Lear. Prithee, away.
Edg. 'Tis noble Kent, your friend.
Lear. A plague upon you, murderers, traitors all!
I might have saved her; now she's gone for ever!
Cordelia, Cordelia! stay a little. Ha!
What is't thou say'st. Her voice was ever soft,
Gentle, and low, an excellent thing in woman.
I kill'd the slave that was a-hanging thee.
Capt. 'Tis true, my lords, he did.
Lear. Did I not, fellow?
I have seen the day, with my good biting falchion
I would have made them skip. I am old now,
And these same crosses spoil me. Who are you?
Mine eyes are not o' the best. I'll tell you straight.
Kent. If fortune brag of two she loved and hated,
One of them we behold.
Lear. This is a dull sight. Are you not Kent?
Kent. The same.
Your servant Kent. Where is your servant Caius?
Lear. He's a good fellow, I can tell you that;
He'll strike, and quickly too. He's dead and rotten.
Kent. No, my good lord; I am the very man—
Lear. I'll see that straight.
Kent. That, from your first of difference and decay,
Have follow'd your sad steps.
Lear. You are welcome hither.
Kent. Nor no man else. All's cheerless, dark, and deadly.
Your eldest daughters have fordone themselves,
And desperately are dead.
Lear. Ay, so I think.
Alb. He knows not what he says; and vain it is
That we present us to him.
Edg. Very bootless.

Enter a CAPTAIN.

Capt. Edmund is dead, my lord.
Alb. That's but a trifle here.
You lords and noble friends, know our intent.
What comfort to this great decay may come
Shall be applied. For us, we will resign,
During the life of this old majesty,
To him our absolute power; [*To* EDGAR *and* KENT] you, to your rights;
With boot, and such addition as your honours
Have more than merited. All friends shall taste
The wages of their virtue, and all foes
The cup of their deservings. O, see, see!
Lear. And my poor fool is hang'd! No, no, no life!
Why should a dog, a horse, a rat, have life,
And thou no breath at all? Thou'lt come no more,
Never, never, never, never, never!
Pray you, undo this button. Thank you, sir.
Do you see this? Look on her, look, her lips,
Look there, look there! [*Dies.*
Edg. He faints! My lord, my lord!
Kent. Break, heart; I prithee, break!

Edg. Look up, my lord.
Kent. Vex not his ghost. O, let him pass! he hates him much
That would upon the rack of this tough world
Stretch him out longer.
Edg. He is gone, indeed.
Kent. The wonder is he hath endured so long.
He but usurp'd his life.
Alb. Bear them from hence. Our present business
Is general woe. [*To* KENT *and* EDGAR] Friends of my soul, you twain
Rule in this realm, and the gored state sustain.
Kent. I have a journey, sir, shortly to go;
My master calls me, I must not say no.
Alb. The weight of this sad time we must obey;
Speak what we feel, not what we ought to say.
The oldest hath borne most; we that are young
Shall never see so much, nor live so long.
[*Exeunt, with a dead march.*

MACBETH

DRAMATIS PERSONÆ

DUNCAN, *King of Scotland*
MALCOLM, DONALBAIN — *his sons*
MACBETH, BANQUO — *generals of the King's army*
MACDUFF, LENNOX, ROSS, MENTEITH, ANGUS, CAITHNESS — *noblemen of Scotland*
FLEANCE, *son to Banquo*
SIWARD, *Earl of Northumberland, general of the English forces*
YOUNG SIWARD, *his son*
SEYTON, *an officer attending on Macbeth*
BOY, *son to Macduff*
AN ENGLISH DOCTOR
A SCOTCH DOCTOR
A LORD
A PORTER
AN OLD MAN
A SERGEANT
TWO MESSENGERS
AN ATTENDANT *on Macbeth*
A SERVANT *to Lady Macbeth*
THREE MURDERERS

LADY MACBETH
LADY MACDUFF
A GENTLEWOMAN, *attending on Lady Macbeth*

HECATE
THREE WITCHES
THREE APPARITIONS

NON-SPEAKING: *Lords, Ladies, Officers, Soldiers, Ghosts, and Attendants*

SCENE: *Scotland; England*

ACT I

SCENE I. *A desert place*

Thunder and lightning. Enter THREE WITCHES.

1st Witch. When shall we three meet again
In thunder, lightning, or in rain?
2nd Witch. When the hurlyburly's done,
When the battle's lost and won.
3rd Witch. That will be ere the set of sun.
1st Witch. Where the place?
2nd Witch. Upon the heath.
3rd Witch. There to meet with Macbeth.
1st Witch. I come, Graymalkin!
2nd Witch. Paddock calls.
3rd Witch. Anon.
All. Fair is foul, and foul is fair;
Hover through the fog and filthy air. [*Exeunt.*

SCENE II. *A camp near Forres*

Alarum within. Enter DUNCAN, MALCOLM, DONALBAIN, LENNOX, *with Attendants, meeting a bleeding* SERGEANT.

Dun. What bloody man is that? He can report,
As seemeth by his plight, of the revolt
The newest state.
Mal. This is the sergeant
Who like a good and hardy soldier fought
'Gainst my captivity. Hail, brave friend!
Say to the King the knowledge of the broil
As thou didst leave it.
Ser. Doubtful it stood;
As two spent swimmers that do cling together
And choke their art. The merciless Macdonwald—
Worthy to be a rebel, for to that
The multiplying villanies of nature
Do swarm upon him—from the western isles
Of kerns and gallowglasses is supplied;
And Fortune, on his damned quarrel smiling,
Show'd like a rebel's whore. But all's too weak;
For brave Macbeth—well he deserves that name—
Disdaining Fortune, with his brandish'd steel,
Which smoked with bloody execution,
Like valour's minion carved out his passage
Till he faced the slave;
Which ne'er shook hands, nor bade farewell to him,
Till he unseam'd him from the nave to the chaps,
And fix'd his head upon our battlements.
Dun. O valiant cousin! worthy gentleman!
Ser. As whence the sun 'gins his reflection
Shipwrecking storms and direful thunders break,
So from that spring whence comfort seem'd to come
Discomfort swells. Mark, King of Scotland, mark!
No sooner justice had, with valour arm'd,
Compell'd these skipping kerns to trust their heels,
But the Norweyan lord surveying vantage,
With furbish'd arms and new supplies of men
Began a fresh assault.

Dun. Dismay'd not this
Our captains, Macbeth and Banquo?
Ser. Yes;
As sparrows eagles, or the hare the lion.
If I say sooth, I must report they were
As cannons overcharged with double cracks, so they
Doubly redoubled strokes upon the foe.
Except they meant to bathe in reeking wounds,
Or memorize another Golgotha,
I cannot tell.
But I am faint, my gashes cry for help.
Dun. So well thy words become thee as thy wounds;
They smack of honour both. Go get him surgeons. [*Exit* SERGEANT *attended.*
Who comes here?

Enter ROSS.

Mal. The worthy thane of Ross.
Len. What a haste looks through his eyes! So should he look
That seems to speak things strange.
Ross. God save the King!
Dun. Whence camest thou, worthy thane?
Ross. From Fife, great King;
Where the Norweyan banners flout the sky
And fan our people cold. Norway himself,
With terrible numbers,
Assisted by that most disloyal traitor
The thane of Cawdor, began a dismal conflict;
Till that Bellona's bridegroom, lapp'd in proof,
Confronted him with self-comparisons,
Point against point rebellious, arm 'gainst arm,
Curbing his lavish spirit; and, to conclude,
The victory fell on us.
Dun. Great happiness!
Ross. That now
Sweno, the Norways' king, craves composition;
Nor would we deign him burial of his men
Till he disbursed at Saint Colme's inch
Ten thousand dollars to our general use.
Dun. No more that thane of Cawdor shall deceive
Our bosom interest. Go pronounce his present death,
And with his former title greet Macbeth.
Ross. I'll see it done.
Dun. What he hath lost, noble Macbeth hath won. [*Exeunt.*

SCENE III. *A heath near Forres*

Thunder. Enter the THREE WITCHES.

1st Witch. Where hast thou been, sister?
2nd Witch. Killing swine.
3rd Witch. Sister, where thou?
1st Witch. A sailor's wife had chestnuts in her lap,
And munch'd, and munch'd, and munch'd. "Give me," quoth I.
"Aroint thee, witch!" the rump-fed ronyon cries.
Her husband's to Aleppo gone, master o' the Tiger;
But in a sieve I'll thither sail,
And, like a rat without a tail,
I'll do, I'll do, and I'll do.
2nd Witch. I'll give thee a wind.
1st Witch. Thou 'rt kind.
3rd Witch. And I another.
1st Witch. I myself have all the other,
And the very ports they blow,
All the quarters that they know
I' the shipman's card.
I will drain him dry as hay.
Sleep shall neither night nor day
Hang upon his pent-house lid;
He shall live a man forbid.
Weary se'nnights nine times nine
Shall he dwindle, peak and pine.
Though his bark cannot be lost,
Yet it shall be tempest-tost.
Look what I have.
2nd Witch. Show me, show me.
1st Witch. Here I have a pilot's thumb,
Wreck'd as homeward he did come.
Drum within.
3rd Witch. A drum, a drum!
Macbeth doth come.
All. The weird sisters, hand in hand,
Posters of the sea and land,
Thus do go about, about;
Thrice to thine and thrice to mine
And thrice again, to make up nine.
Peace! the charm's wound up.

Enter MACBETH *and* BANQUO.

Macb. So foul and fair a day I have not seen.
Ban. How far is't call'd to Forres? What are these
So wither'd and so wild in their attire,
That look not like the inhabitants o' the earth,
And yet are on't? Live you? or are you aught
That man may question? You seem to understand me,
By each at once her choppy finger laying
Upon her skinny lips. You should be women,
And yet your beards forbid me to interpret
That you are so.
Macb. Speak, if you can. What are you?
1st Witch. All hail, Macbeth! hail to thee, thane of Glamis!

2nd Witch. All hail, Macbeth! hail to thee, thane of Cawdor!
3rd Witch. All hail, Macbeth, that shalt be King hereafter!
Ban. Good sir, why do you start, and seem to fear
Things that do sound so fair? I' the name of truth,
Are ye fantastical, or that indeed
Which outwardly ye show? My noble partner
You greet with present grace and great prediction
Of noble having and of royal hope,
That he seems rapt withal. To me you speak not.
If you can look into the seeds of time,
And say which grain will grow and which will not,
Speak then to me, who neither beg nor fear
Your favours nor your hate.
1st Witch. Hail!
2nd Witch. Hail!
3rd Witch. Hail!
1st Witch. Lesser than Macbeth, and greater.
2nd Witch. Not so happy, yet much happier.
3rd Witch. Thou shalt get kings, though thou be none.
So all hail, Macbeth and Banquo!
1st Witch. Banquo and Macbeth, all hail!
Macb. Stay, you imperfect speakers, tell me more.
By Sinel's death I know I am thane of Glamis;
But how of Cawdor? the thane of Cawdor lives,
A prosperous gentleman; and to be king
Stands not within the prospect of belief,
No more than to be Cawdor. Say from whence
You owe this strange intelligence? or why
Upon this blasted heath you stop our way
With such prophetic greeting? Speak, I charge you. [WITCHES *vanish*.
Ban. The earth hath bubbles, as the water has,
And these are of them. Whither are they vanish'd?
Macb. Into the air; and what seem'd corporal melted
As breath into the wind. Would they had stay'd!
Ban. Were such things here as we do speak about?
Or have we eaten on the insane root
That takes the reason prisoner?
Macb. Your children shall be kings.
Ban. You shall be King.
Macb. And thane of Cawdor too; went it not so?
Ban. To the selfsame tune and words. Who's here?

Enter ROSS *and* ANGUS.

Ross. The King hath happily received, Macbeth,
The news of thy success; and when he reads
Thy personal venture in the rebels' fight,
His wonders and his praises do contend
Which should be thine or his. Silenced with that,
In viewing o'er the rest o' the selfsame day,
He finds thee in the stout Norweyan ranks,
Nothing afeard of what thyself didst make,
Strange images of death. As thick as hail
Came post with post; and every one did bear
Thy praises in his kingdom's great defence,
And pour'd them down before him.
Ang. We are sent
To give thee from our royal master thanks;
Only to herald thee into his sight,
Not pay thee.
Ross. And, for an earnest of a greater honour,
He bade me, from him, call thee thane of Cawdor;
In which addition, hail, most worthy thane!
For it is thine.
Ban. What, can the devil speak true?
Macb. The thane of Cawdor lives. Why do you dress me
In borrow'd robes?
Ang. Who was the thane lives yet;
But under heavy judgement bears that life
Which he deserves to lose. Whether he was combined
With those of Norway, or did line the rebel
With hidden help and vantage, or that with both
He labour'd in his country's wreck, I know not;
But treasons capital, confess'd, and proved,
Have overthrown him.
Macb. [*Aside*] Glamis, and thane of Cawdor!
The greatest is behind. [*To* ROSS *and* ANGUS] Thanks for your pains.
[*To* BANQUO] Do you not hope your children shall be kings,
When those that gave the thane of Cawdor to me
Promised no less to them?
Ban. That trusted home
Might yet enkindle you unto the crown,
Besides the thane of Cawdor. But 'tis strange;
And oftentimes, to win us to our harm,
The instruments of darkness tell us truths,
Win us with honest trifles, to betray's
In deepest consequence.
Cousins, a word, I pray you.
Macb. [*Aside*] Two truths are told,
As happy prologues to the swelling act
Of the imperial theme.—I thank you, gentlemen.
[*Aside*] This supernatural soliciting
Cannot be ill, cannot be good. If ill,

Why hath it given me earnest of success,
Commencing in a truth? I am thane of Cawdor.
If good, why do I yield to that suggestion
Whose horrid image doth unfix my hair
And make my seated heart knock at my ribs,
Against the use of nature? Present fears
Are less than horrible imaginings.
My thought, whose murder yet is but fantastical,
Shakes so my single state of man that function
Is smother'd in surmise, and nothing is
But what is not.

Ban. Look, how our partner's rapt.

Macb. [*Aside*] If chance will have me King, why, chance may crown me
Without my stir.

Ban. New honours come upon him,
Like our strange garments, cleave not to their mould
But with the aid of use.

Macb. [*Aside*] Come what come may,
Time and the hour runs through the roughest day.

Ban. Worthy Macbeth, we stay upon your leisure.

Macb. Give me your favour. My dull brain was wrought
With things forgotten. Kind gentlemen, your pains
Are register'd where every day I turn
The leaf to read them. Let us toward the King.
[*To* BANQUO] Think upon what hath chanced, and, at more time,
The interim having weigh'd it, let us speak
Our free hearts each to other.

Ban. Very gladly.

Macb. Till then, enough. Come, friends.

[*Exeunt.*

SCENE IV. *Forres: the palace*

Flourish. Enter DUNCAN, MALCOLM, DONALBAIN, LENNOX, *and Attendants.*

Dun. Is execution done on Cawdor? Are not
Those in commission yet return'd?

Mal. My liege,
They are not yet come back. But I have spoke
With one that saw him die; who did report
That very frankly he confess'd his treasons,
Implor'd your Highness' pardon, and set forth
A deep repentance. Nothing in his life
Became him like the leaving it; he died
As one that had been studied in his death
To throw away the dearest thing he owed,
As 'twere a careless trifle.

Dun. There's no art
To find the mind's construction in the face.
He was a gentleman on whom I built
An absolute trust.

Enter MACBETH, BANQUO, ROSS, *and* ANGUS.

O worthiest cousin!
The sin of my ingratitude even now
Was heavy on me. Thou art so far before
That swiftest wing of recompense is slow
To overtake thee. Would thou hadst less deserved,
That the proportion both of thanks and payment
Might have been mine! only I have left to say,
More is thy due than more than all can pay.

Macb. The service and the loyalty I owe,
In doing it, pays itself. Your Highness' part
Is to receive our duties; and our duties
Are to your throne and state children and servants,
Which do but what they should, by doing everything
Safe toward your love and honour.

Dun. Welcome hither.
I have begun to plant thee, and will labour
To make thee full of growing. Noble Banquo,
That hast no less deserved, nor must be known
No less to have done so, let me infold thee
And hold thee to my heart.

Ban. There if I grow,
The harvest is your own.

Dun. My plenteous joys,
Wanton in fulness, seek to hide themselves
In drops of sorrow. Sons, kinsmen, thanes,
And you whose places are the nearest, know
We will establish our estate upon
Our eldest, Malcolm, whom we name hereafter
The Prince of Cumberland; which honour must
Not unaccompanied invest him only,
But signs of nobleness, like stars, shall shine
On all deservers. From hence to Inverness,
And bind us further to you.

Macb. The rest is labour, which is not used for you.
I'll be myself the harbinger and make joyful
The hearing of my wife with your approach;
So humbly take my leave.

Dun. My worthy Cawdor!

Macb. [*Aside*] The Prince of Cumberland! that is a step
On which I must fall down, or else o'erleap,
For in my way it lies. Stars, hide your fires;
Let not light see my black and deep desires;
The eye wink at the hand; yet let that be
Which the eye fears, when it is done, to see.

[*Exit.*

Dun. True, worthy Banquo; he is full so valiant,
And in his commendations I am fed;
It is a banquet to me. Let's after him,
Whose care is gone before to bid us welcome.

It is a peerless kinsman. [*Flourish. Exeunt.*

SCENE V. *Inverness: Macbeth's castle*

Enter LADY MACBETH, *reading a letter.*

Lady M. "They met me in the day of success; and I have learned by the perfectest report, they have more in them than mortal knowledge. When I burned in desire to question them further, they made themselves air, into which they vanished. Whiles I stood rapt in the wonder of it, came missives from the King, who all-hailed me 'Thane of Cawdor'; by which title, before, these weird sisters saluted me, and referred me to the coming on of time with 'Hail, King that shalt be!' This have I thought good to deliver thee, my dearest partner of greatness, that thou mightst not lose the dues of rejoicing by being ignorant of what greatness is promised thee. Lay it to thy heart, and farewell."

Glamis thou art, and Cawdor; and shalt be
What thou art promised. Yet do I fear thy nature;
It is too full o' the milk of human kindness
To catch the nearest way. Thou wouldst be great;
Art not without ambition, but without
The illness should attend it. What thou wouldst highly,
That wouldst thou holily; wouldst not play false,
And yet wouldst wrongly win. Thou'dst have, great Glamis,
That which cries "Thus thou must do, if thou have it;
And that which rather thou dost fear to do
Than wishest should be undone." Hie thee hither,
That I may pour my spirits in thine ear;
And chastise with the valour of my tongue
All that impedes thee from the golden round,
Which fate and metaphysical aid doth seem
To have thee crown'd withal.

Enter a MESSENGER.

What is your tidings?

Mess. The King comes here to-night.

Lady M. Thou'rt mad to say it!
Is not thy master with him? who, were't so,
Would have inform'd for preparation.

Mess. So please you, it is true; our thane is coming.
One of my fellows had the speed of him,
Who, almost dead for breath, had scarcely more
Than would make up his message.

Lady M. Give him tending;
He brings great news. [*Exit* MESSENGER.
The raven himself is hoarse
That croaks the fatal entrance of Duncan
Under my battlements. Come, you spirits
That tend on mortal thoughts, unsex me here,
And fill me from the crown to the toe top-full
Of direst cruelty! make thick my blood;
Stop up the access and passage to remorse.
That no compunctious visitings of nature
Shake my fell purpose, nor keep peace between
The effect and it! Come to my woman's breasts,
And take my milk for gall, you murdering ministers,
Wherever in your sightless substances
You wait on nature's mischief! Come, thick night,
And pall thee in the dunnest smoke of hell,
That my keen knife see not the wound it makes,
Nor heaven peep through the blanket of the dark,
To cry, "Hold, hold!"

Enter MACBETH.

Great Glamis! worthy Cawdor!
Greater than both, by the all-hail hereafter!
Thy letters have transported me beyond
This ignorant present, and I feel now
The future in the instant.

Macb. My dearest love,
Duncan comes here to-night.

Lady M. And when goes hence?

Macb. To-morrow, as he purposes.

Lady M. O, never
Shall sun that morrow see!
Your face, my thane, is as a book where men
May read strange matters. To beguile the time,
Look like the time; bear welcome in your eye,
Your hand, your tongue; look like the innocent flower,
But be the serpent under't. He that's coming
Must be provided for; and you shall put
This night's great business into my dispatch;
Which shall to all our nights and days to come
Give solely sovereign sway and masterdom.

Macb. We will speak further.

Lady M. Only look up clear;
To alter favour ever is to fear.
Leave all the rest to me. [*Exeunt.*

SCENE VI. *Before Macbeth's castle*

Hautboys and torches. Enter DUNCAN, MALCOLM, DONALBAIN, BANQUO, LENNOX, MACDUFF, ROSS, ANGUS, *and Attendants.*

Dun. This castle hath a pleasant seat; the air
Nimbly and sweetly recommends itself
Unto our gentle senses.

Ban. This guest of summer,
The temple-haunting martlet, does approve,
By his loved mansionry, that the heaven's breath
Smells wooingly here; no jutty, frieze,

Buttress, nor coign of vantage, but this bird
Hath made his pendent bed and procreant cradle.
Where they most breed and haunt, I have observed,
The air is delicate.

Enter LADY MACBETH.

Dun. See, see, our honour'd hostess!
The love that follows us sometime is our trouble,
Which still we thank as love. Herein I teach you
How you shall bid God 'ild us for your pains,
And thank us for your trouble.

Lady M. All our service
In every point twice done and then done double
Were poor and single business to contend
Against those honours deep and broad wherewith
Your Majesty loads our house. For those of old,
And the late dignities heap'd up to them,
We rest your hermits.

Dun. Where's the thane of Cawdor?
We coursed him at the heels, and had a purpose
To be his purveyor; but he rides well,
And his great love, sharp as his spur, hath holp him
To his home before us. Fair and noble hostess,
We are your guest to-night.

Lady M. Your servants ever
Have theirs, themselves, and what is theirs, in compt,
To make their audit at your Highness' pleasure,
Still to return your own.

Dun. Give me your hand;
Conduct me to mine host. We love him highly,
And shall continue our graces towards him.
By your leave, hostess. [*Exeunt.*

SCENE VII. *Macbeth's castle*

Hautboys and torches. Enter a SEWER, *and divers Servants with dishes and service, and pass over the stage. Then enter* MACBETH.

Macb. If it were done when 'tis done, then 'twere well
It were done quickly. If the assassination
Could trammel up the consequence, and catch
With his surcease success; that but this blow
Might be the be-all and the end-all here,
But here, upon this bank and shoal of time,
We'd jump the life to come. But in these cases
We still have judgement here; that we but teach
Bloody instructions, which, being taught, return
To plague the inventor. This even-handed justice
Commends the ingredients of our poison'd chalice
To our own lips. He's here in double trust;
First, as I am his kinsman and his subject,
Strong both against the deed; then, as his host,
Who should against his murderer shut the door,
Not bear the knife myself. Besides, this Duncan
Hath borne his faculties so meek, hath been
So clear in his great office, that his virtues
Will plead like angels, trumpet-tongued, against
The deep damnation of his taking-off;
And pity, like a naked new-born babe,
Striding the blast, or heaven's cherubim, horsed
Upon the sightless couriers of the air,
Shall blow the horrid deed in every eye,
That tears shall drown the wind. I have no spur
To prick the sides of my intent, but only
Vaulting ambition, which o'erleaps itself
And falls on the other.

Enter LADY MACBETH.

How now! what news?

Lady M. He has almost supp'd. Why have you left the chamber?

Macb. Hath he ask'd for me?

Lady M. Know you not he has?

Macb. We will proceed no further in this business.
He hath honour'd me of late; and I have bought
Golden opinions from all sorts of people,
Which would be worn now in their newest gloss,
Not cast aside so soon.

Lady M. Was the hope drunk
Wherein you dress'd yourself? Hath it slept since?
And wakes it now, to look so green and pale
At what it did so freely? From this time
Such I account thy love. Art thou afeard
To be the same in thine own act and valour
As thou art in desire? Wouldst thou have that
Which thou esteem'st the ornament of life,
And live a coward in thine own esteem,
Letting "I dare not" wait upon "I would,"
Like the poor cat i' the adage?

Macb. Prithee, peace.
I dare do all that may become a man;
Who dares do more is none.

Lady M. What beast was't, then,
That made you break this enterprise to me?
When you durst do it, then you were a man;
And, to be more than what you were, you would
Be so much more the man. Nor time nor place
Did then adhere, and yet you would make both.
They have made themselves, and that their fitness now
Does unmake you. I have given suck, and know
How tender 'tis to love the babe that milks me;
I would, while it was smiling in my face,
Have pluck'd my nipple from his boneless gums

And dash'd the brains out, had I so sworn as you
Have done to this.

Macb. If we should fail?

Lady M. We fail!
But screw your courage to the sticking-place,
And we'll not fail. When Duncan is asleep—
Whereto the rather shall his day's hard journey
Soundly invite him—his two chamberlains
Will I with wine and wassail so convince
That memory, the warder of the brain,
Shall be a fume, and the receipt of reason
A limbeck only. When in swinish sleep
Their drenched natures lie as in a death,
What cannot you and I perform upon
The unguarded Duncan? what not put upon
His spongy officers, who shall bear the guilt
Of our great quell?

Macb. Bring forth men-children only;
For thy undaunted mettle should compose
Nothing but males. Will it not be received,
When we have mark'd with blood those sleepy two
Of his own chamber and used their very daggers,
That they have done 't?

Lady M. Who dares receive it other,
As we shall make our griefs and clamour roar
Upon his death?

Macb. I am settled, and bend up
Each corporal agent to this terrible feat.
Away, and mock the time with fairest show;
False face must hide what the false heart doth know [*Exeunt.*

ACT II

SCENE I. *Court of Macbeth's castle*

Enter BANQUO, *and* FLEANCE *bearing a torch before him.*

Ban. How goes the night, boy?

Fle. The moon is down; I have not heard the clock.

Ban. And she goes down at twelve.

Fle. I take't, 'tis later, sir.

Ban. Hold, take my sword. There's husbandry in heaven;
Their candles are all out. Take thee that too.
A heavy summons lies like lead upon me,
And yet I would not sleep. Merciful powers,
Restrain in me the cursed thoughts that nature
Gives way to in repose!

Enter MACBETH, *and a Servant with a torch.*

Give me my sword.
Who's there?

Macb. A friend.

Ban. What, sir, not yet at rest? The King's a-bed.
He hath been in unusual pleasure, and
Sent forth great largess to your offices.
This diamond he greets your wife withal,
By the name of most kind hostess; and shut up
In measureless content.

Macb. Being unprepared,
Our will became the servant to defect;
Which else should free have wrought.

Ban. All's well.
I dreamt last night of the three weird sisters.
To you they have show'd some truth.

Macb. I think not of them:
Yet, when we can entreat an hour to serve,
We would spend it in some words upon that business,
If you would grant the time.

Ban. At your kind'st leisure.

Macb. If you shall cleave to my consent, when 'tis,
It shall make honour for you.

Ban. So I lose none
In seeking to augment it, but still keep
My bosom franchised and allegiance clear,
I shall be counsell'd.

Macb. Good repose the while!

Ban. Thanks, sir; the like to you!
[*Exeunt* BANQUO *and* FLEANCE.

Macb. Go bid thy mistress, when my drink is ready,
She strike upon the bell. Get thee to bed.
[*Exit Servant.*
Is this a dagger which I see before me,
The handle toward my hand? Come, let me clutch thee.
I have thee not, and yet I see thee still.
Art thou not, fatal vision, sensible
To feeling as to sight? or art thou but
A dagger of the mind, a false creation,
Proceeding from the heat-oppressed brain?
I see thee yet, in form as palpable
As this which now I draw.
Thou marshall'st me the way that I was going;
And such an instrument I was to use.
Mine eyes are made the fools o' the other senses,
Or else worth all the rest; I see thee still,
And on thy blade and dudgeon gouts of blood,
Which was not so before. There's no such thing.
It is the bloody business which informs
Thus to mine eyes. Now o'er the one half-world
Nature seems dead, and wicked dreams abuse
The curtain'd sleep; witchcraft celebrates
Pale Hecate's offerings, and wither'd murder,
Alarum'd by his sentinel, the wolf,

Whose howl's his watch, thus with his stealthy pace,
With Tarquin's ravishing strides, towards his design
Moves like a ghost. Thou sure and firm-set earth,
Hear not my steps, which way they walk, for fear
Thy very stones prate of my whereabout,
And take the present horror from the time,
Which now suits with it. Whiles I threat, he lives:
Words to the heat of deeds too cold breath gives.
A bell rings.
I go, and it is done; the bell invites me.
Hear it not, Duncan; for it is a knell
That summons thee to heaven or to hell. [*Exit.*

SCENE II. *The same*

Enter LADY MACBETH.

Lady M. That which hath made them drunk hath made me bold;
What hath quench'd them hath given me fire. Hark! Peace!
It was the owl that shriek'd, the fatal bellman,
Which gives the stern'st good-night. He is about it.
The doors are open, and the surfeited grooms
Do mock their charge with snores. I have drugg'd their possets,
That death and nature do contend about them,
Whether they live or die.
Macb. [*Within*] Who's there? what, ho!
Lady M. Alack, I am afraid they have awaked,
And 'tis not done. The attempt and not the deed
Confounds us. Hark! I laid their daggers ready;
He could not miss 'em. Had he not resembled
My father as he slept, I had done 't.

Enter MACBETH.

My husband!
Macb. I have done the deed. Didst thou not hear a noise?
Lady M. I heard the owl scream and the crickets cry.
Did not you speak?
Macb. When?
Lady M. Now.
Macb. As I descended?
Lady M. Ay.
Macb. Hark!
Who lies i' the second chamber?
Lady M. Donalbain.
Macb. This is a sorry sight.
Looking on his hands.
Lady M. A foolish thought, to say a sorry sight.
Macb. There's one did laugh in's sleep, and one cried "Murder!"
That they did wake each other. I stood and heard them;
But they did say their prayers, and address'd them
Again to sleep.
Lady M. There are two lodged together.
Macb. One cried "God bless us!" and "Amen" the other;
As they had seen me with these hangman's hands.
Listening their fear, I could not say "Amen,"
When they did say "God bless us!"
Lady M. Consider it not so deeply.
Macb. But wherefore could not I pronounce "Amen"?
I had most need of blessing, and "Amen"
Stuck in my throat
Lady M. These deeds must not be thought
After these ways; so, it will make us mad.
Macb. Methought I heard a voice cry, "Sleep no more!
Macbeth does murder sleep," the innocent sleep,
Sleep that knits up the ravell'd sleave of care,
The death of each day's life, sore labour's bath,
Balm of hurt minds, great nature's second course,
Chief nourisher in life's feast—
Lady M. What do you mean?
Macb. Still it cried, "Sleep no more!" to all the house;
"Glamis hath murder'd sleep, and therefore Cawdor
Shall sleep no more; Macbeth shall sleep no more."
Lady M. Who was it that thus cried? Why, worthy thane,
You do unbend your noble strength, to think
So brainsickly of things. Go get some water,
And wash this filthy witness from your hand.
Why did you bring these daggers from the place?
They must lie there. Go carry them; and smear
The sleepy grooms with blood.
Macb. I'll go no more.
I am afraid to think what I have done;
Look on 't again I dare not.
Lady M. Infirm of purpose!
Give me the daggers. The sleeping and the dead
Are but as pictures; tis the eye of childhood
That fears a painted devil. If he do bleed,
I'll gild the faces of the grooms withal;
For it must seem their guilt.
[*Exit. Knocking within.*
Macb. Whence is that knocking?
How is't with me, when every noise appals me?
What hands are here? ha! they pluck out mine eyes.

Will all great Neptune's ocean wash this blood
Clean from my hand? No, this my hand will rather
The multitudinous seas incarnadine,
Making the green one red.

Re-enter LADY MACBETH.

Lady M. My hands are of your colour; but I shame
To wear a heart so white. [*Knocking within.*] I hear a knocking
At the south entry. Retire we to our chamber.
A little water clears us of this deed;
How easy is it, then! Your constancy
Hath left you unattended. [*Knocking within.*]
Hark! more knocking.
Get on your nightgown, lest occasion call us,
And show us to be watchers. Be not lost
So poorly in your thoughts.

Macb. To know my deed, 'twere best not know myself. [*Knocking within.*
Wake Duncan with thy knocking! I would thou couldst! [*Exeunt.*

SCENE III. *The same*

Knocking within. Enter a PORTER.

Porter. Here's a knocking indeed! If a man were porter of hell-gate, he should have old turning the key. [*Knocking within.*] Knock, knock, knock! Who's there, i' the name of Beelzebub? Here's a farmer, that hanged himself on the expectation of plenty. Come in time; have napkins enow about you; here you'll sweat for't, [*Knocking within.*] Knock, knock! Who's there, in the other devil's name? Faith, here's an equivocator, that could swear in both the scales against either scale; who committed treason enough for God's sake, yet could not equivocate to heaven. O, come in, equivocator. [*Knocking within.*] Knock, knock, knock! Who's there? Faith, here's an English tailor come hither for stealing out of a French hose. Come in, tailor; here you may roast your goose. [*Knocking within.*] Knock, knock; never at quiet! What are you? But this place is too cold for hell. I'll devil-porter it no further. I had thought to have let in some of all professions that go the primrose way to the everlasting bonfire. [*Knocking within.*] Anon, anon! I pray you, remember the porter.
Opens the gate.

Enter MACDUFF *and* LENNOX.

Macd. Was it so late, friend, ere you went to bed,
That you do lie so late?

Port. 'Faith, sir, we were carousing till the second cock. And drink, sir, is a great provoker of three things.

Macd. What three things does drink especially provoke?

Port. Marry, sir, nose-painting, sleep, and urine. Lechery, sir, it provokes, and unprovokes; it provokes the desire but it takes away the performance; therefore, much drink may be said to be an equivocator with lechery: it makes him, and it mars him; it sets him on, and it takes him off; it persuades him, and disheartens him; makes him stand to, and not stand to; in conclusion, equivocates him in a sleep, and, giving him the lie, leaves him.

Macd. I believe drink gave thee the lie last night.

Port. That it did, sir, i' the very throat on me. But I requited him for his lie; and, I think, being too strong for him, though he took up my legs sometime, yet I made a shift to cast him.

Macd. Is thy master stirring?

Enter MACBETH.

Our knocking has awakened him; here he comes.

Len. Good morrow, noble sir.

Macb. Good morrow, both.

Macd. Is the King stirring, worthy thane?

Macb. Not yet.

Macd. He did command me to call timely on him.
I have almost slipp'd the hour.

Macb. I'll bring you to him.

Macd. I know this is a joyful trouble to you;
But yet 'tis one.

Macb. The labour we delight in physics pain.
This is the door.

Macd. I'll make so bold to call,
For 'tis my limited service. [*Exit.*

Len. Goes the King hence to-day?

Macb. He does; he did appoint so.

Len. The night has been unruly. Where we lay,
Our chimneys were blown down; and, as they say,
Lamentings heard i' the air; strange screams of death,
And prophesying with accents terrible
Of dire combustion and confused events
New hatch'd to the woeful time. The obscure bird
Clamour'd the livelong night; some say, the earth
Was feverous and did shake,

Macb. 'Twas a rough night.

Len. My young remembrance cannot parallel
A fellow to it.

Re-enter MACDUFF.

Macd. O horror, horror, horror! Tongue nor heart
Cannot conceive nor name thee.
Macb.
Len. } What's the matter?
Macd. Confusion now hath made his masterpiece!
Most sacrilegious murder hath broke ope
The Lord's anointed temple, and stole thence
The life o' the building!
Macb. What is't you say? the life?
Len. Mean you his Majesty?
Macd. Approach the chamber, and destroy your sight
With a new Gorgon. Do not bid me speak;
See, and then speak yourselves.
[*Exeunt* MACBETH *and* LENNOX.
Awake, awake!
Ring the alarum-bell. Murder and treason!
Banquo and Donalbain! Malcolm! awake!
Shake off this downy sleep, death's counterfeit,
And look on death itself! Up, up, and see
The great doom's image! Malcolm! Banquo!
As from your graves rise up, and walk like sprites,
To countenance this horror! Ring the bell.
Bell rings.

Enter LADY MACBETH.

Lady M. What's the business,
That such a hideous trumpet calls to parley
The sleepers of the house? Speak, speak!
Macd. O gentle lady,
'Tis not for you to hear what I can speak.
The repetition, in a woman's ear,
Would murder as it fell.

Enter BANQUO.

O Banquo, Banquo,
Our royal master's murder'd!
Lady M. Woe, alas!
What, in our house?
Ban. Too cruel anywhere.
Dear Duff, I prithee, contradict thyself,
And say it is not so.

Re-enter MACBETH *and* LENNOX, *with* ROSS.

Macb. Had I but died an hour before this chance,
I had lived a blessed time; for, from this instant,
There's nothing serious in mortality;
All is but toys. Renown and grace is dead;
The wine of life is drawn, and the mere lees
Is left this vault to brag of.

Enter MALCOLM *and* DONALBAIN.

Don. What is amiss?
Macb. You are, and do not know't.
The spring, the head, the fountain of your blood
Is stopp'd; the very source of it is stopp'd.
Macd. Your royal father's murder'd.
Mal. O, by whom?
Len. Those of his chamber, as it seem'd, had done't.
Their hands and faces were all badged with blood;
So were their daggers, which unwiped we found
Upon their pillows.
They stared, and were distracted; no man's life
Was to be trusted with them.
Macb. O, yet I do repent me of my fury,
That I did kill them.
Macd. Wherefore did you so?
Macb. Who can be wise, amazed, temperate and furious,
Loyal and neutral, in a moment? No man.
The expedition of my violent love
Outrun the pauser, reason. Here lay Duncan,
His silver skin laced with his golden blood;
And his gash'd stabs look'd like a breach in nature
For ruin's wasteful entrance; there, the murderers,
Steep'd in the colours of their trade, their daggers
Unmannerly breech'd with gore. Who could refrain,
That had a heart to love, and in that heart
Courage to make 's love known?
Lady M. Help me hence, ho!
Macd. Look to the lady.
Mal. [*Aside to* DONALBAIN] Why do we hold our tongues,
That most may claim this argument for ours?
Don. [*Aside to* MALCOLM] What should be spoken here, where our fate,
Hid in an auger-hole, may rush, and seize us?
Let's away;
Our tears are not yet brew'd.
Mal. [*Aside to* DONALBAIN] Nor our strong sorrow
Upon the foot of motion.
Ban. Look to the lady;
[*Lady* MACBETH *is carried out*.
And when we have our naked frailties hid,
That suffer in exposure, let us meet
And question this most bloody piece of work,
To know it further. Fears and scruples shake us.
In the great hand of God I stand; and thence
Against the undivulged pretence I fight
Of treasonous malice.
Macd. And so do I.
All. So all.
Macb. Let's briefly put on manly readiness,
And meet i' the hall together.
All. Well contented.

[*Exeunt all but* MALCOLM *and* DONALBAIN.

Mal. What will you do? Let's not consort with them;
To show an unfelt sorrow is an office
Which the false man does easy. I'll to England.
Don. To Ireland, I; our separated fortune
Shall keep us both the safer. Where we are,
There's daggers in men's smiles; the near in blood,
The nearer bloody.
Mal. This murderous shaft that's shot
Hath not yet lighted, and our safest way
Is to avoid the aim. Therefore, to horse;
And let us not be dainty of leave-taking,
But shift away. There's warrant in that theft
Which steals itself, when there's no mercy left.
[*Exeunt*.

SCENE IV. *Outside Macbeth's castle*

Enter ROSS *and an* OLD MAN.

Old M. Threescore and ten I can remember well;
Within the volume of which time I have seen
Hours dreadful and things strange; but this sore night
Hath trifled former knowings.
Ross. Ah, good father,
Thou seest, the heavens, as troubled with man's act,
Threaten his bloody stage. By the clock, 'tis day,
And yet dark night strangles the travelling lamp.
Is't night's predominance, or the day's shame,
That darkness does the face of earth entomb,
When living light should kiss it?
Old M. 'Tis unnatural,
Even like the deed that's done. On Tuesday last,
A falcon, towering in her pride of place,
Was by a mousing owl hawk'd at and kill'd.
Ross. And Duncan's horses—a thing most strange and certain—
Beauteous and swift, the minions of their race,
Turn'd wild in nature, broke their stalls, flung out,
Contending 'gainst obedience, as they would make
War with mankind.
Old M. 'Tis said they eat each other.
Ross. They did so, to the amazement of mine eyes
That look'd upon't. Here comes the good Macduff.

Enter MACDUFF.

How goes the world, sir, now?
Macd. Why, see you not?
Ross. Is't known who did this more than bloody deed?
Macd. Those that Macbeth hath slain.
Ross. Alas, the day!
What good could they pretend?
Macd. They were suborn'd.
Malcolm and Donalbain, the King's two sons,
Are stol'n away and fled; which puts upon them
Suspicion of the deed.
Ross. 'Gainst nature still!
Thriftless ambition, that wilt ravin up
Thine own life's means! Then 'tis most like
The sovereignty will fall upon Macbeth.
Macd. He is already named, and gone to Scone
To be invested.
Ross. Where is Duncan's body?
Macd. Carried to Colmekill,
The sacred storehouse of his predecessors,
And guardian of their bones.
Ross. Will you to Scone?
Macd. No, cousin, I'll to Fife.
Ross. Well, I will thither.
Macd. Well, may you see things well done there, adieu!
Lest our old robes sit easier than our new!
Ross. Farewell, father.
Old M. God's benison go with you; and with those
That would make good of bad, and friends of foes!
[*Exeunt*.

ACT III

SCENE I. *Forres: the palace*

Enter BANQUO.

Ban. Thou hast it now: King, Cawdor, Glamis, all,
As the weird women promised, and, I fear,
Thou play'dst most foully for't; yet it was said
It should not stand in thy posterity,
But that myself should be the root and father
Of many kings. If there come truth from them—
As upon thee, Macbeth, their speeches shine—
Why, by the verities on thee made good,
May they not be my oracles as well,
And set me up in hope? But hush! no more.

Sennet sounded. Enter MACBETH, *as King*, LADY MACBETH, *as Queen*, LENNOX, ROSS, *Lords, Ladies, and Attendants*.

Macb. Here's our chief guest.
Lady M. If he had been forgotten,
It had been as a gap in our great feast,
And all-thing unbecoming.
Macb. To-night we hold a solemn supper, sir,
And I'll request your presence.

Ban. Let your Highness
Command upon me; to the which my duties
Are with a most indissoluble tie
For ever knit.
Macb. Ride you this afternoon?
Ban. Ay, my good lord.
Macb. We should have else desired your good advice,
Which still hath been both grave and prosperous,
In this day's council; but we'll take to-morrow.
Is't far you ride?
Ban. As far, my lord, as will fill up the time
'Twixt this and supper. Go not my horse the better,
I must become a borrower of the night
For a dark hour or twain.
Macb. Fail not our feast.
Ban. My lord, I will not.
Macb. We hear, our bloody cousins are bestow'd
In England and in Ireland, not confessing
Their cruel parricide, filling their hearers
With strange invention. But of that to-morrow,
When therewithal we shall have cause of state
Craving us jointly. Hie you to horse; adieu,
Till you return at night. Goes Fleance with you?
Ban. Ay, my good lord. Our time does call upon 's.
Macb. I wish your horses swift and sure of foot;
And so I do commend you to their backs.
Farewell. [*Exit* BANQUO.
Let every man be master of his time
Till seven at night. To make society
The sweeter welcome, we will keep ourself
Till supper-time alone; while then, God be with you!
[*Exeunt all but* MACBETH, *and an* ATTENDANT.
Sirrah, a word with you. Attend those men
Our pleasure?
Atten. They are, my lord, without the palace gate.
Macb. Bring them before us. [*Exit* ATTENDANT.
To be thus is nothing;
But to be safely thus. Our fears in Banquo
Stick deep; and in his royalty of nature
Reigns that which would be fear'd. 'Tis much he dares;
And, to that dauntless temper of his mind,
He hath a wisdom that doth guide his valour
To act in safety. There is none but he
Whose being I do fear; and, under him,
My Genius is rebuked, as, it is said,
Mark Antony's was by Cæsar. He chid the sisters
When first they put the name of king upon me,
And bade them speak to him; then prophet-like
They hail'd him father to a line of kings;
Upon my head they placed a fruitless crown,
And put a barren sceptre in my gripe,
Thence to be wrench'd with an unlineal hand,
No son of mine succeeding. If't be so,
For Banquo's issue have I filed my mind;
For them the gracious Duncan have I murder'd;
Put rancours in the vessel of my peace
Only for them; and mine eternal jewel
Given to the common enemy of man,
To make them kings, the seed of Banquo Kings!
Rather than so, come fate into the list,
And champion me to the utterance! Who's there?
Re-enter Attendant, with TWO MURDERERS.
Now go to the door, and stay there till we call.
[*Exit Attendant.*
Was it not yesterday we spoke together?
1st Mur. It was, so please your Highness.
Macb. Well then, now
Have you consider'd of my speeches? Know
That it was he in the times past which held you
So under fortune, which you thought had been
Our innocent self. This I made good to you
In our last conference, pass'd in probation with you,
How you were borne in hand, how cross'd, the instruments,
Who wrought with them, and all things else that might
To half a soul and to a notion crazed
Say "Thus did Banquo."
1st Mur. You made it known to us.
Macb. I did so, and went further, which is now
Our point of second meeting. Do you find
Your patience so predominant in your nature
That you can let this go? Are you so gospell'd
To pray for this good man and for his issue,
Whose heavy hand hath bow'd you to the grave
And beggar'd yours for ever?
1st Mur. We are men, my liege.
Macb. Ay, in the catalogue ye go for men;
As hounds and greyhounds, mongrels, spaniels, curs,
Shoughs, water-rugs and demi-wolves are clept
All by the name of dogs; the valued file
Distinguishes the swift, the slow, the subtle,
The housekeeper, the hunter, every one
According to the gift which bounteous nature
Hath in him closed, whereby he does receive
Particular addition, from the bill
That writes them all alike; and so of men.
Now, if you have a station in the file,
Not i' the worst rank of manhood, say't;

And I will put that business in your bosoms,
Whose execution takes your enemy off,
Grapples you to the heart and love of us,
Who wear our health but sickly in his life,
Which in his death were perfect.
2nd Mur. I am one, my liege,
Whom the vile blows and buffets of the world
Have so incensed that I am reckless what
I do to spite the world.
1st Mur. And I another
So weary with disasters, tugg'd with fortune,
That I would set my life on any chance,
To mend it, or be rid on't.
Macb. Both of you
Know Banquo was your enemy.
Both Mur. True, my lord.
Macb. So is he mine; and in such bloody distance,
That every minute of his being thrusts
Against my near'st of life; and though I could
With barefaced power sweep him from my sight
And bid my will avouch it, yet I must not,
For certain friends that are both his and mine,
Whose loves I may not drop, but wail his fall
Who I myself struck down; and thence it is,
That I to your assistance do make love,
Masking the business from the common eye
For sundry weighty reasons.
2nd Mur. We shall, my lord,
Perform what you command us.
1st Mur. Though our lives—
Macb. Your spirits shine through you. Within this hour at most
I will advise you where to plant yourselves;
Acquaint you with the perfect spy o' the time,
The moment on't; for't must be done to-night,
And something from the palace; always thought
That I require a clearness: and with him—
To leave no rubs nor botches in the work—
Fleance his son, that keeps him company,
Whose absence is no less material to me
Than is his father's, must embrace the fate
Of that dark hour. Resolve yourselves apart;
I'll come to you anon.
Both Mur. We are resolved, my lord.
Macb. I'll call upon you straight; abide within. [*Exeunt* MURDERERS.
It is concluded. Banquo, thy soul's flight,
If it find heaven, must find it out to-night. [*Exit.*

SCENE II. *The palace*

Enter LADY MACBETH *and a* SERVANT.

Lady M. Is Banquo gone from court?
Serv. Ay, madam, but returns again to-night.
Lady M. Say to the King, I would attend his leisure
For a few words.
Serv. Madam, I will. [*Exit.*
Lady M. Nought's had, all's spent,
Where our desire is got without content.
'Tis safer to be that which we destroy
Than by destruction dwell in doubtful joy.

Enter MACBETH.

How now, my lord! why do you keep alone,
Of sorriest fancies your companions making,
Using those thoughts which should indeed have died
With them they think on? Things without all remedy
Should be without regard; what's done is done.
Macb. We have scotch'd the snake, not kill'd it;
She'll close and be herself, whilst our poor malice
Remains in danger of her former tooth,
But let the frame of things disjoint, both the worlds suffer,
Ere we will eat our meal in fear and sleep
In the affliction of these terrible dreams
That shake us nightly. Better be with the dead,
Whom we, to gain our peace, have sent to peace,
Than on the torture of the mind to lie
In restless ecstasy. Duncan is in his grave;
After life's fitful fever he sleeps well;
Treason has done his worst; nor steel, nor poison,
Malice domestic, foreign levy, nothing,
Can touch him further.
Lady M. Come on;
Gentle my lord, sleek o'er your rugged looks;
Be bright and jovial among your guests to-night.
Macb. So shall I, love; and so, I pray, be you.
Let your remembrance apply to Banquo;
Present him eminence, both with eye and tongue.
Unsafe the while, that we
Must lave our honours in these flattering streams,
And make our faces vizards to our hearts,
Disguising what they are.
Lady M. You must leave this.
Macb. O, full of scorpions is my mind, dear wife!
Thou know'st that Banquo, and his Fleance, lives.
Lady M. But in them nature's copy's not eterne.
Macb. There's comfort yet; they are assailable;
Then be thou jocund; ere the bat hath flown
His cloister'd flight, ere to black Hecate's summons
The shard-borne beetle with his drowsy hums
Hath rung night's yawning peal, there shall be done
A deed of dreadful note.
Lady M. What's to be done?

Macb. Be innocent of the knowledge, dearest chuck,
Till thou applaud the deed. Come, seeling night,
Scarf up the tender eye of pitiful day;
And with thy bloody and invisible hand
Cancel and tear to pieces that great bond
Which keeps me pale! Light thickens; and the crow
Makes wing to the rooky wood;
Good things of day begin to droop and drowse;
Whiles night's black agents to their preys do rouse.
Thou marvell'st at my words, but hold thee still;
Things bad begun make strong themselves by ill.
So, prithee, go with me. [*Exeunt.*

SCENE III. *A park near the palace*

Enter THREE MURDERERS.

1st Mur. But who did bid thee join with us?
3rd Mur. Macbeth.
2nd Mur. He needs not our mistrust, since he delivers
Our offices and what we have to do
To the direction just.
1st Mur. Then stand with us.
The west yet glimmers with some streaks of day;
Now spurs the lated traveller apace
To gain the timely inn; and near approaches
The subject of our watch.
3rd Mur. Hark! I hear horses.
Ban. [*Within*] Give us a light there, ho!
2nd Mur. Then 'tis he; the rest
That are within the note of expectation
Already are i' the court.
1st Mur. His horses go about.
3rd Mur. Almost a mile; but he does usually,
So all men do, from hence to the palace gate
Make it their walk.
2nd Mur. A light, a light!

Enter BANQUO, *and* FLEANCE *with a torch.*

3rd Mur. 'Tis he.
1st Mur. Stand to't.
Ban. It will be rain to-night.
1st Mur. Let it come down.

They set upon BANQUO.

Ban. O, treachery! Fly, good Fleance, fly, fly, fly!
Thou mayst revenge. O slave!
[*Dies.* FLEANCE *escapes.*
3rd Mur. Who did strike out the light?
1st Mur. Was't not the way?
3rd Mur. There's but one down; the son is fled.
2nd Mur. We have lost
Best half of our affair.
1st Mur. Well, let's away, and say how much is done. [*Exeunt.*

SCENE IV. *The same: hall in the palace*

A banquet prepared. Enter MACBETH, LADY MACBETH, ROSS, LENNOX, *Lords, and Attendants.*

Macb. You know your own degrees; sit down. At first
And last the hearty welcome.
Lords. Thanks to your Majesty.
Macb. Ourself will mingle with society,
And play the humble host.
Our hostess keeps her state, but in best time
We will require her welcome.
Lady M. Pronounce it for me, sir, to all our friends;
For my heart speaks they are welcome.

FIRST MURDERER *appears at the door.*

Macb. See, they encounter thee with their hearts' thanks.
Both sides are even; here I'll sit i' the midst.
Be large in mirth; anon we'll drink a measure
The table round. [*Approaching the door.*] There's blood upon thy face.
1st Mur. 'Tis Banquo's then.
Macb. 'Tis better thee without than he within.
Is he dispatch'd?
1st Mur. My lord, his throat is cut; that I did for him.
Macb. Thou art the best o' the cut-throats; yet he's good
That did the like for Fleance. If thou didst it,
Thou art the nonpareil.
1st Mur. Most royal sir,
Fleance is 'scaped.
Macb. Then comes my fit again. I had else been perfect,
Whole as the marble, founded as the rock,
As broad and general as the casing air;
But now I am cabin'd, cribb'd, confined, bound in
To saucy doubts and fears. But Banquo's safe?
1st Mur. Ay, my good lord; safe in a ditch he bides,
With twenty trenched gashes on his head;
The least a death to nature.
Macb. Thanks for that.
There the grown serpent lies; the worm that's fled
Hath nature that in time will venom breed,
No teeth for the present. Get thee gone; to-morrow
We'll hear, ourselves, again. [*Exit* MURDERER.
Lady M. My royal lord,
You do not give the cheer. The feast is sold
That is not often vouch'd, while 'tis a-making,

'Tis given with welcome. To feed were best at home;
From thence the sauce to meat is ceremony;
Meeting were bare without it.
Macb. Sweet remembrancer!
Now, good digestion wait on appetite,
And health on both!
Len. May't please your Highness sit.

The Ghost of Banquo enters, and sits in Macbeth's place.

Macb. Here had we now our country's honour roof'd,
Were the graced person of our Banquo present;
Who may I rather challenge for unkindness
Than pity for mischance!
Ross. His absence, sir,
Lays blame upon his promise. Please't your Highness
To grace us with your royal company.
Macb. The table's full.
Len. Here is a place reserved, sir.
Macb. Where?
Len. Here, my good lord. What is't that moves your Highness?
Macb. Which of you have done this?
Lords. What, my good lord?
Macb. Thou canst not say I did it. Never shake
Thy gory locks at me.
Ross. Gentlemen, rise: his Highness is not well.
Lady M. Sit, worthy friends; my lord is often thus,
And hath been from his youth. Pray you, keep seat;
The fit is momentary; upon a thought
He will again be well. If much you note him,
You shall offend him and extend his passion.
Feed, and regard him not. Are you a man?
Macb. Ay, and a bold one, that dare look on that
Which might appal the devil.
Lady M. O proper stuff!
This is the very painting of your fear;
This is the air-drawn dagger which, you said,
Led you to Duncan. O, these flaws and starts,
Impostors to true fear, would well become
A woman's story at a winter's fire,
Authorized by her grandam. Shame itself!
Why do you make such faces? When all's done,
You look but on a stool.
Macb. Prithee, see there! behold! look! lo! how say you?
Why, what care I? If thou canst nod, speak too.
If charnel-houses and our graves must send
Those that we bury back, our monuments
Shall be the maws of kites. [*Ghost vanishes.*
Lady M. What, quite unmann'd in folly?
Macb. If I stand here, I saw him.
Lady M. Fie, for shame!
Macb. Blood hath been shed ere now, i' the olden time,
Ere humane statute purged the gentle weal;
Ay, and since too, murders have been perform'd
Too terrible for the ear. The time has been
That, when the brains were out, the man would die,
And there an end; but now they rise again,
With twenty mortal murders on their crowns,
And push us from our stools. This is more strange
Than such a murder is.
Lady M. My worthy lord,
Your noble friends do lack you.
Macb. I do forget.
Do not muse at me, my most worthy friends;
I have a strange infirmity, which is nothing
To those that know me. Come, love and health to all;
Then I'll sit down. Give me some wine; fill full.
I drink to the general joy o' the whole table,
And to our dear friend Banquo, whom we miss;
Would he were here! to all, and him, we thirst,
And all to all.
Lords. Our duties, and the pledge.

Re-enter Ghost.

Macb. Avaunt! and quit my sight! let the earth hide thee!
Thy bones are marrowless, thy blood is cold;
Thou hast no speculation in those eyes
Which thou dost glare with!
Lady M. Think of this, good peers,
But as a thing of custom; 'tis no other.
Only it spoils the pleasure of the time.
Macb. What man dare, I dare.
Approach thou like the rugged Russian bear,
The arm'd rhinoceros, or the Hyrcan tiger;
Take any shape but that, and my firm nerves
Shall never tremble. Or be alive again,
And dare me to the desert with thy sword;
If trembling I inhabit then, protest me
The baby of a girl. Hence, horrible shadow!
Unreal mockery, hence! [*Ghost vanishes.*
Why, so; being gone,
I am a man again. Pray you, sit still.
Lady M. You have displaced the mirth, broke the good meeting,
With most admired disorder.
Macb. Can such things be,
And overcome us like a summer's cloud,
Without our special wonder? You make me strange
Even to the disposition that I owe,

When now I think you can behold such sights,
And keep the natural ruby of your cheeks,
When mine is blanch'd with fear.

Ross. What sights, my lord?

Lady M. I pray you, speak not; he grows worse and worse;
Question enrages him. At once, good night.
Stand not upon the order of your going,
But go at once.

Len. Good night; and better health
Attend his Majesty!

Lady M. A kind good night to all!

[*Exeunt all but* MACBETH *and* LADY MACBETH.

Macb. It will have blood; they say, blood will have blood.
Stones have been known to move and trees to speak;
Augurs and understood relations have
By magot-pies and choughs and rooks brought forth
The secret'st man of blood. What is the night?

Lady M. Almost at odds with morning, which is which.

Macb. How say'st thou, that Macduff denies his person
At our great bidding?

Lady M. Did you send to him, sir?

Macb. I hear it by the way; but I will send.
There's not a one of them but in his house
I keep a servant fee'd. I will to-morrow,
And betimes I will, to the weird sisters.
More shall they speak; for now I am bent to know,
By the worst means, the worst. For mine own good,
All causes shall give way. I am in blood
Stepp'd in so far that, should I wade no more,
Returning were as tedious as go o'er.
Strange things I have in head, that will to hand;
Which must be acted ere they may be scann'd.

Lady M. You lack the season of all natures, sleep.

Macb. Come, we'll to sleep. My strange and self-abuse
Is the initiate fear that wants hard use.
We are yet but young in deed. [*Exeunt.*

SCENE V. *A Heath*

Thunder. Enter the THREE WITCHES, *meeting* HECATE.

1st Witch. Why, how now, Hecate! you look angerly.

Hec. Have I not reason, beldams as you are,
Saucy and overbold? How did you dare
To trade and traffic with Macbeth
In riddles and affairs of death;
And I, the mistress of your charms,
The close contriver of all harms,
Was never call'd to bear my part,
Or show the glory of our art?
And, which is worse, all you have done
Hath been but for a wayward son,
Spiteful and wrathful, who, as others do,
Loves for his own ends, not for you.
But make amends now; get you gone,
And at the pit of Acheron
Meet me i' the morning; thither he
Will come to know his destiny.
Your vessels and your spells provide,
Your charms and everything beside.
I am for the air; this night I'll spend
Unto a dismal and a fatal end;
Great business must be wrought ere noon.
Upon the corner of the moon
There hangs a vaporous drop profound;
I'll catch it ere it come to ground;
And that distill'd by magic sleights
Shall raise such artificial sprites
As by the strength of their illusion
Shall draw him on to his confusion.
He shall spurn fate, scorn death, and bear
His hopes 'bove wisdom, grace and fear;
And you all know, security
Is mortals' chiefest enemy.

Music and a song within: "Come away, come away," &c.

Hark! I am call'd; my little spirit, see,
Sits in a foggy cloud, and stays for me. [*Exit.*

1st Witch. Come, let's make haste; she'll soon be back again. [*Exeunt.*

SCENE VI. *Forres: the palace*

Enter LENNOX *and another* LORD.

Len. My former speeches have but hit your thoughts,
Which can interpret further; only, I say,
Things have been strangely borne. The gracious Duncan
Was pitied of Macbeth; marry, he was dead.
And the right-valiant Banquo walk'd too late;
Whom, you may say, if't please you, Fleance kill'd,
For Fleance fled. Men must not walk too late.
Who cannot want the thought how monstrous
It was for Malcolm and for Donalbain
To kill their gracious father? damned fact!
How it did grieve Macbeth! did he not straight
In pious rage the two delinquents tear,
That were the slaves of drink and thralls of sleep?
Was not that nobly done? Ay, and wisely too;
For 'twould have anger'd any heart alive
To hear the men deny't. So that, I say,

He has borne all things well; and I do think
That had he Duncan's sons under his key—
As, an't please heaven, he shall not—they should find
What 'twere to kill a father; so should Fleance.
But, peace! for from broad words and 'cause he fail'd
His presence at the tyrant's feast, I hear
Macduff lives in disgrace. Sir, can you tell
Where he bestows himself?

Lord. The son of Duncan,
From whom this tyrant holds the due of birth,
Lives in the English court, and is received
Of the most pious Edward with such grace
That the malevolence of Fortune nothing
Takes from his high respect. Thither Macduff
Is gone to pray the holy King, upon his aid
To wake Northumberland and warlike Siward;
That, by the help of these—with Him above
To ratify the work—we may again
Give to our tables meat, sleep to our nights,
Free from our feasts and banquets bloody knives,
Do faithful homage, and receive free honours;
All which we pine for now. And this report
Hath so exasperate the King that he
Prepares for some attempt of war.

Len. Sent he to Macduff?

Lord. He did; and with an absolute "Sir, not I,"
The cloudy messenger turns me his back,
And hums, as who should say, "You'll rue the time
That clogs me with this answer."

Len. And that well might
Advise him to a caution, to hold what distance
His wisdom can provide. Some holy angel
Fly to the court of England and unfold
His message ere he come, that a swift blessing
May soon return to this our suffering country
Under a hand accursed!

Lord. I'll send my prayers with him.
[*Exeunt.*

ACT IV

Scene I. *A cavern: in the middle, a boiling cauldron*

Thunder. Enter the THREE WITCHES.

1st Witch. Thrice the brinded cat hath mew'd.

2nd Witch. Thrice and once the hedge-pig whined.

3rd Witch. Harpier cries; 'tis time, 'tis time.

1st Witch. Round about the cauldron go;
In the poison'd entrails throw.
Toad, that under cold stone
Days and nights has thirty-one
Swelter'd venom sleeping got,
Boil thou first i' the charmed pot.

All. Double, double, toil and trouble;
Fire burn and cauldron bubble.

2nd Witch. Fillet of a fenny snake,
In the cauldron boil and bake;
Eye of newt and toe of frog,
Wool of bat and tongue of dog,
Adder's fork and blind-worm's sting,
Lizard's leg and howlet's wing,
For a charm of powerful trouble,
Like a hell-broth boil and bubble.

All. Double, double, toil and trouble;
Fire burn and cauldron bubble.

3rd Witch. Scale of dragon, tooth of wolf,
Witches' mummy, maw and gulf
Of the ravin'd salt-sea shark,
Root of hemlock digg'd i' the dark,
Liver of blaspheming Jew,
Gall of goat, and slips of yew
Sliver'd in the moon's eclipse,
Nose of Turk and Tartar's lips,
Finger of birth-strangled babe
Ditch-deliver'd by a drab,
Make the gruel thick and slab.
Add thereto a tiger's chaudron,
For the ingredients of our cauldron.

All. Double, double, toil and trouble;
Fire burn and cauldron bubble.

2nd Witch. Cool it with a baboon's blood,
Then the charm is firm and good.

Enter HECATE *to the other* THREE WITCHES.

Hec. O, well done! I commend your pains;
And every one shall share i' the gains.
And now about the cauldron sing,
Like elves and fairies in a ring,
Enchanting all that you put in.

Music and a song: "Black spirits," &c.
[HECATE *retires.*

2nd Witch. By the pricking of my thumbs,
Something wicked this way comes.
Open, locks,
Whoever knocks!

Enter MACBETH.

Macb. How now, you secret, black, and midnight hags!
What is't you do?

All. A deed without a name.

Macb. I conjure you by that which you profess,
Howe'er you come to know it, answer me:
Though you untie the winds and let them fight
Against the churches; though the yesty waves
Confound and swallow navigation up;
Though bladed corn be lodged and trees blown down;

Though castles topple on their warders' heads;
Though palaces and pyramids do slope
Their heads to their foundations; though the treasure
Of nature's germens tumble all together,
Even till destruction sicken; answer me
To what I ask you.

1st Witch. Speak.

2nd Witch. Demand.

3rd Witch. We'll answer.

1st Witch. Say, if thou'dst rather hear it from our mouths,
Or from our masters?

Macb. Call 'em; let me see 'em.

1st Witch. Pour in sow's blood, that hath eaten
Her nine farrow; grease that's sweaten
From the murderer's gibbet throw
Into the flame.

All. Come, high or low;
Thyself and office deftly show!

Thunder. FIRST APPARITION: *an armed Head.*

Macb. Tell me, thou unknown power—

1st Witch. He knows thy thought.
Hear his speech, but say thou nought.

1st App. Macbeth! Macbeth! Macbeth! beware Macduff;
Beware the thane of Fife. Dismiss me. Enough. [*Descends.*

Macb. Whate'er thou art, for thy good caution, thanks;
Thou hast harp'd my fear aright. But one word more—

1st Witch. He will not be commanded. Here's another,
More potent than the first.

Thunder. SECOND APPARITION: *a bloody Child.*

2nd App. Macbeth! Macbeth! Macbeth!

Macb. Had I three ears, I'd hear thee.

2nd App. Be bloody, bold, and resolute; laugh to scorn
The power of man, for none of woman born
Shall harm Macbeth. [*Descends.*

Macb. Then live, Macduff; what need I fear of thee?
But yet I'll make assurance double sure,
And take a bond of fate. Thou shalt not live;
That I may tell pale-hearted fear it lies,
And sleep in spite of thunder.

Thunder. THIRD APPARITION: *a Child crowned, with a tree in his hand.*

What is this
That rises like the issue of a king,
And wears upon his baby-brow the round
And top of sovereignty?

All. Listen, but speak not to 't.

3rd App. Be lion-mettled, proud; and take no care
Who chafes, who frets, or where conspirers are.
Macbeth shall never vanquish'd be until
Great Birnam wood to high Dunsinane hill
Shall come against him. [*Descends.*

Macb. That will never be.
Who can impress the forest, bid the tree
Unfix his earth-bound root? Sweet bodements! good!
Rebellion's head, rise never till the wood
Of Birnam rise, and our high-placed Macbeth
Shall live the lease of nature, pay his breath
To time and mortal custom. Yet my heart
Throbs to know one thing. Tell me, if your art
Can tell so much: shall Banquo's issue ever
Reign in this kingdom?

All. Seek to know no more.

Macb. I will be satisfied; deny me this,
And an eternal curse fall on you! Let me know.
Why sinks that cauldron? and what noise is this?

Hautboys.

1st Witch. Show!

2nd Witch. Show!

3rd Witch. Show!

All. Show his eyes, and grieve his heart;
Come like shadows, so depart!

A show of EIGHT KINGS, *the last with a glass in his hand; Banquo's Ghost following.*

Macb. Thou art too like the spirit of Banquo; down!
Thy crown does sear mine eye-balls. And thy hair,
Thou other gold-bound brow, is like the first.
A third is like the former. Filthy hags!
Why do you show me this? A fourth! Start, eyes!
What, will the line stretch out to the crack of doom?
Another yet! A seventh! I'll see no more.
And yet the eighth appears, who bears a glass
Which shows me many more; and some I see
That two-fold balls and treble sceptres carry.
Horrible sight! Now, I see, 'tis true;
For the blood-bolter'd Banquo smiles upon me,
And points at them for his. [*Apparitions vanish.*]
What, is this so?

1st Witch. Ay, sir, all this is so. But why
Stands Macbeth thus amazedly?
Come, sisters, cheer we up his sprites,
And show the best of our delights.
I'll charm the air to give a sound,
While you perform your antic round;
That this great king may kindly say,

Our duties did his welcome pay.
[*Music. The* WITCHES *dance, and then vanish, with* HECATE.

Macb. Where are they? Gone? Let this pernicious hour
Stand aye accursed in the calendar!
Come in, without there!

Enter LENNOX.

Len. What's your Grace's will?
Macb. Saw you the weird sisters?
Len. No, my lord.
Macb. Came they not by you?
Len. No, indeed, my lord.
Macb. Infected be the air whereon they ride;
And damn'd all those that trust them! I did hear
The galloping of horse; who was't came by?
Len. 'Tis two or three, my lord, that bring you word
Macduff is fled to England.
Macb. Fled to England!
Len. Ay, my good lord.
Macb. Time, thou anticipatest my dread exploits;
The flighty purpose never is o'ertook
Unless the deed go with it. From this moment
The very firstlings of my heart shall be
The firstlings of my hand. And even now,
To crown my thoughts with acts, be it thought and done.
The castle of Macduff I will surprise;
Seize upon Fife; give to the edge o' the sword
His wife, his babes, and all unfortunate souls
That trace him in his line. No boasting like a fool;
This deed I'll do before this purpose cool.
But no more sights! Where are these gentlemen?
Come, bring me where they are. [*Exeunt.*

SCENE II. *Fife: Macduff's castle*

Enter LADY MACDUFF, *her* SON, *and* ROSS.

L. Macd. What had he done, to make him fly the land?
Ross. You must have patience, madam.
L. Macd. He had none;
His flight was madness. When our actions do not,
Our fears do make us traitors.
Ross. You know not
Whether it was his wisdom or his fear.
L. Macd. Wisdom! to leave his wife, to leave his babes,
His mansion, and his titles in a place
From whence himself does fly? He loves us not;
He wants the natural touch; for the poor wren,
The most diminutive of birds, will fight,
Her young ones in her nest, against the owl.
All is the fear and nothing is the love;
As little is the wisdom, where the flight
So runs against all reason.
Ross. My dearest coz,
I pray you, school yourself; but for your husband,
He is noble, wise, judicious, and best knows
The fits o' the season. I dare not speak much further;
But cruel are the times, when we are traitors
And do not know ourselves, when we hold rumour
From what we fear, yet know not what we fear,
But float upon a wild and violent sea
Each way and move. I take my leave of you;
Shall not be long but I'll be here again.
Things at the worst will cease, or else climb upward
To what they were before. My pretty cousin,
Blessing upon you!
L. Macd. Father'd he is, and yet he's fatherless.
Ross. I am so much a fool, should I stay longer,
It would be my disgrace and your discomfort.
I take my leave at once. [*Exit.*
L. Macd. Sirrah, your father's dead;
And what will you do now? How will you live?
Son. As birds do, mother.
L. Macd. What, with worms and flies?
Son. With what I get, I mean; and so do they.
L. Macd. Poor bird! thou'dst never fear the net nor lime,
The pitfall nor the gin.
Son. Why should I, mother? Poor birds they are not set for.
My father is not dead, for all your saying.
L. Macd. Yes, he is dead. How wilt thou do for a father?
Son. Nay, how will you do for a husband?
L. Macd. Why, I can buy me twenty at any market.
Son. Then you'll buy 'em to sell again.
L. Macd. Thou speak'st with all thy wit; and yet, i' faith,
With wit enough for thee.
Son. Was my father a traitor, mother?
L. Macd. Ay, that he was.
Son. What is a traitor?
L. Macd. Why, one that swears and lies.
Son. And be all traitors that do so?

L. Macd. Every one that does so is a traitor, and must be hanged.

Son. And must they all be hanged that swear and lie?

L. Macd. Every one.

Son. Who must hang them?

L. Macd. Why, the honest men.

Son. Then the liars and swearers are fools, for there are liars and swearers enow to beat the honest men and hang up them.

L. Macd. Now, God help thee, poor monkey!
But how wilt thou do for a father?

Son. If he were dead, you'd weep for him; if you would not, it were a good sign that I should quickly have a new father.

L. Macd. Poor prattler, how thou talk'st!

Enter a MESSENGER.

Mess. Bless you, fair dame! I am not to you known,
Though in your state of honour I am perfect.
I doubt some danger does approach you nearly.
If you will take a homely man's advice,
Be not found here; hence, with your little ones.
To fright you thus, methinks, I am too savage;
To do worse to you were fell cruelty,
Which is too nigh your person. Heaven preserve you!
I dare abide no longer. [*Exit*.

L. Macd. Whither should I fly?
I have done no harm. But I remember now
I am in this earthly world; where to do harm
Is often laudable, to do good sometime
Accounted dangerous folly. Why then, alas,
Do I put up that womanly defence,
To say I have done no harm?

Enter MURDERERS.

What are these faces?

1st Mur. Where is your husband?

L. Macd. I hope, in no place so unsanctified
Where such as thou mayst find him.

1st Mur. He's a traitor.

Son. Thou liest, thou shag-hair'd villain!

1st Mur. What, you egg!
Stabbing him.
Young fry of treachery!

Son. He has kill'd me, mother.
Run away, I pray you! [*Dies*.
[*Exit* LADY MACDUFF, *crying* "Murder!"
Exeunt MURDERERS, *following her*.

SCENE III. *England: before the King's palace*

Enter MALCOLM *and* MACDUFF.

Mal. Let us seek out some desolate shade, and there
Weep our sad bosoms empty.

Macd. Let us rather
Hold fast the mortal sword, and like good men
Bestride our down-fall'n birthdom. Each new morn
New widows howl, new orphans cry, new sorrows
Strike heaven on the face, that it resounds
As if it felt with Scotland and yell'd out
Like syllable of dolour.

Mal. What I believe I'll wail,
What know believe, and what I can redress,
As I shall find the time to friend, I will.
What you have spoke, it may be so perchance.
This tyrant, whose sole name blisters our tongues,
Was once thought honest; you have loved him well.
He hath not touch'd you yet. I am young; but something
You may deserve of him through me, and wisdom
To offer up a weak poor innocent lamb
To appease an angry god.

Macd. I am not treacherous.

Mal. But Macbeth is.
A good and virtuous nature may recoil
In an imperial charge. But I shall crave your pardon;
That which you are my thoughts cannot transpose.
Angels are bright still, though the brightest fell.
Though all things foul would wear the brows of grace,
Yet grace must still look so.

Macd. I have lost my hopes.

Mal. Perchance even there where I did find my doubts.
Why in that rawness left you wife and child,
Those precious motives, those strong knots of love,
Without leave-taking? I pray you,
Let not my jealousies be your dishonours,
But mine own safeties. You may be rightly just,
Whatever I shall think.

Macd. Bleed, bleed, poor country!
Great tyranny! lay thou thy basis sure,
For goodness dare not check thee. Wear thou thy wrongs;
The title is affeer'd! Fare thee well, lord.
I would not be the villain that thou think'st
For the whole space that's in the tyrant's grasp,
And the rich East to boot.

Mal. Be not offended.
I speak not as in absolute fear of you.
I think our country sinks beneath the yoke;
It weeps, it bleeds; and each new day a gash
Is added to her wounds. I think withal
There would be hands uplifted in my right;
And here from gracious England have I offer
Of goodly thousands. But, for all this,
When I shall tread upon the tyrant's head,
Or wear it on my sword, yet my poor country
Shall have more vices than it had before,
More suffer and more sundry ways than ever,

By him that shall succeed.
Macd. What should he be?
Mal. It is myself I mean; in whom I know
All the particulars of vice so grafted
That, when they shall be open'd, black Macbeth
Will seem as pure as snow, and the poor state
Esteem him as a lamb, being compared
With my confineless harms.
Macd. Not in the legions
Of horrid hell can come a devil more damn'd
In evils to top Macbeth.
Mal. I grant him bloody,
Luxurious, avaricious, false, deceitful,
Sudden, malicious, smacking of every sin
That has a name; but there's no bottom, none,
In my voluptuousness. Your wives, your daughters,
Your matrons, and your maids, could not fill up
The cistern of my lust, and my desire
All continent impediments would o'erbear
That did oppose my will. Better Macbeth
Than such an one to reign.
Macd. Boundless intemperance
In nature is a tyranny; it hath been
The untimely emptying of the happy throne
And fall of many kings. But fear not yet
To take upon you what is yours; you may
Convey your pleasures in a spacious plenty,
And yet seem cold, the time you may so hoodwink.
We have willing dames enough; there cannot be
That vulture in you, to devour so many
As will to greatness dedicate themselves,
Finding it so inclined.
Mal. With this there grows
In my most ill-composed affection such
A stanchless avarice that, were I king,
I should cut off the nobles for their lands,
Desire his jewels and this other's house;
And my more-having would be as a sauce
To make me hunger more; that I should forge
Quarrels unjust against the good and loyal,
Destroying them for wealth.
Macd. This avarice
Sticks deeper, grows with more pernicious root
Than summer-seeming lust, and it hath been
The sword of our slain kings. Yet do not fear;
Scotland hath foisons to fill up your will,
Of your mere own. All these are portable,
With other graces weigh'd.
Mal. But I have none. The king-becoming graces,
As justice, verity, temperance, stableness,
Bounty, perseverance, mercy, lowliness,
Devotion, patience, courage, fortitude,
I have no relish of them, but abound
In the division of each several crime,
Acting it many ways. Nay, had I power, I should
Pour the sweet milk of concord into hell,
Uproar the universal peace, confound
All unity on earth.
Macd. O Scotland, Scotland!
Mal. If such a one be fit to govern, speak.
I am as I have spoken.
Macd. Fit to govern!
No, not to live. O nation miserable,
With an untitled tyrant bloody-scepter'd,
When shalt thou see thy wholesome days again,
Since that the truest issue of thy throne
By his own interdiction stands accursed,
And does blaspheme his breed? Thy royal father
Was a most sainted king; the queen that bore thee,
Oftener upon her knees than on her feet,
Died every day she lived. Fare thee well!
These evils thou repeat'st upon thyself
Have banish'd me from Scotland. O my breast,
Thy hope ends here!
Mal. Macduff, this noble passion,
Child of integrity, hath from my soul
Wiped the black scruples, reconciled my thoughts
To thy good truth and honour. Devilish Macbeth
By many of these trains hath sought to win me
Into his power, and modest wisdom plucks me
From over-credulous haste. But God above
Deal between thee and me! for even now
I put myself to thy direction, and
Unspeak mine own detraction, here abjure
The taints and blames I laid upon myself,
For strangers to my nature. I am yet
Unknown to woman, never was forsworn,
Scarcely have coveted what was mine own,
At no time broke my faith, would not betray
The devil to his fellow, and delight
No less in truth than life. My first false speaking
Was this upon myself; what I am truly,
Is thine and my poor country's to command.
Whither indeed, before thy here-approach,
Old Siward, with ten thousand warlike men,
Already at a point, was setting forth.
Now we'll together; and the chance of goodness
Be like our warranted quarrel! Why are you silent?
Macd. Such welcome and unwelcome things at once
'Tis hard to reconcile.

Enter a DOCTOR.

Mal. Well; more anon.—Comes the King forth, I pray you?
Doct. Ay, sir; there are a crew of wretched souls
That stay his cure. Their malady convinces

The great assay of art; but at his touch—
Such sanctity hath heaven given his hand—
They presently amend.
Mal. I thank you, doctor. [*Exit* DOCTOR.
Macd. What's the disease he means?
Mal. 'Tis call'd the evil;
A most miraculous work in this good king;
Which often, since my here-remain in England,
I have seen him do. How he solicits Heaven,
Himself best knows; but strangely-visited people,
All swoln and ulcerous, pitiful to the eye,
The mere despair of surgery, he cures,
Hanging a golden stamp about their necks,
Put on with holy prayers. And 'tis spoken,
To the succeeding royalty he leaves
The healing benediction. With this strange virtue,
He hath a heavenly gift of prophecy,
And sundry blessings hang about his throne
That speak him full of grace.

Enter ROSS.

Macd. See, who comes here?
Mal. My countryman; but yet I know him not.
Macd. My ever-gentle cousin, welcome hither.
Mal. I know him now. Good God, betimes remove
The means that makes us strangers!
Ross. Sir, amen.
Macd. Stands Scotland where it did?
Ross. Alas, poor country!
Almost afraid to know itself. It cannot
Be call'd our mother, but our grave; where nothing,
But who knows nothing, is once seen to smile;
Where sighs and groans and shrieks that rend the air
Are made, not mark'd; where violent sorrow seems
A modern ecstasy. The dead man's knell
Is there scarce ask'd for who; and good men's lives
Expire before the flowers in their caps,
Dying or ere they sicken.
Macd. O, relation
Too nice, and yet too true!
Mal. What's the newest grief?
Ross. That of an hour's age doth hiss the speaker;
Each minute teems a new one.
Macd. How does my wife?
Ross. Why, well.
Macd. And all my children?
Ross. Well too.
Macd. The tyrant has not batter'd at their peace?
Ross. No; they were well at peace when I did leave 'em.
Macd. Be not a niggard of your speech; how goes't?
Ross. When I came hither to transport the tidings,
Which I have heavily borne, there ran a rumour
Of many worthy fellows that were out;
Which was to my belief witness'd the rather,
For that I saw the tyrant's power a-foot.
Now is the time of help; your eye in Scotland
Would create soldiers, make our women fight,
To doff their dire distresses.
Mal. Be't their comfort
We are coming thither. Gracious England hath
Lent us good Siward and ten thousand men;
An older and a better soldier none
That Christendom gives out.
Ross. Would I could answer
This comfort with the like! But I have words
That would be howl'd out in the desert air,
Where hearing should not latch them.
Macd. What concern they?
The general cause? or is it a fee-grief
Due to some single breast?
Ross. No mind that's honest
But in it shares some woe; though the main part
Pertains to you alone.
Macd. If it be mine,
Keep it not from me, quickly let me have it.
Ross. Let not your ears despise my tongue for ever,
Which shall possess them with the heaviest sound
That ever yet they heard.
Macd. Hum! I guess at it.
Ross. Your castle is surprised; your wife and babes
Savagely slaughter'd. To relate the manner
Were, on the quarry of these murder'd deer,
To add the death of you.
Mal. Merciful heaven!
What, man! ne'er pull your hat upon your brows;
Give sorrow words. The grief that does not speak
Whispers the o'er-fraught heart and bids it break.
Macd. My children too?
Ross. Wife, children, servants, all
That could be found.
Macd. And I must be from thence!
My wife kill'd too?
Ross. I have said.
Mal. Be comforted.
Let's make us medicines of our great revenge

To cure this deadly grief.

Macd. He has no children. All my pretty ones?
Did you say all? O hell-kite! All?
What, all my pretty chickens and their dam
At one fell swoop?

Mal. Dispute it like a man.

Macd. I shall do so;
But I must also feel it as a man.
I cannot but remember such things were,
That were most precious to me. Did heaven look on,
And would not take their part? Sinful Macduff,
They were all struck for thee! naught that I am,
Not for their own demerits, but for mine,
Fell slaughter on their souls. Heaven rest them now!

Mal. Be this the whetstone of your sword; let grief
Convert to anger; blunt not the heart, enrage it.

Macd. O, I could play the woman with mine eyes
And braggart with my tongue! But, gentle heavens,
Cut short all intermission; front to front
Bring thou this fiend of Scotland and myself;
Within my sword's length set him; if he 'scape,
Heaven forgive him too!

Mal. This tune goes manly.
Come, go we to the King; our power is ready;
Our lack is nothing but our leave. Macbeth
Is ripe for shaking, and the powers above
Put on their instruments. Receive what cheer you may;
The night is long that never finds the day.
[*Exeunt.*

ACT V

SCENE I. *Dunsinane: ante-room in the castle*

Enter a DOCTOR OF PHYSIC *and a* WAITING-GENTLEWOMAN.

Doct. I have two nights watched with you, but can perceive no truth in your report. When was it she last walked?

Gent. Since his Majesty went into the field, I have seen her rise from her bed, throw her night-gown upon her, unlock her closet, take forth paper, fold it, write upon't, read it, afterwards seal it, and again return to bed; yet all this while in a most fast sleep.

Doct. A great perturbation in nature, to receive at once the benefit of sleep, and do the effects of watching! In this slumbery agitation, besides her walking and other actual performances, what, at any time, have you heard her say?

Gent. That, sir, which I will not report after her.

Doct. You may to me; and 'tis most meet you should.

Gent. Neither to you nor any one; having no witness to confirm my speech.

Enter LADY MACBETH, *with a taper.*

Lo you, here she comes! This is her very guise; and, upon my life, fast asleep. Observe her; stand close.

Doct. How came she by that light?

Gent. Why, it stood by her. She has light by her continually; 'tis her command.

Doct. You see, her eyes are open.

Gent. Ay, but their sense is shut.

Doct. What is it she does now? Look, how she rubs her hands.

Gent. It is an accustomed action with her, to seem thus washing her hands. I have known her continue in this a quarter of an hour.

Lady M. Yet here's a spot.

Doct. Hark! she speaks. I will set down what comes from her, to satisfy my remembrance the more strongly.

Lady M. Out, damned spot! out, I say! One; two. Why, then 'tis time to do't. Hell is murky! Fie, my lord, fie! a soldier, and afeard? What need we fear who knows it, when none can call our power to account? Yet who would have thought the old man to have had so much blood in him.

Doct. Do you mark that?

Lady M. The thane of Fife had a wife. Where is she now? What, will these hands ne'er be clean? No more o' that, my lord, no more o' that! You mar all with this starting.

Doct. Go to, go to; you have known what you should not.

Gent. She has spoke what she should not, I am sure of that. Heaven knows what she has known.

Lady M. Here's the smell of the blood still. All the perfumes of Arabia will not sweeten this little hand. Oh, oh, oh!

Doct. What a sigh is there! The heart is sorely charged.

Gent. I would not have such a heart in my bosom for the dignity of the whole body.

Doct. Well, well, well—

Gent. Pray God it be, sir.

Doct. This disease is beyond my practice. Yet I have known those which have walked in their sleep who have died holily in their beds.

Lady M. Wash your hands, put on your night-gown; look not so pale. I tell you yet again, Banquo's buried; he cannot come out on's grave.

Doct. Even so?

Lady M. To bed, to bed! there's knocking at

the gate. Come, come, come, come, give me your hand. What's done cannot be undone. To bed, to bed, to bed! [*Exit.*

Doct. Will she go now to bed?

Gent. Directly.

Doct. Foul whisperings are abroad. Unnatural deeds
Do breed unnatural troubles. Infected minds
To their deaf pillows will discharge their secrets.
More needs she the divine than the physician.
God, God forgive us all! Look after her;
Remove from her the means of all annoyance,
And still keep eyes upon her. So, good night.
My mind she has mated, and amazed my sight.
I think, but dare not speak.

Gent. Good night, good doctor.
[*Exeunt.*

SCENE II. *The country near Dunsinane*

Drum and colours. Enter MENTEITH, CAITHNESS, ANGUS, LENNOX, *and Soldiers.*

Ment. The English power is near, led on by Malcolm,
His uncle Siward, and the good Macduff.
Revenges burn in them; for their dear causes
Would to the bleeding and the grim alarm
Excite the mortified man.

Ang. Near Birnam wood
Shall we well meet them; that way are they coming.

Caith. Who knows if Donalbain be with his brother?

Len. For certain, sir, he is not; I have a file
Of all the gentry. There is Siward's son,
And many unrough youths that even now
Protest their first of manhood.

Ment. What does the tyrant?

Caith. Great Dunsinane he strongly fortifies.
Some say he's mad; others that lesser hate him
Do call it valiant fury; but, for certain,
He cannot buckle his distemper'd cause
Within the belt of rule.

Ang. Now does he feel
His secret murders sticking on his hands;
Now minutely revolts upbraid his faith-breach;
Those he commands move only in command,
Nothing in love; now does he feel his title
Hang loose about him, like a giant's robe
Upon a dwarfish thief.

Ment. Who then shall blame
His pester'd senses to recoil and start,
When all that is within him does condemn
Itself for being there?

Caith. Well, march we on,
To give obedience where 'tis truly owed.
Meet we the medicine of the sickly weal,
And with him pour we in our country's purge
Each drop of us.

Len. Or so much as it needs,
To dew the sovereign flower and drown the weeds.
Make we our march towards Birnam.
[*Exeunt, marching.*

SCENE III. *Dunsinane: a room in the castle*

Enter MACBETH, DOCTOR, *and Attendants.*

Macb. Bring me no more reports; let them fly all.
Till Birnam wood remove to Dunsinane,
I cannot taint with fear. What's the boy Malcolm?
Was he not born of woman? The spirits that know
All mortal consequences have pronounced me thus:
"Fear not, Macbeth; no man that's born of woman
Shall e'er have power upon thee." Then fly, false thanes,
And mingle with the English epicures.
The mind I sway by and the heart I bear
Shall never sag with doubt nor shake with fear.

Enter a SERVANT.

The devil damn thee black, thou cream-faced loon!
Where got'st thou that goose look?

Serv. There is ten thousand—

Macb. Geese, villain?

Serv. Soldiers, sir.

Macb. Go prick thy face, and over-red thy fear,
Thou lily-liver'd boy. What soldiers, patch?
Death of thy soul! those linen cheeks of thine
Are counsellors to fear. What soldiers, whey-face?

Serv. The English force, so please you.

Macb. Take thy face hence. [*Exit* SERVANT.
Seyton!—I am sick at heart,
When I behold—Seyton, I say!—This push
Will cheer me ever, or disseat me now.
I have lived long enough; my way of life
Is fall'n into the sear, the yellow leaf;
And that which should accompany old age,
As honour, love, obedience, troops of friends,
I must not look to have; but, in their stead,
Curses, not loud but deep, mouth-honour, breath,
Which the poor heart would fain deny, and dare not.
Seyton!

Enter SEYTON.

Sey. What is your gracious pleasure?

Macb. What news more?
Sey. All is confirm'd, my lord, which was reported.
Macb. I'll fight till from my bones my flesh be hack'd.
Give me my armour.
Sey. 'Tis not needed yet.
Macb. I'll put it on.
Send out more horses; skirr the country round;
Hang those that talk of fear. Give me mine armour.
How does your patient, doctor?
Doct. Not so sick, my lord.
As she is troubled with thick-coming fancies,
That keep her from her rest.
Macb. Cure her of that.
Canst thou not minister to a mind diseased,
Pluck from the memory a rooted sorrow,
Raze out the written troubles of the brain,
And with some sweet oblivious antidote
Cleanse the stuff'd bosom of that perilous stuff
Which weighs upon the heart?
Doct. Therein the patient
Must minister to himself.
Macb. Throw physic to the dogs; I'll none of it.
Come, put mine armour on; give me my staff.
Seyton, send out. Doctor, the thanes fly from me.
Come, sir, dispatch. If thou couldst, doctor, cast
The water of my land, find her disease,
And purge it to a sound and pristine health,
I would applaud thee to the very echo,
That should applaud again.—Pull't off, I say.—
What rhubarb, senna, or what purgative drug,
Would scour these English hence? Hear'st thou of them?
Doct. Ay, my good lord; your royal preparation
Makes us hear something.
Macb. Bring it after me.
I will not be afraid of death and bane,
Till Birnam forest come to Dunsinane.
Doct. [*Aside*] Were I from Dunsinane away and clear,
Profit again should hardly draw me here.
[*Exeunt.*

SCENE IV. *Country near Birnam wood*

Drum and colours. Enter MALCOLM, OLD SIWARD *and his son*, MACDUFF, MENTEITH, CAITHNESS, ANGUS, LENNOX, ROSS, *and Soldiers, marching.*

Mal. Cousins, I hope the days are near at hand
That chambers will be safe.
Ment. We doubt it nothing.
Siw. What wood is this before us?
Ment. The wood of Birnam.
Mal. Let every soldier hew him down a bough
And bear't before him; thereby shall we shadow
The numbers of our host and make discovery
Err in report of us.
Soldiers. It shall be done.
Siw. We learn no other but the confident tyrant
Keeps still in Dunsinane, and will endure
Our setting down before 't.
Mal. 'Tis his main hope;
For where there is advantage to be given,
Both more and less have given him the revolt,
And none serve with him but constrained things
Whose hearts are absent too.
Macd. Let our just censures
Attend the true event, and put we on
Industrious soldiership.
Siw. The time approaches
That will with due decision make us know
What we shall say we have and what we owe.
Thoughts speculative their unsure hopes relate,
But certain issue strokes must arbitrate;
Towards which advance the war.
[*Exeunt, marching.*

SCENE V. *Dunsinane: within the castle*

Enter MACBETH, SEYTON, *and Soldiers, with drum and colours.*

Macb. Hang out our banners on the outward walls;
The cry is still "They come." Our castle's strength
Will laugh a siege to scorn; here let them lie
Till famine and the ague eat them up.
Were they not forced with those that should be ours,
We might have met them dareful, beard to beard,
And beat them backward home.
A cry of women within.
What is that noise?
Sey. It is the cry of women, my good lord.
[*Exit.*
Macb. I have almost forgot the taste of fears.
The time has been, my senses would have cool'd
To hear a night-shriek; and my fell of hair
Would at a dismal treatise rouse and stir
As life were in 't. I have supp'd full with horrors;
Direness, familiar to my slaughterous thoughts,
Cannot once start me.

Re-enter SEYTON.

Wherefore was that cry?
Sey. The Queen, my lord, is dead.
Macb. She should have died hereafter;
There would have been a time for such a word.
To-morrow, and to-morrow, and to-morrow,

Creeps in this petty pace from day to day
To the last syllable of recorded time,
And all our yesterdays have lighted fools
The way to dusty death. Out, out, brief candle!
Life's but a walking shadow, a poor player
That struts and frets his hour upon the stage
And then is heard no more. It is a tale
Told by an idiot, full of sound and fury,
Signifying nothing.

Enter a MESSENGER.

Thou comest to use thy tongue; thy story quickly.
Mess. Gracious my lord,
I should report that which I say I saw,
But know not how to do it.
Macb. Well, say, sir.
Mess. As I did stand my watch upon the hill,
I look'd toward Birnam, and anon, methought,
The wood began to move.
Macb. Liar and slave!
Mess. Let me endure your wrath, if 't be not so.
Within this three mile may you see it coming;
I say, a moving grove.
Macb. If thou speak'st false,
Upon the next tree shalt thou hang alive,
Till famine cling thee. If thy speech be sooth,
I care not if thou dost for me as much.
I pull in resolution, and begin
To doubt the equivocation of the fiend
That lies like truth: "Fear not, till Birnam wood
Do come to Dunsinane"; and now a wood
Comes toward Dunsinane. Arm, arm, and out!
If this which he avouches does appear,
There is nor flying hence nor tarrying here.
I gin to be aweary of the sun,
And wish the estate o' the world were now undone.
Ring the alarum-bell! Blow, wind! come, wrack!
At least we'll die with harness on our back.
[*Exeunt.*

SCENE VI. *Dunsinane: before the castle*

Drum and colours. Enter MALCOLM, OLD SIWARD, MACDUFF, *and their Army, with boughs.*

Mal. Now near enough. Your leavy screens throw down,
And show like those you are. You, worthy uncle,
Shall, with my cousin, your right-noble son,
Lead our first battle. Worthy Macduff and we
Shall take upon 's what else remains to do,
According to our order.
Siw. Fare you well.
Do we but find the tyrant's power to-night,
Let us be beaten, if we cannot fight.
Macd. Make all our trumpets speak; give them all breath
Those clamorous harbingers of blood and death.
[*Exeunt.*

SCENE VII. *Another part of the field*

Alarums. Enter MACBETH.

Macb. They have tied me to a stake; I cannot fly,
But, bear-like, I must fight the course. What's he
That was not born of woman? Such a one
Am I to fear, or none.

Enter YOUNG SIWARD.

Yo. Siw. What is thy name?
Macb. Thou'lt be afraid to hear it.
Yo. Siw. No; though thou call'st thyself a hotter name
Than any is in hell.
Macb. My name's Macbeth.
Yo. Siw. The devil himself could not pronounce a title
More hateful to mine ear.
Macb. No, nor more fearful.
Yo. Siw. Thou liest, abhorred tyrant; with my sword
I'll prove the lie thou speak'st.
They fight and YOUNG SIWARD *is slain.*
Macb. Thou wast born of woman.
But swords I smile at, weapons laugh to scorn,
Brandish'd by man that's of a woman born.
[*Exit.*

Alarums. Enter MACDUFF.

Macd. That way the noise is. Tyrant, show thy face!
If thou be'st slain and with no stroke of mine,
My wife and children's ghosts will haunt me still.
I cannot strike at wretched kerns, whose arms
Are hired to bear their staves. Either thou, Macbeth,
Or else my sword with an unbatter'd edge
I sheathe again undeeded. There thou shouldst be;
By this great clatter, one of greatest note
Seems bruited. Let me find him, fortune!
And more I beg not. [*Exit. Alarums.*

Enter MALCOLM *and* OLD SIWARD.

Siw. This way, my lord; the castle's gently render'd.
The tyrant's people on both sides do fight;
The noble thanes do bravely in the war;
The day almost itself professes yours,
And little is to do.

Mal. We have met with foes
That strike beside us.
Siw. Enter, sir, the castle.
[*Exeunt. Alarums.*

SCENE VIII. *Another part of the field*

Enter MACBETH.

Macb. Why should I play the Roman fool, and die
On mine own sword? whiles I see lives, the gashes
Do better upon them.

Enter MACDUFF.

Macd. Turn, hell-hound, turn!
Macb. Of all men else I have avoided thee.
But get thee back; my soul is too much charged
With blood of thine already.
Macd. I have no words;
My voice is in my sword. Thou bloodier villain
Than terms can give thee out!
They fight.
Macb. Thou losest labour.
As easy mayst thou the intrenchant air
With thy keen sword impress as make me bleed.
Let fall thy blade on vulnerable crests;
I bear a charmed life, which must not yield
To one of woman born.
Macd. Despair thy charm;
And let the angel whom thou still hast served
Tell thee, Macduff was from his mother's womb
Untimely ripp'd.
Macb. Accursed be that tongue that tells me so,
For it hath cow'd my better part of man!
And be these juggling fiends no more believed
That palter with us in a double sense;
That keep the word of promise to our ear,
And break it to our hope. I'll not fight with thee.
Macd. Then yield thee, coward,
And live to be the show and gaze o' the time!
We'll have thee, as our rarer monsters are,
Painted upon a pole, and underwrit,
"Here may you see the tyrant."
Macb. I will not yield,
To kiss the ground before young Malcolm's feet
And to be baited with the rabble's curse.
Though Birnam wood be come to Dunsinane,
And thou opposed, being of no woman born,
Yet I will try the last. Before my body
I throw my warlike shield. Lay on, Macduff,
And damn'd be him that first cries, "Hold, enough!"
[*Exeunt, fighting. Alarums.*

Retreat. Flourish. Enter, with drum and colours, MALCOLM, OLD SIWARD, ROSS, *the other Thanes, and Soldiers.*

Mal. I would the friends we miss were safe arrived.
Siw. Some must go off; and yet, by these I see,
So great a day as this is cheaply bought.
Mal. Macduff is missing, and your noble son.
Ross. Your son, my lord, has paid a soldier's debt.
He only lived but till he was a man;
The which no sooner had his prowess confirm'd
In the unshrinking station where he fought,
But like a man he died.
Siw. Then he is dead?
Ross. Ay, and brought off the field. Your cause of sorrow
Must not be measured by his worth, for then
It hath no end.
Siw. Had he his hurts before?
Ross. Ay, on the front.
Siw. Why then, God's soldier be he!
Had I as many sons as I have hairs,
I would not wish them to a fairer death.
And so, his knell is knoll'd.
Mal. He's worth more sorrow,
And that I'll spend for him.
Siw. He's worth no more.
They say he parted well, and paid his score;
And so, God be with him! Here comes newer comfort.

Re-enter MACDUFF, *with* MACBETH'S *head.*

Macd. Hail, King! for so thou art. Behold, where stands
The usurper's cursed head. The time is free.
I see thee compass'd with thy kingdom's pearl,
That speak my salutation in their minds;
Whose voices I desire aloud with mine:
Hail, King of Scotland!
All. Hail, King of Scotland! [*Flourish.*
Mal. We shall not spend a large expense of time
Before we reckon with your several loves,
And make us even with you. My thanes and kinsmen,
Henceforth be earls, the first that ever Scotland
In such an honour named. What's more to do,
Which would be planted newly with the time,
As calling home our exiled friends abroad
That fled the snares of watchful tyranny;
Producing forth the cruel ministers
Of this dead butcher and his fiend-like queen,
Who, as 'tis thought, by self and violent hands
Took off her life; this, and what needful else
That calls upon us, by the grace of Grace,
We will perform in measure, time and place.
So, thanks to all at once and to each one,
Whom we invite to see us crown'd at Scone.
[*Flourish. Exeunt.*

ANTONY AND CLEOPATRA

DRAMATIS PERSONÆ

Mark Antony Octavius Cæsar M. Æmilius Lepidus	*triumvirs*
Sextus Pompeius Domitius Enobarbus Ventidius Eros Scarus Dercetas Demetrius Philo	*friends to Antony*
Mecænas Agrippa Dolabella Proculeius Thyreus Gallus	*friends to Cæsar*
Menas Menecrates Varrius	*friends to Pompey*

Taurus, *lieutenant-general to Cæsar*
Canidius, *lieutenant-general to Antony*
Silius, *an officer in Ventidius' army*
Euphronius, *an ambassador from Antony to Cæsar*

Alexas Mardian, *a eunuch* Seleucus Diomedes	*attendants on Cleopatra*

A Soothsayer
A Clown
Five Messengers
An Egyptian
Two Servants *to Pompey*
A Captain *of Antony's army*
Four Soldiers *of Antony's army*
Four Soldiers *of Cæsar's army*
Two Guards *to Cleopatra*
Three Guards *of Antony's army*
Two Attendants *on Antony*
One Attendant *on Cleopatra*

Cleopatra, *Queen of Egypt*
Octavia, *sister to Cæsar and wife to Antony*

Charmian Iras	*attendants on Cleopatra*

Non-Speaking: *Officers, Soldiers, Guards, Servitors, and Attendants*

Scene: *In several parts of the Roman Empire*

ACT I

Scene i. *Alexandria: a room in Cleopatra's palace*

Enter DEMETRIUS *and* PHILO.

Phi. Nay, but this dotage of our general's
O'erflows the measure. Those his goodly eyes,
That o'er the files and musters of the war
Have glow'd like plated Mars, now bend, now turn,
The office and devotion of their view
Upon a tawny front; his captain's heart,
Which in the scuffles of great fights hath burst
The buckles on his breast, reneges all temper,
And is become the bellows and the fan
To cool a gipsy's lust.

Flourish. Enter ANTONY, CLEOPATRA, *her Ladies, the Train, with Eunuchs fanning her.*

Look, where they come!
Take but good note, and you shall see in him
The triple pillar of the world transform'd
Into a strumpet's fool. Behold and see.
Cleo. If it be love indeed, tell me how much.
Ant. There's beggary in the love that can be reckon'd.
Cleo. I'll set a bourn how far to be beloved.
Ant. Then must thou needs find out new heaven, new earth.

Enter an ATTENDANT.

Att. News, my good lord, from Rome.
Ant. Grates me: the sum.
Cleo. Nay, hear them, Antony.
Fulvia perchance is angry; or, who knows
If the scarce-bearded Cæsar have not sent
His powerful mandate to you, "Do this, or this;
Take in that kingdom, and enfranchise that;
Perform 't, or else we damn thee."
Ant. How, my love!
Cleo. Perchance! nay, and most like.
You must not stay here longer, your dismission
Is come from Cæsar; therefore hear it, Antony.
Where's Fulvia's process? Cæsar's I would say? Both?
Call in the messengers. As I am Egypt's queen,
Thou blushest, Antony; and that blood of thine
Is Cæsar's homager; else so thy cheek pays shame
When shrill-tongued Fulvia scolds. The messengers!
Ant. Let Rome in Tiber melt, and the wide arch
Of the ranged empire fall! Here is my space.
Kingdoms are clay; our dungy earth alike

Feeds beast as man; the nobleness of life
Is to do thus; when such a mutual pair
Embracing.
And such a twain can do't, in which I bind,
On pain of punishment, the world to weet
We stand up peerless.

Cleo. Excellent falsehood!
Why did he marry Fulvia, and not love her?
I'll seem the fool I am not. Antony
Will be himself.

Ant. But stirr'd by Cleopatra.
Now, for the love of Love and her soft hours,
Let's not confound the time with conference harsh.
There's not a minute of our lives should stretch
Without some pleasure now. What sport to-night?

Cleo. Hear the ambassadors.

Ant. Fie, wrangling queen!
Whom everything becomes, to chide, to laugh,
To weep; whose every passion fully strives
To make itself, in thee, fair and admired!
No messenger, but thine; and all alone
To-night we'll wander through the streets and note
The qualities of people. Come, my queen;
Last night you did desire it. Speak not to us.
[*Exeunt* ANTONY *and* CLEOPATRA *with their train.*

Dem. Is Cæsar with Antonius prized so slight?

Phi. Sir, sometimes, when he is not Antony,
He comes too short of that great property
Which still should go with Antony.

Dem. I am full sorry
That he approves the common liar, who
Thus speaks of him at Rome; but I will hope
Of better deeds to-morrow. Rest you happy!
[*Exeunt.*

SCENE II. *The same: another room*

Enter CHARMIAN, IRAS, ALEXAS, *and a* SOOTHSAYER.

Char. Lord Alexas, sweet Alexas, most anything Alexas, almost most absolute Alexas, where's the soothsayer that you praised so to the Queen? O, that I knew this husband, which, you say, must charge his horns with garlands!

Alex. Soothsayer!

Sooth. Your will?

Char. Is this the man? Is't you, sir, that know things?

Sooth. In nature's infinite book of secrecy
A little I can read.

Alex. Show him your hand.

Enter ENOBARBUS.

Eno. Bring in the banquet quickly; wine enough Cleopatra's health to drink.

Char. Good sir, give me good fortune.

Sooth. I make not, but foresee.

Char. Pray, then, foresee me one.

Sooth. You shall be yet far fairer than you are.

Char. He means in flesh.

Iras. No, you shall paint when you are old.

Char. Wrinkles forbid!

Alex. Vex not his prescience; be attentive.

Char. Hush!

Sooth. You shall be more beloving than beloved.

Char. I had rather heat my liver with drinking.

Alex. Nay, hear him.

Char. Good now, some excellent fortune! Let me be married to three kings in a forenoon, and widow them all. Let me have a child at fifty, to whom Herod of Jewry may do homage. Find me to marry me with Octavius Cæsar, and companion me with my mistress.

Sooth. You shall outlive the lady whom you serve.

Char. O excellent! I love long life better than figs.

Sooth. You have seen and proved a fairer former fortune
Than that which is to approach.

Char. Then belike my children shall have no names. Prithee, how many boys and wenches must I have?

Sooth. If every of your wishes had a womb,
And fertile every wish, a million.

Char. Out, fool! I forgive thee for a witch.

Alex. You think none but your sheets are privy to your wishes.

Char. Nay, come, tell Iras hers.

Alex. We'll know all our fortunes.

Eno. Mine, and most of our fortunes, to-night, shall be—drunk to bed.

Iras. There's a palm presages chastity, if nothing else.

Char. E'en as the o'erflowing Nilus presageth famine.

Iras. Go, you wild bedfellow, you cannot soothsay.

Char. Nay, if an oily palm be not a fruitful prognostication, I cannot scratch mine ear. Prithee, tell her but a worky-day fortune.

Sooth. Your fortunes are alike.

Iras. But how, but how? give me particulars.

Sooth. I have said.

Iras. Am I not an inch of fortune better than she?

Char. Well, if you were but an inch of fortune better than I, where would you choose it?

Iras. Not in my husband's nose.

Char. Our worser thoughts heavens mend! Alexas—come, his fortune, his fortune! O, let him marry a woman that cannot go, sweet Isis, I beseech thee! and let her die too, and give him a worse! and let worse follow worse, till the worst of all follow him laughing to his grave, fifty-fold a cuckold! Good Isis, hear me this prayer, though thou deny me a matter of more weight; good Isis, I beseech thee!

Iras. Amen. Dear goddess, hear that prayer of the people! for, as it is a heart-breaking to see a handsome man loose-wived, so it is a deadly sorrow to behold a foul knave uncuckolded; therefore, dear Isis, keep decorum, and fortune him accordingly!

Char. Amen.

Alex. Lo, now, if it lay in their hands to make me a cuckold, they would make themselves whores, but they'd do 't!

Eno. Hush! here comes Antony.
Char. Not he; the Queen.

Enter CLEOPATRA.

Cleo. Saw you my lord?
Eno. No, lady.
Cleo. Was he not here?
Char. No, madam.
Cleo. He was disposed to mirth; but on the sudden
A Roman thought hath struck him. Enobarbus!
Eno. Madam?
Cleo. Seek him, and bring him hither. Where's Alexas?
Alex. Here, at your service. My lord approaches.
Cleo. We will not look upon him. Go with us.
[*Exeunt*.

Enter ANTONY *with a* MESSENGER *and* ATTENDANTS.

Mess. Fulvia thy wife first came into the field.
Ant. Against my brother Lucius?
Mess. Ay.
But soon that war had end, and the time 's state
Made friends of them, jointing their force 'gainst Cæsar;
Whose better issue in the war, from Italy,
Upon the first encounter, drave them.
Ant. Well, what worst?
Mess. The nature of bad news infects the teller.
Ant. When it concerns the fool or coward. On:
Things that are past are done with me. 'Tis thus;
Who tells me true, though in his tale lie death,
I hear him as he flatter'd.
Mess. Labienus—
This is stiff news—hath with his Parthian force
Extended Asia from Euphrates;
His conquering banner shook from Syria
To Lydia and to Ionia;
Whilst—
Ant. Antony, thou wouldst say—
Mess. O, my lord!
Ant. Speak to me home, mince not the general tongue.
Name Cleopatra as she is call'd in Rome;
Rail thou in Fulvia's phrase; and taunt my faults
With such full license as both truth and malice
Have power to utter. O, then we bring forth weeds,
When our quick minds lie still; and our ills told us
Is as our earing. Fare thee well awhile.
Mess. At your noble pleasure. [*Exit*.
Ant. From Sicyon, ho, the news! Speak there!
1st Att. The man from Sicyon—is there such an one?
2nd Att. He stays upon your will.
Ant. Let him appear.
These strong Egyptian fetters I must break,
Or lose myself in dotage.

Enter another MESSENGER.

What are you?
2nd Mess. Fulvia thy wife is dead.
Ant. Where died she?
2nd Mess. In Sicyon.
Her length of sickness, with what else more serious
Importeth thee to know, this bears.
Gives a letter.
Ant. Forbear me.
[*Exit* SECOND MESSENGER.
There's a great spirit gone! Thus did I desire it.
What our contempt doth often hurl from us,
We wish it ours again; the present pleasure,
By revolution lowering, does become
The opposite of itself. She's good, being gone;
The hand could pluck her back that shoved her on.
I must from this enchanting queen break off;
Ten thousand harms, more than the ills I know,
My idleness doth hatch. How now! Enobarbus!

Re-enter ENOBARBUS.

Eno. What's your pleasure, sir?
Ant. I must with haste from hence.
Eno. Why, then, we kill all our women. We see how mortal an unkindness is to them; if they suffer our departure, death's the word.
Ant. I must be gone.
Eno. Under a compelling occasion, let women die. It were pity to cast them away for nothing; though, between them and a great cause, they

should be esteemed nothing. Cleopatra, catching but the least noise of this, dies instantly; I have seen her die twenty times upon far poorer moment. I do think there is mettle in death, which commits some loving act upon her, she hath such a celerity in dying.

Ant. She is cunning past man's thought.

Eno. Alack, sir, no; her passions are made of nothing but the finest part of pure love. We cannot call her winds and waters sighs and tears; they are greater storms and tempests than almanacs can report. This cannot be cunning in her; if it be, she makes a shower of rain as well as Jove.

Ant. Would I had never seen her!

Eno. O, sir, you had then left unseen a wonderful piece of work; which not to have been blest withal would have discredited your travel.

Ant. Fulvia is dead.

Eno. Sir?

Ant. Fulvia is dead.

Eno. Fulvia!

Ant. Dead.

Eno. Why, sir, give the gods a thankful sacrifice. When it pleaseth their deities to take the wife of a man from him, it shows to man the tailors of the earth; comforting therein, that when old robes are worn out, there are members to make new. If there were no more women but Fulvia, then had you indeed a cut, and the case to be lamented. This grief is crowned with consolation; your old smock brings forth a new petticoat; and indeed the tears live in an onion that should water this sorrow.

Ant. The business she hath broached in the state
Cannot endure my absence.

Eno. And the business you have broached here cannot be without you; especially that of Cleopatra's, which wholly depends on your abode.

Ant. No more light answers. Let our officers
Have notice what we purpose. I shall break
The cause of our expedience to the Queen,
And get her leave to part. For not alone
The death of Fulvia, with more urgent touches,
Do strongly speak to us; but the letters too
Of many our contriving friends in Rome
Petition us at home. Sextus Pompeius
Hath given the dare to Cæsar, and commands
The empire of the sea. Our slippery people,
Whose love is never link'd to the deserver
Till his deserts are past, begin to throw
Pompey the Great and all his dignities
Upon his son; who, high in name and power,
Higher than both in blood and life, stands up
For the main soldier; whose quality, going on,
The sides o' the world may danger. Much is breeding,
Which, like the courser's hair, hath yet but life,
And not a serpent's poison. Say, our pleasure,
To such whose place is under us, requires
Our quick remove from hence.

Eno. I shall do 't. [*Exeunt.*

SCENE III. *The same: another room*

Enter CLEOPATRA, CHARMIAN, IRAS, *and* ALEXAS.

Cleo. Where is he?

Char. I did not see him since.

Cleo. See where he is, who's with him, what he does.
I did not send you. If you find him sad,
Say I am dancing; if in mirth, report
That I am sudden sick. Quick, and return.
[*Exit* ALEXAS.

Char. Madam, methinks, if you did love him dearly,
You do not hold the method to enforce
The like from him.

Cleo. What should I do, I do not?

Char. In each thing give him way, cross him in nothing.

Cleo. Thou teachest like a fool; the way to lose him.

Char. Tempt him not so too far; I wish, forbear.
In time we hate that which we often fear.
But here comes Antony.

Enter ANTONY.

Cleo. I am sick and sullen.

Ant. I am sorry to give breathing to my purpose—

Cleo. Help me away, dear Charmian; I shall fall.
It cannot be thus long, the sides of nature
Will not sustain it.

Ant. Now, my dearest queen—

Cleo. Pray you, stand farther from me.

Ant. What's the matter?

Cleo. I know, by that same eye, there's some good news.
What says the married woman? You may go.
Would she had never given you leave to come!
Let her not say 'tis I that keep you here;
I have no power upon you; hers you are.

Ant. The gods best know—

Cleo. O, never was there queen
So mightily betray'd! yet at the first
I saw the treasons planted.

Ant. Cleopatra—

Cleo. Why should I think you can be mine and true,
Though you in swearing shake the throned gods,

Who have been false to Fulvia? Riotous madness,
To be entangled with those mouth-made vows,
Which break themselves in swearing!
Ant. Most sweet queen—
Cleo. Nay, pray you, seek no colour for your going,
But bid farewell, and go. When you sued staying,
Then was the time for words; no going then;
Eternity was in our lips and eyes,
Bliss in our brows' bent; none our parts so poor,
But was a race of heaven. They are so still,
Or thou, the greatest soldier of the world,
Art turn'd the greatest liar.
Ant. How now, lady!
Cleo. I would I had thy inches; thou shouldst know
There were a heart in Egypt.
Ant. Hear me, Queen.
The strong necessity of time commands
Our services awhile; but my full heart
Remains in use with you. Our Italy
Shines o'er with civil swords; Sextus Pompeius
Makes his approaches to the port of Rome;
Equality of two domestic powers
Breed scrupulous faction; the hated, grown to strength,
Are newly grown to love; the condemn'd Pompey,
Rich in his father's honour, creeps apace
Into the hearts of such as have not thrived
Upon the present state, whose numbers threaten;
And quietness, grown sick of rest, would purge
By any desperate change. My more particular,
And that which most with you should safe my going,
Is Fulvia's death.
Cleo. Though age from folly could not give me freedom,
It does from childishness. Can Fulvia die?
Ant. She's dead, my queen.
Look here, and at thy sovereign leisure read
The garboils she awaked; at the last, best;
See when and where she died.
Cleo. O most false love!
Where be the sacred vials thou shouldst fill
With sorrowful water? Now I see, I see,
In Fulvia's death, how mine received shall be.
Ant. Quarrel no more, but be prepared to know
The purposes I bear; which are, or cease,
As you shall give the advice. By the fire
That quickens Nilus' slime, I go from hence
Thy soldier, servant; making peace or war
As thou affect'st.
Cleo. Cut my lace, Charmian, come!
But let it be; I am quickly ill, and well,
So Antony loves.
Ant. My precious queen, forbear;
And give true evidence to his love, which stands
An honourable trial.
Cleo. So Fulvia told me.
I prithee, turn aside and weep for her;
Then bid adieu to me, and say the tears
Belong to Egypt. Good now, play one scene
Of excellent dissembling; and let it look
Like perfect honour.
Ant. You'll heat my blood. No more.
Cleo. You can do better yet; but this is meetly.
Ant. Now, by my sword—
Cleo. And target. Still he mends;
But this is not the best. Look, prithee, Charmian,
How this Herculean Roman does become
The carriage of his chafe.
Ant. I'll leave you, lady.
Cleo. Courteous lord, one word.
Sir, you and I must part, but that's not it;
Sir, you and I have loved, but there's not it;
That you know well. Something it is I would—
O, my oblivion is a very Antony,
And I am all forgotten.
Ant. But that your royalty
Holds idleness your subject, I should take you
For idleness itself.
Cleo. 'Tis sweating labour
To bear such idleness so near the heart
As Cleopatra this. But, sir, forgive me;
Since my becomings kill me, when they do not
Eye well to you. Your honour calls you hence;
Therefore be deaf to my unpitied folly,
And all the gods go with you! Upon your sword
Sit laurel victory! and smooth success
Be strew'd before your feet!
Ant. Let us go. Come;
Our separation so abides, and flies,
That thou, residing here, go'st yet with me,
And I, hence fleeting, here remain with thee.
Away! [*Exeunt.*

SCENE IV. *Rome: Cæsar's house*

Enter OCTAVIUS CÆSAR, *reading a letter,* LEPIDUS, *and their Train.*

Cæs. You may see, Lepidus, and henceforth know,
It is not Cæsar's natural vice to hate
Our great competitor. From Alexandria
This is the news: he fishes, drinks, and wastes
The lamps of night in revel; is not more manlike
Than Cleopatra; nor the queen of Ptolemy
More womanly than he; hardly gave audience, or
Vouchsafed to think he had partners. You shall find there

A man who is the abstract of all faults
That all men follow.
Lep. I must not think there are
Evils enow to darken all his goodness.
His faults in him seem as the spots of heaven,
More fiery by night's blackness; hereditary,
Rather than purchased; what he cannot change,
Than what he chooses.
Cæs. You are too indulgent. Let us grant, it is not
Amiss to tumble on the bed of Ptolemy;
To give a kingdom for a mirth; to sit
And keep the turn of tippling with a slave;
To reel the streets at noon, and stand the buffet
With knaves that smell of sweat: say this becomes him—
As his composure must be rare indeed
Whom these things cannot blemish—yet must Antony
No way excuse his soils, when we do bear
So great weight in his lightness. If he fill'd
His vacancy with his voluptuousness,
Full surfeits and the dryness of his bones,
Call on him for't; but to confound such time,
That drums him from his sport and speaks as loud
As his own state and ours—'tis to be chid
As we rate boys, who, being mature in knowledge,
Pawn their experience to their present pleasure,
And so rebel to judgement.

Enter a MESSENGER.

Lep. Here's more news.
Mess. Thy biddings have been done; and every hour,
Most noble Cæsar, shalt thou have report
How 'tis abroad. Pompey is strong at sea;
And it appears he is beloved of those
That only have fear'd Cæsar. To the ports
The discontents repair, and men's reports
Give him much wrong'd.
Cæs. I should have known no less.
It hath been taught us from the primal state,
That he which is was wish'd until he were;
And the ebb'd man, ne'er loved till ne'er worth love,
Comes dear'd by being lack'd. This common body,
Like to a vagabond flag upon the stream,
Goes to and back, lackeying the varying tide,
To rot itself with motion.
Mess. Cæsar, I bring thee word,
Menecrates and Menas, famous pirates,
Make the sea serve them, which they ear and wound
With keels of every kind. Many hot inroads
They make in Italy; the borders maritime
Lack blood to think on't, and flush youth revolt;
No vessel can peep forth, but 'tis as soon
Taken as seen; for Pompey's name strikes more
Than could his war resisted.
Cæs. Antony,
Leave thy lascivious wassails. When thou once
Wast beaten from Modena, where thou slew'st
Hirtius and Pansa, consuls, at thy heel
Did famine follow; whom thou fought'st against,
Though daintily brought up, with patience more
Than savages could suffer. Thou didst drink
The stale of horses, and the gilded puddle
Which beasts would cough at; thy palate then did deign
The roughest berry on the rudest hedge;
Yea, like the stag, when snow the pasture sheets,
The barks of trees thou browsed'st; on the Alps
It is reported thou didst eat strange flesh,
Which some did die to look on; and all this—
It wounds thine honour that I speak it now—
Was borne so like a soldier, that thy cheek
So much as lank'd not.
Lep. 'Tis pity of him.
Cæs. Let his shames quickly
Drive him to Rome. 'Tis time we twain
Did show ourselves i' the field; and to that end
Assemble we immediate council. Pompey
Thrives in our idleness.
Lep. To-morrow, Cæsar,
I shall be furnish'd to inform you rightly
Both what by sea and land I can be able
To front this present time.
Cæs. Till which encounter,
It is my business too. Farewell.
Lep. Farewell, my lord. What you shall know meantime
Of stirs abroad, I shall beseech you, sir,
To let me be partaker.
Cæs. Doubt not, sir;
I knew it for my bond. [*Exeunt.*

SCENE V. *Alexandria: Cleopatra's palace*

Enter CLEOPATRA, CHARMIAN, IRAS, *and* MARDIAN.

Cleo. Charmian!
Char. Madam?
Cleo. Ha, ha!
Give me to drink mandragora.
Char. Why, madam?
Cleo. That I might sleep out this great gap of time
My Antony is away.
Char. You think of him too much.
Cleo. O, 'tis treason!
Char. Madam, I trust, not so.

Cleo. Thou, eunuch Mardian!
Mar. What's your Highness' pleasure?
Cleo. Not now to hear thee sing; I take no pleasure
In aught an eunuch has. 'Tis well for thee,
That, being unseminar'd, thy freer thoughts
May not fly forth of Egypt. Hast thou affections?
Mar. Yes, gracious madam.
Cleo. Indeed!
Mar. Not in deed, madam; for I can do nothing
But what indeed is honest to be done;
Yet have I fierce affections, and think
What Venus did with Mars.
Cleo. O Charmian,
Where, think'st thou he is now? Stands he, or sits he?
Or does he walk? or is he on his horse?
O happy horse, to bear the weight of Antony!
Do bravely, horse! for wot'st thou whom thou movest?
The demi-Atlas of this earth, the arm
And burgonet of men. He's speaking now,
Or murmuring, "Where's my serpent of old Nile?"
For so he calls me. Now I feed myself
With most delicious poison. Think on me,
That am with Phoebus' amorous pinches black,
And wrinkled deep in time? Broad-fronted Cæsar,
When thou wast here above the ground, I was
A morsel for a monarch; and great Pompey
Would stand and make his eyes grow in my brow;
There would he anchor his aspect and die
With looking on his life.

Enter ALEXAS.

Alex. Sovereign of Egypt, hail!
Cleo. How much unlike art thou Mark Antony!
Yet, coming from him, that great medicine hath
With his tinct gilded thee.
How goes it with my brave Mark Antony?
Alex. Last thing he did, dear queen,
He kiss'd—the last of many doubled kisses—
This orient pearl. His speech sticks in my heart.
Cleo. Mine ear must pluck it thence.
Alex. "Good friend," quoth he,
"Say, the firm Roman to great Egypt sends
This treasure of an oyster; at whose foot,
To mend the petty present, I will piece
Her opulent throne with kingdoms; all the East,
Say thou, shall call her mistress." So he nodded,
And soberly did mount an arm-gaunt steed,
Who neigh'd so high that what I would have spoke
Was beastly dumb'd by him.
Cleo. What, was he sad or merry?
Alex. Like to the time o' the year between the extremes
Of hot and cold, he was nor sad nor merry.
Cleo. O well-divided disposition! Note him,
Note him, good Charmian, 'tis the man; but note him:
He was not sad, for he would shine on those
That make their looks by his; he was not merry,
Which seem'd to tell them his remembrance lay
In Egypt with his joy; but between both.
O heavenly mingle! Be'st thou sad or merry,
The violence of either thee becomes,
So does it no man else. Met'st thou my posts?
Alex. Ay, madam, twenty several messengers.
Why do you send so thick?
Cleo. Who's born that day
When I forget to send to Antony,
Shall die a beggar. Ink and paper, Charmian.
Welcome, my good Alexas. Did I, Charmian,
Ever love Cæsar so?
Char. O that brave Cæsar!
Cleo. Be choked with such another emphasis!
Say, the brave Antony.
Char. The valiant Cæsar!
Cleo. By Isis, I will give thee bloody teeth,
If thou with Cæsar paragon again
My man of men.
Char. By your most gracious pardon,
I sing but after you.
Cleo. My salad days,
When I was green in judgement, cold in blood,
To say as I said then! But, come, away;
Get me ink and paper.
He shall have every day a several greeting,
Or I'll unpeople Egypt. [*Exeunt.*

ACT II

SCENE I. *Messina: Pompey's house*

Enter POMPEY, MENECRATES, *and* MENAS, *in warlike manner.*

Pom. If the great gods be just, they shall assist
The deeds of justest men.
Mene. Know, worthy Pompey,
That what they do delay, they not deny.
Pom. Whiles we are suitors to their throne, decays
The thing we sue for.
Mene. We, ignorant of ourselves,
Beg often our own harms, which the wise powers
Deny us for our good; so find we profit
By losing of our prayers.
Pom. I shall do well.
The people love me, and the sea is mine;
My powers are crescent, and my auguring hope

Says it will come to the full. Mark Antony
In Egypt sits at dinner, and will make
No wars without doors. Cæsar gets money where
He loses hearts. Lepidus flatters both,
Of both is flatter'd; but he neither loves,
Nor either cares for him.

Men. Cæsar and Lepidus
Are in the field; a mighty strength they carry.

Pom. Where have you this? 'tis false.

Men. From Silvius, sir.

Pom. He dreams. I know they are in Rome together,
Looking for Antony. But all the charms of love,
Salt Cleopatra, soften thy waned lip!
Let witchcraft join with beauty, lust with both!
Tie up the libertine in a field of feasts,
Keep his brain fuming; Epicurean cooks
Sharpen with cloyless sauce his appetite;
That sleep and feeding may prorogue his honour
Even till a Lethe'd dulness!

Enter VARRIUS.

How now, Varrius!

Var. This is most certain that I shall deliver:
Mark Antony is every hour in Rome
Expected; since he went from Egypt 'tis
A space for further travel.

Pom. I could have given less matter
A better ear. Menas, I did not think
This amorous surfeiter would have donn'd his helm
For such a petty war. His soldiership
Is twice the other twain; but let us rear
The higher our opinion, that our stirring
Can from the lap of Egypt's widow pluck
The ne'er-lust-wearied Antony.

Men. I cannot hope
Cæsar and Antony shall well greet together.
His wife that's dead did trespasses to Cæsar;
His brother warr'd upon him; although, I think,
Not moved by Antony.

Pom. I know not, Menas,
How lesser enmities may give way to greater.
Were't not that we stand up against them all,
'Twere pregnant they should square between themselves;
For they have entertained cause enough
To draw their swords; but how the fear of us
May cement their divisions and bind up
The petty difference, we yet not know.
Be't as our gods will have't! It only stands
Our lives upon to use our strongest hands.
Come, Menas. [*Exeunt.*

SCENE II. *Rome: the house of Lepidus*

Enter ENOBARBUS *and* LEPIDUS.

Lep. Good Enobarbus, 'tis a worthy deed,
And shall become you well, to entreat your captain
To soft and gentle speech.

Eno. I shall entreat him
To answer like himself. If Cæsar move him,
Let Antony look over Cæsar's head
And speak as loud as Mars. By Jupiter,
Were I the wearer of Antonius' beard,
I would not shave't to-day.

Lep. 'Tis not a time
For private stomaching.

Eno. Every time
Serves for the matter that is then born in't.

Lep. But small to greater matters must give way.

Eno. Not if the small come first.

Lep. Your speech is passion;
But, pray you, stir no embers up. Here comes
The noble Antony.

Enter ANTONY *and* VENTIDIUS.

Eno. And yonder, Cæsar.

Enter CÆSAR, MECÆNAS, *and* AGRIPPA.

Ant. If we compose well here, to Parthia!
Hark, Ventidius.

Cæs. I do not know,
Mecænas; ask Agrippa.

Lep. Noble friends,
That which combined us was most great, and let not
A leaner action rend us. What's amiss,
May it be gently heard; when we debate
Our trivial difference loud, we do commit
Murder in healing wounds; then, noble partners,
The rather, for I earnestly beseech,
Touch you the sourest points with sweetest terms,
Nor curstness grow to the matter.

Ant. 'Tis spoken well.
Were we before our armies, and to fight,
I should do thus.

Flourish.

Cæs. Welcome to Rome.

Ant. Thank you.

Cæs. Sit.

Ant. Sit, sir.

Cæs. Nay, then.

Ant. I learn, you take things ill which are not so,
Or being, concern you not.

Cæs. I must be laugh'd at
If, or for nothing or a little, I

Should say myself offended, and with you
Chiefly i' the world; more laugh'd at that I should
Once name you derogately, when to sound your name
It not concern'd me.
Ant. My being in Egypt, Cæsar,
What was't to you?
Cæs. No more than my residing here at Rome
Might be to you in Egypt; yet, if you there
Did practise on my state, your being in Egypt
Might be my question.
Ant. How intend you, practised?
Cæs. You may be pleased to catch at mine intent.
By what did here befal me. Your wife and brother
Made wars upon me; and their contestation
Was theme for you, you were the word of war.
Ant. You do mistake your business; my brother never
Did urge me in his act. I did inquire it;
And have my learning from some true reports,
That drew their swords with you. Did he not rather
Discredit my authority with yours;
And make the wars alike against my stomach,
Having alike your cause? Of this my letters
Before did satisfy you. If you'll patch a quarrel,
As matter whole you have not to make it with,
It must not be with this.
Cæs. You praise yourself
By laying defects of judgement to me; but
You patch'd up your excuses.
Ant. Not so, not so;
I know you could not lack, I am certain on't,
Very necessity of this thought, that I,
Your partner in the cause 'gainst which he fought,
Could not with graceful eyes attend those wars
Which fronted mine own peace. As for my wife,
I would you had her spirit in such another.
The third o' the world is yours; which with a snaffle
You may pace easy, but not such a wife.
Eno. Would we had all such wives, that the men might go to wars with the women!
Ant. So much uncurbable, her garboils, Cæsar,
Made out of her impatience, which not wanted
Shrewdness of policy too, I grieving grant
Did you too much disquiet. For that you must
But say, I could not help it.
Cæs. I wrote to you
When rioting in Alexandria; you
Did pocket up my letters, and with taunts
Did gibe my missive out of audience.
Ant. Sir,
He fell upon me ere admitted. Then
Three kings I had newly feasted, and did want
Of what I was i' the morning; but next day
I told him of myself; which was as much
As to have ask'd him pardon. Let this fellow
Be nothing of our strife; if we contend,
Out of our question wipe him.
Cæs. You have broken
The article of your oath; which you shall never
Have tongue to charge me with.
Lep. Soft, Cæsar!
Ant. No,
Lepidus, let him speak.
The honour is sacred which he talks on now,
Supposing that I lack'd it. But, on, Cæsar;
The article of my oath.
Cæs. To lend me arms and aid when I required them;
The which you both denied.
Ant. Neglected, rather;
And then when poison'd hours had bound me up
From mine own knowledge. As nearly as I may,
I'll play the penitent to you; but mine honesty
Shall not make poor my greatness, nor my power
Work without it. Truth is that Fulvia,
To have me out of Egypt, made wars here;
For which myself, the ignorant motive, do
So far ask pardon as befits mine honour
To stoop in such a case.
Lep. 'Tis noble spoken.
Mec. If it might please you, to enforce no further
The griefs between ye: to forget them quite
Were to remember that the present need
Speaks to atone you.
Lep. Worthily spoken, Mecænas.
Eno. Or, if you borrow one another's love for the instant, you may, when you hear no more words of Pompey, return it again. You shall have time to wrangle in when you have nothing else to do.
Ant. Thou art a soldier only; speak no more.
Eno. That truth should be silent I had almost forgot.
Ant. You wrong this presence; therefore speak no more.
Eno. Go to, then; your considerate stone.
Cæs. I do not much dislike the matter, but
The manner of his speech; for't cannot be
We shall remain in friendship, our conditions
So differing in their acts. Yet, if I knew
What hoop should hold us stanch, from edge to edge
O' the world I would pursue it.

Agr. Give me leave, Cæsar—
Cæs. Speak, Agrippa.
Agr. Thou hast a sister by the mother's side,
Admired Octavia. Great Mark Antony
Is now a widower.
Cæs. Say not so, Agrippa.
If Cleopatra heard you, your reproof
Were well deserved of rashness.
Ant. I am not married, Cæsar. Let me hear
Agrippa further speak.
Agr. To hold you in perpetual amity,
To make you brothers, and to knit your hearts
With an unslipping knot, take Antony
Octavia to his wife; whose beauty claims
No worse a husband than the best of men;
Whose virtue and whose general graces speak
That which none else can utter. By this marriage,
All little jealousies, which now seem great,
And all great fears, which now import their dangers,
Would then be nothing. Truths would be tales,
Where now half tales be truths. Her love to both
Would, each to other and all loves to both,
Draw after her. Pardon what I have spoke;
For 'tis a studied, not a present thought,
By duty ruminated.
Ant. Will Cæsar speak?
Cæs. Not till he hears how Antony is touch'd
With what is spoke already.
Ant. What power is in Agrippa,
If I would say, "Agrippa, be it so,"
To make this good?
Cæs. The power of Cæsar, and
His power unto Octavia.
Ant. May I never
To this good purpose, that so fairly shows,
Dream of impediment! Let me have thy hand.
Further this act of grace; and from this hour
The heart of brothers govern in our loves
And sway our great designs!
Cæs. There is my hand.
A sister I bequeath you, whom no brother
Did ever love so dearly. Let her live
To join our kingdoms and our hearts; and never
Fly off our loves again!
Lep. Happily, amen!
Ant. I did not think to draw my sword 'gainst Pompey;
For he hath laid strange courtesies and great
Of late upon me. I must thank him only,
Lest my remembrance suffer ill report;
At heel of that, defy him.
Lep. Time calls upon's.
Of us must Pompey presently be sought,
Or else he seeks out us.
Ant. Where lies he?
Cæs About the mount Misenum.
Ant. What is his strength by land?
Cæs. Great and increasing; but by sea
He is an absolute master.
Ant. So is the fame.
Would we had spoke together! Haste we for it;
Yet, ere we put ourselves in arms, dispatch we
The business we have talk'd of.
Cæs. With most gladness;
And do invite you to my sister's view,
Whither straight I'll lead you.
Ant. Let us, Lepidus,
Not lack your company.
Lep. Noble Antony,
Not sickness should detain me.
[*Flourish*. *Exeunt* CÆSAR, ANTONY, *and* LEPIDUS.

Mec. Welcome from Egypt, sir.

Eno. Half the heart of Cæsar, worthy Mecænas! My honourable friend, Agrippa!

Agr. Good Enobarbus!

Mec. We have cause to be glad that matters are so well digested. You stayed well by't in Egypt.

Eno. Ay, sir; we did sleep day out of countenance, and made the night light with drinking.

Mec. Eight wild-boars roasted whole at a breakfast, and but twelve persons there; is this true?

Eno. This was but as a fly by an eagle. We had much more monstrous matter of feast, which worthily deserved noting.

Mec. She's a most triumphant lady, if report be square to her.

Eno. When she first met Mark Antony, she pursed up his heart, upon the river of Cydnus.

Agr. There she appeared indeed; or my reporter devised well for her.

Eno. I will tell you.
The barge she sat in, like a burnish'd throne,
Burn'd on the water. The poop was beaten gold;
Purple the sails, and so perfumed that
The winds were love-sick with them; the oars were silver,
Which to the tune of flutes kept stroke, and made
The water which they beat to follow faster,
As amorous of their strokes. For her own person,
It beggar'd all description: she did lie
In her pavilion—cloth-of-gold of tissue—
O'er-picturing that Venus where we see
The fancy outwork nature. On each side her
Stood pretty dimpled boys, like smiling Cupids,
With divers-colour'd fans, whose wind did seem
To glow the delicate cheeks which they did cool,
And what they undid did.
Agr. O, rare for Antony!
Eno. Her gentlewomen, like the Nereides,
So many mermaids, tended her i' the eyes,

And made their bends adornings. At the helm
A seeming mermaid steers; the silken tackle
Swell with the touches of those flower-soft hands,
That yarely frame the office. From the barge
A strange invisible perfume hits the sense
Of the adjacent wharfs. The city cast
Her people out upon her; and Antony,
Enthroned i' the market-place, did sit alone,
Whistling to the air; which, but for vacancy,
Had gone to gaze on Cleopatra too
And made a gap in nature.
Agr. Rare Egyptian!
Eno. Upon her landing, Antony sent to her,
Invited her to supper. She replied,
It should be better he became her guest;
Which she entreated. Our courteous Antony,
Whom ne'er the word of "No" woman heard speak,
Being barber'd ten times o'er, goes to the feast,
And for his ordinary pays his heart
For what his eyes eat only.
Agr. Royal wench!
She made great Cæsar lay his sword to bed.
He plough'd her and she cropp'd.
Eno. I saw her once
Hop forty paces through the public street;
And having lost her breath, she spoke, and panted,
That she did make defect perfection,
And, breathless, power breathe forth.
Mec. Now Antony must leave her utterly.
Eno. Never; he will not.
Age cannot wither her, not custom stale
Her infinite variety. Other women cloy
The appetites they feed, but she makes hungry
Where most she satisfies; for vilest things
Become themselves in her, that the holy priests
Bless her when she is riggish.
Mec. If beauty, wisdom, modesty, can settle
The heart of Antony, Octavia is
A blessed lottery to him.
Agr. Let us go.
Good Enobarbus, make yourself my guest
Whilst you abide here.
Eno. Humbly, sir, I thank you. [*Exeunt.*

SCENE III. *The same: Cæsar's house*

Enter ANTONY, CÆSAR, OCTAVIA *between them, and Attendants.*

Ant. The world and my great office will sometimes
Divide me from your bosom.
Octa. All which time
Before the gods my knee shall bow my prayers
To them for you.
Ant. Good night, sir. My Octavia,
Read not my blemishes in the world's report.
I have not kept my square; but that to come
Shall all be done by the rule. Good night, dear lady.
Good night, sir.
Cæs. Good night.
[*Exeunt* CÆSAR *and* OCTAVIA.

Enter SOOTHSAYER.

Ant. Now, sirrah; you do wish yourself in Egypt?
Sooth. Would I had never come from thence, nor you
Thither!
Ant. If you can, your reason?
Sooth. I see it in
My motion, have it not in my tongue; but yet
Hie you to Egypt again.
Ant. Say to me,
Whose fortunes shall rise higher, Cæsar's or mine?
Sooth. Cæsar's.
Therefore, O Antony, stay not by his side.
Thy demon, that's thy spirit which keeps thee, is
Noble, courageous, high, unmatchable,
Where Cæsar's is not; but, near him, thy angel
Becomes a fear, as being o'erpower'd: therefore
Make space enough between you.
Ant. Speak this no more.
Sooth. To none but thee; no more, but when to thee.
If thou dost play with him at any game,
Thou art sure to lose; and, of that natural luck,
He beats thee 'gainst the odds. Thy lustre thickens,
When he shines by. I say again, thy spirit
Is all afraid to govern thee near him;
But, he away, 'tis noble.
Ant. Get thee gone.
Say to Ventidius I would speak with him.
[*Exit* SOOTHSAYER.
He shall to Parthia. Be it art or hap,
He hath spoken true. The very dice obey him;
And in our sports my better cunning faints
Under his chance. If we draw lots, he speeds;
His cocks do win the battle still of mine,
When it is all to nought; and his quails ever
Beat mine, inhoop'd, at odds. I will to Egypt;
And though I make this marriage for my peace,
I' the East my pleasure lies.

Enter VENTIDIUS.

O, come, Ventidius,
You must to Parthia. Your commission's ready;
Follow me, and receive't. [*Exeunt.*

SCENE IV. *The same: a street*

Enter LEPIDUS, MECÆNAS, *and* AGRIPPA.

Lep. Trouble yourselves no further; pray you, hasten
Your generals after.
Agr. Sir, Mark Antony
Will e'en but kiss Octavia, and we'll follow.
Lep. Till I shall see you in your soldier's dress,
Which will become you both, farewell.
Mec. We shall,
As I conceive the journey, be at the Mount
Before you, Lepidus.
Lep. Your way is shorter;
My purposes do draw me much about.
You'll win two days upon me.
Mec. }
Agr. } Sir, good success!
Lep. Farewell. [*Exeunt.*

SCENE V. *Alexandria: Cleopatra's palace*

Enter CLEOPATRA, CHARMIAN, IRAS, *and* ALEXAS.

Cleo. Give me some music; music, moody food
Of us that trade in love.
Attend. The music, ho!

Enter MARDIAN *the eunuch.*

Cleo. Let it alone; let's to billiards. Come, Charmian.
Char. My arm is sore; best play with Mardian.
Cleo. As well a woman with an eunuch play'd
As with a woman. Come, you'll play with me, sir?
Mar. As well as I can, madam.
Cleo. And when good will is show'd, though't come too short,
The actor may plead pardon. I'll none now.
Give me mine angle; we'll to the river; there,
My music playing far off, I will betray
Tawny-finn'd fishes; my bended hook shall pierce
Their slimy jaws; and, as I draw them up,
I'll think them every one an Antony,
And say, "Ah, ha! you're caught."
Char. 'Twas merry when
You wager'd on your angling; when your diver
Did hang a salt-fish on his hook, which he
With fervency drew up.
Cleo. That time—O times!—
I laugh'd him out of patience; and that night
I laugh'd him into patience; and next morn,
Ere the ninth hour, I drunk him to his bed;
Then put my tires and mantles on him, whilst
I wore his sword Philippan.

Enter a MESSENGER.

O, from Italy!
Ram thou thy fruitful tidings in mine ears,
That long time have been barren.
Mess. Madam, madam—
Cleo. Antonius dead!—If thou say so, villain,
Thou kill'st thy mistress; but well and free,
If thou so yield him, there is gold, and here
My bluest veins to kiss; a hand that kings
Have lipp'd, and trembled kissing.
Mess. First, madam, he is well.
Cleo. Why, there's more gold.
But, sirrah, mark, we use
To say the dead are well. Bring it to that,
The gold I give thee will I melt and pour
Down thy ill-uttering throat.
Mess. Good madam, hear me.
Cleo. Well, go to, I will;
But there's no goodness in thy face. If Antony
Be free and healthful—so tart a favour
To trumpet such good tidings! If not well,
Thou shouldst come like a Fury crown'd with snakes,
Not like a formal man.
Mess. Will't please you hear me?
Cleo. I have a mind to strike thee ere thou speak'st.
Yet, if thou say Antony lives, is well,
Or friends with Cæsar, or not captive to him,
I'll set thee in a shower of gold, and hail
Rich pearls upon thee.
Mess. Madam, he's well.
Cleo. Well said.
Mess. And friends with Cæsar.
Cleo. Thou'rt an honest man.
Mess. Cæsar and he are greater friends than ever.
Cleo. Make thee a fortune from me.
Mess. But yet, madam—
Cleo. I do not like "But yet," it does allay
The good precedence; fie upon "But yet"!
"But yet" is as a gaoler to bring forth
Some monstrous malefactor. Prithee, friend,
Pour out the pack of matter to mine ear,
The good and bad together. He's friends with Cæsar;
In state of health thou say'st; and thou say'st free.
Mess. Free, madam! no; I made no such report.
He's bound unto Octavia.
Cleo. For what good turn?
Mess. For the best turn i' the bed.
Cleo. I am pale, Charmian.
Mess. Madam, he's married to Octavia.

Cleo. The most infectious pestilence upon thee!
Strikes him down.
Mess. Good madam, patience.
Cleo. What say you? Hence,
Strikes him again.
Horrible villain! or I'll spurn thine eyes
Like balls before me; I'll unhair thy head.
She hales him up and down.
Thou shalt be whipp'd with wire, and stew'd in brine,
Smarting in lingering pickle.
Mess. Gracious madam,
I that do bring the news made not the match.
Cleo. Say 'tis not so, a province I will give thee,
And make thy fortunes proud; the blow thou hadst
Shall make thy peace for moving me to rage;
And I will boot thee with what gift beside
Thy modesty can beg.
Mess. He's married, madam.
Cleo. Rogue, thou hast lived too long.
Draws a knife.
Mess. Nay, then I'll run.
What mean you, madam? I have made no fault.
[*Exit.*
Char. Good madam, keep yourself within yourself.
The man is innocent.
Cleo. Some innocents 'scape not the thunderbolt.
Melt Egypt into Nile! and kindly creatures
Turn all to serpents! Call the slave again.
Though I am mad, I will not bite him. Call.
Char. He is afeard to come.
Cleo. I will not hurt him.
[*Exit* CHARMIAN.
These hands do lack nobility that they strike
A meaner than myself; since I myself
Have given myself the cause.

Re-enter CHARMIAN *and* MESSENGER.

Come hither, sir.
Though it be honest, it is never good
To bring bad news. Give to a gracious message
An host of tongues; but let ill tidings tell
Themselves when they be felt.
Mess. I have done my duty.
Cleo. Is he married?
I cannot hate thee worser than I do,
If thou again say "Yes."
Mess. He's married, madam.
Cleo. The gods confound thee! dost thou hold there still?
Mess. Should I lie, madam?
Cleo. O, I would thou didst,
So half my Egypt were submerged and made
A cistern for scaled snakes! Go, get thee hence.
Hadst thou Narcissus in thy face, to me
Thou wouldst appear most ugly. He is married?
Mess. I crave your Highness' pardon.
Cleo. He is married?
Mess. Take no offence that I would not offend you.
To punish me for what you make me do
Seems much unequal. He's married to Octavia.
Cleo. O, that his fault should make a knave of thee,
That art not what thou'rt sure of! Get thee hence.
The merchandise which thou hast brought from Rome
Are all too dear for me; lie they upon thy hand,
And be undone by 'em! [*Exit* MESSENGER.
Char. Good your Highness, patience.
Cleo. In praising Antony, I have dispraised Cæsar.
Char. Many times, madam.
Cleo. I am paid for't now.
Lead me from hence;
I faint. O Iras, Charmian! 'tis no matter.
Go to the fellow, good Alexas; bid him
Report the feature of Octavia, her years,
Her inclination, let him not leave out
The colour of her hair. Bring me word quickly.
[*Exit* ALEXAS.
Let him for ever go; let him not—Charmian,
Though he be painted one way like a Gorgon,
The other way's a Mars. Bid you Alexas
[*To* MARDIAN.
Bring me word how tall she is. Pity me, Charmian,
But do not speak to me. Lead me to my chamber.
[*Exeunt.*

SCENE VI. *Near Misenum*

Flourish. Enter POMPEY *and* MENAS *at one side, with drum and trumpet; at another,* CÆSAR, ANTONY, LEPIDUS, ENOBARBUS, MECÆNAS *with Soldiers marching.*

Pom. Your hostages I have, so have you mine;
And we shall talk before we fight.
Cæs. Most meet
That first we come to words; and therefore have we
Our written purposes before us sent;
Which, if thou hast consider'd, let us know
If 'twill tie up thy discontented sword,
And carry back to Sicily much tall youth
That else must perish here.
Pom. To you all three,
The senators alone of this great world,
Chief factors for the gods, I do not know
Wherefore my father should revengers want,
Having a son and friends; since Julius Cæsar,

Who at Philippi the good Brutus ghosted,
There saw you labouring for him. What was't
That moved pale Cassius to conspire; and what
Made the all-honour'd, honest Roman, Brutus,
With the arm'd rest, courtiers of beauteous freedom,
To drench the Capitol; but that they would
Have one man but a man? And that is it
Hath made me rig my navy; at whose burthen
The anger'd ocean foams; with which I meant
To scourge the ingratitude that despiteful Rome
Cast on my noble father.
Cæs. Take your time.
Ant. Thou canst not fear us, Pompey, with thy sails;
We'll speak with thee at sea. At land, thou know'st
How much we do o'er-count thee.
Pom. At land, indeed,
Thou dost o'er-count me of my father's house;
But, since the cuckoo builds not for himself,
Remain in't as thou mayst.
Lep. Be pleased to tell us—
For this is from the present—how you take
The offers we have sent you.
Cæs. There's the point.
Ant. Which do not be entreated to, but weigh
What it is worth embraced.
Cæs. And what may follow,
To try a larger fortune.
Pom. You have made me offer
Of Sicily, Sardinia; and I must
Rid all the sea of pirates; then, to send
Measures of wheat to Rome; this 'greed upon,
To part with unhack'd edges, and bear back
Our targes undinted.
Cæs. Ant. Lep. That's our offer.
Pom. Know, then,
I came before you here a man prepared
To take this offer; but Mark Antony
Put me to some impatience. Though I lose
The praise of it by telling, you must know,
When Cæsar and your brother were at blows,
Your mother came to Sicily and did find
Her welcome friendly.
Ant. I have heard it, Pompey;
And am well studied for a liberal thanks
Which I do owe you.
Pom. Let me have your hand.
I did not think, sir, to have met you here.
Ant. The beds i' the East are soft; and thanks to you,
That call'd me timelier than my purpose hither;
For I have gain'd by't.
Cæs. Since I saw you last,
There is a change upon you.
Pom. Well, I know not
What counts harsh Fortune casts upon my face;
But in my bosom shall she never come,
To make my heart her vassal.
Lep. Well met here.
Pom. I hope so, Lepidus. Thus we are agreed.
I crave our composition may be written,
And seal'd between us.
Cæs. That's the next to do.
Pom. We'll feast each other ere we part; and let's
Draw lots who shall begin.
Ant. That will I, Pompey.
Pom. No, Antony, take the lot; but, first
Or last, your fine Egyptian cookery
Shall have the fame. I have heard that Julius Cæsar
Grew fat with feasting there.
Ant. You have heard much.
Pom. I have fair meanings, sir.
Ant. And fair words to them.
Pom. Then so much have I heard;
And I have heard, Apollodorus carried—
Eno. No more of that; he did so.
Pom. What, I pray you?
Eno. A certain queen to Cæsar in a mattress.
Pom. I know thee now. How farest thou, soldier?
Eno. Well;
And well am like to do; for, I perceive,
Four feasts are toward.
Pom. Let me shake thy hand;
I never hated thee. I have seen thee fight,
When I have envied thy behaviour.
Eno. Sir,
I never loved you much; but I ha' praised ye,
When you have well deserved ten times as much
As I have said you did.
Pom. Enjoy thy plainness,
It nothing ill becomes thee.
Aboard my galley I invite you all.
Will you lead, lords?
Cæs. Ant. Lep. Show us the way, sir.
Pom. Come.
[*Exeunt all but* MENAS *and* ENOBARBUS.

Men. [*Aside*] Thy father, Pompey, would ne'er have made this treaty. You and I have known, sir.

Eno. At sea, I think.

Men. We have, sir.

Eno. You have done well by water.

Men. And you by land.

Eno. I will praise any man that will praise me; though it cannot be denied what I have done by land.

Men. Nor what I have done by water.

Eno. Yes, something you can deny for your own safety. You have been a great thief by sea.

Men. And you by land.

Eno. There I deny my land service. But give me your hand, Menas. If our eyes had authority, here they might take two thieves kissing.

Men. All men's faces are true, whatsome'er their hands are.

Eno. But there is never a fair woman has a true face.

Men. No slander; they steal hearts.

Eno. We came hither to fight with you.

Men. For my part, I am sorry it is turned to a drinking. Pompey doth this day laugh away his fortune.

Eno. If he do, sure, he cannot weep't back again.

Men. You've said, sir. We looked not for Mark Antony here. Pray you, is he married to Cleopatra?

Eno. Cæsar's sister is called Octavia.

Men. True, sir; she was the wife of Caius Marcellus.

Eno. But she is now the wife of Marcus Antonius.

Men. Pray ye, sir?

Eno. 'Tis true.

Men. Then is Cæsar and he for ever knit together.

Eno. If I were bound to divine of this unity, I would not prophesy so.

Men. I think the policy of that purpose made more in the marriage than the love of the parties.

Eno. I think so too. But you shall find the band that seems to tie their friendship together will be the very strangler of their amity. Octavia is of a holy, cold, and still conversation.

Men. Who would not have his wife so?

Eno. Not he that himself is not so; which is Mark Antony. He will to his Egyptian dish again. Then shall the sighs of Octavia blow the fire up in Cæsar; and, as I said before, that which is the strength of their amity shall prove the immediate author of their variance. Antony will use his affection where it is; he married but his occasion here.

Men. And thus it may be. Come, sir, will you aboard? I have a health for you.

Eno. I shall take it, sir. We have used our throats in Egypt.

Men. Come, let's away. [*Exeunt*.

SCENE VII. *On board Pompey's galley, off Misenum*

Music plays. Enter two or three SERVANTS *with a banquet*.

1st Serv. Here they'll be, man. Some o' their plants are ill-rooted already; the least wind i' the world will blow them down.

2nd Serv. Lepidus is high-coloured.

1st Serv. They have made him drink alms-drink.

2nd Serv. As they pinch one another by the disposition, he cries out "No more"; reconciles them to his entreaty, and himself to the drink.

1st Serv. But it raises the greater war between him and his discretion.

2nd Serv. Why, this it is to have a name in great men's fellowship. I had as lief have a reed that will do me no service as a partisan I could not heave.

1st Serv. To be called into a huge sphere, and not to be seen to move in't, are the holes where eyes should be, which pitifully disaster the cheeks.

A sennet sounded. Enter CÆSAR, ANTONY, LEPIDUS POMPEY, AGRIPPA, MECÆNAS, ENOBARBUS, MENAS, *with other captains*.

Ant. [*To* CÆSAR] Thus do they, sir: they take the flow o' the Nile
By certain scales i' the pyramid; they know,
By the height, the lowness, or the mean, if dearth
Or foison follow. The higher Nilus swells,
The more it promises; as it ebbs, the seedsman
Upon the slime and ooze scatters his grain,
And shortly comes to harvest.

Lep. You've strange serpents there.

Ant. Ay, Lepidus.

Lep. Your serpent of Egypt is bred now of your mud by the operation of your sun. So is your crocodile.

Ant. They are so.

Pom. Sit—and some wine! A health to Lepidus!

Lep. I am not so well as I should be, but I'll ne'er out.

Eno. Not till you have slept; I fear me you'll be in till then.

Lep. Nay, certainly, I have heard the Ptolemies' pyramises are very goodly things; without contradiction, I have heard that.

Men. [*Aside to* POMPEY] Pompey, a word.

Pom. [*Aside to Menas*] Say in mine ear: what is't?

Men. [*Aside to* POMPEY] Forsake thy seat, I do beseech thee, captain,
And hear me speak a word.

Pom. [*Aside to* MENAS] Forbear me till anon.
This wine for Lepidus!

Lep. What manner o' thing is your crocodile?

Ant. It is shaped, sir, like itself; and it is as broad as it hath breadth; it is just so high as it is, and moves with it own organs; it lives by that which nourisheth it; and the elements once out of it, it transmigrates.

Lep. What colour is it of?

Ant. Of it own colour too.

Lep. 'Tis a strange serpent.

Ant. 'Tis so. And the tears of it are wet.

Cæs. Will this description satisfy him?

Ant. With the health that Pompey gives him, else he is a very epicure.

Pom. [*Aside to* MENAS] Go hang, sir, hang!
Tell me of that? away!
Do as I bid you. Where's this cup I call'd for?

Men. [*Aside to* POMPEY] If for the sake of merit thou wilt hear me,
Rise from thy stool.

Pom. [*Aside to* MENAS] I think thou'rt mad.
The matter? [*Rises, and walks aside.*]

Men. I have ever held my cap off to thy fortunes.

Pom. Thou hast served me with much faith.
What's else to say?
Be jolly, lords.

Ant. These quick-sands, Lepidus,
Keep off them, for you sink.

Men. Wilt thou be lord of all the world?

Pom. What say'st thou?

Men. Wilt thou be lord of the whole world?
That's twice.

Pom. How should that be?

Men. But entertain it,
And, though thou think me poor, I am the man
Will give thee all the world.

Pom. Hast thou drunk well?

Men. No, Pompey, I have kept me from the cup.
Thou art, if thou darest be, the earthly Jove.
Whate'er the ocean pales, or sky inclips,
Is thine, if thou wilt ha't.

Pom. Show me which way.

Men. These three world-sharers, these competitors,
Are in thy vessel. Let me cut the cable;
And, when we are put off, fall to their throats.
All there is thine.

Pom. Ah, this thou shouldst have done,
And not have spoke on 't! In me 'tis villainy;
In thee 't had been good service. Thou must know,
'Tis not my profit that does lead mine honour;
Mine honour, it. Repent that e'er thy tongue
Hath so betray'd thine act; being done unknown,
I should have found it afterwards well done;
But must condemn it now. Desist, and drink.

Men. [*Aside*] For this,
I'll never follow thy pall'd fortunes more.
Who seeks, and will not take when once 'tis offer'd,
Shall never find it more.

Pom. This health to Lepidus!

Ant. Bear him ashore. I'll pledge it for him, Pompey.

Eno. Here's to thee, Menas!

Men. Enobarbus, welcome!

Pom. Fill till the cup be hid.

Eno. There's a strong fellow, Menas.
[*Pointing to the Attendant who carries off* LEPIDUS.

Men. Why?

Eno. A' bears the third part of the world, man; see'st not?

Men. The third part, then, is drunk. Would it were all,
That it might go on wheels!

Eno. Drink thou; increase the reels.

Men. Come.

Pom. This is not yet an Alexandrian feast.

Ant. It ripens towards it. Strike the vessels, ho!
Here is to Cæsar!

Cæs. I could well forbear 't.
It's monstrous labour, when I wash my brain,
And it grows fouler.

Ant. Be a child o' the time.

Cæs. Possess it, I'll make answer.
But I had rather fast from all four days
Than drink so much in one.

Eno. Ha, my brave emperor! [*To* ANTONY.
Shall we dance now the Egyptian Bacchanals,
And celebrate our drink?

Pom. Let's ha't, good soldier.

Ant. Come, let's all take hands,
Till that the conquering wine hath steep'd our sense
In soft and delicate Lethe.

Eno. All take hands.
Make battery to our ears with the loud music;
The while I'll place you; then the boy shall sing;
The holding every man shall bear as loud
As his strong sides can volley.

Music plays. ENOBARBUS *places them hand in hand.*

THE SONG

Come, thou monarch of the vine,
Plumpy Bacchus with pink eyne!
In thy fats our cares be drown'd,
With thy grapes our hairs be crown'd.
Cup us, till the world go round,
Cup us, till the world go round!

Cæs. What would you more? Pompey, good night. Good brother,

Let me request you off; our graver business
Frowns at this levity. Gentle lords, let's part;
You see we have burnt our cheeks. Strong Enobarb
Is weaker than the wine; and mine own tongue
Splits what it speaks; the wild disguise hath almost
Antick'd us all. What needs more words? Good night.
Good Antony, your hand.
Pom. I'll try you on the shore.
Ant. And shall, sir; give's your hand.
Pom. O Antony,
You have my father's house—But, what? we are friends.
Come, down into the boat.
Eno. Take heed you fall not.
[*Exeunt all but* ENOBARBUS *and* MENAS.
Menas, I'll not on shore.
Men. No, to my cabin.
These drums! these trumpets, flutes! what!
Let Neptune hear we bid a loud farewell
To these great fellows. Sound and be hang'd, sound out!
Sound a flourish, with drums.
Eno. Ho! says a'. There's my cap.
Men. Ho! Noble captain, come. [*Exeunt.*

ACT III

SCENE I. *A plain in Syria*

Enter VENTIDIUS *as it were in triumph, with* SILIUS, *and other Romans, Officers, and Soldiers; the dead body of* PACORUS *borne before him.*

Ven. Now, darting Parthia, art thou struck; and now
Pleased fortune does of Marcus Crassus' death
Make me revenger. Bear the King's son's body
Before our army. Thy Pacorus, Orodes,
Pays this for Marcus Crassus.
Sil. Noble Ventidius,
Whilst yet with Parthian blood thy sword is warm,
The fugitive Parthians follow; spur through Media,
Mesopotamia, and the shelters whither
The routed fly; so thy grand captain Antony
Shall set thee on triumphant chariots and
Put garlands on thy head.
Ven. O Silius, Silius,
I have done enough; a lower place, note well,
May make too great an act; for learn this, Silius;
Better to leave undone, than by our deed
Acquire too high a fame when him we serve's away.
Cæsar and Antony have ever won
More in their officer than person. Sossius,
One of my place in Syria, his lieutenant,
For quick accumulation of renown,
Which he achieved by the minute, lost his favour.
Who does i' the wars more than his captain can
Becomes his captain's captain; and ambition,
The soldier's virtue, rather makes choice of loss,
Than gain which darkens him.
I could do more to do Antonius good,
But 'twould offend him; and in his offence
Should my performance perish.
Sil. Thou hast, Ventidius, that
Without the which a soldier, and his sword,
Grants scarce distinction. Thou wilt write to Antony?
Ven. I'll humbly signify what in his name,
That magical word of war, we have effected;
How, with his banners and his well-paid ranks,
The ne'er-yet-beaten horse of Parthia
We have jaded out o' the field.
Sil. Where is he now?
Ven. He purposeth to Athens; whither, with what haste
The weight we must convey with 's will permit,
We shall appear before him. On, there; pass along! [*Exeunt.*

SCENE II. *Rome: an ante-chamber in Cæsar's house*

Enter AGRIPPA *at one door,* ENOBARBUS *at another.*

Agr. What, are the brothers parted?
Eno. They have dispatch'd with Pompey, he is gone;
The other three are sealing. Octavia weeps
To part from Rome; Cæsar is sad; and Lepidus,
Since Pompey's feast, as Menas says, is troubled
With the green sickness.
Agr. 'Tis a noble Lepidus.
Eno. A very fine one. O, how he loves Cæsar!
Agr. Nay, but how dearly he adores Mark Antony!
Eno. Cæsar? Why, he's the Jupiter of men.
Agr. What's Antony? The god of Jupiter.
Eno. Spake you of Cæsar? How! the nonpareil!
Agr. O Antony! O thou Arabian bird!
Eno. Would you praise Cæsar, say "Cæsar"; go no further.
Agr. Indeed, he plied them both with excellent praises.
Eno. But he loves Cæsar best; yet he loves Antony.
Ho! hearts, tongues, figures, scribes, bards, poets, cannot
Think, speak, cast, write, sing, number, ho!
His love to Antony. But as for Cæsar,

Kneel down, kneel down, and wonder.
Agr. Both he loves.
Eno. They are his shards, and he their beetle.
[*Trumpets within.*] So;
This is to horse. Adieu, noble Agrippa.
Agr. Good fortune, worthy soldier; and farewell.

Enter CÆSAR, ANTONY, LEPIDUS, *and* OCTAVIA.

Ant. No further, sir.
Cæs. You take from me a great part of myself;
Use me well in 't. Sister, prove such a wife
As my thoughts make thee, and as my farthest band
Shall pass on thy approof. Most noble Antony,
Let not the piece of virtue, which is set
Betwixt us as the cement of our love,
To keep it builded, be the ram to batter
The fortress of it; for better might we
Have loved without this mean, if on both parts
This be not cherish'd.
Ant. Make me not offended.
In your distrust.
Cæs. I have said.
Ant. You shall not find,
Though you be therein curious, the least cause
For what you seem to fear. So, the gods keep you,
And make the hearts of Romans serve your ends!
We will here part.
Cæs. Farewell, my dearest sister, fare thee well.
The elements be kind to thee, and make
Thy spirits all of comfort! fare thee well.
Oct. My noble brother!
Ant. The April's in her eyes; it is love's spring,
And these the showers to bring it on. Be cheerful.
Oct. Sir, look well to my husband's house; and—
Cæs. What,
Octavia?
Oct. I'll tell you in your ear.
Ant. Her tongue will not obey her heart, nor can
Her heart inform her tongue—the swan's down-feather,
That stands upon the swell at full of tide,
And neither way inclines.
Eno. [*Aside to* AGRIPPA] Will Cæsar weep?
Agr. [*Aside to* ENOBARBUS] He has a cloud in's face.
Eno. [*Aside to* AGRIPPA] He were the worse for that, were he a horse;
So is he, being a man.
Agr. [*Aside to* ENOBARBUS] Why, Enobarbus,
When Antony found Julius Cæsar dead
He cried almost to roaring; and he wept
When at Philippi he found Brutus slain.
Eno. [*Aside to* AGRIPPA] That year, indeed, he was troubled with a rheum;
What willingly he did confound he wail'd,
Believe 't, till I wept too.
Cæs. No, sweet Octavia,
You shall hear from me still; the time shall not
Out-go my thinking on you.
Ant. Come, sir, come;
I'll wrestle with you in my strength of love.
Look, here I have you; thus I let you go,
And give you to the gods.
Cæs. Adieu; be happy!
Lep. Let all the number of the stars give light
To thy fair way!
Cæs. Farewell, farewell! [*Kisses* OCTAVIA.
Ant. Farewell!
[*Trumpets sound. Exeunt.*

SCENE III. *Alexandria: Cleopatra's palace*

Enter CLEOPATRA, CHARMIAN, IRAS, *and* ALEXAS.

Cleo. Where is the fellow?
Alex. Half afeard to come.
Cleo. Go to, go to.

Enter the MESSENGER *as before.*

Come hither, sir.
Alex. Good Majesty,
Herod of Jewry dare not look upon you
But when you are well pleased.
Cleo. That Herod's head
I'll have; but how, when Antony is gone
Through whom I might command it? Come thou near.
Mess. Most gracious Majesty—
Cleo. Didst thou behold Octavia?
Mess. Ay, dread queen.
Cleo. Where?
Mess. Madam, in Rome;
I look'd her in the face, and saw her led
Between her brother and Mark Antony.
Cleo. Is she as tall as me?
Mess. She is not, madam.
Cleo. Didst hear her speak? is she shrill-tongued or low?
Mess. Madam, I heard her speak; she is low-voiced.
Cleo. That's not so good. He cannot like her long?
Char. Like her! O Isis! 'tis impossible.
Cleo. I think so, Charmian. Dull of tongue, and dwarfish!
What majesty is in her gait? Remember,
If e'er thou look'dst on majesty.
Mess. She creeps;
Her motion and her station are as one;

She shows a body rather than a life,
A statue than a breather.
Cleo. Is this certain?
Mess. Or I have no observance.
Char. Three in Egypt
Cannot make better note.
Cleo. He's very knowing;
I do perceive 't. There's nothing in her yet.
The fellow has good judgement.
Char. Excellent.
Cleo. Guess at her years, I prithee.
Mess. Madam,
She was a widow—
Cleo. Widow! Charmian, hark.
Mess. And I do think she's thirty.
Cleo. Bear'st thou her face in mind? is't long or round?
Mess. Round even to faultiness.
Cleo. For the most part, too, they are foolish that are so.
Her hair, what colour?
Mess. Brown, madam; and her forehead
As low as she would wish it.
Cleo. There's gold for thee.
Thou must not take my former sharpness ill.
I will employ thee back again; I find thee
Most fit for business. Go make thee ready;
Our letters are prepared. [*Exit* MESSENGER.
Char. A proper man.
Cleo. Indeed, he is so. I repent me much
That so I harried him. Why, methinks, by him,
This creature's no such thing.
Char. Nothing, madam.
Cleo. The man hath seen some majesty, and should know.
Char. Hath he seen majesty? Isis else defend,
And serving you so long!
Cleo. I have one thing more to ask him yet, good Charmian;
But 'tis no matter; thou shalt bring him to me
Where I will write. All may be well enough.
Char. I warrant you, madam. [*Exeunt.*

SCENE IV. *Athens: A room in Antony's house*

Enter ANTONY *and* OCTAVIA.

Ant. Nay, nay, Octavia, not only that—
That were excusable, that, and thousands more
Of semblable import—but he hath waged
New wars 'gainst Pompey; made his will, and read it
To public ear;
Spoke scantly of me; when perforce he could not
But pay me terms of honour, cold and sickly
He vented them; most narrow measure lent me;
When the best hint was given him, he not took 't,
Or did it from his teeth.
Oct. O my good lord,
Believe not all; or, if you must believe,
Stomach not all. A more unhappy lady,
If this division chance, ne'er stood between,
Praying for both parts.
The good gods will mock me presently,
When I shall pray, "O, bless my lord and husband!"
Undo that prayer, by crying out as loud,
"O, bless my brother!" Husband win, win brother,
Prays, and destroys the prayer; no midway
'Twixt these extremes at all.
Ant. Gentle Octavia,
Let your best love draw to that point which seeks
Best to preserve it. If I lose mine honour,
I lose myself; better I were not yours
Than yours so branchless. But, as you requested,
Yourself shall go between's. The mean time, lady,
I'll raise the preparation of a war
Shall stain your brother. Make your soonest haste;
So your desires are yours.
Oct. Thanks to my lord.
The Jove of power make me most weak, most weak,
Your reconciler! Wars 'twixt you twain would be
As if the world should cleave, and that slain men
Should solder up the rift.
Ant. When it appears to you where this begins,
Turn your displeasure that way; for our faults
Can never be so equal that your love
Can equally move with them. Provide your going;
Choose your own company, and command what cost
Your heart has mind to. [*Exeunt.*

SCENE V. *The same: another room*

Enter ENOBARBUS *and* EROS, *meeting.*

Eno. How now, friend Eros!
Eros. There's strange news come, sir.
Eno. What, man?
Eros. Cæsar and Lepidus have made wars upon Pompey.
Eno. This is old. What is the success?
Eros. Cæsar, having made use of him in the wars 'gainst Pompey, presently denied him rivality; would not let him partake in the glory of the action; and not resting here, accuses him of letters he had formerly wrote to Pompey; upon his own appeal, seizes him. So the poor third is up, till death enlarge his confine.

Eno. Then, world, thou hast a pair of chaps, no more;
And throw between them all the food thou hast,
They'll grind the one the other. Where's Antony?
Eros. He's walking in the garden—thus; and spurns
The rush that lies before him; cries, "Fool Lepidus!"
And threats the throat of that his officer
That murder'd Pompey.
Eno. Our great navy's rigg'd.
Eros. For Italy and Cæsar. More, Domitius;
My lord desires you presently; my news
I might have told hereafter.
Eno. 'Twill be naught;
But let it be. Bring me to Antony.
Eros. Come, sir. [*Exeunt.*

SCENE VI. *Rome: Cæsar's house*

Enter CÆSAR, AGRIPPA, *and* MECÆNAS.

Cæs. Contemning Rome, he has done all this and more
In Alexandria. Here's the manner of't:
I' the market-place, on a tribunal silver'd,
Cleopatra and himself in chairs of gold
Were publicly enthroned. At the feet sat
Cæsarion, whom they call my father's son,
And all the unlawful issue that their lust
Since then hath made between them. Unto her
He gave the stablishment of Egypt; made her
Of lower Syria, Cyprus, Lydia,
Absolute queen.
Mec. This in the public eye?
Cæs. I' the common show-place, where they exercise.
His sons he there proclaim'd the kings of kings:
Great Media, Parthia, and Armenia,
He gave to Alexander; to Ptolemy he assign'd
Syria, Cilicia, and Phœnicia. She
In the habiliments of the goddess Isis
That day appear'd; and oft before gave audience,
As 'tis reported, so.
Mec. Let Rome be thus
Inform'd.
Agr. Who, queasy with his insolence
Already, will their good thoughts call from him.
Cæs. The people know it; and have now received
His accusations.
Agr. Who does he accuse?
Cæs. Cæsar; and that, having in Sicily
Sextus Pompeius spoil'd, we had not rated him
His part o' the isle. Then does he say he lent me
Some shipping unrestored. Lastly, he frets
That Lepidus of the triumvirate
Should be deposed; and, being, that we detain
All his revenue.
Agr. Sir, this should be answer'd.
Cæs. 'Tis done already, and the messenger gone.
I have told him Lepidus was grown too cruel;
That he his high authority abused,
And did deserve his change. For what I have conquer'd,
I grant him part; but then, in his Armenia,
And other of his conquer'd kingdoms, I
Demand the like.
Mec. He'll never yield to that.
Cæs. Nor must not then be yielded to in this.

Enter OCTAVIA *with her train.*

Oct. Hail, Cæsar, and my lord! hail, most dear Cæsar!
Cæs. That ever I should call thee castaway!
Oct. You have not call'd me so, nor have you cause.
Cæs. Why have you stol'n upon us thus? You come not
Like Cæsar's sister. The wife of Antony
Should have an army for an usher, and
The neighs of horse to tell of her approach
Long ere she did appear; the trees by the way
Should have borne men; and expectation fainted,
Longing for what it had not; nay, the dust
Should have ascended to the roof of heaven,
Raised by your populous troops. But you are come
A market-maid to Rome; and have prevented
The ostentation of our love, which, left unshown,
Is often left unloved. We should have met you
By sea and land; supplying every stage
With an augmented greeting.
Oct. Good my lord,
To come thus was I not constrain'd, but did it
On my free will. My lord, Mark Antony,
Hearing that you prepared for war, acquainted
My grieved ear withal; whereon, I begg'd
His pardon for return.
Cæs. Which soon he granted,
Being an obstruct 'tween his lust and him.
Oct. Do not say so, my lord.
Cæs. I have eyes upon him,
And his affairs come to me on the wind.
Where is he now?
Oct. My lord, in Athens.
Cæs. No, my most wronged sister; Cleopatra
Hath nodded him to her. He hath given his empire
Up to a whore; who now are levying
The kings o' the earth for war. He hath assembled
Bocchus, the King of Libya; Archelaus,

Of Cappadocia; Philadelphos, King
Of Paphlagonia; the Thracian king, Adallas;
King Malchus of Arabia; King of Pont;
Herod of Jewry; Mithridates, King
Of Comagene; Polemon and Amyntas,
The Kings of Mede and Lycaonia,
With a more larger list of sceptres.

Oct. Ay me, most wretched,
That have my heart parted betwixt two friends
That do afflict each other!

Cæs. Welcome hither.
Your letters did withhold our breaking forth;
Till we perceived, both how you were wrong led,
And we in negligent danger. Cheer your heart;
Be you not troubled with the time, which drives
O'er your content these strong necessities;
But let determined things to destiny
Hold unbewail'd their way. Welcome to Rome;
Nothing more dear to me. You are abused
Beyond the mark of thought: and the high gods,
To do you justice, make them ministers
Of us and those that love you. Best of comfort;
And ever welcome to us.

Agr. Welcome, lady.

Mec. Welcome, dear madam.
Each heart in Rome does love and pity you.
Only the adulterous Antony, most large
In his abominations, turns you off,
And gives his potent regiment to a trull,
That noises it against us.

Oct. Is it so, sir?

Cæs. Most certain. Sister, welcome. Pray you,
Be ever known to patience. My dear'st sister!
[*Exeunt.*

SCENE VII. *Near Actium: Antony's camp*

Enter CLEOPATRA *and* ENOBARBUS.

Cleo. I will be even with thee, doubt it not.

Eno. But why, why, why?

Cleo. Thou hast forspoke my being in these wars,
And say'st it is not fit.

Eno. Well, is it, is it?

Cleo. If not denounced against us, why should not we
Be there in person?

Eno. [*Aside*] Well, I could reply:
If we should serve with horse and mares together,
The horse were merely lost; the mares would bear
A soldier and his horse.

Cleo. What is't you say?

Eno. Your presence needs must puzzle Antony;
Take from his heart, take from his brain, from's time,
What should not then be spared. He is already
Traduced for levity; and 'tis said in Rome
That Photinus an eunuch and your maids
Manage this war.

Cleo. Sink Rome, and their tongues rot
That speak against us! A charge we bear i' the war,
And, as the president of my kingdom, will
Appear there for a man. Speak not against it;
I will not stay behind.

Eno. Nay, I have done.
Here comes the Emperor.

Enter ANTONY *and* CANIDIUS.

Ant. Is it not strange, Canidius,
That from Tarentum and Brundusium
He could so quickly cut the Ionian sea,
And take in Toryne? You have heard on 't, sweet?

Cleo. Celerity is never more admired
Than by the negligent.

Ant. A good rebuke,
Which might have well becomed the best of men,
To taunt at slackness. Canidius, we
Will fight with him by sea.

Cleo. By sea! what else?

Can. Why will my lord do so?

Ant. For that he dares us to 't.

Eno. So hath my lord dared him to single fight.

Can. Ay, and to wage this battle at Pharsalia,
Where Cæsar fought with Pompey; but these offers,
Which serve not for his vantage, he shakes off;
And so should you.

Eno. Your ships are not well mann'd;
Your mariners are muleters, reapers, people
Ingross'd by swift impress; in Cæsar's fleet
Are those that often have 'gainst Pompey fought.
Their ships are yare; yours, heavy. No disgrace
Shall fall you for refusing him at sea,
Being prepared for land.

Ant. By sea, by sea.

Eno. Most worthy sir, you therein throw away
The absolute soldiership you have by land;
Distract your army, which doth most consist
Of war-mark'd footmen; leave unexecuted
Your own renowned knowledge; quite forego
The way which promises assurance; and
Give up yourself merely to chance and hazard,
From firm security.

Ant. I'll fight at sea.

Cleo. I have sixty sails, Cæsar none better.

Ant. Our overplus of shipping will we burn;
And, with the rest full-mann'd, from the head of Actium

Beat the approaching Cæsar. But if we fail,
We then can do't at land.

Enter a MESSENGER.

Thy business?
Mess. The news is true, my lord; he is descried;
Cæsar has taken Toryne.
Ant. Can he be there in person? 'tis impossible;
Strange that his power should be. Canidius,
Our nineteen legions thou shalt hold by land,
And our twelve thousand horse. We'll to our ship.
Away, my Thetis!

Enter a SOLDIER.

How now, worthy soldier!
Sold. O noble emperor, do not fight by sea;
Trust not to rotten planks. Do you misdoubt
This sword and these my wounds? Let the Egyptians
And the Phœnicians go a-ducking; we
Have used to conquer, standing on the earth,
And fighting foot to foot.
Ant. Well, well; away!
[*Exeunt* ANTONY, CLEOPATRA, *and* ENOBARBUS.
Sold. By Hercules, I think I am i' the right.
Can. Soldier, thou art; but his whole action grows
Not in the power on't. So our leader's led,
And we are women's men.
Sold. You keep by land
The legions and the horse whole, do you not?
Can. Marcus Octavius, Marcus Justeius,
Publicola, and Cælius, are for sea;
But we keep whole by land. This speed of Cæsar's
Carries beyond belief.
Sold. While he was yet in Rome,
His power went out in such distractions as
Beguiled all spies.
Can. Who's his lieutenant, hear you?
Sold. They say, one Taurus.
Can. Well I know the man.

Enter a MESSENGER.

Mess. The Emperor calls Canidius.
Can. With news the time's with labour, and throes forth,
Each minute, some. [*Exeunt*.

SCENE VIII. *A plain near Actium*

Enter CÆSAR, *and* TAURUS, *with his army, marching*.

Cæs. Taurus!
Taur. My Lord?
Cæs. Strike not by land; keep whole; provoke not battle,
Till we have done at sea. Do not exceed
The prescript of this scroll; our fortune lies
Upon this jump. [*Exeunt*.

SCENE IX. *Another part of the plain*

Enter ANTONY *and* ENOBARBUS.

Ant. Set we our squadrons on yond side o' the hill,
In eye of Cæsar's battle; from which place
We may the number of the ships behold,
And so proceed accordingly. [*Exeunt*.

SCENE X. *Another part of the plain*

CANIDIUS *marcheth with his land army one way over the stage; and* TAURUS, *the lieutenant of* CÆSAR, *the other way. After their going in, is heard the noise of a sea-fight*.

Alarum. Enter ENOBARBUS.

Eno. Naught, naught, all naught! I can behold no longer.
The Antoniad, the Egyptian admiral,
With all their sixty, fly and turn the rudder.
To see't mine eyes are blasted.

Enter SCARUS.

Scar. Gods and goddesses,
All the whole synod of them!
Eno. What's thy passion?
Scar. The greater cantle of the world is lost
With very ignorance; we have kiss'd away
Kingdoms and provinces.
Eno. How appears the fight?
Scar. On our side like the token'd pestilence,
Where death is sure. Yon ribaudred nag of Egypt—
Whom leprosy o'ertake!—i' the midst o' the fight,
When vantage like a pair of twins appear'd,
Both as the same, or rather ours the elder,
The breese upon her, like a cow in June,
Hoists sails and flies.
Eno. That I beheld.
Mine eyes did sicken at the sight, and could not
Endure a further view.
Scar. She once being loof'd,
The noble ruin of her magic, Antony,
Claps on his sea-wing, and, like a doting mallard,
Leaving the fight in height, flies after her.
I never saw an action of such shame;
Experience, manhood, honour, ne'er before
Did violate so itself.
Eno. Alack, alack!

Enter CANIDIUS.

Can. Our fortune on the sea is out of breath
And sinks most lamentably. Had our general
Been what he knew himself, it had gone well.
O, he has given example for our flight,
Most grossly, by his own!
Eno. Ay, are you thereabouts?
Why, then, good night indeed.
Can. Toward Peloponnesus are they fled.
Scar. 'Tis easy to't; and there I will attend
What further comes.
Can. To Cæsar will I render
My legions and my horse. Six kings already
Show me the way of yielding.
Eno. I'll yet follow
The wounded chance of Antony, though my reason
Sits in the wind against me. [*Exeunt.*

SCENE XI. *Alexandria: Cleopatra's palace*

Enter ANTONY *with* ATTENDANTS.

Ant. Hark! the land bids me tread no more upon't;
It is ashamed to bear me! Friends, come hither.
I am so lated in the world, that I
Have lost my way for ever. I have a ship
Laden with gold; take that, divide it; fly,
And make your peace with Cæsar.
All. Fly! not we.
Ant. I have fled myself; and have instructed cowards
To run and show their shoulders. Friends, be gone;
I have myself resolved upon a course
Which has no need of you; be gone.
My treasure's in the harbour, take it. O,
I follow'd that I blush to look upon.
My very hairs do mutiny; for the white
Reprove the brown for rashness, and they them
For fear and doting. Friends, be gone; you shall
Have letters from me to some friends that will
Sweep your way for you. Pray you, look not sad,
Nor make replies of loathness. Take the hint
Which my despair proclaims; let that be left
Which leaves itself. To the sea-side straightway;
I will possess you of that ship and treasure.
Leave me, I pray, a little; pray you now.
Nay, do so; for, indeed, I have lost command,
Therefore I pray you. I'll see you by and by.
Sits down.

Enter CLEOPATRA *led by* CHARMIAN *and* IRAS; EROS *following.*

Eros. Nay, gentle madam, to him, comfort him.
Iras. Do, most dear queen.
Char. Do! why, what else?
Cleo. Let me sit down. O Juno!
Ant. No, no, no, no, no.
Eros. See you here, sir?
Ant. O fie, fie, fie!
Char. Madam!
Iras. Madam, O good empress!
Eros. Sir, sir—
Ant. Yes, my lord, yes; he at Philippi kept
His sword e'en like a dancer; while I struck
The lean and wrinkled Cassius; and 'twas I
That the mad Brutus ended. He alone
Dealt on lieutenantry, and no practice had
In the brave squares of war; yet now—No matter.
Cleo. Ah, stand by.
Eros. The Queen, my lord, the Queen.
Iras. Go to him, madam, speak to him;
He is unqualitied with very shame.
Cleo. Well then, sustain me. O!
Eros. Most noble sir, arise; the Queen approaches.
Her head's declined, and death will seize her, but
Your comfort makes the rescue.
Ant. I have offended reputation,
A most unnoble swerving.
Eros. Sir, the Queen.
Ant. O, whither hast thou led me, Egypt? See,
How I convey my shame out of thine eyes
By looking back what I have left behind
'Stroy'd in dishonour.
Cleo. O my lord, my lord,
Forgive my fearful sails! I little thought
You would have follow'd.
Ant. Egypt, thou knew'st too well
My heart was to thy rudder tied by the strings,
And thou shouldst tow me after. O'er my spirit
Thy full supremacy thou knew'st, and that
Thy beck might from the bidding of the gods
Command me.
Cleo. O, my pardon!
Ant. Now I must
To the young man send humble treaties, dodge
And palter in the shifts of lowness; who
With half the bulk o' the world play'd as I pleased,
Making and marring fortunes. You did know
How much you were my conqueror; and that
My sword, made weak by my affection, would
Obey it on all cause.
Cleo. Pardon, pardon!
Ant. Fall not a tear, I say; one of them rates
All that is won and lost. Give me a kiss;
Even this repays me. We sent our schoolmaster;
Is he come back? Love, I am full of lead.

Some wine, within there, and our viands! Fortune knows
We scorn her most when most she offers blows.
[*Exeunt.*

SCENE XII. *Egypt. Cæsar's camp*

Enter CÆSAR, DOLABELLA, THYREUS, *with others.*

Cæs. Let him appear that's come from Antony.
Know you him?
Dol. Cæsar, 'tis his schoolmaster;
An argument that he is pluck'd, when hither
He sends so poor a pinion of his wing,
Which had superfluous kings for messengers
Not many moons gone by.

Enter EUPHRONIUS, *ambassador from Antony.*

Cæs. Approach, and speak.
Euph. Such as I am, I come from Antony.
I was of late as petty to his ends
As is the morn-dew on the myrtle-leaf
To his grand sea.
Cæs. Be't so; declare thine office.
Euph. Lord of his fortunes he salutes thee, and
Requires to live in Egypt; which not granted,
He lessens his requests; and to thee sues
To let him breathe between the heavens and earth,
A private man in Athens. This for him.
Next, Cleopatra does confess thy greatness;
Submits her to thy might; and of thee craves
The circle of the Ptolemies for her heirs,
Now hazarded to thy grace.
Cæs. For Antony,
I have no ears to his request. The Queen
Of audience nor desire shall fail, so she
From Egypt drive her all-disgraced friend,
Or take his life there. This if she perform,
She shall not sue unheard. So to them both.
Euph. Fortune pursue thee!
Cæs. Bring him through the bands.
[*Exit* EUPHRONIUS.
[*To* THYREUS] To try thy eloquence, now 'tis time; dispatch.
From Antony win Cleopatra; promise,
And in our name, what she requires; add more,
From thine invention, offers. Women are not
In their best fortunes strong; but want will perjure
The ne'er-touch'd vestal. Try thy cunning, Thyreus;
Make thine own edict for thy pains, which we
Will answer as a law.
Thyr. Cæsar, I go.
Cæs. Observe how Antony becomes his flaw,
And what thou think'st his very action speaks
In every power that moves.
Thyr. Cæsar, I shall. [*Exeunt.*

SCENE XIII. *Alexandria: Cleopatra's palace*

Enter CLEOPATRA, ENOBARBUS, CHARMIAN, *and* IRAS.

Cleo. What shall we do, Enobarbus?
Eno. Think, and die.
Cleo. Is Antony or we in fault for this?
Eno. Antony only, that would make his will
Lord of his reason. What though you fled
From that great face of war, whose several ranges
Frighted each other? why should he follow?
The itch of his affection should not then
Have nick'd his captainship; at such a point,
When half to half the world opposed, he being
The meered question. 'Twas a shame no less
Than was his loss, to course your flying flags,
And leave his navy gazing.
Cleo. Prithee, peace.

Enter ANTONY *with* EUPHRONIUS, *the Ambassador.*

Ant. Is that his answer?
Euph. Ay, my lord.
Ant. The Queen shall then have courtesy, so she
Will yield us up.
Euph. He says so.
Ant. Let her know't.
To the boy Cæsar send this grizzled head,
And he will fill thy wishes to the brim
With principalities.
Cleo. That head, my lord?
Ant. To him again. Tell him he wears the rose
Of youth upon him; from which the world should note
Something particular. His coin, ships, legions,
May be a coward's; whose ministers would prevail
Under the service of a child as soon
As i' the command of Cæsar. I dare him therefore
To lay his gay comparisons apart,
And answer me declined, sword against sword,
Ourselves alone. I'll write it. Follow me.
[*Exeunt* ANTONY *and* EUPHRONIUS.
Eno. [*Aside*] Yes, like enough, high-battled Cæsar will
Unstate his happiness, and be staged to the show,
Against a sworder! I see men's judgements are
A parcel of their fortunes; and things outward
Do draw the inward quality after them,
To suffer all alike. That he should dream,
Knowing all measures, the full Cæsar will
Answer his emptiness! Cæsar, thou hast subdued
His judgement too.

Enter an ATTENDANT.

Att. A messenger from Cæsar.
Cleo. What, no more ceremony? See, my women!
Against the blown rose may they stop their nose
That kneel'd unto the buds. Admit him, sir.
[*Exit* ATTENDANT.
Eno. [*Aside*] Mine honesty and I begin to square.
The loyalty well held to fools does make
Our faith mere folly; yet he that can endure
To follow with allegiance a fall'n lord
Does conquer him that did his master conquer,
And earns a place i' the story.

Enter THYREUS.

Cleo. Cæsar's will?
Thyr. Hear it apart.
Cleo. None but friends; say boldly.
Thyr. So, haply, are they friends to Antony.
Eno. He needs as many, sir, as Cæsar has;
Or needs not us. If Cæsar please, our master
Will leap to be his friend. For us, you know
Whose he is we are, and that is, Cæsar's.
Thyr. So.
Thus then, thou most renown'd: Cæsar entreats,
Not to consider in what case thou stand'st,
Further than he is Cæsar.
Cleo. Go on: right royal.
Thyr. He knows that you embrace not Antony
As you did love, but as you fear'd him.
Cleo. O!
Thyr. The scars upon your honour, therefore, he
Does pity, as constrained blemishes,
Not as deserved.
Cleo. He is a god and knows
What is most right. Mine honour was not yielded,
But conquer'd merely.
Eno. [*Aside*] To be sure of that,
I will ask Antony. Sir, sir, thou art so leaky,
That we must leave thee to thy sinking, for
Thy dearest quit thee. [*Exit.*
Thyr. Shall I say to Cæsar
What you require of him? for he partly begs
To be desired to give. It much would please him
That of his fortunes you should make a staff
To lean upon; but it would warm his spirits
To hear from me you had left Antony,
And put yourself under his shroud,
The universal landlord.
Cleo. What's your name?
Thyr. My name is Thyreus.
Cleo. Most kind messenger,
Say to great Cæsar this: in deputation
I kiss his conquering hand. Tell him, I am prompt
To lay my crown at's feet, and there to kneel.
Tell him, from his all-obeying breath I hear
The doom of Egypt.
Thyr. 'Tis your noblest course.
Wisdom and fortune combating together,
If that the former dare but what it can,
No chance may shake it. Give me grace to lay
My duty on your hand.
Cleo. Your Cæsar's father oft,
When he hath mused of taking kingdoms in,
Bestow'd his lips on that unworthy place,
As it rain'd kisses.

Re-enter ANTONY *and* ENOBARBUS.

Ant. Favours, by Jove that thunders!
What art thou, fellow?
Thyr. One that but performs
The bidding of the fullest man, and worthiest
To have command obey'd.
Eno. [*Aside*] You will be whipp'd.
Ant. Approach, there! Ah, you kite! Now, gods and devils!
Authority melts from me. Of late, when I cried "Ho!"
Like boys unto a muss, kings would start forth,
And cry "Your will?" Have you no ears? I am
Antony yet.

Enter Attendants.

Take hence this Jack, and whip him.
Eno. [*Aside*] 'Tis better playing with a lion's whelp
Than with an old one dying.
Ant. Moon and stars!
Whip him. Were't twenty of the greatest tributaries
That do acknowledge Cæsar, should I find them
So saucy with the hand of she here—what's her name,
Since she was Cleopatra? Whip him, fellows,
Till, like a boy, you see him cringe his face.
And whine aloud for mercy. Take him hence.
Thyr. Mark Antony!
Ant. Tug him away. Being whipp'd,
Bring him again; this Jack of Cæsar's shall
Bear us an errand to him.
[*Exeunt Attendants with* THYREUS.
You were half blasted ere I knew you; ha!
Have I my pillow left unpress'd in Rome,
Forborne the getting of a lawful race,
And by a gem of women, to be abused
By one that looks on feeders?
Cleo. Good my lord—
Ant. You have been a boggler ever;
But when we in our viciousness grow hard—

O misery on't!—the wise gods seel our eyes;
In our own filth drop our clear judgements; make us
Adore our errors; laugh at's, while we strut
To our confusion.
Cleo. O, is't come to this?
Ant. I found you as a morsel cold upon
Dead Cæsar's trencher; nay, you were a fragment
Of Cneius Pompey's; besides what hotter hours,
Unregister'd in vulgar fame, you have
Luxuriously pick'd out; for, I am sure,
Though you can guess what temperance should be,
You know not what it is.
Cleo. Wherefore is this?
Ant. To let a fellow that will take rewards
And say' "God quit you!" be familiar with
My playfellow, your hand, this kingly seal
And plighter of high hearts! O, that I were
Upon the hill of Basan, to outroar
The horned herd! for I have savage cause;
And to proclaim it civilly were like
A halter'd neck which does the hangman thank
For being yare about him.

Re-enter ATTENDANTS *with* THYREUS.

Is he whipp'd?
1st Att. Soundly, my lord.
Ant. Cried he? and begg'd a' pardon?
1st Att. He did ask favour.
Ant. If that thy father live, let him repent
Thou wast not made his daughter; and be thou sorry
To follow Cæsar in his triumph, since
Thou hast been whipp'd for following him; henceforth
The white hand of a lady fever thee,
Shake thou to look on 't. Get thee back to Cæsar,
Tell him thy entertainment. Look, thou say
He makes me angry with him; for he seems
Proud and disdainful, harping on what I am,
Not what he knew I was. He makes me angry;
And at this time most easy 'tis to do't,
When my good stars, that were my former guides,
Have empty left their orbs, and shot their fires
Into the abysm of hell. If he mislike
My speech and what is done, tell him he has
Hipparchus, my enfranched bondman, whom
He may at pleasure whip, or hang, or torture,
As he shall like, to quit me. Urge it thou.
Hence with thy stripes, begone! [*Exit* THYREUS.
Cleo. Have you done yet?
Ant. Alack, our terrene moon
Is now eclipsed; and it portends alone
The fall of Antony!
Cleo. I must stay his time.
Ant. To flatter Cæsar, would you mingle eyes
With one that ties his points?
Cleo. Not know me yet?
Ant. Cold-hearted toward me?
Cleo. Ah, dear, if I be so,
From my cold heart let heaven engender hail,
And poison it in the source; and the first stone
Drop in my neck; as it determines, so
Dissolve my life! The next Cæsarion smite!
Till by degrees the memory of my womb,
Together with my brave Egyptians all,
By the discandying of this pelleted storm,
Lie graveless, till the flies and gnats of Nile
Have buried them for prey!
Ant. I am satisfied.
Cæsar sits down in Alexandria, where
I will oppose his fate. Our force by land
Hath nobly held; our sever'd navy too
Have knit again, and fleet, threatening most sea-like.
Where hast thou been, my heart? Dost thou hear, lady?
If from the field I shall return once more
To kiss these lips, I will appear in blood;
I and my sword will earn our chronicle.
There's hope in't yet.
Cleo. That's my brave lord!
Ant. I will be treble-sinew'd, hearted, breathed,
And fight maliciously; for when mine hours
Were nice and lucky, men did ransom lives
Of me for jests; but now I'll set my teeth,
And send to darkness all that stop me. Come,
Let's have one other gaudy night. Call to me
All my sad captains; fill our bowls once more;
Let's mock the midnight bell.
Cleo. It is my birth-day.
I had thought to have held it poor; but, since my lord
Is Antony again, I will be Cleopatra.
Ant. We will yet do well.
Cleo. Call all his noble captains to my lord.
Ant. Do so, we'll speak to them; and to-night I'll force
The wine peep through their scars. Come on, my queen;
There's sap in't yet. The next time I do fight,
I'll make death love me; for I will contend
Even with his pestilent scythe.
[*Exeunt all but* ENOBARBUS.
Eno. Now he'll outstare the lightning. To be furious,
Is to be frighted out of fear; and in that mood
The dove will peck the estridge; and I see still,

A diminution in our captain's brain
Restores his heart. When valour preys on reason,
It eats the sword it fights with. I will seek
Some way to leave him. [*Exit.*

ACT IV

SCENE I. *Before Alexandria: Cæsar's camp*

Enter CÆSAR, AGRIPPA, *and* MECÆNAS, *with his Army;* CÆSAR *reading a letter.*

Cæs. He calls me boy; and chides, as he had power
To beat me out of Egypt; my messenger
He hath whipp'd with rods; dares me to personal combat,
Cæsar to Antony. Let the old ruffian know
I have many other ways to die; meantime
Laugh at his challenge.
Mec. Cæsar must think,
When one so great begins to rage, he's hunted
Even to falling. Give him no breath, but now
Make boot of his distraction. Never anger
Made good guard for itself.
Cæs. Let our best heads
Know that to-morrow the last of many battles
We mean to fight. Within our files there are,
Of those that served Mark Antony but late,
Enough to fetch him in. See it done,
And feast the army; we have store to do't,
And they have earn'd the waste. Poor Antony!
[*Exeunt.*

SCENE II. *Alexandria: Cleopatra's palace*

Enter ANTONY, CLEOPATRA, ENOBARBUS, CHARMIAN, IRAS, ALEXAS, *with others.*

Ant. He will not fight with me, Domitius.
Eno. No.
Ant. Why should he not?
Eno. He thinks, being twenty times of better fortune,
He is twenty men to one.
Ant. To-morrow, soldier,
By sea and land I'll fight; or I will live,
Or bathe my dying honour in the blood
Shall make it live again. Woo't thou fight well?
Eno. I'll strike, and cry, "Take all."
Ant. Well said; come on.
Call forth my household servants; let's to-night
Be bounteous at our meal.

Enter three or four Servitors.

Give me thy hand,
Thou hast been rightly honest; so hast thou,
Thou, and thou, and thou; you have served me well,
And kings have been your fellows.
Cleo. [*Aside to* ENOBARBUS] What means this?
Eno. [*Aside to* CLEOPATRA] 'Tis one of those odd tricks which sorrow shoots
Out of the mind.
Ant. And thou art honest too.
I wish I could be made so many men,
And all of you clapp'd up together in
An Antony, that I might do you service
So good as you have done.
All. The gods forbid!
Ant. Well, my good fellows, wait on me to-night;
Scant not my cups; and make as much of me
As when mine empire was your fellow too,
And suffer'd my command.
Cleo. [*Aside to* ENOBARBUS] What does he mean?
Eno. [*Aside to* CLEOPATRA] To make his followers weep.
Ant. Tend me to-night;
May be it is the period of your duty;
Haply you shall not see me more; or if,
A mangled shadow; perchance to-morrow
You'll serve another master. I look on you
As one that takes his leave. Mine honest friends,
I turn you not away; but, like a master
Married to your good service, stay till death.
Tend me to-night two hours, I ask no more,
And the gods yield you for't!
Eno. What mean you, sir,
To give them this discomfort? Look, they weep,
And I, an ass, am onion-eyed. For shame,
Transform us not to women.
Ant. Ho, ho, ho!
Now the witch take me, if I meant it thus!
Grace grow where those drops fall! My hearty friends,
You take me in too dolorous a sense;
For I spake to you for your comfort; did desire you
To burn this night with torches. Know, my hearts,
I hope well of to-morrow, and will lead you
Where rather I'll expect victorious life
Than death and honour. Let's to supper, come,
And drown consideration. [*Exeunt.*

SCENE III. *The same: before the palace.*

Enter TWO SOLDIERS *to their guard.*

1st Sold. Brother, good night; to-morrow is the day.
2nd Sold. It will determine one way; fare you well.
Heard you of nothing strange about the streets?
1st Sold. Nothing. What news?

2nd Sold. Belike 'tis but a rumour. Good night to you.
1st Sold. Well, sir, good night.

Enter TWO *other* SOLDIERS.

2nd. Sold. Soldiers, have careful watch.
3rd Sold. And you. Good night, good night.
They place themselves in every corner of the stage.
4th Sold. Here we. And if to-morrow
Our navy thrive, I have an absolute hope
Our landmen will stand up.
3rd Sold. 'Tis a brave army,
And full of purpose.
Music of the hautboys as under the stage.
4th Sold. Peace! what noise?
1st Sold. List, List!
2nd Sold. Hark!
1st Sold. Music i' the air.
3rd Sold. Under the earth.
4th Sold. It signs well, does it not?
3rd Sold. No.
1st Sold. Peace, I say!
What should this mean?
2nd Sold. 'Tis the god Hercules, whom Antony loved,
Now leaves him.
1st Sold. Walk; let's see if other watchmen
Do hear what we do.
They advance to another post.
2nd Sold. How now, masters!
All. [*Speaking together*] How now!
How now! do you hear this?
1st Sold. Ay; is't not strange?
3rd Sold. Do you hear, masters? do you hear?
1st Sold. Follow the noise so far as we have quarter;
Let's see how it will give off.
All. Content. 'Tis strange. [*Exeunt.*

SCENE IV. *The same: a room in the palace*

Enter ANTONY *and* CLEOPATRA, CHARMIAN, *and others attending.*

Ant. Eros! mine armour, Eros!
Cleo. Sleep a little.
Ant. No, my chuck. Eros, come; mine armour, Eros!

Enter EROS *with armour.*

Come, good fellow, put mine iron on.
If fortune be not ours to-day, it is
Because we brave her. Come.
Cleo. Nay, I'll help too
What's this for?
Ant. Ah, let be, let be! thou art
The armourer of my heart. False, false; this, this.
Cleo. Sooth, la, I'll help. Thus it must be.
Ant. Well, well;
We shall thrive now. Seest thou, my good fellow?
Go put on thy defences.
Eros. Briefly, sir.
Cleo. Is not this buckled well?
Ant. Rarely, rarely.
He that unbuckles this, till we do please
To daff't for our repose, shall hear a storm.
Thou fumblest, Eros; and my queen's a squire
More tight at this than thou. Dispatch. O love,
That thou couldst see my wars to-day, and knew'st
The royal occupation! thou shouldst see
A workman in't.

Enter an armed SOLDIER.

Good morrow to thee; welcome.
Thou look'st like him that knows a warlike charge.
To business that we love we rise betime,
And go to't with delight.
Sold. A thousand, sir,
Early though't be, have on their riveted trim,
And at the port expect you.
Shout. Trumpets flourish.
Enter CAPTAINS *and* SOLDIERS.
Capt. The morn is fair. Good morrow, general.
All. Good morrow, general.
Ant. 'Tis well blown, lads.
This morning, like the spirit of a youth
That means to be of note, begins betimes.
So, so; come, give me that. This way; well said.
Fare thee well, dame, whate'er becomes of me.
This is a soldier's kiss; rebukeable [*Kisses her.*]
And worthy shameful check it were, to stand
On more mechanic compliment; I'll leave thee
Now, like a man of steel. You that will fight,
Follow me close; I'll bring you to 't. Adieu.
[*Exeunt* ANTONY, EROS, CAPTAINS, *and* SOLDIERS.

Char. Please you, retire to your chamber.
Cleo. Lead me.
He goes forth gallantly. That he and Cæsar might
Determine this great war in single fight!
Then, Antony—but now—Well, on. [*Exeunt.*

SCENE V. *Alexandria: Antony's camp*

Trumpets sound. Enter ANTONY *and* EROS; *a* SOLDIER *meeting them.*

Sold. The gods make this a happy day to Antony!
Ant. Would thou and those thy scars had once prevail'd
To make me fight at land!

Sold. Hadst thou done so,
The kings that have revolted, and the soldier
That has this morning left thee, would have still
Follow'd thy heels.
Ant. Who's gone this morning?
Sold. Who!
One ever near thee. Call for Enobarbus,
He shall not hear thee; or from Cæsar's camp
Say, "I am none of thine."
Ant. What say'st thou?
Sold. Sir,
He is with Cæsar.
Eros. Sir, his chests and treasure
He has not with him.
Ant. Is he gone?
Sold. Most certain.
Ant. Go, Eros, send his treasure after; do it;
Detain no jot, I charge thee. Write to him—
I will subscribe—gentle adieus and greetings;
Say that I wish he never find more cause
To change a master. O, my fortunes have
Corrupted honest men! Dispatch. Enobarbus!
[*Exeunt.*

SCENE VI. *Alexandria: Cæsar's camp*

Flourish. Enter CÆSAR, AGRIPPA, *with* ENOBARBUS, *and others.*

Cæs. Go forth, Agrippa, and begin the fight.
Our will is Antony be took alive;
Make it so known.
Agr. Cæsar, I shall. [*Exit.*
Cæs. The time of universal peace is near.
Prove this a prosperous day, the three-nook'd world
Shall bear the olive freely.

Enter a MESSENGER.

Mess. Antony
Is come into the field.
Cæs. Go charge Agrippa
Plant those that have revolted in the van,
That Antony may seem to spend his fury
Upon himself. [*Exeunt all but* ENOBARBUS.
Eno. Alexas did revolt; and went to Jewry on
Affairs of Antony; there did persuade
Great Herod to incline himself to Cæsar,
And leave his master Antony; for this pains
Cæsar hath hang'd him. Canidius and the rest
That fell away have entertainment, but
No honourable trust. I have done ill;
Of which I do accuse myself so sorely,
That I will joy no more.

Enter a SOLDIER *of* CÆSAR'S.

Sold. Enobarbus, Antony
Hath after thee sent all thy treasure, with
His bounty overplus. The messenger
Came on my guard, and at thy tent is now
Unloading of his mules.
Eno. I give it you.
Sold. Mock not, Enobarbus.
I tell you true. Best you safed the bringer
Out of the host; I must attend mine office,
Or would have done 't myself. Your emperor
Continues still a Jove. [*Exit.*
Eno. I am alone the villain of the earth,
And feel I am so most. O Antony,
Thou mine of bounty, how wouldst thou have paid
My better service, when my turpitude
Thou dost so crown with gold! This blows my heart.
If swift thought break it not, a swifter mean
Shall outstrike thought; but thought will do 't, I feel
I fight against thee! No! I will go seek
Some ditch wherein to die; the foul'st best fits
My latter part of life. [*Exit.*

SCENE VII. *Field of battle between the camps*

Alarum. Drums and trumpets. Enter AGRIPPA *and others.*

Agr. Retire, we have engaged ourselves too far.
Cæsar himself has work, and our oppression
Exceeds what we expected. [*Exeunt.*

Alarums. Enter ANTONY, *and* SCARUS *wounded.*

Scar. O my brave emperor, this is fought indeed!
Had we done so at first, we had droven them home
With clouts about their heads.
Ant. Thou bleed'st apace.
Scar. I had a wound here that was like a *T*,
But now 'tis made an *H*.
Ant. They do retire.
Scar. We'll beat 'em into bench-holes. I have yet
Room for six scotches more.

Enter EROS.

Eros. They are beaten, sir; and our advantage serves
For a fair victory.
Scar. Let us score their backs,
And snatch 'em up, as we take hares, behind.
'Tis sport to maul a runner.
Ant. I will reward thee
Once for thy spritely comfort, and ten-fold
For thy good valour. Come thee on.
Scar. I'll halt after. [*Exeunt.*

SCENE VIII. *Under the walls of Alexandria*

Alarum. Enter ANTONY, *in a march;* SCARUS, *with others.*

Ant. We have beat him to his camp. Run one before,
And let the Queen know of our gests. To-morrow,
Before the sun shall see 's, we'll spill the blood
That has to-day escaped. I thank you all;
For doughty-handed are you, and have fought
Not as you served the cause, but as 't had been
Each man's like mine; you have shown all Hectors.
Enter the city, clip your wives, your friends,
Tell them your feats; whilst they with joyful tears
Wash the congealment from your wounds, and kiss
The honour'd gashes whole. [*To* SCARUS] Give me thy hand;

Enter CLEOPATRA, *attended.*

To this great fairy I'll commend thy acts,
Make her thanks bless thee. [*To* CLEOPATRA] O thou day o' the world,
Chain mine arm'd neck; leap thou, attire and all,
Through proof of harness to my heart, and there
Ride on the pants triumphing!
Cleo. Lord of lords!
O infinite virtue, comest thou smiling from
The world's great snare uncaught?
Ant. My nightingale,
We have beat them to their beds. What, girl! though grey
Do something mingle with our younger brown, yet ha' we
A brain that nourishes our nerves, and can
Get goal for goal of youth. Behold this man;
Commend unto his lips thy favouring hand.
Kiss it, my warrior. He hath fought to-day
As if a god, in hate of mankind, had
Destroy'd in such a shape.
Cleo. I'll give thee, friend,
An armour all of gold; it was a king's.
Ant. He has deserved it, were it carbuncled
Like holy Phœbus' car. Give me thy hand.
Through Alexandria make a jolly march;
Bear our hack'd targets like the men that owe them.
Had our great palace the capacity
To camp this host, we all would sup together,
And drink carouses to the next day's fate,
Which promises royal peril. Trumpeters,
With brazen din blast you the city's ear;
Make mingle with our rattling tabourines,
That heaven and earth may strike their sounds together,
Applauding our approach. [*Exeunt.*

SCENE IX. *Cæsar's camp*

Sentinels at their post.

1st Sold. If we be not relieved within this hour,
We must return to the court of guard. The night
Is shiny, and they say we shall embattle
By the second hour i' the morn.
2nd Sold. This last day was
A shrewd one to 's.

Enter ENOBARBUS.

Eno. O, bear me witness, night—
3rd Sold. What man is this?
2nd Sold. Stand close, and list him.
Eno. Be witness to me, O thou blessed moon,
When men revolted shall upon record
Bear hateful memory, poor Enobarbus did
Before thy face repent!
1st Sold. Enobarbus!
3rd Sold. Peace!
Hark further.
Eno. O sovereign mistress of true melancholy,
The poisonous damp of night disponge upon me,
That life, a very rebel to my will,
May hang no longer on me. Throw my heart
Against the flint and hardness of my fault;
Which, being dried with grief, will break to powder,
And finish all foul thoughts. O Antony,
Nobler than my revolt is infamous,
Forgive me in thine own particular;
But let the world rank me in register
A master-leaver and a fugitive.
O Antony! O Antony! [*Dies.*
2nd Sold. Let's speak
To him.
1st Sold. Let's hear him, for the things he speaks
May concern Cæsar.
3rd Sold. Let's do so. But he sleeps.
1st Sold. Swoons rather; for so bad a prayer as his
Was never yet for sleep.
2nd Sold. Go we to him.
3rd Sold. Awake, sir, awake; speak to us.
2nd Sold. Hear you, sir?
1st Sold. The hand of death hath raught him.
[*Drums afar off.*] Hark! the drums
Demurely wake the sleepers. Let us bear him
To the court of guard; he is of note. Our hour
Is fully out.
3rd Sold. Come on, then;
He may recover yet. [*Exeunt with the body.*

SCENE X. *Between the two camps*

Enter ANTONY *and* SCARUS, *with their Army.*

Ant. Their preparation is to-day by sea;
We please them not by land.
Scar. For both, my lord.
Ant. I would they'd fight i' the fire or i' the air;
We'd fight there too. But this it is; our foot
Upon the hills adjoining to the city
Shall stay with us; order for sea is given;
They have put forth the haven. [Go we up.]
Where their appointment we may best discover,
And look on their endeavour. [*Exeunt.*

SCENE XI. *Another part of the same*

Enter CÆSAR, *and his Army.*

Cæs. But being charged, we will be still by land,
Which, as I take 't, we shall; for his best force
Is forth to man his galleys. To the vales,
And hold our best advantage. [*Exeunt.*

SCENE XII. *Another part of the same*

Enter ANTONY *and* SCARUS.

Ant. Yet they are not join'd. Where yond pine does stand,
I shall discover all. I'll bring thee word
Straight, how 'tis like to go. [*Exit.*
Scar. Swallows have built
In Cleopatra's sails their nests. The augurers
Say they know not, they cannot tell; look grimly,
And dare not speak their knowledge. Antony
Is valiant, and dejected; and, by starts,
His fretted fortunes give him hope, and fear,
Of what he has, and has not.

Alarum afar off, as at a sea-fight.

Re-enter ANTONY.

Ant. All is lost;
This foul Egyptian hath betrayed me.
My fleet hath yielded to the foe; and yonder
They cast their caps up and carouse together
Like friends long lost. Triple-turn'd whore! 'tis thou
Hast sold me to this novice; and my heart
Makes only wars on thee. Bid them all fly;
For when I am revenged upon my charm,
I have done all. Bid them all fly; begone.
[*Exit* SCARUS.
O sun, thy uprise shall I see no more;
Fortune and Antony part here; even here
Do we shake hands. All come to this? The hearts
That spaniel'd me at heels, to whom I gave
Their wishes, do discandy, melt their sweets
On blossoming Cæsar; and this pine is bark'd,
That overtopp'd them all. Betray'd I am.
O this false soul of Egypt! this grave charm—
Whose eye beck'd forth my wars, and call'd them home;
Whose bosom was my crownet, my chief end—
Like a right gipsy, hath at fast and loose
Beguiled me to the very heart of loss.
What, Eros, Eros!

Enter CLEOPATRA.

Ah, thou spell! Avaunt!
Cleo. Why is my lord enraged against his love?
Ant. Vanish, or I shall give thee thy deserving
And blemish Cæsar's triumph. Let him take thee
And hoist thee up to the shouting plebeians.
Follow his chariot, like the greatest spot
Of all thy sex; most monster-like, be shown
For poor'st diminutives, for dolts; and let
Patient Octavia plough thy visage up
With her prepared nails.
[*Exit* CLEOPATRA.
'Tis well thou'rt gone,
If it be well to live; but better 'twere
Thou fell'st into my fury, for one death
Might have prevented many. Eros, ho!
The shirt of Nessus is upon me. Teach me,
Alcides, thou mine ancestor, thy rage.
Let me lodge Lichas on the horns o' the moon;
And with those hands, that grasp'd the heaviest club,
Subdue my worthiest self. The witch shall die.
To the young Roman boy she hath sold me, and I fall
Under this plot; she dies for 't. Eros, ho! [*Exit.*

SCENE XIII. *Alexandria: Cleopatra's palace*

Enter CLEOPATRA, CHARMIAN, IRAS, *and* MARDIAN.

Cleo. Help me, my women! O, he is more mad
Than Telamon for his shield; the boar of Thessaly
Was never so emboss'd.
Char. To the monument!
There lock yourself, and send him word you are dead.
The soul and body rive not more in parting
Than greatness going off.
Cleo. To the monument!
Mardian, go tell him I have slain myself;
Say, that the last I spoke was "Antony,"
And word it, prithee, piteously. Hence, Mardian,
And bring me how he takes my death. To the monument! [*Exeunt.*

SCENE XIV. *The same: another room*

Enter ANTONY *and* EROS.

Ant. Eros, thou yet behold'st me?
Eros. Ay, noble lord.
Ant. Sometime we see a cloud that's dragonish;

A vapour sometime like a bear or lion,
A tower'd citadel, a pendent rock,
A forked mountain, or blue promontory
With trees upon 't, that nod unto the world,
And mock our eyes with air. Thou hast seen these signs;
They are black vesper's pageants.

Eros. Ay, my lord.

Ant. That which is now a horse, even with a thought
The rack dislimns, and makes it indistinct,
As water is in water.

Eros. It does, my lord.

Ant. My good knave Eros, now thy captain is
Even such a body. Here I am Antony;
Yet cannot hold this visible shape, my knave.
I made these wars for Egypt; and the Queen—
Whose heart I thought I had, for she had mine;
Which whilst it was mine had annex'd unto 't
A million more, now lost—she, Eros, has
Pack'd cards with Cæsar, and false-play'd my glory
Unto an enemy's triumph.
Nay, weep not, gentle Eros; there is left us
Ourselves to end ourselves.

Enter MARDIAN.

O, thy vile lady!
She has robb'd me of my sword.

Mar. No, Antony;
My mistress loved thee, and her fortunes mingled
With thine entirely.

Ant. Hence, saucy eunuch; peace!
She hath betray'd me and shall die the death.

Mar. Death of one person can be paid but once,
And that she has discharged. What thou wouldst do
Is done unto thy hand. The last she spake
Was, "Antony! most noble Antony!"
Then in the midst a tearing groan did break
The name of Antony; it was divided
Between her heart and lips. She render'd life,
Thy name so buried in her.

Ant. Dead, then?

Mar. Dead.

Ant. Unarm, Eros; the long day's task is done,
And we must sleep. [*To* MARDIAN] That thou depart'st hence safe,
Does pay thy labour richly; go. [*Exit* MARDIAN.
Off, pluck off!
The seven-fold shield of Ajax cannot keep
The battery from my heart. O, cleave, my sides!
Heart, once be stronger than thy continent,
Crack thy frail case! Apace, Eros, apace.
No more a soldier. Bruised pieces, go;
You have been nobly borne. From me awhile.
[*Exit* EROS.
I will o'ertake thee, Cleopatra, and
Weep for my pardon. So it must be, for now
All length is torture; since the torch is out,
Lie down, and stray no farther. Now all labour
Mars what it does; yea, very force entangles
Itself with strength. Seal then, and all is done.
Eros!—I come, my queen.—Eros!—Stay for me!
Where souls do couch on flowers, we'll hand in hand,
And with our sprightly port make the ghosts gaze.
Dido and her Æneas shall want troops,
And all the haunt be ours. Come, Eros, Eros!

Re-enter EROS.

Eros. What would my lord?

Ant. Since Cleopatra died,
I have lived in such dishonour that the gods
Detest my baseness. I, that with my sword
Quarter'd the world, and o'er green Neptune's back
With ships made cities, condemn myself to lack
The courage of a woman; less noble mind
Than she which by her death our Cæsar tells,
"I am conqueror of myself." Thou art sworn, Eros,
That, when the exigent should come, which now
Is come indeed, when I should see behind me
The inevitable prosecution of
Disgrace and horror, that, on my command,
Thou then wouldst kill me. Do 't; the time is come.
Thou strikest not me, 'tis Cæsar thou defeat'st.
Put colour in thy cheek.

Eros. The gods withhold me!
Shall I do that which all the Parthian darts,
Though enemy, lost aim and could not?

Ant. Eros,
Wouldst thou be window'd in great Rome and see
Thy master thus with pleach'd arms, bending down
His corrigible neck, his face subdued
To penetrative shame, whilst the wheel'd seat
Of fortunate Cæsar, drawn before him, branded
His baseness that ensued?

Eros. I would not see 't.

Ant. Come, then; for with a wound I must be cured.
Draw that thy honest sword, which thou hast worn
Most useful for thy country.

Eros. O, sir, pardon me!

Ant. When I did make thee free, sworest thou not then
To do this when I bade thee? Do it at once;
Or thy precedent services are all
But accidents unpurposed. Draw, and come.
Eros. Turn from me, then, that noble countenance,
Wherein the worship of the whole world lies.
Ant. Lo thee! [*Turning from him.*]
Eros. My sword is drawn.
Ant. Then let it do at once
The thing why thou hast drawn it.
Eros. My dear master,
My captain, and my emperor, let me say,
Before I strike this bloody stroke, farewell.
Ant. 'Tis said, man; and farewell.
Eros. Farewell, great chief. Shall I strike now?
Ant. Now, Eros.
Eros. Why, there then. [*Kills himself.*] Thus I do escape the sorrow
Of Antony's death.
Ant. Thrice-nobler than myself!
Thou teachest me, O valiant Eros, what
I should, and thou couldst not. My queen and Eros
Have by their brave instruction got upon me
A nobleness in record; but I will be
A bridegroom in my death, and run into 't
As to a lover's bed. Come, then; and, Eros,
Thy master dies thy scholar: to do thus
Falling on his sword.
I learn'd of thee. How! not dead? not dead?
The guard, ho! O, dispatch me!

Enter DERCETAS *and* GUARD.

1st Guard. What's the noise?
Ant. I have done my work ill, friends. O, make an end
Of what I have begun.
2nd Guard. The star is fall'n.
1st Guard. And time is at his period.
All. Alas, and woe!
Ant. Let him that loves me strike me dead.
1st Guard. Not I.
2nd Guard. Nor I.
3rd Guard. Nor any one. [*Exeunt* GUARD.
Der. Thy death and fortunes bid thy followers fly.
This sword but shown to Cæsar, with this tidings,
Shall enter me with him.

Enter DIOMEDES.

Dio. Where's Antony?
Der. There, Diomed, there.
Dio. Lives he?
Wilt thou not answer, man? [*Exit* DERCETAS.
Ant. Art thou there, Diomed? Draw thy sword, and give me
Sufficing strokes for death.
Dio. Most absolute lord,
My mistress Cleopatra sent me to thee.
Ant. When did she send thee?
Dio. Now, my lord.
Ant. Where is she?
Dio. Lock'd in her monument. She had a prophesying fear
Of what hath come to pass; for when she saw—
Which never shall be found—you did suspect
She had disposed with Cæsar, and that your rage
Would not be purged, she sent you word she was dead;
But, fearing since how it might work, hath sent
Me to proclaim the truth; and I am come,
I dread, too late.
Ant. Too late, good Diomed. Call my guard, I prithee.
Dio. What, ho, the Emperor's guard! The guard, what, ho!
Come, your lord calls!

Enter four or five of the GUARD *of Antony.*

Ant. Bear me, good friends, where Cleopatra bides;
'Tis the last service that I shall command you.
1st Guard. Woe, woe are we, sir, you may not live to wear
All your true followers out.
All. Most heavy day!
Ant. Nay, good my fellows, do not please sharp fate
To grace it with your sorrows. Bid that welcome
Which comes to punish us, and we punish it
Seeming to bear it lightly. Take me up.
I have led you oft; carry me now, good friends,
And have my thanks for all.
[*Exeunt, bearing* ANTONY.

SCENE XV. *The same: a monument*

Enter CLEOPATRA, *and her maids aloft, with* CHARMIAN *and* IRAS.

Cleo. O Charmian, I will never go from hence.
Char. Be comforted, dear madam.
Cleo. No, I will not.
All strange and terrible events are welcome,
But comforts we despise; our size of sorrow,
Proportion'd to our cause, must be as great
As that which makes it.

Enter, below, DIOMEDES.

How now! is he dead?
Dio. His death's upon him, but not dead.

Look out o' the other side your monument;
His guard have brought him thither.

Enter, below, ANTONY, *borne by the* GUARD.

Cleo. O sun,
Burn the great sphere thou movest in! darkling stand
The varying shore o' the world. O Antony,
Antony, Antony! Help, Charmian, help, Iras, help;
Help, friends below; let's draw him hither.

Ant. Peace!
Not Cæsar's valour hath o'erthrown Antony,
But Antony's hath triumph'd on itself.

Cleo. So it should be, that none but Antony
Should conquer Antony; but woe 'tis so!

Ant. I am dying, Egypt, dying; only
I here importune death awhile, until
Of many thousand kisses the poor last
I lay upon thy lips.

Cleo. I dare not, dear—
Dear my lord, pardon—I dare not,
Lest I be taken. Not the imperious show
Of the full-fortuned Cæsar ever shall
Be brooch'd with me; if knife, drugs, serpents, have
Edge, sting, or operation, I am safe.
Your wife Octavia, with her modest eyes
And still conclusion, shall acquire no honour
Demuring upon me. But come, come, Antony—
Help me, my women—we must draw thee up.
Assist, good friends. 31

Ant. O, quick, or I am gone.

Cleo. Here's sport indeed! How heavy weighs my lord!
Our strength is all gone into heaviness,
That makes the weight. Had I great Juno's power,
The strong-wing'd Mercury should fetch thee up,
And set thee by Jove's side. Yet come a little—
Wishers were ever fools—O, come, come, come;

They heave ANTONY *aloft to* CLEOPATRA.

And welcome, welcome! die where thou hast lived;
Quicken with kissing. Had my lips that power,
Thus would I wear them out.

All. A heavy sight!

Ant. I am dying, Egypt, dying.
Give me some wine, and let me speak a little.

Cleo. No, let me speak; and let me rail so high,
That the false housewife Fortune break her wheel,
Provoked by my offence.

Ant. One word, sweet queen:
Of Cæsar seek your honour, with your safety. O!

Cleo. They do not go together.

Ant. Gentle, hear me:
None about Cæsar trust but Proculeius.

Cleo. My resolution and my hands I'll trust;
None about Cæsar.

Ant. The miserable change now at my end
Lament nor sorrow at; but please your thoughts
In feeding them with those my former fortunes
Wherein I lived, the greatest prince o' the world,
The noblest; and do now not basely die,
Not cowardly put off my helmet to
My countryman—a Roman by a Roman
Valiantly vanquish'd. Now my spirit is going;
I can no more.

Cleo. Noblest of men, woo't die?
Hast thou no care of me? shall I abide
In this dull world, which in thy absence is
No better than a sty? O, see, my women,

[ANTONY *dies.*

The crown o' the earth doth melt. My lord!
O, wither'd is the garland of the war,
The soldier's pole is fall'n; young boys and girls
Are level now with men; the odds is gone,
And there is nothing left remarkable
Beneath the visiting moon. [*Faints.*

Char. O, quietness, lady!

Iras. She is dead too, our sovereign.

Char. Lady!

Iras. Madam!

Char. O madam, madam, madam!

Iras. Royal Egypt,
Empress!

Char. Peace, peace, Iras!

Cleo. No more, but e'en a woman, and commanded
By such poor passion as the maid that milks
And does the meanest chares. It were for me
To throw my sceptre at the injurious gods;
To tell them that this world did equal theirs
Till they had stol'n our jewel. All's but naught;
Patience is sottish, and impatience does
Become a dog that's mad. Then is it sin
To rush into the secret house of death,
Ere death dare come to us? How do you, women?
What, what! good cheer! Why, how now, Charmian!
My noble girls! Ah, women, women, look,
Our lamp is spent, it's out! Good sirs, take heart.
We'll bury him; and then, what's brave, what's noble,
Let's do it after the high Roman fashion,
And make death proud to take us. Come, away;
This case of that huge spirit now is cold.
Ah, women, women! come; we have no friend

But resolution and the briefest end.
[*Exeunt; those above bearing off Antony's body.*

ACT V

SCENE I. *Alexandria: Cæsar's camp*

Enter CÆSAR, AGRIPPA, DOLABELLA, MECÆNAS, GALLUS, PROCULEIUS, *and others, his council of war.*

Cæs. Go to him, Dolabella, bid him yield;
Being so frustrate, tell him he mocks
The pauses that he makes.
Dol. Cæsar, I shall. [*Exit.*

Enter DERCETAS, *with the sword of* ANTONY.

Cæs. Wherefore is that? and what art thou that darest
Appear thus to us?
Der. I am call'd Dercetas;
Mark Antony I served, who best was worthy
Best to be served. Whilst he stood up and spoke,
He was my master; and I wore my life
To spend upon his haters. If thou please
To take me to thee, as I was to him
I'll be to Cæsar; if thou pleasest not,
I yield thee up my life.
Cæs. What is 't thou say'st?
Der. I say, O Cæsar, Antony is dead.
Cæs. The breaking of so great a thing should make
A greater crack. The round world
Should have shook lions into civil streets,
And citizens to their dens. The death of Antony
Is not a single doom; in the name lay
A moiety of the world.
Der. He is dead, Cæsar.
Not by a public minister of justice,
Nor by a hired knife; but that self hand
Which writ his honour in the acts it did
Hath, with the courage which the heart did lend it,
Splitted the heart. This is his sword;
I robb'd his wound of it; behold it stain'd
With his most noble blood.
Cæs. Look you sad, friends?
The gods rebuke me, but it is tidings
To wash the eyes of kings.
Agr. And strange it is,
That nature must compel us to lament
Our most persisted deeds.
Mec. His taints and honours
Waged equal with him.
Agr. A rarer spirit never
Did steer humanity; but you, gods, will give us
Some faults to make us men. Cæsar is touch'd.
Mec. When such a spacious mirror's set before him,
He needs must see himself.
Cæs. O Antony!
I have follow'd thee to this; but we do lance
Diseases in our bodies. I must perforce
Have shown to thee such a declining day,
Or look on thine; we could not stall together
In the whole world. But yet let me lament,
With tears as sovereign as the blood of hearts,
That thou, my brother, my competitor
In top of all design, my mate in empire,
Friend and companion in the front of war,
The arm of mine own body, and the heart
Where mine his thoughts did kindle—that our stars,
Unreconciliable, should divide
Our equalness to this. Hear me, good friends—
But I will tell you at some meeter season.

Enter an EGYPTIAN.

The business of this man looks out of him;
We'll hear him what he says. Whence are you?
Egyp. A poor Egyptian yet. The Queen my mistress,
Confined in all she has, her monument,
Of thy intents desires instruction,
That she preparedly may frame herself
To the way she's forced to.
Cæs. Bid her have good heart.
She soon shall know of us, by some of ours,
How honourable and how kindly we
Determine for her; for Cæsar cannot live
To be ungentle.
Egyp. So the gods preserve thee! [*Exit.*
Cæs. Come hither, Proculeius. Go and say,
We purpose her no shame. Give her what comforts
The quality of her passion shall require,
Lest, in her greatness, by some mortal stroke
She do defeat us; for her life in Rome
Would be eternal in our triumph. Go,
And with your speediest bring us what she says,
And how you find of her.
Pro. Cæsar, I shall. [*Exit.*
Cæs. Gallus, go you along. [*Exit* GALLUS.]
Where's Dolabella,
To second Proculeius?
All. Dolabella!
Cæs. Let him alone, for I remember now
How he's employ'd; he shall in time be ready.
Go with me to my tent; where you shall see
How hardly I was drawn into this war;
How calm and gentle I proceeded still
In all my writings. Go with me, and see
What I can show in this. [*Exeunt.*

SCENE II. *Alexandria: a room in the monument*

Enter CLEOPATRA, CHARMIAN, *and* IRAS.

Cleo. My desolation does begin to make
A better life. 'Tis paltry to be Cæsar;
Not being Fortune, he's but Fortune's knave,
A minister of her will; and it is great
To do that thing that ends all other deeds;
Which shackles accidents and bolts up change;
Which sleeps, and never palates more the dug,
The beggar's nurse and Cæsar's.

Enter, to the gates of the monument, PROCULEIUS, GALLUS, *and Soldiers.*

Pro. Cæsar sends greeting to the Queen of
Egypt;
And bids thee study on what fair demands
Thou mean'st to have him grant thee.
Cleo. What's thy name?
Pro. My name is Proculeius.
Cleo. Antony
Did tell me of you, bade me trust you; but
I do not greatly care to be deceived,
That have no use for trusting. If your master
Would have a queen his beggar, you must tell
him
That majesty, to keep decorum, must
No less beg than a kingdom. If he please
To give me conquer'd Egypt for my son,
He gives me so much of mine own as I
Will kneel to him with thanks.
Pro. Be of good cheer;
You're fall'n into a princely hand, fear nothing.
Make your full reference freely to my lord,
Who is so full of grace that it flows over
On all that need. Let me report to him
Your sweet dependency; and you shall find
A conqueror that will pray in aid for kindness,
Where he for grace is kneel'd to.
Cleo. Pray you, tell him
I am his fortune's vassal, and I send him
The greatness he has got. I hourly learn
A doctrine of obedience; and would gladly
Look him i' the face.
Pro. This I'll report, dear lady.
Have comfort, for I know your plight is pitied
Of him that caused it.
Gal. You see how easily she may be surprised.

Here PROCULEIUS *and two of the Guard ascend the monument by a ladder placed against a window, and, having descended, come behind* CLEOPATRA. *Some of the Guard unbar and open the gates.*

[*To* PROCULEIUS *and the Guard*] Guard her till
Cæsar come. [*Exit.*

Iras. Royal queen!
Char. O Cleopatra! thou art taken, Queen.
Cleo. Quick, quick, good hands.
Drawing a dagger.
Pro. Hold, worthy lady, hold
Seizes and disarms her.
Do not yourself such wrong, who are in this
Relieved, but not betray'd.
Cleo. What, of death too,
That rids our dogs of languish?
Pro. Cleopatra,
Do not abuse my master's bounty by
The undoing of yourself. Let the world see
His nobleness well acted, which your death
Will never let come forth.
Cleo. Where art thou, Death?
Come hither, come! Come, come, and take a
queen
Worth many babes and beggars!
Pro. O, temperance, lady!
Cleo. Sir, I will eat no meat, I'll not drink, sir;
If idle talk will once be necessary,
I'll not sleep neither. This mortal house I'll
ruin,
Do Cæsar what he can. Know, sir, that I
Will not wait pinion'd at your master's court;
Nor once be chastised with the sober eye
Of dull Octavia. Shall they hoist me up
And show me to the shouting varletry
Of censuring Rome? Rather a ditch in Egypt
Be gentle grave unto me! rather on Nilus' mud
Lay me stark naked, and let the water-flies
Blow me into abhorring! rather make
My country's high pyramids my gibbet,
And hang me up in chains!
Pro. You do extend
These thoughts of horror further than you
shall
Find cause in Cæsar.

Enter DOLABELLA.

Dol. Proculeius,
What thou hast done thy master Cæsar knows,
And he hath sent for thee. For the Queen,
I'll take her to my guard.
Pro. So, Dolabella,
It shall content me best. Be gentle to her.
[*To* CLEOPATRA] To Cæsar I will speak what you
shall please,
If you'll employ me to him.
Cleo. Say, I would die.
[*Exeunt* PROCULEIUS *and Soldiers.*
Dol. Most noble empress, you have heard of
me?
Cleo. I cannot tell.
Dol. Assuredly you know me.

Cleo. No matter, sir, what I have heard or known.
You laugh when boys or women tell their dreams;
Is 't not your trick?
Dol. I understand not, madam.
Cleo. I dream'd there was an Emperor Antony.
O, such another sleep, that I might see
But such another man!
Dol. If it might please ye—
Cleo. His face was as the heavens; and therein stuck
A sun and moon, which kept their course, and lighted
The little O, the earth.
Dol. Most sovereign creature—
Cleo. His legs bestrid the ocean; his rear'd arm
Crested the world; his voice was propertied
As all the tuned spheres, and that to friends;
But when he meant to quail and shake the orb,
He was as rattling thunder. For his bounty,
There was no winter in 't; an autumn 'twas
That grew the more by reaping. His delights
Were dolphin-like; they show'd his back above
The element they lived in. In his livery
Walk'd crowns and crownets; realms and islands were
As plates dropp'd from his pocket.
Dol. Cleopatra!
Cleo. Think you there was, or might be, such a man
As this I dream'd of?
Dol. Gentle madam, no.
Cleo. You lie, up to the hearing of the gods.
But, if there be, or ever were, one such,
It's past the size of dreaming. Nature wants stuff
To vie strange forms with fancy; yet, to imagine
An Antony, were nature's piece 'gainst fancy,
Condemning shadows quite.
Dol. Hear me, good madam.
Your loss is as yourself great; and you bear it
As answering to the weight. Would I might never
O'ertake pursued success, but I do feel,
By the rebound of yours, a grief that smites
My very heart at root.
Cleo. I thank you, sir.
Know you what Cæsar means to do with me?
Dol. I am loath to tell you what I would you knew.
Cleo. Nay, pray you, sir—
Dol. Though he be honourable—
Cleo. He'll lead me, then, in triumph?
Dol. Madam, he will; I know 't.
Flourish, and shout within, "Make way there. Cæsar!"
Enter CÆSAR, GALLUS, PROCULEIUS, MECÆNAS, SELEUCUS, *and others of his train*.
Cæs. Which is the Queen of Egypt?
Dol. It is the Emperor, madam.
CLEOPATRA *kneels*.
Cæs. Arise, you shall not kneel.
I pray you, rise; rise, Egypt.
Cleo. Sir, the gods
Will have it thus; my master and my lord
I must obey.
Cæs. Take to you no hard thoughts.
The record of what injuries you did us,
Though written in our flesh, we shall remember
As things but done by chance.
Cleo. Sole sir o' the world,
I cannot project mine own cause so well
To make it clear; but do confess I have
Been laden with like frailties which before
Have often shamed our sex.
Cæs. Cleopatra, know,
We will extenuate rather than enforce.
If you apply yourself to our intents,
Which towards you are most gentle, you shall find
A benefit in this change; but if you seek
To lay on me a cruelty, by taking
Antony's course, you shall bereave yourself
Of my good purposes, and put your children
To that destruction which I'll guard them from,
If thereon you rely. I'll take my leave.
Cleo. And may, through all the world; 'tis yours; and we,
Your scutcheons and your signs of conquest, shall
Hang in what place you please. Here, my good lord.
Cæs. You shall advise me in all for Cleopatra.
Cleo. This is the brief of money, plate, and jewels,
I am possess'd of; 'tis exactly valued;
Not petty things admitted. Where's Seleucus?
Sel. Here, madam.
Cleo. This is my treasurer; let him speak, my lord,
Upon his peril, that I have reserved
To myself nothing. Speak the truth, Seleucus.
Sel. Madam,
I had rather seal my lips, than, to my peril,
Speak that which is not.
Cleo. What have I kept back?
Sel. Enough to purchase what you have made known.
Cæs. Nay, blush not, Cleopatra; I approve
Your wisdom in the deed.
Cleo. See, Cæsar! O, behold,

How pomp is follow'd! mine will now be yours;
And, should we shift estates, yours would be mine.
The ingratitude of this Seleucus does
Even make me wild. O slave, of no more trust
Than love that's hired! What, goest thou back? thou shalt
Go back, I warrant thee; but I'll catch thine eyes,
Though they had wings. Slave, soulless villain, dog!
O rarely base!

Cæs. Good queen, let us entreat you.

Cleo. O Cæsar, what a wounding shame is this,
That thou, vouchsafing here to visit me,
Doing the honour of thy lordliness
To one so meek, that mine own servant should
Parcel the sum of my disgraces by
Addition of his envy! Say, good Cæsar,
That I some lady trifles have reserved,
Immoment toys, things of such dignity
As we greet modern friends withal; and say,
Some nobler token I have kept apart
For Livia and Octavia, to induce
Their mediation; must I be unfolded
With one that I have bred? The gods! it smites me
Beneath the fall I have. [*To* SELEUCUS] Prithee, go hence;
Or I shall show the cinders of my spirits
Through the ashes of my chance. Wert thou a man,
Thou wouldst have mercy on me.

Cæs. Forbear, Seleucus.
[*Exit* SELEUCUS.

Cleo. Be it known that we, the greatest, are misthought
For things that others do; and, when we fall,
We answer others' merits in our name,
Are therefore to be pitied.

Cæs. Cleopatra,
Not what you have reserved, nor what acknowledged,
Put we i' the roll of conquest. Still be 't yours,
Bestow it at your pleasure; and believe,
Cæsar's no merchant, to make prize with you
Of things that merchants sold. Therefore be cheer'd;
Make not your thoughts your prisons; no, dear queen;
For we intend so to dispose you as
Yourself shall give us counsel. Feed, and sleep.
Our care and pity is so much upon you
That we remain your friend; and so, adieu.

Cleo. My master, and my lord!

Cæs. Not so. Adieu.
[*Flourish. Exeunt* CÆSAR *and his train.*

Cleo. He words me, girls, he words me, that I should not
Be noble to myself. But, hark thee, Charmian.
Whispers CHARMIAN.

Iras. Finish, good lady; the bright day is done,
And we are for the dark.

Cleo. Hie thee again.
I have spoke already, and it is provided;
Go put it to the haste.

Char. Madam, I will.

Re-enter DOLABELLA.

Dol. Where is the Queen?

Char. Behold, sir. [*Exit.*

Cleo. Dolabella!

Dol. Madam, as thereto sworn by your command,
Which my love makes religion to obey,
I tell you this: Cæsar through Syria
Intends his journey; and within three days
You with your children will he send before.
Make your best use of this. I have perform'd
Your pleasure and my promise.

Cleo. Dolabella,
I shall remain your debtor.

Dol. I your servant.
Adieu, good queen; I must attend on Cæsar.

Cleo. Farewell, and thanks. [*Exit* DOLABELLA.
Now, Iras, what think'st thou?
Thou, an Egyptian puppet, shalt be shown
In Rome, as well as I. Mechanic slaves
With greasy aprons, rules, and hammers, shall
Uplift us to the view; in their thick breaths,
Rank of gross diet, shall we be enclouded,
And forced to drink their vapour.

Iras. The gods forbid!

Cleo. Nay, 'tis most certain, Iras. Saucy lictors
Will catch at us, like strumpets; and scald rhymers
Ballad us out o' tune. The quick comedians
Extemporally will stage us, and present
Our Alexandrian revels; Antony
Shall be brought drunken forth, and I shall see
Some squeaking Cleopatra boy my greatness
I' the posture of a whore.

Iras. O the good gods!

Cleo. Nay, that's certain.

Iras. I'll never see 't; for, I am sure, my nails
Are stronger than mine eyes.

Cleo. Why, that's the way
To fool their preparation, and to conquer
Their most absurd intents.

Re-enter CHARMIAN.

Now, Charmian!
Show me, my women, like a queen. Go fetch

My best attires. I am again for Cydnus,
To meet Mark Antony. Sirrah Iras, go.
Now, noble Charmian, we'll dispatch indeed;
And, when thou hast done this chare, I'll give thee leave
To play till doomsday. Bring our crown and all.
Wherefore's this noise?
[*Exit* IRAS. *A noise within.*

Enter a GUARDSMAN.

Guard. Here is a rural fellow
That will not be denied your highness' presence:
He brings you figs.
Cleo. Let him come in. [*Exit* GUARDSMAN.
What poor an instrument
May do a noble deed! he brings me liberty.
My resolution's placed, and I have nothing
Of woman in me. Now from head to foot
I am marble-constant; now the fleeting moon
No planet is of mine.

Re-enter GUARDSMAN, *with* CLOWN *bringing in a basket.*

Guard. This is the man.
Cleo. Avoid, and leave him.
[*Exit* GUARDSMAN.
Hast thou the pretty worm of Nilus there,
That kills and pains not?

Clown. Truly, I have him; but I would not be the party that should desire you to touch him, for his biting is immortal; those that do die of it do seldom or never recover.

Cleo. Rememberest thou any that have died on 't?

Clown. Very many, men and women too. I heard of one of them no longer than yesterday; a very honest woman, but something given to lie; as a woman should not do, but in the way of honesty; how she died of the biting of it, what pain she felt; truly, she makes a very good report o' the worm. But he that will believe all that they say, shall never be saved by half that they do. But this is most fallible, the worm's an odd worm.

Cleo. Get thee hence; farewell.

Clown. I wish you all joy of the worm.
Setting down his basket.

Cleo. Farewell.

Clown. You must think this, look you, that the worm will do his kind.

Cleo. Ay, ay; farewell.

Clown. Look you, the worm is not to be trusted but in the keeping of wise people; for, indeed, there is no goodness in the worm.

Cleo. Take thou no care; it shall be heeded.

Clown. Very good. Give it nothing, I pray you, for it is not worth the feeding.

Cleo. Will it eat me?

Clown. You must not think I am so simple but I know the devil himself will not eat a woman. I know that a woman is a dish for the gods, if the devil dress her not. But, truly, these same whoreson devils do the gods great harm in their women; for in every ten that they make, the devils mar five.

Cleo. Well, get thee gone; farewell.

Clown. Yes, forsooth; I wish you joy o' the worm. [*Exit.*

Re-enter IRAS *with a robe, crown, &c.*

Cleo. Give me my robe, put on my crown; I have
Immortal longings in me. Now no more
The juice of Egypt's grape shall moist this lip.
Yare, yare, good Iras; quick. Methinks I hear
Antony call; I see him rouse himself
To praise my noble act; I hear him mock
The luck of Cæsar, which the gods give men
To excuse their after wrath. Husband, I come:
Now to that name my courage prove my title!
I am fire and air; my other elements
I give to baser life. So; have you done?
Come then, and take the last warmth of my lips.
Farewell, kind Charmian; Iras, long farewell.
Kisses them. Iras falls and dies.
Have I the aspic in my lips? Dost fall?
If thou and nature can so gently part,
The stroke of death is as a lover's pinch,
Which hurts, and is desired. Dost thou lie still?
If thus thou vanishest, thou tell'st the world
It is not worth leave-taking.
Char. Dissolve, thick cloud, and rain; that I may say,
The gods themselves do weep!
Cleo. This proves me base.
If she first meet the curled Antony,
He'll make demand of her, and spend that kiss
Which is my heaven to have. Come, thou mortal wretch,
To an asp, which she applies to her breast.
With thy sharp teeth this knot intrinsicate
Of life at once untie. Poor venomous fool,
Be angry, and dispatch. O, couldst thou speak,
That I might hear thee call great Cæsar ass
Unpolicied!
Char. O eastern star!
Cleo. Peace, peace!
Dost thou not see my baby at my breast,
That sucks the nurse asleep?
Char. O, break! O, break!
Cleo. As sweet as balm, as soft as air, as gentle—
O Antony!—Nay, I will take thee too.

Applying another asp to her arm.

What should I stay— [*Dies.*

Char. In this vile world? So, fare thee well.
Now boast thee, Death, in thy possession lies
A lass unparallel'd. Downy windows, close;
And golden Phœbus never be beheld
Of eyes again so royal! Your crown's awry;
I'll mend it, and then play.

Enter the GUARD, *rushing in.*

1st Guard. Where is the Queen?
Char. Speak softly, wake her not.
1st Guard. Cæsar hath sent—
Char. Too slow a messenger.

Applies an asp.

O, come apace, dispatch! I partly feel thee.
1st Guard. Approach, ho! All's not well; Cæsar's beguiled.
2nd Guard. There's Dolabella sent from Cæsar; call him.
1st Guard. What work is here! Charmian, is this well done?
Char. It is well done, and fitting for a princess
Descended of so many royal kings.
Ah, soldier! [*Dies.*

Re-enter DOLABELLA.

Dol. How goes it here?
2nd Guard. All dead.
Dol. Cæsar, thy thoughts
Touch their effects in this. Thyself art coming
To see perform'd the dreaded act which thou
So sought'st to hinder.

Within, "A way there, a way for Cæsar!"

Re-enter CÆSAR *and all his train, marching.*

Dol. O sir, you are too sure an augurer;
That you did fear is done.
Cæs. Bravest at the last,
She levell'd at our purposes, and, being royal,
Took her own way. The manner of their deaths?
I do not see them bleed.
Dol. Who was last with them?
1st Guard. A simple countryman, that brought her figs:
This was his basket.
Cæs. Poison'd, then.
1st Guard. O Cæsar,
This Charmian lived but now; she stood and spake.
I found her trimming up the diadem
On her dead mistress; tremblingly she stood
And on the sudden dropp'd.
Cæs. O noble weakness!
If they had swallow'd poison, 'twould appear
By external swelling; but she looks like sleep,
As she would catch another Antony
In her strong toil of grace.
Dol. Here, on her breast,
There is a vent of blood and something blown.
The like is on her arm.
1st Guard. This is an aspic's trail; and these fig-leaves
Have slime upon them, such as the aspic leaves
Upon the caves of Nile.
Cæs. Most probable
That so she died; for her physician tells me
She hath pursued conclusions infinite
Of easy ways to die. Take up her bed;
And bear her women from the monument.
She shall be buried by her Antony.
No grave upon the earth shall clip in it
A pair so famous. High events as these
Strike those that make them; and their story is
No less in pity than his glory which
Brought them to be lamented. Our army shall
In solemn show attend this funeral;
And then to Rome. Come, Dolabella, see
High order in this great solemnity. [*Exeunt.*

CORIOLANUS

DRAMATIS PERSONÆ

CAIUS MARCIUS, *afterwards* CAIUS MARCIUS CORIOLANUS
TITUS LARTIUS, COMINIUS — *generals against the Volscians*
MENENIUS AGRIPPA, *friend to Coriolanus*
SICINIUS VELUTUS, JUNIUS BRUTUS — *tribunes of the people*
YOUNG MARCIUS, *son to Coriolanus*
A ROMAN HERALD
NICANOR, *a Roman*
AN ÆDILE
TWO PATRICIANS
TWO OFFICERS
A LIEUTENANT *to Lartius*
TWO SENATORS
SEVEN CITIZENS
THREE MESSENGERS
THREE SOLDIERS

TULLUS AUFIDIUS, *general of the Volscians*

A LIEUTENANT *to Aufidius*
THREE CONSPIRATORS *with Aufidius*
A CITIZEN *of Antium*
TWO LORDS
TWO SENTRIES
TWO SENATORS
THREE SOLDIERS
ADRIAN, *A Volscian*
THREE SERVANTS *to Aufidius*

VOLUMNIA, *mother to Coriolanus*
VIRGILIA, *wife to Coriolanus*
VALERIA, *friend to Virgilia*
GENTLEWOMAN, *attending on Virgilia*

NON-SPEAKING: *Roman and Volscian Senators, Patricians, Soldiers, Citizens, Lictors, and Attendants*

SCENE: *Rome and the neighbourhood; Corioli and the neighbourhood; Antium*

ACT I

SCENE I. *Rome: a street*

Enter a company of mutinous CITIZENS, *with staves, clubs, and other weapons.*

1st Cit. Before we proceed any further, hear me speak.

All. Speak, speak.

1st Cit. You are all resolved rather to die than to famish?

All. Resolved, resolved.

1st Cit. First, you know Caius Marcius is chief enemy to the people.

All. We know't, we know't.

1st Cit. Let us kill him, and we'll have corn at our own price. Is't a verdict? 11

All. No more talking on't; let it be done. Away, away!

2nd Cit. One word, good citizens.

1st Cit. We are accounted poor citizens, the patricians good. What authority surfeits on would relieve us; if they would yield us but the superfluity, while it were wholesome, we might guess they relieved us humanely; but they think we are too dear. The leanness that afflicts us, the object of our misery, is as an inventory to particularize their abundance; our sufferance is a gain to them. Let us revenge this with our pikes, ere we become rakes; for the gods know I speak this in hunger for bread, not in thirst for revenge.

2nd Cit. Would you proceed especially against Caius Marcius?

All. Against him first; he's a very dog to the commonalty. 29

2nd. Cit. Consider you what services he has done for his country?

1st Cit. Very well; and could be content to give him good report for't, but that he pays himself with being proud.

2nd Cit. Nay, but speak not maliciously.

1st Cit. I say unto you, what he hath done famously, he did it to that end. Though soft-conscienced men can be content to say it was for his country, he did it to please his mother, and to be partly proud; which he is, even to the altitude of his virtue. 41

2nd Cit. What he cannot help in his nature, you account a vice in him. You must in no way say he is covetous.

1st Cit. If I must not, I need not be barren of accusations; he hath faults, with surplus, to tire in repetition. [*Shouts within.*] What shouts are these? The other side o' the city is risen; why stay we prating here? To the Capitol!

All. Come, come. 50

1st Cit. Soft! who comes here?

Enter MENENIUS AGRIPPA.

2nd Cit. Worthy Menenius Agrippa; one that hath always loved the people.

1st Cit. He's one honest enough; would all the rest were so!

Men. What work's, my countrymen, in hand? where go you
With bats and clubs? The matter? speak, I pray you.

1st Cit. Our business is not unknown to the Senate; they have had inkling this fortnight what we intend to do, which now we'll show 'em in deeds. They say poor suitors have strong breaths; they shall know we have strong arms too.

Men. Why, masters, my good friends, mine honest neighbours,
Will you undo yourselves?

1st Cit. We cannot, sir, we are undone already.

Men. I tell you, friends, most charitable care
Have the patricians of you. For your wants,
Your suffering in this dearth, you may as well
Strike at the heaven with your staves as lift them
Against the Roman state, whose course will on
The way it takes, cracking ten thousand curbs
Of more strong link asunder than can ever
Appear in your impediment. For the dearth,
The gods, not the patricians, make it, and
Your knees to them, not arms, must help. Alack,
You are transported by calamity
Thither where more attends you, and you slander
The helms o' the state, who care for you like fathers
When you curse them as enemies.

1st Cit. Care for us! True, indeed! they ne'er cared for us yet: suffer us to famish, and their store-houses crammed with grain; make edicts for usury, to support usurers; repeal daily any wholesome act established against the rich, and provide more piercing statutes daily, to chain up and restrain the poor. If the wars eat us not up, they will; and there's all the love they bear us.

Men. Either you must
Confess yourselves wondrous malicious,
Or be accused of folly. I shall tell you
A pretty tale. It may be you have heard it;
But, since it serves my purpose, I will venture
To stale 't a little more.

1st Cit. Well, I'll hear it, sir; yet you must not think to fob off our disgrace with a tale. But, an 't please you, deliver.

Men. There was a time when all the body's members
Rebell'd against the belly, thus accused it:
That only like a gulf it did remain
I' the midst o' the body, idle and unactive,
Still cupboarding the viand, never bearing
Like labour with the rest, where the other instruments
Did see and hear, devise, instruct, walk, feel,
And mutually participate, did minister
Unto the appetite and affection common
Of the whole body. The belly answer'd—

1st Cit. Well, sir, what answer made the belly?

Men. Sir, I shall tell you. With a kind of smile,
Which ne'er came from the lungs, but even thus—
For, look you, I may make the belly smile
As well as speak—it tauntingly replied
To the discontented members, the mutinous parts
That envied his receipt; even so most fitly
As you malign our senators for that
They are not such as you.

1st Cit. Your belly's answer? What?
The kingly-crowned head, the vigilant eye,
The counsellor heart, the arm our soldier,
Our steed the leg, the tongue our trumpeter,
With other muniments and petty helps
In this our fabric, if that they—

Men. What then?
'Fore me, this fellow speaks: What then? what then?

1st Cit. Should by the cormorant belly be restrain'd,
Who is the sink o' the body—

Men. Well, what then?

1st Cit. The former agents, if they did complain,
What could the belly answer?

Men. I will tell you;
If you'll bestow a small—of what you have little—
Patience awhile, you'll hear the belly's answer.

1st Cit. Ye're long about it.

Men. Note me this, good friend;
Your most grave belly was deliberate,
Not rash like his accusers, and thus answer'd:
"True is it, my incorporate friends," quoth he,
"That I receive the general food at first,
Which you do live upon; and fit it is,
Because I am the store-house and the shop
Of the whole body. But, if you do remember,
I send it through the rivers of your blood,
Even to the court, the heart, to the seat o' the brain;
And, through the cranks and offices of man,
The strongest nerves and small inferior veins
From me receive that natural competency
Whereby they live: and though that all at once,
You, my good friends"—this says the belly, mark me—

1st Cit. Ay, sir; well, well.

Men. "Though all at once cannot
See what I do deliver out to each,
Yet I can make my audit up, that all

From me do back receive the flour of all,
And leave me but the bran." What say you to't?
1st Cit. It was an answer. How apply you this?
Men. The senators of Rome are this good belly,
And you the mutinous members; for examine
Their counsels and their cares, digest things rightly
Touching the weal o'the common, you shall find
No public benefit which you receive
But it proceeds or comes from them to you
And no way from yourselves. What do you think,
You, the great toe of this assembly?
1st Cit. I the great toe! Why the great toe?
Men. For that, being one o' the lowest, basest, poorest,
Of this most wise rebellion, thou go'st foremost;
Thou rascal, that art worst in blood to run,
Lead'st first to win some vantage.
But make you ready your stiff bats and clubs;
Rome and her rats are at the point of battle;
The one side must have bale.

Enter CAIUS MARCIUS.

Hail, noble Marcius!
Mar. Thanks. What's the matter, you dissentious rogues,
That, rubbing the poor itch of your opinion,
Make yourselves scabs?
1st Cit. We have ever your good word.
Mar. He that will give good words to thee will flatter
Beneath abhorring. What would you have, you curs,
That like nor peace nor war? the one affrights you,
The other makes you proud. He that trusts to you,
Where he should find you lions, finds you hares;
Where foxes, geese. You are no surer, no,
Than is the coal of fire upon the ice,
Or hailstone in the sun. Your virtue is
To make him worthy whose offence subdues him
And curse that justice did it. Who deserves greatness
Deserves your hate; and your affections are
A sick man's appetite, who desires most that
Which would increase his evil. He that depends
Upon your favours swims with fins of lead
And hews down oaks with rushes. Hang ye! Trust ye?
With every minute you do change a mind,
And call him noble that was now your hate,
Him vile that was your garland. What's the matter,
That in these several places of the city
You cry against the noble Senate, who,
Under the gods, keep you in awe, which else
Would feed on one another? What's their seeking?
Men. For corn at their own rates; whereof, they say,
The city is well stored.
Mar. Hang 'em! They say!
They'll sit by the fire, and presume to know
What's done i' the Capitol; who's like to rise,
Who thrives, and who declines; side factions and give out
Conjectural marriages; making parties strong
And feebling such as stand not in their liking
Below their cobbled shoes. They say there's grain enough!
Would the nobility lay aside their ruth,
And let me use my sword, I'd make a quarry
With thousands of these quarter'd slaves as high
As I could pick my lance.
Men. Nay, these are almost thoroughly persuaded;
For though abundantly they lack discretion,
Yet are they passing cowardly. But, I beseech you,
What says the other troop?
Mar. They are dissolved, hang 'em!
They said they were an-hungry; sigh'd forth proverbs,
That hunger broke stone walls, that dogs must eat,
That meat was made for mouths, that the gods sent not
Corn for the rich men only. With these shreds
They vented their complainings; which being answer'd,
And a petition granted them, a strange one—
To break the heart of generosity,
And make bold power look pale—they threw their caps
As they would hang them on the horns o' the moon,
Shouting their emulation.
Men. What is granted them?
Mar. Five tribunes to defend their vulgar wisdoms,
Of their own choice. One's Junius Brutus,
Sicinius Velutus, and I know not—'Sdeath!
The rabble should have first unroof'd the city,
Ere so prevail'd with me. It will in time
Win upon power and throw forth greater themes
For insurrection's arguing.
Men. This is strange.
Mar. Go, get you home, you fragments!

Enter a MESSENGER, *hastily*.

Mess. Where's Caius Marcius?
Mar. Here. What's the matter?
Mess. The news is, sir, the Volsces are in arms.
Mar. I am glad on 't. Then we shall ha' means to vent
Our musty superfluity. See, our best elders.

Enter COMINIUS, TITUS LARTIUS, *and other* SENATORS; JUNIUS BRUTUS *and* SICINIUS VELUTUS.

1st Sen. Marcius, 'tis true that you have lately told us;
The Volsces are in arms.
Mar. They have a leader,
Tullus Aufidius, that will put you to 't.
I sin in envying his nobility,
And were I anything but what I am,
I would wish me only he.
Com. You have fought together.
Mar. Were half to half the world by the ears and he
Upon my party, I'd revolt, to make
Only my wars with him. He is a lion
That I am proud to hunt.
1st Sen. Then, worthy Marcius,
Attend upon Cominius to these wars.
Com. It is your former promise.
Mar. Sir, it is;
And I am constant. Titus Lartius, thou
Shalt see me once more strike at Tullus' face.
What, art thou stiff? stand'st out?
Tit. No, Caius Marcius;
I'll lean upon one crutch and fight with t'other,
Ere stay behind this business.
Men. O, true-bred!
1st Sen. Your company to the Capitol; where, I know,
Our greatest friends attend us.
Tit. [*To* COMINIUS] Lead you on.
[*To* MARCIUS] Follow Cominius; we must follow you;
Right worthy you priority.
Com. Noble Marcius!
1st Sen. [*To the* CITIZENS] Hence to your homes; be gone!
Mar. Nay, let them follow.
The Volsces have much corn; take these rats thither
To gnaw their garners. Worshipful mutiners,
Your valour puts well forth. Pray, follow.
[CITIZENS *steal away*. *Exeunt all but* SICINIUS *and* BRUTUS.

Sic. Was ever man so proud as is this Marcius?
Bru. He has no equal.
Sic. When we were chosen tribunes for the people—
Bru. Mark'd you his lip and eyes?
Sic. Nay, but his taunts.
Bru. Being moved, he will not spare to gird the gods.
Sic. Be-mock the modest moon.
Bru. The present wars devour him. He is grown
Too proud to be so valiant.
Sic. Such a nature,
Tickled with good success, disdains the shadow
Which he treads on at noon. But I do wonder
His insolence can brook to be commanded
Under Cominius.
Bru. Fame, at the which he aims,
In whom already he's well graced, can not
Better be held nor more attain'd than by
A place below the first; for what miscarries
Shall be the general's fault, though he perform
To the utmost of a man, and giddy censure
Will then cry out of Marcius "O, if he
Had borne the business!"
Sic. Besides, if things go well,
Opinion that so sticks on Marcius shall
Of his demerits rob Cominius.
Bru. Come.
Half all Cominius' honours are to Marcius,
Though Marcius earn'd them not, and all his faults
To Marcius shall be honours, though indeed
In aught he merit not.
Sic. Let's hence, and hear
How the dispatch is made, and in what fashion,
More than his singularity, he goes
Upon this present action.
Bru. Let's along. [*Exeunt*.

SCENE II. *Corioli: the Senate-house*

Enter TULLUS AUFIDIUS *and certain* SENATORS *of Corioli*.

1st Sen. So, your opinion is, Aufidius,
That they of Rome are enter'd in our counsels
And know how we proceed.
Auf. Is it not yours?
What ever have been thought on in this state,
That could be brought to bodily act ere Rome
Had circumvention? 'Tis not four days gone
Since I heard thence; these are the words; I think
I have the letter here; yes, here it is:
[*Reads*] "They have press'd a power, but it is not known
Whether for east or west. The dearth is great;
The people mutinous; and it is rumour'd,
Cominius, Marcius your old enemy,
Who is of Rome worse hated than of you,
And Titus Lartius, a most valiant Roman,

These three lead on this preparation
Whither 'tis bent. Most likely 'tis for you;
Consider of it."

1st Sen. Our army's in the field.
We never yet made doubt but Rome was ready
To answer us.

Auf. Nor did you think it folly
To keep your great pretences veil'd till when
They needs must show themselves; which in the hatching,
It seem'd, appear'd to Rome. By the discovery
We shall be shorten'd in our aim, which was
To take in many towns ere almost Rome
Should know we were afoot.

2nd Sen. Noble Aufidius,
Take your commission; hie you to your bands;
Let us alone to guard Corioli.
If they set down before 's, for the remove
Bring up your army; but, I think, you'll find
They've not prepared for us.

Auf. O, doubt not that;
I speak from certainties. Nay, more,
Some parcels of their power are forth already,
And only hitherward. I leave your honours.
If we and Caius Marcius chance to meet,
'Tis sworn between us we shall ever strike
Till one can do no more.

All. The gods assist you!

Auf. And keep your honours safe!

1st Sen. Farewell.

2nd Sen. Farewell.

All. Farewell. [*Exeunt.*

SCENE III. *Rome: a room in Marcius' house*

Enter VOLUMNIA *and* VIRGILIA. *They set them down on two low stools, and sew.*

Vol. I pray you, daughter, sing; or express yourself in a more comfortable sort. If my son were my husband, I should freelier rejoice in that absence wherein he won honour than in the embracements of his bed where he would show most love. When yet he was but tender-bodied and the only son of my womb, when youth with comeliness plucked all gaze his way, when for a day of kings' entreaties a mother should not sell him an hour from her beholding, I, considering how honour would become such a person, that it was no better than picture-like to hang by the wall, if renown made it not stir, was pleased to let him seek danger where he was like to find fame. To a cruel war I sent him; from whence he returned, his brows bound with oak. I tell thee, daughter, I sprang not more in joy at first hearing he was a man-child than now in first seeing he had proved himself a man.

Vir. But had he died in the business, madam; how then?

Vol. Then his good report should have been my son; I therein would have found issue. Hear me profess sincerely: had I a dozen sons, each in my love alike and none less dear than thine and my good Marcius, I had rather had eleven die nobly for their country than one voluptuously surfeit out of action.

Enter a GENTLEWOMAN.

Gent. Madam, the Lady Valeria is come to visit you.

Vir. Beseech you, give me leave to retire myself.

Vol. Indeed, you shall not.
Methinks I hear hither your husband's drum,
See him pluck Aufidius down by the hair,
As children from a bear, the Volsces shunning him.
Methinks I see him stamp thus, and call thus:
"Come on, you cowards! you were got in fear,
Though you were born in Rome." His bloody brow
With his mail'd hand then wiping, forth he goes,
Like to a harvest-man that's task'd to mow
Or all or lose his hire.

Vir. His bloody brow! O Jupiter, no blood!

Vol. Away, you fool! it more becomes a man
Than gilt his trophy. The breasts of Hecuba,
When she did suckle Hector, look'd not lovelier
Than Hector's forehead when it spit forth blood
At Grecian sword, contemning. Tell Valeria,
We are fit to bid her welcome.
[*Exit* GENTLEWOMAN.

Vir. Heavens bless my lord from fell Aufidius!

Vol. He'll beat Aufidius' head below his knee
And tread upon his neck.

Enter VALERIA, *with an Usher and* GENTLEWOMAN.

Val. My ladies both, good day to you.

Vol. Sweet madam.

Vir. I am glad to see your ladyship.

Val. How do you both? you are manifest housekeepers. What are you sewing here? A fine spot, in good faith. How does your little son?

Vir. I thank your ladyship; well, good madam.

Vol. He had rather see the swords and hear a drum than look upon his schoolmaster.

Val. O' my word, the father's son. I'll swear, 'tis a very pretty boy. O' my troth, I looked upon him o' Wednesday half an hour together; has such a confirmed countenance. I saw him run after a gilded butterfly; and when he caught it, he let it go again; and after it again; and over and over he comes, and up again; catched it again; or whether his fall enraged him, or how 'twas, he did so set his teeth and tear it; O, I warrant, how he mammocked it!

Vol. One on's father's moods.

Val. Indeed, la, 'tis a noble child.

Vir. A crack, madam.

Val. Come, lay aside your stitchery; I must have you play the idle huswife with me this afternoon.

Vir. No, good madam; I will not out of doors.

Val. Not out of doors!

Vol. She shall, she shall.

Vir. Indeed, no, by your patience; I'll not over the threshold till my lord return from the wars.

Val. Fie, you confine yourself most unreasonably. Come, you must go visit the good lady that lies in.

Vir. I will wish her speedy strength, and visit her with my prayers; but I cannot go thither.

Vol. Why, I pray you?

Vir. 'Tis not to save labour, nor that I want love.

Val. You would be another Penelope. Yet, they say, all the yarn she spun in Ulysses' absence did but fill Ithaca full of moths. Come; I would your cambric were sensible as your finger, that you might leave pricking it for pity. Come, you shall go with us.

Vir. No, good madam, pardon me; indeed, I will not forth.

Val. In truth, la, go with me; and I'll tell you excellent news of your husband.

Vir. O, good madam, there can be none yet.

Val. Verily, I do not jest with you; there came news from him last night.

Vir. Indeed, madam?

Val. In earnest, it's true; I heard a senator speak it. Thus it is: the Volsces have an army forth; against whom Cominius the general is gone, with one part of our Roman power. Your lord and Titus Lartius are set down before their city Corioli; they nothing doubt prevailing and to make it brief wars. This is true, on mine honour; and so, I pray, go with us.

Vir. Give me excuse, good madam; I will obey you in everything hereafter.

Vol. Let her alone, lady. As she is now, she will but disease our better mirth.

Val. In troth, I think she would. Fare you well, then. Come, good sweet lady. Prithee, Virgilia, turn thy solemness out o' door, and go aong with us.

Vir. No, at a word, madam; indeed, I must not. I wish you much mirth.

Val. Well, then, farewell. [*Exeunt.*

SCENE IV. *Before Corioli*

Enter, with drum and colours, MARCIUS, TITUS LARTIUS, *Captains and Soldiers. To them a* MESSENGER.

Mar. Yonder comes news. A wager they have met.

Lart. My horse to yours, no.

Mar. 'Tis done.

Lart. Agreed.

Mar. Say, has our general met the enemy?

Mess. They lie in view; but have not spoke as yet.

Lart. So, the good horse is mine.

Mar. I'll buy him of you.

Lart. No, I'll nor sell nor give him; lend you him I will
For half a hundred years. Summon the town.

Mar. How far off lie these armies?

Mess. Within this mile and half.

Mar. Then shall we hear their 'larum, and they ours.
Now, Mars, I prithee, make us quick in work,
That we with smoking swords may march from hence,
To help our fielded friends! Come, blow thy blast.

They sound a parley. Enter TWO SENATORS *with others on the walls.*

Tullus Aufidius, is he within your walls?

1st Sen. No, nor a man that fears you less than he,
That's lesser than a little. [*Drums afar off.*]
Hark! our drums
Are bringing forth our youth. We'll break our walls,
Rather than they shall pound us up. Our gates,
Which yet seem shut, we have put pinn'd with rushes;
They'll open of themselves. [*Alarum afar off.*]
Hark you, far off!
There is Aufidius; list, what work he makes
Amongst your cloven army.

Mar. O, they are at it!

Lart. Their noise be our instruction. Ladders, ho!

Enter the army of the Volsces.

Mar. They fear us not, but issue forth their city.
Now put your shields before your hearts, and fight
With hearts more proof than shields. Advance, brave Titus.
They do disdain us much beyond our thoughts,

Which makes me sweat with wrath. Come on, my fellows!
He that retires, I'll take him for a Volsce,
And he shall feel mine edge.

Alarum. The Romans are beat back to their trenches. Re-enter MARCIUS, *cursing.*

Mar. All the contagion of the south light on you,
You shames of Rome! you herd of—Boils and plagues
Plaster you o'er, that you may be abhorr'd
Further than seen and one infect another
Against the wind a mile! You souls of geese,
That bear the shapes of men, how have you run
From slaves that apes would beat! Pluto and hell!
All hurt behind; backs red, and faces pale
With flight and agued fear! Mend and charge home,
Or, by the fires of heaven, I'll leave the foe
And make my wars on you. Look to't; come on!
If you'll stand fast, we'll beat them to their wives,
As they us to our trenches followed.

Another alarum. The Volsces fly, and MARCIUS *follows them to the gates.*

So, now the gates are ope. Now prove good seconds;
'Tis for the followers fortune widens them,
Not for the fliers. Mark me, and do the like.
Enters the gates.

1st Sol. Fool-hardiness; not I.
2nd Sol. Nor I.
MARCIUS *is shut in.*
1st Sol. See, they have shut him in.
All. To the pot, I warrant him.
Alarum continues.

Re-enter TITUS LARTIUS.

Lart. What is become of Marcius?
All. Slain, sir, doubtless.
1st Sol. Following the fliers at the very heels,
With them he enters; who, upon the sudden,
Clapp'd to their gates. He is himself alone,
To answer all the city.
Lart. O noble fellow!
Who sensibly outdares his senseless sword,
And, when it bows, stands up. Thou art left, Marcius.
A carbuncle entire, as big as thou art,
Were not so rich a jewel. Thou wast a soldier
Even to Cato's wish, not fierce and terrible
Only in strokes; but, with thy grim looks and
The thunder-like percussion of thy sounds,
Thou madest thine enemies shake, as if the world
Were feverous and did tremble.

Re-enter MARCIUS, *bleeding, assaulted by the enemy.*

1st Sol. Look, sir.
Lart. O, 'tis Marcius!
Let's fetch him off, or make remain alike.
[*They fight, and all enter the city.*

SCENE V. *Corioli: a street*

Enter certain ROMANS, *with spoils.*

1st Rom. This will I carry to Rome.
2nd Rom. And I this.
3rd Rom. A murrain on't! I took this for silver.
Alarum continues still afar off.

Enter MARCIUS *and* TITUS LARTIUS *with a trumpet.*

Mar. See here these movers that do prize their hours
At a crack'd drachma! Cushions, leaden spoons,
Irons of a doit, doublets that hangmen would
Bury with those that wore them, these base slaves,
Ere yet the fight be done, pack up. Down with them!
And hark, what noise the general makes! To him!
There is the man of my soul's hate, Aufidius,
Piercing our Romans; then, valiant Titus, take
Convenient numbers to make good the city;
Whilst I, with those that have the spirit, will haste
To help Cominius.
Lart. Worthy sir, thou bleed'st;
Thy exercise hath been too violent
For a second course of fight.
Mar. Sir, praise me not;
My work hath yet not warm'd me; fare you well.
The blood I drop is rather physical
Than dangerous to me. To Aufidius thus
I will appear, and fight.
Lart. Now the fair goddess, Fortune,
Fall deep in love with thee; and her great charms
Misguide thy opposers' swords! Bold gentleman,
Prosperity be thy page!
Mar. Thy friend no less
Than those she placeth highest! So, farewell.
Lart. Thou worthiest Marcius!
[*Exit* MARCIUS.
Go sound thy trumpet in the market-place;
Call thither all the officers o' the town,
Where they shall know our mind. Away!
[*Exeunt.*

SCENE VI. *Near the camp of Cominius*

Enter COMINIUS, *as it were in retire, with soldiers.*

Com. Breathe you, my friends. Well fought; we are come off

Like Romans, neither foolish in our stands,
Nor cowardly in retire. Believe me, sirs,
We shall be charged again. Whiles we have struck,
By interims and conveying gusts we have heard
The charges of our friends. Ye Roman gods!
Lead their successes as we wish our own,
That both our powers, with smiling fronts encountering,
May give you thankful sacrifice.

Enter a MESSENGER.

Thy news?

Mess. The citizens of Corioli have issued,
And given to Lartius and to Marcius battle.
I saw our party to their trenches driven,
And then I came away.

Com. Though thou speak'st truth,
Methinks thou speak'st not well. How long is't since?

Mess. Above an hour, my lord.

Com. 'Tis not a mile; briefly we heard their drums.
How couldst thou in a mile confound an hour,
And bring thy news so late?

Mess. Spies of the Volsces
Held me in chase, that I was forced to wheel
Three or four miles about, else had I, sir,
Half an hour since brought my report.

Com. Who's yonder,
That does appear as he were flay'd? O gods!
He has the stamp of Marcius; and I have
Before-time seen him thus.

Mar. [*Within*] Come I too late?

Com. The shepherd knows not thunder from a tabor
More than I know the sound of Marcius' tongue
From every meaner man.

Enter MARCIUS.

Mar. Come I too late?

Com. Ay, if you come not in the blood of others,
But mantled in your own.

Mar. O, let me clip ye
In arms as sound as when I woo'd, in heart
As merry as when our nuptial day was done,
And tapers burn'd to bedward!

Com. Flower of warriors,
How is't with Titus Lartius?

Mar. As with a man busied about decrees:
Condemning some to death, and some to exile;
Ransoming him, or pitying, threatening the other;
Holding Corioli in the name of Rome,
Even like a fawning greyhound in the leash,
To let him slip at will.

Com. Where is that slave
Which told me they had beat you to your trenches?
Where is he? call him hither.

Mar. Let him alone;
He did inform the truth. But for our gentlemen,
The common file—a plague! tribunes for them!—
The mouse ne'er shunn'd the cat as they did budge
From rascals worse than they.

Com. But how prevail'd you?

Mar. Will the time serve to tell? I do not think.
Where is the enemy? are you lords o' the field?
If not, why cease you till you are so?

Com. Marcius,
We have at disadvantage fought and did
Retire to win our purpose.

Mar. How lies their battle? Know you on which side
They have placed their men of trust?

Com. As I guess, Marcius,
Their bands i' the vaward are the Antiates,
Of their best trust; o'er them Aufidius,
Their very heart of hope.

Mar. I do beseech you,
By all the battles wherein we have fought,
By the blood we have shed together, by the vows
We have made to endure friends, that you directly
Set me against Aufidius and his Antiates;
And that you not delay the present, but,
Filling the air with swords advanced and darts,
We prove this very hour.

Com. Though I could wish
You were conducted to a gentle bath
And balms applied to you, yet dare I never
Deny your asking. Take your choice of those
That best can aid your action.

Mar. Those are they
That most are willing. If any such be here—
As it were sin to doubt—that love this painting
Wherein you see me smear'd; if any fear
Lesser his person than an ill report;
If any think brave death outweighs bad life
And that his country's dearer than himself;
Let him alone, or so many so minded,
Wave thus, to express his disposition,
And follow Marcius.

They all shout and wave their swords, take him up in their arms, and cast up their caps.

O, me alone! make you a sword of me?
If these shows be not outward, which of you
But is four Volsces? none of you but is

Able to bear against the great Aufidius
A shield as hard as his. A certain number,
Though thanks to all, must I select from all; the rest
Shall bear the business in some other fight,
As cause will be obey'd. Please you to march;
And four shall quickly draw out my command,
Which men are best inclined.
Com. March on, my fellows.
Make good this ostentation, and you shall
Divide in all with us. [*Exeunt.*

SCENE VII. *The gates of Corioli*

TITUS LARTIUS, *having set a guard upon Corioli, going with drum and trumpet toward* COMINIUS *and* CAIUS MARCIUS, *enters with a* LIEUTENANT, *other Soldiers, and a Scout.*

Lart. So, let the ports be guarded; keep your duties,
As I have set them down. If I do send, dispatch
Those centuries to our aid; the rest will serve
For a short holding. If we lose the field,
We cannot keep the town.
Lieu. Fear not our care, sir.
Lart. Hence, and shut your gates upon's.
Our guider, come; to the Roman camp conduct us. [*Exeunt.*

SCENE VIII. *A field of battle*

Alarum as in battle. Enter, from opposite sides, MARCIUS *and* AUFIDIUS.

Mar. I'll fight with none but thee; for I do hate thee
Worse than a promise-breaker.
Auf. We hate alike.
Not Afric owns a serpent I abhor
More than thy fame and envy. Fix thy foot.
Mar. Let the first budger die the other's slave,
And the gods doom him after!
Auf. If I fly, Marcius,
Holloa me like a hare.
Mar. Within these three hours, Tullus,
Alone I fought in your Corioli walls,
And made what work I pleased. 'Tis not my blood
Wherein thou seest me mask'd; for thy revenge
Wrench up thy power to the highest.
Auf. Wert thou the Hector
That was the whip of your bragg'd progeny,
Thou shouldst not scape me here.

They fight, and certain Volsces come in the aid of AUFIDIUS. MARCIUS *fights till they be driven in breathless.*

Officious, and not valiant, you have shamed me
In your condemned seconds. [*Exeunt.*

SCENE IX. *The Roman camp.*

Flourish. Alarum. A retreat is sounded. Flourish. Enter, from one side, COMINIUS *with the* ROMANS; *from the other side,* MARCIUS, *with his arm in a scarf.*

Com. If I should tell thee o'er this thy day's work,
Thou'dst not believe thy deeds; but I'll report it
Where senators shall mingle tears with smiles,
Where great patricians shall attend and shrug,
I' the end admire, where ladies shall be frighted,
And, gladly quaked, hear more; where the dull tribunes,
That, with the fusty plebeians, hate thine honours,
Shall say against their hearts, "We thank the gods
Our Rome hath such a soldier."
Yet camest thou to a morsel of this feast,
Having fully dined before.

Enter TITUS LARTIUS, *with his power, from the pursuit.*

Lart. O general,
Here is the steed, we the caparison.
Hadst thou beheld—
Mar. Pray now, no more. My mother,
Who has a charter to extol her blood,
When she does praise me grieves me. I have done
As you have done; that's what I can; induced
As you have been; that's for my country.
He that has but effected his good will
Hath overta'en mine act.
Com. You shall not be
The grave of your deserving; Rome must know
The value of her own. 'Twere a concealment
Worse than a theft, no less than a traducement,
To hide your doings; and to silence that,
Which, to the spire and top of praises vouch'd,
Would seem but modest; therefore, I beseech you—
In sign of what you are, not to reward
What you have done—before our army hear me.
Mar. I have some wounds upon me, and they smart
To hear themselves remember'd.
Com. Should they not,
Well might they fester 'gainst ingratitude,
And tent themselves with death. Of all the horses,
Whereof we have ta'en good and good store, of all
The treasure in this field achieved and city,
We render you the tenth, to be ta'en forth,
Before the common distribution, at
Your only choice.

Mar. I thank you, general;
But cannot make my heart consent to take
A bribe to pay my sword. I do refuse it;
And stand upon my common part with those
That have beheld the doing.

A long flourish. They all cry, "Marcius! Marcius!" *cast up their caps and lances.* COMINIUS *and* LARTIUS *stand bare.*

Mar. May these same instruments, which you profane,
Never sound more! when drums and trumpets shall
I' the field prove flatterers, let courts and cities be
Made all of false-faced soothing!
When steel grows soft as the parasite's silk,
Let him be made a coverture for the wars!
No more, I say! For that I have not wash'd
My nose that bled, or foil'd some debile wretch—
Which, without note, here's many else have done—
You shout me forth
In acclamations hyperbolical;
As if I loved my little should be dieted
In praises sauced with lies.

Com. Too modest are you;
More cruel to your good report than grateful
To us that give you truly. By your patience,
If 'gainst yourself you be incensed, we'll put you,
Like one that means his proper harm, in manacles,
Then reason safely with you. Therefore, be it known,
As to us, to all the world, that Caius Marcius
Wears this war's garland; in token of the which,
My noble steed, know to the camp, I give him,
With all his trim belonging; and from this time,
For what he did before Corioli, call him,
With all the applause and clamour of the host,
Caius Marcius Coriolanus! Bear
The addition nobly ever!

Flourish. Trumpets sound, and drums.

All. Caius Marcius Coriolanus!

Cor. I will go wash;
And when my face is fair, you shall perceive
Whether I blush or no. Howbeit, I thank you.
I mean to stride your steed, and at all times
To undercrest your good addition
To the fairness of my power.

Com. So, to our tent;
Where, ere we do repose us, we will write
To Rome of our success. You, Titus Lartius,
Must to Corioli back. Send us to Rome
The best, with whom we may articulate,
For their own good and ours.

Lart. I shall, my lord.

Cor. The gods begin to mock me. I, that now
Refused most princely gifts, am bound to beg
Of my lord general.

Com. Take't; 'tis yours. What is't?

Cor. I sometime lay here in Corioli
At a poor man's house; he used me kindly.
He cried to me; I saw him prisoner;
But then Aufidius was within my view,
And wrath o'erwhelm'd my pity. I request you
To give my poor host freedom.

Com. O, well begg'd!
Were he the butcher of my son, he should
Be free as is the wind. Deliver him, Titus.

Lart. Marcius, his name?

Cor. By Jupiter! forgot.
I am weary; yea, my memory is tired.
Have we no wine here?

Com. Go we to our tent.
The blood upon your visage dries; 'tis time
It should be look'd to. Come. [*Exeunt.*

SCENE X. *The camp of the Volsces*

A flourish. Cornets. Enter TULLUS AUFIDIUS, *bloody, with two or three* SOLDIERS.

Auf. The town is ta'en!

1st Sol. 'Twill be deliver'd back on good condition.

Auf. Condition!
I would I were a Roman; for I cannot,
Being a Volsce, be that I am. Condition!
What good condition can a treaty find
I' the part that is at mercy? Five times, Marcius,
I have fought with thee; so often hast thou beat me,
And wouldst do so, I think, should we encounter
As often as we eat. By the elements,
If e'er again I meet him beard to beard,
He's mine, or I am his. Mine emulation
Hath not that honour in't it had; for where
I thought to crush him in an equal force,
True sword to sword, I'll potch at him some way
Or wrath or craft may get him.

1st Sol. He's the devil.

Auf. Bolder, though not so subtle. My valour's poison'd
With only suffering stain by him; for him
Shall fly out of itself. Nor sleep nor sanctuary,
Being naked, sick, nor fane nor Capitol,
The prayers of priests nor times of sacrifice,
Embarquements all of fury, shall lift up
Their rotten privilege and custom 'gainst
My hate to Marcius. Where I find him, were it
At home, upon my brother's guard, even there,
Against the hospitable canon, would I
Wash my fierce hand in's heart. Go you to the city;

Learn how 'tis held; and what they are that must
Be hostages for Rome.
1st Sol. Will not you go?
Auf. I am attended at the cypress grove. I pray you—
'Tis south the city mills—bring me word thither
How the world goes, that to the pace of it
I may spur on my journey.
1st Sol. I shall, sir.
[*Exeunt.*

ACT II

SCENE I. *Rome: a public place*

Enter MENENIUS *with the two Tribunes of the people,* SICINIUS *and* BRUTUS.

Men. The augurer tells me we shall have news to-night.

Bru. Good or bad?

Men. Not according to the prayer of the people, for they love not Marcius.

Sic. Nature teaches beasts to know their friends.

Men. Pray you, who does the wolf love?

Sic. The lamb.

Men. Ay, to devour him; as the hungry plebeians would the noble Marcius.

Bru. He's a lamb indeed, that baes like a bear.

Men. He's a bear indeed, that lives like a lamb. You two are old men; tell me one thing that I shall ask you.

Both. Well, sir.

Men. In what enormity is Marcius poor in, that you two have not in abundance?

Bru. He's poor in no one fault, but stored with all.

Sic. Especially in pride.

Bru. And topping all others in boasting.

Men. This is strange now. Do you two know how you are censured here in the city, I mean of us o' the right-hand file? do you?

Both. Why, how are we censured?

Men. Because you talk of pride now—will you not be angry?

Both. Well, well, sir, well.

Men. Why, 'tis no great matter; for a very little thief of occasion will rob you of a great deal of patience. Give your dispositions the reins, and be angry at your pleasures; at the least, if you take it as a pleasure to you in being so. You blame Marcius for being proud?

Bru. We do it not alone, sir.

Men. I know you can do very little alone; for your helps are many, or else your actions would grow wondrous single; your abilities are too infant-like for doing much alone. You talk of pride. O that you could turn your eyes toward the napes of your necks, and make but an interior survey of your good selves! O that you could!

Bru. What then, sir?

Men. Why, then you should discover a brace of unmeriting, proud, violent, testy magistrates, alias fools, as any in Rome.

Sic. Menenius, you are known well enough too.

Men. I am known to be a humorous patrician, and one that loves a cup of hot wine with not a drop of allaying Tiber in 't; said to be something imperfect in favouring the first complaint; hasty and tinder-like upon too trivial motion; one that converses more with the buttock of the night than with the forehead of the morning. What I think I utter, and spend my malice in my breath. Meeting two such wealsmen as you are—I cannot call you Lycurguses—if the drink you give me touch my palate adversely, I make a crooked face at it. I can't say your worships have delivered the matter well, when I find the ass in compound with the major part of your syllables; and though I must be content to bear with those that say you are reverend grave men, yet they lie deadly that tell you you have good faces. If you see this in the map of my microcosm, follows it that I am known well enough too? what harm can your bisson conspectuities glean out of this character, if I be known well enough too?

Bru. Come, sir, come, we know you well enough.

Men. You know neither me, yourselves, nor anything. You are ambitious for poor knaves' caps and legs. You wear out a good wholesome forenoon in hearing a cause between an orange-wife and a fosset-seller; and then rejourn the controversy of three pence to a second day of audience. When you are hearing a matter between party and party, if you chance to be pinched with the colic, you make faces like mummers; set up the bloody flag against all patience; and, in roaring for a chamber-pot, dismiss the controversy bleeding, the more entangled by your hearing. All the peace you make in their cause is calling both the parties knaves. You are a pair of strange ones.

Bru. Come, come, you are well understood to be a perfecter giber for the table than a necessary bencher in the Capitol.

Men. Our very priests must become mockers, if they shall encounter such ridiculous subjects as you are. When you speak best unto the purpose, it is not worth the wagging of your beards; and your beards deserve not so honourable a grave as to stuff a botcher's cushion, or to be entombed in an ass's pack-saddle. Yet you must be saying Marcius is proud; who, in a cheap estimation, is worth all your predecessors since Deucalion, though peradventure some of the best of 'em were hereditary hangmen. God-den to your worships. More of your conversation would infect my brain, being the herdsmen of the beastly plebeians. I will be bold to take my leave of you.

[BRUTUS *and* SICINIUS *go aside*.

Enter VOLUMNIA, VIRGILIA, *and* VALERIA.

How now, my as fair as noble ladies—and the moon, were she earthly, no nobler—whither do you follow your eyes so fast?

Vol. Honourable Menenius, my boy Marcius approaches; for the love of Juno, let's go.

Men. Ha! Marcius coming home!

Vol. Ay, worthy Menenius; and with most prosperous approbation.

Men. Take my cap, Jupiter, and I thank thee. Hoo! Marcius coming home!

Vol. *Vir*. Nay, 'tis true.

Vol. Look, here's a letter from him; the state hath another, his wife another; and, I think, there's one at home for you.

Men. I will make my very house reel tonight. A letter for me!

Vir. Yes, certain, there's a letter for you; I saw't.

Men. A letter for me! it gives me an estate of seven years' health; in which time I will make a lip at the physician. The most sovereign prescription in Galen is but empiricutic, and, to this preservative, of no better report than a horse-drench. Is he not wounded? he was wont to come home wounded.

Vir. O, no, no, no.

Vol. O, he is wounded; I thank the gods for 't.

Men. So do I too, if it be not too much. Brings a' victory in his pocket? the wounds become him.

Vol. On's brows. Menenius, he comes the third time home with the oaken garland.

Men. Has he disciplined Aufidius soundly?

Vol. Titus Lartius writes they fought together, but Aufidius got off.

Men. And 'twas time for him too, I'll warrant him that. An he had stayed by him, I would not have been so fidiused for all the chests in Corioli and the gold that's in them. Is the Senate possessed of this?

Vol. Good ladies, let's go. Yes, yes, yes; the Senate has letters from the general, wherein he gives my son the whole name of the war. He hath in this action outdone his former deeds doubly.

Val. In troth, there's wondrous things spoke of him.

Men. Wondrous! ay, I warrant you, and not without his true purchasing.

Vir. The gods grant them true!

Vol. True! pow, wow.

Men. True! I'll be sworn they are true. Where is he wounded? [*To the* TRIBUNES] God save your good worships! Marcius is coming home; he has more cause to be proud. Where is he wounded?

Vol. I' the shoulder and i' the left arm. There will be large cicatrices to show the people, when he shall stand for his place. He received in the repulse of Tarquin seven hurts i' the body.

Men. One i' the neck, and two i' the thigh—there's nine that I know.

Vol. He had, before this last expedition, twenty-five wounds upon him.

Men. Now it's twenty-seven. Every gash was an enemy's grave. [*A shout and flourish*.] Hark! the trumpets.

Vol. These are the ushers of Marcius. Before him he carries noise, and behind him he leaves tears.
Death, that dark spirit, in's nervy arm doth lie;
Which, being advanced, declines, and then men die.

A sennet. Trumpets sound. Enter COMINIUS *the general, and* TITUS LARTIUS; *between them*, CORIOLANUS, *crowned with an oaken garland; with Captains and Soldiers, and a* HERALD.

Her. Know, Rome, that all alone Marcius did fight
Within Corioli gates, where he hath won,
With fame, a name to Caius Marcius; these
In honour follows Coriolanus.
Welcome to Rome, renowned Coriolanus!
Flourish.

All. Welcome to Rome, renowned Coriolanus!

Cor. No more of this; it does offend my heart.
Pray now, no more.

Com. Look, sir, your mother!

Cor. O,
You have, I know, petition'd all the gods
For my prosperity! [*Kneels*.]

Vol. Nay, my good soldier, up;
My gentle Marcius, worthy Caius, and
By deed-achieving honour newly named—
What is it? Coriolanus must I call thee?
But, O, thy wife!

Cor. My gracious silence, hail!
Wouldst thou have laugh'd had I come coffin'd home,
That weep'st to see me triumph? Ah, my dear,
Such eyes the widows in Corioli wear,
And mothers that lack sons.

Men. Now, the gods crown thee!

Cor. And live you yet? [*To* VALERIA] O my sweet lady, pardon.
Vol. I know not where to turn. O, welcome home;
And welcome, general; and ye're welcome all.
Men. A hundred thousand welcomes. I could weep
And I could laugh, I am light and heavy. Welcome.
A curse begin at very root on's heart,
That is not glad to see thee! You are three
That Rome should dote on; yet, by the faith of men,
We have some old crab-trees here at home that will not
Be grafted to your relish. Yet welcome, warriors.
We call a nettle but a nettle and
The faults of fools but folly.
Com. Ever right.
Cor. Menenius ever, ever.
Her. Give way there, and go on!
Cor. [*To* VOLUMNIA *and* VIRGILIA] Your hand, and yours.
Ere in our own house I do shade my head,
The good patricians must be visited;
From whom I have received not only greetings,
But with them change of honours.
Vol. I have lived
To see inherited my very wishes
And the buildings of my fancy. Only
There's one thing wanting, which I doubt not but
Our Rome will cast upon thee.
Cor. Know, good mother,
I had rather be their servant in my way
Than sway with them in theirs.
Com. On, to the Capitol!
[*Flourish. Cornets. Exeunt in state, as before.* BRUTUS *and* SICINIUS *come forward.*
Bru. All tongues speak of him, and the bleared sights
Are spectacled to see him. Your prattling nurse
Into a rapture lets her baby cry
While she chats him; the kitchen malkin pins
Her richest lockram 'bout her reechy neck,
Clambering the walls to eye him; stalls, bulks, windows,
Are smother'd up, leads fill'd, and ridges horsed
With variable complexions, all agreeing
In earnestness to see him. Seld-shown flamens
Do press among the popular throngs and puff
To win a vulgar station; our veil'd dames
Commit the war of white and damask in
Their nicely-gawded cheeks to the wanton spoil
Of Phœbus' burning kisses; such a pother
As if that whatsoever god who leads him
Were slily crept into his human powers
And gave him graceful posture.
Sic. On the sudden,
I warrant him consul.
Bru. Then our office may,
During his power, go sleep.
Sic. He cannot temperately transport his honours
From where he should begin and end, but will
Lose those he hath won.
Bru. In that there's comfort.
Sic. Doubt not
The commoners, for whom we stand, but they
Upon their ancient malice will forget
With the least cause these his new honours, which
That he will give them make I as little question
As he is proud to do't.
Bru. I heard him swear,
Were he to stand for consul, never would he
Appear i' the market-place nor on him put
The napless vesture of humility;
Nor, showing, as the manner is, his wounds
To the people, beg their stinking breaths.
Sic. 'Tis right.
Bru. It was his word. O, he would miss it rather
Than carry it but by the suit of the gentry to him
And the desire of the nobles.
Sic. I wish no better
Than have him hold that purpose and to put it
In execution.
Bru. 'Tis most like he will.
Sic. It shall be to him then as our good wills,
A sure destruction.
Bru. So it must fall out
To him or our authorities. For an end,
We must suggest the people in what hatred
He still hath held them; that to's power he would
Have made them mules, silenced their pleaders, and
Dispropertied their freedoms, holding them,
In human action and capacity,
Of no more soul nor fitness for the world
Than camels in the war, who have their provand
Only for bearing burdens, and sore blows
For sinking them.
Sic. This, as you say, suggested
At some time when his soaring insolence
Shall touch the people—which time shall not want,
If he be put upon 't; and that's as easy
As to set dogs on sheep—will be his fire
To kindle their dry stubble; and their blaze

Shall darken him for ever.

Enter a MESSENGER.

Bru. What's the matter?
Mess. You are sent for to the Capitol. 'Tis thought
That Marcius shall be consul.
I have seen the dumb men throng to see him and
The blind to hear him speak. Matrons flung gloves,
Ladies and maids their scarfs and handkerchers,
Upon him as he pass'd. The nobles bended,
As to Jove's statue, and the commons made
A shower and thunder with their caps and shouts.
I never saw the like.
Bru. Let's to the Capitol;
And carry with us ears and eyes for the time,
But hearts for the event.
Sic. Have with you. [*Exeunt.*

SCENE II. *The same: the Capitol*

Enter TWO OFFICERS, *to lay cushions.*

1st Off. Come, come, they are almost here. How many stand for consulships?

2nd Off. Three, they say; but 'tis thought of every one Coriolanus will carry it.

1st Off. That's a brave fellow; but he's vengeance proud, and loves not the common people.

2nd Off. Faith, there have been many great men that have flattered the people, who ne'er loved them; and there be many that they have loved, they know not wherefore; so that, if they love they know not why, they hate upon no better a ground; therefore, for Coriolanus neither to care whether they love or hate him manifests the true knowledge he has in their disposition; and out of his noble carelessness lets them plainly see 't.

1st Off. If he did not care whether he had their love or no, he waved indifferently 'twixt doing them neither good nor harm; but he seeks their hate with greater devotion than they can render it him; and leaves nothing undone that may fully discover him their opposite. Now, to seem to affect the malice and displeasure of the people is as bad as that which he dislikes, to flatter them for their love.

2nd Off. He hath deserved worthily of his country; and his ascent is not by such easy degrees as those who, having been supple and courteous to the people, bonneted, without any further deed to have them at all into their estimation and report. But he hath so planted his honours in their eyes and his actions in their hearts that for their tongues to be silent and not confess so much were a kind of ingrateful injury; to report otherwise were a malice that, giving itself the lie, would pluck reproof and rebuke from every ear that heard it.

1st Off. No more of him; he's a worthy man. Make way, they are coming.

A sennet. Enter, with Lictors before them, COMINIUS *the consul,* MENENIUS, CORIOLANUS, SENATORS, SICINIUS *and* BRUTUS. *The* SENATORS *take their places; the Tibunes take their places by themselves.* CORIOLANUS *stands.*

Men. Having determined of the Volsces and
To send for Titus Lartius, it remains,
As the main point of this our after-meeting,
To gratify his noble service that
Hath thus stood for his country; therefore, please you,
Most reverend and grave elders, to desire
The present consul and last general
In our well-found successes, to report
A little of that worthy work perform'd
By Caius Marcius Coriolanus, whom
We met here both to thank and to remember
With honours like himself.
1st Sen. Speak, good Cominius.
Leave nothing out for length, and make us think
Rather our state's defective for requital
Than we to stretch it out. [*To the Tribunes*] Masters o' the people,
We do request your kindest ears, and after,
Your loving motion toward the common body,
To yield what passes here.
Sic. We are convented
Upon a pleasing treaty, and have hearts
Inclinable to honour and advance
The theme of our assembly.
Bru. Which the rather
We shall be blest to do, if he remember
A kinder value of the people than
He hath hereto prized them at.
Men. That's off, that's off;
I would you rather had been silent. Please you
To hear Cominius speak?
Bru. Most willingly;
But yet my caution was more pertinent
Than the rebuke you give it.
Men. He loves your people;
But tie him not to be their bedfellow.
Worthy Cominius, speak. [CORIOLANUS *offers to go away.*] Nay, keep your place.
1st Sen. Sit, Coriolanus; never shame to hear
What you have nobly done.
Cor. Your honours' pardon.
I had rather have my wounds to heal again
Than hear say how I got them.
Bru. Sir, I hope
My words disbench'd you not.

Cor. No, sir; yet oft,
When blows have made me stay, I fled from words.
You soothed not, therefore hurt not; but your people,
I love them as they weigh.
Men. Pray now, sit down.
Cor. I had rather have one scratch my head i' the sun
When the alarum were struck than idly sit
To hear my nothings monster'd. [*Exit.*
Men. Masters of the people,
Your multiplying spawn how can he flatter—
That's thousand to one good one—when you now see
He had rather venture all his limbs for honour
Than one on's ears to hear it? Proceed, Cominius.
Com. I shall lack voice; the deeds of Coriolanus
Should not be utter'd feebly. It is held
That valour is the chiefest virtue and
Most dignifies the haver; if it be,
The man I speak of cannot in the world
Be singly counterpoised. At sixteen years,
When Tarquin made a head for Rome, he fought
Beyond the mark of others. Our then dictator,
Whom with all praise I point at, saw him fight,
When with his Amazonian chin he drove
The bristled lips before him. He bestrid
An o'er-press'd Roman and i' the consul's view
Slew three opposers. Tarquin's self he met,
And struck him on his knee. In that day's feats,
When he might act the woman in the scene,
He proved best man i' the field, and for his meed
Was brow-bound with the oak. His pupil age
Man-enter'd thus, he waxed like a sea,
And in the brunt of seventeen battles since
He lurch'd all swords of the garland. For this last,
Before and in Corioli, let me say,
I cannot speak him home. He stopp'd the fliers;
And by his rare example made the coward
Turn terror into sport; as weeds before
A vessel under sail, so men obey'd
And fell below his stem. His sword, death's stamp,
Where it did mark, it took; from face to foot
He was a thing of blood, whose every motion
Was timed with dying cries. Alone he enter'd
The mortal gate of the city, which he painted
With shunless destiny; aidless came off,
And with a sudden reinforcement struck
Corioli like a planet; now all's his.
When, by and by, the din of war gan pierce
His ready sense, then straight his doubled spirit
Re-quicken'd what in flesh was fatigate,
And to the battle came he; where he did
Run reeking o'er the lives of men, as if
'Twere a perpetual spoil; and till we call'd
Both field and city ours, he never stood
To ease his breast with panting.
Men Worthy man!
1st Sen. He cannot but with measure fit the honours
Which we devise him.
Com. Our spoils he kick'd at,
And look'd upon things precious as they were
The common muck of the world. He covets less
Than misery itself would give; rewards
His deeds with doing them, and is content
To spend the time to end it.
Men. He's right noble.
Let him be call'd for.
1st Sen. Call Coriolanus.
1st Off. He doth appear.

Re-enter CORIOLANUS.

Men. The Senate, Coriolanus, are well pleased
To make thee consul.
Cor. I do owe them still
My life and services.
Men. It then remains
That you do speak to the people.
Cor. I do beseech you,
Let me o'erleap that custom, for I cannot
Put on the gown, stand naked and entreat them
For my wounds' sake to give their suffrage.
Please you
That I may pass this doing.
Sic. Sir, the people
Must have their voices; neither will they bate
One jot of ceremony.
Men. Put them not to 't.
Pray you, go fit you to the custom and
Take to you, as your predecessors have,
Your honour with your form.
Cor. It is a part
That I shall blush in acting, and might well
Be taken from the people.
Bru. Mark you that?
Cor. To brag unto them, "Thus I did, and thus";
Show them the unaching scars which I should hide,
As if I had received them for the hire
Of their breath only!
Men. Do not stand upon 't.
We recommend to you, tribunes of the people,
Our purpose to them; and to our noble consul
Wish we all joy and honour.
Senators. To Coriolanus come all joy and honour! [*Flourish of cornets. Exeunt all but* SICINIUS *and* BRUTUS.
Bru. You see how he intends to use the people.

Sic. May they perceive 's intent! He will require them,
As if he did contemn what he requested
Should be in them to give.
Bru. Come, we'll inform them
Of our proceedings here. On the market-place,
I know, they do attend us. [*Exeunt.*

SCENE III. *The same: the Forum*

Enter seven or eight CITIZENS.

1st Cit. Once, if he do require our voices, we ought not to deny him.

2nd Cit. We may, sir, if we will.

3rd Cit. We have power in ourselves to do it, but it is a power that we have no power to do; for if he show us his wounds and tell us his deeds, we are to put our tongues into those wounds and speak for them; so, if he tell us his noble deeds, we must also tell him our noble acceptance of them. Ingratitude is monstrous, and for the multitude to be ingrateful were to make a monster of the multitude; of the which we being members, should bring ourselves to be monstrous members.

1st Cit. And to make us no better thought of, a little help will serve; for once we stood up about the corn, he himself stuck not to call us the many-headed multitude.

3rd Cit. We have been called so of many; not that our heads are some brown, some black, some auburn, some bald, but that our wits are so diversely coloured; and truly I think if all our wits were to issue out of one skull, they would fly east, west, north, south, and their consent of one direct way should be at once to all the points o' the compass.

2nd Cit. Think you so? Which way do you judge my wit would fly?

3rd Cit. Nay, your wit will not so soon out as another man's will; 'tis strongly wedged up in a block-head, but if it were at liberty, 'twould, sure, southward.

2nd Cit. Why that way?

3rd Cit. To lose itself in a fog, where being three parts melted away with rotten dews, the fourth would return for conscience sake, to help to get thee a wife.

2nd Cit. You are never without your tricks; you may, you may.

3rd Cit. Are you all resolved to give your voices? But that's no matter, the greater part carries it. I say, if he would incline to the people, there was never a worthier man.

Enter CORIOLANUS *in a gown of humility, with* MENENIUS.

Here he comes, and in the gown of humility; mark his behaviour. We are not to stay all together, but to come by him where he stands, by ones, by twos, and by threes. He's to make his requests by particulars; wherein every one of us has a single honour, in giving him our own voices with our own tongues; therefore follow me, and I'll direct you how you shall go by him.

All. Content, content. [*Exeunt* CITIZENS.

Men. O sir, you are not right. Have you not known
The worthiest men have done 't?
Cor. What must I say?
"I pray, sir"—Plague upon 't! I cannot bring
My tongue to such a pace. "Look, sir. My wounds!
I got them in my country's service, when
Some certain of your brethren roar'd and ran
From the noise of our own drums."
Men. O me, the gods!
You must not speak of that. You must desire them
To think upon you.
Cor. Think upon me! Hang 'em!
I would they would forget me, like the virtues
Which our divines lose by 'em.
Men. You'll mar all.
I'll leave you. Pray you, speak to 'em, I pray you,
In wholesome manner. [*Exit.*
Cor. Bid them wash their faces
And keep their teeth clean. [*Re-enter two of the* CITIZENS.] So, here comes a brace. [*Re-enter a* THIRD CITIZEN.]
You know the cause, sir, of my standing here.

3rd Cit. We do, sir; tell us what hath brought you to 't.

Cor. Mine own desert.

2nd Cit. Your own desert!

Cor. Ay, but not mine own desire.

3rd Cit. How not your own desire?

Cor. No, sir, 'twas never my desire yet to trouble the poor with begging.

3rd Cit. You must think, if we give you anything, we hope to gain by you.

Cor. Well then, I pray, your price o' the consulship?

1st Cit. The price is to ask it kindly.

Cor. Kindly! Sir, I pray, let me ha 't. I have wounds to show you, which shall be yours in private. Your good voice, sir; what say you?

2nd Cit. You shall ha 't, worthy sir.

Cor. A match, sir. There's in all two worthy voices begged. I have your alms; adieu.

3rd Cit. But this is something odd.

2nd Cit. An 'twere to give again—but 'tis no matter. [*Exeunt the* THREE CITIZENS.

Re-enter two other CITIZENS.

Cor. Pray you now, if it may stand with the tune of your voices that I may be consul, I have here the customary gown.

4th Cit. You have deserved nobly of your country, and you have not deserved nobly.

Cor. Your enigma?

4th Cit. You have been a scourge to her enemies, you have been a rod to her friends; you have not indeed loved the common people.

Cor. You should account me the more virtuous that I have not been common in my love. I will, sir, flatter my sworn brother, the people, to earn a dearer estimation of them; 'tis a condition they account gentle. And since the wisdom of their choice is rather to have my hat than my heart, I will practise the insinuating nod and be off to them most counterfeitly; that is, sir, I will counterfeit the bewitchment of some popular man and give it bountiful to the desirers. Therefore, beseech you, I may be consul.

5th Cit. We hope to find you our friend; and therefore give you our voices heartily.

4th Cit. You have received many wounds for your country.

Cor. I will not seal your knowledge with showing them. I will make much of your voices, and so trouble you no further.

Both Cit. The gods give you joy, sir, heartily!

[*Exeunt.*

Cor. Most sweet voices!
Better it is to die, better to starve,
Than crave the hire which first we do deserve.
Why in this woolvish toge should I stand here,
To beg of Hob and Dick, that do appear,
Their needless vouches? Custom calls me to 't.
What custom wills, in all things should we do 't,
The dust on antique time would lie unswept,
And mountainous error be too highly heapt
For truth to o'er-peer. Rather than fool it so,
Let the high office and the honour go
To one that would do thus. I am half through;
The one part suffer'd, the other will I do.

Re-enter three CITIZENS *more.*

Here come more voices.
Your voices! For your voices I have fought;
Watch'd for your voices; for your voices bear
Of wounds two dozen odd; battles thrice six
I have seen and heard of; for your voices have
Done many things, some less, some more. Your voices.
Indeed, I would be consul.

6th Cit. He has done nobly, and cannot go without any honest man's voice.

7th Cit. Therefore let him be consul. The gods give him joy, and make him good friend to the people!

All Cit. Amen, amen. God save thee, noble consul!

[*Exeunt.*

Cor. Worthy voices!

Re-enter MENENIUS, *with* BRUTUS *and* SICINIUS.

Men. You have stood your limitation; and the tribunes
Endue you with the people's voice. Remains
That, in the official marks invested, you
Anon do meet the Senate.

Cor. Is this done?

Sic. The custom of request you have discharged.
The people do admit you, and are summon'd
To meet anon, upon your approbation.

Cor. Where? at the Senate-house?

Sic. There, Coriolanus.

Cor. May I change these garments?

Sic. You may, sir.

Cor. That I'll straight do; and, knowing myself again,
Repair to the Senate-house.

Men. I'll keep you company. Will you along?

Bru. We stay here for the people.

Sic. Fare you well.

[*Exeunt* CORIOLANUS *and* MENENIUS.

He has it now, and by his looks methinks
'Tis warm at 's heart.

Bru. With a proud heart he wore his humble weeds.
Will you dismiss the people?

Re-enter CITIZENS.

Sic. How now, my masters! have you chose this man?

1st Cit. He has our voices, sir.

Bru. We pray the gods he may deserve your loves.

2nd Cit. Amen, sir. To my poor unworthy notice,
He mock'd us when he begg'd our voices.

3rd Cit. Certainly
He flouted us downright.

1st Cit. No, 'tis his kind of speech. He did not mock us.

2nd Cit. Not one amongst us, save yourself, but says
He used us scornfully. He should have show'd us
His marks of merit, wounds received for 's country.

Sic. Why, so he did, I am sure.

Citizens. No, no; no man saw 'em.

3rd Cit. He said he had wounds, which he could show in private;

And with his hat, thus waving it in scorn,
"I would be consul," says he; "aged custom,
But by your voices, will not so permit me;
Your voices therefore." When we granted that,
Here was "I thank you for your voices: thank you:
Your most sweet voices. Now you have left your voices,
I have no further with you." Was not this mockery?

Sic. Why either were you ignorant to see 't,
Or, seeing it, of such childish friendliness
To yield your voices?

Bru. Could you not have told him
As you were lesson'd, when he had no power,
But was a petty servant to the state,
He was your enemy, ever spake against
Your liberties and the charters that you bear
I' the body of the weal; and now, arriving
A place of potency and sway o' the state,
If he should still malignantly remain
Fast foe to the *plebeii*, your voices might
Be curses to yourselves? You should have said
That as his worthy deeds did claim no less
Than what he stood for, so his gracious nature
Would think upon you for your voices and
Translate his malice towards you into love,
Standing your friendly lord.

Sic. Thus to have said,
As you were fore-advised, had touch'd his spirit
And tried his inclination; from him pluck'd
Either his gracious promise, which you might,
As cause had call'd you up, have held him to;
Or else it would have gall'd his surly nature,
Which easily endures not article
Tying him to aught; so putting him to rage,
You should have ta'en the advantage of his choler
And pass'd him unelected.

Bru. Did you perceive
He did solicit you in free contempt
When he did need your loves, and do you think
That his contempt shall not be bruising to you,
When he hath power to crush? Why, had your bodies
No heart among you? or had you tongues to cry
Against the rectorship of judgement?

Sic. Have you
Ere now denied the asker? and now again
Of him that did not ask, but mock, bestow
Your sued-for tongues?

3rd Cit. He's not confirm'd; we may deny him yet.

2nd Cit. And will deny him.
I'll have five hundred voices of that sound.

1st Cit. I twice five hundred and their friends to piece 'em.

Bru. Get you hence instantly, and tell those friends,
They have chose a consul that will from them take
Their liberties; make them of no more voice
Than dogs that are as often beat for barking
As therefore kept to do so.

Sic. Let them assemble,
And on a safer judgement all revoke
Your ignorant election; enforce his pride,
And his old hate unto you; besides, forget not
With what contempt he wore the humble weed,
How in his suit he scorn'd you; but your loves,
Thinking upon his services, took from you
The apprehension of his present portance,
Which most gibingly, ungravely, he did fashion
After the inveterate hate he bears you.

Bru. Lay
A fault on us, your tribunes; that we labour'd,
No impediment between, but that you must
Cast your election on him.

Sic. Say, you chose him
More after our commandment than as guided
By your own true affections, and that your minds,
Pre-occupied with what you rather must do
Than what you should, made you against the grain
To voice him consul. Lay the fault on us.

Bru. Ay, spare us not. Say we read lectures to you,
How youngly he began to serve his country,
How long continued, and what stock he springs of,
The noble house o' the Marcians, from whence came
That Ancus Marcius, Numa's daughter's son,
Who, after great Hostilius, here was king;
Of the same house Publius and Quintus were,
That our best water brought by conduits hither;
And [Censorinus,] nobly named so,
Twice being [by the people chosen] censor,
Was his great ancestor.

Sic. One thus descended,
That hath beside well in his person wrought
To be set high in place, we did commend
To your remembrances; but you have found,
Scaling his present bearing with his past,
That he's your fixed enemy, and revoke
Your sudden approbation.

Bru. Say, you ne'er had done't—
Harp on that still—but by our putting on;
And presently, when you have drawn your number,
Repair to the Capitol.

All. We will so. Almost all
Repent in their election. [*Exeunt* CITIZENS.

Bru. Let them go on;
This mutiny were better put in hazard
Than stay, past doubt, for greater.
If, as his nature is, he fall in rage
With their refusal, both observe and answer
The vantage of his anger.
Sic. To the Capitol, come.
We will be there before the stream o' the people;
And this shall seem, as partly 'tis, their own,
Which we have goaded onward. [*Exeunt.*

ACT III

SCENE I. *Rome: a street*

Cornets. Enter CORIOLANUS, MENENIUS, *all the Gentry*, COMINIUS, TITUS LARTIUS, *and other* SENATORS.

Cor. Tullus Aufidius then had made new head?
Lart. He had, my lord; and that it was which caused
Our swifter composition.
Cor. So then the Volsces stand but as at first,
Ready, when time shall prompt them, to make road
Upon's again.
Com. They are worn, Lord Consul, so,
That we shall hardly in our ages see
Their banners wave again.
Cor. Saw you Aufidius?
Lart. On safe-guard he came to me; and did curse
Against the Volsces, for they had so vilely
Yielded the town. He is retired to Antium.
Cor. Spoke he of me?
Lart. He did, my lord,
Cor. How? what?
Lart. How often he had met you, sword to sword;
That of all things upon the earth he hated
Your person most, that he would pawn his fortunes
To hopeless restitution, so he might
Be call'd your vanquisher.
Cor. At Antium lives he?
Lart. At Antium.
Cor. I wish I had a cause to seek him there,
To oppose his hatred fully. Welcome home.

Enter SICINIUS *and* BRUTUS.

Behold, these are the tribunes of the people,
The tongues o' the common mouth. I do despise them;
For they do prank them in authority,
Against all noble sufferance.
Sic. Pass no further.
Cor. Ha! what is that?
Bru. It will be dangerous to go on. No further.
Cor. What makes this change?
Men. The matter?
Com. Hath he not pass'd the noble and the common?
Bru. Cominius, no.
Cor. Have I had children's voices?
1st Sen. Tribunes, give way; he shall to the market-place.
Bru. The people are incensed against him.
Sic. Stop,
Or all will fall in broil.
Cor. Are these your herd?
Must these have voices, that can yield them now
And straight disclaim their tongues? What are your offices?
You being their mouths, why rule you not their teeth?
Have you not set them on?
Men. Be calm, be calm.
Cor. It is a purposed thing, and grows by plot,
To curb the will of the nobility.
Suffer't, and live with such as cannot rule
Nor ever will be ruled.
Bru. Call't not a plot.
The people cry you mock'd them, and of late,
When corn was given them gratis, you repined;
Scandal'd the suppliants for the people, call'd them
Time-pleasers, flatterers, foes to nobleness.
Cor. Why, this was known before.
Bru. Not to them all.
Cor. Have you inform'd them sithence?
Bru. How! I inform them!
Com. You are like to do such business.
Bru. Not unlike,
Each way, to better yours.
Cor. Why then should I be consul? By yond clouds,
Let me deserve so ill as you, and make me
Your fellow tribune.
Sic. You show too much of that
For which the people stir. If you will pass
To where you are bound, you must inquire your way,
Which you are out of, with a gentler spirit,
Or never be so noble as a consul,
Nor yoke with him for tribune.
Men. Let's be calm.
Com. The people are abused; set on. This paltering
Becomes not Rome, nor has Coriolanus
Deserved this so dishonour'd rub, laid falsely
I' the plain way of his merit.
Cor. Tell me of corn!
This was my speech, and I will speak't again—

Men. Not now, not now.
1st Sen. Not in this heat, sir, now.
Cor. Now, as I live, I will. My nobler friends,
I crave their pardons;
For the mutable rank-scented many, let them
Regard me as I do not flatter, and
Therein behold themselves. I say again,
In soothing them we nourish 'gainst our Senate
The cockle of rebellion, insolence, sedition,
Which we ourselves have plough'd for, sow'd, and scatter'd,
By mingling them with us, the honour'd number,
Who lack not virtue, no, nor power, but that
Which they have given to beggars.
Men. Well, no more.
1st Sen. No more words, we beseech you.
Cor. How! no more!
As for my country I have shed my blood,
Not fearing outward force, so shall my lungs
Coin words till their decay against those measles,
Which we disdain should tetter us, yet sought
The very way to catch them.
Bru. You speak o' the people
As if you were a god to punish, not
A man of their infirmity.
Sic. 'Twere well
We let the people know't.
Men. What, what? His choler?
Cor. Choler!
Were I as patient as the midnight sleep,
By Jove, 'twould be my mind!
Sic. It is a mind
That shall remain a poison where it is,
Not poison any further.
Cor. Shall remain!
Hear you this Triton of the minnows? mark you
His absolute "shall"?
Com. 'Twas from the canon.
Cor. "Shall"!
O good but most unwise patricians! why,
You grave but reckless senators, have you thus
Given Hydra here to choose an officer,
That with his peremptory "shall," being but
The horn and noise o' the monster's, wants not spirit
To say he'll turn your current in a ditch,
And make your channel his? If he have power,
Then vail your ignorance; if none, awake
Your dangerous lenity. If you are learn'd,
Be not as common fools; if you are not,
Let them have cushions by you. You are plebeians,
If they be senators; and they are no less,
When, both your voices blended, the great'st taste
Most palates theirs. They choose their magistrate,
And such a one as he, who puts his "shall,"
His popular "shall," against a graver bench
Than ever frown'd in Greece. By Jove himself!
It makes the consuls base. And my soul aches
To know, when two authorities are up,
Neither supreme, how soon confusion
May enter 'twixt the gap of both and take
The one by the other.
Com. Well, on to the market-place.
Cor. Whoever gave that counsel, to give forth
The corn o' the storehouse gratis, as 'twas used
Sometime in Greece—
Men. Well, well, no more of that.
Cor. Though there the people had more absolute power,
I say, they nourish'd disobedience, fed
The ruin of the state.
Bru. Why, shall the people give
One that speaks thus their voice?
Cor. I'll give my reasons,
More worthier than their voices. They know the corn
Was not our recompense, resting well assured
They ne'er did service for't; being press'd to the war,
Even when the navel of the state was touch'd,
They would not thread the gates. This kind of service
Did not deserve corn gratis. Being i' the war,
Their mutinies and revolts, wherein they show'd
Most valour, spoke not for them. The accusation
Which they have often made against the Senate,
All cause unborn, could never be the motive
Of our so frank donation. Well, what then?
How shall this bisson multitude digest
The Senate's courtesy? Let deeds express
What's like to be their words: "We did request it;
We are the greater poll, and in true fear
They gave us our demands." Thus we debase
The nature of our seats and make the rabble
Call our cares fears; which will in time
Break ope the locks o' the Senate and bring in
The crows to peck the eagles.
Men. Come, enough.
Bru. Enough, with over-measure.
Cor. No, take more.
What may be sworn by, both divine and human,
Seal what I end withal! This double worship,
Where one part does disdain with cause, the other
Insult without all reason, where gentry, title, wisdom,
Cannot conclude but by the yea and no

Of general ignorance—it must omit
Real necessities, and give way the while
To unstable slightness; purpose so barr'd, it follows,
Nothing is done to purpose. Therefore, beseech you—
You that will be less fearful than discreet,
That love the fundamental part of state
More than you doubt the change on't, that prefer
A noble life before a long, and wish
To jump a body with a dangerous physic
That's sure of death without it, at once pluck out
The multitudinous tongue; let them not lick
The sweet which is their poison. Your dishonour
Mangles true judgement and bereaves the state
Of that integrity which should become't,
Not having the power to do the good it would,
For the ill which doth control't.

Bru. Has said enough.

Sic. Has spoken like a traitor, and shall answer
As traitors do.

Cor. Thou wretch, despite o'erwhelm thee!
What should the people do with these bald tribunes?
On whom depending, their obedience fails
To the greater bench. In a rebellion,
When what's not meet, but what must be, was law,
Then were they chosen. In a better hour,
Let what is meet be said it must be meet,
And throw their power i' the dust.

Bru. Manifest treason!

Sic. This a consul? no.

Bru. The ædiles, ho!

Enter an ÆDILE.

Let him be apprehended.

Sic. Go, call the people: [*Exit* ÆDILE] in whose name myself
Attach thee as a traitorous innovator,
A foe to the public weal. Obey, I charge thee,
And follow to thine answer.

Cor. Hence, old goat!

Senators, &c. We'll surety him.

Com. Aged sir, hands off.

Cor. Hence, rotten thing! or I shall shake thy bones
Out of thy garments.

Sic. Help, ye citizens!

Enter a rabble of CITIZENS (*Plebeians*), *with the* ÆDILES.

Men. On both sides more respect.

Sic. Here's he that would take from you all your power.

Bru. Seize him, ædiles!

Citizens. Down with him! down with him!

Senators, &c. Weapons, weapons, weapons!

They all bustle about Coriolanus, crying:

Tribunes! Patricians! Citizens! What, ho!
Sicinius! Brutus! Coriolanus! Citizens!
Peace, peace, peace! Stay, hold, peace!

Men. What is about to be? I am out of breath;
Confusion's near; I cannot speak. You, tribunes
To the people! Coriolanus, patience!
Speak, good Sicinius.

Sic. Hear me, people; peace!

Citizens. Let's hear our tribune; peace!
Speak, speak, speak.

Sic. You are at point to lose your liberties.
Marcius would have all from you; Marcius,
Whom late you have named for consul.

Men. Fie, fie, fie!
This is the way to kindle, not to quench,

1st Sen. To unbuild the city and to lay all flat.

Sic. What is the city but the people?

Citizens. True,
The people are the city.

Bru. By the consent of all, we were establish'd
The people's magistrates.

Citizens. You so remain.

Men. And so are like to do.

Com. That is the way to lay the city flat;
To bring the roof to the foundation
And bury all, which yet distinctly ranges,
In heaps and piles of ruin.

Sic. This deserves death.

Bru. Or let us stand to our authority,
Or let us lose it. We do here pronounce,
Upon the part o' the people, in whose power
We were elected theirs, Marcius is worthy
Of present death.

Sic. Therefore lay hold of him;
Bear him to the rock Tarpeian, and from thence
Into destruction cast him.

Bru. Ædiles, seize him!

Citizens. Yield, Marcius, yield!

Men. Hear me one word;
Beseech you, tribunes, hear me but a word.

Æd. Peace, peace!

Men. [*To* BRUTUS] Be that you seem, truly your country's friend,
And temperately proceed to what you would
Thus violently redress.

Bru. Sir, those cold ways
That seem like prudent helps are very poisonous
Where the disease is violent. Lay hands upon him,
And bear him to the rock.

Cor. No, I'll die here.

Drawing his sword.

There's some among you have beheld me fighting.

Come, try upon yourselves what you have seen me.
Men. Down with that sword! Tribunes, withdraw awhile.
Bru. Lay hands upon him.
Men. Help Marcius, help,
You that be noble; help him, young and old!
Citizens. Down with him, down with him!
[*In this mutiny, the* TRIBUNES, *the* ÆDILES, *and the People, are beat in.*
Men. Go, get you to your house; be gone, away!
All will be naught else.
2nd Sen. Get you gone.
Com. Stand fast;
We have as many friends as enemies.
Men. Shall it be put to that?
1st Sen. The gods forbid!
I prithee, noble friend, home to thy house;
Leave us to cure this cause.
Men. For 'tis a sore upon us,
You cannot tent yourself. Be gone, beseech you.
Com. Come, sir, along with us.
Cor. I would they were barbarians—as they are,
Though in Rome litter'd—not Romans—as they are not,
Though calved i' the porch o' the Capitol—
Men. Be gone;
Put not your worthy rage into your tongue;
One time will owe another.
Cor. On fair ground
I could beat forty of them.
Men. I could myself
Take up a brace o' the best of them; yea, the two tribunes.
Com. But now 'tis odds beyond arithmetic;
And manhood is call'd foolery when it stands
Against a falling fabric. Will you hence,
Before the tag return, whose rage doth rend
Like interrupted waters and o'erbear
What they are used to bear?
Men. Pray you, be gone.
I'll try whether my old wit be in request
With those that have but little. This must be patch'd
With cloth of any colour.
Com. Nay, come away.
[*Exeunt* CORIOLANUS, COMINIUS, *and others.*
1st Patrician. This man has marr'd his fortune.
Men. His nature is too noble for the world.
He would not flatter Neptune for his trident,
Or Jove for's power to thunder. His heart's his mouth.
What his breast forges, that his tongue must vent;
And, being angry, does forget that ever
He heard the name of death. [*A noise within.*]
Here's goodly work!
2nd Pat. I would they were a-bed!
Men. I would they were in Tiber! What the vengeance!
Could he not speak 'em fair?

Re-enter BRUTUS *and* SICINIUS, *with the rabble.*

Sic. Where is this viper
That would depopulate the city and
Be every man himself?
Men. You worthy tribunes—
Sic. He shall be thrown down the Tarpeian rock
With rigorous hands. He hath resisted law,
And therefore law shall scorn him further trial
Than the severity of the public power
Which he so sets at nought.
1st Cit. He shall well know
The noble tribunes are the people's mouths,
And we their hands.
Citizens. He shall, sure on't.
Men. Sir, sir—
Sic. Peace!
Men. Do not cry havoc, where you should but hunt
With modest warrant.
Sic. Sir, how comes 't that you
Have holp to make this rescue?
Men. Hear me speak.
As I do know the consul's worthiness,
So can I name his faults—
Sic. Consul! what consul?
Men. The consul Coriolanus.
Bru. He consul!
Citizens. No, no, no, no, no.
Men. If, by the tribunes' leave, and yours, good people,
I may be heard, I would crave a word or two;
The which shall turn you to no further harm
Than so much loss of time.
Sic. Speak briefly then;
For we are peremptory to dispatch
This viperous traitor. To eject him hence
Where but one danger, and to keep him here
Our certain death; therefore it is decreed
He dies to-night.
Men. Now the good gods forbid
That our renowned Rome, whose gratitude
Towards her deserved children is enroll'd
In Jove's own book, like an unnatural dam
Should now eat up her own!
Sic. He's a disease that must be cut away.
Men. O, he's a limb that has but a disease;
Mortal, to cut it off; to cure it, easy.
What has he done to Rome that's worthy death?

Killing our enemies, the blood he hath lost—
Which, I dare vouch, is more than that he hath,
By many an ounce—he dropp'd it for his country;
And what is left, to lose it by his country,
Were to us all, that do't and suffer it,
A brand to the end o' the world.

Sic. This is clean kam.

Bru. Merely awry. When he did love his country,
It honour'd him.

Men. The service of the foot
Being once gangrened is not then respected
For what before it was.

Bru. We'll hear no more.
Pursue him to his house and pluck him thence;
Lest his infection, being of catching nature,
Spread further.

Men. One word more, one word.
This tiger-footed rage, when it shall find
The harm of unscann'd swiftness, will too late
Tie leaden pounds to's heels. Proceed by process;
Lest parties, as he is beloved, break out,
And sack great Rome with Romans.

Bru. If it were so—

Sic. What do ye talk?
Have we not had a taste of his obedience?
Our ædiles smote? ourselves resisted? Come.

Men. Consider this: he has been bred i' the wars
Since he could draw a sword, and is ill school'd
In bolted language; meal and bran together
He throws without distinction. Give me leave,
I'll go to him, and undertake to bring him
Where he shall answer, by a lawful form,
In peace, to his utmost peril.

1st Sen. Noble tribunes,
It is the humane way. The other course
Will prove too bloody, and the end of it
Unknown to the beginning.

Sic. Noble Menenius,
Be you then as the people's officer.
Masters, lay down your weapons.

Bru. Go not home.

Sic. Meet on the market-place. We'll attend you there;
Where, if you bring not Marcius, we'll proceed
In our first way.

Men. I'll bring him to you.
[*To the* SENATORS] Let me desire your company.
He must come,
Or what is worst will follow.

1st Sen. Pray you, let's to him.
[*Exeunt.*

SCENE II. *A room in Coriolanus's house*

Enter CORIOLANUS *with* PATRICIANS.

Cor. Let them pull all about mine ears, present me
Death on the wheel or at wild horses' heels,
Or pile ten hills on the Tarpeian rock,
That the precipitation might down stretch
Below the beam of sight, yet will I still
Be thus to them.

1st Patrician. You do the nobler.

Cor. I muse my mother
Does not approve me further, who was wont
To call them woollen vassals, things created
To buy and sell with groats, to show bare heads
In congregations, to yawn, be still and wonder
When one but of my ordinance stood up
To speak of peace or war.

Enter VOLUMNIA.

I talk of you.
Why did you wish me milder? Would you have me
False to my nature? Rather say I play
The man I am.

Vol. O, sir, sir, sir,
I would have had you put your power well on,
Before you had worn it out.

Cor. Let go.

Vol. You might have been enough the man you are,
With striving less to be so. Lesser had been
The thwartings of your dispositions, if
You had not show'd them how ye were disposed
Ere they lack'd power to cross you.

Cor. Let them hang.

1st Patrician. Ay, and burn too.

Enter MENENIUS *and Senators.*

Men. Come, come, you have been too rough, something too rough;
You must return and mend it.

1st Sen. There's no remedy;
Unless, by not so doing, our good city
Cleave in the midst, and perish.

Vol. Pray, be counsell'd.
I have a heart as little apt as yours,
But yet a brain that leads my use of anger
To better vantage.

Men. Well said, noble woman!
Before he should thus stoop to the herd, but that
The violent fit o' the time craves it as physic
For the whole state, I would put mine armour on,
Which I can scarcely bear.

Cor. What must I do?

Men. Return to the tribunes.

Cor. Well, what then? what then?
Men. Repent what you have spoke.
Cor. For them! I cannot do it to the gods;
Must I then do't to them?
Vol. You are too absolute;
Though therein you can never be too noble,
But when extremities speak. I have heard you say,
Honour and policy, like unsever'd friends,
I' the war do grow together. Grant that, and tell me,
In peace what each of them by the other lose,
That they combine not there.
Cor. Tush, tush!
Men. A good demand.
Vol. If it be honour in your wars to seem
The same you are not, which, for your best ends,
You adopt your policy, how is it less or worse,
That it shall hold companionship in peace
With honour, as in war, since that to both
It stands in like request?
Cor. Why force you this?
Vol. Because that now it lies you on to speak
To the people; not by your own instruction,
Nor by the matter which your heart prompts you,
But with such words that are but roted in
Your tongue, though but bastards and syllables
Of no allowance to your bosom's truth.
Now, this no more dishonours you at all
Than to take in a town with gentle words,
Which else would put you to your fortune and
The hazard of much blood.
I would dissemble with my nature where
My fortunes and my friends at stake required
I should do so in honour. I am in this,
Your wife, your son, these senators, the nobles;
And you will rather show our general louts
How you can frown than spend a fawn upon 'em,
For the inheritance of their loves and safeguard
Of what that want might ruin.
Men. Noble lady!
Come, go with us; speak fair. You may salve so,
Not what is dangerous present, but the loss
Of what is past.
Vol. I prithee now, my son,
Go to them, with this bonnet in thy hand;
And thus far having stretch'd it—here be with them—
Thy knee bussing the stones—for in such business
Action is eloquence, and the eyes of the ignorant
More learned than the ears—waving thy head,
Which often, thus, correcting thy stout heart,
Now humble as the ripest mulberry
That will not hold the handling; or say to them,
Thou art their soldier, and being bred in broils
Hast not the soft way which, thou dost confess,
Were fit for thee to use as they to claim,
In asking their good loves, but thou wilt frame
Thyself, forsooth, hereafter theirs, so far
As thou hast power and person.
Men. This but done,
Even as she speaks, why, their hearts were yours;
For they have pardons, being ask'd, as free
As words to little purpose.
Vol. Prithee now,
Go, and be ruled; although I know thou hadst rather
Follow thine enemy in a fiery gulf
Than flatter him in a bower. Here is Cominius.

Enter COMINIUS.

Com. I have been i' the market-place; and, sir, 'tis fit
You make strong party, or defend yourself
By calmness or by absence. All's in anger.
Men. Only fair speech.
Com. I think 'twill serve, if he
Can thereto frame his spirit.
Vol. He must, and will.
Prithee now, say you will, and go about it.
Cor. Must I go show them my unbarbed sconce?
Must I with base tongue give my noble heart
A lie that it must bear? Well, I will do't;
Yet, were there but this single plot to lose,
This mould of Marcius, they to dust should grind it
And throw 't against the wind. To the market-place!
You have put me now to such a part which never
I shall discharge to the life.
Com. Come, come, we'll prompt you.
Vol. I prithee now, sweet son, as thou hast said
My praises made thee first a soldier, so,
To have my praise for this, perform a part
Thou hast not done before.
Cor. Well, I must do 't.
Away, my disposition, and possess me
Some harlot's spirit! my throat of war be turn'd,
Which quired with my drum, into a pipe
Small as an eunuch, or the virgin voice
That babies lulls asleep! the smiles of knaves
Tent in my cheeks, and schoolboys' tears take up
The glasses of my sight! a beggar's tongue
Make motion through my lips, and my arm'd knees,
Who bow'd but in my stirrup, bend like his
That hath received an alms! I will not do 't,
Lest I surcease to honour mine own truth
And by my body's action teach my mind
A most inherent baseness.
Vol. At thy choice, then.

To beg of thee, it is my more dishonour
Than thou of them. Come all to ruin; let
Thy mother rather feel thy pride than fear
Thy dangerous stoutness, for I mock at death
With as big heart as thou. Do as thou list.
Thy valiantness was mine, thou suck'dst it from me,
But owe thy pride thyself.
Cor. Pray, be content.
Mother, I am going to the market-place;
Chide me no more. I'll mountebank their loves,
Cog their hearts from them, and come home beloved
Of all the trades in Rome. Look, I am going.
Commend me to my wife. I'll return consul,
Or never trust to what my tongue can do
I' the way of flattery further.
Vol. Do your will. [*Exit.*
Com. Away! the tribunes do attend you. Arm yourself
To answer mildly; for they are prepared
With accusations, as I hear, more strong
Than are upon you yet.
Cor. The word is "mildly." Pray you, let us go:
Let them accuse me by invention, I
Will answer in mine honour.
Men. Ay, but mildly.
Cor. Well, mildly be it then. Mildly! [*Exeunt.*

SCENE III. *The same: the Forum*

Enter SICINIUS *and* BRUTUS.

Bru. In this point charge him home, that he affects
Tyrannical power. If he evade us there,
Enforce him with his envy to the people,
And that the spoil got on the Antiates
Was ne'er distributed.

Enter an ÆDILE.

What, will he come?
Æd. He's coming.
Bru. How accompanied?
Æd. With old Menenius, and those senators
That always favour'd him.
Sic. Have you a catalogue
Of all the voices that we have procured
Set down by the poll?
Æd. I have; 'tis ready.
Sic. Have you collected them by tribes?
Æd. I have.
Sic. Assemble presently the people hither;
And when they hear me say, "It shall be so
I' the right and strength o' the commons," be it either
For death, for fine, or banishment, then let them,
If I say fine, cry "Fine!" if death, cry "Death!"
Insisting on the old prerogative
And power i' the truth o' the cause.
Æd. I shall inform them.
Bru. And when such time they have begun to cry,
Let them not cease, but with a din confused
Enforce the present execution
Of what we chance to sentence.
Æd. Very well.
Sic. Make them be strong and ready for this hint,
When we shall hap to give't them.
Bru. Go about it. [*Exit* ÆDILE.
Put him to choler straight. He hath been used
Ever to conquer, and to have his worth
Of contradiction. Being once chafed, he cannot
Be rein'd again to temperance; then he speaks
What's in his heart; and that is there which looks
With us to break his neck.
Sic. Well, here he comes.

Enter CORIOLANUS, MENENIUS, *and* COMINIUS, *with* SENATORS *and* PATRICIANS.

Men. Calmly, I do beseech you.
Cor. Ay, as an ostler, that for the poorest piece
Will bear the knave by the volume. The honour'd gods
Keep Rome in safety, and the chairs of justice
Supplied with worthy men! plant love among 's!
Throng our large temples with the shows of peace,
And not our streets with war!
1st Sen. Amen, amen.
Men. A noble wish.

Re-enter ÆDILE, *with* CITIZENS.

Sic. Draw near, ye people.
Æd. List to your tribunes. Audience! peace, I say!
Cor. First, hear me speak.
Both Tri. Well, say. Peace, ho!
Cor. Shall I be charged no further than this present?
Must all determine here?
Sic. I do demand,
If you submit you to the people's voices,
Allow their officers, and are content
To suffer lawful censure for such faults
As shall be proved upon you?
Cor. I am content.
Men. Lo, citizens, he says he is content.
The warlike service he has done, consider; think
Upon the wounds his body bears, which show
Like graves i' the holy churchyard.
Cor. Scratches with briers,

Scars to move laughter only.

Men. Consider further,
That when he speaks not like a citizen,
You find him like a soldier. Do not take
His rougher accents for malicious sounds,
But, as I say, such as become a soldier
Rather than envy you.

Com. Well, well, no more.

Cor. What is the matter
That being pass'd for consul with full voice,
I am so dishonour'd that the very hour
You take it off again?

Sic. Answer to us.

Cor. Say, then. 'Tis true, I ought so.

Sic. We charge you that you have contrived to take
From Rome all season'd office and to wind
Yourself into a power tyrannical;
For which you are a traitor to the people.

Cor. How! traitor!

Men. Nay, temperately; your promise.

Cor. The fires i' the lowest hell fold-in the people!
Call me their traitor! Thou injurious tribune!
Within thine eyes sat twenty thousand deaths,
In thy hands clutch'd as many millions, in
Thy lying tongue both numbers, I would say
"Thou liest" unto thee with a voice as free
As I do pray the gods.

Sic. Mark you this, people?

Citizens. To the rock, to the rock with him!

Sic. Peace!
We need not put new matter to his charge.
What you have seen him do and heard him speak,
Beating your officers, cursing yourselves,
Opposing laws with strokes, and here defying
Those whose great power must try him; even this,
So criminal and in such capital kind,
Deserves the extremest death.

Bru. But since he hath
Served well for Rome—

Cor. What do you prate of service?

Bru. I talk of that, that know it.

Cor. You?

Men. Is this the promise that you made your mother?

Com. Know, I pray you—

Cor. I'll know no further.
Let them pronounce the steep Tarpeian death,
Vagabond exile, flaying, pent to linger
But with a grain a day, I would not buy
Their mercy at the price of one fair word;
Nor check my courage for what they can give,
To have't with saying "Good morrow."

Sic. For that he has,
As much as in him lies, from time to time
Envied against the people, seeking means
To pluck away their power, as now at last
Given hostile strokes, and that not in the presence
Of dreaded justice, but on the ministers
That do distribute it; in the name o' the people
And in the power of us the tribunes, we,
Even from this instant, banish him our city,
In peril of precipitation
From off the rock Tarpeian never more
To enter our Rome gates. I' the people's name,
I say it shall be so.

Citizens. It shall be so, it shall be so; let him away.
He's banish'd, and it shall be so.

Com. Hear me, my masters, and my common friends—

Sic. He's sentenced; no more hearing.

Com. Let me speak.
I have been consul, and can show for Rome
Her enemies' marks upon me. I do love
My country's good with a respect more tender,
More holy and profound, than mine own life,
My dear wife's estimate, her womb's increase,
And treasure of my loins; then if I would
Speak that—

Sic. We know your drift; speak what?

Bru. There's no more to be said, but he is banish'd,
As enemy to the people and his country.
It shall be so.

Citizens. It shall be so, it shall be so.

Cor. You common cry of curs! whose breath I hate
As reek o' the rotten fens, whose loves I prize
As the dead carcasses of unburied men
That do corrupt my air, I banish you;
And here remain with your uncertainty!
Let every feeble rumour shake your hearts!
Your enemies, with nodding of their plumes,
Fan you into despair! Have the power still
To banish your defenders; till at length
Your ignorance, which finds not till it feels,
Making not reservation of yourselves,
Still your own foes, deliver you as most
Abated captives to some nation
That won you without blows! Despising,
For you, the city, thus I turn my back;
There is a world elsewhere.

[*Exeunt* CORIOLANUS, COMINIUS, MENENIUS, SENATORS, *and* PATRICIANS.

Æd. The people's enemy is gone, is gone!

Citizens. Our enemy is banish'd! he is gone!
Hoo! hoo! [*Shouting, and throwing up their caps.*]

Sic. Go, see him out at gates, and follow him,
As he hath follow'd you, with all despite;
Give him deserved vexation. Let a guard
Attend us through the city.
Citizens. Come, come; let's see him out at gates; come.
The gods preserve our noble tribunes! Come.
[*Exeunt.*

ACT IV

SCENE I. *Rome: before a gate of the city*

Enter CORIOLANUS, VOLUMNIA, VIRGILIA, MENENIUS, COMINIUS, *with the young Nobility of Rome.*

Cor. Come, leave your tears: a brief farewell. The beast
With many heads butts me away. Nay, mother,
Where is your ancient courage? You were used
To say extremity was the trier of spirits;
That common chances common men could bear;
That when the sea was calm all boats alike
Show'd mastership in floating; fortune's blows,
When most struck home, being gentle wounded, craves
A noble cunning. You were used to load me
With precepts that would make invincible
The heart that conn'd them.
Vir. O heavens! O heavens!
Cor. Nay, I prithee, woman—
Vol. Now the red pestilence strike all trades in Rome,
And occupations perish!
Cor. What, what, what!
I shall be loved when I am lack'd. Nay, mother,
Resume that spirit when you were wont to say,
If you had been the wife of Hercules,
Six of his labours you'd have done, and saved
Your husband so much sweat. Cominius,
Droop not; adieu. Farewell, my wife, my mother.
I'll do well yet. Thou old and true Menenius,
Thy tears are salter than a younger man's,
And venomous to thine eyes. My sometime general,
I have seen thee stern, and thou hast oft beheld
Heart-hardening spectacles; tell these sad women
'Tis fond to wail inevitable strokes,
As 'tis to laugh at 'em. My mother, you wot well
My hazards still have been your solace; and
Believe't not lightly—though I go alone,
Like to a lonely dragon, that his fen
Makes fear'd and talk'd of more than seen—your son
Will or exceed the common or be caught
With cautelous baits and practice.
Vol. My first son,
Whither wilt thou go? Take good Cominius
With thee awhile. Determine on some course,
More than a wild exposture to each chance
That starts i' the way before thee.
Cor. O the gods!
Com. I'll follow thee a month, devise with thee
Where thou shalt rest, that thou mayst hear of us
And we of thee. So if the time thrust forth
A cause for thy repeal, we shall not send
O'er the vast world to seek a single man,
And lose advantage, which doth ever cool
I' the absence of the needer.
Cor. Fare ye well.
Thou hast years upon thee; and thou art too full
Of the wars' surfeits to go rove with one
That's yet unbruised; bring me but out at gate.
Come, my sweet wife, my dearest mother, and
My friends of noble touch, when I am forth,
Bid me farewell, and smile. I pray you, come.
While I remain above the ground, you shall
Hear from me still, and never of me aught
But what is like me formerly.
Men. That's worthily
As any ear can hear. Come, let's not weep.
If I could shake off but one seven years
From these old arms and legs, by the good gods,
I'd with thee every foot.
Cor. Give me thy hand.
Come.
[*Exeunt.*

SCENE II. *The same: a street near the gate*

Enter SICINIUS, BRUTUS, *and an* ÆDILE.

Sic. Bid them all home; he's gone, and we'll no further.
The nobility are vex'd, whom we see have sided
In his behalf.
Bru. Now we have shown our power,
Let us seem humbler after it is done
Than when it was a-doing.
Sic. Bid them home.
Say their great enemy is gone, and they
Stand in their ancient strength.
Bru. Dismiss them home. [*Exit* ÆDILE.
Here comes his mother.
Sic. Let's not meet her.
Bru. Why?
Sic. They say she's mad.
Bru. They have ta'en note of us; keep on your way.

Enter VOLUMNIA, VIRGILIA, *and* MENENIUS.

Vol. O, ye're well met. The hoarded plague o' the gods
Requite your love!
Men. Peace, peace; be not so loud.

Vol. If that I could for weeping, you should hear—
Nay, and you shall hear some. [*To* BRUTUS] Will you be gone?
Vir. [*To* SICINIUS] You shall stay too. I would I had the power
To say so to my husband.
Sic. Are you mankind?
Vol. Ay, fool; is that a shame? Note but this fool.
Was not a man my father? Hadst thou foxship
To banish him that struck more blows for Rome
Than thou hast spoken words?
Sic. O blessed heavens!
Vol. More noble blows than ever thou wise words;
And for Rome's good. I'll tell thee what; yet go.
Nay, but thou shalt stay too. I would my son
Were in Arabia, and thy tribe before him,
His good sword in his hand.
Sic. What then?
Vir. What then!
He'd make an end of thy posterity.
Vol. Bastards and all.
Good man, the wounds that he does bear for Rome!
Men. Come, come, peace.
Sic. I would he had continued to his country
As he began, and not unknit himself
The noble knot he made.
Bru. I would he had.
Vol. "I would he had"! 'Twas you incensed the rabble;
Cats, that can judge as fitly of his worth
As I can of those mysteries which heaven
Will not have earth to know.
Bru. Pray, let us go.
Vol. Now, pray, sir, get you gone;
You have done a brave deed. Ere you go, hear this:
As far as doth the Capitol exceed
The meanest house in Rome, so far my son—
This lady's husband here, this, do you see—
Whom you have banish'd, does exceed you all.
Bru. Well, well, we'll leave you.
Sic. Why stay we to be baited
With one that wants her wits?
Vol. Take my prayers with you.
[*Exeunt* TRIBUNES.
I would the gods had nothing else to do
But to confirm my curses! Could I meet 'em
But once a-day, it would unclog my heart
Of what lies heavy to't.
Men. You have told them home;
And, by my troth, you have cause. You'll sup with me?
Vol. Anger's my meat; I sup upon myself,
And so shall starve with feeding. Come, let's go.
Leave this faint puling and lament as I do,
In anger, Juno-like. Come, come, come.
Men. Fir, fie, fie! [*Exeunt*.

SCENE III. *A highway between Rome and Antium*

Enter a ROMAN *and a* VOLSCE, *meeting*.

Rom. I know you well, sir, and you know me. Your name, I think, is Adrian.

Vols. It is so, sir. Truly, I have forgot you.

Rom. I am a Roman; and my services are, as you are, against 'em. Know you me yet?

Vols. Nicanor? no.

Rom. The same, sir.

Vols. You had more beard when I last saw you; but your favour is well approved by your tongue. What's the news in Rome? I have a note from the Volscian state, to find you out there. You have well saved me a day's journey.

Rom. There hath been in Rome strange insurrections; the people against the senators, partricians, and nobles.

Vols. Hath been! Is it ended, then? Our state thinks not so. They are in a most warlike preparation, and hope to come upon them in the heat of their division.

Rom. The main blaze of it is past, but a small thing would make it flame again; for the nobles receive so to heart the banishment of that worthy Coriolanus, that they are in a ripe aptness to take all power from the people and to pluck from them their tribunes for ever. This lies glowing, I can tell you, and is almost mature for the violent breaking out.

Vols. Coriolanus banished!

Rom. Banished, sir.

Vols. You will be welcome with this intelligence, Nicanor.

Rom.The day serves well for them now. I have heard it said, the fittest time to corrupt a man's wife is when she's fallen out with her husband. Your noble Tullus Aufidius will appear well in these wars, his great opposer, Coriolanus, being now in no request of his country.

Vols. He cannot choose. I am most fortunate, thus accidentally to encounter you. You have ended my business, and I will merrily accompany you home.

Rom. I shall, between this and supper, tell you most strange things from Rome; all tending to the good of their adversaries. Have you an army ready, say you?

Vols. A most royal one; the centurions and their charges, distinctly billeted, already in the entertainment, and to be on foot at an hour's warning.

Rom. I am joyful to hear of their readiness, and am the man, I think, that shall set them in present action. So, sir, heartily well met, and most glad of your company.

Vols. You take my part from me, sir; I have the most cause to be glad of yours.

Rom. Well, let us go together. [*Exeunt.*

SCENE IV. *Antium: before Aufidius's house*

Enter CORIOLANUS *in mean apparel, disguised and muffled.*

Cor. A goodly city is this Antium. City,
'Tis I that made thy widows; many an heir
Of these fair edifices 'fore my wars
Have I heard groan and drop. Then know me not,
Lest that thy wives with spits and boys with stones
In puny battle slay me.

Enter a CITIZEN.

Save you, sir.

Cit. And you.

Cor. Direct me, if it be your will,
Where great Aufidius lies. Is he in Antium?

Cit. He is, and feasts the nobles of the state
At his house this night.

Cor. Which is his house, beseech you?

Cit. This, here before you.

Cor. Thank you, sir; farewell.
[*Exit* CITIZEN.
O world, thy slippery turns! Friends now fast sworn,
Whose double bosoms seem to wear one heart,
Whose hours, whose bed, whose meal, and exercise,
Are still together, who twin, as 'twere, in love
Unseparable, shall within this hour,
On a dissension of a doit, break out
To bitterest enmity; so, fellest foes,
Whose passions and whose plots have broke their sleep
To take the one the other, by some chance,
Some trick not worth an egg, shall grow dear friends
And interjoin their issues. So with me;
My birth-place hate I, and my love's upon
This enemy town. I'll enter. If he slay me,
He does fair justice; if he give me way,
I'll do his country service. [*Exit.*

SCENE V. *The same: a hall in Aufidius's house*

Music within. Enter a SERVINGMAN.

1st Serv. Wine, wine, wine! What service is here! I think our fellows are asleep. [*Exit.*

Enter a SECOND SERVINGMAN.

2nd Serv. Where's Cotus? my master calls for him. Cotus! [*Exit.*

Enter CORIOLANUS.

Cor. A goodly house! the feast smells well; but I
Appear not like a guest.

Re-enter the FIRST SERVINGMAN.

1st Serv. What would you have, friend?
Whence are you? Here's no place for you; pray, go to the door. [*Exit.*

Cor. I have deserved no better entertainment,
In being Coriolanus.

Re-enter SECOND SERVINGMAN.

2nd Serv. Whence are you, sir? Has the porter his eyes in his head, that he gives entrance to such companions? Pray, get you out.

Cor. Away!

2nd Serv. Away! get you away.

Cor. Now thou'rt troublesome.

2nd Serv. Are you so brave? I'll have you talked with anon.

Enter a THIRD SERVINGMAN. *The* FIRST *meets him.*

3rd Serv. What fellow's this?

1st Serv. A strange one as ever I looked on. I cannot get him out o' the house; prithee call my master to him. [*Retires*

3rd Serv. What have you to do here, fellow? Pray you, avoid the house.

Cor. Let me but stand; I will not hurt your hearth.

3rd Serv. What are you?

Cor. A gentleman.

3rd Serv. A marvellous poor one.

Cor. True, so I am.

3rd Serv. Pray you, poor gentleman, take up some other station; here's no place for you; pray you, avoid. Come.

Cor. Follow your function, go, and batten on cold bits. [*Pushes him away.*]

3rd. Serv. What, you will not? Prithee, tell my master what a strange guest he has here.

2nd Serv. And I shall. [*Exit.*

3rd Serv. Where dwellest thou?

Cor. Under the canopy.

3rd Serv. Under the canopy?

Cor. Ay.

3rd Serv. Where's that?

Cor. I' the city of kites and crows.

3rd Serv. I' the city of kites and crows! What an ass it is! Then thou dwellest with daws too?

Cor. No, I serve not thy master.

3rd Serv. How, sir! do you meddle with my master?

Cor. Ay; 'tis an honester service than to meddle with thy mistress.
Thou pratest, and pratest; serve with thy trencher, hence!

[*Beats him away. Exit* THIRD SERVINGMAN.

Enter AUFIDIUS *with the* SECOND SERVINGMAN.

Auf. Where is this fellow?

2nd Serv. Here, sir: I'd have beaten him like a dog, but for disturbing the lords within. [*Retires.*

Auf. Whence comest thou? What wouldst thou? Thy name?
Why speak'st not? Speak, man. What's thy name?

Cor. If, Tullus, [*Unmuffling.*]
Not yet thou knowest me, and, seeing me, dost not
Think me for the man I am, necessity
Commands me name myself.

Auf. What is thy name?

Cor. A name unmusical to the Volscians' ears,
And harsh in sound to thine.

Auf. Say, what's thy name?
Thou hast a grim appearance, and thy face
Bears a command in 't; though thy tackle's torn,
Thou show'st a noble vessel. What's thy name?

Cor. Prepare thy brow to frown. Know'st thou me yet?

Auf. I know thee not. Thy name?

Cor. My name is Caius Marcius, who hath done
To thee particularly and to all the Volsces
Great hurt and mischief; thereto witness may
My surname, Coriolanus. The painful service,
The extreme dangers, and the drops of blood
Shed for my thankless country are requited
But with that surname; a good memory,
And witness of the malice and displeasure
Which thou shouldst bear me. Only that name remains;
The cruelty and envy of the people
Permitted by our dastard nobles, who
Have all forsook me, hath devour'd the rest;
And suffer'd me by the voice of slaves to be
Whoop'd out of Rome. Now this extremity
Hath brought me to thy hearth; not out of hope—
Mistake me not—to save my life, for if
I had fear'd death, of all the men i' the world
I would have 'voided thee, but in mere spite
To be full quit of those my banishers,
Stand I before thee here. Then if thou hast
A heart of wreak in thee, that wilt revenge
Thine own particular wrongs and stop those maims
Of shame seen through thy country, speed thee straight,
And make my misery serve thy turn. So use it
That my revengeful services may prove
As benefits to thee, for I will fight
Against my canker'd country with the spleen
Of all the under fiends. But if so be
Thou darest not this and that to prove more fortunes
Thou'rt tired, then, in a word, I also am
Longer to live most weary, and present
My throat to thee and to thy ancient malice;
Which not to cut would show thee but a fool,
Since I have ever follow'd thee with hate,
Drawn tuns of blood out of thy country's breast,
And cannot live but to thy shame, unless
It be to do thee service.

Auf. O Marcius, Marcius!
Each word thou hast spoke hath weeded from my heart
A root of ancient envy. If Jupiter
Should from yond cloud speak divine things,
And say "'Tis true," I'd not believe them more
Than thee, all noble Marcius. Let me twine
Mine arms about that body, where against
My grained ash an hundred times hath broke
And scarr'd the moon with splinters. Here I clip
The anvil of my sword, and do contest
As hotly and as nobly with thy love
As ever in ambitious strength I did
Contend against thy valour. Know thou first,
I loved the maid I married; never man
Sigh'd truer breath; but that I see thee here,
Thou noble thing! more dances my rapt heart
Than when I first my wedded mistress saw
Bestride my threshold. Why, thou Mars! I tell thee,
We have a power on foot; and I had purpose
Once more to hew thy target from thy brawn,
Or lose mine arm for 't. Thou hast beat me out
Twelve several times, and I have nightly since
Dreamt of encounters 'twixt thyself and me;
We have been down together in my sleep,
Unbuckling helms, fisting each other's throat,
And waked half dead with nothing. Worthy Marcius,
Had we no quarrel else to Rome, but that
Thou art thence banish'd, we would muster all
From twelve to seventy, and pouring war
Into the bowels of ungrateful Rome,
Like a bold flood o'er-bear. O, come, go in,
And take our friendly senators by the hands;
Who now are here, taking their leaves of me,
Who am prepared against your territories.

Though not for Rome itself.
Cor. You bless me, gods!
Auf. Therefore, most absolute sir, if thou wilt have
The leading of thine own revenges, take
The one half of my commission; and set down—
As best thou art experienced, since thou know'st
Thy country's strength and weakness—thine own ways;
Whether to knock against the gates of Rome,
Or rudely visit them in parts remote,
To fright them, ere destroy. But come in;
Let me commend thee first to those that shall
Say yea to thy desires. A thousand welcomes!
And more a friend than e'er an enemy;
Yet, Marcius, that was much. Your hand; most welcome!

[*Exeunt* CORIOLANUS *and* AUFIDIUS. *The* TWO SERVINGMEN *come forward.*

1st Serv. Here's a strange alteration!

2nd Serv. By my hand, I had thought to have strucken him with a cudgel; and yet my mind gave me his clothes made a false report of him.

1st Serv. What an arm he has! he turned me about with his finger and his thumb, as one would set up a top.

2nd Serv. Nay, I knew by his face that there was something in him. He had, sir, a kind of face, methought—I cannot tell how to term it.

1st Serv. He had so; looking as it were—would I were hanged, but I thought there was more in him than I could think.

2nd Serv. So did I, I'll be sworn. He is simply the rarest man i' the world.

1st Serv. I think he is; but a greater soldier than he you wot one.

2nd Serv. Who, my master?

1st Serv. Nay, it's no matter for that.

2nd Serv. Worth six on him.

1st Serv. Nay, not so neither; but I take him to be the greater soldier.

2nd Serv. Faith, look you, one cannot tell how to say that. For the defence of a town, our general is excellent.

1st Serv. Ay, and for an assault too.

Re-enter THIRD SERVINGMAN.

3rd Serv. O slaves, I can tell you news—news, you rascals!

1st and 2nd Serv. What, what, what? Let's partake.

3rd Serv. I would not be a Roman, of all nations; I had as lieve be a condemned man.

1st and 2nd Serv. Wherefore? Wherefore?

3rd Serv. Why, here's he that was wont to thwack our general, Caius Marcius.

1st Serv. Why do you say "thwack our general"?

3rd Serv. I do not say "thwack our general"; but he was always good enough for him.

2nd Serv. Come, we are fellows and friends; he was ever too hard for him; I have heard him say so himself.

1st Serv. He was too hard for him directly, to say the troth on 't. Before Corioli he scotched him and notched him like a carbonado.

2nd Serv. An he had been cannibally given, he might have broiled and eaten him too.

1st Serv. But, more of thy news?

3rd Serv. Why, he is so made on here within, as if he were son and heir to Mars; set at upper end o' the table; no question asked him by any of the senators, but they stand bald before him. Our general himself makes a mistress of him; sanctifies himself with 's hand and turns up the white o' the eye to his discourse. But the bottom of the news is, our general is cut i' the middle and but one half of what he was yesterday; for the other has half, by the entreaty and grant of the whole table. He'll go, he says, and sowl the porter of Rome gates by the ears. He will mow all down before him, and leave his passage polled.

2nd Serv. And he's as like to do 't as any man I can imagine.

3rd Serv. Do 't! he will do 't; for, look you, sir, he has as many friends as enemies; which friends, sir, as it were, durst not, look you, sir, show themselves, as we term it, his friends whilst he's in directitude.

1st Serv. Directitude! what's that?

3rd Serv. But when they shall see, sir, his crest up again, and the man in blood, they will out of their burrows, like conies after rain, and revel all with him.

1st Serv. But when goes this forward?

3rd Serv. To-morrow; to-day; presently; you shall have the drum struck up this afternoon. 'Tis, as it were, a parcel of their feast, and to be executed ere they wipe their lips.

2nd Serv. Why, then we shall have a stirring world again. This peace is nothing but to rust iron, increase tailors, and breed ballad-makers.

1st Serv. Let me have war, say I; it exceeds peace as far as day does night; it's spritely, waking, audible, and full of vent. Peace is a very apoplexy, lethargy; mulled, deaf, sleepy, insensible; a getter of more bastard children than war's a destroyer of men.

2nd Serv. 'Tis so; and as war, in some sort, may be said to be a ravisher, so it cannot be denied but peace is a great maker of cuckolds.

1st Serv. Ay, and it makes men hate one another.

3rd Serv. Reason; because they then less need one another. The wars for my money. I hope to see Romans as cheap as Volscians. They are rising, they are rising.

All. In, in, in, in! [*Exeunt.*

SCENE VI. *Rome: a public place*

Enter SICINIUS *and* BRUTUS.

Sic. We hear not of him, neither need we fear him;
His remedies are tame i' the present peace
And quietness of the people, which before
Were in wild hurry. Here do we make his friends
Blush that the world goes well, who rather had,
Though they themselves did suffer by 't, behold
Dissentious numbers pestering streets than see
Our tradesmen singing in their shops and going
About their functions friendly.

Bru. We stood to 't in good time. [*Enter* MENENIUS.] Is this Menenius?

Sic. 'Tis he, 'tis he. O, he is grown most kind of late.

Both Tri. Hail, sir!

Men. Hail to you both!

Sic. Your Coriolanus
Is not much miss'd, but with his friends.
The commonwealth doth stand, and so would do,
Were he more angry at it.

Men. All's well; and might have been much better, if
He could have temporized.

Sic. Where is he, hear you?

Men. Nay, I hear nothing; his mother and his wife
Hear nothing from him.

Enter three or four CITIZENS.

Citizens. The gods preserve you both!

Sic. God-den, our neighbours.

Bru. God-den to you all, god-den to you all.

1st Cit. Ourselves, our wives, and children, on our knees,
Are bound to pray for you both.

Sic. Live, and thrive!

Bru. Farewell, kind neighbours. We wish'd Coriolanus
Had loved you as we did.

Citizens. Now the gods keep you!

Both Tri. Farewell, farewell. [*Exeunt* CITIZENS.

Sic. This is a happier and more comely time
Than when these fellows ran about the streets,
Crying confusion.

Bru. Caius Marcius was
A worthy officer i' the war; but insolent,
O'ercome with pride, ambitious past all thinking,
Self-loving—

Sic. And affecting one sole throne,
Without assistance.

Men. I think not so.

Sic. We should by this, to all our lamentation,
If he had gone forth consul, found it so.

Bru. The gods have well prevented it, and Rome
Sits safe and still without him.

Enter an ÆDILE.

Æd. Worthy tribunes,
There is a slave, whom we have put in prison,
Reports, the Volsces with two several powers
Are enter'd in the Roman territories,
And with the deepest malice of the war
Destroy what lies before 'em.

Men. 'Tis Aufidius,
Who, hearing of our Marcius' banishment,
Thrusts forth his horns again into the world;
Which were inshell'd when Marcius stood for Rome,
And durst not once peep out.

Sic. Come, what talk you
Of Marcius?

Bru. Go see this rumourer whipp'd. It cannot be
The Volsces dare break with us.

Men. Cannot be!
We have record that very well it can,
And three examples of the like have been
Within my age. But reason with the fellow,
Before you punish him, where he heard this,
Lest you shall chance to whip your information
And beat the messenger who bids beware
Of what is to be dreaded.

Sic. Tell not me.
I know this cannot be.

Bru. Not possible.

Enter a MESSENGER.

Mess. The nobles in great earnestness are going
All to the Senate-house. Some news is come
That turns their countenances.

Sic. 'Tis this slave—
Go whip him 'fore the people's eyes—his raising;
Nothing but his report.

Mess. Yes, worthy sir,
The slave's report is seconded; and more,
More fearful, is deliver'd.

Sic. What more fearful?

Mess. It is spoke freely out of many mouths—
How probable I do not know—that Marcius,

Join'd with Aufidius, leads a power 'gainst Rome,
And vows revenge as spacious as between
The young'st and oldest thing.
Sic. This is most likely!
Bru. Raised only, that the weaker sort may wish
Good Marcius home again.
Sic. The very trick on 't.
Men. This is unlikely;
He and Aufidius can no more atone
Than violentest contrariety.

Enter a SECOND MESSENGER.

2nd Mess. You are sent for to the Senate.
A fearful army, led by Caius Marcius
Associated with Aufidius, rages
Upon our territories; and have already
O'erborne their way, consumed with fire, and took
What lay before them.

Enter COMINIUS.

Com. O, you have made good work!
Men. What news? what news?
Com. You have holp to ravish your own daughters and
To melt the city leads upon your pates,
To see your wives dishonour'd to your noses—
Men. What's the news? what's the news?
Com. Your temples burned in their cement, and
Your franchises, whereon you stood, confined
Into an auger's bore.
Men. Pray now, your news?
You have made fair work, I fear me. Pray, your news?
If Marcius should be join'd with Volscians—
Com. If!
He is their god. He leads them like a thing
Made by some other deity than nature,
That shapes man better; and they follow him,
Against us brats with no less confidence
Than boys pursuing summer butterflies,
Or butchers killing flies.
Men. You have made good work,
You and your apron-men; you that stood so much
Upon the voice of occupation and
The breath of garlic-eaters!
Com. He will shake
Your Rome about your ears.
Men. As Hercules
Did shake down mellow fruit. You have made fair work!
Bru. But is this true, sir?
Com. Ay; and you'll look pale
Before you find it other. All the regions
Do smilingly revolt; and who resist
Are mock'd for valiant ignorance,
And perish constant fools. Who is 't can blame him?
Your enemies and his find something in him.
Men. We are all undone, unless
The noble man have mercy.
Com. Who shall ask it?
The tribunes cannot do 't for shame; the people
Deserve such pity of him as the wolf
Does of the shepherds. For his best friends, if they
Should say, "Be good to Rome," they charged him even
As those should do that had deserved his hate,
And therein show'd like enemies.
Men. 'Tis true.
If he were putting to my house the brand
That should consume it, I have not the face
To say, "Beseech you, cease." You have made fair hands,
You and your crafts! you have crafted fair!
Com. You have brought
A trembling upon Rome, such as was never
So incapable of help.
Both Tri. Say not we brought it.
Men. How! Was it we? We loved him; but, like beasts
And cowardly nobles, gave way unto your clusters,
Who did hoot him out o' the city.
Com. But I fear
They'll roar him in again. Tullus Aufidius,
The second name of men, obeys his points
As if he were his officer. Desperation
Is all the policy, strength, and defence,
That Rome can make against them.

Enter a troop of CITIZENS.

Men. Here come the clusters.
And is Aufidius with him? You are they
That made the air unwholesome, when you cast
Your stinking greasy caps in hooting at
Coriolanus' exile. Now he's coming;
And not a hair upon a soldier's head
Which will not prove a whip. As many coxcombs
As you threw caps up will he tumble down,
And pay you for your voices. 'Tis no matter;
If he could burn us all into one coal,
We have deserved it.
Citizens. Faith, we hear fearful news.
1st Cit. For mine own part,
When I said banish him, I said 'twas pity.
2nd Cit. And so did I.
3rd Cit. And so did I; and, to say the truth, so did very many of us. That we did, we did for the

best; and though we willingly consented to his banishment, yet it was against our will.

Com. Ye're goodly things, you voices!

Men. You have made
Good work, you and your cry! Shall's to the Capitol?

Com. O, ay, what else?

[*Exeunt* COMINIUS *and* MENENIUS.

Sic. Go, masters, get you home; be not dismay'd.
These are a side that would be glad to have
This true which they so seem to fear. Go home,
And show no sign of fear.

1st Cit. The gods be good to us! Come, masters, let's home. I ever said we were i' the wrong when we banished him.

2nd Cit. So did we all. But, come, let's home.

[*Exeunt* CITIZENS.

Bru. I do not like this news.

Sic. Nor I.

Bru. Let's to the Capitol. Would half my wealth
Would buy this for a lie!

Sic. Pray, let us go.

[*Exeunt.*

SCENE VII. *A camp, at a small distance from Rome*

Enter AUFIDIUS *and his* LIEUTENANT.

Auf. Do they still fly to the Roman?

Lieu. I do not know what witchcraft's in him, but
Your soldiers use him as the grace 'fore meat,
Their talk at table, and their thanks at end;
And you are darken'd in this action, sir,
Even by your own.

Auf. I cannot help it now,
Unless, by using means, I lame the foot
Of our design. He bears himself more proudlier,
Even to my person, than I thought he would
When first I did embrace him. Yet his nature
In that's no changeling; and I must excuse
What cannot be amended.

Lieu. Yet I wish, sir—
I mean for your particular—you had not
Join'd in commission with him; but either
Had borne the action of yourself, or else
To him had left it solely.

Auf. I understand thee well; and be thou sure,
When he shall come to his account, he knows not
What I can urge against him. Although it seems,
And so he thinks, and is no less apparent
To the vulgar eye, that he bears all things fairly,
And shows good husbandry for the Volscian state,
Fights dragon-like, and does achieve as soon
As draw his sword; yet he hath left undone
That which shall break his neck or hazard mine,
Whene'er we come to our account.

Lieu. Sir, I beseech you, think you he'll carry Rome?

Auf. All places yield to him ere he sits down;
And the nobility of Rome are his;
The senators and patricians love him too;
The tribunes are no soldiers; and their people
Will be as rash in the repeal, as hasty
To expel him thence. I think he'll be to Rome
As is the osprey to the fish, who takes it
By sovereignty of nature. First he was
A noble servant to them; but he could not
Carry his honours even. Whether 'twas pride,
Which out of daily fortune ever taints
The happy man; whether defect of judgement,
To fail in the disposing of those chances
Which he was lord of; or whether nature,
Not to be other than one thing, not moving
From the casque to the cushion, but commanding peace
Even with the same austerity and garb
As he controll'd the war; but one of these—
As he hath spices of them all, not all,
For I dare so far free him—made him fear'd,
So hated, and so banish'd; but he has a merit,
To choke it in the utterance. So our virtues
Lie in the interpretation of the time;
And power, unto itself most commendable,
Hath not a tomb so evident as a chair
To extol what it hath done.
One fire drives out one fire; one nail, one nail;
Rights by rights falter, strengths by strengths do fail.
Come, let's away. When, Caius, Rome is thine,
Thou art poor'st of all; then shortly art thou mine.

[*Exeunt.*

ACT V

SCENE I. *Rome: a public place*

Enter MENENIUS, COMINIUS, SICINIUS, BRUTUS, *and others.*

Men. No, I'll not go. You hear what he hath said
Which was sometime his general; who loved him
In a most dear particular. He call'd me father;
But what o' that? Go, you that banish'd him;
A mile before his tent fall down, and knee
The way into his mercy. Nay, if he coy'd
To hear Cominius speak, I'll keep at home.

Com. He would not seem to know me.

Men. Do you hear?

Com. Yet one time he did call me by my name.

I urged our old acquaintance, and the drops
That we have bled together. Coriolanus
He would not answer to; forbad all names;
He was a kind of nothing, titleless,
Till he had forged himself a name o' the fire
Of burning Rome.
Men. Why, so; you have made good work!
A pair of tribunes that have rack'd fair Rome
To make coals cheap—a noble memory!
Com. I minded him how royal 'twas to pardon
When it was less expected. He replied
It was a bare petition of a state
To one whom they had punish'd.
Men. Very well;
Could he say less?
Com. I offer'd to awaken his regard
For 's private friends. His answer to me was
He could not stay to pick them in a pile
Of noisome musty chaff. He said 'twas folly,
For one poor grain or two, to leave unburnt,
And still to nose the offence.
Men. For one poor grain or two!
I am one of those; his mother, wife, his child,
And this brave fellow too, we are the grains.
You are the musty chaff; and you are smelt
Above the moon. We must be burnt for you.
Sic. Nay, pray, be patient. If you refuse your aid
In this so never-needed help, yet do not
Upbraid's with our distress. But, sure, if you
Would be your country's pleader, your good tongue,
More than the instant army we can make,
Might stop our countryman.
Men. No, I'll not meddle.
Sic. Pray you, go to him.
Men. What should I do?
Bru. Only make trial what your love can do
For Rome, towards Marcius.
Men. Well, and say that Marcius
Return me, as Cominius is return'd,
Unheard; what then?
But as a discontented friend, grief-shot
With his unkindness? say 't be so?
Sic. Yet your good will
Must have that thanks from Rome, after the measure
As you intended well.
Men. I'll undertake 't;
I think he'll hear me. Yet, to bite his lip
And hum at good Cominius, much unhearts me.
He was not taken well; he had not dined.
The veins unfill'd, our blood is cold, and then
We pout upon the morning, are unapt
To give or to forgive; but when we have stuff'd
These pipes and these conveyances of our blood
With wine and feeding, we have suppler souls
Than in our priest-like fasts. Therefore I'll watch him
Till he be dieted to my request,
And then I'll set upon him.
Bru. You know the very road into his kindness,
And cannot lose your way.
Men. Good faith, I'll prove him,
Speed how it will. I shall ere long have knowledge
Of my success. [*Exit.*
Com. He'll never hear him.
Sic. Not?
Com. I tell you, he does sit in gold, his eye
Red as 'twould burn Rome; and his injury
The gaoler to his pity. I kneel'd before him;
'Twas very faintly he said "Rise"; dismiss'd me
Thus, with his speechless hand. What he would do
He sent in writing after me; what he would not,
Bound with an oath to yield to his conditions.
So that all hope is vain,
Unless his noble mother, and his wife;
Who, as I hear, mean to solicit him
For mercy to his country. Therefore, let's hence,
And with our fair entreaties haste them on.
[*Exeunt.*

SCENE II. *Entrance of the Volscian camp before Rome*

TWO SENTINELS *on guard. Enter to them,* MENENIUS.

1st Sen. Stay! Whence are you?
2nd Sen. Stand, and go back.
Men. You guard like men; 'tis well. But, by your leave,
I am an officer of state, and come
To speak with Coriolanus.
1st Sen. From whence?
Men. From Rome.
1st Sen. You may not pass, you must return. Our general
Will no more hear from thence.
2nd Sen. You'll see your Rome embraced with fire before
You'll speak with Coriolanus.
Men. Good my friends,
If you have heard your general talk of Rome,
And of his friends there, it is lots to blanks,
My name hath touch'd your ears: it is Menenius.
1st Sen. Be it so; go back. The virtue of your name
Is not here passable.
Men. I tell thee, fellow,
Thy general is my lover. I have been

The book of his good acts, whence men have read
His fame unparallel'd, haply amplified;
For I have ever verified my friends,
Of whom he's chief, with all the size that verity
Would without lapsing suffer; nay, sometimes,
Like to a bowl upon a subtle ground,
I have tumbled past the throw; and in his praise
Have almost stamp'd the leasing: therefore, fellow,
I must have leave to pass.

1st Sen. Faith, sir, if you had told as many lies in his behalf as you have uttered words in your own, you should not pass here; no, though it were as virtuous to lie as to live chastely. Therefore, go back.

Men. Prithee, fellow, remember my name is Menenius, always factionary on the party of your general.

2nd Sen. Howsoever you have been his liar, as you say you have, I am one that, telling true under him, must say, you cannot pass. Therefore, go back.

Men. Has he dined, canst thou tell? for I would not speak with him till after dinner.

1st Sen. You are a Roman, are you?

Men. I am, as thy general is.

1st Sen. Then you should hate Rome, as he does. Can you, when you have pushed out your gates the very defender of them, and, in a violent popular ignorance, given your enemy your shield, think to front his revenges with the easy groans of old women, the virginal palms of your daughters, or with the palsied intercession of such a decayed dotant as you seem to be? Can you think to blow out the intended fire your city is ready to flame in, with such weak breath as this? No, you are deceived; therefore, back to Rome, and prepare for your execution. You are condemned, our general has sworn you out of reprieve and pardon.

Men. Sirrah, if thy captain knew I were here, he would use me with estimation.

1st Sen. Come, my captain knows you not.

Men. I mean, thy general.

1st Sen. My general cares not for you. Back, I say, go; lest I let forth your half-pint of blood; back—that's the utmost of your having. Back.

Men. Nay, but, fellow, fellow—

Enter CORIOLANUS *and* AUFIDIUS.

Cor. What's the matter?

Men. Now, you companion, I'll say an errand for you; you shall know now that I am in estimation; you shall perceive that a Jack guardant cannot office me from my son Coriolanus. Guess, but by my entertainment with him, if thou standest not i' the state of hanging, or of some death more long in spectatorship, and crueller in suffering; behold now presently, and swoon for what's to come upon thee. [*To* CORIOLANUS] The glorious gods sit in hourly synod about thy particular prosperity, and love thee no worse than thy old father Menenius does! O my son, my son! thou art preparing fire for us; look thee, here's water to quench it. I was hardly moved to come to thee; but being assured none but myself could move thee, I have been blown out of your gates with sighs; and conjure thee to pardon Rome, and thy petitionary countrymen. The good gods assuage thy wrath, and turn the dregs of it upon this varlet here—this, who, like a block, hath denied my access to thee.

Cor. Away!

Men. How! Away!

Cor. Wife, mother, child, I know not. My affairs
Are servanted to others. Though I owe
My revenge properly, my remission lies
In Volscian breasts. That we have been familiar,
Ingrate forgetfulness shall poison, rather
Than pity note how much. Therefore, be gone.
Mine ears against your suits are stronger than
Your gates against my force. Yet, for I loved thee,
Take this along; I writ it for thy sake,
Gives a letter.
And would have sent it. Another word, Menenius,
I will not hear thee speak. This man, Aufidius,
Was my beloved in Rome; yet thou behold'st!

Auf. You keep a constant temper.
[*Exeunt* CORIOLANUS *and* AUFIDIUS.

1st Sen. Now, sir, is your name Menenius?

2nd Sen. 'Tis a spell, you see, of much power. You know the way home again.

1st Sen. Do you hear how we are shent for keeping your greatness back?

2nd Sen. What cause, do you think, I have to swoon?

Men. I neither care for the world nor your general. For such things as you, I can scarce think there's any, ye're so slight. He that hath a will to die by himself fears it not from another. Let your general do his worst. For you, be that you are, long; and your misery increase with your age! I say to you, as I was said to, "Away!"
[*Exit.*

1st Sen. A noble fellow, I warrant him.

2nd Sen. The worthy fellow is our general.
He's the rock, the oak not to be wind-shaken.
[*Exeunt.*

SCENE III. *The tent of* CORIOLANUS

Enter CORIOLANUS, AUFIDUS, *and others.*

Cor. We will before the walls of Rome to-morrow
Set down our host. My partner in this action,
You must report to the Volscian lords how plainly
I have borne this business.
Auf. Only their ends
You have respected; stopp'd your ears against
The general suit of Rome; never admitted
A private whisper, no, not with such friends
That thought them sure of you.
Cor. This last old man,
Whom with a crack'd heart I have sent to Rome,
Loved me above the measure of a father;
Nay, godded me, indeed. Their latest refuge
Was to send him; for whose old love I have,
Though I show'd sourly to him, once more offer'd
The first conditions, which they did refuse
And cannot now accept; to grace him only
That thought he could do more, a very little
I have yielded to. Fresh embassies and suits,
Nor from the state nor private friends, hereafter
Will I lend ear to. Ha! what shout is this?
Shout within.
Shall I be tempted to infringe my vow
In the same time 'tis made? I will not.

Enter, in mourning habits, VIRGILIA, VOLUMNIA *leading young* MARCIUS, VALERIA, *and Attendants.*

My wife comes foremost; then the honour'd mould
Wherein this trunk was framed, and in her hand
The grandchild to her blood. But, out, affection!
All bond and privilege of nature, break!
Let it be virtuous to be obstinate.
What is that curt'sy worth? or those doves' eyes,
Which can make gods forsworn? I melt, and am not
Of stronger earth than others. My mother bows;
As if Olympus to a molehill should
In supplication nod; and my young boy
Hath an aspect of intercession, which
Great nature cries "Deny not." Let the Volsces
Plough Rome, and harrow Italy, I'll never
Be such a gosling to obey instinct, but stand,
As if a man were author of himself
And knew no other kin.
Vir. My lord and husband!
Cor. These eyes are not the same I wore in Rome.
Vir. The sorrow that delivers us thus changed
Makes you think so.
Cor. Like a dull actor now,
I have forgot my part, and I am out,
Even to a full disgrace. Best of my flesh,
Forgive my tyranny; but do not say
For that "Forgive our Romans." O, a kiss
Long as my exile, sweet as my revenge!
Now, by the jealous queen of heaven, that kiss
I carried from thee, dear, and my true lip
Hath virgin'd it e'er since. You gods! I prate,
And the most noble mother of the world
Leave unsaluted. Sink, my knee, i' the earth;
Kneels.
Of thy deep duty more impression show
Than that of common sons.
Vol. O, stand up blest!
Whilst, with no softer cushion than the flint,
I kneel before thee; and unproperly
Show duty, as mistaken all this while
Between the child and parent. [*Kneels.*]
Cor. What is this?
Your knees to me? to your corrected son?
Then let the pebbles on the hungry beach
Fillip the stars; then let the mutinous winds
Strike the proud cedars 'gainst the fiery sun;
Murdering impossibility, to make
What cannot be, slight work.
Vol. Thou art my warrior;
I holp to frame thee. Do you know this lady?
Cor. The noble sister of Publicola,
The moon of Rome, chaste as the icicle
That's curdied by the frost from purest snow
And hangs on Dian's temple. Dear Valeria!
Vol. This is a poor epitome of yours,
Which by the interpretation of full time
May show like all yourself.
Cor. The god of soldiers,
With the consent of supreme Jove, inform
Thy thoughts with nobleness; that thou mayst prove
To shame unvulnerable, and stick i' the wars
Like a great sea-mark, standing every flaw,
And saving those that eye thee!
Vol. Your knee, sirrah.
Cor. That's my brave boy!
Vol. Even he, your wife, this lady, and myself,
Are suitors to you.
Cor. I beseech you, peace;
Or, if you'd ask, remember this before:
The thing I have forsworn to grant may never
Be held by you denials. Do not bid me
Dismiss my soldiers, or capitulate
Again with Rome's mechanics. Tell me not
Wherein I seem unnatural. Desire not
To allay my rages and revenges with
Your colder reasons.
Vol. O, no more, no more!

You have said you will not grant us anything;
For we have nothing else to ask, but that
Which you deny already. Yet we will ask;
That, if you fail in our request, the blame
May hang upon your hardness; therefore hear us.
Cor. Aufidius, and you Volsces, mark; for we'll
Hear nought from Rome in private. Your request?
Vol. Should we be silent and not speak, our raiment
And state of bodies would bewray what life
We have led since thy exile. Think with thyself
How more unfortunate than all living women
Are we come hither; since that thy sight, which should
Make our eyes flow with joy, hearts dance with comforts,
Constrains them weep and shake with fear and sorrow;
Making the mother, wife, and child to see
The son, the husband, and the father tearing
His country's bowels out. And to poor we
Thine enmity's most capital; thou barr'st us
Our prayers to the gods, which is a comfort
That all but we enjoy; for how can we,
Alas, how can we for our country pray,
Whereto we are bound, together with thy victory,
Whereto we are bound? alack, or we must lose
The country, our dear nurse, or else thy person,
Our comfort in the country. We must find
An evident calamity, though we had
Our wish, which side should win; for either thou
Must, as a foreign recreant, be led
With manacles through our streets, or else
Triumphantly tread on thy country's ruin,
And bear the palm for having bravely shed
Thy wife and children's blood. For myself, son,
I purpose not to wait on fortune till
These wars determine. If I cannot persuade thee
Rather to show a noble grace to both parts
Than seek the end of one, thou shalt no sooner
March to assault thy country than to tread—
Trust to 't, thou shalt not—on thy mother's womb,
That brought thee to this world.
Vir. Ay, and mine,
That brought you forth this boy, to keep your name
Living to time.
Young Mar. A' shall not tread on me;
I'll run away till I am bigger, but then I'll fight.
Cor. Not of a woman's tenderness to be,
Requires nor child nor woman's face to see.
I have sat too long. [*Rising*.]
Vol. Nay, go not from us thus.
If it were so that our request did tend
To save the Romans, thereby to destroy
The Volsces whom you serve, you might condemn us,
As poisonous of your honour. No; our suit
Is that you reconcile them: while the Volsces
May say, "This mercy we have show'd"; the Romans,
"This we received"; and each in either side
Give the all-hail to thee, and cry, "Be blest
For making up this peace!" Thou know'st, great son,
The end of war's uncertain, but this certain,
That, if thou conquer Rome, the benefit
Which thou shalt thereby reap is such a name,
Whose repetition will be dogg'd with curses;
Whose chronicle thus writ: "The man was noble,
But with his last attempt he wiped it out;
Destroy'd his country, and his name remains
To the ensuing age abhorr'd." Speak to me, son.
Thou hast affected the fine strains of honour,
To imitate the graces of the gods;
To tear with thunder the wide cheeks o' the air,
And yet to charge thy sulphur with a bolt
That should but rive an oak. Why dost not speak?
Think'st thou it honourable for a noble man
Still to remember wrongs? Daughter, speak you;
He cares not for your weeping. Speak thou, boy;
Perhaps thy childishness will move him more
Than can our reasons. There's no man in the world
More bound to 's mother; yet here he lets me prate
Like one i' the stocks. Thou hast never in thy life
Show'd thy dear mother any courtesy,
When she, poor hen, fond of no second brood,
Has cluck'd thee to the wars and safely home,
Loaden with honour. Say my request's unjust,
And spurn me back. But if it be not so,
Thou art not honest; and the gods will plague thee
That thou restrain'st from me the duty which
To a mother's part belongs. He turns away.
Down, ladies; let us shame him with our knees.
To his surname Coriolanus 'longs more pride
Than pity to our prayers. Down! an end;
This is the last. So we will home to Rome,
And die among our neighbours. Nay, behold 's!
This boy, that cannot tell what he would have,
But kneels and holds up hands for fellowship,
Does reason our petition with more strength
Than thou hast to deny 't. Come, let us go.
This fellow had a Volscian to his mother;
His wife is in Corioli, and his child
Like him by chance. Yet give us our dispatch.
I am hush'd until our city be afire,
And then I'll speak a little.

He holds her by the hand, silent.

Cor. O mother, mother!
What have you done? Behold, the heavens do ope,
The gods look down, and this unnatural scene
They laugh at. O my mother, mother! O!
You have won a happy victory to Rome;
But, for your son—believe it, O, believe it,
Most dangerously you have with him prevail'd,
If not most mortal to him. But, let it come.
Aufidius, though I cannot make true wars,
I'll frame convenient peace. Now, good Aufidius,
Were you in my stead, would you have heard
A mother less? or granted less, Aufidius?

Auf. I was moved withal.

Cor. I dare be sworn you were:
And, sir, it is no little thing to make
Mine eyes to sweat compassion. But, good sir,
What peace you'll make, advise me. For my part,
I'll not to Rome, I'll back with you; and pray you,
Stand to me in this cause. O mother! wife!

Auf. [*Aside.*] I am glad thou hast set thy mercy and thy honour
At difference in thee. Out of that I'll work
Myself a former fortune.

The Ladies make signs to CORIOLANUS.

Cor. Ay, by and by;
[*To* VOLUMNIA, VIRGILIA, *&c.*
But we will drink together; and you shall bear
A better witness back than words, which we,
On like conditions, will have counter-seal'd.
Come, enter with us. Ladies, you deserve
To have a temple built you. All the swords
In Italy, and her confederate arms,
Could not have made this peace. [*Exeunt.*

SCENE IV. *Rome: a public place*

Enter MENENIUS *and* SICINIUS.

Men. See you yond coign o' the Capitol, yond corner-stone?

Sic. Why, what of that?

Men. If it be possible for you to displace it with your little finger, there is some hope the ladies of Rome, especially his mother, may prevail with him. But I say there is no hope in't. Our throats are sentenced and stay upon execution.

Sic. Is't possible that so short a time can alter the condition of a man?

Men. There is differency between a grub and a butterfly; yet your butterfly was a grub. This Marcius is grown from man to dragon; he has wings; he's more than a creeping thing.

Sic. He loved his mother dearly.

Men. So did he me; and he no more remembers his mother now than an eight-year-old horse. The tartness of his face sours ripe grapes; when he walks, he moves like an engine and the ground shrinks before his treading. He is able to pierce a corslet with his eye; talks like a knell, and his hum is a battery. He sits in his state, as a thing made for Alexander. What he bids be done is finished with his bidding. He wants nothing of a god but eternity and a heaven to throne in.

Sic. Yes, mercy, if you report him truly.

Men. I paint him in the character. Mark what mercy his mother shall bring from him. There is no more mercy in him than there is milk in a male tiger; that shall our poor city find; and all this is long of you.

Sic. The gods be good unto us!

Men. No, in such a case the gods will not be good unto us. When we banished him, we respected not them; and, he returning to break our necks, they respect not us.

Enter a MESSENGER

Mess. Sir, if you'd save your life, fly to your house.
The plebeians have got your fellow-tribune
And hale him up and down, all swearing, if
The Roman ladies bring not comfort home,
They'll give him death by inches.

Enter a SECOND MESSENGER.

Sic. What's the news?

2nd Mess. Good news, good news; the ladies have prevail'd,
The Volscians are dislodged, and Marcius gone.
A merrier day did never yet greet Rome,
No, not the expulsion of the Tarquins.

Sic. Friend,
Art thou certain this is true? is it most certain?

2nd Mess. As certain as I know the sun is fire.
Where have you lurk'd, that you make doubt of it?
Ne'er through an arch so hurried the blown tide,
As the recomforted through the gates. Why, hark you! *Trumpets; hautboys; drums beat; all together.*
The trumpets, sackbuts, psalteries and fifes,
Tabors and cymbals and the shouting Romans,
Make the sun dance. Hark you!

A shout within.

Men. This is good news;
I will go meet the ladies. This Volumnia
Is worth of consuls, senators, patricians,
A city full; of tribunes, such as you,
A sea and land full. You have pray'd well to-day.
This morning for ten thousand of your throats

I'd not have given a doit. Hark, how they joy!
Music still, with shouts.
Sic. First, the gods bless you for your tidings; next,
Accept my thankfulness.
2nd Mess. Sir, we have all
Great cause to give great thanks.
Sic. They are near the city?
2nd Mess. Almost at point to enter.
Sic. We will meet them,
And help the joy. [*Exeunt.*

SCENE V. *The same: a street near the gate*

Enter two SENATORS *with* VOLUMNIA, VIRGILIA, VALERIA, *&c. passing over the stage, followed by Patricians, and others.*

1st Sen. Behold our patroness, the life of Rome!
Call all your tribes together, praise the gods,
And make triumphant fires; strew flowers before them!
Unshout the noise that banish'd Marcius,
Repeal him with the welcome of his mother;
Cry, "Welcome, ladies, welcome!"
All. Welcome, ladies,
Welcome! [*A flourish with drums and trumpets.*
Exeunt.

SCENE VI. *Antium: a public place*

Enter TULLUS AUFIDIUS, *with Attendants.*

Auf. Go tell the lords o' the city I am here;
Deliver them this paper. Having read it,
Bid them repair to the market-place; where I,
Even in theirs and in the commons' ears,
Will vouch the truth of it. Him I accuse
The city ports by this hath enter'd and
Intends to appear before the people, hoping
To purge himself with words. Dispatch.
[*Exeunt Attendants.*

Enter three or four CONSPIRATORS *of* AUFIDIUS' *faction.*

Most welcome!
1st Con. How is it with our general?
Auf. Even so
As with a man by his own alms empoison'd,
And with his charity slain.
2nd Con. Most noble sir,
If you do hold the same intent wherein
You wish'd us parties, we'll deliver you
Of your great danger.
Auf. Sir, I cannot tell.
We must proceed as we do find the people.
3rd Con. The people will remain uncertain whilst
'Twixt you there's difference; but the fall of either
Makes the survivor heir of all.
Auf. I know it;
And my pretext to strike at him admits
A good construction. I raised him, and I pawn'd
Mine honour for his truth; who being so heighten'd,
He water'd his new plants with dews of flattery,
Seducing so my friends; and, to this end,
He bow'd his nature, never known before
But to be rough, unswayable, and free.
3rd Con. Sir, his stoutness
When he did stand for consul, which he lost
By lack of stooping—
Auf. That I would have spoke of.
Being banish'd for't, he came unto my hearth;
Presented to my knife his throat. I took him;
Made him joint-servant with me; gave him way
In all his own desires; nay, let him choose
Out of my files, his projects to accomplish,
My best and freshest men, served his designments
In mine own person; holp to reap the fame
Which he did end all his; and took some pride
To do myself this wrong; till, at the last,
I seem'd his follower, not partner, and
He waged me with his countenance, as if
I had been mercenary.
1st Con. So he did, my lord.
The army marvell'd at it, and, in the last,
When he had carried Rome and that we look'd
For no less spoil than glory—
Auf. There was it,
For which my sinews shall be stretch'd upon him.
At a few drops of women's rheum, which are
As cheap as lies, he sold the blood and labour
Of our great action. Therefore shall he die,
And I'll renew me in his fall. But, hark!
Drums and trumpets sound, with great shouts of the People.
1st Con. Your native town you enter'd like a post,
And had no welcomes home; but he returns,
Splitting the air with noise.
2nd Con. And patient fools,
Whose children he hath slain, their base throats tear
With giving him glory.
3rd Con. Therefore, at your vantage,
Ere he express himself, or move the people
With what he would say, let him feel your sword,
Which we will second. When he lies along,
After your way his tale pronounced shall bury
His reasons with his body.
Auf. Say no more.
Here come the lords.

Enter the LORDS *of the city.*

All the Lords. You are most welcome home.

Auf. I have not deserved it.
But, worthy lords, have you with heed perused
What I have written to you?
Lords. We have.
1st Lord. And grieve to hear't.
What faults he made before the last, I think
Might have found easy fines; but there to end
Where he was to begin and give away
The benefit of our levies, answering us
With our own charge, making a treaty where
There was a yielding—this admits no excuse.
Auf. He approaches. You shall hear him.

Enter CORIOLANUS, *marching with drum and colours; Commoners being with him.*

Cor. Hail, lords! I am return'd your soldier,
No more infected with my country's love
Than when I parted hence, but still subsisting
Under your great command. You are to know
That prosperously I have attempted and
With bloody passage led your wars even to
The gates of Rome. Our spoils we have brought home
Do more than counterpoise a full third part
The charges of the action. We have made peace
With no less honour to the Antiates
Than shame to the Romans; and we here deliver,
Subscribed by the consuls and patricians,
Together with the seal o' the Senate, what
We have compounded on.
Auf. Read it not, noble lords;
But tell the traitor, in the high'st degree
He hath abused your powers.
Cor. "Traitor!" how now!
Auf. Ay, traitor, Marcius!
Cor. "Marcius!"
Auf. Ay, Marcius, Caius Marcius. Dost thou think
I'll grace thee with that robbery, thy stol'n name,
Coriolanus, in Corioli?
You lords and heads o' the state, perfidiously
He has betray'd your business, and given up,
For certain drops of salt, your city Rome,
I say "your city," to his wife and mother;
Breaking his oath and resolution like
A twist of rotten silk, never admitting
Counsel o' the war, but at his nurse's tears
He whined and roar'd away your victory,
That pages blush'd at him and men of heart
Look'd wondering each at other.
Cor. Hear'st thou, Mars?
Auf. Name not the god, thou boy of tears!
Cor. Ha!
Auf. No more.
Cor. Measureless liar, thou hast made my heart
Too great for what contains it. "Boy!" O slave!
Pardon me, lords, 'tis the first time that ever
I was forced to scold. Your judgements, my grave lords,
Must give this cur the lie; and his own notion—
Who wears my stripes impress'd upon him; that
Must bear my beating to his grave—shall join
To thrust the lie unto him.
1st Lord. Peace, both, and hear me speak.
Cor. Cut me to pieces, Volsces; men and lads,
Stain all your edges on me. "Boy!" False hound!
If you have writ your annals true, 'tis there,
That, like an eagle in a dove-cote, I
Flutter'd your Volscians in Corioli.
Alone I did it. "Boy!"
Auf. Why, noble lords,
Will you be put in mind of his blind fortune,
Which was your shame, by this unholy braggart,
'Fore your own eyes and ears?
All Consp. Let him die for't.
All the people. Tear him to pieces. Do it presently. He killed my son. My daughter. He killed my cousin Marcus. He killed my father.
2nd Lord. Peace, ho! no outrage; peace!
The man is noble and his fame folds-in
This orb o' the earth. His last offences to us
Shall have judicious hearing. Stand, Aufidius,
And trouble not the peace.
Cor. O that I had him,
With six Aufidiuses, or more, his tribe,
To use my lawful sword!
Auf. Insolent villain!
All Consp. Kill, kill, kill, kill, kill him!

The CONSPIRATORS *draw, and* KILL CORIOLANUS. AUFIDIUS *stands on his body.*

Lords. Hold, hold, hold, hold!
Auf. My noble masters, hear me speak.
1st Lord. O Tullus—
2nd Lord. Thou hast done a deed whereat valour will weep.
3rd Lord. Tread not upon him. Masters all, be quiet;
Put up your swords.
Auf. My lords, when you shall know—as in this rage,
Provoked by him, you cannot—the great danger
Which this man's life did owe you, you'll rejoice
That he is thus cut off. Please it your honours
To call me to your Senate, I'll deliver
Myself your loyal servant, or endure
Your heaviest censure.
1st Lord. Bear from hence his body;
And mourn you for him. Let him be regarded
As the most noble corse that ever herald
Did follow to his urn.
2nd Lord. His own impatience

Takes from Aufidius a great part of blame.
Let's make the best of it.
Auf. My rage is gone;
And I am struck with sorrow. Take him up. 149
Help, three o' the chiefest soldiers; I'll be one.
Beat thou the drum, that it speak mournfully;
Trail your steel pikes. Though in this city he
Hath widow'd and unchilded many a one,
Which to this hour bewail the injury,
Yet he shall have a noble memory.
Assist. [*Exeunt, bearing the body of Coriolanus. A dead march sounded.*

TIMON OF ATHENS

DRAMATIS PERSONÆ

TIMON *of Athens*
LUCIUS, LUCULLUS, SEMPRONIUS — *flattering lords*
VENTIDIUS, *one of Timon's false friends*
ALCIBIADES, *an Athenian captain*
APEMANTUS, *a churlish philosopher*
FLAVIUS, *steward to Timon*
A POET
A PAINTER
A JEWELLER
A MERCHANT
AN OLD ATHENIAN
A PAGE
A FOOL
THREE STRANGERS
A SOLDIER
THREE BANDITTI
FOUR SENATORS
FOUR LORDS
THREE MESSENGERS
FLAMINIUS, LUCILIUS, SERVILIUS — *Servants to Timon*
CAPHIS, PHILOTUS, TITUS, HORTENSIUS — *Servants to Timon's creditors*
THREE SERVANTS *to Timon*
TWO SERVANTS *to Varro*
A SERVANT *to Isidore*
A SERVANT *to Lucullus*
A SERVANT *to Lucius*

PHRYNIA, TIMANDRA — *mistresses to Alcibiades*

CUPID, AMAZONS — *in the mask*

NON-SPEAKING: *Lords, Senators, Officers, Soldiers, Banditti, and Attendants*

SCENE: *Athens, and the neighbouring woods*

ACT I

SCENE I. *Athens: A hall in Timon's house*

Enter POET, PAINTER, JEWELLER, MERCHANT, *and others, at several doors.*

Poet. Good day, sir.
Pain. I am glad you're well.
Poet. I have not seen you long. How goes the world?
Pain. It wears, sir, as it grows.
Poet. Ay, that's well known;
But what particular rarity? What strange,
Which manifold record not matches? See,
Magic of bounty! all these spirits thy power
Hath conjured to attend. I know the merchant.
Pain. I know them both; th' other's a jeweller.
Mer. O, 'tis a worthy lord.
Jew. Nay, that's most fix'd.
Mer. A most incomparable man, breathed, as it were,
To an untirable and continuate goodness;
He passes.
Jew. I have a jewel here—
Mer. O, pray, let's see't. For the Lord Timon, sir?
Jew. If he will touch the estimate: but, for that—
Poet. [*Reciting to himself*] "When we for recompense have praised the vile,
It stains the glory in that happy verse
Which aptly sings the good."
Mer. 'Tis a good form.
Looking at the jewel.
Jew. And rich. Here is a water, look ye.
Pain. You are rapt, sir, in some work, some dedication
To the great lord.
Poet. A thing slipp'd idly from me.
Our poesy is as a gum, which oozes
From whence 'tis nourish'd. The fire i' the flint
Shows not till it be struck; our gentle flame
Provokes itself and like the current flies
Each bound it chafes. What have you there?
Pain. A picture, sir. When comes your book forth?
Poet. Upon the heels of my presentment, sir.
Let's see your piece.
Pain. 'Tis a good piece.
Poet. So 'tis; this comes off well and excellent.
Pain. Indifferent.
Poet. Admirable. How this grace
Speaks his own standing! What a mental power
This eye shoots forth! How big imagination
Moves in this lip! to the dumbness of the gesture
One might interpret.
Pain. It is a pretty mocking of the life.
Here is a touch; is't good?
Poet. I will say of it,

It tutors nature. Artificial strife
Lives in these touches, livelier than life.

Enter certain Senators, and pass over.

Pain. How this lord is follow'd!
Poet. The senators of Athens; happy man!
Pain. Look, more!
Poet. You see this confluence, this great flood of visitors.
I have, in this rough work, shaped out a man,
Whom this beneath world doth embrace and hug
With amplest entertainment. My free drift
Halts not particularly, but moves itself
In a wide sea of wax. No levell'd malice
Infects one comma in the course I hold;
But flies an eagle flight,bold and forth on,
Leaving no tract behind.
Pain. How shall I understand you?
Poet. I will unbolt to you.
You see how all conditions, how all minds,
As well of glib and slippery creatures as
Of grave and austere quality, tender down
Their services to Lord Timon. His large fortune
Upon his good and gracious nature hanging
Subdues and properties to his love and tendance
All sorts of hearts; yea, from the glass-faced flatterer
To Apemantus, that few things loves better
Than to abhor himself. Even he drops down
The knee before him and returns in peace
Most rich in Timon's nod.
Pain. I saw them speak together.
Poet. Sir, I have upon a high and pleasant hill
Feign'd Fortune to be throned. The base o' the mount
Is rank'd with all deserts, all kind of natures,
That labour on the bosom of this sphere
To propagate their states. Amongst them all,
Whose eyes are on this sovereign lady fixed,
One do I personate of Lord Timons' frame,
Whom Fortune with her ivory hand wafts to her;
Whose present grace to present slaves and servants
Translates his rivals.
Pain. 'Tis conceived to scope.
This throne, this Fortune, and this hill, methinks,
With one man beckon'd from the rest below,
Bowing his head against the steepy mount
To climb his happiness, would be well express'd
In our condition.
Poet. Nay, sir, but hear me on.
All those which were his fellows but of late,
Some better than his value, on the moment
Follow his strides, his lobbies fill with tendance,
Rain sacrificial whisperings in his ear,
Make sacred even his stirrup, and through him
Drink the free air.
Pain. Ay, marry, what of these?
Poet. When Fortune in her shift and change of mood
Spurns down her late beloved, all his dependants
Which labour'd after him to the mountain's top
Even on their knees and hands, let him slip down,
Not one accompanying his declining foot.
Pain. 'Tis common.
A thousand moral paintings I can show
That shall demonstrate these quick blows of Fortune's
More pregnantly than words. Yet you do well
To show Lord Timon that mean eyes have seen
The foot above the head.

Trumpets sound. Enter LORD TIMON, *addressing himself courteously to every suitor; a* MESSENGER *from* VENTIDIUS *talking with him;* LUCILIUS *and other servants following.*

Tim. Imprison'd is he, say you?
Mess. Ay, my good lord. Five talents is his debt,
His means most short, his creditors most strait.
Your honourable letter he desires
To those have shut him up; which failing,
Periods his comfort.
Tim. Noble Ventidius! Well;
I am not of that feather to shake off
My friend when he must need me. I do know him
A gentleman that well deserves a help,
Which he shall have. I'll pay the debt, and free him.
Mess. Your lordship ever binds him.
Tim. Commend me to him. I will send his ransom;
And being enfranchised, bid him come to me.
'Tis not enough to help the feeble up,
But to support him after. Fare you well.
Mess. All happiness to your honour! [*Exit.*

Enter an old ATHENIAN.

Old Ath. Lord Timon, hear me speak.
Tim. Freely, good father.
Old Ath. Thou hast a servant named Lucilius.
Tim. I have so. What of him?
Old Ath. Most noble Timon, call the man before thee.
Tim. Attends he here, or no? Lucilius!
Luc. Here, at your lordship's service.
Old Ath. This fellow here, Lord Timon, this thy creature,

By night frequents my house. I am a man
That from my first have been inclined to thrift;
And my estate deserves an heir more raised
Than one which holds a trencher.

Tim. Well; what further?

Old Ath. One only daughter have I, no kin else,
On whom I may confer what I have got.
The maid is fair, o' the youngest for a bride,
And I have bred her at my dearest cost
In qualities of the best. This man of thine
Attempts her love. I prithee, noble lord,
Join with me to forbid him her resort;
Myself have spoke in vain.

Tim. The man is honest.

Old Ath. Therefore he will be, Timon.
His honesty rewards him in itself;
It must not bear my daughter.

Tim. Does she love him?

Old Ath. She is young and apt.
Our own precedent passions do instruct us
What levity's in youth.

Tim. [*To* LUCILIUS] Love you the maid?

Luc. Ay, my good lord, and she accepts of it.

Old Ath. If in her marriage my consent be missing,
I call the gods to witness, I will choose
Mine heir from forth the beggars of the world,
And dispossess her all.

Tim. How shall she be endow'd,
If she be mated with an equal husband?

Old Ath. Three talents on the present; in future, all.

Tim. This gentleman of mine hath served me long.
To build his fortune I will strain a little,
For 'tis a bond in men. Give him thy daughter.
What you bestow, in him I'll counterpoise,
And make him weigh with her.

Old Ath. Most noble lord,
Pawn me to this your honour, she is his.

Tim. My hand to thee; mine honour on my promise.

Luc. Humbly I thank your lordship. Never may
That state or fortune fall into my keeping,
Which is not owed to you!

[*Exeunt* LUCILIUS *and* OLD ATHENIAN.

Poet. Vouchsafe my labour, and long live your lordship!

Tim. I thank you; you shall hear from me anon;
Go not away. What have you there, my friend?

Pain. A piece of painting, which I do beseech
Your lordship to accept.

Tim. Painting is welcome.
The painting is almost the natural man;
For since dishonour traffics with man's nature,
He is but outside. These pencill'd figures are
Even such as they give out. I like your work;
And you shall find I like it. Wait attendance
Till you hear further from me.

Pain. The gods preserve ye!

Tim. Well fare you, gentleman. Give me your hand;
We must needs dine together. Sir, your jewel
Hath suffer'd under praise.

Jew. What, my lord! dispraise?

Tim. A mere satiety of commendations.
If I should pay you for't as 'tis extoll'd,
It would unclew me quite.

Jew. My lord, 'tis rated
As those which sell would give. But you well know,
Things of like value differing in the owners
Are prized by their masters. Believe't, dear lord,
You mend the jewel by the wearing it.

Tim. Well mock'd.

Mer. No, my good lord; he speaks the common tongue,
Which all men speak with him.

Tim. Look, who comes here; will you be chid?

Enter APEMANTUS.

Jew. We'll bear, with your lordship.

Mer. He'll spare none.

Tim. Good morrow to thee, gentle Apemantus!

Apem. Till I be gentle, stay thou for thy good morrow;
When thou art Timons' dog, and these knaves honest.

Tim. Why dost thou call them knaves? Thou know'st them not.

Apem. Are they not Athenians?

Tim. Yes.

Apem. Then I repent not.

Jew. You know me, Apemantus?

Apem. Thou know'st I do. I call'd thee by thy name.

Tim. Thou art proud, Apemantus.

Apem. Of nothing so much as that I am not like Timon.

Tim. Whither art going?

Apem. To knock out an honest Athenian's brains.

Tim. That's a deed thou'lt die for.

Apem. Right, if doing nothing be death by the law.

Tim. How likest thou this picture, Apemantus?

Apem. The best, for the innocence.

Tim. Wrought he not well that painted it?

Apem. He wrought better that made the painter; and yet he's but a filthy piece of work.

Pain. You're a dog.

Apem. Thy mother's of my generation. What's she, if I be a dog?

Tim. Wilt dine with me, Apemantus?

Apem. No; I eat not lords.

Tim. An thou shouldst, thou'dst anger ladies.

Apem. O, they eat lords; so they come by great bellies.

Tim. That's a lascivious apprehension.

Apem. So thou apprehendest it; take it for thy labour.

Tim. How dost thou like this jewel, Apemantus?

Apem. Not so well as plain-dealing, which will not cost a man a doit.

Tim. What dost thou think 'tis worth?

Apem. Not worth my thinking. How now poet!

Poet. How now, philosopher!

Apem. Thou liest.

Poet. Art not one?

Apem. Yes.

Poet. Then I lie not.

Apem. Art not a poet?

Poet. Yes.

Apem. Then thou liest. Look in thy last work, where thou hast feigned him a worthy fellow.

Poet. That's not feigned; he is so.

Apem. Yes, he is worthy of thee, and to pay thee for thy labour. He that loves to be flattered is worthy o' the flatterer. Heavens, that I were a lord!

Tim. What wouldst do then, Apemantus?

Apem. E'en as Apemantus does now; hate a lord with my heart.

Tim. What, thyself?

Apem. Ay.

Tim. Wherefore?

Apem. That I had no angry wit to be a lord. Art not thou a merchant?

Mer. Ay, Apemantus.

Apem. Traffic confound thee, if the gods will not!

Mer. If traffic do it, the gods do it.

Apem. Traffic's thy god; and thy god confound thee!

Trumpet sounds. Enter a MESSENGER.

Tim. What trumpet's that?

Mess. 'Tis Alcibiades, and some twenty horse,
All of companionship. 251

Tim. Pray, entertain them; give them guide to
us. [*Exeunt some Attendants.*
You must needs dine with me; go not you
hence
Till I have thank'd you. When dinner's done,
Show me this piece. I am joyful of your sights.

Enter ALCIBIADES, *with the rest.*

Most welcome, sir!

Apem. So, so, there!
Aches contract and starve your supple joints!
That there should be small love 'mongst these
sweet knaves,
And all this courtesy! The strain of man's bred
out
Into baboon and monkey.

Alcib. Sir, you have saved my longing, and I
feed
Most hungerly on your sight.

Tim. Right welcome, sir!
Ere we depart, we'll share a bounteous time
In different pleasures. Pray you, let us in.
[*Exeunt all except* APEMANTUS.

Enter TWO LORDS.

1st Lord. What time o'day is't, Apemantus?

Apem. Time to be honest.

1st Lord. That time serves still.

Apem. The more accursed thou, that still
omitt'st it.

2nd Lord. Thou art going to Lord Timon's
feast?

Apem. Ay, to see meat fill knaves and wine
heat fools.

2nd Lord. Fare thee well, fare thee well.

Apem. Thou art a fool to bid me farewell twice.

2nd Lord. Why, Apemantus?

Apem. Shouldst have kept one to thyself, for I mean to give thee none.

1st Lord. Hang thyself!

Apem. No, I will do nothing at thy bidding. Make thy requests to thy friend.

2nd Lord. Away, unpeaceable dog, or I'll spurn thee hence! 281

Apem. I will fly, like a dog, the heels o' the ass.
[*Exit.*

1st Lord. He's opposite to humanity.
Come, shall we in
And taste Lord Timon's bounty? He outgoes
The very heart of kindness.

2nd Lord. He pours it out; Plutus, the god of
gold,
Is but his steward. No meed but he repays
Sevenfold above itself; no gift to him,
But breeds the giver a return exceeding
All use of quittance.

1st Lord. The noblest mind he carries
That ever govern'd man.

2nd Lord. Long may he live in fortunes!
Shall we in?

1st Lord. I'll keep you company. [*Exeunt.*

SCENE II. *A banqueting-room in Timon's house. Hautboys playing loud music. A great banquet served in;* FLAVIUS *and others attending, then enter* LORD TIMON, ALCIBIADES, LORDS, SENATORS, *and* VENTIDIUS. *Then comes, dropping after all,* APEMANTUS, *discontentedly, like himself.*

Ven. Most honour'd Timon,
It hath pleased the gods to remember my father's age,
And call him to long peace.
He is gone happy, and has left me rich.
Then, as in grateful virtue I am bound
To your free heart, I do return those talents,
Doubled with thanks and service, from whose help
I derived liberty.

Tim. O, by no means,
Honest Ventidius; you mistake my love.
I gave it freely ever; and there's none
Can truly say he gives, if he receives.
If our betters play at that game, we must not dare
To imitate them; faults that are rich are fair.

Ven. A noble spirit!

Tim. Nay, my lords,

They all stand ceremoniously looking on TIMON.

Ceremony was but devised at first
To set a gloss on faint deeds, hollow welcomes,
Recanting goodness, sorry ere 'tis shown;
But where there is true friendship, there needs none.
Pray, sit; more welcome are ye to my fortunes
Than my fortunes to me.

They sit.

1st Lord. My lord, we always have confess'd it.

Apem. Ho, ho, confess'd it! Hang'd it, have you not?

Tim. O, Apemantus, you are welcome.

Apem. No;
You shall not make me welcome.
I come to have thee thrust me out of doors.

Tim. Fie, thou'rt a churl; ye've got a humour there
Does not become a man; 'tis much to blame.
They say, my lords, "*ira furor brevis est*"; but yond man is ever angry. Go, let him have a table by himself, for he does neither affect company, nor is he fit for't, indeed.

Apem. Let me stay at thine apperil, Timon.
I come to observe; I give thee warning on't.

Tim. I take no heed of thee; thou 'rt an Athenian, therefore welcome. I myself would have no power; prithee, let my meat make thee silent.

Apem. I scorn thy meat; 'twould choke me, for I should ne'er flatter thee. O you gods, what a number of men eat Timon, and he sees 'em not! It grieves me to see so many dip their meat in one man's blood; and all the madness is, he cheers them up too.
I wonder men dare trust themselves with men.
Methinks they should invite them without knives;
Good for their meat, and safer for their lives.
There's much example for't; the fellow that sits next him now, parts bread with him, pledges the breath of him in a divided draught, is the readiest man to kill him; 't has been proved. If I were a huge man, I should fear to drink at meals;
Lest they should spy my windpipe's dangerous notes.
Great men should drink with harness on their throats.

Tim. My lord, in heart; and let the health go round.

2nd Lord. Let it flow this way, my good lord.

Apem. Flow this way! A brave fellow! he keeps his tides well. Those healths will make thee and thy state look ill, Timon. Here's that which is too weak to be a sinner, honest water, which ne'er left man i' the mire.
This and my food are equals; there's no odds.
Feasts are too proud to give thanks to the gods.

Apemantus' grace

Immortal gods, I crave no pelf;
I pray for no man but myself.
Grant I may never prove so fond,
To trust man on his oath or bond;
Or a harlot, for her weeping;
Or a dog, that seems a-sleeping;
Or a keeper with my freedom;
Or my friends, if I should need 'em.
Amen. So fall to 't.
Rich men sin, and I eat root.

Eats and drinks.

Much good dich thy good heart, Apemantus!

Tim. Captain Alcibiades, your heart's in the field now.

Alcib. My heart is ever at your service, my lord.

Tim. You had rather be at a breakfast of enemies than a dinner of friends.

Alcib. So they were bleeding-new, my lord, there's no meat like 'em. I could wish my best friend at such a feast.

Apem. Would all those flatterers were thine enemies then, that then thou mightst kill 'em and bid me to 'em!

1st Lord. Might we but have that happiness, my lord, that you would once use our hearts, whereby we might express some part of our zeals, we should think ourselves for ever perfect.

Tim. O, no doubt, my good friends, but the gods themselves have provided that I shall have much help from you. How had you been my friends else? Why have you that charitable title from thousands, did not you chiefly belong to my heart? I have told more of you to myself than you can with modesty speak in your own behalf; and thus far I confirm you. O you gods, think I, what need we have any friends, if we should ne'er have need of 'em? They were the most needless creatures living, should we ne'er have use for 'em, and would most resemble sweet instruments hung up in cases that keep their sounds to themselves. Why, I have often wished myself poorer, that I might come nearer to you. We are born to do benefits; and what better or properer can we call our own than the riches of our friends? O, what a precious comfort 'tis, to have so many, like brothers, commanding one another's fortunes! O joy, e'en made away ere 't can be born! Mine eyes cannot hold out water, methinks; to forget their faults, I drink to you.

Apem. Thou weepest to make them drink, Timon.

2nd Lord. Joy had the like conception in our eyes
And at that instant like a babe sprung up.

Apem. Ho, ho! I laugh to think that babe a bastard.

3rd Lord. I promise you, my lord, you moved me much.

Apem. Much!

Tucket, within.

Tim. What means that trump?

Enter a SERVANT.

How now?

Serv. Please you, my lord, there are certain ladies most desirous of admittance.

Tim. Ladies! what are their wills?

Serv. There comes with them a forerunner, my lord, which bears that office, to signify their pleasures.

Tim. I pray, let them be admitted.

Enter CUPID.

Cup. Hail to thee, worthy Timon, and to all
That of his bounties taste! The five best senses
Acknowledge thee their patron: and come freely
To gratulate thy plenteous bosom. Th' ear,
Taste, touch and smell, pleased from thy table rise;
They only now come but to feast thine eyes.

Tim. They're welcome all; let 'em have kind admittance:
Music, make their welcome! [*Exit* CUPID.

1st Lord. You see, my lord, how ample you're beloved.

Music. Re-enter CUPID, *with a mask of* LADIES *as Amazons with lutes in their hands, dancing and playing.*

Apem. Hoy-day, what a sweep of vanity comes this way!
They dance! they are mad women.
Like madness is the glory of this life,
As this pomp shows to a little oil and root.
We make ourselves fools to disport ourselves;
And spend our flatteries to drink those men
Upon whose age we void it up again,
With poisonous spite and envy.
Who lives that's not depraved or depraves?
Who dies, that bears not one spurn to their graves
Of their friends' gift?
I should fear those that dance before me now
Would one day stamp upon me. 'T has been done;
Men shut their doors against a setting sun.

The LORDS *rise from table, with much adoring of* TIMON; *and to show their loves, each singles out an* AMAZON, *and all dance, men with women, a lofty strain or two to the hautboys, and cease.*

Tim. You have done our pleasures much grace, fair ladies,
Set a fair fashion on our entertainment,
Which was not half so beautiful and kind;
You have added worth unto 't and lustre,
And entertain'd me with mine own device;
I am to thank you for 't.

1st Lady. My lord, you take us even at the best.

Apem. 'Faith, for the worst is filthy; and would not hold taking, I doubt me.

Tim. Ladies, there is an idle banquet attends you.
Please you to dispose yourselves.

All Ladies. Most thankfully, my lord.

[*Exeunt* CUPID *and* LADIES.

Tim. Flavius.

Flav. My lord?

Tim. The little casket bring me hither.

Flav. Yes, my lord. More jewels yet! [*Aside.*]
There is no crossing him in 's humour;
Else I should tell him—well, i' faith, I should,
When all's spent, he'd be cross'd then, an he could.
'Tis pity bounty had not eyes behind,
That man might ne'er be wretched for his mind.

[*Exit.*

1st Lord. Where be our men?

Serv. Here, my lord, in readiness.

2nd Lord. Our horses!

Re-enter FLAVIUS, *with the casket.*

Tim. O my friends,
I have one word to say to you. Look you, my good lord,
I must entreat you, honour me so much
As to advance this jewel; accept it and wear it,
Kind my lord.

1st Lord. I am so far already in your gifts—

All. So are we all.

Enter a SERVANT.

Serv. My lord, there are certain nobles of the Senate
Newly alighted, and come to visit you.

Tim. They are fairly welcome.

Flav. I beseech your honour,
Vouchsafe me a word; it does concern you near.

Tim. Near! why then, another time I'll hear thee.
I prithee, let's be provided to show them entertainment.

Flav. [*Aside*] I scarce know how.

Enter a SECOND SERVANT.

2nd Serv. May it please your honour, Lord Lucius,
Out of his free love, hath presented to you
Four milk-white horses, trapp'd in silver.

Tim. I shall accept them fairly; let the presents
Be worthily entertain'd.

Enter a THIRD SERVANT.

How now! what news?

3rd Serv. Please you, my lord, that honourable gentleman, Lord Lucullus, entreats your company to-morrow to hunt with him, and has sent your honour two brace of greyhounds.

Tim. I'll hunt with him; and let them be received,
Not without fair reward.

Flav. [*Aside*] What will this come to?
He commands us to provide, and give great gifts,
And all out of an empty coffer.
Nor will he know his purse, or yield me this,
To show him what a beggar his heart is,
Being of no power to make his wishes good.
His promises fly so beyond his state
That what he speaks is all in debt; he owes
For every word. He is so kind that he now
Pays interest for't; his land's put to their books.
Well, would I were gently put out of office
Before I were forced out!
Happier is he that has no friend to feed
Than such that do e'en enemies exceed.
I bleed inwardly for my lord. *Exit.*

Tim. You do yourselves
Much wrong, you bate too much of your own merits.
Here, my lord, a trifle of our love.

2nd Lord. With more than common thanks I will receive it.

3rd Lord. O, he's the very soul of bounty!

Tim. And now I remember, my lord, you gave
Good words the other day of a bay courser
I rode on. It is yours, because you liked it.

2nd Lord. O, I beseech you, pardon me, my lord, in that.

Tim. You may take my word, my lord; I know, no man
Can justly praise but what he does affect.
I weigh my friend's affection with mine own;
I'll tell you true. I'll call to you.

All Lords. O, none so welcome.

Tim. I take all and your several visitations
So kind to heart, 'tis not enough to give;
Methinks, I could deal kingdoms to my friends,
And ne'er be weary. Alcibiades,
Thou art a soldier, therefore seldom rich;
It comes in charity to thee. For all thy living
Is 'mongst the dead, and all the lands thou hast
Lie in a pitch'd field.

Alcib. Ay, defiled land, my lord.

1st Lord. We are so virtuously bound—

Tim. And so
Am I to you.

2nd Lord. So infinitely endear'd—

Tim. All to you. Lights, more lights!

1st Lord. The best of happiness,
Honour and fortunes, keep with you, Lord Timon!

Tim. Ready for his friends.

[*Exeunt all but* APEMANTUS *and* TIMON.

Apem. What a coil's here!
Serving of becks and jutting-out of bums!
I doubt whether their legs be worth the sums
That are given for 'em. Friendship's full of dregs.
Methinks, false hearts should never have sound legs.
Thus honest fools lay out their wealth on court'sies.

Tim. Now, Apemantus, if thou wert not sullen,
I would be good to thee.

Apem. No, I'll nothing. For if I should be bribed too, there would be none left to rail upon thee, and then thou wouldst sin the faster. Thou givest so long, Timon, I fear me thou wilt give away thyself in paper shortly. What need these feasts, pomps, and vain-glories?

Tim. Nay, an you begin to rail on society once, I am sworn not to give regard to you.

Farewell; and come with better music. [*Exit.*
Apem. So;
Thou wilt not hear me now; thou shalt not then;
I'll lock thy heaven from thee.
O, that men's ears should be
To counsel deaf, but not to flattery! [*Exit.*

ACT II

SCENE I. *A Senator's house*

Enter SENATOR, *with papers in his hand.*

Sen. And late, five thousand; to Varro and to Isidore
He owes nine thousand; besides my former sum,
Which makes it five and twenty. Still in motion
Of raging waste? It cannot hold; it will not.
If I want gold, steal but a beggar's dog,
And give it Timon, why, the dog coins gold.
If I would sell my horse, and buy twenty more
Better than he, why, give my horse to Timon,
Ask nothing, give it him, it foals me, straight,
And able horses. No porter at his gate,
But rather one that smiles and still invites
All that pass by. It cannot hold; no reason
Can found his state in safety. Caphis, ho!
Caphis, I say!

Enter CAPHIS.

Caph. Here, sir; what is your pleasure?
Sen. Get on your cloak, and haste you to Lord Timon;
Importune him for my moneys; be not ceased
With slight denial, nor then silenced when—
"Commend me to your master," and the cap
Plays in the right hand, thus; but tell him,
My uses cry to me, I must serve my turn
Out of mine own; his days and times are past
And my reliances on his fracted dates
Have smit my credit. I love and honour him,
But must not break my back to heal his finger;
Immediate are my needs, and my relief
Must not be toss'd and turn'd to me in words,
But find supply immediate. Get you gone.
Put on a most importunate aspect,
A visage of demand; for, I do fear,
When every feather sticks in his own wing,
Lord Timon will be left a naked gull,
Which flashes now a phœnix. Get you gone.
Caph. I go, sir.
Sen. "I go, sir!" Take the bonds along with you,
And have the dates in compt.
Caph. I will, sir.
Sen. Go. [*Exeunt.*

SCENE II. *The same: a hall in Timon's house*

Enter FLAVIUS, *with many bills in his hand.*

Flavius. No care, no stop! so senseless of expense,
That he will neither know how to maintain it,
Nor cease his flow of riot; takes no account
How things go from him, nor resumes no care
Of what is to continue; never mind
Was to be so unwise, to be so kind.
What shall be done? He will not hear, till feel.
I must be round with him, now he comes from hunting.
Fie, fie, fie, fie!

Enter CAPHIS, *and the* SERVANTS *of* ISIDORE *and* VARRO.

Caph. Good even, Varro. What,
You come for money?
Var. Serv. Is 't not your business too?
Caph. It is; and yours too, Isidore?
Isid. Serv. It is so.
Caph. Would we were all discharged!
Var. Serv. I fear it.
Caph. Here comes the lord.

Enter TIMON, ALCIBIADES, *and* LORDS, *&c.*

Tim. So soon as dinner's done, we'll forth again,
My Alcibiades. With me? What is your will?
Caph. My lord, here is a note of certain dues.
Tim. Dues! Whence are you?
Caph. Of Athens here, my lord.
Tim. Go to my steward.
Caph. Please it your lordship, he hath put me off
To the succession of new days this month.
My master is awaked by great occasion
To call upon his own, and humbly prays you
That with your other noble parts you'll suit
In giving him his right.
Tim. Mine honest friend,
I prithee, but repair to me next morning.
Caph. Nay, good my lord—
Tim. Contain thyself, good friend.
Var. Serv. One Varro's servant, my good lord—
Isid. Serv. From Isidore;
He humbly prays your speedy payment.
Caph. If you did know, my lord, my master's wants—
Var. Serv. 'Twas due on forfeiture, my lord, six weeks
And past.
Isid. Serv. Your steward puts me off, my lord;
And I am sent expressly to your lordship.
Tim. Give me breath.

I do beseech you, good my lords, keep on;
I'll wait upon you instantly.
[*Exeunt* ALCIBIADES *and* LORDS.
[*To* FLAVIUS] Come hither. Pray you,
How goes the world, that I am thus encounter'd
With clamorous demands of date-broke bonds,
And the detention of long-since-due debts,
Against my honour?

Flav. Please you, gentlemen,
The time is unagreeable to this business.
Your importunacy cease till after dinner,
That I may make his lordship understand
Wherefore you are not paid.

Tim. Do so, my friends. See them well entertain'd. [*Exit.*

Flav. Pray, draw near. [*Exit.*

Enter APEMANTUS *and* FOOL.

Caph. Stay, stay, here comes the Fool with Apemantus. Let's ha' some sport with 'em.

Var. Serv. Hang him, he'll abuse us.

Isid. Serv. A plague upon him, dog!

Var. Serv. How dost, Fool?

Apem. Dost dialogue with thy shadow?

Var. Serv. I speak not to thee.

Apem. No, 'tis to thyself. [*To the* FOOL] Come away.

Isid. Serv. There's the Fool hangs on your back already.

Apem. No, thou stand'st single, thou'rt not on him yet.

Caph. Where's the Fool now?

Apem. He last asked the question. Poor rogues, and usurers' men! bawds between gold and want!

All Serv. What are we, Apemantus?

Apem. Asses.

All Serv. Why?

Apem. That you ask me what you are, and do not know yourselves. Speak to 'em, Fool.

Fool. How do you, gentlemen?

All Serv. Gramercies, good Fool; how does your mistress?

Fool. She's e'en setting on water to scald such chickens as you are. Would we could see you at Corinth!

Apem. Good! gramercy.

Enter PAGE.

Fool. Look you, here comes my mistress' page.

Page. [*To the* FOOL] Why, how now, captain! what do you in this wise company? How dost thou, Apemantus?

Apem. Would I had a rod in my mouth, that I might answer thee profitably.

Page. Prithee, Apemantus, read me the superscription of these letters; I know not which is which.

Apem. Canst not read?

Page. No.

Apem. There will little learning die then, that day thou art hanged. This is to Lord Timon; this to Alcibiades. Go; thou wast born a bastard, and thou't die a bawd.

Page. Thou wast whelped a dog, and thou shalt famish a dog's death. Answer not; I am gone. [*Exit.*

Apem. E'en so thou outrunnest grace. Fool, I will go with you to Lord Timon's.

Fool. Will you leave me there?

Apem. If Timon stay at home. You three serve three usurers?

All Serv. Ay; would they served us!

Apem. So would I—as good a trick as ever hangman served thief.

Fool. Are you three usurers' men?

All Serv. Ay, Fool.

Fool. I think no usurer but has a fool to his servant; my mistress is one, and I am her fool. When men come to borrow of your masters, they approach sadly, and go away merry; but they enter my mistress' house merrily, and go away sadly. The reason of this?

Var. Serv. I could render one.

Apem. Do it then, that we may account thee a whoremaster and a knave; which notwithstanding, thou shalt be no less esteemed.

Var. Serv. What is a whoremaster, Fool?

Fool. A fool in good clothes, and something like thee. 'Tis a spirit; sometime 't appears like a lord; sometime like a lawyer; sometime like a philosopher, with two stones more than's artificial one. He is very often like a knight; and, generally, in all shapes that man goes up and down in from fourscore to thirteen, this spirit walks in.

Var. Serv. Thou art not altogether a fool.

Fool. Nor thou altogether a wise man. As much foolery as I have, so much wit thou lackest.

Apem. That answer might have become Apemantus.

All Serv. Aside, aside; here comes Lord Timon.

Re-enter TIMON *and* FLAVIUS.

Apem. Come with me, Fool, come.

Fool. I do not always follow lover, elder brother, and woman; sometime the philosopher.
[*Exeunt* APEMANTUS *and* FOOL.

Flav. Pray you, walk near. I'll speak with you anon. [*Exeunt* SERVANTS.

Tim. You make me marvel. Wherefore ere this time
Had you not fully laid my state before me,

That I might so have rated my expense,
As I had leave of means?
Flav. You would not hear me,
At many leisures I proposed.
Tim. Go to.
Perchance some single vantages you took,
When my indisposition put you back;
And that unaptness made your minister,
Thus to excuse yourself.
Flav. O my good lord,
At many times I brought in my accounts,
Laid them before you; you would throw them off,
And say you found them in mine honesty.
When, for some trifling present, you have bid me
Return so much, I have shook my head and wept;
Yea, 'gainst the authority of manners, pray'd you
To hold your hand more close. I did endure
Not seldom, nor no slight checks, when I have
Prompted you in the ebb of your estate
And your great flow of debts. My loved lord,
Though you hear now, too late—yet now's a time—
The greatest of your having lacks a half
To pay your present debts.
Tim. Let all my land be sold.
Flav. 'Tis all engaged, some forfeited and gone;
And what remains will hardly stop the mouth
Of present dues. The future comes apace;
What shall defend the interim? and at length
How goes our reckoning?
Tim. To Lacedæmon did my land extend.
Flav. O my good lord, the world is but a word;
Were it all yours to give it in a breath,
How quickly were it gone!
Tim. You tell me true.
Flav. If you suspect my husbandry or falsehood,
Call me before the exactest auditors
And set me on the proof. So the gods bless me,
When all our offices have been oppress'd
With riotous feeders, when our vaults have wept
With drunken spilth of wine, when every room
Hath blazed with lights and bray'd with minstrelsy,
I have retired me to a wasteful cock,
And set mine eyes at flow.
Tim. Prithee, no more.
Flav. Heavens, have I said, the bounty of this lord!
How many prodigal bits have slaves and peasants
This night englutted! Who is not Timon's?
What heart, head, sword, force, means, but is Lord Timon's?
Great Timon, noble, worthy, royal Timon!
Ah, when the means are gone that buy this praise,
The breath is gone whereof this praise is made.
Feast-won, fast-lost; one cloud of winter showers,
These flies are couch'd.
Tim. Come, sermon me no further.
No villainous bounty yet hath pass'd my heart;
Unwisely, not ignobly, have I given.
Why dost thou weep? Canst thou the conscience lack,
To think I shall lack friends? Secure thy heart;
If I would broach the vessels of my love,
And try the argument of hearts by borrowing,
Men and men's fortunes could I frankly use
As I can bid thee speak.
Flav. Assurance bless your thoughts!
Tim. And, in some sort, these wants of mine are crown'd,
That I account them blessings; for by these
Shall I try friends. You shall perceive how you
Mistake my fortunes; I am wealthy in my friends.
Within there! Flaminius! Servilius!

Enter FLAMINIUS, SERVILIUS, *and other* SERVANTS.

Servants. My lord? my lord?
Tim. I will dispatch you severally; you to Lord Lucius; to Lord Lucullus you, I hunted with his honour to-day; you, to Sempronius. Commend me to their loves, and, I am proud, say, that my occasions have found time to use 'em toward a supply of money. Let the request be fifty talents.
Flam. As you have said, my lord.
Flav. [*Aside*] Lord Lucius and Lucullus? hum!
Tim. Go you, sir, to the senators—
Of whom, even to the state's best health, I have
Deserved this hearing—bid 'em send o' the instant
A thousand talents to me.
Flav. I have been bold—
For that I knew it the most general way—
To them to use your signet and your name;
But they do shake their heads, and I am here
No richer in return.
Tim. Is't true? can't be?
Flav. They answer, in a joint and corporate voice,
That now they are at fall, want treasure, cannot
Do what they would; are sorry—you are honourable—
But yet they could have wish'd—they know not—
Something hath been amiss—a noble nature
May catch a wrench—would all were well—'tis pity—

And so, intending other serious matters,
After distasteful looks and these hard fractions,
With certain half-caps and cold-moving nods
They froze me into silence.

Tim. You gods, reward them!
Prithee, man, look cheerly. These old fellows
Have their ingratitude in them hereditary.
Their blood is caked, 'tis cold, it seldom flows;
'Tis lack of kindly warmth they are not kind;
And nature, as it grows again toward earth,
Is fashion'd for the journey, dull and heavy.
[*To a* SERVANT] Go to Ventidius. [*To* FLAVIUS]
Prithee, be not sad,
Thou art true and honest; ingeniously I speak,
No blame belongs to thee. [*To* SERVANT] Ventidius lately
Buried his father; by whose death he's stepp'd
Into a great estate. When he was poor,
Imprison'd, and in scarcity of friends,
I clear'd him with five talents. Greet him from me;
Bid him suppose some good necessity
Touches his friend, which craves to be remember'd
With those five talents [*Exit* SERVANT]. [*To* FLAVIUS] That had, give 't these fellows
To whom 'tis instant due. Ne'er speak, or think,
That Timon's fortunes 'mong his friends can sink.

Flav. I would I could not think it. That thought is bounty's foe;
Being free itself, it thinks all others so. [*Exeunt.*

ACT III

SCENE I. *A room in Lucullus' house*

FLAMINIUS *waiting. Enter a* SERVANT *to him.*

Serv. I have told my lord of you; he is coming down to you.

Flam. I thank you, sir.

Enter LUCULLUS.

Serv. Here's my lord.

Lucul. [*Aside*] One of Lord Timon's men? a gift, I warrant. Why, this hits right; I dreamt of a silver basin and ewer to-night. Flaminius, honest Flaminius; you are very respectively welcome, sir. Fill me some wine. [*Exit* SERVANT.] And how does that honourable, complete, free-hearted gentleman of Athens, thy very bountiful good lord and master?

Flam. His health is well, sir.

Lucul. I am right glad that his health is well, sir. And what hast thou there under thy cloak, pretty Flaminius?

Flam. 'Faith, nothing but an empty box, sir; which, in my lord's behalf, I come to entreat your honour to supply; who, having great and instant occasion to use fifty talents, hath sent to your lordship to furnish him, nothing doubting your present assistance therein.

Lucul. La, la, la, la! "nothing doubting," says he? Alas, good lord! a noble gentleman 'tis, if he would not keep so good a house. Many a time and often I ha' dined with him, and told him on't, and come again to supper to him, of purpose to have him spend less, and yet he would embrace no counsel, take no warning by my coming. Every man has his fault, and honesty is his. I ha' told him on 't, but I could ne'er get him from 't.

Re-enter SERVANT, *with wine.*

Serv. Please your lordship, here is the wine.

Lucul. Flaminius, I have noted thee always wise. Here's to thee.

Flam. Your lordship speaks your pleasure.

Lucul. I have observed thee always for a towardly prompt spirit—give thee thy due—and one that knows what belongs to reason; and canst use the time well, if the time use thee well; good parts in thee. [*To* SERVANT] Get you gone, sirrah [*Exit* SERVANT]. Draw nearer, honest Flaminius. Thy lord's a bountiful gentleman; but thou art wise; and thou knowest well enough, although thou comest to me, that this is no time to lend money, especially upon bare friendship, without security. Here's three solidares for thee; good boy, wink at me, and say thou sawest me not. Fare thee well.

Flam. Is 't possible the world should so much differ,
And we alive that lived? Fly, damned baseness,
To him that worships thee!
Throwing the money back.

Lucul. Ha! now I see thou art a fool, and fit for thy master. [*Exit.*

Flam. May these add to the number that may scald thee!
Let molten coin be thy damnation,
Thou disease of a friend, and not himself!
Has friendship such a faint and milky heart,
It turns in less than two nights? O you gods,
I feel my master's passion! this slave,
Unto his honour, has my lord's meat in him.
Why should it thrive and turn to nutriment,
When he is turn'd to poison?
O, may diseases only work upon 't!
And, when he's sick to death, let not that part of nature
Which my lord paid for, be of any power
To expel sickness, but prolong his hour! [*Exit.*

Scene ii. *A public place*

Enter Lucius, *with* three strangers.

Luc. Who, the Lord Timon? He is my very good friend, and an honourable gentleman.

1st Stran. We know him for no less, though we are but strangers to him. But I can tell you one thing, my lord, and which I hear from common rumours: now Lord Timon's happy hours are done and past, and his estate shrinks from him.

Luc. Fie, no, do not believe it; he cannot want for money.

2nd Stran. But believe you this, my lord, that, not long ago, one of his men was with the Lord Lucullus to borrow so many talents, nay, urged extremely for 't and showed what necessity belonged to 't, and yet was denied.

Luc. How!

2nd Stran. I tell you, denied, my lord.

Luc. What a strange case was that! now, before the gods, I am ashamed on 't. Denied that honourable man! there was very little honour showed in 't. For my own part, I must needs confess, I have received some small kindnesses from him, as money, plate, jewels, and such-like trifles, nothing comparing to his; yet, had he mistook him and sent to me, I should ne'er have denied his occasion so many talents.

Enter Servilius.

Ser. See, by good hap, yonder's my lord; I have sweat to see his honour. My honoured lord— [*To* Lucius.]

Luc. Servilius! you are kindly met, sir. Fare thee well. Commend me to thy honourable virtuous lord, my very exquisite friend.

Ser. May it please your honour, my lord hath sent—

Luc. Ha! what has he sent? I am so much endeared to that lord; he's ever sending. How shall I thank him, thinkest thou? And what has he sent now?

Ser. Has only sent his present occasion now, my lord; requesting your lordship to supply his instant use with so many talents.

Luc. I know his lordship is but merry with me;
He cannot want fifty-five hundred talents.

Ser. But in the mean time he wants less, my lord.
If his occasion were not virtuous,
I should not urge it half so faithfully.

Luc. Dost thou speak seriously, Servilius?

Ser. Upon my soul, 'tis true, sir.

Luc. What a wicked beast was I to disfurnish myself against such a good time, when I might ha' shown myself honourable! How unluckily it happened that I should purchase the day before for a little part, and undo a great deal of honour! Servilius, now, before the gods, I am not able to do—the more beast, I say. I was sending to use Lord Timon myself, these gentlemen can witness; but I would not, for the wealth of Athens, I had done 't now. Commend me bountifully to his good lordship; and I hope his honour will conceive the fairest of me, because I have no power to be kind; and tell him this from me, I count it one of my greatest afflictions, say, that I cannot pleasure such an honourable gentleman. Good Servilius, will you befriend me so far as to use mine own words to him?

Ser. Yes, sir, I shall.

Luc. I'll look you out a good turn, Servilius.
[*Exit* Servilius.
True, as you said, Timon is shrunk indeed;
And he that's once denied will hardly speed.
[*Exit.*

1st Stran. Do you observe this, Hostilius?

2nd Stran. Ay, too well.

1st Stran. Why, this is the world's soul; and just of the same piece
Is every flatterer's spirit. Who can call him
His friend that dips in the same dish? for, in
My knowing, Timon has been this lord's father,
And kept his credit with his purse,
Supported his estate; nay, Timon's money
Has paid his men their wages. He ne'er drinks,
But Timon's silver treads upon his lip;
And yet—O, see the monstrousness of man
When he looks out in an ungrateful shape!—
He does deny him, in respect of his,
What charitable men afford to beggars.

3rd Stran. Religion groans at it.

1st Stran. For mine own part,
I never tasted Timon in my life,
Nor came any of his bounties over me,
To mark me for his friend; yet, I protest,
For his right noble mind, illustrious virtue
And honourable carriage,
Had his necessity made use of me,
I would have put my wealth into donation,
And the best half should have return'd to him,
So much I love his heart. But I perceive
Men must learn now with pity to dispense,
For policy sits above conscience. [*Exeunt.*

Scene iii. *A room in Sempronius' house*

Enter Sempronius, *and a* servant *of* Timon's.

Sem. Must he needs trouble me in 't—hum!— 'bove all others?
He might have tried Lord Lucius or Lucullus;
And now Ventidius is wealthy too,
Whom he redeem'd from prison. All these
Owe their estates unto him.

Serv. My lord,
They have all been touch'd and found base metal, for
They have all denied him.
Sem. How! have they denied him?
Has Ventidius and Lucullus denied him?
And does he send to me? Three? hum!
It shows but little love or judgement in him.
Must I be his last refuge? His friends, like physicians,
Thrice give him over; must I take the cure upon me?
Has much disgraced me in 't; I'm angry at him,
That might have known my place. I see no sense for 't,
But his occasions might have woo'd me first;
For, in my conscience, I was the first man
That e'er received gift from him;
And does he think so backwardly of me now,
That I'll requite it last? No!
So it may prove an argument of laughter
To the rest, and 'mongst lords I be thought a fool.
I'd rather than the worth of thrice the sum,
Had sent to me first, but for my mind's sake;
I'd such a courage to do him good. But now return,
And with their faint reply this answer join;
Who bates mine honour shall not know my coin.
[*Exit.*

Serv. Excellent! Your lordship's a goodly villain. The devil knew not what he did when he made man politic; he crossed himself by 't; and I cannot think but, in the end, the villanies of man will set him clear. How fairly this lord strives to appear foul! takes virtuous copies to be wicked, like those that under hot ardent zeal would set whole realms on fire;
Of such a nature is his politic love.
This was my lord's best hope; now all are fled,
Save only the gods. Now his friends are dead,
Doors, that were ne'er acquainted with their wards
Many a bounteous year, must be employ'd
Now to guard sure their master.
And this is all a liberal course allows;
Who cannot keep his wealth must keep his house. [*Exit.*

SCENE IV. *The same: a hall in Timon's house*

Enter TWO SERVANTS *of* VARRO, *and the* SERVANT *of* LUCIUS, *meeting* TITUS, HORTENSIUS, *and other* SERVANTS *of* TIMON'S *creditors, waiting his coming out.*

1st Var. Serv. Well met; good morrow, Titus and Hortensius.
Tit. The like to you, kind Varro.
Hor. Lucius!
What, do we meet together?
Luc. Serv. Ay, and I think
One business does command us all; for mine
Is money.
Tit. So is theirs and ours.

Enter PHILOTUS.

Luc. Serv. And Sir Philotus too!
Phi. Good day at once.
Luc. Serv. Welcome, good brother.
What do you think the hour?
Phi. Labouring for nine.
Luc. Serv. So much?
Phi. Is not my lord seen yet?
Luc. Serv. Not yet.
Phi. I wonder on 't; he was wont to shine at seven.
Luc. Serv. Ay, but the days are wax'd shorter with him.
You must consider that a prodigal course
Is like the sun's; but not, like his, recoverable.
I fear 'tis deepest winter in Lord Timon's purse;
That is, one may reach deep enough, and yet
Find little.
Phi. I am of your fear for that.
Tit. I'll show you how to observe a strange event.
Your lord sends now for money.
Hor. Most true, he does.
Tit. And he wears jewels now of Timon's gift,
For which I wait for money.
Hor. It is against my heart.
Luc. Serv. Mark, how strange it shows,
Timon in this should pay more than he owes;
And e'en as if your lord should wear rich jewels,
And send for money for 'em.
Hor. I'm weary of this charge, the gods can witness.
I know my lord hath spent of Timon's wealth,
And now ingratitude makes it worse than stealth.
1st Var. Serv. Yes, mine's three thousand crowns. What's yours?
Luc. Serv. Five thousand mine.
1st Var. Serv. 'Tis much deep; and it should seem by the sum,
Your master's confidence was above mine;
Else, surely, his had equall'd.

Enter FLAMINIUS.

Tit. One of Lord Timon's men.
Luc. Serv. Flaminius! Sir, a word. Pray, is my lord ready to come forth?
Flam. No, indeed, he is not.
Tit. We attend his lordship; pray, signify so much.

Flam. I need not tell him that; he knows you are too diligent. [*Exit.*

Enter FLAVIUS *in a cloak, muffled.*

Luc. Serv. Ha! is not that his steward muffled so?
He goes away in a cloud. Call him, call him.

Tit. Do you hear, sir?

2nd Var. Serv. By your leave, sir—

Flav. What do ye ask of me, my friend?

Tit. We wait for certain money here, sir.

Flav. Ay,
If money were as certain as your waiting,
'Twere sure enough.
Why then preferr'd you not your sums and bills,
When your false masters eat of my lord's meat?
Then they could smile and fawn upon his debts
And take down the interest into their gluttonous maws.
You do yourselves but wrong to stir me up;
Let me pass quietly.
Believe't, my lord and I have made an end;
I have no more to reckon, he to spend.

Luc. Serv. Ay, but this answer will not serve.

Flav. If 'twill not serve, 'tis not so base as you;
For you serve knaves. [*Exit.*

1st Var. Serv. How! what does his cashiered worship mutter?

2nd Var. Serv. No matter what; he's poor, and that's revenge enough. Who can speak broader than he that has no house to put his head in? such may rail against great buildings.

Enter SERVILIUS.

Tit. O, here's Servilius; now we shall know some answer.

Ser. If I might beseech you, gentlemen, to repair some other hour, I should derive much from 't; for, take 't of my soul, my lord leans wondrously to discontent. His comfortable temper has forsook him; he's much out of health, and keeps his chamber.

Luc. Serv. Many do keep their chambers are not sick:
And, if it be so far beyond his health,
Methinks he should the sooner pay his debts,
And make a clear way to the gods.

Ser. Good gods!

Tit. We cannot take this for answer, sir.

Flam. [*Within*] Servilius, help! My lord! my lord!

Enter TIMON, *in a rage;* FLAMINIUS *following.*

Tim. What, are my doors opposed against my passage?
Have I been ever free, and must my house
Be my retentive enemy, my gaol?
The place which I have feasted, does it now,
Like all mankind, show me an iron heart?

Luc. Serv. Put in now, Titus.

Tit. My lord, here is my bill.

Luc. Serv. Here's mine.

Hor. And mine, my lord.

Both Var. Serv. And ours, my lord.

Phi. All our bills.

Tim. Knock me down with 'em! Cleave me to the girdle.

Luc. Serv. Alas, my lord—

Tim. Cut my heart in sums.

Tit. Mine, fifty talents.

Tim. Tell out my blood.

Luc. Serv. Five thousand crowns, my lord.

Tim. Five thousand drops pays that. What yours? and yours?

1st Var. Serv. My lord—

2nd Var. Serv. My lord—

Tim. Tear me, take me, and the gods fall upon you! [*Exit.*

Hor. 'Faith, I perceive our masters may throw their caps at their money. These debts may well be called desperate ones, for a madman owes 'em. [*Exeunt.*

Re-enter TIMON *and* FLAVIUS.

Tim. They have e'en put my breath from me, the slaves.
Creditors? devils!

Flav. My dear lord—

Tim. What if it should be so?

Flav. My lord—

Tim. I'll have it so. My steward!

Flav. Here, my lord.

Tim. So fitly? Go, bid all my friends again,
Lucius, Lucullus, and Sempronius;
All, sirrah, all.
I'll once more feast the rascals.

Flav. O my lord,
You only speak from your distracted soul;
There is not so much left, to furnish out
A moderate table.

Tim. Be 't not in thy care; go,
I charge thee, invite them all. Let in the tide
Of knaves once more; my cook and I'll provide. [*Exeunt.*

SCENE V. *The same: the Senate-house*

The Senate sitting.

1st Sen. My lord, you have my voice to it; the fault's
Bloody; 'tis necessary he should die.
Nothing emboldens sin so much as mercy.

2nd Sen. Most true; the law shall bruise him.

Enter ALCIBIADES, *with Attendants.*

Alcib. Honour, health, and compassion to the Senate!
1st Sen. Now, captain?
Alcib. I am an humble suitor to your virtues;
For pity is the virtue of the law,
And none but tyrants use it cruelly.
It pleases time and fortune to lie heavy
Upon a friend of mine, who, in hot blood,
Hath stepp'd into the law, which is past depth
To those that, without heed, do plunge into 't.
He is a man, setting his fate aside,
Of comely virtues.
Nor did he soil the fact with cowardice—
An honour in him which buys out his fault—
But with a noble fury and fair spirit,
Seeing his reputation touch'd to death,
He did oppose his foe;
And with such sober and unnoted passion
He did behave his anger, ere 'twas spent,
As if he had but proved an argument.
1st Sen. You undergo too strict a paradox,
Striving to make an ugly deed look fair.
Your words have took such pains as if they labour'd
To bring manslaughter into form and set quarrelling
Upon the head of valour; which indeed
Is valour misbegot and came into the world
When sects and factions were newly born.
He's truly valiant that can wisely suffer
The worst that man can breathe, and make his wrongs
His outsides, to wear them like his raiment, carelessly,
And ne'er prefer his injuries to his heart,
To bring it into danger.
If wrongs be evils and enforce us kill,
What folly 'tis to hazard life for ill!
Alcib. My lord—
1st Sen. You cannot make gross sins look clear.
To revenge is no valour, but to bear.
Alcib. My lords, then, under favour, pardon me,
If I speak like a captain.
Why do fond men expose themselves to battle,
And not endure all threats? sleep upon 't,
And let the foes quietly cut their throats,
Without repugnancy? If there be
Such valour in the bearing, what make we
Abroad? why then, women are more valiant
That stay at home, if bearing carry it,
And the ass more captain than the lion, the felon
Loaden with irons wiser than the judge,
If wisdom be in suffering. O my lords,
As you are great, be pitifully good.
Who cannot condemn rashness in cold blood?
To kill, I grant, is sin's extremest gust;
But, in defence, by mercy, 'tis most just.
To be in anger is impiety;
But who is man that is not angry?
Weigh but the crime with this.
2nd Sen. You breathe in vain.
Alcib. In vain! his service done
At Lacedæmon and Byzantium
Were a sufficient briber for his life.
1st Sen. What's that?
Alcib. I say, my lords, he has done fair service,
And slain in fight many of your enemies.
How full of valour did he bear himself
In the last conflict, and made plenteous wounds!
2nd Sen. He has made too much plenty with 'em;
He's a sworn rioter; he has a sin that often
Drowns him, and takes his valour prisoner.
If there were no foes, that were enough
To overcome him. In that beastly fury
He has been known to commit outrages
And cherish factions. 'Tis inferr'd to us
His days are foul and his drink dangerous.
1st Sen. He dies.
Alcib. Hard fate! he might have died in war.
My lords, if not for any parts in him—
Though his right arm might purchase his own time
And be in debt to none—yet, more to move you,
Take my deserts to his, and join 'em both;
And, for I know your reverend ages love
Security, I'll pawn my victories, all
My honours to you, upon his good returns.
If by this crime he owes the law his life,
Why, let the war receive 't in valiant gore;
For law is strict, and war is nothing more.
1st Sen. We are for law. He dies. Urge it no more,
On height of our displeasure. Friend or brother,
He forfeits his own blood that spills another.
Alcib. Must it be so? it must not be. My lords,
I do beseech you, know me.
2nd Sen. How!
Alcib. Call me to your remembrances.
3rd Sen. What!
Alcib. I cannot think but your age has forgot me;
It could not else be, I should prove so base,
To sue, and be denied such common grace.
My wounds ache at you.
1st Sen. Do you dare our anger?
'Tis in few words, but spacious in effect;
We banish thee for ever.

Alcib. Banish me!
Banish your dotage; banish usury,
That makes the Senate ugly.

1st Sen. If, after two days' shine, Athens contain thee,
Attend our weightier judgement. And, not to swell our spirit,
He shall be executed presently.

[*Exeunt* SENATORS.

Alcib. Now the gods keep you old enough; that you may live
Only in bone, that none may look on you!
I'm worse than mad. I have kept back their foes,
While they have told their money and let out
Their coin upon large interest, I myself
Rich only in large hurts. All those for this?
Is this the balsam that the usuring Senate
Pours into captains' wounds? Banishment!
It comes not ill; I hate not to be banish'd;
It is a cause worthy my spleen and fury,
That I may strike at Athens. I'll cheer up
My discontented troops, and lay for hearts.
'Tis honour with most lands to be at odds;
Soldiers should brook as little wrongs as gods.

[*Exit.*

SCENE VI. *The same: a banqueting-room in Timon's house*

Music. Tables set out: Servants attending. Enter divers LORDS, SENATORS *and others, at several doors.*

1st Lord. The good time of day to you, sir.

2nd Lord. I also wish it to you. I think this honourable lord did but try us this other day.

1st Lord. Upon that were my thoughts tiring, when we encountered. I hope it is not so low with him as he made it seem in the trial of his several friends.

2nd Lord. It should not be, by the persuasion of his new feasting.

1st Lord. I should think so. He hath sent me an earnest inviting, which many my near occasions did urge me to put off; but he hath conjured me beyond them, and I must needs appear.

2nd Lord. In like manner was I in debt to my importunate business, but he would not hear my excuse. I am sorry, when he sent to borrow of me, that my provision was out.

1st Lord. I am sick of that grief too, as I understand how all things go.

2nd Lord. Every man here's so. What would he have borrowed of you?

1st Lord. A thousand pieces.

2nd Lord. A thousand pieces!

1st Lord. What of you?

2nd Lord. He sent to me, sir—Here he comes.

Enter TIMON *and Attendants.*

Tim. With all my heart, gentlemen both; and how fare you?

1st Lord. Ever at the best, hearing well of your lordship.

2nd Lord. The swallow follows not summer more willing than we your lordship.

Tim. [Aside] Nor more willingly leaves winter; such summer-birds are men. Gentlemen, our dinner will not recompense this long stay. Feast your ears with the music awhile, if they will fare so harshly o' the trumpet's sound; we shall to 't presently.

1st Lord. I hope it remains not unkindly with your lordship that I returned you an empty messenger.

Tim. O, sir, let it not trouble you.

2nd Lord. My noble lord—

Tim. Ah, my good friend, what cheer?

2nd Lord. My most honourable lord, I am e'en sick of shame that, when your lordship this other day sent to me, I was so unfortunate a beggar.

Tim. Think not on 't, sir.

2nd Lord. If you had sent but two hours before—

Tim. Let it not cumber your better remembrance. [*The banquet brought in.*] Come, bring in all together.

2nd Lord. All covered dishes!

1st Lord. Royal cheer, I warrant you.

3rd Lord. Doubt not that, if money and the season can yield it.

1st Lord. How do you? What's the news?

3rd Lord. Alcibiades is banished. Hear you of it?

1st and 2nd Lord. Alcibiades banished!

3rd Lord. 'Tis so, be sure of it.

1st Lord. How! how!

2nd Lord. I pray you, upon what?

Tim. My worthy friends, will you draw near?

3rd Lord. I'll tell you more anon. Here's a noble feast toward.

2nd Lord. This is the old man still.

3rd Lord. Will't hold? will't hold?

2nd Lord. It does; but time will—and so—

3rd Lord. I do conceive.

Tim. Each man to his stool, with that spur as he would to the lip of his mistress; your diet shall be in all places alike. Make not a city feast of it, to let the meat cool ere we can agree upon the first place. Sit, sit. The gods require our thanks.

You great benefactors, sprinkle our society with thankfulness. For your own gifts, make yourselves praised; but reserve still to give, lest your deities be despised. Lend to each man enough, that one need not lend to another; for, were your godheads to borrow of men, men would forsake the gods. Make the meat be beloved more than the man that gives it. Let no assembly of twenty be without a score of villains. If there sit twelve women at the table, let a dozen of them be—as they are. The rest of your foes, O gods—the senators of Athens, together with the common lag of people—what is amiss in them, you gods, make suitable for destruction. For these my present friends, as they are to me nothing, so in nothing bless them, and to nothing are they welcome.

Uncover, dogs, and lap.

The dishes are uncovered and seen to be full of warm water.

Some speak. What does his lordship mean?
Some other. I know not.
Tim. May you a better feast never behold,
You knot of mouth-friends! Smoke and lukewarm water
Is your perfection. This is Timon's last;
Who, stuck and spangled with your flatteries,
Washes it off, and sprinkles in your faces
Your reeking villany.

Throwing the water in their faces.

Live loathed and long,
Most smiling, smooth, detested parasites,
Courteous destroyers, affable wolves, meek bears,
You fools of fortune, trencher-friends, time's flies,
Cap and knee slaves, vapours, and minute-jacks!
Of man and beast the infinite malady
Crust you quite o'er! What, dost thou go?
Soft! take thy physic first—thou too—and thou;
Stay, I will lend thee money, borrow none.

Throws the dishes at them, and drives them out.

What, all in motion? Henceforth be no feast,
Whereat a villain's not a welcome guest.
Burn, house! sink, Athens! henceforth hated be
Of Timon man and all humanity! [*Exit.*

Re-enter the LORDS, SENATORS, *&c.*

1st Lord. How now, my lords!
2nd Lord. Know you the quality of Lord Timon's fury?
3rd Lord. Push! did you see my cap?
4th Lord. I have lost my gown.
1st Lord. He's but a mad lord, and nought but humour sways him. He gave me a jewel th' other day, and now he has beat it out of my hat. Did you see my jewel?
3rd Lord. Did you see my cap?
2nd Lord. Here 'tis.
4th Lord. Here lies my gown.
1st Lord. Let's make no stay.
2nd Lord. Lord Timon's mad.
3rd Lord. I feel't upon my bones.
4th Lord. One day he gives us diamonds, next day stones. [*Exeunt.*

ACT IV

SCENE I. *Without the walls of Athens*

Enter TIMON.

Tim. Let me look back upon thee. O thou wall
That girdlest in those wolves, dive in the earth
And fence not Athens! Matrons, turn incontinent!
Obedience fail in children! slaves and fools,
Pluck the grave wrinkled Senate from the bench,
And minister in their steads! To general filths
Convert o' the instant, green virginity!
Do't in your parents' eyes! Bankrupts, hold fast;
Rather than render back, out with your knives
And cut your trusters' throats! Bound servants, steal!
Large-handed robbers your grave masters are,
And pill by law. Maid, to thy master's bed;
Thy mistress is o' the brothel! Son of sixteen,
Pluck the lined crutch from thy old limping sire,
With it beat out his brains! Piety, and fear,
Religion to the gods, peace, justice, truth,
Domestic awe, night-rest, and neighbourhood,
Instruction, manners, mysteries, and trades,
Degrees, observances, customs, and laws,
Decline to your confounding contraries,
And let confusion live! Plagues, incident to men,
Your potent and infectious fevers heap
On Athens, ripe for stroke! Thou cold sciatica,
Cripple our senators, that their limbs may halt
As lamely as their manners! Lust and liberty
Creep in the minds and marrows of our youth,
That 'gainst the stream of virtue they may strive,
And drown themselves in riot! Itches, blains,
Sow all the Athenian bosoms; and their crop
Be general leprosy! Breath infect breath,
That their society, as their friendship, may
Be merely poison! Nothing I'll bear from thee,
But nakedness, thou detestable town!
Take thou that too, with multiplying bans!
Timon will to the woods; where he shall find
The unkindest beast more kinder than mankind.
The gods confound—hear me, you good gods all—
The Athenians both within and out that wall!
And grant, as Timon grows, his hate may grow
To the whole race of mankind, high and low!
Amen. [*Exit.*

SCENE II. *Athens: a room in Timon's house*

Enter FLAVIUS, *with two or three* SERVANTS.

1st Serv. Hear you, master steward, where's our master?
Are we undone? cast off? nothing remaining?

Flav. Alack, my fellows, what should I say to you?
Let me be recorded by the righteous gods,
I am as poor as you.

1st Serv. Such a house broke!
So noble a master fall'n! All gone! and not
One friend to take his fortune by the arm,
And go along with him!

2nd Serv. As we do turn out backs
From our companion thrown into his grave,
So his familiars to his buried fortunes
Slink all away, leave their false vows with him,
Like empty purses pick'd; and his poor self,
A dedicated beggar to the air,
With his disease of all-shunn'd poverty,
Walks, like contempt, alone. More of our fellows.

Enter other SERVANTS.

Flav. All broken implements of a ruin'd house.

3rd Serv. Yet do our hearts wear Timon's livery;
That see I by our faces; we are fellows still,
Serving alike in sorrow. Leak'd is our bark,
And we, poor mates, stand on the dying deck,
Hearing the surges threat. We must all part
Into this sea of air.

Flav. Good fellows all,
The latest of my wealth I'll share amongst you.
Wherever we shall meet, for Timon's sake,
Let's yet be fellows; let's shake our heads, and say,
As 'twere a knell unto our master's fortunes,
"We have seen better days." Let each take some;
Nay, put out all your hands. Not one word more.
Thus we part rich in sorrow, parting poor.

[SERVANTS *embrace, and part several ways.*

O, the fierce wretchedness that glory brings us!
Who would not wish to be from wealth exempt,
Since riches point to misery and contempt?
Who would be so mock'd with glory? or to live
But in a dream of friendship?
To have his pomp and all what state compounds
But only painted, like his varnish'd friends?
Poor honest lord, brought low by his own heart,
Undone by goodness! Strange, unusual blood,
When man's worst sin is he does too much good!
Who, then, dares to be half so kind again?
For bounty, that makes gods, does still mar men.
My dearest lord, bless'd, to be most accursed,
Rich, only to be wretched, thy great fortunes
Are made thy chief afflictions. Alas, kind lord!
He's flung in rage from this ingrateful seat
Of monstrous friends, nor has he with him to
Supply his life, or that which can command it.
I'll follow and inquire him out.
I'll ever serve his mind with my best will;
Whilst I have gold, I'll be his steward still.

[*Exit.*

SCENE III. *Woods and cave, near the sea-shore*

Enter TIMON, *from the cave.*

Tim. O blessed breeding sun, draw from the earth
Rotten humidity; below thy sister's orb
Infect the air! Twinn'd brothers of one womb,
Whose procreation, residence, and birth,
Scarce is dividant, touch them with several fortunes;
The greater scorns the lesser. Not nature,
To whom all sores lay siege, can bear great fortune,
But by contempt of nature.
Raise me this beggar, and deny 't that lord;
The senator shall bear contempt hereditary,
The beggar native honour.
It is the pasture lards the rother's sides,
The want that makes him lean. Who dares, who dares,
In purity of manhood stand upright,
And say, "This man's a flatterer"? if one be,
So are they all; for every grise of fortune
Is smooth'd by that below. The learned pate
Ducks to the golden fool. All is oblique;
There's nothing level in our cursed natures,
But direct villainy. Therefore, be abhorr'd
All feasts, societies, and throngs of men!
His semblable, yea, himself, Timon disdains.
Destruction fang mankind! Earth, yield me roots! [*Digging.*]
Who seeks for better of thee, sauce his palate
With thy most operant poison! What is here?
Gold? Yellow, glittering, precious gold? No, gods,
I am no idle votarist: roots, you clear heavens!
Thus much of this will make black white, foul fair,
Wrong right, base noble, old young, coward valiant.
Ha, you gods! why this? what this, you gods?
Why, this
Will lug your priests and servants from your sides,
Pluck stout men's pillows from below their heads.
This yellow slave
Will knit and break religions, bless the accursed,
Make the hoar leprosy adored, place thieves

And give them title, knee, and approbation
With senators on the bench. This is it
That makes the wappen'd widow wed again;
She, whom the spital-house and ulcerous sores
Would cast the gorge at, this embalms and spices
To the April day again. Come, damned earth,
Thou common whore of mankind, that put'st odds
Among the rout of nations, I will make thee
Do thy right nature. [*March afar off.*] Ha! a drum? Thou'rt quick,
But yet I'll bury thee. Thou'lt go, strong thief,
When gouty keepers of thee cannot stand.
Nay, stay thou out for earnest.
Keeping some gold.

Enter ALCIBIADES, *with drum and fife, in warlike manner;* PHRYNIA *and* TIMANDRA.

Alcib. What art thou there? speak.
Tim. A beast, as thou art. The canker gnaw thy heart,
For showing me again the eyes of man!
Alcib. What is thy name? Is man so hateful to thee,
That art thyself a man?
Tim. I am Misanthropos and hate mankind.
For thy part, I do wish thou wert a dog,
That I might love thee something.
Alcib. I know thee well;
But in thy fortunes am unlearn'd and strange.
Tim. I know thee too; and more than that I know thee,
I not desire to know. Follow thy drum;
With man's blood paint the ground, gules, gules!
Religious canons, civil laws are cruel;
Then what should war be? This fell whore of thine
Hath in her more destruction than thy sword,
For all her cherubin look.
Phry. Thy lips rot off!
Tim. I will not kiss thee; then the rot returns
To thine own lips again.
Alcib. How came the noble Timon to this change?
Tim. As the moon does, by wanting light to give.
But then renew I could not, like the moon;
There were no suns to borrow of.
Alcib. Noble Timon,
What friendship may I do thee?
Tim. None, but to
Maintain my opinion.
Alcib. What is it, Timon?
Tim. Promise me friendship, but perform none. If thou wilt not promise, the gods plague thee, for thou art a man! If thou dost perform, confound thee, for thou art a man!
Alcib. I have heard in some sort of thy miseries.
Tim. Thou saw'st them, when I had prosperity.
Alcib. I see them now; then was a blessed time.
Tim. As thine is now, held with a brace of harlots.
Timan. Is this the Athenian minion, whom the world
Voiced so regardfully?
Tim. Art thou Timandra?
Timan. Yes.
Tim. Be a whore still. They love thee not that use thee;
Give them diseases, leaving with thee their lust.
Make use of thy salt hours; season the slaves
For tubs and baths; bring down rose-cheeked youth
To the tub-fast and the diet.
Timan. Hang thee, monster!
Alcib. Pardon him, sweet Timandra; for his wits
Are drown'd and lost in his calamities.
I have but little gold of late, brave Timon,
The want whereof doth daily make revolt
In my penurious band. I have heard, and grieved,
How cursed Athens, mindless of thy worth,
Forgetting thy great deeds, when neighbour states,
But for thy sword and fortune, trod upon them—
Tim. I prithee, beat thy drum, and get thee gone.
Alcib. I am thy friend, and pity thee, dear Timon.
Tim. How dost thou pity him whom thou dost trouble?
I had rather be alone.
Alcib. Why, fare thee well.
Here is some gold for thee.
Tim. Keep it, I cannot eat it.
Alcib. When I have laid proud Athens on a heap—
Tim. Warr'st thou 'gainst Athens?
Alcib. Ay, Timon, and have cause.
Tim. The gods confound them all in thy conquest;
And thee after, when thou hast conquer'd!
Alcib. Why me, Timon?
Tim. That, by killing of villians,
Thou wast born to conquer my country.
Put up thy gold. Go on. Here's gold. Go on.
Be as a planetary plague, when Jove
Will o'er some high-viced city hang his poison
In the sick air. Let not thy sword skip one.
Pity not honour'd age for his white beard;
He is an usurer. Strike me the counterfeit matron;

It is her habit only that is honest,
Herself's a bawd. Let not the virgin's cheek
Make soft thy trenchant sword; for those milk-paps,
That through the window-bars bore at men's eyes,
Are not within the leaf of pity writ,
But set them down horrible traitors. Spare not the babe,
Whose dimpled smiles from fools exhaust their mercy;
Think it a bastard, whom the oracle
Hath doubtfully pronounced thy throat shall cut,
And mince it sans remorse. Swear against objects;
Put armour on thine ears and on thine eyes;
Whose proof, nor yells of mothers, maids, nor babes,
Nor sight of priests in holy vestments bleeding,
Shall pierce a jot. There's gold to pay thy soldiers.
Make large confusion; and, thy fury spent,
Confounded be thyself! Speak not, be gone.

Alcib. Hast thou gold yet? I'll take the gold thou givest me,
Not all thy counsel.

Tim. Dost thou, or dost thou not, heaven's curse upon thee!

Phr. and Timan. Give us some gold, good Timon. Hast thou more?

Tim. Enough to make a whore forswear her trade,
And to make whores, a bawd. Hold up, you sluts,
Your aprons mountant. You are not oathable—
Although, I know, you'll swear, terribly swear
Into strong shudders and to heavenly agues
The immortal gods that hear you—spare your oaths,
I'll trust to your conditions. Be whores still;
And he whose pious breath seeks to convert you,
Be strong in whore, allure him, burn him up;
Let your close fire predominate his smoke,
And be no turncoats. Yet may your pains, six months,
Be quite contrary! And thatch your poor thin roofs
With burthens of the dead—some that were hang'd.
No matter!—Wear them, betray with them. Whore still;
Paint till a horse may mire upon your face.
A pox of wrinkles!

Phr. and Timan. Well, more gold. What then?
Believe't, that we'll do anything for gold.

Tim. Consumptions sow
In hollow bones of man; strike their sharp shins,
And mar men's spurring. Crack the lawyers' voice,
That he may never more false title plead,
Nor sound his quillets shrilly. Hoar the flamen,
That scolds against the quality of flesh,
And not believes himself. Down with the nose,
Down with it flat; take the bridge quite away
Of him that, his particular to foresee,
Smells from the general weal. Make curl'd-pate ruffians bald;
And let the unscarr'd braggarts of the war
Derive some pain from you. Plague all;
That your activity may defeat and quell
The source of all erection. There's more gold.
Do you damn others, and let this damn you,
And ditches grave you all!

Phr. and Timan. More counsel with more money, bounteous Timon.

Tim. More whore, more mischief first; I have given you earnest.

Alcib. Strike up the drum towards Athens! Farewell, Timon.
If I thrive well, I'll visit thee again.

Tim. If I hope well, I'll never see thee more.

Alcib. I never did thee harm.

Tim. Yes, thou spokest well of me.

Alcib. Call'st thou that harm?

Tim. Men daily find it. Get thee away, and take
Thy beagles with thee.

Alcib. We but offend him. Strike!

[*Drum beats, Exeunt* ALCIBIADES, PHRYNIA, *and* TIMANDRA.

Tim. That nature, being sick of man's unkindness,
Should yet be hungry! Common mother, thou, *Digging*.
Whose womb unmeasurable, and infinite breast,
Teems, and feeds all; whose selfsame mettle,
Whereof thy proud child, arrogant man, is puff'd,
Engenders the black toad and adder blue,
The gilded newt and eyeless venom'd worm,
With all the abhorred births below crisp heaven
Whereon Hyperion's quickening fire doth shine;
Yield him, who all thy human sons doth hate,
From forth thy plenteous bosom, one poor root!
Ensear thy fertile and conceptious womb,
Let it no more bring out ingrateful man!
Go great with tigers, dragons, wolves, and bears;
Teem with new monsters, whom thy upward face
Hath to the marbled mansion all above
Never presented!—O, a root. Dear thanks!—
Dry up thy marrows, vines, and plough-torn leas;
Whereof ingrateful man, with liquorish draughts
And morsels unctuous, greases his pure mind,

That from it all consideration slips!

Enter APEMANTUS.

More man? plague, plague!
Apem. I was directed hither. Men report
Thou dost affect my manners, and dost use them.
Tim. 'Tis then because thou dost not keep a dog,
Whom I would imitate. Consumption catch thee!
Apem. This is in thee a nature but infected;
A poor unmanly melancholy sprung
From change of fortune. Why this spade? this place?
This slave-like habit? and these looks of care?
Thy flatters yet wear silk, drink wine, lie soft;
Hug their diseased perfumes, and have forgot
That ever Timon was. Shame not these woods,
By putting on the cunning of a carper.
Be thou a flatterer now, and seek to thrive
By that which has undone thee. Hinge thy knee,
And let his very breath, whom thou'lt observe,
Blow off thy cap; praise his most vicious strain,
And call it excellent. Thou wast told thus;
Thou gavest thine ears like tapsters that bid welcome
To knaves and all approachers. 'Tis most just
That thou turn rascal; hadst thou wealth again,
Rascals should have't. Do not assume my likeness.
Tim. Were I like thee, I'd throw away myself.
Apem. Thou hast cast away thyself, being like thyself;
A madman so long, now a fool. What, think'st
That the bleak air, thy boisterous chamberlain,
Will put thy shirt on warm? Will these moss'd trees,
That have outlived the eagle, page thy heels,
And skip where thou point'st out? Will the cold brook,
Candied with ice, caudle thy morning taste,
To cure thy o'er-night's surfeit? Call the creatures
Whose naked natures live in all the spite
Of wreakful heaven, whose bare unhoused trunks,
To the conflicting elements exposed,
Answer mere nature; bid them flatter thee;
O, thou shalt find—
Tim. A fool of thee. Depart.
Apem. I love thee better now than e'er I did.
Tim. I hate thee worse.
Apem. Why?
Tim. Thou flatter'st misery.
Apem. I flatter not; but say thou art a caitiff.
Tim. Why dost thou seek me out?
Apem. To vex thee.
Tim. Always a villain's office or a fool's.
Dost please thyself in't?
Apem. Ay.
Tim. What! a knave too?
Apem. If thou didst put this sour-cold habit on
To castigate thy pride, 'twere well; but thou
Dost it enforcedly; thou'dst courtier be again,
Wert thou not beggar. Willing misery
Outlives incertain pomp, is crown'd before.
The one is filling still, never complete;
The other, at high wish. Best state, contentless,
Hath a distracted and most wretched being,
Worse than the worst, content.
Thou shouldst desire to die, being miserable.
Tim. Not by his breath that is more miserable.
Thou art a slave, whom Fortune's tender arm
With favour never clasp'd; but bred a dog.
Hadst thou, like us from our first swath, proceeded
The sweet degrees that this brief world affords
To such as may the passive drugs of it
Freely command, thou wouldst have plunged thyself
In general riot; melted down thy youth
In different beds of lust; and never learn'd
The icy precepts of respect, but follow'd
The sugar'd game before thee. But myself,
Who had the world as my confectionary,
The mouths, the tongues, the eyes, and hearts of men
At duty, more than I could frame employment,
That numberless upon me stuck as leaves
Do on the oak, have with one winter's brush
Fell from their boughs and left me open, bare
For every storm that blows. I, to bear this,
That never knew but better, is some burden.
Thy nature did commence in sufferance, time
Hath made thee hard in't. Why shouldst thou hate men?
They never flatter'd thee. What hast thou given?
If thou wilt curse, thy father, that poor rag,
Must be thy subject, who in spite put stuff
To some she beggar and compounded thee
Poor rogue hereditary. Hence, be gone!
If thou hadst not been born the worst of men,
Thou hadst been a knave and flatterer.
Apem. Art thou proud yet?
Tim. Ay, that I am not thee.
Apem. I, that I was
No prodigal.
Tim. I, that I am one now.
Were all the wealth I have shut up in thee,
I'd give thee leave to hang it. Get thee gone.
That the whole life of Athens were in this!
Thus would I eat it. [*Eating a root.*]

Apem. Here; I will mend thy feast.
Offering him a root.

Tim. First mend my company, take away thyself.

Apem. So I shall mend mine own, by the lack of thine.

Tim. 'Tis not well mended so, it is but botch'd;
If not, I would it were.

Apem. What wouldst thou have to Athens?

Tim. Thee thither in a whirlwind. If thou wilt,
Tell them there I have gold; look, so I have.

Apem. Here is no use for gold.

Tim. The best and truest;
For here it sleeps, and does no hired harm.

Apem. Where liest o' nights, Timon?

Tim. Under that's above me.
Where feed'st thou o' days, Apemantus?

Apem. Where my stomach finds meat; or, rather, where I eat it.

Tim. Would poison were obedient and knew my mind!

Apem. Where wouldst thou send it?

Tim. To sauce thy dishes.

Apem. The middle of humanity thou never knewest, but the extremity of both ends. When thou wast in thy gilt and thy perfume, they mocked thee for too much curiosity; in thy rags thou knowest none, but art despised for the contrary. There's a medlar for thee, eat it.

Tim. On what I hate I feed not.

Apem. Dost hate a medlar?

Tim. Ay, though it look like thee.

Apem. An thou hadst hated medlers sooner, thou shouldst have loved thyself better now. What man didst thou ever know unthrift that was beloved after his means?

Tim. Who, without those means thou talkest of, didst thou ever know beloved?

Apem. Myself.

Tim. I understand thee; thou hadst some means to keep a dog.

Apem. What things in the world canst thou nearest compare to thy flatterers?

Tim. Women nearest; but men, men are the things themselves. What wouldst thou do with the world, Apemantus, if it lay in thy power?

Apem. Give it the beasts, to be rid of the men.

Tim. Wouldst thou have thyself fall in the confusion of men, and remain a beast with the beasts?

Apem. Ay, Timon.

Tim. A beastly ambition, which the gods grant thee t' attain to! If thou wert the lion, the fox would beguile thee. If thou wert the lamb, the fox would eat thee. If thou wert the fox, the lion would suspect thee, when peradventure thou wert accused by the ass. If thou wert the ass, thy dulness would torment thee, and still thou livedst but as a breakfast to the wolf. If thou wert the wolf, thy greediness would afflict thee, and oft thou shouldst hazard thy life for thy dinner. Wert thou the unicorn, pride and wrath would confound thee and make thine own self the conquest of thy fury. Wert thou a bear, thou wouldst be killed by the horse. Wert thou a horse, thou wouldst be seized by the leopard. Wert thou a leopard, thou wert german to the lion and the spots of thy kindred were jurors on thy life. All thy safety were remotion and thy defence absence. What beast couldst thou be, that were not subject to a beast? and what a beast art thou already, that seest not thy loss in transformation!

Apem. If thou couldst please me with speaking to me, thou mightst have hit upon it here. The commonwealth of Athens is become a forest of beasts.

Tim. How has the ass broke the wall, that thou art out of the city?

Apem. Yonder comes a poet and a painter; the plague of company light upon thee! I will fear to catch it and give way. When I know not what else to do, I'll see thee again.

Tim. When there is nothing living but thee, thou shalt be welcome. I had rather be a beggar's dog than Apemantus.

Apem. Thou art the cap of all the fools alive.

Tim. Would thou wert clean enough to spit upon!

Apem. A plague on thee! Thou art too bad to curse.

Tim. All villains that do stand by thee are pure.

Apem. There is no leprosy but what thou speak'st.

Tim. If I name thee.
I'll beat thee, but I should infect my hands.

Apem. I would my tongue could rot them off!

Tim. Away, thou issue of a mangy dog!
Choler does kill me that thou art alive;
I swound to see thee.

Apem. Would thou wouldst burst!

Tim. Away,
Thou tedious rogue! I am sorry I shall lose
A stone by thee. [*Throws a stone at him.*]

Apem. Beast!

Tim. Slave!

Apem. Toad!

Tim. Rogue, rogue, rogue!
I am sick of this false world, and will love nought
But even the mere necessities upon't.
Then, Timon, presently prepare thy grave;
Lie where the light foam of the sea may beat

Thy grave-stone daily; make thine epitaph
That death in me at others' lives may laugh.
[*To the gold*] O thou sweet king-killer, and dear divorce
'Twixt natural son and sire! thou bright defiler
Of Hymen's purest bed! thou valiant Mars!
Thou ever young, fresh, loved, and delicate wooer,
Whose blush doth thaw the consecrated snow
That lies in Dian's lap! thou visible god,
That solder'st close impossibilities,
And makest them kiss! that speak'st with every tongue,
To every purpose! O thou touch of hearts!
Think, thy slave man rebels, and by thy virtue
Set them into confounding odds, that beasts
May have the world in empire!

Apem. Would 'twere so!
But not till I am dead. I'll say thou'st gold.
Thou wilt be throng'd to shortly.

Tim. Throng'd to!

Apem. Ay.

Tim. Thy back, I prithee.

Apem. Live, and love thy misery.

Tim. Long live so, and so die. [*Exit* APEMANTUS.] I am quit.
Moe things like men! Eat, Timon, and abhor them.

Enter BANDITTI.

1st Ban. Where should he have this gold? It is some poor fragment, some slender ort of his remainder. The mere want of gold, and the falling-from of his friends, drove him into this melancholy.

2nd Ban. It is noised he hath a mass of treasure.

3rd Ban. Let us make the assay upon him. If he care not for't, he will supply us easily; if he covetously reserve it, how shall's get it?

2nd Ban. True; for he bears it not about him, 'tis hid.

1st Ban. Is not this he?

Banditti. Where?

2nd Ban. 'Tis his description.

3rd Ban. He; I know him.

Banditti. Save thee, Timon.

Tim. Now, thieves?

Banditti. Soldiers, not thieves.

Tim. Both too; and women's sons.

Banditti. We are not thieves, but men that much do want.

Tim. Your greatest want is, you want much of meat.
Why should you want? Behold, the earth hath roots;
Within this mile break forth a hundred springs;
The oaks bear mast, the briers scarlet hips;
The bounteous housewife, Nature, on each bush
Lays her full mess before you. Want! why want?

1st Ban. We cannot live on grass, on berries, water,
As beasts and birds and fishes.

Tim. Nor on the beasts themselves, the birds, and fishes;
You must eat men. Yet thanks I must you con
That you are thieves profess'd, that you work not
In holier shapes: for there is boundless theft
In limited professions. Rascal thieves,
Here's gold. Go, suck the subtle blood o' the grape,
Till the high fever seethe your blood to froth,
And so 'scape hanging. Trust not the physician;
His antidotes are poison, and he slays
Moe than you rob. Take wealth and lives together;
Do villainy, do, since you protest to do't.
Like workmen. I'll example you with thievery:
The sun's a thief, and with his great attraction
Robs the vast sea; the moon's an arrant thief,
And her pale fire she snatches from the sun;
The sea's a thief, whose liquid surge resolves
The moon into salt tears; the earth's a thief,
That feeds and breeds by a composture stolen
From general excrement; each thing's a thief;
The laws, your curb and whip, in their rough power
Have uncheck'd theft. Love not yourselves. Away,
Rob one another. There's more gold. Cut throats.
All that you meet are thieves. To Athens go,
Break open shops; nothing can you steal,
But thieves do lose it. Steal no less for this
I give you; and gold confound you howsoe'er!
Amen.

3rd Ban. Has almost charmed me from my profession, by persuading me to it.

1st Ban. 'Tis in the malice of mankind that he thus advises us; not to have us thrive in our mystery.

2nd Ban. I'll believe him as an enemy, and give over my trade.

1st Ban. Let us first see peace in Athens. There is no time so miserable but a man may be true.
[*Exeunt* BANDITTI.

Enter FLAVIUS.

Flav. O you gods!
Is yond despised and ruinous man my lord?
Full of decay and failing? O monument
And wonder of good deeds evilly bestow'd!
What an alteration of honour

Has desperate want made!
What viler thing upon the earth than friends
Who can bring noblest minds to basest ends!
How rarely does it meet with this time's guise,
When man was wish'd to love his enemies!
Grant I may ever love, and rather woo
Those that would mischief me than those that do!
Has caught me in his eye. I will present
My honest grief unto him; and, as my lord,
Still serve him with my life. My dearest master!

Tim. Away! what art thou?

Flav. Have you forgot me, sir?

Tim. Why dost ask that? I have forgot all men;
Then, if thou grant'st thou'rt a man, I have forgot thee.

Flav. An honest poor servant of yours.

Tim. Then I know thee not.
I never had honest man about me, I; all
I kept were knaves, to serve in meat to villains.

Flav. The gods are witness,
Ne'er did poor steward wear a truer grief
For his undone lord than mine eyes for you.

Tim. What, dost thou weep? Come nearer. Then I love thee,
Because thou art a woman and disclaim'st
Flinty mankind, whose eyes do never give
But thorough lust and laughter. Pity's sleeping:
Strange times, that weep with laughing, not with weeping!

Flav. I beg of you to know me, good my lord,
To accept my grief and whilst this poor wealth lasts
To entertain me as your steward still.

Tim. Had I a steward
So true, so just, and now so comfortable?
It almost turns my dangerous nature mild.
Let me behold thy face. Surely, this man
Was born of woman.
Forgive my general and exceptless rashness,
You perpetual-sober gods! I do proclaim
One honest man—mistake me not—but one;
No more, I pray—and he's a steward.
How fain would I have hated all mankind!
And thou redeem'st thyself; but all, save thee,
I fell with curses.
Methinks thou art more honest now than wise;
For, by oppressing and betraying me,
Thou mightst have sooner got another service;
For many so arrive at second masters,
Upon their first lord's neck. But tell me true—
For I must ever doubt, though ne'er so sure—
Is not thy kindness subtle, covetous,
If not a usuring kindness, and, as rich men deal gifts,
Expecting in return twenty for one?

Flav. No, my most worthy master; in whose breast
Doubt and suspect, alas, are placed too late.
You should have fear'd false times when you did feast;
Suspect still comes where an estate is least.
That which I show, Heaven knows, is merely love,
Duty, and zeal to your unmatched mind,
Care of your food and living; and, believe it,
My most honour'd lord,
For any benefit that points to me,
Either in hope or present, I'd exchange
For this one wish, that you had power and wealth
To requite me, by making rich yourself.

Tim. Look thee, 'tis so! Thou singly honest man,
Here, take. The gods out of my misery
Have sent thee treasure. Go, live rich and happy;
But thus condition'd; thou shalt build from men;
Hate all, curse all, show charity to none,
But let the famish'd flesh slide from the bone
Ere thou relieve the beggar; give to dogs
What thou deny'st to men; let prisons swallow 'em,
Debts wither 'em to nothing; be men like blasted woods,
And may diseases lick up their false bloods!
And so farewell and thrive.

Flav. O, let me stay,
And comfort you, my master.

Tim. If thou hatest curses,
Stay not; fly, whilst thou art blest and free.
Ne'er see thou man, and let me ne'er see thee.

[*Exit* FLAVIUS. TIMON *retires to his cave.*

ACT V

SCENE I. *The woods: Before Timon's cave*

Enter POET *and* PAINTER; TIMON *watching them from his cave.*

Pain. As I took note of the place, it cannot be far where he abides.

Poet. What's to be thought of him? Does the rumour hold for true that he's so full of gold?

Pain. Certain. Alcibiades reports it; Phyrnia and Timandra had gold of him. He likewise enriched poor straggling soldiers with great quantity. 'Tis said he gave unto his steward a mighty sum.

Poet. Then this breaking of his has been but a try for his friends.

Pain. Nothing else. You shall see him a palm in Athens again, and flourish with the highest. Therefore 'tis not amiss we tender our loves to him, in this supposed distress of his. It will show honestly in us; and is very likely to load our purposes with what they travail for, if it be a just and true report that goes of his having.

Poet. What have you now to present unto him?

Pain. Nothing at this time but my visitation; only I will promise him an excellent piece.

Poet. I must serve him so too, tell him of an intent that's coming toward him.

Pain. Good as the best. Promising is the very air o' the time; it opens the eyes of expectation. Performance is ever the duller for his act; and, but in the plainer and simpler kind of people, the deed of saying is quite out of use. To promise is most courtly and fashionable; performance is a kind of will or testament which argues a great sickness in his judgement that makes it.

TIMON *comes from his cave, behind.*

Tim. [*Aside*] Excellent workman! thou canst not paint a man so bad as is thyself.

Poet. I am thinking what I shall say I have provided for him. It must be a personating of himself; a satire against the softness of prosperity, with a discovery of the infinite flatteries that follow youth and opulency.

Tim. [*Aside*] Must thou needs stand for a villain in thine own work? Wilt thou whip thine own faults in other men? Do so, I have gold for thee.

Poet. Nay, let's seek him.
Then do we sin against our own estate,
When we may profit meet, and come too late.

Pain. True;
When the day serves, before black-corner'd night,
Find what thou want'st by free and offer'd light.
Come.

Tim. [*Aside*] I'll meet you at the turn. What a god's gold,
That he is worshipp'd in a baser temple
Than where swine feed!
'Tis thou that rigg'st the bark and plough'st the foam,
Settlest admired reverence in a slave.
To thee be worship! and thy saints for aye
Be crown'd with plagues that thee alone obey!
Fit I meet them. [*Coming forward*.]

Poet. Hail, worthy Timon!

Pain. Our late noble master!

Tim. Have I once lived to see two honest men?

Poet. Sir,
Having often of your open bounty tasted,
Hearing you were retired, your friends fall'n off,
Whose thankless natures—O abhorred spirits!—
Not all the whips of heaven are large enough.
What! to you,
Whose star-like nobleness gave life and influence
To their whole being! I am rapt and cannot cover
The monstrous bulk of this ingratitude
With any size of words.

Tim. Let it go naked, men may see't the better.
You that are honest, by being what you are,
Make them best seen and known.

Pain. He and myself
Have travail'd in the great shower of your gifts,
And sweetly felt it.

Tim. Ay, you are honest men.

Pain. We are hither come to offer you our service.

Tim. Most honest men! Why, how shall I requite you?
Can you eat roots, and drink cold water? no.

Both. What we can do, we'll do, to do you service.

Tim. Ye're honest men. Ye've heard that I have gold;
I am sure you have. Speak truth; ye're honest men.

Pain. So it is said, my noble lord; but therefore
Came not my friend nor I.

Tim. Good honest men! Thou draw'st a counterfeit
Best in all Athens. Thou'rt, indeed, the best;
Thou counterfeit'st most lively.

Pain. So, so, my lord.

Tim. E'en so, sir, as I say. And, for thy fiction,
Why, thy verse swells with stuff so fine and smooth
That thou art even natural in thine art.
But, for all this, my honest-natured friends,
I must needs say you have a little fault.
Marry, 'tis not monstrous in you, neither wish I
You take much pains to mend.

Both. Beseech your honour
To make it known to us.

Tim. You'll take it ill.

Both. Most thankfully, my lord.

Tim. Will you, indeed?

Both. Doubt it not, worthy lord.

Tim. There's never a one of you but trusts a knave,
That mightily deceives you.

Both. Do we, my lord?

Tim. Ay, and you hear him cog, see him dissemble,
Know his gross patchery, love him, feed him,
Keep in your bosom. Yet remain assured
That he's a made-up villain.

Pain. I know none such, my lord.

Poet. Nor I.

Tim. Look you, I love you well; I'll give you gold,
Rid me these villains from your companies.

Hang them or stab them, drown them in a draught,
Confound them by some course, and come to me,
I'll give you gold enough.

Both. Name them, my lord, let's know them.

Tim. You that way and you this, but two in company;
Each man apart, all single and alone,
Yet an arch-villain keeps him company.
If where thou art two villains shall not be,
Come not near him. If thou wouldst not reside
But where one villain is, then him abandon.
Hence, pack! there's gold; you came for gold, ye slaves!
[*To* PAINTER] You have work'd for me; there's payment for you. Hence!
[*To* POET] You are an alchemist; make gold of that.
Out, rascal dogs!

Beats them out, and then retires to his cave.

Enter FLAVIUS *and* TWO SENATORS.

Flav. It is in vain that you would speak with Timon;
For he is set so only to himself
That nothing but himself which looks like man
Is friendly with him.

1st Sen. Bring us to his cave.
It is our part and promise to the Athenians
To speak with Timon.

2nd Sen. At all times alike
Men are not still the same. 'Twas time and griefs
That framed him thus; time, with his fairer hand,
Offering the fortunes of his former days,
The former man may make him. Bring us to him,
And chance it as it may.

Flav. Here is his cave. 129
Peace and content be here! Lord Timon! Timon!
Look out, and speak to friends. The Athenians,
By two of their most reverend Senate, greet thee.
Speak to them, noble Timon.

TIMON *comes from his cave.*

Tim. Thou sun, that comfort'st, burn! Speak, and be hang'd.
For each true word, a blister! and each false
Be as a cauterizing to the root o' the tongue,
Consuming it with speaking!

1st Sen. Worthy Timon—

Tim. Of none but such as you, and you of Timon.

1st Sen. The senators of Athens greet thee, Timon.

Tim. I thank them; and would send them back the plague,
Could I but catch it for them.

1st Sen. O, forget
What we are sorry for ourselves in thee.
The senators with one consent of love
Entreat thee back to Athens; who have thought
On special dignities, which vacant lie
For thy best use and wearing.

2nd Sen. They confess
Toward thee forgetfulness too general, gross;
Which now the public body, which doth seldom
Play the recanter, feeling in itself
A lack of Timon's aid, hath sense withal
Of it own fail, restraining aid to Timon;
And send forth us, to make their sorrow'd render,
Together with a recompense more fruitful
Than their offence can weigh down by the dram;
Ay, even such heaps and sums of love and wealth
As shall to thee blot out what wrongs were theirs
And write in thee the figures of their love,
Ever to read them thine.

Tim. You witch me in it;
Surprise me to the very brink of tears.
Lend me a fool's heart and a woman's eyes,
And I'll beweep these comforts, worthy senators.

1st Sen. Therefore, so please thee to return with us
And of our Athens, thine and ours, to take
The captainship, thou shalt be met with thanks,
Allow'd with absolute power, and thy good name
Live with authority; so soon we shall drive back
Of Alcibiades the approaches wild,
Who, like a boar too savage, doth root up
His country's peace.

2nd Sen. And shakes his threatening sword
Against the walls of Athens.

1st Sen. Therefore, Timon—

Tim. Well, sir, I will; therefore, I will, sir; thus:
If Alcibiades kill my countrymen,
Let Alcibiades know this of Timon,
That Timon care not. But if he sack fair Athens,
And take our goodly aged men by the beards,
Giving our holy virgins to the stain
Of contumelious, beastly, mad-brain'd war,
Then let him know, and tell him Timon speaks it,
In pity of our aged and our youth,
I cannot choose but tell him, that I care not,
And let him take't at worst; for their knives care not,
While you have throats to answer. For myself,
There's not a whittle in the unruly camp
But I do prize it at my love before
The reverend'st throat in Athens. So I leave you
To the protection of the prosperous gods,
As thieves to keepers.

Flav. Stay not, all's in vain.

Tim. Why, I was writing of my epitaph;

It will be seen to-morrow. My long sickness
Of health and living now begins to mend,
And nothing brings me all things. Go, live still;
Be Alcibiades your plague, you his,
And last so long enough!
1st Sen. We speak in vain.
Tim. But yet I love my country, and am not
One that rejoices in the common wreck,
As common bruit doth put it.
1st Sen. That's well spoke.
Tim. Commend me to my loving countrymen—
1st Sen. These words become your lips as they pass through them.
2nd Sen. And enter in our ears like great triumphers
In their applauding gates.
Tim. Commend me to them,
And tell them that, to ease them of their griefs,
Their fears of hostile strokes, their aches, losses,
Their pangs of love, with other incident throes
That nature's fragile vessel doth sustain
In life's uncertain voyage, I will some kindness do them.
I'll teach them to prevent wild Alcibiades' wrath.
1st Sen. I like this well; he will return again.
Tim. I have a tree, which grows here in my close,
That mine own use invites me to cut down,
And shortly must I fell it. Tell my friends,
Tell Athens, in the sequence of degree
From high to low throughout, that whoso please
To stop affliction, let him take his haste,
Come hither, ere my tree hath felt the axe,
And hang himself. I pray you, do my greeting.
Flav. Trouble him no further; thus you still shall find him.
Tim. Come not to me again; but say to Athens,
Timon hath made his everlasting mansion
Upon the beached verge of the salt flood;
Who once a day with his embossed froth
The turbulent surge shall cover. Thither come,
And let my grave-stone be your oracle.
Lips, let sour words go by and language end.
What is amiss plague and infection mend!
Graves only be men's works and death their gain!
Sun, hide thy beams! Timon hath done his reign.
[*Retires to his cave.*
1st Sen. His discontents are unremoveably
Coupled to nature.
2nd Sen. Our hope in him is dead. Let us return
And strain what other means is left unto us
In our dear peril.
1st Sen. It requires swift foot. [*Exeunt.*

SCENE II. *Before the walls of Athens*

Enter TWO SENATORS *and a* MESSENGER.

1st Sen. Thou hast painfully discover'd. Are his files
As full as thy report?
Mess. I have spoke the least.
Besides, his expedition promises
Present approach.
2nd Sen. We stand much hazard, if they bring not Timon.
Mess. I met a courier, one mine ancient friend;
Whom, though in general part we were opposed,
Yet our old love made a particular force,
And made us speak like friends. This man was riding
From Alcibiades to Timon's cave,
With letters of entreaty, which imported
His fellowship i' the cause against your city,
In part for his sake moved.
1st Sen. Here come our brothers.

Enter the SENATORS *from* TIMON.

3rd Sen. No talk of Timon, nothing of him expect.
The enemies' drum is heard, and fearful scouring
Doth choke the air with dust. In, and prepare.
Ours is the fall, I fear; our foes the snare.
[*Exeunt.*

SCENE III. *The woods: Timon's cave, and a rude tomb seen*

Enter a SOLDIER, *seeking* TIMON.

Sold. By all description this should be the place.
Who's here? speak, ho! No answer! What is this?
Timon is dead, who hath outstretch'd his span.
Some beast rear'd this; there does not live a man.
Dead, sure; and this his grave. What's on this tomb
I cannot read; the character I'll take with wax.
Our captain hath in every figure skill,
An aged interpreter, though young in days.
Before proud Athens he's set down by this,
Whose fall the mark of his ambition is. [*Exit.*

SCENE IV. *Before the walls of Athens*

Trumpets sound. Enter ALCIBIADES *with his powers.*

Alcib. Sound to this coward and lascivious town
Our terrible approach.
A parley sounded.

Enter SENATORS *on the walls.*

Till now you have gone on and fill'd the time

With all licentious measure, making your wills
The scope of justice; till now myself and such
As slept within the shadow of your power
Have wander'd with our traversed arms and breathed
Our sufferance vainly. Now the time is flush,
When crouching marrow in the bearer strong
Cries of itself "No more." Now breathless wrong
Shall sit and pant in your great chairs of ease,
And pursy insolence shall break his wind
With fear and horrid flight.

1st Sen. Noble and young,
When thy first griefs were but a mere conceit,
Ere thou hadst power or we had cause of fear,
We sent to thee to give thy rages balm,
To wipe out our ingratitude with loves
Above their quantity.

2nd Sen. So did we woo
Transformed Timon to our city's love
By humble message and by promised means.
We were not all unkind, nor all deserve
The common stroke of war.

1st Sen. These walls of ours
Were not erected by their hands from whom
You have received your griefs; nor are they such
That these great towers, trophies, and schools should fall
For private faults in them.

2nd Sen. Nor are they living
Who were the motives that you first went out;
Shame that they wanted cunning, in excess
Hath broke their hearts. March, noble lord,
Into our city with thy banners spread.
By decimation, and a tithed death—
If thy revenges hunger for that food
Which nature loathes—take thou the destined tenth,
And by the hazard of the spotted die
Let die the spotted.

1st Sen. All have not offended;
For those that were, it is not square to take
On those that are, revenges; crimes, like lands,
Are not inherited. Then, dear countryman,
Bring in thy ranks, but leave without thy rage;
Spare thy Athenian cradle and those kin
Which in the bluster of thy wrath must fall
With those that have offended; like a shepherd,
Approach the fold and cull the infected forth,
But kill not all together.

2nd Sen. What thou wilt,
Thou rather shalt enforce it with thy smile
Than hew to't with thy sword.

1st Sen. Set but thy foot
Against our rampired gates, and they shall ope;
So thou wilt send thy gentle heart before,
To say thou'lt enter friendly.

2nd Sen. Throw thy glove,
Or any token of thine honour else,
That thou wilt use the wars as thy redress
And not as our confusion, all thy powers
Shall make their harbour in our town, till we
Have seal'd thy full desire.

Alcib. Then there's my glove;
Descend, and open your uncharged ports.
Those enemies of Timon's and mine own
Whom you yourselves shall set out for reproof
Fall and no more. And, to atone your fears
With my more noble meaning, not a man
Shall pass his quarter, or offend the stream
Of regular justice in your city's bounds,
But shall be render'd to your public laws
At heaviest answer.

Both. 'Tis most nobly spoken.

Alcib. Descend, and keep your words.

The SENATORS *descend, and open the gates.*
Enter SOLDIER.

Sold. My noble general, Timon is dead;
Entomb'd upon the very hem o' the sea;
And on his grave-stone this insculpture, which
With wax I brought away, whose soft impression
Interprets for my poor ignorance.

Alcib. [*Reads the epitaph*] "Here lies a wretched corse, of wretched soul bereft.
Seek not my name. A plague consume you wicked caitiffs left!
Here lie I, Timon; who, alive, all living men did hate.
Pass by and curse thy fill, but pass and stay not here thy gait."
These well express in thee thy latter spirits.
Though thou abhorr'dst in us our human griefs,
Scorn'dst our brain's flow and those our droplets which
From niggard nature fall, yet rich conceit
Taught thee to make vast Neptune weep for aye
On thy low grave, on faults forgiven. Dead
Is noble Timon, of whose memory
Hereafter more. Bring me into your city,
And I will use the olive with my sword,
Make war breed peace, make peace stint war, make each
Prescribe to other as each other's leech.
Let our drums strike. [*Exeunt.*

PERICLES, Prince of Tyre

DRAMATIS PERSONÆ

GOWER, *as Chorus*
ANTIOCHUS, *King of Antioch*
PERICLES, *Prince of Tyre*
HELICANUS, ESCANES — *two lords of Tyre*
SIMONIDES, *King of Pentapolis*
CLEON, *governor of Tarsus*
LYSIMACHUS, *governor of Mytilene*
CERIMON, *a lord of Ephesus*
THALIARD, *a lord of Antioch*
PHILEMON, *servant to Cerimon*
LEONINE, *servant to Dionyza*
MARSHAL
A PANDAR
BOULT, *his servant*
A MESSENGER
THREE LORDS *of Tyre*
A LORD *of Tarsus*
THREE FISHERMEN
A KNIGHT, *attending on Simonides*
TWO SAILORS *of Pentapolis*
A SERVANT *to Cerimon*
THREE PIRATES
TWO GENTLEMEN *of Mytilene*
A SAILOR *of Tyre*
A SAILOR *of Mytilene*
FIVE KNIGHTS, *suitors to Thaisa*
THE DAUGHTER *of Antiochus*
DIONYZA, *wife to Cleon*
THAISA, *daughter to Simonides*
MARINA, *daughter to Pericles and Thaisa*
LYCHORIDA, *nurse to Marina*
A BAWD
DIANA

NON-SPEAKING: *Lords, Knights, Gentlemen, Sailors, and Attendants*

SCENE: *Antioch, Tyre, Tarsus, Pentapolis and the sea-coast near it, Ephesus, Mytilene and the sea-coast near it, and at sea*

ACT I

Before the palace of Antioch

Enter GOWER.

To sing a song that old was sung,
From ashes ancient Gower is come,
Assuming man's infirmities,
To glad your ear, and please your eyes.
It hath been sung at festivals,
On ember-eves and holy-ales;
And lords and ladies in their lives
Have read it for restoratives.
The purchase is to make men glorious;
Et bonum quo antiquius, eo melius.
If you, born in these latter times
When wit's more ripe, accept my rhymes,
And that to hear an old man sing
May to your wishes pleasure bring,
I life would wish, and that I might
Waste it for you, like taper-light.
This Antioch, then, Antiochus the Great
Built up, this city, for his chiefest seat,
The fairest in all Syria;
I tell you what mine authors say.
This king unto him took a fere,
Who died and left a female heir,
So buxom, blithe, and full of face,
As heaven had lent her all his grace;
With whom the father liking took,
And her to incest did provoke.
Bad child; worse father! to entice his own
To evil should be done by none.
But custom what they did begin
Was with long use account no sin.
The beauty of this sinful dame
Made many princes thither frame,
To seek her as a bed-fellow,
In marriage-pleasures play-fellow;
Which to prevent he made a law
To keep her still, and men in awe,
That whoso ask'd her for his wife,
His riddle told not, lost his life.
So for her many a wight did die,
As yon grim looks do testify.
What now ensues, to the judgement of your eye
I give, my cause who best can justify. [*Exit.*

SCENE I. *Antioch: a room in the palace*

Enter ANTIOCHUS, PRINCE PERICLES, *and followers.*

Ant. Young prince of Tyre, you have at large received
The danger of the task you undertake.
Per. I have, Antiochus, and, with a soul
Embolden'd with the glory of her praise,
Think death no hazard in this enterprise.
Ant. Bring in our daughter, clothed like a bride,
For the embracements even of Jove himself;
At whose conception, till Lucina reign'd,

Nature this dowry gave, to glad her presence,
The senate-house of planets all did sit,
To knit in her their best perfections.

Music. Enter the DAUGHTER *of Antiochus.*

Per. See where she comes, apparell'd like the spring,
Graces her subjects, and her thoughts the king
Of every virtue gives renown to men!
Her face the book of praises, where is read
Nothing but curious pleasures, as from thence
Sorrow were ever razed, and testy wrath
Could never be her mild companion.
You gods that made me man, and sway in love,
That have inflamed desire in my breast
To taste the fruit of yon celestial tree
Or die in the adventure, be my helps,
As I am son and servant to your will,
To compass such a boundless happiness!

Ant. Prince Pericles—

Per. That would be son to great Antiochus.

Ant. Before thee stands this fair Hesperides,
With golden fruit, but dangerous to be touch'd;
For death-like dragons here affright thee hard.
Her face, like heaven, enticeth thee to view
Her countless glory, which desert must gain,
And which, without desert, because thine eye
Presumes to reach, all thy whole heap must die.
Yon sometimes famous princes, like thyself,
Drawn by report, adventurous by desire,
Tell thee, with speechless tongues and semblance pale,
That without covering, save yon field of stars,
Here they stand martyrs, slain in Cupid's wars;
And with dead cheeks advise thee to desist
For going on death's net, whom none resist.

Per. Antiochus, I thank thee, who hath taught
My frail mortality to know itself,
And by those fearful objects to prepare
This body, like to them, to what I must;
For death remember'd should be like a mirror,
Who tells us life's but breath, to trust it error.
I'll make my will then, and, as sick men do
Who know the world, see heaven, but, feeling woe,
Gripe not at earthly joys as erst they did;
So I bequeath a happy peace to you
And all good men, as every prince should do;
My riches to the earth from whence they came;
But my unspotted fire of love to you. [*To the* DAUGHTER *of Antiochus.*]
Thus ready for the way of life or death,
I wait the sharpest blow, Antiochus.

Ant. Scorning advice, read the conclusion, then:
Which read and not expounded, 'tis decreed,
As these before thee, thou thyself shalt bleed.

Daugh. Of all say'd yet, mayst thou prove prosperous!
Of all say'd yet, I wish thee happiness!

Per. Like a bold champion, I assume the lists,
Nor ask advice of any other thought
But faithfulness and courage.
"I am no viper, yet I feed
On mother's flesh which did me breed.
I sought a husband, in which labour
I found that kindness in a father.
He's father, son, and husband mild;
I mother, wife, and yet his child.
How they may be, and yet in two,
As you will live, resolve it you."
Sharp physic is the last; but, O you powers
That give heaven countless eyes to view men's acts,
Why cloud they not their sights perpetually,
If this be true, which makes me pale to read it?
Fair glass of light, I loved you, and could still,

Takes hold of the hand of the PRINCESS.

Were not this glorious casket stored with ill.
But I must tell you, now my thoughts revolt;
For he's no man on whom perfections wait
That, knowing sin within, will touch the gate.
You are a fair viol, and your sense the strings;
Who, finger'd to make man his lawful music,
Would draw heaven down, and all the gods, to hearken;
But being play'd upon before your time,
Hell only danceth at so harsh a chime.
Good sooth, I care not for you.

Ant. Prince Pericles, touch not, upon thy life,
For that's an article within our law,
As dangerous as the rest. Your time's expired.
Either expound now, or receive your sentence.

Per. Great king,
Few love to hear the sins they love to act,
'Twould braid yourself too near for me to tell it.
Who has a book of all that monarchs do,
He's more secure to keep it shut than shown;
For vice repeated is like the wandering wind,
Blows dust in others' eyes, to spread itself;
And yet the end of all is bought thus dear,
The breath is gone, and the sore eyes see clear
To stop the air would hurt them. The blind mole casts
Copp'd hills towards heaven, to tell the earth is throng'd
By man's oppression; and the poor worm doth die for 't.
Kings are earth's gods; in vice their law's their will;
And if Jove stray, who dares say Jove doth ill?
It is enough you know; and it is fit,

What being more known grows worse, to smother it.
All love the womb that their first being bred,
Then give my tongue like leave to love my head.
Ant. [*Aside*] Heaven, that I had thy head! he has found the meaning;
But I will gloze with him.—Young Prince of Tyre,
Though by the tenour of our strict edict,
Your exposition misinterpreting,
We might proceed to cancel of your days;
Yet hope, succeeding from so fair a tree
As your fair self, doth tune us otherwise.
Forty days longer we do respite you;
If by which time our secret be undone,
This mercy shows we'll joy in such a son;
And until then your entertain shall be
As doth befit our honour and your worth.
[*Exeunt all but* PERICLES.
Per. How courtesy would seem to cover sin,
When what is done is like an hypocrite,
The which is good in nothing but in sight!
If it be true that I interpret false,
Then were it certain you were not so bad
As with foul incest to abuse your soul;
Where now you're both a father and a son,
By your untimely claspings with your child,
Which pleasure fits an husband, not a father;
And she an eater of her mother's flesh,
By the defiling of her parent's bed;
And both like serpents are, who though they feed
On sweetest flowers, yet they poison breed.
Antioch, farewell! for wisdom sees, those men
Blush not in actions blacker than the night,
Will shun no course to keep them from the light.
One sin, I know, another doth provoke;
Murder's as near to lust as flame to smoke;
Poison and treason are the hands of sin,
Ay, and the targets, to put off the shame;
Then, lest my life be cropp'd to keep you clear,
By flight I'll shun the danger which I fear. [*Exit*.

Re-enter ANTIOCHUS.

Ant. He hath found the meaning, for which we mean
To have his head.
He must not live to trumpet forth my infamy,
Nor tell the world Antiochus doth sin
In such a loathed manner;
And therefore instantly this prince must die,
For by his fall my honour must keep high.
Who attends us there?

Enter THALIARD.

Thal. Doth your Highness call?
Ant. Thaliard,
You are of our chamber, and our mind partakes
Her private actions to your secrecy;
And for your faithfulness we will advance you.
Thaliard, behold, here's poison, and here's gold;
We hate the Prince of Tyre, and thou must kill him.
It fits thee not to ask the reason why,
Because we bid it. Say, is it done?
Thal. My lord,
'Tis done.
Ant. Enough.

Enter a MESSENGER.

Let your breath cool yourself, telling your haste.
Mess. My lord, Prince Pericles is fled. [*Exit*.
Ant. As thou
Wilt live, fly after; and like an arrow shot
From a well-experienced archer hits the mark
His eye doth level at, so thou ne'er return
Unless thou say, "Prince Pericles is dead."
Thal. My lord,
If I can get him within my pistol's length,
I'll make him sure enough; so, farewell to your Highness.
Ant. Thaliard, adieu! [*Exit* THALIARD.] Till Pericles be dead,
My heart can lend no succour to my head. [*Exit*.

SCENE II. *Tyre: a room in the palace*

Enter PERICLES.

Per. [*To* LORDS *without*] Let none disturb us.—Why should this change of thoughts,
The sad companion, dull-eyed melancholy,
Be my so used a guest as not an hour
In the day's glorious walk or peaceful night,
The tomb where grief should sleep, can breed me quiet?
Here pleasures court mine eyes, and mine eyes shun them,
And danger, which I fear'd, is at Antioch,
Whose arm seems far too short to hit me here.
Yet neither pleasure's art can joy my spirits,
Nor yet the other's distance comfort me.
Then it is thus: the passions of the mind,
That have their first conception by mis-dread,
Have after-nourishment and life by care;
And what was first but fear what might be done,
Grows elder now and cares it be not done.
And so with me. The great Antiochus,
'Gainst whom I am too little to contend,
Since he's so great can make his will his act,
Will think me speaking, though I swear to silence;
Nor boots it me to say I honour him,
If he suspect I may dishonour him;
And what may make him blush in being known,

He'll stop the course by which it might be known;
With hostile forces he'll o'erspread the land,
And with the ostent of war will look so huge,
Amazement shall drive courage from the state;
Our men be vanquish'd ere they do resist,
And subjects punish'd that ne'er thought offence:
Which care of them, not pity of myself,
Who am no more but as the tops of trees,
Which fence the roots they grow by and defend them,
Makes both my body pine and soul to languish,
And punish that before that he would punish.

Enter HELICANUS, *with other* LORDS.

1st Lord. Joy and all comfort in your sacred breast!
2nd Lord. And keep your mind, till you return to us,
Peaceful and comfortable!
Hel. Peace, peace, and give experience tongue.
They do abuse the King that flatter him,
For flattery is the bellows blows up sin;
The thing the which is flatter'd, but a spark
To which that blast gives heat and stronger glowing;
Whereas reproof, obedient and in order,
Fits kings, as they are men, for they may err.
When Signior Sooth here does proclaim a peace,
He flatters you, makes war upon your life.
Prince, pardon me, or strike me, if you please;
I cannot be much lower than my knees.
Per. All leave us else; but let your cares o'erlook
What shipping and what lading's in our haven,
And then return to us. [*Exeunt* LORDS.] Helicanus, thou
Hast moved us. What seest thou in our looks?
Hel. An angry brow, dread lord.
Per. If there be such a dart in princes' frowns,
How durst thy tongue move anger to our face?
Hel. How dare the plants look up to heaven, from whence
They have their nourishment?
Per. Thou know'st I have power
To take thy life from thee.
Hel. [*Kneeling*] I have ground the axe myself;
Do you but strike the blow.
Per. Rise, prithee, rise.
Sit down. Thou art no flatterer.
I thank thee for it; and heaven forbid
That kings should let their ears hear their faults hid!
Fit counsellor and servant for a prince,
Who by thy wisdom makest a prince thy servant,
What wouldst thou have me do?
Hel. To bear with patience
Such griefs as you yourself do lay upon yourself.
Per. Thou speak'st like a physician, Helicanus,
That minister'st a potion unto me
That thou wouldst tremble to receive thyself.
Attend me, then. I went to Antioch,
Where as thou know'st, against the face of death
I sought the purchase of a glorious beauty,
From whence an issue I might propagate
Are arms to princes and bring joys to subjects.
Her face was to mine eye beyond all wonder;
The rest—hark in thine ear—as black as incest;
Which by my knowledge found, the sinful father
Seem'd not to strike, but smooth. But thou know'st this,
'Tis time to fear when tyrants seem to kiss.
Which fear so grew in me, I hither fled,
Under the covering of a careful night,
Who seem'd my good protector; and, being here,
Bethought me what was past, what might succeed.
I knew him tyrannous; and tyrants' fears
Decrease not, but grow faster than the years;
And should he doubt it, as no doubt he doth,
That I should open to the listening air
How many worthy princes' bloods were shed
To keep his bed of blackness unlaid ope,
To lop that doubt, he'll fill this land with arms
And make pretence of wrong that I have done him;
When all, for mine, if I may call offence,
Must feel war's blow, who spares not innocence:
Which love to all, of which thyself art one,
Who now reprovest me for it—
Hel. Alas, sir!
Per. Drew sleep out of mine eyes, blood from my cheeks,
Musings into my mind, with thousand doubts
How I might stop this tempest ere it came;
And finding little comfort to relieve them,
I thought it princely charity to grieve them.
Hel. Well, my lord, since you have given me leave to speak,
Freely will I speak. Antiochus you fear;
And justly too, I think, you fear the tyrant,
Who either by public war or private treason
Will take away your life.
Therefore, my lord, go travel for a while,
Till that his rage and anger be forgot,
Or till the Destinies do cut his thread of life.
Your rule direct to any; if to me,
Day serves not light more faithful than I'll be.
Per. I do not doubt thy faith;
But should he wrong my liberties in my absence?
Hel. We'll mingle our bloods together in the earth,
From whence we had our being and our birth.

Per. Tyre, I now look from thee then, and to Tarsus
Intend my travel, where I'll hear from thee,
And by whose letters I'll dispose myself.
The care I had and have of subjects' good
On thee I lay, whose wisdom's strength can bear it.
I'll take thy word for faith, not ask thine oath;
Who shuns not to break one will sure crack both.
But in our orbs we'll live so round and safe,
That time of both this truth shall ne'er convince,
Thou show'dst a subject's shine, I a true prince.
[*Exeunt.*

SCENE III. *Tyre: an ante-chamber in the palace*

Enter THALIARD.

Thal. So, this is Tyre, and this the court. Here must I kill King Pericles; and if I do it not, I am sure to be hanged at home. 'Tis dangerous. Well, I perceive he was a wise fellow and had good discretion that, being bid to ask what he would of the King, desired he might know none of his secrets. Now do I see he had some reason for 't; for if a king bid a man be a villain, he's bound by the indenture of his oath to be one. Hush! here come the lords of Tyre.

Enter HELICANUS *and* ESCANES, *with other Lords of Tyre.*

Hel. You shall not need, my fellow peers of Tyre,
Further to question me of your king's departure.
His seal'd commission, left in trust with me,
Doth speak sufficiently he's gone to travel.
Thal. [*Aside*] How! the King gone!
Hel. If further yet you will be satisfied,
Why, as it were unlicensed of your loves,
He would depart, I'll give some light unto you.
Being at Antioch—
Thal. [*Aside*] What from Antioch?
Hel. Royal Antiochus—on what cause I know not—
Took some displeasure at him; at least he judged so;
And doubting lest that he had err'd or sinn'd,
To show his sorrow, he'd correct himself;
So puts himself unto the shipman's toil,
With whom each minute threatens life or death.
Thal. [*Aside*] Well, I perceive
I shall not be hang'd now, although I would;
But since he's gone, the king it sure must please,
He 'scaped the land, to perish at the sea.
I'll present myself.—Peace to the lords of Tyre!
Hel. Lord Thaliard from Antiochus is welcome.
Thal. From him I come
With message unto princely Pericles;
But since my landing I have understood
Your lord has betook himself to unknown travels,
My message must return from whence it came.
Hel. We have no reason to desire it,
Commended to our master, not to us.
Yet, ere you shall depart, this we desire,
As friends to Antioch, we may feast in Tyre.
[*Exeunt.*

SCENE IV. *Tarsus: a room in the Governor's house*

Enter CLEON, *the governor of Tarsus, with* DIONYZA, *and others.*

Cle. My Dionyza, shall we rest us here,
And by relating tales of others' griefs,
See if 'twill teach us to forget our own?
Dio. That were to blow at fire in hope to quench it;
For who digs hills because they do aspire
Throws down one mountain to cast up a higher.
O my distressed lord, even such our griefs are;
Here they're but felt, and seen with mischief's eyes,
But like to groves, being topp'd, they higher rise.
Cle. O Dionyza,
Who wanteth food, and will not say he wants it,
Or can conceal his hunger till he famish?
Our tongues and sorrows do sound deep
Our woes into the air; our eyes do weep,
Till tongues fetch breath that may proclaim them louder;
That, if heaven slumber while their creatures want,
They may awake their helps to comfort them.
I'll then discourse our woes, felt several years,
And wanting breath to speak help me with tears.
Dio. I'll do my best, sir.
Cle. This Tarsus, o'er which I have the government,
A city on whom plenty held full hand,
For riches strew'd herself even in the streets;
Whose towers bore heads so high they kiss'd the clouds,
And strangers ne'er beheld but wonder'd at;
Whose men and dames so jetted and adorn'd,
Like one another's glass to trim them by.
Their tables were stored full, to glad the sight,
And not so much to feed on as delight;
All poverty was scorn'd, and pride so great,
The name of help grew odious to repeat.
Dio. O, 'tis too true.
Cle. But see what heaven can do! By this our change,
These mouths, who but of late, earth, sea, and air,
Were all too little to content and please,

Although they gave their creatures in abundance,
As houses are defiled for want of use,
They are now starved for want of exercise.
Those palates who, not yet two summers younger,
Must have inventions to delight the taste,
Would now be glad of bread, and beg for it.
Those mothers who, to nousle up their babes,
Thought nought too curious, are ready now
To eat those little darlings whom they loved.
So sharp are hunger's teeth that man and wife
Draw lots who first shall die to lengthen life.
Here stands a lord, and there a lady weeping;
Here many sink, yet those which see them fall
Have scarce strength left to give them burial.
Is not this true?

Dio. Our cheeks and hollow eyes do witness it.

Cle. O, let those cities that of Plenty's cup
And her prosperities so largely taste
With their superfluous riots, hear these tears!
The misery of Tarsus may be theirs.

Enter a LORD.

Lord. Where's the Lord Governor?

Cle. Here.
Speak out thy sorrows which thou bring'st in haste,
For comfort is too far for us to expect.

Lord. We have descried, upon our neighbouring shore,
A portly sail of ships make hitherward.

Cle. I thought as much.
One sorrow never comes but brings an heir,
That may succeed as his inheritor;
And so in ours. Some neighbouring nation,
Taking advantage of our misery,
Hath stuff'd these hollow vessels with their power,
To beat us down, the which are down already;
And make a conquest of unhappy me,
Whereas no glory's got to overcome.

Lord. That's the least fear; for, by the semblance
Of their white flags display'd, they bring us peace,
And come to us as favourers, not as foes.

Cle. Thou speak'st like him's untutor'd to repeat,
"Who makes the fairest show means most deceit."
But bring they what they will and what they can,
What need we fear?
The ground's the lowest, and we are half way there.
Go tell their general we attend him here,
To know for what he comes, and whence he comes,
And what he craves.

Lord. I go, my lord. [*Exit*.

Cle. Welcome is peace, if he on peace consist;
If wars, we are unable to resist.

Enter PERICLES *with Attendants*.

Per. Lord Governor, for so we hear you are,
Let not our ships and number of our men
Be like a beacon fired to amaze your eyes.
We have heard your miseries as far as Tyre,
And seen the desolation of your streets.
Nor come we to add sorrow to your tears,
But to relieve them of their heavy load;
And these our ships, you happily may think
Are like the Trojan horse was stuff'd within
With bloody veins, expecting overthrow,
Are stored with corn to make your needy bread,
And give them life whom hunger starved half dead.

All. The gods of Greece protect you!
And we'll pray for you.

Per. Arise, I pray you, rise.
We do not look for reverence, but for love,
And harbourage for ourself, our ships, and men.

Cle. The which when any shall not gratify,
Or pay you with unthankfulness in thought,
Be it our wives, our children, or ourselves,
The curse of heaven and men succeed their evils!
Till when—the which I hope shall ne'er be seen—
Your Grace is welcome to our town and us.

Per. Which welcome we'll accept; feast here awhile,
Until our stars that frown lend us a smile.
[*Exeunt*.

ACT II

Enter GOWER.

Gow. Here have you seen a mighty king
His child, I wis, to incest bring;
A better prince and benign lord,
That will prove awful both in deed and word.
Be quiet then as men should be,
Till he hath pass'd necessity.
I'll show you those in troubles reign,
Losing a mite, a mountain gain.
The good in conversation,
To whom I give my benison,
Is still at Tarsus, where each man
Thinks all is writ he speken can;
And, to remember what he does,
Build his statue to make him glorious.
But tidings to the contrary

Are brought your eyes; what need speak I?

DUMB SHOW.

Enter at one door PERICLES *talking with* CLEON; *all the train with them. Enter at another door a* GENTLEMAN, *with a letter to* PERICLES; PERICLES *shows the letter to* CLEON; *gives the* MESSENGER *a reward, and knights him. Exit* PERICLES *at one door, and* CLEON *at another.*

Good Helicane, that stay'd at home,
Not to eat honey like a drone
From others' labours; for though he strive
To killen bad, keep good alive;
And to fulfil his prince' desire,
Sends word of all that haps in Tyre:
How Thaliard came full bent with sin
And had intent to murder him;
And that in Tarsus was not best
Longer for him to make his rest.
He, doing so, put forth to seas,
Where when men been, there's seldom ease;
For now the wind begins to blow;
Thunder above and deeps below
Make such unquiet that the ship
Should house him safe is wreck'd and split;
And he, good prince, having all lost,
By waves from coast to coast is tost.
All perishen of man, of pelf,
Ne aught escapen but himself;
Till fortune, tired with doing bad,
Threw him ashore, to give him glad;
And here he comes. What shall be next,
Pardon old Gower—this longs the text.
[*Exit.*

SCENE I. *Pentapolis: an open place by the sea-side*

Enter PERICLES, *wet.*

Per. Yet cease your ire, you angry stars of heaven!
Wind, rain, and thunder, remember, earthly man
Is but a substance that must yield to you;
And I, as fits my nature, do obey you.
Alas, the sea hath cast me on the rocks,
Wash'd me from shore to shore, and left me breath
Nothing to think on but ensuing death.
Let it suffice the greatness of your powers
To have bereft a prince of all his fortunes;
And having thrown him from your watery grave,
Here to have death in peace is all he'll crave.

Enter THREE FISHERMEN.

1st Fish. What, ho, Pilch!

2nd Fish. Ha, come and bring away the nets!

1st Fish. What, Patch-breech, I say!

3rd Fish. What say you, master?

1st Fish. Look how thou stirrest now! come away, or I'll fetch thee with a wanion.

3rd Fish. 'Faith, master, I am thinking of the poor men that were cast away before us even now.

1st Fish. Alas, poor souls, it grieved my heart to hear what pitiful cries they made to us to help them, when, well-a-day, we could scarce help ourselves.

3rd Fish. Nay, master, said not I as much when I saw the porpoise how he bounced and tumbled? they say they're half fish, half flesh. A plague on them, they ne'er come but I look to be washed. Master, I marvel how the fishes live in the sea.

1st Fish. Why, as men do a-land; the great ones eat up the little ones. I can compare our rich misers to nothing so fitly as to a whale; a' plays and tumbles, driving the poor fry before him, and at last devours them all at a mouthful. Such whales have I heard on o' the land, who never leave gaping till they've swallowed the whole parish, church, steeple, bells, and all.

Per. [*Aside*] A pretty moral.

3rd Fish. But, master, if I had been the sexton, I would have been that day in the belfry.

2nd Fish. Why, man?

3rd Fish. Because he should have swallowed me too. And when I had been in his belly, I would have kept such a jangling of the bells, that he should never have left, till he cast bells, steeple, church, and parish, up again. But if the good King Simonides were of my mind—

Per. [*Aside*] Simonides!

3rd Fish. We would purge the land of these drones, that rob the bee of her honey.

Per. [*Aside*] How from the finny subject of the sea
These fishers tell the infirmities of men;
And from their watery empire recollect
All that may men approve or men detect!
Peace be at your labour, honest fishermen.

2nd Fish. Honest! good fellow, what's that? If it be a day fits you, scratch 't out of the calendar, and nobody look after it.

Per. May see the sea hath cast upon your coast.

2nd Fish. What a drunken knave was the sea to cast thee in our way!

Per. A man whom both the waters and the wind,
In that vast tennis-court, have made the ball
For them to play upon, entreats you pity him;
He asks of you, that never used to beg.

1st Fish. No, friend, cannot you beg? Here's them in our country of Greece gets more with begging than we can do with working.

2nd Fish. Canst thou catch any fishes, then?

Per. I never practised it.

2nd Fish. Nay, then thou wilt starve, sure; for here's nothing to be got now-a-days, unless thou canst fish for 't.

Per. What I have been I have forgot to know;
But what I am, want teaches me to think on.
A man throng'd up with cold; my veins are chill,
And have no more of life than may suffice
To give my tongue that heat to ask your help;
Which if you shall refuse, when I am dead,
For that I am a man, pray see me buried.

1st Fish. Die quoth-a? Now gods forbid! I have a gown here; come, put it on; keep thee warm. Now, afore me, a handsome fellow! Come, thou shalt go home, and we'll have flesh for holidays, fish for fasting-days, and moreo'er puddings and flap-jacks, and thou shalt be welcome.

Per. I thank you, sir.

2nd Fish. Hark you, my friend; you said you could not beg.

Per. I did but crave.

2nd Fish. But crave! Then I'll turn craver too, and so I shall 'scape whipping.

Per. Why, are all your beggars whipped, then?

2nd Fish. O, not all, my friend, not all; for if all your beggars were whipped, I would wish no better office than to be beadle. But, master, I'll go draw up the net.

[*Exit with* THIRD FISHERMAN.

Per. [*Aside*] How well this honest mirth becomes their labour!

1st Fish. Hark you, sir, do you know where ye are?

Per. Not well.

1st Fish. Why, I'll tell you. This is called Pentapolis, and our king the good Simonides.

Per. The good King Simonides, do you call him?

1st Fish. Ay, sir; and he deserves so to be called for his peaceable reign and good government.

Per. He is a happy king, since he gains from his subjects the name of good by his government. How far is his court distant from this shore?

1st Fish. Marry, sir, half a day's journey. And I'll tell you, he hath a fair daughter, and tomorrow is her birthday; and there are princes and knights come from all parts of the world to just and tourney for her love.

Per. Were my fortunes equal to my desires, I could wish to make one there.

1st Fish. O, sir, things must be as they may; and what a man cannot get, he may lawfully deal for —his wife's soul.

Re-enter SECOND *and* THIRD FISHERMEN, *drawing up a net.*

2nd Fish. Help, master, help! here's a fish hangs in the net, like a poor man's right in the law; 'twill hardly come out. Ha! bots on 't, 'tis come at last, and 'tis turned to a rusty armour.

Per. An armour, friends! I pray you, let me see it.
Thanks, fortune, yet, that, after all my crosses,
Thou givest me somewhat to repair myself;
And though it was mine own, part of my heritage,
Which my dead father did bequeath to me,
With this strict charge, even as he left his life,
"Keep it, my Pericles; it hath been a shield
'Twixt me and death"—and pointed to this brace;
"For that it saved me, keep it; in like necessity—
The which the gods protect thee from!—may defend thee."
It kept where I kept, I so dearly loved it;
Till the rough seas, that spare not any man,
Took it in rage, though calm'd have given 't again.
I thank thee for 't. My shipwreck now's no ill,
Since I have here my father's gift in 's will.

1st Fish. What mean you, sir?

Per. To beg of you, kind friends, this coat of worth,
For it was sometime target to a king;
I know it by this mark. He loved me dearly,
And for his sake I wish the having of it;
And that you'd guide me to your sovereign's court,
Where with it I may appear a gentleman;
And if that ever my low fortune's better,
I'll pay your bounties; till then rest your debtor.

1st Fish. Why, wilt thou tourney for the lady?

Per. I'll show the virtue I have borne in arms.

1st Fish. Why, do 'e take it, and the gods give thee good on 't!

2nd Fish. Ay, but hark you, my friend; 'twas we that made up this garment through the rough seams of the waters. There are certain condolements, certain vails. I hope, sir, if you thrive, you'll remember from whence you had it.

Per. Believe 't, I will.
By your furtherance I am clothed in steel;
And, spite of all the rapture of the sea,
This jewel holds his building on my arm.
Unto thy value I will mount myself
Upon a courser, whose delightful steps
Shall make the gazer joy to see him tread.
Only, my friend, I yet am unprovided
Of a pair of bases.

2nd Fish. We'll sure provide. Thou shalt have my best gown to make thee a pair; and I'll bring thee to the court myself.

Per. Then honour be but a goal to my will,

This day I'll rise, or else add ill to ill. [*Exeunt.*

SCENE II. *The same: a public way or platform leading to the lists. A pavilion by the side of it for the reception of the King, Princess, Lords, &c.*

Enter SIMONIDES, THAISA, LORDS, *and Attendants.*

Sim. Are the knights ready to begin the triumph?
1st Lord. They are, my liege;
And stay your coming to present themselves.
Sim. Return them, we are ready; and our daughter,
In honour of whose birth these triumphs are,
Sits here, like beauty's child, whom nature gat
For men to see and, seeing, wonder at.
[*Exit a* LORD.
Thai. It pleaseth you, my royal father, to express
My commendations great, whose merit's less.
Sim. It's fit it should be so; for princes are
A model, which heaven makes like to itself.
As jewels lose their glory if neglected,
So princes their renowns if not respected.
'Tis now your honour, daughter, to explain
The labour of each knight in his device.
Thai. Which, to preserve mine honour, I'll perform.

Enter FIRST KNIGHT; *he passes over, and his Squire presents his shield to the* PRINCESS.

Sim. Who is the first that doth prefer himself?
Thai. A knight of Sparta, my renowned father;
And the device he bears upon his shield
Is a black Ethiope reaching at the sun;
The word, "*Lux tua vita mihi.*"
Sim. He loves you well that holds his life of you.

The SECOND KNIGHT *passes over.*

Who is the second that presents himself?
Thai. A prince of Macedon, my royal father;
And the device he bears upon his shield
Is an arm'd knight that's conquer'd by a lady;
The motto thus, in Spanish, "*Piu por dulzura que por fuerza.*"

The THIRD KNIGHT *passes over.*

Sim. And what's the third?
Thai. The third of Antioch;
And his device, a wreath of chivalry;
The word, "*Me pompæ provexit apex.*"

The FOURTH KNIGHT *passes over.*

Sim. What is the fourth?
Thai. A burning torch that's turned upside down;
The word, "*Quod me alit, me extinguit.*"
Sim. Which shows that beauty hath his power and will,
Which can as well inflame as it can kill.

The FIFTH KNIGHT *passes over.*

Thai. The fifth, an hand environed with clouds,
Holding out gold that's by the touchstone tried;
The motto thus, "*Sic spectanda fides.*"

The Sixth Knight, Pericles, passes over.

Sim. And what's
The sixth and last, the which the knight himself
With such a graceful courtesy deliver'd?
Thai. He seems to be a stranger; but his present is
A wither'd branch, that's only green at top;
The motto, "*In hac spe vivo.*"
Sim. A pretty moral;
From the dejected state wherein he is,
He hopes by you his fortunes yet may flourish.
1st Lord. He had need mean better than his outward show
Can any way speak in his just commend;
For by his rusty outside he appears
To have practised more the whipstock than the lance.
2nd Lord. He well may be a stranger, for he comes
To an honour'd triumph strangely furnished.
3rd Lord. And on set purpose let his armour rust
Until this day, to scour it in the dust.
Sim. Opinion's but a fool, that makes us scan
The outward habit by the inward man.
But stay, the knights are coming. We will withdraw
Into the gallery. [*Exeunt.*
Great shouts within, and all cry, "The mean knight!"

SCENE III. *The same: a hall of state; a banquet prepared*

Enter SIMONIDES, THAISA, LORDS, *Attendants, and* KNIGHTS, *from tilting.*

Sim. Knights,
To say you're welcome were superfluous.
To place upon the volume of your deeds,
As in a title-page, your worth in arms,
Were more than you expect, or more than's fit,
Since every worth in show commends itself.
Prepare for mirth, for mirth becomes a feast.
You are princes and my guests.
Thai. But you, my knight and guest;
To whom this wreath of victory I give,
And crown you king of this day's happiness.
Per. 'Tis more by fortune, lady, than by merit.
Sim. Call it by what you will, the day is yours;

And here, I hope, is none that envies it.
In framing an artist, Art hath thus decreed
To make some good, but others to exceed;
And you are her labour'd scholar. Come, queen o' the feast—
For, daughter, so you are—here take your place.
Marshal the rest as they deserve their grace.

Knights. We are honour'd much by good Simonides.

Sim. Your presence glads our days. Honour we love;
For who hates honour hates the gods above.

Marshal. Sir, yonder is your place.

Per. Some other is more fit.

1st Knight. Contend not, sir; for we are gentlemen
That neither in our hearts nor outward eyes
Envy the great nor do the low despise.

Per. You are right courteous knights.

Sim. Sit, sir, sit.
[*Aside*.] By Jove, I wonder, that is king of thoughts,
These cates resist me, she but thought upon.

Thai. [*Aside*.] By Juno, that is queen of marriage,
All viands that I eat do seem unsavoury,
Wishing him my meat.—Sure, he's a gallant gentleman.

Sim. [*Aside*.] He's but a country gentleman;
Has done no more than other knights have done;
Has broken a staff or so; so let it pass.

Thai. [*Aside*.] To me he seems like diamond to glass.

Per. [*Aside*.] Yon king's to me like to my father's picture,
Which tells me in that glory once he was;
Had princes sit, like stars, about his throne,
And he the sun, for them to reverence;
None that beheld him but, like lesser lights,
Did vail their crowns to his supremacy;
Where now his son's like a glow-worm in the night,
The which hath fire in darkness, none in light;
Whereby I see that Time's the king of men:
He's both their parent, and he is their grave,
And gives them what he will, not what they crave.

Sim. What, are you merry, knights?

Knights. Who can be other in this royal presence?

Sim. Here, with a cup that's stored unto the brim—
As you do love, fill to your mistress' lips—
We drink this health to you.

Knights. We thank your Grace.

Sim. Yet pause awhile;
Yon knight doth sit too melancholy,
As if the entertainment in our court
Had not a show might countervail his worth.
Note it not you, Thaisa?

Thai. What is it
To me, my father?

Sim. O, attend, my daughter.
Princes in this should live like gods above,
Who freely give to every one that comes
To honour them;
And princes not doing so are like to gnats,
Which make a sound, but, kill'd, are wonder'd at.
Therefore to make his entrance more sweet,
Here, say we drink this standing-bowl of wine to him.

Thai. Alas, my father, it befits not me
Unto a stranger knight to be so bold.
He may my proffer take for an offence,
Since men take women's gifts for impudence.

Sim. How!
Do as I bid you, or you'll move me else.

Thai. [*Aside*] Now, by the gods, he could not please me better.

Sim. And furthermore tell him we desire to know of him
Of whence he is, his name, and parentage.

Thai. The King my father, sir, has drunk to you.

Per. I thank him.

Thai. Wishing it so much blood unto your life.

Per. I thank both him and you, and pledge him freely.

Thai. And further he desires to know of you
Of whence you are, your name, and parentage.

Per. A gentleman of Tyre; my name, Pericles;
My education been in arts and arms;
Who, looking for adventures in the world
Was by the rough seas reft of ships and men,
And after shipwreck driven upon this shore.

Thai. He thanks your Grace; names himself Pericles,
A gentleman of Tyre,
Who only by misfortune of the seas
Bereft of ships and men, cast on this shore.

Sim. Now, by the gods, I pity his misfortune,
And will awake him from his melancholy.
Come, gentlemen, we sit too long on trifles,
And waste the time, which looks for other revels.
Even in your armours, as you are address'd,
Will very well become a soldier's dance.
I will not have excuse, with saying this
Loud music is too harsh for ladies' heads,
Since they love men in arms as well as beds.

The KNIGHTS *dance*.

So, this was well ask'd, 'twas so well perform'd.
Come, sir;
Here is a lady that wants breathing too;
And I have heard, you knights of Tyre
Are excellent in making ladies trip;
And that their measures are as excellent.
Per. In those that practise them they are, my lord.
Sim. O, that's as much as you would be denied
Of your fair courtesy.
The KNIGHTS *and Ladies dance.*
Unclasp, unclasp.
Thanks, gentlemen, to all; all have done well,
[*To* PERICLES] But you the best. Pages and lights, to conduct
These knights unto their several lodgings! [*To* PERICLES] Yours, sir,
We have given order to be next our own.
Per. I am at your Grace's pleasure.
Sim. Princes, it is too late to talk of love;
And that's the mark I know you level at.
Therefore each one betake him to his rest;
To-morrow all for speeding do their best.
[*Exeunt.*

SCENE IV. *Tyre: a room in the Governor's house*

Enter HELICANUS *and* ESCANES.

Hel. No, Escanes, know this of me,
Antiochus from incest lived not free;
For which, the most high gods not minding longer
To withhold the vengeance that they had in store,
Due to this heinous capital offence,
Even in the height and pride of all his glory,
When he was seated in a chariot
Of an inestimable value, and his daughter with him,
A fire from heaven came and shrivell'd up
Their bodies, even to loathing; for they so stunk,
That all those eyes adored them ere their fall
Scorn now their hand should give them burial.
Esca. 'Twas very strange.
Hel. And yet but justice; for though
This king were great, his greatness was no guard
To bar heaven's shaft, but sin had his reward.
Esca. 'Tis very true.

Enter THREE LORDS.

1st Lord. See, not a man in private conference
Or council has respect with him but he.
2nd Lord. It shall no longer grieve without reproof.
3rd Lord. And cursed be he that will not second it.
1st Lord. Follow me, then. Lord Helicane, a word.
Hel. With me? and welcome. Happy day, my lords.
1st Lord. Know that our griefs are risen to the top,
And now at length they overflow their banks.
Hel. Your griefs! for what? Wrong not your prince you love.
1st Lord. Wrong not yourself, then, noble Helicane;
But if the Prince do live, let us salute him,
Or know what ground's made happy by his breath.
If in the world he live, we'll seek him out;
If in his grave he rest, we'll find him there;
And be resolved he lives to govern us,
Or, dead, give 's cause to mourn his funeral,
And leave us to our free election.
2nd Lord. Whose death indeed's the strongest in our censure;
And knowing this kingdom is without a head—
Like goodly buildings left without a roof
Soon fall to ruin—your noble self,
That best know how to rule and how to reign,
We thus submit unto—our sovereign.
All. Live, noble Helicane!
Hel. For honour's cause, forbear your suffrages.
If that you love Prince Pericles, forbear.
Take I your wish, I leap into the seas,
Where's hourly trouble for a minute's ease.
A twelvemonth longer, let me entreat you to
Forbear the absence of your king;
If in which time expired he not return,
I shall with aged patience bear your yoke.
But if I cannot win you to this love,
Go search like nobles, like noble subjects,
And in your search spend your adventurous worth;
Whom if you find, and win unto return,
You shall like diamonds sit about his crown.
1st Lord. To wisdom he's a fool that will not yield;
And since Lord Helicane enjoineth us,
We with our travels will endeavour us.
Hel. Then you love us, we you, and we'll clasp hands.
When peers thus knit, a kingdom ever stands.
[*Exeunt.*

SCENE V. *Pentapolis: a room in the palace*

Enter SIMONIDES, *reading a letter, at one door; the* KNIGHTS *meet him.*

1st Knight. Good morrow to the good Simonides.

Sim. Knights, from my daughter this I let you know,
That for this twelvemonth she'll not undertake
A married life.
Her reason to herself is only known,
Which yet from her by no means can I get.
2nd Knight. May we not get access to her, my lord?
Sim. 'Faith, by no means; she hath so strictly tied
Her to her chamber that 'tis impossible.
One twelve moons more she'll wear Diana's livery;
This by the eye of Cynthia hath she vow'd,
And on her virgin honour will not break it.
3rd Knight. Loath to bid farewell, we take our leaves. [*Exeunt* KNIGHTS.
Sim. So,
They are well dispatch'd; now to my daughter's letter.
She tells me here she'll wed the stranger knight,
Or never more to view nor day nor light.
'Tis well, mistress; your choice agrees with mine;
I like that well. Nay, how absolute she's in 't,
Not minding whether I dislike or no!
Well, I do commend her choice;
And will no longer have it be delay'd.
Soft! here he comes. I must dissemble it.

Enter PERICLES.

Per. All fortune to the good Simonides!
Sim. To you as much, sir! I am beholding to you
For your sweet music this last night. I do
Protest my ears were never better fed
With such delightful pleasing harmony.
Per. It is your Grace's pleasure to commend;
Not my desert.
Sim. Sir, you are music's master.
Per. The worst of all her scholars, my good lord.
Sim. Let me ask you one thing.
What do you think of my daughter, sir?
Per. A most virtuous princess.
Sim. And she is fair too, is she not?
Per. As a fair day in summer, wondrous fair.
Sim. Sir, my daughter thinks very well of you;
Ay, so well, that you must be her master,
And she will be your scholar; therefore look to it.
Per. I am unworthy for her schoolmaster.
Sim. She thinks not so; peruse this writing else.
Per. [*Aside*] What's here?
A letter, that she loves the knight of Tyre!
'Tis the King's subtilty to have my life.
O, seek not to entrap me, gracious lord,
A stranger and distressed gentleman,
That never aim'd so high to love your daughter,
But bent all offices to honour her.
Sim. Thou hast bewitch'd my daughter, and thou art
A villain.
Per. By the gods, I have not.
Never did thought of mine levy offence;
Nor never did my actions yet commence
A deed might gain her love or your displeasure.
Sim. Traitor, thou liest.
Per. Traitor!
Sim. Ay, traitor.
Per. Even in his throat—unless it be the King—
That calls me traitor, I return the lie.
Sim. [*Aside*] Now, by the gods, I do applaud his courage.
Per. My actions are as noble as my thoughts,
That never relish'd of a base descent.
I came unto your court for honour's cause,
And not to be a rebel to her state;
And he that otherwise accounts of me,
This sword shall prove he's honour's enemy.
Sim. No?
Here comes my daughter, she can witness it.

Enter THASIA.

Per. Then, as you are as virtuous as fair,
Resolve your angry father, if my tongue
Did e'er solicit, or my hand subscribe
To any syllable that made love to you.
Thai. Why, sir, say if you had,
Who takes offence at that would make me glad?
Sim. Yea, mistress, are you so peremptory?
[*Aside*] I am glad on't with all my heart.—
I'll tame you; I'll bring you in subjection.
Will you, not having my consent,
Bestow your love and your affections
Upon a stranger? [*Aside*] who, for aught I know,
May be, nor can I think the contrary,
As great in blood as I myself.—
Therefore hear you, mistress; either frame
Your will to mine—and you, sir, hear you,
Either be ruled by me, or I will make you—
Man and wife.
Nay, come, your hands and lips must seal it too.
And being join'd, I'll thus your hopes destroy;
And for a further grief—God give you joy!—
What, are you both pleased?
Thai. Yes, if you love me, sir.
Per. Even as my life my blood that fosters it.
Sim. What, are you both agreed?
Both. Yes, if it please your Majesty.
Sim. It pleaseth me so well that I will see you wed;
And then with what haste you can get you to bed. [*Exeunt.*

ACT III

Enter GOWER.

Gow. Now sleep yslaked hath the rout;
No din but snores the house about,
Made louder by the o'er-fed breast
Of this most pompous marriage-feast.
The cat, with eyne of burning coal,
Now couches fore the mouse's hole;
And crickets sing at the oven's mouth,
E'er the blither for their drouth.
Hymen hath brought the bride to bed,
Where, by the loss of maidenhead,
A babe is moulded. Be attent,
And time that is so briefly spent
With your fine fancies quaintly eche.
What's dumb in show I'll plain with speech.

DUMB SHOW

Enter, PERICLES *and* SIMONIDES, *at one door, with Attendants; a* MESSENGER *meets them, kneels, and gives* PERICLES *a letter.* PERICLES *shows it* SIMONIDES; *the* LORDS *kneel to him. Then enter* THAISA *with child, with* LYCHORIDA *a nurse. The* KING *shows her the letter; she rejoices. She and* PERICLES *take leave of her father, and depart with* LYCHORIDA *and their Attendants. Then exeunt* SIMONIDES *and the rest.*

By many a dern and painful perch
Of Pericles the careful search,
By the four opposing coigns
Which the world together joins,
Is made with all due diligence
That horse and sail and high expense
Can stead the quest. At last from Tyre,
Fame answering the most strange inquire,
To the court of King Simonides
Are letters brought, the tenour these:
Antiochus and his daughter dead,
The men of Tyrus on the head
Of Helicanus would set on
The crown of Tyre, but he will none.
The mutiny he there hastes t' oppress;
Says to 'em, if King Pericles
Come not home in twice six moons,
He, obedient to their dooms,
Will take the crown. The sum of this,
Brought hither to Pentapolis,
Y-ravished the regions round,
And every one with claps can sound,
"Out heir-apparent is a king!
Who dream'd, who thought of such a thing?"
Brief, he must hence depart to Tyre:
His queen with child makes her desire—
Which who shall cross?—along to go.
Omit we all their dole and woe.
Lychorida, her nurse, she takes,
And so to sea. Their vessel shakes
On Neptune's billow; half the flood
Hath their keel cut. But fortune's mood
Varies again; the grisled north
Disgorges such a tempest forth
That, as a duck for life that dives,
So up and down the poor ship drives.
The lady shrieks, and well-a-near
Does fall in travail with her fear.
And what ensues in this fell storm
Shall for itself itself perform.
I nill relate, action may
Conveniently the rest convey,
Which might not what by me is told.
In your imagination hold
This stage the ship, upon whose deck
The sea-tost Pericles appears to speak. [*Exit.*

SCENE I

Enter PERICLES, *on shipboard.*

Per. Thou god of this great vast, rebuke these surges,
Which wash both heaven and hell; and thou, that hast
Upon the winds command, bind them in brass,
Having call'd them from the deep! O, still
Thy deafening, dreadful thunders; gently quench
Thy nimble, sulphurous flashes! O, how, Lychorida,
How does my queen? Thou stormest venomously;
Wilt thou spit all thyself? The seaman's whistle
Is as a whisper in the ears of death,
Unheard. Lychorida!—Lucina, O
Divinest patroness, and midwife gentle
To those that cry by night, convey thy deity
Aboard our dancing boat; make swift the pangs
Of my queen's travails!

Enter LYCHORIDA, *with an infant.*

Now, Lychorida!

Lyc. Here is a thing too young for such a place,
Who, if it had conceit, would die, as I
Am like to do. Take in your arms this piece
Of your dead queen.

Per. How, how, Lychorida!

Lyc. Patience, good sir; do not assist the storm.
Here's all that is left living of your queen,
A little daughter. For the sake of it
Be manly, and take comfort.

Per. O you gods!
Why do you make us love your goodly gifts,
And snatch them straight away? We here below

Recall not what we give, and therein may
Use honour with you.

Lyc. Patience, good sir,
Even for this charge.

Per. Now, mild may be thy life!
For a more blustrous birth had never babe.
Quiet and gentle thy conditions! for
Thou art the rudeliest welcome to this world
That ever was prince's child. Happy what follows!
Thou hast as chiding a nativity
As fire, air, water, earth, and heaven can make,
To herald thee from the womb. Even at the first
Thy loss is more than can thy portage quit,
With all thou canst find here. Now, the good gods
Throw their best eyes upon't!

Enter TWO SAILORS.

1st Sail. What courage, sir? God save you!

Per. Courage enough. I do not fear the flaw;
It hath done to me the worst. Yet, for the love
Of this poor infant, this fresh-new sea-farer,
I would it would be quiet.

1st Sail. Slack the bolins there! Thou wilt not, wilt thou? Blow, and split thyself.

2nd Sail. But sea-room, an the brine and cloudy billow kiss the moon, I care not.

1st Sail. Sir, your queen must overboard. The sea works high, the wind is loud, and will not lie till the ship be cleared of the dead.

Per. That's your superstition.

1st Sail. Pardon us, sir; with us at sea it hath been still observed, and we are strong in custom. Therefore briefly yield her; for she must overboard straight.

Per. As you think meet. Most wretched queen!

Lyc. Here she lies, sir.

Per. A terrible childbed hast thou had, my dear;
No light, no fire; the unfriendly elements
Forgot thee utterly; nor have I time
To give thee hallow'd to thy grave, but straight
Must cast thee, scarcely coffin'd, in the ooze,
Where, for a monument upon thy bones,
And e'er-remaining lamps, the belching whale
And humming water must o'erwhelm thy corpse,
Lying with simple shells. O Lychorida,
Bid Nestor bring me spices, ink, and paper,
My casket and my jewels; and bid Nicander
Bring me the satin coffer. Lay the babe
Upon the pillow. Hie thee, whiles I say
A priestly farewell to her. Suddenly, woman.
[*Exit* LYCHORIDA.

2nd Sail. Sir, we have a chest beneath the hatches, caulked and bitumed ready.

Per. I thank thee. Mariner, say what coast is this?

2nd. Sail. We are near Tarsus.

Per. Thither, gentle mariner,
Alter thy course for Tyre. When canst thou reach it?

2nd Sail. By break of day, if the wind cease.

Per. O, make for Tarsus!
There will I visit Cleon, for the babe
Cannot hold out to Tyrus. There I'll leave it
At careful nursing. Go thy ways, good mariner.
I'll bring the body presently. [*Exeunt.*

SCENE II. *Ephesus: a room in Cerimon's house*

Enter CERIMON, *with a* SERVANT, *and some Persons who have been shipwrecked.*

Cer. Philemon, ho!

Enter PHILEMON.

Phil. Doth my lord call?

Cer. Get fire and meat for these poor men.
'T has been a turbulent and stormy night.

Serv. I have been in many; but such a night as this,
Till now, I ne'er endured.

Cer. Your master will be dead ere you return;
There's nothing can be minister'd to nature
That can recover him. [*To* PHILEMON] Give this to the 'pothecary,
And tell me how it works.
[*Exeunt all but* CERIMON.

Enter TWO GENTLEMEN.

1st Gent. Good morrow.

2nd Gent. Good morrow to your lordship.

Cer. Gentlemen,
Why do you stir so early?

1st Gent. Sir,
Our lodgings, standing bleak upon the sea,
Shook as the earth did quake;
The very principals did seem to rend,
And all-to topple. Pure surprise and fear
Made me to quit the house.

2nd Gent. That is the cause we trouble you so early;
'Tis not our husbandry.

Cer. O, you say well.

1st Gent. But I much marvel that your lordship, having
Rich tire about you, should at these early hours
Shake off the golden slumber of repose.
'Tis most strange
Nature should be so conversant with pain,
Being thereto not compell'd.

Cer. I hold it ever
Virtue and cunning were endowments greater

Than nobleness and riches. Careless heirs
May the two latter darken and expend;
But immortality attends the former,
Making a man a god. 'Tis known, I ever
Have studied physic, through which secret art,
By turning o'er authorities, I have,
Together with my practice, made familiar
To me and to my aid the blest infusions
That dwell in vegetives, in metals, stones;
And I can speak of the disturbances
That nature works, and of her cures; which doth give me
A more content in course of true delight
Than to be thirsty after tottering honour,
Or tie my treasure up in silken bags,
To please the fool and Death.

2nd Gent. Your honour has through Ephesus pour'd forth
Your charity, and hundreds call themselves
Your creatures, who by you have been restored.
And not your knowledge, your personal pain, but even
Your purse, still open, hath built Lord Cerimon
Such strong renown as time shall ne'er decay.

Enter two or three SERVANTS *with a chest.*

1st Serv. So; lift there.

Cer. What is that?

1st Serv. Sir, even now
Did the sea toss upon our shore this chest.
'Tis of some wreck.

Cer. Set't down, let's look upon't.

2nd Gent. 'Tis like a coffin, sir.

Cer. Whate'er it be,
'Tis wondrous heavy. Wrench it open straight:
If the sea's stomach be o'ercharged with gold,
'Tis a good constraint of fortune it belches upon us.

2nd Gent. 'Tis so, my lord.

Cer. How close 'tis caulk'd and bitumed!
Did the sea cast it up?

1st Serv. I never saw so huge a billow, sir,
As toss'd it upon shore.

Cer. Wrench it open;
Soft! it smells most sweetly in my sense.

2nd Gent. A delicate odour.

Cer. As ever hit my nostril. So, up with it.
O you most potent gods! what's here? a corse!

1st Gent. Most strange!

Cer. Shrouded in cloth of state; balm'd and entreasured
With full bags of spices! A passport too!
Apollo, perfect me in the characters!

Reads from a scroll.

"Here I give to understand,
If e'er this coffin drive a-land,
I, King Pericles, have lost
This queen, worth all our mundane cost.
Who finds her, give her burying;
She was the daughter of a king.
Besides this treasure for a fee,
The gods requite his charity!"
If thou livest, Pericles, thou hast a heart
That even cracks for woe! This chanced tonight.

2nd Gent. Most likely, sir.

Cer. Nay, certainly to-night;
For look how fresh she looks! They were too rough
That threw her in the sea. Make a fire within.
Fetch hither all my boxes in my closet.

[*Exit a Servant.*

Death may usurp on nature many hours,
And yet the fire of life kindle again
The o'erpress'd spirits. I heard of an Egyptian
That had nine hours lien dead,
Who was by good appliance recovered.

Re-enter a Servant, with boxes, napkins, and fire.

Well said, well said; the fire and cloths.
The rough and woeful music that we have,
Cause it to sound, beseech you.
The viol once more. How thou stirr'st, thou block!
The music there! I pray you, give her air.
Gentlemen,
This queen will live. Nature awakes; a warmth
Breathes out of her. She hath not been entranced
Above five hours. See how she gins to blow
Into life's flower again!

1st Gent. The heavens,
Through you, increase our wonder and set up
Your fame for ever.

Cer. She is alive; behold,
Her eyelids, cases to those heavenly jewels
Which Pericles hath lost,
Begin to part their fringes of bright gold;
The diamonds of a most praised water
Do appear, to make the world twice rich. Live,
And make us weep to hear your fate, fair creature,
Rare as you seem to be. [*She moves.*]

Thai. O dear Diana,
Where am I? Where's my lord? What world is this?

2nd Gent. Is not this strange?

1st Gent. Most rare.

Cer. Hush, my gentle neighbours!
Lend me your hands; to the next chamber bear her.
Get linen. Now this matter must be look'd to,
For her relapse is mortal. Come, come;

And Æsculapius guide us!
[*Exeunt, carrying her away.*

SCENE III. *Tarsus: a room in Cleon's house*

Enter PERICLES, CLEON, DIONYZA, *and* LYCHORIDA *with* MARINA *in her arms.*

Per. Most honour'd Cleon, I must needs be gone;
My twelve months are expired, and Tyrus stands
In a litigious peace. You, and your lady,
Take from my heart all thankfulness! The gods
Make up the rest upon you!
Cle. Your shafts of fortune, though they hurt you mortally,
Yet glance full wanderingly on us.
Dion. O your sweet queen!
That the strict fates had pleased you had brought her hither,
To have bless'd mine eyes with her!
Per. We cannot but obey
The powers above us. Could I rage and roar
As doth the sea she lies in, yet the end
Must be as 'tis. My gentle babe Marina, whom,
For she was born at sea, I have named so, here
I charge your charity withal, leaving her
The infant of your care; beseeching you
To give her princely training, that she may be
Manner'd as she is born.
Cle. Fear not, my lord, but think
Your Grace, that fed my country with your corn,
For which the people's prayers still fall upon you,
Must in your child be thought on. If neglection
Should therein make me vile, the common body,
By you relieved, would force me to my duty.
But if to that my nature need a spur,
The gods revenge it upon me and mine,
To the end of generation!
Per. I believe you;
Your honour and your goodness teach me to't,
Without your vows. Till she be married, madam,
By bright Diana, whom we honour, all
Unscissar'd shall this hair of mine remain,
Though I show ill in't. So I take my leave.
Good madam, make me blessed in your care
In bringing up my child.
Dion. I have one myself,
Who shall not be more dear to my respect
Than yours, my lord.
Per. Madam, my thanks and prayers.
Cle. We'll bring your Grace e'en to the edge o' the shore,
Then give you up to the mask'd Neptune and
The gentlest winds of heaven.
Per. I will embrace
Your offer. Come, dearest madam. O, no tears,
Lychorida, no tears.
Look to your little mistress, on whose grace
You may depend hereafter. Come, my lord.
[*Exeunt.*

SCENE IV. *Ephesus: a room in Cerimon's house*

Enter CERIMON *and* THAISA.

Cer. Madam, this letter, and some certain jewels,
Lay with you in your coffer, which are now
At your command. Know you the character?
Thai. It is my lord's.
That I was shipp'd at sea, I well remember,
Even on my eaning time; but whether there
Deliver'd, by the holy gods,
I cannot rightly say. But since King Pericles,
My wedded lord, I ne'er shall see again,
A vestal livery will I take me to,
And never more have joy.
Cer. Madam, if this you purpose as ye speak,
Diana's temple is not distant far,
Where you may abide till your date expire.
Moreover, if you please, a niece of mine
Shall there attend you.
Thai. My recompense is thanks, that's all;
Yet my good will is great, though the gift small.
[*Exeunt.*

ACT IV

Enter GOWER.

Gow. Imagine Pericles arrived at Tyre,
Welcomed and settled to his own desire.
His woeful queen we leave at Ephesus,
Unto Diana there a votaress.
Now to Marina bend your mind,
Whom our fast-growing scene must find
At Tarsus, and by Cleon train'd
In music, letters; who hath gain'd
Of education all the grace,
Which makes her both the heart and place
Of general wonder. But, alack,
That monster envy, oft the wrack
Of earned praise, Marina's life
Seeks to take off by treason's knife.
And in this kind hath our Cleon
One daughter, and a wench full grown,
Even ripe for marriage-rite; this maid
Hight Philoten; and it is said
For certain in our story, she
Would ever with Marina be.
Be't when she weaved the sleided silk
With fingers long, small, white as milk;
Or when she would with sharp needle wound
The cambric, which she made more sound
By hurting it; or when to the lute
She sung, and made the night-bird mute,
That still records with moan; or when

She would with rich and constant pen
Vail to her mistress Dian; still
This Philoten contends in skill
With absolute Marina: so
With the dove of Paphos might the crow
Vie feathers white. Marina gets
All praises, which are paid as debts,
And not as given. This so darks
In Philoten all graceful marks,
That Cleon's wife, with envy rare,
A present murderer does prepare
For good Mariana, that her daughter
Might stand peerless by this slaughter.
The sooner her vile thoughts to stead,
Lychorida, our nurse, is dead.
And cursed Dionyza hath
The pregnant instrument of wrath
Prest for this blow. The unborn event
I do commend to your content;
Only I carry winged time
Post on the lame feet of my rhyme;
Which never could I so convey,
Unless your thoughts went on my way.
Dionyza does appear,
With Leonine, a murderer. [*Exit*.

SCENE I. *Tarsus. an open place near the sea-shore*

Enter DIONYZA *and* LEONINE.

Dion. Thy oath remember; thou hast sworn to do't.
'Tis but a blow, which never shall be known.
Thou canst not do a thing in the world so soon,
To yield thee so much profit. Let not conscience,
Which is but cold, inflaming love i' thy bosom,
Inflame too nicely; nor let pity, which
Even women have cast off, melt thee, but be
A soldier to thy purpose.

Leon. I will do't; but yet she is a goodly creature.

Dion. The fitter, then, the gods should have her.
Here she comes weeping for her only mistress' death. Thou art resolved?

Leon. I am resolved.

Enter MARINA, *with a basket of flowers*.

Mar. No, I will rob Tellus of her weed,
To strew thy green with flowers. The yellows, blues,
The purple violets, and marigolds,
Shall as a carpet hang upon thy grave,
While summer-days do last. Ay me! poor maid,
Born in a tempest, when my mother died,
This world to me is like a lasting storm,
Whirring me from my friends.

Dion. How now, Marina! why do you keep alone?
How chance my daughter is not with you? Do not
Consume your blood with sorrowing; you have
A nurse of me. Lord, how your favour's changed
With this unprofitable woe!
Come, give me your flowers, ere the sea mar it.
Walk with Leonine; the air is quick there,
And it pierces and sharpens the stomach. Come,
Leonine, take her by the arm, walk with her.

Mar. No, I pray you;
I'll not bereave you of your servant.

Dion. Come, come;
I love the King your father, and yourself,
With more than foreign heart. We every day
Expect him here. When he shall come and find
Our paragon to all reports thus blasted,
He will repent the breadth of his great voyage;
Blame both my lord and me, that we have taken
No care to your best courses. Go, I pray you,
Walk, and be cheerful once again; reserve
That excellent complexion, which did steal
The eyes of young and old. Care not for me;
I can go home alone.

Mar. Well, I will go;
But yet I have no desire to it.

Dion. Come, come, I know 'tis good for you.
Walk half an hour, Leonine, at the least.
Remember what I have said.

Leon. I warrant you, madam.

Dion. I'll leave you, my sweet lady, for a while.
Pray, walk softly, do not heat your blood.
What! I must have a care of you.

Mar. My thanks, sweet madam.
[*Exit* DIONYZA.
Is this wind westerly that blows?

Leon. South-west.

Mar. When I was born, the wind was north.

Leon. Was't so?

Mar. My father, as nurse said, did never fear,
But cried "Good seamen!" to the sailors, galling
His kingly hands, haling ropes;
And, clasping to the mast, endured a sea
That almost burst the deck.

Leon. When was this?

Mar. When I was born.
Never was waves nor wind more violent;
And from the ladder-tackle washes off
A canvas-climber. "Ha!" says one, "wilt out?"
And with a dropping industry they skip
From stem to stern. The boatswain whistles, and
The master calls, and trebles their confusion.

Leon. Come, say your prayers.

Mar. What mean you?

Leon. If you require a little space for prayer,
I grant it. Pray; but be not tedious,
For the gods are quick of ear, and I am sworn

To do my work with haste.
Mar. Why will you kill me?
Leon. To satisfy my lady.
Mar. Why would she have me kill'd?
Now, as I can remember, by my troth,
I never did her hurt in all my life.
I never spake bad word, nor did ill turn
To any living creature. Believe me, la,
I never kill'd a mouse, nor hurt a fly.
I trod upon a worm against my will,
But I wept for it. How have I offended,
Wherein my death might yield her any profit,
Or my life imply her any danger?
Leon. My commission
Is not to reason of the deed, but do it.
Mar. You will not do't for all the world, I hope.
You are well favour'd, and your looks foreshow
You have a gentle heart. I saw you lately,
When you caught hurt in parting two that fought.
Good sooth, it show'd well in you. Do so now.
Your lady seeks my life; come you between,
And save poor me, the weaker.
Leon. I am sworn,
And will dispatch.
He seizes her.

Enter PIRATES.

1st Pirate. Hold, villain!
[LEONINE *runs away.*
2nd Pirate. A prize! a prize!
3rd Pirate. Half-part, mates, half-part.
Come, let's have her aboard suddenly.
[*Exeunt* PIRATES *with* MARINA.

Re-enter LEONINE.

Leon. These roguing thieves serve the great pirate Valdes;
And they have seized Marina. Let her go;
There's no hope she will return. I'll swear she's dead,
And thrown into the sea. But I'll see further.
Perhaps they will but please themselves upon her,
Not carry her aboard. If she remain,
Whom they have ravish'd must by me be slain.
[*Exit.*

SCENE II. *Mytilene: a room in a brothel*

Enter PANDAR, BAWD, *and* BOULT.

Pand. Boult!

Boult. Sir?

Pand. Search the market narrowly; Mytilene is full of gallants. We lost too much money this mart by being too wenchless.

Bawd. We were never so much out of creatures. We have but poor three, and they can do no more than they can do; and they with continual action are even as good as rotten.

Pand. Therefore let's have fresh ones, whate'er we pay for them. If there be not a conscience to be used in every trade, we shall never prosper.

Bawd. Thou sayest true. 'Tis not our bringing up of poor bastards—as, I think, I have brought up some eleven—

Boult. Ay, to eleven; and brought them down again. But shall I search the market?

Bawd. What else, man? The stuff we have, a strong wind will blow it to pieces, they are so pitifully sodden.

Pand. Thou sayest true; they're too unwholesome, o' conscience. The poor Transylvanian is dead, that lay with the little baggage.

Boult. Ay, she quickly pooped him, she made him roast-meat for worms. But I'll go search the market. [*Exit.*

Pand. Three or four thousand chequins were as pretty a proportion to live quietly, and so give over.

Bawd. Why to give over, I pray you? Is it a shame to get when we are old?

Pand. O, our credit comes not in like the commodity, nor the commodity wages not with the danger; therefore, if in our youths we could pick up some pretty estate, 'twere not amiss to keep our door hatched. Besides, the sore terms we stand upon with the gods will be strong with us for giving over.

Bawd. Come, other sorts offend as well as we.

Pand. As well as we! Ay, and better too; we offend worse. Neither is our profession any trade; it's no calling. But here comes Boult.

Re-enter BOULT, *with the* PIRATES *and* MARINA.

Boult [*To* MARINA] Come your ways. My masters, you say she's a virgin?

1st Pirate. O, sir, we doubt it not.

Boult. Master, I have gone through for this piece, you see. If you like her, so; if not, I have lost my earnest.

Bawd. Boult, has she any qualities?

Boult. She has a good face, speaks well, and has excellent good clothes. There's no further necessity of qualities can make her be refused.

Bawd. What's her price, Boult?

Boult. I cannot be bated one doit of a thousand pieces.

Pand. Well, follow me, my masters, you shall have your money presently. Wife, take her in; instruct her what she has to do, that she may not be raw in her entertainment.
[*Exeunt* PANDAR *and* PIRATES.

Bawd. Boult, take you the marks of her, the

colour of her hair, complexion, height, age, with warrant of her virginity; and cry, "He that will give most shall have her first." Such a maidenhead were no cheap thing, if men were as they have been. Get this done as I command you.

Boult. Performance shall follow. [*Exit*.

Mar. Alack that Leonine was so slack, so slow!
He should have struck, not spoke; or that these pirates,
Not enough barbarous, had not o'erboard thrown me
For to seek my mother!

Bawd. Why lament you, pretty one?

Mar. That I am pretty.

Bawd. Come, the gods have done their part in you.

Mar. I accuse them not.

Bawd. You are light into my hands, where you are like to live.

Mar. The more my fault
To scape his hands where I was like to die.

Bawd. Ay, and you shall live in pleasure.

Mar. No.

Bawd. Yes, indeed shall you, and taste gentlemen of all fashions. You shall fare well; you shall have the difference of all complexions. What! do you stop your ears?

Mar. Are you a woman?

Bawd. What would you have me be, an I be not a woman?

Mar. An honest woman, or not a woman.

Bawd. Marry, whip thee, gosling. I think I shall have something to do with you. Come, you're a young foolish sapling, and must be bowed as I would have you.

Mar. The gods defend me!

Bawd. If it please the gods to defend you by men, then men must comfort you, men must feed you, men must stir you up. Boult's returned.

Re-enter BOULT.

Now, sir, hast thou cried her through the market?

Boult. I have cried her almost to the number of her hairs; I have drawn her picture with my voice.

Bawd. And I prithee tell me, how dost thou find the inclination of the people, especially of the younger sort?

Boult. 'Faith, they listened to me as they would have hearkened to their father's testament. There was a Spaniard's mouth so watered, that he went to bed to her very description.

Bawd. We shall have him here to-morrow with his best ruff on.

Boult. To-night, to-night. But, mistress, do you know the French knight that cowers i' the hams?

Bawd. Who, Monsieur Veroles?

Boult. Ay, he. He offered to cut a caper at the proclamation; but he made a groan at it, and swore he would see her to-morrow.

Bawd. Well, well; as for him, he brought his disease hither. Here he does but repair it. I know he will come in our shadow, to scatter his crowns in the sun.

Boult. Well, if we had of every nation a traveller, we should lodge them with this sign.

Bawd. [*To* MARINA] Pray you, come hither awhile. You have fortunes coming upon you. Mark me: you must seem to do that fearfully which you commit willingly, despise profit where you have most gain. To weep that you live as ye do makes pity in your lovers; seldom but that pity begets you a good opinion, and that opinion a mere profit.

Mar. I understand you not.

Boult. O, take her home, mistress, take her home. These blushes of hers must be quenched with some present practice.

Bawd. Thou sayest true, i' faith, so they must; for your bride goes to that with shame which is her way to go with warrant.

Boult. 'Faith, some do, and some do not. But, mistress, if I have bargained for the joint—

Bawd. Thou mayst cut a morsel off the spit.

Boult. I may so.

Bawd. Who should deny it? Come, young one, I like the manner of your garments well.

Boult. Ay, by my faith, they shall not be changed yet.

Bawd. Boult, spend thou that in the town; report what a sojourner we have; you'll lose nothing by custom. When nature framed this piece, she meant thee a good turn; therefore say what a paragon she is, and thou hast the harvest out of thine own report.

Boult. I warrant you, mistress, thunder shall not so awake the beds of eels as my giving out her beauty stir up the lewdly-inclined. I'll bring home some to-night.

Bawd. Come your ways; follow me.

Mar. If fires be hot, knives sharp, or waters deep,
Untied I still my virgin knot will keep.
Diana, aid my purpose!

Bawd. What have we to do with Diana? Pray you, will you go with us? [*Exeunt*.

SCENE III. *Tarsus: a room in Cleon's house*

Enter CLEON *and* DIONYZA.

Dion. Why, are you foolish? Can it be undone?

Cle. O Dionyza, such a piece of slaughter
The sun and moon ne'er look'd upon!
Dion. I think
You'll turn a child again.
Cle. Were I chief lord of all this spacious world,
I'd give it to undo the deed. O lady,
Much less in blood than virtue, yet a princess
To equal any single crown o' the earth
I' the justice of compare! O villain Leonine!
Whom thou hast poison'd too.
If thou hadst drunk to him, 't had been a kindness
Becoming well thy fact. What canst thou say
When noble Pericles shall demand his child?
Dion. That she is dead. Nurses are not the fates,
To foster it, nor ever to preserve.
She died at night; I'll say so. Who can cross it?
Unless you play the pious innocent,
And for an honest attribute cry out,
"She died by foul play."
Cle. O, go to. Well, well,
Of all the faults beneath the heavens, the gods
Do like this worst.
Dion. Be one of those that think
The petty wrens of Tarsus will fly hence
And open this to Pericles. I do shame
To think of what a noble strain you are,
And of how coward a spirit.
Cle. To such proceeding
Who ever but his approbation added,
Though not his prime consent, he did not flow
From honourable sources.
Dion. Be it so, then.
Yet none does know, but you, how she came dead,
Nor none can know, Leonine being gone.
She did distain my child, and stood between
Her and her fortunes. None would look on her,
But cast their gazes on Marina's face;
Whilst ours was blurted at and held a Malkin
Not worth the time of day. It pierced me thorough;
And though you call my course unnatural,
You not your child well loving, yet I find
It greets me as an enterprise of kindness
Perform'd to your sole daughter.
Cle. Heavens forgive it!
Dion. And as for Pericles,
What should he say? We wept after her hearse,
And yet we mourn. Her monument
Is almost finish'd, and her epitaphs
In glittering golden characters express
A general praise to her, and care in us
At whose expense 'tis done.
Cle. Thou art like the harpy,
Which, to betray, dost, with thine angel's face,
Seize with thine eagle's talons.
Dion. You are like one that superstitiously
Doth swear to the gods that winter kills the flies;
But yet I know you'll do as I advise. [*Exeunt.*

SCENE IV

Enter GOWER, *before the monument of Marina at Tarsus.*

Gow. Thus time we waste, and longest leagues make short;
Sail seas in cockles, have an wish but for't;
Making, to take your imagination,
From bourn to bourn, region to region.
By you being pardon'd, we commit no crime
To use one language in each several clime
Where our scenes seem to live. I do beseech you
To learn of me, who stand i' the gaps to teach you,
The stages of our story. Pericles
Is now again thwarting the wayward seas,
Attended on by many a lord and knight,
To see his daughter, all his life's delight.
Old Escanes, whom Helicanus late
Advanced in time to great and high estate,
Is left to govern. Bear you it in mind,
Old Helicanus goes along behind.
Well-sailing ships and bounteous winds have brought
This king to Tarsus—think his pilot thought;
So with his steerage shall your thoughts grow on—
To fetch his daughter home, who first is gone.
Like motes and shadows see them move awhile;
Your ears unto your eyes I'll reconcile.

DUMB SHOW

Enter PERICLES, *at one door, with all his train;* CLEON *and* DIONYZA, *at the other.* CLEON *shows* PERICLES *the tomb; whereat* PERICLES *makes lamentation, puts on sackcloth, and in a mighty passion departs. Then exeunt* CLEON *and* DIONYZA.

See how belief may suffer by foul show!
This borrow'd passion stands for true old woe;
And Pericles, in sorrow all devour'd,
With sighs shot through, and biggest tears o'ershower'd,
Leaves Tarsus and again embarks. He swears
Never to wash his face, nor cut his hairs:
He puts on sackcloth, and to sea. He bears
A tempest, which his mortal vessel tears,
And yet he rides it out. Now please you wit
The epitaph is for Marina writ
By wicked Dionyza.
Reads the inscription on Marina's monument.
"The fairest, sweet'st, and best lies here,

Who wither'd in her spring of year.
She was of Tyrus the King's daughter,
On whom foul death hath made this slaughter;
Marina was she call'd; and at her birth,
Thetis, being proud, swallow'd some part o' the earth:
Therefore the earth, fearing to be o'erflowed,
Hath Thetis' birth-child on the heavens bestow'd;
Wherefore she does, and swears she'll never stint,
Make raging battery upon shores of flint."

No visor does become black villainy
So well as soft and tender flattery.
Let Pericles believe his daughter's dead,
And bear his courses to be ordered
By Lady Fortune; while our scene must play
His daughter's woe and heavy well-a-day
In her unholy service. Patience, then,
And think you now are all in Mytilene. [*Exit.*

SCENE V. *Mytilene: a street before the brothel*

Enter, from the brothel, TWO GENTLEMAN.

1st Gent. Did you ever hear the like?

2nd Gent. No, nor ever shall do in such a place as this, she being once gone.

1st Gent. But to have divinity preached there! did you ever dream of such a thing?

2nd Gent. No, no. Come, I am for no more bawdy-houses. Shall's go hear the vestals sing?

1st Gent. I'll do anything now that is virtuous; but I am out of the road of rutting for ever.

[*Exeunt.*

SCENE VI. *The same: a room in the brothel*

Enter PANDAR, BAWD, *and* BOULT.

Pand. Well, I had rather than twice the worth of her she had ne'er come her.

Bawd. Fie, fie upon her! she's able to freeze the god Priapus and undo a whole generation. We must either get her ravished, or be rid of her. When she should do for clients her fitment, and do me the kindness of our profession, she has me her quirks, her reasons, her master reasons, her prayers, her knees; that she would make a puritan of the devil, if he should cheapen a kiss of her.

Boult. 'Faith, I must ravish her, or she'll disfurnish us of all our cavaliers, and make our swearers priests.

Pand. Now, the pox upon her green-sickness for me!

Bawd. 'Faith, there's no way to be rid on't but by the way to the pox. Here comes the Lord Lysimachus disguised.

Boult. We should have both lord and lown, if the peevish baggage would but give way to customers.

Enter LYSIMACHUS.

Lys. How now! How a dozen of virginities?

Bawd. Now, the gods to bless your honour!

Boult. I am glad to see your honour in good health.

Lys. You may so; 'tis the better for you that your resorters stand upon sound legs. How now! Wholesome iniquity have you that a man may deal withal, and defy the surgeon?

Bawd. We have here one, sir, if she would—but there never came her like in Mytilene.

Lys. If she'd do the deed of darkness, thou wouldst say.

Bawd. Your honour knows what 'tis to say well enough.

Lys. Well, call forth, call forth.

Boult. For flesh and blood, sir, white and red, you shall see a rose; and she were a rose indeed, if she had but—

Lys. What, prithee?

Boult. O, sir, I can be modest.

Lys. That dignifies the renown of a bawd, no less than it gives a good report to a number to be chaste. [*Exit* BOULT.

Bawd. Here comes that which grows to the stalk; never plucked yet, I can assure you.

Re-enter BOULT *with* MARINA.

Is she not a fair creature?

Lys. 'Faith, she would serve after a long voyage at sea. Well, there's for you. Leave us.

Bawd. I beseech your honour, give me leave. A word, and I'll have done presently.

Lys. I beseech you, do.

Bawd. [*To* MARINA] First, I would have you note, this is an honourable man.

Mar. I desire to find him so, that I may worthily note him.

Bawd. Next, he's the governor of this country, and a man whom I am bound to.

Mar. If he govern the country, you are bound to him indeed; but how honourable he is in that, I know not.

Bawd. Pray you, without any more virginal fencing, will you use him kindly? He will line your apron with gold.

Mar. What he will do graciously, I will thankfully receive.

Lys. Ha' you done?

Bawd. My lord, she's not paced yet. You must take some pains to work her to your manage. Come, we will leave his honour and her together. Go thy ways.

[*Exeunt* BAWD, PANDAR, *and* BOULT.

Lys. Now, pretty one, how long have you been at this trade?

Mar. What trade, sir?

Lys. Why, I cannot name't but I shall offend.

Mar. I cannot be offended with my trade. Please you to name it.

Lys. How long have you been of this profession?

Mar. E'er since I can remember.

Lys. Did you go to't so young? Were you a gamester at five or at seven?

Mar. Earlier too, sir, if now I be one.

Lys. Why, the house you dwell in proclaims you to be a creature of sale.

Mar. Do you know this house to be a place of such resort, and will come into't? I hear say you are of honourable parts, and are the governor of this place.

Lys. Why, hath your principal made known unto you who I am?

Mar. Who is my principal?

Lys. Why, your herb-woman; she that sets seeds and roots of shame and iniquity. O, you have heard something of my power, and so stand aloof for more serious wooing. But I protest to thee, pretty one, my authority shall not see thee, or else look friendly upon thee. Come, bring me to some private place. Come, come.

Mar. If you were born to honour, show it now;
If put upon you, make the judgement good
That thought you worthy of it.

Lys. How's this? how's this? Some more; be sage.

Mar. For me,
That am a maid, though most ungentle fortune
Have placed me in this sty, where, since I came,
Diseases have been sold dearer than physic,
O, that the gods
Would set me free from this unhallow'd place,
Though they did change me to the meanest bird
That flies i' the purer air!

Lys. I did not think
Thou couldst have spoke so well; ne'er dream'd thou couldst.
Had I brought hither a corrupted mind,
Thy speech had alter'd it. Hold, here's gold for thee.
Persever in that clear way thou goest,
And the gods strengthen thee!

Mar. The good gods preserve you!

Lys. For me, be you thoughten
That I came with no ill intent; for to me
The very doors and windows savour vilely.
Fare thee well. Thou art a piece of virtue, and
I doubt not but thy training hath been noble.
Hold, here's more gold for thee.
A curse upon him, die he like a thief,
That robs thee of thy goodness! If thou dost
Hear from me, it shall be for thy good.

Re-enter BOULT

Boult. I beseech your honour, one piece for me.

Lys. Avaunt, thou damned door-keeper!
Your house, but for this virgin that doth prop it,
Would sink and overwhelm you. Away! [*Exit.*

Boult. How's this? We must take another course with you. If your peevish chastity, which is not worth a breakfast in the cheapest country under the cope, shall undo a whole household, let me be gelded like a spaniel. Come your ways.

Mar. Whither would you have me?

Boult. I must have your maidenhead taken off, or the common hangman shall execute it. Come your ways. We'll have no more gentlemen driven away. Come your ways, I say.

Re-enter BAWD.

Bawd. How now! what's the matter?

Boult. Worse and worse, mistress; she has here spoken holy words to the Lord Lysimachus.

Bawd. O abominable!

Boult. She makes our profession as it were to stink afore the face of the gods.

Bawd. Marry, hang her up for ever!

Boult. The nobleman would have dealt with her like a nobleman, and she sent him away as cold as a snowball; saying his prayers too.

Bawd. Boult, take her away; use her at thy pleasure. Crack the glass of her virginity, and make the rest malleable.

Boult. An if she were a thornier piece of ground than she is, she shall be ploughed.

Mar. Hark, hark, you gods!

Bawd. She conjures. Away with her! Would she had never come within my doors! Marry, hang you! She's born to undo us. Will you not go the way of women-kind? Marry, come up, my dish of chastity with rosemary and bays! [*Exit.*

Boult. Come, mistress; come your ways with me.

Mar. Whither wilt thou have me?

Boult. To take from you the jewel you hold so dear.

Mar. Prithee, tell me one thing first.

Boult. Come now, your one thing.

Mar. What canst thou wish thine enemy to be?

Boult. Why, I could wish him to be my master, or rather, my mistress.

Mar. Neither of these are so bad as thou art,
Since they do better thee in their command.

Thou hold'st a place, for which the pained'st fiend
Of hell would not in reputation change.
Thou art the damned doorkeeper to every
Coistrel that comes inquiring for his Tib;
To the choleric fisting of every rogue
Thy ear is liable; thy food is such
As hath been belch'd on by infected lungs.

Boult. What would you have me do? go to the wars, would you? where a may may serve seven years for the loss of a leg, and have not money enough in the end to buy him a wooden one?

Mar. Do anything but this thou doest. Empty
Old receptacles, or common shores, of filth;
Serve by indenture to the common hangman.
Any of these ways are yet better than this;
For what thou professest, a baboon, could he speak,
Would own a name too dear. O, that the gods
Would safely deliver me from this place!
Here, here's gold for thee.
If that thy master would gain by me,
Proclaim that I can sing, weave, sew, and dance,
With other virtues, which I'll keep from boast;
And I will undertake all these to teach.
I doubt not but this populous city will
Yield many scholars.

Boult. But can you teach all this you speak of?

Mar. Prove that I cannot, take me home again,
And prostitute me to the basest groom
That doth frequent your house.

Boult. Well, I will see what I can do for thee. If I can place thee, I will.

Mar. But amongst honest women.

Boult. 'Faith, my acquaintance lies little amongst them. But since my master and mistress have bought you, there's no going but by their consent; therefore I will make them acquainted with your purpose, and I doubt not but I shall find them tractable enough. Come, I'll do for thee what I can; come your ways.

[*Exeunt.*

ACT V

Enter GOWER.

Gow. Marina thus the brothel 'scapes, and chances
Into an honest house, our story says.
She sings like one immortal, and she dances
As goddess-like to her admired lays;
Deep clerks she dumbs; and with her neeld composes
Nature's own shape, of bud, bird, branch, or berry,
That even her art sisters the natural roses;
Her inkle, silk, twin with the rubied cherry,
That pupils lacks she none of noble race,
Who pour their bounty on her; and her gain
She gives the cursed bawd. Here we her place;
And to her father turn our thoughts again,
Where we left him, on the sea. We there him lost;
Whence, driven before the winds, he is arrived
Here where his daughter dwells; and on this coast
Suppose him now at anchor. The city strived
God Neptune's annual feast to keep; from whence
Lysimachus our Tyrian ship espies,
His banners sable, trimm'd with rich expense;
And to him in his barge with fervour hies.
In your supposing once more put your sight
Of heavy Pericles; think this his bark.
Where what is done in action, more, if might,
Shall be discover'd; please you, sit and hark.

[*Exit.*

SCENE I. *On board Pericles' ship, off Mytilene. A close pavilion on deck, with a curtain before it, Pericles within it, reclined on a couch. A barge lying beside the Tyrian vessel*

Enter TWO SAILORS, *one belonging to the Tyrian vessel, the other to the barge; to them* HELICANUS.

Tyr. Sail. [*To the* SAILOR *of Mytilene*]
Where is lord Helicanus? He can resolve you.
O, here he is.
Sir, there's a barge put off from Mytilene,
And in it is Lysimachus the governor,
Who craves to come aboard. What is your will?

Hel. That he have his. Call up some gentlemen.

Tyr. Sail. Ho, gentlemen! my lord calls.

Enter two or three GENTLEMEN.

1st Gent. Doth your lordship call?

Hel. Gentlemen, there's some of worth would come aboard;
I pray ye, greet them fairly.

[*The* GENTLEMEN *and the* TWO SAILORS *descend, and go on board the barge.*

Enter, from thence, LYSIMACHUS *and* LORDS; *with the* GENTLEMEN *and the* TWO SAILORS.

Tyr. Sail. Sir,
This is the man that can, in aught you would,
Resolve you.

Lys. Hail, reverend sir! the gods preserve you!

Hel. And you, sir, to outlive the age I am,
And die as I would do.

Lys. You wish me well.
Being on shore, honouring of Neptune's triumphs,
Seeing this goodly vessel ride before us,
I made to it, to know of whence you are.

Hel. First, what is your place?

Lys. I am the governor of this place you lie before.

Hel. Sir,
Our vessel is of Tyre, in it the King;
A man who for this three months hath not spoken
To any one, nor taken sustenance
But to prorogue his grief.

Lys. Upon what ground is his distemperature?

Hel. 'Twould be too tedious to repeat;
But the main grief springs from the loss
Of a beloved daughter and a wife.

Lys. May we not see him?

Hel. You may;
But bootless is your sight. He will not speak
To any.

Lys. Yet let me obtain my wish.

Hel. Behold him. [PERICLES *discovered.*] This was a goodly person,
Till the disaster that, one mortal night,
Drove him to this.

Lys. Sir king, all hail! the gods preserve you!
Hail, royal sir!

Hel. It is in vain; he will not speak to you.

1st Lord. Sir,
We have a maid in Mytilene, I durst wager,
Would win some words of him.

Lys. 'Tis well bethought.
She questionless with her sweet harmony
And other chosen attractions, would allure,
And make a battery through his deafen'd parts,
Which now are midway stopp'd.
She is all happy as the fairest of all,
And, with her fellow maids, is now upon
The leafy shelter that abuts against
The island's side.

[*Whispers a* LORD, *who goes off in the barge of Lysimachus.*

Hel. Sure, all's effectless; yet nothing we'll omit
That bears recovery's name. But, since your kindness
We have stretch'd thus far, let us beseech you
That for our gold we may provision have,
Wherein we are not destitute for want,
But weary for the staleness.

Lys. O, sir, a courtesy
Which if we should deny, the most just gods
For every graff would send a caterpillar,
And so afflict our province. Yet once more
Let me entreat to know at large the cause
Of your king's sorrow.

Hel. Sit, sir, I will recount it to you.
But, see, I am prevented.

Re-enter, from the barge, LORD, *with* MARINA, *and a young Lady.*

Lys. O, here is
The lady that I sent for. Welcome, fair one!
Is't not a goodly presence?

Hel. She's a gallant lady.

Lys. She's such a one, that, were I well assured
Came of a gentle kind and noble stock,
I'd wish no better choice, and think me rarely wed.
Fair one, all goodness that consists in bounty
Expect even here, where is a kingly patient.
If that thy prosperous and artificial feat
Can draw him but to answer thee in aught,
Thy sacred physic shall receive such pay
As thy desires can wish.

Mar. Sir, I will use
My utmost skill in his recovery,
Provided
That none but I and my companion maid
Be suffer'd to come near him.

Lys. Come, let us leave her;
And the gods make her prosperous!

Marina sings.

Lys. Mark'd he your music?

Mar. No, nor look'd on us.

Lys. See, she will speak to him.

Mar. Hail, sir! my lord, lend ear.

Per. Hum, ha! [*Pushing her back.*]

Mar. I am a maid,
My lord, that ne'er before invited eyes,
But have been gazed on like a comet. She speaks,
My lord, that, may be, hath endured a grief
Might equal yours, if both were justly weigh'd.
Though wayward fortune did malign my state,
My derivation was from ancestors
Who stood equivalent with mighty kings.
But time hath rooted out my parentage,
And to the world and awkward casualties
Bound me in servitude. [*Aside*] I will desist;
But there is something glows upon my cheek,
And whispers in mine ear, "Go not till he speak."

Per. My fortunes—parentage—good parentage—
To equal mine!—was it not thus? what say you?

Mar. I said, my lord, if you did know my parentage,
You would not do me violence.

Per. I do think so. Pray you, turn your eyes upon me.
You are like something that—What countrywoman?
Here of these shores?

Mar. No, nor of any shores.
Yet I was mortally brought forth, and am
No other than I appear.

Per. I am great with woe, and shall deliver weeping.

My dearest wife was like this maid, and such a one
My daughter might have been. My queen's square brows;
Her stature to an inch; as wand-like straight;
As silver-voiced; her eyes as jewel-like
And cased as richly; in pace another Juno;
Who starves the ears she feeds, and makes them hungry,
The more she gives them speech. Where do you live?
Mar. Where I am but a stranger. From the deck
You may discern the place.
Per. Where were you bred?
And how achieved you these endowments, which
You make more rich to owe?
Mar. If I should tell my history, it would seem
Like lies disdain'd in the reporting.
Per. Prithee, speak.
Falseness cannot come from thee; for thou look'st
Modest as Justice, and thou seem'st a palace
For the crown'd Truth to dwell in. I will believe thee,
And make my senses credit thy relation
To points that seem impossible; for thou look'st
Like one I loved indeed. What were thy friends?
Didst thou not say, when I did push thee back—
Which was when I perceived thee— that thou camest
From good descending?
Mar. So indeed I did.
Per. Report thy parentage. I think thou said'st
Thou hadst been toss'd from wrong to injury,
And that thou thought'st thy griefs might equal mine,
If both were open'd.
Mar. Some such thing
I said, and said no more but what my thoughts
Did warrant me was likely.
Per. Tell thy story;
If thine consider'd prove the thousandth part
Of my endurance, thou art a man, and I
Have suffer'd like a girl. Yet thou dost look
Like Patience gazing on kings' graves, and smiling
Extremity out of act. What were thy friends?
How lost thou them? Thy name, my most kind virgin?
Recount, I do beseech thee. Come, sit by me.
Mar. My name is Marina.
Per. O, I am mock'd,
And thou by some incensed god sent hither
To make the world to laugh at me.
Mar. Patience, good sir,
Or here I'll cease.
Per. Nay, I'll be patient.
Thou little know'st how thou dost startle me,
To call thyself Marina.
Mar. The name
Was given me by one that had some power,
My father, and a king.
Per. How! a king's daughter?
And call'd Marina?
Mar. You said you would believe me;
But, not to be troubler of your peace,
I will end here.
Per. But are you flesh and blood?
Have you a working pulse? and are no fairy?
Motion! Well; speak on. Where were you born?
And wherefore call'd Marina?
Mar. Call'd Marina
For I was born at sea.
Per. At sea! what mother?
Mar. My mother was the daughter of a king;
Who died the minute I was born,
As my good nurse Lychorida hath oft
Deliver'd weeping.
Per. O, stop there a little!
[*Aside*] This is the rarest dream that e'er dull sleep
Did mock sad fools withal. This cannot be;
My daughter's buried. Well, where were you bred?
I'll hear you more, to the bottom of your story,
And never interrupt you.
Mar. You scorn. Believe me, 'twere best I did give o'er.
Per. I will believe you by the syllable
Of what you shall deliver. Yet, give me leave:
How came you in these parts? where were you bred?
Mar. The King my father did in Tarsus leave me;
Till cruel Cleon, with his wicked wife,
Did seek to murder me; and having woo'd
A villain to attempt it, who having drawn to do 't,
A crew of pirates came and rescued me;
Brought me to Mytilene. But, good sir,
Whither will you have me? Why do you weep? It may be,
You think me an impostor. No, good faith;
I am the daughter to King Pericles,
If good King Pericles be.
Per. Ho, Helicanus!
Hel. Calls my lord?
Per. Thou art a grave and noble counsellor,
Most wise in general. Tell me, if thou canst,
What this maid is, or what is like to be,
That thus hath made me weep?

Hel. I know not; but
Here is the regent, sir, of Mytilene
Speaks nobly of her.
Lys. She would never tell
Her parentage; being demanded that,
She would sit still and weep.
Per. O Helicanus, strike me, honour'd sir;
Give me a gash, put me to present pain;
Lest this great sea of joys rushing upon me
O'erbear the shores of my mortality,
And drown me with their sweetness. O, come hither,
Thou that beget'st him that did thee beget;
Thou that wast born at sea, buried at Tarsus,
And found at sea again! O Helicanus,
Down on thy knees, thank the holy gods as loud
As thunder threatens us. This is Marina.
What was thy mother's name? tell me but that,
For truth can never be confirm'd enough,
Though doubts did ever sleep.
Mar. First, sir, I pray,
What is your title?
Per. I am Pericles of Tyre; but tell me now
My drown'd queen's name, as in the rest you said
Thou hast been godlike perfect,
The heir of kingdoms and another like
To Pericles thy father.
Mar. Is it no more to be your daughter than
To say my mother's name was Thaisa?
Thaisa was my mother, who did end
The minute I began.
Per. Now, blessing on thee! Rise; thou art my child.
Give me fresh garments. Mine own, Helicanus;
She is not dead at Tarsus, as she should have been,
By savage Cleon. She shall tell thee all;
When thou shalt kneel, and justify in knowledge
She is thy very princess. Who is this?
Hel. Sir, 'tis the governor of Mytilene,
Who, hearing of your melancholy state,
Did come to see you.
Per. I embrace you.
Give me my robes. I am wild in my beholding.
O heavens bless my girl! But, hark, what music?
Tell Helicanus, my Marina, tell him
O'er, point by point, for yet he seems to doubt,
How sure you are my daughter. But, what music?
Hel. My lord, I hear none.
Per. None!
The music of the spheres! List, my Marina.
Lys. It is not good to cross him; give him way.
Per. Rarest sounds! Do ye not hear?
Lys. My lord, I hear.
Music.
Per. Most heavenly music!
It nips me unto listening, and thick slumber
Hangs upon mine eyes. Let me rest. [*Sleeps.*]
Lys. A pillow for his head.
So, leave him all. Well, my companion friends,
If this but answer to my just belief,
I'll well remember you.
[*Exeunt all but* PERICLES.

DIANA *appears to* PERICLES *as in a vision.*

Dia. My temple stands in Ephesus. Hie thee thither,
And do upon mine altar sacrifice.
There, when my maiden priests are met together,
Before the people all,
Reveal how thou at sea didst lose thy wife.
To mourn thy crosses, with thy daughter's, call
And give them repetition to the life.
Or perform my bidding, or thou livest in woe;
Do it, and happy; by my silver bow!
Awake, and tell thy dream. [*Disappears.*
Per. Celestial Dian, goddess argentine,
I will obey thee. Helicanus!

Re-enter HELICANUS, LYSIMACHUS, *and* MARINA.

Hel. Sir?
Per. My purpose was for Tarsus, there to strike
The inhospitable Cleon; but I am
For other service first. Toward Ephesus
Turn our blown sails; eftsoons I'll tell thee why.
[*To* LYSIMACHUS] Shall we refresh us, sir, upon your shore,
And give you gold for such provision
As our intents will need?
Lys. Sir,
With all my heart; and, when you come ashore,
I have another suit.
Per. You shall prevail,
Were it to woo my daughter; for it seems
You have been noble towards her.
Lys. Sir, lend me your arm.
Per. Come, my Marina. [*Exeunt.*

SCENE II. *Enter* GOWER, *before the temple of* DIANA *at Ephesus.*

Gow. Now our sands are almost run;
More a little, and then dumb.
This, my last boon, give me,
For such kindness must relieve me,
That you aptly will suppose
What pageantry, what feats, what shows,
What minstrelsy, and pretty din,
The regent made in Mytilene
To greet the King. So he thrived,

That he is promised to be wived
To fair Marina; but in no wise
Till he had done his sacrifice,
As Dian bade; whereto being bound,
The interim, pray you, all confound.
In feather'd briefness sails are fill'd,
And wishes fall out as they're will'd.
At Ephesus, the temple see,
Our king and all his company.
That he can hither come so soon,
Is by your fancy's thankful doom. [*Exit.*

SCENE III. *The temple of Diana at Ephesus;* THAISA *standing near the altar, as high priestess; a number of Virgins on each side;* CERIMON *and other inhabitants of Ephesus attending.*

Enter PERICLES, *with his train;* LYSIMACHUS, HELICANUS, MARINA, *and a Lady.*

Per. Hail, Dian! to perform thy just command,
I here confess myself the King of Tyre;
Who, frighted from my country, did wed
At Pentapolis the fair Thaisa.
At sea in childbed died she, but brought forth
A maid-child call'd Marina; who, O goddess,
Wears yet thy silver livery. She at Tarsus
Was nursed with Cleon; who at fourteen years
He sought to murder; but her better stars
Brought her to Mytilene; 'gainst whose shore
Riding, her fortunes brought the maid aboard us,
Where, by her own most clear remembrance, she
Made known herself my daughter.
Thai. Voice and favour!
You are, you are—O royal Pericles! [*Faints.*]
Per. What means the nun? she dies! help, gentlemen!
Cer. Noble sir,
If you have told Diana's altar true,
This is your wife.
Per. Reverend appearer, no;
I threw her overboard with these very arms.
Cer. Upon this coast, I warrant you.
Per. 'Tis most certain.
Cer. Look to the lady; O, she's but o'erjoy'd.
Early in blustering morn this lady was
Thrown upon this shore. I oped the coffin,
Found there rich jewels; recover'd her, and placed her
Here in Diana's temple.
Per. May we see them?
Cer. Great sir, they shall be brought you to my house,
Whither I invite you. Look, Thaisa is
Recovered.
Thai. O, let me look!
If he be none of mine, my sanctity
Will to my sense bend no licentious ear,
But curb it, spite of seeing. O, my lord,
Are you not Pericles? Like him you spake,
Like him you are. Did you not name a tempest,
A birth, and death?
Per. The voice of dead Thaisa!
Thai. That Thaisa am I, supposed dead
And drown'd.
Per. Immortal Dian!
Thai. Now I know you better.
When we with tears parted Pantapolis,
The King my father gave you such a ring.
Shows a ring.
Per. This, this. No more, you gods! your present kindness
Makes my past miseries sports. You shall do well,
That on the touching of her lips I may
Melt and no more be seen. O, come, be buried
A second time within these arms.
Mar. My heart
Leaps to be gone into my mother's bosom.
Kneels to THAISA.
Per. Look, who kneels here! Flesh of thy flesh, Thaisa;
Thy burden at the sea, and call'd Marina
For she was yielded there.
Thai. Blest, and mine own!
Hel. Hail, madam, and my queen!
Thai. I know you not.
Per. You have heard me say, when I did fly from Tyre,
I left behind an ancient substitute.
Can you remember what I call'd the man?
I have named him oft.
Thai. 'Twas Helicanus then.
Per. Still confirmation.
Embrace him, dear Thaisa; this is he.
Now do I long to hear how you were found;
How possibly preserved; and who to thank,
Besides the gods, for this great miracle.
Thai. Lord Cerimon, my lord; this man,
Through whom the gods have shown their power; that can
From first to last resolve you.
Per. Reverend sir,
The gods can have no mortal officer
More like a god than you. Will you deliver
How this dead queen re-lives?
Cer. I will, my lord.
Beseech you, first go with me to my house,
Where shall be shown you all was found with her;
How she came placed here in the temple;
No needful thing omitted.
Per. Pure Dian, bless thee for thy vision! I

Will offer night-oblations to thee. Thaisa,
This prince, the fair-betrothed of your daughter,
Shall marry her at Pentapolis. And now,
This ornament
Makes me look dismal will I clip to form;
And what this fourteen years, no razor touch'd,
To grace thy marriage-day, I'll beautify.

Thai. Lord Cerimon hath letters of good credit, sir,
My father's dead.

Per. Heavens make a star of him! Yet there, my queen,
We'll celebrate their nuptials, and ourselves
Will in that kingdom spend our following days.
Our son and daughter shall in Tyrus reign.
Lord Cerimon, we do our longing stay
To hear the rest untold. Sir, lead's the way.
[*Exeunt.*

Enter GOWER.

Gow. In Antiochus and his daughter you have heard
Of monstrous lust the due and just reward.
In Pericles, his queen and daughter, seen,
Although assail'd with fortune fierce and keen,
Virtue preserved from fell destruction's blast,
Led on by heaven, and crown'd with joy at last:
In Helicanus may you well descry
A figure of truth, of faith, of loyalty.
In reverend Cerimon there well appears
The worth that learned charity aye wears.
For wicked Cleon and his wife, when fame
Had spread their cursed deed, and honour'd name
Of Pericles, to rage the city turn,
That him and his they in his palace burn;
The gods for murder seemed so content
To punish them; although not done, but meant.
So, on your patience evermore attending,
New joy wait on you! Here our play has ending.
[*Exit.*

CYMBELINE

DRAMATIS PERSONÆ

CYMBELINE, *King of Britain*
CLOTEN, *son to the Queen by a former husband*
POSTHUMUS LEONATUS, *a gentleman, husband to Imogen*
BELARIUS, *a banished lord, disguised under the name of Morgan*
GUIDERIUS, ARVIRAGUS — *sons to Cymbeline, disguised under the names of Polydore and Cadwal, supposed sons to Morgan*
PHILARIO, *friend to Posthumus*, IACHIMO, *friend to Philario* — *Italians*
CAIUS LUCIUS, *general of the Roman forces*
PISANIO, *servant to Posthumus*
CORNELIUS, *a physician*
A ROMAN CAPTAIN
TWO BRITISH CAPTAINS
A FRENCHMAN, A SPANIARD, A DUTCHMAN — *friends to Philario*
TWO LORDS *of Cymbeline's court*
TWO GENTLEMEN *of Cymbeline's court*
TWO GAOLERS
A SOOTHSAYER
A TRIBUNE
TWO SENATORS
AN ATTENDANT *on Cymbeline*
TWO MESSENGERS

QUEEN, *wife to Cymbeline*
IMOGEN, *daughter to Cymbeline by a former Queen*
HELEN, *a lady attending on Imogen*
A LADY *attending on the Queen*

SICILIUS LEONATUS, *father to Posthumus*, TWO LEONATI, *brothers to Posthumus*, MOTHER *to Posthumus*, JUPITER — *Apparitions*

NON-SPEAKING: *Lords, Ladies, Roman Senators and Tribunes, Musicians, Officers, Captains, Soldiers, and Attendants*

SCENE: *Britain, and Rome*

ACT I

SCENE I. *Britain: the garden of Cymbeline's palace*

Enter TWO GENTLEMEN.

1st Gent. You do not meet a man but frowns. Our bloods
No more obey the heavens than our courtiers
Still seem as does the King.
2nd Gent. But what's the matter?
1st Gent. His daughter, and the heir of's kingdom, whom
He purposed to his wife's sole son—a widow
That late he married—hath referr'd herself
Unto a poor but worthy gentleman. She's wedded;
Her husband banish'd; she imprison'd. All
Is outward sorrow; though I think the King
Be touch'd at very heart.
2nd Gent. None but the King?
1st Gent. He that hath lost her too; so is the Queen,
That most desired the match; but not a courtier,
Although they wear their faces to the bent
Of the King's looks, hath a heart that is not
Glad at the thing they scowl at.
2nd Gent. And why so?
1st Gent. He that hath miss'd the Princess is a thing
Too bad for bad report. And he that hath her—
I mean, that married her, alack, good man!
And therefore banish'd—is a creature such
As, to seek through the regions of the earth
For one his like, there would be something failing
In him that should compare. I do not think
So fair an outward and such stuff within
Endows a man but he.
2nd Gent. You speak him far.
1st Gent. I do extend him, sir, within himself,
Crush him together rather than unfold
His measure duly.
2nd Gent. What's his name and birth?
1st Gent. I cannot delve him to the root. His father
Was called Sicilius, who did join his honour
Against the Romans with Cassibelan,
But had his titles by Tenantius whom
He served with glory and admired success,
So gain'd the sur-addition Leonatus;
And had, besides this gentleman in question,
Two other sons, who in the wars o' the time
Died with their swords in hand; for which their father,
Then old and fond of issue, took such sorrow
That he quit being, and his gentle lady,
Big of this gentleman our theme, deceased
As he was born. The King he takes the babe
To his protection, calls him Posthumus Leonatus,
Breeds him and makes him of his bed-chamber,
Puts to him all the learnings that his time

Could make him the receiver of; which he took,
As we do air, fast as 'twas minister'd,
And in's spring became a harvest, lived in court—
Which rare it is to do—most praised, most loved,
A sample to the youngest, to the more mature
A glass that feated them, and to the graver
A child that guided dotards; to his mistress,
For whom he now is banish'd, her own price
Proclaims how she esteem'd him and his virtue;
By her election may be truly read
What kind of man he is.
2nd Gent. I honour him
Even out of your report. But, pray you, tell me,
Is she sole child to the King?
1st Gent. His only child.
He had two sons. If this be worth your hearing,
Mark it: the eldest of them at three years old,
I' the swathing-clothes the other, from their nursery
Were stol'n, and to this hour no guess in knowledge
Which way they went.
2nd Gent. How long is this ago?
1st Gent. Some twenty years.
2nd Gent. That a king's children should be so convey'd,
So slackly guarded, and the search so slow,
That could not trace them!
1st Gent. Howsoe'er 'tis strange,
Or that the negligence may well be laugh'd at,
Yet it is true, sir.
2nd Gent. I do well believe you.
1st Gent. We must forbear; here comes the gentleman,
The Queen, and Princess. [*Exeunt.*

Enter the QUEEN, POSTHUMUS, *and* IMOGEN.

Queen. No, be assured you shall not find me, daughter,
After the slander of most stepmothers,
Evil-eyed unto you. You're my prisoner, but
Your gaoler shall deliver you the keys
That lock up your restraint. For you, Posthumus,
So soon as I can win the offended King,
I will be known your advocate. Marry, yet
The fire of rage is in him, and 'twere good
You lean'd unto his sentence with what patience
Your wisdom may inform you.
Post. Please your Highness,
I will from hence to-day.
Queen. You know the peril.
I'll fetch a turn about the garden, pitying
The pangs of barr'd affections, though the King
Hath charged you should not speak together.
[*Exit.*
Imo. O
Dissembling courtesy! How fine this tyrant
Can tickle where she wounds! My dearest husband,
I something fear my father's wrath; but nothing—
Always reserved my holy duty—what
His rage can do on me. You must be gone;
And I shall here abide the hourly shot
Of angry eyes, not comforted to live,
But that there is this jewel in the world
That I may see again.
Post. My queen! my mistress!
O lady, weep no more, lest I give cause
To be suspected of more tenderness
Than doth become a man. I will remain
The loyal'st husband that did e'er plight troth.
My residence in Rome at one Philario's,
Who to my father was a friend, to me
Known but by letter. Thither write, my queen,
And with mine eyes I'll drink the words you send,
Though ink be made of gall.

Re-enter QUEEN.

Queen. Be brief, I pray you.
If the king come, I shall incur I know not
How much of his displeasure. [*Aside*] Yet I'll move him
To walk this way. I never do him wrong,
But he does buy my injuries, to be friends;
Pays dear for my offences. [*Exit.*
Post. Should we be taking leave
As long a term as yet we have to live,
The loathness to depart would grow. Adieu!
Imo. Nay, stay a little.
Were you but riding forth to air yourself,
Such parting were too petty. Look here, love;
This diamond was my mother's. Take it, heart;
But keep it till you woo another wife,
When Imogen is dead.
Post. How, how! another?
You gentle gods, give me but this I have,
And sear up my embracements from a next
With bonds of death! [*Putting on the ring.*]
Remain, remain thou here
While sense can keep it on. And, sweetest, fairest,
As I my poor self did exchange for you,
To your so infinite loss, so in our trifles
I still win of you. For my sake wear this;
It is a manacle of love; I'll place it
Upon this fairest prisoner.
Putting a bracelet upon her arm.
Imo. O the gods!
When shall we see again?

Enter CYMBELINE *and Lords.*

Post. Alack, the King!
Cym. Thou basest thing, avoid! Hence, from my sight!
If after this command thou fraught the court
With thy unworthiness, thou diest. Away!
Thou'rt poison to my blood.
Post. The gods protect you!
And bless the good remainders of the court!
I am gone. [*Exit.*
Imo. There cannot be a pinch in death
More sharp than this is.
Cym. O disloyal thing,
That shouldst repair my youth, thou heap'st
A year's age on me.
Imo. I beseech you, sir,
Harm not yourself with your vexation.
I am senseless of your wrath; a touch more rare
Subdues all pangs, all fears.
Cym. Past grace? obedience?
Imo. Past hope, and in despair; that way, past grace.
Cym. That mightst have had the sole son of my queen!
Imo. O blest, that I might not! I chose an eagle,
And did avoid a puttock.
Cym. Thou took'st a beggar; wouldst have made my throne
A seat for baseness.
Imo. No; I rather added
A lustre to it.
Cym. O thou vile one!
Imo. Sir,
It is your fault that I have loved Posthumus.
You bred him as my playfellow, and he is
A man worth any woman, overbuys me
Almost the sum he pays.
Cym. What, art thou mad?
Imo. Almost sir; heaven restore me! Would I were
A neat-herd's daughter, and my Leonatus
Our neighbour shepherd's son!
Cym. Thou foolish thing!

Re-enter QUEEN.

They were again together. You have done
Not after our command. Away with her,
And pen her up.
Queen. Beseech your patience. Peace,
Dear lady daughter, peace! Sweet sovereign,
Leave us to ourselves; and make yourself some comfort
Out of your best advice.
Cym. Nay, let her languish
A drop of blood a day; and, being aged,
Die of this folly! [*Exeunt* CYMBELINE *and Lords.*
Queen. Fie! you must give way.

Enter PISANIO.

Here is your servant. How now, sir! What news?
Pis. My lord your son drew on my master.
Queen. Ha!
No harm, I trust, is done?
Pis. There might have been,
But that my master rather play'd than fought
And had no help of anger. They were parted
By gentlemen at hand.
Queen. I am very glad on't.
Imo. Your son's my father's friend; he takes his part.
To draw upon an exile! O brave sir!
I would they were in Afric both together;
Myself by with a needle, that I might prick
The goer-back. Why came you from your master?
Pis. On his command. He would not suffer me
To bring him to the haven; left these notes
Of what commands I should be subject to,
When 't pleased you to employ me.
Queen. This hath been
Your faithful servant. I dare lay mine honour
He will remain so.
Pis. I humbly thank your Highness.
Queen. Pray, walk awhile.
Imo. About some half-hour hence,
I pray you, speak with me. You shall at least
Go see my lord aboard. For this time leave me.
[*Exeunt.*

SCENE II. *The same: a public place*

Enter CLOTEN *and* TWO LORDS.

1st Lord. Sir, I would advise you to shift a shirt; the violence of action hath made you reek as a sacrifice. Where air comes out, air comes in. There's none abroad so wholesome as that you vent.

Clo. If my shirt were bloody, then to shift it. Have I hurt him?

2nd Lord. [*Aside*] No, 'faith; not so much as his patience.

1st Lord. Hurt him! his body's a passable carcass, if he be not hurt. It is a throughfare for steel, if it be not hurt.

2nd Lord. [*Aside*] His steel was in debt; it went o' the backside the town.

Clo. The villain would not stand me.

2nd Lord. [*Aside*] No; but he fled forward still, toward your face.

1st Lord. Stand you! You have land enough of your own; but he added to your having; gave you some ground.

2nd Lord. [*Aside*] As many inches as you have oceans. Puppies!

Clo. I would they had not come between us.

2nd Lord. [*Aside*] So would I, till you had measured how long a fool you were upon the ground.

Clo. And that she should love this fellow and refuse me!

2nd Lord. [*Aside*] If it be a sin to make a true election, she is damned.

1st Lord. Sir, as I told you always, her beauty and her brain go not together. She's a good sign, but I have seen small reflection of her wit.

2nd Lord. [*Aside*] She shines not upon fools, lest the reflection should hurt her.

Clo. Come, I'll to my chamber. Would there had been some hurt done!

2nd Lord. [*Aside*] I wish not so; unless it had been the fall of an ass, which is no great hurt.

Clo. You'll go with us?

1st Lord. I'll attend your lordship.

Clo. Nay, come, let's go together.

2nd Lord. Well, my lord. [*Exeunt*.

SCENE III. *A room in Cymbeline's palace*

Enter IMOGEN *and* PISANIO.

Imo. I would thou grew'st unto the shores o' the haven,
And question'dst every sail. If he should write,
And I not have it, 'twere a paper lost,
As offer'd mercy is. What was the last
That he spake to thee?

Pis. It was his queen, his queen!

Imo. Then waved his handkerchief?

Pis. And kiss'd it, madam.

Imo. Senseless linen! happier therein than I!
And that was all?

Pis. No, madam; for so long
As he could make me with this eye or ear
Distinguish him from others, he did keep
The deck, with glove, or hat, or handkerchief,
Still waving, as the fits and stirs of's mind
Could best express how slow his soul sail'd on,
How swift his ship.

Imo. Thou shouldst have made him
As little as a crow, or less, ere left
To after-eye him.

Pis. Madam, so I did.

Imo. I would have broke mine eye-strings; crack'd them, but
To look upon him, till the diminution
Of space had pointed him sharp as my needle;
Nay, follow'd him till he had melted from
The smallness of a gnat to air, and then
Have turn'd mine eye and wept. But, good Pisanio,
When shall we hear from him?

Pis. Be assured, madam,
With his next vantage.

Imo. I did not take my leave of him, but had
Most pretty things to say. Ere I could tell him
How I would think on him at certain hours
Such thoughts and such, or I could make him swear
The shes of Italy should not betray
Mine interest and his honour, or have charged him,
At the sixth hour of morn, at noon, at midnight,
To encounter me with orisons, for then
I am in heaven for him; or ere I could
Give him that parting kiss which I had set
Betwixt two charming words, comes in my father
And like the tyrannous breathing of the north
Shakes all our buds from growing.

Enter a LADY.

Lady. The Queen madam,
Desires your Highness' company.

Imo. Those things I bid you do, get them dispatch'd.
I will attend the Queen.

Pis. Madam, I shall. [*Exeunt*.

SCENE IV. *Rome: Philario's house*

Enter PHILARIO, IACHIMO, *a* FRENCHMAN, *a* DUTCHMAN, *and a* SPANIARD.

Iach. Believe it, sir, I have seen him in Britain. He was then of a crescent note, expected to prove so worthy as since he hath been allowed the name of; but I could then have looked on him without the help of admiration, though the catalogue of his endowments had been tabled by his side and I to peruse him by items.

Phi. You speak of him when he was less furnished than now he is with that which makes him both without and within.

French. I have seen him in France. We had very many there could behold the sun with as firm eyes as he.

Iach. This matter of marrying his king's daughter, wherein he must be weighed rather by her value than his own, words him, I doubt not, a great deal from the matter.

French. And then his banishment.

Iach. Ay, and the approbation of those that weep this lamentable divorce under her colours are wonderfully to extend him; be it but to fortify her judgement, which else an easy battery might lay flat, for taking a beggar without less quality. But how comes it he is to sojourn with you? How creeps acquaintance?

Phi. His father and I were soldiers together; to whom I have been often bound for no less than my life. Here comes the Briton. Let him be so entertained amongst you as suits, with gentlemen of your knowing, to a stranger of his quality.

Enter POSTHUMUS.

I beseech you all, be better known to this gentleman, whom I commend to you as a noble friend of mine. How worthy he is I will leave to appear hereafter, rather than story him in his own hearing.

French. Sir, we have known together in Orleans.

Post. Since when I have been debtor to you for courtesies, which I will be ever to pay and yet pay still.

French. Sir, you o'er-rate my poor kindness. I was glad I did atone my countryman and you; it had been pity you should have been put together with so mortal a purpose as then each bore, upon importance of so slight and trivial a nature.

Post. By your pardon, sir, I was then a young traveller; rather shunned to go even with what I heard than in my every action to be guided by others' experiences. But upon my mended judgement—if I offend not to say it is mended—my quarrel was not altogether slight.

French. 'Faith, yes, to be put to the arbitrement of swords, and by such two that would by all likelihood have confounded one the other, or have fallen both.

Iach. Can we, with manners, ask what was the difference?

French. Safely, I think. 'Twas a contention in public, which may, without contradiction, suffer the report. It was much like an argument that fell out last night, where each of us fell in praise of our country mistresses; this gentleman at that time vouching—and upon warrant of bloody affirmation—his to be more fair, virtuous, wise, chaste, constant-qualified and less attemptable than any the rarest of our ladies in France.

Iach. That lady is not now living, or this gentleman's opinion by this worn out.

Post. She holds her virtue still and I my mind.

Iach. You must not so far prefer her 'fore ours of Italy.

Post. Being so far provoked as I was in France, I would abate her nothing, though I profess myself her adorer, not her friend.

Iach. As fair and as good—a kind of hand-in-hand comparison—had been something too fair and too good for any lady in Britain. If she went before others I have seen, as that diamond of yours outlustres many I have beheld, I could not but believe she excelled many. But I have not seen the most precious diamond that is, nor you the lady.

Post. I praised her as I rated her. So do I my stone.

Iach. What do you esteem it at?

Post. More than the world enjoys.

Iach. Either your unparagoned mistress is dead, or she's outprized by a trifle.

Post. You are mistaken. The one may be sold, or given, if there were wealth enough for the purchase, or merit for the gift. The other is not a thing for sale, and only the gift of the gods.

Iach. Which the gods have given you?

Post. Which, by their graces, I will keep.

Iach. You may wear her in title yours; but, you know, strange fowl light upon neighbouring ponds. Your ring may be stolen too; so your brace of unprizable estimations; the one is but frail and the other casual; a cunning thief, or a that way accomplished courtier, would hazard the winning both of first and last.

Post. Your Italy contains none so accomplished a courtier to convince the honour of my mistress, if, in the holding or loss of that, you term her frail. I do nothing doubt you have store of thieves; notwithstanding, I fear not my ring.

Phi. Let us leave here, gentlemen.

Post. Sir, with all my heart. This worthy signior, I thank him, makes no stranger of me; we are familiar at first.

Iach. With five times so much conversation, I should get ground of your fair mistress, make her go back, even to the yielding, had I admittance and opportunity to friend.

Post. No, no.

Iach. I dare thereupon pawn the moiety of my estate to your ring; which, in my opinion, o'ervalues it something. But I make my wager rather against your confidence than her reputation. And, to bar your offence herein too, I durst attempt it against any lady in the world.

Post. You are a great deal abused in too bold a persuasion; and I doubt not you sustain what you're worthy of by your attempt.

Iach. What's that?

Post. A repulse; though your attempt, as you call it, deserve more; a punishment too.

Phi. Gentlemen, enough of this. It came in too suddenly; let it die as it was born, and, I pray you, be better acquainted.

Iach. Would I had put my estate and my neighbour's on the approbation of what I have spoke!

Post. What lady would you choose to assail?

Iach. Yours; whom in constancy you think

stands so safe. I will lay you ten thousand ducats to your ring that, commend me to the court where your lady is, with no more advantage than the opportunity of a second conference, and I will bring from thence that honour of hers which you imagine so reserved.

Post. I will wage against your gold, gold to it. My ring I hold dear as my finger; 'tis part of it.

Iach. You are afraid, and therein the wiser. If you buy ladies' flesh at a million a dram, you cannot preserve it from tainting. But I see you have some religion in you, that you fear.

Post. This is but a custom in your tongue; you bear a graver purpose, I hope.

Iach. I am the master of my speeches, and would undergo what's spoken, I swear.

Post. Will you? I shall but lend my diamond till your return. Let there be covenants drawn between's. My mistress exceeds in goodness the hugeness of your unworthy thinking. I dare you to this match; here's my ring.

Phi. I will have it no lay.

Iach. By the gods, it is one. If I bring you no sufficient testimony that I have enjoyed the dearest bodily part of your mistress, my ten thousand ducats are yours; so is your diamond too. If I come off, and leave her in such honour as you have trust in, she your jewel, this your jewel, and my gold are yours; provided I have your commendation for my more free entertainment.

Post. I embrace these conditions; let us have articles betwixt us. Only, thus far you shall answer. If you make your voyage upon her and give me directly to understand you have prevailed, I am no further your enemy; she is not worth our debate. If she remain unseduced, you not making it appear otherwise, for your ill opinion and the assault you have made to her chastity you shall answer me with your sword.

Iach. Your hand; a covenant. We will have these things set down by lawful counsel, and straight away for Britain, lest the bargain should catch cold and starve. I will fetch my gold and have our two wagers recorded.

Post. Agreed.

[*Exeunt* POSTHUMUS *and* IACHIMO.

French. Will this hold, think you?

Phi. Signior Iachimo will not from it. Pray, let us follow 'em. [*Exeunt.*

SCENE V. *Britain: a room in Cymbeline's palace*

Enter QUEEN, LADIES, *and* CORNELIUS.

Queen. Whiles yet the dew's on ground, gather those flowers;
Make haste. Who has the note of them?
1st Lady. I, madam.
Queen. Dispatch. [*Exeunt* LADIES.
Now, master doctor, have you brought those drugs?
Cor. Pleaseth your highness, ay. Here they are, madam. [*Presenting a small box.*]
But I beseech your Grace, without offence—
My conscience bids me ask—wherefore you have
Commanded of me these most poisonous compounds,
Which are the movers of a languishing death;
But, though slow, deadly?
Queen. I wonder, doctor,
Thou ask'st me such a question. Have I not been
Thy pupil long? Hast thou not learn'd me how
To make perfumes? distil? preserve? yea, so
That our great king himself doth woo me oft
For my confections? Having thus far proceeded—
Unless thou think'st me devilish—is't not meet
That I did amplify my judgement in
Other conclusions? I will try the forces
Of these thy compounds on such creatures as
We count not worth the hanging, but none human,
To try the vigour of them and apply
Allayments to their act, and by them gather
Their several virtues and effects.
Cor. Your Highness
Shall from this practice but make hard your heart.
Besides, the seeing these effects will be
Both noisome and infectious.
Queen. O, content thee.

Enter PISANIO.

[*Aside*] Here comes a flattering rascal; upon him
Will I first work. He's for his master,
And enemy to my son. How now, Pisanio!
Doctor, your service for this time is ended;
Take your own way.
Cor. [*Aside*] I do suspect you, madam;
But you shall do no harm.
Queen. [*To* PISANIO] Hark thee, a word.
Cor. [*Aside*] I do not like her. She doth think she has
Strange lingering poisons. I do know her spirit,
And will not trust one of her malice with
A drug of such damn'd nature. Those she has
Will stupefy and dull the sense awhile;
Which first, perchance, she'll prove on cats and dogs,
Then afterward up higher. But there is
No danger in what show of death it makes,
More than the locking-up the spirits a time,
To be more fresh, reviving. She is fool'd

With a most false effect; and I the truer,
So to be false with her.
Queen. No further service, doctor,
Until I send for thee.
Cor. I humbly take my leave. [*Exit.*
Queen. Weeps she still, say'st thou? Dost thou think in time
She will not quench and let instructions enter
Where folly now possesses? Do thou work.
When thou shalt bring me word she loves my son,
I'll tell thee on the instant thou art then
As great as is thy master, greater, for
His fortunes all lie speechless and his name
Is at last gasp. Return he cannot, nor
Continue where he is. To shift his being
Is to exchange one misery with another,
And every day that comes comes to decay
A day's work in him. What shalt thou expect,
To be depender on a thing that leans,
Who cannot be new built, nor has no friends,
So much as but to prop him? [*The* QUEEN *drops the box.* PISANIO *takes it up.*] Thou takest up
Thou know'st not what; but take it for thy labour.
It is a thing I made, which hath the King
Five times redeem'd from death. I do not know
What is more cordial. Nay, I prithee, take it;
It is an earnest of a further good
That I mean to thee. Tell thy mistress how
The case stands with her; do't as from thyself.
Think what a chance thou changest on, but think
Thou hast thy mistress still, to boot, my son,
Who shall take notice of thee. I'll move the King
To any shape of thy preferment such
As thou'lt desire; and then myself, I chiefly,
That set thee on to this desert, am bound
To load thy merit richly. Call my women:
Think on my words. [*Exit* PISANIO.
A sly and constant knave,
Not to be shaked; the agent for his master
And the remembrancer of her to hold
The hand-fast to her lord. I have given him that
Which, if he take, shall quite unpeople her
Of liegers for her sweet, and which she after,
Except she bend her humour, shall be assured
To taste of too.

Re-enter PISANIO *and* LADIES.

So, so; well done, well done.
The violets, cowslips, and the primroses,
Bear to my closet. Fare thee well, Pisanio;
Think on my words. [*Exeunt* QUEEN *and* LADIES.
Pis. And shall do.
But when to my good lord I prove untrue,
I'll choke myself; there's all I'll do for you.
[*Exit.*

SCENE VI. *The same: another room in the palace*

Enter IMOGEN.

Imo. A father cruel, and a step-dame false;
A foolish suitor to a wedded lady,
That hath her husband banish'd—O, that husband!
My supreme crown of grief! and those repeated
Vexations of it! Had I been thief-stol'n,
As my two brothers, happy! but most miserable
Is the desire that's glorious. Blest be those,
How mean soe'er, that have their honest wills,
Which seasons comfort. Who may this be? Fie!

Enter PISANIO *and* IACHIMO.

Pis. Madam, a noble gentleman of Rome
Comes from my lord with letters.
Iach. Change you, madam?
The worthy Leonatus is in safety
And greets your Highness dearly.
Presents a letter.
Imo. Thanks, good sir;
You're kindly welcome.
Iach. [*Aside*] All of her that is out of door most rich!
If she be furnish'd with a mind so rare,
She is alone the Arabian bird, and I
Have lost the wager. Boldness be my friend!
Arm me, audacity, from head to foot!
Or, like the Parthian, I shall flying fight;
Rather, directly fly.
Imo. [*Reads*] "He is one of the noblest note, to whose kindnesses I am most infinitely tied. Reflect upon him accordingly, as you value your trust— Leonatus"
So far I read aloud;
But even the very middle of my heart
Is warm'd by the rest, and takes it thankfully.
You are as welcome, worthy sir, as I
Have words to bid you, and shall find it so
In all that I can do.
Iach. Thanks, fairest lady.
What are men mad? Hath nature given them eyes
To see this vaulted arch, and the rich crop
Of sea and land, which can distinguish 'twixt
The fiery orbs above and the twinn'd stones
Upon the number'd beach? and can we not
Partition make with spectacles so precious
'Twixt fair and foul?
Imo. What makes your admiration?
Iach. It cannot be i' the eye, for apes and monkeys
'Twixt two such shes would chatter this way and

Contemn with mows the other; nor i' the judgement,
For idiots in this case of favour would
Be wisely definite; nor i' the appetite;
Sluttery to such neat excellence opposed
Should make desire vomit emptiness,
Not so allured to feed.

Imo. What is the matter, trow?

Iach. The cloyed will,
That satiate yet unsatisfied desire, that tub
Both fill'd and running, ravening first the lamb
Longs after for the garbage.

Imo. What, dear sir,
Thus raps you? Are you well?

Iach. Thanks, madam; well. [*To* PISANIO] Beseech you, sir, desire
My man's abode where I did leave him. He
Is strange and peevish.

Pis. I was going, sir,
To give him welcome. [*Exit.*

Imo. Continues well my lord? His health, beseech you?

Iach. Well, madam.

Imo. Is he disposed to mirth? I hope he is.

Iach. Exceeding pleasant; none a stranger there
So merry and so gamesome. He is call'd
The Briton reveller.

Imo. When he was here,
He did incline to sadness, and oft-times
Not knowing why.

Iach. I never saw him sad.
There is a Frenchman his companion, one
An eminent monsieur, that, it seems, much loves
A Gallian girl at home; he furnaces
The thick sighs from him, whiles the jolly Briton—
Your lord, I mean—laughs from's free lungs, cries, "O,
Can my sides hold, to think that man, who knows
By history, report, or his own proof,
What woman is, yea, what she cannot choose
But must be, will his free hours languish for
Assured bondage?"

Imo. Will my lord say so?

Iach. Ay, madam, with his eyes in flood with laughter.
It is a recreation to be by
And hear him mock the Frenchman. But, heavens know,
Some men are much to blame.

Imo. Not he, I hope.

Iach. Not he; but yet heaven's bounty towards him might
Be used more thankfully. In himself, 'tis much;
In you, which I account his beyond all talents,
Whilst I am bound to wonder, I am bound
To pity too.

Imo. What do you pity, sir?

Iach. Two creatures heartily.

Imo. Am I one, sir?
You look on me. What wreck discern you in me
Deserves your pity?

Iach. Lamentable! What,
To hide me from the radiant sun and solace
I' the dungeon by a snuff?

Imo. I pray you, sir,
Deliver with more openness your answers
To my demands. Why do you pity me?

Iach. That others do—
I was about to say—enjoy your—But
It is an office of the gods to venge it,
Not mine to speak on 't.

Imo. You do seem to know
Something of me, or what concerns me. Pray you—
Since doubting things go ill often hurts more
Than to be sure they do; for certainties
Either are past remedies, or, timely knowing,
The remedy then born—discover to me
What both you spur and stop.

Iach. Had I this cheek
To bathe my lips upon; this hand, whose touch,
Whose every touch, would force the feeler's soul
To the oath of loyalty; this object, which
Takes prisoner the wild motion of mine eye,
Fixing it only here; should I, damn'd then,
Slaver with lips as common as the stairs
That mount the Capitol; join gripes with hands
Made hard with hourly falsehood—falsehood, as
With labour; then by-peeping in an eye
Base and unlustrous as the smoky light
That's fed with stinking tallow; it were fit
That all the plagues of hell should at one time
Encounter such revolt.

Imo. My lord, I fear,
Has forgot Britain.

Iach. And himself. Not I,
Inclined to this intelligence, pronounce
The beggary of his change; but 'tis your graces
That from my mutest conscience to my tongue
Charms this report out.

Imo. Let me hear no more.

Iach. O dearest soul! your cause doth strike my heart
With pity, that doth make me sick. A lady
So fair, and fasten'd to an empery,
Would make the great'st king double—to be partner'd
With tomboys hired with that self exhibition
Which your own coffers yield! with diseased ventures

That play with all infirmities for gold
Which rottenness can lend nature! such boil'd stuff
As well might poison poison! Be revenged;
Or she that bore you was no queen, and you
Recoil from your great stock.
Imo. Revenged!
How should I be revenged? If this be true—
As I have such a heart that both mine ears
Must not in haste abuse—if it be true,
How should I be revenged?
Iach. Should he make me
Live, like Diana's priest, betwixt cold sheets,
Whiles he is vaulting variable ramps,
In your despite, upon your purse? Revenge it.
I dedicate myself to your sweet pleasure,
More noble than that runagate to your bed,
And will continue fast to your affection,
Still close as sure.
Imo. What, ho, Pisanio!
Iach. Let me my service tender on your lips.
Imo. Away! I do condemn mine ears that have
So long attended thee. If thou wert honourable,
Thou wouldst have told this tale for virtue, not
For such an end thou seek'st—as base as strange.
Thou wrong'st a gentleman, who is as far
From thy report as thou from honour, and
Solicit'st here a lady that disdains
Thee and the devil alike. What ho, Pisanio!
The King my father shall be made acquainted
Of thy assault. If he shall think it fit,
A saucy stranger in his court to mart
As in a Romish stew and to expound
His beastly mind to us, he hath a court
He little cares for and a daughter who
He not respects at all. What, ho, Pisanio!
Iach. O happy Leonatus! I may say.
The credit that thy lady hath of thee
Deserves thy trust, and thy most perfect goodness
Her assured credit. Blessed live you long!
A lady to the worthiest sir that ever
Country call'd his! and you his mistress, only
For the most worthiest fit! Give me your pardon.
I have spoke this to know if your affiance
Were deeply rooted, and shall make your lord,
That which he is, new o'er; and he is one
The truest manner'd, such a holy witch
That he enchants societies into him;
Half all men's hearts are his.
Imo. You make amends.
Iach. He sits 'mongst men like a descended god.
He hath a kind of honour sets him off,
More than a mortal seeming. Be not angry,
Most mighty princess, that I have adventured
To try your taking of a false report; which hath
Honour'd with confirmation your great judgement
In the election of a sir so rare,
Which you know cannot err. The love I bear him
Made me to fan you thus, but the gods made you,
Unlike all others, chaffless. Pray, your pardon.
Imo. All's well, sir. Take my power i' the court for yours.
Iach. My humble thanks. I had almost forgot
To entreat your Grace but in a small request,
And yet of moment too, for it concerns
Your lord; myself and other noble friends
Are partners in the business.
Imo. Pray, what is 't?
Iach. Some dozen Romans of us and your lord—
The best feather of our wing—have mingled sums
To buy a present for the Emperor;
Which I, the factor for the rest, have done
In France. 'Tis plate of rare device, and jewels
Of rich and exquisite form; their values great;
And I am something curious, being strange,
To have them in safe stowage. May it please you
To take them in protection?
Imo. Willingly;
And pawn mine honour for their safety. Since
My lord hath interest in them, I will keep them
In my bedchamber.
Iach. They are in a trunk,
Attended by my men. I will make bold
To send them to you, only for this night;
I must aboard to-morrow.
Imo. O, no, no.
Iach. Yes, I beseech; or I shall short my word
By lengthening my return. From Gallia
I cross'd the seas on purpose and on promise
To see your Grace.
Imo. I thank you for your pains;
But not away to-morrow!
Iach. O, I must, madam;
Therefore I shall beseech you, if you please
To greet your lord with writing, do 't to-night.
I have outstood my time; which is material
To the tender of our present.
Imo. I will write.
Send your trunk to me; it shall safe be kept,
And truly yielded you. You're very welcome.
[*Exeunt.*

ACT II

SCENE I. *Britain: before Cymbeline's palace*

Enter CLOTEN *and* TWO LORDS.

Clo. Was there ever man had such luck! when I kissed the jack, upon an up-cast to be hit away! I had a hundred pound on 't; and then a whoreson jackanapes must take me up for swearing; as if I borrowed mine oaths of him and might not spend them at my pleasure.

1st Lord. What got he by that? You have broke his pate with your bowl.

2nd Lord. [*Aside*] If his wit had been like him that broke it, it would have run all out.

Clo. When a gentleman is disposed to swear, it is not for any standers-by to curtail his oaths, ha?

2nd Lord. No, my lord; [*Aside*] nor crop the ears of them.

Clo. Whoreson dog! I give him satisfaction? Would he had been one of my rank!

2nd Lord. [*Aside*] To have smelt like a fool.

Clo. I am not vexed more at anything in the earth; a pox on 't! I had rather not be so noble as I am; they dare not fight with me, because of the Queen my mother. Every Jack-slave hath his bellyful of fighting, and I must go up and down like a cock that nobody can match.

2nd Lord. [*Aside*] You are cock and capon too; and you crow, cock, with your comb on.

Clo. Sayest thou?

2nd Lord. It is not fit your lordship should undertake every companion that you give offence to.

Clo. No, I know that. But it is fit I should commit offence to my inferiors.

2nd Lord. Ay, it is fit for your lordship only.

Clo. Why, so I say.

1st Lord. Did you hear of a stranger that's come to court to-night?

Clo. A stranger, and I not know on 't!

2nd Lord. [*Aside*] He's a strange fellow himself, and knows it not.

1st Lord. There's an Italian come; and, 'tis thought, one of Leonatus' friends.

Clo. Leonatus! a banished rascal; and he's another, whatsoever he be. Who told you of this stranger?

1st Lord. One of your lordship's pages.

Clo. Is it fit I went to look upon him? is there no derogation in 't?

2nd Lord. You cannot derogate, my lord.

Clo. Not easily, I think.

2nd Lord. [*Aside*] You are a fool granted; therefore your issues, being foolish, do not derogate.

Clo. Come, I'll go see this Italian. What I have lost to-day at bowls I'll win to-night of him. Come, go.

2nd Lord. I'll attend your lordship.

[*Exeunt* CLOTEN *and* FIRST LORD.

That such a crafty devil as is his mother
Should yield the world this ass! a woman that
Bears all down with her brain; and this her son
Cannot take two from twenty, for his heart,
And leave eighteen. Alas, poor princess,
Thou divine Imogen, what thou endurest,
Betwixt a father by thy step-dame govern'd,
A mother hourly coining plots, a wooer
More hateful than the foul expulsion is
Of thy dear husband, than that horrid act
Of the divorce he'd make! The heavens hold firm
The walls of thy dear honour, keep unshaked
That temple, thy fair mind, that thou mayst stand,
To enjoy thy banish'd lord and this great land!

[*Exit*.

SCENE II. *Imogen's bedchamber in Cymbeline's palace; a trunk in one corner of it*

IMOGEN *in bed, reading;* HELEN, *a Lady, attending*.

Imo. Who's there? my woman Helen?
Hel. Please you, madam.
Imo. What hour is it?
Hel. Almost midnight, madam.
Imo. I have read three hours then. Mine eyes are weak.
Fold down the leaf where I have left. To bed.
Take not away the taper, leave it burning;
And if thou canst awake by four o' the clock,
I prithee, call me. Sleep hath seized me wholly.

[*Exit* HELEN.

To your protection I commend me, gods.
From fairies and the tempters of the night
Guard me, beseech ye.

[*Sleeps*. IACHIMO *comes from the trunk*.

Iach. The crickets sing, and man's o'er-labour'd sense
Repairs itself by rest. Our Tarquin thus
Did softly press the rushes, ere he waken'd
The chastity he wounded. Cytherea,
How bravely thou becomest thy bed, fresh lily,
And whiter than the sheets! That I might touch!
But kiss; one kiss! Rubies unparagon'd,
How dearly they do 't! 'Tis her breathing that
Perfumes the chamber thus. The flame o' the taper
Bows toward her, and would under-peep her lids,
To see the enclosed lights, now canopied
Under these windows, white and azure laced
With blue of heaven's own tinct. But my design,
To note the chamber. I will write all down.
Such and such pictures; there the window; such

The adornment of her bed; the arras; figures,
Why, such and such; and the contents o' the story.
Ah, but some natural notes about her body,
Above ten thousand meaner moveables
Would testify, to enrich mine inventory.
O sleep, thou ape of death, lie dull upon her!
And be her sense but as a monument,
Thus in a chapel lying! Come off, come off.
Taking off her bracelet.
As slippery as the Gordian knot was hard!
'Tis mine; and this will witness outwardly,
As strongly as the conscience does within,
To the madding of her lord. On her left breast
A mole cinque-spotted, like the crimson drops
I' the bottom of a cowslip. Here's a voucher,
Stronger than ever law could make. This secret
Will force him think I have pick'd the lock and ta'en
The treasure of her honour. No more. To what end?
Why should I write this down, that's riveted,
Screw'd to my memory? She hath been reading late
The tale of Tereus; here the leaf's turn'd down
Where Philomel gave up. I have enough.
To the trunk again, and shut the spring of it.
Swift, swift, you dragons of the night, that dawning
May bare the raven's eye! I lodge in fear;
Though this a heavenly angel, hell is here.
Clock strikes.
One, two, three; time, time!
[*Goes into the trunk. The scene closes.*

SCENE III. *An ante-chamber adjoining Imogen's apartments*

Enter CLOTEN *and* LORDS.

1st Lord. Your lordship is the most patient man in loss, the most coldest that ever turned up ace.

Clo. It would make any man cold to lose.

1st Lord. But not every man patient after the noble temper of your lordship. You are most hot and furious when you win.

Clo. Winning will put any man into courage. If I could get this foolish Imogen, I should have gold enough. It's almost morning, is 't not?

1st Lord. Day, my lord.

Clo. I would this music would come. I am advised to give her music o' mornings; they say it will penetrate.

Enter Musicians.

Come on; tune. If you can penetrate her with your fingering, so; we'll try with tongue too. If none will do, let her remain; but I'll never give o'er. First, a very excellent good-conceited thing; after, a wonderful sweet air, with admirable rich words to it; and then let her consider.

SONG

Hark, hark! the lark at heaven's gate sings,
And Phœbus 'gins arise,
His steeds to water at those springs
On chaliced flowers that lies;
And winking Mary-buds begin
To ope their golden eyes;
With every thing that pretty is,
My lady sweet, arise,
Arise, arise.

Clo. So, get you gone. If this penetrate, I will consider your music the better; if it do not, it is a vice in her ears, which horse-hairs and calves'-guts, nor the voice of unpaved eunuch to boot, can never amend. [*Exeunt Musicians.*

2nd Lord. Here comes the King.

Clo. I am glad I was up so late; for that's the reason I was up so early. He cannot choose but take this service I have done fatherly.

Enter CYMBELINE *and* QUEEN.

Good morrow to your Majesty and to my gracious mother.

Cym. Attend you here the door of our stern daughter?
Will she not forth?

Clo. I have assailed her with music, but she vouchsafes no notice.

Cym. The exile of her minion is too new;
She hath not yet forgot him. Some more time
Must wear the print of his remembrance out,
And then she's yours.

Queen. You are most bound to the King,
Who lets go by no vantages that may
Prefer you to his daughter. Frame yourself
To orderly soliciting, and be friended
With aptness of the season; make denials
Increase your services; so seem as if
You were inspired to do those duties which
You tender to her; that you in all obey her,
Save when command to your dismission tends,
And therein you are senseless.

Clo. Senseless! not so.

Enter a MESSENGER.

Mess. So like you, sir, ambassadors from Rome;
The one is Caius Lucius.

Cym. A worthy fellow,
Albeit he comes on angry purpose now;
But that's no fault of his. We must receive him
According to the honour of his sender;

And towards himself, his goodness forespent on us,
We must extend our notice. Our dear son,
When you have given good morning to your mistress,
Attend the Queen and us; we shall have need
To employ you towards this Roman. Come, our queen. [*Exeunt all but* CLOTEN.
Clo. If she be up, I'll speak with her; if not,
Let her lie still and dream. [*Knocks*] By your leave, ho!
I know her women are about her. What
If I do line one of their hands? 'Tis gold
Which buys admittance; oft it doth; yea, and makes
Diana's rangers false themselves, yield up
Their deer to the stand o' the stealer; and 'tis gold
Which makes the true man kill'd and saves the thief;
Nay, sometime hangs both thief and true man. What
Can it not do and undo? I will make
One of her women lawyer to me, for
I yet not understand the case myself.
[*Knocks*] By your leave.

Enter HELEN.

Hel. Who's there that knocks?
Clo. A gentleman.
Hel. No more?
Clo. Yes, and a gentlewoman's son.
Hel. That's more
Than some, whose tailors are as dear as yours,
Can justly boast of. What's your lordship's pleasure?
Clo. Your lady's person. Is she ready?
Hel. Ay,
To keep her chamber.
Clo. There is gold for you;
Sell me your good report.
Hel. How! my good name? or to report of you
What I shall think is good?—The Princess!

Enter IMOGEN.

Clo. Good morrow, fairest. Sister, your sweet hand. [*Exit* HELEN.
Imo. Good morrow, sir. You lay out too much pains
For purchasing but trouble. The thanks I give
Is telling you that I am poor of thanks
And scarce can spare them.
Clo. Still, I swear I love you.
Imo. If you but said so, 'twere as deep with me.
If you swear still, your recompense is still
That I regard it not.
Clo. This is no answer.
Imo. But that you shall not say I yield being silent,
I would not speak. I pray you, spare me. 'Faith,
I shall unfold equal discourtesy
To your best kindness. One of your great knowing
Should learn, being taught, forbearance.
Clo. To leave you in your madness, 'twere my sin.
I will not.
Imo. Fools are not mad folks.
Clo. Do you call me fool?
Imo. As I am mad, I do.
If you'll be patient, I'll no more be mad;
That cures us both. I am much sorry, sir,
You put me to forget a lady's manners,
By being so verbal. And learn now, for all,
That I, which know my heart, do here pronounce,
By the very truth of it, I care not for you,
And am so near the lack of charity—
To accuse myself—I hate you; which I had rather
You felt than make 't my boast.
Clo. You sin against
Obedience, which you owe your father. For
The contract you pretend with that base wretch,
One bred of alms and foster'd with cold dishes,
With scraps o' the court, it is no contract, none.
And though it be allow'd in meaner parties—
Yet who than he more mean?—to knit their souls,
On whom there is no more dependency
But brats and beggary, in self-figured knot;
Yet you are curb'd from that enlargement by
The consequence o' the crown, and must not soil
The precious note of it with a base slave,
A hilding for a livery, a squire's cloth,
A pantler, not so eminent.
Imo. Profane fellow!
Wert thou the son of Jupiter and no more
But what thou art besides, thou wert too base
To be his groom. Thou wert dignified enough,
Even to the point of envy, if 'twere made
Comparative for your virtues, to be styled
The under-hangman of his kingdom, and hated
For being preferr'd so well.
Clo. The south-fog rot him!
Imo. He never can meet more mischance than come
To be but named of thee. His meanest garment,
That ever hath but clipp'd his body, is dearer
In my respect than all the hairs above thee,
Were they all made such men. How now, Pisanio!

Enter PISANIO.

Clo. "His garment!" Now the devil—
Imo. To Dorothy my woman hie thee presently—
Clo. "His garment!"
Imo. I am sprited with a fool,
Frighted, and anger'd worse. Go bid my woman
Search for a jewel that too casually
Hath left mine arm. It was thy master's; 'shrew me,
If I would lose it for a revenue
Of any king's in Europe. I do think
I saw't this morning. Confident I am
Last night 'twas on mine arm; I kiss'd it.
I hope it be not gone to tell my lord
That I kiss aught but he.
Pis. 'Twill not be lost.
Imo. I hope so. Go and search.
[*Exit* PISANIO.
Clo. You have abused me.
"His meanest garment!"
Imo. Ay, I said so, sir.
If you will make 't an action, call witness to 't.
Clo. I will inform your father.
Imo. Your mother too.
She's my good lady, and will conceive, I hope,
But the worst of me. So, I leave you, sir,
To the worst of discontent. [*Exit.*
Clo. I'll be revenged.
"His meanest garment!" Well. [*Exit.*

SCENE IV. *Rome: Philario's house*

Enter POSTHUMUS *and* PHILARIO.

Post. Fear it not, sir. I would I were so sure
To win the King as I am bold her honour
Will remain hers.
Phi. What means do you make to him?
Post. Not any, but abide the change of time,
Quake in the present winter's state and wish
That warmer days would come. In these sear'd hopes,
I barely gratify your love; they failing,
I must die much your debtor.
Phi. Your very goodness and your company
O'erpays all I can do. By this, your king
Hath heard of great Augustus. Caius Lucius
Will do's commission throughly; and I think
He'll grant the tribute, send the arrearages,
Or look upon our Romans, whose remembrance
Is yet fresh in their grief.
Post. I do believe,
Statist though I am none, nor like to be,
That this will prove a war; and you shall hear
The legions now in Gallia sooner landed
In our not-fearing Britain than have tidings
Of any penny tribute paid. Our countrymen
Are men more order'd than when Julius Cæsar
Smiled at their lack of skill, but found their courage
Worthy his frowning at. Their discipline,
Now mingled with their courages, will make known
To their approvers they are people such
That mend upon the world.

Enter IACHIMO.

Phi. See! Iachimo!
Post. The swiftest harts have posted you by land;
And winds of all the corners kiss'd your sails,
To make your vessel nimble.
Phi. Welcome, sir.
Post. I hope the briefness of your answer made
The speediness of your return.
Iach. Your lady 31
Is one of the fairest that I have look'd upon.
Post. And therewithal the best; or let her beauty
Look through a casement to allure false hearts
And be false with them.
Iach. Here are letters for you.
Post. Their tenour good, I trust.
Iach. 'Tis very like.
Phi. Was Caius Lucius in the Britain court
When you were there?
Iach. He was expected then,
But not approach'd.
Post. All is well yet.
Sparkles this stone as it was wont? or is 't not
Too dull for your good wearing?
Iach. If I had lost it,
I should have lost the worth of it in gold.
I'll make a journey twice as far, to enjoy
A second night of such sweet shortness which
Was mine in Britain, for the ring is won.
Post. The stone's too hard to come by.
Iach. Not a whit,
Your lady being so easy.
Post. Make not, sir,
Your loss your sport. I hope you know that we
Must not continue friends.
Iach. Good sir, we must,
If you keep covenant. Had I not brought
The knowledge of your mistress home, I grant
We were to question further; but I now
Profess myself the winner of her honour,
Together with your ring; and not the wronger
Of her or you, having proceeded but
By both your wills.
Post. If you can make 't apparent
That you have tasted her in bed, my hand
And ring is yours; if not, the foul opinion

You had of her pure honour gains or loses
Your sword or mine, or masterless leaves both
To who shall find them.
Iach. Sir, my circumstances,
Being so near the truth as I will make them,
Must first induce you to believe; whose strength
I will confirm with oath; which, I doubt not,
You'll give me leave to spare, when you shall find
You need it not.
Post. Proceed.
Iach. First, her bedchamber—
Where, I confess, I slept not, but profess
Had that was well worth watching—it was hang'd
With tapestry of silk and silver; the story
Proud Cleopatra, when she met her Roman,
And Cydnus swell'd above the banks, or for
The press of boats or pride; a piece of work
So bravely done, so rich, that it did strive
In workmanship and value; which I wonder'd
Could be so rarely and exactly wrought,
Since the true life on 't was—
Post. This is true;
And this you might have heard of here, by me,
Or by some other.
Iach. More particulars
Must justify my knowledge.
Post. So they must,
Or do your honour injury.
Iach. The chimney
Is south the chamber, and the chimney-piece
Chaste Dian bathing. Never saw I figures
So likely to report themselves. The cutter
Was as another Nature, dumb; outwent her,
Motion and breath left out.
Post. This is a thing
Which you might from relation likewise reap,
Being, as it is, much spoke of.
Iach. The roof o' the chamber
With golden cherubins is fretted. Her andirons—
I had forgot them—were two winking Cupids
Of silver, each on one foot standing, nicely
Depending on their brands.
Post. This is her honour!
Let it be granted you have seen all this—and praise
Be given to your remembrance—the description
Of what is in her chamber nothing saves
The wager you have laid.
Iach. Then, if you can,
Showing the bracelet.
Be pale. I beg but leave to air this jewel; see!
And now 'tis up again. It must be married
To that your diamond; I'll keep them.
Post. Jove!
Once more let me behold it. Is it that
Which I left with her?
Iach. Sir—I thank her—that.
She stripp'd it from her arm; I see her yet;
Her pretty action did outsell her gift,
And yet enrich'd it too. She gave it me, and said
She prized it once.
Post. May be she pluck'd it off
To send it me.
Iach. She writes so to you, doth she?
Post. O, no, no, no! 'tis true. Here, take this too; [*Gives the ring*.]
It is a basilisk unto mine eye,
Kills me to look on 't. Let there be no honour
Where there is beauty; truth, where semblance; love,
Where there's another man. The vows of women
Of no more bondage be to where they are made
Than they are to their virtues; which is nothing.
O, above measure false!
Phi. Have patience, sir,
And take your ring again; 'tis not yet won.
It may be probable she lost it; or
Who knows if one of her women, being corrupted,
Hath stol'n it from her?
Post. Very true;
And so, I hope, he came by 't. Back my ring.
Render to me some corporal sign about her,
More evident than this; for this was stolen.
Iach. By Jupiter, I had it from her arm.
Post. Hark you, he swears; by Jupiter he swears.
'Tis true—nay, keep the ring—'tis true. I am sure
She would not lose it. Her attendants are
All sworn and honourable. They induced to steal it!
And by a stranger! No, he hath enjoy'd her.
The cognizance of her incontinency
Is this: she hath bought the name of whore thus dearly.
There, take thy hire; and all the fiends of hell
Divide themselves between you!
Phi. Sir, be patient.
This is not strong enough to be believed
Of one persuaded well of—
Post. Never talk on 't;
She hath been colted by him.
Iach. If you seek
For further satisfying, under her breast—
Worthy the pressing—lies a mole, right proud
Of that most delicate lodging. By my life,
I kiss'd it; and it gave me present hunger
To feed again, though full. You do remember
This stain upon her?
Post. Ay, and it doth confirm

Another stain, as big as hell can hold,
Were there no more but it.
Iach. Will you hear more?
Post. Spare your arithmetic; never count the turns;
Once, and a million!
Iach. I'll be sworn—
Post. No swearing.
If you will swear you have not done 't, you lie;
And I will kill thee, if thou dost deny
Thou'st made me cuckold.
Iach. I'll deny nothing.
Post. O, that I had her here, to tear her limb-meal!
I will go there and do 't, i' the court, before
Her father. I'll do something— [*Exit.*
Phi. Quite besides
The government of patience! You have won.
Let's follow him and pervert the present wrath
He hath against himself.
Iach. With all my heart. [*Exeunt.*

SCENE V. *Another room in Philario's house*

Enter POSTHUMUS.

Post. Is there no way for men to be but women
Must be half-workers? We are all bastards;
And that most venerable man which I
Did call my father, was I know not where
When I was stamp'd; some coiner with his tools
Made me a counterfeit. Yet my mother seem'd
The Dian of that time; so doth my wife
The nonpareil of this. O, vengeance, vengeance!
Me of my lawful pleasure she restrain'd
And pray'd me oft forbearance; did it with
A pudency so rosy the sweet view on 't
Might well have warm'd old Saturn; that I thought her
As chaste as unsunn'd snow. O, all the devils!
This yellow Iachimo, in an hour—was 't not?—
Or less—at first?—perchance he spoke not, but,
Like a full-acorn'd boar, a German one,
Cried "O!" and mounted; found no opposition
But what he look'd for should oppose and she
Should from encounter guard. Could I find out
The woman's part in me! For there's no motion
That tends to vice in man, but I affirm
It is the woman's part: be it lying, note it,
The woman's; flattering, hers; deceiving, hers;
Lust and rank thoughts, hers, hers; revenges, hers;
Ambitions, covetings, change of prides, disdain,
Nice longing, slanders, mutability,
All faults that may be named, nay, that hell knows,
Why, hers, in part or all; but rather, all;
For even to vice
They are not constant, but are changing still
One vice, but of a minute old, for one
Not half so old as that. I'll write against them,
Detest them, curse them. Yet 'tis greater skill
In a true hate, to pray they have their will;
The very devils cannot plague them better.
[*Exit.*

ACT III

SCENE I. *Britain: a hall in Cymbeline's palace*

Enter in state, CYMBELINE, QUEEN, CLOTEN, *and* LORDS *at one door, and at another,* CAIUS LUCIUS *and Attendants.*

Cym. Now say, what would Augustus Cæsar with us?
Luc. When Julius Cæsar, whose remembrance yet
Lives in men's eyes and will to ears and tongues
Be theme and hearing ever, was in this Britain
And conquer'd it, Cassibelan, thine uncle—
Famous in Cæsar's praises, no whit less
Than in his feats deserving it—for him
And his succession granted Rome a tribute,
Yearly three thousand pounds, which by thee lately
Is left untender'd.
Queen. And, to kill the marvel,
Shall be so ever.
Clo. There be many Cæsars,
Ere such another Julius. Britain is
A world by itself; and we will nothing pay
For wearing our own noses.
Queen. That opportunity
Which then they had to take from 's, to resume
We have again. Remember, sir, my liege,
The kings your ancestors, together with
The natural bravery of your isle, which stands
As Neptune's park, ribbed and paled in
With rocks unscaleable and roaring waters,
With sands that will not bear your enemies' boats,
But suck them up to the topmast. A kind of conquest
Cæsar made here; but made not here his brag
Of "Came and saw and overcame." With shame—
The first that ever touch'd him—he was carried
From off our coast, twice beaten; and his shipping—
Poor ignorant baubles!—on our terrible seas,
Like egg-shells moved upon their surges, crack'd
As easily 'gainst our rocks; for joy whereof
The famed Cassibelan, who was once at point—
O giglot fortune!—to master Cæsar's sword,
Made Lud's town with rejoicing fires bright

And Britons strut with courage.

Clo. Come, there's no more tribute to be paid. Our kingdom is stronger than it was at that time; and, as I said, there is no moe such Cæsars. Other of them may have crook'd noses, but to owe such straight arms, none.

Cym. Son, let your mother end.

Clo. We have yet many among us can gripe as hard as Cassibelan. I do not say I am one; but I have a hand. Why tribute? why should we pay tribute? If Cæsar can hide the sun from us with a blanket, or put the moon in his pocket, we will pay him tribute for light; else, sir, no more tribute, pray you now.

Cym. You must know,
Till the injurious Romans did extort
This tribute from us, we were free. Cæsar's ambition,
Which swell'd so much that it did almost stretch
The sides o' the world, against all colour here
Did put the yoke upon 's; which to shake off
Becomes a warlike people, whom we reckon
Ourselves to be.

Clo. and Lords. We do.

Cym. Say, then, to Cæsar,
Our ancestor was that Mulmutius which
Ordain'd our laws, whose use the sword of Cæsar
Hath too much mangled; whose repair and franchise
Shall, by the power we hold, be our good deed,
Though Rome be therefore angry. Mulmutius made our laws,
Who was the first of Britain which did put
His brows within a golden crown and call'd
Himself a king.

Luc. I am sorry, Cymbeline,
That I am to pronounce Augustus Cæsar—
Cæsar, that hath more kings his servants than
Thyself domestic officers—thine enemy.
Receive it from me, then: war and confusion
In Cæsar's name pronounce I 'gainst thee. Look
For fury not to be resisted. Thus defied,
I thank thee for myself.

Cym. Thou art welcome, Caius.
Thy Cæsar knighted me; my youth I spent
Much under him; of him I gather'd honour;
Which he to seek of me again, perforce,
Behoves me keep at utterance. I am perfect
That the Pannonians and Dalmatians for
Their liberties are now in arms; a precedent
Which not to read would show the Britons cold.
So Cæsar shall not find them.

Luc. Let proof speak.

Clo. His Majesty bids you welcome. Make pastime with us a day or two, or longer. If you seek us afterwards in other terms, you shall find us in our salt-water girdle. If you beat us out of it, it is yours; if you fall in the adventure, our crows shall fare the better for you; and there's an end.

Luc. So, sir.

Cym. I know your master's pleasure and he mine;
All the remain is "Welcome!" [*Exeunt*.

SCENE II. *Another room in the palace*

Enter PISANIO, *with a letter*.

Pis. How! of adultery? Wherefore write you not
What monster's her accuser? Leonatus!
O master! what a strange infection
Is fall'n into thy ear! What false Italian,
As poisonous-tongued as handed, hath prevail'd
On thy too ready hearing? Disloyal! No.
She's punish'd for her truth, and undergoes,
More goddess-like than wife-like, such assaults
As would take in some virtue. O my master!
Thy mind to her is now as low as were
Thy fortunes. How! that I should murder her?
Upon the love and truth and vows which I
Have made to thy command? I, her? her blood?
If it be so to do good service, never
Let me be counted serviceable. How look I
That I should seem to lack humanity
So much as this fact comes to? [*Reading*] "Do 't. the letter
That I have sent her, by her own command
Shall give thee opportunity." O damn'd paper!
Black as the ink that's on thee! Senseless bauble,
Art thou a fedary for this act, and look'st
So virgin-like without? Lo, here she comes.
I am ignorant in what I am commanded.

Enter IMOGEN.

Imo. How now, Pisanio!

Pis. Madam, here is a letter from my lord.

Imo. Who? thy lord? that is my lord, Leonatus!
O, learn'd indeed were that astronomer
That knew the stars as I his characters;
He'd lay the future open. You good gods,
Let what is here contain'd relish of love,
Of my lord's health, of his content, yet not
That we two are asunder; let that grieve him.
Some griefs are med'cinable; that is one of them,
For it doth physic love; of his content,
All but in that! Good wax, thy leave. Blest be
You bees that make these locks of counsel. Lovers
And men in dangerous bonds pray not alike.
Though forfeiters you cast in prison, yet
You clasp young Cupid's tables. Good news, gods!

[*Reads*] "Justice, and your father's wrath, should he take me in his dominion, could not be so cruel to me as you, O the dearest of creatures, would even renew me with your eyes. Take notice that I am in Cambria, at Milford-Haven; what your own love will out of this advise you, follow. So he wishes you all happiness, that remains loyal to his vow, and your increasing in love,

Leonatus Posthumus"

O, for a horse with wings! Hear'st thou, Pisanio?
He is at Milford-Haven. Read, and tell me
How far 'tis thither. If one of mean affairs
May plod it in a week, why may not I
Glide thither in a day? Then, true Pisanio—
Who long'st, like me, to see thy lord; who long'st—
O, let me bate—but not like me—yet long'st,
But in a fainter kind.—O, not like me;
For mine's beyond beyond—say, and speak thick;
Love's counsellor should fill the bores of hearing,
To the smothering of the sense—how far it is
To this same blessed Milford; and by the way
Tell me how Wales was made so happy as
To inherit such a haven; but first of all,
How we may steal from hence, and for the gap
That we shall make in time, from our hencegoing
And our return, to excuse. But first, how get hence?
Why should excuse be born or e'er begot?
We'll talk of that hereafter. Prithee, speak,
How many score of miles may we well ride
'Twixt hour and hour?

Pis. One score 'twixt sun and sun,
Madam, 's enough for you; [*Aside*] and too much too.

Imo. Why, one that rode to's execution, man,
Could never go so slow. I have heard of riding wagers,
Where horses have been nimbler than the sands
That run i' the clock's behalf. But this is foolery.
Go bid my woman feign a sickness; say
She'll home to her father; and provide me presently
A riding-suit, no costlier than would fit
A franklin's housewife.

Pis. Madam, you're best consider.

Imo. I see before me, man; nor here, nor here,
Nor what ensues, but have a fog in them,
That I cannot look through. Away, I prithee;
Do as I bid thee. There's no more to say;
Accessible is none but Milford way. [*Exeunt.*

SCENE III. *Wales: a mountainous country with a cave*

Enter, from the cave, BELARIUS; GUIDERIUS, *and* ARVIRAGUS *following.*

Bel. A goodly day not to keep house, with such
Whose roof's as low as ours! Stoop, boys; this gate
Instructs you how to adore the heavens and bows you
To a morning's holy office. The gates of monarchs
Are arch'd so high that giants may jet through
And keep their impious turbans on, without
Good morrow to the sun. Hail, thou fair heaven!
We house i' the rock, yet use thee not so hardly
As proud livers do.

Gui. Hail, heaven!

Arv. Hail, heaven!

Bel. Now for our mountain sport. Up to yond hill;
Your legs are young; I'll tread these flats. Consider,
When you above perceive me like a crow,
That it is place which lessens and sets off;
And you may then revolve what tales I have told you
Of courts, of princes, of the tricks in war.
This service is not service, so being done,
But being so allow'd. To apprehend thus
Draws us a profit from all things we see;
And often, to our comfort, shall we find
The sharded beetle in a safer hold
Than is the full-wing'd eagle. O, this life
Is nobler than attending for a check,
Richer than doing nothing for a bauble,
Prouder than rustling in unpaid-for silk.
Such gain the cap of him that makes 'em fine,
Yet keeps his book uncross'd. No life to ours.

Gui. Out of your proof you speak. We, poor unfledged,
Have never wing'd from view o' the nest, nor know not
What air's from home. Haply this life is best,
If quiet life be best; sweeter to you
That have a sharper known; well corresponding
With your stiff age. But unto us it is
A cell of ignorance; travelling a-bed;
A prison for a debtor that not dares
To stride a limit.

Arv. What should we speak of
When we are old as you? When we shall hear
The rain and wind beat dark December, how,
In this our pinching cave, shall we discourse
The freezing hours away? We have seen nothing;
We are beastly, subtle as the fox for prey,

Like warlike as the wolf for what we eat;
Our valour is to chase what flies; our cage
We make a quire, as doth the prison'd bird,
And sing our bondage freely.

Bel. How you speak!
Did you but know the city's usuries
And felt them knowingly; the art o' the court,
As hard to leave as keep; whose top to climb
Is certain falling, or so slippery that
The fear's as bad as falling; the toil o' the war,
A pain that only seems to seek out danger
I' the name of fame and honour; which dies i' the search,
And hath as oft a slanderous epitaph
As record of fair act; nay, many times,
Doth ill deserve by doing well; what's worse.
Must court'sy at the censure. O boys, this story
The world may read in me. My body's mark'd
With Roman swords, and my report was once
First with the best of note. Cymbeline loved me,
And when a soldier was the theme, my name
Was not far off. Then was I as a tree
Whose boughs did bend with fruit. But in one night,
A storm or robbery, call it what you will,
Shook down my mellow hangings, nay, my leaves,
And left me bare to weather.

Gui. Uncertain favour!

Bel. My fault being nothing—as I have told you oft—
But that two villains, whose false oaths prevail'd
Before my perfect honour, swore to Cymbeline
I was confederate with the Romans. So
Follow'd my banishment, and this twenty years
This rock and these demesnes have been my world,
Where I have lived at honest freedom, paid
More pious debts to heaven than in all
The fore-end of my time. But up to the mountains!
This is not hunters' language. He that strikes
The venison first shall be the lord o' the feast;
To him the other two shall minister;
And we will fear no poison, which attends
In place of greater state. I'll meet you in the valleys. [*Exeunt* GUIDERIUS *and* ARVIRAGUS.
How hard it is to hide the sparks of nature!
These boys know little they are sons to the King;
Nor Cymbeline dreams that they are alive.
They think they are mine; and though train'd up thus meanly
I' the cave wherein they bow, their thoughts do hit
The roofs of palaces, and nature prompts them
In simple and low things to prince it much
Beyond the trick of others. This Polydore,
The heir of Cymbeline and Britain, who
The King his father call'd Guiderius—Jove!
When on my three-foot stool I sit and tell
The warlike feats I have done, his spirits fly out
Into my story; say "Thus mine enemy fell,
And thus I set my foot on's neck"; even then
The princely blood flows in his cheek, he sweats,
Strains his young nerves, and puts himself in posture
That acts my words. The younger brother, Cadwal,
Once Arviragus, in as like a figure,
Strikes life into my speech and shows much more
His own conceiving.—Hark, the game is roused!—
O Cymbeline! Heaven and my conscience knows
Thou didst unjustly banish me; whereon,
At three and two years old, I stole these babes;
Thinking to bar thee of succession, as
Thou reft'st me of my lands. Euriphile,
Thou wast their nurse; they took thee for their mother,
And every day do honour to her grave.
Myself, Belarius, that am Morgan call'd,
They take for natural father.—The game is up.
[*Exit.*

SCENE IV. *Country near Milford-Haven*

Enter PISANIO *and* IMOGEN.

Imo. Thou told'st me, when we came from horse, the place
Was near at hand. ne'er long'd my mother so
To see me first, as I have now. Pisanio! man!
Where is Posthumus? What is in thy mind,
That makes thee stare thus? Wherefore breaks that sigh
From the inward of thee? One but painted thus
Would be interpreted a thing perplex'd
Beyond self-explication. Put thyself
Into a haviour of less fear, ere wildness
Vanquish my staider senses. What's the matter?
Why tender'st thou that paper to me, with
A look untender? If't be summer news,
Smile to't before; if winterly, thou need'st
But keep that countenance still. My husband's hand!
That drug-damn'd Italy hath out-craftied him,
And he's at some hard point. Speak, man. Thy tongue
May take off some extremity, which to read
Would be even mortal to me.

Pis. Please you, read;
And you shall find me, wretched man, a thing
The most disdain'd of fortune.

Imo. [*Reads*] "Thy mistress, Pisanio, hath played the strumpet in my bed; the testimonies whereof lie bleeding in me. I speak not out of weak surmises, but from proof as strong as my grief and as certain as I expect my revenge. That part thou, Pisanio, must act for me, if thy faith be not tainted with the breach of hers. Let thine own hands take away her life. I shall give thee opportunity at Milford-Haven. She hath my letter for the purpose; where, if thou fear to strike and to make me certain it is done, thou art the pandar to her dishonour and equally to me disloyal."

Pis. What shall I need to draw my sword? the paper
Hath cut her throat already. No, 'tis slander,
Whose edge is sharper than the sword, whose tongue
Outvenoms all the worms of Nile, whose breath
Rides on the posting winds and doth belie
All corners of the world. Kings, queens and states,
Maids, matrons, nay, the secrets of the grave
This viperous slander enters. What cheer, madam?

Imo. False to his bed! What is it to be false?
To lie in watch there and to think on him?
To weep 'twixt clock and clock? if sleep charge nature,
To break it with a fearful dream of him
And cry myself awake? that's false to's bed, is it?

Pis. Alas, good lady!

Imo. I false! Thy conscience witness. Iachimo,
Thou didst accuse him of incontinency;
Thou then look'dst like a villain; now methinks
Thy favour's good enough. Some jay of Italy
Whose mother was her painting, hath betray'd him.
Poor I am stale, a garment out of fashion;
And, for I am richer than to hang by the walls,
I must be ripp'd—To pieces with me! O,
Men's vows are women's traitors! All good seeming,
By thy revolt, O husband, shall be thought
Put on for villainy; not born where 't grows,
But worn a bait for ladies.

Pis. Good madam, hear me.

Imo. True honest men being heard, like false Æneas,
Were in his time thought false, and Sinon's weeping
Did scandal many a holy tear, took pity
From most true wretchedness. So thou, Posthumus,
Wilt lay the leaven on all proper men;
Goodly and gallant shall be false and perjured
From thy great fail. Come, fellow, be thou honest.
Do thou thy master's bidding. When thou see'st him,
A little witness my obedience. Look!
I draw the sword myself. Take it, and hit
The innocent mansion of my love, my heart.
Fear not; 'tis empty of all things but grief.
Thy master is not there, who was indeed
The riches of it. Do his bidding; strike.
Thou mayst be valiant in a better cause;
But now thou seem'st a coward.

Pis. Hence, vile instrument!
Thou shalt not damn my hand.

Imo. Why, I must die;
And if I do not by thy hand, thou art
No servant of thy master's. Against self-slaughter
There is a prohibition so divine
That cravens my weak hand. Come, here's my heart.
Something's afore't. Soft, soft! we'll no defence;
Obedient as the scabbard. What is here?
The scriptures of the loyal Leonatus,
All turn'd to heresy? Away, away,
Corrupters of my faith! you shall no more
Be stomachers to my heart. Thus may poor fools
Believe false teachers. Though those that are betray'd
Do feel the treason sharply, yet the traitor
Stands in worse case of woe.
And thou, Posthumus, thou that didst set up
My disobedience 'gainst the King my father
And make me put into contempt the suits
Of princely fellows, shalt hereafter find
It is no act of common passage, but
A strain of rareness; and I grieve myself
To think, when thou shalt be disedged by her
That now thou tirest on, how thy memory
Will then be pang'd by me. Prithee, dispatch;
The lamb entreats the butcher; where's thy knife?
Thou art too slow to do thy master's bidding,
When I desire it too.

Pis. O gracious lady,
Since I received command to do this business
I have not slept one wink.

Imo. Do't, and to bed then.

Pis. I'll wake mine eye-balls blind first.

Imo. Wherefore then
Didst undertake it? Why hast thou abused
So many miles with a pretence? this place?
Mine action and thine own? our horses' labour?
The time inviting thee? the perturb'd court,
For my being absent? whereunto I never
Purpose return. Why hast thou gone so far,
To be unbent when thou hast ta'en thy stand,
The elected deer before thee?

Pis. But to win time
To lose so bad employment; in the which

I have consider'd of a course. Good lady,
Hear me with patience.
Imo. Talk thy tongue weary; speak.
I have heard I am a strumpet; and mine ear,
Therein false struck, can take no greater wound,
Nor tent to bottom that. But speak.
Pis. Then, madam,
I thought you would not back again.
Imo. Most like;
Bringing me here to kill me.
Pis. Not so, neither.
But if I were as wise as honest, then
My purpose would prove well. It cannot be
But that my master is abused.
Some villain, ay, and singular in his art,
Hath done you both this cursed injury.
Imo. Some Roman courtezan.
Pis. No, on my life.
I'll give but notice you are dead and send him
Some bloody sign of it; for 'tis commanded
I should do so. You shall be miss'd at court,
And that will well confirm it.
Imo. Why, good fellow,
What shall I do the while? where bide? how live?
Or in my life what comfort, when I am
Dead to my husband?
Pis. If you'll back to the court—
Imo. No court, no father; nor no more ado
With that harsh, noble, simple nothing,
That Cloten, whose love-suit hath been to me
As fearful as a siege.
Pis. If not at court,
Then not in Britain must you bide.
Imo. Where then?
Hath Britain all the sun that shines? Day, night,
Are they not but in Britain? I' the world's volume
Our Britain seems as of it, but not in't;
In a great pool a swan's nest. Prithee, think
There's livers out of Britain.
Pis. I am most glad
You think of other place. The ambassador,
Lucius the Roman, comes to Milford-Haven
To-morrow. Now, if you could wear a mind
Dark as your fortune is, and but disguise
That which, to appear itself, must not yet be
But by self-danger, you should tread a course
Pretty and full of view; yea, haply, near
The residence of Posthumus; so nigh at least
That though his actions were not visible, yet
Report should render him hourly to your ear
As truly as he moves.
Imo. O, for such means!
Though peril to my modesty, not death on't,
I would adventure.
Pis. Well, then, here's the point.
You must forget to be a woman; change
Command into obedience; fear and niceness—
The handmaids of all women, or, more truly,
Woman it pretty self—into a waggish courage;
Ready in gibes, quick-answer'd, saucy, and
As quarrelous as the weasel; nay, you must
Forget that rarest treasure of your cheek,
Exposing it—but, O, the harder heart!
Alack, no remedy!—to the greedy touch
Of common-kissing Titan, and forget
Your laboursome and dainty trims, wherein
You made great Juno angry.
Imo. Nay, be brief.
I see into thy end and am almost
A man already.
Pis. First, make yourself but like one.
Fore-thinking this, I have already fit—
'Tis in my cloak-bag—doublet, hat, hose, all
That answer to them. Would you in their serving,
And with what imitation you can borrow
From youth of such a season, 'fore noble Lucius
Present yourself, desire his service, tell him
Wherein you're happy—which you'll make him know,
If that his head have ear in music—doubtless
With joy he will embrace you, for he's honourable
And, doubling that, most holy. Your means abroad,
You have me, rich; and I will never fail
Beginning nor supplyment.
Imo. Thou art all the comfort
The gods will diet me with. Prithee, away.
There's more to be consider'd; but we'll even
All that good time will give us. This attempt
I am soldier to, and will abide it with
A prince's courage. Away, I prithee.
Pis. Well, madam, we must take a short farewell,
Lest, being miss'd, I be suspected of
Your carriage from the court. My noble mistress,
Here is a box; I had it from the Queen.
What's in 't is precious; if you are sick at sea,
Or stomach-qualm'd at land, a dram of this
Will drive away distemper. To some shade,
And fit you to your manhood. May the gods
Direct you to the best!
Imo. Amen! I thank thee. [*Exeunt, severally.*

SCENE V. *A room in Cymbeline's palace*

Enter CYMBELINE, QUEEN, CLOTEN, LUCIUS, LORDS, *and* ATTENDANTS.

Cym. Thus far; and so farewell.
Luc. Thanks, royal sir.
My emperor hath wrote, I must from hence;
And am right sorry that I must report ye
My master's enemy.

Cym. Our subjects, sir,
Will not endure his yoke; and for ourself
To show less sovereignty than they, must needs
Appear unkinglike.
Luc. So, sir. I desire of you
A conduct over-land to Milford-Haven.
Madam, all joy befal your Grace!
Queen. And you!
Cym. My lords, you are appointed for that office;
The due of honour in no point omit.
So farewell, noble Lucius.
Luc. Your hand, my lord.
Clo. Receive it friendly; but from this time forth
I wear it as your enemy.
Luc. Sir, the event
Is yet to name the winner. Fare you well.
Cym. Leave not the worthy Lucius, good my lords,
Till he have cross'd the Severn. Happiness!
[*Exeunt* LUCIUS *and* LORDS.
Queen. He goes hence frowning; but it honours us
That we have given him cause.
Clo. 'Tis all the better;
Your valiant Britons have their wishes in it.
Cym. Lucius hath wrote already to the Emperor
How it goes here. It fits us therefore ripely
Out chariots and our horsemen be in readiness.
The powers that he already hath in Gallia
Will soon be drawn to head, from whence he moves
His war for Britain.
Queen. 'Tis not sleepy business;
But must be look'd to speedily and strongly.
Cym. Our expectation that it would be thus
Hath made us forward. But, my gentle queen,
Where is our daughter? She hath not appear'd
Before the Roman, nor to us hath tender'd
The duty of the day. She looks us like
A thing more made of malice than of duty;
We have noted it. Call her before us; for
We have been too slight in sufferance.
[*Exit an* ATTENDANT.
Queen. Royal sir,
Since the exile of Posthumus, most retired
Hath her life been; the cure whereof, my lord,
'Tis time must do. Beseech your Majesty,
Forbear sharp speeches to her. She's a lady
So tender of rebukes that words are strokes
And strokes death to her.

Re-enter ATTENDANT.

Cym. Where is she, sir? How
Can her contempt be answer'd?
Atten. Please you, sir,
Her chambers are all lock'd; and there's no answer
That will be given to the loudest noise we make.
Queen. My lord, when last I went to visit her,
She pray'd me to excuse her keeping close,
Whereto constrain'd by her infirmity,
She should that duty leave unpaid to you,
Which daily she was bound to proffer. This
She wish'd me to make known; but our great court
Made me to blame in memory.
Cym. Her doors lock'd?
Not seen of late? Grant, heavens, that which I fear
Prove false! [*Exit.*
Queen. Son, I say, follow the King.
Clo. That man of hers, Pisanio, her old servant,
I have not seen these two days.
Queen. Go, look after. [*Exit* CLOTEN.
Pisanio, thou that stand'st so for Posthumus!
He hath a drug of mine; I pray his absence
Proceed by swallowing that, for he believes
It is a thing most precious. But for her,
Where is she gone? Haply, despair hath seized her,
Or, wing'd with fervour of her love, she's flown
To her desired Posthumus. Gone she is
To death or to dishonour; and my end
Can make good use of either. She being down,
I have the placing of the British crown.

Re-enter CLOTEN.

How now, my son!
Clo. 'Tis certain she is fled.
Go in and cheer the King. He rages; none
Dare come about him.
Queen. [*Aside*] All the better. May
This night forestall him of the coming day! [*Exit.*
Clo. I love and hate her; for she's fair and royal,
And that she hath all courtly parts more exquisite
Than lady, ladies, woman; from every one
The best she hath, and she, of all compounded,
Outsells them all. I love her therefore; but
Disdaining me and throwing favours on
The low Posthumus slanders so her judgement
That what's else rare is choked; and in that point
I will conclude to hate her, nay, indeed,
To be revenged upon her. For when fools
Shall—

Enter PISANIO.

Who is here? What, are you packing, sirrah?
Come hither. Ah, you precious pandar! Villain,
Where is thy lady? In a word; or else

Thou art straightway with the fiends.

Pis. O, good my lord!

Clo. Where is thy lady? or, by Jupiter,
I will not ask again. Close villain,
I'll have this secret from thy heart, or rip
Thy heart to find it. Is she with Posthumus?
From whose so many weights of baseness cannot
A dram of worth be drawn.

Pis. Alas, my lord,
How can she be with him? When was she miss'd?
He is in Rome.

Clo. Where is she, sir? Come nearer;
No further halting. Satisfy me home
What is become of her.

Pis. O, my all-worthy lord!

Clo. All-worthy villain!
Discover where thy mistress is at once,
At the next word. No more of "worthy lord!"
Speak, or thy silence on the instant is
Thy condemnation and thy death.

Pis. Then, sir,
This paper is the history of my knowledge
Touching her flight. [*Presenting a letter*.]

Clo. Let's see't. I will pursue her
Even to Augustus' throne.

Pis. [*Aside*] Or this, or perish.
She's far enough; and what he learns by this
May prove his travel, not her danger.

Clo. Hum!

Pis. [*Aside*] I'll write to my lord she's dead.
O Imogen,
Safe mayst thou wander, safe return again!

Clo. Sirrah, is this letter true?

Pis. Sir, as I think.

Clo. It is Posthumus' hand; I know't. Sirrah, if thou wouldst not be a villain, but do me true service, undergo those employments wherein I should have cause to use thee with a serious industry, that is, what villainy soe'er I bid thee do, to perform it directly and truly, I would think thee an honest man. Thou shouldst neither want my means for thy relief nor my voice for thy preferment.

Pis. Well, my good lord.

Clo. Wilt thou serve me? for since patiently and constantly thou hast stuck to the bare fortune of that beggar Posthumus, thou canst not, in the course of gratitude, but be a diligent follower of mine. Wilt thou serve me?

Pis. Sir, I will.

Clo. Give me thy hand; here's my purse. Hast any of thy late master's garments in thy possession?

Pis. I have, my lord, at my lodging, the same suit he wore when he took leave of my lady and mistress.

Clo. The first service thou dost me, fetch that suit hither. Let it be thy first service; go.

Pis. I shall, my lord. [*Exit.*

Clo. Meet thee at Milford-Haven!—I forgot to ask him one thing; I'll remember't anon.—even there, thou villain Posthumus, will I kill thee. I would these garments were come. She said upon a time—the bitterness of it I now belch from my heart—that she held the very garment of Posthumus in more respect than my noble and natural person, together with the adornment of my qualities. With that suit upon my back will I ravish her; first kill him, and in her eyes; there shall she see my valour, which will then be a torment to her contempt. He on the ground, my speech of insultment ended on his dead body, and when my lust hath dined—which, as I say, to vex her I will execute in the clothes that she so praised—to the court I'll knock her back, foot her home again. She hath despised me rejoicingly, and I'll be merry in my revenge.

Re-enter PISANIO, *with the clothes.*

Be those the garments?

Pis. Ay, my noble lord.

Clo. How long is't since she went to Milford-Haven?

Pis. She can scarce be there yet.

Clo. Bring this apparel to my chamber; that is the second thing that I have commanded thee. The third is that thou wilt be a voluntary mute to my design. Be but duteous, and true preferment shall tender itself to thee. My revenge is now at Milford. Would I had wings to follow it! Come, and be true. [*Exit.*

Pis. Thou bid'st me to my loss; for true to thee
Were to prove false, which I will never be,
To him that is most true. To Milford go,
And find not her whom thou pursuest. Flow, flow,
You heavenly blessings, on her! This fool's speed
Be cross'd with slowness; labour be his meed!
[*Exit.*

SCENE VI. *Wales before the cave of Belarius*

Enter IMOGEN, *in boy's clothes.*

Imo. I see a man's life is a tedious one.
I have tired myself, and for two nights together
Have made the ground my bed. I should be sick,
But that my resolution helps me. Milford,
When from the mountain-top Pisanio show'd thee,
Thou wast within a ken. O Jove! I think
Foundations fly the wretched; such, I mean,

Where they should be relieved. Two beggars told me
I could not miss my way. Will poor folks lie,
That have afflictions on them, knowing 'tis
A punishment or trial? Yes; no wonder,
When rich ones scarce tell true. To lapse in fulness
Is sorer than to lie for need, and falsehood
Is worse in kings than beggars. My dear lord!
Thou art one o' the false ones. Now I think on thee,
My hunger's gone; but even before, I was
At point to sink for food. But what is this?
Here is a path to't. 'Tis some savage hold.
I were best not call; I dare not call; yet famine,
Ere clean it o'erthrow nature, makes it valiant.
Plenty and peace breeds cowards; hardness ever
Of hardiness is mother. Ho! who's here?
If anything that's civil, speak; if savage,
Take or lend. Ho! No answer? Then I'll enter.
Best draw my sword; and if mine enemy
But fear the sword like me, he'll scarcely look on't.
Such a foe, good heavens! [*Exit, to the cave.*

Enter BELARIUS, GUIDERIUS, *and* ARVIRAGUS.

Bel. You, Polydore, have proved best woodman and
Are master of the feast. Cadwal and I
Will play the cook and servant; 'tis our match.
The sweat of industry would dry and die,
But for the end it works to. Come; our stomachs
Will make what's homely savoury. Weariness
Can snore upon the flint, when resty sloth
Finds the down pillow hard. Now peace be here,
Poor house, that keep'st thyself!
Gui. I am throughly weary.
Arv. I am weak with toil, yet strong in appetite.
Gui. There is cold meat i' the cave; we'll browse on that,
Whilst what we have kill'd be cook'd.
Bel. [*Looking into the cave*] Stay; come not in.
But that it eats our victuals, I should think
Here were a fairy.
Gui. What's the matter, sir?
Bel. By Jupiter, an angel! or, if not,
An earthly paragon! Behold divineness
No elder than a boy!

Re-enter IMOGEN.

Imo. Good masters, harm me not.
Before I enter'd here, I call'd; and thought
To have begg'd or bought what I have took. Good troth,
I have stol'n nought, nor would not, though I had found
Gold strew'd i' the floor. Here's money for my meat.
I would have left it on the board so soon
As I had made my meal, and parted
With prayers for the provider.
Gui. Money, youth?
Arv. All gold and silver rather turn to dirt!
As 'tis no better reckon'd, but of those
Who worship dirty gods.
Imo. I see you're angry.
Know, if you kill me for my fault, I should
Have died had I not made it.
Bel. Whither bound?
Imo. To Milford-Haven.
Bel. What's your name?
Imo. Fidele, sir. I have a kinsman who
Is bound for Italy; he embark'd at Milford;
To whom being going, almost spent with hunger,
I am fall'n in this offence.
Bel. Prithee, fair youth,
Think us no churls, nor measure our good minds
By this rude place we live in. Well encounter'd!
'Tis almost night; you shall have better cheer
Ere you depart; and thanks to stay and eat it.
Boys, bid him welcome.
Gui. Were you a woman, youth,
I should woo hard but be your groom. In honesty,
I bid for you as I'd buy.
Arv. I'll make 't my comfort
He is a man; I'll love him as my brother;
And such a welcome as I'd give to him
After long absence, such is yours. Most welcome!
Be sprightly, for you fall 'mongst friends.
Imo. 'Mongst friends,
If brothers. [*Aside*] Would it had been so, that they
Had been my father's sons! Then had my prize
Been less, and so more equal ballasting
To thee, Posthumus.
Bel. He wrings at some distress.
Gui. Would I could free 't!
Arv. Or I, whate'er it be,
What pain it cost, what danger. Gods!
Bel. Hark, boys.
Whispering.
Imo. [*Aside.*] Great men,
That had a court no bigger than this cave,
That did attend themselves and had the virtue
Which their own conscience seal'd them—laying by
That nothing-gift of differing multitudes—
Could not out-peer these twain. Pardon me, gods!
I'd change my sex to be companion with them,
Since Leonatus's false.

Bel. It shall be so.
Boys, we'll go dress our hunt. Fair youth, come in.
Discourse is heavy, fasting; when we have supp'd,
We'll mannerly demand thee of thy story,
So far as thou wilt speak it.
Gui. Pray, draw near.
Arv. The night to the owl and morn to the lark less welcome.
Imo. Thanks, sir.
Arv. I pray, draw near. [*Exeunt.*

SCENE VII. *Rome: a public place*

Enter TWO SENATORS *and* TRIBUNES.

1st Sen. This is the tenour of the Emperor's writ:
That since the common men are now in action
'Gainst the Pannonians and Dalmatians,
And that the legions now in Gallia are
Full weak to undertake our wars against
The fall'n-off Britons, that we do incite
The gentry to this business. He creates
Lucius proconsul; and to you the tribunes,
For this immediate levy, he commends
His absolute commission. Long live Cæsar!
1st Tri. Is Lucius general of the forces?
2nd Sen. Ay.
1st Tri. Remaining now in Gallia?
1st Sen. With those legions
Which I have spoke of, whereunto your levy
Must be supplyant. The words of your commission
Will tie you to the numbers and the time
Of their dispatch.
1st Tri. We will discharge our duty.
[*Exeunt.*

ACT IV

SCENE I. *Wales: near the cave of Belarius*

Enter CLOTEN.

Clo. I am near to the place where they should meet, if Pisanio have mapped it truly. How fit his garments serve me! Why should his mistress, who was made by him that made the tailor, not be fit too? the rather—saving reverence of the word—for 'tis said a woman's fitness comes by fits. Therein I must play the workman. I dare speak it to myself—for it is not vain-glory for a man and his glass to confer in his own chamber—I mean, the lines of my body are as well drawn as his; no less young, more strong, not beneath him in fortunes, beyond him in the advantage of the time, above him in birth, alike conversant in general services, and more remarkable in single oppositions; yet this imperceiverant thing loves him in my despite. What mortality is! Posthumus, thy head, which now is growing upon thy shoulders, shall within this hour be off; thy mistress enforced; thy garments cut to pieces before thy face: and all this done, spurn her home to her father; who may haply be a little angry for my so rough usage; but my mother, having power of his testiness, shall turn all into my commendations. My horse is tied up safe. Out, sword, and to a sore purpose! Fortune, put them into my hand! This is the very description of their meeting-place; and the fellow dares not deceive me. [*Exit.*

SCENE II. *Before the cave of Belarius*

Enter, from the cave, BELARIUS, GUIDERIUS, ARVIRAGUS, *and* IMOGEN.

Bel. [*To* IMOGEN] You are not well. Remain here in the cave;
We'll come to you after hunting.
Arv. [*To* IMOGEN] Brother, stay here.
Are we not brothers?
Imo. So man and man should be;
But clay and clay differs in dignity,
Whose dust is both alike. I am very sick.
Gui. Go you to hunting; I'll abide with him.
Imo. So sick I am not, yet I am not well;
But not so citizen a wanton as
To seem to die ere sick. So please you, leave me;
Stick to your journal course. The breach of custom
Is breach of all. I am ill, but your being by me
Cannot amend me; society is no comfort
To one not sociable. I am not very sick,
Since I can reason of it. Pray you, trust me here.
I'll rob none but myself; and let me die,
Stealing so poorly.
Gui. I love thee; I have spoke it.
How much the quantity, the weight as much,
As I do love my father.
Bel. What! how! how!
Arv. If it be sin to say so, sir, I yoke me
In my good brother's fault. I know not why
I love this youth; and I have heard you say,
Love's reason's without reason. The bier at door,
And a demand who is 't shall die, I'd say,
"My father, not this youth."
Bel. [*Aside*] O noble strain!
O worthiness of nature! breed of greatness!
Cowards father cowards and base things sire base;
Nature hath meal and bran, contempt and grace.
I'm not their father; yet who this should be,
Doth miracle itself, loved before me.
'Tis the ninth hour o' the morn.

Arv. Brother, farewell.
Imo. I wish ye sport.
Arv. You health. So please you, sir.
Imo. [*Aside*] These are kind creatures. Gods, what lies I have heard!
Our courtiers say all's savage but at court.
Experience, O, thou disprovest report!
The imperious seas breed monsters, for the dish
Poor tributary rivers as sweet fish.
I am sick still; heart-sick. Pisanio,
I'll now taste of thy drug. [*Swallows some.*]
Gui. I could not stir him.
He said he was gentle, but unfortunate;
Dishonestly afflicted, but yet honest.
Arv. Thus did he answer me; yet said, hereafter
I might know more.
Bel. To the field, to the field!
We'll leave you for this time. Go in and rest.
Arv. We'll not be long away.
Bel. Pray, be not sick,
For you must be our housewife.
Imo. Well or ill,
I am bound to you.
Bel. And shalt be ever.
[*Exit* IMOGEN, *to the cave.*
This youth, howe'er distress'd, appears he hath had
Good ancestors.
Arv. How angel-like he sings!
Gui. But his neat cookery! he cut our roots
In characters,
And sauced our broths, as Juno had been sick
And he her dieter.
Arv. Nobly he yokes
A smiling with a sigh, as if the sigh
Was that it was, for not being such a smile;
The smile mocking the sigh, that it would fly
From so divine a temple, to commix
With winds that sailors rail at.
Gui. I do note
That grief and patience, rooted in him both,
Mingle their spurs together.
Arv. Grow, patience!
And let the stinking elder, grief, untwine
His perishing root with the increasing vine!
Bel. It is great morning. Come, away!—Who's there?

Enter CLOTEN.

Clo. I cannot find those runagates; that villain
Hath mock'd me. I am faint.
Bel. "Those runagates!"
Means he not us? I partly know him. 'Tis
Cloten, the son o' the Queen. I fear some ambush.
I saw him not these many years, and yet
I know 'tis he. We are held as outlaws; hence!
Gui. He is but one. You and my brother search
What companies are near. Pray you, away;
Let me alone with him.
[*Exeunt* BELARIUS *and* ARVIRAGUS.
Clo. Soft! What are you
That fly me thus? some villain mountaineers?
I have heard of such. What slave art thou?
Gui. A thing
More slavish did I ne'er than answering
A slave without a knock.
Clo. Thou art a robber,
A law-breaker, a villain. Yield thee, thief.
Gui. To who? to thee? What art thou? Have not I
An arm as big as thine? a heart as big?
Thy words, I grant, are bigger, for I wear not
My dagger in my mouth. Say what thou art,
Why I should yield to thee?
Clo. Thou villain base,
Know'st me not by my clothes?
Gui. No, nor thy tailor, rascal,
Who is thy grandfather. He made those clothes,
Which, as it seems, make thee.
Clo. Thou precious varlet,
My tailor made them not.
Gui. Hence, then, and thank
The man that gave them thee. Thou art some fool;
I am loath to beat thee.
Clo. Thou injurious thief,
Hear but my name, and tremble.
Gui. What's thy name?
Clo. Cloten, thou villain.
Gui. Cloten, thou double villain, be thy name,
I cannot tremble at it. Were it Toad, or Adder, Spider,
'Twould move me sooner.
Clo. To thy further fear,
Nay, to thy mere confusion, thou shalt know
I am son to the Queen.
Gui. I am sorry for 't; not seeming
So worthy as thy birth.
Clo. Art not afeard?
Gui. Those that I reverence those I fear, the wise.
At fools I laugh, not fear them.
Clo. Die the death!
When I have slain thee with my proper hand,
I'll follow those that even now fled hence,
And on the gates of Lud's-town set your heads.
Yield, rustic mountaineer. [*Exeunt, fighting.*

Re-enter BELARIUS *and* ARVIRAGUS.

Bel. No companies abroad?

Arv. None in the world. You did mistake him, sure.
Bel. I cannot tell. Long is it since I saw him,
But time hath nothing blurr'd those lines of favour
Which then he wore; the snatches in his voice,
And burst of speaking, were as his. I am absolute
'Twas very Cloten.
Arv. In this place we left them.
I wish my brother make good time with him,
You say he is so fell.
Bel. Being scarce made up,
I mean, to man, he had not apprehension
Of roaring terrors; for the effect of judgement
Is oft the cause of fear. But, see, thy brother.

Re-enter GUIDERIUS, *with Cloten's head.*

Gui. This Cloten was a fool, an empty purse;
There was no money in 't. Not Hercules
Could have knock'd out his brains, for he had none.
Yet I not doing this, the fool had borne
My head as I do his.
Bel. What hast thou done?
Gui. I am perfect what; cut off one Cloten's head,
Son to the Queen, after his own report;
Who call'd me traitor, mountaineer, and swore
With his own single hand he'd take us in,
Displace our heads where—thank the gods!—they grow,
And set them on Lud's-town.
Bel. We are all undone.
Gui. Why, worthy father, what have we to lose,
But that he swore to take, our lives? The law
Protects not us. Then why should we be tender
To let an arrogant piece of flesh threat us,
Play judge and executioner all himself,
For we do fear the law? What company
Discover you abroad?
Bel. No single soul
Can we set eye on; but in all safe reason
He must have some attendants. Though his humour
Was nothing but mutation, ay, and that
From one bad thing to worse; not frenzy, not
Absolute madness could so far have raved
To bring him here alone; although perhaps
It may be heard at court that such as we
Cave here, hunt here, are outlaws, and in time
May make some stronger head; the which he hearing—
As it is like him—might break out, and swear
He'd fetch us in; yet is 't not probable
To come alone, either he so undertaking,
Or they so suffering. Then on good ground we fear,
If we do fear this body hath a tail
More perilous than the head.
Arv. Let ordinance
Come as the gods foresay it. Howsoe'er,
My brother hath done well.
Bel. I had no mind
To hunt this day. The boy Fidele's sickness
Did make my way long forth.
Gui. With his own sword,
Which he did wave against my throat, I have ta'en
His head from him. I'll throw 't into the creek
Behind our rock; and let it to the sea,
And tell the fishes he's the Queen's son, Cloten.
That's all I reck. [*Exit.*
Bel. I fear 'twill be revenged.
Would, Polydore, thou hadst not done 't! though valour
Becomes thee well enough.
Arv. Would I had done 't,
So the revenge alone pursued me! Polydore,
I love thee brotherly, but envy much
Thou hast robb'd me of this deed. I would revenges,
That possible strength might meet, would seek us through
And put us to our answer.
Bel. Well, 'tis done.
We'll hunt no more to-day, nor seek for danger
Where there's no profit. I prithee, to our rock;
You and Fidele play the cooks. I'll stay
Till hasty Polydore return, and bring him
To dinner presently.
Arv. Poor sick Fidele!
I'll willingly to him. To gain his colour
I'd let a parish of such Clotens blood,
And praise myself for charity. [*Exit.*
Bel. O thou goddess,
Thou divine Nature, how thyself thou blazon'st
In these two princely boys! They are as gentle
As zephyrs blowing below the violet,
Not wagging his sweet head; and yet as rough,
Their royal blood enchafed, as the rudest wind,
That by the top doth take the mountain pine
And make him stoop to the vale. 'Tis wonder
That an invisible instinct should frame them
To royalty unlearn'd, honour untaught,
Civility not seen from other, valour
That wildly grows in them, but yields a crop
As if it had been sow'd. Yet still it's strange
What Cloten's being here to us portends,
Or what his death will bring us.

Re-enter GUIDERIUS.

Gui. Where's my brother?
I have sent Cloten's clotpoll down the stream,
In embassy to his mother. His body's hostage
For his return.
Solemn music.
Bel. My ingenious instrument!
Hark, Polydore, it sounds! But what occasion
Hath Cadwal now to give it motion? Hark!
Gui. Is he at home?
Bel. He went hence even now.
Gui. What does he mean? since death of my dear'st mother
It did not speak before. All solemn things
Should answer solemn accidents. The matter?
Triumphs for nothing and lamenting toys
Is jollity for apes and grief for boys.
Is Cadwal mad?
Bel. Look, here he comes,
And brings the dire occasion in his arms
Of what we blame him for.

Re-enter ARVIRAGUS, *with* IMOGEN, *as dead, bearing her in his arms.*

Arv. The bird is dead
That we have made so much on. I had rather
Have skipp'd from sixteen years of age to sixty,
To have turn'd my leaping-time into a crutch,
Than have seen this.
Gui. O sweetest, fairest lily!
My brother wears thee not the one half so well
As when thou grew'st thyself.
Bel. O melancholy!
Who ever yet could sound thy bottom? find
The ooze, to show what coast thy sluggish crare
Might easiliest harbour in? Thou blessed thing!
Jove knows what man thou mightst have made; but I,
Thou diedst, a most rare boy, of melancholy.
How found you him?
Arv. Stark, as you see.
Thus smiling, as some fly had tickled slumber,
Not as death's dart, being laugh'd at; his right cheek
Reposing on a cushion.
Gui. Where?
Arv. O' the floor;
His arms thus leagued: I thought he slept, and put
My clouted brogues from off my feet, whose rudeness
Answer'd my steps too loud.
Gui. Why, he but sleeps.
If he be gone, he'll make his grave a bed;
With female fairies will his tomb be haunted,
And worms will not come to thee.
Arv. With fairest flowers
Whilst summer lasts and I live here, Fidele,
I'll sweeten thy sad grave. Thou shalt not lack
The flower that's like thy face, pale primrose, nor
The azured harebell, like thy veins, no, nor
The leaf of eglantine, whom not to slander,
Out-sweeten'd not thy breath. The ruddock would,
With charitable bill—O bill, sore-shaming
Those rich-left heirs that let their fathers lie
Without a monument!—bring thee all this;
Yea, and furr'd moss besides, when flowers are none,
To winter-ground thy corse.
Gui. Prithee, have done;
And do not play in wench-like words with that
Which is so serious. Let us bury him,
And not protract with admiration what
Is now due debt. To the grave!
Arv. Say, where shall's lay him?
Gui. By good Euriphile, our mother.
Arv. Be 't so.
And let us, Polydore, though now our voices
Have got the mannish crack, sing him to the ground,
As once our mother; use like note and words,
Save that Euriphile must be Fidele.
Gui. Cadwal,
I cannot sing. I'll weep, and word it with thee;
For notes of sorrow out of tune are worse
Than priests and fanes that lie.
Arv. We'll speak it, then.
Bel. Great griefs, I see, medicine the less; for Cloten
Is quite forgot. He was a queen's son, boys;
And though he came our enemy, remember
He was paid for that. Though mean and mighty, rotting
Together, have one dust, yet reverence,
That angel of the world, doth make distinction
Of place 'tween high and low. Our foe was princely;
And though you took his life, as being our foe,
Yet bury him as a prince.
Gui. Pray you, fetch him hither.
Thersites' body is as good as Ajax',
When neither are alive.
Arv. If you'll go fetch him,
We'll say our song the whilst. Brother, begin.
[*Exit* BELARIUS.
Gui. Nay, Cadwal, we must lay his head to the east;
My father hath a reason for 't.
Arv. 'Tis true.

Gui. Come on then, and remove him.
Arv. So. Begin.

SONG

Gui. Fear no more the heat o' the sun,
Nor the furious winter's rages;
Thou thy worldly task hast done,
Home art gone, and ta'en thy wages.
Golden lads and girls all must,
As chimney-sweepers, come to dust.

Arv. Fear no more the frown o' the great;
Thou art past the tyrant's stroke;
Care no more to clothe and eat;
To thee the reed is as the oak.
The sceptre, learning, physic, must
All follow this, and come to dust.

Gui. Fear no more the lightning-flash,
Arv. Nor the all-dreaded thunder-stone;
Gui. Fear not slander, censure rash;
Arv. Thou hast finish'd joy and moan.
Both. All lovers young, all lovers must
Consign to thee, and come to dust.

Gui. No exorciser harm thee!
Arv. Nor no witchcraft charm thee!
Gui. Ghost unlaid forbear thee!
Arv. Nothing ill come near thee!
Both. Quiet consummation have;
And renowned be thy grave!

Re-enter BELARIUS, *with the body of* CLOTEN.

Gui. We have done our obsequies. Come, lay him down.
Bel. Here's a few flowers; but 'bout midnight, more.
The herbs that have on them cold dew o' the night
Are strewings fitt'st for graves. Upon their faces.
You were as flowers, now wither'd; even so
These herblets shall, which we upon you strew.
Come on, away; apart upon our knees.
The ground that gave them first has them again.
Their pleasures here are past, so is their pain.
[*Exeunt* BELARIUS, GUIDERIUS, *and* ARVIRAGUS.
Imo. [*Awaking*] Yes, sir, to Milford-Haven; which is the way?
I thank you.—By yond bush?—Pray, how far thither?
'Ods pittikins! can it be six mile yet?
I have gone all night. 'Faith, I'll lie down and sleep.
But, soft! no bedfellow!—O gods and goddesses!
Seeing the body of CLOTEN.
These flowers are like the pleasures of the world;
This bloody man, the care on 't. I hope I dream;
For so I thought I was a cave-keeper
And cook to honest creatures. But 'tis not so.
'Twas but a bolt of nothing, shot at nothing,
Which the brain makes of fumes. Our very eyes
Are sometimes like our judgements, blind. Good faith,
I tremble still with fear; but if there be
Yet left in heaven as small a drop of pity
As a wren's eye, fear'd gods, a part of it!
The dream's here still; even when I wake, it is
Without me, as within me; not imagined, felt.
A headless man! The garments of Posthumus!
I know the shape of's leg. This is his hand;
His foot Mercurial; his Martial thigh;
The brawns of Hercules: but his Jovial face—
Murder in heaven?—How!—'Tis gone. Pisanio,
All curses madded Hecuba gave the Greeks,
And mine to boot, be darted on thee! Thou,
Conspired with that irregulous devil, Cloten,
Hast here cut off my lord. To write and read
Be henceforth treacherous! Damn'd Pisanio
Hath with his forged letters—damn'd Pisanio—
From this most bravest vessel of the world
Struck the main-top! O Posthumus! alas,
Where is thy head? where's that? Ay me! where's that?
Pisanio might have kill'd thee at the heart,
And left this head on. How should this be? Pisanio?
'Tis he and Cloten. Malice and lucre in them
Have laid this woe here. O, 'tis pregnant, pregnant!
The drug he gave me, which he said was precious
And cordial to me, have I not found it
Murderous to the senses? That confirms it home.
This is Pisanio's deed, and Cloten's. O!
Give colour to my pale cheek with thy blood,
That we the horrider may seem to those
Which chance to find us. O, my lord, my lord!
Falls on the body.

Enter LUCIUS, *a* CAPTAIN *and other Officers, and a* SOOTHSAYER.

Cap. To them the legions garrison'd in Gallia,
After your will, have cross'd the sea, attending
You here at Milford-Haven with your ships.
They are in readiness.
Luc. But what from Rome?
Cap. The Senate hath stirr'd up the confiners
And gentlemen of Italy, most willing spirits,
That promise noble service; and they come
Under the conduct of bold Iachimo,
Syenna's brother.
Luc. When expect you them?
Cap. With the next benefit o' the wind.

Luc. This forwardness
Makes our hopes fair. Command our present numbers
Be muster'd; bid the captains look to 't. Now, sir,
What have you dream'd of late of this war's purpose?
Sooth. Last night the very gods show'd me a vision—
I fast and pray'd for their intelligence—thus.
I saw Jove's bird, the Roman eagle, wing'd
From the spongy south to this part of the west,
There vanish'd in the sunbeams; which portends—
Unless my sins abuse my divination—
Success to the Roman host.
Luc. Dream often so,
And never false. Soft, ho! what trunk is here
Without his top? The ruin speaks that sometime
It was a worthy building. How! a page!
Or dead, or sleeping on him? But dead rather;
For nature doth abhor to make his bed
With the defunct, or sleep upon the dead.
Let's see the boy's face.
Cap. He's alive, my lord.
Luc. He'll then instruct us of this body. Young one,
Inform us of thy fortunes, for it seems
They crave to be demanded. Who is this
Thou makest thy bloody pillow? Or who was he
That, otherwise than noble nature did,
Hath alter'd that good picture? What's thy interest
In this sad wreck? How came it? Who is it?
What art thou?
Imo. I am nothing: or if not,
Nothing to be were better. This was my master,
A very valiant Briton and a good,
That here by mountaineers lies slain. Alas!
There is no more such masters. I may wander
From east to occident, cry out for service,
Try many, all good, serve truly, never
Find such another master.
Luc. 'Lack, good youth!
Thou movest no less with thy complaining than
Thy master in bleeding. Say his name, good friend.
Imo. Richard du Champ. [*Aside*] If I do lie and do
No harm by it, though the gods hear, I hope
They'll pardon it.—Say you, sir?
Luc. Thy name?
Imo. Fidele, sir.
Luc. Thou dost approve thyself the very same;
Thy name well fits thy faith, thy faith thy name.
Wilt take thy chance with me? I will not say
Thou shalt be so well master'd, but, be sure,
No less beloved. The Roman Emperor's letters,
Sent by a consul to me, should not sooner
Than thine own worth prefer thee. Go with me.
Imo. I'll follow, sir. But first, an't please the gods,
I'll hide my master from the flies, as deep
As these poor pickaxes can dig; and when
With wild wood-leaves and weeds I ha' strew'd his grave,
And on it said a century of prayers,
Such as I can, twice o'er, I'll weep and sigh;
And leaving so his service, follow you,
So please you entertain me.
Luc. Ay, good youth;
And rather father thee than master thee.
My friends,
The boy hath taught us manly duties. Let us
Find out the prettiest daisied plot we can,
And make him with our pikes and partisans
A grave. Come, arm him. Boy, he is preferr'd
By thee to us, and he shall be interr'd
As soldiers can. Be cheerful; wipe thine eyes.
Some falls are means the happier to arise.
[*Exeunt.*

SCENE III. *A room in Cymbeline's palace*

Enter CYMBELINE, LORDS, PISANIO, *and Attendants.*

Cym. Again; and bring me word how 'tis with her. [*Exit an Attendant.*
A fever with the absence of her son,
A madness, of which her life's in danger. Heavens,
How deeply you at once do touch me! Imogen,
The great part of my comfort, gone; my queen
Upon a desperate bed, and in a time
When fearful wars point at me; her son gone,
So needful for this present. It strikes me, past
The hope of comfort. But for thee, fellow,
Who needs must know of her departure and
Dost seem so ignorant, we'll enforce it from thee
By a sharp torture.
Pis. Sir, my life is yours;
I humbly set it at your will; but, for my mistress,
I nothing know where she remains, why gone,
Nor when she purposes return. Beseech your Highness,
Hold me your loyal servant.
1st Lord. Good my liege,
The day that she was missing he was here.
I dare be bound he's true and shall perform
All parts of his subjection loyally. For Cloten,
There wants no diligence in seeking him,
And will, no doubt, be found.
Cym. The time is troublesome.

[*To* PISANIO] We'll slip you for a season; but our jealousy
Does yet depend.
1st Lord. So please your Majesty,
The Roman legions, all from Gallia drawn,
Are landed on your coast, with a supply
Of Roman gentlemen, by the Senate sent.
Cym. Now for the counsel of my son and queen!
I am amazed with matter.
1st Lord. Good my liege,
Your preparation can affront no less
Than what you hear of. Come more, for more you're ready.
The want is but to put those powers in motion
That long to move.
Cym. I thank you. Let's withdraw;
And meet the time as it seeks us. We fear not
What can from Italy annoy us; but
We grieve at chances here. Away!
[*Exeunt all but* PISANIO.
Pis. I heard no letter from my master since
I wrote him Imogen was slain. 'Tis strange.
Nor hear I from my mistress, who did promise
To yield me often tidings; neither know I
What is betid to Cloten; but remain
Perplex'd in all. The heavens still must work.
Wherein I am false I am honest; not true, to be true.
These present wars shall find I love my country,
Even to the note o' the King, or I'll fall in them.
All other doubts, by time let them be clear'd.
Fortune brings in some boats that are not steer'd.
[*Exit*.

SCENE IV. *Wales: before the cave of Belarius*

Enter BELARIUS, GUIDERIUS, *and* ARVIRAGUS.

Gui. The noise is round about us.
Bel. Let us from it.
Arv. What pleasure, sir, find we in life, to lock it
From action and adventure?
Gui. Nay, what hope
Have we in hiding us? This way, the Romans
Must or for Britons slay us, or receive us
For barbarous and unnatural revolts
During their use, and slay us after.
Bel. Sons,
We'll higher to the mountains; there secure us.
To the King's party there's no going. Newness
Of Cloten's death—we being not known, not muster'd
Among the bands—may drive us to a render
Where we have lived, and so extort from 's that
Which we have done, whose answer would be death
Drawn on with torture.
Gui. This is, sir, a doubt
In such a time nothing becoming you,
Nor satisfying us.
Arv. It is not likely
That when they hear the Roman horses neigh,
Behold their quarter'd fires, have both their eyes
And ears so cloy'd importantly as now,
That they will waste their time upon our note,
To know from whence we are.
Bel. O, I am known
Of many in the army. Many years,
Though Cloten then but young, you see, not wore him
From my remembrance. And, besides, the King
Hath not deserved my service nor your loves;
Who find in my exile the want of breeding,
The certainty of this hard life; aye hopeless
To have the courtesy your cradle promised,
But to be still hot summer's tanlings and
The shrinking slaves of winter.
Gui. Than be so
Better to cease to be. Pray, sir, to the army.
I and my brother are not known; yourself
So out of thought, and thereto so o'ergrown,
Cannot be question'd.
Arv. By this sun that shines,
I'll thither. What thing is it that I never
Did see man die! scarce ever look'd on blood,
But that of coward hares, hot goats, and venison!
Never bestrid a horse, save one that had
A rider like myself, who ne'er wore rowel
Nor iron on his heel! I am ashamed
To look upon the holy sun, to have
The benefit of his blest beams, remaining
So long a poor unknown.
Gui. By heavens, I'll go.
If you will bless me, sir, and give me leave,
I'll take the better care, but if you will not,
The hazard therefore due fall on me by
The hands of Romans!
Arv. So say I; amen.
Bel. No reason I, since of your lives you set
So slight a valuation, should reserve
My crack'd one to more care. Have with you, boys!
If in your country wars you chance to die,
That is my bed too, lads, and there I'll lie.
Lead, lead. [*Aside*] The time seems long; their blood thinks scorn,
Till it fly out and show them princes born.
[*Exeunt*.

ACT V

SCENE I. *Britain: the Roman camp*

Enter POSTHUMUS, *with a bloody handkerchief.*

Post. Yea, bloody cloth, I'll keep thee, for I wish'd
Thou shouldst be colour'd thus. You married ones,
If each of you should take this course, how many
Must murder wives much better than themselves
For wrying but a little! O Pisanio!
Every good servant does not all commands;
No bond but to do just ones. Gods! if you
Should have ta'en vengeance on my faults, I never
Had lived to put on this. So had you saved
The noble Imogen to repent, and struck
Me, wretch more worth your vengeance. But, alack,
You snatch some hence for little faults; that's love,
To have them fall no more. You some permit
To second ills with ills, each elder worse,
And make them dread it, to the doers' thrift.
But Imogen is your own; do your best wills,
And make me blest to obey! I am brought hither
Among the Italian gentry, and to fight
Against my lady's kingdom. 'Tis enough
That, Britain, I have kill'd thy mistress; peace!
I'll give no wound to thee. Therefore, good heavens,
Hear patiently my purpose: I'll disrobe me
Of these Italian weeds and suit myself
As does a Briton peasant; so I'll fight
Against the part I come with; so I'll die
For thee, O Imogen, even for whom my life
Is every breath a death; and thus, unknown,
Pitied nor hated, to the face of peril
Myself I'll dedicate. Let me make men know
More valour in me than my habits show.
Gods, put the strength o' the Leonati in me!
To shame the guise o' the world, I will begin
The fashion, less without and more within. [*Exit.*

SCENE II. *Field of battle between the British and Roman camps*

Enter, from one side, LUCIUS, IACHIMO, *and the Roman Army; from the other side, the British Army;* LEONATUS POSTHUMUS *following, like a poor soldier. They march over and go out. Then enter again, in skirmish,* IACHIMO *and* POSTHUMUS; *he vanquisheth and disarmeth* IACHIMO, *and then leaves him.*

Iach. The heaviness and guilt within my bosom
Takes off my manhood. I have belied a lady,
The princess of this country, and the air on't
Revengingly enfeebles me; or could this carl,
A very drudge of nature's, have subdued me
In my profession? Knighthoods and honours, borne
As I wear mine, are titles but of scorn.
If that thy gentry, Britain, go before
This lout as he exceeds our lords, the odds
Is that we scarce are men and you are gods.
[*Exit.*

The battle continues; the Britons fly; CYMBELINE *is taken: then enter, to his rescue,* BELARIUS, GUIDERIUS, *and* ARVIRAGUS.

Bel. Stand, stand! We have the advantage of the ground;
The lane is guarded. Nothing routs us but
The villainy of our fears.
Gui., *Arv.* Stand, stand, and fight!

Re-enter POSTHUMUS, *and seconds the Britons; they rescue* CYMBELINE, *and exeunt. Then re-enter* LUCIUS, *and* IACHIMO, *with* IMOGEN.

Luc. Away, boy, from the troops, and save thyself;
For friends kill friends, and the disorder's such
As war were hoodwink'd.
Iach. 'Tis their fresh supplies.
Luc. It is a day turn'd strangely. Or betimes
Let's re-inforce, or fly. [*Exeunt.*

SCENE III. *Another part of the field*

Enter POSTHUMUS *and a* BRITISH LORD.

Lord. Camest thou from where they made the stand?
Post. I did;
Though you, it seems, come from the fliers.
Lord. I did.
Post. No blame be to you, sir; for all was lost,
But that the heavens fought. The king himself
Of his wings destitute, the army broken,
And but the backs of Britons seen, all flying
Through a strait lane; the enemy full-hearted,
Lolling the tongue with slaughtering, having work
More plentiful than tools to do 't, struck down
Some mortally, some slightly touch'd, some falling
Merely through fear; that the strait pass was damm'd
With dead men hurt behind, and cowards living
To die with lengthen'd shame.
Lord. Where was this lane?
Post. Close by the battle, ditch'd, and wall'd with turf;

Which gave advantage to an ancient soldier,
An honest one, I warrant; who deserved
So long a breeding as his white beard came to,
In doing this for's country. Athwart the lane,
He, with two striplings—lads more like to run
The country base than to commit such slaughter;
With faces fit for masks, or rather fairer
Than those for preservation cased, or shame—
Made good the passage; cried to those that fled,
"Our Britain's harts die flying, not our men.
To darkness fleet souls that fly backwards. Stand;
Or we are Romans and will give you that
Like beasts which you shun beastly, and may save,
But to look back in frown. Stand, stand." These three,
Three thousand confident, in act as many—
For three performers are the file when all
The rest do nothing—with this word "Stand, stand,"
Accommodated by the place, more charming
With their own nobleness, which could have turn'd
A distaff to a lance, gilded pale looks,
Part shame, part spirit renew'd; that some, turn'd coward
But by example—O, a sin in war,
Damn'd in the first beginners!—gan to look
The way that they did, and to grin like lions
Upon the pikes o' the hunters. Then began
A stop i' the chaser, a retire, anon
A rout, confusion thick; forthwith they fly
Chickens, the way which they stoop'd eagles; slaves,
The strides they victors made. And now our cowards,
Like fragments in hard voyages, became
The life o' the need. Having found the back-door open
Of the unguarded hearts, heavens, how they wound!
Some slain before; some dying; some their friends
O'er-borne i' the former wave. Ten, chased by one,
Are now each one the slaughter-man of twenty.
Those that would die or ere resist are grown
The mortal bugs o' the field.

Lord. This was strange chance.
A narrow lane, an old man, and two boys.

Post. Nay, do not wonder at it. You are made
Rather to wonder at the things you hear
Than to work any. Will you rhyme upon 't,
And vent it for a mockery? Here is one:
"Two boys, an old man twice a boy, a lane,
Preserved the Britons, was the Romans' bane."

Lord. Nay, be not angry, sir.

Post. 'Lack, to what end?
Who dares not stand his foe, I'll be his friend;
For if he'll do as he is made to do,
I know he'll quickly fly my friendship too.
You have put me into rhyme.

Lord. Farewell; you're angry.

Post. Still going? [*Exit* LORD.] This is a lord! O noble misery,
To be i' the field, and ask "what news?" of me!
To-day how many would have given their honours
To have saved their carcases! took heel to do 't,
And yet died too! I, in mine own woe charm'd,
Could not find death where I did hear him groan,
Nor feel him where he struck. Being an ugly monster,
'Tis strange he hides him in fresh cups, soft beds,
Sweet words; or hath more ministers than we
That draw his knives i' the war. Well, I will find him;
For being now a favourer to the Briton,
No more a Briton, I have resumed again
The part I came in. Fight I will no more,
But yield me to the veriest hind that shall
Once touch my shoulder. Great the slaughter is
Here made by the Roman; great the answer be
Britons must take. For me, my ransom's death;
On either side I come to spend my breath;
Which neither here I'll keep nor bear again,
But end it by some means for Imogen.

Enter TWO BRITISH CAPTAINS *and Soldiers.*

1st Cap. Great Jupiter be praised! Lucius is taken.
'Tis thought the old man and his sons were angels.

2nd Cap. There was a fourth man, in a silly habit,
That gave the affront with them.

1st Cap. So 'tis reported;
But none of 'em can be found. Stand! who's there?

Post. A Roman,
Who had not now been drooping here, if seconds
Had answer'd him.

2nd Cap. Lay hands on him; a dog!
A leg of Rome shall not return to tell
What crows have peck'd them here. He brags his service
As if he were of note. Bring him to the King.

Enter CYMBELINE, BELARIUS, GUIDERIUS, ARVIRAGUS, PISANIO, *Soldiers, Attendants, and Roman Captives. The* CAPTAINS *present* POSTHUMUS *to* CYMBELINE, *who delivers him over to a Gaoler; then exeunt omnes.*

SCENE IV. *A British prison*

Enter POSTHUMUS *and* TWO GAOLERS.

1st Gaol. You shall not now be stol'n, you have locks upon you;
So graze as you find pasture.
2nd Gaol. Ay, or a stomach.
[*Exeunt* GAOLERS.
Post. Most welcome, bondage! for thou art a way,
I think, to liberty. Yet am I better
Than one that's sick o' the gout; since he had rather
Groan so in perpetuity than be cured
By the sure physician, Death, who is the key
To unbar these locks. My conscience, thou art fetter'd
More than my shanks and wrists. You good gods, give me
The penitent instrument to pick that bolt,
Then, free for ever! Is 't enough I am sorry?
So children temporal fathers do appease;
Gods are more full of mercy. Must I repent?
I cannot do it better than in gyves,
Desired more than constrain'd; to satisfy,
If of my freedom 'tis the main part, take
No stricter render of me than my all.
I know you are more clement than vile men,
Who of their broken debtors take a third,
A sixth, a tenth, letting them thrive again
On their abatement. That's not my desire.
For Imogen's dear life take mine; and though
'Tis not so dear, yet 'tis a life; you coin'd it.
'Tween man and man they weigh not every stamp;
Though light, take pieces for the figure's sake;
You rather mine, being yours; and so, great powers,
If you will take this audit, take this life,
And cancel these cold bonds. O Imogen!
I'll speak to thee in silence. [*Sleeps.*]

Solemn music. Enter, as in an apparition, SICILIUS LEONATUS, *father to Posthumus, an old man, attired like a warrior; leading in his hand an ancient matron, his wife, and mother to Posthumus, with music before them: then, after other music, follow the two young* LEONATI, *brothers to Posthumus, with wounds as they died in the wars. They circle* POSTHUMUS *round, as he lies sleeping.*

Sici. No more, thou thunder-master, show
Thy spite on mortal flies.
With Mars fall out, with Juno chide,
That thy adulteries
Rates and revenges.
Hath my poor boy done aught but well,
Whose face I never saw?
I died whilst in the womb he stay'd
Attending nature's law;
Whose father then, as men report
Thou orphans' father art,
Thou shouldst have been, and shielded him
From this earth-vexing smart.
Moth. Lucina lent not me her aid,
But took me in my throes;
That from me was Posthumus ript,
Came crying 'mongst his foes,
A thing of pity!
Sici. Great nature, like his ancestry,
Moulded the stuff so fair,
That he deserved the praise o' the world,
As great Sicilius' heir.
1st Bro. When once he was mature for man,
In Britain where was he
That could stand up his parallel;
Or fruitful object be
In eye of Imogen, that best
Could deem his dignity?
Moth. With marriage wherefore was he mock'd,
To be exiled, and thrown
From Leonati seat, and cast
From her his dearest one,
Sweet Imogen?
Sici. Why did you suffer Iachimo,
Slight thing of Italy,
To taint his nobler heart and brain
With needless jealousy;
And to become the geck and scorn
O' th' other's villainy?
2nd Bro. For this from stiller seats we came,
Our parents and us twain,
That striking in our country's cause
Fell bravely and were slain,
Our fealty and Tenantius' right
With honour to maintain.
1st Bro. Like hardiment Posthumus hath
To Cymbeline perform'd.
Then, Jupiter, thou king of gods,
Why hast thou thus adjourn'd
The graces for his merits due,
Being all to dolours turn'd?
Sici. Thy crystal window ope; look out;
No longer exercise
Upon a valiant race thy harsh
And potent injuries.
Moth. Since, Jupiter, our son is good,

Take off his miseries.
Sici. Peep through thy marble mansion; help;
Or we poor ghosts will cry
To the shining synod of the rest
Against thy deity.
Both Bro. Help, Jupiter; or we appeal,
And from thy justice fly.

JUPITER *descends in thunder and lightning, sitting upon an eagle; he throws a thunderbolt. The Ghosts fall on their knees.*

Jup. No more, you petty spirits of region low,
Offend our hearing; hush! How dare you ghosts
Accuse the thunderer, whose bolt, you know,
Sky-planted batters all rebelling coasts?
Poor shadows of Elysium, hence, and rest
Upon your never-withering banks of flowers.
Be not with mortal accidents opprest;
No care of yours it is; you know 'tis ours.
Whom best I love I cross; to make my gift,
The more delay'd, delighted. Be content;
Your low-laid son our godhead will uplift.
His comforts thrive, his trials well are spent.
Our Jovial star reign'd at his birth, and in
Our temple was he married. Rise, and fade.
He shall be lord of lady Imogen,
And happier much by his affliction made.
This tablet lay upon his breast, wherein
Our pleasure his full fortune doth confine.
And so, away! No further with your din
Express impatience, lest you stir up mine.
Mount, eagle, to my palace crystalline.
[*Ascends*.
Sici. He came in thunder; his celestial breath
Was sulphurous to smell. The holy eagle
Stoop'd, as to foot us. His ascension is
More sweet than our blest fields. His royal bird
Prunes the immortal wing and cloys his beak,
As when his god is pleased.
All. Thanks, Jupiter!
Sici. The marble pavement closes, he is enter'd
His radiant roof. Away! and, to be blest,
Let us with care perform his great behest.
[*The Ghosts vanish*.
Post. [*Waking*] Sleep, thou hast been a grandsire and begot
A father to me; and thou hast created
A mother and two brothers; but, O scorn!
Gone! they went hence so soon as they were born.
And so I am awake. Poor wretches that depend
On greatness' favour dream as I have done,
Wake and find nothing. But, alas, I swerve.
Many dream not to find, neither deserve,
And yet are steep'd in favours; so am I,
That have this golden chance and know not why.
What fairies haunt this ground? A book? O rare one!
Be not, as is our fangled world, a garment
Nobler than that it covers! Let thy effects
So follow, to be most unlike our courtiers,
As good as promise.

[*Reads*] "When as a lion's whelp shall, to himself unknown, without seeking find, and be embraced by a piece of tender air; and when from a stately cedar shall be lopped branches, which, being dead many years, shall after revive, be jointed to the old stock and freshly grow; then shall Posthumus end his miseries, Britain be fortunate and flourish in peace and plenty."
'Tis still a dream or else such stuff as madmen
Tongue and brain not; either both or nothing;
Or senseless speaking or a speaking such
As sense cannot untie. Be what it is,
The action of my life is like it, which
I'll keep, if but for sympathy.

Re-enter GAOLERS.

1st Gaol. Come, sir, are you ready for death?

Post. Over-roasted rather; ready long ago.

1st Gaol. Hanging is the word, sir. If you be ready for that, you are well cooked.

Post. So, if I prove a good repast to the spectators, the dish pays the shot.

1st Gaol. A heavy reckoning for you, sir. But the comfort is, you shall be called to no more payments, fear no more tavern-bills; which are often the sadness of parting, as the procuring of mirth. You come in faint for want of meat, depart reeling with too much drink; sorry that you have paid too much, and sorry that you are paid too much; purse and brain both empty; the brain the heavier for being too light, the purse too light, being drawn of heaviness. Of this contradiction you shall now be quit. O, the charity of a penny cord! it sums up thousands in a trice. You have no true debitor and creditor but it; of what's past, is, and to come, the discharge. Your neck, sir, is pen, book, and counters; so the acquittance follows.

Post. I am merrier to die than thou art to live.

1st Gaol. Indeed, sir, he that sleeps feels not the tooth-ache; but a man that were to sleep your sleep, and a hangman to help him to bed, I think he would change places with his officer; for, look you, sir, you know not which way you shall go.

Post. Yes, indeed do I, fellow.

1st Gaol. Your death has eyes in 's head then; I have not seen him so pictured. You must either be directed by some that take upon them to know, or to take upon yourself that which I am sure you do not know, or jump the after inquiry on your own peril. And how you shall speed in your journey's end, I think you'll never return to tell one.

Post. I tell thee, fellow, there are none want eyes to direct them the way I am going, but such as wink and will not use them.

1st Gaol. What an infinite mock is this, that a man should have the best use of eyes to see the way of blindness! I am sure hanging's the way of winking.

Enter a MESSENGER.

Mess. Knock off his manacles; bring your prisoner to the King.

Post. Thou bring'st good news; I am called to be made free.

1st Gaol. I'll be hang'd then.

Post. Thou shalt be then freer than a gaoler; no bolts for the dead.

[*Exeunt all but the* FIRST GAOLER.

1st Gaol. Unless a man would marry a gallows and beget young gibbets, I never saw one so prone. Yet, on my conscience, there are verier knaves desire to live, for all he be a Roman; and there be some of them too that die against their wills; so should I, if I were one. I would we were all of one mind, and one mind good; O, there were desolation of gaolers and gallowses! I speak against my present profit, but my wish hath a preferment in't. [*Exit.*

SCENE V. *Cymbeline's tent*

Enter CYMBELINE, BELARIUS, GUIDERIUS, ARVIRAGUS, PISANIO, LORDS, OFFICERS, *and Attendants.*

Cym. Stand by my side, you whom the gods have made
Preservers of my throne. Woe is my heart
That the poor soldier that so richly fought,
Whose rags shamed gilded arms, whose naked breast
Stepp'd before targes of proof, cannot be found.
He shall be happy that can find him, if
Our grace can make him so.
Bel. I never saw
Such noble fury in so poor a thing;
Such precious deeds in one that promised nought
But beggary and poor looks.
Cym. No tidings of him?
Pis. He hath been search'd among the dead and living,
But no trace of him.
Cym. To my grief, I am
The heir of his reward; [*To* BELARIUS, GUIDERIUS, *and* ARVIRAGUS] which I will add
To you, the liver, heart and brain of Britain,
By whom I grant she lives. 'Tis now the time
To ask of whence you are. Report it.
Bel. Sir,
In Cambria are we born, and gentlemen.
Further to boast were neither true nor modest,
Unless I add, we are honest.
Cym. Bow your knees.
Arise my knights o' the battle. I create you
Companions to our person and will fit you
With dignities becoming your estates.

Enter CORNELIUS *and* LADIES.

There's business in these faces. Why so sadly
Greet you our victory? you look like Romans,
And not o' the court of Britain.
Cor. Hail, great king!
To sour your happiness, I must report
The queen is dead.
Cym. Who worse than a physician
Would this report become? But I consider,
By medicine life may be prolong'd, yet death
Will seize the doctor too. How ended she?
Cor. With horror, madly dying, like her life,
Which, being cruel to the world, concluded
Most cruel to herself. What she confess'd
I will report, so please you. These her women
Can trip me, if I err; who with wet cheeks
Were present when she finish'd.
Cym. Prithee, say.
Cor. First, she confess'd she never loved you, only
Affected greatness got by you, not you;
Married your royalty, was wife to your place;
Abhorr'd your person.
Cym. She alone knew this;
And, but she spoke it dying, I would not
Believe her lips in opening it. Proceed.
Cor. Your daughter, whom she bore in hand to love
With such integrity, she did confess
Was as a scorpion to her sight; whose life,
But that her flight prevented it, she had
Ta'en off by poison.
Cym. O most delicate fiend!
Who is't can read a woman? Is there more?
Cor. More, sir, and worse. She did confess she had
For you a mortal mineral; which, being took,
Should by the minute feed on life and lingering
By inches waste you; in which time she purposed,
By watching, weeping, tendance, kissing, to
O'ercome you with her show, and in time,
When she had fitted you with her craft, to work

Her son into the adoption of the crown;
But, failing of her end by this strange absence,
Grew shameless-desperate; open'd, in despite
Of heaven and men, her purposes; repented
The evils she hatch'd were not effected; so
Despairing died.
Cym. Heard you all this, her women?
1st Lady. We did, so please your Highness.
Cym. Mine eyes
Were not in fault, for she was beautiful;
Mine ears, that heard her flattery; nor my heart,
That thought her like her seeming; it had been vicious
To have mistrusted her; yet, O my daughter!
That it was folly in me, thou mayst say,
And prove it in thy feeling. Heaven mend all!

Enter LUCIUS, IACHIMO, *the* SOOTHSAYER, *and other Roman Prisoners, guarded;* POSTHUMUS *behind, and* IMOGEN.

Thou comest not, Caius, now for tribute; that
The Britons have razed out, though with the loss
Of many a bold one; whose kinsmen have made suit
That their good souls may be appeased with slaughter
Of you their captives, which ourself have granted.
So think of your estate.
Luc. Consider, sir, the chance of war. The day
Was yours by accident; had it gone with us,
We should not, when the blood was cool, have threaten'd
Our prisoners with the sword. But since the gods
Will have it thus, that nothing but our lives
May be call'd ransom, let it come. Sufficeth
A Roman with a Roman's heart can suffer.
Augustus lives to think on't; and so much
For my peculiar care. This one thing only
I will entreat; my boy, a Briton born,
Let him be ransom'd. Never master had
A page so kind, so duteous, diligent,
So tender over his occasions, true,
So feat, so nurse-like. Let his virtue join
With my request, which I'll make bold your Highness
Cannot deny; he hath done no Briton harm,
Though he have served a Roman. Save him, sir,
And spare no blood beside.
Cym. I have surely seen him;
His favour is familiar to me. Boy,
Thou hast look'd thyself into my grace,
And art mine own. I know not why, wherefore,
To say "live, boy." Ne'er thank thy master; live
And ask of Cymbeline what boon thou wilt,
Fitting my bounty and thy state, I'll give it;
Yea, though thou do demand a prisoner,
The noblest ta'en.
Imo. I humbly thank your Highness.
Luc. I do not bid thee beg my life, good lad;
And yet I know thou wilt.
Imo. No, no; alack,
There's other work in hand. I see a thing
Bitter to me as death. Your life, good master,
Must shuffle for itself.
Luc. The boy disdains me,
He leaves me, scorns me. Briefly die their joys
That place them on the truth of girls and boys.
Why stands he so perplexed?
Cym. What wouldst thou, boy?
I love thee more and more. Think more and more
What's best to ask. Know'st him thou look'st on? speak,
Wilt have him live? Is he thy kin? thy friend?
Imo. He is a Roman; no more kin to me
Than I to your Highness; who, being born your vassal,
Am something nearer.
Cym. Wherefore eyest him so?
Imo. I'll tell you, sir, in private, if you please
To give me hearing.
Cym. Ay, with all my heart,
And lend my best attention. What's thy name?
Imo. Fidele, sir.
Cym. Thou'rt my good youth, my page;
I'll be thy master. Walk with me; speak freely.

CYMBELINE *and* IMOGEN *converse apart.*

Bel. Is not this boy revived from death?
Arv. One sand another
Not more resembles that sweet rosy lad
Who died, and was Fidele. What think you?
Gui. The same dead thing alive.
Bel. Peace, peace! see further; he eyes us not; forbear;
Creatures may be alike. Were't he, I am sure
He would have spoke to us.
Gui. But we saw him dead.
Bel. Be silent; let's see further.
Pis. [*Aside*] It is my mistress.
Since she is living, let the time run on
To good or bad.

CYMBELINE *and* IMOGEN *come forward.*

Cym. Come, stand thou by our side;
Make thy demand aloud. [*To* IACHIMO] Sir, step you forth;
Give answer to this boy, and do it freely;
Or, by our greatness and the grace of it,
Which is our honour, bitter torture shall
Winnow the truth from falsehood. On, speak to him.
Imo. My boon is that this gentleman may render
Of whom he had this ring.

Post. [*Aside*] What's that to him?
Cym. That diamond upon your finger, say
How came it yours?
Iach. Thou'lt torture me to leave unspoken that
Which, to be spoke, would torture thee.
Cym. How! me?
Iach. I am glad to be constrain'd to utter that
Which torments me to conceal. By villainy
I got this ring. 'Twas Leonatus' jewel;
Whom thou didst banish; and—which more may grieve thee,
As it doth me—a nobler sir ne'er lived
'Twixt sky and ground. Wilt thou hear more, my lord?
Cym. All that belongs to this.
Iach. That paragon, thy daughter—
For whom my heart drops blood, and my false spirits
Quail to remember—Give me leave; I faint.
Cym. My daughter! what of her? Renew thy strength.
I had rather thou shouldst live while nature will
Than die ere I hear more. Strive, man, and speak.
Iach. Upon a time—unhappy was the clock
That struck the hour!—it was in Rome—accursed
The mansion where!—'twas at a feast—O, would
Our viands had been poison'd, or at least
Those which I heaved to head!—the good Posthumus—
What should I say? He was too good to be
Where ill men were; and was the best of all
Amongst the rarest of good ones—sitting sadly,
Hearing us praise our loves of Italy
For beauty that made barren the swell'd boast
Of him that best could speak, for feature, laming
The shrine of Venus, or straight-pight Minerva,
Postures beyond brief nature, for condition,
A shop of all the qualities that man
Loves woman for, besides that hook of wiving,
Fairness which strikes the eye—
Cym. I stand on fire.
Come to the matter.
Iach. All too soon I shall,
Unless thou wouldst grieve quickly. This Posthumus,
Most like a noble lord in love and one
That had a royal lover, took his hint;
And, not dispraising whom we praised—therein
He was as calm as virtue—he began
His mistress' picture; which by his tongue being made,
And then a mind put in't, either our brags
Were crack'd of kitchen-trulls, or his description
Proved us unspeaking sots.
Cym. Nay, nay, to the purpose.
Iach. Your daughter's chastity—there it begins.
He spake of her, as Dian had hot dreams,
And she alone were cold. Whereat I, wretch,
Made scruple of his praise; and wager'd with him
Pieces of gold 'gainst this which then he wore
Upon his honour'd finger, to attain
In suit the place of's bed and win this ring
By hers and mine adultery. He, true knight,
No lesser of her honour confident
Than I did truly find her, stakes this ring;
And would so, had it been a carbuncle
Of Phoebus' wheel, and might so safely, had it
Been all the worth of's car. Away to Britain
Post I in this design. Well may you, sir,
Remember me at court; where I was taught
Of your chaste daughter the wide difference
'Twixt amorous and villainous. Being thus quench'd
Of hope, not longing, mine Italian brain
'Gan in your duller Britain operate
Most vilely; for my vantage, excellent;
And, to be brief, my practice so prevail'd,
That I return'd with simular proof enough
To make the noble Leonatus mad,
By wounding his belief in her renown
With tokens thus, and thus; averring notes
Of chamber-hanging, pictures, this her bracelet—
O cunning, how I got it!—nay, some marks
Of secret on her person, that he could not
But think her bond of chastity quite crack'd,
I having ta'en the forfeit. Whereupon—
Methinks, I see him now—
Post. [*Advancing*] Ay, so thou dost,
Italian fiend! Ay me, most credulous fool,
Egregious murderer, thief, anything
That's due to all the villains past, in being,
To come! O, give me cord, or knife, or poison,
Some upright justicer! Thou, King, send out
For torturers ingenious. It is I
That all the abhorred things o' the earth amend
By being worse than they. I am Posthumus,
That kill'd thy daughter—villain-like, I lie—
That caused a lesser villain than myself,
A sacrilegious thief, to do't. The temple
Of virtue was she; yea, and she herself.
Spit, and throw stones, cast mire upon me, set
The dogs o' the street to bay me. Every villain
Be call'd Posthumus Leonatus; and
Be villainy less than 'twas! O Imogen!
My queen, my life, my wife! O Imogen,
Imogen, Imogen!
Imo. Peace, my lord; hear, hear—
Post. Shall's have a play of this? Thou scornful page,
There lie thy part. [*Striking her: she falls.*]
Pis. O, gentlemen, help!

Mine and your mistress! O, my lord Posthumus!
You ne'er kill'd Imogen till now. Help, help!
Mine honour'd lady!
Cym. Does the world go round?
Post. How come these staggers on me?
Pis. Wake, my mistress!
Cym. If this be so, the gods do mean to strike me
To death with mortal joy.
Pis. How fares my mistress?
Imo. O, get thee from my sight;
Thou gavest me poison. Dangerous fellow, hence!
Breathe not where princes are.
Cym. The tune of Imogen!
Pis. Lady,
The gods throw stones of sulphur on me, if
That box I gave you was not thought by me
A precious thing. I had it from the Queen.
Cym. New matter still?
Imo. It poison'd me.
Cor. O gods!
I left out one thing which the Queen confess'd,
Which must approve thee honest: "If Pisanio
Have," said she, "given his mistress that confection
Which I gave him for cordial, she is served
As I would serve a rat."
Cym. What's this, Cornelius?
Cor. The Queen, sir, very oft importuned me
To temper poisons for her, still pretending
The satisfaction of her knowledge only
In killing creatures vile, as cats and dogs,
Of no esteem. I, dreading that her purpose
Was of more danger, did compound for her
A certain stuff, which, being ta'en, would cease
The present power of life, but in short time
All offices of nature should again
Do their due functions. Have you ta'en of it?
Imo. Most like I did, for I was dead.
Bel. My boys,
There was our error.
Gui. This is, sure, Fidele.
Imo. Why did you throw your wedded lady from you?
Think that you are upon a rock; and now
Throw me again. [*Embracing him.*]
Post. Hang there like fruit, my soul,
Till the tree die!
Cym. How now, my flesh, my child!
What, makest thou me a dullard in this act?
Wilt thou not speak to me?
Imo. [*Kneeling*] Your blessing sir.
Bel. [*To* GUIDERIUS *and* ARVIRAGUS] Though you did love this youth, I blame ye not;
You had a motive for't.
Cym. My tears that fall
Prove holy water on thee! Imogen,
Thy mother's dead.
Imo. I am sorry for't, my lord.
Cym. O, she was naught; and long of her it was
That we meet here so strangely. But her son
Is gone, we know not how nor where.
Pis. My lord,
Now fear is from me, I'll speak troth. Lord Cloten,
Upon my lady's missing, came to me
With his sword drawn; foam'd at the mouth, and swore,
If I discover'd not which way she was gone,
It was my instant death. By accident,
I had a feigned letter of my master's
Then in my pocket; which directed him
To seek her on the mountains near to Milford;
Where, in a frenzy, in my master's garments,
Which he enforced from me, away he posts
With unchaste purpose and with oath to violate
My lady's honour. What became of him
I further know not.
Gui. Let me end the story;
I slew him there.
Cym. Marry, the gods forfend!
I would not thy good deeds should from my lips
Pluck a hard sentence. Prithee, valiant youth,
Deny't again.
Gui. I have spoke it, and I did it.
Cym. He was a prince.
Gui. A most incivil one. The wrongs he did me
Were nothing prince-like; for he did provoke me
With language that would make me spurn the sea,
If it could so roar to me. I cut off's head;
And am right glad he is not standing here
To tell this tale of mine.
Cym. I am sorry for thee.
By thine own tongue thou art condemn'd, and must
Endure our law. Thou'rt dead.
Imo. That headless man
I thought had been my lord.
Cym. Bind the offender,
And take him from our presence.
Bel. Stay, sir King.
This man is better than the man he slew,
As well descended as thyself; and hath
More of thee merited than a band of Clotens
Had ever scar for. [*To the Guard*] Let his arms alone;
They were not born for bondage.
Cym. Why, old soldier,
Wilt thou undo the worth thou art unpaid for,
By tasting of our wrath? How of descent
As good as we?

Arv. In that he spake too far.
Cym. And thou shalt die for't.
Bel. We will die all three,
But I will prove that two on's are as good
As I have given out him. My sons, I must,
For mine own part, unfold a dangerous speech,
Though, haply, well for you.
Arv. Your danger's ours.
Gui. And our good his.
Bel. Have at it then, by leave.
Thou hadst, great King, a subject who
Was call'd Belarius.
Cym. What of him? he is
A banish'd traitor.
Bel. He it is that hath
Assumed this age; indeed a banish'd man;
I know not how a traitor.
Cym. Take him hence.
The whole world shall not save him.
Bel. Not too hot.
First pay me for the nursing of thy sons;
And let it be confiscate all, so soon
As I have received it.
Cym. Nursing of my sons!
Bel. I am too blunt and saucy; here's my knee.
Ere I arise, I will prefer my sons;
Then spare not the old father. Mighty sir,
These two young gentlemen, that call me father
And think they are my sons, are none of mine;
They are the issue of your loins, my liege,
And blood of your begetting.
Cym. How! my issue!
Bel. So sure as you your father's. I, old Morgan,
Am that Belarius whom you sometime banish'd.
Your pleasure was my mere offence, my punishment
Itself, and all my treason; that I suffer'd
Was all the harm I did. These gentle princes—
For such and so they are—these twenty years
Have I train'd up. Those arts they have as I
Could put into them; my breeding was, sir, as
Your Highness knows. Their nurse, Euriphile,
Whom for the theft I wedded, stole these children
Upon my banishment. I moved her to't,
Having received the punishment before,
For that which I did then. Beaten for loyalty
Excited me to treason. Their dear loss,
The more of you 'twas felt, the more it shaped
Unto my end of stealing them. But, gracious sir,
Here are your sons again; and I must lose
Two of the sweet'st companions in the world.
The benediction of these covering heavens
Fall on their heads like dew! for they are worthy
To inlay heaven with stars.
Cym. Thou weep'st, and speak'st.
The service that you three have done is more
Unlike than this thou tell'st. I lost my children.
If these be they, I know not how to wish
A pair of worthier sons.
Bel. Be pleased awhile.
This gentleman, whom I call Polydore,
Most worthy prince, as yours, is true Guiderius.
This gentleman, my Cadwal, Arviragus,
Your younger princely son; he, sir, was lapp'd
In a most curious mantle, wrought by the hand
Of his queen mother, which for more probation
I can with ease produce.
Cym. Guiderius had
Upon his neck a mole, a sanguine star;
It was a mark of wonder.
Bel. This is he;
Who hath upon him still that natural stamp.
It was wise nature's end in the donation,
To be his evidence now.
Cym. O, what, am I
A mother to the birth of three? Ne'er mother
Rejoiced deliverance more. Blest pray you be,
That, after this strange starting from your orbs,
You may reign in them now! O Imogen,
Thou hast lost by this a kingdom.
Imo. No, my lord;
I have got two worlds by't. O my gentle brothers,
Have we thus met? O, never say hereafter
But I am truest speaker. You call'd me brother,
When I was but your sister; I you brothers,
When ye were so indeed.
Cym. Did you e'er meet?
Arv. Ay, my good lord.
Gui. And at first meeting loved;
Continued so, until we thought he died.
Cor. By the Queen's dram she swallow'd.
Cym. O rare instinct!
When shall I hear all through? This fierce abridgement
Hath to it circumstantial branches, which
Distinction should be rich in. Where? how lived you?
And when came you to serve our Roman captive?
How parted with your brothers? how first met them?
Why fled you from the court? and whither? These,
And your three motives to the battle, with
I know not how much more, should be demanded;
And all the other by-dependencies,
From chance to chance; but nor the time nor place
Will serve our long inter'gatories. See,
Posthumus anchors upon Imogen,
And she, like harmless lightning, throws her eye
On him, her brothers, me, her master, hitting
Each object with a joy; the counterchange

Is severally in all. Let's quit this ground,
And smoke the temple with our sacrifices.
[*To* BELARIUS] Thou art my brother; so we'll hold thee ever.
Imo. You are my father too, and did relieve me
To see this gracious season.
Cym. All o'erjoy'd,
Save these in bonds. Let them be joyful too,
For they shall taste our comfort.
Imo. My good master,
I will yet do you service.
Luc. Happy be you!
Cym. The forlorn soldier, that so nobly fought,
He would have well becomed this place, and graced
The thankings of a king.
Post. I am, sir,
The soldier that did company these three
In poor beseeming; 'twas a fitment for
The purpose I then follow'd. That I was he,
Speak, Iachimo. I had you down and might
Have made you finish.
Iach. [*Kneeling*] I am down again;
But now my heavy conscience sinks my knee,
As then your force did. Take that life, beseech you,
Which I so often owe; but your ring first;
And here the bracelet of the truest princess
That ever swore her faith.
Post. Kneel not to me.
The power that I have on you is to spare you;
The malice towards you to forgive you. Live,
And deal with others better.
Cym. Nobly doom'd!
We'll learn our freeness of a son-in-law;
Pardon's the word to all.
Arv. You holp us, sir,
As you did mean indeed to be our brother;
Joy'd are we that you are.
Post. Your servant, Princes. Good my lord of Rome,
Call forth your soothsayer. As I slept, methought
Great Jupiter, upon his eagle back'd,
Appear'd to me, with other spritely shows
Of mine own kindred. When I waked, I found
This label on my bosom; whose containing
Is so from sense in hardness, that I can
Make no collection of it. Let him show
His skill in the construction.
Luc. Philarmonus!
Sooth. Here, my good lord.
Luc. Read, and declare the meaning.

Sooth. [*Reads*] "When as a lion's whelp shall, to himself unknown, without seeking find, and be embraced by a piece of tender air; and when from a stately cedar shall be lopped branches, which, being dead many years, shall after revive, be jointed to the old stock, and freshly grow; then shall Posthumus end his miseries, Britain be fortunate and flourish in peace and plenty."

Thou, Leonatus, art the lion's whelp;
The fit and apt construction of thy name,
Being *leo-natus*, doth import so much.
[*To* CYMBELINE] The piece of tender air, thy virtuous daughter,
Which we call *mollis aer*; and *mollis aer*
We term it *mulier*; which *mulier* I divine
Is this most constant wife; who, even now,
Answering the letter of the oracle,
Unknown to you, unsought, were clipp'd about
With this most tender air.
Cym. This hath some seeming.
Sooth. The lofty cedar, royal Cymbeline,
Personates thee; and thy lopp'd branches point
Thy two sons forth; who, by Belarius stol'n,
For many years thought dead, are now revived,
To the majestic cedar join'd, whose issue
Promises Britain peace and plenty.
Cym. Well;
My peace we will begin. And, Caius Lucius,
Although the victor, we submit to Cæsar,
And to the Roman empire; promising
To pay our wonted tribute, from the which
We were dissuaded by our wicked queen;
Whom heavens, in justice, both on her and hers,
Have laid most heavy hand.
Sooth. The fingers of the powers above do tune
The harmony of this peace. The vision
Which I made known to Lucius, ere the stroke
Of this yet scarce-cold battle, at this instant
Is full accomplish'd; for the Roman eagle,
From south to west on wing soaring aloft,
Lessen'd herself, and in the beams o' the sun
So vanish'd; which foreshow'd our princely eagle,
The imperial Cæsar, should again unite
His favour with the radiant Cymbeline,
Which shines here in the west.
Cym. Laud we the gods;
And let our crooked smokes climb to their nostrils
From our blest altars. Publish we this peace
To all our subjects. Set we forward. Let
A Roman and a British ensign wave
Friendly together. So through Lud's-town march;
And in the temple of great Jupiter
Our peace we'll ratify; seal it with feasts.
Set on there! Never was a war did cease,
Ere bloody hands were wash'd, with such a peace. [*Exeunt*.

THE WINTER'S TALE

DRAMATIS PERSONÆ

TIME, *as Chorus*

LEONTES, *King of Sicilia*
MAMILLIUS, *young Prince of Sicilia*
CAMILLO
ANTIGONUS
CLEOMENES
DION — *four Lords of Sicilia*
POLIXENES, *King of Bohemia*
FLORIZEL, *Prince of Bohemia*
ARCHIDAMUS, *a Lord of Bohemia*
OLD SHEPHERD, *reputed father of Perdita*
CLOWN, *his son*
AUTOLYCUS, *a rogue*
A MARINER
A GAOLER
THREE GENTLEMEN

A LORD, *attending on Leontes*
THREE SERVANTS *to Leontes*
AN OFFICER
A SERVANT *to the Old Shepherd*

HERMIONE, *Queen to Leontes*
PERDITA, *daughter to Leontes and Hermione*
PAULINA, *wife to Antigonus*
EMILIA, *a lady attending on Hermione*
MOPSA
DORCAS — *shepherdesses*
TWO LADIES *attending on Hermione*

NON-SPEAKING: *Lords, Ladies, Gentlemen, Officers Servants, Shepherds, Shepherdesses, and Attendants*

SCENE: *Sicilia, and Bohemia*

ACT I

SCENE I. *Antechamber in Leontes' palace*

Enter CAMILLO *and* ARCHIDAMUS.

Arch. If you shall chance, Camillo, to visit Bohemia, on the like occasion whereon my services are now on foot, you shall see, as I have said, great difference betwixt our Bohemia and your Sicilia.

Cam. I think, this coming summer, the King of Sicilia means to pay Bohemia the visitation which he justly owes him.

Arch. Wherein our entertainment shall shame us we will be justified in our loves; for indeed—

Cam. Beseech you,—

Arch. Verily, I speak it in the freedom of my knowledge. We cannot with such magnificence—in so rare—I know not what to say. We will give you sleepy drinks, that your senses, unintelligent of our insufficience, may, though they cannot praise us, as little accuse us.

Cam. You pay a great deal too dear for what's given freely.

Arch. Believe me, I speak as my understanding instructs me and as mine honesty puts it to utterance.

Cam. Sicilia cannot show himself over-kind to Bohemia. They were trained together in their childhoods; and there rooted betwixt them then such an affection, which cannot choose but branch now. Since their more mature dignities and royal necessities made separation of their society, their encounters, though not personal, have been royally attorneyed with interchange of gifts, letters, loving embassies; that they have seemed to be together, though absent, shook hands, as over a vast, and embraced, as it were, from the ends of opposed winds. The heavens continue their loves!

Arch. I think there is not in the world either malice or matter to alter it. You have an unspeakable comfort of your young prince Mamillius. It is a gentleman of the greatest promise that ever came into my note.

Cam. I very well agree with you in the hopes of him. It is a gallant child; one that indeed physics the subject, makes old hearts fresh. They that went on crutches ere he was born desire yet their life to see him a man.

Arch. Would they else be content to die?

Cam. Yes; if there were no other excuse why they should desire to live.

Arch. If the King had no son, they would desire to live on crutches till he had one.

[*Exeunt.*

SCENE II. *A room of state in the same*

Enter LEONTES, HERMIONE, MAMILLIUS, POLIXENES, CAMILLO, *and Attendants.*

Pol. Nine changes of the watery star hath been
The shepherd's note since we have left our throne
Without a burthen; time as long again
Would be fill'd up, my brother, with our thanks;
And yet we should, for perpetuity,
Go hence in debt; and therefore, like a cipher,
Yet standing in rich place, I multiply

With one "We thank you" many thousands moe
That go before it.
Leon. Stay your thanks a while;
And pay them when you part.
Pol. Sir, that's to-morrow.
I am question'd by my fears of what may chance
Or breed upon our absence; that may blow
No sneaping winds at home, to make us say,
"This is put forth too truly." Besides, I have stay'd
To tire your royalty.
Leon. We are tougher, brother,
Than you can put us to't.
Pol. No longer stay.
Leon. One seven-night longer.
Pol. Very sooth, to-morrow.
Leon. We'll part the time between's then; and in that
I'll no gainsaying.
Pol. Press me not, beseech you, so.
There is no tongue that moves, none, none i' the world,
So soon as yours could win me. So it should now,
Were there necessity in your request, although
'Twere needful I denied it. My affairs
Do even drag me homeward; which to hinder
Were in your love a whip to me; my stay
To you a charge and trouble. To save both,
Farewell, our brother.
Leon. Tongue-tied our Queen? speak you.
Her. I had thought, sir, to have held my peace until
You had drawn oaths from him not to stay. You, sir,
Charge him too coldly. Tell him, you are sure
All in Bohemia's well; this satisfaction
The by-gone day proclaim'd. Say this to him,
He's beat from his best ward.
Leon. Well said, Hermione.
Her. To tell he longs to see his son were strong;
But let him say so then, and let him go;
But let him swear so, and he shall not stay,
We'll thwack him hence with distaffs.
Yet of your royal presence I'll adventure
The borrow of a week. When at Bohemia
You take my lord, I'll give him my commission
To let him there a month behind the gest
Prefix'd for's parting; yet, good deed, Leontes,
I love thee not a jar o' the clock behind
What lady she her lord. You'll stay?
Pol. No, madam.
Her. Nay, but you will?
Pol. I may not, verily.
Her. Verily!
You put me off with limber vows; but I,
Though you would seek to unsphere the stars with oaths,
Should yet say, "Sir, no going." Verily,
You shall not go; a lady's "Verily" 's
As potent as a lord's. Will you go yet?
Force me to keep you as a prisoner,
Not like a guest; so you shall pay your fees
When you depart, and save your thanks. How say you?
My prisoner or my guest? by your dread "Verily,"
One of them you shall be.
Pol. Your guest, then, madam.
To be your prisoner should import offending;
Which is for me less easy to commit
Than you to punish.
Her. Not your gaoler, then,
But your kind hostess. Come, I'll question you
Of my lord's tricks and yours when you were boys.
You were pretty lordings then?
Pol. We were, fair Queen,
Two lads that thought there was no more behind
But such a day to-morrow as to-day,
And to be boy eternal.
Her. Was not my lord
The verier wag o' the two?
Pol. We were as twinn'd lambs that did frisk i' the sun,
And bleat the one at the other. What we changed
Was innocence for innocence; we knew not
The doctrine of ill-doing, nor dream'd
That any did. Had we pursued that life,
And our weak spirits ne'er been higher rear'd
With stronger blood, we should have answer'd heaven
Boldly, "Not guilty"; the imposition clear'd
Hereditary ours.
Her. By this we gather
You have tripp'd since.
Pol. O my most sacred lady!
Temptations have since then been born to's; for
In those unfledged days was my wife a girl;
Your precious self had then not cross'd the eyes
Of my young play-fellow.
Her. Grace to boot!
Of this make no conclusion, lest you say
Your Queen and I are devils. Yet go on;
The offences we have made you do we'll answer,
If you first sinn'd with us and that with us
You did continue fault and that you slipp'd not
With any but with us.
Leon. Is he won yet?
Her. He'll stay, my lord.
Leon. At my request he would not.

Hermione, my dearest, thou never spokest
To better purpose.
Her. Never?
Leon. Never, but once.
Her. What! have I twice said well? when was't before?
I prithee tell me; cram 's with praise, and make 's
As fat as tame things. One good deed dying tongueless
Slaughters a thousand waiting upon that.
Our praises are our wages. You may ride's
With one soft kiss a thousand furlongs ere
With spur we heat an acre. But to the goal:
My last good deed was to entreat his stay;
What was my first? It has an elder sister,
Or I mistake you. O, would her name were Grace!
But once before I spoke to the purpose; when?
Nay, let me have't; I long.
Leon. Why, that was when
Three crabbed months had sour'd themselves to death,
Ere I could make thee open thy white hand
And clap thyself my love. Then didst thou utter,
"I am yours for ever."
Her. 'Tis grace indeed.
Why, lo you now, I have spoke to the purpose twice:
The one for ever earn'd a royal husband;
The other for some while a friend.
Leon. [*Aside*] Too hot, too hot!
To mingle friendship far is mingling bloods.
I have *tremor cordis* on me; my heart dances;
But not for joy; not joy. This entertainment
May a free face put on, derive a liberty
From heartiness, from bounty, fertile bosom,
And well become the agent; 't may, I grant;
But to be paddling palms and pinching fingers,
As now they are, and making practised smiles,
As in a looking-glass, and then to sigh, as 'twere
The mort o' the deer; O, that is entertainment
My bosom likes not, nor my brows! Mamillius,
Art thou my boy?
Mam. Ay, my good lord.
Leon. I' fecks!
Why, that's my bawcock. What, hast smutch'd thy nose?
They say it is a copy out of mine. Come, captain,
We must be neat; not neat, but cleanly, captain.
And yet the steer, the heifer and the calf
Are all call'd neat.—Still virginalling
Upon his palm!—How now, you wanton calf!
Art thou my calf?
Mam. Yes, if you will, my lord.
Leon. Thou want'st a rough pash and the shoots that I have,
To be full like me; yet they say we are
Almost as like as eggs; women say so,
That will say any thing. But were they false
As o'er-dyed blacks, as wind, as waters, false
As dice are to be wish'd by one that fixes
No bourn 'twixt his and mine, yet were it true
To say this boy were like me. Come, sir page,
Look on me with your welkin eye. Sweet villain!
Most dear'st! my collop! Can thy dam?—may't be?—
Affection! thy intention stabs the centre.
Thou dost make possible things not so held,
Communicatest with dreams—how can this be?—
With what's unreal thou coactive art,
And fellow'st nothing. Then 'tis very credent
Thou mayst co-join with something; and thou dost,
And that beyond commission, and I find it,
And that to the infection of my brains
And hardening of my brows.
Pol. What means Sicilia?
Her. He something seems unsettled.
Pol. How, my lord!
What cheer? how is't with you, best brother?
Her. You look
As if you held a brow of much distraction.
Are you moved, my lord?
Leon. No, in good earnest.
How sometimes nature will betray its folly,
Its tenderness, and make itself a pastime
To harder bosoms! Looking on the lines
Of my boy's face, methoughts I did recoil
Twenty-three years, and saw myself unbreech'd,
In my green velvet coat, my dagger muzzled,
Lest it should bite its master, and so prove,
As ornaments oft do, too dangerous.
How like, methought, I then was to this kernel,
This squash, this gentleman. Mine honest friend,
Will you take eggs for money?
Mam. No, my lord, I'll fight.
Leon. You will! why, happy man be's dole! My brother,
Are you so fond of your young prince as we
Do seem to be of ours?
Pol. If at home, sir,
He's all my exercise, my mirth, my matter,
Now my sworn friend and then mine enemy,
My parasite, my soldier, statesman, all.
He makes a July's day short as December,
And with his varying childness cures in me
Thoughts that would thick my blood.
Leon. So stands this squire
Officed with me. We two will walk, my lord,
And leave you to your graver steps. Hermione,

How thou lovest us, show in our brother's welcome;
Let what is dear in Sicily be cheap.
Next to thyself and my young rover, he's
Apparent to my heart.

Her. If you would seek us,
We are yours i' the garden. Shall's attend you there?

Leon. To your own bents dispose you; you'll be found,
Be you beneath the sky. [*Aside*] I am angling now,
Though you perceive me not how I give line.
Go to, go to!
How she holds up the neb, the bill to him!
And arms her with the boldness of a wife
To her allowing husband!

[*Exeunt* POLIXENES, HERMIONE, *and Attendants.*

Gone already!
Inch-thick, knee-deep, o'er head and ears a fork'd one!
Go, play, boy, play. Thy mother plays, and I
Play too, but so disgraced a part, whose issue
Will hiss me to my grave; contempt and clamour
Will be my knell. Go, play, boy, play. There have been,
Or I am much deceived, cuckolds ere now;
And many a man there is, even at this present,
Now while I speak this, holds his wife by the arm,
That little thinks she has been sluiced in's absence
And his pond fish'd by his next neighbour, by
Sir Smile, his neighbour. Nay, there's comfort in 't
Whiles other men have gates and those gates open'd,
As mine, against their will. Should all despair
That have revolted wives, the tenth of mankind
Would hang themselves. Physic for 't there is none;
It is a bawdy planet, that will strike
Where 'tis predominant; and 'tis powerful, think it,
From east, west, north and south. Be it concluded,
No barricado for a belly; know't;
It will let in and out the enemy
With bag and baggage. Many thousand on's
Have the disease, and feel't not. How now, boy!

Mam. I am like you, they say.

Leon. Why, that's some comfort.
What, Camillo there?

Cam. Ay, my good lord.

Leon. Go play, Mamillius; thou'rt an honest man. [*Exit* MAMILLIUS.
Camillo, this great sir will yet stay longer.

Cam. You had much ado to make his anchor hold.
When you cast out, it still came home.

Leon. Didst note it?

Cam. He would not stay at your petitions; made
His business more material.

Leon. Didst perceive it?
[*Aside*] They're here with me already, whispering, rounding,
"Sicilia is a so-forth." 'Tis far gone,
When I shall gust it last. How came't, Camillo,
That he did stay?

Cam. At the good Queen's entreaty.

Leon. At the Queen's be't: "good" should be pertinent;
But, so it is, it is not. Was this taken
By any understanding pate but thine?
For thy conceit is soaking, will draw in
More than the common blocks. Not noted, is't,
But of the finer natures? By some severals
Of head-piece extraordinary? Lower messes
Perchance are to this business purblind? Say.

Cam. Business, my lord! I think most understand
Bohemia stays here longer.

Leon. Ha!

Cam. Stays here longer.

Leon. Ay, but why?

Cam. To satisfy your Highness and the entreaties
Of our most gracious mistress.

Leon. Satisfy!
The entreaties of your mistress! Satisfy!
Let that suffice. I have trusted thee, Camillo,
With all the nearest things to my heart, as well
My chamber-councils, wherein, priest-like, thou
Hast cleansed my bosom, I from thee departed
Thy penitent reform'd; but we have been
Deceived in thy integrity, deceived
In that which seems so.

Cam. Be it forbid, my lord!

Leon. To bide upon't, thou art not honest, or,
If thou inclinest that way, thou art a coward,
Which hoxes honesty behind, restraining
From course required; or else thou must be counted
A servant grafted in my serious trust
And therein negligent; or else a fool
That seest a game play'd home, the rich stake drawn,
And takest it all for jest.

Cam. My gracious lord,
I may be negligent, foolish and fearful;
In every one of these no man is free,
But that his negligence, his folly, fear,

Among the infinite doings of the world,
Sometime puts forth. In your affairs, my lord,
If ever I were wilful-negligent,
It was my folly; if industriously
I play'd the fool, it was my negligence,
Not weighing well the end; if ever fearful
To do a thing, where I the issue doubted,
Whereof the execution did cry out
Against the non-performance, 'twas a fear
Which oft infects the wisest. These, my lord,
Are such allow'd infirmities that honesty
Is never free of. But, beseech your Grace,
Be plainer with me; let me know my trespass
By its own visage. If I then deny it,
'Tis none of mine.

Leon. Ha' not you seen, Camillo—
But that's past doubt, you have, or your eye-glass
Is thicker than a cuckold's horn—or heard—
For to a vision so apparent rumour
Cannot be mute—or thought—for cogitation
Resides not in that man that does not think—
My wife is slippery? If thou wilt confess,
Or else be impudently negative,
To have nor eyes nor ears nor thought, then say
My wife's a hobby-horse, deserves a name
As rank as any flax-wench that puts to
Before her troth-plight; say't and justify't.

Cam. I would not be a stander-by to hear
My sovereign mistress clouded so, without
My present vengeance taken. 'Shrew my heart,
You never spoke what did become you less
Than this; which to reiterate were sin
As deep as that, though true.

Leon. Is whispering nothing?
Is leaning cheek to cheek? is meeting noses?
Kissing with inside lip? stopping the career
Of laughter with a sigh?—a note infallible
Of breaking honesty—horsing foot on foot?
Skulking in corners? wishing clocks more swift?
Hours, minutes? noon, midnight? and all eyes
Blind with the pin and web but theirs, theirs only,
That would unseen be wicked? Is this nothing?
Why, then the world and all that's in't is nothing;
The covering sky is nothing; Bohemia nothing;
My wife is nothing; nor nothing have these nothings,
If this be nothing.

Cam. Good my lord, be cured
Of this diseased opinion, and betimes;
For 'tis most dangerous.

Leon. Say it be, 'tis true.

Cam. No, no, my lord.

Leon. It is; you lie, you lie.
I say thou liest, Camillo, and I hate thee,
Pronounce thee a gross lout, a mindless slave,
Or else a hovering temporizer, that
Canst with thine eyes at once see good and evil,
Inclining to them both. Were my wife's liver
Infected as her life, she would not live
The running of one glass.

Cam. Who does infect her?

Leon. Why, he that wears her like her medal, hanging
About his neck, Bohemia; who, if I
Had servants true about me, that bare eyes
To see alike mine honour as their profits,
Their own particular thrifts, they would do that
Which should undo more doing; ay, and thou,
His cupbearer—whom I from meaner form
Have bench'd and rear'd to worship, who mayst see
Plainly as heaven sees earth and earth sees heaven,
How I am galled—mightst bespice a cup,
To give mine enemy a lasting wink;
Which draught to me were cordial.

Cam. Sir, my lord,
I could do this, and that with no rash potion,
But with a lingering dram that should not work
Maliciously like poison; but I cannot
Believe this crack to be in my dread mistress,
So sovereignly being honourable.
I have loved thee—

Leon. Make that thy question, and go rot!
Dost think I am so muddy, so unsettled,
To appoint myself in this vexation, sully
The purity and whiteness of my sheets,
Which to preserve is sleep, which being spotted
Is goads, thorns, nettles, tails of wasps,
Give scandal to the blood o' the prince my son,
Who I do think is mine and love as mine,
Without ripe moving to't? Would I do this?
Could man so blench?

Cam. I must believe you, sir;
I do; and will fetch off Bohemia for 't;
Provided that, when he's removed, your Highness
Will take again your Queen as yours at first,
Even for your son's sake; and thereby for sealing
The injury of tongues in courts and kingdoms
Known and allied to yours.

Leon. Thou dost advise me
Even so as I mine own course have set down.
I'll give no blemish to her honour, none.

Cam. My lord,
Go then; and with a countenance as clear
As friendship wears at feasts, keep with Bohemia
And with your Queen. I am his cupbearer:
If from me he have wholesome beverage,

Account me not your servant.
Leon. This is all.
Do 't and thou hast the one half of my heart;
Do 't not, thou split'st thine own.
Cam. I'll do 't, my lord.
Leon. I will seem friendly, as thou hast advised me. [*Exit.*
Cam. O miserable lady! But, for me,
What case stand I in? I must be the poisoner
Of good Polixenes; and my ground to do 't
Is the obedience to a master, one
Who in rebellion with himself will have
All that are his so too. To do this deed,
Promotion follows. If I could find example
Of thousands that had struck anointed kings
And flourish'd after, I'd not do 't; but since
Nor brass nor stone nor parchment bears not one,
Let villainy itself forswear 't. I must
Forsake the court. To do 't, or no, is certain
To me a break-neck. Happy star reign now!
Here comes Bohemia.

Re-enter POLIXENES.

Pol. This is strange; methinks
My favour here begins to warp. Not speak?
Good day, Camillo.
Cam. Hail, most royal sir!
Pol. What is the news i' the court?
Cam. None rare, my lord.
Pol. The King hath on him such a countenance
As he had lost some province and a region
Loved as he loves himself. Even now I met him
With customary compliment; when he,
Wafting his eyes to the contrary and falling
A lip of much contempt, speeds from me and
So leaves me to consider what is breeding
That changeth thus his manners.
Cam. I dare not know, my lord.
Pol. How! dare not! Do not. Do you know, and dare not?
Be intelligent to me: 'tis thereabouts;
For, to yourself, what you do know, you must,
And cannot say you dare not. Good Camillo,
Your changed complexions are to me a mirror
Which shows me mine changed too; for I must be
A party in this alteration, finding
Myself thus alter'd with 't.
Cam. There is a sickness
Which puts some of us in distemper, but
I cannot name the disease; and it is caught
Of you that yet are well.
Pol. How! caught of me!
Make me not sighted like the basilisk.
I have look'd on thousands, who have sped the better
By my regard, but kill'd none so. Camillo—
As you are certainly a gentleman, thereto
Clerk-like experienced, which no less adorns
Our gentry than our parents' noble names,
In whose success we are gentle—I beseech you,
If you know aught which does behove my knowledge
Thereof to be inform'd, imprison 't not
In ignorant concealment.
Cam. I may not answer.
Pol. A sickness caught of me, and yet I well!
I must be answer'd. Dost thou hear, Camillo?
I conjure thee, by all the parts of man
Which honour does acknowledge, whereof the least
Is not this suit of mine, that thou declare
What incidency thou dost guess of harm
Is creeping toward me; how far off, how near;
Which way to be prevented, if to be;
If not, how best to bear it.
Cam. Sir, I will tell you;
Since I am charged in honour and by him
That I think honourable; therefore mark my counsel,
Which must be even as swiftly follow'd as
I mean to utter it, or both yourself and me
Cry lost, and so good night!
Pol. On, good Camillo.
Cam. I am appointed him to murder you.
Pol. By whom, Camillo?
Cam. By the King.
Pol. For what?
Cam. He thinks, nay, with all confidence he swears,
As he had seen 't or been an instrument
To vice you to 't, that you have touch'd his Queen
Forbiddenly.
Pol. O, then my best blood turn
To an infected jelly and my name
Be yoked with his that did betray the Best!
Turn then my freshest reputation to
A savour that may strike the dullest nostril
Where I arrive, and my approach be shunn'd,
Nay, hated too, worse than the great'st infection
That e'er was heard or read!
Cam. Swear his thought over
By each particular star in heaven and
By all their influences, you may as well
Forbid the sea for to obey the moon
As or by oath remove or counsel shake
The fabric of his folly, whose foundation
Is piled upon his faith and will continue
The standing of his body.
Pol. How should this grow?
Cam. I know not; but I am sure 'tis safer to

Avoid what's grown than question how 'tis born.
If therefore you dare trust my honesty,
That lies enclosed in this trunk which you
Shall bear along impawn'd, away to-night!
Your followers I will whisper to the business,
And will by twos and threes at several posterns
Clear them o' the city. For myself, I'll put
My fortunes to your service, which are here
By this discovery lost. Be not uncertain;
For, by the honour of my parents, I
Have utter'd truth; which if you seek to prove,
I dare not stand by; nor shall you be safer
Than one condemn'd by the King's own mouth, thereon
His execution sworn.

Pol. I do believe thee;
I saw his heart in's face. Give me thy hand.
Be pilot to me and thy places shall
Still neighbour mine. My ships are ready and
My people did expect my hence departure
Two days ago. This jealousy
Is for a precious creature. As she's rare,
Must it be great, and as his person's mighty,
Must it be violent, and as he does conceive
He is dishonour'd by a man which ever
Profess'd to him, why, his revenges must
In that be made more bitter. Fear o'ershades me.
Good expedition be my friend, and comfort
The gracious Queen, part of his theme, but nothing
Of his ill-ta'en suspicion! Come, Camillo;
I will respect thee as a father if
Thou bear'st my life off hence. Let us avoid.

Cam. It is in mine authority to command
The keys of all the posterns. Please your Highness
To take the urgent hour. Come, sir, away.
[*Exeunt.*

ACT II

SCENE I. *A room in Leontes' palace*

Enter HERMIONE, MAMILLIUS, *and* LADIES.

Her. Take the boy to you; he so troubles me,
'Tis past enduring.

1st Lady. Come, my gracious lord,
Shall I be your playfellow?

Mam. No, I'll none of you.

1st Lady. Why, my sweet lord?

Mam. You'll kiss me hard and speak to me as if
I were a baby still. I love you better.

2nd Lady. And why so, my lord?

Mam. Not for because
Your brows are blacker; yet black brows, they say,
Become some women best, so that there be not
Too much hair there, but in a semicircle,
Or a half-moon made with a pen.

2nd Lady. Who taught you this?

Mam. I learnt it out of women's faces. Pray now
What colour are your eyebrows?

1st Lady. Blue, my lord.

Mam. Nay, that's a mock. I have seen a lady's nose
That has been blue, but not her eyebrows.

1st Lady. Hark ye;
The Queen your mother rounds apace. We shall
Present our services to a fine new prince
One of these days; and then you'd wanton with us,
If we would have you.

2nd Lady. She is spread of late
Into a goodly bulk. Good time encounter her!

Her. What wisdom stirs amongst you? Come, sir, now
I am for you again. Pray you, sit by us,
And tell's a tale.

Mam. Merry or sad shall 't be?

Her. As merry as you will.

Mam. A sad tale's best for winter. I have one
Of sprites and goblins.

Her. Let's have that, good sir.
Come on, sit down; come on, and do your best
To fright me with your sprites; you're powerful at it.

Mam. There was a man—

Her. Nay, come, sit down; then on.

Mam. Dwelt by a churchyard. I will tell it softly;
Yond crickets shall not hear it.

Her. Come on, then,
And give 't me in mine ear.

Enter LEONTES, *with* ANTIGONUS, LORDS, *and others.*

Leon. Was he met there? his train? Camillo with him?

1st Lord. Behind the tuft of pines I met them; never
Saw I men scour so on their way. I eyed them
Even to their ships.

Leon. How blest am I
In my just censure, in my true opinion!
Alack, for lesser knowledge! how accursed
In being so blest! There may be in the cup
A spider steep'd, and one may drink, depart,
And yet partake no venom, for his knowledge
Is not infected; but if one present
The abhorr'd ingredient to his eye, make known
How he hath drunk, he cracks his gorge, his sides,

With violent hefts. I have drunk, and seen the spider.
Camillo was his help in this, his pandar.
There is a plot against my life, my crown;
All's true that is mistrusted. That false villain
Whom I employ'd was pre-employ'd by him.
He has discover'd my design, and I
Remain a pinch'd thing; yea, a very trick
For them to play at will. How came the posterns
So easily open?

1st Lord. By his great authority;
Which often hath no less prevail'd than so
On your command.

Leon. I know 't too well.
Give me the boy. I am glad you did not nurse him.
Though he does bear some signs of me, yet you
Have too much blood in him.

Her. What is this? sport?

Leon. Bear the boy hence; he shall not come about her;
Away with him! and let her sport herself
With that she's big with; for 'tis Polixenes
Has made thee swell thus.

Her. But I'd say he had not,
And I'll be sworn you would believe my saying,
Howe'er you lean to the nayward.

Leon. You, my lords,
Look on her, mark her well; be but about
To say "she is a goodly lady," and
The justice of your hearts will thereto add
"'Tis pity she's not honest, honourable."
Praise her but for this her without-door form,
Which on my faith deserves high speech, and straight
The shrug, the hum or ha, these petty brands
That calumny doth use—O, I am out—
That mercy does, for calumny will sear
Virtue itself; these shrugs, these hums and ha's,
When you have said "She's goodly," come between
Ere you can say, "She's honest." But be 't known,
From him that has most cause to grieve it should be,
She's an adulteress.

Her. Should a villain say so,
The most replenish'd villain in the world,
He were as much more villain. You, my lord,
Do but mistake.

Leon. You have mistook, my lady,
Polixenes for Leontes. O thou thing!
Which I'll not call a creature of thy place,
Lest barbarism, making me the precedent,
Should a like language use to all degrees
And mannerly distinguishment leave out
Betwixt the prince and beggar. I have said
She's an adulteress; I have said with whom.
More, she's a traitor and Camillo is
A federary with her, and one that knows
What she should shame to know herself
But with her most vile principal, that she's
A bed-swerver, even as bad as those
That vulgars give bold'st titles, ay, and privy
To this their late escape.

Her. No, by my life,
Privy to none of this. How will this grieve you,
When you shall come to clearer knowledge, that
You thus have publish'd me! Gentle my lord,
You scarce can right me throughly then to say
You did mistake.

Leon. No; if I mistake
In those foundations which I build upon,
The centre is not big enough to bear
A school-boy's top. Away with her! to prison!
He who shall speak for her is afar off guilty
But that he speaks.

Her. There's some ill planet reigns.
I must be patient till the heavens look
With an aspect more favourable. Good my lords,
I am not prone to weeping, as our sex
Commonly are, the want of which vain dew
Perchance shall dry your pities; but I have
That honourable grief lodged here which burns
Worse than tears drown. Beseech you all, my lords,
With thoughts so qualified as your charities
Shall best instruct you, measure me; and so
The King's will be perform'd!

Leon. Shall I be heard?

Her. Who is 't that goes with me? Beseech your Highness,
My women may be with me; for you see
My plight requires it. Do not weep, good fools;
There is no cause. When you shall know your mistress
Has deserved prison, then abound in tears
As I come out. This action I now go on
Is for my better grace. Adieu, my lord.
I never wish'd to see you sorry; now
I trust I shall. My women, come; you have leave.

Leon. Go, do our bidding; hence!

[*Exit* QUEEN, *guarded; with* LADIES.

1st Lord. Beseech your Highness, call the Queen again.

Ant. Be certain what you do, sir, lest your justice
Prove violence; in the which three great ones suffer,
Yourself, your queen, your son.

1st Lord. For her, my lord,
I dare my life lay down and will do 't, sir,
Please you to accept it, that the Queen is spotless

I' the eyes of heaven and to you; I mean,
In this which you accuse her.
Ant. If it prove
She's otherwise, I'll keep my stables where
I lodge my wife; I'll go in couples with her;
Than when I feel and see her no farther trust her;
For every inch of woman in the world,
Ay, every dram of woman's flesh is false,
If she be.
Leon. Hold your peaces.
1st Lord. Good my lord—
Ant. It is for you we speak, not for ourselves:
You are abused and by some putter-on
That will be damn'd for 't; would I knew the villain,
I would land-damn him. Be she honour-flaw'd,
I have three daughters; the eldest is eleven;
The second and the third, nine, and some five;
If this prove true, they'll pay for 't. By mine honour,
I'll geld 'em all; fourteen they shall not see,
To bring false generations. They are co-heirs;
And I had rather glib myself than they
Should not produce fair issue.
Leon. Cease; no more.
You smell this business with a sense as cold
As is a dead man's nose; but I do see 't and feel 't,
As you feel doing thus, and see withal
The instruments that feel.
Ant. If it be so,
We need no grave to bury honesty.
There's not a grain of it the face to sweeten
Of the whole dungy earth.
Leon. What! lack I credit?
1st Lord. I had rather you did lack than I, my lord,
Upon this ground; and more it would content me
To have her honour true than your suspicion,
Be blamed for 't how you might.
Leon. Why, what need we
Commune with you of this, but rather follow
Our forceful instigation? Our prerogative
Calls not your counsels, but our natural goodness
Imparts this; which if you, or stupified
Or seeming so in skill, cannot or will not
Relish a truth like us, inform yourselves
We need no more of your advice. The matter,
The loss, the gain, the ordering on 't, is all
Properly ours.
Ant. And I wish, my liege,
You had only in your silent judgment tried it,
Without more overture.
Leon. How could that be?
Either thou art most ignorant by age,
Or thou wert born a fool. Camillo's flight,
Added to their familiarity,
Which was as gross as ever touch'd conjecture,
That lack'd sight only, nought for approbation
But only seeing, all other circumstances
Made up to the deed, doth push on this proceeding.
Yet, for a greater confirmation,
For in an act of this importance 'twere
Most piteous to be wild, I have dispatch'd in post
To sacred Delphos, to Apollo's temple,
Cleomenes and Dion, whom you know
Of stuff'd sufficiency. Now from the oracle
They will bring all; whose spiritual counsel had,
Shall stop or spur me. Have I done well?
1st Lord. Well done, my lord.
Leon. Though I am satisfied and need no more
Than what I know, yet shall the oracle
Give rest to the minds of others, such as he
Whose ignorant credulity will not
Come up to the truth. So have we thought it good
From our free person she should be confined,
Lest that the treachery of the two fled hence
Be left her to perform. Come, follow us;
We are to speak in public; for this business
Will raise us all.
Ant. [*Aside*] To laughter, as I take it,
If the good truth were known. [*Exeunt.*

SCENE II. *A prison*

Enter PAULINA, *a Gentleman, and Attendants.*

Paul. The keeper of the prison, call to him;
Let him have knowledge who I am.
[*Exit Gentleman.*
Good lady,
No court in Europe is too good for thee;
What dost thou then in prison?

Re-enter Gentleman, with the GAOLER.

Now, good sir,
You know me, do you not?
Gaol. For a worthy lady
And one whom much I honour.
Paul. Pray you then,
Conduct me to the Queen.
Gaol. I may not, madam.
To the contrary I have express commandment.
Paul. Here's ado,
To lock up honesty and honour from
The access of gentle visitors! Is 't lawful, pray you,
To see her women? any of them? Emilia?
Gaol. So please you, madam,
To put apart these your attendants, I
Shall bring Emilia forth.
Paul. I pray now, call her.
Withdraw yourselves.
[*Exeunt Gentleman and Attendants.*

Gaol. And, madam,
I must be present at your conference.
Paul. Well, be 't so, prithee. [*Exit* GAOLER.
Here's such ado to make no stain a stain
As passes colouring.

Re-enter GAOLER, *with* EMILIA.

Dear gentlewoman,
How fares our gracious lady?
Emil. As well as one so great and so forlorn
May hold together. On her frights and griefs,
Which never tender lady hath borne greater,
She is something before her time deliver'd.
Paul. A boy?
Emil. A daughter, and a goodly babe,
Lusty and like to live. The queen receives
Much comfort in 't; says "My poor prisoner,
I am innocent as you."
Paul. I dare be sworn.
These dangerous unsafe lunes i' the King, beshrew them!
He must be told on 't, and he shall. The office
Becomes a woman best; I'll take 't upon me.
If I prove honey-mouth'd, let my tongue blister
And never to my red-look'd anger be
The trumpet any more. Pray you, Emilia,
Commend my best obedience to the queen.
If she dares trust me with her little babe,
I'll show 't the King and undertake to be
Her advocate to the loud'st. We do not know
How he may soften at the sight o' the child.
The silence often of pure innocence
Persuades when speaking fails.
Emil. Most worthy madam,
Your honour and your goodness is so evident
That your free undertaking cannot miss
A thriving issue. There is no lady living
So meet for this great errand. Please your ladyship
To visit the next room, I'll presently
Acquaint the Queen of your most noble offer;
Who but to-day hammer'd of this design,
But durst not tempt a minister of honour,
Lest she should be denied.
Paul. Tell her, Emilia,
I'll use that tongue I have. If wit flow from 't
As boldness from my bosom, let 't not be doubted
I shall do good.
Emil. Now be you blest for it!
I'll to the Queen. Please you, come something nearer.
Gaol. Madam, if 't please the Queen to send the babe,
I know not what I shall incur to pass it,
Having no warrant.
Paul. You need not fear it, sir.
This child was prisoner to the womb and is
By law and process of great nature thence
Freed and enfranchised, not a party to
The anger of the King nor guilty of,
If any be, the trespass of the Queen.
Gaol. I do believe it.
Paul. Do not you fear. Upon mine honour, I
Will stand betwixt you and danger. [*Exeunt.*

SCENE III. *A room in Leontes' palace*

Enter LEONTES, ANTIGONUS, LORDS, *and* SERVANTS.

Leon. Nor night nor day no rest. It is but weakness
To bear the matter thus; mere weakness. If
The cause were not in being—part o' the cause,
She the adulteress; for the harlot king
Is quite beyond mine arm, out of the blank
And level of my brain, plot-proof; but she
I can hook to me. Say that she were gone,
Given to the fire, a moiety of my rest
Might come to me again. Who's there?
1st Serv. My lord?
Leon. How does the boy?
1st Serv. He took good rest to-night;
'Tis hoped his sickness is discharged.
Leon. To see his nobleness!
Conceiving the dishonour of his mother,
He straight declined, droop'd, took it deeply,
Fasten'd and fix'd the shame on 't in himself,
Threw off his spirit, his appetite, his sleep,
And downright languish'd. Leave me solely. Go,
See how he fares. [*Exit* SERVANT] Fie, fie! no thought of him.
The very thought of my revenges that way
Recoil upon me. In himself too mighty,
And in his parties, his alliance; let him be
Until a time may serve. For present vengeance,
Take it on her. Camillo and Polixenes
Laugh at me, make their pastime at my sorrow;
They should not laugh if I could reach them, nor
Shall she within my power.

Enter PAULINA, *with a child.*

1st Lord. You must not enter.
Paul. Nay, rather, good my lords, be second to me.
Fear you his tyrannous passion more, alas,
Than the Queen's life? a gracious innocent soul,
More free than he is jealous.
Ant. That's enough.
2nd Serv. Madam, he hath not slept to-night; commanded
None should come at him.
Paul. Not so hot, good sir.
I come to bring him sleep. 'Tis such as you,

That creep like shadows by him and do sigh
At each his needless heavings, such as you
Nourish the cause of his awaking. I
Do come with words as medicinal as true,
Honest as either, to purge him of that humour
That presses him from sleep.
Leon. What noise there, ho?
Paul. No noise, my lord; but needful conference
About some gossips for your Highness.
Leon. How!
Away with that audacious lady! Antigonus,
I charged thee that she should not come about
me.
I knew she would.
Ant. I told her so, my lord,
On your displeasure's peril and on mine,
She should not visit you.
Leon. What, canst not rule her?
Paul. From all dishonesty he can. In this,
Unless he take the course that you have done,
Commit me for committing honour, trust it,
He shall not rule me.
Ant. La you now, you hear.
When she will take the rein I let her run;
But she'll not stumble.
Paul. Good my liege, I come;
And, I beseech you, hear me, who profess
Myself your loyal servant, your physician,
Your most obedient counsellor, yet that dare
Less appear so in comforting your evils,
Than such as most seem yours. I say, I come
From your good queen.
Leon. Good queen!
Paul. Good queen, my lord,
Good queen; I say good queen;
And would by combat make her good, so were I
A man, the worst about you.
Leon. Force her hence.
Paul. Let him that makes but trifles of his eyes
First hand me. On mine own accord I'll off;
But first I'll do my errand. The good queen,
For she is good, hath brought you forth a daugh-
ter;
Here 'tis; commends it to your blessing.
Laying down the child.
Leon. Out!
A mankind witch! Hence with her, out o' door!
A most intelligencing bawd!
Paul. Not so.
I am as ignorant in that as you
In so entitling me, and no less honest
Than you are mad; which is enough, I'll warrant,
As this world goes, to pass for honest.
Leon. Traitors!
Will you not push her out? Give her the bastard.
Thou dotard! thou art woman-tired, unroosted
By thy dame Partlet here. Take up the bastard;
Take 't up, I say; give 't to thy crone.
Paul. For ever
Unvenerable be thy hands, if thou
Takest up the princess by that forced baseness
Which he has put upon 't!
Leon. He dreads his wife.
Paul. So I would you did; then 'twere past all
doubt
You'd call your children yours.
Leon. A nest of traitors!
Ant. I am none, by this good light.
Paul. Nor I, nor any
But one that's here, and that's himself, for he
The sacred honour of himself, his queen's,
His hopeful son's, his babe's, betrays to slander,
Whose sting is sharper than the sword's; and
will not—
For, as the case now stands, it is a curse
He cannot be compell'd to 't—once remove
The root of his opinion, which is rotten
As ever oak or stone was sound.
Leon. A callet
Of boundless tongue, who late hath beat her hus-
band
And now baits me! This brat is none of mine;
It is the issue of Polixenes.
Hence with it, and together with the dam
Commit them to the fire!
Paul. It is yours;
And, might we lay the old proverb to your
charge,
So like you, 'tis the worse. Behold, my lords,
Although the print be little, the whole matter
And copy of the father, eye, nose, lip,
The trick of's frown, his forehead, nay, the val-
ley,
The pretty dimples of his chin and cheek,
His smiles,
The very mould and frame of hand, nail, finger.
And thou, good goddess Nature, which hast
made it
So like to him that got it, if thou hast
The ordering of the mind too, 'mongst all colours
No yellow in 't, lest she suspect, as he does,
Her children not her husband's!
Leon. A gross hag!
And, lozel, thou art worthy to be hang'd,
That wilt not stay her tongue.
Ant. Hang all the husbands
That cannot do that feat, you'll leave yourself
Hardly one subject.
Leon. Once more, take her hence.
Paul. A most unworthy and unnatural lord
Can do no more.
Leon. I'll ha' thee burnt.

Paul. I care not.
It is an heretic that makes the fire,
Not she which burns in 't. I'll not call you tyrant;
But this most cruel usage of your queen,
Not able to produce more accusation
Than your own weak-hinged fancy, something savours
Of tyranny and will ignoble make you,
Yea, scandalous to the world.
Leon. On your allegiance,
Out of the chamber with her! Were I a tyrant,
Where were her life? she durst not call me so,
If she did know me one. Away with her!
Paul. I pray you, do not push me; I'll be gone.
Look to your babe, my lord; 'tis yours. Jove send her
A better guiding spirit! What needs these hands?
You, that are thus so tender o'er his follies,
Will never do him good, not one of you.
So, so; farewell; we are gone. [*Exit.*
Leon. Thou, traitor, hast set on thy wife to this.
My child? away with 't! Even thou, that hast
A heart so tender o'er it, take it hence
And see it instantly consumed with fire;
Even thou and none but thou. Take it up straight:
Within this hour bring me word 'tis done,
And by good testimony, or I'll seize thy life,
With what thou else call'st thine. If thou refuse
And wilt encounter with my wrath, say so;
The bastard brains with these my proper hands
Shall I dash out. Go, take it to the fire;
For thou set'st on thy wife.
Ant. I did not, sir.
These lords, my noble fellows, if they please,
Can clear me in 't.
Lords. We can. My royal liege,
He is not guilty of her coming hither.
Leon. You're liars all.
1st Lord. Beseech your Highness, give us better credit.
We have always truly served you, and beseech you
So to esteem of us, and on our knees we beg,
As recompense of our dear services
Past and to come, that you do change this purpose,
Which being so horrible, so bloody, must
Lead on to some foul issue: we all kneel.
Leon. I am a feather for each wind that blows.
Shall I live on to see this bastard kneel
And call me father? Better burn it now
Than curse it then. But be it; let it live.
It shall not neither. You, sir, come you hither;
You that have been so tenderly officious
With Lady Margery, your midwife there,
To save this bastard's life—for 'tis a bastard,
So sure as this beard's grey—what will you adventure
To save this brat's life?
Ant. Anything, my lord,
That my ability may undergo
And nobleness impose; at least thus much:
I'll pawn the little blood which I have left
To save the innocent. Anything possible.
Leon. It shall be possible. Swear by this sword
Thou wilt perform my bidding.
Ant. I will, my lord!
Leon. Mark and perform it, see'st thou? for the fail
Of any point in 't shall not only be
Death to thyself but to thy lewd-tongued wife,
Whom for this time we pardon. We enjoin thee,
As thou art liege-man to us, that thou carry
This female bastard hence and that thou bear it
To some remote and desert place quite out
Of our dominions, and that there thou leave it,
Without more mercy, to its own protection
And favour of the climate. As by strange fortune
It came to us, I do in justice charge thee,
On thy soul's peril and thy body's torture,
That thou commend it strangely to some place
Where chance may nurse or end it. Take it up.
Ant. I swear to do this, though a present death
Had been more merciful. Come on, poor babe.
Some powerful spirit instruct the kites and ravens
To be thy nurses! Wolves and bears, they say,
Casting their savageness aside have done
Like offices of pity. Sir, be prosperous
In more than this deed does require! And blessing
Against this cruelty fight on thy side,
Poor thing, condemn'd to loss!
[*Exit with the child.*
Leon. No, I'll not rear
Another's issue.

Enter a SERVANT.

Serv. Please your Highness, posts
From those you sent to the oracle are come
An hour since. Cleomenes and Dion,
Being well arrived from Delphos, are both landed,
Hasting to the court.
1st Lord. So please you, sir, their speed
Hath been beyond account.
Leon. Twenty three days
They have been absent. 'Tis good speed; foretells
The great Apollo suddenly will have
The truth of this appear. Prepare you, lords;
Summon a session, that we may arraign
Our most disloyal lady, for, as she hath
Been publicly accused, so shall she have

A just and open trial. While she lives
My heart will be a burthen to me. Leave me,
And think upon my bidding. [*Exeunt.*

ACT III

Scene i. *A sea-port in Sicilia*

Enter CLEOMENES *and* DION.

Cleo. The climate's delicate, the air most sweet,
Fertile the isle, the temple much surpassing
The common praise it bears.
Dion. I shall report,
For most it caught me, the celestial habits,
Methinks I so should term them, and the reverence
Of the grave wearers. O, the sacrifice!
How ceremonious, solemn, and unearthly
It was i' the offering!
Cleo. But of all, the burst
And the ear-deafening voice o' the oracle,
Kin to Jove's thunder, so surprised my sense
That I was nothing.
Dion. If the event o' the journey
Prove as successful to the Queen—O be 't so!—
As it hath been to us rare, pleasant, speedy,
The time is worth the use on 't.
Cleo. Great Apollo
Turn all to the best! These proclamations,
So forcing faults upon Hermione,
I little like.
Dion. The violent carriage of it
Will clear or end the business. When the oracle,
Thus by Apollo's great divine seal'd up,
Shall the contents discover, something rare
Even then will rush to knowledge. Go; fresh horses!
And gracious be the issue! [*Exeunt.*

Scene ii. *A court of Justice*

Enter LEONTES, LORDS, *and* OFFICERS.

Leon. This sessions, to our great grief we pronounce,
Even pushes 'gainst our heart: the party tried
The daughter of a king, our wife, and one
Of us too much beloved. Let us be clear'd
Of being tyrannous, since we so openly
Proceed in justice, which shall have due course,
Even to the guilt or the purgation.
Produce the prisoner.
Officer. It is his Highness' pleasure that the Queen
Appear in person here in court. Silence!

Enter HERMIONE *guarded;* PAULINA *and* LADIES *attending.*

Leon. Read the indictment.

Off. [*Reads*] "Hermione, Queen to the worthy Leontes, King of Sicilia, thou art here accused and arraigned of high treason, in committing adultery with Polixenes, King of Bohemia, and conspiring with Camillo to take away the life of our sovereign lord the King, thy royal husband: the pretence whereof being by circumstances partly laid open, thou, Hermione, contrary to the faith and allegiance of a true subject, didst counsel and aid them, for their better safety, to fly away by night."

Her. Since what I am to say must be but that
Which contradicts my accusation and
The testimony on my part no other
But what comes from myself, it shall scarce boot me
To say "Not guilty." Mine integrity,
Being counted falsehood, shall, as I express it,
Be so received. But thus: if powers divine
Behold our human actions, as they do,
I doubt not then but innocence shall make
False accusation blush and tyranny
Tremble at patience. You, my lord, best know,
Who least will seem to do so, my past life
Hath been as continent, as chaste, as true,
As I am now unhappy; which is more
Than history can pattern, though devised
And play'd to take spectators. For behold me
A fellow of the royal bed, which owe
A moiety of the throne, a great king's daughter,
The mother to a hopeful prince, here standing
To prate and talk for life and honour 'fore
Who please to come and hear. For life, I prize it
As I weigh grief, which I would spare; for honour,
'Tis a derivative from me to mine,
And only that I stand for. I appeal
To your own conscience, sir, before Polixenes
Came to your court, how I was in your grace,
How merited to be so; since he came,
With what encounter so uncurrent I
Have strain'd to appear thus; if one jot beyond
The bound of honour, or in act or will
That way inclining, harden'd be the hearts
Of all that hear me, and my near'st of kin
Cry fie upon my grave!
Leon. I ne'er heard yet
That any of these bolder vices wanted
Less impudence to gainsay what they did
Than to perform it first.
Her. That's true enough;
Though 'tis a saying, sir, not due to me.
Leon. You will not own it.
Her. More than mistress of
Which comes to me in name of fault, I must not
At all acknowledge. For Polixenes,

With whom I am accused, I do confess
I loved him as in honour he required,
With such a kind of love as might become
A lady like me, with a love even such,
So and no other, as yourself commanded;
Which not to have done I think had been in me
Both disobedience and ingratitude
To you and toward your friend, whose love had spoke,
Even since it could speak, from an infant, freely
That it was yours. Now, for conspiracy,
I know not how it tastes; though it be dish'd
For me to try how. All I know of it
Is that Camillo was an honest man;
And why he left your court, the gods themselves,
Wotting no more than I, are ignorant.
Leon. You knew of his departure, as you know
What you have underta'en to do in's absence.
Her. Sir,
You speak a language that I understand not.
My life stands in the level of your dreams,
Which I'll lay down.
Leon. Your actions are my dreams;
You had a bastard by Polixenes,
And I but dream'd it. As you were past all shame—
Those of your fact are so—so past all truth,
Which to deny concerns more than avails; for as
Thy brat hath been cast out, like to itself,
No father owning it—which is, indeed,
More criminal in thee than it—so thou
Shalt feel our justice, in whose easiest passage
Look for no less than death.
Her. Sir, spare your threats.
The bug which you would fright me with I seek.
To me can life be no commodity.
The crown and comfort of my life, your favour,
I do give lost; for I do feel it gone,
But know not how it went. My second joy
And first-fruits of my body, from his presence
I am barr'd, like one infectious. My third comfort,
Starr'd most unluckily, is from my breast,
The innocent milk in it most innocent mouth,
Haled out to murder; myself on every post
Proclaim'd a strumpet; with immodest hatred
The child-bed privilege denied, which 'longs
To women of all fashion; lastly, hurried
Here to this place, i' the open air, before
I have got strength of limit. Now, my liege,
Tell me what blessings I have here alive,
That I should fear to die? Therefore proceed.
But yet hear this; mistake me not; no life,
I prize it not a straw, but for mine honour,
Which I would free, if I shall be condemn'd
Upon surmises, all proofs sleeping else
But what your jealousies awake, I tell you
'Tis rigour and not law. Your honours all,
I do refer me to the oracle.
Apollo be my judge!
1st Lord. This your request
Is altogether just; therefore bring forth,
And in Apollo's name, his oracle.
[*Exeunt certain Officers*.
Her. The Emperor of Russia was my father.
O that he were alive, and here beholding
His daughter's trial! that he did but see
The flatness of my misery, yet with eyes
Of pity, not revenge!

Re-enter OFFICERS, *with* CLEOMENES *and* DION.

Off. You here shall swear upon this sword of justice,
That you, Cleomenes and Dion, have
Been both at Delphos, and from thence have brought
This seal'd-up oracle, by the hand deliver'd
Of great Apollo's priest and that since then
You have not dared to break the holy seal
Nor read the secrets in 't.
Cleo. Dion. All this we swear.
Leon. Break up the seals and read.
Off. [*Reads*] "Hermione is chaste; Polixenes blameless; Camillo a true subject; Leontes a jealous tyrant; his innocent babe truly begotten; and the King shall live without an heir, if that which is lost be not found."
Lords. Now blessed be the great Apollo!
Her. Praised!
Leon. Hast thou read truth?
Off. Ay, my lord; even so
As it is here set down.
Leon. There is no truth at all i' the oracle.
The sessions shall proceed. This is mere falsehood.

Enter SERVANT.

Serv. My lord the King, the King!
Leon. What is the business?
Serv. O sir, I shall be hated to report it!
The Prince your son, with mere conceit and fear
Of the Queen's speed, is gone.
Leon. How! gone!
Serv. Is dead.
Leon. Apollo's angry; and the heavens themselves
Do strike at my injustice. [HERMIONE *swoons*.]
How now there!
Paul. This news is mortal to the Queen. Look down
And see what death is doing.
Leon. Take her hence.

Her heart is but o'ercharged; she will recover.
I have too much believed mine own suspicion.
Beseech you, tenderly apply to her
Some remedies for life.
[*Exeunt* PAULINA *and* LADIES, *with* HERMIONE.
Apollo, pardon
My great profaneness 'gainst thine oracle!
I'll reconcile me to Polixenes,
New woo my queen, recall the good Camillo,
Whom I proclaim a man of truth, of mercy;
For, being transported by my jealousies
To bloody thoughts and to revenge, I chose
Camillo for the minister to poison
My friend Polixenes; which had been done,
But that the good mind of Camillo tardied
My swift command, though I with death and with
Reward did threaten and encourage him,
Not doing 't and being done. He, most humane
And fill'd with honour, to my kingly guest
Unclasp'd my practice, quit his fortunes here,
Which you knew great, and to the hazard
Of all incertainties himself commended,
No richer than his honour. How he glisters
Thorough my rust! and how his piety
Does my deeds make the blacker!

Re-enter PAULINA.

Paul. Woe the while!
O, cut my lace, lest my heart, cracking it,
Break too!
1st Lord. What fit is this, good lady?
Paul. What studied torments, tyrant, hast for me?
What wheels? racks? fires? what flaying? boiling?
In leads or oils? what old or newer torture
Must I receive, whose every word deserves
To taste of thy most worst? Thy tyranny
Together working with thy jealousies,
Fancies too weak for boys, too green and idle
For girls of nine, O, think what they have done
And then run mad indeed, stark mad! for all
Thy by-gone fooleries were but spices of it.
That thou betray'dst Polixenes, 'twas nothing;
That did but show thee of a fool, inconstant
And damnable ingrateful; nor was 't much,
Thou wouldst have poison'd good Camillo's honour,
To have him kill a king; poor trespasses,
More monstrous standing by; whereof I reckon
The casting forth to crows thy baby-daughter
To be or none or little; though a devil
Would have shed water out of fire ere done 't;
Nor is 't directly laid to thee, the death
Of the young prince, whose honourable thoughts,
Thoughts high for one so tender, cleft the heart
That could conceive a gross and foolish sire
Blemish'd his gracious dam; this is not, no,
Laid to thy answer: but the last—O lords,
When I have said, cry "woe!"—the Queen, the Queen,
The sweet'st, dear'st creature's dead, and vengeance for 't
Not dropp'd down yet.
1st Lord. The higher powers forbid!
Paul. I say she's dead; I'll swear 't. If word nor oath
Prevail not, go and see. If you can bring
Tincture or lustre in her lip, her eye,
Heat outwardly or breath within, I'll serve you
As I would do the gods. But, O thou tyrant!
Do not repent these things, for they are heavier
Than all thy woes can stir; therefore betake thee
To nothing but despair. A thousand knees
Ten thousand years together, naked, fasting,
Upon a barren mountain, and still winter
In storm perpetual, could not move the gods
To look that way thou wert.
Leon. Go on, go on;
Thou canst not speak too much. I have deserved
All tongues to talk their bitterest.
1st Lord. Say no more.
Howe'er the business goes, you have made fault
I' the boldness of your speech.
Paul. I am sorry for 't.
All faults I make, when I shall come to know them,
I do repent. Alas! I have show'd too much
The rashness of a woman; he is touch'd
To the noble heart. What's gone and what's past help
Should be past grief. Do not receive affliction
At my petition; I beseech you, rather
Let me be punish'd, that have minded you
Of what you should forget. Now, good my liege,
Sir, royal sir, forgive a foolish woman.
The love I bore your queen—lo, fool again!—
I'll speak of her no more, nor of your children;
I'll not remember you of my own lord,
Who is lost too. Take your patience to you,
And I'll say nothing.
Leon. Thou didst speak but well
When most the truth; which I receive much better
Than to be pitied of thee. Prithee, bring me
To the dead bodies of my queen and son.
One grave shall be for both; upon them shall
The causes of their death appear, unto
Our shame perpetual. Once a day I'll visit
The chapel where they lie, and tears shed there
Shall be my recreation. So long as nature

Will bear up with this exercise, so long
I daily vow to use it. Come and lead me
Unto these sorrows. [*Exeunt.*

SCENE III. *Bohemia: a desert country near the sea*

Enter ANTIGONUS *with a Child, and a* MARINER.

Ant. Thou art perfect then, our ship hath touch'd upon
The deserts of Bohemia?
Mar. Ay, my lord; and fear
We have landed in ill time. The skies look grimly
And threaten present blusters. In my conscience,
The heavens with that we have in hand are angry
And frown upon 's.
Ant. Their sacred wills be done! Go, get aboard;
Look to thy bark. I'll not be long before
I call upon thee.
Mar. Make your best haste, and go not
Too far i' the land; 'tis like to be loud weather.
Besides, this place is famous for the creatures
Of prey that keep upon 't.
Ant. Go thou away.
I'll follow instantly.
Mar. I am glad at heart
To be so rid o' the business. [*Exit.*
Ant. Come, poor babe.
I have heard, but not believed, the spirits o' the dead
May walk again. If such thing be, thy mother
Appear'd to me last night, for ne'er was dream
So like a waking. To me comes a creature,
Sometimes her head on one side, some another;
I never saw a vessel of like sorrow,
So fill'd and so becoming. In pure white robes,
Like very sanctity, she did approach
My cabin where I lay; thrice bow'd before me,
And gasping to begin some speech, her eyes
Became two spouts; the fury spent, anon
Did this break from her: "Good Antigonus,
Since fate, against thy better disposition,
Hath made thy person for the thrower-out
Of my poor babe, according to thine oath,
Places remote enough are in Bohemia,
There weep and leave it crying; and, for the babe
Is counted lost for ever, Perdita,
I prithee, call 't. For this ungentle business,
Put on thee by my lord, thou ne'er shalt see
Thy wife Paulina more." And so, with shrieks,
She melted into air. Affrighted much,
I did in time collect myself and thought
This was so and no slumber. Dreams are toys;
Yet for this once, yea, superstitiously,
I will be squared by this. I do believe
Hermione hath suffer'd death, and that
Apollo would, this being indeed the issue
Of King Polixenes, it should here be laid,
Either for life or death, upon the earth
Of its right father. Blossom, speed thee well!
There lie, and there thy character; there these;
Which may, if fortune please, both breed thee, pretty,
Laying down the babe, with a paper and a bundle.]
And still rest thine. The storm begins. Poor wretch,
That for thy mother's fault art thus exposed
To loss and what may follow! Weep I cannot,
But my heart bleeds; and most accursed am I
To be by oath enjoin'd to this. Farewell!
The day frowns more and more; thou'rt like to have
A lullaby too rough. I never saw
The heavens so dim by day. A savage clamour!
Well may I get aboard! This is the chase:
I am gone for ever. [*Exit, pursued by a bear.*

Enter a SHEPHERD.

Shep. I would there were no age between sixteen and three-and-twenty, or that youth would sleep out the rest; for there is nothing in the between but getting wenches with child, wronging the ancientry, stealing, fighting—Hark you now! Would any but these boiled brains of nineteen and two-and-twenty hunt this weather? They have scared away two of my best sheep, which I fear the wolf will sooner find than the master: if anywhere I have them, 'tis by the seaside, browsing of ivy. Good luck, an 't be thy will! what have we here? Mercy on 's, a barne; a very pretty barne! A boy or a child, I wonder? A pretty one; a very pretty one: sure, some 'scape. Though I am not bookish, yet I can read waiting-gentlewoman in the 'scape. This has been some stair-work, some trunk-work, some behind-door-work; they were warmer that got this than the poor thing is here. I'll take it up for pity; yet I'll tarry till my son come; he hallooed but even now. Whoa, ho, hoa!

Enter CLOWN.

Clo. Hilloa, loa!
Shep. What, art so near? If thou'lt see a thing to talk on when thou art dead and rotten, come hither. What ailest thou, man?
Clo. I have seen two such sights, by sea and by land! but I am not to say it is a sea, for it is now

the sky: betwixt the firmament and it you cannot thrust a bodkin's point.

Shep. Why, boy, how is it?

Clo. I would you did but see how it chafes, how it rages, how it takes up the shore! but that's not to the point. O, the most piteous cry of the poor souls! sometimes to see 'em, and not to see 'em; now the ship boring the moon with her mainmast, and anon swallowed with yest and froth, as you'd thrust a cork into a hogshead. And then for the land-service, to see how the bear tore out his shoulder-bone; how he cried to me for help and said his name was Antigonus, a nobleman. But to make an end of the ship, to see how the sea flap-dragoned it; but, first, how the poor souls roared, and the sea mocked them; and how the poor gentleman roared and the bear mocked him, both roaring louder than the sea or weather.

Shep. Name of mercy, when was this, boy?

Clo. Now, now; I have not winked since I saw these sights. The men are not yet cold under water, nor the bear half dined on the gentleman. He's at it now.

Shep. Would I had been by, to have helped the old man!

Clo. I would you had been by the ship side, to have helped her; there your charity would have lacked footing.

Shep. Heavy matters! heavy matters! but look thee here, boy. Now bless thyself; thou mettest with things dying, I with things new-born. Here's a sight for thee; look thee, a bearing-cloth for a squire's child! look thee here; take up, take up, boy; open 't. So, let's see. It was told me I should be rich by the fairies. This is some changeling; open 't. What's within, boy?

Clo. You're a made old man; if the sins of your youth are forgiven you, you're well to live. Gold! all gold!

Shep. This is fairy gold, boy, and 'twill prove so. Up with 't, keep it close. Home, home, the next way. We are lucky, boy; and to be so still requires nothing but secrecy. Let my sheep go. Come, good boy, the next way home.

Clo. Go you the next way with your findings. I'll go see if the bear be gone from the gentleman and how much he hath eaten. They are never curst but when they are hungry. If there be any of him left, I'll bury it.

Shep. That's a good deed. If thou mayest discern by that which is left of him what he is, fetch me to the sight of him.

Clo. Marry, will I; and you shall help to put him i' the ground.

Shep. 'Tis a lucky day, boy, and we'll do good deeds on 't. [*Exeunt.*

ACT IV

SCENE I.

Enter TIME, *the* Chorus.

Time. I, that please some, try all, both joy and terror
Of good and bad, that makes and unfolds error,
Now take upon me, in the name of Time,
To use my wings. Impute it not a crime
To me or my swift passage, that I slide
O'er sixteen years and leave the growth untried
Of that wide gap, since it is in my power
To o'erthrow law and in one self-born hour
To plant and o'erwhelm custom. Let me pass
The same I am, ere ancient'st order was
Or what is now received. I witness to
The times that brought them in; so shall I do
To the freshest things now reigning and make stale
The glistering of this present, as my tale
Now seems to it. Your patience this allowing,
I turn my glass and give my scene such growing
As you had slept between. Leontes leaving,
The effects of his fond jealousies so grieving
That he shuts up himself, imagine me,
Gentle spectators, that I now may be
In fair Bohemia; and remember well,
I mentioned a son o' the King's, which Florizel
I now name to you; and with speed so pace
To speak of Perdita, now grown in grace
Equal with wondering. What of her ensues
I list not prophesy; but let Time's news
Be known when 'tis brought forth. A shepherd's daughter,
And what to her adheres, which follows after,
Is the argument of Time. Of this allow,
If ever you have spent time worse ere now;
If never, yet that Time himself doth say
He wishes earnestly you never may. [*Exit.*

SCENE II. *Bohemia: the palace of Polixenes*

Enter POLIXENES *and* CAMILLO.

Pol. I pray thee, good Camillo, be no more importunate. 'Tis a sickness denying thee any thing; a death to grant this.

Cam. It is fifteen years since I saw my country; though I have for the most part been aired abroad, I desire to lay my bones there. Besides, the penitent king, my master, hath sent for me; to whose feeling sorrows I might be some allay, or I o'erween to think so, which is another spur to my departure.

Pol. As thou lovest me, Camillo, wipe not out the rest of thy services by leaving me now. The need I have of thee thine own goodness hath made; better not to have had thee than thus to want thee. Thou, having made me businesses which none without thee can sufficiently manage, must either stay to execute them thyself or take away with thee the very services thou hast done; which if I have not enough considered, as too much I cannot, to be more thankful to thee shall be my study, and my profit therein the heaping friendships. Of that fatal country, Sicilia, prithee speak no more; whose very naming punishes me with the remembrance of that penitent, as thou callest him, and reconciled king, my brother; whose loss of his most precious queen and children are even now to be afresh lamented. Say to me, when sawest thou the Prince Florizel, my son? Kings are no less unhappy, their issue not being gracious, than they are in losing them when they have approved their virtues.

Cam. Sir, it is three days since I saw the Prince. What his happier affairs may be, are to me unknown; but I have missingly noted, he is of late much retired from court and is less frequent to his princely exercises than formerly he hath appeared.

Pol. I have considered so much, Camillo, and with some care; so far that I have eyes under my service which look upon his removedness; from whom I have this intelligence, that he is seldom from the house of a most homely shepherd; a man, they say, that from very nothing, and beyond the imagination of his neighbours, is grown into an unspeakable estate.

Cam. I have heard, sir, of such a man, who hath a daughter of most rare note. The report of her is extended more than can be thought to begin from such a cottage.

Pol. That's likewise part of my intelligence; but, I fear, the angle that plucks our son thither. Thou shalt accompany us to the place; where we will, not appearing what we are, have some question with the shepherd; from whose simplicity I think it not uneasy to get the cause of my son's resort thither. Prithee, be my present partner in this business, and lay aside the thoughts of Sicilia.

Cam. I willingly obey your command.

Pol. My best Camillo! We must disguise ourselves. [*Exeunt.*

SCENE III. *A road near the Shepherd's cottage*

Enter AUTOLYCUS, *singing.*

"When daffodils begin to peer,
With heigh! the doxy over the dale,
Why, then comes in the sweet o' the year;
For the red blood reigns in the winter's pale.

"The white sheet bleaching on the hedge,
With heigh! the sweet birds, O, how they sing!
Doth set my pugging tooth on edge;
For a quart of ale is a dish for a king.

"The lark, that tirra-lyra chants,
With heigh! with heigh! the thrush and the jay,
Are summer songs for me and my aunts,
While we lie tumbling in the hay."

I have served Prince Florizel and in my time wore three-pile; but now I am out of service.

"But shall I go mourn for that, my dear?
The pale moon shines by night:
And when I wander here and there,
I then do most go right.

"If tinkers may have leave to live,
And bear the sow-skin budget,
Then my account I well may give,
And in the stocks avouch it."

My traffic is sheets; when the kite builds, look to lesser linen. My father named me Autolycus; who being, as I am, littered under Mercury, was likewise a snapper-up of unconsidered trifles. With die and drab I purchased this caparison, and my revenue is the silly cheat. Gallows and knock are too powerful on the highway; beating and hanging are terrors to me; for the life to come, I sleep out the thought of it. A prize! a prize!

Enter CLOWN.

Clo. Let me see: every 'leven wether tods; every tod yields pound and odd shilling; fifteen hundred shorn, what comes the wool to?

Aut. [*Aside*] If the springe hold, the cock's mine.

Clo. I cannot do 't without counters. Let me see; what am I to buy for our sheep-shearing feast? Three pound of sugar, five pound of currants, rice—what will this sister of mine do with rice? But my father hath made her mistress of the feast, and she lays it on. She hath made me four and twenty nosegays for the shearers, three-man song-men all, and very good ones; but they are most of them means and bases; but one puritan amongst them, and he sings psalms to hornpipes. I must have saffron to colour the warden pies; mace; dates?—none, that's out of my note; nutmegs, seven; a race or two of ginger, but that I may beg; four pound of prunes, and as many of raisins o' the sun.

Aut. O that ever I was born!

Grovelling on the ground.

Clo. I' the name of me—

Aut. O, help me, help me! pluck but off these rags; and then, death, death!

Clo. Alack, poor soul! thou hast need of more rags to lay on thee, rather than have these off.

Aut. O sir, the loathsomeness of them offends me more than the stripes I have received, which are mighty ones and millions.

Clo. Alas, poor man! a million of beating may come to a great matter.

Aut. I am robbed, sir, and beaten; my money and apparel ta'en from me, and these detestable things put upon me.

Clo. What, by a horseman, or a footman?

Aut. A footman, sweet sir, a footman.

Clo. Indeed, he should be a footman by the garments he has left with thee. If this be a horseman's coat, it hath seen very hot service. Lend me thy hand, I'll help thee. Come, lend me thy hand.

Aut. O, good sir, tenderly, O!

Clo. Alas, poor soul!

Aut. O, good sir, softly, good sir! I fear, sir, my shoulder-blade is out.

Clo. How now! canst stand?

Aut. [*Picking his pocket*] Softly, dear sir; good sir, softly. You ha' done me a charitable office.

Clo. Dost lack any money? I have a little money for thee.

Aut. No, good sweet sir; no, I beseech you, sir. I have a kinsman not past three quarters of a mile hence, unto whom I was going; I shall there have money, or anything I want. Offer me no money, I pray you; that kills my heart.

Clo. What manner of fellow was he that robbed you?

Aut. A fellow, sir, that I have known to go about with troll-my-dames. I knew him once a servant of the Prince. I cannot tell, good sir, for which of his virtues it was, but he was certainly whipped out of the court.

Clo. His vices, you would say; there's no virtue whipped out of the court. They cherish it to make it stay there; and yet it will no more but abide.

Aut. Vices, I would say, sir. I know this man well. He hath been since an ape-bearer; then a process-server, a bailiff; then he compassed a motion of the Prodigal Son, and married a tinker's wife within a mile where my land and living lies; and, having flown over many knavish professions, he settled only in rogue. Some call him Autolycus.

Clo. Out upon him! prig, for my life, prig. He haunts wakes, fairs and bear-baitings.

Aut. Very true, sir; he, sir, he; that's the rogue that put me into this apparel.

Clo. Not a more cowardly rogue in all Bohemia. If you had but looked big and spit at him, he'd have run.

Aut. I must confess to you, sir, I am no fighter. I am false of heart that way; and that he knew, I warrant him.

Clo. How do you now?

Aut. Sweet sir, much better than I was; I can stand and walk. I will even take my leave of you, and pace softly towards my kinsman's.

Clo. Shall I bring thee on the way?

Aut. No, good-faced sir; no, sweet sir.

Clo. Then fare thee well. I must go buy spices for our sheep-shearing.

Aut. Prosper you, sweet sir! [*Exit* CLOWN.] Your purse is not hot enough to purchase your spice. I'll be with you at your sheep-shearing too. If I make not this cheat bring out another and the shearers prove sheep, let me be unrolled and my name put in the book of virtue!

[*Sings*] "Jog on, jog on, the foot-path way,
And merrily hent the stile-a;
A merry heart goes all the day,
Your sad tires in a mile-a." [*Exit.*

SCENE IV. *The Shepherd's cottage*

Enter FLORIZEL *and* PERDITA.

Flo. These your unusual weeds to each part of you
Do give a life; no shepherdess, but Flora
Peering in April's front. This your sheep-shearing
Is as a meeting of the petty gods,
And you the queen on 't.

Per. Sir, my gracious lord,
To chide at your extremes it not becomes me.
O, pardon, that I name them! Your high self,
The gracious mark o' the land, you have obscured
With a swain's wearing, and me, poor lowly maid,
Most goddess-like prank'd up. But that our feasts
In every mess have folly and the feeders
Digest it with a custom, I should blush
To see you so attired, sworn, I think,
To show myself a glass.

Flo. I bless the time
When my good falcon made her flight across
Thy father's ground.

Per. Now Jove afford you cause!
To me the difference forges dread; your greatness
Hath not been used to fear. Even now I tremble
To think your father, by some accident,

Should pass this way as you did. O, the Fates!
How would he look, to see his work so noble
Vilely bound up? What would he say? Or how
Should I, in these my borrow'd flaunts, behold
The sternness of his presence?

Flo. Apprehend
Nothing but jollity. The gods themselves,
Humbling their deities to love, have taken
The shapes of beasts upon them. Jupiter
Became a bull, and bellow'd; the green Neptune
A ram, and bleated; and the fire-robed god,
Golden Apollo, a poor humble swain,
As I seem now. Their transformations
Were never for a piece of beauty rarer,
Nor in a way so chaste, since my desires
Run not before mine honour, nor my lusts
Burn hotter than my faith.

Per. O, but, sir,
Your resolution cannot hold, when 'tis
Opposed, as it must be, by the power of the King.
One of these two must be necessities,
Which then will speak, that you must change this purpose,
Or I my life.

Flo. Thou dearest Perdita,
With these forced thoughts, I prithee, darken not
The mirth o' the feast. Or I'll be thine, my fair,
Or not my father's. For I cannot be
Mine own, nor anything to any, if
I be not thine. To this I am most constant,
Though destiny say no. Be merry, gentle;
Strangle such thoughts as these with anything
That you behold the while. Your guests are coming.
Lift up your countenance, as it were the day
Of celebration of that nuptial which
We two have sworn shall come.

Per. O lady Fortune,
Stand you auspicious!

Flo. See, your guests approach.
Address yourself to entertain them sprightly,
And let's be red with mirth.

Enter SHEPHERD, CLOWN, MOPSA, DORCAS, *and others, with* POLIXENES *and* CAMILLO *disguised.*

Shep. Fie, daughter! when my old wife lived, upon
This day she was both pantler, butler, cook,
Both dame and servant; welcomed all, served all;
Would sing her song and dance her turn; now here,
At upper end o' the table, now i' the middle;
On his shoulder, and his; her face o' fire
With labour and the thing she took to quench it,
She would to each one sip. You are retired,
As if you were a feasted one and not
The hostess of the meeting. Pray you, bid
These unknown friends to 's welcome; for it is
A way to make us better friends, more known.
Come, quench your blushes and present yourself
That which you are, mistress o' the feast. Come on,
And bid us welcome to your sheep-shearing,
As your good flock shall prosper.

Per. [*To* POLIXENES] Sir, welcome.
It is my father's will I should take on me
The hostess-ship o' the day. [*To* CAMILLO] You're welcome, sir.
Give me those flowers there, Dorcas. Reverend sirs,
For you there's rosemary and rue; these keep
Seeming and savour all the winter long.
Grace and remembrance be to you both,
And welcome to our shearing!

Pol. Shepherdess—
A fair one are you—well you fit our ages
With flowers of winter.

Per. Sir, the year growing ancient,
Not yet on summer's death, nor on the birth
Of trembling winter, the fairest flowers o' the season
Are our carnations and streak'd gillyvors,
Which some call Nature's bastards. Of that kind
Our rustic garden's barren; and I care not
To get slips of them.

Pol. Wherefore, gentle maiden,
Do you neglect them?

Per. For I have heard it said
There is an art which in their piedness shares
With great creating Nature.

Pol. Say there be;
Yet Nature is made better by no mean
But Nature makes that mean; so, over that art
Which you say adds to Nature, is an art
That Nature makes. You see, sweet maid, we marry
A gentler scion to the wildest stock,
And make conceive a bark of baser kind
By bud of nobler race. This is an art
Which does mend Nature, change it rather, but
The art itself is Nature.

Per. So it is.

Pol. Then make your garden rich in gillyvors,
And do not call them bastards.

Per. I'll not put
The dibble in earth to set one slip of them;
No more than were I painted I would wish
This youth should say 'twere well and only therefore
Desire to breed by me. Here's flowers for you;

Hot lavender, mints, savory, marjoram;
The marigold, that goes to bed wi' the sun
And with him rises weeping. These are flowers
Of middle summer, and I think they are given
To men of middle age. You're very welcome.
Cam. I should leave grazing, were I of your flock,
And only live by gazing.
Per. Out, alas!
You'd be so lean, that blasts of January
Would blow you through and through. Now, my fair'st friend,
I would I had some flowers o' the spring that might
Become your time of day; and yours, and yours,
That wear upon your virgin branches yet
Your maidenheads growing. O Proserpina,
For the flowers now, that frighted thou let'st fall
From Dis's waggon! daffodils,
That come before the swallow dares, and take
The winds of March with beauty; violets dim,
But sweeter than the lids of Juno's eyes
Or Cytherea's breath; pale primroses,
That die unmarried, ere they can behold
Bright Phœbus in his strength—a malady
Most incident to maids; bold oxlips and
The crown imperial; lilies of all kinds,
The flower-de-luce being one! O, these I lack,
To make you garlands of, and my sweet friend,
To strew him o'er and o'er!
Flo. What, like a corse?
Per. No, like a bank for love to lie and play on;
Not like a corse; or if, not to be buried,
But quick and in mine arms. Come, take your flowers.
Methinks I play as I have seen them do
In Whitsun pastorals. Sure this robe of mine
Does change my disposition.
Flo. What you do
Still betters what is done. When you speak, sweet,
I'd have you do it ever. When you sing,
I'd have you buy and sell so, so give alms,
Pray so; and, for the ordering your affairs,
To sing them too. When you do dance, I wish you
A wave o' the sea, that you might ever do
Nothing but that; move still, still so,
And own no other function. Each your doing,
So singular in each particular,
Crowns what you are doing in the present deed,
That all your acts are queens.
Per. O Doricles,
Your praises are too large. But that your youth,
And the true blood which peepeth fairly through 't,
Do plainly give you out an unstain'd shepherd,
With wisdom I might fear, my Doricles,
You woo'd me the false way.
Flo. I think you have
As little skill to fear as I have purpose
To put you to 't. But come; our dance, I pray.
Your hand, my Perdita. So turtles pair,
That never mean to part.
Per. I'll swear for 'em.
Pol. This is the prettiest low-born lass that ever
Ran on the green-sward. Nothing she does or seems
But smacks of something greater than herself,
Too noble for this place.
Cam. He tells her something
That makes her blood look out. Good sooth, she is
The queen of curds and cream.
Clo. Come on, strike up!
Dor. Mopsa must be your mistress; marry, garlic,
To mend her kissing with!
Mop. Now, in good time!
Clo. Not a word, a word; we stand upon our manners.
Come, strike up!

Music. Here a dance of Shepherds and Shepherdesses.

Pol. Pray, good shepherd, what fair swain is this
Which dances with your daughter?
Shep. They call him Doricles; and boasts himself
To have a worthy feeding; but I have it
Upon his own report and I believe it;
He looks like sooth. He says he loves my daughter.
I think so too; for never gazed the moon
Upon the water as he'll stand and read
As 'twere my daughter's eyes; and, to be plain,
I think there is not half a kiss to choose
Who loves another best.
Pol. She dances featly.
Shep. So she does anything; though I report it,
That should be silent. If young Doricles
Do light upon her, she shall bring him that
Which he not dreams of.

Enter SERVANT.

Serv. O master, if you did but hear the pedlar at the door, you would never dance again after a tabor and pipe; no, the bagpipe could not move you. He sings several tunes faster than you'll tell money; he utters them as he had eaten ballads and all men's ears grew to his tunes.

Clo. He could never come better; he shall come in. I love a ballad but even too well, if it be doleful matter merrily set down, or a very pleasant thing indeed and sung lamentably.

Serv. He hath songs for man or woman, of all sizes; no milliner can so fit his customers with gloves. He has the prettiest love-songs for maids; so without bawdry, which is strange; with such delicate burthens of dildos and fadings, "jump her and thump her"; and where some stretch-mouthed rascal would, as it were, mean mischief and break a foul gap into the matter, he makes the maid to answer "Whoop, do me no harm good man"; puts him off, slights him, with "Whoop, do me no harm, good man."

Pol. This is a brave fellow.

Clo. Believe me, thou talkest of an admirable conceited fellow. Has he any unbraided wares?

Serv. He hath ribbons of all the colours i' the rainbow; points more than all the lawyers in Bohemia can learnedly handle, though they come to him by the gross; inkles, caddisses, cambrics, lawns. Why, he sings 'em over as they were gods or goddesses; you would think a smock were a she-angel, he so chants to the sleeve-hand and the work about the square on 't.

Clo. Prithee bring him in; and let him approach singing.

Per. Forewarn him that he use no scurrilous words in 's tunes. [*Exit* SERVANT.

Clo. You have of these pedlars, that have more in them than you'd think, sister.

Per. Ay, good brother, or go about to think.

Enter AUTOLYCUS, *singing.*

"Lawn as white as driven snow;
Cyprus black as e'er was crow;
Gloves as sweet as damask roses;
Masks for faces and for noses;
Bugle bracelet, necklace amber,
Perfume for a lady's chamber;
Golden quoifs and stomachers,
For my lads to give their dears;
Pins and poking-sticks of steel,
What maids lack from head to heel.
Come buy of me, come; come buy, come
buy;
Buy, lads, or else your lasses cry.
Come buy."

Clo. If I were not in love with Mopsa, thou shouldst take no money of me; but being enthralled as I am, it will also be the bondage of certain ribbons and gloves.

Mop. I was promised them against the feast; but they come not too late now.

Dor. He hath promised you more than that, or there be liars.

Mop. He hath paid you all he promised you. May be, he has paid you more, which will shame you to give him again.

Clo. Is there no manners left among maids? will they wear their plackets where they should bear their faces? Is there not milking-time, when you are going to bed, or kiln-hole, to whistle off these secrets, but you must be tittle-tattling before all our guests? 'tis well they are whispering. Clamour your tongues, and not a word more.

Mop. I have done. Come, you promised me a tawdry-lace and a pair of sweet gloves.

Clo. Have I not told thee how I was cozened by the way and lost all my money?

Aut. And indeed, sir, there are cozeners abroad; therefore it behoves men to be wary.

Clo. Fear not thou, man, thou shalt lose nothing here.

Aut. I hope so, sir; for I have about me many parcels of charge.

Clo. What hast here? ballads?

Mop. Pray now, buy some. I love a ballad in print o' life, for then we are sure they are true.

Aut. Here's one to a very doleful tune, how a usurer's wife was brought to bed of twenty money-bags at a burthen and how she longed to eat adders' heads and toads carbonadoed.

Mop. Is it true, think you?

Aut. Very true, and but a month old.

Dor. Bless me from marrying a usurer!

Aut. Here's the midwife's name to 't, one Mistress Tale-porter, and five or six honest wives that were present. Why should I carry lies abroad?

Mop. Pray you now, buy it.

Clo. Come on, lay it by, and let's first see moe ballads. We'll buy the other things anon.

Aut. Here's another ballad of a fish, that appeared upon the coast on Wednesday the fourscore of April, forty thousand fathom above water, and sung this ballad against the hard hearts of maids. It was thought she was a woman and was turned into a cold fish for she would not exchange flesh with one that loved her. The ballad is very pitiful and as true.

Dor. Is it true too, think you?

Aut. Five justices' hands at it, and witnesses more than my pack will hold.

Clo. Lay it by too. Another.

Aut. This is a merry ballad, but a very pretty one.

Mop. Let's have some merry ones.

Aut. Why, this is a passing merry one and goes to the tune of "Two maids wooing a man." There's scarce a maid westward but she sings it; 'tis in request, I can tell you.

Mop. We can both sing it. If thou'lt bear a part,

thou shalt hear; 'tis in three parts.

Dor. We had the tune on 't a month ago.

Aut. I can bear my part; you must know 'tis my occupation; have at it with you.

SONG

Aut. Get you hence, for I must go
Where it fits not you to know.
Dor. Whither? *Mop.* O, whither? *Dor.* Whither?
Mop. It becomes thy oath full well,
Thou to me thy secrets tell.
Dor. Me too, let me go thither.
Mop. Or thou goest to the grange or mill.
Dor. If to either, thou dost ill.
Aut. Neither. *Dor.* What, neither? *Aut.* Neither.
Dor. Thou hast sworn my love to be.
Mop. Thou hast sworn it more to me.
Then whither goest? say, whither?

Clo. We'll have this song out anon by ourselves. My father and the gentlemen are in sad talk, and we'll not trouble them. Come, bring away thy pack after me. Wenches, I'll buy for you both. Pedlar, let's have the first choice. Follow me, girls. [*Exit with* DORCAS *and* MOPSA.

Aut. And you shall pay well for 'em.

Follows singing.
"Will you buy any tape,
Or lace for your cape,
My dainty duck, my dear-a?
Any silk, any thread,
Any toys for your head,
Of the new'st and finest, finest wear-a?
Come to the pedlar;
Money's a medler,
That doth utter all men's ware-a."
[*Exit.*

Re-enter SERVANT.

Serv. Master, there is three carters, three shepherds, three neat-herds, three swine-herds, that have made themselves all men of hair, they call themselves Saltiers, and they have a dance which the wenches say is a gallimaufry of gambols, because they are not in 't; but they themselves are o' the mind, if it be not too rough for some that know little but bowling, it will please plentifully.

Shep. Away! we'll none on't. Here has been too much homely foolery already. I know, sir, we weary you.

Pol. You weary those that refresh us. Pray, let's see these four threes of herdsmen.

Serv. One three of them, by their own report, sir, hath danced before the King; and not the worst of the three but jumps twelve foot and a half by the squire.

Shep. Leave your prating. Since these good men are pleased, let them come in; but quickly now.

Serv. Why, they stay at door, sir. [*Exit.*

Here a dance of twelve Satyrs.

Pol. O, father, you'll know more of that hereafter.
[*To* CAMILLO] Is it not too far gone? 'Tis time to part them.
He's simple and tells much. [*To* FLORIZEL] How now, fair shepherd!
Your heart is full of something that does take
Your mind from feasting. Sooth, when I was young
And handed love as you do, I was wont
To load my she with knacks. I would have ransack'd
The pedlar's silken treasury and have pour'd it
To her acceptance; you have let him go
And nothing marted with him. If your lass
Interpretation should abuse and call this
Your lack of love or bounty, you were straited
For a reply, at least if you make a care
Of happy holding her.

Flo. Old sir, I know
She prizes not such trifles as these are.
The gifts she looks from me are pack'd and lock'd
Up in my heart; which I have given already,
But not deliver'd. O, hear me breathe my life
Before this ancient sir, who, it should seem,
Hath sometime loved! I take thy hand, this hand,
As soft as dove's down and as white as it,
Or Ethiopian's tooth, or the fann'd snow that's bolted
By the northern blasts twice o'er.

Pol. What follows this?
How prettily the young swain seems to wash
The hand was fair before! I have put you out.
But to your protestation; let me hear
What you profess.

Flo. Do, and be witness to 't

Pol. And this my neighbour too?

Flo. And he, and more
Than he, and men, the earth, the heavens, and all:
That, were I crown'd the most imperial monarch,
Thereof most worthy, were I the fairest youth
That ever made eye swerve, had force and knowledge
More than was ever man's, I would not prize them
Without her love; for her employ them all;
Commend them and condemn them to her service

Or to their own perdition.
Pol. Fairly offer'd.
Cam. This shows a sound affection.
Shep. But, my daughter,
Say you the like to him?
Per. I cannot speak
So well, nothing so well; no, nor mean better.
By the pattern of mine own thoughts I cut out
The purity of his.
Shep. Take hands, a bargain!
And, friends unknown, you shall bear witness to 't.
I give my daughter to him, and will make
Her portion equal his.
Flo. O, that must be
I' the virtue of your daughter. One being dead,
I shall have more than you can dream of yet;
Enough then for your wonder. But, come on,
Contract us 'fore these witnesses.
Shep. Come, your hand;
And, daughter, yours.
Pol. Soft, swain, awhile, beseech you;
Have you a father?
Flo. I have; but what of him?
Pol. Knows he of this?
Flo. Ne neither does nor shall.
Pol. Methinks a father
Is at the nuptial of his son a guest
That best becomes the table. Pray you once more,
Is not your father grown incapable
Of reasonable affairs? is he not stupid
With age and altering rheums? can he speak? hear?
Know man from man? dispute his own estate?
Lies he not bed-rid? and again does nothing
But what he did being childish?
Flo. No, good sir;
He has his health and ampler strength indeed
Than most have of his age.
Pol. By my white beard,
You offer him, if this be so, a wrong
Something unfilial. Reason my son
Should choose himself a wife, but as good reason
The father, all whose joy is nothing else
But fair posterity, should hold some counsel
In such a business.
Flo. I yield all this;
But for some other reasons, my grave sir,
Which 'tis not fit you know, I not acquaint
My father of this business.
Pol. Let him know't.
Flo. He shall not.
Pol. Prithee, let him.
Flo. No, he must not.
Shep. Let him, my son. He shall not need to grieve
At knowing of thy choice.
Flo. Come, come, he must not.
Mark our contract.
Pol. Mark your divorce, young sir,
Discovering himself.
Whom son I dare not call. Thou art too base
To be acknowledged. Thou a sceptre's heir,
That thus affect'st a sheep-hook! Thou old traitor,
I am sorry that by hanging thee I can
But shorten thy life one week. And thou, fresh piece
Of excellent witchcraft, who of force must know
The royal fool thou copest with—
Shep. O, my heart!
Pol. I'll have thy beauty scratch'd with briers, and made
More homely than thy state. For thee, fond boy,
If I may ever know thou dost but sigh
That thou no more shalt see this knack, as never
I mean thou shalt, we'll bar thee from succession;
Not hold thee of our blood, no, not our kin,
Far than Deucalion off. Mark thou my words.
Follow us to the court. Thou churl, for this time,
Though full of our displeasure, yet we free thee
From the dead blow of it. And you, enchantment—
Worthy enough a herdsman; yea, him too,
That makes himself, but for our honour therein,
Unworthy thee—if ever henceforth thou
These rural latches to his entrance open,
Or hoop his body more with thy embraces,
I will devise a death as cruel for thee
As thou art tender to 't. [*Exit.*
Per. Even here undone!
I was not much afeard; for once or twice
I was about to speak and tell him plainly,
The selfsame sun that shines upon his court
Hides not his visage from our cottage but
Looks on alike. Will't please you, sir, be gone?
I told you what would come of this. Beseech you,
Of your own state take care. This dream of mine—
Being now awake, I'll queen it no inch farther,
But milk my ewes and weep.
Cam. Why, how now, father!
Speak ere thou diest.
Shep. I cannot speak, nor think,
Nor dare to know that which I know. O sir!
You have undone a man of fourscore three,
That thought to fill his grave in quiet, yea,
To die upon the bed my father died,
To lie close by his honest bones; but now
Some hangman must put on my shroud and lay me

Where no priest shovels in dust. O cursed wretch,
That knew'st this was the Prince, and wouldst adventure
To mingle faith with him! Undone! undone!
If I might die within this hour, I have lived
To die when I desire. [*Exit.*
Flo. Why look you so upon me?
I am but sorry, not afeard; delay'd,
But nothing alter'd. What I was, I am;
More straining on for plucking back, not following
My leash unwillingly.
Cam. Gracious my lord,
You know your father's temper. At this time
He will allow no speech, which I do guess
You do not purpose to him; and as hardly
Will he endure your sight as yet, I fear.
Then, till the fury of his Highness settle,
Come not before him.
Flo. I not purpose it.
I think, Camillo?
Cam. Even he, my lord.
Per. How often have I told you 'twould be thus!
How often said, my dignity would last
But till 'twere known!
Flo. It cannot fail but by
The violation of my faith; and then
Let Nature crush the sides o' the earth together
And mar the seeds within! Lift up thy looks.
From my succession wipe me, father; I
Am heir to my affection.
Cam. Be advised.
Flo. I am, and by my fancy. If my reason
Will thereto be obedient, I have reason;
If not, my senses, better pleased with madness,
Do bid it welcome.
Cam. This is desperate, sir.
Flo. So call it, but it does fulfil my vow;
I needs must think it honesty. Camillo,
Not for Bohemia, nor the pomp that may
Be thereat glean'd, for all the sun sees or
The close earth wombs or the profound seas hide
In unknown fathoms, will I break my oath
To this my fair beloved; therefore, I pray you,
As you have ever been my father's honour'd friend,
When he shall miss me—as, in faith, I mean not
To see him any more—cast your good counsels
Upon his passion. Let myself and fortune
Tug for the time to come. This you may know
And so deliver: I am put to sea
With her whom here I cannot hold on shore;
And most opportune to our need I have
A vessel rides fast by, but nor prepared
For this design. What course I mean to hold
Shall nothing benefit your knowledge, nor
Concern me the reporting.
Cam. O my lord!
I would your spirit were easier for advice,
Or stronger for your need.
Flo. Hark, Perdita. [*Drawing her aside.*]
I'll hear you by and by.
Cam. He's irremoveable,
Resolved for flight. Now were I happy, if
His going I could frame to serve my turn,
Save him from danger, do him love and honour,
Purchase the sight again of dear Sicilia
And that unhappy king, my master, whom
I so much thirst to see.
Flo. Now, good Camillo;
I am so fraught with curious business that
I leave out ceremony.
Cam. Sir, I think
You have heard of my poor services, i' the love
That I have borne your father?
Flo. Very nobly
Have you deserved. It is my father's music
To speak your deeds, not little of his care
To have them recompensed as thought on.
Cam. Well, my lord,
If you may please to think I love the King
And through him what is nearest to him, which is
Your gracious self, embrace but my direction.
If your more ponderous and settled project
May suffer alteration, on mine honour,
I'll point you where you shall have such receiving
As shall become your Highness; where you may
Enjoy your mistress, from the whom, I see,
There's no disjunction to be made, but by—
As heavens forfend!—your ruin; marry her,
And, with my best endeavours in your absence,
Your discontenting father strive to qualify
And bring him up to liking.
Flo. How, Camillo,
May this, almost a miracle, be done?
That I may call thee something more than man
And after that trust to thee.
Cam. Have you thought on
A place whereto you'll go?
Flo. Not any yet;
But as the unthought-on accident is guilty
To what we wildly do, so we profess
Ourselves to be the slaves of chance and flies
Of every wind that blows.
Cam. Then list to me.
This follows, if you will not change your purpose
But undergo this flight, make for Sicilia,
And there present yourself and your fair princess,
For so I see she must be, 'fore Leontes.
She shall be habited as it becomes
The partner of your bed. Methinks I see

Leontes opening his free arms and weeping
His welcomes forth; asks thee the son forgiveness,
As 'twere i' the father's person; kisses the hands
Of your fresh princess; o'er and o'er divides him
'Twixt his unkindness and his kindness; the one
He chides to hell and bids the other grow
Faster than thought or time.

Flo. Worthy Camillo,
What colour for my visitation shall I
Hold up before him?

Cam. Sent by the King your father
To greet him and to give him comforts. Sir,
The manner of your bearing towards him, with
What you as from your father shall deliver,
Things known betwixt us three, I'll write you down;
The which shall point you forth at every sitting
What you must say; that he shall not perceive
But that you have your father's bosom there
And speak his very heart.

Flo. I am bound to you.
There is some sap in this.

Cam. A course more promising
Than a wild dedication of yourselves
To unpath'd waters, undream'd shores, most certain
To miseries enough; no hope to help you,
But as you shake off one to take another;
Nothing so certain as your anchors, who
Do their best office, if they can but stay you
Where you'll be loath to be. Besides you know
Prosperity's the very bond of love,
Whose fresh complexion and whose heart together
Affliction alters.

Per. One of these is true.
I think affliction may subdue the cheek,
But not take in the mind.

Cam. Yea, say you so?
There shall not at your father's house these seven years
Be born another such.

Flo. My good Camillo,
She is as forward of her breeding as
She is i' the rear our birth.

Cam. I cannot say 'tis pity
She lacks instructions, for she seems a mistress
To most that teach.

Per. Your pardon, sir; for this
I'll blush you thanks.

Flo. My prettiest Perdita!
But O, the thorns we stand upon! Camillo,
Preserver of my father, now of me,
The medicine of our house, how shall we do?
We are not furnish'd like Bohemia's son,
Nor shall appear in Sicilia.

Cam. My lord,
Fear none of this. I think you know my fortunes
Do all lie there. It shall be so my care
To have you royally appointed as if
The scene you play were mine. For instance, sir,
That you may know you shall not want, one word.

They talk aside.

Re-enter AUTOLYCUS.

Aut. Ha, ha! what a fool Honesty is! and Trust, his sworn brother, a very simple gentleman! I have sold all my trumpery; not a counterfeit stone, not a ribbon, glass, pomander, brooch, table-book, ballad, knife, tape, glove, shoe-tie, bracelet, horn-ring, to keep my pack from fasting. They throng who should buy first, as if my trinkets had been hallowed and brought a benediction to the buyer; by which means I saw whose purse was best in picture; and what I saw, to my good use I remembered. My clown, who wants but something to be a reasonable man, grew so in love with the wenches' song, that he would not stir his pettitoes till he had both tune and words; which so drew the rest of the herd to me that all their other senses stuck in ears. You might have pinched a placket, it was senseless; 'twas nothing to geld a codpiece of a purse; I could have filed keys off that hung in chains. No hearing, no feeling, but my sir's song, and admiring the nothing of it. So that in this time of lethargy I picked and cut most of their festival purses; and had not the old man come in with a whoo-bub against his daughter and the King's son and scared my choughs from the chaff, I had not left a purse alive in the whole army.

[CAMILLO, FLORIZEL, *and* PERDITA *come forward.*

Cam. Nay, but my letters, by this means being there
So soon as you arrive, shall clear that doubt.

Flo. And those that you'll procure from King Leontes—

Cam. Shall satisfy your father.

Per. Happy be you!
All that you speak shows fair.

Cam. Who have we here?

Seeing AUTOLYCUS.

We'll make an instrument of this, omit
Nothing may give us aid.

Aut. If they have overheard me now, why, hanging.

Cam. How now, good fellow! why shakest thou so? Fear not, man; here's no harm intended to thee.

Aut. I am a poor fellow, sir.

Cam. Why, be so still; here's nobody will steal that from thee. Yet for the outside of thy poverty we must make an exchange; therefore disease thee instantly—thou must think there's a necessity in't—and change garments with this gentleman. Though the pennyworth on his side be the worst, yet hold thee, there's some boot.

Aut. I am a poor fellow, sir. [*Aside*] I know ye well enough.

Cam. Nay, prithee, dispatch. The gentleman is half flayed already.

Aut. Are you in earnest, sir? [*Aside*] I smell the trick on't.

Flo. Dispatch, I prithee.

Aut. Indeed, I have had earnest; but I cannot with conscience take it.

Cam. Unbuckle, unbuckle.

FLORIZEL *and* AUTOLYCUS *exchange garments*.

Fortunate mistress—let my prophecy
Come home to ye!—you must retire yourself
Into some covert. Take your sweetheart's hat
And pluck it o'er your brows, muffle your face,
Dismantle you, and, as you can, disliken
The truth of your own seeming; that you may—
For I do fear eyes over—to shipboard
Get undescried.

Per. I see the play so lies
That I must bear a part.

Cam. No remedy.
Have you done there?

Flo. Should I now meet my father,
He would not call me son.

Cam. Nay, you shall have no hat.

Giving it to PERDITA.

Come, lady, come. Farewell, my friend,

Aut. Adieu, sir.

Flo. O Perdita, what have we twain forgot!
Pray you, a word.

Cam. [*Aside*] What I do next, shall be to tell the King.
Of this escape and whither they are bound;
Wherein my hope is I shall so prevail
To force him after; in whose company
I shall review Sicilia, for whose sight
I have a woman's longing.

Flo. Fortune speed us!
Thus we set on, Camillo, to the sea-side.

Cam. The swifter speed the better.

[*Exeunt* FLORIZEL, PERDITA, *and* CAMILLO.

Aut. I understand the business, I hear it. To have an open ear, a quick eye, and a nimble hand, is necessary for a cut-purse; a good nose is requisite also, to smell out work for the other senses. I see this is the time that the unjust man doth thrive. What an exchange had this been without boot! What a boot is here with this exchange! Sure the gods do this year connive at us, and we may do anything extempore. The Prince himself is about a piece of iniquity, stealing away from his father with his clog at his heels. If I thought it were a piece of honesty to acquaint the king withal, I would not do 't. I hold it the more knavery to conceal it; and therein am I constant to my profession.

Re-enter CLOWN *and* SHEPHERD.

Aside, aside; here is more matter for a hot brain. Every lane's end, every shop, church, session, hanging, yields a careful man work.

Clo. See, see; what a man you are now! There is no other way but to tell the King she's a changeling and none of your flesh and blood.

Shep. Nay, but hear me.

Clo. Nay but hear me.

Shep. Go to, then.

Clo. She being none of your flesh and blood, your flesh and blood has not offended the king; and so your flesh and blood is not to be punished by him. Show those things you found about her, those secret things, all but what she has with her. This being done, let the law go whistle. I warrant you.

Shep. I will tell the King all, every word, yea, and his son's pranks too; who, I may say, is no honest man, neither to his father nor to me, to go about to make me the King's brother-in-law.

Clo. Indeed, brother-in-law was the farthest off you could have been to him and then your blood had been the dearer by I know how much an ounce.

Aut. [*Aside*] Very wisely, puppies!

Shep. Well, let us to the King. There is that in this fardel will make him scratch his beard.

Aut. [*Aside*] I know not what impediment this complaint may be to the flight of my master.

Clo. Pray heartily he be at palace.

Aut. [*Aside*] Though I am not naturally honest, I am so sometimes by chance. Let me pocket up my pedlar's excrement. [*Takes off his false beard*.] How now, rustics! whither are you bound?

Shep. To the palace, an it like your worship.

Aut. Your affairs there, what, with whom, the condition of that fardel, the place of your dwelling, your names, your ages, of what having, breeding, and anything that is fitting to be known, discover.

Clo. We are but plain fellows, sir.

Aut. A lie; you are rough and hairy. Let me have no lying. It becomes none but tradesmen, and they often give us soldiers the lie; but we pay them for it with stamped coin, not stabbing steel; therefore they do not give us the lie.

Clo. Your worship had like to have given us one, if you had not taken yourself with the manner.

Shep. Are you a courtier, an't like you, sir?

Aut. Whether it like me or no, I am a courtier. Seest thou not the air of the court in these enfoldings? hath not my gait in it the measure of the court? receives not thy nose court-odour from me? reflect I not on thy baseness court-contempt? Thinkest thou, for that I insinuate, or toaze from thee thy business, I am therefore no courtier? I am courtier cap-a-pe; and one that will either push on or pluck back thy business there; whereupon I command thee to open thy affair.

Shep. My business, sir, is to the King.

Aut. What advocate hast thou to him?

Shep. I know not, an't like you.

Clo. Advocate's the court-word for a pheasant. Say you have none.

Shep. None, sir; I have no pheasant, cock nor hen.

Aut. How blessed are we that are not simple men!
Yet nature might have made me as these are,
Therefore I will not disdain.

Clo. This cannot be but a great courtier.

Shep. His garments are rich, but he wears them not handsomely.

Clo. He seems to be the more noble in being fantastical. A great man, I'll warrant; I know by the picking on's teeth.

Aut. The fardel there? what's i' the fardel? Wherefore that box?

Shep. Sir, there lies such secrets in this fardel and box, which none must know but the King; and which he shall know within this hour, if I may come to the speech of him.

Aut. Age, thou hast lost thy labour.

Shep. Why, sir?

Aut. The King is not at the palace; he is gone aboard a new ship to purge melancholy and air himself; for, if thou beest capable of things serious, thou must know the King is full of grief.

Shep. So 'tis said, sir; about his son, that should have married a shepherd's daughter.

Aut. If that shepherd be not in hand-fast, let him fly. The curses he shall have, the tortures he shall feel, will break the back of man, the heart of monster.

Clo. Think you so, sir?

Aut. Not he alone shall suffer what wit can make heavy and vengeance bitter; but those that are germane to him, though removed fifty times, shall all come under the hangman; which though it be great pity, yet it is necessary. An old sheep-whistling rogue, a ram-tender, to offer to have his daughter come into grace! Some say he shall be stoned; but that death is too soft for him, say I. Draw our throne into a sheep-cote! all deaths are too few, the sharpest too easy.

Clo. Has the old man e'er a son, sir, do you hear, an't like you, sir?

Aut. He has a son, who shall be flayed alive; then 'nointed over with honey, set on the head of a wasp's nest; then stand till he be three quarters and a dram dead; then recovered again with aqua-vitae or some other hot infusion; then, raw as he is, and in the hottest day prognostication proclaims, shall he be set against a brick-wall, the sun looking with a southward eye upon him, where he is to behold him with flies blown to death. But what talk we of these traitorly rascals, whose miseries are to be smiled at, their offences being so capital? Tell me, for you seem to be honest plain men, what you have to the King. Being something gently considered, I'll bring you where he is aboard, tender your persons to his presence, whisper him in your behalfs; and if it be in man besides the King to effect your suits, here is man shall do it.

Clo. He seems to be of great authority. Close with him, give him gold; and though authority be a subborn bear, yet he is oft led by the nose with gold. Show the inside of your purse to the outside of his hand, and no more ado. Remember "stoned," and "flayed alive."

Shep. An't please you, sir, to undertake the business for us, here is that gold I have. I'll make it as much more and leave this young man in pawn till I bring it you.

Aut. After I have done what I promised?

Shep. Ay, sir.

Aut. Well, give me the moiety. Are you a party in this business?

Clo. In some sort, sir; but though my case be a pitiful one, I hope I shall not be flayed out of it.

Aut. O, that's the case of the shepherd's son. Hang him, he'll be made an example.

Clo. Comfort, good comfort! We must to the King and show our strange sights. He must know 'tis none of your daughter nor my sister; we are gone else. Sir, I will give you as much as this old man does when the business is performed, and remain, as he says, your pawn till it be brought you.

Aut. I will trust you. Walk before toward the sea-side; go on the right hand. I will but look upon the hedge and follow you.

Clo. We are blest in this man, as I may say, even blest.

Shep. Let's before as he bids us. He was provided to do us good.

[*Exeunt* SHEPHERD *and* CLOWN.

Aut. If I had a mind to be honest, I see Fortune would not suffer me. She drops booties in my mouth. I am courted now with a double occasion, gold and a means to do the Prince my master good; which who knows how that may turn back to my advancement? I will bring these two moles, these blind ones, aboard him. If he think it fit to shore them again and that the complaint they have to the King concerns him nothing, let him call me rogue for being so far officious; for I am proof against that title and what shame else belongs to't. To him will I present them. There may be matter in it. [*Exit*.

ACT V

SCENE I. *A room in Leontes' palace*

Enter LEONTES, CLEOMENES, DION, PAULINA, *and Servants*.

Cleo. Sir, you have done enough, and have perform'd
A saint-like sorrow. No fault could you make,
Which you have not redeem'd; indeed, paid down
More penitence than done trespass. At the last,
Do as the heavens have done, forget your evil;
With them forgive yourself.
Leon. Whilst I remember
Her and her virtues, I cannot forget
My blemishes in them, and so still think of
The wrong I did myself; which was so much,
That heirless it hath made my kingdom and
Destroy'd the sweet'st companion that e'er man
Bred his hopes out of.
Paul. True, too true, my lord.
If, one by one, you wedded all the world,
Or from the all that are took something good,
To make a perfect woman, she you kill'd
Would be unparallel'd.
Leon. I think so. Kill'd!
She I kill'd! I did so; but thou strikest me
Sorely, to say I did; it is as bitter
Upon thy tongue as is my thought. Now, good now,
Say so but seldom.
Cleo. Not at all, good lady:
You might have spoken a thousand things that would
Have done the time more benefit and graced
Your kindness better.
Paul. You are one of those
Would have him wed again.
Dion. If you would not so,
You pity not the state, nor the remembrance
Of his most sovereign name; consider little
What dangers, by his Highness' fail of issue,
May drop upon his kingdom and devour
Incertain lookers on. What were more holy
Than to rejoice the former queen is well?
What holier than, for royalty's repair,
For present comfort and for future good,
To bless the bed of majesty again
With a sweet fellow to 't?
Paul. There is none worthy,
Respecting her that's gone. Besides, the gods
Will have fulfill'd their secret purposes;
For has not the divine Apollo said,
Is't not the tenour of his oracle,
That King Leontes shall not have an heir
Till his lost child be found? which that it shall,
Is all as monstrous to our human reason
As my Antigonus to break his grave
And come again to me; who, on my life,
Did perish with the infant. 'Tis your counsel
My lord should to the heavens be contrary,
Oppose against their wills. [*To* LEONTES.] Care not for issue;
The crown will find an heir. Great Alexander
Left his to the worthiest; so his successor
Was like to be the best.
Leon. Good Paulina,
Who hast the memory of Hermione,
I know, in honour, O, that ever I
Had squared me to thy counsel! then, even now,
I might have look'd upon my queen's full eyes,
Have taken treasure from her lips—
Paul. And left them
More rich for what they yielded.
Leon. Thou speak'st truth.
No more such wives; therefore, no wife. One worse,
And better used, would make her sainted spirit
Again possess her corpse, and on this stage,
Where we're offenders now, appear soul-vex'd,
And begin, "Why to me?"
Paul. Had she such power,
She had just cause.
Leon. She had; and would incense me
To murder her I married.
Paul. I should so.
Were I the ghost that walk'd, I'd bid you mark
Her eye, and tell me for what dull part in't
You chose her; then I'd shriek, that even your ears
Should rift to hear me; and the words that follow'd
Should be, "Remember mine."
Leon. Stars, stars,

And all eyes else dead coals! Fear thou no wife;
I'll have no wife, Paulina.
Paul. Will you swear
Never to marry but by my free leave?
Leon. Never, Paulina; so be blest my spirit!
Paul. Then, good my lords, bear witness to his oath.
Cleo. You tempt him over-much.
Paul. Unless another,
As like Hermione as is her picture,
Affront his eye.
Cleo. Good madam—
Paul. I have done.
Yet, if my lord will marry—if you will, sir,
No remedy, but you will—give me the office
To choose you a queen. She shall not be so young
As was your former; but she shall be such
As, walk'd your first queen's ghost, it should take joy
To see her in your arms.
Leon. My true Paulina,
We shall not marry till thou bid'st us.
Paul. That
Shall be when your first queen's again in breath;
Never till then.

Enter a GENTLEMAN.

Gent. One that gives out himself Prince Florizel,
Son of Polixenes, with his princess, she
The fairest I have yet beheld, desires access
To your high presence.
Leon. What with him? he comes not
Like to his father's greatness. His approach,
So out of circumstance and sudden, tells us
'Tis not a visitation framed, but forced
By need and accident. What train?
Gent. But few,
And those but mean.
Leon. His princess, say you, with him?
Gent. Ay, the most peerless piece of earth, I think,
That e'er the sun shone bright on.
Paul. O Hermione,
As every present time doth boast itself
Above a better gone, so must thy grave
Give way to what's seen now! Sir, you yourself
Have said and writ so, but your writing now
Is colder than that theme, "She had not been,
Nor was not to be equall'd." Thus your verse
Flow'd with her beauty once." 'Tis shrewdly ebb'd,
To say you have seen a better.
Gent. Pardon, madam.
The one I have almost forgot—your pardon—
The other, when she has obtain'd your eye,
Will have your tongue too. This is a creature,
Would she begin a sect, might quench the zeal
Of all professors else, make proselytes
Of who she but bid follow.
Paul. How! not women?
Gent. Women will love her, that she is a woman
More worth than any man; men, that she is
The rarest of all women.
Leon. Go, Cleomenes;
Yourself, assisted with your honour'd friends,
Bring them to our embracement. Still, 'tis strange
[*Exeunt* CLEOMENES *and others*.
He thus should steal upon us.
Paul. Had our prince,
Jewel of children, seen this hour, he had pair'd
Well with this lord. There was not full a month
Between their births.
Leon. Prithee, no more; cease; thou know'st
He dies to me again when talk'd of. Sure,
When I shall see this gentleman, thy speeches
Will bring me to consider that which may
Unfurnish me of reason. They are come.

Re-enter CLEOMENES *and others, with* FLORIZEL *and* PERDITA.

Your mother was most true to wedlock, prince;
For she did print your royal father off,
Conceiving you. Were I but twenty one,
Your father's image is so hit in you,
His very air, that I should call you brother,
As I did him, and speak of something wildly
By us perform'd before. Most dearly welcome!
And your fair princess—goddess!—O, alas! 131
I lost a couple, that 'twixt heaven and earth
Might thus have stood begetting wonder as
You, gracious couple, do; and then I lost—
All mine own folly—the society,
Amity too, of your brave father, whom,
Though bearing misery, I desire my life
Once more to look on him.
Flo. By his command
Have I here touch'd Sicilia and from him
Give you all greetings that a king, at friend,
Can send his brother; and, but infirmity
Which waits upon worn times hath something seized
His wish'd ability, he had himself
The lands and waters 'twixt your throne and his
Measured to look upon you; whom he loves—
He bade me say so—more than all the sceptres
And those that bear them living.
Leon. O my brother,
Good gentleman! the wrongs I have done thee stir
Afresh within me, and these thy offices,
So rarely kind, are as interpreters

Of my behind-hand slackness. Welcome hither,
As is the spring to the earth. And hath he too
Exposed this paragon to the fearful usage,
At least ungentle, of the dreadful Neptune,
To greet a man not worth her pains, much less
The adventure of her person?
Flo. Good my lord,
She came from Libya.
Leon. Where the warlike Smalus,
That noble honour'd lord, is fear'd and loved?
Flo. Most royal sir, from thence; from him, whose daughter
His tears proclaim'd his, parting with her. Thence,
A prosperous south-wind friendly, we have cross'd,
To execute the charge my father gave me
For visiting your Highness. My best train
I have from your Sicilian shores dismiss'd;
Who for Bohemia bend, to signify
Not only my success in Libya, sir,
But my arrival and my wife's in safety
Here where we are.
Leon. The blessed gods
Purge all infection from our air whilst you
Do climate here! You have a holy father,
A graceful gentleman; against whose person,
So sacred as it is, I have done sin;
For which the heavens, taking angry note,
Have left me issueless; and your father's blest,
As he from heaven merits it, with you
Worthy his goodness. What might I have been,
Might I a son and daughter now have look'd on,
Such goodly things as you!

Enter a LORD.

Lord. Most noble sir,
That which I shall report will bear no credit,
Were not the proof so nigh. Please you, great sir,
Bohemia greets you from himself by me;
Desires you to attach his son, who has—
His dignity and duty both cast off—
Fled from his father, from his hopes, and with
A shepherd's daughter.
Leon. Where's Bohemia? speak.
Lord. Here in your city; I now came from him.
I speak amazedly; and it becomes
My marvel and my message. To your court
Whiles he was hastening, in the chase, it seems,
Of this fair couple, meets he on the way
The father of this seeming lady and
Her brother, having both their country quitted
With this young prince.
Flo. Camillo has betray'd me;
Whose honour and whose honesty till now
Endured all weathers.
Lord. Lay't so to his charge;
He's with the King your father.
Leon. Who? Camillo?
Lord. Camillo, sir; I spake with him; who now
Has these poor men in question. Never saw I
Wretches so quake. They kneel, they kiss the earth;
Forswear themselves as often as they speak.
Bohemia stops his ears, and threatens them
With divers deaths in death.
Per. O my poor father!
The heaven sets spies upon us, will not have
Our contract celebrated.
Leon. You are married?
Flo. We are not sir, nor are we like to be;
The stars, I see, will kiss the valleys first.
The odds for high and low's alike.
Leon. My lord,
Is this the daughter of a king?
Flo. She is,
When once she is my wife.
Leon. That "once," I see by your good father's speed,
Will come on very slowly. I am sorry,
Most sorry, you have broken from his liking
Where you were tied in duty, and as sorry
Your choice is not so rich in worth as beauty,
That you might well enjoy her.
Flo. Dear, look up.
Though Fortune, visible an enemy,
Should chase us with my father, power no jot
Hath she to change our loves. Beseech you, sir,
Remember since you owed no more to time
Than I do now. With thought of such affections,
Step forth mine advocate; at your request
My father will grant precious things as trifles.
Leon. Would he do so, I'd beg your precious mistress,
Which he counts but a trifle.
Paul. Sir, my liege,
Your eye hath too much youth in 't. Not a month
'Fore your queen died, she was more worth such gazes
Than what you look on now.
Leon. I thought of her,
Even in these looks I made. [*To* FLORIZEL] But your petition
Is yet unanswer'd. I will to your father.
Your honour not o'erthrown by your desires,
I am friend to them and you; upon which errand
I now go toward him; therefore follow me
And mark what way I make. Come, good my lord. [*Exeunt.*

SCENE II. *Before Leontes' palace*

Enter AUTOLYCUS *and a* GENTLEMAN.

Aut. Beseech you, sir, were you present at this relation?

1st Gent. I was by at the opening of the fardel, heard the old shepherd deliver the manner how he found it; whereupon, after a little amazedness, we were all commanded out of the chamber; only this methought I heard the shepherd say, he found the child.

Aut. I would most gladly know the issue of it.

1st Gent. I make a broken delivery of the business; but the changes I perceived in the King and Camillo were very notes of admiration. They seemed almost, with staring on one another, to tear the cases of their eyes; there was speech in their dumbness, language in their very gesture; they looked as they had heard of a world ransomed, or one destroyed. A notable passion of wonder appeared in them; but the wisest beholder, that knew no more but seeing, could not say if the importance were joy or sorrow; but in the extremity of the one, it must needs be.

Enter SECOND GENTLEMAN.

Here comes a gentleman that haply knows more. The news, Rogero?

2nd Gent. Nothing but bonfires. The oracle is fulfilled; the King's daughter is found. Such a deal of wonder is broken out within this hour that ballad-makers cannot be able to express it.

Enter a THIRD GENTLEMAN.

Here comes the Lady Paulina's steward. He can deliver you more. How goes it now, sir? this news which is called true is so like an old tale, that the verity of it is in strong suspicion. Has the King found his heir?

3rd Gent. Most true, if ever truth were pregnant by circumstance. That which you hear you'll swear you see, there is such unity in the proofs. The mantle of Queen Hermione's, her jewel about the neck of it, the letters of Antigonus found with it which they know to be his character, the majesty of the creature in resemblance of the mother, the affection of nobleness which nature shows above her breeding, and many other evidences proclaim her with all certainty to be the King's daughter. Did you see the meeting of the two kings?

2nd Gent. No.

3rd Gent. Then have you lost a sight, which was to be seen, cannot be spoken of. There might you have beheld one joy crown another, so and in such manner that it seemed sorrow wept to take leave of them, for their joy waded in tears. There was casting up of eyes, holding up of hands, with countenance of such distraction that they were to be known by garment, not by favour. Our king, being ready to leap out of himself for joy of his found daughter, as if that joy were now become a loss, cries, "O, thy mother, thy mother!" then asks Bohemia forgiveness; then embraces his son-in-law; then again worries he his daughter with clipping her; now he thanks the old shepherd, which stands by like a weather-bitten conduit of many kings' reigns. I never heard of such another encounter, which lames report to follow it and undoes description to do it.

2nd Gent. What, pray you, became of Antigonus, that carried hence the child?

3rd Gent. Like an old tale still, which will have matter to rehearse, though credit be asleep and not an ear open. He was torn to pieces with a bear. This avouches the shepherd's son; who has not only his innocence, which seems much, to justify him, but a handkerchief and rings of his that Paulina knows.

1st Gent. What became of his bark and his followers?

3rd Gent. Wrecked the same instant of their master's death and in the view of the shepherd; so that all the instruments which aided to expose the child were even then lost when it was found. But O, the noble combat that 'twixt joy and sorrow was fought in Paulina! She had one eye declined for the loss of her husband, another elevated that the oracle was fulfilled. She lifted the Princess from the earth, and so locks her in embracing, as if she would pin her to her heart that she might no more be in danger of losing.

1st Gent. The dignity of this act was worth the audience of kings and princes; for by such was it acted.

3rd Gent. One of the prettiest touches of all and that which angled for mine eyes, caught the water though not the fish, was when, at the relation of the Queen's death, with the manner how she came to't bravely confessed and lamented by the King, how attentiveness wounded his daughter; till, from one sign of dolour to another, she did, with an "Alas," I would fain say, bleed tears, for I am sure my heart wept blood. Who was most marble there changed colour; some swooned, all sorrowed. If all the world could have seen't, the woe had been universal.

1st Gent. Are they returned to the court?

3rd Gent. No; the Princess hearing of her mother's statue, which is in the keeping of Paulina—

a piece many years in doing and now newly performed by that rare Italian master, Julio Romano, who, had he himself eternity and could put breath into his work, would beguile Nature of her custom, so perfectly he is her ape. He so near to Hermione hath done Hermione that they say one would speak to her and stand in hope of answer. Thither with all greediness of affection are they gone, and there they intend to sup.

2nd Gent. I thought she had some great matter there in hand; for she hath privately twice or thrice a day, ever since the death of Hermione, visited that removed house. Shall we thither and with our company piece the rejoicing?

1st Gent. Who would be thence that has the benefit of access? every wink of an eye some new grace will be born. Our absence makes us unthrifty to our knowledge. Let's along.

[*Exeunt* GENTLEMEN.

Aut. Now, had I not the dash of my former life in me, would preferment drop on my head. I brought the old man and his son aboard the Prince; told him I heard them talk of a fardel and I know not what. But he at that time, over-fond of the shepherd's daughter, so he then took her to be, who began to be much sea-sick, and himself little better, extremity of weather continuing, this mystery remained undiscovered. But 'tis all one to me; for had I been the finder out of this secret, it would not have relished among my other discredits.

Enter SHEPHERD *and* CLOWN.

Here come those I have done good to against my will, and already appearing in the blossoms of their fortune.

Shep. Come, boy; I am past moe children, but thy sons and daughters will be all gentlemen born.

Clo. You are well met, sir. You denied to fight with me this other day, because I was no gentleman born. See you these clothes? say you see them not and think me still no gentleman born. You were best say these robes are not gentlemen born. Give me the lie, do, and try whether I am not now a gentleman born.

Aut. I know you are now, sir, a gentleman born.

Clo. Ay, and have been so any time these four hours.

Shep. And so have I, boy.

Clo. So you have; but I was a gentleman born before my father; for the King's son took me by the hand, and called me brother; and then the two kings called my father brother; and then the Prince my brother and the Princess my sister called my father father; and so we wept, and there was the first gentleman-like tears that ever we shed.

Shep. We may live, son, to shed many more.

Clo. Ay; or else 'twere hard luck, being in so preposterous estate as we are.

Aut. I humbly beseech you, sir, to pardon me all the faults I have committed to your worship and to give me your good report to the Prince my master.

Shep. Prithee, son, do; for we must be gentle, now we are gentlemen.

Clo. Thou wilt amend thy life?

Aut. Ay, an it like your good worship.

Clo. Give me thy hand. I will swear to the Prince thou art as honest a true fellow as any is in Bohemia.

Shep. You may say it, but not swear it.

Clo. Not swear it; now I am a gentleman? Let boors and franklins say it, I'll swear it.

Shep. How if it be false, son?

Clo. If it be ne'er so false, a true gentleman may swear it in the behalf of his friend; and I'll swear to the Prince thou art a tall fellow of thy hands and that thou wilt not be drunk; but I know thou art no tall fellow of thy hands and that thou wilt be drunk; but I'll swear it, and I would thou wouldst be a tall fellow of thy hands.

Aut. I will prove so, sir, to my power.

Clo. Ay, by any means prove a tall fellow. If I do not wonder how thou darest venture to be drunk, not being a tall fellow, trust me not. Hark! the kings and the princes, our kindred, are going to see the Queen's picture. Come, follow us; we'll be thy good masters. [*Exeunt.*

SCENE III. *A chapel in Paulina's house*

Enter LEONTES, POLIXENES, FLORIZEL, PERDITA, CAMILLO, PAULINA, *Lords, and Attendants.*

Leon. O grave and good Paulina, the great comfort
That I have had of thee!
Paul. What, sovereign sir,
I did not well I meant well. All my services
You have paid home; but that you have vouchsafed,
With your crown'd brother and these your contracted
Heirs of your kingdoms, my poor house to visit,
It is a surplus of your grace, which never
My life may last to answer.
Leon. O Paulina,
We honour you with trouble; but we came
To see the statue of our queen. Your gallery
Have we pass'd through, not without much content
In many singularities; but we saw not

That which my daughter came to look upon,
The statue of her mother.
Paul. As she lived peerless,
So her dead likeness, I do well believe,
Excels whatever yet you look'd upon
Or hand of man hath done; therefore I keep it
Lonely, apart. But here it is. Prepare
To see the life as lively mock'd as ever
Still sleep mock'd death. Behold, and say 'tis
well.

PAULINA *draws a curtain, and discovers* HERMIONE *standing like a statue.*

I like your silence, it the more shows off
Your wonder. But yet speak; first, you, my liege.
Comes it not something near?
Leon. Her natural posture!
Chide me, dear stone, that I may say indeed
Thou art Hermione; or rather, thou art she
In thy not chiding, for she was as tender
As infancy and grace. But yet, Paulina,
Hermione was not so much wrinkled, nothing
So aged as this seems.
Pol. O, not by much.
Paul. So much the more our carver's excellence;
Which lets go by some sixteen years and makes
her
As she lived now.
Leon. As now she might have done,
So much to my good comfort, as it is
Now piercing to my soul. O, thus she stood,
Even with such life of majesty, warm life,
As now it coldly stands, when first I woo'd her!
I am ashamed. Does not the stone rebuke me
For being more stone than it? O royal piece,
There's magic in thy majesty, which has
My evils conjured to remembrance and
From thy admiring daughter took the spirits,
Standing like stone with thee.
Per. And give me leave,
And do not say 'tis superstition, that
I kneel and then implore her blessing. Lady,
Dear queen, that ended when I but began,
Give me that hand of yours to kiss.
Paul. O, patience!
The statue is but newly fix'd, the colour's
Not dry.
Cam. My lord, your sorrow was too sore laid
on,
Which sixeen winters cannot blow away,
So many summers dry. Scarce any joy
Did ever so long live; no sorrow
But kill'd itself much sooner.
Pol. Dear my brother,
Let him that was the cause of this have power
To take off so much grief from you as he
Will piece up in himself.
Paul. Indeed, my lord,
If I had thought the sight of my poor image
Would thus have wrought you—for the stone is
mine—
I'd not have show'd it.
Leon. Do not draw the curtain.
Paul. No longer shall you gaze on 't, lest your
fancy
May think anon it moves.
Leon. Let be, let be.
Would I were dead, but that, methinks, already—
What was he that did make it? See, my lord,
Would you not deem it breathed? and that those
veins
Did verily bear blood?
Pol. Masterly done.
The very life seems warm upon her lip.
Leon. The fixture of her eye has motion in 't,
As we are mock'd with art.
Paul. I'll draw the curtain.
My lord's almost so far transported that
He'll think anon it lives.
Leon. O sweet Paulina,
Make me to think so twenty years together!
No settled senses of the world can match
The pleasure of that madness. Let 't alone.
Paul. I am sorry, sir, I have thus far stirr'd you;
but
I could afflict you farther.
Leon. Do, Paulina;
For this affliction has a taste as sweet
As any cordial comfort. Still, methinks,
There is an air comes from her. What fine chisel
Could ever yet cut breath? Let no man mock me,
For I will kiss her.
Paul. Good my lord, forbear.
The ruddiness upon her lip is wet;
You'll mar it if you kiss it, stain your own
With oily painting. Shall I draw the curtain?
Leon. No, not these twenty years.
Per. So long could I
Stand by, a looker on.
Paul. Either forbear,
Quit presently the chapel, or resolve you
For more amazement. If you can behold it,
I'll make the statue move indeed, descend
And take you by the hand. But then you'll think—
Which I protest against—I am assisted
By wicked powers.
Leon. What you can make her do,
I am content to look on; what to speak,
I am content to hear; for 'tis as easy
To make her speak as move.
Paul. It is required
You do awake your faith. Then all stand still;
On; those that think it is unlawful business

I am about, let them depart.
Leon. Proceed;
No foot shall stir.
Paul. Music, awake her; strike!
Music.
'Tis time; descend; be stone no more; approach;
Strike all that look upon with marvel. Come,
I'll fill your grave up: stir, nay, come away,
Bequeath to death your numbness, for from him
Dear life redeems you. You perceive she stirs.
HERMIONE *comes down.*
Start not; her actions shall be holy as
You hear my spell is lawful. Do not shun her
Until you see her die again; for then
You kill her double. Nay, present your hand.
When she was young you woo'd her; now in age
Is she become the suitor?
Leon. O, she's warm!
If this be magic, let it be an art
Lawful as eating.
Pol. She embraces him.
Cam. She hangs about his neck.
If she pertain to life let her speak too.
Pol. Ay, and make 't manifest where she has lived,
Or how stolen from the dead.
Paul. That she is living,
Were it but told you, should be hooted at
Like an old tale. But it appears she lives,
Though yet she speak not. Mark a little while.
Please you to interpose, fair madam; kneel
And pray your mother's blessing. Turn, good lady;
Our Perdita is found.
Her. You gods, look down
And from your sacred vials pour your graces
Upon my daughter's head! Tell me, mine own,
Where hast thou been preserved? where lived? how found
Thy father's court? for thou shalt hear that I,
Knowing by Paulina that the oracle
Gave hope thou wast in being, have preserved
Myself to see the issue.
Paul. There's time enough for that;
Lest they desire upon this push to trouble
Your joys with like relation. Go together,
You precious winners all; your exultation
Partake to every one. I, an old turtle,
Will wing me to some wither'd bough and there
My mate, that's never to be found again,
Lament till I am lost.
Leon. O, peace, Paulina!
Thou shouldst a husband take by my consent,
As I by thine a wife. This is a match,
And made between 's by vows. Thou hast found mine;
But how, is to be question'd; for I saw her,
As I thought, dead, and have in vain said many
A prayer upon her grave. I'll not seek far—
For him, I partly know his mind—to find thee
An honourable husband. Come, Camillo,
And take her by the hand, whose worth and honesty
Is richly noted and here justified
By us, a pair of kings. Let's from this place.
What! look upon my brother. Both your pardons,
That e'er I put between your holy looks
My ill suspicion. This is your son-in-law
And son unto the King, who, heavens directing,
Is troth-plight to your daughter. Good Paulina,
Lead us from hence, where we may leisurely
Each one demand and answer to his part
Perform'd in this wide gap of time since first
We were dissever'd. Hastily lead away. [*Exeunt.*

THE TEMPEST

DRAMATIS PERSONÆ

ALONSO, *King of Naples*
SEBASTIAN, *his brother*
PROSPERO, *the right Duke of Milan*
ANTONIO, *his brother, the usurping Duke of Milan*
FERDINAND, *son to the King of Naples*
GONZALO, *an honest old counsellor*
ADRIAN | FRANCISCO — *Lords*
CALIBAN, *a savage and deformed slave*
TRINCULO, *a jester*
STEPHANO, *a drunken butler*
MASTER *of a ship*
BOATSWAIN

MARINERS

MIRANDA, *daughter to Prospero*

ARIEL, *an airy spirit*
IRIS | CERES | JUNO — *Spirits*

NON-SPEAKING: *Nymphs and Reapers, presented by spirits; and other Spirits attending on Prospero*

SCENE: *A ship at sea, and an island*

ACT I

SCENE I. *On a ship at sea: a tempestuous noise of thunder and lightning heard*

Enter a SHIP-MASTER *and a* BOATSWAIN.

Mast. Boatswain!

Boats. Here, master; what cheer?

Mast. Good, speak to the mariners. Fall to 't, yarely, or we run ourselves aground. Bestir, bestir. [*Exit.*

Enter MARINERS.

Boats. Heigh, my hearts! cheerly, cheerly, my hearts! yare, yare! Take in the topsail. Tend to the master's whistle. Blow, till thou burst thy wind, if room enough!

Enter ALONSO, SEBASTIAN, ANTONIO, FERDINAND, GONZALO, *and others.*

Alon. Good boatswain, have care. Where's the master? Play the men.

Boats. I pray now, keep below.

Ant. Where is the master, boatswain?

Boats. Do you not hear him? You mar our labour. Keep your cabins; you do assist the storm.

Gon. Nay, good, be patient.

Boats. When the sea is. Hence! What cares these roarers for the name of king? To cabin. Silence! trouble us not.

Gon. Good, yet remember whom thou hast aboard.

Boats. None that I more love than myself. You are a counsellor; if you can command these elements to silence, and work the peace of the present, we will not hand a rope more; use your authority. If you cannot, give thanks you have lived so long, and make yourself ready in your cabin for the mischance of the hour, if it so hap. Cheerly, good hearts! Out of our way, I say. [*Exit.*

Gon. I have great comfort from this fellow: Methinks he hath no drowning mark upon him; his complexion is perfect gallows. Stand fast, good Fate, to his hanging. Make the rope of his destiny our cable, for our own doth little advantage. If he be not born to be hanged, our case is miserable. [*Exeunt.*

Re-enter BOATSWAIN.

Boats. Down with the topmast! yare! lower, lower! Bring her to try with main-course. [*A cry within.*] A plague upon this howling! they are louder than the weather or our office.

Re-enter SEBASTIAN, ANTONIO, *and* GONZALO.

Yet again! what do you here? Shall we give o'er and drown? Have you a mind to sink?

Seb. A pox o' your throat, you bawling, blasphemous, incharitable dog!

Boats. Work you then.

Ant. Hang, cur! hang, you whoreson, insolent noisemaker! We are less afraid to be drowned than thou art.

Gon. I'll warrant him for drowning; though the ship were no stronger than a nutshell and as leaky as an unstanched wench.

Boats. Lay her a-hold, a-hold! set her two courses off to sea again; lay her off.

Enter MARINERS *wet.*

Mariners. All lost! to prayers, to prayers! all lost!

Boats. What, must our mouths be cold?

Gon. The King and Prince at prayers! let's assist them,
For our case is as theirs.
Seb. I'm out of patience.
Ant. We are merely cheated of our lives by drunkards.
This wide-chapp'd rascal—would thou mightst lie drowning
The washing of ten tides!
Gon. He'll be hang'd yet,
Though every drop of water swear against it
And gape at widest to glut him.
A confused noise within: Mercy on us!—
We split, we split!—Farewell, my wife and children!—
Farewell, brother!—We split, we split, we split!
Ant. Let's all sink with the King.
Seb. Let's take leave of him.
[*Exeunt* ANTONIO *and* SEBASTIAN.

Gon. Now would I give a thousand furlongs of sea for an acre of barren ground, long heath, brown furze, anything. The wills above be done! but I would fain die a dry death. [*Exeunt.*

SCENE II. *The island: before Prospero's cell*

Enter PROSPERO *and* MIRANDA.

Mir. If by your art, my dearest father, you have
Put the wild waters in this roar, allay them.
The sky, it seems, would pour down stinking pitch,
But that the sea, mounting to the welkin's cheek,
Dashes the fire out. O, I have suffer'd
With those that I saw suffer. A brave vessel,
Who had, no doubt, some noble creature in her,
Dash'd all to pieces. O, the cry did knock
Against my very heart. Poor souls, they perish'd.
Had I been any god of power, I would
Have sunk the sea within the earth or ere
It should the good ship so have swallow'd and
The fraughting souls within her.
Pros. Be collected;
No more amazement. Tell your piteous heart
There's no harm done.
Mir. O, woe the day!
Pros. No harm.
I have done nothing but in care of thee,
Of thee, my dear one, thee, my daughter, who
Art ignorant of what thou art, nought knowing
Of whence I am, nor that I am more better
Than Prospero, master of a full poor cell,
And thy no greater father.
Mir. More to know
Did never meddle with my thoughts.
Pros. 'Tis time
I should inform thee farther. Lend thy hand,
And pluck my magic garment from me. So;
Lays down his mantle.
Lie there, my art. Wipe thou thine eyes; have comfort.
The direful spectacle of the wreck, which touch'd
The very virtue of compassion in thee,
I have with such provision in mine art
So safely ordered that there is no soul—
No, not so much perdition as an hair
Betid to any creature in the vessel
Which thou heard'st cry, which thou saw'st sink. Sit down;
For thou must now know farther.
Mir. You have often
Begun to tell me what I am, but stopp'd
And left me to a bootless inquisition,
Concluding, "Stay; not yet."
Pros. The hour's now come;
The very minute bids thee ope thine ear;
Obey and be attentive. Canst thou remember
A time before we came unto this cell?
I do not think thou canst, for then thou wast not
Out three years old.
Mir. Certainly, sir, I can.
Pros. By what? by any other house or person?
Of anything the image tell me that
Hath kept with thy remembrance.
Mir. 'Tis far off
And rather like a dream than an assurance
That my remembrance warrants. Had I not
Four or five women once that tended me?
Pros. Thou hadst, and more, Miranda. But how is it
That this lives in thy mind? What seest thou else
In the dark backward and abysm of time?
If thou remember'st aught ere thou camest here,
How thou camest here thou mayst.
Mir. But that I do not.
Pros. Twelve year since, Miranda, twelve year since,
Thy father was the Duke of Milan and
A prince of power.
Mir. Sir, are not you my father?
Pros. Thy mother was a piece of virtue, and
She said thou wast my daughter; and thy father
Was Duke of Milan; and thou his only heir
And princess no worse issued.
Mir. O the heavens!
What foul play had we, that we came from thence?
Or blessed was 't we did?
Pros. Both, both, my girl.
By foul play, as thou say'st, were we heaved thence,
But blessedly holp hither.

Mir. O, my heart bleeds
To think o' the teen that I have turn'd you to,
Which is from my remembrance! Please you, farther.
Pros. My brother and thy uncle, call'd Antonio—
I pray thee, mark me—that a brother should
Be so perfidious!—he whom next thyself
Of all the world I loved and to him put
The manage of my state; as at that time
Through all the signories it was the first
And Prospero the prime duke, being so reputed
In dignity, and for the liberal arts
Without a parallel; those being all my study,
The government I cast upon my brother
And to my state grew stranger, being transported
And rapt in secret studies. Thy false uncle—
Dost thou attend me?
Mir. Sir, most heedfully.
Pros. Being once perfected how to grant suits,
How to deny them, who to advance and who
To trash for over-topping, new created
The creatures that were mine, I say, or changed 'em,
Or else new form'd 'em; having both the key
Of officer and office, set all hearts i' the state
To what tune pleased his ear; that now he was
The ivy which had hid my princely trunk,
And suck'd my verdure out on 't. Thou attend'st not.
Mir. O, good sir, I do.
Pros. I pray thee, mark me.
I, thus neglecting worldly ends, all dedicated
To closeness and the bettering of my mind
With that which, but by being so retired,
O'er-prized all popular rate, in my false brother
Awaked an evil nature; and my trust,
Like a good parent, did beget of him
A falsehood in its contrary as great
As my trust was; which had indeed no limit,
A confidence sans bound. He being thus lorded,
Not only with what my revenue yielded,
But what my power might else exact, like one
Who having into truth, by telling of it,
Made such a sinner of his memory,
To credit his own lie, he did believe
He was indeed the Duke. Out o' the substitution,
And executing the outward face of royalty,
With all prerogative, hence his ambition growing—
Dost thou hear?
Mir. Your tale, sir, would cure deafness.
Pros. To have no screen between this part he play'd
And him he play'd it for, he needs will be
Absolute Milan. Me, poor man, my library
Was dukedom large enough. Of temporal royalties
He thinks me now incapable; confederates—
So dry he was for sway—wi' the King of Naples
To give him annual tribute, do him homage,
Subject his coronet to his crown and bend
The dukedom yet unbow'd—alas, poor Milan!—
To most ignoble stooping.
Mir. O the heavens!
Pros. Mark his condition and the event; then tell me
If this might be a brother.
Mir. I should sin
To think but nobly of my grandmother.
Good wombs have borne bad sons.
Pros. Now the condition.
This King of Naples, being an enemy
To me inveterate, hearkens my brother's suit;
Which was, that he, in lieu o' the premises
Of homage and I know not how much tribute,
Should presently extirpate me and mine
Out of the dukedom and confer fair Milan
With all the honours on my brother; whereon,
A treacherous army levied, one midnight
Fated to the purpose did Antonio open
The gates of Milan, and, i' the dead of darkness,
The ministers for the purpose hurried thence
Me and thy crying self.
Mir. Alack, for pity!
I, not remembering how I cried out then,
Will cry it o'er again. It is a hint
That wrings mine eyes to 't.
Pros. Hear a little further
And then I'll bring thee to the present business
Which now's upon 's; without the which this story
Were most impertinent.
Mir. Wherefore did they not
That hour destroy us?
Pros. Well demanded, wench;
My tale provokes that question. Dear, they durst not,
So dear the love my people bore me, nor set
A mark so bloody on the business, but
With colours fairer painted their foul ends.
In few, they hurried us aboard a bark,
Bore us some leagues to sea; where they prepared
A rotten carcass of a boat, not rigg'd,
Nor tackle, sail, nor mast; the very rats
Instinctively have quit it. There they hoist us,
To cry to the sea that roar'd to us, to sigh
To the winds whose pity, sighing back again,
Did us but loving wrong.
Mir. Alack, what trouble
Was I then to you!

Pros. O, a cherubin
Thou wast that did preserve me. Thou didst smile,
Infused with a fortitude from heaven,
When I have deck'd the sea with drops full salt,
Under my burthen groan'd; which raised in me
An undergoing stomach, to bear up
Against what should ensue.
Mir. How came we ashore?
Pros. By Providence divine.
Some food we had and some fresh water that
A noble Neapolitan, Gonzalo,
Out of his charity, who being then appointed
Master of this design, did give us, with
Rich garments, linens, stuffs and necessaries,
Which since have steaded much; so, of his gentleness,
Knowing I loved my books, he furnish'd me
From mine own library with volumes that
I prize above my dukedom.
Mir. Would I might
But ever see that man!
Pros. Now I arise. [*Resumes his mantle.*]
Sit still, and hear the last of our sea-sorrow.
Here in this island we arrived; and here
Have I, thy schoolmaster, made thee more profit
Than other princesses can that have more time
For vainer hours and tutors not so careful.
Mir. Heavens thank you for 't! And now, I pray you, sir,
For still 'tis beating in my mind, your reason
For raising this sea-storm?
Pros. Know thus far forth.
By accident most strange, bountiful Fortune,
Now my dear lady, hath mine enemies
Brought to this shore; and by my prescience
I find my zenith doth depend upon
A most auspicious star, whose influence
If now I court not but omit, my fortunes
Will ever after droop. Here cease more questions.
Thou art inclined to sleep; 'tis a good dulness,
And give it way; I know thou canst not choose.
MIRANDA *sleeps.*
Come away, servant, come. I am ready now.
Approach, my Ariel, come.

Enter ARIEL.

Ari. All hail, great master! grave sir, hail! I come
To answer thy best pleasure, be 't to fly,
To swim, to dive into the fire, to ride
On the curl'd clouds, to thy strong bidding task
Ariel and all his quality.
Pros. Hast thou, spirit,
Perform'd to point the tempest that I bade thee?
Ari. To every article.
I boarded the King's ship; now on the beak,
Now in the waist, the deck, in every cabin,
I flamed amazement. Sometime I'd divide,
And burn in many places; on the topmast,
The yards and bowsprit, would I flame distinctly,
Then meet and join. Jove's lightnings, the precursors
O' the dreadful thunder-claps, more momentary
And sight-outrunning were not; the fire and cracks
Of sulphurous roaring the most mighty Neptune
Seem to besiege and make his bold waves tremble,
Yea, his dread trident shake.
Pros. My brave spirit!
Who was so firm, so constant, that this coil
Would not infect his reason?
Ari. Not a soul
But felt a fever of the mad and play'd
Some tricks of desperation. All but mariners
Plunged in the foaming brine and quit the vessel,
Then all afire with me. The King's son, Ferdinand,
With hair up-staring—then like reeds, not hair—
Was the first man that leap'd; cried, "Hell is empty,
And all the devils are here."
Pros. Why, that's my spirit!
But was not this nigh shore?
Ari. Close by, my master.
Pros. But are they, Ariel, safe?
Ari. Not a hair perish'd;
On their sustaining garments not a blemish,
But fresher than before; and, as thou badest me,
In troops I have dispersed them 'bout the isle.
The King's son have I landed by himself;
Whom I left cooling of the air with sighs
In an odd angle of the isle and sitting,
His arms in this sad knot.
Pros. Of the King's ship
The mariners say how thou hast disposed
And all the rest o' the fleet.
Ari. Safely in harbour
Is the King's ship; in the deep nook, where once
Thou call'dst me up at midnight to fetch dew
From the still-vex'd Bermoothes, there she's hid.
The mariners all under hatches stow'd;
Who, with a charm join'd to their suffer'd labour,
I have left asleep; and for the rest o' the fleet
Which I dispersed, they all have met again
And are upon the Mediterranean float,
Bound sadly home for Naples,
Supposing that they saw the King's ship wreck'd

And his great person perish.
Pros. Ariel, thy charge
Exactly is perform'd; but there's more work.
What is the time o' the day?
Ari. Past the mid season.
Pros. At least two glasses. The time 'twixt six and now
Must by us both be spent most preciously.
Ari. Is there more toil? Since thou dost give me pains,
Let me remember thee what thou hast promised,
Which is not yet perform'd me.
Pros. How now? moody?
What is 't thou canst demand?
Ari. My liberty.
Pros. Before the time be out? no more!
Ari. I prithee,
Remember I have done thee worthy service;
Told thee no lies, made thee no mistakings, served
Without or grudge or grumblings. Thou didst promise
To bate me a full year.
Pros. Dost thou forget
From what a torment I did free thee?
Ari. No.
Pros. Thou dost, and think'st it much to tread the ooze
Of the salt deep,
To run upon the sharp wind of the north,
To do me business in the veins o' the earth
When it is baked with frost.
Ari. I do not, sir.
Pros. Thou liest, malignant thing! Hast thou forgot
The foul witch Sycorax, who with age and envy
Was grown into a hoop? Hast thou forgot her?
Ari. No, sir.
Pros. Thou hast. Where was she born? speak; tell me.
Ari. Sir, in Argier.
Pros. O, was she so? I must
Once in a month recount what thou hast been,
Which thou forget'st. This damn'd witch Sycorax,
For mischiefs manifold and sorceries terrible
To enter human hearing, from Argier,
Thou know'st, was banish'd; for one thing she did
They would not take her life. Is not this true?
Ari. Ay, sir.
Pros. This blue-eyed hag was hither brought with child
And here was left by the sailors. Thou, my slave,
As thou report'st thyself, wast then her servant;
And, for thou wast a spirit too delicate
To act her earthy and abhorr'd commands,
Refusing her grand hests, she did confine thee,
By help of her more potent ministers
And in her most unmitigable rage,
Into a cloven pine; within which rift
Imprison'd thou didst painfully remain
A dozen years; within which space she died
And left thee there; where thou didst vent thy groans
As fast as mill-wheels strike. Then was this island—
Save for the son that she did litter here,
A freckled whelp hag-born—not honour'd with
A human shape.
Ari. Yes, Caliban her son.
Pros. Dull thing, I say so; he, that Caliban
Whom now I keep in service. Thou best know'st
What torment I did find thee in; thy groans
Did make wolves howl and penetrate the breasts
Of ever angry bears. It was a torment
To lay upon the damn'd, which Sycorax
Could not again undo. It was mine art,
When I arrived and heard thee, that made gape
The pine and let thee out.
Ari. I thank thee, master.
Pros. If thou more murmur'st, I will rend an oak
And peg thee in his knotty entrails till
Thou hast howl'd away twelve winters.
Ari. Pardon, master;
I will be correspondent to command
And do my spiriting gently.
Pros. Do so, and after two days
I will discharge thee.
Ari. That's my noble master!
What shall I do? Say what; what shall I do?
Pros. Go make thyself like a nymph o' the sea; be subject
To no sight but thine and mine, invisible
To every eyeball else. Go take this shape
And hither come in 't. Go, hence with diligence!
[*Exit* ARIEL.
Awake, dear heart, awake! thou hast slept well;
Awake!
Mir. The strangeness of your story put
Heaviness in me.
Pros. Shake it off. Come on;
We'll visit Caliban my slave, who never
Yields us kind answer.
Mir. 'Tis a villain, sir,
I do not love to look on.
Pros. But, as 'tis,
We cannot miss him: he does make our fire,
Fetch in our wood, and serves in offices
That profit us. What, ho! slave! Caliban!
Thou earth, thou! speak.

Cal. [*Within*] There's wood enough within.
Pros. Come forth, I say! there's other business for thee.
Come, thou tortoise! when?

Re-enter ARIEL *like a water-nymph.*

Fine apparition! My quaint Ariel,
Hark in thine ear.
Ari. My lord, it shall be done. [*Exit.*
Pros. Thou poisonous slave, got by the devil himself
Upon thy wicked dam, come forth!

Enter CALIBAN.

Cal. As wicked dew as e'er my mother brush'd
With raven's feather from unwholesome fen
Drop on you both! a south-west blow on ye
And blister you all o'er!
Pros. For this, be sure, to-night thou shalt have cramps,
Side-stitches that shall pen thy breath up; urchins
Shall, for that vast of night that they may work,
All exercise on thee; thou shalt be pinch'd
As thick as honeycomb, each pinch more stinging
Than bees that made 'em.
Cal. I must eat my dinner.
This island's mine, by Sycorax my mother,
Which thou takest from me. When thou camest first,
Thou strokedst me and madest much of me, wouldst give me
Water with berries in 't, and teach me how
To name the bigger light, and how the less,
That burn by day and night; and then I loved thee
And show'd thee all the qualities o' the isle,
The fresh springs, brine-pits, barren place and fertile.
Cursed be I that did so! All the charms
Of Sycorax, toads, beetles, bats, light on you!
For I am all the subjects that you have,
Which first was mine own king; and here you sty me
In this hard rock, whiles you do keep from me
The rest o' the island.
Pros. Thou most lying slave,
Whom stripes may move, not kindness! I have used thee,
Filth as thou art, with human care, and lodged thee
In mine own cell, till thou didst seek to violate
The honour of my child.
Cal. O ho, O ho! would 't had been done!
Thou didst prevent me; I had peopled else
This isle with Calibans.
Pros. Abhorred slave,
Which any print of goodness wilt not take,
Being capable of all ill! I pitied thee,
Took pains to make thee speak, taught thee each hour
One thing or other. When thou didst not, savage,
Know thine own meaning, but wouldst gabble like
A thing most brutish, I endow'd thy purposes
With words that made them known. But thy vile race,
Though thou didst learn, had that in 't which good natures
Could not abide to be with; therefore wast thou
Deservedly confined into this rock,
Who hadst deserved more than a prison.
Cal. You taught me language; and my profit on 't
Is, I know how to curse. The red plague rid you
For learning me your language!
Pros. Hag-seed, hence!
Fetch us in fuel; and be quick, thou'rt best,
To answer other business. Shrug'st thou, malice?
If thou neglect'st or dost unwillingly
What I command, I'll rack thee with old cramps,
Fill all thy bones with aches, make thee roar
That beasts shall tremble at thy din.
Cal. No, pray thee.
[*Aside*] I must obey. His art is of such power,
It would control my dam's god, Setebos,
And make a vassal of him.
Pros. So, slave; hence! [*Exit* CALIBAN.

Re-enter ARIEL, *invisible, playing and singing;* FERDINAND *following.*

ARIEL'S SONG

Come unto these yellow sands,
And then take hands.
Courtsied when you have and kiss'd
The wild waves whist,
Foot it featly here and there;
And, sweet sprites, the burthen bear.
Burden (*dispersedly*) Hark, hark!
Bow-wow.
The watch-dogs bark!
Bow-wow.
Ari. Hark, hark! I hear
The strain of strutting chanticleer
Cry, Cock-a-diddle-dow.

Fer. Where should this music be? i' the air or the earth?
It sounds no more; and, sure, it waits upon

Some god o' the island. Sitting on a bank,
Weeping again the King my father's wreck,
This music crept by me upon the waters,
Allaying both their fury and my passion
With its sweet air. Thence I have follow'd it,
Or it hath drawn me rather. But 'tis gone.
No, it begins again.

ARIEL'S SONG

Full fathom five thy father lies;
Of his bones are coral made;
Those are pearls that were his eyes:
Nothing of him that doth fade
But doth suffer a sea-change
Into something rich and strange.
Sea-nymphs hourly ring his knell:
Burden. Ding-dong.

Ari. Hark! now I hear them—Ding-dong, bell.

Fer. The ditty does remember my drown'd father.
This is no mortal business, nor no sound
That the earth owes. I hear it now above me.

Pros. The fringed curtains of thine eye advance
And say what thou seest yond.

Mir. What is 't? a spirit?
Lord, how it looks about! Believe me, sir,
It carries a brave form. But 'tis a spirit.

Pros. No, wench; it eats and sleeps and hath such senses
As we have, such. This gallant which thou seest
Was in the wreck; and, but he's something stain'd
With grief that's beauty's canker, thou mightst call him
A goodly person. He hath lost his fellows
And strays about to find 'em.

Mir. I might call him
A thing divine, for nothing natural
I ever saw so noble.

Pros. [*Aside*] It goes on, I see,
As my soul prompts it. Spirit, fine spirit! I'll free thee
Within two days for this.

Fer. Most sure, the goddess
On whom these airs attend! Vouchsafe my prayer
May know if you remain upon this island;
And that you will some good instruction give
How I may bear me here. My prime request,
Which I do last pronounce, is, O you wonder!
If you be maid or no?

Mir. No wonder, sir;
But certainly a maid.

Fer. My language! heavens!
I am the best of them that speak this speech,
Were I but where 'tis spoken.

Pros. How? the best?
What wert thou, if the King of Naples heard thee?

Fer. A single thing, as I am now, that wonders
To hear thee speak of Naples. He does hear me;
And that he does I weep. Myself am Naples,
Who with mine eyes, never since at ebb, beheld
The King my father wreck'd.

Mir. Alack, for mercy!

Fer. Yes, faith, and all his lords; the Duke of Milan
And his brave son being twain.

Pros. [*Aside*] The Duke of Milan
And his more braver daughter could control thee,
If now 'twere fit to do 't. At the first sight
They have changed eyes. Delicate Ariel,
I'll set thee free for this. [*To* FERDINAND] A word, good sir;
I fear you have done yourself some wrong; a word.

Mir. Why speaks my father so ungently? This
Is the third man that e'er I saw, the first
That e'er I sigh'd for. Pity move my father
To be inclined my way!

Fer. O, if a virgin,
And your affection not gone forth, I'll make you
The Queen of Naples.

Pros. Soft, sir! one word more.
[*Aside*] They are both in either's powers; but this swift business
I must uneasy make, lest too light winning
Make the prize light. [*To* FERDINAND] One word more; I charge thee
That thou attend me. Thou dost here usurp
The name thou owest not; and hast put thyself
Upon this island as a spy, to win it
From me, the lord on 't.

Fer. No, as I am a man.

Mir. There's nothing ill can dwell in such a temple.
If the ill spirit have so fair a house,
Good things will strive to dwell with 't.

Pros. Follow me.
Speak not you for him; he's a traitor. Come;
I'll manacle thy neck and feet together;
Sea-water shalt thou drink; thy food shall be
The fresh-brook muscles, wither'd roots, and husks
Wherein the acorn cradled. Follow.

Fer. No;
I will resist such entertainment till
Mine enemy has more power.

Draws, and is charmed from moving.

Mir. O dear father,
Make not too rash a trial of him, for
He's gentle and not fearful.
Pros. What? I say,
My foot my tutor? Put thy sword up, traitor;
Who makest a show but darest not strike, thy conscience
Is so possess'd with guilt. Come from thy ward,
For I can here disarm thee with this stick
And make thy weapon drop.
Mir. Beseech you, father.
Pros. Hence! hang not on my garments.
Mir. Sir, have pity;
I'll be his surety.
Pros. Silence! one word more
Shall make me chide thee, if not hate thee. What!
An advocate for an impostor! hush!
Thou think'st there is no more such shapes as he,
Having seen but him and Caliban. Foolish wench!
To the most of men this is a Caliban
And they to him are angels.
Mir. My affections
Are then most humble; I have no ambition
To see a goodlier man.
Pros. Come on; obey.
Thy nerves are in their infancy again
And have no vigour in them.
Fer. So they are;
My spirits, as in a dream, are all bound up.
My father's loss, the weakness which I feel,
The wreck of all my friends, nor this man's threats,
To whom I am subdued, are but light to me,
Might I but through my prison once a day
Behold this maid. All corners else o' the earth
Let liberty make use of; space enough
Have I in such a prison.
Pros. [*Aside*] It works. [*To* FERDINAND] Come on.
Thou hast done well, fine Ariel! [*To* FERDINAND] Follow me.
[*To* ARIEL] Hark what thou else shalt do me.
Mir. Be of comfort;
My father's of a better nature, sir,
Than he appears by speech. This is unwonted
Which now came from him.
Pros. Thou shalt be as free
As mountain winds. But then exactly do
All points of my command.
Ari. To the syllable.
Pros. Come, follow. Speak not for him.
[*Exeunt.*

ACT II

SCENE I. *Another part of the island*

Enter ALONSO, SEBASTIAN, ANTONIO, GONZALO, ADRIAN, FRANCISCO, *and others*.

Gon. Beseech you, sir, be merry; you have cause,
So have we all, of joy; for our escape
Is much beyond our loss. Our hint of woe
Is common; every day some sailor's wife,
The masters of some merchant, and the merchant
Have just our theme of woe; but for the miracle,
I mean our preservation, few in millions
Can speak like us. Then wisely, good sir, weigh
Our sorrow with our comfort.
Alon. Prithee, peace.
Seb. He receives comfort like cold porridge.
Ant. The visitor will not give him o'er so.
Seb. Look, he's winding up the watch of his wit; by and by it will strike.
Gon. Sir—
Seb. One. Tell.
Gon. When every grief is entertain'd that's offer'd,
Comes to the entertainer—
Seb. A dollar.
Gon. Dolour comes to him, indeed; you have spoken truer than you purposed.
Seb. You have taken it wiselier than I meant you should.
Gon. Therefore, my lord—
Ant. Fie, what a spendthrift is he of his tongue!
Alon. I prithee, spare.
Gon. Well, I have done. But yet—
Seb. He will be talking.
Ant. Which, of he or Adrian, for a good wager, first begins to crow?
Seb. The old cock.
Ant. The cockerel.
Seb. Done. The wager?
Ant. A laughter.
Seb. A match!
Adr. Though this island seem to be desert—
Seb. Ha, ha, ha! So, you're paid.
Adr. Uninhabitable and almost inaccessible—
Seb. Yet—
Adr. Yet—
Ant. He could not miss 't.
Adr. It must needs be of subtle, tender, and delicate temperance.
Ant. Temperance was a delicate wench.
Seb. Ay, and a subtle; as he most learnedly delivered.
Adr. The air breathes upon us here most sweetly.
Seb. As if it had lungs and rotten ones.

Ant. Or as 'twere perfumed by a fen.

Gon. Here is everything advantageous to life.

Ant. True; save means to live.

Seb. Of that there's none, or little.

Gon. How lush and lusty the grass looks! how green!

Ant. The ground indeed is tawny.

Seb. With an eye of green in 't.

Ant. He misses not much.

Seb. No; he doth but mistake the truth totally.

Gon. But the rarity of it is—which is indeed almost beyond credit—

Seb. As many vouched rarities are.

Gon. That our garments, being, as they were, drenched in the sea, hold notwithstanding their freshness and glosses, being rather new-dyed than stained with salt water.

Ant. If but one of his pockets could speak, would it not say he lies?

Seb. Ay, or very falsely pocket up his report.

Gon. Methinks our garments are now as fresh as when we put them on first in Afric, at the marriage of the King's fair daughter Claribel to the King of Tunis.

Seb. 'Twas a sweet marriage, and we prosper well in our return.

Adr. Tunis was never graced before with such a paragon to their queen.

Gon. Not since widow Dido's time.

Ant. Widow! a pox o' that! How came that widow in? widow Dido!

Seb. What if he had said "widower Æneas" too? Good Lord, how you take it!

Adr. "Widow Dido" said you? you make me study of that. She was of Carthage, not of Tunis.

Gon. This Tunis, sir, was Carthage.

Adr. Carthage?

Gon. I assure you, Carthage.

Seb. His word is more than the miraculous harp; he hath raised the wall and houses too.

Ant. What impossible matter will he make easy next?

Seb. I think he will carry this island home in his pocket and give it his son for an apple.

Ant. And, sowing the kernels of it in the sea, bring forth more islands.

Gon. Ay.

Ant. Why, in good time.

Gon. Sir, we were talking that our garments seem now as fresh as when we were at Tunis at the marriage of your daughter, who is now Queen.

Ant. And the rarest that e'er came there.

Seb. Bate, I beseech you, widow Dido.

Ant. O, widow Dido! ay, widow Dido.

Gon. Is not, sir, my doublet as fresh as the first day I wore it? I mean, in a sort.

Ant. That sort was well fished for.

Gon. When I wore it at your daughter's marriage?

Alon. You cram these words into mine ears against
The stomach of my sense. Would I had never
Married my daughter there! for, coming thence,
My son is lost and, in my rate, she too,
Who is so far from Italy removed
I ne'er again shall see her. O thou mine heir
Of Naples and of Milan, what strange fish
Hath made his meal on thee?

Fran. Sir, he may live.
I saw him beat the surges under him
And ride upon their backs; he trod the water,
Whose enmity he flung aside, and breasted
The surge most swoln that met him; his bold head
'Bove the contentious waves he kept, and oar'd
Himself with his good arms in lusty stroke
To the shore, that o'er his wave-worn basis bow'd,
As stooping to relieve him. I not doubt
He came alive to land.

Alon. No, no, he's gone.

Seb. Sir, you may thank yourself for this great loss,
That would not bless our Europe with your daughter,
But rather lose her to an African;
Where she at least is banish'd from your eye,
Who hath cause to wet the grief on 't.

Alon. Prithee, peace.

Seb. You were kneel'd to and importuned otherwise
By all of us, and the fair soul herself
Weigh'd between loathness and obedience, at
Which end o' the beam should bow. We have lost your son,
I fear, for ever. Milan and Naples have
Moe widows in them of this business' making
Than we bring men to comfort them.
The fault's your own.

Alon. So is the dear'st o' the loss.

Gon. My lord Sebastian,
The truth you speak doth lack some gentleness
And time to speak it in. You rub the sore,
When you should bring the plaster.

Seb. Very well.

Ant. And most chirurgeonly.

Gon. It is foul weather in us all, good sir,
When you are cloudy.

Seb. Foul weather?

Ant. Very foul.

Gon. Had I plantation of this isle, my lord—

Ant. He'd sow 't with nettle-seed.
Seb. Or docks, or mallows.
Gon. And were the king on 't, what would I do?
Seb. 'Scape being drunk for want of wine.
Gon. I' the commonwealth I would by contraries
Execute all things; for no kind of traffic
Would I admit; no name of magistrate;
Letters should not be known; riches, poverty,
And use of service, none; contract, succession,
Bourn, bound of land, tilth, vineyard, none;
No use of metal, corn, or wine, or oil;
No occupation; all men idle, all;
And women too, but innocent and pure;
No sovereignty—
Seb. Yet he would be king on 't.
Ant. The latter end of his commonwealth forgets the beginning.
Gon. All things in common nature should produce
Without sweat or endeavour. Treason, felony,
Sword, pike, knife, gun, or need of any engine,
Would I not have; but nature should bring forth,
Of it own kind, all foison, all abundance,
To feed my innocent people.
Seb. No marrying 'mong his subjects?
Ant. None, man; all idle. Whores and knaves.
Gon. I would with such perfection govern, sir,
To excel the golden age.
Seb. God save his Majesty!
Ant. Long live Gonzalo!
Gon. And—do you mark me, sir?
Alon. Prithee, no more. Thou dost talk nothing to me.
Gon. I do well believe your Highness; and did it to minister occasion to these gentlemen, who are of such sensible and nimble lungs that they always use to laugh at nothing.
Ant. 'Twas you we laughed at.
Gon. Who in this kind of merry fooling am nothing to you. So you may continue and laugh at nothing still.
Ant. What a blow was there given!
Seb. An it had not fallen flatlong.
Gon. You are gentlemen of brave mettle; you would lift the moon out of her sphere, if she would continue in it five weeks without changing.

Enter ARIEL, *invisible, playing solemn music.*

Seb. We would so, and then go a bat-fowling.
Ant. Nay, good my lord, be not angry.
Gon. No, I warrant you; I will not adventure my discretion so weakly. Will you laugh me asleep, for I am very heavy?
Ant. Go sleep, and hear us.

All sleep except ALONSO, SEBASTIAN, *and* ANTONIO.

Alon. What, all so soon asleep! I wish mine eyes
Would, with themselves, shut up my thoughts. I find
They are inclined to do so.
Seb. Please you, sir,
Do not omit the heavy offer of it.
It seldom visits sorrow; when it doth,
It is a comforter.
Ant. We two, my lord,
Will guard your person while you take your rest,
And watch your safety.
Alon. Thank you. Wondrous heavy.
[ALONSO *sleeps. Exit* ARIEL.
Seb. What a strange drowsiness possesses them!
Ant. It is the quality o' the climate.
Seb. Why
Doth it not then our eyelids sink? I find not
Myself disposed to sleep.
Ant. Nor I; my spirits are nimble.
They fell together all, as by consent;
They dropp'd, as by a thunder-stroke. What might,
Worthy Sebastian? O, what might? No more;
And yet methinks I see it in thy face,
What thou shouldst be. The occasion speaks thee, and
My strong imagination sees a crown
Dropping upon thy head.
Seb. What, art thou waking?
Ant. Do you not hear me speak?
Seb. I do; and surely
It is a sleepy language and thou speak'st
Out of thy sleep. What is it thou didst say?
This is a strange repose, to be asleep
With eyes wide open; standing, speaking, moving,
And yet so fast asleep.
Ant. Noble Sebastian,
Thou let'st thy fortune sleep—die, rather; wink'st
Whiles thou art waking.
Seb. Thou dost snore distinctly;
There's meaning in thy snores.
Ant. I am more serious than my custom. You
Must be so too, if heed me; which to do
Trebles thee o'er.
Seb. Well, I am standing water.
Ant. I'll teach you how to flow.
Seb. Do so. To ebb
Hereditary sloth instructs me.
Ant. O,
If you but knew how you the purpose cherish
Whiles thus you mock it! how, in stripping it,

You more invest it! Ebbing men, indeed,
Most often do so near the bottom run
By their own fear or sloth.

Seb. Prithee, say on.
The setting of thine eye and cheek proclaim
A matter from thee, and a birth indeed
Which throes thee much to yield.

Ant. Thus, sir:
Although this lord of weak remembrance, this,
Who shall be of as little memory
When he is earth'd, hath here almost persuaded—
For he's a spirit of persuasion, only
Professes to persuade—the King his son's alive,
'Tis as impossible that he's undrown'd
As he that sleeps here swims.

Seb. I have no hope
That he's undrown'd.

Ant. O, out of that "no hope"
What great hope have you! no hope that way is
Another way so high a hope that even
Ambition cannot pierce a wink beyond,
But doubt discovery there. Will you grant with me
That Ferdinand is drown'd?

Seb. He's gone.

Ant. Then, tell me,
Who's the next heir of Naples?

Seb. Claribel.

Ant. She that is Queen of Tunis; she that dwells
Ten leagues beyond man's life; she that from Naples
Can have no note, unless the sun were post—
The man i' the moon's too slow—till new-born chins
Be rough and razorable; she that—from whom?
We all were sea-swallow'd, though some cast again,
And by that destiny to perform an act
Whereof what's past is prologue, what to come
In yours and my discharge.

Seb. What stuff is this! how say you?
'Tis true, my brother's daughter's Queen of Tunis;
So is she heir of Naples; 'twixt which regions
There is some space.

Ant. A space whose every cubit
Seems to cry out, "How shall that Claribel
Measure us back to Naples? Keep in Tunis,
And let Sebastian wake." Say, this were death
That now hath seized them; why, they were no worse
Than now they are. There be that can rule Naples
As well as he that sleeps; lords that can prate
As amply and unnecessarily
As this Gonzalo; I myself could make
A chough of as deep chat. O, that you bore
The mind that I do! what a sleep were this
For your advancement! Do you understand me?

Seb. Methinks I do.

Ant. And how does your content
Tender your own good fortune?

Seb. I remember
You did supplant your brother Prospero.

Ant. True;
And look how well my garments sit upon me;
Much feater than before. My brother's servants
Were then my fellows; now they are my men.

Seb. But, for your conscience?

Ant. Ay, sir; where lies that? if 'twere a kibe,
'Twould put me to my slipper: but I feel not
This deity in my bosom. Twenty consciences,
That stand 'twixt me and Milan, candied be they
And melt ere they molest! Here lies your brother,
No better than the earth he lies upon,
If he were that which now he's like, that's dead;
Whom I, with this obedient steel, three inches of it,
Can lay to bed for ever; whiles you, doing thus,
To the perpetual wink for aye might put
This ancient morsel, this Sir Prudence, who
Should not upbraid our course. For all the rest,
They'll take suggestion as a cat laps milk;
They'll tell the clock to any business that
We say befits the hour.

Seb. Thy case, dear friend,
Shall be my precedent; as thou got'st Milan,
I'll come by Naples. Draw thy sword. One stroke
Shall free thee from the tribute which thou payest;
And I the King shall love thee.

Ant. Draw together;
And when I rear my hand, do you the like,
To fall it on Gonzalo.

Seb. O, but one word. [*They talk apart.*]

Re-enter ARIEL, *invisible.*

Ari. My master through his art foresees the danger
That you, his friend, are in; and sends me forth—
For else his project dies—to keep them living.

Sings in GONZALO'S *ear.*

While you here do snoring lie,
Open-eyed conspiracy
His time doth take.
If of life you keep a care,
Shake off slumber, and beware;
Awake, awake!

Ant. Then let us both be sudden.
Gon. Now, good angels
Preserve the King.
They wake.
Alon. Why, how now? ho, awake! Why are you drawn?
Wherefore this ghastly looking?
Gon. What's the matter?
Seb. Whiles we stood here securing your repose,
Even now, we heard a hollow burst of bellowing
Like bulls, or rather lions. Did 't not wake you?
It struck mine ear most terribly.
Alon. I heard nothing.
Ant. O, 'twas a din to fright a monster's ear,
To make an earthquake! sure, it was the roar
Of a whole herd of lions.
Alon. Heard you this, Gonzalo?
Gon. Upon mine honour, sir, I heard a humming,
And that a strange one too, which did awake me.
I shaked you, sir, and cried. As mine eyes open'd,
I saw their weapons drawn. There was a noise,
That's verily. 'Tis best we stand upon our guard,
Or that we quit this place. Let's draw our weapons.
Alon. Lead off this ground; and let's make further search
For my poor son.
Gon. Heavens keep him from these beasts!
For he is, sure, i' the island.
Alon. Lead away.
Ari. Prospero my lord shall know what I have done.
So, King, go safely to seek thy son. [*Exeunt.*

SCENE II. *Another part of the island*

Enter CALIBAN *with a burden of wood. A noise of thunder heard.*

Cal. All the infections that the sun sucks up
From bogs, fens, flats, on Prosper fall and make him
By inch-meal a disease! His spirits hear me
And yet I needs must curse. But they'll nor pinch,
Fright me with urchin-shows, pitch me i' the mire,
Nor lead me, like a firebrand, in the dark
Out of my way, unless he bid 'em; but
For every trifle are they set upon me;
Sometime like apes that mow and chatter at me
And after bite me, then like hedgehogs which
Lie tumbling in my barefoot way and mount
Their pricks at my footfall; sometime am I
All wound with adders who with cloven tongues
Do hiss me into madness.

Enter TRINCULO.

Lo, now, lo!
Here comes a spirit of his, and to torment me
For bringing wood in slowly. I'll fall flat;
Perchance he will not mind me.

Trin. Here's neither bush nor shrub, to bear off any weather at all, and another storm brewing; I hear it sing i' the wind. Yond same black cloud, yond huge one, looks like a foul bombard that would shed his liquor. If it should thunder as it did before, I know not where to hide my head; yond same cloud cannot choose but fall by pailfuls. What have we here? a man or a fish? Dead or alive? A fish; he smells like a fish; a very ancient and fish-like smell; a kind of not-of-the newest Poor-John. A strange fish! Were I in England now, as once I was, and had but this fish painted, not a holiday fool there but would give a piece of silver. There would this monster make a man; any strange beast there makes a man; when they will not give a doit to relieve a lame beggar, they will lay out ten to see a dead Indian. Legged like a man! and his fins like arms! Warm o' my troth! I do now let loose my opinion; hold it no longer. This is no fish, but an islander, that hath lately suffered by a thunderbolt. [*Thunder.*] Alas, the storm is come again! my best way is to creep under his garberdine; there is no other shelter hereabout. Misery acquaints a man with strange bedfellows. I will here shroud till the dregs of the storm be past.

Enter STEPHANO, *singing, a bottle in his hand.*

Ste. "I shall no more to sea, to sea,
Here shall I die ashore—"

This is a very scurvy tune to sing at a man's funeral. Well, here's my comfort. [*Drinks.*]
[*Sings*] "The master, the swabber, the boatswain and I,
The gunner and his mate
Loved Mall, Meg, and Marian, and Margery,
But none of us cared for Kate;
For she had a tongue with a tang,
Would cry to a sailor, 'Go hang!'
She loved not the savour of tar nor of pitch,
Yet a tailor might scratch her where'er she did itch;
Then to sea, boys, and let her go hang!"

This is a scurvy tune too; but here's my comfort.
Drinks.
Cal. Do not torment me! Oh!
Ste. What's the matter? Have we devils here?
Do you put tricks upon's with savages and men

of Ind, ha? I have not 'scaped drowning to be afeard now of your four legs; for it hath been said, "As proper a man as ever went on four legs cannot make him give ground"; and it shall be said so again while Stephano breathes at nostrils.

Cal. The spirit torments me; Oh!

Ste. This is some monster of the isle with four legs, who hath got, as I take it, an ague. Where the devil should he learn our language? I will give him some relief, if it be but for that. If I can recover him and keep him tame and get to Naples with him, he's a present for any emperor that ever trod on neat's-leather.

Cal. Do not torment me, prithee; I'll bring my wood home faster.

Ste. He's in his fit now and does not talk after the wisest. He shall taste of my bottle. If he have never drunk wine afore, it will go near to remove his fit. If I can recover him and keep him tame, I will not take too much for him; he shall pay for him that hath him, and that soundly.

Cal. Thou dost me yet but little hurt; thou wilt anon, I know it by thy trembling. Now, Prosper works upon thee.

Ste. Come on your ways; open your mouth; here is that which will give language to you, cat. Open your mouth; this will shake your shaking, I can tell you, and that soundly. You cannot tell who's your friend. Open your chaps again.

Trin. I should know that voice. It should be—but he is drowned; and these are devils. O defend me!

Ste. Four legs and two voices; a most delicate monster! His forward voice now is to speak well of his friend; his backward voice is to utter foul speeches and to detract. If all the wine in my bottle will recover him, I will help his ague. Come. Amen! I will pour some in thy other mouth.

Trin. Stephano!

Ste. Doth thy other mouth call me? Mercy, mercy! This is a devil, and no monster. I will leave him; I have no long spoon.

Trin. Stephano! If thou beest Stephano, touch me and speak to me; for I am Trinculo—be not afeard—thy good friend Trinculo.

Ste. If thou beest Trinculo, come forth. I'll pull thee by the lesser legs. If any be Trinculo's legs, these are they. Thou art very Trinculo indeed! How camest thou to be the siege of this moon-calf? can he vent Trinculos?

Trin. I took him to be killed with a thunder-stroke. But art thou not drowned, Stephano? I hope now thou art not drowned. Is the storm overblown? I hid me under the dead moon-calf's gaberdine for fear of the storm. And art thou living, Stephano? O Stephano, two Neapolitans 'scaped!

Ste. Prithee, do not turn me about; my stomach is not constant.

Cal. [*Aside*] These be fine things, an if they be not sprites.
That's a brave god and bears celestial liquor.
I will kneel to him.

Ste. How didst thou 'scape? How camest thou hither? swear by this bottle how thou camest hither. I escaped upon a butt of sack which the sailors heaved o'erboard, by this bottle, which I made of the bark of a tree with mine own hands since I was cast ashore.

Cal. I'll swear upon that bottle to be thy true subject; for the liquor is not earthly.

Ste. Here; swear then how thou escapedst.

Trin. Swum ashore, man, like a duck. I can swim like a duck, I'll be sworn.

Ste. Here, kiss the book. [*Passing the bottle.*] Though thou canst swim like a duck, thou art made like a goose.

Trin. O Stephano, hast any more of this?

Ste. The whole butt, man. My cellar is in a rock by the sea-side where my wine is hid. How now, moon-calf! how does thine ague?

Cal. Hast thou not dropp'd from heaven?

Ste. Out o' the moon, I do assure thee. I was the man i' the moon when time was.

Cal. I have seen thee in her and I do adore thee.
My mistress show'd me thee and thy dog and thy bush.

Ste. Come, swear to that; kiss the book. I will furnish it anon with new contents. Swear.

Trin. By this good light, this is a very shallow monster! I afeard of him! A very weak monster! The man i' the moon! A most poor credulous monster! Well drawn, monster, in good sooth!

Cal. I'll show thee every fertile inch o' th' island;
And I will kiss thy foot. I prithee, be my god.

Trin. By this light, a most perfidious and drunken monster! When's god's asleep, he'll rob his bottle.

Cal. I'll kiss thy foot; I'll swear myself thy subject.

Ste. Come on then; down, and swear.

Trin. I shall laugh myself to death at this puppy-headed monster. A most scurvy monster! I could find in my heart to beat him—

Ste. Come, kiss.

Trin. But that the poor monster's in drink. An abominable monster!

Cal. I'll show thee the best springs; I'll pluck thee berries;
I'll fish for thee and get thee wood enough.

A plague upon the tyrant that I serve!
I'll bear him no more sticks, but follow thee,
Thou wondrous man.

Trin. A most ridiculous monster, to make a wonder of a poor drunkard!

Cal. I prithee, let me bring thee where crabs grow;
And I with my long nails will dig thee pig-nuts;
Show thee a jay's nest and instruct thee how
To snare the nimble marmoset; I'll bring thee
To clustering filberts and sometimes I'll get thee
Young scamels from the rock. Wilt thou go with me?

Ste. I prithee now, lead the way without any more talking. Trinculo, the King and all our company else being drowned, we will inherit here. Here; bear my bottle. Fellow Trinculo, we'll fill him by and by again.

Cal. [*Sings drunkenly*]
Farewell, master; farewell, farewell!

Trin. A howling monster; a drunken monster!

Cal. No more dams I'll make for fish;
Nor fetch in firing
At requiring;
Nor scrape trencher, nor wash dish.
'Ban, 'Ban, Cacaliban
Has a new master, get a new man.
Freedom, hey-day! hey-day, freedom! freedom, hey-day, freedom!

Ste. O brave monster! Lead the way. [*Exeunt.*

ACT III

SCENE I. *Before Prospero's cell*

Enter FERDINAND, *bearing a log.*

Fer. There be some sports are painful, and their labour
Delight in them sets off; some kinds of baseness
Are nobly undergone and most poor matters
Point to rich ends. This my mean task
Would be as heavy to me as odious, but
The mistress which I serve quickens what's dead
And makes my labours pleasures. O, she is
Ten times more gentle than her father's crabbed,
And he's composed of harshness. I must remove
Some thousands of these logs and pile them up,
Upon a sore injunction. My sweet mistress
Weeps when she sees me work, and says, such baseness
Had never like executor. I forget;
But these sweet thoughts do even refresh my labours
Most busiest when I do it.

Enter MIRANDA; *and* PROSPERO *at a distance, unseen.*

Mir. Alas, now, pray you,
Work not so hard. I would the lightning had
Burnt up those logs that you are enjoin'd to pile!
Pray, set it down and rest you. When this burns,
'Twill weep for having wearied you. My father
Is hard at study; pray now, rest yourself;
He's safe for these three hours.

Fer. O most dear mistress,
The sun will set before I shall discharge
What I must strive to do.

Mir. If you'll sit down,
I'll bear your logs the while. Pray, give me that;
I'll carry it to the pile.

Fer. No, precious creature;
I had rather crack my sinews, break my back,
Than you should such dishonour undergo,
While I sit lazy by.

Mir. It would become me
As well as it does you; and I should do it
With much more ease; for my good will is to it,
And yours it is against.

Pros. Poor worm, thou art infected!
This visitation shows it.

Mir. You look wearily.

Fer. No, noble mistress; 'tis fresh morning with me
When you are by at night. I do beseech you—
Chiefly that I might set it in my prayers—
What is your name?

Mir. Miranda.—O my father,
I have broke your hest to say so!

Fer. Admired Miranda!
Indeed the top of admiration! worth
What's dearest to the world! Full many a lady
I have eyed with best regard and many a time
The harmony of their tongues hath into bondage
Brought my too diligent ear; for several virtues
Have I liked several women; never any
With so full soul, but some defect in her
Did quarrel with the noblest grace she owed
And put it to the foil; but you, O you,
So perfect and so peerless, are created
Of every creature's best!

Mir. I do not know
One of my sex; no woman's face remember,
Save, from my glass, mine own; nor have I seen
More that I may call men than you, good friend,
And my dear father. How features are abroad,
I am skilless of; but, by my modesty,
The jewel in my dower, I would not wish
Any companion in the world but you,
Nor can imagination form a shape,
Besides yourself, to like of. But I prattle

Something too wildly and my father's precepts
I therein do forget.

Fer. I am in my condition
A prince, Miranda; I do think, a king;
I would, not so!—and would no more endure
This wooden slavery than to suffer
The flesh-fly blow my mouth. Hear my soul speak.
The very instant that I saw you, did
My heart fly to your service; there resides,
To make me slave to it; and for your sake
Am I this patient log-man.

Mir. Do you love me?

Fer. O heaven, O earth, bear witness to this sound
And crown what I profess with kind event
If I speak true! if hollowly, invert
What best is boded me to mischief! I
Beyond all limit of what else i' the world
Do love, prize, honour you.

Mir. I am a fool
To weep at what I am glad of.

Pros. Fair encounter
Of two most rare affections! Heavens rain grace
On that which breeds between 'em!

Fer. Wherefore weep you?

Mir. At mine unworthiness that dare not offer
What I desire to give, and much less take
What I shall die to want. But this is trifling;
And all the more it seeks to hide itself,
The bigger bulk it shows. Hence, bashful cunning!
And prompt me, plain and holy innocence!
I am your wife, if you will marry me;
If not, I'll die your maid. To be your fellow
You may deny me; but I'll be your servant,
Whether you will or no.

Fer. My mistress, dearest;
And I thus humble ever.

Mir. My husband, then?

Fer. Ay, with a heart as willing
As bondage e'er of freedom. Here's my hand.

Mir. And mine, with my heart in 't. And now farewell
Till half an hour hence.

Fer. A thousand thousand!

[*Exeunt* FERDINAND *and* MIRANDA *severally*.

Pros. So glad of this as they I cannot be,
Who are surprised withal; but my rejoicing
At nothing can be more. I'll to my book,
For yet ere supper-time must I perform
Much business appertaining. [*Exit*.

SCENE II. *Another part of the island*

Enter CALIBAN, STEPHANO, *and* TRINCULO.

Ste. Tell not me; when the butt is out, we will drink water; not a drop before; therefore bear up, and board 'em. Servant-monster, drink to me.

Trin. Servant-monster! the folly of this island! They say there's but five upon this isle; we are three of them; if th' other two be brained like us, the state totters.

Ste. Drink, servant-monster, when I bid thee. Thy eyes are almost set in thy head.

Trin. Where should they be set else? He were a brave monster indeed, if they were set in his tail.

Ste. My man-monster hath drown'd his tongue in sack. For my part, the sea cannot drown me; I swam, ere I could recover the shore, five and thirty leagues off and on. By this light, thou shalt be my lieutenant, monster, or my standard.

Trin. Your lieutenant, if you list; he's no standard.

Ste. We'll not run, Monsieur Monster.

Trin. Nor go neither; but you'll lie like dogs and yet say nothing neither.

Ste. Moon-calf, speak once in thy life, if thou beest a good moon-calf.

Cal. How does thy honour? Let me lick thy shoe.
I'll not serve him; he is not valiant.

Trin. Thou liest, most ignorant monster. I am in case to justle a constable. Why, thou deboshed fish, thou, was there ever man a coward that hath drunk so much sack as I to-day? Wilt thou tell a monstrous lie, being but half a fish and half a monster?

Cal. Lo, how he mocks me! wilt thou let him, my lord?

Trin. "Lord" quoth he! That a monster should be such a natural!

Cal. Lo, lo, again! bite him to death, I prithee.

Ste. Trinculo, keep a good tongue in your head. If you prove a mutineer—the next tree! The poor monster's my subject, and he shall not suffer indignity.

Cal. I thank my noble lord. Wilt thou be pleased to hearken once again to the suit I made to thee?

Ste. Marry, will I; kneel and repeat it; I will stand, and so shall Trinculo.

Enter ARIEL, *invisible*.

Cal. As I told thee before, I am subject to a tyrant, a sorcerer, that by his cunning hath cheated me of the island.

Ari. Thou liest.

Cal. Thou liest, thou jesting monkey, thou. I would my valiant master would destroy thee! I do not lie.

Ste. Trinculo, if you trouble him any more in's tale, by this hand, I will supplant some of your teeth.

Trin. Why, I said nothing.
Ste. Mum, then, and no more. Proceed.
Cal. I say, by sorcery he got this isle;
From me he got it. If thy greatness will
Revenge it on him—for I know thou darest,
But this thing dare not—
Ste. That's most certain.
Cal. Thou shalt be lord of it and I'll serve thee.
Ste. How now shall this be compassed? Canst thou bring me to the party?
Cal. Yea, yea, my lord. I'll yield him thee asleep,
Where thou mayst knock a nail into his head.
Ari. Thou liest; thou canst not.
Cal. What a pied ninny's this! Thou scurvy patch!
I do beseech thy greatness, give him blows
And take his bottle from him. When that's gone
He shall drink nought but brine; for I'll not show him
Where the quick freshes are.
Ste. Trinculo, run into no further danger. Interrupt the monster one word further, and, by this hand, I'll turn my mercy out o' doors and make a stock-fish of thee.
Trin. Why, what did I? I did nothing. I'll go farther off.
Ste. Didst thou not say he lied?
Ari. Thou liest.
Ste. Do I so? take thou that. [*Beats* TRINCULO]
As you like this, give me the lie another time.
Trin. I did not give the lie. Out o' your wits and hearing too? A pox o' your bottle! this can sack and drinking do. A murrain on your monster, and the devil take your fingers!
Cal. Ha, ha, ha!
Ste. Now, forward with your tale. Prithee, stand farther off.
Cal. Beat him enough. After a little time
I'll beat him too.
Ste. Stand farther. Come, proceed.
Cal. Why, as I told thee, 'tis a custom with him,
I' th' afternoon to sleep. There thou mayst brain him,
Having first seized his books, or with a log
Batter his skull, or paunch him with a stake,
Or cut his wezand with thy knife. Remember
First to possess his books; for without them
He's but a sot, as I am, nor hath not
One spirit to command. They all do hate him
As rootedly as I. Burn but his books.
He has brave utensils—for so he calls them—
Which, when he has a house, he'll deck withal.
And that most deeply to consider is
The beauty of his daughter; he himself
Calls her a nonpareil. I never saw a woman,
But only Sycorax my dam and she;
But she as far surpasseth Sycorax
As great'st does least.
Ste. Is it so brave a lass?
Cal. Ay, lord; she will become thy bed, I warrant.
And bring thee forth brave brood.
Ste. Monster, I will kill this man. His daughter and I will be king and queen—save our graces!—and Trinculo and thyself shall be viceroys. Dost thou like the plot, Trinculo?
Trin. Excellent.
Ste. Give me thy hand. I am sorry I beat thee; but, while thou livest, keep a good tongue in thy head.
Cal. Within this half hour will he be asleep.
Wilt thou destroy him then?
Ste. Ay, on mine honour.
Ari. This will I tell my master.
Cal. Thou makest me merry; I am full of pleasure.
Let us be jocund. Will you troll the catch
You taught me but while-ere?
Ste. At thy request, monster, I will do reason, any reason. Come on, Trinculo, let us sing. [*Sings*]
"Flout 'em and scout 'em
And scout 'em and flout 'em;
Thought is free."
Cal. That's not the tune.
ARIEL *plays the tune on a tabor and pipe.*
Ste. What is this same?
Trin. This is the tune of our catch, played by the picture of Nobody.
Ste. If thou beest a man, show thyself in thy likeness. If thou beest a devil, take 't as thou list.
Trin. O, forgive me my sins!
Ste. He that dies pays all debts. I defy thee.
Mercy upon us!
Cal. Art thou afeard?
Ste. No, monster, not I.
Cal. Be not afeard; the isle is full of noises,
Sounds and sweet airs, that give delight and hurt not.
Sometimes a thousand twangling instruments
Will hum about mine ears, and sometimes voices
That, if I then had waked after long sleep,
Will make me sleep again; and then, in dreaming,
The clouds methought would open and show riches
Ready to drop upon me, that, when I waked,
I cried to dream again.
Ste. This will prove a brave kingdom to me, where I shall have my music for nothing.
Cal. When Prospero is destroyed.
Ste. That shall be by and by. I remember the story.

Trin. The sound is going away; let's follow it, and after do our work.

Ste. Lead, monster; we'll follow. I would I could see this taborer; he lays it on.

Trin. Wilt come? I'll follow, Stephano.

[*Exeunt.*

SCENE III. *Another part of the island*

Enter ALONSO, SEBASTIAN, ANTONIO, GONZALO, ADRIAN, FRANCISCO, *and others.*

Gon. By'r lakin, I can go no further, sir;
My old bones ache. Here's a maze trod indeed
Through forth-rights and meanders! By your patience,
I needs must rest me.
Alon. Old lord, I cannot blame thee,
Who am myself attach'd with weariness,
To the dulling of my spirits. Sit down, and rest.
Even here I will put off my hope and keep it
No longer for my flatterer. He is drown'd
Whom thus we stray to find, and the sea mocks
Our frustrate search on land. Well, let him go.
Ant. [*Aside to* SEBASTIAN] I am right glad that he's so out of hope.
Do not, for one repulse, forego the purpose
That you resolved to effect.
Seb. [*Aside to* ANTONIO] The next advantage
Will we take throughly.
Ant. [*Aside to* SEBASTIAN] Let it be to-night;
For, now they are oppress'd with travel, they
Will not, nor cannot, use such vigilance
As when they are fresh.
Seb. [*Aside to* ANTONIO] I say, to-night. No more.

Solemn and strange music.

Alon. What harmony is this? My good friends, hark!
Gon. Marvellous sweet music!

Enter PROSPERO *above, invisible. Enter several strange Shapes, bringing in a banquet; they dance about it with gentle actions of salutation; and, inviting the* KING, *&c. to eat, they depart.*

Alon. Give us kind keepers, heavens! What were these?
Seb. A living drollery. Now I will believe
That there are unicorns, that in Arabia
There is one tree, the phœnix' throne, one phœnix
At this hour reigning there.
Ant. I'll believe both;
And what does else want credit, come to me,
And I'll be sworn 'tis true. Travellers ne'er did lie,
Though fools at home condemn 'em.
Gon. If in Naples
I should report this now, would they believe me?
If I should say, I saw such islanders—
For, certes, these are people of the island—
Who, though they are of monstrous shape, yet, note,
Their manners are more gentle-kind than of
Our human generation you shall find
Many, nay, almost any.
Pros. [*Aside*] Honest lord,
Thou hast said well; for some of you there present
Are worse than devils.
Alon. I cannot too much muse
Such shapes, such gesture and such sound, expressing,
Although they want the use of tongue, a kind
Of excellent dumb discourse.
Pros. [*Aside*] Praise in departing.
Fran. They vanish'd strangely.
Seb. No matter, since
They have left their viands behind; for we have stomachs.
Will 't please you taste of what is here?
Alon. Not I.
Gon. Faith, sir, you need not fear. When we were boys,
Who would believe that there were mountaineers
Dew-lapp'd like bulls, whose throats had hanging at 'em
Wallets of flesh? or that there were such men
Whose heads stood in their breasts? which now we find
Each putter-out of five for one will bring us
Good warrant of.
Alon. I will stand to and feed,
Although my last. No matter, since I feel
The best is past. Brother, my lord the Duke,
Stand to and do as we.

Thunder and lightning. Enter ARIEL, *like a harpy; claps his wings upon the table; and, with a quaint device, the banquet vanishes.*

Ari. You are three men of sin, whom Destiny,
That hath to instrument this lower world
And what is in 't, the never-surfeited sea
Hath caused to belch up you; and on this island
Where man doth not inhabit; you 'mongst men
Being most unfit to live. I have made you mad;
And even with such-like valour men hang and drown
Their proper selves.

ALONSO, SEBASTIAN, *&c. draw their swords.*

You fools! I and my fellows
Are ministers of Fate. The elements,
Of whom your swords are temper'd, may as well
Wound the loud winds, or with bemock'd-at-stabs

Kill the still-closing waters, as diminish
One dowle that's in my plume. My fellow-ministers
Are like invulnerable. If you could hurt,
Your swords are now too massy for your strengths
And will not be uplifted. But remember—
For that's my business to you—that you three
From Milan did supplant good Prospero;
Exposed unto the sea, which hath requit it,
Him and his innocent child; for which foul deed
The powers, delaying, not forgetting, have
Incensed the seas and shores, yea, all the creatures,
Against your peace. Thee of thy son, Alonso,
They have bereft; and do pronounce by me
Lingering perdition, worse than any death
Can be at once, shall step by step attend
You and your ways; whose wraths to guard you from—
Which here, in this most desolate isle, else falls
Upon your heads—is nothing but heart-sorrow
And a clear life ensuing.

He vanishes in thunder; then, to soft music, enter the Shapes again, and dance, with mocks and mows, and carrying out the table.

Pros. Bravely the figure of this harpy hast thou
Perform'd, my Ariel; a grace it had, devouring.
Of my instruction hast thou nothing bated
In what thou hadst to say. So, with good life
And observation strange, my meaner ministers
Their several kinds have done. My high charms work
And these mine enemies are all knit up
In their distractions; they now are in my power;
And in these fits I leave them, while I visit
Young Ferdinand, whom they suppose is drown'd,
And his and mine loved darling. [*Exit above.*
Gon. I' the name of something holy, sir, why stand you
In this strange stare?
Alon. O, it is monstrous, monstrous!
Methought the billows spoke and told me of it;
The winds did sing it to me, and the thunder,
That deep and dreadful organ-pipe, pronounced
The name of Prosper; it did bass my trespass.
Therefore my son i' the ooze is bedded, and
I'll seek him deeper than e'er plummet sounded
And with him there lie mudded. [*Exit.*
Seb. But one fiend at a time,
I'll fight their legions o'er.
Ant. I'll be thy second.
[*Exeunt* SEBASTIAN *and* ANTONIO.
Gon. All three of them are desperate. Their great guilt,
Like poison given to work a great time after,
Now 'gins to bite the spirits. I do beseech you
That are of suppler joints, follow them swiftly
And hinder them from what this ecstasy
May now provoke them to.
Adr. Follow, I pray you. [*Exeunt.*

ACT IV

SCENE I. *Before Prospero's cell*

Enter PROSPERO, FERDINAND, *and* MIRANDA.

Pros. If I have too austerely punish'd you,
Your compensation makes amends, for I
Have given you here a thrid of mine own life,
Or that for which I live; who once again
I tender to thy hand. All thy vexations
Were but my trials of thy love, and thou
Hast strangely stood the test. Here, afore Heaven,
I ratify this my rich gift. O Ferdinand,
Do not smile at me that I boast her off,
For thou shalt find she will outstrip all praise
And make it halt behind her.
Fer. I do believe it
Against an oracle.
Pros. Then, as my gift and thine own acquisition
Worthily purchased, take my daughter; but
If thou dost break her virgin-knot before
All sanctimonious ceremonies may
With full and holy rite be minister'd,
No sweet aspersion shall the heavens let fall
To make this contract grow; but barren hate,
Sour-eyed disdain, and discord shall bestrew
The union of your bed with weeds so loathly
That you shall hate it both. Therefore take heed,
As Hymen's lamps shall light you.
Fer. As I hope
For quiet days, fair issue, and long life,
With such love as 'tis now, the murkiest den,
The most opportune place, the strong'st suggestion
Our worser genius can, shall never melt
Mine honour into lust, to take away
The edge of that day's celebration
When I shall think, or Phœbus' steeds are founder'd,
Or Night kept chain'd below.
Pros. Fairly spoke.
Sit then and talk with her; she is thine own.
What, Ariel! my industrious servant, Ariel!

Enter ARIEL.

Ari. What would my potent master? here I am.
Pros. Thou and thy meaner fellows your last service

Did worthily perform; and I must use you
In such another trick. Go bring the rabble,
O'er whom I give thee power, here to this place;
Incite them to quick motion; for I must
Bestow upon the eyes of this young couple
Some vanity of mine art. It is my promise,
And they expect it from me.

Ari. Presently?

Pros. Ay, with a twink.

Ari. Before you can say "come" and "go,"
And breathe twice and cry "so, so,"
Each one, tripping on his toe,
Will be here with mop and mow.
Do you love me, master? No?

Pros. Dearly, my delicate Ariel. Do not approach
Till thou dost hear me call.

Ari. Well, I conceive. [*Exit.*

Pros. Look thou be true; do not give dalliance
Too much the rein. The strongest oaths are straw
To the fire i' the blood. Be more abstemious,
Or else, good night your vow!

Fer. I warrant you, sir;
The white cold virgin snow upon my heart
Abates the ardour of my liver.

Pros. Well.
Now come, my Ariel! bring a corollary,
Rather than want a spirit. Appear, and pertly!
No tongue! all eyes! be silent.

Soft music.

Enter IRIS.

Iris. Ceres, most bounteous lady, thy rich leas
Of wheat, rye, barley, vetches, oats, and pease;
Thy turfy mountains, where live nibbling sheep,
And flat meads thatch'd with stover, them to keep;
Thy banks with pioned and twilled brims,
Which spongy April at thy hest betrims,
To make cold nymphs chaste crowns; and thy broom-groves,
Whose shadow the dismissed bachelor loves,
Being lass-lorn; thy pole-clipt vineyard;
And thy sea-marge, sterile and rocky-hard,
Where thou thyself dost air—the queen o' the sky,
Whose watery arch and messenger am I,
Bids thee leave these, and with her sovereign grace,
Here on this grass-plot, in this very place,
To come and sport; here peacocks fly amain.
Approach, rich Ceres, her to entertain.

Enter CERES.

Cer. Hail, many-colour'd messenger, that ne'er
Dost disobey the wife of Jupiter;
Who with thy saffron wings upon my flowers
Diffusest honey-drops, refreshing showers,
And with each end of thy blue bow dost crown
My bosky acres and my unshrubb'd down,
Rich scarf to my proud earth; why hath thy queen
Summon'd me hither, to this short-grass'd green?

Iris. A contract of true love to celebrate;
And some donation freely to estate
On the blest lovers.

Cer. Tell me, heavenly bow,
If Venus or her son, as thou dost know,
Do now attend the Queen? Since they did plot
The means that dusky Dis my daughter got,
Her and her blind boy's scandal'd company
I have forsworn.

Iris. Of her society
Be not afraid. I met her deity
Cutting the clouds towards Paphos and her son
Dove-drawn with her. Here thought they to have done
Some wanton charm upon this man and maid,
Whose vows are, that no bed-right shall be paid
Till Hymen's torch be lighted; but in vain;
Mar's hot minion is return'd again;
Her waspish-headed son has broke his arrows,
Swears he will shoot no more but play with sparrows
And be a boy right out.

Cer. High'st queen of state,
Great Juno, comes; I know her by her gait.

Enter JUNO.

Juno. How does my bounteous sister? Go with me
To bless this twain, that they may prosperous be
And honour'd in their issue. [*They sing.*]

Juno. Honour, riches, marriage-blessing,
Long continuance, and increasing,
Hourly joys be still upon you!
Juno sings her blessings on you.

Cer. Earth's increase, foison plenty,
Barns and garners never empty,
Vines with clustering bunches growing,
Plants with goodly burthen bowing;

Spring come to you at the farthest
In the very end of harvest!
Scarcity and want shall shun you;
Ceres' blessing so is on you.

Fer. This is a most majestic vision, and
Harmonious charmingly. May I be bold
To think these spirits?

Pros. Spirits, which by mine art
I have from their confines call'd to enact
My present fancies.
Fer. Let me live here ever;
So rare a wonder'd father and a wife
Makes this place Paradise.

JUNO *and* CERES *whisper, and send* IRIS *on employment.*

Pros. Sweet, now, silence!
Juno and Ceres whisper seriously;
There's something else to do. Hush, and be mute,
Or else our spell is marr'd.
Iris. You nymphs, call'd Naiads, of the windring brooks,
With your sedged crowns and ever-harmless looks,
Leave your crisp channels and on this green land
Answer your summons; Juno does command.
Come, temperate nymphs, and help to celebrate
A contract of true love; be not too late.

Enter certain Nymphs.

You sunburnt sicklemen, of August weary,
Come hither from the furrow and be merry;
Make holiday; your rye-straw hats put on
And these fresh nymphs encounter every one
In country footing.

Enter certain Reapers, properly habited; they join with the Nymphs in a graceful dance; towards the end whereof PROSPERO *starts suddenly, and speaks; after which, to a strange, hollow, and confused noise, they heavily vanish.*

Pros. [*Aside*] I had forgot that foul conspiracy
Of the beast Caliban and his confederates
Against my life; the minute of their plot
Is almost come. [*To the Spirits.*] Well done! avoid; no more!
Fer. This is strange. Your father's in some passion
That works him strongly.
Mir. Never till this day
Saw I him touch'd with anger so distemper'd.
Pros. You do look, my son, in a moved sort,
As if you were dismay'd; be cheerful, sir.
Our revels now are ended. These our actors,
As I foretold you, were all spirits and
Are melted into air, into thin air,
And, like the baseless fabric of this vision,
The cloud-capp'd towers, the gorgeous palaces,
The solemn temples, the great globe itself,
Yea, all which it inherit, shall dissolve
And, like this insubstantial pageant faded,
Leave not a rack behind. We are such stuff
As dreams are made on, and our little life
Is rounded with a sleep. Sir, I am vex'd;
Bear with my weakness; my old brain is troubled.
Be not disturb'd with my infirmity.
If you be pleased, retire into my cell
And there repose. A turn or two I'll walk,
To still my beating mind.
Fer. Mir. We wish your peace. [*Exeunt.*
Pros. Come with a thought. I thank thee, Ariel; come.

Enter ARIEL.

Ari. Thy thoughts I cleave to. What's thy pleasure?
Pros. Spirit,
We must prepare to meet with Caliban.
Ari. Ay, my commander. When I presented Ceres,
I thought to have told thee of it, but I fear'd
Lest I might anger thee.
Pros. Say again, where didst thou leave these varlets?
Ari. I told you, sir, they were red-hot with drinking;
So full of valour that they smote the air
For breathing in their faces; beat the ground
For kissing of their feet; yet always bending
Towards their project. Then I beat my tabor;
At which, like unback'd colts, they prick'd their ears,
Advanced their eyelids, lifted up their noses
As they smelt music. So I charm'd their ears
That calf-like they my lowing follow'd through
Tooth'd briers, sharp furzes, pricking goss, and thorns,
Which enter'd their frail shins. At last I left them
I' the filthy-mantled pool beyond your cell,
There dancing up to the chins, that the foul lake
O'erstunk their feet.
Pros. This was well done, my bird.
Thy shape invisible retain thou still.
The trumpery in my house, go bring it hither,
For stale to catch these thieves.
Ari. I go, I go. [*Exit.*
Pros. A devil, a born devil, on whose nature
Nurture can never stick, on whom my pains,
Humanely taken, all, all lost, quite lost;
And as with age his body uglier grows,
So his mind cankers. I will plague them all,
Even to roaring.

Re-enter ARIEL, *loaden with glistering apparel, &c.*

Come, hang them on this line.

PROSPERO *and* ARIEL *remain, invisible. Enter* CALIBAN, STEPHANO, *and* TRINCULO, *all wet.*

Cal. Pray you, tread softly, that the blind mole may not
Hear a foot fall. We now are near his cell.

Ste. Monster, your fairy, which you say is a harmless fairy, has done little better than played the Jack with us.

Trin. Monster, I do smell all horse-piss; at which my nose is in great indignation.

Ste. So is mine. Do you hear, monster? If I should take a displeasure against you, look you—

Trin. Thou wert but a lost monster.

Cal. Good my lord, give me thy favour still.
Be patient, for the prize I'll bring thee to
Shall hoodwink this mischance; therefore speak softly.
All's hush'd as midnight yet.

Trin. Ay, but to lose our bottles in the pool—

Ste. There is not only disgrace and dishonour in that, monster, but an infinite loss.

Trin. That's more to me than my wetting; yet this is your harmless fairy, monster.

Ste. I will fetch off my bottle, though I be o'er ears for my labour.

Cal. Prithee, my king, be quiet. See'st thou here,
This is the mouth o' the cell. No noise, and enter.
Do that good mischief which may make this island
Thine own for ever, and I, thy Caliban,
For aye thy foot-licker.

Ste. Give me thy hand. I do begin to have bloody thoughts. 221

Trin. O King Stephano! O peer! O worthy Stephano! look what a wardrobe here is for thee!

Cal. Let it alone, thou fool; it is but trash.

Trin. O, ho, monster! we know what belongs to a frippery. O King Stephano!

Ste. Put off that gown, Trinculo; by this hand, I'll have that gown.

Trin. Thy grace shall have it.

Cal. The dropsy drown this fool! what do you mean
To dote thus on such luggage? Let's alone
And do the murder first. If he awake,
From toe to crown he'll fill our skins with pinches,
Make us strange stuff.

Ste. Be you quiet, monster. Mistress line, is not this my jerkin? Now is the jerkin under the line. Now, jerkin, you are like to lose your hair and prove a bald jerkin.

Trin. Do, do; we steal by line and level, an't like your Grace.

Ste. I thank thee for that jest; here's a garment for 't. Wit shall not go unrewarded while I am king of this country. "Steal by line and level" is an excellent pass of pate; there's another garment for 't.

Trin. Monster, come, put some lime upon your fingers, and away with the rest.

Cal. I will have none on 't. We shall lose our time,
And all be turn'd to barnacles, or to apes
With foreheads villainous low.

Ste. Monster, lay-to your fingers. Help to bear this away where my hogshead of wine is, or I'll turn you out of my kingdom. Go to, carry this.

Trin. And this.

Ste. Ay, and this.

A noise of hunters heard. Enter divers Spirits, in shapes of dogs and hounds, and hunt them about, PROSPERO *and* ARIEL *setting them on.*

Pros. Hey, Mountain, hey!

Ari. Silver! there it goes, Silver!

Pros. Fury, Fury! there, Tyrant, there! hark! hark! [CALIBAN, STEPHANO, *and* TRINCULO *are driven out.*
Go charge my goblins that they grind their joints
With dry convulsions, shorten up their sinews
With aged cramps, and more pinch-spotted make them
Than pard or cat o' mountain.

Ari. Hark, they roar!

Pros. Let them be hunted soundly. At this hour
Lie at my mercy all mine enemies.
Shortly shall all my labours end, and thou
Shalt have the air at freedom. For a little
Follow, and do me service. [*Exeunt.*

ACT V

SCENE I. *Before Prospero's cell*

Enter PROSPERO *in his magic robes, and* ARIEL.

Pros. Now does my project gather to a head.
My charms crack not; my spirits obey; and time
Goes upright with his carriage. How's the day?

Ari. On the sixth hour; at which time, my lord,
You said our work should cease.

Pros. I did say so,
When first I raised the tempest. Say, my spirit,
How fares the King and's followers?

Ari. Confined together
In the same fashion as you gave in charge,
Just as you left them; all prisoners, sir,
In the line-grove which weather-fends your cell;
They cannot budge till your release. The King,
His brother, and yours, abide all three distracted
And the remainder mourning over them,
Brimful of sorrow and dismay; but chiefly
Him that you term'd, sir, "The good old lord, Gonzalo";

His tears run down his beard, like winter's drops
From eaves of reeds. Your charm so strongly works 'em
That if you now beheld them, your affections
Would become tender.

Pros. Dost thou think so, spirit?

Ari. Mine would, sir, were I human.

Pros. And mine shall.
Hast thou, which art but air, a touch, a feeling
Of their afflictions, and shall not myself,
One of their kind, that relish all as sharply,
Passion as they, be kindlier moved than thou art?
Though with their high wrongs I am struck to the quick,
Yet with my nobler reason 'gainst my fury
Do I take part. The rarer action is
In virtue than in vengeance. They being penitent,
The sole drift of my purpose doth extend
Not a frown further. Go release them, Ariel.
My charms I'll break, their senses I'll restore,
And they shall be themselves.

Ari. I'll fetch them, sir. [*Exit.*

Pros. Ye elves of hills, brooks, standing lakes, and groves,
And ye that on the sands with printless foot
Do chase the ebbing Neptune and do fly him
When he comes back; you demi-puppets that
By moonshine do the green sour ringlets make,
Whereof the ewe not bites, and you whose pastime
Is to make midnight mushrooms, that rejoice
To hear the solemn curfew; by whose aid,
Weak masters though ye be, I have bedimm'd
The noontide sun, call'd forth the mutinous winds,
And 'twixt the green sea and the azured vault
Set roaring war; to the dread rattling thunder
Have I given fire and rifted Jove's stout oak
With his own bolt; the strong-based promontory
Have I made shake and by the spurs pluck'd up
The pine and cedar; graves at my command
Have waked their sleepers, oped, and let 'em forth
By my so potent art. But this rough magic
I here abjure, and, when I have required
Some heavenly music, which even now I do,
To work mine end upon their senses that
This airy charm is for, I'll break my staff,
Bury it certain fathoms in the earth,
And deeper than did ever plummet sound
I'll drown my book.
Solemn music.

Re-enter ARIEL *before; then* ALONSO, *with a frantic gesture, attended by* GONZALO; SEBASTIAN *and* ANTONIO *in like manner, attended by* ADRIAN *and* FRANCISCO. *They all enter the circle which* PROSPERO *had made, and there stand charmed; which* PROSPERO *observing, speaks.*

A solemn air and the best comforter
To an unsettled fancy cure thy brains,
Now useless, boil'd within thy skull! There stand,
For you are spell-stopp'd.
Holy Gonzalo, honourable man,
Mine eyes, even sociable to the show of thine,
Fall fellowly drops. The charm dissolves apace,
And as the morning steals upon the night,
Melting the darkness, so their rising senses
Begin to chase the ignorant fumes that mantle
Their clearer reason. O good Gonzalo,
My true preserver, and a loyal sir
To him thou follow'st! I will pay thy graces
Home both in word and deed. Most cruelly
Didst thou, Alonso, use me and my daughter;
Thy brother was a furtherer in the act.
Thou art pinch'd for 't now, Sebastian. Flesh and blood,
You, brother mine, that entertain'd ambition,
Expell'd remorse and nature; who, with Sebastian,
Whose inward pinches therefore are most strong,
Would here have kill'd your king, I do forgive thee,
Unnatural though thou art. Their understanding
Begins to swell, and the approaching tide
Will shortly fill the reasonable shore
That now lies foul and muddy. Not one of them
That yet looks on me, or would know me. Ariel,
Fetch me the hat and rapier in my cell.
I will discase me, and myself present
As I was sometime Milan. Quickly, spirit;
Thou shalt ere long be free.

ARIEL *sings and helps to attire him.*

Where the bee sucks, there suck I.
In a cowslip's bell I lie;
There I couch when owls do cry.
On the bat's back I do fly
After summer merrily.
Merrily, merrily shall I live now
Under the blossom that hangs on the bough.

Pros. Why, that's my dainty Ariel! I shall miss thee;
But yet thou shalt have freedom. So, so, so.
To the King's ship, invisible as thou art;
There shalt thou find the mariners asleep
Under the hatches; the master and the boatswain
Being awake, enforce them to this place,

And presently, I prithee.
Ari. I drink the air before me, and return
Or ere your pulse twice beat. [*Exit.*
Gon. All torment, trouble, wonder, and amazement
Inhabits here. Some heavenly power guide us
Out of this fearful country!
Pros. Behold, sir King,
The wronged Duke of Milan, Prospero.
For more assurance that a living prince
Does now speak to thee, I embrace thy body;
And to thee and thy company I bid
A hearty welcome.
Alon. Whether thou be'st he or no,
Or some enchanted trifle to abuse me,
As late I have been, I not know. Thy pulse
Beats as of flesh and blood; and, since I saw thee,
The affliction of my mind amends, with which,
I fear, a madness held me. This must crave,
An if this be at all, a most strange story.
Thy dukedom I resign and do entreat
Thou pardon me my wrongs. But how should Prospero
Be living and be here?
Pros. First, noble friend,
Let me embrace thine age, whose honour cannot
Be measured or confined.
Gon. Whether this be
Or be not, I'll not swear.
Pros. You do yet taste
Some subtilties o' the isle, that will not let you
Believe things certain. Welcome, my friends all!
[*Aside to* SEBASTIAN *and* ANTONIO] But you, my brace of lords, were I so minded,
I here could pluck his Highness' frown upon you
And justify you traitors. At this time
I will tell no tales.
Seb. [*Aside*] The devil speaks in him.
Pros. No.
For you, most wicked sir, whom to call brother
Would even infect my mouth, I do forgive
Thy rankest fault; all of them; and require
My dukedom of thee, which perforce, I know,
Thou must restore.
Alon. If thou be'st Prospero,
Give us particulars of thy preservation;
How thou hast met us here, who three hours since
Were wreck'd upon this shore; where I have lost—
How sharp the point of this remembrance is!—
My dear son Ferdinand.
Pros. I am woe for 't, sir.
Alon. Irreparable is the loss, and Patience
Says it is past her cure.
Pros. I rather think
You have not sought her help, of whose soft grace
For the like loss I have her sovereign aid
And rest myself content.
Alon. You the like loss!
Pros. As great to me as late; and, supportable
To make the dear loss, have I means much weaker
Than you may call to comfort you, for I
Have lost my daughter.
Alon. A daughter?
O heavens, that they were living both in Naples,
The King and Queen there! that they were, I wish
Myself were mudded in that oozy bed
Where my son lies. When did you lose your daughter?
Pros. In this last tempest. I perceive, these lords
At this encounter do so much admire
That they devour their reason and scarce think
Their eyes do offices of truth, their words
Are natural breath; but, howsoe'er you have
Been justled from your senses, know for certain
That I am Prospero and that very duke
Which was thrust forth of Milan, who most strangely
Upon this shore, where you were wreck'd, was landed,
To be the lord on 't. No more yet of this;
For 'tis a chronicle of day by day,
Not a relation for a breakfast nor
Befitting this first meeting. Welcome, sir;
This cell's my court. Here have I few attendants
And subjects none abroad. Pray you, look in.
My dukedom since you have given me again,
I will requite you with as good a thing;
At least bring forth a wonder, to content ye
As much as me my dukedom.

Here PROSPERO *discovers* FERDINAND *and* MIRANDA *playing at chess.*

Mir. Sweet lord, you play me false.
Fer. No, my dear'st love,
I would not for the world.
Mir. Yes, for a score of kingdoms you should wrangle,
And I would call it fair play.
Alon. If this prove
A vision of the island, one dear son
Shall I twice lose.
Seb. A most high miracle!
Fer. Though the seas threaten, they are merciful;
I have cursed them without cause. [*Kneels.*]
Alon. Now all the blessings
Of a glad father compass thee about!
Arise, and say how thou camest here.

Mir. O, wonder!
How many goodly creatures are there here!
How beauteous mankind is! O brave new world,
That has such people in 't!
Pros. 'Tis new to thee.
Alon. What is this maid with whom thou wast at play?
Your eld'st acquaintance cannot be three hours.
Is she the goddess that hath sever'd us,
And brought us thus together?
Fer. Sir, she is mortal;
But by immortal Providence she's mine.
I chose her when I could not ask my father
For his advice, nor thought I had one. She
Is daughter to this famous Duke of Milan,
Of whom so often I have heard renown,
But never saw before; of whom I have
Received a second life; and second father
This lady makes him to me.
Alon. I am hers.
But, O, how oddly will it sound that I
Must ask my child forgiveness!
Pros. There, sir, stop.
Let us not burthen our remembrance with
A heaviness that's gone.
Gon. I have inly wept,
Or should have spoke ere this. Look down, you gods,
And on this couple drop a blessed crown!
For it is you that have chalk'd forth the way
Which brought us hither.
Alon. I say, Amen, Gonzalo!
Gon. Was Milan thrust from Milan, that his issue
Should become king of Naples? O, rejoice
Beyond a common joy, and set it down
With gold on lasting pillars. In one voyage
Did Claribel her husband find at Tunis
And Ferdinand, her brother, found a wife
Where he himself was lost, Prospero his dukedom
In a poor isle, and all of us ourselves
When no man was his own.
Alon. [*To* FERDINAND *and* MIRANDA] Give me your hands.
Let grief and sorrow still embrace his heart
That doth not wish you joy!
Gon. Be it so! Amen!

Re-enter ARIEL, *with the* MASTER *and* BOATSWAIN *amazedly following.*

O, look, sir, look, sir! here is more of us.
I prophesied, if a gallows were on land,
This fellow could not drown. Now, blasphemy,
That swear'st grace o'erboard, not an oath on shore?
Hast thou no mouth by land? What is the news?
Boats. The best news is that we have safely found
Our King and company; the next, our ship—
Which, but three glasses since, we gave out split—
Is tight and yare and bravely rigg'd as when
We first put out to sea.
Ari. [*Aside to* PROSPERO.] Sir, all this service
Have I done since I went.
Pros. [*Aside to* ARIEL] My tricksy spirit!
Alon. These are not natural events; they strengthen
From strange to stranger. Say, how came you hither?
Boats. If I did think, sir, I were well awake,
I'd strive to tell you. We were dead of sleep,
And—how we know not—all clapp'd under hatches;
Where but even now with strange and several noises
Of roaring, shrieking, howling, jingling chains,
And moe diversity of sounds, all horrible,
We were awaked; straightway, at liberty;
Where we, in all her trim, freshly beheld
Our royal, good, and gallant ship, our master
Capering to eye her. On a trice, so please you,
Even in a dream, were we divided from them
And were brought moping hither.
Ari. [*Aside to* PROSPERO] Was 't well done?
Pros. [*Aside to* ARIEL] Bravely, my diligence. Thou shalt be free.
Alon. This is as strange a maze as e'er men trod;
And there is in this business more than nature
Was ever conduct of. Some oracle
Must rectify our knowledge.
Pros. Sir, my liege,
Do not infest your mind with beating on
The strangeness of this business; at pick'd leisure
Which shall be shortly, single I'll resolve you,
Which to you shall seem probable, of every
These happen'd accidents; till when, be cheerful
And think of each thing well. [*Aside to* ARIEL] Come hither, spirit.
Set Caliban and his companions free;
Untie the spell. [*Exit* ARIEL.] How fares my gracious sir?
There are yet missing of your company
Some few odd lads that you remember not.

Re-enter ARIEL, *driving in* CALIBAN, STEPHANO *and* TRINCULO, *in their stolen apparel.*

Ste. Every man shift for all the rest, and let no man take care for himself; for all is but fortune. Coragio, bully-monster, coragio!

Trin. If these be true spies which I wear in my head, here's a goodly sight.

Cal. O Setebos, these be brave spirits indeed!
How fine my master is! I am afraid
He will chastise me.

Seb. Ha, ha!
What things are these, my lord Antonio?
Will money buy 'em?

Ant. Very like; one of them
Is a plain fish, and, no doubt, marketable.

Pros. Mark but the badges of these men, my lords,
Then say if they be true. This mis-shapen knave,
His mother was a witch, and one so strong
That could control the moon, make flows and ebbs,
And deal in her command without her power.
These three have robb'd me; and this demi-devil—
For he's a bastard one—had plotted with them
To take my life. Two of these fellows you
Must know and own; this thing of darkness I
Acknowledge mine.

Cal. I shall be pinch'd to death.

Alon. Is not this Stephano, my drunken butler?

Seb. He is drunk now. Where had he wine?

Alon. And Trinculo is reeling ripe. Where should they
Find this grand liquor that hath gilded 'em?
How camest thou in this pickle?

Trin. I have been in such a pickle since I saw you last that, I fear me, will never out of my bones. I shall not fear fly-blowing.

Seb. Why, how now, Stephano!

Ste. O, touch me not; I am not Stephano, but a cramp.

Pros. You'd be king o' the isle, sirrah?

Ste. I should have been a sore one then.

Alon. [*Pointing to* CALIBAN] This is a strange thing as e'er I look'd on.

Pros. He is as disproportion'd in his manners
As in his shape. Go, sirrah, to my cell;
Take with you your companions; as you look
To have my pardon, trim it handsomely.

Cal. Ay, that I will; and I'll be wise hereafter
And seek for grace. What a thrice-double ass
Was I, to take this drunkard for a god
And worship this dull fool!

Pros. Go to; away!

Alon. Hence, and bestow your luggage where you found it.

Seb. Or stole it, rather.

[*Exeunt* CALIBAN, STEPHANO, *and* TRINCULO.

Pros. Sir, I invite your Highness and your train
To my poor cell, where you shall take your rest
For this one night; which, part of it, I'll waste
With such discourse as, I not doubt, shall make it
Go quick away; the story of my life
And the particular accidents gone by
Since I came to this isle. And in the morn
I'll bring you to your ship and so to Naples,
Where I have hope to see the nuptial
Of these our dear-beloved solemnized;
And thence retire me to my Milan, where
Every third thought shall be my grave.

Alon. I long
To hear the story of your life, which must
Take the ear strangely.

Pros. I'll deliver all;
And promise you calm seas, auspicious gales,
And sail so expeditious that shall catch
Your royal fleet far off. [*Aside to* ARIEL] My Ariel, chick,
That is thy charge. Then to the elements
Be free, and fare thou well! Please you, draw near.

[*Exeunt.*

EPILOGUE

SPOKEN BY PROSPERO

Now my charms are all o'erthrown,
And what strength I have's mine own,
Which is most faint. Now, 'tis true,
I must be here confined by you,
Or sent to Naples. Let me not,
Since I have my dukedom got
And pardon'd the deceiver, dwell
In this bare island by your spell;
But release me from my bands
With the help of your good hands.
Gentle breath of yours my sails
Must fill, or else my project fails,
Which was to please. Now I want
Spirits to enforce, art to enchant,
And my ending is despair,
Unless I be relieved by prayer,
Which pierces so that it assaults
Mercy itself and frees all faults.
As you from crimes would pardon'd be,
Let your indulgence set me free.

The Famous History of the Life of KING HENRY THE EIGHTH

DRAMATIS PERSONÆ

King Henry the Eighth
Cardinal Wolsey
Cardinal Campeius
Capucius, *ambassador from the Emperor Charles V*
Cranmer, *Archbishop of Canterbury*
Duke of Norfolk
Duke of Buckingham
Duke of Suffolk
Earl of Surrey
Lord Chamberlain
Lord Chancellor
Gardiner, *Bishop of Winchester*
Bishop of Lincoln
Lord Abergavenny
Lord Sands
Sir Henry Guildford
Sir Thomas Lovell
Sir Anthony Denny
Sir Nicholas Vaux
Two Secretaries *to Wolsey*
Cromwell, *servant to Wolsey*
Griffith, *gentleman-usher to Queen Katharine*
Three Gentlemen
Doctor Butts, *physician to the King*
Garter King-at-Arms
Surveyor *to the Duke of Buckingham*
Brandon
Sergeant-at-Arms
Door-Keeper *of the Council-chamber*
Porter
Man, *to the Porter*
Page *to Gardiner*
A Crier
A Messenger
A Scribe
A Servant *to Wolsey*

Queen Katharine, *wife to King Henry, afterwards divorced*
Anne Bullen, *her Maid of Honour, afterwards Queen*
An Old Lady, *friend to Anne Bullen*
Patience, *woman to Queen Katharine*

Non-Speaking: *Lords and Ladies in the Dumb Shows, Women attending on the Queen, Scribes, Officers, Guards, Attendants, and Six Spirits appearing to Queen Katharine*

Scene: *London, Westminister, and Kimbolton*

THE PROLOGUE

I come no more to make you laugh; things now,
That bear a weighty and a serious brow,
Sad, high, and working, full of state and woe,
Such noble scenes as draw the eye to flow,
We now present. Those that can pity, here
May, if they think it well, let fall a tear;
The subject will deserve it. Such as give
Their money out of hope they may believe,
May here find truth too. Those that come to see
Only a show or two, and so agree
The play may pass, if they be still and willing,
I'll undertake may see away their shilling
Richly in two short hours. Only they
That come to hear a merry bawdy play,
A noise of targets, or to see a fellow
In a long motley coat guarded with yellow,
Will be deceived; for, gentle hearers, know,
To rank our chosen truth with such a show
As fool and fight is, beside forfeiting
Our own brains and the opinion that we bring,
To make that only true we now intend,
Will leave us never an understanding friend.
Therefore, for goodness' sake, and as you are known
The first and happiest hearers of the town,
Be sad, as we would make ye. Think ye see
The very persons of our noble story
As they were living; think you see them great,
And follow'd with the general throng and sweat
Of thousand friends; then, in a moment, see
How soon this mightiness meets misery;
And, if you can be merry then, I'll say
A man may weep upon his wedding-day.

ACT I

Scene i. *London: an ante-chamber in the palace*

Enter the Duke of Norfolk *at one door; at the other, the* Duke of Buckingham *and the* Lord Abergavenny.

Buck. Good morrow, and well met. How have ye done
Since last we saw in France?
Nor. I thank your Grace,
Healthful; and ever since a fresh admirer
Of what I saw there.

Buck. An untimely ague
Stay'd me a prisoner in my chamber when
Those suns of glory, those two lights of men,
Met in the vale of Andren.
Nor. 'Twixt Guynes and Arde.
I was then present, saw them salute on horse-
back;
Beheld them, when they lighted, how they clung
In their embracement, as they grew together;
Which had they, what four throned ones could
have weigh'd
Such a compounded one?
Buck. All the whole time
I was my chamber's prisoner.
Nor. Then you lost
The view of earthly glory. Men might say
Till this time pomp was single, but now married
To one above itself. Each following day
Became the next day's master, till the last
Made former wonders its. To-day the French,
All clinquant, all in gold, like heathen gods, 19
Shone down the English; and, to-morrow, they
Made Britain India: every man that stood
Show'd like a mine. Their dwarfish pages were
As cherubins, all gilt; the madams too,
Not used to toil, did almost sweat to bear
The pride upon them, that their very labour
Was to them as a painting. Now this masque
Was cried incomparable; and the ensuing night
Made it a fool and beggar. The two kings,
Equal in lustre, were now best, now worst,
As presence did present them; him in eye,
Still him in praise; and, being present both,
'Twas said they saw but one; and no discerner
Durst wag his tongue in censure. When these
suns—
For so they phrase 'em—by their heralds chal-
lenged
The noble spirits to arms, they did perform
Beyond thought's compass; that former fabulous
story,
Being now seen possible enough, got credit,
That Bevis was believed.
Buck. O, you go far.
Nor. As I belong to worship and affect
In honour honesty, the tract of everything
Would by a good discourser lose some life,
Which action's self was tongue to. All was royal;
To the disposing of it nought rebell'd,
Order gave each thing view; the office did
Distinctly his full function.
Buck. Who did guide,
I mean, who set the body and the limbs
Of this great sport together, as you guess?
Nor. One, certes, that promises no element
In such a business.
Buck. I pray you, who, my lord?
Nor. All this was order'd by the good discre-
tion
Of the right reverend Cardinal of York.
Buck. The devil speed him! No man's pie is
freed
From his ambitious finger. What had he
To do in these fierce vanities? I wonder
That such a keech can with his very bulk
Take up the rays o' the beneficial sun
And keep it from the earth.
Nor. Surely, sir,
There's in him stuff that puts him to these ends;
For, being not propp'd by ancestry, whose grace
Chalks successors their way, nor call'd upon
For high feats done to the crown; neither allied
To eminent assistants; but, spider-like,
Out of his self-drawing web, he gives us note,
The force of his own merit makes his way;
A gift that heaven gives for him, which buys
A place next to the King.
Aber. I cannot tell
What heaven hath given him—let some graver
eye
Pierce into that; but I can see his pride
Peep through each part of him. Whence has he
that,
If not from hell? the devil is a niggard,
Or has given all before, and he begins
A new hell in himself.
Buck. Why the devil,
Upon this French going out, took he upon him,
Without the privity o' the King, to appoint
Who should attend on him? He makes up the file
Of all the gentry; for the most part such
To whom as great a charge as little honour
He meant to lay upon; and his own letter,
The honourable board of council out,
Must fetch him in the papers.
Aber. I do know
Kinsmen of mine, three at the least, that have
By this so sicken'd their estates, that never
They shall abound as formerly.
Buck. O, many
Have broke their backs with laying manors on
'em
For this great journey. What did this vanity
But minister communication of
A most poor issue?
Nor. Grievingly I think,
The peace between the French and us not values
The cost that did conclude it.
Buck. Every man,
After the hideous storm that follow'd, was
A thing inspired; and, not consulting, broke
Into a general prophecy, that this tempest,

Dashing the garment of this peace, aboded
The sudden breach on 't.
Nor. Which is budded out;
For France hath flaw'd the league, and hath attach'd
Our merchants' goods at Bourdeaux.
Aber. Is it therefore
The ambassador is silenced?
Nor. Marry, is 't.
Aber. A proper title of a peace; and purchased
At a superfluous rate!
Buck. Why, all this business
Our reverend Cardinal carried.
Nor. Like it your Grace,
The state takes notice of the private difference
Betwixt you and the Cardinal. I advise you—
And take it from a heart that wishes towards you
Honour and plenteous safety—that you read
The Cardinal's malice and his potency
Together; to consider further that
What his high hatred would effect wants not
A minister in his power. You know his nature,
That he's revengeful, and I know his sword
Hath a sharp edge; it's long and, 't may be said,
It reaches far, and where 'twill not extend,
Thither he darts it. Bosom up my counsel,
You'll find it wholesome. Lo, where comes that rock
That I advise your shunning.

Enter CARDINAL WOLSEY, *the purse borne before him, certain of the Guard, and* TWO SECRETARIES *with papers. The* CARDINAL *in his passage fixeth his eye on* BUCKINGHAM, *and* BUCKINGHAM *on him, both full of disdain.*

Wol. The Duke of Buckingham's surveyor, ha?
Where's his examination?
1st Secr. Here, so please you.
Wol. Is he in person ready?
1st Secr. Ay, please your Grace.
Wol. Well, we shall then know more; and Buckingham
Shall lessen this big look.
[*Exeunt* WOLSEY *and his train.*
Buck. This butcher's cur is venom-mouth'd, and I
Have not the power to muzzle him; therefore best
Not wake him in his slumber. A beggar's book
Outworths a noble's blood.
Nor. What, are you chafed?
Ask God for temperance; that's the appliance only
Which your disease requires.
Buck. I read in's looks
Matter against me; and his eye reviled
Me as his abject object. At this instant
He bores me with some trick. He's gone to the King;
I'll follow and outstare him.
Nor. Stay, my lord,
And let your reason with your choler question
What 'tis you go about. To climb steep hills
Requires slow pace at first. Anger is like
A full hot horse, who being allow'd his way,
Self-mettle tires him. Not a man in England
Can advise me like you; be to yourself
As you would to your friend.
Buck. I'll to the King;
And from a mouth of honour quite cry down
This Ipswich fellow's insolence; or proclaim
There's difference in no persons.
Nor. Be advised;
Heat not a furnace for your foe so hot
That it do singe yourself. We may outrun,
By violent swiftness, that which we run at,
And lose by over-running. Know you not
The fire that mounts the liquor till 't run o'er
In seeming to augment it wastes it? Be advised.
I say again, there is no English soul
More stronger to direct you than yourself,
If with the sap of reason you would quench,
Or but allay, the fire of passion.
Buck. Sir,
I am thankful to you; and I'll go along
By your prescription. But this top-proud fellow,
Whom from the flow of gall I name not but
From sincere motions, by intelligence,
And proofs as clear as founts in July when
We see each grain of gravel, I do know
To be corrupt and treasonous.
Nor. Say not "treasonous."
Buck. To the King I'll say 't; and make my vouch as strong
As shore of rock. Attend. This holy fox,
Or wolf, or both—for he is equal ravenous
As he is subtle, and as prone to mischief
As able to perform 't; his mind and place
Infecting one another, yea, reciprocally—
Only to show his pomp as well in France
As here at home, suggests the King our master
To this last costly treaty, the interview,
That swallow'd so much treasure, and like a glass
Did break i' the rinsing.
Nor. Faith, and so it did.
Buck. Pray, give me favour, sir. This cunning Cardinal
The articles o' the combination drew
As himself pleased; and they were ratified
As he cried, "Thus let be:" to as much end
As give a crutch to the dead. But our count-cardinal

Has done this, and 'tis well; for worthy Wolsey,
Who cannot err, he did it. Now this follows—
Which, as I take it, is a kind of puppy
To the old dam, treason—Charles the Emperor,
Under pretence to see the Queen his aunt—
For 'twas indeed his colour, but he came
To whisper Wolsey—here makes visitation.
His fears were that the interview betwixt
England and France might, through their amity,
Breed him some prejudice; for from this league
Peep'd harms that menaced him. He privily
Deals with our Cardinal; and, as I trow—
Which I do well; for I am sure the Emperor
Paid ere he promised; whereby his suit was granted
Ere it was ask'd; but when the way was made,
And paved with gold, the Emperor thus desired,
That he would please to alter the King's course,
And break the foresaid peace. Let the King know,
As soon he shall by me, that thus the Cardinal
Does buy and sell his honour as he pleases,
And for his own advantage.

Nor. I am sorry
To hear this of him, and could wish he were
Something mistaken in 't.

Buck. No, not a syllable.
I do pronounce him in that very shape
He shall appear in proof.

Enter BRANDON, *a* SERGEANT-AT-ARMS *before him, and two or three of the Guard.*

Bran. Your office, sergeant; execute it.

Serg. Sir,
My lord the Duke of Buckingham, and Earl
Of Hereford, Stafford, and Northampton, I
Arrest thee of high treason, in the name
Of our most sovereign King.

Buck. Lo, you, my lord,
The net has fall'n upon me! I shall perish
Under device and practice.

Bran. I am sorry
To see you ta'en from liberty, to look on
The business present. 'Tis his Highness' pleasure
You shall to the Tower.

Buck. It will help me nothing
To plead mine innocence; for that dye is on me
Which makes my whitest part black. The will of heaven
Be done in this and all things! I obey.
O my Lord Abergavenny, fare you well!

Bran. Nay, he must bear you company. The King [*To* ABERGAVENNY.]
Is pleased you shall to the Tower, till you know
How he determines further.

Aber. As the Duke said,
The will of heaven be done, and the King's pleasure
By me obey'd!

Bran. Here is a warrant from
The king to attach Lord Montacute; and the bodies
Of the Duke's confessor, John de la Car,
One Gilbert Peck, his chancellor—

Buck. So; so;
These are the limbs o' the plot. No more, I hope.

Bran. A monk o' the Chartreux.

Buck. O, Nicholas Hopkins?

Bran. He.

Buck. My surveyor is false; the o'er-great Cardinal
Hath show'd him gold; my life is spann'd already.
I am the shadow of poor Buckingham,
Whose figure even this instant cloud puts on,
By darkening my clear sun. My lord, farewell.
[*Exeunt.*

SCENE II. *The same: the council-chamber*

Cornets. Enter the KING, *leaning on the* CARDINAL'S *shoulder, the Nobles, and* SIR THOMAS LOVELL; *the* CARDINAL *places himself under the* KING'S *feet on his right side.*

King. My life itself, and the best heart of it,
Thanks you for this great care. I stood i' the level
Of a full-charged confederacy, and give thanks
To you that choked it. Let be call'd before us
That gentleman of Buckingham's; in person
I'll hear him his confessions justify;
And point by point the treasons of his master
He shall again relate.

A noise within, crying, "Room for the Queen!" *Enter* QUEEN KATHARINE, *ushered by the* DUKE OF NORFOLK, *and the* DUKE OF SUFFOLK; *she kneels. The* KING *riseth from his state, takes her up, kisses and placeth her by him.*

Q. Kath. Nay, we must longer kneel. I am a suitor.

King. Arise, and take place by us. Half your suit
Never name to us; you have half our power.
The other moiety, ere you ask, is given;
Repeat your will and take it.

Q. Kath. Thank your Majesty.
That you would love yourself, and in that love
Not unconsider'd leave your honour, nor
The dignity of your office, is the point
Of my petition.

King. Lady mine, proceed.

Q. Kath. I am solicited, not by a few,

And those of true condition, that your subjects
Are in great grievance. There have been commissions
Sent down among 'em, which hath flaw'd the heart
Of all their loyalties; wherein, although,
My good lord Cardinal, they vent reproaches
Most bitterly on you, as putter on
Of these exactions, yet the King our master—
Whose honour heaven shield from soil!—even he escapes not
Language unmannerly, yea, such which breaks
The sides of loyalty, and almost appears
In loud rebellion.

Nor. Not almost appears,
It doth appear; for, upon these taxations,
The clothiers all, not able to maintain
The many to them 'longing, have put off
The spinsters, carders, fullers, weavers, who,
Unfit for other life, compell'd by hunger
And lack of other means, in desperate manner
Daring the event to the teeth, are all in uproar,
And danger serves among them.

King. Taxation!
Wherein? and what taxation? My lord Cardinal,
You that are blamed for it alike with us,
Know you of this taxation?

Wol. Please you, sir,
I know but of a single part, in aught
Pertains to the state; and front but in that file
Where others tell steps with me.

Q. Kath. No, my lord,
You know no more than others; but you frame
Things that are known alike; which are not wholesome
To those which would not know them, and yet must
Perforce be their acquaintance. These exactions,
Whereof my sovereign would have note, they are
Most pestilent to the hearing; and, to bear 'em,
The back is sacrifice to the load. They say
They are devised by you; or else you suffer
Too hard an exclamation.

King. Still exaction!
The nature of it? in what kind, let's know,
Is this exaction?

Q. Kath. I am much too venturous
In tempting of your patience; but am bolden'd
Under your promised pardon. The subjects' grief
Comes through commissions, which compel from each
The sixth part of his substance, to be levied
Without delay; and the pretence for this
Is named, your wars in France. This makes bold mouths.
Tongues spit their duties out, and cold hearts freeze
Allegiance in them; their curses now
Live where their prayers did; and it's come to pass,
This tractable obedience is a slave
To each incensed will. I would your Highness
Would give it quick consideration, for
There is no primer business.

King. By my life,
This is against our pleasure.

Wol. And for me,
I have no further gone in this than by
A single voice; and that not pass'd me but
By learned approbation of the judges. If I am
Traduced by ignorant tongues, which neither know
My faculties nor person, yet will be
The chronicles of my doing, let me say
'Tis but the fate of place, and the rough brake
That virtue must go through. We must not stint
Our necessary actions, in the fear
To cope malicious censurers; which ever,
As ravenous fishes, do a vessel follow
That is new-trimm'd, but benefit no further
Than vainly longing. What we oft do best,
By sick interpreters, once weak ones, is
Not ours, or not allow'd; what worst, as oft,
Hitting a grosser quality, is cried up
For our best act. If we shall stand still,
In fear our motion will be mock'd or carp'd at,
We should take root here where we sit, or sit
State-statues only.

King. Things done well,
And with a care, exempt themselves from fear;
Things done without example, in their issue
Are to be fear'd. Have you a precedent
Of this commission? I believe, not any.
We must not rend our subjects from our laws,
And stick them in our will. Sixth part of each?
A trembling contribution! Why, we take
From every tree lop, bark, and part o' the timber;
And, though we leave it with a root, thus hack'd,
The air will drink the sap. To every county
Where this is question'd send our letters, with
Free pardon to each man that has denied
The force of this commission. Pray, look to 't;
I put it to your care.

Wol. A word with you.
To the SECRETARY.
Let there be letters writ to every shire,
Of the King's grace and pardon. The grieved commons
Hardly conceive of me; let it be noised
That through our intercession this revokement

And pardon comes. I shall anon advise you
Further in the proceeding. [*Exit* SECRETARY.

Enter SURVEYOR.

Q. Kath. I am sorry that the Duke of Buckingham
Is run in your displeasure.
King. It grieves many.
The gentleman is learn'd, and a most rare speaker;
To nature none more bound; his training such,
That he may furnish and instruct great teachers,
And never seek for aid out of himself. Yet see,
When these so noble benefits shall prove
Not well disposed, the mind growing once corrupt,
They turn to vicious forms, ten times more ugly
Than ever they were fair. This man so complete,
Who was enroll'd 'mongst wonders, and when we,
Almost with ravish'd listening, could not find
His hour of speech a minute; he, my lady,
Hath into monstrous habits put the graces
That once were his, and is become as black
As if besmear'd in hell. Sit by us; you shall hear—
This was his gentleman in trust—of him
Things to strike honour sad. Bid him recount
The fore-recited practices; whereof
We cannot feel too little, hear too much.
Wol. Stand forth, and with bold spirit relate what you,
Most like a careful subject, have collected
Out of the Duke of Buckingham.
King. Speak freely.
Surv. First, it was usual with him, every day
It would infect his speech, that if the King
Should without issue die, he'll carry it so
To make the sceptre his. These very words
I've heard him utter to his son-in-law,
Lord Abergavenny; to whom by oath he menaced
Revenge upon the Cardinal.
Wol. Please your Highness, note
This dangerous conception in this point.
Not friended by his wish, to your high person
His will is most malignant; and it stretches
Beyond you, to your friends.
Q. Kath. My learn'd lord Cardinal,
Deliver all with charity.
King. Speak on.
How grounded he his title to the crown,
Upon our fail? to this point hast thou heard him
At any time speak aught?
Surv. He was brought to this
By a vain prophecy of Nicholas Hopkins.
King. What was that Hopkins?
Surv. Sir, a Chartreux friar,
His confessor, who fed him every minute
With words of sovereignty.
King. How know'st thou this?
Surv. Not long before your Highness sped to France,
The Duke being at the Rose, within the parish
Saint Lawrence Poultney, did of me demand
What was the speech among the Londoners
Concerning the French journey. I replied,
Men fear'd the French would prove perfidious,
To the King's danger. Presently the Duke
Said, 'twas the fear, indeed; and that he doubted
'Twould prove the verity of certain words
Spoke by a holy monk; "that oft," says he,
"Hath sent to me, wishing me to permit
John de la Car, my chaplain, a choice hour
To hear from him a matter of some moment;
Whom after under the confession's seal
He solemnly had sworn that what he spoke
My chaplain to no creature living, but
To me, should utter, with demure confidence
This pausingly ensued: "Neither the King nor's heirs,
Tell you the Duke, shall prosper. Bid him strive
To gain the love o' the commonalty. The Duke
Shall govern England."
Q. Kath. If I know you well,
You were the Duke's surveyor, and lost your office
On the complaint o' the tenants. Take good heed
You charge not in your spleen a noble person
And spoil your nobler soul. I say, take heed;
Yes, heartily beseech you.
King. Let him on.
Go forward.
Surv. On my soul, I'll speak but truth.
I told my lord the Duke, by the devil's illusions
The monk might be deceived; and that 'twas dangerous for him
To ruminate on this so far, until
It forged him some design, which, being believed,
It was much like to do. He answer'd, "Tush,
It can do me no damage"; adding further,
That, had the King in his last sickness fail'd,
The Cardinal's and Sir Thomas Lovell's heads
Should have gone off.
King. Ha! what, so rank? Ah ha!
There's mischief in this man. Canst thou say further?
Surv. I can, my liege.
King. Proceed.
Surv. Being at Greenwich,
After your Highness had reproved the Duke

About Sir William Bulmer—
King. I remember
Of such a time. Being my sworn servant,
The Duke retain'd him his. But on; what hence?
Surv. "If," quoth he, "I for this had been committed,
As, to the Tower, I thought, I would have play'd
The part my father meant to act upon
The usurper Richard; who, being at Salisbury,
Made suit to come in 's presence; which if granted,
As he made semblance of his duty, would
Have put his knife into him."
King. A giant traitor!
Wol. Now, madam, may his Highness live in freedom,
And this man out of prison?
Q. Kath. God mend all!
King. There's something more would out of thee; what say'st?
Surv. After "the Duke his father," with "the knife,"
He stretch'd him, and, with one hand on his dagger,
Another spread on 's breast, mounting his eyes,
He did discharge a horrible oath; whose tenour
Was—were he evil used, he would outgo
His father by as much as a performance
Does an irresolute purpose.
King. There's his period,
To sheathe his knife in us. He is attach'd;
Call him to present trial. If he may
Find mercy in the law, 'tis his; if none,
Let him not seek 't of us. By day and night,
He's traitor to the height. [*Exeunt.*

SCENE III. *An antechamber in the palace*

Enter the LORD CHAMBERLAIN *and* LORD SANDS.

Cham. Is 't possible the spells of France should juggle
Men into such strange mysteries?
Sands. New customs,
Though they be never so ridiculous,
Nay, let 'em be unmanly, yet are follow'd.
Cham. As far as I see, all the good our English
Have got by the late voyage is but merely
A fit or two o' the face; but they are shrewd ones;
For when they hold 'em, you would swear directly
Their very noses had been counsellors
To Pepin or Clotharius, they keep state so.
Sands. They have all new legs, and lame ones. One would take it,
That never saw 'em pace before, the spavin
Or springhalt reign'd among 'em.
Cham. Death! my lord,
Their clothes are after such a pagan cut too,
That, sure, they've worn out Christendom.

Enter SIR THOMAS LOVELL.

How now!
What news, Sir Thomas Lovell?
Lov. Faith, my lord,
I hear of none, but the new proclamation
That's clapp'd upon the court-gate.
Cham. What is 't for?
Lov. The reformation of our travell'd gallants,
That fill the court with quarrels, talk, and tailors.
Cham. I'm glad 'tis there. Now I would pray our monsieurs
To think an English courtier may be wise
And never see the Louvre.
Lov. They must either,
For so run the conditions, leave those remnants
Of fool and feather that they got in France,
With all their honourable points of ignorance
Pertaining thereunto, as fights and fireworks,
Abusing better men than they can be,
Out of a foreign wisdom, renouncing clean
The faith they have in tennis, and tall stockings,
Short blister'd breeches, and those types of travel,
And understand again like honest men;
Or pack to their old playfellows. There, I take it,
They may, "*cum privilegio*," wear away
The lag end of their lewdness and be laugh'd at.
Sands. 'Tis time to give 'em physic, their diseases
Are grown so catching.
Cham. What a loss our ladies
Will have of these trim vanities!
Lov. Ay, marry,
There will be woe indeed, lords. The sly whoresons
Have got a speeding trick to lay down ladies;
A French song and a fiddle has no fellow.
Sands. The devil fiddle 'em! I am glad they are going,
For, sure, there's no converting of 'em. Now
An honest country lord, as I am, beaten
A long time out of play, may bring his plain-song
And have an hour of hearing; and, by'r lady,
Held current music too.
Cham. Well said, Lord Sands;
Your colt's tooth is not cast yet.
Sands. No, my lord;
Nor shall not, while I have a stump.
Cham. Sir Thomas,
Whither were you a-going?
Lov. To the Cardinal's;
Your lordship is a guest too.

Cham. O, 'tis true:
This night he makes a supper, and a great one,
To many lords and ladies; there will be
The beauty of this kingdom, I'll assure you.
Lov. That churchman bears a bounteous mind indeed,
A hand as fruitful as the land that feeds us;
His dews fall everywhere.
Cham. No doubt he's noble;
He had a black mouth that said other of him.
Sands. He may, my lord; has wherewithal; in him
Sparing would show a worse sin than ill doctrine.
Men of his way should be most liberal;
They are set here for examples.
Cham. True, they are so;
But few now give so great ones. My barge stays;
Your lordship shall along. Come, good Sir Thomas,
We shall be late else; which I would not be,
For I was spoke to, with Sir Henry Guildford
This night to be comptrollers.
Sands. I am your lordship's. [*Exeunt.*

SCENE IV. *A Hall in York Place*

Hautboys. A small table under a state for the CARDINAL, *a longer table for the guests. Then enter* ANNE BULLEN *and divers other Ladies and Gentlemen as guests, at one door; at another door, enter* SIR HENRY GUILDFORD.

Guild. Ladies, a general welcome from his Grace
Salutes ye all; this night he dedicates
To fair content and you. None here, he hopes,
In all this noble bevy, has brought with her
One care abroad; he would have all as merry
As, first, good company, good wine, good welcome,
Can make good people. O, my lord, you're tardy.

Enter LORD CHAMBERLAIN, LORD SANDS, *and* SIR THOMAS LOVELL.

The very thought of this fair company
Clapp'd wings to me.
Cham. You are young, Sir Harry Guildford.
Sands. Sir Thomas Lovell, had the Cardinal
But half my lay thoughts in him, some of these
Should find a running banquet ere they rested,
I think would better please 'em. By my life,
They are a sweet society of fair ones.
Lov. O, that your lordship were but now confessor
To one or two of these!
Sands. I would I were;
They should find easy penance.
Lov. Faith, how easy?
Sands. As easy as a down-bed would afford it.
Cham. Sweet ladies, will it please you sit? Sir Harry,
Place you that side; I'll take the charge of this.
His Grace is entering. Nay, you must not freeze;
Two women placed together makes cold weather.
My Lord Sands, you are one will keep 'em waking;
Pray, sit between these ladies.
Sands. By my faith,
And thank your lordship. By your leave, sweet ladies.
If I chance to talk a little wild, forgive me;
I had it from my father.
Anne. Was he mad, sir?
Sands. O, very mad, exceeding mad, in love too;
But he would bite none; just as I do now,
He would kiss you twenty with a breath.
Kisses her.
Cham. Well said, my lord.
So, now you're fairly seated. Gentlemen,
The penance lies on you, if these fair ladies
Pass away frowning.
Sands. For my little cure,
Let me alone.

Hautboys. Enter CARDINAL WOLSEY, *and takes his state.*

Wol. You're welcome, my fair guests. That noble lady,
Or gentleman, that is not freely merry,
Is not my friend. This, to confirm my welcome;
And to you all, good health. [*Drinks.*]
Sands. Your Grace is noble:
Let me have such a bowl may hold my thanks,
And save me so much talking.
Wol. My Lord Sands,
I am beholding to you; cheer your neighbours.
Ladies, you are not merry. Gentlemen,
Whose fault is this?
Sands. The red wine first must rise
In their fair cheeks, my lord; then we shall have 'em
Talk us to silence.
Anne. You are a merry gamester,
My Lord Sands.
Sands. Yes, if I make my play.
Here's to your ladyship; and pledge it, madam,
For 'tis to such a thing—
Anne. You cannot show me.
Sands. I told your Grace they would talk anon.
Drum and trumpet, chambers discharged.
Wol. What's that?
Cham. Look out there, some of ye.
[*Exit* SERVANT.

Wol. What warlike voice,
And to what end, is this? Nay, ladies, fear not;
By all the laws of war you're privileged.

Re-enter SERVANT.

Cham. How now! what is 't?
Serv. A noble troop of strangers;
For so they seem. They've left their barge and landed;
And hither make, as great ambassadors
From foreign princes.
Wol. Good Lord Chamberlain,
Go, give 'em welcome; you can speak the French tongue;
And, pray, receive 'em nobly, and conduct 'em
Into our presence, where this heaven of beauty
Shall shine at full upon them. Some attend him.
[*Exit* CHAMBERLAIN, *attended. All rise, and tables removed.*
You have now a broken banquet; but we'll mend it.
A good digestion to you all. And once more
I shower a welcome on ye; welcome all.

Hautboys. Enter the KING *and others, as masquers, habited like shepherds, ushered by the* LORD CHAMBERLAIN. *They pass directly before the* CARDINAL, *and gracefully salute him.*

A noble company! what are their pleasures?
Cham. Because they speak no English, thus they pray'd
To tell your Grace, that, having heard by fame
Of this so noble and so fair assembly
This night to meet here, they could do no less,
Out of the great respect they bear to beauty,
But leave their flocks; and, under your fair conduct,
Crave leave to view these ladies and entreat
An hour of revels with 'em.
Wol. Say, Lord Chamberlain,
They have done my poor house grace; for which I pay 'em
A thousand thanks, and pray 'em take their pleasures.

They choose Ladies for the dance. The KING *chooses* ANNE BULLEN.

King. The fairest hand I ever touch'd! O beauty,
Till now I never knew thee!
Music. Dance.
Wol. My lord!
Cham. Your Grace?
Wol. Pray, tell 'em thus much from me:
There should be one amongst 'em, by his person,
More worthy this place than myself; to whom,
If I but knew him, with my love and duty
I would surrender it.
Cham. I will, my lord.
Whispers the Masquers.
Wol. What say they?
Cham. Such a one, they all confess,
There is indeed; which they would have your Grace
Find out, and he will take it.
Wol. Let me see, then.
By all your good leaves, gentlemen; here I'll make
My royal choice.
King. Ye have found him, Cardinal.
Unmasking.
You hold a fair assembly; you do well, lord.
You are a churchman, or, I'll tell you, Cardinal,
I should judge now unhappily.
Wol. I am glad
Your Grace is grown so pleasant.
King. My Lord Chamberlain,
Prithee, come hither. What fair lady's that?
Cham. An't please your Grace, Sir Thomas Bullen's daughter—
The Viscount Rochford—one of her Highness' women.
King. By heaven, she is a dainty one. Sweetheart,
I were unmannerly to take you out
And not to kiss you. A health, gentlemen!
Let it go round.
Wol. Sir Thomas Lovell, is the banquet ready
I' the privy chamber?
Lov. Yes, my lord.
Wol. Your Grace,
I fear, with dancing is a little heated.
King. I fear, too much.
Wol. There's fresher air, my lord,
In the next chamber.
King. Lead in your ladies, every one. Sweet partner,
I must not yet forsake you; let's be merry.
Good my lord Cardinal, I have half a dozen healths
To drink to these fair ladies, and a measure
To lead 'em once again; and then let's dream
Who's best in favour. Let the music knock it.
[*Exeunt with trumpets.*

ACT II

SCENE I. *Westminster: a street*

Enter TWO GENTLEMEN, *meeting.*

1st Gent. Whither away so fast?
2nd Gent. O, God save ye!

Even to the hall, to hear what shall become
Of the great Duke of Buckingham.
1st Gent. I'll save you
That labour, sir. All's now done, but the ceremony
Of bringing back the prisoner.
2nd Gent. Were you there?
1st Gent. Yes, indeed, was I.
2nd Gent. Pray, speak what has happen'd.
1st Gent. You may guess quickly what.
2nd Gent. Is he found guilty?
1st Gent. Yes, truly is he, and condemn'd upon 't.
2nd Gent. I am sorry for 't.
1st Gent. So are a number more.
2nd Gent. But, pray, how pass'd it?
1st Gent. I'll tell you in a little. The great Duke
Came to the bar; where to his accusations
He pleaded still not guilty and alleged
Many sharp reasons to defeat the law.
The King's attorney on the contrary
Urged on the examinations, proofs, confessions
Of divers witnesses; which the Duke desired
To have brought *vivâ voce* to his face;
At which appear'd against him his surveyor;
Sir Gilbert Peck his chancellor; and John Car,
Confessor to him; with that devil-monk,
Hopkins, that made this mischief.
2nd Gent. That was he
That fed him with his prophecies?
1st Gent. The same.
All these accused him strongly; which he fain
Would have flung from him, but, indeed, he could not.
And so his peers, upon this evidence,
Have found him guilty of high treason. Much
He spoke, and learnedly, for life; but all
Was either pitied in him or forgotten.
2nd Gent. After all this, how did he bear himself?
1st Gent. When he was brought again to the bar, to hear
His knell rung out, his judgement, he was stirr'd
With such an agony, he sweat extremely,
And something spoke in choler, ill, and hasty.
But he fell to himself again, and sweetly
In all the rest show'd a most noble patience.
2nd Gent. I do not think he fears death.
1st Gent. Sure, he does not;
He never was so womanish. The cause
He may a little grieve at.
2nd Gent. Certainly
The Cardinal is the end of this.
1st Gent. 'Tis likely,
By all conjectures: first, Kildare's attainder,
Then deputy of Ireland; who removed,
Earl Surrey was sent thither, and in haste too,
Lest he should help his father.
2nd Gent. That trick of state
Was a deep envious one.
1st Gent. At his return
No doubt he will requite it. This is noted,
And generally, whoever the King favours,
The Cardinal instantly will find employment,
And far enough from court too.
2nd Gent. All the commons
Hate him perniciously, and, o' my conscience,
Wish him ten fathom deep. This Duke as much
They love and dote on, call him bounteous Buckingham,
The mirror of all courtesy—
1st Gent. Stay there, sir,
And see the noble ruin'd man you speak of.

Enter BUCKINGHAM *from his arraignment; tipstaves before him; the axe with the edge towards him; halberds on each side; accompanied with* SIR THOMAS LOVELL, SIR NICHOLAS VAUX, SIR WILLIAM SANDS, *and common people.*

2nd Gent. Let's stand close, and behold him.
Buck. All good people,
You that thus far have come to pity me,
Hear what I say, and then go home and lose me.
I have this day received a traitor's judgement,
And by that name must die. Yet, heaven bear witness,
And if I have a conscience, let it sink me,
Even as the axe falls, if I be not faithful!
The law I bear no malice for my death;
'T has done, upon the premises, but justice;
But those that sought it I could wish more Christians.
Be what they will, I heartily forgive 'em;
Yet let 'em look they glory not in mischief,
Nor build their evils on the graves of great men;
For then my guiltless blood must cry against 'em.
For further life in this world I ne'er hope,
Nor will I sue, although the King have mercies
More than I dare make faults. You few that loved me,
And dare be bold to weep for Buckingham,
His noble friends and fellows, whom to leave
Is only bitter to him, only dying,
Go with me, like good angels, to my end;
And, as the long divorce of steel falls on me,
Make of your prayers one sweet sacrifice,
And lift my soul to heaven. Lead on, o' God's name.
Lov. I do beseech your Grace, for charity,
If ever any malice in your heart
Were hid against me, now to forgive me frankly.
Buck. Sir Thomas Lovell, I as free forgive you
As I would be forgiven. I forgive all;

There cannot be those numberless offences
'Gainst me, that I cannot take peace with. No black envy
Shall mark my grave. Commend me to his Grace;
And, if he speak of Buckingham, pray, tell him
You met him half in heaven. My vows and prayers
Yet are the king's; and, till my soul forsake,
Shall cry for blessings on him. May he live
Longer than I have time to tell his years!
Ever beloved and loving may his rule be!
And when old time shall lead him to his end,
Goodness and he fill up one monument!

Lov. To the water side I must conduct your Grace;
Then give my charge up to Sir Nicholas Vaux,
Who undertakes you to your end.

Vaux. Prepare there,
The Duke is coming. See the barge be ready;
And fit it with such furniture as suits
The greatness of his person.

Buck. Nay, Sir Nicholas,
Let it alone; my state now will but mock me.
When I came hither, I was Lord High Constable
And Duke of Buckingham; now, poor Edward Bohun.
Yet I am richer than my base accusers,
That never knew what truth meant. I now seal it;
And with that blood will make 'em one day groan for 't.
My noble father, Henry of Buckingham,
Who first raised head against usurping Richard,
Flying for succour to his servant Banister,
Being distress'd, was by that wretch betray'd,
And without trial fell; God's peace be with him!
Henry the Seventh succeeding, truly pitying
My father's loss, like a most royal prince,
Restored me to my honours, and, out of ruins,
Made my name once more noble. Now his son,
Henry the Eighth, life, honour, name, and all
That made me happy at one stroke has taken
For ever from the world. I had my trial,
And, must needs say, a noble one; which makes me
A little happier than my wretched father.
Yet thus far we are one in fortunes: both
Fell by our servants, by those men we loved most,
A most unnatural and faithless service!
Heaven has an end in all; yet, you that hear me,
This from a dying man receive as certain:
Where you are liberal of your loves and counsels
Be sure you be not loose; for those you make friends
And give your hearts to, when they once perceive
The least rub in your fortunes, fall away
Like water from ye, never found again
But where they mean to sink ye. All good people,
Pray for me! I must now forsake ye. The last hour
Of my long weary life is come upon me.
Farewell!
And when you would say something that is sad,
Speak how I fell. I have done; and God forgive me! [*Exeunt* DUKE *and Train.*

1st Gent. O, this is full of pity! Sir, it calls,
I fear, too many curses on their heads
That were the authors.

2nd Gent. If the Duke be guiltless,
'Tis full of woe. Yet I can give you inkling
Of an ensuing evil, if it fall,
Greater than this.

1st Gent. Good angels keep it from us!
What may it be? You do not doubt my faith, sir?

2nd Gent. This secret is so weighty, 'twill require
A strong faith to conceal it.

1st Gent. Let me have it;
I do not talk much.

2nd Gent. I am confident;
You shall, sir. Did you not of late days hear
A buzzing of a separation
Between the King and Katharine?

1st Gent. Yes, but it held not;
For when the King once heard it, out of anger
He sent command to the Lord Mayor straight
To stop the rumour, and allay those tongues
That durst disperse it.

2nd Gent. But that slander, sir,
Is found a truth now; for it grows again
Fresher than e'er it was; and held for certain
The King will venture at it. Either the Cardinal,
Or some about him near, have, out of malice
To the good Queen, possess'd him with a scruple
That will undo her. To confirm this too,
Cardinal Campeius is arrived, and lately;
As all think, for this business.

1st Gent. 'Tis the Cardinal;
And merely to revenge him on the Emperor
For not bestowing on him, at his asking,
The archbishopric of Toledo, this is purposed.

2nd Gent. I think you have hit the mark; but is 't not cruel
That she should feel the smart of this? The Cardinal
Will have his will, and she must fall.

1st Gent. 'Tis woeful.
We are too open here to argue this;
Let's think in private more. [*Exeunt.*

SCENE II. *An ante-chamber in the palace*

Enter the LORD CHAMBERLAIN, *reading a letter.*

Cham. "My lord, the horses your lordship sent for, with all the care I had, I saw well chosen, ridden, and furnished. They were young and handsome, and of the best breed in the north. When they were ready to set out for London, a man of my Lord Cardinal's, by commission and main power, took 'em from me; with this reason: His master would be served before a subject, if not before the King; which stopped our mouths, sir."
I fear he will indeed. Well, let him have them;
He will have all, I think.

Enter, to the LORD CHAMBERLAIN, *the* DUKES OF NORFOLK *and* SUFFOLK.

Nor. Well met, my Lord Chamberlain.
Cham. Good day to both your Graces.
Suf. How is the King employ'd?
Cham. I left him private,
Full of sad thoughts and troubles.
Nor. What's the cause?
Cham. It seems the marriage with his brother's wife
Has crept too near his conscience.
Suf. No, his conscience
Has crept too near another lady.
Nor. 'Tis so.
This is the Cardinal's doing, the king-cardinal.
That blind priest, like the eldest son of Fortune,
Turns what he list. The King will know him one day.
Suf. Pray God he do! He'll never know himself else.
Nor. How holily he works in all his business!
And with what zeal! for, now he has crack'd the league
Between us and the Emperor, the Queen's great nephew,
He dives into the King's soul, and there scatters
Dangers, doubts, wringing of the conscience,
Fears, and despairs; and all these for his marriage.
And out of all these to restore the King,
He counsels a divorce; a loss of her
That, like a jewel, has hung twenty years
About his neck, yet never lost her lustre;
Of her that loves him with that excellence
That angels love good men with; even of her
That, when the greatest stroke of fortune falls,
Will bless the King. And is not this course pious?
Cham. Heaven keep me from such counsel! 'Tis most true
These news are everywhere; every tongue speaks 'em,
And every true heart weeps for 't. All that dare
Look into these affairs see this main end,
The French king's sister. Heaven will one day open
The King's eyes, that so long have slept upon
This bold bad man.
Suf. And free us from his slavery.
Nor. We had need pray,
And heartily, for our deliverance;
Or this imperious man will work us all
From princes into pages. All men's honours
Lie like one lump before him, to be fashion'd
Into what pitch he please.
Suf. For me, my lords,
I love him not, nor fear him; there's my creed.
As I am made without him, so I'll stand,
If the King please; his curses and his blessings
Touch me alike, they're breath I not believe in.
I knew him, and I know him; so I leave him
To him that made him proud, the Pope.
Nor. Let's in;
And with some other business put the King
From these sad thoughts, that work too much upon him.
My lord, you'll bear us company?
Cham. Excuse me;
The king has sent me otherwhere: besides,
You'll find a most unfit time to disturb him:
Health to your lordships.
Nor. Thanks, my good Lord Chamberlain.
[*Exit* LORD CHAMBERLAIN; *and the* KING *draws the curtain, and sits reading pensively.*
Suf. How sad he looks! sure, he is much afflicted.
King. Who's there, ha?
Nor. Pray God he be not angry.
King. Who's there, I say? How dare you thrust yourselves
Into my private meditations?
Who am I? ha?
Nor. A gracious king that pardons all offences
Malice ne'er meant. Our breach of duty this way
Is business of estate; in which we come
To know your royal pleasure.
King. Ye are too bold.
Go to; I'll make ye know your times of business.
Is this an hour for temporal affairs, ha?

Enter WOLSEY *and* CAMPEIUS, *with a commission.*

Who's there? my good Lord Cardinal? O my Wolsey,
The quiet of my wounded conscience;

Thou art a cure fit for a king. [*To* CAMPEIUS] You're welcome,
Most learned reverend sir, into our kingdom;
Use us and it. [*To* WOLSEY] My good lord, have great care
I be not found a talker.
Wol. Sir, you cannot.
I would your Grace would give us but an hour
Of private conference.
King. [*To* NORFOLK *and* SUFFOLK] We are busy; go.
Nor. [*Aside to* SUFFOLK] This priest has no pride in him?
Suf. [*Aside to* NORFOLK] Not to speak of.
I would not be so sick though for his place.
But this cannot continue.
Nor. [*Aside to* SUFFOLK] If it do,
I'll venture one have-at-him.
Suf. [*Aside to* NORFOLK] I another.
[*Exeunt* NORFOLK *and* SUFFOLK.
Wol. Your Grace has given a precedent of wisdom
Above all princes, in committing freely
Your scruple to the voice of Christendom.
Who can be angry now? What envy reach you?
The Spaniard, tied by blood and favour to her,
Must now confess, if they have any goodness,
The trial just and noble. All the clerks,
I mean the learned ones, in Christian kingdoms
Have their free voices. Rome, the nurse of judgement,
Invited by your noble self, hath sent
One general tongue unto us, this good man,
This just and learned priest, Cardinal Campeius;
Whom once more I present unto your Highness.
King. And once more in mine arms I bid him welcome,
And thank the holy conclave for their loves.
They have sent me such a man I would have wish'd for.
Cam. Your Grace must needs deserve all strangers' loves,
You are so noble. To your Highness' hand
I tender my commission; by whose virtue,
The court of Rome commanding, you, my lord
Cardinal of York, are join'd with me their servant
In the unpartial judging of this business.
King. Two equal men. The Queen shall be acquainted
Forthwith for what you come. Where's Gardiner?
Wol. I know your Majesty has always loved her
So dear in heart not to deny her that
A woman of less place might ask by law,
Scholars allow'd freely to argue for her.
King. Ay, and the best she shall have; and my favour
To him that does best; God forbid else. Cardinal,
Prithee, call Gardiner to me, my new secretary.
I find him a fit fellow. [*Exit* WOLSEY.

Re-enter WOLSEY, *with* GARDINER.

Wol. [*Aside to* GARDINER] Give me your hand.
Much joy and favour to you;
You are the King's now.
Gard. [*Aside to* WOLSEY] But to be commanded
For ever by your Grace, whose hand has raised me.
King. Come hither, Gardiner.
Walks and whispers.
Cam. My Lord of York, was not one Doctor Pace
In this man's place before him?
Wol. Yes, he was.
Cam. Was he not held a learned man?
Wol. Yes, surely.
Cam. Believe me, there's an ill opinion spread then
Even of yourself, Lord Cardinal.
Wol. How! of me?
Cam. They will not stick to say you envied him,
And fearing he would rise, he was so virtuous,
Kept him a foreign man still; which so grieved him,
That he ran mad and died.
Wol. Heaven's peace be with him!
That's Christian care enough; for living murmurers
There's places of rebuke. He was a fool;
For he would needs be virtuous. That good fellow,
If I command him, follows my appointment.
I will have none so near else. Learn this, brother,
We live not to be griped by meaner persons.
King. Deliver this with modesty to the Queen.
[*Exit* GARDINER.
The most convenient place that I can think of
For such receipt of learning is Black-Friars;
There ye shall meet about this weighty business.
My Wolsey, see it furnish'd. O, my lord,
Would it not grieve an able man to leave
So sweet a bedfellow? But, conscience, conscience!
O, 'tis a tender place; and I must leave her.
[*Exeunt.*

SCENE III. *An ante-chamber of the Queen's apartments*

Enter ANNE BULLEN *and an* OLD LADY.

Anne. Not for that neither. Here's the pang that pinches;

His highness having lived so long with her, and she
So good a lady that no tongue could ever
Pronounce dishonour of her; by my life,
She never knew harm-doing. O, now, after
So many courses of the sun enthroned,
Still growing in a majesty and pomp, the which
To leave a thousand-fold more bitter than
'Tis sweet at first to acquire—after this process,
To give her the avaunt! it is a pity
Would move a monster.
Old L. Hearts of most hard temper
Melt and lament for her.
Anne. O, God's will! much better
She ne'er had known pomp. Though 't be temporal,
Yet, if that quarrel, fortune, do divorce
It from the bearer, 'tis a sufferance panging
As soul and body's severing.
Old L. Alas, poor lady!
She's a stranger now again.
Anne. So much the more
Must pity drop upon her. Verily,
I swear, 'tis better to be lowly born,
And range with humble livers in content,
Than to be perk'd up in a glistering grief,
And wear a golden sorrow.
Old L. Our content
Is our best having.
Anne. By my troth and maidenhead,
I would not be a queen.
Old L. Beshrew me, I would,
And venture maidenhead for 't; and so would you,
For all this spice of your hypocrisy.
You, that have so fair parts of woman on you,
Have too a woman's heart; which ever yet
Affected eminence, wealth, sovereignty;
Which, to say sooth, are blessings; and which gifts,
Saving your mincing, the capacity
Of your soft cheveril conscience would receive,
If you might please to stretch it.
Anne. Nay, good troth.
Old L. Yes, troth, and troth; you would not be a queen?
Anne. No, not for all the riches under heaven.
Old L. 'Tis strange. A three-pence bow'd would hire me,
Old as I am, to queen it. But, I pray you,
What think you of a duchess? have you limbs
To bear that load of title?
Anne. No, in truth.
Old L. Then you are weakly made. Pluck off a little;
I would not be a young count in your way,
For more than blushing comes to. If your back
Cannot vouchsafe this burthen, 'tis too weak
Ever to get a boy.
Anne. How you do talk!
I swear again, I would not be a queen
For all the world.
Old L. In faith, for little England
You'd venture an emballing. I myself
Would for Carnarvonshire, although there 'long'd
No more to the crown but that. Lo, who comes here?

Enter the LORD CHAMBERLAIN.

Cham. Good morrow, ladies. What were't worth to know
The secret of your conference?
Anne. My good lord,
Not your demand; it values not your asking.
Our mistress' sorrows we were pitying.
Cham. It was a gentle business, and becoming
The action of good women. There is hope
All will be well.
Anne. Now, I pray God, amen!
Cham. You bear a gentle mind, and heavenly blessings
Follow such creatures. That you may, fair lady,
Perceive I speak sincerely, and high note's
Ta'en of your many virtues, the King's Majesty
Commends his good opinion of you, and
Does purpose honour to you no less flowing
Than Marchioness of Pembroke; to which title
A thousand pound a year, annual support,
Out of his grace he adds.
Anne. I do not know
What kind of my obedience I should tender;
More than my all is nothing; nor my prayers
Are not words duly hallow'd, nor my wishes
More worth than empty vanities; yet prayers and wishes
Are all I can return. Beseech your lordship,
Vouchsafe to speak my thanks and my obedience,
As from a blushing handmaid, to his Highness;
Whose health and royalty I pray for.
Cham. Lady,
I shall not fail to approve the fair conceit
The King hath of you. [*Aside*] I have perused her well;
Beauty and honour in her are so mingled
That they have caught the King; and who knows yet
But from this lady may proceed a gem
To lighten all this isle? I'll to the King,
And say I spoke with you.
[*Exit* LORD CHAMBERLAIN.
Anne. My honour'd lord.

Old. L. Why, this it is; see, see!
I have been begging sixteen years in court,
Am yet a courtier beggarly, nor could
Come pat betwixt too early and too late
For any suit of pounds; and you, O fate!
A very fresh fish here—fie, fie, fie upon
This compell'd fortune!—have your mouth fill'd up
Before you open it.
Anne. This is strange to me.
Old L. How tastes it? is it bitter? forty pence, no.
There was a lady once, 'tis an old story,
That would not be a queen, that would she not,
For all the mud in Egypt. Have you heard it?
Anne. Come, you are pleasant.
Old L. With your theme, I could
O'ermount the lark. The Marchioness of Pembroke!
A thousand pounds a year for pure respect!
No other obligation! By my life,
That promises moe thousands; Honour's train
Is longer than his foreskirt. By this time
I know your back will bear a duchess. Say,
Are you not stronger than you were?
Anne. Good lady,
Make yourself mirth with your particular fancy,
And leave me out on't. Would I had no being,
If this salute my blood a jot. It faints me,
To think what follows.
The Queen is comfortless, and we forgetful
In our long absence. Pray, do not deliver
What here you've heard to her.
Old L. What do you think me?
[*Exeunt.*

SCENE IV. *A hall in Black-Friars*

Trumpets, sennet, and cornets. Enter two Vergers, with short silver wands; next them, two SCRIBES, *in the habit of doctors; after them, the* ARCHBISHOP OF CANTERBURY *alone; after him, the* BISHOPS OF LINCOLN, ELY, ROCHESTER, *and* SAINT ASAPH; *next them, with some small distance, follows a Gentleman bearing the purse, with the great seal, and a cardinal's hat; then two Priests, bearing each a silver cross; then a Gentleman-usher, bareheaded, accompanied with a Sergeant-at-arms bearing a silver mace; then two Gentlemen bearing two great silver pillars; after them, side by side, the two* CARDINALS; *two Noblemen with the sword and mace. The* KING *takes place under the cloth of state; the two* CARDINALS *sit under him as judges. The* QUEEN *takes place some distance from the* KING. *The Bishops place themselves on each side the court, in manner of a consistory; below them, the Scribes. The Lords sit next the Bishops. The rest of the Attendants stand in convenient order about the stage.*

Wol. Whilst our commission from Rome is read,
Let silence be commanded.
King. What's the need?
It hath already publicly been read,
And on all sides the authority allow'd;
You may, then, spare that time.
Wol. Be't so. Proceed.
Scribe. Say, Henry King of England, come into the court.
Crier. Henry King of England, &c.
King. Here.
Scribe. Say, Katharine Queen of England, come into the court.
Crier. Katharine Queen of England, &c.

The QUEEN *makes no answer, rises out of her chair, goes about the court, comes to the* KING, *and kneels at his feet; then speaks.*

Q. Kath. Sir, I desire you do me right and justice;
And to bestow your pity on me; for
I am a most poor woman, and a stranger,
Born out of your dominions; having here
No judge indifferent, nor no more assurance
Of equal friendship and proceeding. Alas, sir,
In what have I offended you? what cause
Hath my behaviour given to your displeasure
That thus you should proceed to put me off
And take your good grace from me? Heaven witness
I have been to you a true and humble wife,
At all times to your will conformable;
Ever in fear to kindle your dislike,
Yea, subject to your countenance, glad or sorry
As I saw it inclined. When was the hour
I ever contradicted your desire,
Or made it not mine too? Or which of your friends
Have I not strove to love, although I knew
He were mine enemy? what friend of mine
That had to him derived your anger, did I
Continue in my liking? nay, gave notice
He was from thence discharged? Sir, call to mind
That I have been your wife in this obedience
Upward of twenty years, and have been blest
With many children by you. If, in the course
And process of this time, you can report,
And prove it too, against mine honour aught,
My bond to wedlock, or my love and duty,
Against your sacred person, in God's name,
Turn me away; and let the foul'st contempt
Shut door upon me, and so give me up

To the sharp'st kind of justice. Please you, sir,
The King, your father, was reputed for
A prince most prudent, of an excellent
And unmatch'd wit and judgement; Ferdinand,
My father, King of Spain, was reckon'd one
The wisest prince that there had reign'd by many
A year before. It is not to be question'd
That they had gather'd a wise council to them
Of every realm, that did debate this business,
Who deem'd our marriage lawful; wherefore I humbly
Beseech you, sir, to spare me, till I may
Be by my friends in Spain advised; whose counsel
I will implore. If not, i' the name of God,
Your pleasure be fulfill'd!

Wol. You have here, lady,
And of your choice, these reverend fathers; men
Of singular integrity and learning,
Yea, the elect o' the land, who are assembled
To plead your cause. It shall be therefore bootless
That longer you desire the court; as well
For your own quiet, as to rectify
What is unsettled in the King.

Cam. His Grace
Hath spoken well and justly; therefore, madam,
It's fit this royal session do proceed;
And that without delay their arguments
Be now produced and heard.

Q. Kath. Lord Cardinal,
To you I speak.

Wol. Your pleasure, madam?

Q. Kath. Sir,
I am about to weep; but, thinking that
We are a queen, or long have dream'd so, certain
The daughter of a king, my drops of tears
I'll turn to sparks of fire.

Wol. Be patient yet.

Q. Kath. I will, when you are humble; nay, before,
Or God will punish me. I do believe,
Induced by potent circumstances, that
You are mine enemy, and make my challenge
You shall not be my judge; for it is you
Have blown this coal betwixt my lord and me;
Which God's dew quench! Therefore I say again,
I utterly abhor, yea, from my soul
Refuse you for my judge; whom, yet once more,
I hold my most malicious foe, and think not
At all a friend to truth.

Wol. I do profess
You speak not like yourself; who ever yet
Have stood to charity, and display'd the effects
Of disposition gentle, and of wisdom
O'ertopping woman's power. Madam, you do me wrong.
I have no spleen against you; nor injustice
For you or any. How far I have proceeded,
Or how far further shall, is warranted
By a commission from the consistory,
Yea, the whole consistory of Rome. You charge me
That I have blown this coal. I do deny it.
The King is present; if it be known to him
That I gainsay my deed, how may he wound,
And worthily, my falsehood! yea, as much
As you have done my truth. If he know
That I am free of your report, he knows
I am not of your wrong. Therefore in him
It lies to cure me; and the cure is to
Remove these thoughts from you; the which before
His Highness shall speak in, I do beseech
You, gracious madam, to unthink your speaking
And to say so no more.

Q. Kath. My lord, my lord,
I am a simple woman, much too weak
To oppose your cunning. You're meek and humble-mouth'd;
You sign your place and calling, in full seeming,
With meekness and humility; but your heart
Is cramm'd with arrogancy, spleen, and pride.
You have, by fortune and his Highness' favours,
Gone slightly o'er low steps and now are mounted
Where powers are your retainers, and your words,
Domestics to you, serve your will as 't please
Yourself pronounce their office. I must tell you,
You tender more your person's honour than
Your high profession spiritual; that again
I do refuse you for my judge; and here,
Before you all, appeal unto the Pope,
To bring my whole cause 'fore his Holiness,
And to be judged by him.

She curtsies to the KING, *and offers to depart.*

Cam. The Queen is obstinate,
Stubborn to justice, apt to accuse it, and
Disdainful to be tried by 't. 'Tis not well.
She's going away.

King. Call her again.

Crier. Katharine Queen of England, come into the court.

Grif. Madam, you are call'd back.

Q. Kath. What need you note it? pray you, keep your way.
When you are call'd, return. Now, the Lord help,
They vex me past my patience! Pray you, pass on.
I will not tarry; no, nor ever more

Upon this business my appearance make
In any of their courts.
[*Exeunt* QUEEN, *and her Attendants*.
King. Go thy ways, Kate.
That man i' the world who shall report he has
A better wife, let him in nought be trusted,
For speaking false in that. Thou art alone
If thy rare qualities, sweet gentleness,
Thy meekness saint-like, wife-like government,
Obeying in commanding, and thy parts
Sovereign and pious else, could speak thee out,
The queen of earthly queens. She's noble born;
And like her true nobility she has
Carried herself towards me.
Wol. Most gracious sir,
In humblest manner I require your Highness
That it shall please you to declare, in hearing
Of all these ears—for where I am robb'd and bound,
There must I be unloosed, although not there
At once and fully satisfied—whether ever I
Did broach this business to your Highness; or
Laid any scruple in your way, which might
Induce you to the question on 't? or ever
Have to you, but with thanks to God for such
A royal lady, spake one the least word that might
Be to the prejudice of her present state,
Or touch of her good person?
King. My Lord Cardinal,
I do excuse you; yea, upon mine honour,
I free you from 't. You are not to be taught
That you have many enemies, that know not
Why they are so, but, like to village-curs,
Bark when their fellows do. By some of these
The Queen is put in anger. You're excused;
But will you be more justified? you ever
Have wish'd the sleeping of this business; never desired
It to be stirr'd; but oft have hinder'd, oft,
The passages made toward it. On my honour,
I speak my good Lord Cardinal to this point,
And thus far clear him. Now, what moved me to 't,
I will be bold with time and your attention:
Then mark the inducement. Thus it came; give heed to 't:
My conscience first received a tenderness,
Scruple, and prick, on certain speeches utter'd
By the Bishop of Bayonne, then French ambassador;
Who had been hither sent on the debating
A marriage 'twixt the Duke of Orleans and
Our daughter Mary. I' the progress of this business,
Ere a determinate resolution, he,
I mean the Bishop, did require a respite;
Wherein he might the King his lord advertise
Whether our daughter were legitimate,
Respecting this our marriage with the dowager,
Sometimes our brother's wife. This respite shook
The bosom of my conscience, enter'd me,
Yea, with a splitting power, and made to tremble
The region of my breast; which forced such way,
That many mazed considerings did throng
And press'd in with this caution. First, methought
I stood not in the smile of Heaven; who had
Commanded nature, that my lady's womb,
If it conceived a male child by me, should
Do no more offices of life to 't than
The grave does to the dead; for her male issue
Or died where they were made, or shortly after
This world had air'd them. Hence I took a thought
This was a judgement on me; that my kingdom,
Well worthy the best heir o' the world, should not
Be gladded in 't by me. Then follows, that
I weigh'd the danger which my realms stood in
By this my issue's fail; and that gave to me
Many a groaning throe. Thus hulling in
The wild sea of my conscience, I did steer
Toward this remedy, whereupon we are
Now present here together; that's to say,
I meant to rectify my conscience—which
I then did feel full sick, and yet not well—
By all the reverend fathers of the land
And doctors learn'd. First I began in private
With you, my Lord of Lincoln; you remember
How under my oppression I did reek,
When I first moved you.
Lin. Very well, my liege.
King. I have spoke long. Be pleased yourself to say
How far you satisfied me.
Lin. So please your Highness,
The question did at first so stagger me,
Bearing a state of mighty moment in 't
And consequence of dread, that I committed
The daring'st counsel which I had to doubt;
And did entreat your Highness to this course
Which you are running here.
King. I then moved you,
My Lord of Canterbury; and got your leave
To make this present summons. Unsolicited
I left no reverend person in this court;
But by particular consent proceeded
Under your hands and seals. Therefore, go on;
For no dislike i' the world against the person
Of the good queen, but the sharp thorny points

Of my alleged reasons, drive this forward.
Prove but our marriage lawful, by my life
And kingly dignity, we are contented
To wear our mortal state to come with her,
Katharine our queen, before the primest creature
That's paragon'd o' the world.

Cam. So please your Highness,
The Queen being absent, 'tis a needful fitness
That we adjourn this court till further day.
Meanwhile must be an earnest motion
Made to the Queen to call back her appeal
She intends unto his Holiness.

King. [*Aside*] I may perceive
These Cardinals trifle with me; I abhor
This dilatory sloth and tricks of Rome.
My learn'd and well-beloved servant, Cranmer,
Prithee, return. With thy approach, I know,
My comfort comes along. Break up the court!
I say, set on.

[*Exeunt in manner as they entered.*

ACT III

Scene I. *London: The Queen's apartments*

The QUEEN *and her women, as at work.*

Q. Kath. Take thy lute, wench: my soul grows sad with troubles.
Sing, and disperse 'em, if thou canst. Leave working.

SONG

Orpheus with his lute made trees
And the mountain tops that freeze
Bow themselves when he did sing.
To his music plants and flowers
Ever sprung; as sun and showers
There had made a lasting spring.

Everything that heard him play,
Even the billows of the sea,
Hung their heads, and then lay by.
In sweet music is such art,
Killing care and grief of heart
Fall asleep, or hearing, die.

Enter a GENTLEMAN.

Q. Kath. How now!

Gent. An 't please your Grace, the two great Cardinals
Wait in the presence.

Q. Kath. Would they speak with me?

Gent. They will'd me say so, madam.

Q. Kath. Pray their Graces
To come near. [*Exit* GENTLEMAN.] What can be their business
With me, a poor weak woman, fall'n from favour?
I do not like their coming. Now I think on 't,
They should be good men; their affairs as righteous.
But all hoods make not monks.

Enter the two CARDINALS, WOLSEY *and* CAMPEIUS.

Wol. Peace to your Highness!

Q. Kath. Your Graces find me here part of a housewife;
I would be all, against the worst may happen.
What are your pleasures with me, reverend lords?

Wol. May it please you, noble madam, to withdraw
Into your private chamber, we shall give you
The full cause of our coming.

Q. Kath. Speak it here;
There's nothing I have done yet, o' my conscience,
Deserves a corner. Would all other women
Could speak this with as free a soul as I do!
My lords, I care not, so much I am happy
Above a number, if my actions
Were tried by every tongue, every eye saw 'em,
Envy and base opinion set against 'em,
I know my life so even. If your business
Seek me out, and that way I am wife in,
Out with it boldly. Truth loves open dealing.

Wol. Tanta est erga te mentis integritas, regina serenissima—

Q. Kath. O, good my lord, no Latin;
I am not such a truant since my coming,
As not to know the language I have lived in.
A strange tongue makes my cause more strange, suspicious;
Pray, speak in English. Here are some will thank you,
If you speak truth, for their poor mistress' sake;
Believe me, she has had much wrong. Lord Cardinal,
The willing'st sin I ever yet committed
May be absolved in English.

Wol. Noble lady,
I am sorry my integrity should breed,
And service to his Majesty and you,
So deep suspicion, where all faith was meant.
We come not by the way of accusation,
To taint that honour every good tongue blesses,
Nor to betray you any way to sorrow,
You have too much, good lady; but to know
How you stand minded in the weighty difference
Between the King and you; and to deliver,
Like free and honest men, our just opinions
And comforts to your cause.

Cam. Most honour'd madam,
My Lord of York, out of his noble nature,
Zeal, and obedience he still bore your Grace,
Forgetting, like a good man, your late censure
Both of his truth and him, which was too far,
Offers, as I do, in a sign of peace,
His service and his counsel.
Q. Kath. [*Aside*] To betray me.—
My lords, I thank you both for your good wills;
Ye speak like honest men; pray God, ye prove so!
But how to make ye suddenly an answer,
In such a point of weight, so near mine honour—
More near my life, I fear—with my weak wit,
And to such men of gravity and learning,
In truth, I know not. I was set at work
Among my maids full little, God knows, looking
Either for such men or such business.
For her sake that I have been—for I feel
The last fit of my greatness—good your Graces,
Let me have time and counsel for my cause.
Alas, I am a woman, friendless, hopeless!
Wol. Madam, you wrong the King's love with these fears.
Your hopes and friends are infinite.
Q. Kath. In England
But little for my profit. Can you think, lords,
That any Englishman dare give me counsel?
Or be a known friend, 'gainst his Highness' pleasure,
Though he be grown so desperate to be honest,
And live a subject? Nay, forsooth, my friends,
They that must weigh out my afflictions,
They that my trust must grow to, live not here.
They are, as all my other comforts, far hence
In mine own country, lords.
Cam. I would your Grace
Would leave your griefs, and take my counsel.
Q. Kath. How, sir?
Cam. Put your main cause into the King's protection;
He's loving and most gracious. 'Twill be much
Both for your honour better and your cause;
For if the trial of the law o'ertake ye,
You'll part away disgraced.
Wol. He tells you rightly.
Q. Kath. Ye tell me what ye wish for both—my ruin.
Is this your Christian counsel? Out upon ye!
Heaven is above all yet; there sits a judge
That no king can corrupt.
Cam. Your rage mistakes us.
Q. Kath. The more shame for ye. Holy men I thought ye,
Upon my soul, two reverend cardinal virtues;
But cardinal sins and hollow hearts I fear ye.
Mend 'em, for shame, my lords. Is this your comfort?
The cordial that ye bring a wretched lady,
A woman lost among ye, laugh'd at, scorn'd?
I will not wish ye half my miseries;
I have more charity; but say, I warn'd ye.
Take heed, for heaven's sake, take heed, lest at once
The burden of my sorrows fall upon ye.
Wol. Madam, this is a mere distraction;
You turn the good we offer into envy.
Q. Kath. Ye turn me into nothing. Woe upon ye
And all such false professors! Would you have me—
If you have any justice, any pity;
If ye be anything but churchmen's habits—
Put my sick cause into his hands that hates me?
Alas, has banish'd me his bed already,
His love, too long ago! I am old, my lords,
And all the fellowship I hold now with him
Is only my obedience. What can happen
To me above this wretchedness? all your studies
Make me a curse like this.
Cam. Your fears are worse.
Q. Kath. Have I lived thus long—let me speak myself,
Since virtue finds no friends—a wife, a true one?
A woman, I dare say without vain-glory,
Never yet branded with suspicion?
Have I with all my full affections
Still met the King? loved him next heaven? obey'd him?
Been, out of fondness, superstitious to him?
Almost forgot my prayers to content him?
And am I thus rewarded? 'tis not well, lords.
Bring me a constant woman to her husband,
One that ne'er dream'd a joy beyond his pleasure;
And to that woman, when she has done most,
Yet will I add an honour, a great patience.
Wol. Madam, you wander from the good we aim at.
Q. Kath. My lord, I dare not make myself so guilty
To give up willingly that noble title
Your master wed me to. Nothing but death
Shall e'er divorce my dignities.
Wol. Pray, hear me.
Q. Kath. Would I had never trod this English earth,
Or felt the flatteries that grow upon it!
Ye have angels' faces, but heaven knows your hearts.
What will become of me now, wretched lady!
I am the most unhappy woman living.
Alas, poor wenches, where are now your fortunes!

Shipwreck'd upon a kingdom, where no pity,
No friends, no hope; no kindred weep for me;
Almost no grave allow'd me. Like the lily,
That once was mistress of the field and flourish'd,
I'll hang my head and perish.
Wol. If your Grace
Could but be brought to know our ends are honest,
You'd feel more comfort. Why should we, good lady,
Upon what cause, wrong you? alas, our places,
The way of our profession is against it.
We are to cure such sorrows, not to sow 'em.
For goodness' sake, consider what you do;
How you may hurt yourself, ay, utterly
Grow from the King's acquaintance, by this carriage.
The hearts of princes kiss obedience,
So much they love it; but to stubborn spirits
They swell, and grow as terrible as storms.
I know you have a gentle, noble temper,
A soul as even as a calm. Pray, think us
Those we profess, peace-makers, friends, and servants.
Cam. Madam, you'll find it so. You wrong your virtues
With these weak women's fears. A noble spirit,
As yours was put into you, ever casts
Such doubts, as false coin, from it. The King loves you;
Beware you lose it not. For us, if you please
To trust us in your business, we are ready
To use our utmost studies in your service.
Q. Kath. Do what ye will, my lords; and, pray, forgive me,
If I have used myself unmannerly.
You know I am a woman, lacking wit
To make a seemly answer to such persons.
Pray, do my service to his Majesty.
He has my heart yet; and shall have my prayers
While I shall have my life. Come, reverend fathers,
Bestow your counsels on me. She now begs,
That little thought, when she set footing here,
She should have bought her dignities so dear.
[*Exeunt.*

SCENE II. *Ante-chamber to the King's apartment*

Enter the DUKE OF NORFOLK, *the* DUKE OF SUFFOLK, *the* EARL OF SURREY, *and the* LORD CHAMBERLAIN.

Nor. If you will now unite in your complaints,
And force them with a constancy, the Cardinal
Cannot stand under them. If you omit
The offer of this time, I cannot promise
But that you shall sustain moe new disgraces,
With these you bear already.
Sur. I am joyful
To meet the least occasion that may give me
Remembrance of my father-in-law, the Duke,
To be revenged on him.
Suf. Which of the peers
Have uncontemn'd gone by him, or at least
Strangely neglected? When did he regard
The stamp of nobleness in any person
Out of himself?
Cham. My lords, you speak your pleasures.
What he deserves of you and me I know;
What we can do to him, though now the time
Gives way to us, I much fear. If you cannot
Bar his access to the King, never attempt
Anything on him; for he hath a witchcraft
Over the King in 's tongue.
Nor. O, fear him not;
His spell in that is out. The King hath found
Matter against him that for ever mars
The honey of his language. No, he's settled,
Not to come off, in his displeasure.
Sur. Sir,
I should be glad to hear such news as this
Once every hour.
Nor. Believe it, this is true.
In the divorce his contrary proceedings
Are all unfolded; wherein he appears
As I would wish mine enemy.
Sur. How came
His practices to light?
Suf. Most strangely.
Sur. O, how, how?
Suf. The Cardinal's letters to the Pope miscarried,
And came to the eye o' the King; wherein was read,
How that the Cardinal did entreat his Holiness
To stay the judgement o' the divorce; for if
It did take place, "I do," quoth he, "perceive
My King is tangled in affection to
A creature of the Queen's, Lady Anne Bullen."
Sur. Has the King this?
Suf. Believe it.
Sur. Will this work?
Cham. The King in this perceives him, how he coasts
And hedges his own way. But in this point
All his tricks founder, and he brings his physic
After his patient's death. The King already
Hath married the fair lady.
Sur. Would he had!
Suf. May you be happy in your wish, my lord!
For, I profess, you have it.
Sur. Now, all my joy
Trace the conjunction!

Suf. My amen to 't!
Nor. All men's!
Suf. There's order given for her coronation.
Marry, this is yet but young, and may be left
To some ears unrecounted. But, my lords,
She is a gallant creature, and complete
In mind and feature. I persuade me, from her
Will fall some blessing to this land, which shall
In it be memorized.
Sur. But, will the King
Digest this letter of the Cardinal's?
The Lord forbid!
Nor. Marry, amen!
Suf. No, no;
There be moe wasps that buzz about his nose
Will make this sting the sooner. Cardinal Campeius
Is stol'n away to Rome; hath ta'en no leave;
Has left the cause o' the King unhandled; and
Is posted, as the agent of our Cardinal,
To second all his plot. I do assure you
The King cried "Ha!" at this.
Cham. Now, God incense him,
And let him cry "Ha!" louder!
Nor. But, my lord,
When returns Cranmer?
Suf. He is return'd in his opinions; which
Have satisfied the King for his divorce,
Together with all famous colleges
Almost in Christendom. Shortly, I believe,
His second marriage shall be publish'd, and
Her coronation. Katharine no more
Shall be call'd Queen, but Princess Dowager
And widow to Prince Arthur.
Nor. This same Cranmer's
A worthy fellow, and hath ta'en much pain
In the King's business.
Suf. He has; and we shall see him
For it an archbishop.
Nor. So I hear.
Suf. 'Tis so.
The Cardinal!

Enter WOLSEY *and* CROMWELL.

Nor. Observe, observe, he's moody.
Wol. The packet, Cromwell,
Gave 't you the King?
Crom. To his own hand, in's bedchamber.
Wol. Look'd he o' the inside of the paper?
Crom. Presently
He did unseal them; and the first he view'd,
He did it with a serious mind; a heed
Was in his countenance. You he bade
Attend him here this morning.
Wol. Is he ready
To come abroad?
Crom. I think, by this he is.
Wol. Leave me awhile. [*Exit* CROMWELL.
[*Aside*] It shall be to the Duchess of Alençon,
The French king's sister; he shall marry her.
Anne Bullen! No; I'll no Anne Bullens for him;
There's more in 't than fair visage. Bullen!
No, we'll no Bullens. Speedily I wish
To hear from Rome. The Marchioness of Pembroke!
Nor. He's discontented.
Suf. May be, he hears the King
Does whet his anger to him.
Sur. Sharp enough,
Lord, for thy justice!
Wol. [*Aside*] The late queen's gentlewoman, a knight's daughter,
To be her mistress' mistress! the Queen's queen!
This candle burns not clear; 'tis I must snuff it;
Then out it goes. What though I know her virtuous
And well deserving? yet I know her for
A spleeny Lutheran; and not wholesome to
Our cause, that she should lie i' the bosom of
Our hard-ruled king. Again, there is sprung up
An heretic, an arch one, Cranmer; one
Hath crawl'd into the favour of the King,
And is his oracle.
Nor. He is vex'd at something.
Sur. I would 'twere something that would fret the string,
The master-cord on 's heart!

Enter the KING, *reading of a schedule, and* LOVELL.

Suf. The King, the King!
King. What piles of wealth hath he accumulated
To his own portion! and what expense by the hour
Seems to flow from him! How, i' the name of thrift,
Does he rake this together! Now, my lords,
Saw you the Cardinal?
Nor. My lord, we have
Stood here observing him. Some strange commotion
Is in his brain; he bites his lip, and starts;
Stops on a sudden, looks upon the ground,
Then lays his finger on his temple; straight
Springs out into fast gait; then stops again,
Strikes his breast hard, and anon he casts
His eye against the moon. In most strange postures
We have seen him set himself.
King. It may well be;
There is a mutiny in 's mind. This morning
Papers of state he sent me to peruse,

As I required; and wot you what I found
There—on my conscience, put unwittingly?
Forsooth, an inventory, thus importing;
The several parcels of his plate, his treasure,
Rich stuffs, and ornaments of household; which
I find at such proud rate that it out-speaks
Possession of a subject.
Nor. It's Heaven's will.
Some spirit put this paper in the packet,
To bless your eye withal.
King. If we did think
His contemplation were above the earth,
And fix'd on spiritual object, he should still
Dwell in his musings; but I am afraid
His thinkings are below the moon, not worth
His serious considering.
KING *takes his seat; whispers* LOVELL, *who goes to the* CARDINAL.
Wol. Heaven forgive me!
Ever God bless your Highness!
King. Good my lord,
You are full of heavenly stuff, and bear the inventory
Of your best graces in your mind; the which
You were now running o'er. You have scarce time
To steal from spiritual leisure a brief span
To keep your earthly audit. Sure, in that
I deem you an ill husband, and am glad
To have you therein my companion.
Wol. Sir,
For holy offices I have a time; a time
To think upon the part of business which
I bear i' the state; and nature does require
Her times of preservation, which perforce
I, her frail son, amongst my brethren mortal,
Must give my tendance to.
King. You have said well.
Wol. And ever may your Highness yoke together,
As I will lend you cause, my doing well
With my well saying!
King. 'Tis well said again;
And 'tis a kind of good deed to say well;
And yet words are no deeds. My father loved you.
He said he did; and with his deed did crown
His word upon you. Since I had my office,
I have kept you next my heart; have not alone
Employ'd you where high profits might come home,
But pared my present havings, to bestow
My bounties upon you.
Wol. [*Aside*] What should this mean?
Sur. [*Aside*] The Lord increase this business!
King. Have I not made you
The prime man of the state? I pray you, tell me,
If what I now pronounce you have found true;
And, if you may confess it, say withal,
If you are bound to us or no. What say you?
Wol. My sovereign, I confess your royal graces,
Shower'd on me daily, have been more than could
My studied purposes requite; which went
Beyond all man's endeavours. My endeavours
Have ever come too short of my desires,
Yet fil'd with my abilities. Mine own ends
Have been mine so that evermore they pointed
To the good of your most sacred person and
The profit of the state. For your great graces
Heap'd upon me, poor undeserver, I
Can nothing render but allegiant thanks,
My prayers to heaven for you, my loyalty,
Which ever has and ever shall be growing,
Till death, that winter, kill it.
King. Fairly answer'd;
A loyal and obedient subject is
Therein illustrated. The honour of it
Does pay the act of it; as, i' the contrary,
The foulness is the punishment. I presume
That, as my hand has open'd bounty to you,
My heart dropp'd love, my power rain'd honour, more
On you than any; so your hand and heart,
Your brain, and every function of your power,
Should, notwithstanding that your bond of duty,
As 'twere in love's particular, be more
To me, your friend, than any.
Wol. I do profess
That for your Highness' good I ever labour'd
More than mine own, that am, have, and will be—
Though all the world should crack their duty to you
And throw it from their soul; though perils did
Abound, as thick as thought could make 'em, and
Appear in forms more horrid—yet my duty,
As doth a rock against the chiding flood,
Should the approach of this wild river break,
And stand unshaken yours.
King. 'Tis nobly spoken.
Take notice, lords, he has a loyal breast,
For you have seen him open 't. Read o'er this;
Giving him papers.
And after, this. And then to breakfast with
What appetite you have.
[*Exit* KING, *frowning upon* CARDINAL WOLSEY. *The Nobles throng after him, smiling and whispering.*
Wol. What should this mean?
What sudden anger's this? how have I reap'd it?
He parted frowning from me, as if ruin

Leap'd from his eyes. So looks the chafed lion
Upon the daring huntsman that has gall'd him;
Then makes him nothing. I must read this paper;
I fear, the story of his anger. 'Tis so;
This paper has undone me. 'Tis the account
Of all that world of wealth I have drawn together
For mine own ends; indeed, to gain the popedom,
And fee my friends in Rome. O negligence!
Fit for a fool to fall by. What cross devil
Made me put this main secret in the packet
I sent the King? Is there no way to cure this?
No new device to beat this from his brains?
I know 'twill stir him strongly; yet I know
A way, if it take right, in spite of fortune
Will bring me off again. What's this? "To the Pope!"
The letter, as I live, with all the business
I writ to's Holiness. Nay then, farewell!
I have touch'd the highest point of all my greatness;
And, from that full meridian of my glory,
I haste now to my setting. I shall fall
Like a bright exhalation in the evening,
And no man see me more.

Re-enter to WOLSEY, *the* DUKES OF NORFOLK *and* SUFFOLK, *the* EARL OF SURREY, *and the* LORD CHAMBERLAIN.

Nor. Hear the King's pleasure, Cardinal! who commands you
To render up the great seal presently
Into our hands; and to confine yourself
To Asher House, my Lord of Winchester's,
Till you hear further from his Highness.
Wol. Stay!
Where's your commission, lords? words cannot carry
Authority so weighty.
Suf. Who dare cross 'em,
Bearing the King's will from his mouth expressly?
Wol. Till I find more than will or words to do it,
I mean your malice, know, officious lords,
I dare and must deny it. Now I feel
Of what coarse metal ye are moulded, envy.
How eagerly ye follow my disgraces,
As if it fed ye! and how sleek and wanton
Ye appear in everything may bring my ruin!
Follow your envious courses, men of malice;
You have Christian warrant for 'em, and, no doubt,
In time will find their fit rewards. That seal,
You ask with such a violence, the King,
Mine and your master, with his own hand gave me;
Bade me enjoy it, with the place and honours,
During my life; and, to confirm his goodness,
Tied it by letters-patents. Now, who'll take it?
Sur. The King, that gave it.
Wol. It must be himself, then.
Sur. Thou art a proud traitor, priest.
Wol. Proud lord, thou liest.
Within these forty hours Surrey durst better
Have burnt that tongue than said so.
Sur. Thy ambition,
Thou scarlet sin, robb'd this bewailing land
Of noble Buckingham, my father-in-law.
The heads of all thy brother cardinals,
With thee and all thy best parts bound together,
Weigh'd not a hair of his. Plague of your policy!
You sent me deputy for Ireland;
Far from his succour, from the King, from all
That might have mercy on the fault thou gavest him;
Whilst your great goodness, out of holy pity,
Absolved him with an axe.
Wol. This, and all else
This talking lord can lay upon my credit,
I answer is most false. The Duke by law
Found his deserts. How innocent I was
From any private malice in his end,
His noble jury and foul cause can witness.
If I loved many words, lord, I should tell you
You have as little honesty as honour,
That in the way of loyalty and truth
Toward the King, my ever royal master,
Dare mate a sounder man than Surrey can be,
And all that love his follies.
Sur. By my soul,
Your long coat, priest, protects you; thou shouldst feel
My sword i' the life-blood of thee else. My lords,
Can ye endure to hear this arrogance?
And from this fellow? If we live thus tamely,
To be thus jaded by a piece of scarlet,
Farewell nobility; let his Grace go forward,
And dare us with his cap like larks.
Wol. All goodness
Is poison to thy stomach.
Sur. Yes, that goodness
Of gleaning all the land's wealth into one,
Into your own hands, Cardinal, by extortion;
The goodness of your intercepted packets
You writ to the Pope against the King. Your goodness,
Since you provoke me, shall be most notorious.
My Lord of Norfolk, as you are truly noble,
As you respect the common good, the state
Of our despised nobility, our issues,

Who, if he live, will scarce be gentlemen,
Produce the grand sum of his sins, the articles
Collected from his life. I'll startle you
Worse than the sacring bell, when the brown wench
Lay kissing in your arms, Lord Cardinal.
Wol. How much, methinks, I could despise this man,
But that I am bound in charity against it!
Nor. Those articles, my lord, are in the King's hand;
But, thus much, they are foul ones.
Wol. So much fairer
And spotless shall mine innocence arise,
When the King knows my truth.
Sur. This cannot save you.
I thank my memory, I yet remember
Some of these articles; and out they shall.
Now, if you can blush and cry "guilty," Cardinal,
You'll show a little honesty.
Wol. Speak on, sir;
I dare your worst objections. If I blush,
It is to see a nobleman want manners.
Sur. I had rather want those than my head. Have at you!
First, that, without the King's assent or knowledge,
You wrought to be a legate; by which power
You maim'd the jurisdiction of all bishops.
Nor. Then, that in all you writ to Rome, or else
To foreign princes, "*Ego et Rex meus*"
Was still inscribed; in which you brought the King
To be your servant.
Suf. Then that, without the knowledge
Either of king or council, when you went
Ambassador to the Emperor, you made bold
To carry into Flanders the great seal.
Sur. Item, you sent a large commission
To Gregory de Cassado, to conclude,
Without the King's will or the state's allowance,
A league between his Highness and Ferrara.
Suf. That, out of mere ambition, you have caused
Your holy hat to be stamp'd on the king's coin.
Sur. Then that you have sent innumerable substance—
By what means got, I leave to your own conscience—
To furnish Rome, and to prepare the ways
You have for dignities; to the mere undoing
Of all the kingdom. Many more there are;
Which, since they are of you, and odious,
I will not taint my mouth with.
Cham. O my lord,
Press not a falling man too far! 'tis virtue.
His faults lie open to the laws; let them,
Not you, correct him. My heart weeps to see him
So little of his great self.
Sur. I forgive him.
Suf. Lord Cardinal, the King's further pleasure is,
Because all those things you have done of late,
By your power legatine, within this kingdom,
Fall into the compass of a *præmunire*,
That therefore such a writ be sued against you;
To forfeit all your goods, lands, tenements,
Chattels, and whatsoever, and to be
Out of the King's protection. This is my charge.
Nor. And so we'll leave you to your meditations
How to live better. For your stubborn answer
About the giving back the great seal to us,
The King shall know it, and, no doubt, shall thank you.
So fare you well, my little good Lord Cardinal.
[*Exeunt all but* WOLSEY.
Wol. So farewell to the little good you bear me.
Farewell! a long farewell, to all my greatness!
This is the state of man: to-day he puts forth
The tender leaves of hopes; to-morrow blossoms,
And bears his blushing honours thick upon him;
The third day comes a frost, a killing frost,
And, when he thinks, good easy man, full surely
His greatness is a-ripening, nips his root,
And then he falls, as I do. I have ventured,
Like little wanton boys that swim on bladders,
This many summers in a sea of glory,
But far beyond my depth. My high-blown pride
At length broke under me and now has left me,
Weary and old with service, to the mercy
Of a rude stream that must for ever hide me.
Vain pomp and glory of this world, I hate ye.
I feel my heart new open'd. O, how wretched
Is that poor man that hangs on princes' favours!
There is, betwixt that smile we would aspire to,
That sweet aspect of princes, and their ruin,
More pangs and fears than wars or women have;
And when he falls, he falls like Lucifer,
Never to hope again.

Enter CROMWELL, *and stands amazed*.

Why, how now, Cromwell!
Crom. I have no power to speak, sir.
Wol. What, amazed
At my misfortunes? can thy spirit wonder
A great man should decline? Nay, an you weep,
I am fall'n indeed.
Crom. How does your Grace?
Wol. Why, well;
Never so truly happy, my good Cromwell.
I know myself now; and I feel within me

A peace above all earthly dignities,
A still and quiet conscience. The King has cured me,
I humbly thank his Grace; and from these shoulders,
These ruin'd pillars, out of pity, taken
A load would sink a navy, too much honour.
O, 'tis a burden, Cromwell, 'tis a burden
Too heavy for a man that hopes for heaven!

Crom. I am glad your Grace has made that right use of it.

Wol. I hope I have. I am able now, methinks,
Out of a fortitude of soul I feel,
To endure more miseries and greater far
Than my weak-hearted enemies dare offer.
What news abroad?

Crom. The heaviest and the worst
Is your displeasure with the King.

Wol. God bless him!

Crom. The next is that Sir Thomas More is chosen
Lord Chancellor in your place.

Wol. That's somewhat sudden;
But he's a learned man. May he continue
Long in his Highness' favour, and do justice
For truth's sake and his conscience; that his bones,
When he has run his course and sleeps in blessings,
May have a tomb of orphans' tears wept on 'em!
What more?

Crom. That Cranmer is return'd with welcome,
Install'd Lord Archbishop of Canterbury.

Wol. That's news indeed.

Crom. Last, that the Lady Anne,
Whom the King hath in secrecy long married,
This day was view'd in open as his queen,
Going to chapel; and the voice is now
Only about her coronation.

Wol. There was the weight that pull'd me down. O Cromwell,
The King has gone beyond me! All my glories
In that one woman I have lost for ever.
No sun shall ever usher forth mine honours,
Or gild again the noble troops that waited
Upon my smiles. Go, get thee from me, Cromwell;
I am a poor fall'n man, unworthy now
To be thy lord and master. Seek the King;
That sun, I pray, may never set! I have told him
What and how true thou art; he will advance thee;
Some little memory of me will stir him—
I know his noble nature—not to let
Thy hopeful service perish too. Good Cromwell,
Neglect him not; make use now, and provide
For thine own future safety.

Crom. O my lord,
Must I, then, leave you? must I needs forgo
So good, so noble, and so true a master?
Bear witness, all that have not hearts of iron,
With what a sorrow Cromwell leaves his lord.
The King shall have my service; but my prayers
For ever and for ever shall be yours.

Wol. Cromwell, I did not think to shed a tear
In all my miseries; but thou hast forced me,
Out of thy honest truth, to play the woman.
Let's dry our eyes; and thus far hear me, Cromwell;
And, when I am forgotten, as I shall be,
And sleep in dull cold marble, where no mention
Of me more must be heard of, say, I taught thee,
Say, Wolsey, that once trod the ways of glory,
And sounded all the depths and shoals of honour,
Found thee a way, out of his wreck, to rise in;
A sure and safe one, though thy master miss'd it.
Mark but my fall, and that that ruin'd me.
Cromwell, I charge thee, fling away ambition.
By that sin fell angels; how can man, then,
The image of his Maker, hope to win by it?
Love thyself last. Cherish those hearts that hate thee;
Corruption wins not more than honesty.
Still in thy right hand carry gentle peace.
To silence envious tongues. Be just, and fear not.
Let all the ends thou aim'st at be thy country's,
Thy God's, and truth's; then if thou fall'st, O Cromwell,
Thou fall'st a blessed martyr! Serve the King;
And—prithee, lead me in.
There take an inventory of all I have,
To the last penny; 'tis the King's. My robe,
And my integrity to heaven, is all
I dare now call mine own. O Cromwell, Cromwell!
Had I but served my God with half the zeal
I served my King, he would not in mine age
Have left me naked to mine enemies.

Crom. Good sir, have patience.

Wol. So I have. Farewell
The hopes of court! my hopes in heaven do dwell.
[*Exeunt.*

ACT IV

SCENE I. *A street in Westminster*

Enter TWO GENTLEMEN, *meeting one another.*

1st Gent. You're well met once again.

2nd Gent. So are you.

1st Gent. You come to take your stand here, and behold
The Lady Anne pass from her coronation?

2nd Gent. 'Tis all my business. At our last encounter,
The Duke of Buckingham came from his trial.
1st Gent. 'Tis very true. But that time offer'd sorrow;
This, general joy.
2nd Gent. 'Tis well. The citizens,
I am sure, have shown at full their royal minds—
As, let 'em have their rights, they are ever forward—
In celebration of this day with shows,
Pageants, and sights of honour.
1st Gent. Never greater,
Nor, I'll assure you, better taken, sir.
2nd Gent. May I be bold to ask what that contains,
That paper in your hand?
1st Gent. Yes; 'tis the list
Of those that claim their offices this day
By custom of the coronation.
The Duke of Suffolk is the first, and claims
To be High Steward; next, the Duke of Norfolk,
He to be Earl Marshal. You may read the rest.
2nd Gent. I thank you, sir. Had I not known those customs,
I should have been beholding to your paper.
But, I beseech you, what's become of Katharine,
The Princess Dowager? how goes her business?
1st Gent. That I can tell you too. The Archbishop
Of Canterbury, accompanied with other
Learned and reverend fathers of his order,
Held a late court at Dunstable, six miles off
From Ampthill where the Princess lay; to which
She was often cited by them, but appear'd not;
And, to be short, for not appearance and
The King's late scruple, by the main assent
Of all these learned men she was divorced,
And the late marriage made of none effect;
Since which she was removed to Kimbolton,
Where she remains now sick.
2nd Gent. Alas, good lady!
Trumpets.
The trumpets sound: stand close, the queen is coming.
Hautboys.

THE ORDER OF THE CORONATION

1. *A lively flourish of Trumpets.*
2. *Then, two Judges.*
3. *Lord Chancellor, with the purse and mace before him.*
4. *Choristers, singing.* [*Music.*
5. *Mayor of London, bearing the mace. Then Garter, in his coat of arms, and on his head a gilt copper crown.*
6. *Marquess Dorset, bearing a sceptre of gold, on his head a demi-coronal of gold. With him, the* EARL OF SURREY, *bearing the rod of silver with the dove, crowned with an earl's coronet. Collars of SS.*
7. DUKE OF SUFFOLK, *in his robe of estate, his coronet on his head, bearing a long white wand, as high-steward. With him, the* DUKE OF NORFOLK, *with the rod of marshalship, a coronet on his head. Collars of SS.*
8. *A canopy borne by four of the Cinque-ports; under it, the* QUEEN *in her robe; in her hair richly adorned with pearl, crowned. On each side her, the Bishops of London and Winchester.*
9. *The old Duchess of Norfolk, in a coronal of gold, wrought with flowers, bearing the Queen's train.*
10. *Certain Ladies or Countesses, with plain circlets of gold without flowers.*

They pass over the stage in order and state.

2nd Gent. A royal train, believe me. These I know.
Who's that that bears the sceptre?
1st Gent. Marquess Dorset;
And that the Earl of Surrey, with the rod.
2nd Gent. A bold brave gentleman. That should be
The Duke of Suffolk?
1st Gent. 'Tis the same; High Steward.
2nd Gent. And that my Lord of Norfolk?
1st Gent. Yes.
2nd Gent. Heaven bless thee!
Looking on the QUEEN.
Thou hast the sweetest face I ever look'd on.
Sir, as I have a soul, she is an angel;
Our King has all the Indies in his arms,
And more and richer, when he strains that lady.
I cannot blame his conscience.
1st Gent. They that bear
The cloth of honour over her are four barons
Of the Cinque-ports.
2nd Gent. Those men are happy; and so are all are near her.
I take it, she that carries up the train
Is that old noble lady, Duchess of Norfolk.
1st Gent. It is; and all the rest are countesses.
2nd Gent. Their coronets say so. These are stars indeed;
And sometimes falling ones.
1st Gent. No more of that.
[*Exit procession, and then a great flourish of trumpets.*

Enter a THIRD GENTLEMAN.

1st Gent. God save you, sir! where have you been broiling?
3rd Gent. Among the crowd i' the Abbey; where a finger
Could not be wedged in more. I am stifled
With the mere rankness of their joy.
2nd Gent. You saw
The ceremony?
3rd Gent. That I did.
1st Gent. How was it?
3rd Gent. Well worth the seeing.
2nd Gent. Good sir, speak it to us.
3rd Gent. As well as I am able. The rich stream
Of lords and ladies, having brought the Queen
To a prepared place in the choir, fell off
A distance from her; while her Grace sat down
To rest awhile, some half an hour or so,
In a rich chair of state, opposing freely
The beauty of her person to the people.
Believe me, sir, she is the goodliest woman
That ever lay by man; which when the people
Had the full view of, such a noise arose
As the shrouds make at sea in a stiff tempest,
As loud, and to as many tunes. Hats, cloaks—
Doublets, I think—flew up; and had their faces
Been loose, this day they had been lost. Such joy
I never saw before. Great-bellied women,
That had not half a week to go, like rams
In the old time of war, would shake the press,
And make 'em reel before 'em. No man living
Could say "This is my wife" there; all were woven
So strangely in one piece.
2nd Gent. But, what follow'd?
3rd Gent. At length her Grace rose and with modest paces
Came to the altar, where she kneel'd, and saint-like
Cast her fair eyes to heaven and pray'd devoutly.
Then rose again and bow'd her to the people.
When by the Archbishop of Canterbury
She had all the royal makings of a queen;
As holy oil, Edward Confessor's crown,
The rod, and bird of peace, and all such emblems
Laid nobly on her; which perform'd, the choir,
With all the choicest music of the kingdom,
Together sung "*Te Deum.*" So she parted,
And with the same full state paced back again
To York Place, where the feast is held.
1st Gent. Sir,
You must no more call it York Place, that's past;
For, since the Cardinal fell, that title's lost.
'Tis now the King's, and call'd Whitehall.
3rd Gent. I know it;
But 'tis so lately alter'd that the old name
Is fresh about me.
2nd Gent. What two reverend bishops
Were those that went on each side of the Queen?
3rd Gent. Stokesly and Gardiner; the one of Winchester,
Newly preferr'd from the King's secretary,
The other, London.
2nd Gent. He of Winchester
Is held no great good lover of the archbishop's,
The virtuous Cranmer.
3rd Gent. All the land knows that.
However, yet there is no great breach; when it comes,
Cranmer will find a friend will not shrink from him.
2nd Gent. Who may that be, I pray you?
3rd Gent. Thomas Cromwell;
A man in much esteem with the King, and truly
A worthy friend. The King has made him master
O' the jewel house,
And one, already, of the privy council.
2nd Gent. He will deserve more.
3rd Gent. Yes, without all doubt.
Come, gentlemen, ye shall go my way, which
Is to the court, and there ye shall be my guests;
Something I can command. As I walk thither,
I'll tell ye more.
Both. You may command us, sir. [*Exeunt.*

SCENE II. *Kimbolton*

Enter KATHARINE, *Dowager, sick; led between* GRIFFITH, *her gentleman usher, and* PATIENCE, *her woman.*

Grif. How does your Grace?
Kath. O Griffith, sick to death!
My legs, like loaden branches, bow to the earth,
Willing to leave their burthen. Reach a chair;
So; now, methinks, I feel a little ease.
Didst thou not tell me, Griffith, as thou led'st me,
That the great child of honour, Cardinal Wolsey,
Was dead?
Grif. Yes, madam; but I think your Grace,
Out of the pain you suffer'd, gave no ear to't.
Kath. Prithee, good Griffith, tell me how he died.
If well, he stepp'd before me, happily
For my example.
Grif. Well, the voice goes, madam.
For after the stout Earl Northumberland
Arrested him at York, and brought him forward,
As a man sorely tainted, to his answer,
He fell sick suddenly, and grew so ill
He could not sit his mule.
Kath. Alas, poor man!

Grif. At last, with easy roads, he came to Leicester,
Lodged in the abbey; where the reverend abbot,
With all his covent, honourably received him;
To whom he gave these words, "O, father abbot,
An old man, broken with the storms of state,
Is come to lay his weary bones among ye;
Give him a little earth for charity!"
So went to bed, where eagerly his sickness
Pursued him still; and, three nights after this,
About the hour of eight, which he himself
Foretold should be his last, full of repentance,
Continual meditations, tears, and sorrows,
He gave his honours to the world again,
His blessed part to heaven, and slept in peace.
Kath. So may he rest; his faults lie gently on him!
Yet thus far, Griffith, give me leave to speak him,
And yet with charity. He was a man
Of an unbounded stomach, ever ranking
Himself with princes; one that, by suggestion,
Tied all the kingdom. Simony was fair-play;
His own opinion was his law; i' the presence
He would say untruths; and be ever double
Both in his words and meaning. He was never,
But where he meant to ruin, pitiful.
His promises were, as he then was, mighty;
But his performance, as he is now, nothing.
Of his own body he was ill, and gave
The clergy ill example.
Grif. Noble madam,
Men's evil manners live in brass; their virtues
We write in water. May it please your Highness
To hear me speak his good now?
Kath. Yes, good Griffith;
I were malicious else.
Grif. This Cardinal,
Though from an humble stock, undoubtedly
Was fashion'd to much honour from his cradle.
He was a scholar, and a ripe and good one;
Exceeding wise, fair-spoken, and persuading;
Lofty and sour to them that loved him not;
But to those men that sought him sweet as summer.
And though he were unsatisfied in getting,
Which was a sin, yet in bestowing, madam,
He was most princely. Ever witness for him
Those twins of learning that he raised in you,
Ipswich and Oxford! one of which fell with him,
Unwilling to outlive the good that did it;
The other, though unfinish'd, yet so famous,
So excellent in art, and still so rising,
That Christendom shall ever speak his virtue.
His overthrow heap'd happiness upon him;
For then, and not till then, he felt himself,
And found the blessedness of being little.
And, to add greater honours to his age
Than man could give him, he died fearing God.
Kath. After my death I wish no other herald,
No other speaker of my living actions,
To keep mine honour from corruption,
But such an honest chronicler as Griffith.
Whom I most hated living, thou hast made me,
With thy religious truth and modesty,
Now in his ashes honour. Peace be with him!
Patience, be near me still; and set me lower.
I have not long to trouble thee. Good Griffith,
Cause the musicians play me that sad note
I named my knell, whilst I sit meditating
On that celestial harmony I go to.
Sad and solemn music.
Grif. She is asleep; good wench, let's sit down quiet,
For fear we wake her. Softly, gentle Patience.

The vision. Enter, solemnly tripping one after another, six personages, clad in white robes, wearing on their heads garlands of bays, and golden vizards on their faces; branches of bays or palm in their hands. They first congee unto her, then dance; and, at certain changes, the first two hold a spare garland over her head; at which the other four make reverent curtsies; then the two that held the garland deliver the same to the other next two, who observe the same order in their changes, and holding the garland over her head: which done, they deliver the same garland to the last two, who likewise observe the same order: at which, as it were by inspiration, she makes in her sleep signs of rejoicing, and holdeth up her hands to heaven: and so in their dancing vanish, carrying the garland with them. The music continues.

Kath. Spirits of peace, where are ye? are ye all gone
And leave me here in wretchedness behind ye?
Grif. Madam, we are here.
Kath. It is not you I call for.
Saw ye none enter since I slept?
Grif. None, madam.
Kath. No? Saw you not, even now, a blessed troop
Invite me to a banquet; whose bright faces
Cast thousand beams upon me, like the sun?
They promised me eternal happiness
And brought me garlands, Griffith, which I feel
I am not worthy yet to wear. I shall, assuredly.
Grif. I am most joyful, madam, such good dreams
Possess your fancy.
Kath. Bid the music leave,
They are harsh and heavy to me. [*Music ceases.*

Pat. Do you note
How much her Grace is alter'd on the sudden?
How long her face is drawn? how pale she looks,
And of an earthy cold? Mark her eyes!
Grif. She is going, wench. Pray, pray.
Pat. Heaven comfort her!

Enter a MESSENGER.

Mess. An't like your Grace—
Kath. You are a saucy fellow.
Deserve we no more reverence?
Grif. You are to blame,
Knowing she will not lose her wonted greatness,
To use so rude behaviour; go to, kneel.
Mess. I humbly do entreat your Highness' pardon;
My haste made me unmannerly. There is staying
A gentleman, sent from the King, to see you.
Kath. Admit him entrance, Griffith; but this fellow
Let me ne'er see again.
[*Exeunt* GRIFFITH *and* MESSENGER.

Re-enter GRIFFITH, *with* CAPUCIUS.

If my sight fail not,
You should be lord ambassador from the Emperor,
My royal nephew, and your name Capucius.
Cap. Madam, the same; your servant.
Kath. O, my lord,
The times and titles now are alter'd strangely
With me since first you knew me. But, I pray you,
What is your pleasure with me?
Cap. Noble lady,
First, mine own service to your Grace; the next,
The King's request that I would visit you;
Who grieves much for your weakness, and by me
Sends you his princely commendations,
And heartily entreats you take good comfort.
Kath. O my good lord, that comfort comes too late;
'Tis like a pardon after execution.
That gentle physic, given in time, had cured me;
But now I am past all comforts here, but prayers.
How does his Highness?
Cap. Madam, in good health.
Kath. So may he ever do! and ever flourish,
When I shall dwell with worms, and my poor name
Banish'd the kingdom! Patience, is that letter,
I caused you write, yet sent away?
Pat. No, madam.
Giving it to KATHARINE.
Kath. Sir, I most humbly pray you to deliver
This to my lord the King.
Cap. Most willing, madam.
Kath. In which I have commended to his goodness
The model of our chaste loves, his young daughter;
The dews of heaven fall thick in blessings on her!
Beseeching him to give her virtuous breeding—
She is young, and of a noble modest nature,
I hope she will deserve well—and a little
To love her for her mother's sake, that loved him,
Heaven knows how dearly. My next poor petition
Is that his noble grace would have some pity
Upon my wretched women, that so long
Have follow'd both my fortunes faithfully;
Of which there is not one, I dare avow,
And now I should not lie, but will deserve,
For virtue and true beauty of the soul,
For honesty and decent carriage,
A right good husband, let him be a noble;
And, sure, those men are happy that shall have 'em.
The last is, for my men; they are the poorest,
But poverty could never draw 'em from me;
That they may have their wages duly paid 'em,
And something over to remember me by.
If heaven had pleased to have given me longer life
And able means, we had not parted thus.
These are the whole contents; and, good my lord,
By that you love the dearest in this world,
As you wish Christian peace to souls departed,
Stand these poor people's friend, and urge the King
To do me this last right.
Cap. By heaven, I will,
Or let me lose the fashion of a man!
Kath. I thank you, honest lord. Remember me
In all humility unto his Highness.
Say his long trouble now is passing
Out of this world; tell him, in death I bless'd him,
For so I will. Mine eyes grow dim. Farewell,
My lord. Griffith, farewell. Nay, Patience,
You must not leave me yet. I must to bed;
Call in more women. When I am dead, good wench,
Let me be used with honour. Strew me over
With maiden flowers, that all the world may know
I was a chaste wife to my grave. Embalm me,
Then lay me forth. Although unqueen'd, yet like
A queen, and daughter to a king, inter me.
I can no more. [*Exeunt, leading* KATHARINE.

ACT V

SCENE I. *London: a gallery in the palace*

Enter GARDINER, BISHOP OF WINCHESTER, *a* PAGE *with a torch before him, met by* SIR THOMAS LOVELL.

Gar. It's one o'clock, boy, is 't not?
Boy. It hath struck.
Gar. These should be hours for necessities,
Not for delights; times to repair our nature
With comforting repose, and not for us
To waste these times. Good hour of night, Sir Thomas!
Whither so late?
Lov. Came you from the King, my lord?
Gar. I did, Sir Thomas; and left him at primero
With the Duke of Suffolk.
Lov. I must to him too,
Before he go to bed. I'll take my leave.
Gar. Not yet, Sir Thomas Lovell. What's the matter?
It seems you are in haste; an if there be
No great offence belongs to 't, give your friend
Some touch of your late business. Affairs, that walk,
As they say spirits do, at midnight, have
In them a wilder nature than the business
That seeks dispatch by day.
Lov. My lord, I love you;
And durst commend a secret to your ear
Much weightier than this work. The Queen's in labour,
They say, in great extremity; and fear'd
She'll with the labour end.
Gar. The fruit she goes with
I pray for heartily, that it may find
Good time, and live: but for the stock, Sir Thomas,
I wish it grubb'd up now.
Lov. Methinks I could
Cry the amen; and yet my conscience says
She's a good creature, and, sweet lady, does
Deserve our better wishes.
Gar. But, sir, sir,
Hear me, Sir Thomas. You're a gentleman
Of mine own way; I know you wise, religious;
And, let me tell you, it will ne'er be well,
'Twill not, Sir Thomas Lovell, take 't of me,
Till Cranmer, Cromwell, her two hands, and she,
Sleep in their graves.
Lov. Now, sir, you speak of two
The most remark'd i' the kingdom. As for Cromwell,
Beside that of the jewel house, is made master
O' the rolls, and the King's secretary; further, sir,
Stands in the gap and trade of moe preferments,
With which the time will load him. The archbishop
Is the King's hand and tongue; and who dare speak
One syllable against him?
Gar. Yes, yes, Sir Thomas,
There are that dare; and I myself have ventured
To speak my mind of him; and indeed this day,
Sir, I may tell it you, I think I have
Incensed the lords o' the council that he is,
For so I know he is, they know he is,
A most arch heretic, a pestilence
That does infect the land: with which they moved
Have broken with the King; who hath so far
Given ear to our complaint, of his great grace
And princely care foreseeing those fell mischiefs
Our reasons laid before him, hath commanded
To-morrow morning to the council-board
He be convented. He's a rank weed, Sir Thomas,
And we must root him out. From your affairs
I hinder you too long. Good night, Sir Thomas.
Lov. Many good nights, my lord. I rest your servant. [*Exeunt* GARDINER *and* PAGE.

Enter the KING *and* SUFFOLK.

King. Charles, I will play no more to-night;
My mind's not on 't; you are too hard for me.
Suf. Sir, I did never win of you before.
King. But little, Charles;
Nor shall not, when my fancy's on my play.
Now, Lovell, from the Queen what is the news?
Lov. I could not personally deliver to her
What you commanded me, but by her woman
I sent your message; who return'd her thanks
In the great'st humbleness, and desired your Highness
Most heartily to pray for her.
King. What say'st thou, ha?
To pray for her? what, is she crying out?
Lov. So said her woman; and that her sufferance made
Almost each pang a death.
King. Alas, good lady!
Suf. God safely quit her of her burthen, and
With gentle travail, to the gladding of
Your Highness with an heir!
King. 'Tis midnight, Charles;
Prithee, to bed; and in thy prayers remember
The estate of my poor queen. Leave me alone;
For I must think of that which company
Would not be friendly to.
Suf. I wish your Highness
A quiet night; and my good mistress will
Remember in my prayers.
King. Charles, good night. [*Exit* SUFFOLK.

Enter SIR ANTHONY DENNY.

Well, sir, what follows?
Den. Sir, I have brought my lord the archbishop,
As you commanded me.
King. Ha! Canterbury?
Den. Ay, my good lord.
King 'Tis true; where is he, Denny?
Den. He attends your Highness' pleasure.
King. Bring him to us.
[*Exit* DENNY.
Lov. [*Aside*] This is about that which the bishop spake.
I am happily come hither.

Re-enter DENNY, *with* CRANMER.

King. Avoid the gallery. [LOVELL *seems to stay*.]
Ha! I have said. Be gone.
What! [*Exeunt* LOVELL *and* DENNY.
Cran. [*Aside*] I am fearful. Wherefore frowns he thus?
'Tis his aspect of terror. All's not well.
King. How now, my lord! you do desire to know
Wherefore I sent for you.
Cran. [*Kneeling*] It is my duty
To attend your Highness' pleasure.
King. Pray you, arise,
My good and gracious Lord of Canterbury.
Come, you and I must walk a turn together;
I have news to tell you. Come, come, give me your hand.
Ah, my good lord, I grieve at what I speak,
And am right sorry to repeat what follows.
I have, and most unwillingly, of late
Heard many grievous, I do say, my lord,
Grievous complaints of you; which, being consider'd,
Have moved us and our council that you shall
This morning come before us; where, I know,
You cannot with such freedom purge yourself,
But that, till further trial in those charges
Which will require your answer, you must take
Your patience to you and be well contented
To make your house our Tower. You a brother of us,
It fits we thus proceed, or else no witness
Would come against you.
Cran. [*Kneeling*] I humbly thank your Highness;
And am right glad to catch this good occasion
Most throughly to be winnow'd, where my chaff
And corn shall fly asunder; for, I know,
There's none stands under more calumnious tongues
Than I myself, poor man.
King. Stand up, good Canterbury.
Thy truth and thy integrity is rooted
In us, thy friend. Give me thy hand, stand up.
Prithee, let's walk. Now, by my holidame,
What manner of man are you? My lord, I look'd
You would have given me your petition, that
I should have ta'en some pains to bring together
Yourself and your accusers; and to have heard you,
Without indurance, further.
Cran. Most dread liege,
The good I stand on is my truth and honesty.
If they shall fail, I, with mine enemies,
Will triumph o'er my person; which I weigh not,
Being of those virtues vacant. I fear nothing
What can be said against me.
King. Know you not
How your state stands i' the world, with the whole world?
Your enemies are many, and not small; their practices
Must bear the same proportion; and not ever
The justice and the truth o' the question carries
The due o' the verdict with it. At what ease
Might corrupt minds procure knaves as corrupt
To swear against you? such things have been done.
You are potently opposed; and with a malice
Of as great size. Ween you of better luck,
I mean, in perjured witness, than your master,
Whose minister you are, whiles here he lived
Upon this naughty earth? Go to, go to;
You take a precipice for no leap of danger,
And woo your own destruction.
Cran. God and your Majesty
Protect mine innocence, or I fall into
The trap is laid for me!
King. Be of good cheer;
They shall no more prevail than we give way to.
Keep comfort to you; and this morning see
You do appear before them. If they shall chance,
In charging you with matters, to commit you,
The best persuasions to the contrary
Fail not to use, and with that vehemency
The occasion shall instruct you. If entreaties
Will render you no remedy, this ring
Deliver them, and your appeal to us
There make before them. Look, the good man weeps!
He's honest, on mine honour. God's blest mother!
I swear he is true-hearted; and a soul
None better in my kingdom. Get you gone,
And do as I have bid you. [*Exit* CRANMER.] He has strangled
His language in his tears.

Enter OLD LADY, LOVELL *following*.

Gent. [*Within*] Come back! What mean you?
Old L. I'll not come back; the tidings that I bring
Will make my boldness manners. Now, good angels
Fly o'er thy royal head and shade thy person
Under their blessed wings!
King. Now, by thy looks
I guess thy message. Is the Queen deliver'd?
Say, ay; and of a boy.
Old L. Ay, ay, my liege;
And of a lovely boy. The God of heaven
Both now and ever bless her! 'tis a girl,
Promises boys hereafter. Sir, your queen
Desires your visitation, and to be
Acquainted with this stranger. 'Tis as like you
As cherry is to cherry.
King. Lovell!
Lov. Sir?
King. Give her an hundred marks. I'll to the Queen. [*Exit*.
Old L. An hundred marks! By this light, I'll ha' more.
An ordinary groom is for such payment.
I will have more, or scold it out of him.
Said I for this, the girl was like to him?
I will have more, or else unsay 't; and now,
While it is hot, I'll put it to the issue.
[*Exeunt*.

SCENE II. *Before the council-chamber*
Pursuivants, Pages, &c. attending.

Enter CRANMER, ARCHBISHOP OF CANTERBURY.

Cran. I hope I am not too late; and yet the gentleman
That was sent to me from the council pray'd me
To make great haste. All fast? what means this? Ho!
Who waits there? Sure, you know me?

Enter KEEPER.

Keep. Yes, my lord;
But yet I cannot help you.
Cran. Why?

Enter DOCTOR BUTTS.

Keep. Your Grace must wait till you be call'd for.
Cran. So.
Butts. [*Aside*] This is a piece of malice. I am glad
I came this way so happily. The King
Shall understand it presently. [*Exit*.
Cran. [*Aside*] 'Tis Butts,
The king's physician; as he pass'd along,
How earnestly he cast his eyes upon me!
Pray heaven, he sound not my disgrace! For certain,
This is of purpose laid by some that hate me—
God turn their hearts! I never sought their malice—
To quench mine honour. They would shame to make me
Wait else at door, a fellow-counsellor,
'Mong boys, grooms, and lackeys. But their pleasures
Must be fulfill'd, and I attend with patience.

Enter the KING *and* BUTTS *at a window above*.

Butts. I'll show your Grace the strangest sight—
King. What's that, Butts?
Butts. I think your Highness saw this many a day.
King. Body o' me, where is it?
Butts. There, my lord;
The high promotion of his grace of Canterbury;
Who holds his state at door, 'mongst pursuivants,
Pages, and footboys.
King. Ha! 'tis he, indeed.
Is this the honour they do one another?
'Tis well there's one above 'em yet. I had thought
They had parted so much honesty among 'em,
At least, good manners, as not thus to suffer
A man of his place, and so near our favour,
To dance attendance on their lordships' pleasures,
And at the door too, like a post with packets.
By holy Mary, Butts, there's knavery.
Let 'em alone, and draw the curtain close;
We shall hear more anon. [*Exeunt*.

SCENE III. *The Council-chamber*

Enter LORD CHANCELLOR; *places himself at the upper end of the table on the left hand; a seat being left void above him, as for* CANTERBURY'S *seat*. DUKE OF SUFFOLK, DUKE OF NORFOLK, SURREY, LORD CHAMBERLAIN, GARDINER, *seat themselves in order on each side*. CROMWELL *at lower end, as secretary*. KEEPER *at the door*.

Chan. Speak to the business, master secretary.
Why are we met in council?
Crom. Please your honours,
The chief cause concerns his Grace of Canterbury.
Gar. Has he had knowledge of it?
Crom. Yes.
Nor. Who waits there?
Keep. Without, my noble lords?
Gar. Yes.
Keep. My Lord Archbishop;

And has done half an hour, to know your pleasures.
Chan. Let him come in.
Keep. Your Grace may enter now.

CRANMER *enters and approaches the council-table.*

Chan. My good Lord Archbishop, I'm very sorry
To sit here at this present and behold
That chair stand empty; but we all are men,
In our own natures frail, and capable
Of our flesh; few are angels; out of which frailty
And want of wisdom, you, that best should teach us,
Have misdemean'd yourself, and not a little,
Toward the King first, then his laws, in filling
The whole realm, by your teaching and your chaplains,
For so we are inform'd, with new opinions,
Divers and dangerous; which are heresies,
And, not reform'd, may prove pernicious.
Gar. Which reformation must be sudden too,
My noble lords; for those that tame wild horses
Pace 'em not in their hands to make 'em gentle,
But stop their mouths with stubborn bits, and spur 'em,
Till they obey the manage. If we suffer,
Out of our easiness and childish pity
To one man's honour, this contagious sickness,
Farewell all physic; and what follows then?
Commotions, uproars, with a general taint
Of the whole state, as, of late days, our neighbours,
The upper Germany, can dearly witness,
Yet freshly pitied in our memories.
Cran. My good lords, hitherto, in all the progress
Both of my life and office, I have labour'd,
And with no little study, that my teaching
And the strong course of my authority
Might go one way, and safely; and the end
Was ever to do well. Nor is there living,
I speak it with a single heart, my lords,
A man that more detests, more stirs against,
Both in his private conscience and his place,
Defacers of a public peace, than I do.
Pray heaven, the King may never find a heart
With less allegiance in it! Men that make
Envy and crooked malice nourishment
Dare bite the best. I do beseech your lordships
That, in this case of justice, my accusers,
Be what they will, may stand forth face to face
And freely urge against me.
Suf. Nay, my lord,
That cannot be. You are a counsellor,
And, by that virtue, no man dare accuse you.
Gar. My lord, because we have business of more moment,
We will be short with you. 'Tis his Highness' pleasure,
And our consent, for better trial of you,
From hence you be committed to the Tower;
Where, being but a private man again,
You shall know many dare accuse you boldly,
More than, I fear, you are provided for.
Cran. Ah, my good Lord of Winchester, I thank you;
You are always my good friend; if your will pass,
I shall both find your lordship judge and juror,
You are so merciful. I see your end;
'Tis my undoing. Love and meekness, lord,
Become a churchman better than ambition.
Win straying souls with modesty again,
Cast none away. That I shall clear myself,
Lay all the weight ye can upon my patience,
I make as little doubt as you do conscience
In doing daily wrongs. I could say more,
But reverence to your calling makes me modest.
Gar. My lord, my lord, you are a sectary,
That's the plain truth. Your painted gloss discovers,
To men that understand you, words and weakness.
Crom. My Lord of Winchester, you are a little,
By your good favour, too sharp; men so noble,
However faulty, yet should find respect
For what they have been. 'Tis a cruelty
To load a falling man.
Gar. Good master secretary,
I cry your honour mercy; you may, worst
Of all this table, say so.
Crom. Why, my lord?
Gar. Do not I know you for a favourer
Of this new sect? ye are not sound.
Crom. Not sound?
Gar. Not sound, I say.
Crom. Would you were half so honest!
Men's prayers then would seek you, not their fears.
Gar. I shall remember this bold language.
Crom. Do.
Remember your bold life too.
Chan. This is too much;
Forbear, for shame, my lords.
Gar. I have done.
Crom. And I.
Chan. Then thus for you, my lord: it stands agreed,
I take it, by all voices, that forthwith
You be convey'd to the Tower a prisoner;
There to remain till the King's further pleasure

Be known unto us. Are you all agreed, lords?
All. We are.
Cran. Is there no other way of mercy,
But I must needs to the Tower, my lords?
Gar. What other
Would you expect? you are strangely troublesome.
Let some o' the guard be ready there.

Enter GUARD.

Cran. For me?
Must I go like a traitor thither?
Gar. Receive him,
And see him safe i' the Tower.
Cran. Stay, good my lords,
I have a little yet to say. Look there, my lords;
By virtue of that ring, I take my cause
Out of the gripes of cruel men, and give it
To a most noble judge, the King my master.
Cham. This is the King's ring.
Sur. 'Tis no counterfeit.
Suf. 'Tis the right ring, by heaven. I told ye all,
When we first put this dangerous stone a-rolling,
'Twould fall upon ourselves.
Nor. Do you think, my lords,
The King will suffer but the little finger
Of this man to be vex'd?
Chan. 'Tis now too certain.
How much more is his life in value with him?
Would I were fairly out on 't!
Crom. My mind gave me,
In seeking tales and informations
Against this man, whose honesty the devil
And his disciples only envy at,
Ye blew the fire that burns ye. Now have at ye!

Enter KING, *frowning on them; takes his seat.*

Gar. Dread sovereign, how much are we bound to heaven
In daily thanks, that gave us such a prince;
Not only good and wise, but most religious;
One that, in all obedience, makes the church
The chief aim of his honour; and, to strengthen
That holy duty, out of dear respect,
His royal self in judgement come to hear
The cause betwixt her and this great offender.
King. You were ever good at sudden commendations,
Bishop of Winchester. But know, I come not
To hear such flattery now, and in my presence;
They are too thin and bare to hide offences.
To me you cannot reach, you play the spaniel,
And think with wagging of your tongue to win me;
But, whatsoe'er thou takest me for, I'm sure
Thou hast a cruel nature and a bloody.
[*To* CRANMER] Good man, sit down. Now let me see the proudest
He, that dares most, but wag his finger at thee.
By all that's holy, he had better starve
Than but once think this place becomes thee not.
Sur. May it please your Grace—
King. No, sir, it does not please me.
I had thought I had had men of some understanding
And wisdom of my council; but I find none.
Was it discretion, lords, to let this man,
This good man—few of you deserve that title—
This honest man, wait like a lousy footboy
At chamber-door? and one as great as you are?
Why, what a shame was this! Did my commission
Bid ye so far forget yourselves? I gave ye
Power as he was a counsellor to try him,
Not as a groom. There's some of ye, I see,
More out of malice than integrity,
Would try him to the utmost, had ye mean;
Which ye shall never have while I live.
Chan. Thus far,
My most dread sovereign, may it like your Grace
To let my tongue excuse all. What was purposed
Concerning his imprisonment was rather,
If there be faith in men, meant for his trial
And fair purgation to the world, than malice,
I'm sure, in me.
King. Well, well, my lords, respect him;
Take him, and use him well, he's worthy of it.
I will say thus much for him, if a prince
May be beholding to a subject, I
Am, for his love and service, so to him.
Make me no more ado, but all embrace him.
Be friends, for shame, my lords! My Lord of Canterbury,
I have a suit which you must not deny me;
That is, a fair young maid that yet wants baptism,
You must be godfather, and answer for her.
Cran. The greatest monarch now alive may glory
In such an honour. How may I deserve it,
That am a poor and humble subject to you?
King. Come, come, my lord, you'd spare your spoons. You shall have two noble partners with you; the old Duchess of Norfolk, and Lady Marquess Dorset. Will these please you?
Once more, my Lord of Winchester, I charge you,
Embrace and love this man.
Gar. With a true heart
And brother-love I do it.
Cran. And let Heaven

Witness how dear I hold this confirmation.

King. Good man, those joyful tears show thy true heart.
The common voice, I see, is verified
Of thee, which says thus, "Do my Lord of Canterbury
A shrewd turn, and he is your friend for ever."
Come, lords, we trifle time away; I long
To have this young one made a Christian.
As I have made ye one, lords, one remain;
So I grow stronger, you more honour gain.
[*Exeunt*.

SCENE IV. *The palace yard*

Noise and tumult within. Enter PORTER *and his* MAN.

Port. You'll leave your noise anon, ye rascals. Do you take the court for Paris-garden? ye rude slaves, leave your gaping.

[*Within*] Good master porter, I belong to the larder.

Port. Belong to the gallows, and be hanged, ye rogue! is this a place to roar in? Fetch me a dozen crab-tree staves, and strong ones; these are but switches to 'em. I'll scratch your heads. You must be seeing christenings? do you look for ale and cakes here, you rude rascals?

Man. Pray, sir, be patient. 'Tis as much impossible—
Unless we sweep 'em from the door with cannons—
To scatter 'em, as 'tis to make 'em sleep
On May-day morning; which will never be.
We may as well push against Powle's, as stir 'em.

Port. How got they in, and be hang'd?

Man. Alas, I know not; how gets the tide in?
As much as one sound cudgel of four foot—
You see the poor remainder—could distribute,
I made no spare, sir.

Port. You did nothing, sir.

Man. I am not Samson, nor Sir Guy, nor Colbrand,
To mow 'em down before me; but if I spared any
That had a head to hit, either young or old,
He or she, cuckold or cuckold-maker,
Let me ne'er hope to see a chine again;
And that I would not for a cow, God save her!

[*Within*] Do you hear, master porter?

Port. I shall be with you presently, good master puppy. Keep the door close, sirrah.

Man. What would you have me do?

Port. What should you do, but knock 'em down by the dozens? Is this Moorfields to muster in? or have we some strange Indian with the great tool come to court, the women so besiege us? Bless me, what a fry of fornication is at door! On my Christian conscience, this one christening will beget a thousand; here will be father, godfather, and all together.

Man. The spoons will be the bigger, sir. There is a fellow somewhat near the door, he should be a brazier by his face, for, o' my conscience, twenty of the dog-days now reign in's nose; all that stand about him are under the line, they need no other penance. That fire-drake did I hit three times on the head, and three times was his nose discharged against me; he stands there, like a mortar-piece, to blow us. There was a haberdasher's wife of small wit near him, that railed upon me till her pinked porringer fell off her head, for kindling such a combustion in the state. I missed the meteor once, and hit that woman; who cried out "Clubs!" when I might see from far some forty truncheoners draw to her succour, which were the hope o' the Strand, where she was quartered. They fell on; I made good my place. At length they came to the broomstaff to me; I defied 'em still; when suddenly a file of boys behind 'em, loose shot, delivered such a shower of pebbles that I was fain to draw mine honour in and let 'em win the work. The devil was amongst 'em, I think, surely.

Port. These are the youths that thunder at a playhouse, and fight for bitten apples; that no audience, but the tribulation of Tower-hill, or the limbs of Limehouse, their dear brothers, are able to endure. I have some of 'em in *Limbo Patrum*, and there they are like to dance these three days; besides the running banquet of two beadles that is to come.

Enter LORD CHAMBERLAIN.

Cham. Mercy o' me, what a multitude are here!
They grow still too; from all parts they are coming,
As if we kept a fair here! Where are these porters,
These lazy knaves? Ye have made a fine hand, fellows;
There's a trim rabble let in. Are all these
Your faithful friends o' the suburbs? We shall have
Great store of room, no doubt, left for the ladies,
When they pass back from the christening.

Port. An't please your honour,
We are but men; and what so many may do,
Not being torn a-pieces, we have done.
An army cannot rule 'em.

Cham. As I live,
If the King blame me for 't, I'll lay ye all
By the heels, and suddenly; and on your heads

Clap round fines for neglect. Ye are lazy knaves;
And here ye lie baiting of bombards, when
Ye should do service. Hark! the trumpets sound;
They're come already from the christening.
Go, break among the press, and find a way out
To let the troop pass fairly; or I'll find
A Marshalsea shall hold ye play these two months.

Port. Make way there for the Princess.

Man. You great fellow,
Stand close up, or I'll make your head ache.

Port. You i' the camlet, get up o' the rail;
I'll peck you o'er the pales else. [*Exeunt.*

SCENE V. *The palace*

Enter trumpets, sounding; then two ALDERMEN, LORD MAYOR, GARTER, CRANMER, DUKE OF NORFOLK *with his marshal's staff*, DUKE OF SUFFOLK, *two Noblemen bearing great standing-bowls for the christening-gifts; then four Noblemen bearing a canopy, under which the Duchess of Norfolk, godmother, bearing the child richly habited in a mantle, &c., train borne by a Lady; then follows the Marchioness Dorset, the other godmother, and Ladies. The troop pass once about the stage, and* GARTER *speaks.*

Gart. Heaven, from thy endless goodness, send prosperous life, long, and ever happy, to the high and mighty Princess of England, Elizabeth!

Flourish. Enter KING *and Guard.*

Cran. [*Kneeling*] And to your royal Grace, and the good queen,
My noble partners, and myself, thus pray:
All comfort, joy, in this most gracious lady,
Heaven ever laid up to make parents happy,
May hourly fall upon ye!

King. Thank you, good Lord Archbishop.
What is her name?

Cran. Elizabeth.

King. Stand up, lord.

The KING *kisses the child.*

With this kiss take my blessing. God protect thee!
Into whose hand I give thy life.

Cran. Amen.

King. My noble gossips, ye have been too prodigal.
I thank ye heartily; so shall this lady,
When she has so much English.

Cran. Let me speak, sir,
For heaven now bids me; and the words I utter
Let none think flattery, for they'll find 'em truth.
This royal infant—heaven still move about her!—
Though in her cradle, yet now promises
Upon this land a thousand thousand blessings,
Which time shall bring to ripeness. She shall be—
But few now living can behold that goodness—
A pattern to all princes living with her,
And all that shall succeed. Saba was never
More covetous of wisdom and fair virtue
Than this pure soul shall be. All princely graces,
That mould up such a mighty piece as this is,
With all the virtues that attend the good,
Shall still be doubled on her. Truth shall nurse her,
Holy and heavenly thoughts still counsel her.
She shall be loved and fear'd; her own shall bless her;
Her foes shake like a field of beaten corn,
And hang their heads with sorrow. Good grows with her.
In her days every man shall eat in safety,
Under his own vine, what he plants; and sing
The merry songs of peace to all his neighbours.
God shall be truly known; and those about her
From her shall read the perfect ways of honour,
And by those claim their greatness, not by blood.
Nor shall this peace sleep with her; but as when
The bird of wonder dies, the maiden phœnix,
Her ashes new create another heir,
As great in admiration as herself;
So shall she leave her blessedness to one,
When Heaven shall call her from this cloud of darkness,
Who from the sacred ashes of her honour
Shall star-like rise, as great in fame as she was,
And so stand fix'd. Peace, plenty, love, truth, terror,
That were the servants to this chosen infant,
Shall then be his, and like a vine grow to him.
Wherever the bright sun of heaven shall shine,
His honour and the greatness of his name
Shall be, and make new nations. He shall flourish,
And, like a mountain cedar, reach his branches
To all the plains about him. Our children's children
Shall see this, and bless Heaven.

King. Thou speakest wonders.

Cran. She shall be, to the happiness of England,
An aged princess; many days shall see her,
And yet no day without a deed to crown it.
Would I had known no more! but she must die,
She must, the saints must have her; yet a virgin,
A most unspotted lily shall she pass
To the ground, and all the world shall mourn her.

King. O Lord Archbishop,
Thou hast made me now a man! never, before
This happy child, did I get anything.
This oracle of comfort has so pleased me
That when I am in heaven I shall desire
To see what this child does, and praise my Maker.
I thank ye all. To you, my good Lord Mayor,
And your good brethren, I am much beholding;
I have received much honour by your presence,
And ye shall find me thankful. Lead the way, lords.
Ye must all see the Queen, and she must thank ye,
She will be sick else. This day, no man think
Has business at his house; for all shall stay.
This little one shall make it holiday. [*Exeunt*.

EPILOGUE

'Tis ten to one this play can never please
All that are here. Some come to take their ease,
And sleep an act or two; but those, we fear,
We have frighted with our trumpets; so, 'tis clear,
They'll say 'tis naught; others, to hear the city
Abused extremely, and to cry, "That's witty!"
Which we have not done neither. That, I fear,
All the expected good we're like to hear
For this play at this time is only in
The merciful construction of good women;
For such a one we show'd 'em. If they smile,
And say 'twill do, I know, within a while
All the best men are ours; for 'tis ill hap,
If they hold when their ladies bid 'em clap.

SONNETS

TO THE ONLIE BEGETTER OF
THESE INSUING SONNETS
MR. W. H. ALL HAPPINESSE
AND THAT ETERNITIE
PROMISED BY
OUR EVER-LIVING POET
WISHETH
THE WELL WISHING
ADVENTURER IN
SETTING
FORTH

T. T.

I

From fairest creatures we desire increase,
That thereby beauty's rose might never die,
But as the riper should by time decease,
His tender heir might bear his memory;
But thou, contracted to thine own bright eyes,
Feed'st thy light's flame with self-substantial fuel,
Making a famine where abundance lies,
Thyself thy foe, to thy sweet self too cruel.
Thou that art now the world's fresh ornament
And only herald to the gaudy spring,
Within thine own bud buriest thy content
And, tender churl, makest waste in niggarding.
Pity the world, or else this glutton be,
To eat the world's due, by the grave and thee.

II

When forty winters shall besiege thy brow
And dig deep trenches in thy beauty's field,
Thy youth's proud livery, so gazed on now,
Will be a tatter'd weed, of small worth held.
Then being ask'd where all thy beauty lies,
Where all the treasure of thy lusty days,
To say, within thine own deep-sunken eyes,
Were an all-eating shame and thriftless praise.
How much more praise deserved thy beauty's use,
If thou couldst answer, "This fair child of mine
Shall sum my count and make my old excuse,"
Proving his beauty by succession thine!
This were to be new made when thou art old,
And see thy blood warm when thou feel'st it cold.

III

Look in thy glass and tell the face thou viewest
Now is the time that face should form another;
Whose fresh repair if now thou not renewest,
Thou dost beguile the world, unbless some mother.
For where is she so fair whose unear'd womb
Disdains the tillage of thy husbandry?
Or who is he so fond will be the tomb
Of his self-love, to stop posterity?
Thou art thy mother's glass, and she in thee
Calls back the lovely April of her prime.
So thou through windows of thine age shalt see
Despite of wrinkles this thy golden time.
But if thou live, remember'd not to be,
Die single, and thine image dies with thee.

IV

Unthrifty loveliness, why dost thou spend
Upon thyself thy beauty's legacy?
Nature's bequest gives nothing but doth lend,
And, being, frank, she lends to those are free.
Then, beauteous niggard, why dost thou abuse
The bounteous largess given thee to give?
Profitless usurer, why dost thou use
So great a sum of sums, yet canst not live?
For having traffic with thyself alone,
Thou of thyself thy sweet self dost deceive.
Then how, when nature calls thee to be gone,
What acceptable audit canst thou leave?
Thy unused beauty must be tomb'd with thee,
Which, used, lives th' executor to be.

V

Those hours, that with gentle work did frame
The lovely gaze where every eye doth dwell,
Will play the tyrants to the very same
And that unfair which fairly doth excel;
For never-resting time leads summer on
To hideous winter and confounds him there;
Sap check'd with frost and lusty leaves quite gone,
Beauty o'ersnow'd and bareness every-where.
Then, were not summer's distillation left,
A liquid prisoner pent in walls of glass,
Beauty's effect with beauty were bereft,
Nor it nor no remembrance what it was;

But flowers distill'd, though they with winter meet,
Leese but their show; their substance still lives sweet.

VI

Then let not winter's ragged hand deface
In thee thy summer, ere thou be distill'd.
Make sweet some vial; treasure thou some place
With beauty's treasure, ere it be self-kill'd.
That use is not forbidden usury
Which happies those that pay the willing loan;
That's for thyself to breed another thee,
Or ten times happier, be it ten for one;
Ten times thyself were happier than thou art,
If ten of thine ten times refigured thee.
Then what could death do, if thou shouldst depart,
Leaving thee living in posterity?
Be not self-will'd, for thou art much too fair
To be death's conquest and make worms thine heir.

VII

Lo! in the orient when the gracious light
Lifts up his burning head, each under eye
Doth homage to his new-appearing sight,
Serving with looks his sacred majesty;
And having climb'd the steep-up heavenly hill,
Resembling strong youth in his middle age,
Yet mortal looks adore his beauty still,
Attending on his golden pilgrimage;
But when from highmost pitch, with weary car,
Like feeble age he reeleth from the day,
The eyes, 'fore duteous, now converted are
From his low tract and look another way.
So thou, thyself out-going in thy noon,
Unlook'd on diest, unless thou get a son.

VIII

Music to hear, why hear'st thou music sadly?
Sweets with sweets war not, joy delights in joy.
Why lovest thou that which thou receivest not gladly,
Or else receivest with pleasure thine annoy?
If the true concord of well-tuned sounds,
By unions married, do offend thine ear,
They do but sweetly chide thee, who confounds
In singleness the parts that thou shouldst bear.
Mark how one string, sweet husband to another,
Strikes each in each by mutual ordering,
Resembling sire and child and happy mother
Who all in one, one pleasing note do sing;
Whose speechless song, being many, seeming one,
Sings this to thee: "Thou single wilt prove none."

IX

Is it for fear to wet a widow's eye
That thou consumest thyself in single life?
Ah! if thou issueless shalt hap to die,
The world will wail thee like a makeless wife;
The world will be thy widow and still weep
That thou no form of thee hast left behind,
When every private widow well may keep
By children's eyes her husband's shape in mind.
Look, what an unthrift in the world doth spend
Shifts but his place, for still the world enjoys it;
But beauty's waste hath in the world an end,
And kept unused, the user so destroys it.
No love toward others in that bosom sits
That on himself such murderous shame commits.

X

For shame! deny that thou bear'st love to any,
Who for thyself art so unprovident.
Grant, if thou wilt, thou art beloved of many,
But that thou none lovest is most evident;
For thou art so possess'd with murderous hate
That 'gainst thyself thou stick'st not to conspire,
Seeking that beauteous roof to ruinate
Which to repair should be thy chief desire.
O, change thy thought, that I may change my mind!
Shall hate be fairer lodged than gentle love?
Be, as thy presence is, gracious and kind,
Or to thyself at least kind-hearted prove.
Make thee another self, for love of me,
That beauty still may live in thine or thee.

XI

As fast as thou shalt wane, so fast thou growest
In one of thine, from that which thou departest;
And that fresh blood which youngly thou bestowest
Thou mayst call thine when thou from youth convertest.
Herein lives wisdom, beauty, and increase;
Without this, folly, age, and cold decay.
If all were minded so, the times should cease
And threescore year would make the world away.
Let those whom Nature hath not made for store,
Harsh, featureless and rude, barrenly perish.
Look, whom she best endow'd she gave the more;
Which bounteous gift thou shouldst in bounty cherish.
She carved thee for her seal, and meant thereby
Thou shouldst print more, not let that copy die.

XII

When I do count the clock that tells the time,
And see the brave day sunk in hideous night;
When I behold the violet past prime,
And sable curls all silver'd o'er with white;
When lofty trees I see barren of leaves
Which erst from heat did canopy the herd,
And summer's green all girded up in sheaves
Borne on the bier with white and bristly beard,
Then of thy beauty do I question make,
That thou among the wastes of time must go,
Since sweets and beauties do themselves forsake
And die as fast as they see others grow;
And nothing 'gainst Time's scythe can make defence
Save breed, to brave him when he takes thee hence.

XIII

O, that you were yourself! but, love, you are
No longer yours than you yourself here live.
Against this coming end you should prepare,
And your sweet semblance to some other give.
So should that beauty which you hold in lease
Find no determination; then you were
Yourself again after yourself's decease,
When your sweet issue your sweet form should bear.
Who lets so fair a house fall to decay,
Which husbandry in honour might uphold
Against the stormy gusts of winter's day
And barren rage of death's eternal cold?
O, none but unthrifts! Dear my love, you know
You had a father—let your son say so.

XIV

Not from the stars do I my judgement pluck,
And yet methinks I have astronomy;
But not to tell of good or evil luck,
Of plagues, of dearths, or seasons' quality;
Nor can I fortune to brief minutes tell,
Pointing to each his thunder, rain, and wind,
Or say with princes if it shall go well
By oft predict that I in heaven find;
But from thine eyes my knowledge I derive,
And, constant stars, in them I read such art
As truth and beauty shall together thrive,
If from thyself to store thou wouldst convert;
Or else of thee this I prognosticate:
Thy end is truth's and beauty's doom and date.

XV

When I consider every thing that grows
Holds in perfection but a little moment,
That this huge stage presenteth nought but shows
Whereon the stars in secret influence comment;
When I perceive that men as plants increase,
Cheered and check'd even by the self-same sky,
Vaunt in their youthful sap, at height decrease,
And wear their brave state out of memory;
Then the conceit of this inconstant stay
Sets you most rich in youth before my sight,
Where wasteful Time debateth with Decay,
To change your day of youth to sullied night;
And, all in war with Time for love of you,
As he takes from you, I engraft you new.

XVI

But wherefore do not you a mightier way
Make war upon this bloody tyrant, Time?
And fortify yourself in your decay
With means more blessed than my barren rhyme?
Now stand you on the top of happy hours;
And many maiden gardens, yet unset,
With virtuous wish would bear your living flowers,
Much liker than your painted counterfeit.
So should the lines of life that life repair,
Which this Time's pencil, or my pupil pen,
Neither in inward worth nor outward fair,
Can make you live yourself in eyes of men.
To give away yourself keeps yourself still,
And you must live, drawn by your own sweet skill.

XVII

Who will believe my verse in time to come
If it were fill'd with your most high deserts?
Though yet, heaven knows, it is but as a tomb
Which hides your life and shows not half your parts.
If I could write the beauty of your eyes
And in fresh numbers number all your graces,
The age to come would say, "This poet lies;
Such heavenly touches ne'er touch'd earthly faces."
So should my papers yellow'd with their age
Be scorn'd like old men of less truth than tongue,
And your true rights be term'd a poet's rage
And stretched metre of an antique song.
But were some child of yours alive that time,
You should live twice—in it and in my rhyme.

XVIII

Shall I compare thee to a summer's day?
Thou art more lovely and more temperate.
Rough winds do shake the darling buds of May,
And summer's lease hath all too short a date.
Sometime too hot the eye of heaven shines,
And often is his gold complexion dimm'd;

And every fair from fair sometime declines,
By chance or nature's changing course untrimm'd;
But thy eternal summer shall not fade
Nor lose possession of that fair thou owest;
Nor shall Death brag thou wander'st in his shade,
When in eternal lines to time thou growest.
  So long as men can breathe or eyes can see,
  So long lives this and this gives life to thee.

XIX

Devouring Time, blunt thou the lion's paws,
And make the earth devour her own sweet brood;
Pluck the keen teeth from the fierce tiger's jaws,
And burn the long-lived phœnix in her blood;
Make glad and sorry seasons as thou fleets,
And do whate'er thou wilt, swift-footed Time,
To the wide world and all her fading sweets;
But I forbid thee one most heinous crime:
O, carve not with thy hours my love's fair brow,
Nor draw no lines there with thine antique pen;
Him in thy course untainted do allow
For beauty's pattern to succeeding men.
  Yet, do thy worst, old Time! despite thy wrong,
  My love shall in my verse ever live young.

XX

A woman's face, with Nature's own hand painted,
Hast thou, the master-mistress of my passion;
A woman's gentle heart, but not acquainted
With shifting change, as is false women's fashion;
An eye more bright than theirs, less false in rolling,
Gilding the object whereupon it gazeth;
A man in hue, all "hues" in his controlling,
Which steals men's eyes and women's souls amazeth.
And for a woman wert thou first created,
Till Nature, as she wrought thee, fell a-doting,
And by addition me of thee defeated,
By adding one thing to my purpose nothing.
  But since she prick'd thee out for women's pleasure,
  Mine be thy love, and thy love's use their treasure.

XXI

So is it not with me as with that Muse
Stirr'd by a painted beauty to his verse,
Who heaven itself for ornament doth use
And every fair with his fair doth rehearse;
Making a couplement of proud compare,
With sun and moon, with earth and sea's rich gems,
With April's first-born flowers, and all things rare
That heaven's air in this huge rondure hems.
O, let me, true in love, but truly write,
And then believe me, my love is as fair
As any mother's child, though not so bright
As those gold candles fix'd in heaven's air.
  Let them say more that like of hearsay well;
  I will not praise that purpose not to sell.

XXII

My glass shall not persuade me I am old
So long as youth and thou are of one date;
But when in thee time's furrows I behold,
Then look I death my days should expiate.
For all that beauty that doth cover thee
Is but the seemly raiment of my heart,
Which in thy breast doth live, as thine in me.
How can I then be elder than thou art?
O, therefore, love, be of thyself so wary
As I, not for myself, but for thee will;
Bearing thy heart, which I will keep so chary
As tender nurse her babe from faring ill.
  Presume not on thy heart when mine is slain;
  Thou gavest me thine, not to give back again.

XXIII

As an unperfect actor on the stage
Who with his fear is put besides his part,
Or some fierce thing replete with too much rage,
Whose strength's abundance weakens his own heart,
So I, for fear of trust, forget to say
The perfect ceremony of love's rite,
And in mine own love's strength seem to decay,
O'ercharged with burden of mine own love's might.
O, let my books be then the eloquence
And dumb presagers of my speaking breast,
Who plead for love and look for recompense
More than that tongue that more hath more express'd.
  O, learn to read what silent love hath writ:
  To hear with eyes belongs to love's fine wit.

XXIV

Mine eye hath play'd the painter and hath stell'd
Thy beauty's form in table of my heart;
My body is the frame wherein 'tis held,
And perspective it is best painter's art.
For through the painter must you see his skill,
To find where your true image pictured lies;
Which in my bosom's shop is hanging still,
That hath his windows glazed with thine eyes.
Now see what good turns eyes for eyes have done:

Mine eyes have drawn thy shape, and thine for me
Are windows to my breast, wherethrough the sun
Delights to peep, to gaze therein on thee.
Yet eyes this cunning want to grace their art—
They draw but what they see, know not the heart.

XXV

Let those who are in favour with their stars
Of public honour and proud titles boast,
Whilst I, whom fortune of such triumph bars,
Unlook'd for joy in that I honour most.
Great princes' favourites their fair leaves spread
But as the marigold at the sun's eye;
And in themselves their pride lies buried,
For at a frown they in their glory die.
The painful warrior famoused for fight,
After a thousand victories once foil'd,
Is from the book of honour razed quite,
And all the rest forgot for which he toil'd.
Then happy I, that love and am beloved
Where I may not remove nor be removed.

XXVI

Lord of my love, to whom in vassalage
Thy merit hath my duty strongly knit,
To thee I send this written embassage,
To witness duty, not to show my wit:
Duty so great, which wit so poor as mine
May make seem bare, in wanting words to show it,
But that I hope some good conceit of thine
In thy soul's thought, all naked, will bestow it;
Till whatsoever star that guides my moving
Points on me graciously with fair aspect
And puts apparel on my tatter'd loving,
To show me worthy of thy sweet respect.
Then may I dare to boast how I do love thee;
Till then not show my head where thou mayst prove me.

XXVII

Weary with toil, I haste me to my bed,
The dear repose for limbs with travel tired;
But then begins a journey in my head
To work my mind, when body's work's expired.
For then my thoughts, from far where I abide,
Intend a zealous pilgrimage to thee,
And keep my drooping eyelids open wide,
Looking on darkness which the blind do see;
Save that my soul's imaginary sight
Presents thy shadow to my sightless view,
Which, like a jewel hung in ghastly night,
Makes black night beauteous and her old face new.
Lo! thus, by day my limbs, by night my mind,
For thee and for myself no quiet find.

XXVIII

How can I then return in happy plight,
That am debarr'd the benefit of rest?
When day's oppression is not eased by night,
But day by night and night by day oppress'd?
And each, though enemies to either's reign,
Do in consent shake hands to torture me,
The one by toil, the other to complain
How far I toil, still farther off from thee.
I tell the day, to please him, thou art bright
And dost him grace when clouds do blot the heaven;
So flatter I the swart-complexion'd night,
When sparkling stars twire not thou gild'st the even.
But day doth daily draw my sorrows longer,
And night doth nightly make grief's strength seem stronger.

XXIX

When, in disgrace with Fortune and men's eyes,
I all alone beweep my outcast state
And trouble deaf heaven with my bootless cries
And look upon myself and curse my fate,
Wishing me like to one more rich in hope,
Featured like him, like him with friends possess'd,
Desiring this man's art and that man's scope,
With what I most enjoy contented least;
Yet in these thoughts myself almost despising,
Haply I think on thee, and then my state,
Like to the lark at break of day arising
From sullen earth, sings hymns at heaven's gate;
For thy sweet love remember'd such wealth brings
That then I scorn to change my state with kings.

XXX

When to the sessions of sweet silent thought
I summon up remembrance of things past,
I sigh the lack of many a thing I sought,
And with old woes new wail my dear time's waste.
Then can I drown an eye, unused to flow,
For precious friends hid in death's dateless night,
And weep afresh love's long since cancell'd woe,
And moan the expense of many a vanish'd sight.
Then can I grieve at grievances foregone,
And heavily from woe to woe tell o'er
The sad account of fore-bemoaned moan,

Which I new pay as if not paid before.
  But if the while I think on thee, dear friend,
  All losses are restored and sorrows end.

XXXI

Thy bosom is endeared with all hearts
Which I by lacking have supposed dead;
And there reigns love and all love's loving parts,
And all those friends which I thought buried.
How many a holy and obsequious tear
Hath dear religious love stol'n from mine eye
As interest of the dead, which now appear
But things removed that hidden in thee lie!
Thou art the grave where buried love doth live,
Hung with the trophies of my lovers gone,
Who all their parts of me to thee did give;
That due of many now is thine alone.
  Their images I loved I view in thee,
  And thou, all they, hast all the all of me.

XXXII

If thou survive my well-contented day,
When that churl Death my bones with dust shall cover,
And shalt by fortune once more re-survey
These poor rude lines of thy deceased lover,
Compare them with the bettering of the time,
And though they be outstripp'd by every pen,
Reserve them for my love, not for their rhyme,
Exceeded by the height of happier men.
O, then vouchsafe me but this loving thought:
"Had my friend's Muse grown with this growing age,
A dearer birth than this his love had brought,
To march in ranks of better equipage;
  But since he died, and poets better prove,
  Theirs for their style I'll read, his for his love."

XXXIII

Full many a glorious morning have I seen
Flatter the mountain-tops with sovereign eye,
Kissing with golden face the meadows green,
Gilding pale streams with heavenly alchemy;
Anon permit the basest clouds to ride
With ugly rack on his celestial face,
And from the forlorn world his visage hide,
Stealing unseen to west with this disgrace.
Even so my sun one early morn did shine
With all-triumphant splendour on my brow;
But out, alack! he was but one hour mine,
The region cloud hath mask'd him from me now.
  Yet him for this my love no whit disdaineth;
  Suns of the world may stain when heaven's sun staineth.

XXXIV

Why didst thou promise such a beauteous day
And make me travel forth without my cloak,
To let base clouds o'ertake me in my way,
Hiding thy bravery in their rotten smoke?
'Tis not enough that through the cloud thou break
To dry the rain on my storm-beaten face,
For no man well of such a salve can speak
That heals the wound and cures not the disgrace;
Nor can thy shame give physic to my grief;
Though thou repent, yet I have still the loss.
The offender's sorrow lends but weak relief
To him that bears the strong offence's cross.
  Ah! but those tears are pearl which thy love sheds,
  And they are rich and ransom all ill deeds.

XXXV

No more be grieved at that which thou hast done:
Roses have thorns, and silver fountains mud;
Clouds and eclipses stain both moon and sun,
And loathsome canker lives in sweetest bud.
All men make faults, and even I in this,
Authorizing thy trespass with compare,
Myself corrupting, salving thy amiss,
Excusing thy sins more than thy sins are;
For to thy sensual fault I bring in sense—
Thy adverse party is thy advocate—
And 'gainst myself a lawful plea commence.
Such civil war is in my love and hate
  That I an accessary needs must be
  To that sweet thief which sourly robs from me.

XXXVI

Let me confess that we two must be twain,
Although our undivided loves are one.
So shall those blots that do with me remain
Without thy help by me be borne alone.
In our two loves there is but one respect,
Though in our lives a separable spite,
Which though it alter not love's sole effect,
Yet doth it steal sweet hours from love's delight.
I may not evermore acknowledge thee,
Lest my bewailed guilt should do thee shame,
Nor thou with public kindness honour me,
Unless thou take that honour from thy name.
  But do not so; I love thee in such sort
  As, thou being mine, mine is thy good report.

XXXVII

As a decrepit father takes delight
To see his active child do deeds of youth,
So I, made lame by Fortune's dearest spite,

Take all my comfort of thy worth and truth.
For whether beauty, birth, or wealth, or wit,
Or any of these all, or all, or more,
Entitled in thy parts do crowned sit,
I make my love engrafted to this store.
So then I am not lame, poor, nor despised,
Whilst that this shadow doth such substance give
That I in thy abundance am sufficed
And by a part of all thy glory live.
Look, what is best, that best I wish in thee.
This wish I have; then ten times happy me!

XXXVIII

How can my Muse want subject to invent,
While thou dost breathe, that pour'st into my verse
Thine own sweet argument, too excellent
For every vulgar paper to rehearse?
O, give thyself the thanks, if aught in me
Worthy perusal stand against thy sight;
For who's so dumb that cannot write to thee,
When thou thyself dost give invention light?
Be thou the tenth Muse, ten times more in worth
Than those old nine which rhymers invocate;
And he that calls on thee, let him bring forth
Eternal numbers to outlive long date.
If my slight Muse do please these curious days,
The pain be mine, but thine shall be the praise.

XXXIX

O, how thy worth with manners may I sing,
When thou art all the better part of me?
What can mine own praise to mine own self bring?
And what is 't but mine own when I praise thee?
Even for this let us divided live,
And our dear love lose name of single one,
That by this separation I may give
That due to thee which thou deservest alone.
O absence, what a torment wouldst thou prove,
Were it not thy sour leisure gave sweet leave
To entertain the time with thoughts of love,
Which time and thoughts so sweetly doth deceive,
And that thou teachest how to make one twain,
By praising him here who doth hence remain!

XL

Take all my loves, my love, yea, take them all;
What hast thou then more than thou hadst before?
No love, my love, that thou mayst true love call;
All mine was thine before thou hadst this more.
Then if for my love thou my love receivest,
I cannot blame thee for my love thou usest;
But yet be blamed, if thou thyself deceivest
By wilful taste of what thyself refusest.
I do forgive thy robbery, gentle thief,
Although thou steal thee all my poverty;
And yet love knows it is a greater grief
To bear love's wrong than hate's known injury.
Lascivious grace, in whom all ill well shows,
Kill me with spites; yet we must not be foes.

XLI

Those pretty wrongs that liberty commits
When I am sometime absent from thy heart,
Thy beauty and thy years full well befits,
For still temptation follows where thou art.
Gentle thou art and therefore to be won,
Beauteous thou art, therefore to be assailed;
And when a woman woos, what woman's son
Will sourly leave her till she have prevailed?
Ay me! but yet thou mightst my seat forbear,
And chide thy beauty and thy straying youth,
Who lead thee in their riot even there
Where thou art forced to break a twofold truth,
Hers, by thy beauty tempting her to thee,
Thine, by thy beauty being false to me.

XLII

That thou hast her, it is not all my grief,
And yet it may be said I loved her dearly;
That she hath thee is of my wailing chief,
A loss in love that touches me more nearly.
Loving offenders, thus I will excuse ye:
Thou dost love her because thou know'st I love her,
And for my sake even so doth she abuse me,
Suffering my friend for my sake to approve her.
If I lose thee, my loss is my love's gain,
And losing her, my friend hath found that loss;
Both find each other, and I lose both twain,
And both for my sake lay on me this cross.
But here's the joy; my friend and I are one.
Sweet flattery! then she loves but me alone.

XLIII

When most I wink, then do mine eyes best see,
For all the day they view things unrespected;
But when I sleep, in dreams they look on thee,
And darkly bright are bright in dark directed.
Then thou, whose shadow shadows doth make bright,
How would thy shadow's form form happy show
To the clear day with thy much clearer light,
When to unseeing eyes thy shade shines so!
How would, I say, mine eyes be blessed made
By looking on thee in the living day,
When in dead night thy fair imperfect shade
Through heavy sleep on sightless eyes doth stay!
All days are nights to see till I see thee,

And nights bright days when dreams do show
thee me.

XLIV

If the dull substance of my flesh were thought,
Injurious distance should not stop my way;
For then despite of space I would be brought,
From limits far remote, where thou dost stay.
No matter then although my foot did stand
Upon the farthest earth removed from thee;
For nimble thought can jump both sea and land
As soon as think the place where he would be.
But, ah! thought kills me that I am not thought,
To leap large lengths of miles when thou art gone,
But that, so much of earth and water wrought,
I must attend time's leisure with my moan,
Receiving nought by elements so slow
But heavy tears, badges of either's woe.

XLV

The other two, slight air and purging fire,
Are both with thee, wherever I abide;
The first my thought, the other my desire,
These present-absent with swift motion slide.
For when these quicker elements are gone
In tender embassy of love to thee,
My life, being made of four, with two alone
Sinks down to death, oppress'd with melancholy;
Until life's composition be recured
By those swift messengers return'd from thee,
Who even but now come back again, assured
Of thy fair health, recounting it to me.
This told, I joy; but then no longer glad,
I send them back again and straight grow sad.

XLVI

Mine eye and heart are at a mortal war
How to divide the conquest of thy sight;
Mine eye my heart thy picture's sight would bar,
My heart mine eye the freedom of that right.
My heart doth plead that thou in him dost lie,
A closet never pierced with crystal eyes,
But the defendant doth that plea deny
And says in him thy fair appearance lies.
To 'cide this title is impanneled
A quest of thoughts, all tenants to the heart,
And by their verdict is determined
The clear eye's moiety and the dear heart's part:
As thus—mine eye's due is thy outward part,
And my heart's right thy inward love of heart.

XLVII

Betwixt mine eye and heart a league is took,
And each doth good turns now unto the other.
When that mine eye is famish'd for a look,
Or heart in love with sighs himself doth smother,
With my love's picture then my eye doth feast
And to the painted banquet bids my heart.
Another time mine eye is my heart's guest
And in his thoughts of love doth share a part.
So, either by thy picture or my love,
Thyself away art present still with me;
For thou not farther than my thoughts canst
move,
And I am still with them, and they with thee;
Or, if they sleep, thy picture in my sight
Awakes my heart to heart's and eye's delight.

XLVIII

How careful was I, when I took my way,
Each trifle under truest bars to thrust,
That to my use it might unused stay
From hands of falsehood, in sure wards of trust!
But thou, to whom my jewels trifles are,
Most worthy comfort, now my greatest grief,
Thou, best of dearest and mine only care,
Art left the prey of every vulgar thief.
Thee have I not lock'd up in any chest,
Save where thou art not, though I feel thou art,
Within the gentle closure of my breast,
From whence at pleasure thou mayst come and
part;
And even thence thou wilt be stol'n, I fear,
For truth proves thievish for a prize so dear.

XLIX

Against that time, if ever that time come,
When I shall see thee frown on my defects,
When as thy love hath cast his utmost sum,
Call'd to that audit by advised respects;
Against that time when thou shalt strangely pass
And scarcely greet me with that sun, thine eye,
When love, converted from the thing it was,
Shall reasons find of settled gravity—
Against that time do I ensconce me here
Within the knowledge of mine own desert,
And this my hand against myself uprear,
To guard the lawful reasons on thy part.
To leave poor me thou hast the strength of
laws,
Since why to love I can allege no cause.

L

How heavy do I journey on the way
When what I seek, my weary travel's end,
Doth teach that ease and that repose to say,
"Thus far the miles are measured from thy
friend!"
The beast that bears me, tired with my woe,
Plods dully on, to bear that weight in me,
As if by some instinct the wretch did know
His rider loved not speed, being made from thee.

The bloody spur cannot provoke him on
That sometimes anger thrusts into his hide;
Which heavily he answers with a groan,
More sharp to me than spurring to his side;
  For that same groan doth put this in my mind—
  My grief lies onward and my joy behind.

LI

Thus can my love excuse the slow offence
Of my dull bearer when from thee I speed:
From where thou art why should I haste me thence?
Till I return, of posting is no need.
O, what excuse will my poor beast then find,
When swift extremity can seem but slow?
Then should I spur, though mounted on the wind,
In winged speed no motion shall I know.
Then can no horse with my desire keep pace;
Therefore desire, of perfect'st love being made,
Shall neigh—no dull flesh—in his fiery race;
But love, for love, thus shall excuse my jade—
  Since from thee going he went wilful-slow,
  Towards thee I'll run, and give him leave to go.

LII

So am I as the rich whose blessed key
Can bring him to his sweet up-locked treasure,
The which he will not every hour survey,
For blunting the fine point of seldom pleasure.
Therefore are feasts so solemn and so rare,
Since, seldom coming, in the long year set,
Like stones of worth they thinly placed are,
Or captain jewels in the carcanet.
So is the time that keeps you as my chest,
Or as the wardrobe which the robe doth hide,
To make some special instant special blest
By new unfolding his imprison'd pride.
  Blessed are you, whose worthiness gives scope,
  Being had, to triumph, being lack'd, to hope.

LIII

What is your substance, whereof are you made,
That millions of strange shadows on you tend?
Since every one hath, every one, one shade,
And you, but one, can every shadow lend.
Describe Adonis, and the counterfeit
Is poorly imitated after you;
On Helen's cheek all art of beauty set,
And you in Grecian tires are painted new.
Speak of the spring and foison of the year;
The one doth shadow of your beauty show,
The other as your bounty doth appear;
And you in every blessed shape we know.
  In all external grace you have some part,
  But you like none, none you, for constant heart.

LIV

O, how much more doth beauty beauteous seem
By that sweet ornament which truth doth give!
The rose looks fair, but fairer we it deem
For that sweet odour which doth in it live.
The canker-blooms have full as deep a dye
As the perfumed tincture of the roses,
Hang on such thorns and play as wantonly
When summer's breath their masked buds discloses;
But, for their virtue only is their show,
They live unwoo'd and unrespected fade,
Die to themselves. Sweet roses do not so;
Of their sweet deaths are sweetest odours made.
  And so of you, beauteous and lovely youth,
  When that shall fade, my verse distills your truth.

LV

Not marble nor the gilded monuments
Of princes shall outlive this powerful rhyme;
But you shall shine more bright in these contents
Than unswept stone besmear'd with sluttish time.
When wasteful war shall statues overturn,
And broils root out the work of masonry,
Nor Mars his sword nor war's quick fire shall burn
The living record of your memory.
'Gainst death and all-oblivious enmity
Shall you pace forth; your praise shall still find room
Even in the eyes of all posterity
That wear this world out to the ending doom.
  So, till the judgement that yourself arise,
  You live in this, and dwell in lovers' eyes.

LVI

Sweet love, renew thy force; be it not said
Thy edge should blunter be than appetite,
Which but to-day by feeding is allay'd,
To-morrow sharpen'd in his former might.
So, love, be thou; although to-day thou fill
Thy hungry eyes even till they wink with fullness,
To-morrow see again, and do not kill
The spirit of love with a perpetual dullness.
Let this sad interim like the ocean be
Which parts the shore, where two contracted new
Come daily to the banks, that, when they see
Return of love, more blest may be the view;
  Else call it winter, which, being full of care,
  Makes summer's welcome thrice more wish'd, more rare.

LVII

Being your slave, what should I do but tend
Upon the hours and times of your desire?
I have no precious time at all to spend,
Nor services to do, till you require.
Nor dare I chide the world-without-end hour
Whilst I, my sovereign, watch the clock for you,
Nor think the bitterness of absence sour
When you have bid your servant once adieu;
Nor dare I question with my jealous thought
Where you may be, or your affairs suppose,
But, like a sad slave, stay and think of nought
Save where you are how happy you make those.
So true a fool is love that in your will,
Though you do anything, he thinks no ill.

LVIII

That god forbid that made me first your slave,
I should in thought control your times of pleasure,
Or at your hand the account of hours to crave,
Being your vassal, bound to stay your leisure!
O, let me suffer, being at your beck,
The imprison'd absence of your liberty;
And patience, tame to sufferance, bide each check
Without accusing you of injury.
Be where you list, your charter is so strong
That you yourself may privilege your time
To what you will; to you it doth belong
Yourself to pardon of self-doing crime.
I am to wait, though waiting so be hell;
Not blame your pleasure, be it ill or well.

LIX

If there be nothing new, but that which is
Hath been before, how are our brains beguiled,
Which, labouring for invention, bear amiss
The second burthen of a former child!
O, that record could with a backward look,
Even of five hundred courses of the sun,
Show me your image in some antique book,
Since mind at first in character was done!
That I might see what the old world could say
To this composed wonder of your frame;
Whether we are mended, or whether better they,
Or whether revolution be the same.
O, sure I am, the wits of former days
To subjects worse have given admiring praise.

LX

Like as the waves make towards the pebbled shore,
So do our minutes hasten to their end;
Each changing place with that which goes before,
In sequent toil all forwards do contend.
Nativity, once in the main of light,
Crawls to maturity, wherewith being crown'd,
Crooked eclipses 'gainst his glory fight,
And Time that gave doth now his gift confound.
Time doth transfix the flourish set on youth
And delves the parallels in beauty's brow,
Feeds on the rarities of nature's truth,
And nothing stands but for his scythe to mow;
And yet to times in hope my verse shall stand,
Praising thy worth, despite his cruel hand.

LXI

Is it thy will thy image should keep open
My heavy eyelids to the weary night?
Dost thou desire my slumbers should be broken,
While shadows like to thee do mock my sight?
Is it thy spirit that thou send'st from thee
So far from home into my deeds to pry,
To find out shames and idle hours in me,
The scope and tenour of thy jealousy?
O, no! thy love, though much, is not so great.
It is my love that keeps mine eye awake;
Mine own true love that doth my rest defeat,
To play the watchman ever for thy sake.
For thee watch I whilst thou dost wake elsewhere,
From me far off, with others all too near.

LXII

Sin of self-love possesseth all mine eye
And all my soul and all my every part;
And for this sin there is no remedy,
It is so grounded inward in my heart.
Methinks no face so gracious is as mine,
No shape so true, no truth of such account;
And for myself mine own worth do define,
As I all other in all worths surmount.
But when my glass shows me myself indeed,
Beated and chopp'd with tann'd antiquity,
Mine own self-love quite contrary I read;
Self so self-loving were iniquity.
'Tis thee, myself, that for myself I praise,
Painting my age with beauty of thy days.

LXIII

Against my love shall be, as I am now,
With Time's injurious hand crush'd and o'erworn;
When hours have drain'd his blood and fill'd his brow
With lines and wrinkles; when his youthful morn
Hath travell'd on to age's steepy night,
And all those beauties whereof now he's king
Are vanishing or vanish'd out of sight,
Stealing away the treasure of his spring;
For such a time do I now fortify
Against confounding age's cruel knife,

That he shall never cut from memory
My sweet love's beauty, though my lover's life.
  His beauty shall in these black lines be seen,
  And they shall live, and he in them still green.

LXIV

When I have seen by Time's fell hand defaced
The rich proud cost of outworn buried age;
When sometime lofty towers I see down-razed
And brass eternal slave to mortal rage;
When I have seen the hungry ocean gain
Advantage on the kingdom of the shore,
And the firm soil win of the watery main,
Increasing store with loss and loss with store;
When I have seen such interchange of state,
Or state itself confounded to decay;
Ruin hath taught me thus to ruminate,
That Time will come and take my love away.
  This thought is as a death, which cannot choose
  But weep to have that which it fears to lose.

LXV

Since brass, nor stone, nor earth, nor boundless sea,
But sad mortality o'er-sways their power,
How with this rage shall beauty hold a plea,
Whose action is no stronger than a flower?
O, how shall summer's honey breath hold out
Against the wreckful siege of battering days,
When rocks impregnable are not so stout,
Nor gates of steel so strong, but Time decays?
O fearful meditation! where, alack,
Shall Time's best jewel from Time's chest lie hid?
Or what strong hand can hold his swift foot back?
Or who his spoil of beauty can forbid?
  O, none, unless this miracle have might,
  That in black ink my love may still shine bright.

LXVI

Tired with all these, for restful death I cry:
As, to behold desert a beggar born,
And needy nothing trimm'd in jollity,
And purest faith unhappily forsworn,
And gilded honour shamefully misplaced,
And maiden virtue rudely strumpeted,
And right perfection wrongfully disgraced,
And strength by limping sway disabled,
And art made tongue-tied by authority,
And folly doctor-like controlling skill,
And simple truth miscall'd simplicity,
And captive good attending captain ill.
  Tired with all these, from these would I be gone,
  Save that, to die, I leave my love alone.

LXVII

Ah! wherefore with infection should he live
And with his presence grace impiety,
That sin by him advantage should achieve
And lace itself with his society?
Why should false painting imitate his cheek
And steal dead seeing of his living hue?
Why should poor beauty indirectly seek
Roses of shadow, since his rose is true?
Why should he live, now Nature bankrupt is,
Beggar'd of blood to blush through lively veins?
For she hath no exchequer now but his,
And, proud of many, lives upon his gains.
  O, him she stores, to show what wealth she had
  In days long since, before these last so bad.

LXVIII

Thus is his cheek the map of days outworn,
When beauty lived and died as flowers do now,
Before these bastard signs of fair were born,
Or durst inhabit on a living brow;
Before the golden tresses of the dead,
The right of sepulchres, were shorn away
To live a second life on second head;
Ere beauty's dead fleece made another gay.
In him those holy antique hours are seen,
Without all ornament, itself and true,
Making no summer of another's green,
Robbing no old to dress his beauty new;
  And him as for a map doth Nature store,
  To show false Art what beauty was of yore.

LXIX

Those parts of thee that the world's eye doth view
Want nothing that the thought of hearts can mend;
All tongues, the voice of souls, give thee that due,
Uttering bare truth, even so as foes commend.
Thy outward thus with outward praise is crown'd;
But those same tongues that give thee so thine own
In other accents do this praise confound
By seeing farther than the eye hath shown.
They look into the beauty of thy mind,
And that, in guess, they measure by thy deeds;
Then, churls, their thoughts, although their eyes were kind,
To thy fair flower add the rank smell of weeds;
  But why thy odour matcheth not thy show,
  The solve is this—that thou dost common grow.

LXX

That thou art blamed shall not be thy defect,
For slander's mark was ever yet the fair;
The ornament of beauty is suspect,
A crow that flies in heaven's sweetest air.
So thou be good, slander doth but approve
Thy worth the greater, being woo'd of time;
For canker vice the sweetest buds doth love,
And thou present'st a pure unstained prime.
Thou hast pass'd by the ambush of young days,
Either not assail'd or victor being charged;
Yet this thy praise cannot be so thy praise,
To tie up envy, evermore enlarged.
If some suspect of ill mask'd not thy show,
Then thou alone kingdoms of hearts shouldst owe.

LXXI

No longer mourn for me when I am dead
Than you shall hear the surly sullen bell
Give warning to the world that I am fled
From this vile world, with vilest worms to dwell.
Nay, if you read this line, remember not
The hand that writ it; for I love you so
That I in your sweet thoughts would be forgot
If thinking on me then should make you woe.
O, if, I say, you look upon this verse
When I perhaps compounded am with clay,
Do not so much as my poor name rehearse,
But let your love even with my life decay,
Lest the wise world should look into your moan
And mock you with me after I am gone.

LXXII

O, lest the world should task you to recite
What merit lived in me, that you should love
After my death, dear love, forget me quite,
For you in me can nothing worthy prove;
Unless you would devise some virtuous lie,
To do more for me than mine own desert,
And hang more praise upon deceased I
Than niggard truth would willingly impart.
O, lest your true love may seem false in this,
That you for love speak well of me untrue,
My name be buried where my body is,
And live no more to shame nor me nor you.
For I am shamed by that which I bring forth,
And so should you, to love things nothing worth.

LXXIII

That time of year thou mayst in me behold
When yellow leaves, or none, or few, do hang
Upon those boughs which shake against the cold,
Bare ruin'd choirs, where late the sweet birds sang.
In me thou see'st the twilight of such day
As after sunset fadeth in the west,
Which by and by black night doth take away,
Death's second self, that seals up all in rest.
In me thou see'st the glowing of such fire
That on the ashes of his youth doth lie,
As the death-bed whereon it must expire
Consumed with that which it was nourish'd by.
This thou perceivest, which makes thy love more strong,
To love that well which thou must leave ere long.

LXXIV

But be contented. When that fell arrest
Without all bail shall carry me away,
My life hath in this line some interest,
Which for memorial still with thee shall stay.
When thou reviewest this, thou dost review
The very part was consecrate to thee.
The earth can have but earth, which is his due;
My spirit is thine, the better part of me.
So then thou hast but lost the dregs of life,
The prey of worms, my body being dead,
The coward conquest of a wretch's knife,
Too base of thee to be remembered.
The worth of that is that which it contains,
And that is this, and this with thee remains.

LXXV

So are you to my thoughts as food to life,
Or as sweet-season'd showers are to the ground;
And for the peace of you I hold such strife
As 'twixt a miser and his wealth is found;
Now proud as an enjoyer and anon
Doubting the filching age will steal his treasure,
Now counting best to be with you alone,
Then better'd that the world may see my pleasure;
Sometime all full with feasting on your sight
And by and by clean starved for a look;
Possessing or pursuing no delight
Save what is had or must from you be took.
Thus do I pine and surfeit day by day,
Or gluttoning on all, or all away.

LXXVI

Why is my verse so barren of new pride,
So far from variation or quick change?
Why with the time do I not glance aside
To new-found methods and to compounds strange?
Why write I still all one, ever the same,
And keep invention in a noted weed,

That every word doth almost tell my name,
Showing their birth and where they did proceed?
O, know, sweet love, I always write of you,
And you and love are still my argument;
So all my best is dressing old words new,
Spending again what is already spent;
For as the sun is daily new and old,
So is my love still telling what is told.

LXXVII

Thy glass will show thee how thy beauties wear,
Thy dial how thy precious minutes waste;
The vacant leaves thy mind's imprint will bear,
And of this book this learning mayst thou taste.
The wrinkles which thy glass will truly show
Of mouthed graves will give thee memory;
Thou by thy dial's shady stealth mayst know
Time's thievish progress to eternity.
Look, what thy memory can not contain
Commit to these waste blanks, and thou shalt find
Those children nursed, deliver'd from thy brain,
To take a new acquaintance of thy mind.
These offices, so oft as thou wilt look,
Shall profit thee and much enrich thy book.

LXXVIII

So oft have I invoked thee for my Muse
And found such fair assistance in my verse
As every alien pen hath got my use
And under thee their poesy disperse.
Thine eyes that taught the dumb on high to sing
And heavy ignorance aloft to fly
Have added feathers to the learned's wing
And given grace a double majesty.
Yet be most proud of that which I compile,
Whose influence is thine and born of thee.
In others' works thou dost but mend the style,
And arts with thy sweet graces graced be;
But thou art all my art and dost advance
As high as learning my rude ignorance.

LXXIX

Whilst I alone did call upon thy aid,
My verse alone had all thy gentle grace,
But now my gracious numbers are decay'd
And my sick Muse doth give another place.
I grant, sweet love, thy lovely argument
Deserves the travail of a worthier pen,
Yet what of thee thy poet doth invent
He robs thee of and pays it thee again.
He lends thee virtue and he stole that word
From thy behaviour; beauty doth he give
And found it in thy cheek; he can afford
No praise to thee but what in thee doth live.
Then thank him not for that which he doth say,
Since what he owes thee thou thyself dost pay.

LXXX

O, how I faint when I of you do write,
Knowing a better spirit doth use your name
And in the praise thereof spends all his might
To make me tongue-tied, speaking of your fame!
But since your worth, wide as the ocean is,
The humble as the proudest sail doth bear,
My saucy bark inferior far to his
On your broad main doth wilfully appear.
Your shallowest help will hold me up afloat
Whilst he upon your soundless deep doth ride;
Or, being wreck'd, I am a worthless boat,
He of tall building and of goodly pride.
Then if he thrive and I be cast away,
The worst was this: my love was my decay.

LXXXI

Or I shall live your epitaph to make,
Or you survive when I in earth am rotten.
From hence your memory death cannot take,
Although in me each part will be forgotten.
Your name from hence immortal life shall have,
Though I, once gone, to all the world must die.
The earth can yield me but a common grave,
When you entombed in men's eyes shall lie.
Your monument shall be my gentle verse,
Which eyes not yet created shall o'er-read,
And tongues to be your being shall rehearse
When all the breathers of this world are dead.
You still shall live—such virtue hath my pen—
Where breath most breathes, even in the mouths of men.

LXXXII

I grant thou wert not married to my Muse
And therefore mayst without attaint o'erlook
The dedicated words which writers use
Of their fair subject, blessing every book.
Thou art as fair in knowledge as in hue,
Finding thy worth a limit past my praise,
And therefore art enforced to seek anew
Some fresher stamp of the time-bettering days.
And do so, love; yet when they have devised
What strained touches rhetoric can lend,
Thou truly fair wert truly sympathized
In true plain words by thy true-telling friend;
And their gross painting might be better used
Where cheeks need blood; in thee it is abused.

LXXXIII

I never saw that you did painting need
And therefore to your fair no painting set;
I found, or thought I found, you did exceed
The barren tender of a poet's debt;
And therefore have I slept in your report,

That you yourself being extant well might show
How far a modern quill doth come too short,
Speaking of worth, what worth in you doth grow.
This silence for my sin you did impute,
Which shall be most my glory, being dumb;
For I impair not beauty being mute,
When others would give life and bring a tomb.
There lives more life in one of your fair eyes
Than both your poets can in praise devise.

LXXXIV

Who is it that says most which can say more
Than this rich praise, that you alone are you?
In whose confine immured is the store
Which should example where your equal grew.
Lean penury within that pen doth dwell
That to his subject lends not some small glory;
But he that writes of you, if he can tell
That you are you, so dignifies his story.
Let him but copy what in you is writ,
Not making worse what nature made so clear,
And such a counterpart shall fame his wit,
Making his style admired everywhere.
You to your beauteous blessings add a curse,
Being fond on praise, which makes your praises worse.

LXXXV

My tongue-tied Muse in manners holds her still,
While comments of your praise, richly compiled,
Reserve their character with golden quill
And precious phrase by all the Muses filed.
I think good thoughts whilst other write good words,
And like unletter'd clerk still cry "Amen"
To every hymn that able spirit affords
In polish'd form of well-refined pen.
Hearing you praised, I say "'Tis so, 'tis true,"
And to the most of praise add something more;
But that is in my thought, whose love to you,
Though words come hindmost, holds his rank before.
Then others for the breath of words respect;
Me for my dumb thoughts, speaking in effect.

LXXXVI

Was it the proud full sail of his great verse,
Bound for the prize of all too precious you,
That did my ripe thoughts in my brain inhearse,
Making their tomb the womb wherein they grew?
Was it his spirit, by spirits taught to write
Above a mortal pitch, that struck me dead?
No, neither he, nor his compeers by night
Giving him aid, my verse astonished.
He, nor that affable familiar ghost
Which nightly gulls him with intelligence,
As victors of my silence cannot boast—
I was not sick of any fear from thence;
But when your countenance fill'd up his line,
Then lack'd I matter; that enfeebled mine.

LXXXVII

Farewell! thou art too dear for my possessing,
And like enough thou know'st thy estimate.
The charter of thy worth gives thee releasing;
My bonds in thee are all determinate.
For how do I hold thee but by thy granting?
And for that riches where is my deserving?
The cause of this fair gift in me is wanting,
And so my patent back again is swerving.
Thyself thou gavest, thy own worth then not knowing,
Or me, to whom thou gavest it, else mistaking;
So thy great gift, upon misprision growing,
Comes home again, on better judgement making.
Thus have I had thee, as a dream doth flatter—
In sleep a king, but waking no such matter.

LXXXVIII

When thou shalt be disposed to set me light
And place my merit in the eye of scorn,
Upon thy side against myself I'll fight
And prove thee virtuous, though thou art forsworn.
With mine own weakness being best acquainted,
Upon thy part I can set down a story
Of faults conceal'd, wherein I am attainted,
That thou in losing me shalt win much glory.
And I by this will be a gainer too;
For bending all my loving thoughts on thee,
The injuries that to myself I do,
Doing thee vantage, double-vantage me.
Such is my love, to thee I so belong,
That for thy right myself will bear all wrong.

LXXXIX

Say that thou didst forsake me for some fault,
And I will comment upon that offence;
Speak of my lameness, and I straight will halt,
Against thy reasons making no defence.
Thou canst not, love, disgrace me half so ill,
To set a form upon desired change,
As I'll myself disgrace, knowing thy will.
I will acquaintance strangle and look strange,
Be absent from thy walks, and in my tongue
Thy sweet beloved name no more shall dwell,
Lest I, too much profane, should do it wrong
And haply of our old acquaintance tell.
For thee against myself I'll vow debate,
For I must ne'er love him whom thou dost hate.

XC

Then hate me when thou wilt! if ever, now!
Now, while the world is bent my deeds to cross,
Join with the spite of fortune, make me bow,
And do not drop in for an after-loss.
Ah, do not, when my heart hath 'scaped this sorrow,
Come in the rearward of a conquer'd woe;
Give not a windy night a rainy morrow,
To linger out a purposed overthrow.
If thou wilt leave me, do not leave me last,
When other petty griefs have done their spite,
But in the onset come. So shall I taste
At first the very worst of fortune's might;
And other strains of woe, which now seem woe,
Compared with loss of thee will not seem so.

XCI

Some glory in their birth, some in their skill,
Some in their wealth, some in their bodies' force,
Some in their garments, though new-fangled ill,
Some in their hawks and hounds, some in their horse;
And every humour hath his adjunct pleasure,
Wherein it finds a joy above the rest.
But these particulars are not my measure;
All these I better in one general best.
Thy love is better than high birth to me,
Richer than wealth, prouder than garments' cost,
Of more delight than hawks or horses be;
And having thee, of all men's pride I boast—
Wretched in this alone, that thou mayst take
All this away and me most wretched make.

XCII

But do thy worst to steal thyself away,
For term of life thou art assured mine;
And life no longer than thy love will stay,
For it depends upon that love of thine.
Then need I not to fear the worst of wrongs,
When in the least of them my life hath end.
I see a better state to me belongs
Than that which on thy humour doth depend;
Thou canst not vex me with inconstant mind,
Since that my life on thy revolt doth lie.
O, what a happy title do I find,
Happy to have thy love, happy to die!
But what's so blessed-fair that fears no blot?
Thou mayst be false, and yet I know it not.

XCIII

So shall I live, supposing thou art true,
Like a deceived husband; so love's face
May still seem love to me, though alter'd new;
Thy looks with me, thy heart in other place.
For there can live no hatred in thine eye,
Therefore in that I cannot know thy change.
In many's looks the false heart's history
Is writ in moods and frowns and wrinkles strange,
But heaven in thy creation did decree
That in thy face sweet love should ever dwell;
Whate'er thy thoughts or thy heart's workings be,
Thy looks should nothing thence but sweetness tell.
How like Eve's apple doth thy beauty grow,
If thy sweet virtue answer not thy show!

XCIV

They that have power to hurt and will do none,
That do not do the thing they most do show,
Who, moving others, are themselves as stone,
Unmoved, cold, and to temptation slow,
They rightly do inherit heaven's graces
And husband nature's riches from expense;
They are the lords and owners of their faces,
Others but stewards of their excellence.
The summer's flower is to the summer sweet,
Though to itself it only live and die;
But if that flower with base infection meet,
The basest weed outbraves his dignity:
For sweetest things turn sourest by their deeds;
Lilies that fester smell far worse than weeds.

XCV

How sweet and lovely dost thou make the shame
Which, like a canker in the fragrant rose,
Doth spot the beauty of thy budding name!
O, in what sweets dost thou thy sins enclose!
That tongue that tells the story of thy days,
Making lascivious comments on thy sport,
Cannot dispraise but in a kind of praise;
Naming thy name blesses an ill report.
O, what a mansion have those vices got
Which for their habitation chose out thee,
Where beauty's veil doth cover every blot,
And all things turn to fair that eyes can see!
Take heed, dear heart, of this large privilege.
The hardest knife ill-used doth lose his edge.

XCVI

Some say thy fault is youth, some wantonness;
Some say thy grace is youth and gentle sport;
Both grace and faults are loved of more and less;
Thou makest faults graces that to thee resort.
As on the finger of a throned queen
The basest jewel will be well esteem'd,
So are those errors that in thee are seen
To truths translated and for true things deem'd.
How many lambs might the stern wolf betray,

If like a lamb he could his looks translate!
How many gazers mightst thou lead away,
If thou wouldst use the strength of all thy state!
But do not so; I love thee in such sort
As, thou being mine, mine is thy good report.

XCVII

How like a winter hath my absence been
From thee, the pleasure of the fleeting year!
What freezings have I felt, what dark days seen!
What old December's bareness everywhere!
And yet this time removed was summer's time,
The teeming autumn, big with rich increase,
Bearing the wanton burthen of the prime,
Like widow'd wombs after their lord's decease;
Yet this abundant issue seem'd to me
But hope of orphans and unfather'd fruit;
For summer and his pleasures wait on thee,
And, thou away, the very birds are mute;
Or, if they sing, 'tis with so dull a cheer
That leaves look pale, dreading the winter's near.

XCVIII

From you have I been absent in the spring,
When proud-pied April, dress'd in all his trim,
Hath put a spirit of youth in everything,
That heavy Saturn laugh'd and leap'd with him.
Yet nor the lays of birds, nor the sweet smell
Of different flowers in odour and in hue,
Could make me any summer's story tell,
Or from their proud lap pluck them where they grew;
Nor did I wonder at the lily's white,
Nor praise the deep vermilion in the rose;
They were but sweet, but figures of delight,
Drawn after you, you pattern of all those.
Yet seem'd it winter still, and, you away,
As with your shadow I with these did play:

XCIX

The forward violet thus did I chide:
Sweet thief, whence didst thou steal thy sweet that smells,
If not from my love's breath? The purple pride
Which on thy soft cheek for complexion dwells
In my love's veins thou hast too grossly dyed.
The lily I condemned for thy hand,
And buds of marjoram had stol'n thy hair.
The roses fearfully on thorns did stand,
One blushing shame, another white despair;
A third, nor red nor white, had stol'n of both,
And to his robbery had annex'd thy breath;
But, for his theft, in pride of all his growth
A vengeful canker eat him up to death.
More flowers I noted, yet I none could see
But sweet or colour it had stol'n from thee.

C

Where art thou, Muse, that thou forget'st so long
To speak of that which gives thee all thy might?
Spend'st thou thy fury on some worthless song,
Darkening thy power to lend base subjects light?
Return, forgetful Muse, and straight redeem
In gentle numbers time so idly spent;
Sing to the ear that doth thy lays esteem
And gives thy pen both skill and argument.
Rise, resty Muse, my love's sweet face survey,
If Time have any wrinkle graven there;
If any, be a satire to decay,
And make Time's spoils despised everywhere.
Give my love fame faster than Time wastes life;
So thou prevent'st his scythe and crooked knife.

CI

O truant Muse, what shall be thy amends
For thy neglect of truth in beauty dyed?
Both truth and beauty on my love depends;
So dost thou too, and therein dignified.
Make answer, Muse. Wilt thou not haply say,
"Truth needs no colour, with his colour fix'd;
Beauty no pencil, beauty's truth to lay;
But best is best, if never intermix'd?"
Because he needs no praise, wilt thou be dumb?
Excuse not silence so; for 't lies in thee
To make him much outlive a gilded tomb,
And to be praised of ages yet to be.
Then do thy office, Muse; I teach thee how
To make him seem long hence as he shows now.

CII

My love is strengthen'd, though more weak in seeming;
I love not less, though less the show appear.
That love is merchandized whose rich esteeming
The owner's tongue doth publish everywhere.
Our love was new and then but in the spring
When I was wont to greet it with my lays,
As Philomel in summer's front doth sing
And stops her pipe in growth of riper days;
Not that the summer is less pleasant now
Than when her mournful hymns did hush the night,
But that wild music burthens every bough,
And sweets grown common lose their dear delight.
Therefore like her I sometime hold my tongue,
Because I would not dull you with my song.

CIII

Alack, what poverty my Muse brings forth,
That, having such a scope to show her pride,
The argument all bare is of more worth
Than when it hath my added praise beside!
O, blame me not, if I no more can write!
Look in your glass, and there appears a face
That over-goes my blunt invention quite,
Dulling my lines and doing me disgrace.
Were it not sinful then, striving to mend,
To mar the subject that before was well?
For to no other pass my verses tend
Than of your graces and your gifts to tell;
And more, much more, than in my verse can sit
Your own glass shows you when you look in it.

CIV

To me, fair friend, you never can be old,
For as you were when first your eye I eyed,
Such seems your beauty still. Three winters cold
Have from the forests shook three summers' pride,
Three beauteous springs to yellow autumn turn'd
In process of the seasons have I seen,
Three April perfumes in three hot Junes burn'd,
Since first I saw you fresh, which yet are green.
Ah! yet doth beauty, like a dial-hand,
Steal from his figure and no pace perceived;
So your sweet hue, which methinks still doth stand,
Hath motion, and mine eye may be deceived;
For fear of which, hear this, thou age unbred;
Ere you were born was beauty's summer dead.

CV

Let not my love be call'd idolatry,
Nor my beloved as an idol show,
Since all alike my songs and praises be
To one, of one, still such, and ever so.
Kind is my love to-day, to-morrow kind,
Still constant in a wondrous excellence;
Therefore my verse to constancy confined,
One thing expressing, leaves out difference.
"Fair, kind, and true," is all my argument,
"Fair, kind, and true," varying to other words;
And in this change is my invention spent,
Three themes in one, which wondrous scope affords.
"Fair, kind, and true," have often lived alone,
Which three till now never kept seat in one.

CVI

When in the chronicle of wasted time
I see descriptions of the fairest wights,
And beauty making beautiful old rhyme
In praise of ladies dead and lovely knights,
Then, in the blazon of sweet beauty's best,
Of hand, of foot, of lip, of eye, of brow,
I see their antique pen would have express'd
Even such a beauty as you master now.
So all their praises are but prophecies
Of this our time, all you prefiguring;
And, for they look'd but with divining eyes,
They had not skill enough your worth to sing;
For we, which now behold these present days,
Have eyes to wonder, but lack tongues to praise.

CVII

Not mine own fears, nor the prophetic soul
Of the wide world dreaming on things to come,
Can yet the lease of my true love control,
Supposed as forfeit to a confined doom.
The mortal moon hath her eclipse endured,
And the sad augurs mock their own presage;
Incertainties now crown themselves assured,
And peace proclaims olives of endless age.
Now with the drops of this most balmy time
My love looks fresh, and Death to me subscribes,
Since, spite of him, I'll live in this poor rhyme,
While he insults o'er dull and speechless tribes;
And thou in this shalt find thy monument,
When tyrants' crests and tombs of brass are spent.

CVIII

What's in the brain that ink may character
Which hath not figured to thee my true spirit?
What's new to speak, what new to register,
That may express my love or thy dear merit?
Nothing, sweet boy; but yet, like prayers divine,
I must each day say o'er the very same,
Counting no old thing old, thou mine, I thine,
Even as when first I hallow'd thy fair name.
So that eternal love in love's fresh case
Weighs not the dust and injury of age,
Nor gives to necessary wrinkles place,
But makes antiquity for aye his page,
Finding the first conceit of love there bred
Where time and outward form would show it dead.

CIX

O, never say that I was false of heart,
Though absence seem'd my flame to qualify.
As easy might I from myself depart
As from my soul, which in thy breast doth lie.
That is my home of love. If I have ranged,
Like him that travels I return again,
Just to the time, not with the time exchanged,

So that myself bring water for my stain.
Never believe, though in my nature reign'd
All frailties that besiege all kinds of blood,
That it could so preposterously be stain'd,
To leave for nothing all thy sum of good;
For nothing this wide universe I call,
Save thou, my rose; in it thou art my all.

CX

Alas, 'tis true I have gone here and there
And made myself a motley to the view,
Gored mine own thoughts, sold cheap what is most dear,
Made old offences of affections new.
Most true it is that I have look'd on truth
Askance and strangely; but, by all above,
These blenches gave my heart another youth,
And worse essays proved thee my best of love.
Now all is done, have what shall have no end!
Mine appetite I never more will grind
On newer proof, to try an older friend,
A god in love, to whom I am confined.
Then give me welcome, next my heaven the best,
Even to thy pure and most most loving breast.

CXI

O, for my sake do you with Fortune chide,
The guilty goddess of my harmful deeds,
That did not better for my life provide
Than public means which public manners breeds.
Thence comes it that my name receives a brand,
And almost thence my nature is subdued
To what it works in, like the dyer's hand.
Pity me then and wish I were renew'd,
Whilst, like a willing patient, I will drink
Potions of eisel 'gainst my strong infection;
No bitterness that I will bitter think,
Nor double penance, to correct correction.
Pity me then, dear friend, and I assure ye
Even that your pity is enough to cure me.

CXII

Your love and pity doth the impression fill
Which vulgar scandal stamp'd upon my brow;
For what care I who calls me well or ill,
So you o'er-green my bad, my good allow?
You are my all the world, and I must strive
To know my shames and praises from your tongue—
None else to me, nor I to none alive,
That my steel'd sense or changes right or wrong.
In so profound abysm I throw all care
Of others' voices, that my adder's sense
To critic and to flatterer stopped are.
Mark how with my neglect I do dispense:
You are so strongly in my purpose bred
That all the world besides methinks are dead.

CXIII

Since I left you, mine eye is in my mind;
And that which governs me to go about
Doth part his function and is partly blind,
Seems seeing, but effectually is out;
For it no form delivers to the heart
Of bird, of flower, or shape, which it doth latch;
Of his quick objects hath the mind no part,
Nor his own vision holds what it doth catch;
For if it see the rudest or gentlest sight,
The most sweet favour or deformed'st creature,
The mountain or the sea, the day or night,
The crow or dove, it shapes them to your feature.
Incapable of more, replete with you,
My most true mind thus makes mine eye untrue.

CXIV

Or whether doth my mind, being crown'd with you,
Drink up the monarch's plague, this flattery?
Or whether shall I say mine eye saith true,
And that your love taught it this alchemy,
To make of monsters and things indigest
Such cherubins as your sweet self resemble,
Creating every bad a perfect best,
As fast as objects to his beams assemble?
O, 'tis the first; 'tis flattery in my seeing,
And my great mind most kingly drinks it up.
Mine eye well knows what with his gust is 'greeing,
And to his palate doth prepare the cup.
If it be poison'd, 'tis the lesser sin
That mine eye loves it and doth first begin.

CXV

Those lines that I before have writ do lie,
Even those that said I could not love you dearer.
Yet then my judgement knew no reason why
My most full flame should afterwards burn clearer.
But reckoning time, whose million'd accidents
Creep in 'twixt vows and change decrees of kings,
Tan sacred beauty, blunt the sharp'st intents,
Divert strong minds to the course of altering things—
Alas, why, fearing of Time's tyranny,
Might I not then say, "Now I love you best,"
When I was certain o'er incertainty,
Crowning the present, doubting of the rest?
Love is a babe; then might I not say so,
To give full growth to that which still doth grow?

CXVI

Let me not to the marriage of true minds
Admit impediments. Love is not love
Which alters when it alteration finds,
Or bends with the remover to remove.
O, no! it is an ever-fixed mark
That looks on tempests and is never shaken;
It is the star to every wandering bark,
Whose worth's unknown, although his height be taken.
Love's not Time's fool, though rosy lips and cheeks
Within his bending sickle's compass come;
Love alters not with his brief hours and weeks,
But bears it out even to the edge of doom.
If this be error and upon me proved,
I never writ, nor no man ever loved.

CXVII

Accuse me thus: that I have scanted all
Wherein I should your great deserts repay,
Forget upon your dearest love to call,
Whereto all bonds do tie me day by day;
That I have frequent been with unknown minds
And given to time your own dear-purchased right;
That I have hoisted sail to all the winds
Which should transport me farthest from your sight.
Book both my wilfulness and errors down
And on just proof surmise accumulate;
Bring me within the level of your frown,
But shoot not at me in your waken'd hate;
Since my appeal says I did strive to prove
The constancy and virtue of your love.

CXVIII

Like as, to make our appetites more keen,
With eager compounds we our palate urge,
As, to prevent our maladies unseen,
We sicken to shun sickness when we purge,
Even so, being full of your ne'er-cloying sweetness,
To bitter sauces did I frame my feeding
And, sick of welfare, found a kind of meetness
To be diseased ere that there was true needing.
Thus policy in love, to anticipate
The ills that were not, grew to faults assured
And brought to medicine a healthful state
Which, rank of goodness, would by ill be cured.
But thence I learn, and find the lesson true,
Drugs poison him that so fell sick of you.

CXIX

What potions have I drunk of Siren tears,
Distill'd from limbecks foul as hell within,
Applying fears to hopes and hopes to fears,
Still losing when I saw myself to win!
What wretched errors hath my heart committed,
Whilst it hath thought itself so blessed never!
How have mine eyes out of their spheres been fitted
In the distraction of this madding fever!
O benefit of ill! now I find true
That better is by evil still made better;
And ruin'd love, when it is built anew,
Grows fairer than at first, more strong, far greater.
So I return rebuked to my content
And gain by ill thrice more than I have spent.

CXX

That you were once unkind befriends me now,
And for that sorrow which I then did feel
Needs must I under my transgression bow,
Unless my nerves were brass or hammer'd steel.
For if you were by my unkindness shaken
As I by yours, you've pass'd a hell of time,
And I, a tyrant, have no leisure taken
To weigh how once I suffer'd in your crime.
O, that our night of woe might have remember'd
My deepest sense, how hard true sorrow hits,
And soon to you, as you to me, then tender'd
The humble salve which wounded bosoms fits!
But that your trespass now becomes a fee;
Mine ransoms yours, and yours must ransom me.

CXXI

'Tis better to be vile than vile esteem'd,
When not to be receives reproach of being,
And the just pleasure lost, which is so deem'd
Not by our feeling but by others' seeing.
For why should others' false adulterate eyes
Give salutation to my sportive blood?
Or on my frailties why are frailer spies,
Which in their wills count bad what I think good?
No, I am that I am, and they that level
At my abuses reckon up their own.
I may be straight, though they themselves be bevel;
By their rank thoughts my deeds must not be shown;
Unless this general evil they maintain—
All men are bad and in their badness reign.

CXXII

Thy gift, thy tables, are within my brain
Full character'd with lasting memory,
Which shall above that idle rank remain

Beyond all date, even to eternity;
Or at the least, so long as brain and heart
Have faculty by nature to subsist,
Till each to razed oblivion yield his part
Of thee, thy record never can be miss'd.
That poor retention could not so much hold,
Nor need I tallies thy dear love to score;
Therefore to give them from me was I bold,
To trust those tables that receive thee more.
To keep an adjunct to remember thee
Were to import forgetfulness in me.

CXXIII

No, Time, thou shalt not boast that I do change!
Thy pyramids built up with newer might
To me are nothing novel, nothing strange;
They are but dressings of a former sight.
Our dates are brief, and therefore we admire
What thou dost foist upon us that is old,
And rather make them born to our desire
Than think that we before have heard them told.
Thy registers and thee I both defy,
Not wondering at the present nor the past,
For thy records and what we see doth lie,
Made more or less by thy continual haste.
This I do vow, and this shall ever be—
I will be true, despite thy scythe and thee.

CXXIV

If my dear love were but the child of state,
It might for Fortune's bastard be unfather'd,
As subject to Time's love or to Time's hate,
Weeds among weeds, or flowers with flowers gather'd.
No, it was builded far from accident;
It suffers not in smiling pomp, nor falls
Under the blow of thralled discontent,
Whereto the inviting time our fashion calls.
It fears not policy, that heretic,
Which works on leases of short-number'd hours,
But all alone stands hugely politic,
That it nor grows with heat nor drowns with showers.
To this I witness call the fools of time,
Which die for goodness, who have lived for crime.

CXXV

Were 't aught to me I bore the canopy,
With my extern the outward honouring,
Or laid great bases for eternity,
Which prove more short than waste or ruining?
Have I not seen dwellers on form and favour
Lose all, and more, by paying too much rent,
For compound sweet forgoing simple savour—
Pitiful thrivers, in their gazing spent?
No, let me be obsequious in thy heart,
And take thou my oblation, poor but free,
Which is not mix'd with seconds, knows no art
But mutual render, only me for thee.
Hence, thou suborn'd informer! a true soul
When most impeach'd stands least in thy control.

CXXVI

O thou, my lovely boy, who in thy power
Dost hold Time's fickle glass, his sickle, hour;
Who hast by waning grown, and therein show'st
Thy lovers withering as thy sweet self grow'st;
If Nature, sovereign mistress over wrack,
As thou goest onwards, still will pluck thee back,
She keeps thee to this purpose, that her skill
May time disgrace and wretched minutes kill.
Yet fear her, O thou minion of her pleasure!
She may detain, but not still keep, her treasure;
Her audit, though delay'd, answer'd must be,
And her quietus is to render thee.

CXXVII

In the old age black was not counted fair,
Or if it were, it bore not beauty's name;
But now is black beauty's successive heir,
And beauty slander'd with a bastard shame;
For since each hand hath put on nature's power,
Fairing the foul with art's false borrow'd face,
Sweet beauty hath no name, no holy bower,
But is profaned, if not lives in disgrace.
Therefore my mistress' brows are raven black,
Her eyes so suited, and they mourners seem
At such who, not born fair, no beauty lack,
Slandering creation with a false esteem.
Yet so they mourn, becoming of their woe,
That every tongue says beauty should look so.

CXXVIII

How oft, when thou, my music, music play'st,
Upon that blessed wood whose motion sounds
With thy sweet fingers, when thou gently sway'st
The wiry concord that mine ear confounds,
Do I envy those jacks that nimble leap
To kiss the tender inward of thy hand,
Whilst my poor lips, which should that harvest reap,
At the wood's boldness by thee blushing stand!
To be so tickled, they would change their state
And situation with those dancing chips,
O'er whom thy fingers walk with gentle gait,
Making dead wood more blest than living lips.
Since saucy jacks so happy are in this,
Give them thy fingers, me thy lips to kiss.

CXXIX

The expense of spirit in a waste of shame
Is lust in action; and till action, lust
Is perjured, murderous, bloody, full of blame,
Savage, extreme, rude, cruel, not to trust,
Enjoy'd no sooner but despised straight,
Past reason hunted, and no sooner had,
Past reason hated, as a swallow'd bait
On purpose laid to make the taker mad;
Mad in pursuit, and in possession so;
Had, having, and in quest to have, extreme;
A bliss in proof, and proved, a very woe;
Before, a joy proposed; behind, a dream.
  All this the world well knows; yet none knows well
  To shun the heaven that leads men to this hell.

CXXX

My mistress' eyes are nothing like the sun;
Coral is far more red than her lips' red;
If snow be white, why then her breasts are dun;
If hairs be wires, black wires grow on her head.
I have seen roses damask'd, red and white,
But no such roses see I in her cheeks;
And in some perfumes is there more delight
Than in the breath that from my mistress reeks.
I love to hear her speak, yet well I know
That music hath a far more pleasing sound;
I grant I never saw a goddess go;
My mistress, when she walks, treads on the ground.
  And yet, by heaven, I think my love as rare
  As any she belied with false compare.

CXXXI

Thou art as tyrannous, so as thou art,
As those whose beauties proudly make them cruel;
For well thou know'st to my dear doting heart
Thou art the fairest and most precious jewel.
Yet, in good faith, some say that thee behold,
Thy face hath not the power to make love groan.
To say they err I dare not be so bold,
Although I swear it to myself alone.
And, to be sure that is not false I swear,
A thousand groans, but thinking on thy face,
One on another's neck, do witness bear
Thy black is fairest in my judgement's place.
  In nothing art thou black save in thy deeds,
  And thence this slander, as I think, proceeds.

CXXXII

Thine eyes I love, and they, as pitying me,
Knowing thy heart torments me with disdain,
Have put on black and loving mourners be,
Looking with pretty ruth upon my pain.
And truly not the morning sun of heaven
Better becomes the grey cheeks of the east,
Nor that full star that ushers in the even
Doth half that glory to the sober west,
As those two mourning eyes become thy face.
O, let it then as well beseem thy heart
To mourn for me, since mourning doth thee grace,
And suit thy pity like in every part.
  Then will I swear beauty herself is black
  And all they foul that thy complexion lack.

CXXXIII

Beshrew that heart that makes my heart to groan
For that deep wound it gives my friend and me!
Is 't not enough to torture me alone,
But slave to slavery my sweet'st friend must be?
Me from myself thy cruel eye hath taken,
And my next self thou harder hast engross'd.
Of him, myself, and thee, I am forsaken;
A torment thrice threefold thus to be cross'd.
Prison my heart in thy steel bosom's ward,
But then my friend's heart let my poor heart bail;
Whoe'er keeps me, let my heart be his guard;
Thou canst not then use rigour in my gaol.
  And yet thou wilt; for I, being pent in thee,
  Perforce am thine, and all that is in me.

CXXXIV

So, now I have confess'd that he is thine,
And I myself am mortgaged to thy will,
Myself I'll forfeit, so that other mine
Thou wilt restore, to be my comfort still.
But thou wilt not, nor he will not be free,
For thou art covetous and he is kind;
He learn'd but surety-like to write for me
Under that bond that him as fast doth bind.
The statute of thy beauty thou wilt take,
Thou usurer, that put'st forth all to use,
And sue a friend came debtor for my sake;
So him I lose through my unkind abuse.
  Him have I lost; thou hast both him and me;
  He pays the whole, and yet am I not free.

CXXXV

Whoever hath her wish, thou hast thy Will,
And Will to boot, and Will in overplus;
More than enough am I that vex thee still,
To thy sweet will making addition thus.
Wilt thou, whose will is large and spacious,
Not once vouchsafe to hide my will in thine?
Shall will in others seem right gracious,
And in my will no fair acceptance shine?
The sea, all water, yet receives rain still
And in abundance addeth to his store;

So thou, being rich in Will, add to thy Will
One will of mine, to make thy large Will more.
  Let no unkind, no fair beseechers kill;
  Think all but one, and me in that one Will.

CXXXVI

If thy soul check thee that I come so near,
Swear to thy blind soul that I was thy Will,
And will, thy soul knows, is admitted there;
Thus far for love my love-suit, sweet, fulfil.
Will will fulfil the treasure of thy love,
Ay, fill it full with wills, and my will one.
In things of great receipt with ease we prove
Among a number one is reckon'd none.
Then in the number let me pass untold,
Though in thy stores' account I one must be;
For nothing hold me, so it please thee hold
That nothing me, a something sweet to thee.
  Make but my name thy love, and love that still,
  And then thou lovest me, for my name is Will.

CXXXVII

Thou blind fool, Love, what dost thou to mine eyes,
That they behold, and see not what they see?
They know what beauty is, see where it lies,
Yet what the best is take the worst to be.
If eyes corrupt by over-partial looks,
Be anchor'd in the bay where all men ride,
Why of eyes' falsehood hast thou forged hooks,
Whereto the judgement of my heart is tied?
Why should my heart think that a several plot
Which my heart knows the wide world's common place?
Or mine eyes seeing this, say this is not,
To put fair truth upon so foul a face?
  In things right true my heart and eyes have err'd,
  And to this false plague are they now transferr'd.

CXXXVIII

When my love swears that she is made of truth
I do believe her, though I know she lies,
That she might think me some untutor'd youth,
Unlearned in the world's false subtleties.
Thus vainly thinking that she thinks me young,
Although she knows my days are past the best,
Simply I credit her false-speaking tongue:
On both sides thus is simple truth suppress'd.
But wherefore says she not she is unjust?
And wherefore say not I that I am old?
O, love's best habit is in seeming trust,
And age in love loves not to have years told.
  Therefore I lie with her and she with me,
  And in our faults by lies we flatter'd be.

CXXXIX

O, call not me to justify the wrong
That thy unkindness lays upon my heart;
Wound me not with thine eye, but with thy tongue;
Use power with power, and slay me not by art.
Tell me thou lovest elsewhere, but in my sight,
Dear heart, forbear to glance thine eye aside.
What need'st thou wound with cunning when thy might
Is more than my o'er-press'd defence can bide?
Let me excuse thee—ah! my love well knows
Her pretty looks have been mine enemies,
And therefore from my face she turns my foes,
That they elsewhere might dart their injuries.
  Yet do not so; but since I am near slain,
  Kill me outright with looks and rid my pain.

CXL

Be wise as thou art cruel; do not press
My tongue-tied patience with too much disdain;
Lest sorrow lend me words, and words express
The manner of my pity-wanting pain.
If I might teach thee wit, better it were,
Though not to love, yet, love, to tell me so;
As testy sick men, when their deaths be near,
No news but health from their physicians know;
For if I should despair, I should grow mad,
And in my madness might speak ill of thee.
Now this ill-wresting world is grown so bad
Mad slanderers by mad ears believed be.
  That I may not be so, nor thou belied,
  Bear thine eyes straight, though thy proud heart go wide.

CXLI

In faith, I do not love thee with mine eyes,
For they in thee a thousand errors note;
But 'tis my heart that loves what they despise,
Who in despite of view is pleased to dote.
Nor are mine ears with thy tongue's tune delighted,
Nor tender feeling, to base touches prone,
Nor taste, nor smell, desire to be invited
To any sensual feast with thee alone;
But my five wits nor my five senses can
Dissuade one foolish heart from serving thee,
Who leaves unsway'd the likeness of a man,
Thy proud heart's slave and vassal wretch to be:
  Only my plague thus far I count my gain,
  That she that makes me sin awards me pain.

CXLII

Love is my sin, and thy dear virtue hate,
Hate of my sin, grounded on sinful loving.
O, but with mine compare thou thine own state,
And thou shalt find it merits not reproving!
Or, if it do, not from those lips of thine,
That have profaned their scarlet ornaments
And seal'd false bonds of love as oft as mine,
Robb'd others' beds' revenues of their rents.
Be it lawful I love thee, as thou lovest those
Whom thine eyes woo as mine importune thee.
Root pity in thy heart, that, when it grows,
Thy pity may deserve to pitied be.
If thou dost seek to have what thou dost hide,
By self-example mayst thou be denied!

CXLIII

Lo! as a careful housewife runs to catch
One of her feather'd creatures broke away,
Sets down her babe, and makes all swift dispatch
In pursuit of the thing she would have stay;
Whilst her neglected child holds her in chase,
Cries to catch her whose busy care is bent
To follow that which flies before her face,
Not prizing her poor infant's discontent—
So runn'st thou after that which flies from thee,
Whilst I thy babe chase thee afar behind;
But if thou catch thy hope, turn back to me
And play the mother's part, kiss me, be kind.
So will I pray that thou mayst have thy Will,
If thou turn back and my loud crying still.

CXLIV

Two loves I have of comfort and despair,
Which like two spirits do suggest me still.
The better angel is a man right fair,
The worser spirit a woman colour'd ill.
To win me soon to hell, my female evil
Tempteth my better angel from my side,
And would corrupt my saint to be a devil,
Wooing his purity with her foul pride.
And whether that my angel be turn'd fiend
Suspect I may, yet not directly tell;
But being both from me, both to each friend,
I guess one angel in another's hell.
Yet this shall I ne'er know, but live in doubt,
Till my bad angel fire my good one out.

CXLV

Those lips that Love's own hand did make
Breathed forth the sound that said "I hate"
To me that languish'd for her sake;
But when she saw my woeful state,
Straight in her heart did mercy come,
Chiding that tongue that ever sweet
Was used in giving gentle doom,
And taught it thus anew to greet:
"I hate" she alter'd with an end
That follow'd it as gentle day
Doth follow night, who, like a fiend,
From heaven to hell is flown away.
"I hate" from hate away she threw,
And saved my life, saying "not you."

CXLVI

Poor soul, the centre of my sinful earth,
. . . . these rebel powers that thee array,
Why dost thou pine within and suffer dearth,
Painting thy outward walls so costly gay?
Why so large cost, having so short a lease,
Dost thou upon thy fading mansion spend?
Shall worms, inheritors of this excess,
Eat up thy charge? Is this thy body's end?
Then, soul, live thou upon thy servant's loss,
And let that pine to aggravate thy store;
Buy terms divine in selling hours of dross;
Within be fed, without be rich no more.
So shalt thou feed on Death, that feeds on men,
And Death once dead, there's no more dying then.

CXLVII

My love is as a fever, longing still
For that which longer nurseth the disease,
Feeding on that which doth preserve the ill,
The uncertain sickly appetite to please.
My Reason, the physician to my love,
Angry that his prescriptions are not kept,
Hath left me, and I desperate now approve
Desire is death, which physic did except.
Past cure I am, now reason is past care,
And frantic-mad with evermore unrest;
My thoughts and my discourse as madmen's are,
At random from the truth vainly express'd;
For I have sworn thee fair and thought thee bright,
Who art as black as hell, as dark as night.

CXLVIII

O me, what eyes hath Love put in my head,
Which have no correspondence with true sight!
Or, if they have, where is my judgement fled,
That censures falsely what they see aright?
If that be fair whereon my false eyes dote,
What means the world to say it is not so?
If it be not, then love doth well denote
Love's eye is not so true as all men's "No."
How can it? O, how can Love's eye be true,
That is so vex'd with watching and with tears?
No marvel then, though I mistake my view;
The sun itself sees not till heaven clears.

O cunning Love! with tears thou keep'st me blind,
Lest eyes well-seeing thy foul faults should find.

CXLIX

Canst thou, O cruel! say I love thee not,
When I against myself with thee partake?
Do I not think on thee, when I forgot
Am of myself, all tyrant, for thy sake?
Who hateth thee that I do call my friend?
On whom frown'st thou that I do fawn upon?
Nay, if thou lour'st on me, do I not spend
Revenge upon myself with present moan?
What merit do I in myself respect,
That is so proud thy service to despise,
When all my best doth worship thy defect,
Commanded by the motion of thine eyes?
But, love, hate on, for now I know thy mind;
Those that can see thou lovest, and I am blind.

CL

O, from what power hast thou this powerful might
With insufficiency my heart to sway?
To make me give the lie to my true sight,
And swear that brightness doth not grace the day?
Whence hast thou this becoming of things ill,
That in the very refuse of thy deeds
There is such strength and warrantise of skill
That in my mind thy worst all best exceeds?
Who taught thee how to make me love thee more,
The more I hear and see just cause of hate?
O, though I love what others do abhor,
With others thou shouldst not abhor my state:
If thy unworthiness raised love in me,
More worthy I to be beloved of thee.

CLI

Love is too young to know what conscience is;
Yet who knows not conscience is born of love?
Then, gentle cheater, urge not my amiss,
Lest guilty of my faults thy sweet self prove.
For, thou betraying me, I do betray
My nobler part to my gross body's treason;
My soul doth tell my body that he may
Triumph in love; flesh stays no farther reason,
But, rising at thy name, doth point out thee
As his triumphant prize. Proud of this pride,
He is contented thy poor drudge to be,
To stand in thy affairs, fall by thy side.
No want of conscience hold it that I call
Her "love" for whose dear love I rise and fall.

CLII

In loving thee thou know'st I am forsworn,
But thou art twice forsworn, to me love swearing;
In act thy bed-vow broke and new faith torn
In vowing new hate after new love bearing.
But why of two oaths' breach do I accuse thee,
When I break twenty? I am perjured most;
For all my vows are oaths but to misuse thee,
And all my honest faith in thee is lost;
For I have sworn deep oaths of thy deep kindness,
Oaths of thy love, thy truth, thy constancy,
And, to enlighten thee, gave eyes to blindness,
Or made them swear against the thing they see;
For I have sworn thee fair—more perjured I,
To swear against the truth so foul a lie!

CLIII

Cupid laid by his brand and fell asleep.
A maid of Dian's this advantage found,
And his love-kindling fire did quickly steep
In a cold valley-fountain of that ground;
Which borrow'd from this holy fire of Love
A dateless lively heat, still to endure,
And grew a seething bath, which yet men prove
Against strange maladies a sovereign cure.
But at my mistress' eye Love's brand new-fired,
The boy for trial needs would touch my breast.
I, sick withal, the help of bath desired,
And thither hied, a sad distemper'd guest,
But found no cure. The bath for my help lies
Where Cupid got new fire—my mistress' eyes.

CLIV

The little Love-god, lying once asleep,
Laid by his side his heart-inflaming brand,
Whilst many nymphs that vow'd chaste life to keep
Came tripping by; but in her maiden hand
The fairest votary took up that fire
Which many legions of true hearts had warm'd;
And so the general of hot desire
Was sleeping by a virgin hand disarm'd.
This brand she quenched in a cool well by,
Which from Love's fire took heat perpetual,
Growing a bath and healthful remedy
For men diseased; but I, my mistress' thrall,
Came there for cure, and this by that I prove—
Love's fire heats water, water cools not love.

PRINTED IN THE U.S.A.